EUROPE

Fodor's Europe:

Editorial Contributors: Nicholas Allen, Barbara Walsh Angelillo, Ned Blackmer, Robert Brown, Sheila Brownlee, Robin and Maren Dannhorn, Andrea Dutton, Francis Goodman, George W. Hamilton, Alannah Hopkin, Kristin Helga, Frances Howell, Günther Leidolf, Susan Lowndes, George Maddocks, Ira Mayer, John Mayor, Nina Nelson, Sylvie Nickels, Witek Radwanski, Philip Ray, Peter Sheldon, Zena Støp, Paul Strathern, David Tennant, Roger Thomas, Penny Visman

Editor: Richard Moore

Deputy Editor: Thomas Cussans

Editorial Assistants: Caz Philcox, Margaret Sinclair

Drawings: Lorraine Calaora

Maps: Brian Denyer, Jeremy Ford, Alex Murphy, Swanston Graphics, Bryan Woodfield

FODOR'S

EUROPE

1987

FODOR'S TRAVEL GUIDES
New York & London

The following Fodor's Guides are current; most are also available in a British
edition published by Hodder & Stoughton.

Country and Area Guides

Australia, New Zealand
& the South Pacific
Austria
Bahamas
Belgium & Luxembourg
Bermuda
Brazil
Canada
Canada's Maritime
Provinces
Caribbean
Central America
Eastern Europe
Egypt
Europe
France
Germany
Great Britain
Greece
Holland
India, Nepal &
Sri Lanka
Ireland
Israel
Italy
Japan
Jordan & the Holy Land
Kenya
Korea
Mexico
New Zealand
North Africa
People's Republic
of China
Portugal
Province of Quebec
Scandinavia
Scotland
South America
South Pacific
Southeast Asia
Soviet Union
Spain
Sweden
Switzerland
Turkey
Yugoslavia

City Guides

Amsterdam
Beijing, Guangzhou,
Shanghai
Boston
Chicago
Dallas & Fort Worth
Greater Miami & the
Gold Coast
Hong Kong
Houston & Galveston
Lisbon
London
Los Angeles
Madrid
Mexico City &
Acapulco
Munich
New Orleans
New York City
Paris
Philadelphia
Rome
San Diego
San Francisco
Singapore
Stockholm, Copenhagen,
Oslo, Helsinki &
Reykjavik
Sydney
Tokyo
Toronto
Vienna
Washington, D.C.

U.S.A. Guides

Alaska
Arizona
California
Cape Cod
Chesapeake
Colorado
Far West
Florida
Hawaii
I–95: Maine to Miami
New England

New Mexico
New York State
Pacific North Coast
South
Texas
U.S.A.
Virginia

Budget Travel

American Cities (30)
Britain
Canada
Caribbean
Europe
France
Germany
Hawaii
Italy
Japan
London
Mexico
Spain

Fun Guides

Acapulco
Bahamas
Las Vegas
London
Maui
Montreal
New Orleans
New York City
The Orlando Area
Paris
Puerto Rico
Rio
St. Martin/Sint Maarten
San Francisco
Waikiki

Special-Interest Guides

Selected Hotels of Europe
Ski Resorts of North
America
Views to Dine by around
the World

CONTENTS

CONTENTS

FOREWORD

Europe may be the Old World, but she is very far from senile. Whatever problems may attend her, she can still offer a kaleidoscope of intriguing variety, as more and more tourists discover every year. Likewise, though the sheer popularity of Europe can make the act of travel, especially air travel, something to be endured rather than enjoyed, the excitement of a foreign land and a different way of life still more than justifies the inevitable delays and hassles.

As a series of guidebooks proud to be celebrating over half-a-century of existence, we hope this new, fact-filled edition will help turn your vacation into a voyage of discovery. And if you want to learn more about the background, culture, and sights of the countries covered in this volume, we also publish individual guides that will help you explore Europe in even greater depth.

* * *

We would like to stress, however, that this book can be no more than a *guide*. Our hotel and restaurant listings, for example, are not exhaustive: We do not profess to provide complete listings of either accommodations or places to eat. Instead, we aim to give a general picture of the type and range of establishments available.

Similarly, all prices quoted are based on those available at the time of writing (Easter '86). It is not possible to predict with any hope of exactitude those costs that will be current in 1987. We trust, therefore, that you will take all prices we give as indicators only and will be sure to double-check the latest figures.

It is not only costs that are unpredictable. Hotels and restaurants can become rip-off joints just by a change of ownership, or even the temporary illness of a manager. Museum opening hours alter drastically, buildings close for restoration, masterpieces are stolen, companies go out of business, ferries sink, whole regions are devastated by earthquakes. . . . All the confusion and complexity of life can and on occasion does render out-of-date almost overnight the contents of a travel guide.

For these, and a whole host of other reasons, we greatly appreciate letters from our readers telling us of their experiences and, not least, supplying us with that "traveler's eye view" that our foot-sore writers and editors may miss.

Our addresses are:
In the U.K.—Fodor's Travel Guides, 9–10 Market Place, London, W.1.
In the U.S.—Fodor's Travel Guides, 2 Park Avenue, New York, N.Y. 10016.

Discover the Europe only the natives know.

Avis features GM cars.
Opel Corsa

Get a free "Personally Yours" itinerary when you rent from Avis.

Highlights of Germany. Undiscovered Spain. Irish castles and palaces. And much more.

Personally Yours^{SM} is a customized itinerary, tailored to your own special interests, featuring detailed driving instructions, hotel and restaurant suggestions...plus out-of-the-way places only the natives know about. Be sure to ask for *Personally Yours* when you reserve in advance.

Avis tries harder to make you feel right at home in Europe. Starting with low SuperValue Rates on a wide variety of cars. And your very own personalized itinerary. No wonder we're Europe's largest car rental company. Call your travel consultant, or Avis at **1-800-331-2112.**

Avis. So easy.^{SM}

ONE MAN'S EUROPE

by
GEORGE HAMILTON

U.S.-born George Hamilton has lived in and traveled extensively around Europe and the Middle East. Today he edits a publication on East–West trade from his permanent base in Austria. He is also Fodor's Area Editor for East Germany.

Surely the Eurailpass, that magic identity card that offers access by rail and ship to virtually all western Europe, must qualify as one of the great postwar inventions. I confess to being a rail enthusiast. European rail travel is clean, efficient and fast. And a prime feature of the Eurailpass is that you won't waste valuable time waiting in line for tickets. Just get on the train, bus or ship and go about anywhere you want. That's the way I tackled my first major European vacation, and several trips since, when enough city-hopping was involved to make the pass more economical than a handful of regular tickets.

Another splendid feature of Europe's trains is that you can get a quick overview of a lot of countries in a hurry—not that that's necessarily the best way to see Europe. But it's one way, of course, and on the assumption that the world is small enough and that you'll make the trip again, the quick once-over lets you get enough of a feel for countries and cities to give you a much clearer idea of your targets next time. The "if it's Tuesday, this must be Brussels" syndrome isn't quite the horror story it might seem. You may find instead that your own response is, "if it's Brussels, this must be Tuesday," making a note to come back for more later.

Where to Begin?

For decades London has been the traditional starting point for most travelers from North America to Europe. In a way this makes little sense unless your primary goal is England. Not only must you cope with the semi-organized chaos of Heathrow—Gatwick is a little better —but access to the rest of the Continent, with the formidable Channel still to be crossed, can be awkward.

In fact Brussels, not least that it too can now be reached at budget prices, is perhaps a much better starting point for a European visit, either an extended trip or a whistle-stop tour. From the Belgian capital you can easily head south to Paris and on to Spain and Portugal, or bear southeast to the French Riviera and thence to Italy, or go straight to Switzerland: the French T.G.V. super-express train will take you on to Geneva. Alternatively, you can hop over into Germany to Cologne and catch the Rhine steamers south and then train on to Munich and Austria. Or head north from Cologne to Scandinavia. The possibilities are limited only by the amount of time you can spare.

My other suggestion would be to try heading for another of Europe's prize cities as a starting point. Although if you start from, say, Amsterdam you run the risk of falling utter and complete victim to the abundant charms of your first stop. You may never get to Paris at all. Discipline! Discipline! This is supposed to be a once-over view of Europe. Tear yourself away from Amsterdam if it kills you and plan to come back and next time spend your whole vacation in Holland.

There are other fine starting points as well. Paris, for example, although I find its multiplicity of airports confusing. Or try Rome. Frankfurt isn't much of a city to visit, but it's a good central point from which to start. If you want to start at the extreme easterly point, head for Vienna and either work your way back west through Austria, Switzerland and France, or up through Germany and on to Scandinavia or over into Holland. (I would never manage to leave Vienna, but that's another story.) Alternatively, start in Copenhagen and head south, although again be warned: the city and the Danes have a charm which works its magic on the visitor with an ease you won't even notice until you realize your vacation is half over and you haven't even left Denmark.

Schedules? Yes, but . . .

In fact, half the trick of a successful trip to Europe is in the scheduling. My advice is be flexible. My preference is not to fix a schedule in advance, but, when I've landed in a hotel I like, to ask their advice regarding my next stop and call ahead for a reservation. I've generally had considerable success with this technique, although it doesn't work for major centers like London, where bookings are a must.

Flexibility is useful since so much of Europe can be hopelessly seductive. On my first real exploratory tour of Europe, I decided to head all the way south in Italy, down the east coast of Sicily to Siracusa. A young Italian on the train was astonished I knew so little about Sicily. "Tomorrow head straight back and get off the train at Taormina and you will never forget Sicily or my advice." He was right. Taormina, perched on a bluff high above the sea, was then accessible only by a tortuously narrow road. Little did I know, when approached by one of the frequent "hotel agents" at the railroad station, that our trip to the proffered pension would be accomplished on his Lambretta motor bike, my suitcase perilously wedged between us, constantly threatening to unseat us as we spun dizzily round the hairpin turns.

But the risk was worth it. At sunrise next morning any thoughts I'd had of "a day or two maybe" vanished. Suddenly one of those "too stunning to be real" illustrations out of the *National Geographic* had come to life in three dimensions: an azure expanse of Mediterranean, a backdrop of a mistily smoking Mount Etna behind an ancient Greek amphitheater, flowers everywhere. It was carnival time as well, just before the start of Lent, early for the "season." The few tourists were selective and knowledgeable, the town the focal point for celebrations throughout the area, with folklore, float parades, costumes, a greased-pole climb in the town square, already ankle-deep in confetti brought in by the truckload. These recollections all came back nearly 20 years later when I went back to Taormina at carnival time. The celebrations hadn't changed, nor had that image of a smoking Etna behind the amphitheater or the blaze of flowers in the town gardens. They were impressions never to be forgotten.

Discovery, of course, is one of the prime reasons why anybody would want to see Europe in the first place. Discoveries there are. Take pizza and Naples. Sometime, somewhere, I recall a legend in a U.S. pizzeria attributing the origin of the dish to Naples. Indeed, Naples is ablaze with neon signs proclaiming, suspiciously often in English, to mark the home of the original pizza. Unless your travel pharmacy is well stocked with Alka-Seltzer, resist the temptation. In my quest to verify the claim of originality, I tackled no less than three of Naples' "Home of" pizzerias. Whoever popularized the recipe in the States ought to have done the Neopolitans a favor and shared the secret.

What? It's Closed!

Seasonal timing can make a big difference in Europe. Probably, it's just as well that not everybody is able to rush to Europe during April and May. But I do feel sorry for those who arrive in Vienna in July to find the State Opera taking its own vacation and the famous Lippizaner horses out to pasture. Just as unfortunate are those who hit Paris in August with the whole city seemingly on holiday and many shops and restaurants "Fermé" for the month.

On the other hand, if you can arrange your vacations to take advantage of spring in Europe you are in for a magnificent treat. For those with an eye for color, London is worth a visit almost alone for the sweeps of brilliant daffodils swaying in the parks; Vienna for the broad pedestrian boulevards of the Prater arched with chestnut trees boasting candelabra blossoms ranging from pure white to deepest crimson; the tulip fields of Holland exploding in a spectrum of color; and Paris, of course Paris, as the first cafe tables appear tentatively on the sidewalks. Spring is a glorious time to experience Europe's reawakening from what in some of its countries is a drab, depressing winter.

Perhaps the biggest plus for anyone touring Europe is simply that there is so much *not* to be missed. Headed north from Rome during any season and pressed for time, do you pass up Florence or Venice? A tough choice. Were I to have unlimited time to re-explore Europe, I think I'd do it again more or less the same way. By starting in the south—Greece or Italy—in early spring, it is possible to follow that magic season up through the Continent into Scandinavia, with the best of all possible worlds along the way.

Some reservations notwithstanding, I'd still recommend Greece, if you're prepared to move out on your own. Athens is interesting for the Parthenon and the other compulsory tourist sights both in the city and within a day's bus outing. But alas, as soon as you get very far from civilization's cradle, unless you speak fairly fluent Greek you'll find yourself quite unable to establish contact with the Greeks themselves.

The language barrier reduces the traveler to a mere observer. I recall the exasperation of trying to get coffee at a cafe well away from the better-traveled tourist routes. Efforts in English, French, German and finally Arabic gave way pointing to a neighboring table. But part of the fun of Athens is in the exploring. Take the "subway" out to the port of Piraeus and sample your coffee or tea, or lunch on *moussaka* or *oktapodi* (fried octopus) washed down with ouzo or a cold beer, at one of the fishermen's cafes overlooking the harbor.

Put on Your Walking Shoes

Italy begins—but certainly doesn't end—in Rome. If you tackle Rome after Athens, you may suffer an overdose of antiquity, but the sight of St. Peter's Square and the Vatican will draw you quickly enough into the present. Rome, like most other cities in Europe, is best explored on foot. The banning of cars from much of the city's center has made life for the pedestrian tourist infinitely safer. You can stand back to admire a square or fountain without the fear of instant death at the hands of an excited Italian driver paying far more attention to an attractive female at a cafe than to you.

Relax and enjoy Rome. It is a city that lends itself easily to intentional idleness. The sidewalk cafes throughout the city have a hypnotic attraction for you to relax, rest your feet, scan the *Herald Tribune* over a glass of Campari and let the rest of Rome go by. Now that's a *real* vacation!

If you can tear yourself away from such glorious luxury, then head for Florence and a side trip to Pisa, recommended because you have to see the tower to believe it. Those with any feeling for heights will have the good sense not to attempt the climb, but those inclined to tackle the spiral, beware! Due to the tilt of the tower, at points you have the decided feeling of going down as you go up, a most disconcerting situation, particularly as at the same time the relative absence of guardrails encourages a presumably unwanted launch into space. If only I could say the view from the top is superb. I don't remember. My concern over the return trip obliterated all other perceptions. I certainly wouldn't do it again on a bet and I'm not even sure I want to say that I'm glad I did it even once.

Of Menus and Mountains

One fascinating discovery while traveling through Italy is the variety of regional cooking. Alas, in North America, anything that comes from Italy is referred to simply as Italian, ignoring regional origins. Yet these come into sharp focus even over such relatively short distances as Rome–Florence or Florence–Milan. From the most expensive noble restaurant to the simple trattoria, waiters will be particularly pleased if you ask about regional specialties. In the process you will be rewarded with thoroughly authentic dishes you never knew existed, even if your mother *is* Italian. Much Italian cuisine is much more than just pasta. The sensible Italians start out with a modest portion of pasta and then get on to the more serious and interesting parts of dining.

Heading north from Italy, Switzerland was my next stop. My first target was Lucerne, a small city I had met on my first, limited trip to Europe. Over the years it had lost none of its picturesque charm: the covered bridge crossing the lake; the lake steamers; the Alps in the background. Again for old time's sake, I made the side trip to Interlaken and took a trip up the Rigi cog railway and up the Jungfrau, an expedition that years earlier had left a permanent vision of vast, snow-swept expanses on the top of the Alps, and in August no less. The acquaintanceship of a pleasant older British woman on the trip back down provided practical advice as well. Never, she insisted, use a Continental hotel lift between 4 and 6 P.M. The most power failures occur between those hours, she assured me. Confined to a stranded elevator at that hour one could easily miss tea, and possibly cocktails and dinner as well! I have not in practice found her precaution necessary, but have never forgotten the well-intended advice.

One of the fascinations of compact Switzerland is the diversity to be found in an area only twice the size of Massachusetts: four official languages and a three-way cultural split into Italian, French and German. Try visiting Zurich and Geneva one after the other. It's hard to believe you're in the same country. Not only do the people speak and think differently, they even look dissimilar. But that's just one more of the discoveries that makes the trip so worthwhile.

Food, quite naturally, is another. Suffering a monumental hangover after an excess of *Dôle*—a superb Swiss red wine—I was invited by some friends to join them at Sunday brunch, where at their recommendation I first had beefsteak tartare, raw fillet of beef, spiced and topped with a raw egg. The idea seemed to me as distressing as the hangover. But their advice was excellent. The beefsteak tartare, some good Swiss beer, and the hangover was gone. My taste for the tartare remains to this day, preferably without the hangover, however.

Austrian Approaches

Switzerland for me is a prelude to Austria. Heading across Austria from west to east isn't a bad approach. Each step is one up from the one before. Innsbruck is compact and charming, at its liveliest during the winter ski season. Ah, but Salzburg! A jewel among cities, no matter what the season. I have experienced Salzburg on an early winter morning when the city's ornaments showed in quiet gray under a pristine blanket of snow—and have sat transfixed halfway up the hill to the Festung on a spring afternoon, eavesdropping on a broadcast of a Mozart concerto through an open apartment window. I have stood impatiently in the famous Salzburg showers under the arches by the cathedral waiting for the skies to clear. (Whatever the forecast, always carry an umbrella in Salzburg). Lunch on the terrace of the Festung, overlooking the city, will leave an unforgettable impression no matter what you eat: here it's the experience of place, not the food, that makes the difference. Climb the Kapuziner hill opposite and you will be rewarded with an equally unforgettable view of the Festung itself. Salzburg is a compact city, one for climbing and walking, and one for discoveries.

As if in a celluloid romance, I had fallen in love with Vienna before I set eyes on the city, but that first visit sealed a love affair that holds to this day. Is it my contagious enthusiasm alone that makes visiting friends equally responsive? I doubt it. Here walk the ghosts of Mozart, Beethoven, Schubert, Brahms and Strauss; Klimt and Loos; Freud, Wittgenstein and Herzl. Hitler too, if you will. Wander through the open-air Naschmarkt vegetable stands and, on a Saturday, on to the flea market, looking up at the Jugendstil buildings flanking the streets. Or explore the narrow streets behind the great cathedral to find the rooms where Mozart lived and worked. And do as the Viennese do— take a break for coffee or tea at any of the hundreds of cafes, indoor or out. I was expecting, and found, all of this on my first trip, plus overwhelming friendliness. I couldn't believe it and swore to come back to prove it wasn't really so. Come back I did, and Vienna surpassed itself the second and third times. At that point I promised myself there'd never be a year in my life when I didn't visit Vienna at least once, an oath not yet and not likely to be broken. The hazards of a trip to Europe!

Then there are the environs of Vienna. The city is unusual in that the surrounding countryside is so easy to reach. At the end of a street-car line you can be in the Vienna Woods, in the vineyards, or on the banks of the Danube, where city recreation areas offer everything from picnic areas and bicycle trails to windsurfing and nude sunbathing. Via suburban railway or bus, you can easily reach the spa of Baden. Or the restored castle of Burg Kreuzenstein. A friend and I once climbed the path through the woods to the castle. Somewhat unprepared for the trek, she suggested we follow the road rather than the woodland path back down. I assured her we would be offered a ride by the first car that passed. "Your Camelot," she replied. The first car was full. But the driver of the second offered to take us all the way back to Vienna. We had intended to stop for wine at one of the excellent private wine gardens, or *Heuriger,* at the bottom of the hill. We invited our benefactors to join us. They did so happily.

Camelot? My friend's eyes grow misty still when we speak of that Vienna holiday. The wine gardens at Nussdorf and Sievering, the museums, the experience of coming out of a splendid performance of *Wiener Blut* in the jewel of a theater at Schönbrunn to find the palace complex swept with moonlight . . .

Nordic Variations

There are indeed those who prefer Munich to Vienna, claiming the German city has far more life. They may be right, but I have never found the Bavarian capital to have the same charm as Vienna. If you prefer boisterousness, though, you'll like Munich, from the beer halls to the people themselves. Certainly Munich is a city to be visited, for the remarkable technical museum and the art collections.

Romantic that I am, I find the German towns of Rothenburg ob der Tauber and Heidelberg irresistible. Rothenburg has been lovingly restored and is well worth the effort needed to wander from the beaten path to reach it. Heidelburg is on that main path, easier to reach. Strictly speaking, the town ought to be visited only in spring when the cherry and apple trees are in blossom. For those who recall Sigmund Romberg's *Student Prince,* this is the setting of it all. From the castle above to the drinking halls in the town, Heidelburg will capture every bit of your imagination.

I'll go back to Mainz at any time for the Gutenberg Museum—complete with bible, of course—although the town itself has a certain medieval charm. From Mainz it is a simple matter to catch a Rhine steamer downstream through hills and vineyards, a glorious trip even if the weather doesn't oblige. A logical stop is Cologne, for the cathedral and the museums.

Other than Bremen and Hamburg, I find little of interest in north Germany. But the port cities do have an attraction; certainly the reputation of Hamburg's Reeperbahn is earned as well as deserved. At the other end of the scale, the city's opera, concerts and museums are the equal of any in Germany.

If you can spare the time, include Scandinavia on your itinerary. Not only does Copenhagen hold surprises—such as women enjoying hefty cigars over coffee—but Oslo and Stockholm, too, are thoroughly worthy of visits. Nowhere does the Norwegian gift for sailing and exploring come closer than at the two museums on the outskirts of Oslo housing Amundsen's polar ship *Fram* and Thor Heyerdahl's *Kon Tiki.* But of the trio of Scandinavian capitals, my favorite is Copenhagen. There always seems to be that extra corner to explore. But beware: the goods in the shops are seductive, a guaranteed risk for those with credit cards and a weakness for Danish design.

Amsterdam Ale and London Canals

If you're saving the best—second only, that is, to my own prejudices for Vienna—until last, you'll be heading for Amsterdam and then on to London. Allow enough time for each. These are cities to be savored. The charms of Amsterdam are legendary, ranging from the barely-clad young ladies in their red-lit front parlors, to the brewery tours (catch the 100-year-old Heineken brewery before it's closed down), and the network of canals and the boats which provide housing for a remarkable number of Amsterdamers. Photographers go mad: at every bend in a canal or street there's a view to be captured, day or night.

The main problem of going on to London afterwards is simply that it's too much of a good thing. I cherish London, its squares, mews, flea markets, antique shops, intimate restaurants, excellent theater, its sensible subway, its mad traffic jams, its sense—even if now somewhat jaded—of being the center of the universe. London, too, is a city for exploring on foot. I'd reschedule a trip to manage the Portobello Road market on a Saturday, and devote a full day to the pleasure. Or cross the Thames and explore the area around Southwark cathedral. Try wandering round the City, the financial district, on a Sunday just to look at the buildings. Or—surprise!—take a canal boat ride from Regent's Park to Little Venice. Also on Sunday mornings, the Camden Town pub "entertainments" are great fun, if you can squeeze inside. Weekdays, try a sandwich-and-wine lunch at El Vino's in Fleet Street, but get there well before the 3 P.M. closing time.

The biggest problem in London is simply that there is always too much going on. I have happily spent entire vacations there and still haven't begun to exhaust the possibilities of that fascinating city. I envy those who have taken the time to explore the rest of Britain.

But on the sad assumption that even the best things come to an end, so too do vacations. When we children urged our grandmother to extend her visit, her standard reply was, "If I don't leave, I can't come back." If your first trip to Europe has been a "once over lightly," you'll already be counting on a return, to spend more time in your favorite city or country. I envy you the fun of planning, discovering and, most of all, sharing.

CALL TOLL-FREE
1 800 4-EURAIL
TO ORDER ANY EURAIL OR BRITRAIL PASS

U.S., AK, HI (800) 438-7245   Calif (800) 556-4018

The BEST way to see Europe is with a **Eurailpass** or **Eurail Youthpass**. Good for unlimited rail travel thru 16 countries and 100,000 miles of European Railways. Order today and get a **FREE** rail guide worth $18.45.

All Visitors to Britain should consider the Britrail Pass. Valid for unlimited rail travel thru England, Scotland and Wales. Please note: Eurailpass is **not valid** in Britain.

Normal Delivery in 14 days. 3-day **RUSH SERVICE** available for only $4 extra. For additional Britrail, Eurail, or individual country rail pass information just write or call.

Credit card users may order by phone. Or xerox this page and send it with your payment to:

EUROPEAN RAIL AUTHORITY
1821 Wilshire Boulevard
Santa Monica, CA 90403
(213) 453-3553

Eurailpass

	1st-class Adult	1st-class Child (4-11)	Youth (12-25) 2nd class
15 day	☐ $260	☐ $130	N/A
21 day	☐ $330	☐ $165	N/A
1 mon.	☐ $410	☐ $205	☐ $290
2 mon.	☐ $560	☐ $280	☐ $370
3 mon.	☐ $680	☐ $340	N/A

3 or more 15-day passes ☐ $199 each!

Britrail Pass
(Free Map of England with Order)

	1st-class	2nd-class	Youth (16-25)
7 day	☐ $160	☐ $115	☐ $ 95
14 day	☐ $245	☐ $175	☐ $150
21 day	☐ $310	☐ $220	☐ $190
1 mon.	☐ $365	☐ $260	☐ $225

Full Name _____

Address _____

Address _____

Day Phone ( ) _____ Eve Phone ( ) _____

Birthdate _____ Departure date from U.S. _____

I enclose payment by: ☐ Check ☐ Credit Card

Acct. # _____ Exp. Date _____

Signature _____

Prices subject to change   ©1986 European Rail Authority

FACTS AT YOUR
FINGERTIPS

LANGUAGE/30

For the Business or Vacationing International Traveler

In 30 languages! A basic language course on 2 cassettes and a phrase book . . . Only $14.95 ea. + shipping

Nothing flatters people more than to hear visitors try to speak their language and LANGUAGE/30, used by thousands of satisfied travelers, gets you speaking the basics quickly and easily. Each LANGUAGE/30 course offers:

- approximately 1½ hours of guided practice in greetings, asking questions and general conversation
- special section on social customs and etiquette

Order yours today. Languages available: YIDDISH (available fall '86)

ARABIC	INDONESIAN	PORTUGUESE
CHINESE	IRISH	VIETNAMESE
DANISH	ITALIAN	RUSSIAN
DUTCH	TURKISH	SERBO-CROATIAN
FINNISH	JAPANESE	SPANISH
FRENCH	KOREAN	SWAHILI
GERMAN	LATIN	SWEDISH
GREEK	NORWEGIAN	TAGALOG
HEBREW	PERSIAN	THAI
HINDI	POLISH	

To order send $14.95 per course + shipping $2.00 1st course, $1 ea. add. course. In Canada $3 1st course, $2.00 ea. add. course. NY and CA residents add state sales tax. Outside USA and Canada $14.95 (U.S.) + air mail shipping: $8 for 1st course, $5 ea. add. course. MasterCard, VISA and Am. Express card users give brand, account number (all digits), expiration date and signature.
SEND TO: FODOR'S, Dept. LC 760, 2 Park Ave., NY 10016-5677, USA.

FACTS AT YOUR FINGERTIPS

PLANNING YOUR TRIP

How to Use This Guide

For the reader's convenience and easy reference, we have organized this book in two streamlined sections:

SECTION ONE—Planning Your Trip is designed to supply you with all the information relevant to planning your trip in the broad sense. This includes detailed indications as to necessary documents, travel agents; how to reach Europe by air and sea; and touring by car, bus, train, plane or boat.

Six of the sub-sections will be of particular interest.

Planning Pointers. The most important question—and the hardest to answer—What Will It Cost?, is tackled in this book on a country-by-country basis; but we have started to look at it in this section. This first coverage of the problem is then followed by a series of useful items on such topics as Travel Documents, Student and Budget Youth Travel, Travel Agents, National Tourist Offices, Handicapped Travel and Baggage Tips.

Special Interest Travel helps you to avoid the overcrowded, run-of-the-mill tours by telling you where to find trips arranged for people with special interests—whether the interest be auto-racing, gardening, mountaineering or bird-watching.

Rail Travel in Europe tells you what you already know—Europe has better trains than America. Luxury and comfort, plus incredible speed, are the key-notes. You'll be tempted to take the lazy man's way of traveling after seeing all the sleek trains and their routes listed here.

Motoring in Europe reflects the latest information on Europe's roads and where they can lead you. Especially designed for the man and woman who like leisurely travel with not-too-rigid a timetable, this sub-section is full of helpful hints for charting your itinerary.

On the Water in Europe points out the variety and unhurried enjoyment of water-borne vacations—on the seas, rivers, canals, and lakes—with prices and destinations to suit everyone.

Bus Travel in Europe highlights the economy and ease with which you can enjoy some of the most beautiful scenery in Europe from the depths of a comfortable seat—and without having to worry about filling the tank.

SECTION TWO—Europe Country by Country comprises specific facts on costs, daily budgets and other practical information for each nation, plus a descriptive guide to the people, sights, hotels, restaurants, nightlife and other attractions of the countries of Europe, alphabetically arranged.

PLANNING HINTS

We've tried to bring you the latest price information throughout this book, but because of the continuing instability in world currency markets, we have to point out that all prices herein are subject to change without notice. To a considerable extent, the prices we quote are those obtaining as we go to press— Easter 1986. Every week brings news of radical change in the currencies of Europe against the dollar, and there is no likelihood that these changes are going to slow down between now and the beginning of 1987. We therefore have to ask you to check all prices before starting out on your travels. Some European countries, such as Austria and Switzerland, have fairly stable currencies, others, long thought stable, such as West Germany and Great Britain, are feeling the pressure of the current international situation making them cheaper than ever for American visitors.

We have quoted prices in dollars and pounds for those items that you are likely to invest in before leaving home. Elsewhere, we have tried always to quote in the local currency, to cover the expenditures made in the destination country.

PACKAGE TOURS. If you wish for a fair degree of certainty as to what your trip to Europe will cost you, there is no substitute for the package tour. Apart from money for shopping, extra evening entertainment, drinks and snacks along the way, all the basic costs of your trip—transport, hotels, most food—may already have been covered. Of course, when booking a package tour it is always wise to check with your travel agent on the extent of the "package". Some really are inclusive—down to tips and taxis, nightclubs and theaters; others cover all your transportation, accommodation and meals but leave you to pay on the spot for trips, excursions, etc.

Under *Special Interest Travel,* later in this section, we suggest some of the tours that are available for those who wish to combine their vacation with their hobby. These constitute only a part of the vast number of package tours that are available, the majority being those which provide either the chance to laze on a beach, or the opportunity for visiting some of the really fascinating places that Europe has to offer.

At press time there was some speculation as to whether the cut throat battle for ever-lower trans-Atlantic air fares might not be coming to an end. With the arrival of *People Express, Virgin Atlantic* and *Highland Express* the transatlantic cheap fare situation has once more radically changed to a rough approximation of what it was in the days of Freddy Laker's popularity. The approach of the new services, which treat transatlantic flying in the spirit of the New York/ Washington shuttle, has our whole-hearted support. They are realistic and, if you will pardon the expression, down-to-earth. They once more open the route to free-and-easy flying, and make it possible to take advantage of the fact that the U.K. is still the best place for booking European packages. North Americans will probably still find it most economical to catch a budget flight across to Britain and take a package from there on to the continent.

Among the hundreds of packages available from the **United States,** a fair sampling of quality trips are offered by *Globus-Gateway* 95–25 Queens Blvd., Rego Park, NY 11374—nine days in England, Wales & Southern Scotland from $408–$458; 15 days in England, France, Switzerland, Italy, Austria, Germany and Holland, $698–$798; and 15 days in Denmark, Sweden & Norway from $768 up. Prices, as throughout this section, are approximate and meant to be representative. They are per person/double occupancy, London to London. Full prices will be plus airfare.

Cosmos, 95–25 Queens Blvd., Rego Park, NY 11374, features tours similar to those above but specifically designed for the budget-minded. Typical is a

23-day package stopping in 11 European countries for $774–$804. Other tours begin at $518–$558 for 15 days/8 countries.

Maupintour, 1515 St. Andrews Dr., Lawrence, Kansas 66046, is another organization whose reliability and careful handling of all arrangements have given it an outstanding reputation. Tours span the globe, including 16-day journeys to Spain and Portugal for approximately $1,600, and 22 days in France for about $3,000.

Percival Tours, One Tandy Ctr. Plaza, Fort Worth, TX 76102, is noted primarily for its deluxe packages, but recent years have seen the addition of a series of equally excellent budget trips. Typical multi-city tours for 16 and 25 days run about $799 and $1,299 respectively, and come well recommended for first-timers to the continent.

Changing almost as rapidly as airfares themselves are the packages offered by such international carriers as *TWA, Pan Am* and *British Airways.* Each has a wide array of tours at various price levels and catering to many interests. Best to contact a travel agent for the specifics on these. Similarly, *American Express,* Travel Division, 822 Lexington Ave., New York, N.Y. 10021, has numerous tours for both the novice and experienced traveler.

Travel expenses from **Britain** are suggested by the following package tours: Crete, from £282–758 for 14 nights; to the Costa del Sol, 7 nights from £269–595, 14 from £372–970; skiing in Switzerland, 7 nights from £179–379, 14 from £267–595; and 7 nights in Majorca from £149–338, 14 from £209–505. Prices for half board, sharing double room. All available from *Thomas Cook,* P.O. Box 36, Thorpe Wood, Peterborough PE3 6SB.

Thomson Holidays, Greater London House, Hampstead Rd., London N.W.1 have a huge selection of tours available. Among them are—7 nights in Majorca from £94 (half board); 14 nights at Torremolinos on the Costa del Sol from £165 (full board); 14 nights in Malta from £213 (half board); and a 7-day package split between three days in Athens and three on the island of Rhodes from £230 (half board), including flight from Athens to Rhodes.

D.E.R. Travel Ltd., 18 Conduit St., London W.1, offer a wide choice of motoring holidays on the Continent—Germany and Austria in particular. In all cases, you go by boat across the Channel. With their "Go as you please" package, you select the number of nights you wish to go for, they issue you with a booklet of hotel vouchers, and you make your choice from the selection of Silence Hotels scattered over Austria and Germany. Cost for 7 nights, including accommodations (breakfast only), cross-Channel ferry, A.A. cover, from £207.

Generally speaking, airfares in off-season (mid-September to mid-June) can be about $110 less than usual. However, if you decide to do the land portion of your trip independently, remember that most of the charter flights operate in summer. See "Getting to Europe" section, for more details about air fares.

Eastern European countries are currently high on the list of budget destinations. When visiting Eastern Europe individual travel is certainly possible, even camping, but most tourists prefer a package tour and the variety of these available is rapidly increasing. *Peltours Ltd.,* Mappin House, 4 Winsley St., London W.1, and *Kompas Yugoslavia,* 630 Fifth Ave., New York, N.Y. 10111, offer the following holidays (prices inclusive from London), all B&B only unless otherwise stated: 7 nights Bulgaria from £346–449; 7 nights in Romania from £320–417; 6 nights in East Germany from £337–474 (choice of three centers); 6 nights in Hungary from £255–420 (latter room only); 6 nights in Poland from £334–435; and 6 nights in Czechoslovakia from £293 (half board) to £417. Note that 3-day packages are also available in Hungary and Czechoslovakia.

To visit certain of the Eastern European countries you still must *plan* ahead and *pay* ahead. To obtain from them your tourist visa, you must first make all your hotel reservations. To secure a hotel reservation (foreigners being admitted to specified hotels only), you must pay in advance, in dollars or pounds, for your entire stay. You make this pre-payment to the accredited travel agent in your country acting for the various national tourist bureaux. (These, incidentally, are empowered to represent each other, so you may set up a multi-country tour through a single agent).

You must pre-pay hotel rooms and meals, and may also pay in advance for guide and interpreter services, private cars or buses, even theater tickets. In exchange for your hard-earned hard currency, your travel agent will hand you a tourist voucher, which is simply a receipt itemizing the services you have paid for, at the prevailing legal rate of exchange.

But, as soon as you arrive, the local tourist bureau will redeem your voucher at a special favorable tourist exchange rate. This "bonus" varies from country to country (as do the details of the procedure itself), but can be twice the original exchange rate. You can use this extra cash to order special dishes, upgrade your hotel accommodation, buy souvenirs, or alter your tour itinerary (if hotel space is available). Any traveler's checks or banknotes you cash inside the country will also be exchanged at the bonus rate.

Your voucher also enables your travel agent to obtain your tourist visa. This is more than a permit to cross the frontier and stay in the country. It is an official guarantee that fully paid-up hotel accommodation has been reserved in your name.

For the individual requirements of the different countries of Eastern Europe see the various country chapters in this volume or the separate volume entitled *Fodor's Eastern Europe* in this series.

LESS THAN YOU MIGHT THINK. Some countries have a reputation for being pricey destinations and many would-be visitors flinch from trying them, put off by financial oldwives' tales. The Scandinavian countries and Switzerland all have been thought to be expensive countries to visit, but the actual case is quite the reverse now. On various fronts they have managed to keep down the costs that most affect the traveler; they have had their hotels under rigid control during the years when those of Britain, say, were running out of control. They have tourist menus, which give excellent value for money. They have good budget travel offers and, especially in Switzerland, some of the best trains anywhere in the world, at some of the world's lowest rates.

Among the other countries of Europe, Italy and Portugal are both very light on the tourist's pocket, while, sadly, Britain has rapidly rocketed its way up the cost spiral to become one of Europe's priciest destinations. In most countries there is one rule of thumb that you can rely on—the capital will be more expensive than the country areas. If you add certain up-market centers to the capital, you will have a very good basic rule to work by. Add, for example, some Riviera resorts to Paris, Venice to Rome, or Salzburg to Vienna. This means, for the individual traveler, that he should divide his time between the capital of his chosen country and a trip out into the rural areas.

Year-round Travel. Off-season travel does have advantages over touring during the peak summer months. In cases where prices remain the same, the pressure is off, and you will have a wider choice of accommodations.

The choicest hotel rooms, the very best tables in the restaurants, will not have been pre-empted by fellow tourists, and you will gain a more intimate knowledge of the countries you visit, seeing their inhabitants in their normal routine. The great cities and capitals of Europe bloom in the fall and winter, rather than in the summer. The theaters open, the concert and opera seasons begin, the new shows are presented in the night clubs. The celebrations of Christmas and the New Year are even livelier than they are at home, and the fun continues *crescendo* through the carnivals preceding Lent. Even if you are not a member of that mass movement that converges annually with the first fall of snow on the ski slopes of the Alps, think about "out-of-season" travel this year.

 VACATION TRAVEL INSURANCE. Travel insurance can cover everything from health and accident costs, to lost baggage and trip cancellation. Sometimes they can all be obtained with one blanket policy; other times they overlap with existing coverage you might have for health and/or home; still other times it is best to buy policies that are tailored to very specific needs. But, insurance is available from many sources and many travelers unwittingly end up with redundant coverage. Before purchasing separate travel insurance of any kind, be sure to check your regular policies carefully.

Generally, it is best to take care of your insurance needs *before* embarking on your trip. You'll pay more for less coverage—and have less chance to read the fine print—if you wait until the last minute and make your purchases from, say, an airport vending machine or insurance company counter. Best of all, if you have a regular insurance agent, he is the person to consult first. Flight insurance, often included in the price of the ticket when the fare is paid via American Express, Visa or certain other major credit cards, is also often included in package policies providing accident coverage as well. These policies are available from most tour operators and insurance companies. While it is a good idea to have health and accident insurance when traveling, be careful not to spend money to duplicate coverage you may already have . . . or to neglect some eventuality which could end up costing a small fortune. For example, basic Blue Cross Blue Shield policies cover health costs incurred while traveling. They will not, however, cover the cost of emergency transportation, which can often add up to several thousand dollars. Emergency transportation *is* covered, in part at least, by many major medical policies such as those underwritten by *Prudential, Metropolitan* and *New York Life.* Again, we can't urge too strongly that you check any policy carefully before buying. Another important example: Most insurance issued specifically for travel does not cover pre-existing conditions, such as a heart problem. See also under *Medical Insurance.*

Several organizations offer coverage designed to supplement existing health insurance and to help defray costs not covered by many standard policies, such as emergency transportation. Some of the more prominent are:

NEAR, (Nationwide Emergency Ambulance Return) 1900 N. McArthur Blvd., Suite 210, Oklahoma City, OK 73127. Rates are on a per day basis at $5 for the first day and $3 for each subsequent day, with a minimum of ten days and a maximum of 60.

Carefree Travel Insurance, c/o ARM Coverage Inc., 120 Mineola Blvd., Box 310, Mineola, NY 11501, offers medical evacuation arranged through Europe Assistance of Paris (tel. 212–517–7911). *Carefree* coverage is available from many travel agents.

International SOS Assistance Inc., P.O. Box 11568, Philadelphia, PA, 19116, has fees from $15 a person for seven days, to $195 for a year (tel. 800–523–8930).

IAMAT (International Association for Medical Assistance to Travelers), 736 Center St., Lewiston, NY 14092 in the U.S.; or 188 Nicklin Rd., Guelph, Ontario, N1H 7L5 in Canada.

Travel Assistance International, the American arm of Europ Assistance, offers a comprehensive program offering immediate, on-the-spot medical, personal and financial help. Annual membership is from around $5 and trip protection ranges from $30 for an individual for up to eight days to $220 for an entire family for a year. (These figures may be revised before 1987). For full details, contact your travel agent or insurance broker, or write Europ Assistance World-wide Services Inc., 1333 F St., N.W., Washington, D.C. 20004 (800–821–2828). In the U.K., contact Europ Assistance Ltd., 252 High St., Croydon, Surrey (tel. 01–680 1234).

The British Insurance Association, Aldermary House, 10–15 Queen St., London E.C.4 (tel. 01–248 4477), will give comprehensive advice on all aspects of vacation travel insurance from the U.K.

Loss of baggage is another frequent inconvenience to travelers. It is possible, though often complicated, to insure your luggage against loss through theft or negligence. Insurance companies are reluctant to sell such coverage alone, however, since it is often a losing proposition for them. Instead, this type of coverage is usually included as part of a package that also covers accidents or health. Remuneration is often determined by weight, regardless of the value of the specific contents of the luggage. Should you lose your luggage or some other personal possession, it is essential to report it to the local police immediately. Without documentation of such a report, your insurance company might be very stingy. Also, before buying baggage insurance, check your home-owners policy. Some such policies offer "off-premises theft" coverage, including the loss of luggage while traveling.

The last major area of traveler's insurance is trip cancellation coverage. This is especially important to travelers on APEX or charter flights. Should you get sick abroad, or for some other reason be unable to continue your trip, you may be stuck having to buy a new one-way fare home, plus paying for the charter you're not using. You can guard against this with "trip cancellation insurance," usually available from travel agents. Most of these policies will also cover last minute cancellations.

 MONEY MATTERS. Travelers' checks are the best way to safeguard travel funds. They are sold by various banks and companies in terms of American and Canadian dollars, pounds sterling, German marks, Swiss francs and other foreign currencies. We recommend buying them in the local currency you will be using, whenever possible. These are called *destination-currency* checks, and have the advantage of protecting you against loss on exchange rates.

Those issued by *American Express, Citibank* and *Bank of America* are best known and their offices are most widespread. Note that in the U.S., only *Barclays* and *Thomas Cook* do not charge commission for issuing checks.

Best known and easily exchanged British travelers' checks are those issued by *Thos. Cook & Son* and the main banks *(Barclays, Lloyds, Midland, National Westminster)*.

Changing travelers' checks or cash is easiest at your hotel, but will cost you more (and it will be worse in shops and restaurants!). So change at banks, if you can afford the extra time, and try to avoid doing so at weekends, when rates are less advantageous. Rates at main downtown banks are often better than those at airport branches.

Get most of your travelers' checks in smaller denominations so that you lose as little as possible when you reconvert your unspent remainder. Reconvert before you leave a country, but be sure to check on whether there are any departure taxes first. Get rid of coins because they are hard to reconvert; and keep a few U.S. $1 bills handy for unforeseen expenses. It's also a good idea to keep a record of check serial numbers. In the event of loss or theft, this will make replacement a much simpler matter.

You will find it convenient to have with you a small amount of foreign currency when you arrive, to use for porters, buses or taxis, bellhops, etc. Small packets of currency for this purpose are sold by some larger banks, and by a number of private firms that buy and sell foreign money; look under *Foreign Money Brokers and Dealers* in the Yellow Pages of large-city phone books. In New York, *Deak Perera Co.*, 630 Fifth Ave., and *Deak-Perera International* at Kennedy Airport are among the over two dozen listed.

It is now possible for British travelers to cash personal checks abroad on production of a Barclaycard or one of the many Eurocheque Encashment Cards participating in the scheme in over 19 countries. It can be cheaper than exchanging travelers' checks. Note that not all cards are acceptable everywhere in Europe and that it is essential to check the validity of any cards you may have *before* starting out.

In Eastern Europe. You usually cannot bring any local currency with you into a communist country (except Yugoslavia and Hungary, small amounts). If caught you may be subject to a prison term (some tourists have been imprisoned), or at best, embarrassment, confiscation of your money, and expulsion from the country.

CREDIT CARDS. Credit Cards are now an integral part of the Western Financial Way of Life, and, in theory at least, are accepted all over Europe. But, while the use of credit cards can smooth the traveler's path considerably, they should not be thought of as a universal answer to every problem.

Firstly, there is growing resistance in Europe to the use of credit cards, or rather to the percentage which the credit card organizations demand from establishments taking part in their schemes. Not so long ago, 200 restaurants in Paris refused to accept credit cards—and some of them still refuse—simply because they felt that the benefit credit cards bring is all on the side of the customer. So if you intend to use your credit card in Europe, you would be well advised to get one of the directories that the companies put out and which list the firms that will accept their particular piece of plastic. And keep an eye open for those little signs in the window; you could easily find yourself in an embarrassing situation otherwise.

Another point that should be watched with those useful pieces of plastic is the problem of the rate at which your purchase may be converted into your home currency. If you want to be certain of the rate at which you will pay, insist on the establishment entering the current rate onto your credit card charge at the time you sign it—this will prevent the management from holding your charge until a more favorable rate (to them) comes along, something which could cost you more dollars than you counted on.

We would advise you, also, to check your monthly statement very carefully indeed against the counterfoils you got at the time of your purchase. It has become increasingly common for shops, hotels or restaurants to change the amounts on the original you signed, if they find they have made an error in the original bill. Sometimes, also, unscrupulous employees make this kind of change to their own advantage. The onus is on you to report the change to the credit card firm and insist on sorting the problem out.

While credit cards are easily usable in most of Europe, there are two fairly weak spots, Austria and Germany, where acceptance is less general.

Finally, you can borrow money specifically for travel, from your bank or from special firms handling travel loans.

TRAVEL DOCUMENTS. There actually was a time when you could decide to go to Europe one day and leave the next. Before World War I, you didn't even need a passport. Those days are gone, presumably forever. Today every traveler, even an infant, needs a passport, or to be on a passport. The U.S. Government issues both individual and joint family passports. Individual passports cost more but they offer flexibility. It is not always convenient, or possible, to cross frontiers as a group. You may need to separate—for business, illness, or special-interest sightseeing. Plan for maximum freedom of movement. It may be a good idea, too, to have children wear identification bracelets listing their names and U.S. passport numbers. Another tip: keep extra photos on hand in case you change your plans and need visas for additional countries.

PASSPORTS. U.S. citizens. Apply several months in advance of your expected departure date. U.S. residents must apply in person to the U.S. Passport Agency in Boston, Chicago, Honolulu, Houston, Los Angeles, Miami, New Orleans, New York, Philadelphia, San Francisco, Seattle, Stamford (Conn.), or Washington DC, or to their local County Courthouse. In addition, some 900 First Class post offices around the country are also equipped to handle passport applications. If you still have your latest passport issued within the past eight years you may use this to apply by mail. (Ask for Form DSP–82.) Otherwise, take with you: 1) a birth certificate or certified copy thereof, or other proof of citizenship. A baptismal certificate, record of elementary school enrollment, or certificate from the Bureau of the Census is also acceptable; 2) two identical photographs 2 inches square, full face, black and white or color, on nonglossy paper and taken within the past six months; 3) $35 for the passport itself plus a $7 processing fee if you are applying in person (no processing fee when applying by mail) for those 18 years and older, or, if you are under 18, $20 for the passport plus a $7 processing fee if you are applying in person (again, no extra fee when applying by mail). Adult passports are valid for 10 years, others for five years; 4) proof of identity such as a driver's license, previous passport, any governmental ID card, or a copy of an income tax return. When you receive your passport, write down its number, date and place of issue separately; if it is later lost or stolen, notify either the nearest American Consul or the Passport Office, Department of State, Washington DC 20524, as well as the local police.

If a non-citizen, you need a Treasury Sailing Permit, Form 1040C, certifying that Federal taxes have been paid; apply to your District Director of Internal Revenue for this. You will have to present various documents: 1) blue or green alien registration card; 2) passport; 3) travel tickets; 4) most recently filed Form 1040; 5) W–2 forms for the most recent full year; 6) most recent current payroll stubs or letter; 7) check to be sure this is all! To return to the United States you need a re-entry permit if you intend to remain abroad longer than 1 year. Apply for it in person at least six weeks before departure at the nearest office of the Immigration and Naturalization Service, or by mail to the Immigration and Naturalization Service, Washington, D.C.

British subjects must apply for passports on special forms obtainable from main post offices or a travel agent. The application should be sent or taken to the Passport Office according to residential area (as indicated on the guidance form) or lodged with them through a travel agent. It is best to apply for the passport 4–5 weeks before it is required, although in some cases it will be issued sooner. The regional Passport Offices are located in London, Liverpool, Peterborough, Glasgow and Newport. The application must be countersigned by your bank manager or by a solicitor, barrister, doctor, clergyman or justice of the peace who knows you personally. You will need two full-face photos. The fee is £15; passport valid for 10 years.

British Visitor's Passport. This simplified form of passport has advantages for the once-in-a-while tourist to most European countries (Yugoslavia and Eastern European countries presently excepted). Valid for one year and not renewable, it costs £7.50. Application may be made at main post offices in England, Scotland and Wales, and in Northern Ireland at the Passport Office in Belfast. Birth certificate or medical card for identification and two passport photographs are required—no other formalities.

Canadian citizens must have a valid passport. In Canada, apply in person to regional passport offices in: Edmonton, Halifax, Montreal, Toronto, Fredericton, Hamilton, London, Ottawa, Hull, Quebec, St. John's, Saskatoon, North York, Victoria, Windsor, Vancouver or Winnipeg. Or, write to: The Passport Office, 200 DuPortage, 6th Floor, Place du Center, Hull, P.Q. K1A 0G3. A \$21 fee, two photos, and evidence of citizenship are required. Canadian citizens living in the U.S. need special forms from their nearest Canadian Consulate.

VISAS. Of the countries covered in this guide, the following require a visa from American citizens: Albania, Czechoslovakia, East Germany, Hungary, Poland, Romania, and Yugoslavia (in Romania and Yugoslavia, you get a free visa on arrival). Since the U.S. has no direct diplomatic relations with Albania, Americans must apply for visas through Albanian embassies in Paris or Rome but should be warned that Americans are not often admitted.

British subjects and Canadians must have visas for Albania, Czechoslovakia, East Germany, Hungary, Poland, Romania and Bulgaria. Generally speaking, British-passport holders should apply for visas in the U.K. prior to departure, when they have booked their holiday and are in receipt of (pre-paid) service vouchers. However, certain Eastern European countries will issue visas at the border provided you have the correct documentation. Check with the official tourist bureau for the latest situation. Some evidence of identity is required (with photograph), so always carry your passport and spare passport photographs. Also, Vienna is a particularly convenient jumping-off place for Eastern Europe and has a number of tour agencies specializing in package visits to places like Prague, Cracow and Budapest, and cruises down the Danube.

Potential visitors to communist countries should ask their passport agency to provide them with the addresses of consular offices of the countries they intend to visit in order to check on last-minute details concerning documentation, though visa regulations are considerably eased in some of these countries.

Commonwealth citizens sometimes require visas where United Kingdom "patrial" residents do not. Visas may usually be procured through the consulates of the countries you wish to visit, either in your country or abroad.

HEALTH CERTIFICATES. Not needed for entry to any European country covered in this book. However, any country may demand vaccination certificates periodically and temporarily, especially if there has been a minor outbreak of smallpox or cholera anywhere in Europe. Best check in advance of your trip.

Smallpox vaccination is no longer required for U.S. and Canadian citizens returning from Western Europe, but it is "if you come from an infected area". British residents face the same kind of uncertain regulations.

Rabies. Being an island, Britain is one of the few rabies-free areas in the world, and intends to stay that way. Dogs, cats, and other warm-blooded animals arriving from abroad must be put in quarantine for six months. Persons attempting to smuggle pets into Britain face huge fines and up to one year's imprisonment, and their pets will be destroyed. These regulations are strictly enforced.

Ireland is equally strict on rabies prevention; arrivals from Britain are exempt.

 STUDENT AND BUDGET YOUTH TRAVEL. To know a country well you must live with its people; and learning a foreign language is always easier on the spot. If you are a teacher, student, or young traveler going overseas for the first time, you have a wide and exciting range of possibilities ahead of you. Many American colleges and universities sponsor language and study programs abroad, although the logistical details are usually contracted out to commercial tour operators. However, one of the major developments in the travel field in the last few years is the fact that study and special-interest travel has spread to people of all ages, interests, and walks of life, and now includes not only traditional academic subjects but a wide and increasing range of hobbies, career-oriented experience, self-fulfillment, and public service opportunities, especially for older persons who have already finished ordinary undergraduate programs and who have also done a good deal of conventional tourism and who now want something deeper, more purposeful and more concentrated. (There may sometimes be tax write-off advantages as well.) Thus, in addition to such obvious things as opera in Italy, and historic homes of England, you may travel to study accounting in Switzerland, the operation of the welfare state in Denmark, intercellular communication in France, glassmaking in Ireland, and public relations in Israel. The *Institute of International Education* (see below) offers information on about 800 programs for academic years abroad and about 900 vacation/study programs.

If you are looking for any sort of specialized and/or credit-bearing study experience, it is important to choose a program that is well-organized, experienced, and responsible. Some good sources of general information and certain administrative services (scholarships, charter flights, I.D. cards, etc.) are:

The Council on International Educational Exchange, 205 East 42 Street, New York City 10017, for summer study, travel and work programs and travel services for college and high school students, and a free Charter Flights Guide booklet.

The Institute of International Education, 809 United Nations Plaza, New York, N.Y. 10017, provides information on study opportunities abroad and administers scholarships and fellowships for international study and training.

Travel Delegates Corp., 801 Second Avenue, New York, N.Y. 10017, provides information and help on all aspects of student travel.

A few of the many specific programs available are:

The Experiment in International Living, Kipling Rd., Brattleboro, Vermont 05301, offers high school students summer programs in 25 countries; a month with a foreign family and another month of travel around the country with the hosts.

AFS International/Intercultural Program (formerly the American Field Service), 313 E. 43rd St., New York, 10017, sends over 6,000 students, ages 15 to 18, every year to live either a summer or a full school year with families in nearly 58 countries. Cost for an academic year runs to about $4,450, for a summer about $2,375. They also offer language study programs for about $2,700.

Academic Travel Abroad, 1346 Connecticut Ave. N.W., Washington, D.C. 20036, arranges academic credit-bearing study tours year-round for teachers, students and educational institutions such as museums.

AIESEC (Association International des Etudiants en Sciences Economiques et Commerciales), U.S. National Committee, 14 West 23rd St., New York, N.Y. 10010, is a student-run organization which finds work for college students majoring in business or economics.

IAESTE (International Association for the Exchange of Students for Technical Experience), American City Building, Suite 217, Columbia, Maryland 21044, does the same thing for engineering, science, architecture and agriculture majors.

The American Institute for Foreign Study, 102 Greenwich Avenue, Greenwich, Conn. 06830, offers tours, accompanied by lecturers, for high school and college students and teachers. Academic credit offered.

New York University, 19 University Place, New York, N.Y. 10003, offers both undergraduate and graduate academic years in both France and Spain.

Agencies offering inexpensive, non-academic travel possibilities include:

American Youth Hostels, Inc., 1332 I St., Suite 800, Washington, D.C. 20005, has low-cost overseas activity arrangements. Membership in AYH makes you eligible for the entire network of youth hostels in 50 countries all over the world. In addition to its Directory, AYH also handles hosteling and camping equipment, and runs conducted hosteling tours.

The above is by no means a complete list, and what is available changes from year to year. Also, while the organizations listed above have been in business for some time, some newer ones sending groups to the British Isles, Scandinavia, Western and Central Europe and the Mediterranean are: *Adventure Center,* 5540 College Ave., Oakland, Cal. 94618; *Harwood Tours & Travel,* 2428 Guadalupe St., Austin, Texas 78705; *Students Abroad,* 2378 NE 28 St., Lighthouse Point, Fla. 33064; and *Your World Travel,* 2050 West Goodhope Rd., Milwaukee, Wisc. 53209. The principal clearinghouses for information, the best places to start, remain the first two listed, the C.I.E.E. and the I.I.E. Begin by writing for free lists of all their publications in the field, then narrow your focus from there.

TRAVEL AGENTS. Travel agents are experts in the increasingly complicated business of tourism. A good travel agent (and they are located everywhere) can save you time and money through his knowledge of details which you could not be expected to know about. He can help you take advantage of special reductions in rail fares and the like, save you *time* by making it unnecessary for you to waste precious days abroad trying to get tickets and reservations. In the all-important phase of planning your trip, even if you wish to travel independently, it is wise to take advantage of the services of these specialists. (Travel to certain Eastern European countries can be arranged *only* through special tourist agencies—see above.) Whether you select *Maupintour Associates, American Express, Thomas Cook,* or a smaller organization is only a matter of your preference. But you should be sure he is reliable.

If you wish him merely to arrange a steamship or airline ticket or to book you on a package tour, his services should cost you nothing as he almost certainly has a commission from the tour operator.

If, on the other hand, you wish him to plan for you an individual itinerary he will make a service charge on the total cost of the work he does. This may amount to 10 or 15 percent, but it will *save* you money on balance. If your travel budget is limited, you should frankly explain this to your agent and he will work out an interesting itinerary accordingly.

If you cannot locate a travel agent near your home, write, if in America, to the *American Society of Travel Agents,* 4400 MacArthur Blvd. N.W., Washington D.C. 20007; *A.S.T.A.-West Coast,* Travel Wise, 127 C St., San Diego, CA 92101; in Canada, to *A.S.T.A. Canada,* Royal City Travel Ltd., 450 Sixth St., New Westminster, B.C. V3L 3B3; and in Britain to the *Association of British Travel Agents,* 55 Newman St., London W.1. Any agency affiliated with these organizations is likely to be reliable. The *United States Tour Operators Association,* 211 E. 51st St., Suite 4B, New York, N.Y. 10022 will send you a list of its members, all of whom are bonded for your protection. (In the last few years, the upheavals in airfares particularly have caused the failure of a number of smaller tour operators, leaving their customers stranded and with no recourse. This cannot happen with U.S.T.O.A. members.)

NATIONAL TOURIST OFFICES. All the major tourist countries maintain official information bureaux in important cities—New York, San Francisco, London, Toronto and many others. They have a wealth of free printed matter to help you in planning your trip and they are at your service to give you any additional special information you may require. There is no charge for any of this. They do *not,* however, issue tickets or make hotel reservations.

Addresses of some of the principal European tourist offices in the United States, Canada, and Gt. Britain are as follows:

United States

Austrian National Tourist Office, 500 Fifth Ave., New York City 10110; 3440 Wilshire Blvd., Los Angeles, Calif. 90010; 500 N. Michigan Ave., Chicago, Ill. 60611; 4800 San Felipe, Houston, Tex. 77056.

Belgian National Tourist Office, 745 Fifth Ave., New York City 10022.

British Tourist Authority, 40 West 57th St., New York City 10019; 875 N. Michigan Ave., Chicago, Ill. 60611; 612 S. Flower St., Los Angeles, Calif. 90017; Plaza of the Americas, North Tower, Suite 750, Box 346, Dallas, Tex. 75201.

Bulgarian Tourist Office (Balkantourist), 161 East 86th St., New York, N.Y. 10028.

Cyprus Tourism Organization, 13 E. 40th St., New York, N.Y. 10016.

Czechoslovak Travel Bureau (Cedok), 10 E. 40th St., New York City 10016.

Danish National Tourist Office, 655 Third Ave., New York, N.Y. 10017.

Finnish Tourist Board, 655 Third Ave., New York, N.Y. 10017.

French Government Tourist Office, 610 Fifth Ave., New York City 10022; 645 N. Michigan Ave., Chicago, Ill. 60611; 9401 Wilshire Blvd., Suite 314, Beverly Hills, Calif. 90212; 103 World Trade Center, Dallas, Texas 75258.

German Tourist Information Office, 747 Third Ave., New York, N.Y. 10017; 444 S. Flower St., Los Angeles, Calif. 90071.

Greek National Tourist Organization, 5th floor, Olympic Tower, 645 Fifth Avenue, New York, N.Y. 10022; 611 W. Sixth Street, Los Angeles, Calif. 90017; 168 N. Michigan Ave., Chicago, Ill. 60601.

Hungarian Travel Bureau (IBUSZ), 630 Fifth Avenue, New York, N.Y. 10111.

Icelandic National Tourist Office, 610b Fifth Ave., Rockefeller Center, New York, N.Y. 10017; 908 17th St., N.W., Washington, D.C. 20036.

Irish Tourist Board, 757 Third Ave., New York City 10017; 230 N. Michigan Ave., Chicago, Ill. 60601; 625 Market St., San Francisco, Calif. 94105.

Italian Government (ENIT) Travel Office, 630 Fifth Ave., New York City 10111; 500 N. Michigan Ave., Chicago, Ill. 60611; 360 Post Street, San Francisco, Calif. 94108.

Luxembourg Tourist Information Office, 801 Second Ave., New York City 10017.

Maltese Consulate, 249 E. 35th St., New York, N.Y. 10016.

Monaco Gov't Tourist Office, 845 Third Ave., New York, N.Y. 10022.

Netherlands Board of Tourism, 355 Lexington Ave., New York, N.Y. 10017; 605 Market St., San Francisco, Calif. 94105.

Norwegian National Tourist Office, 655 Third Ave., New York, N.Y. 10017.

Polish Travel Bureau (Orbis), 500 Fifth Ave., New York, N.Y. 10110.

Portuguese Tourist & Information Office (Casa de Portugal), 548 Fifth Ave., New York, N.Y. 10036.

Spanish National Tourist Office, 665 Fifth Ave., New York, N.Y. 10016; 845 Michigan Ave., Chicago, Ill., 60611; 1 Hallidie Plaza 801, San Francisco, Calif. 94102; Casa de Hidalgo, Hypolita St. George, St. Augustine, Fla. 32084; 4800 The Galleria, 5085 Westheimer, Houston, Tex. 77056.

Swedish National Tourist Office, 655 Third Ave., New York, N.Y. 10017.

Swiss National Tourist Office, 608 Fifth Ave., New York, N.Y. 10020; 250 Stockton St., San Francisco, Calif. 94108.

Turkish Tourism and Information Office, 821 U.N. Plaza, New York, N.Y. 10017.

Yugoslav State Tourism Office, 630 Fifth Ave., Rockefeller Center, Suite 280, New York, N.Y. 10111.

Canada

Austrian National Tourist Office, 1010 Sherbrooke St. W., Suite 1410, Montreal, P.Q. H3A 2R7; 2 Bloor St. E., Suite 3330, Toronto, Ont. M4W 1A8; 736 Granville St., Suite 1220, Vancouver, B.C. V6Z 1J2.

British Tourist Authority, 94 Cumberland St., Suite 600, Toronto, Ont. M5R 3N3; 409 Granville St., Suite 451, Vancouver, B.C. V6C 1T2.

Danish National Tourist Office, Box 115, Station N, Toronto, Ont. M8V 3S4.

Finland, c/o Scandinavian National Tourist Office, 655 Third Ave., New York, N.Y. 10017.

French Government Tourist Office, 1981 McGill College Ave., Montreal, P.Q. H3A 2W9; 1 Dundas St. W., Suite 2405, Box 8, Toronto, Ont. M5G 1Z3.

German National Tourist Office, 2 Fundy, P.O. Box 417, Place Bonaventure, Montreal, P.Q. H5A 1B8.

Greek National Tourist Organization, 1233 de la Montague, Montreal, P.Q. H3G 1Z2.

Irish Tourist Board, 10 King St. E., Toronto, Ont., M5C 1C3.

Italian Government Travel Office (ENIT), 3 Place Ville Marie, Montreal, P.Q. H3B 2E3.

Netherlands Board of Tourism, 25 Adelaide St. E., Toronto, Ont., M5Z 1Y2.

Norway, c/o Scandinavian National Tourist Office, 655 Third Ave., New York, N.Y. 10017.

Spanish National Tourist Office, 60 Bloor St. W., Suite 201, Toronto, Ont. M4W 3B8.

Sweden, c/o Scandinavian National Tourist Office, 655 Third Ave., New York, N.Y. 10017.

Swiss National Tourist Office, Commerce Court West, Box 215, Commerce Court Postal Station, Toronto, Ont. M5L 1E8.

Great Britain

Andorran Delegation, 63 Westover Rd., London S.W.18.
Austrian National Tourist Office, 30 St. George St., London W.1.
Belgian National Tourist Office, 38 Dover St., London W.1.
British Tourist Authority, Thames Tower, Blacks Rd., London W.6.
Bulgarian National Tourist Office, 18 Princes St., London W.1.
Czechoslovak Travel Bureau (Cedok), 17–18 Old Bond St., London W.1.
Danish Tourist Board, 169–173 Regent St. (6th Floor), London W.1.
Finnish Tourist Board, 66–68 Haymarket, London S.W.1.
French Tourist Office, 178 Piccadilly, London W.1.
German National Tourist Office, 61 Conduit St., London W.1.
Gibraltar Tourist Office, Arundel Great Court, 179 Strand, London W.C.2.
Greek National Tourist Organization, 195–197 Regent St., London W.1.
Hungarian, Danube Travel, 6 Conduit St., London W.1.
Iceland Tourist Information Bureau, 73 Grosvenor St., London W.1.
Irish Tourist Board, (Eire), 150 New Bond St., London W.1.
Italian State Tourist Office, 1 Princes St., London W.1.
Liechtenstein (see Switzerland).
Luxembourg National Tourist Office, 36–37 Piccadilly, London W.1.
Malta Government Tourist Office, Suite 207, College House, Wright's Lane, London W.8.
Netherlands Board of Tourism, 25–28 Buckingham Gate, London S.W.1.
Norwegian National Tourist Office, 20 Pall Mall, London S.W.1.
Polorbis Travel Ltd. (Poland), 82 Mortimer St., London W.1.
Portuguese National Tourist Office, New Bond St. House, 1–5 New Bond St., London W.1.
Rumanian National Tourist Office (Carpati), New Bond St. House, 1–5 New Bond St., London W.1.
Spanish National Tourist Office, 57 St. James's St., London S.W.1.
Swedish Tourist Board, 3 Cork St., London W.1.
Swiss National Tourist Office, 1 New Coventry St., London W.1.
Turkish Tourism Information Office, Egyptian House (1st Floor), 170–173 Piccadilly, London W.1.
Yugoslavian National Tourist Office, 143 Regent St., London W.1.
Many countries also maintain National Tourist Offices in principal cities within Continental Europe, which may prove useful if you suddenly decide to change your itinerary and want to collect last-minute information.

HANDICAPPED TRAVEL. One of the newest, and largest, groups to enter the travel scene is the handicapped, literally millions of people who are in fact physically able to travel and who do so enthusiastically when they know that they can move about with safety and comfort. Generally these tours parallel those of the non-handicapped traveler, but at a more leisurely pace, with everything checked out in advance to eliminate all inconvenience, whether the traveler happens to be deaf, blind or in a wheelchair.

For a complete list of tour operators who arrange such travel write to the *Society for the Advancement of Travel for the Handicapped,* 26 Court St., Brooklyn, N.Y. 11242. An excellent source of information in this field is the book, *Access to the World: A Travel Guide for the Handicapped,* by Louise Weiss, available from *Facts on File,* 460 Park Ave. South, New York, N.Y. 10016. This book covers travel by air, ship, train, bus, car, recreational vehicle; hotels and motels; travel agents and tour operators; destinations; access guides; health and medical problems; and travel organizations. Another major source of help is the Travel Information Center, Moss Rehabilitation Hospital, 12th St. and Tabor Road, Philadelphia, Penn. 19141. And for an international directory of access guides, write to *Rehabilitation International,* 1123 Broadway, New York, N.Y. 10010, for their listing of sources of information on facilities for the handicapped all over the world.

From the U.K.: The *Airline Transport Users Committee,* 129 Kingsway, London W.C.2, publish a very useful booklet for handicapped passengers entitled *Care in the Air,* available free of charge.

But one of the very best guides is a book published by the *Royal Association for Disability and Rehabilitation,* 25 Mortimer St., London W.1, called *Holidays for the Physically Disabled.* Available from either W.H. Smith or R.A.D.A.R. direct for £2 (no charge for post or packing), its 668 pages provide an in-depth coverage of the length and breadth of the United Kingdom. Another R.A.D.A.R. publication is *Motoring and Mobility,* which gives details of facilities available to the handicapped motorist in Britain and on car ferries to the Continent. Latest edition now available, price £4, direct from R.A.D.A.R. only (again, no post or packing cost).

Also very useful are the *Access* series of booklets, giving details of a wide range of accommodations for the handicapped, as well as of restaurants and theaters and other tourist attractions, and also travel options for the place in question. At the time of writing, the following booklets were available: *Paris* (new edition now available), *Loire, Brittany* (including access to beaches), *Channel Ports, Jersey,* and an extensive *London.* Details from Access, 39 Bradley Gardens, West Ealing, London W.13.

 PRACTICAL BAGGAGE TIPS. Always pack your passport separately, enough money (both travelers' checks and some local currency to use upon arrival) and any medications you may need, and have them readily available, preferably on your person. Take along copies of all medical prescriptions, including eyeglasses, in case you need a refill. Pack film separately or in special lined bags for protection against airport-security X-rays.

Don't buy cheap luggage. Borrow if you must, but have bags whose construction and locks you can trust. Never leave your luggage unlocked anywhere, anytime. Airlines will not take luggage that is not tagged with your name and home address. Put on your destination address as well, with dates of arrival and departure, in case your bags go astray and have to be forwarded. Put your identification inside, too; special stickers are free from any airline. Remove all old tags; they just confuse things. Near the handle put a piece of some bright-colored tape to help pick out your bag from all the similar models on your plane, train, or bus.

With porters very thin on the ground—in fact they should be registered as a nearly extinct species—it is wise to have two small bags rather than one large one. This will mean an evenly distributed load when you are forced to carry them for any distance.

At airports, watch to be sure that your bags go on the conveyor belt, and keep your stubs until you have carefully compared the numbers; those stubs are your receipts. Lost luggage must be reported within four hours after arrival. Remember that the carrier's liability is limited, so carry extra baggage insurance if you need it. It's available from travel agents.

If your baggage is oversize on your return trip, get the rates for shipping the excess separately by Air Freight instead of paying the higher rates for excess baggage.

Whenever you can, on short sections of your trip, try to make do with just your on-flight bag. If you are on a weekend jaunt, this will save you having to wait around for hours to claim your baggage at the airport.

LANGUAGES. Perhaps you already know a smattering of Spanish, French, Greek or some other European language, and even if it's just enough to let you order a meal, ask directions, and say "please" and "thank you", you'll find that it makes your trip that much more enjoyable. It will also, in most parts of Europe, please the locals when they hear you trying to communicate. Although the use of English is very widespread, there are always situations where it will help to have a smattering of the native tongue.

If your command of a foreign language needs some brushing up, or even if there's nothing there to brush up, it would be well worth your while to purchase a packaged course, or, better yet, attend a live one before you go. Most universities and junior and community colleges offer the level and scope that you will need as part of their adult and continuing education programs. You might alternatively want to investigate the numerous recorded language courses available on disc and cassette.

Britons can least expensively learn a language by attending classes at a school of further education run by their local education authority, or otherwise attend one of the numerous private language schools throughout the country.

Whichever method you follow, remember that what you are after is a conversational course. Don't get yourself immersed in the deep technicalities of a language, to the extent that you are petrified to speak in case you get the grammar wrong.

SPECIAL INTEREST TRAVEL

TOURING WITH A PURPOSE. More and more people are looking for unusual methods of travel and off-beat, but purposeful, pastimes. The standard Grand Tour of the Continent's sights is still popular, particularly among those with limited time and those who expect to see Europe only once in their lives. But among younger holidaymakers, or anyone who plans to return, the special interest tour is rocketing in popularity. If you don't like packages, you can still go it alone, putting purpose into travel by fixing up special visits before you leave, and if you don't want to plan ahead, you can even wait till you get to Europe before choosing a special interest tour.

To get the best from a holiday, try to live a life of complete contrast to your normal routine. Off-beat arrangements which bring an extra dimension to travel should be just the thing to give your vacation an added zip.

To be off-beat, you don't have to don oxygen bottles and flippers to explore bedrock beneath the ocean. It's just as off-beat to go trailering around Ireland in a horse-drawn gypsy caravan. If you are interested in comfort, how about the kind which you find in a European castle? Eighteen countries of Europe have some hundreds of castles where paying guests are welcome. Travel agents and the national tourist offices of these countries can provide details. Contentment can be found visiting European gardens or when listening to great music beautifully played or sung at one of Europe's international music festivals. Younger travelers wanting something less sophisticated should be happy on a bachelor's tour or at a house party, pony-trekking, cycling or working abroad in return for board and lodging.

Increasingly in recent years, specialty tours have been designed for specific groups or organizations, rather than for the general public. Those with a keen interest in, say, bird-watching or archeology, are encouraged to seek out professional or amateur associations. These will either have tours themselves, or will be able to guide you to others who do.

The more ambitious of the special interest tours start and finish in the United States or Canada. Those you can book in Europe, though covering a wider range of interests, are usually shorter (seven or fourteen days being the popular length), which enables them to be slotted into a standard European touring itinerary for a few days' fun. While following a favorite hobby or pastime, share your vacation on these shorter tours with Europeans, who will extend a warmer welcome for no other reason than your interest in enjoying a European special interest holiday in their company in preference to one surrounded by fellow Americans.

Though the selection of special interest tours in, and starting from, Great Britain is wide, arrangements are either in the hands of (almost) non-profit travel associations or a small number of specialist tour operators happy to concentrate on providing something a little different. Most British travel agents and operators, naturally, are happier featuring two-week package holidays to European bathing resorts and the like, for a reasonable profit, but you will find many suggestions in the following pages for firms that have made a particular subject their specialty and come up every year with fresh and exciting tours to interest those who wish to use their vacations to indulge their hobby.

Because of Britain's proximity to the Continent and the greater flow of tourist traffic between the U.S. and the rest of Europe, special interest tours from there are more numerous (and often better organized) than those from the U.S.A. If you spot a tour in the following pages which you'd like to join from the U.S.A., therefore, ask your travel agent if it is possible . . . he may be able to arrange it for you.

ART AND ARCHEOLOGY. From the U.S.: One of the leading Art Tour operators is *Exprinter Tours*, 500 Fifth Ave., New York, N.Y. 10110, with about 30 different tours to art treasures the world over, including such lesser known parts as Macedonia, Transylvania and Sicily. Most European tours are 17 days.

Another well-established and experienced firm in this field is *Maupintour*, 1515 St. Andrews Dr., Lawrence, Kan. 66044, with tours to Eastern Europe and the Mediterranean.

A recent entry in this field is *Unique Travel Experiences*, 1043 E. Green St., Pasadena, California 91106.

In archeology a leading specialist is *Sunnyland Tours*, 166 Main Street, Hackensack, N.J. 07601, with packages around the Mediterranean, the Aegean and the Holy Land, lasting 10, 15 or 22 days.

From the U.K.: Long the leaders in the field of guided art and archeology tours are *Swan Hellenic Art Treasure Tours Ltd.*, Canberra House, 47 Middlesex St., London E.1 7AL. Each tour is accompanied by a guest lecturer, as well as a tour manager, and itineraries include some of the most glorious reminders of Europe's rich heritage. Not all the holidays follow the beaten path; for example, there is a 14-day journey through the Italian hill towns starting at £1,138, or 15 days in Thrace and Macedonia from £1,061.

Serenissima and Heritage, 2 Lower Sloane St., London S.W.1, do a couple of splendid Italian tours: one, The Villas and Gardens of Northern Italy, lasts 11 days and starts at £1,385; the other is The Medieval Towns of Tuscany, and the 10 days start at £1,175. All of their tours are accompanied by a native or long-time-resident expert on the culture of the area. Other subjects include Florence, The Painted Churches of Romania, Byzantine Venice and Ravenna, The Bernese Oberland, and Prague and Budapest. Note, however, that itineraries do change from year to year.

For the vacationer who wishes to paint, rather than just look, the specialists are *Galleon World Travel Association Ltd.*, Galleon House, 52 High St., Sevenoaks, Kent TN13 1JG, who arrange painting holidays on the Continent. Choice of centers includes Bruges in Belgium (10 days from £248, 8 from £222; both return coach from London). Galleon also offers painting holidays in Britain, for example at Chichester from £219 for a week, at Keswick from £185 (also a week). Though most packages last 7 days, they also do some weekend vacations. These practical holidays are led by an expert in either oil or water colors. Group numbers are limited so that everyone can get attention.

Another specialist in this field is *Cox and Kings*, 46 Marshall St., London W.1. Tutorage and basic equipment are included with all their packages, and locations include: the Spanish Pyrenees (9 nights from £363, 14 from £475); the Midi-Pyrenees, Le Delmazou and Souel in France (7 nights from £375, 14 from £593), and Montecastello in Italy (14 nights from £597). All prices include flight London–London and full-board accommodations.

Prospect Art Tours Ltd., 10 Barley Mow Passage, London W.4, have developed a fine reputation for their art-historian-conducted tours which cover a multitude of destinations, and touch on a variety of different areas of interest, from London's Smaller Galleries (3 days/2 nights, £116), to French Gothic (5 nights, £282), which concentrates on the best of the Gothic architecture of Northern France, to Renaissance Art in Florence (4 nights, £249). Prices all-inclusive.

The aptly-named *Tour de Force*, 251 Brompton Rd., London S.W.3, are newcomers to the art-and-architecture field. They offer escorted tours—claiming to open doors otherwise closed to the general public—to Hungary, to Poland, and to East Germany and West Berlin. *Note:* Tour de Force holidays can be booked in the U.S. via *Tiberti Travel Inc.*, 177 East 87th St., New York, NY 10128.

BLACK CULTURE. For the black traveler to Europe (or indeed any other part of the world), *Henderson Travel Service*, 931 Martin Luther King Jr. Dr., Atlanta, Georgia 30314, specializes in tours for both individuals and groups that combine Europe's traditional sights with stops that spotlight the influence of black art, theater, history and culture.

CLUB MÉDITERRANÉE. The leading operator of "summer villages" for sun-seekers is *Club Méditerranée International, Inc.*, 3 East 54th St., New York,

N.Y. 10022; Box 4660, Scottsdale, Ariz. 85261; 5 Place Ville Marie, Suite 1401, Montreal, P.Q. H3B 2G2, Canada; and 106 Brompton Rd., London S.W.3, England. Villages all around the Mediterranean, including the Near East and North Africa, as well as in the mountains of France and Switzerland. Tours include transfers, double occupancy rooms, three meals daily, wine with all meals, free use of sports facilities (water skiing, sailboats, scuba-diving, etc.) and evening entertainment. For an untrammeled holiday these villages are hard to beat, they represent what is almost a new way of life.

 FLORA AND FAUNA. From the U.S.: *Questers Tours and Travel, Inc.*, 257 Park Ave. S., New York, N.Y. 10010, have an exciting program of worldwide nature tours. Among their offerings for Europe are—16 days in Iceland, looking at rare birds and exciting landscape, land cost $2,475; a visit to the Outer Islands and Highlands of Scotland, 21 days, $2,485, visiting the birds, Stone Age remains and many other intriguing features of this attractive region; 17 days to Switzerland, $2,405 total cost, paying particular attention to the Alpine rarities of the country; Greece, 16 days for $2,025 and 20 days in Spain for $2,485 viewing birds and rare animals as well as the ancient sites in both countries.

From the U.K.: The British are great lovers of wildlife and natural scenery, so it is no surprise that you can select from numerous tours which concentrate on these subjects. Bird-watching is just one interest. *Sunbird,* at P.O. Box 76, Sandy, Bedfordshire SG19 1DF (tel. 0767 82969), offer ornithology holidays in France, Spain, Greece, Poland, Austria, and many other parts of the world. Two weeks touring Fontainebleau, the Camargue, the environs of Provence, and the Pyrenees costs about $1795 (this price is ex-Paris—getting there is extra). 7 days in Majorca starts at around £560, including flight. All Sunbird tours are led by an expert and co-ordinated with the ornithological calendar. *Note:* Sunbird holidays can be booked **in the U.S.** via parent company *Wings Inc.,* Box 889, N.E. Harbor, ME 04662.

Cox and Kings (address, see under *Art and Archeology* above) do a wide range of botany and wildflower holidays throughout Europe—taking in Spain, Corsica, Austria, Sweden, Italy, Switzerland, and the Aegean Islands. For example, 2 weeks based at Saas Fee in the Swiss Alps start at £535, at Kandersteg £559 (also 2 weeks). Both include flight London–London and half-board accommodations.

Swan Hellenic (again, see under *Art and Archeology*) might also have a selection of packages in this field on offer in 1987, but their plans were still to be finalized as we went to press, so check.

 GOURMET FOOD AND DRINK. From the U.S.: *Floating Through Europe,* 271 Madison Ave., New York, N.Y. 10016, which courses a fleet of luxuriously equipped barges through European inland waterways year-round, offers several tours for wine and champagne aficionados. Among them are the "Champagne Country Cruise," the "Burgundy Wine Country Cruise," the "Royal Thames," and the "Shakespeare Country Cruise." Expeditions last 3 or 6 days; costs run from approximately $600 to well over $3,000 (not including airfare).

For those interested in cooking gourmet food as well as eating it, *Society Expeditions,* 723 Broadway E., Seattle, WA 98102, offer "Secrets of Burgundy," an 8-day tour of Paris and the surrounding wine-country: Dijon, Burgundy, and the Côte d'Or. Travelers are housed in Chez Camille, an inn equipped with its own restaurant, and are instructed in the art of fine cuisine by owner/chef Armand Poinsot. Cost runs about $2,000 (not including airfare).

Wine and Gourmet Tours of France are offered by *Travel Plans International,* 1200 Harger Rd., Oak Brook, Ill. 60521. Allows you enough time in Paris to do the gourmet bit at special restaurants.

A very intriguing group of tours is offered by the *Bombard Society,* 6727 Curran St., McLean, VA 22101 (tel. 1–800–862–8537). This establishment boasts the world's largest fleet of hot-air balloons which, in the Champagne Balloon Tour, will float the traveler over the wine regions of France, touching down at various sacred spots to sample the glories of French wine and cuisine. Balloon tours are also offered over the Loire and Burgundy. Austria's Salzburg and Siena (Italy) and Lucerne (Switzerland). Accommodations are all deluxe and the cost proves it: 6½ days at approximately $3,800, not including airfare. Pricey, but very popular.

And *The World of Oz*, 3 E. 54 St., New York, N.Y. 10022 offers one- and two-week gourmet and culture tours to Paris, the south of France and Burgundy that include wine-tasting, cooking demonstrations and participation lessons as well as both general and food-related sightseeing.

From the U.K.: Autumn is the best time for wine and beer lovers, for then Europe resounds with the gaiety of drinking festivals. A number of travel agents offer short tours of vineyards in Burgundy, Bordeaux, Alsace and the Rhine Valley, often coinciding with the fall festivals. Among them is *World Wine Tours Ltd.*, of 70 North St., London S.W.4 OHE, who do two packages to the Loire Valley; both last 6 days and cost £350 all-inclusive (coach travel, accommodations, all meals). Four days is the allocation for their Champagne Wine Tour, for £250. All tours are led by experts of the very highest repute.

Page and Moy, 136–140 London Rd., Leicester, cater for the vacationer who wishes to learn some of the nuances of French cuisine with their course and demonstrations in Brittany, which range from £129 (ex-Portsmouth) and £139–149 (ex-London), depending on time of year, for the 5 days (4 nights); transport is by boat, then coach. Excursions can be arranged, but at additional cost.

Newcomers in the gastronomy field are *Tour de Force* (address, see *Art and Archeology*), who as we went to press had just introduced their first package, to Belgium, but who may well have expanded their program by 1987.

Tourist offices in the wine districts of West Germany can provide details of tastings in the vineyards of their district, while the German Wine Academy organizes wine seminars (leaflet available from the National Tourist Office).

 MEET THE PEOPLE. Although there are enough museums, scenery, historic monuments and shops in Europe to keep the average tourist panting, many travelers want to penetrate beneath the surface and know what foreign people are really like in their own homes. A number of organized meet-the-people projects exist to satisfy this natural and laudable curiosity.

The prototype of all these schemes for promoting closer international relationships among people is the celebrated *Experiment in International Living*. Founded in 1932, The Experiment introduced the "homestay" experience as the vital educational method of in-depth, cross-cultural communication. High school and college students interested in a summer of semester-length Experiment programs should write The Experiment, Brattleboro, Vermont 05301.

Plan your own trip using lists of hosts with similar interests throughout Europe. *The U.S. Servas Committee, Inc.,* Room 706, 11 John St., New York, N.Y. 10038, is a non-profit, non-governmental, interracial and interfaith organization of approved hosts and travelers whose purpose is to promote peace through understanding and friendship. Travelers are invited to share in the life of the home and the community. Stays are usually for two nights, and no money is exchanged between host and traveler. Membership is $30 per person per year, plus a $15 refundable deposit for the list of hosts. You are asked to supply a written application, and you must receive orientation and approval by a Servas interviewer. Servas now has hosts in more than 100 countries. This is definitely not meant as a cheap way to travel, but as a rewarding experience through the sharing of ideas and daily life.

Austrian American Society, Stallburggasse 2, 1010 Vienna, will help you contact local families. Also offices in Salzburg and Innsbruck. Please write in advance if possible.

Meet the British. A folder listing various private organizations which make arrangements for this program is available from the British Tourist Authority, 40 W. 57 St., New York, N.Y. 10019.

Visitors to Bulgaria wishing to experience life as lived by the Bulgarians should visit the tourist bureaux found in main towns, and some smaller ones, where arrangements can be made.

A very useful organization for Americans wishing to meet Scandinavians is *Friends Overseas,* 68–04 Dartmouth St., Forest Hills, N.Y. 11375. They cater mostly for the professional classes, but can make arrangements for anyone wishing to meet, and learn more about, Scandinavians. Send a self-addressed, stamped envelope.

In Denmark, local tourist offices in nine provincial cities will arrange an evening in a Danish home for you on 24 hours notice under the "Meet the Danes" program. In Copenhagen, through the famous Kiosk P in the Central Station you can arrange lodging in private homes. And the Danish National Tourist Office will supply information on farm vacations, where you live on and take part in the life of working farms.

In Greece, your best bet is to contact the tourist police in whichever town you wish to stay. They will be able to put you in touch with households offering accommodations; though you will find you probably will not be able to eat with the family, as the custom is to eat out.

The Irish Tourist Board, 757 Third Ave., New York, NY 10017, has applications to *Meet the Irish* programs.

For an extended stay—a minimum of one week—with a local Italian host, contact: *Ente Provinciale Turismo* in the city in which you are interested or *Azienda Autonoma Soggiorno Turismo.* Not all local tourist offices offer such arrangements.

There is no organized scheme in Spain, but if you wish to stay with a local family the local papers usually include a list of suitable establishments.

Information on the *Don't Miss the Swiss* program can be obtained from the Swiss National Tourist Office, 608 Fifth Ave., New York 10020, or the Zurich Tourist Office, Bahnhofplatz 15, 8001 Zurich.

Most Yugoslavs are keen on meeting Americans. Contact local tourist offices in each particular city.

 MUSIC AND DRAMA. From the U.S.: Between May and October each year there are about 45 *major* music festivals in Europe plus at least 70 others. Many of them sell out well in advance, so it is obviously wise to plan ahead. One agency with much experience in this field is:

Dailey-Thorp Inc., 315 West 57th St., New York, NY 10019 (tel. 212–307–1555), runs tours to all the major centers (Vienna, Budapest, Munich, Salzburg, Bayreuth, London, Edinburgh) as well as many others. They offer a very wide range of tours particularly emphasizing opera. All accommodations are deluxe, seat reservations are the best. Most tours are about 2 weeks.

Both *TWA* and *British Airways* offer theater packages to London. The details of these vary from year to year, but they are always an excellent way for the theater addict to get a concentrated drama fix at very competitive rates.

From the U.K.: *Specialised Travel P.A. Ltd.,* 4 Hanger Green, London W.5, are agents for the *European Association of Music Festivals* and carry information on some 43 music festivals, from the major ones like Bayreuth to the smaller ones like Perugia and Bath. They do *not* hold tickets themselves, but will make bookings provided they are given sufficient notice; they will also set up a package deal for you, including travel and accommodations. Many of these festivals include drama as well as music on their programs, and nearly all of them are held in surroundings of the utmost interest. The headquarters of the European Association of Music Festivals is at 122 rue de Lausanne, 1202 Geneva, Switzerland.

Sovereign Enterprise Holidays, P.O. Box 410, West London Terminal, Cromwell Rd., London S.W.7, offers opera and music tours to just about every major center in the world, among them, Venice, Verona, Vienna, Wexford, New York, Moscow and Leningrad. Cost includes tickets and guaranteed seats, plus airfare and accommodations.

 SKINNY-DIP HOLIDAYS. From the U.S.: The ultimate in sun worship is to be had in the naturist or nudist holiday. These are very popular throughout Europe. Among the tours offered from the U.S. are those of *Skinny-Dip Tours,* R.D. 1 Box 294, Bloomingburg, New York, N.Y. 12721. Vacation villages and cruise ship vacations are featured; the main areas are France, Corsica, Yugoslavia and Spain; and the Caribbean in the Western Hemisphere.

From the U.K.: Whether you call yourself a naturist or a nudist, the up and coming place to take off your clothes is along Yugoslavia's sunny Adriatic coast. *Yugotours* (150 Regent St., London, W.1) will fly you there and back for £191–215 (1 week) or £280–308 (2 weeks). Yugotours have a wide choice of naturist centers on the Adriatic at a corresponding range of prices.

Peng Travel, 86 Station Rd., Gidea Park, Essex, also has visits to Yugoslav naturist resorts, as well as to France, mainland Spain and the Canaries. One of the largest naturist centers in the Mediterranean is the *Club Corsicana,* where Peng offer holidays starting at £201 for 7 days (very basic facilities) up to £335 for 14 nights (with all comforts) in high season; flights and transfers are included. It has 3 miles of private sandy beach and is an ideal resort for families with children. It is located on the east coast of Corsica, sharing the dune-backed beaches with the naturist resorts of Tropica and La Bagheera.

 PILGRIMAGES. Certain travel agents specialize in pilgrimage tours. Major destinations are Portugal, Spain, Ireland, France and Italy. Departures are mostly between April and October, and a 15-day itinerary will cost around $1500. *Travelink Tours Int'l,* 401 S. Milwaukee Ave., Wheeling, IL 60090, runs pilgrimage tours chiefly to Palestine but including Rome and important sites in Greece.

Trips to sites of special importance in the Jewish heritage are run by *Rabbi Frederick E. Werbell Tours* and *Scandinavian-Jewish Experience Tours,* 45 W. 34 St., Suite 712, New York, N.Y. 10001.

Pilgrims International, c/o 36 Mark Mansions, Westville Rd., London W12 9PS, is a nonsectarian organization that arranges pilgrimages across northern Spain following the medieval pilgrims' route to Santiago de Compostela. They also do pilgrimages to British holy sites.

SINGLES OF ALL AGES. More and more people, of all ages and social situations, are choosing to travel by themselves. The great disadvantage is the punishing extra expense of the single supplement, a surcharge that can run up to as much as 50% above the basic price of the trip on an overseas tour. Because most accommodation is still designed for couples, several travel agencies now specialize in finding ways to beat the extra expense and to introduce people of similar tastes and interests. The largest of these is *Gramercy Travel Systems,* Inc., 444 Madison Ave., New York City 10022, with its *Singleworld* Tours. Some others are: *Single Party Tours,* 480 Seventh Ave., New York, N.Y. 10018; *Travel Mates,* 49 West 44th St., New York, N.Y. 10036; and *Travel Companion Exchange,* Box 833, Amityville, N.Y. 11701. Some of these agencies charge small membership fees ($5–$25).

 SPORTS (GENERAL). Boating. The Norwegian Coastal Voyage is a popular coast-hugging journey from Bergen, Norway, up to the North Cape beyond the Arctic Circle in the land of the Midnight Sun. June departures are best, though the holiday is available throughout the summer. Cost of the 12-night package (11 on the boat, 1 in Bergen) ranges from about £800 in October (less in Nov. and Dec.) up to around £1,000 in the peak May-thru-August period (this is if you fly to Norway; going by boat costs more). These prices are per person sharing a double cabin—other size cabins are available at varying rates. For details contact *Norwegian Travel Office,* 20 Pall Mall, London S.W.1, or *Fred Olsen Travel Ltd.,* 11 Conduit St., London W.1.

For cruises along the canals of the English countryside try *Blakes Holidays Ltd.,* Wroxham, Norwich, Britain's biggest boat holiday operators. They also carry waterway vacations in Ireland, Scotland, France and Holland. Offering the same kind of thing in Denmark, Holland and France, as well as Britain, are *Hoseasons Holidays,* Sunway House, Lowestoft, Suffolk.

More adventurous, and somewhat more energetic, is a holiday combining canoeing down the gorges of the Ardèche, a tributary of France's mighty River Rhone, and exploring the caves of the region, with dinghy sailing and wind surfing (and snorkeling as an ancillary activity) at Lou Village near Marseille en Plage, on the Mediterranean. This involves camping in 2-person tents and full board; also plenty of excitement, variety and fun. The round trip from London costs from £199 (coach) or £299 (air) for 15 days; you can choose just the Ardèche portion, from £139 for 8 days (coach travel only). *P.G.L. Young Adventure Ltd.,* Station St., Ross-on-Wye, Herefordshire.

(See also On Inland Waters under *Traveling in Europe.*)

Golf and Tennis. We once asked Tom Scott, editor of *Golf Illustrated,* to name the 12 best courses on the Continent. At the risk of being "decidedly unpopular" with his many European friends, he named the following links: Three in *Belgium;* the Golf Club des Fagnes, at Spa; the Royal Zoute Golf Club, at Le Zoute-sur-Mer; the Royal Antwerp Golf Club. Two each in *France, Germany and Holland:* the clubs of Morfontaine and Chantilly in France; those of Wiesbaden and Frankfurt in Germany; the Haagsche Golf Club, The Hague, and the Kennemer Golf and Country Club at Zandvoort in Holland. Three other countries get one each—the Milan club for *Italy,* the Stockholm club for *Sweden,* and the Club Puerto de Hierro of Madrid for *Spain.*

Tom Scott obliged us again by listing what he considered the 12 best links in Britain. He names three in Scotland, St. Andrews, Carnoustie and Muirfield; three in the Cheshire-Lancashire area, Royal Liverpool, Royal Birkdale and Royal Lytham-St. Anne's; one in Kent, Royal St. George's; two in the London area, the West Course at Wentworth and the Old Course at Sunningdale; one outside of the main golfing areas, Woodhall Spa, in Lincolnshire; and two in Northern Ireland, Royal Portrush and Royal County Down.

As for golf in Eire, the 20-odd courses in and around Dublin include such internationally known venues as Portmarnock, Dollymount, and Woodbrook.

Golf in Scandinavia has made rapid strides in recent years and there are no less than 66 courses, most of them in Southern Sweden. Portugal's Algarve area is an up and coming golf center with a combination of fine courses and a chance to relax on the beautiful beaches, and Greece has good courses in (conveniently!) the tourist centers of Athens, Rhodes and Corfu.

Bestway Holidays, Inc., 84–14 Jamaica Ave., Woodhaven, N.Y. 11421, has golf tours in Spain, Portugal, England, Ireland and Scotland. Golfing in Ireland is offered by *C.I.E. Tours International Inc.,* 122 E. 42nd St., New York, N.Y. 10017, *Lismore Travel,* 106 E. 31 St., New York, N.Y. 10016, and by *Irish Airlines (Aer Lingus)* with various operators. *B.T.H. Holidays,* the U.S. representative of the British Transport Hotels chain, offers tours in Ireland, England and Scotland, 185 Madison Ave., New York, N.Y. 10016.

In Canada, *International Golf,* 4150 St. Catherine St. W., Suite 390, Montreal, P.Q. H3Z 2Y5, runs golf tours (surprise!) to Scotland, Morocco, Spain, and the French Riviera, among other destinations. 8–11 day trip, including airfare, runs about $1,100–$1,600.

Recent years saw a healthy growth in the number and range of golfing and tennis holidays—sometimes the 2 sports combined in one package—on offer to the U.K.-based traveler. However, there has been something of a leveling off in the last couple of years. Two operators we can still recommend, though, are *Caravela Golf and Tennis,* of 38 Gillingham St., London S.W.1 (serving Portugal), and *Crystal Holidays,* Alexandra House, Alexandra Rd., London S.W.19 (also both golf and tennis, this time in Austria). One of the major British firms dealing with golfing holidays is *Eurogolf,* 41 Watford Way, Hendon, London N.W.4. They carry a huge variety of packages, ranging in duration from weekends to as long as you wish in several countries (France, Spain, Portugal and Britain among them), with all sorts of useful extras—airfares, pension, rental cars, concessionary green fees—and all backed up by solid professionalism, both in golf and in tourism. They also offer tailor-made holidays to suit individual preferences.

Hang gliding. Those wishing to get the hang of this testing and exciting sport can practise 1000 metre glides down into the valleys of the Black Forest. Lessons, equipment, accommodations, and, of course, insurance can all be obtained from *Drachenfliegerschule Peter Uhlig,* D 7292 Baiersbronn, Murgtalstrasse 167, Germany.

Horseback riding vacations are available in several European countries, notably Ireland, Spain, Iceland, and Hungary. In Spain they are conducted as treks into mountain areas (ask *Rutas a Caballo,* Agustina de Aragón 14, 28006 Madrid), in Hungary as extended tours across the plains around Lake Balaton, in Iceland for one or several days across some of Europe's most extraordinary landscapes, and in Ireland around particular riding schools or castles. Details on Ireland from the *Irish Tourist Board,* (address above), or from *Lismore Travel,* 106 E. 31 St., New York, N.Y. 10016. For Hungary, write to: *Hungarian Consulate General,* 8 E. 75 St., New York, N.Y. 10021. For Iceland, write to *Icelandic Airlines,* 21 Penn Plaza, New York, N.Y. 10001.

The British love for horses is reflected in the variety of special interest riding and trekking holidays. Pony-trekking is carried out in all parts of scenic Britain. The *Youth Hostels Association* (14 Southampton St., London W.C.2) looks after travelers of all ages. 7 days of High Peak Action Trekking for 12–15-year-olds starts at £149. Based at Edale in Derbyshire. The 7-day Dales Trail Ride for adults starts and finishes at Kettlewell and costs from £149. This is actually a continuous 7-day ride, with a different halting point every night. Based throughout at Kettlewell is the one-week Children's Pony Trekking package, with tuition in everything you need to know about riding, including pony-care and stable-management. From £135.

Those leaders in the special-interest-holidays field, *Cox and Kings* (address, see under *Art and Archeology* above), offer escorted riding packages in Hungary, Italy, Spain, Iceland, Portugal and Austria. For example, 7 nights (5 riding days) on the Portuguese Algarve range £426–516, depending on the season; while the same duration at a choice of two Hungarian destinations (Hortobagy–Tokaj or Balatonfenyves) is £647. Both include flight London–London; the former just B&B, the latter full board.

Recent additions to the U.K. riding scene are *Northumbria Horse Holidays*, of East Castle, Stanley, Co. Durham, where a 5-day/4-night "post trail riding" package starts at £149.

Hunting and Fishing. When it comes to field sports, you will find splendid opportunities in almost every European country. Throughout Eastern Europe, hunting ranks high on the list of tourist attractions—in price as well as quality (bear hunts in Poland and Romania, stag hunts in Hungary, and birds everywhere).

Aer Lingus, 52 Poland St., London W.1, have many fishing holidays in Ireland, all at extremely competitive rates; prices include return air fare from London. 7 days' sea angling will set you back anything from £200–250, depending on the nature of the accommodations. Price includes flight from London, then self-drive car with unlimited mileage from Dublin. A week's coarse fishing runs from, again, £200–250. *Note,* though, that once you are there you are on your own: there are no special facilities laid on or permits supplied, you must make your own arrangements. Aer Lingus do offer shorter-duration holidays, or can set up a package to suit your fancy.

Best fishing regions for mountain-trout are Scotland, Iceland, Sweden, Norway, Austria, Yugoslavia, Czechoslovakia and France. Facilities for deep-sea fishing exist in Great Britain, South of France, Iceland, Norway, Sweden, Yugoslavia and Greece.

Motor Racing. If you're an addict of motor racing, you will see more of this thrilling sport in Europe than anywhere else in the world. The Big Four of European racing countries are Britain, France, Italy and Germany, but Sweden is right in there on the suicide circuit with its Rally of the Midnight Sun, and Austria with its Österreichring World Championship in Styria. Each year there are more than 100 racing events listed by the International Auto Federation (FIA) in Europe. Among the most exciting: The French Grand Prix at Dijon or the Paul Ricard circuit in early July; the Le Mans twenty-four hour classic; the British Grand Prix (in July); Italy's Grand Prix in September at Monza (near Milan); Monaco's Grand Prix in May, and the famous Monte Carlo Rally, held in January with several hundred drivers starting out from a dozen points between Paris and Athens and fighting through snow and ice to fame and glory on the Riviera.

Page and Moy, 136–140 London Road, Leicester, are the British specialists in speed holidays. They have trips to all the major Grand Prix races—for example, the Belgian Grand Prix, at Spa, from £29 ("fast-and-cheap" 1-day roundtrip) to £209 (includes 3 nights in 4-star accommodations); the Monaco Grand Prix, several packages ranging from £69 to £1289 up (latter includes 8 nights in Loews Monte Carlo hotel); and Le Mans, £47 to £189 (latter including executive-class flight etc.). A combined Belgian Grand Prix and Le Mans package starts at £189. Though entrance is not included, Page and Moy can arrange this as an extra.

Scuba diving flourishes wherever there's a Mediterranean coastline. *Club Méditerranée* provides excellent facilities and instruction at Santa Teresa in Sardinia and at Cadaques; while **snorkeling** can be enjoyed at Club Med centers on the Portuguese coast, at Cargese on Corsica, Helios on Corfu, Porto Petro on Majorca, and off the Yugoslav island of Sveti Marko.

WINTER SPORTS. There are hundreds of beautifully-equipped resorts in the skiing centers of Austria, Switzerland, France, Germany and Italy. Switzerland probably leads the field in amenities, Austria and Italy in economies. Specific information will be found under the country chapters.

The Alpine areas of Europe—an 800-mile arc of majestic mountains—are bustling with hundreds of special events and competitions each winter and advance reservations in the smarter resorts are always advisable.

The Alpine winter playgrounds can be easily reached overnight by plane from the States. Accommodations for every taste and budget abound. Your best direct source of information is usually the national airline of the country you prefer, since the airline has the flight arrangements for a number of tour packagers. However, a number of 3–14-day tours to the Alps are offered by *Goligers Tours Ltd.*, 40 St. Clair Ave. W., Toronto, Ontario M4V 1M2. *Europeacar*, 3 East 54th St., New York, N.Y. 10022, in cooperation with Lufthansa offers skiing packages to Austria.

Starting from London, one of the leading British tour operators in this field is *Inghams*, Snowsports, 329 Putney Bridge Rd., London S.W.15, with dozens of offers all over Europe—Austria and Switzerland in particular (they're actually Swiss owned)—every one highly attractive and competitively priced. *Supertravel* (22 Hans Place, London, S.W.1.) organize chalet parties for groups ranging in size from 6 to 57, in France, Switzerland and Austria.

Here is a list of the best known winter-sports resorts in the five-country Alpine region:

Austria. Igls-Innsbruck, Kitzbühel, Seefeld, Bad Gastein, Saalbach and the Semmering, near Vienna. For would-be champions it's the Arlberg district: Lech, Zürs and St. Anton. For early and late season skiing, Obergurgl, Hoch-Sölden and the Dachstein region are recommended. Over 2,650 lifts and cable cars (about 25 of which take you to the heights between 8,200 ft. and 10,000 ft.), over 200 skating rinks and other amenities, spread throughout more than 450 resorts.

France. Chamonix, at the foot of the Mont Blanc, is an old favorite. New favorites include the futuristic resorts of Flaine, La Plagne and Avoriaz. Most fashionable are Courchevel, Megève, Val d'Isère, l'Alpe d'Huez, Flaine and La Plagne. For an unusual winter thrill you can sunbathe at Cannes in the morning and descend the slopes at Valberg or Auron in the afternoon. Lac de Tignes, along with Val d'Isere, provides the biggest and most varied skiing area in France. En route to Spain, one might sample the Pyrenees resorts of Barèges, Superbagnères and Font-Romeu, though they are "family and friendly", not for the international set. Metabief and Les Rousses are well-equipped and inexpensive Jura Mountain ski towns, though again these are mainly for the locals, not for sophisticates from abroad.

Germany. The Bavarian and Allgäu Alps are the best area. Garmisch-Partenkirchen, (where the Ski World Championships were held in 1978), Oberstdorf, Füssen, Mittenwald, Reichenhall and Bayrischzel, are well known resorts. The Black Forest offers good skiing at Hornisgrinde-Kandel, Feldberg and Blauen. Arnoldshain-Sandplacken in the Taunus Mountains is convenient to Frankfurt.

Italy. The southern slopes of the Alps offer the sunniest winter playground. The western spots are Sestriere, Courmayeur, Cervinia-Breuil while the foremost center in the Dolomites is Cortina d'Ampezzo. In the Trentino region, Madonna di Campiglio is noteworthy. Abetone is close to Florence, while Rieti-Terminillo is handy to Rome. Far south in Calabria is San Giovanni in Fiore, with a November-March season.

Switzerland has over 125 resorts, so it's not easy to choose. Statistics of their equipment are impressive; nearly 1,200 assorted lifts and cableways, 175 places with ice rinks, about 3,000 licensed ski instructors, and around 7,000 hotels and pensions in every price range.

In the southwest our pick is Villars, Verbier and fashionable Gstaad. In the shadow of Matterhorn there are Zermatt and Saas-Fee, while Jungfrau dominates Wengen, Grindelwald and Mürren. The most fashionable spots in the Grisons are St. Moritz, Davos and Arosa, all world famous. Beginners are often referred to Crans, Lenzerheide, Pontresina, Saas Fee or Zweisimmen, to name but five. Spring skiing is commonplace, and there are many places where you can ski throughout the summer. List from Swiss National Tourist Office.

Non-Alpine Areas

Andorra. This tiny Pyrennean country is an up-and-coming winter sports destination, especially for budget-minded skiers. The slopes in its seven or so ski resorts are ideal for beginners or intermediate skiers, though there are one or two tougher runs too. Hotels are generally modern, comfortable, and reasonably equipped. Ski clothes, books, and skis can be bought at bargain prices in Andorran shops.

Scandinavia. This is the home of cross-country skiing. You can ski in the parks of Helsinki, *Finland,* but an hour by bus to Nuuksio or by train to Hyvinkää gets you to popular and more extensive terrains. Many possibilities include reindeer safaris in Finnish Lapland. In *Norway,* the best-equipped ski resorts are Lillehammer, Voss and Geilo. Dalarna is the southernmost skiing terrain of *Sweden* and the easiest accessible, with Sälen and Grövelsjon in the north. But Jämtland is the top skiing region for experts and long distance enthusiasts, and in Lapland you can ski under the rays of the Midnight Sun in May-June. You will not find a plethora of winter sports amenities in Scandinavia because the Scandinavians prefer overland, long-distance skiing, now also called ski-touring.

Spain. Spain has some excellent winter sports areas. By far the best equipped are the Pyrenees resorts from Burguete and Isaba in Navarre, Astun, Candanchú, Cerler, El Formigal, Guarrinza and Panticosa in Aragón, to Espot, La Molina, Nuria, Port del Compte, Salardú and Viella in Catalonia. In the Sierra Nevada, only 35 km. from Granada, is the big Sol y Nieve complex, one of the most fashionable regions. 50 km. from Madrid are the Guadarrama mountains with resorts at Navacerrada, Valcotos and Pinilla; and in the north in the Picos de Europa are the resorts of Pajares, San Isidro, Reinosa and Alto Campóo.

Others. *Yugoslavia* is the best value, for little money. Kranjska Gora, Bled and Ratece Planica are nearest, in Slovenia. Some fine skiing awaits you on the Jahorina plateau near Sarajevo. *Czechoslovakia's* long established resorts are Spindleruv Mlyn in Bohemia; Strbské Pleso, Stary Smokovec and many others in the Tatra Mountains. On the *Polish* slopes of this chain Zakopane and Krynica are the best.

GETTING TO EUROPE

BY PLANE FROM NORTH AMERICA. Flying time from New York to most of the major European cities is between 5½ and 7 hours, long enough to disrupt your normal daily body rhythms and produce jet lag. This may be impossible to avoid, but our advice can help minimize it: get a good sleep before leaving, go easy on food and drink in flight, try to sleep on the plane, and get plenty of rest the first few days in Europe. Time in Britain and Ireland is five hours ahead of U.S. EDST; Portugal is also five hours ahead, while the remainder of Europe runs six hours ahead with the exception of Bulgaria, Romania, Greece, and Finland which are seven hours ahead, and Turkey, which is eight hours ahead.

The supersonic Concorde and the jumbo Boeing 747 try to soften the present ordeal; Concorde by getting you there in less than half the normal time, the 747 by managing to carry 360–390 passengers, nine abreast, yet in seats which are a comfortable two inches wider than on ordinary jets (though the "pitch", the distance between your seat and the one in front, is the same).

On all scheduled services there are now three classes—first, business class and economy. The "full fare" class is for those paying the top economy-class fare; the class is given different names by airlines such as Club, Executive, Ambassador and Clipper. "Full fare" get more space, better food and free drinks and entertainment. The free baggage allowance is based on *size* rather than weight: in first class, 2 pieces up to 62 inches overall measure each piece; in economy class, 2 pieces, neither one over 62 inches, both together no more than 106 inches. Underseat baggage up to 45 inches.

Since the deregulation of air travel came about in 1979/80 the whole business of trans-Atlantic flying—and not the least the fare structure—continues to be complicated and changeable. Indeed even the most expert travel agent has a major problem in keeping up with what is going on, with fares changing constantly, often at the shortest notice. This is not the place to go into the economics of all this, but it is safe to say that the traveler has never been better off from both the viewpoint of services available and the fare structure. From the budget Standby to Concorde there are fares to suit every type of traveler. But a word of warning. Do not choose the cheapest fare simply because it is that. Compare the conditions that each has to offer. By paying say 10% to 20% more for your ticket you could easily get the better bargain than if you opted for the lowest available. In the following paragraphs we have given the basic information as to what is available as we went to press. We must stress however that parts of this may well—almost certainly will—have changed by the time you come around to make your travel plans. Take our advice and consult a good travel agent or the airline of your choice before you make any definite plans.

With deregulation airlines have more or less been allowed to fix their own fare levels. As far as first class and full fare economy is concerned these tickets are inter-changeable among certain but not all airlines on the trans-Atlantic route. On the cheaper tickets you are generally required to fly both ways by the same airline if you have a return ticket. In some circumstances however you can switch from one airline to another either at no cost, or for a small extra payment. If this sounds rather vague the reason is that the position does not stay static on this matter and there are as many variations as there are airlines operating these routes.

The problem of stop-overs does not arise if you are flying non-stop from the U.S. or Canadian gateway to your European destination. Most of the cheapest fares do not allow stop-overs where applicable other than on additional payment. For example take a Pan Am flight from New York to London which then goes on to Frankfurt. With an Advance Booking Excursion Fare (APEX) to Frankfurt you would not be able to make a stop-over in London. But with an ordinary economy class ticket (full fare) you would. Indeed with a full fare ticket you could use other airlines, and, say, stop over in Amsterdam and Cologne before going on to Frankfurt. But not, we repeat, with the cheapest fares.

Here, then, are the basic details about the types of fares. Remember to check with your travel agent for the latest situation.

1. Concorde—most expensive, available from New York and Washington to London and Paris (from N.Y. only). Single fare $2,552 (N.Y.)/$2,423 (Wash.). Return is double. British Airways services have been offering reduced rates at certain times for wives when traveling with their husbands.

2. First class—available on all flights (barring a very few all-economy services) from the U.S.A. and Canada to Europe. No restrictions on these tickets, book anytime, travel anytime, change dates anytime, stop-overs as and when required. All on-board amenities free of charge. Sample fare New York—London $1,998 single, return is double but check on this as some airlines offer reduced return fares under certain conditions.

3. Business class—falls between First and Economy, and now touted by most airlines under various guises.

4. Economy—available on all flights from U.S.A. and Canada. Virtually no restrictions although in some cases there is an additional charge for stop-overs. No advance booking required and dates of travel can be changed. Seats are generally in the regular part of the plane. Sample fare New York–London round trip $800. Amenities vary between airlines.

5. APEX and Super-APEX. This is the most popular fare. You must book 21 days in advance, and if you alter your flying dates the penalties are heavy. The difference between APEX and Super-APEX is minimal, usually just the dates of travel. Sample Super-APEX New York–London round trip fare is $450–$550 according to time of travel.

Note: The number of APEX seats is limited on each flight with the ratio varying from one airline and one route to another and also according to time of year. This ratio is usually a closely kept commercial secret; after all, the airlines really want as many full-fare passengers as possible. As far as APEX goes the earlier you book the better chance you have of getting the seat you want when you want it.

Children's fares. Most airlines charge 10% of the appropriate adult fare for children under two not occupying a seat. Children two to 12 and occupying a seat pay half the appropriate adult fare. But there are no reductions on Stand-by fares for children between two and 12. The ratio for the half fare is one child to one adult.

All fares, except for Concorde and first class, vary according to the season with a variation in respect of route and airline. Roughly speaking the low season for flying to Europe (eastbound) is September to May but for flying the other way (westbound) it is October to June.

Where a return is involved and it overlaps these periods the cost is the sum of half the return in each season. The operative dates are always those of departure, not arrival.

People Express. This has been a big success since starting in 1983 with daily flights between Newark and London (Gatwick). As a budget scheme this service has a lot going for it. The price is around $130 one way for the transatlantic flight, with a pay-on-board system operating. The Newark-based carrier has cut down on frills and brought the simplicity of a shuttle service to the outmoded and rarely-effective "luxury-in-the-sky" concept of transoceanic flight. You can expect to pay $3 extra for each piece of luggage, around $5 for a hot platter or snack-type meal, 50¢ for drinks. Or, you can bring your own food on board.

Virgin Atlantic. Less well-known than People Express, this British airline also offers budget fares across the Atlantic ($175 Newark or Miami to London, Gatwick), but a much higher level of service. In addition, rock videos and cartoons complement the usual in-flight movie. Virgin also offer an excellent, and expensive, first-class service.

A new British airline, *Highland Express*, announced plans to operate a regular Newark–Prestwick (Scotland) service in January 1986. Fares will be low, and service somewhere between People's and Virgin; check for details.

Advance Booking Charters. Known as ABCs, these flights are a good bit less common than they have been, though some charter airlines such as Transamerica or CalAir operate regular services. Some are privately arranged by groups (e.g. teachers' associations or college fraternities) or are operated by charter companies or charter airlines. Sometimes these charters are flown by scheduled airline aircraft. All are subject to advance booking conditions which are usually 21 days in advance from the U.S.A. and Canada. But there are variations on this. Most travel agents can give you details. These services are intermittent, with more available from Canada than the U.S.

In-flight hints. Although the free baggage allowance is quite generous and is now based on size of baggage carried and not weight, you can take excess baggage and pay for it. But this is expensive being based on the ratio of 1% of the single first class fare on the route per kilogram (2.2 lbs) of weight. On, say, the New York route this could mean an extra $50 to $75 one way for an additional suitcase. Keep your baggage to a minimum.

Officially you are allowed one handbag or shoulder bag (e.g. an airline bag) to carry on board with you. This is not included in the free baggage allowance but is extra. However it *must* be able to fit under an aircraft seat. In addition to this an umbrella, overcoat, portable camera, binoculars, reading material, ladies purse etc. are also permitted as extras.

Always keep your passport, tickets, cash, travelers' checks, credit cards, personal documents of any kind, immunisation certificates where applicable and driving license, with you at all times. *Do not pack them in your suitcase.*

As all airports now have strict security checks (very thorough in some, regrettably less so in others) keep your camera and films handy to take out of your handbag in case the X-ray unit is of the strong type which can damage film. Always ask at the security check if it is safe or not to take films through the X-ray units there.

 BY BOAT FROM NORTH AMERICA. The chances of traveling by ship across the Atlantic reduce each year. In the past, sea-lovers had a choice between ocean liners —the number of these in service on trans-Atlantic routes has now diminished to one: Cunard's *Queen Elizabeth 2*—and freighters. The possibilities in the latter category have dwindled almost as drastically. The few cargo ships making the trip and accepting passengers are booked several years ahead.

One agent very familiar with developments in this area cautions that the details surrounding trans-Atlantic travel change rapidly. No sooner are the latest schedules off the presses, he claims, than they are outdated. Nonetheless, the persistent can be rewarded with passage on the rare freighter offering relatively comfortable one-class accommodations for a maximum of 12 people. What they lack in the way of entertainment and refinement these ships make up for by way of informality, relaxation and cost (though flying is almost always cheaper). For details consult either of the following specialists: *Air Marine Travel Service,* 501 Madison Ave., New York, N.Y. 10022, or *Pearl's Freighter Tips,* 175 Great Neck Rd, Great Neck, N.Y. 11021.

Crossing time may take from 5 to 11 days, depending on the route and the speed of your particular vessel. This leisurely tempo affords a way of living that, for many, is equally as appealing as the land part of their trip. If you have any apprehension about motion sickness, provide yourself with Dramamine, Marzine, tranquilizing Nautamine, a French product, or one of the other wellknown "stabilizers". All ocean-going ships with capacity for more than 12 passengers must by law carry a doctor, and the *QE2* has hospital and nursing facilities.

Luggage is far less of a problem to ocean travelers than to those who fly. Although you are limited to a specified number of cubic feet of baggage (the figure varies from class to class and line to line), the allowance is so generous that you are unlikely to exceed it. Pack the clothing you will use on shipboard in one or two bags and mark the rest of your luggage for storage in the hold; it's a nuisance to have your cabin cluttered with suitcases you don't need en route.

Cost. When you travel by sea, your cost is an elusive quality. Tips and incidentals will add to your expenses. There are many and varied fares for ship travel depending not only on cabin but also on dates of travel with peak, intermediate, and off-peak sailings. On the *QE2* you can combine flying one way with traveling the other on the ship; Cunard also have many Concorde–QE2 voyages. Full details from your travel agent.

Tipping on board. Don't be overawed by the problems of tipping at the end of the voyage. Treat it exactly as you would in a hotel—tip for service. The cabin steward and the dining room steward will have helped you most, and perhaps the deck steward. The ship's officers, from the purser up, are not for tipping, of course.

Port taxes. These vary from year to year and from country to country; like airport exit taxes, know that they exist, be prepared for them, and check to see whether they are not included in the fare. These now average $20 to $50 per head.

Cruising In and Around Europe

Cunard has had ships on the North Atlantic route since 1839. The company's flagship *QE2* now maintains regular service from April to October between New York, Cherbourg (France) and Southampton (England). Fares are subject to change, but are always cheaper off-season than during the peak summer months. Among special promotions are air/sea combination tickets, with Cunard providing service in one direction on the *QE2* and in the other by jet. Other tour programs and special land arrangements can be made through *Cunard,* 555 Fifth Ave., New York, N.Y. 10017.

An alternative to trans-Atlantic travel for those who wish to spend some time on the water would be cruises emanating from a variety of British and European ports. Alas, these too change with some frequency, and it is best to consult a travel agent for the latest information. However, many of these offer attractive fly/cruise package rates. Among the possibilities: *Royal Viking's* 8–19 day one-way trip from New York to Southampton begins at $1,592 for deluxe two-bedroom accommodations per person, double occupancy. Their 14-day Fort Lauderdale to Barcelona cruise begins at $2,774. The bulk of such cruises can be found headed for Scandinavia or in combination with trips covering the Mediterranean.

Another possibility would be the canal and river barge trips to be found in England, France, Holland and Scandinavia or the Rhine cruises in Germany. Rates vary according to the trip taken, but the service and cuisine can be first-rate while the size of most of the barges, at least, limits the number of passengers to an intimate group. Contact *Floating Through Europe,* 271 Madison Ave., New York, N.Y. 10016.

The Rhine cruises, which operate from early April to mid-October, tend to be aboard larger vessels and run from 3 to 7 days at prices beginning around $398. A typical jaunt might run downstream for 4 days from Basel, Switzerland through France and Germany to Amsterdam (Holland); cost is about $650, including all meals. Advance booking for first-class or Europa-class trips, some including wine tasting cruises can be made from the U.S. through the *Rhine Cruise Agency,* Suite 317, 170 Hamilton Ave., White Plains, New York 10601; or Suite 619, 323 Geary St., San Francisco, California 94102.

BY PLANE FROM BRITAIN TO THE CONTINENT.

The European continent is very well served from the United Kingdom and to a lesser extent from the Republic of Ireland with flights to all European capitals (other than to Tirana in Albania) from London, which has two main airports, Heathrow and Gatwick, and several lesser ones of which Luton and Stansted are the most used. However, the bulk of all scheduled flights go from Heathrow or Gatwick.

In recent years the number of direct flights from regional airports to European destinations has increased dramatically with flights from cities like Birmingham, Manchester, Newcastle, Cardiff, Bristol, Norwich, Edinburgh, Glasgow, Aberdeen and—in Ireland—from Dublin. (See section on *Traveling in Europe* later in this chapter.)

BY TRAIN FROM BRITAIN TO THE CONTINENT.

For the foot passenger there are three ways to cross that stretch of water—the English Channel and the North Sea—from England to the Continent. The first is the longest-established, namely the ferry which in most cases is a car-carrying vessel. The second is the Hovercraft, the amazing British invention which skims across the surface of the sea. And the third is the newest, the Jetfoil which with its "water skis" just below the surface of the water gives a thrilling ride. And all of these have excellent train connections from London.

The most popular routes using the train to get to the Continent are from London (Victoria and Charing Cross Stations) to Folkestone, Dover and Ramsgate. For Paris the best route is now from Charing Cross Station, then by train to Dover Priory where a bus takes you to the Hoverspeed Terminal. You then skim across the Channel to Boulogne Hoverport where a fast connecting train whisks you to Paris—approximately six-and-a-half hours, city center to city center. Four or five services daily each way.

There is a similar route—but using conventional ferries—leaving London (Victoria Station) at about 9:30 A.M. (time varies according to season) which goes via Dover with direct connection to the ferry and then across to Boulogne (some go to Calais), then by train to Paris. Again about six to six-and-a-half hours.

The sea crossing by Hovercraft takes about 35 to 40 minutes; by ferry 1 hour 15 minutes to 1 hour 30 minutes.

For Belgium, Germany, Austria and beyond (including Poland) use the route from Dover to Ostend. For the Netherlands, Germany, Scandinavia and again Eastern Europe use the longer Harwich (trains from London, Liverpool St. Station) to Hook of Holland service, where there are excellent rail connections linking with all ferry sailings. For north Germany, Denmark and Sweden there are excellent ferry sailings from Harwich with linking trains from Liverpool St. Station. For the Netherlands, the Olau Line from Sheerness (train from Victoria) to Flushing with day or night service is another good route.

Fares vary greatly on the routes, with many permutations and special "bargains" at various times. Roughly speaking a 2nd class return from London to Paris by rail and Hovercraft or ferry costs around £65 to £75. But always check as it is often cheaper to travel at certain times.

For further details of services see under individual countries.

Full details of services by rail and ferry or Hovercraft can be obtained in London at the *Travel Centers* at Victoria, Charing Cross, Waterloo and Liverpool Street Stations, or from the *British Rail Travel Office* in Lower Regent Street, London S.W.1, only two minutes' walk from Piccadilly Circus.

BY CAR FROM BRITAIN TO THE CONTINENT.

Some of the larger ferries on the longer crossings have very acceptable accommodation with reserved seating, and comfortable cabins, and are, in fact, mini-liners even offering 4- to 6-day cruises at certain times of the year, at most reasonable prices.

It is also possible to hire camping equipment, even a tow-caravan when booking your passage. All ferries these days have drive on/off systems for cars.

The fares listed below are the standard summer rates for 2 adult passengers, single journey, and a 4.5m car. The fare can be cheaper if you choose your crossing time carefully, or more costly if you insist on traveling at peak weekends. Children are mostly carried at half price, but the age at which they are deemed to become adult varies between 13 and 18 according to the inspiration of the ferry operators. Astonishing bargains are available for short excursions, ie. 1–5 days, or longer period packages from nearly every company.

France

Dover–Calais. Sealink. 90 mins. Up to 17 day sailings. £62.
Dover–Calais. Townsend Thoresen. 75 mins. Up to 15 sailings daily. £66.
Dover–Calais. Hoverspeed. 35 mins. Up to 19 day sailings. £58.
Dover–Boulogne. Townsend Thoresen. 100 mins. Up to 8 day sailings. £66.
Dover–Boulogne. Hoverspeed. 40 mins. Up to 6 day sailings. £65.
Dover-Dunkerque. Sealink. 2¼ hours. Up to 2 day, 1 night sailings. £66.
Folkestone–Boulogne. Sealink. 105 mins. Up to 13 day sailings. £66.
Newhaven–Dieppe. Sealink. 4 hours. Up to 4 day, 2 night sailings. £77.
Poole–Cherbourg. Truck Line. 4½ hours. 2 night sailings, 1 day. £93 with berth in 4-berth cabin, £79 for day sailing without cabin.
Portsmouth–Caen. Brittany Ferries. 5½ hours. 2 day sailings, £81; 1 night sailing, £103.
Portsmouth–Cherbourg. Sealink. 4¾ hours. 6–7 day sailings weekly. £105.
Portsmouth–Cherbourg. Townsend Thoresen. 4¾–6½ hours. 2 day sailings, £81; 1 night £103.
Portsmouth–Le Havre. Townsend Thoresen. 5½–8½ hours. 3 day sailings, 1 night, £90. Cabin £19.
Portsmouth–St.-Malo. Britanny Ferries. 10 hours. 1 day, 1 night sailing. £91 for day sailings, £117 for night.
Plymouth–Roscoff. Brittany Ferries. 6–7 hours. 3 day, 1 night sailing. £89 for day sailings, £115 for night.
Ramsgate–Dunkerque. Sally Viking. 2½ hours. Up to 3 day, 1 night sailings. £100.
Weymouth–Cherbourg. Sealink. 4½ hours. 6–7 day sailings weekly. £92. Some berths available.

Belgium

Dover–Zeebrugge. Townsend Thoresen. 4¼ hours. Up to 4 day, 2 night sailings.
Felixstowe–Zeebrugge. Townsend Thoresen. 5–9 hours. Up to 2 day, 1 night sailings. £71. 2-berth cabin £19.
Hull–Zeebrugge. North Sea Ferries. 13 hours. 1 night sailing. £116, including 2-berth cabin and meals.

Holland

Harwich–Hook of Holland. Sealink. 6¾–8 hours. 1 day, 1 night sailing. £58 for day sailings, £76 night. 2-berth cabin £19, plus £10 1st.class supplement for two.
Hull–Rotterdam. North Sea Ferries. 13 hours. 1 night sailing. £116, including 2-berth cabin and meals.
Sheerness–Flushing. Olau Line. 7½–8½ hours. 1 day, 1 night sailing. £54 day sailing, £87 night including 2-berth cabin.

Germany

Harwich–Hamburg. DFDS. 20 hours. Alternate night sailings. £184, including 2-berth cabin. £154 economy.

Denmark

Harwich–Esbjerg. DFDS. 19 hours. 3–7 sailings weekly. £198, including 2-berth cabin.

Harwich–Hirtshals. Fred Olsen Lines. 27 hours. 1 sailing weekly. £72 including cabin.

Newcastle–Esbjerg. DFDS. 19–22 hours. 3 sailings weekly May–Sept. £212 including cabin.

Sweden

Harwich–Gothenburg. DFDS. 23½ hours. Up to 3 sailings weekly. £242 including 2-berth cabin; £202 economy cabin.

Newcastle–Gothenburg. DFDS. 26½ hours. 2 sailings weekly June–Aug. £260 including cabin.

Norway

Harwich–Kristiansand. Fred Olsen Lines. 22 hours. 1 sailing weekly June–Aug. £187 including 2-berth cabin.

Newcastle–Stavanger, Bergen. Norway Line. 19½–26 hours. 3 sailings weekly May–Oct. £226 with cabin, £118 with sleeperette.

Spain

Plymouth–Santander. Brittany Ferries. 24 hours. Up to 2 sailings weekly. £190; 2-berth cabin £31.

FARES FACTS. Complete information on fares and sailings is available from the AA, RAC, and the *Continental Car Ferry Center,* 52 Grosvenor Gardens, London S.W.1.

For information on *Townsend Thoresen,* the address is 127 Regent St., London W.1. For *Brittany Ferries,* Millbay Docks, Plymouth, PL1 3EF, England.

STAYING IN EUROPE

CUSTOMS UPON ARRIVAL. Thanks to the efforts of the United Nations, this vexatious problem has been eased by an agreement among most tourist-receiving nations on a standardized list of items which travelers may bring into their territories without paying duty. It includes portable typewriters, radios or phonographs, cameras with a reasonable amount of film, sports equipment and clothing, provided it is only imported in such quantities as would be normal for personal use. The amounts accepted are minimums; thus the countries which have signed the convention all agree to permit tourists to bring in 200 cigarettes, but actually most of them individually set larger quotas. For these variations, see individual chapters of this book. In general, the rule is that you can bring in almost anything for normal personal use while traveling, and it is unlikely that you will have any difficulty with such belongings.

THE SUNSHINE CALENDAR. A rough guide to maximum sunshine from May through September is given here for sun-worshippers. In each case, you will find, based on averages from past years, a minimum of 8 hours of sunshine per day in the following areas:

May: Denmark, Finland, Riviera of France, northern Germany, Greece, southern Italy, Portugal, Spain (except the Atlantic coast), Sweden, Switzerland, southern Yugoslavia.

June: the same as May, plus France's Atlantic coast, all of Italy, Norway, Finland, Sweden, and Iceland for the Midnight Sun (at its peak in June, though dramatic throughout the summer), all of Yugoslavia.

July: Finland, France, Greece, Italy, Portugal, Spain (except Atlantic coast), Sweden, Switzerland, Yugoslavia.

August: France (except Channel coast), Greece, Italy, Portugal, Spain (except Atlantic coast), Sweden, Switzerland, Yugoslavia.

September: French Riviera, Greece, southern Portugal, southern Spain, and best of all, *everywhere* in the Alps.

If you prefer to winter on a beach rather than a ski slope, we suggest two areas in Europe. In the Greek islands winter temperatures are in the upper 50s and 60s, and spring begins around the end of January. Rhodes claims 300 days of sun a year and to its treasurehouse of Greek, Roman, Byzantine, Arabic and Crusader art and architecture has added luxury hotels open year round and with heated swimming pools.

Portugal's southernmost province, the Algarve, has over 100 miles of coast where a warm-water current keeps mid-winter temperatures in the 60s, flowers out year round and spring beginning in late January, when the almond trees bloom. Golf, tennis, water sports and deep sea fishing add to the natural attractions of this area.

SHOPPING. Shopping will be one of the thrills of your trip, and you'll find European stores full of beautiful things and impressive bargains.

Here's a tip for tourists resident *outside* the Common Market countries of Britain, Denmark, France, Germany, Holland, Belgium, Luxembourg, Italy, Ireland, Greece, and—as of 1986—Spain and Portugal, that could save you up to 15% on most of your purchases. In these countries, V.A.T. (value added tax) is tacked onto most prices. You can avoid this tax by having the shop send your purchases home, or by having them delivered to your point of departure, or by promising that you will leave that particular country within three months. Since the shop will have to pay the tax until you have actually left the country, when it will receive a refund from customs, your promise will sometimes have to be a deposit on the tax, which will be returned to you when you have filled out the customs declaration at the point of departure. Some countries are more generous, allowing you to remain with them six months before V.A.T. is payable, and all Common Market countries will allow you one year in the case of car purchase. In Sweden, V.A.T. can be refunded at airports, or ports, when you leave, but only if the goods were bought in a number of specially designated shops. They can be recognized by the sign they display.

This is the time to warn you about those duty-free, tax-free shops. While they *can* offer bargains, especially in liquor, cigarettes, cosmetics and perfume—because of the huge taxes these attract in the normal shops—the "DUTY FREE" signs can often be unpleasant hoaxes. You may not be paying tax on your bottle of whiskey or perfume, but you are certainly contributing to somebody's profits. Duty-free shops are big business these days and mark ups are often around 100 to 200%. So don't be seduced by the idea that because it's duty free it's a bargain. Very often prices are not much different from your local discount store and in the case of perfume or jewelry they can be even higher.

As a general rule of thumb, duty-free stores on the ground offer better value than buying in the air. Also, if you buy duty-free goods on a plane, remember that the range is likely to be limited and that if you are paying in a different currency to that of the airline, their rate of exchange often bears only a passing resemblance to the official one.

MEDICAL SERVICES. The *I.A.M.A.T.* (International Assoc. for Medical Assistance to Travelers) offers you a list of approved English-speaking doctors who have had postgraduate training in the U.S., Canada or Gt. Britain. Membership is free; the scheme is world-wide with many European countries participating. For information apply in the U.S. to 736 Center St., Lewiston, N.Y. 14092; in Canada, 188 Nicklin Rd., Guelph, Ont. N1H 7L5; in Europe, 17 Gotthardstrasse, 6300 Zug, Switzerland. A similar service is provided by *Intermedic*, 777 Third Ave., New York, N.Y. 10017, but there is an initial membership charge of $6 per person, or $10 per family; there is a subsequent schedule of prices for house and hotel calls, etc. *Intermedic* is affiliated with Carte Blanche.

Travel Assistance International, 1333 F St., N.W., Washington, D.C. 20004 (800–821–2828), offer comprehensive medical insurance throughout the globe. For full details see *Vaction Travel Insurance* on page 4. British travelers should contact *Europ Assistance Ltd.,* 252 High St., Croydon, Surrey, (tel. 01–680 1234).

Physically disabled travelers have had trouble in the past arranging travel insurance. But now, British travelers can obtain standard insurance cover at a premium in line with normal market rates. One company that specializes in travel insurance of all kinds—including medical—is named, appropriately enough, *Travelsurance Limited* (210–212 Borough High St., London S.E.1).

Certain countries, Gt. Britain and Sweden, for instance, offer free treatment and hospitalization to visitors, provided the problem arose, or became severely exacerbated, during your stay there.

Free medical services in urgent cases are available for British travelers in other E.E.C. countries. Provided you are neither unemployed nor self-employed (all employed people, pensioners and their dependents *are* eligible), you can go to any local office of the Department of Health and Social Security or any employment exchange and obtain form CM1. Post it to the nearest social security office and a form E111 will be issued to you by post. It is essential to take it with you when you go abroad; it is your certificate of entitlement to medical benefits during your stay in other E.E.C. countries (Belgium, France, West Germany, Greece, Italy, Luxembourg, The Netherlands, Denmark, Ireland—and, since January 1986, Spain and Portugal).

CONVERSION CHARTS. Simplified: 1 inch = 2.54 centimeters; 1 foot = 12 inches = 30.48 centimeters; 1 yard = 3 feet = 0.9144 meters.

Simplified: 1 ounce = 28.35 grams; 1 pound = 453.5924 grams. 2.2 pounds = 1 kilo.

Simplified: 1 U.S. gallon = 3¾ liters; 1 English gallon = 4½ liters.

Length		Weights	
centimeters	*inches*	*gram(me)s*	*ounces*
5	2	100	3.33
10	4 (under)	200	6.67
20	8 (under)	250	8.03
30	11¾	500	16.07
40	15¾	1 kilogram (kilo) = 2.2046 lbs.	
50	19¾		

1 meter = 39.37 inches

Clothing

Although you may see several charts with comparative U.S.-British-Continental sizings, in our experience these are not truly standardized. Best take along a tape measure, or rely on the shop assistant's assessment (in the first place) of your sizing. Always try on a garment before purchasing: an apparently correct sizing may prove to have arm-holes too wide or too narrow, sleeves too long or too short. After all, each country sizes according to the average measurements and proportions of its nationals, just as in the States and Gt. Britain. Dress fabrics, usually 1 meter (100 cm.) wide.

Kilometers Into Miles

This simple chart will help you to convert to both miles and kilometers. If you want to convert from miles into kilometers read from the center column to the right, if from kilometers into miles, from the center column to the left. Example: 5 miles = 8.0 kilometers, 5 kilometers = 3.1 miles.

Miles		*Kilometers*	*Miles*		*Kilometers*
0.6	1	1.6	3.7	6	9.6
1.2	2	3.2	4.3	7	11.3
1.9	3	4.8	5.0	8	12.9
2.5	4	6.3	5.6	9	14.5
3.1	5	8.0	6.2	10	16.1

Miles		Kilometers	Miles		Kilometers
12.4	20	32.2	124.3	200	321.9
18.6	30	48.3	186.4	300	482.8
24.8	40	64.4	248.5	400	643.7
31.0	50	80.5	310.7	500	804.7
37.3	60	96.6	372.8	600	965.6
43.5	70	112.3	434.9	700	1,126.5
49.7	80	128.7	497.1	800	1,287.5
55.9	90	144.8	559.2	900	1,448.4
62.1	100	160.9	621.1	1,000	1,609.03

Tire Pressure Converter

Pounds per Square Inch	16	18	20	22	24	26	28	30	32
Kilogrammes per Square Centimeter	1.12	1.26	1.40	1.54	1.68	1.82	1.96	2.10	2.24

Gallons Into Liters

U.S. Gallon	Liters	Imperial (British) Gallon	Liters
1	3.78	1	4.54
2	7.57	2	9.09
3	11.36	3	13.63
4	15.14	4	18.18
5	18.93	5	22.73
6	22.71	6	27.27
7	26.50	7	31.82
8	30.28	8	36.36
9	34.07	9	40.91
10	37.85	10	45.46

There are 5 Imperial (British) gallons to 6 U.S. gallons.

VILLAS. A stay-put vacation can have definite advantages. Accommodations rented at weekly, fortnightly or monthly rates can be cheaper than staying in hotels, for one or two nights at a time. By doing your own shopping and cooking you obviously save a great deal over eating in restaurants. In addition, you get to meet your neighbors, the people of the country you are visiting, and to see and participate in their daily life. In Finland, for example, you can rent a camp cottage on the shore of a lake surrounded by forests, but in a camp where nearly everyone else will be Finnish.

In resort areas like the French Riviera most of the places for rent will hardly present any budget advantage, whereas in Portugal you may do very well indeed. Because the commercial agencies which handle such rentals from the United States or Britain tend both to specialize in only certain countries and to go into and out of business too easily, your wisest first step is to contact the national tourist office of the country you have in mind and ask either for the names of specific agencies that it can recommend as dependable or for the name of a central clearing house or association of such agencies. A reliable and well-established private company is *Tayling's*, 14 High St., Godalming, Surrey, who handle properties in the U.K. only; in the U.S. c/o *Interchange* (address below). For France there is the *Fédération Nationale des Gîtes de France,* 34 rue Godot de Mauroy, 75009 Paris, which publishes an annual directory of families all over France which rent out rooms, apartments, cottages, camps, villas and chalets.

In the U.S., try the following:

At Home Abroad, Inc., 405 East 56 St., New York, N.Y. 10022, which has properties in England, Scotland, France, Italy, Spain, Portugal, Greece, Ireland and Tunisia.

Rent-a-Villa, Ltd., 422 Madison Ave., New York, N.Y. 10017, operates primarily in Greece and on the Mediterranean coasts of France and Spain.

TAP, the Portuguese national airline (U.S. office at 1140 Ave. of the Americas, New York, N.Y. 10036), arranges apartment rentals in the Estoril and

Algarve resort areas at remarkably low rates in one of Europe's few remaining bargain countries.

Villas International, 71 West 23rd St., New York, N.Y. 10016, has over 20,000 privately owned rental properties available, many of them along the Mediterranean or Atlantic coasts of Europe, or in Britain and Scotland. They also arrange air travel and car rentals.

Two British agencies with many attractive possibilities on their books: *OSL Holidays (Owners' Services Ltd.),* OSL House, High Road, Broxbourne, Herts. EN10 7JD, who have villas and apartments available over much of Europe (*not* U.K. though), including in Spain, Portugal, Greece, Italy, Turkey, Corsica, Madeira, Canary and Greek islands; and *Inter-Home,* 383 Richmond Rd., Twickenham, Middx., who like OSL have properties throughout most of Europe—but *including* the U.K.

 CAMPING. If going by car is the most economical way of traveling, for two or more people, camping is in many respects the most rewarding one, especially if you are the outdoor-type. Some of Europe's favorite camping regions (Scandinavia, the Mediterranean shores, the Alps) have highly organized camps with electricity, shower baths, playgrounds, restaurants and even dancing. You will find a new and different world here, with interesting people and leisurely living. Also it offers the healthiest and cheapest vacation for families with children.

To pitch your tent in a European camp—owned more often than not by a club—you will have to produce the *International Camping Carnet* which is also your third party (public liability) insurance. If you wish to obtain your carnet before leaving home, write to the *National Campers and Hikers Association,* 7172 Transit Road, Buffalo, N.Y., 14221 or *Camping and Caravan Club Ltd.,* 11 Lower Grosvenor Place, London S.W.1. In Europe, try the *Federation International de Camping et de Caravanning,* 78 rue de Rivoli, Paris. If you intend to camp with your family apply for a family carnet, which is more economical (cost varies from country to country: in Britain it costs £1.10, and is available to Camping Club members only). You can also become a member on arrival at the local branch of one of the European camping clubs (apply in person) and receive the carnet which entitles your party to use camps anywhere in Europe—at reduced rates.

You are probably an old hand at camping and know what to take on a trip abroad. Remember however that your free baggage allowance is now limited to two pieces, neither one more than 62 inches overall, and totaling 106 in. in Economy Class, plus underseat baggage up to 45 inches. Excess baggage charges to Western Europe can run $50 to $70. Northwest Orient offers special rates for bicycles. Tents are cheaper to buy in the U.S. than in Europe (there are facilities for renting, including from several of the Channel car ferry operators); and because camping on all levels of comfort or simplicity is so highly developed in Europe, you can find whatever else you need there if you don't have it already.

Your best way to start planning is write to a country's national tourist office; most countries publish directory/guides to their campgrounds. The one for Belgium, for example, lists over 170 sites, with maps and details of equipment, capacity, and classification for each. National camping club offices are listed below:

Austria: Österreichischer Camping Club, Schubert Ring 8, Vienna.

Belgium: Royal Camping et Caravanning Club de Belgique, 51 Rue de Namur, Brussels 1.

Denmark: Densk Camping Union, G1 Konegevej 74, 1850 Copenhagen.

Finland: Camping Committee, Finnish Travel Association, Uudenmaankatu 16A, Helsinki.

France: Federation Française de Camping et de Caravanning (FFCC), 78 rue de Rivoli, Paris.

Germany: Deutscher Camping Club, Mandlstrasse 28, Munich 23.

Great Britain: Camping and Caravan Club Ltd., 11 Lower Grosvenor Place, London S.W.1.

Italy: Federazione Italiana del Campeggio e Caravanning, Casella Postale 649, 50100 Florence.

Netherlands: Koninklijke Nederlandse Toeristenbond, 220 Wassenaarseweg, The Hague.

Norway: Norwegian Campsite Association, Trudvangveien 8, N-3200 Sandefjord.

Portugal: Federacao Portugesa da Campismo e Caravanismo, Rua da Madelena 75, 2 Lisbon.

Spain: Agrupacion Nacional de Campings de España, Calle de Duque de Medinaceli 2, Madrid 14.

Sweden: Swedish Tourist Board, Box 7473, S–103 92 Stockholm.

Switzerland: Swiss Federation of Camping, Hapsburgerstrasse 42, Lucerne.

Yugoslavia: Turisticki Savez Jugoslvije, M. Pijade 8 (P.O.B. 595), Belgrade.

CAMP AND CARAVAN SITES. These are to be found in all European countries. They vary from the extremely good to the absolutely horrible; from highly organized camps with electricity, showers, restaurants, shops, playgrounds and even dancing, to a field with one standpipe. But for the most part they fall between these extremes, are well run and inexpensive. Most state tourist offices can provide lists of sites in their own countries. Germany even operates a radio service for campers and caravaners. During the main holiday season, signs along the motorways tell which radio frequencies to tune in to for details of space available at sites in that region.

Canvas Holidays, Bull Plain, Hertford, Herts. SG14 1DY, England, has its own ready erected tents (around 2,000 at the last count) at some 93 sites in Yugoslavia, France, Germany, Switzerland, Italy, Austria and Spain, offered as part of a complete package (i.e., transport, accommodations en route, etc.) for people who have not or do not wish to be bothered with their own tents.

In Central and Northern Europe the camping season lasts from mid-May to mid-September; around the Mediterranean some of the camps are open all year. But you should be warned that the camping sites along the Mediterranean coast of France have, of recent years, become increasingly congested, with a near breakdown of facilities in some spots caused by the flood tide of campers sweeping in from all parts of Europe during the summer season. If you are thinking of trying this area, you would be well advised to seek current information.

TRAVELING IN EUROPE

JETTING AROUND EUROPE'S AIRWAYS

Europe has a very extensive network of scheduled air services and almost as great a network of charter flight routes, especially in the summer months. Apart from peak routes such as London to Paris, the density of the services is not so great as in many parts of the U.S.A., but the coverage is, by and large, fairly good. Alas, the same cannot be said of the fare structure, which is on a far higher scale than in the U.S., though some routes have come down substantially in the last couple of years. It is, in fact, cheaper to fly the Atlantic than to go, say, between two European capitals which may be only a quarter of the distance apart. The distinction is, perhaps, difficult to draw, since the U.S. situation is one of freely competing airlines, while the European scene is largely a tragicomedy of national airlines maintaining a restricted cartel.

The normal economy fares in Europe (and both Club and first class) are very expensive, there is no denying. But increasingly the European airlines are introducing special fares that make nonsense of their ostensibly rigid maintenance of the overall fare structure. These budget offers consist of weekend rates, or "so-many nights stay", of which one night must be a Saturday, or tickets booked so many days in advance—or booked only a few hours before departure. The permutations of these possibilities would tax even the most sophisticated expert and, as with the trans-Atlantic routes, they are constantly changing. The one thing that is sure is that all these offers exist and should be explored before you dream of paying the full fare.

Major national carriers such as British Airways, Air France, KLM and Lufthansa, have come up with their own "cost cutting" fares, many of which are excellent value if not quite as low as some would like. British Airways for example have abandoned first class on most routes (e.g. to Paris) replacing this with Club class. On other routes there is economy class only. But before we proceed with a discussion of flying around Europe, it is well worth pointing out that for trips of under say 250 miles, and sometimes longer, it is often best to travel by rail. Remember that distances between major points in any one European country are relatively short compared to those in the U.S., and that rail travel in Europe is in any case very much more sophisticated and reliable than in America.

In addition to the scheduled services, the charter network also carry a number of non-package passengers on planes otherwise reserved exclusively for package tourists. This is especially true from the U.K. where all the major tour operators offer "seats only" on many of their flights. The numbers available vary enormously on each flight depending on how well the actual package holiday has sold.

Big tour operators in the U.K. such as *Thomson* and *Cosmos* issue what are in effect timetables of these services under names like "Airfares", "Cheapies" and so forth. These can be booked well in advance but there is no guarantee that they will always be available. They are on the whole cheaper than the cheapest scheduled fares. In addition there are in the U.K. what are called "Bucket Shops". These in effect are non-licensed (i.e. not members of the *Association of British Travel Agents* or holders of *International Air Transport Association— IATA* —licenses) agents who sell tickets for scheduled and some charter flights at cut-rate prices. These shops, most of which are in London, are in a curious "no-man's land" between legality and illegality. Sometimes they go bust and you can lose out. But generally they do offer cheap tickets which have been sold to them by airlines and tour operators anxious to get something back on routes and services which are not doing too well.

The addresses of these "bucket shops" are to be found in the columns of many newspapers in London and also in the weekly magazine *Time Out*. We are not suggesting that you *do* use these shops—but neither are we recommending that you avoid them. They do provide the inexpensive tickets, and they are almost always perfectly reliable. Consequently, although there have been considerable efforts made by regular travel agents and the Civil Aviation Authority to stamp out bucket shops, they still flourish.

Our advice is to check out the position locally at the time you want to travel. Indeed on air travel generally in Europe we strongly advise that you consult either with a good travel agent or with an airline before you make any bookings. In many cases it is much cheaper to take a package tour to a country (especially if you wish to concentrate on one city or resort area) than to go independently. The U.K. has perfected the package tour market and it is certainly worthwhile taking a look at some of these. In the peak summer weeks however the number of these available at short notice is very small.

We are not giving a long list of sample European air fares simply because these are subject to so many changes that most of them would certainly be out of date by the time you want to travel. However, to give you some idea of the variation of many of these—that is the variation on the same route—we have given a few samples which were applicable as we went to press. We have chosen three popular holiday destinations from London and all are returns.

Athens—Club class £650; various excursion fares with different conditions £180–£320; charter flights £110–£180 (must have accommodation attached).

Malaga—Club class £455; various excursion fares with different conditions £120–£340; charter flights £105–£150.

Venice—Club class £420; various excursion fares with different conditions £160–£200; charter flights £110–£140.

Flights in Europe either domestically within one country or internationally range in time between thirty minutes (e.g. Brussels to Amsterdam) and four hours (e.g. Helsinki to Malaga). Service varies depending on the airline, some being very much better than others. But it is essentially a quick, frequently uncomfortable, method of transport and not "the great romantic journey". Flying does enable you to get there in as short a time a possible.

In Eastern Europe service and comfort are not of as high a standard as in Western Europe. Food on East European airlines is generally dull and merely keeps the wolf from the hunger door. Also booking-in time in most East European countries is longer ahead of the flight than in the West. Never be late. It can lead to difficulties. In addition it is often necessary to change local currency back into Western currency—which can take time.

And as for delays—take our advice and accept these as calmly as possible. Time keeping on European air routes has improved substantially in the last couple of years. If you are late—relax. There is after all nothing *you* can do about it. Frequently it will take you as long to get to and from the airports on a trip as the actual flight will take. It is as well to make sure just how long the ground journeys will consume. It might seem you are doing half the distance on the motorway.

Have a good flight!

RAIL TRAVEL IN EUROPE

By David Tennant

The railways of Europe entered the 80s in much better shape and offering infinitely superior services than they had done in their entire 150 years of existence. True the over-all passenger mileage is lower than in the immediate postwar years and all of them have to be subsidised in one way or another by their respective governments, but they are now a highly efficient and indispensable part of the economy and life of Europe. Electrification proceeds apace in virtually every country with new lines and the continued up-grading of those long established. Not only have speeds increased (averages of 90 m.p.h. and more in many expresses is commonplace) but energy efficiency has likewise improved dramatically.

The French *Sud-Est* line from the outskirts of Paris to the suburbs of Lyon is now in full operation, giving a very fast service indeed. It links these two cities in only two hours with appropriate savings to other cities including Dijon, Geneva, St. Etienne, Chambéry, Montpellier and Toulon. These are operated by the *Trains à Grande Vitesse* (TGV), the world's fastest at 168 m.p.h.

In Italy the fast *direttissima* line between Florence and Rome is also in partial operation and by the time this Guide appears should be in a complete state. Here again times have been slashed, the riding quality improved and efficiency and safety raised. In Germany, too, new lines are being built for fast running. The U.K.'s excellent *InterCity High Speed Trains* traveling at up to 125 m.p.h. have been extended and now operate from Aberdeen to Penzance and from Hull on the east coast to the far west of Wales. These High Speed Trains (referred to as HSTs) are also running on cross-country services such as Newcastle to Plymouth and on the Midland route to Sheffield.

International co-operation among all the European railways continues even with the changing political fortunes and attitudes of governments. And work is proceeding in linking the last European country not joined by rail to the rest of the Continent—Albania—with a new line to connect directly with the Yugoslav system. This should come into operation sometime in 1987.

But comfort is just as important as speed, perhaps slightly more so to the leisure traveler. In the last few years there have been remarkable strides in this direction with all the railways of Europe progressively introducing new rolling stock for both day and night services. This new rolling stock offers comfort and spaciousness which a decade ago was restricted to the deluxe first class only trains. Under the UIC agreement second class coaches now have only three seats aside in compartments, as against four previously. Corridors are slightly wider allowing for easier access.

Airconditioning is becoming more common, mainly in first class but increasingly in second class also. Although not visually noticed by the average traveler the "behind the scenes" technical advances in coach design are of equal importance giving smoother and quieter riding all round. Multi-professional teams, including even psychologists and interior decorators, have been employed to make these new coaches more efficient and more attractive for the traveler.

Sadly, there is still quite a lot of older rolling stock in use in many parts of Europe, some well over 50 years of age. This is being phased out, but with the economic recession of the late 1970s and early 1980s, the changeover has slowed down. Do not expect, therefore, to find the latest carriages on all trains, even though the newer stock is well in the majority. Standards of comfort are much better than they were fifteen to twenty years ago, in both first and second and especially second on all expresses.

CLASS CONSCIOUSNESS. The question of which class to choose is often put to me, and the answer is both easy—and difficult. The easy part is "travel first when you can" for there is no doubt at all that it does give substantially more comfort, spaciousness, and generally a more relaxing atmosphere. But it is anything from 30% to 50% dearer than second class. Therefore, if economy is all important, stick to second class. Where you want to economize but not sacrifice too many of life's comforts, then we would recommend traveling second class throughout Scandinavia, on the Benelux expresses in the Netherlands, Belgium and Luxembourg, on the TALGO, ELT and TAF trains in Spain, on "IC" trains in Germany, on the Transalpin express from Basel to Vienna (and also "TS" trains in Austria), on the fast inter-city expresses in Switzerland and on the turbotrains and *Rapides* in France.

Holders of the full Eurailpass do not have to pay any additional surcharges or supplements including the *Trans Europ Express* (T.E.E.) network. On this latter, however, seat reservation is obligatory and this must be paid at the rate of the country in which the train operates.

FOR DAYTIME TRAVEL. The most significant change in the last two years in mainline express rail travel in Europe has been the increase of the Inter-City network, both on national and international bases. These trains now consist almost exclusively of new, airconditioned rolling stock of the most up-to-date design in both first and second class, the latter being almost as good as the old first-class carriages. As we went to press there were over 40 international Inter-City expresses, all with the newest rolling stock, covering much of western and central Europe.

Many of the international expresses no longer require supplementary fares, although in some countries these do still apply and you should always check. Holders of the Eurailpass and other international runabout tickets can use these international and national trains without extra charge.

With the increase in this network there has been a diminution in the Trans Europ Express (TEE) system. This all-first-class high-grade network started in 1957 and was at its peak in the late 1970s. However, it has gradually been reduced. Aimed mainly at business travel it was a big success, but with the economic recession brought on by the 1979 oil crisis the demand for these services was reduced. There are still eight of these running in and/or connecting France, West Germany, Switzerland, Belgium, the Netherlands, and Italy. All continue to offer very high standards and require supplementary fares.

In the U.K. British Rail runs its own InterCity network with a number of routes providing Executive services in first class. All mainline InterCity trains carry first and second class in the U.K. The Eurailpass is not valid in Britain.

FOR OVERNIGHT TRAVEL. Overnight travel by sleeping car on most of Europe's railways is as popular as ever, though many journeys which once required night travel no longer do, because of the faster trains. Night traveling can greatly extend many holiday or business trips—and in comfort. The majority of long-distance overnight trains carry both first- and second-class sleeping cars, and often "couchettes."

A lengthy re-organization of the entire West European sleeping car system has borne fruit in giving much of the Continent an excellent network both on international and internal overnight trains. The various railway systems (excluding those of the U.K. and Ireland) formed the International Sleeping-Car Pool to operate on routes that link two or more countries. Sleeping-cars are staffed and operated by the Wagons-Lit company, by the DSG sleeping-car and dining-car company in Germany, and by the respective railways in Scandinavia. The majority of these sleeping-cars now carry the logo and initials TEN, which stands for Trans Europ Nuit or Nacht or Notte, depending on the language of the country in which they originated.

From the traveler's viewpoint, they offer much the same facilities. Beds are full size, with one, two, or three in each compartment, the last found in the special second-class ("tourist") coaches. Each compartment has a washbasin with hot and cold running water, electric shaving points, coat hangers, mirrors, baggage space, and other amenities. During the day they usually make up into sitting compartments, although this is not always the case. All have toilet and full washroom facilities in each coach. In Germany, around 50 such sleeping-cars also have showers.

The sleeping-cars are all fully staffed, generally with multi-lingual attendants who often can provide refreshments. Each passenger is also provided with a towel and soap. Most trains also carry bottled water.

In the U.K., the first-class sleeping-cars have single berths; second-class has two berths. All have full wash-hand basin facilities, electric shaving points, foot mats, additional blankets, and several lights, as well as individually controlled heating and air ventilation. Most British Rail sleeping-cars can provide limited alcoholic beverages, and all supply morning tea and biscuits as part of the inclusive service. All of British Rail's sleeping cars are of the newest design, very quiet, and fully airconditioned.

If you wish to travel overnight more cheaply, many trains (except in the U.K.) have "couchette" cars. These are more or less simple sleepers with blanket, pillow and small towel provided. In first class, each compartment takes four couchette passengers. In second class, six passengers. Couchettes are certainly more comfortable than sitting up overnight and in the newer coaches—and particularly in first class—they are excellent value for money. But if you require a degree of privacy then opt for a standard sleeper. Apart from the romantic appeal of overnight travel you can save on hotel bills by traveling overnight. Incidentally almost all sleeping car attendants will provide you with a cup of coffee or tea and many also now carry alcoholic refreshments as well.

Always make sleeping car and couchette reservations in advance, but sometimes one can get a last minute cancellation. The cost varies according to the class, the type of sleeper or couchette and the distance traveled. First class single occupancy of sleeper compartments is expensive. For two traveling together, the cost is more or less halved. There are no single sleepers in second class. On many routes where couchettes are used, a standard charge is made whether one is traveling first or second, but of course the appropriate first or second traveling ticket is required.

MEALS ON WHEELS. Every railway system in Europe operates dining cars or refreshment cars of one kind or another. In addition to the standard and traditional dining cars (meals here are always expensive, being anything from about $12 to $25 per head), there are buffet cars (which provide simpler meals from one third to one half the cost of a full dinner meal), self-service "grill" cars, mini bars, and *vendes ambulantes*. The last is a traveling salesperson going through the train with a trolley selling sandwiches, coffee, soft drinks, beer and so on. This is the most economic way of having a meal en route. In some trains you can now get "pre-packed" cold meals at about the same price as on the cafeteria cars. These can be pre-booked or purchased at certain station buffets.

For formal meals in the dining car always book ahead—enquire about this as soon as you get on the train. In many cases you are given a "place card" and told what time the meal starts, or alternatively a dining car attendant comes along the train announcing the meal time.

The tendency on most European railways today is to replace the formal dining-car with a buffet, self-service, or grill car. All T.E.E. trains, however, and most of the prestige expresses in individual countries, will continue to carry full diners for the next few years. But more and more expresses will be providing the simpler eating facilities. Labor costs coupled with the higher speeds of trains (which shorten traveling times) have brought this about. However, be assured that you won't go hungry while traveling by rail.

At most stations, even quite small ones, all over the Continent, there are good buffets (some have top-grade restaurants as well). At all main line stations, trolleys with food and drinks meet most trains. Payment is generally required in the currency of the country, although at frontier stations it has been my experience that they will take several currencies.

The *"Union Internationale des Chemins de Fer,"* or *U.I.C.* as it is generally known, represents almost all of Europe's railways as well as many beyond that continent. Its headquarters are *U.I.C.,* 54, Boulevard Haussmann, F–75436, Paris, France. We would suggest, however, that those planning extensive railway travel in Europe purchase the *Thomas Cook Continental Timetable* published monthly.

SCENIC ROUTES. Many of Europe's top-line expresses push through some of the Continent's finest scenic areas in daylight. It is not possible to list all of these (there are around 200 all told), but we have selected a number which are particularly outstanding. In every case these trains complete all (or the major part) of their journey in the daytime during the summer holiday season, and operate all the year around unless otherwise stated. Those which are T.E.E.-operated are so marked. Dining cars or refreshment services are available on all either for the entire journey or a part of it. All trains listed other than the T.E.E. services carry both first and second-class coaches. Some require supplementary fare for all or part of the way.

Adriatico (T.E.E.). Milan—Bologna—Rimini—Pescara—Bari. Journey time nine and a half hours; partly coastal route. Daylight almost all year. Full dining car throughout journey.

Arlberg Express. Paris—Zurich—Innsbruck—Vienna. Leaves French capital in the evening, travels overnight to Switzerland. Goes through Swiss and Austrian Alps in daylight. Total traveling time 21 hours approx.

Barcelona Talgo. Madrid—Guadalajara—Zaragoza—Taragona—Sitges—Barcelona. Departs from the Spanish capital mid-morning to arrive in the country's second city and main seaport in time for dinner. Approx. 9 hours. Similar service in the afternoon, and about one hour earlier in opposite direction. Full diner throughout.

Linderhof. Bremen—Hannover—Wurzburg—Munich. An all-daylight express (departs around 8:10 A.M.) through the heartland of Germany, passing some very lovely countryside. Arrives at Munich in mid-afternoon. Total traveling time under eight hours.

Cornish Riviera. London—Exeter—Plymouth—Penzance. One of Britain's longest established expresses. Very scenic route, especially after Exeter. Connections for many resorts in Devon and Cornwall. Does not operate on Sundays. Now a high-speed train (InterCity 125) service.

Erasmus. Amsterdam—Dusseldorf—Cologne—Frankfurt—Wurzburg—Nurnberg—Munich—Innsbruck. Morning departures each end; Rhine Valley and the Alps in one day.

Flying Scotsman. London—Newcastle-upon-Tyne—Edinburgh. Perhaps Britain's most famous train; rural scenery for much of way, passing many historic sites. Limited accommodation, reservations advisable. Nearly 400 miles in about 5 hours. Now a High Speed Train.

Foguete. Lisbon—Coimbra—Oporto. Three times daily express between Portugal's two major cities calling at the ancient University city of Coimbra en route. Travels through the heartland of the country. First class only. Reservation strongly advised.

Glasgow-Mallaig. Twice daily (three times May to September), route is through the West Highlands and along the banks of Loch Lomond. One of the most scenic in Britain. Buffet car on all trains. About six leisurely hours for the 165 miles.

Gottardo (T.E.E.). Zurich—Lugano—Como—Milan. A very scenic route passing through the famous St. Gotthard tunnel. Southbound route always in daylight. Excellent connections from/to Basel. Total time approx. 4½ hours.

Glacier Express. Zermatt—Brig—Andermatt—Disentis—Chur—St. Moritz. Across the roof of Switzerland this unique train gives a chance to see the best of the Alps. Dining car part of the way. Not fast but a sheer delight.

Henrik. Bergen—Voss—Finse—Geilo—Oslo. An early (but not too early) start from Norway's second city takes this express through some of the finest of the country's scenery reaching the capital in the early afternoon. Its "twin" the *Pernille* operates at similar timings in the other direction. Dining car on both trains.

Le Catalan. Geneva—Chambéry—Grenoble—Avignon—Narbonne—Perpignan—Barcelona. This is a Talgo train and one of only two to operate outside Spain on an interesting and largely scenic route. Connections at Barcelona to/from Madrid and at Geneva for Lausanne, Berne, Zurich and Basel. Approx. 10 hours Barcelona-Geneva.

Mare Nostrum. Barcelona—Tarragona—Valencia—Alicante. Down much of Spain's Mediterranean coast and then inland. A Talgo train with a buffet car runs through the day, daily. Approx. 10 hours for the journey.

Mediolanum. Munich—Innsbruck—Verona—Milan. Through the Tyrolean Alps and the famous Brenner Pass. Northbound route entirely in daylight throughout the year. Approx. 6 hours.

Norgepilen and Sverigepilen. Oslo—Stockholm. Twin trains connecting the two Scandinavian capitals—lake and woodland scenery most of the way. Approx. 6½ hours.

Peloritano. Palermo—Messina—Salerno—Naples—Rome. Connects the Italian capital with the leading city in Sicily (through coaches also to Catania for Taormina). Runs beside the sea for much of the way. Limited accommodation. Reservation essential. Approx. 11 hours, including train ferry crossing of Straits of Messina.

Rembrandt. Amsterdam—Utrecht—Cologne—Mainz—Darmstadt—Heidelberg—Ulm—Munich. With a mid-afternoon (around 3 P.M.) start, this train travels the Rhine Valley in daylight in summer. Opposite direction is an early start (7 A.M. from Munich) but lets you see Bavaria in daylight.

Rhone-Isar. Geneva—Berne—Zurich—Lindau—Munich. Through Switzerland and part of Bavaria by day most of the way. Dining car in Switzerland. About 9 hours for nearly 400 miles.

Romulus. Vienna—Klagenfurt—Udine—Venice (Mestre)—Bologna—Florence—Rome. An all daylight express (morning departures either end) through the Austrian and Italian Alps and passing through or close to many famous cities. Buffet car most of the way.

Transalpin. Basel—Zurich—Innsbruck—Salzburg—Linz—Vienna. One of the best trains in Europe for mountain scenery, most of which is in daylight throughout the year. Limited accommodation. Reservation essential. Approx. 10 hours.

Vesuvio (T.E.E.). Milan—Bologna—Florence—Rome—Naples. A varied route from northern to southern Italy. Runs south in daylight all the way throughout the year, leaving Milan mid-morning and arriving in Naples late afternoon. Traveling time about 7½ hours.

CITY TO CITY EXPRESSES. In addition to the "scenic routes" mentioned above, there are also many excellent fast expresses connecting most of Europe's main cities, including those in Great Britain and Ireland. Here are a few that are of particular interest to the holiday traveler:

Aberdonian.   London — York — Newcastle — Edinburgh — Dundee — Aberdeen. Daily restaurant car train linking the national capital with the "oil boom" city of Scotland. Total journey takes about eight hours for the 535 miles. Also the "Night Aberdonian" on the same route with first- and second-class sleepers but not serving Newcastle. The daytime train is now a high-speed train (Inter City 125) service.

Le Capitole. Paris—Limoges—Cahors—Toulouse. Twice daily fast *rapides* linking the French capital with the city of Toulouse within sight of the Pyrenees. One departs breakfast time, the other early evening. Opposite services at approx. same times. Takes around 6 hours for the 445 mile journey, one of the fastest in Europe.

Enterprise. Belfast—Dublin. Several-times-daily express connecting the two cities. One in the morning and one in the early evening each way are non-stop—buffet car on each one.

Freccia della Laguna. Rome—Florence—Bologna—Venice. Fastest rail service connecting these cities. Leave Rome at lunch time, arrive Venice for dinner. Runs daily. Reservation essential. Total time under 6 hours.

Galilei. Paris—Dijon—Lausanne—Milan—Verona—Venice or Milan—Bologna—Florence. Overnight train with 1st and 2nd class sleepers and 2nd class couchettes. Buffet Paris to Swiss border and vice versa.

Ile de France and **Rubens** (T.E.E.). Paris—Brussels non-stop, taking just under two and a half hours. Full dining car both ways.

Merkur. Copenhagen—Hamburg—Cologne—Karlsruhe. A daytime express linking many German cities with the Danish capital. Total time about 12½ hours.

Nymphenburg. Munich—Frankfurt—Wiesbaden—Bonn—Cologne—Dortmund—Hannover. One of Germany's "Inter-City" first-class-only expresses. Dining car throughout the entire journey. Takes just under nine hours for the 596 miles. Runs daily.

Palatino. Paris—Rome. Leaves each city in the early evening, arrives just after breakfast—sleeping cars all the way—dining car attached for dinner and breakfast. Inclusive tickets can cover journey, sleeper and meals.

Prinz Eugen. Vienna—Linz—Passau—Nürnberg—Wurzburg—Hannover—Hamburg. An excellent Inter-City service with a dining car all the way. Runs throughout the year. Around 10 hours in all.

Paris-Madrid Talgo. An all-sleeping car (1st and 2nd class) overnight express with dining car and bar all the way. No change at frontier as the wheels are telescopic, adaptable to both the French and Spanish gauges. Takes about 13 hours for complete journey.

Royal Scot. London—Glasgow. A long-established daylight express running every day in the year. Takes 5 hours for the 400-mile journey. Slower on Sundays.

Saphir. Cologne—Aachen—Liege—Brussels—Ostend. Takes just over three and a half hours, with mini-buffet service. Links with ferries at Ostend.

NOSTALGIA RAIL TRAVEL. There are two main trains offering the experience of deluxe rail travel in bygone days, mainly in the 1920s and 30s. The first is Swiss-operated and uses refurbished sleeping, dining, bar, and saloon cars on selected routes in western and central Europe including through trips from Paris to Istanbul and with daytime Pullman cars on the scenic route of the St. Gotthard Pass from Basle to Chiasso in Italy. Details of the 1987 operation were not available as we went to press but this information can be obtained from *Intraflug Ltd.,* CH-8127 Forch, Zurich, Switzerland or many travel agents.

The second is the Venice Simplon-Orient-Express. This is a two part train with one section in England using British Pullman car stock, the other on the continent with 1920s and 30s sleeping, dining, and bar-salon cars from the Wagons-Lits company. All have been totally refurbished in *grande de luxe* style with the sleeping cars also airconditioned. The route is London (Victoria)–Folkestone–Boulogne–Paris–Basle–Zurich–Innsbruck–Verona–Venice, twice weekly to and from London with additional services from Paris according to season. Fares and timings for 1987 were not available as we went to press but the single fare London–Venice including meals in summer 1986 was £520. Full details from *Venice Simplon-Orient Express,* Suite 2841, One World Trade Center, New York, N.Y. 10048 or *Venice Simplon-Orient-Express,* 20 Upper Ground, London S.E.1.

CAR TRAINS. Parallel with the development of the vast network of fast motorways throughout much of Western Europe, the various railway systems have built up a service of "car trains". These fall into two categories—day travel and night travel. In both cases the car travels with you on specially constructed wagons. By night you have the choice of ordinary coaches, couchette cars or full sleeping cars. By day there are both first and second class coaches. Where timings are appropriate these trains carry a dining or buffet car or on some services "mini-bar" facilities.

Some of these trains are international, connecting two or more centers, while others run entirely within one country such as France or Germany. Advance booking is advisable and essential in high season although in the offpeak periods places can often be found on the day of travel. Please note that most of these services run once or twice or in some cases three times a week. A very few offer daily services. All are in full swing in summer while many operate throughout the year. Bookings can be made through the appropriate railway offices in the U.S.A., Canada and Britain or from main travel agents. Last minute bookings are best made at the station of departure.

GENERAL INFORMATION. It is not possible to generalize with any degree of accuracy about cost of rail travel, as rates vary from country to country and according to the type of ticket issued. As a guide rule however, the farther you go, the cheaper the cost per mile becomes. It is more economic to book for long distances, then break your journey en route, than to buy individual tickets for each section of the journey. For example, if you bought a first-class ticket from London to Vienna, this would cost approx. $250 for the entire journey, including the North Sea ferry crossing. With this ticket, you could stop over, for example, in Amsterdam, Cologne, Frankfurt, Munich and Salzburg, all at no extra cost. But if you took individual tickets between each of these places, the total could be nearly half again as much. As you can see, there is a saving!

There are, however, certain restrictions on breaking your journey in some countries, and you should always enquire about these from a travel agent or main line railway station. Certain high-speed expresses such as all the TEE trains require supplementary fares varying according to the distance traveled. But in no cases are these very high. All are clearly marked in the timetables and the supplementary tickets should be purchased before getting on the train, although in some cases this can be done after boarding.

Alas, with increased fares during the last two years the cost of first-class rail travel has gone up noticeably. This now is coming close to economy-class excursion return air fares on many routes and indeed in some cases first-class rail travel (on a return basis) is actually dearer than the equivalent economy air fare. It is however very much cheaper than first-class air travel (but then what is not?). As I stated earlier, second class fares are anything from 30% to 50% cheaper than first-class, but because of the big fare differential in different countries and on different types of tickets this is a wide generalization. Reservations are required on many trains and we would certainly advise it whenever possible, particularly during the busy period. The amount is small, being between the equivalent of £1 and £2.25 depending on the rate of exchange. Reservations can be made at main line stations and many travel agencies.

Concessions on fares are also given to children, the rates varying according to age and from one country to another. Roughly speaking, children under 3 (under 4 or 5 in some countries) travel free and those up to 10, 12, 14 or 15 (according to the country) for half price. On international tickets, travel is usually free under 4 and half rate between 4 and 11 years, inclusive.

The free baggage allowance again varies, but is always very substantial. You can send registered baggage on ahead of you even through international customs. We advise this if you are traveling a long distance by rail and have a lot to carry. Enquire at the station of departure.

In some cases, too, train tickets are interchangeable for bus travel over certain sectors. This also applies to some river steamer services, such as on the Rhine. With the last mentioned, for example, if you had a ticket from Dusseldorf to Frankfurt, you could sail on the Rhine for part of the way. Full information about interchanges (which of course you must arrange in advance) can be got from the mainline stations and leading rail ticket agencies.

In all countries there are special cheap tickets for holiday travel. These sometimes involve using certain trains or traveling at certain times or going by certain routes. In other cases, they allow you unlimited travel within a certain period. Enquire locally on your arrival in the country.

MONEY-SAVING RAIL PASSES. If you plan to do a lot of traveling around in Western Europe, we suggest that you get a *Eurailpass*. This is a convenient, all-inclusive ticket that can save you money on over 100,000 miles of railroads and railroad-operated buses, ferries, river and lake steamers, hydrofoils, and some Mediterranean crossings in 15 countries of Western Europe (excluding the United Kingdom). It provides the holder with unlimited travel at rates of: 15 days for $260; 21 days for $330; 1 month for $410; 2 months for $560; 3 months for $680; and 2nd-class Youthpass (anyone up to age 26) 1 month for $290 and 2 months for $370. Children under 12 go for half-fare, under 4 go free. These prices cover first-class passage for the Trans Europ Express and other services. Available only if you live outside Europe or North Africa. The pass must be bought from an authorized agent in the Western Hemisphere or Japan before you leave for Europe. Apply through your travel agent; or the general agents for North America: French National Railroads, Eurailpass Division, 610 Fifth Avenue, New York, NY 10020; the German Federal Railroad, 747 Third Ave., New York, NY 10017 or 1290 Bay St., Toronto, Ontario M5R 2C3, Canada. Also through the Italian and Swiss railways. To get full value from your pass, be sure not to have it date-stamped until you actually use it for the first time. For complete details, write to Eurailpass, c/o WBA, 51 Ridgefield Ave., Staten Island, NY 10304.

Excellent value as the Eurailpass is it should be remembered that it is essentially for those who plan to do a lot of traveling. If you only want to make say two or three journeys it is best to purchase the tickets as required. In some countries if you travel a certain distance on a return trip or circular trip basis and stay a minimum length of time (generally just a few days) you can get reductions on the standard fares. For example in France if you travel more than 1500 kms. and spend five days or more in the country you get a 20% reduction on the normal fare.

For travel in Great Britain (England, Scotland and Wales only), you can purchase a *BritRailpass,* which again allows you unlimited rail (and associated ferryboat and bus) travel for certain periods. For economy-class travel the cost for 7 days is $115, for 14 days $175, for 21 days $220, and for one month $260. Half-fare for children, special rates for Senior Citizens. In addition to these, young people (ages 16–25) can also obtain *BritRail Youth Passes,* which cost $95 for 7 days, $150 for 14 days, $190 for 21 days and $225 for one month, all for unlimited mileage in 2nd class. (Note: These prices will hold until end March 1987). Ireland is part of the Eurailpass system.

Note. All of these passes and coupons must be purchased in North America or Japan and are for Western Hemisphere and Japan residents only. Apply to BritRail Travel International Ltd., 630 Third Ave., New York, NY 10017; or 800 South Hope St., Los Angeles, CA 90017; 333 N. Michigan Ave., Chicago, IL 60601; Cedar Maple Plaza, Cedar Springs, Dallas, TX 75201; or U.K.

Building, 409 Granville Street, Vancouver 2, B.C.; or 94 Cumberland St., Toronto, Ontario, M5R 1A3.

Young people with a desire to travel extensively in Europe by rail should purchase an *InterRail Card.* This is available to anyone (except, unfortunately, residents of the U.S. and Canada) under 26 years of age and the holder is entitled to unlimited second-class rail travel (along with connecting ferry and in certain cases bus services) in no fewer than 18 countries in Western and central Europe plus Morocco. The card also allows half-fare travel on all rail services in the U.K. and Ireland and on the Sealink ferries connecting the British Isles with the Continent. The InterRail Card is valid for one calendar month and can be purchased at most mainline stations, rail ticket agencies and travel agents. You must show evidence of age on purchase and the card is NOT transferable. The card currently costs around £140 in the U.K.

A *Senior Citizen Pass,* entitling older travelers to discounts of from 1/3 to 1/2, is now offered by many West European countries, with others expected to follow suit; check with each country's tourist bureau. A passport-size photo is required for the card, which must be applied for in each individual country.

Alternatively, students of any age and young people up to the age of 21 wishing to purchase their tickets one at a time should contact *Transalpino Ltd.,* 38 Buckingham Palace Rd., London S.W.1 (tel. 01–630–5232), where, upon proof of age or student status, rail travel can be booked from one to any other of 14 European countries at reductions of up to 50% on normal fares.

If you want to be really knowledgeable about train times in Europe (including Gt. Britain and Ireland), then you should purchase *Cook's Continental Timetable.* Packed with details and lots of information, it is issued monthly. Available in the U.S.A. from: Stephen Forsyth Travel Library, P.O. Box 2975, Shawnee Mission, Kansas 66201. In Britain, order from: Thomas Cook Ltd., Timetable Publishing Office, P.O. Box 36, Peterborough, England PE3 6SB. In either case the price is US $15.95 plus $2.50 postage. Or the timetable is available from any Cook's branch for £4.25, plus postage if required.

USEFUL ADDRESSES. Full information on rail services within the under-mentioned countries can be got from the following addresses (in all other cases, contact the national tourist office of the country concerned):

In the U.S. and Canada: *Belgian National Railroads,* 745 Fifth Avenue, New York City 10151.

BritRail Travel International Inc., 630 Third Avenue, New York City 10017; 333 N. Michigan Ave., Chicago, Ill. 60601; 800 South Hope St., Los Angeles, Cal. 90017; Cedar Maple Plaza, Cedar Springs, Dallas, Tex. 75201; and in Canada: 94 Cumberland St., Suite 601, Toronto, Ontario M5R 1A3; 409 Granville St., Vancouver, B.C. V6C 1T2.

French National Railroads, 610 Fifth Avenue, New York City 10020; 9465 Wilshire Blvd., Beverly Hills, Cal. 90212; 11 E. Adams St., Chicago, Ill. 60603; 2121 Ponce de Leon Blvd., Coral Gables, Fla. 33114; 360 Post St., Union Square, San Francisco, Cal. 94108; and in Canada: 1500 Stanley St., Montreal, P.Q. H3A 1R3, and 409 Granville St., Vancouver, B.C. V6C 1T2.

Germanrail, 747 Third Ave., New York City, 10017; 625 Statler Office Building, Boston, Mass. 02116; 95–75 West Higgins Rd., Suite 505, Rosemont, Ill. 60018; 1121 Walker St., Room 601, Houston, Tex. 77002; 520 Broadway, Room 320, Santa Monica, Cal. 90401; 442 Post St. 6th Floor, San Francisco, Cal. 94102; 8000 Girard Ave., Suite 518, South Denver, Col. 80231; and in Canada, 1290 Bay St., Toronto, Ontario M5R 2C3.

Italian State Railways, (CIT Travel Service, Inc. Official Pass Agent), 666 Fifth Avenue, New York City 10103.

Netherlands Railways, 355 Lexington Ave., New York, N.Y. 10017; 605 Market St., Room 401, San Francisco, Cal. 94105; 25 Adelaide St. East, Suite 710, Toronto, Ont. M5C 1Y2.

Swiss Federal Railways, 608 Fifth Avenue, New York City 10020; Box 215, Commerce Court, Toronto, Ont. M5L 1E8.

In the U.K.: *Austrian Federal Railways,* 30 St. George's St., London W1R 9FA.

Belgian National Railways, 22 Sackville St., London W1X 1DE.

C.I.E. (Irish Railways), 150 New Bond St., London W1Y 9FE; also 35 Lower Abbey St., Dublin 1, Ireland.

Danish State Railways, DFDS Center, 199 Regent St., London W1R 7WA.
Finnish State Railways, Finlandia Travel Agency, 130 Jermyn St., London SW1Y 4UJ.
French Railways, 179 Piccadilly, London W1V 0BA.
German Federal Railways, 10 Old Bond St., London W1X 4EN.
Italian State Railways, C.I.T. Ltd, 50–51 Conduit St., London W1R 9FB.
Luxembourg Railways (CFL), 36 Piccadilly, London W1V 9PA.
Netherlands Railways, 4 New Burlington St., W1X 1FE.
Norwegian State Railways, 21/24 Cockspur St., London SW1Y 5DA.
Portuguese Railways, 1/5 New Bond St., London W1Y 0NP.
Spanish National Railways, 57 St. James's St., London SW1.
Swedish Railways (as for Norwegian Railways).
Swiss Federal Railways, 1 New Coventry St., London W1V 8EE.
Yugoslav Railways, 143 Regent St., London W1R 8AE.
(*Note:* Many of the above offices are for information only, being attached to the respective tourist offices.)

MOTORING ON THE CONTINENT

By Frances Howell

Even people who don't much care for motoring agree that it is the best way to travel in Europe. In other continents, where the distances are greater, the road system perhaps not so extensive or the climate less kindly, other forms of transport may well be preferable—but in Europe, going by car is the thing to do.

The chief reason for this is, in a word, freedom. Freedom from the discipline of public transport schedules; freedom to stop and stare wherever and whenever you wish. Freedom to follow your own, maybe insane, route and at your own speed; to choose your own hotels; freedom from the tyranny of a suitcase which will hold and must weigh just so much and no more. With a car everything goes, even if it has to be carried loose, nor is there any limit set upon your buying something big and bulky if you wish.

This freedom is, however, something more than just a word. Auto travel really does offer the best value in pleasure travel, for in no other way can you see so much for your money. Fly to your destination and you save time and energy, but you see nothing of the land en route. Go by train and you will see much more but will still be moving too fast and are tied to the track, which invariably goes through the seamier side of cities. In a car, you can go by one pleasant route and return by another.

What is possibly more important, you can escape from noise and encourage economy by searching out country hotels away from main roads. Even if your interest lies in a city, it is increasingly worthwhile on both counts to find accommodation just outside it. Anyone who has never endured a night in a room overlooking a narrow street forming a part of some Continental highway route can have no conception of the misery this can mean.

ECONOMY AND CONVENIENCE. Many people question the costs of taking a car abroad, but this need be no barrier, providing that the journey is more than just a short hop. Clearly, to take a car from London to Paris would be an extravagance, and to take it to Italy if your one idea is to get there as fast as possible would be boring and foolish. It used to be possible to make a reasoned comparison between traveling by road or 2nd-class rail, and to find that a journey of, say, 900 miles in a 14 ft. car would be more expensive than rail with one or two people, but less expensive with three or four passengers. (This would be allowing for two overnight stops but no sleeping accommodation on the train, and not including meals which have to be eaten somewhere in either case.) If you elevate the train travel to something approaching the comfort of car travel, say by going 1st-class sleeper, then the car is about half the price. But it is very risky to make comparisons of that sort now, because apart from the surprise fare supplements that are liable to be levied on public transport, higher petrol prices knock the motorist and the speed limits at present operating almost throughout Europe must add, perhaps critically, to journey times. But there remains the money-to-value ratio, which must be subjective.

Then there is the question of parking—what to do with the car when you are not actually using it? This does not often present a problem. If you are staying in a smart hotel in the center of town, it is probable that the porter will be able to direct you to a garage, possibly belonging to the hotel, or take the car himself to park for you. This, of course, always costs a little money. Small hotels in side streets seem to have a facility for producing parking space whenever it is wanted, and naturally, country hotels are surrounded by space, though not always free. When using a car for sight-seeing, there is sometimes a temporary difficulty, but most places of tourist interest have parking places beside them, and arrivals and departures are more or less incessant. It is, naturally, wise to lock the car when leaving it—more so in some countries than others.

Some people also feel that driving long distances is very tiring and not their idea of a holiday. It is, of course, possible to reduce the long distance driving by taking the car on a train, though this can be pretty expensive.

PACKAGE TOURS. For either the first-timer or the idle and luxury-loving, this mode of motor travel has much in its favor. The leading operator in motor touring is now *Car Holidays Abroad* (sister company to *Canvas Holidays*—see p. 34). This company can provide the motorist with anything from a simple channel crossing to a complete holiday. Everything except fuel and personal extras is paid in advance, thus relieving the motorist of any financial anxiety and most of the need to struggle with foreign currencies and languages. Though not for people who want 5-star accommodations, they do offer a wide range of hotels—their forté being the small hotel off the beaten track.

The *AA*, through its subsidiary *Argosy*, offers simple, budget packages, some in Spain but mostly in France, while their British *Country Wanderers* operates a hotel-to-hotel system. Most of the car ferry companies also offer inclusive holidays, as for example DFDS Seaways throughout Scandinavia, Brittany Ferries in France and Spain and all the short-haul companies—Sealink, P&O, Townsend Thoresen, Olau—in those countries within easy reach of Britain.

On the whole, the pre-paid motoring holiday works out well. It is not the cheapest way to travel, but neither is it by any means the most expensive. It deprives the real pioneer of the pleasure of making horrible discoveries, but it saves time and makes everything beautifully easy.

CAR HIRE. Car hire is possible in every country, with *Avis* and *Hertz* operating in all West European countries, plus Yugoslavia (Avis also in all East Europe), and *Godfrey Davis Europcar* in all of Western Europe, plus Yugoslavia, Hungary, Turkey, Israel etc. Local hire firms and their rates are mentioned under each country heading in this book. Some London firms, notably *Lane's Travel Service Ltd.*, 251 Brompton Road, S.W.3, offer a fly- and self-drive holiday consisting of a package varying considerably according to the country concerned, but always economical and well informed.

The cost of car hire with unlimited mileage for cheapest cars varies from around $149.60 a week in Denmark, to $198.45 in Switzerland, at Godfrey Davis Europcar. Third-party insurance and collision damage waiver are included, but not local tax. In Britain it is £175 a week, exc. V.A.T.—collision damage waiver, an additional £19.60. Island cars no longer come cheaper. The hire tax, if included, can be so high that it is worth planning to hire in a low levy country whenever possible. Some firms also offer reduced "holiday hire" rates for 14 days. Each firm has its own ideas about rental terms, and they may vary between countries. The minimum age may be 21 or 25, the max. 69, 70, or no limit. In Britain, a license must have been held for 12 months; in Germany, 6 will do. Endorsed licenses are accepted at the discretion of the company. Notice that insurance cover provided is usually pretty basic and could be costly. Lists of accredited car hire firms can be had from the *AAA* at 28 East 78th Street, New York, N.Y. 10021; Grosvenor Square, London W.1, or 9 rue de la Paix, Paris; *RAC*, 49 Pall Mall, London S.W.1, the *AA*, Fanum House, Leicester Square, London W.C.2 or from branches of *Thomas Cook*.

EUROPEAN ROAD CONDITIONS. Going in search of way-out hotels leads drivers onto secondary, and even lesser, roads. There is no need to fear excursions of this sort in most West European countries; in fact, secondary roads in many are now preferable to their trunk or "A" roads on account of the heavy commercial traffic the latter carry. Apart from the East European countries, where first-class roads tend to be second-class and second-class better left alone, the only countries where unclassified roads should be treated with respect are Spain, Yugoslavia, Greece, Finland and the north of both Sweden and Norway.

In mountainous regions such as Austria, Switzerland, the French Alps and the Italian Dolomites, secondary roads are slow, often narrow, but the surface is usually good.

When planning a route, it is convenient to know that on good, open Continental roads, it is generally accepted that one kilometer per minute (60 km./hour or 37 mph.) is a reasonable average to maintain. When there are long motorways, as in Holland, Germany, France and Italy, the speed will be higher, particularly in Germany, where the Autobahn net is extensive, although often heavy with traffic in summer, particularly on week-ends. The Belgian motorway network is now almost complete and you can speed in all directions on it. The Brussels ring road still has an important gap in the south, but is otherwise now a great help. Rush-hour traffic can, however, be heavy, and frightening.

The great north-south French autoroute is now only a section of the vast European motorway network leading northwards from Paris through Belgium, Holland, Germany to Denmark, and southwards to the toe of Italy. From Dunkerque to the Italian frontier it is 780 miles, costs about £26 in tolls and *can* be covered in 11 hours at legal speeds, including circling Paris on the now complete Boulevard Périphéque. This, however, and the roads feeding into it are often choked with rush hour traffic.

In the southern half of France, many of the roads are winding and not very wide, which, of course, also applies to all mountainous countries, such as Norway, Switzerland, Austria and Northern Italy. All now have speed limits.

All over Europe, there is now a network of International Highways, designated with the letter "E" and then the road number, in black on green. E5, for instance, runs from Ostend, Belgium to Istanbul, Turkey, by way of Germany, Austria, Hungary, Yugoslavia and Greece. Other "E" roads of interest to motorists starting out from Britain or Western Europe are E1, from the UK to Italy; E2, UK to Brindisi (for car ferries to Greece); E8, UK to Poland. These roads are now nearly all expressways or motorways, although not quite all of the same standard.

British roads are not so atrocious as many Americans fear. There are now a couple of thousand miles of excellent motorways; the trunk roads have been greatly improved and the "B"roads, provided that you are not in a hurry, are delightful. They can boast acceptable surfaces even in the wilds of Scotland and Wales. The British, Irish, and Cypriots drive on the left; all the rest on the right.

Road maps are available, free, from every national tourist office, or are on sale in offices of the AA, RAC and the AAA. Several petroleum companies also supply maps cheaply.

Motoring Routes

Here are some outline routes with some idea of the *mileages*. In conjunction with good touring maps, they will enable you to plan a rough touring timetable. To reap the maximum enjoyment from your trip, do not hesitate to make detours from these routes to sample what takes your interest. The suggested time schedules provide ample time for such detours. In most cases, these times can be reduced if you exceed an *average* speed of 30 m.p.h.

Paris—Riviera. This is probably the most popular holiday journey in Europe. There are three separate routes through widely differing regions or autoroute throughout.

(a) *Via Rhône Valley.* One night en route. Fontainebleau via Auxerre, Tournus, Lyon, Bollène, Avignon, Marseille—or Pont St. Esprit, Nîmes, Marseille—St. Raphael, Nice, Menton. Total distance Paris-Marseille, about 495 miles. *Note:* to by-pass Sens and Auxerre you can take a section of the Autoroute du Sud, cutting the distance by about 25 miles and driving time by over an hour.

(b) *Massif Central Route.* About 515 miles. One night. Via Moulin, Vichy, Le Puy, Pont St. Esprit, Remoulins, Avignon, Les Baux, Marseille.

(c) *Route des Alpes.* Two nights. Troyes, Dijon, Geneva, Grenoble, Sisteron, Cannes. Distance about 615 miles.

Paris-Pyrenees-Andorra-Costa Brava. Mileage about 660. Three nights. Via Orleans, Limoges, Toulouse, Foix, Bourg Madame, frontier, Ripoll, Barcelona or eastwards from Toulouse via Carcassone, Perpignan, Côte Vermeille and Rosas.

Paris-Biarritz-Portugal or Malaga. Four nights, Chartres, Tours, Bordeaux, Biarritz, Burgos, Salamanca, Ciudad Rodrigo, frontier, Guarda, Coimbra, Lisbon. For Malaga go south at Burgos through Madrid, Cordoba or Granada to Malaga. Mileage about 1200 and 1100.

Paris-Frankfurt. About 480 miles. One night. Nancy, Strasbourg, Baden-Baden, Stuttgart, Frankfurt.

Paris-Cherbourg. Mileage 200. Autoroute to Evreaux, then Liseaux, Caen, Bayeux, Cherbourg.

Paris-Brussels. Mileage 185. Via Soissons, Laon, Maubeuge, frontier, Mons, Brussels, or autoroute all the way—170 miles.

Channel Coast-Pyrenees (Touring route). Two nights. Approximately 685 miles. Start from Rouen, thence Evreux, Chartres, Vendôme, Blois, Château-roux, Tulle, Albi, Carcassone, Aix-les-Thermes.

Channel Ports-Switzerland. One night. Calais, Arras, Cambrai, St. Quentin, Rheims, Châlons-sur-Marne, Chaumont, Vesoul, then to Basel. Approximately 535 miles.

Black Forest Alternative. From Rheims to Nancy, St. Die, Colmar, Freiburg, Basel. 260 miles.

Channel Coast-Austria. 2 nights. About 700 miles. As to Basel, then Zurich, St. Gallen, Feldkirch, Innsbruck. Alternatively, motorway throughout from Ostend via Germany.

Rotterdam-Frankfurt (Touring route). One night. The Hague, Amsterdam, Utrecht, Arnhem, frontier, Wesel, Duisburg, autobahn to Cologne and cross to west bank of Rhine, Bonn, Koblenz, Mainz, Frankfurt. 357 miles.

Frankfurt-Rome (Touring route). Six nights. Karlsruhe, Freiburg, Titisee, Waldshut, Radolfzell, Konstanz, Meersburg, Füssen, Garmisch, Innsbruck, Brenner Pass, Bolzano, Trento, Verona, Bologna, or Verona, Venice, Bologna, Florence, Siena, Viterbo, Rome. Or motorway all the way.

Rome-Cannes. Two nights. Pisa, Rapallo, Genoa, San Remo, Nice, Cannes 478. *Alternatively,* autostrada throughout.

Rome-Brindisi-Athens. Travel-while-you-sleep route requires one night only and reduces the overland distance by about 1/3. Rome-Naples-Brindisi 370. Overnight car ferry, to Igoumenitsa, continue to Gulf of Corinth ferry (or arrive by longer Brindisi-Patras ferry) then motorway to Athens. Total about 800 miles.

Paris-Barcelona-Madrid-Malaga. Four nights. Route 20 from Paris to Barcelona 630, thence to Zaragoza, Madrid, Malaga. Total mileage: 1,158.

Channel Coast or Paris to Scandinavia. Two nights. Lille, Antwerp, Breda, Arnhem, Hamburg, Flensburg, Kolding, Odense, Copenhagen, 780 miles. Alternative route Hamburg: Lubeck-Puttgarden ferry. On to Stockholm via Halsingborg ferry, Jonkoping and Norrkoping, 400. Ferry direct to Helsinki or via Turku (Abo).

Copenhagen-Oslo-Bergen. Two nights. Ferry to Hälsingborg, Göteborg, Halden, Oslo, Geilo, Bergen. About 655 miles.

Oslo-Arctic Highway-Midnight Sun-Helsinki. 10 to 15 nights. Oslo, Lillehammer, Trondheim, Arctic Circle, Bodø, Narvik, Tromsø, Skibotn 1225. Finnish frontier, Kilpisjärvi, Muonio, Tornio, Oulu, Vaasa, Pori, Turku, Helsinki 2180; or Tromsø-Stockholm. Four nights. To Tornio, Swedish frontier bridge to Sundsvall, Söderhamm, Gävle, Stockholm 1124.

The average speed is rather lower in northern Norway than in most countries owing to ferries across fjords.

London-North Wales. Touring route—Aylesbury, Stratford-on-Avon, Worcester, Rhayader, Aberystwyth, Dolgellau, Caernarvon, Betwys-y-Coed, Llangollen, Ludlow, Hereford, Gloucester, Oxford, London. About 500 miles.

London to West and Southern England. 3 nights touring. Motorway to Taunton, then Exeter, Dartmoor, Plymouth, Torquay, Exeter, Salisbury, Winchester, Tunbridge Wells, Canterbury, London. About 600 miles.

London to Scotland. Motorway to Doncaster, A1 to Darlington, A68 to Edinburgh. 370 miles. Alternatively, by rail night car sleeper, 7½ hours.

Edinburgh to London (Touring route). Two nights. Carlisle, Chester, Shrewsbury, Ludlow, Hereford, Gloucester, Oxford, London 400; or Shrewsbury, Stratford-on-Avon, Oxford.

Vienna-Budapest-Belgrade-Bucharest. Enter Hungary at Nichelsdorf Hegyes Halom, Gyor, Budapest, Szeged, Novisad, Belgrade, 450 miles, 2 nights. Alternatively, continue across Hungary to Oradea in Romania, then Cluj, Brasov, Polesti, Bucharest. 525 miles, 3 nights.

Vienna-Cracow-Warsaw. Three nights. Cross into Czechoslovakia at Bratislava. Then Zilina into Poland at Cieszyn 232. On to Cracow, Kielce, Radom, Warsaw 490.

Berlin-Warsaw. One night. Frankfurt-on-the-Oder, cross into Poland at Slubice, then via Poznan to Warsaw. 341 miles.

Nuremberg-Prague-Uzergod-Kijev-Moscow. Follow International Route E12 into Czechoslovakia to Prague, then E14 into Poland and to Warsaw, then E8 to the Russian frontier at Brest, thence to Minsk, Smolensk to Moscow. About 1525 miles slow going.

Belgrade-Sofia-Istanbul. Two nights. Belgrade (Beograd), Nis, Sofia, Plovdiv, Edirne, Istanbul. Total: 600 miles.

MOUNTAIN PASSES. There are close to a hundred mountain passes in Europe, some of them fantastic feats of road engineering, rising to heights of 9,000 ft. and more. Many of them are obstructed well after the snow season. Below we list some of the more scenic and useful highways, and the annual periods when they may be closed. Their opening depends on the weather, and local guidance should be sought before starting the drive. Asterisks show passes where alternative road or railroad tunnel transportation is available. "Closed occasionally" refers mainly to the winter months.

Austria	Route	Closed to traffic
Arlberg......	St. Anton-Langen...............	Dec–Apr.
	alternative toll tunnel	occasionally*
Grossglockner.	Heiligenblut-Bruck............	Oct. 15–end of May*
	alternative by always-open	
	Felbertauern toll tunnel	
Katschberg...	Spittalradstadt	intermittently closed*
	alternative road tunnel (toll)	
Plöcken......	Carnic Alps	occasionally
		Nov.-Apr.
Tauern	Radstadt-Mautendorf...........	closed occasionally
Timmelsjoch..	Obergugl-Merano (Italy) toll	Oct.-June

France (French Alps)

Allos........	Barcelonette-Colmars...........	early Nov.-late May
Galibier	Valloire—Monetier-Les-Bains.....	Oct.-June
Iseran	Val d'Isère-Lanslebourg..........	mid-Oct.-late June
Izoard.......	Briançon-Arvieux...............	late Oct.-late June
Larche	La Condamine-Argentera (Italy) ..	occasionally
		Nov.-Mar.
Lautaret	Briançon-La Grave	closed occasionally
Mont Cenis ..	Lanslebourg-Susa (Italy)	Nov.-May
	alternatively, rail through tunnel	
Petit St. Bernard	Bourg-Saint-Maurice—Aosta (It.) .	mid-Oct.-late June*

Road tunnel under Mont-Blanc between Chamonix and Courmayeur (It.) takes traffic all year. Toll.

France (Pyrénées)

Pourtalet.....	Laruns-Sallent (Spain)...........	Oct.-June
Puymorens...	Ax-les-Thermes—Bourg Madame .	closed occasionally*
Quillane	Formiguères-Mont Louis.........	occasionally
		Nov.-Mar.
Somport	Oloron-Sainte-Marie—Jaca (Spain)	closed occasionally

Italy

Costalunga...	Bolzano-Vigo di Fassa...........	seldom closed
Falzagero ...	Cortina d'Ampezzo-Andraz	closed occasionally
Monte Croce		
(Plöcken)	Kötschach-Paluzza.............	closed occasionally
Pordoi.......	Canazei-Cortina d'Ampezzo......	closed occasionally

Stelvio.......	Bormio-Gomagoi	usually mid-Oct.-early July
Tre Croci	Cortina d'Ampezzo-Pelos	not closed
Gran San Bar-nardo (Alps)..	Aosta-Martigny (Switz.) .... *alternative* road tunnel, toll	late Oct.-mid June*
Splügen......	Chiavenna-Splügen (Switz.).......	Oct.-June

Spain

| Navacerrada.. | Madrid-La Granja .... | intermittently mid-Nov.-mid-May |

Switzerland

Albula.......	Filisur-La Punt.................	Nov.-early June*
Bernina......	Pontresina-Tirano (Italy).........	open, with chains
Flüela	Davos-Süsch	closed nights, Nov.-May, winter toll
Forclaz......	Martigny-Chamonix (France)	not closed
Furka	Gletsch-Andermatt	mid-Oct.-mid-June
Great St. Bernard	Martigny-Aosta (Italy)	late Oct.-mid-June

(St. Bernard *Tunnel* takes all-year road traffic—toll charge.)

Grimsel......	Gletsch-Meiringen	mid-Oct.-mid-June
Klausen	Altdorf-Glarus Canton (east of Lucerne)	early Nov.-June
Lukmanier ...	Disentis-Biasca.................	Nov.-mid-May
Nufenen	Ul Richen-Airolo...............	Oct.-mid-June
Oberlap......	Andermatt-Disentis	mid-Oct.-mid-May
Pillon	Le Sepey-Gstaad	not closed
San Bernardino	Hinterhein-Mesocco	Nov.-June*
St. Gotthard..	Altdorf-Bellinzona.	
New road tunnel. No toll.		mid Oct.-mid-May*
Simplon	Brigue-Domodossola (Italy)	not closed

TRAFFIC REGULATIONS. For the most part, the old rule, "priority of traffic from the right" *(priorité à droite),* is no longer practised on country roads, but is still maintained to varying degrees in cities. Never, however, rely on a car, cart or bicycle to refrain from darting out in front of you if its driver has a will to do so. Where two country roads of equal importance cross one another, traffic from the right *usually* has right of way, but most such cross roads have signs to indicate who has priority. In France, however, it is *always* priority of traffic from the right (except on roundabouts), country roads or not, *unless* the road coming from the right has a stop signal (or obviously unless a small secondary road crosses a main thoroughfare, but there are *always* signs). For detailed instruction on such matters see the AAA, RAC or AA handbooks. Priority from the right is not accepted in Britain except on roundabouts (rotaries), and then it *is* from the right even though the British drive on the left.

In many countries, it is now obligatory to carry a portable, red reflective triangle, which must be put out on the road well behind a car which has broken down and is in danger of causing an obstruction. Such triangles can be hired at frontiers, but it is cheaper and less trouble to buy one for about $6. In some countries cars with trailers need two.

In many European countries CB radios are completely forbidden, in others they are subject to very strict regulations and limits. Regulations vary so much from one country to another that your best bet is to give up completely any idea you may have had of using a CB in Europe.

CAR FERRIES TO THE CONTINENT. There is an exhaustive list of ferries earlier in this section. All of them now have drive on/off systems. Prices range somewhat, depending on the length of voyage. In some cases return trips are cheaper, or the car rate becomes progressively lower with the number of passengers accompanying it. There are sometimes reduced off-season rates, when there are fewer crossings. *Olau* (Sheerness to Flushing) and *Sally Viking Line* (Dunkerque to Ramsgate) offer some of the most competitive prices around.

CONTINENTAL TRANSPORTATION. Car-sleeper services are also worth considering. But while train service saves both time and energy, it is nonetheless an expensive way to travel. You'll find also that the car-sleeper network, though still covering much of western Europe, is less extensive than it once was. The nearest point you can get to Greece, for example, from northern Europe is now Ljubljana in north Yugoslavia. However, there are still good services across France from Boulogne to various points on the Riviera and to Milan in north Italy. To get to the Atlantic coast of France or Spain and Portugal, car-sleeper services run from Boulogne to Biarritz and from Paris to Madrid and Lisbon. Services also operate from Brussels and S'Hertogen-Bosch to Munich, Salzburg, and Ljubljana, and to Brig in Switzerland.

Sea ferries also play a prominent part in European motor travel. There are around thirty Mediterranean ferries that carry cars to the islands, or between countries, as for example, Italy to Greece or over to Yugoslavia, or from one end of Italy to the other. In Scandinavia, there are two sorts of ferries: the small ones, which virtually form part of a road, particularly in Norway and Denmark, and the inter-country ferries, which connect Norway with Denmark and Sweden, Denmark with Sweden and Finland, Sweden with the other two, and Germany with all of them. Particulars can be had from the motoring associations and the countries concerned (through their tourist offices).

HOTELS FOR THE MOTORIST. There is possibly a wider selection of hotels on the continent of Europe than anywhere else in the world, because they range from the universally common palaces to mountain inns offering no more than two rooms, but perfectly clean and respectable. Obviously, there are some which are neither, and these may be small or large. The point is that in some other parts of the world it simply is not possible to stay in cheap hotels and enjoy it. In Western Europe, you can. For this reason, the motorist can safely go off into the unexplored areas to make his own discoveries. (This advice cannot, however, apply to hotels in Eastern Europe, where the standard is not quite so high, and there is in any case a shortage of accommodation.)

One such discovery is castles. In 17 countries of Western Europe some 500 castles have been converted into castle-hotels. In period and style they range from feudal fortresses complete with moats and drawbridges to elegant, spacious chateaux of the Renaissance and baroque periods. Rates equally range from the surprisingly modest on upwards. One thing that all these castles are likely to have in common, however, is that they were not located so as to be served by modern mass transportation. Hence they are ideal for the motorist, whose car allows him to seek the quiet, out-of-the-way spot that may have the most to offer. Most individual countries' national tourist offices can furnish lists of castle-hotels; but the whole subject is thoroughly covered in Robert Long's book *Castle Hotels of Europe,* published by the author at 634 Bellmore Ave., East Meadow, L.I., N.Y. 11554.

Out of season (that is, other than from mid-July to the first week in September), it is not necessary to pre-book hotel accommodation en route to your holiday destination, and not even when you arrive (unless it happens to be one of exceptional tourist popularity, or such a city as Strasbourg, which is almost permanently occupied with conferences). An exception to this rule has to be made when motoring in winter if the chosen holiday location is a sports center. En route hotels always have plenty of room in winter, but it is as well to check that there will be one open in the place where you are likely to want it. In summer it is advisable to start looking for overnight accommodations not later than six o'clock.

ON THE WATER IN EUROPE

For a very leisurely way of seeing as much of Europe as you can, quite literally "take to the water", whether it be on one of the great rivers, of which the Rhine is the most important, or on a canal, or yet again on a lake, or—and here there are many variations—cruising in European seas such as the Mediterranean, Aegean, Baltic and the coastal regions of Norway. In this section we can only point the way for such holidays, fuller details of which can be obtained from all good travel agents. These water-borne vacations can last from a few hours to several weeks. Some are available all around the year, others operate only in the summer weeks.

 CRUISES BY SEA. A number of leading shipping companies operate cruises on liners from the comparatively small ones, such as the 4,500 tonners popular in the Aegean and Adriatic, to the 35,000 ton giants such as the P&O liner *Canberra* and even the famous *Queen Elizabeth 2*.

From the U.K. there is a series of cruises to the Mediterranean, Atlantic Islands (Canaries and Madeira), the Norwegian fjords and the Baltic. These last from six to 21 days but the majority are in the 12 to 14 day range. Southampton is the most popular port for departure (and return) but some go from Tilbury (near London). They are not cheap holidays, but remember they do include almost everything except your drinks and personal expenses. Costs range from around £600 for a six day "shortie" in a lower grade cabin, to well over £2,800 for the longer voyages in deluxe accommodation.

In addition there are many "fly-cruises" from the U.K., whereby you fly from London (and often provincial airports like Manchester and Birmingham) to the Mediterranean and join the ship there. Ports like Venice, Piraeus (Athens), Malta and Naples are used for these voyages which are usually of a week. Often they are sold with a week on land as a two-center style holiday. These cruises operate from around Easter to November, although there are other longer fly cruises during the winter with inclusive rates from the U.K. The latter, however, are much fewer in number. There are similar "fly-cruises" from other European countries such as Germany, Sweden and Holland.

You can, of course, join these Mediterranean cruises yourself without any flight involved. The Aegean Sea is the busiest area, with cruises mainly from Piraeus from one day to seven days, visiting the islands, available from April to October. These cruises are on smaller ships, some of which are almost like large yachts. Prices again vary tremendously starting at around $50 for a full day to over $1,000 dollars for a week long cruise.

Other Mediterranean cruises go from Trieste and Venice down the Adriatic visiting Yugoslavian ports and islands and on to Greece; they also go from Genoa around the western Mediterranean calling at places like Malta, Palma and Gibraltar.

You can have your own cruise "custom built" by using the network of ferries which operate in both the Aegean and the Mediterranean proper. Piraeus is again the best port for this. For example you can sail from there on a Wednesday, Friday or Sunday morning and call at Syros, Paros, Naxos and Ios ending up at Santorini. Stay the night (you arrive in the early evening) and return the next morning on the same ship—or have a couple of days there and return by another line. A longer trip, staying on the ship, goes from Ancona in southern Italy to Corfu, Piraeus, Rhodes and Haifa in Israel and then return.

In the western Mediterranean there are similar ferry round-trips, as there are up and down the Adriatic. In northern Europe you can use the Baltic ferry system and also sail up the Norwegian coast by the regular steamer service which goes from Bergen to Kirkenes and, in the summer months, makes round trips to Spitzbergen. This is a really exciting voyage—but book ahead as accommodation is very limited.

Often overlooked is the fact that you can make an enjoyable voyage from the U.K. using various ferries; for example, you could sail from Harwich on the *DFDS* (Danish Seaways) ferry to Esbjerg in Denmark, then go by rail to Copenhagen. From there take the overnight ferry (large, comfortable ships on this route) to Oslo. After your stay in Norway, take the Fred Olsen line from Oslo or Kristiansand to Harwich or the Norway line from Bergen to Newcastle. This is just one of many variations possible.

ON INLAND WATERS. The great River Rhine is navigable from the port of Basel (although well inland, it is one of the busiest in Europe) right to the sea. There are several companies offering cruises lasting from three days to nine days on all or part of this famous waterway. The vessels used are as comfortable as ocean liners although naturally with not so much space. If you opt for the round trip from either Rotterdam or Amsterdam then it will take nine days but it is rare to do this, most travelers prefer a one-way voyage going to, or returning from, Basel by train (or air). In addition there are shorter cruises going as far say as Mainz from either Dutch city. In addition, depending on accommodation available, you can also do a part of these voyages, with a 48-hour stay on board the vessel being the usual basic minimum. Services operate from April/May to October. For details of a wide range of Rhine trips, contact *Rhine Cruise Agency,* Dietrich Neuhold Corp., 170 Hamilton Ave., White Plains, NY (914–948–3600).

For shorter trips not involving on board stays the regular sailings of the *Koln Dusseldorfer Line* are available. These operate between Dusseldorf and Mainz with some sailings going up to Frankfurt on the Main. The most scenic stretch of the river is between Koblenz and Mainz.

On the Danube, the Austrians operate between Vienna and Linz taking a full day for the trip. The Russians with the *Soviet Danube Line* operate a service from Passau to Ismail at the mouth of Danube. The vessels are comfortable and well-equipped and take eight days for the entire voyage which calls at Vienna, Bratislava, Budapest, Belgrade and Giurgiu (in Romania). A new deluxe cruise vessel, the *Danube Princess,* a joint German-British enterprise, operates weekly cruises from March to October from Passau to Budapest via Vienna and back. Inclusive fares from London by air is £600–1,100.

There are also holidays on many of Europe's smaller rivers and canals. In Sweden, for example, the delightful trip across the south of the country via the Gota Canal and several lakes en route, takes three days, Gothenberg to Stockholm. The ships are smaller but quite comfortable and operate between May and early September.

On the French canals in Brittany, or on the famous Canal du Midi in the south, there are private motor cruisers for hire. On the Canal du Midi there are also organized cruises by larger vessels—as there are on the River Marne. The French Tourist Office can supply the latest information on these and other expeditions on French waterways.

In the U.K. there are over 3,000 miles of inland navigable waterways—rivers, lakes, lochs (in Scotland) and canals. In addition there are the Norfolk Broads, a unique area of inland lakes, rivers and lagoons. You can hire motor cruisers and other types of vessels on all of these. On the main canals of Britain and on the River Thames there are organized voyages, living on board the vessels and being provided with all meals. The British Tourist Authority, Thames Tower, Blacks Rd., London W.6, can supply details of these.

The Republic of Ireland offers the River Shannon and its adjacent loughs for this type of holiday. Details of hiring and cruises from the Irish Tourist Board.

BUS TRAVEL IN EUROPE

Europe's bus lines and bus touring companies have brought travel by bus to a peak approaching perfection. The physical comfort plus the wide choice of routes accounts for the popularity of exploring Europe by bus. In Turkey and Greece in particular the bus network is better than the railways; and in Britain the inter-city buses may often be as advantageous as the trains. Throughout Europe there is a wide choice of bus companies; and in countries where bus companies are run by the national railways Eurail and InterRail passes are good for those buses as well.

Almost all of them offer inclusive tours lasting as long as 30 days, and a single payment covers transportation, hotels, meals, and tips. Many of them operate regular services that you can pick up or leave at any point, in which case you pay only for transportation. Rates are slightly more than second-class railway fares. As for comfort, you may find yourself in a luxury coach with reclining seats, a hostess to look after you and point out sights, a refrigerator for refreshments, and even a toilet. Generally there are two drivers, who relieve each other periodically. Most tours are offered only in summer. On long, trans-European bus journeys, it is a good idea to bring along a blanket, soap and towel, and a large supply of sandwiches and reading matter.

EUROPABUS/SUPABUS. Europe boasts an excellent, fully-integrated international bus network, owned and operated by a host of different national and international bus companies. Confusingly, in Ireland and the U.K. this is officially known as Supabus. Elsewhere in Europe, the name Europabus is used. Their routes span Europe, from Finland to Portugal, Ireland to Turkey, totalling at least 75,000 miles of services.

On most of the long-haul routes—London to southern Spain, for example, or to Scandinavia—nonstop "through" services are operated. Even so, strict regulations mean that you will have to change buses at least once, while drivers must work in shifts. Comfort stops are made at regular intervals.

However, on some long-haul routes—London to Athens, for instance—an overnight stop will be made. Accommodations are generally in simple hotels and motels. These must be paid for at the start of the journey. You can, if you prefer, arrange your own accommodations, but these will probably be more expensive, and should also be done before you leave.

On almost every route you can stop over en route, catching a later bus as it comes through. Book some way ahead if you plan to do this in a peak period. In less busy periods you can often decide to hop off only at the last minute, confident that you'll be able to get a seat on a later bus. But always check before you do so; the majority of long-distance bus passengers go through to their final destinations.

Of course with such a comprehensive network, almost any permutation of routes is possible. But it's best to have a timetable to do this accurately, and they are not always easy to get hold of in advance, especially at long distance. The major international routes are comparatively straightforward, but routes within individual countries are often more complex and most easily investigated on the spot. Local tourist offices are generally helpful in this.

From the U.K., you can book through to any European destination from hundreds of starting points. There are currently 160 European cities served by Europabus. Bookings can be made at main bus depots and travel agents; enquire locally. In the U.K., contact *Supabus*, 172 Buckingham Palace Rd., London S.W.1 (tel. 01–730 3453). Bookings cannot be made on the telephone. In the U.S. and Canada, details are available from British Tourist Authority offices (see *National Tourist Offices,* page 10, for addresses).

OTHER OPERATORS. There are many coach tour operators and express bus service operators both in the U.K. and on the Continent. Any good travel agent can supply names and addresses of these. Among the more prominent names are *Overland* (part of Global of London), *Frames Tours, Thomas Cook, Thomson Holidays, Trafalgar Travel, Glenton Tours* and *Wallace Arnold (Euroways)*. All these are based in the U.K. The last named has many links with the Continent. *Supabus,* a consortium of around 25 companies, claims the "largest network of International Express Coach services ever assembled." It operates in 12 European countries.

In Europe the *West Belgium Coach Company, Universal Tours* (operating from the Netherlands) and *Generalcar* (another Belgian company) have extensive services.

Apart from trans-European services, the French have introduced the Relais Bus Pass for those who want to see a good deal of the country at reasonable cost. The pass allows unlimited mileage for 15, 21, 30 or 60 days, enabling the traveler to go where he wishes, when he wants, at his own pace. For details, write to the *Federation Inter Jeunes France Europe,* 218 rue St. Jacques, Paris 75005.

The Eastern European tourist bureaux all arrange local bus tours, many of them covering several countries. Their coaches are usually more modern and comfortable than their railroad rolling stock. These tours may be booked through accredited travel agents in the West.

LEAVING EUROPE

CUSTOMS ON RETURNING HOME. If you propose to take on your holiday any *foreign-made* articles, such as cameras, binoculars, expensive timepieces and the like, it is wise to put with your travel documents the receipt from the retailer or some other evidence that the item was bought in your home country. If you bought the article on a previous holiday abroad and have already paid duty on it, carry with you the receipt for this. Otherwise, on returning home, you may be charged duty (for British residents, Value Added Tax as well). In other words, unless you can prove prior possession, foreign-made articles are dutiable *each time* they enter the U.S. The details below are correct as we go to press. It would be wise to check in case of change.

American residents who are out of the U.S.A. at least 48 hours and have claimed no exemption during the previous 30 days are entitled to bring in duty-free up to $400 worth of bona fide gifts or items for their own personal use. Do not think that *already used* will exempt an item. If you buy clothing abroad and wear it during your travels it will nonetheless be dutiable when you reenter the U.S.

The $400 duty free allowance is based on the full fair *retail* value of the goods (previously, the customs' estimation was on the wholesale value). You must now list the items purchased and *they must accompany you when you return.* So keep all receipts handy with the detailed list, and pack the goods together in one case. The $50 mailed gift-scheme (see below) is also based on the retail value. Every member of a family is entitled to this same exemption, regardless of age, and their exemptions can be pooled. Infants and children get the same exemptions as adults, except for alcoholic beverages and tobacco. Beyond the first $400 worth of goods, inspectors now assess a flat 10% duty on the next $1,000 worth; above $1,400 duties vary according to the kind of merchandise.

One quart of alcoholic beverages, 200 cigarettes, and up to 100 cigars (non-Cuban!) may be included in the exemption if you are 21 years of age or older. There is no limitation on the number of cigarettes you bring in for your personal use, regardless of age. Alcoholic beverages in excess of one quart are subject to customs duty and internal revenue tax. Approximate rates are (1/5 gallon); brandy or liquor, $2–$3; champagne, 90¢; wine, 15¢. The importation must not be in violation of the laws of the state of arrival. Furthermore, your tobacco and alcohol may be reported to the authorities in your own home state, to be taxed by them.

Only one bottle of certain perfumes that are trademarked in the United States (Lanvin, Chanel, etc.) may be brought in unless you can completely obliterate the trademark on the bottle, or get written permission from the manufacturer to bring more. Other perfumes are limited by weight or value. The specialized Paris houses will give you the complete list.

Foreign visitors to the U.S. (nonresidents), and U.S. military personnel returning from duty abroad should inquire separately about regulations and exemptions pertaining to them.

You do not have to pay duty on art objects or antiques, provided they are over 100 years old.

Gifts which cost less than $50 may be mailed to friends or relatives at home, but not more than one per day (of receipt) to any one addressee. Mark the package: Unsolicited Gift—value less than $50. These gifts must not include perfumes costing more than $1, tobacco or liquor; however, they do not count as part of your $400 exemption.

Do not bring home foreign meats, fruits, plants, soil, or other agricultural items when you return to the United States. To do so will delay you at the port of entry.

Customs declaration forms are distributed on your plane or ship before you arrive. If your purchases are worth no more than $400 you fill out only the identification portions of the form and make an oral declaration when you pass the inspector. If you have over $400 worth you must make a written declaration. Under the Citizens Bypass Program, American citizens can show their passports to the customs inspector and eliminate the separate inspection by an immigration officer.

Canadian residents: In addition to personal effects, the following articles may be brought in duty free: a maximum of 50 cigars, 200 cigarettes, 2 pounds of tobacco and 40 ounces of liquor, provided these are declared in writing to customs on arrival and accompany the traveler in hand or checked-through baggage. These are included in the basic exemption of $300 a year or $100 per quarter. Personal gifts should be mailed as "Unsolicited Gift—Value Under $40". Canadian customs regulations are strictly enforced; you are recommended to check what your allowances are and to make sure you have kept receipts for whatever you have bought abroad. For details ask for the Canada Customs brochure, "I Declare."

British residents. There are two levels of duty free allowance for people entering the U.K; one, for goods bought outside the EEC or for goods bought in a duty free shop within the EEC; two, for goods bought in an EEC country but not in a duty free shop.

In the first category you may import duty free: 200 cigarettes or 100 cigarillos or 50 cigars or 250 grammes of tobacco (*Note* if you live outside Europe, these allowances are doubled); plus one liter of alcoholic drinks over 22% vol. (38.8% proof) or two liters of alcoholic drinks not over 22% vol. or fortified or sparkling or still table wine; plus two liters of still table wine; plus 50 grammes of perfume; plus nine fluid ounces of toilet water; plus other goods to the value of £28.

In the second category you may import duty free: 300 cigarettes or 150 cigarillos or 75 cigars or 400 grammes of tobacco; plus 1½ liters of alcoholic drinks over 22% vol. (38.8% proof) or three liters of alcoholic drinks not over 22% vol. or fortified or sparkling or still table wine; plus five liters of still table wine; plus 75 grammes of perfume; plus 13 fluid ounces of toilet water; plus other goods to the value of £207 (*Note* though it is not classified as an alcoholic drink by EEC countries for Customs' purposes and is thus considered part of the "other goods" allowance, you may not import more that 50 liters of beer).

In addition, no animals or pets of any kind may be brought into the U.K. The penalties for doing so are severe and are strictly enforced; there are *no* exceptions. Similarly, fresh meats, plants and vegetables, controlled drugs and firearms and ammunition may not be brought into the U.K. There are no restrictions on the import or export of British and foreign currencies.

EUROPE
COUNTRY BY
COUNTRY

ALBANIA

Drop the highlands of Scotland into an area hardly larger than Maryland (10,500 sq. miles) and sprinkle with well over two million feuding Kentucky mountaineers. Season with 20 centuries of warfare against invading Goths, Greeks, Serbs, Turks, Italians and Germans—all of whom have coveted this little country of high mountain passes and sweeping plains. Stir in 450 years of Turkish occupation. Top off with 40 years of communist control by the Soviets, the Chinese and latterly independently. If the resulting mixture of scenery, suspicion and somnolence is your dish, you will find a visit to Shqipëria (the Albanian name for the country, "Land of the Eagles") an offbeat holiday of tremendous interest. But be warned, however, that entry to Albania is by no means a formality and that many people, including *all* United States citizens, are banned completely.

Albania is famed for its fierce tribal people, a race apart speaking a language all their own. Descended from the original Illyrians, these rugged and extraordinarily single-minded people have remained almost wholly cut off from the rest of the world. Lord Byron compared them to Scottish highlanders, not because of the craggy mountains among which they live but because of the religious and tribal differences that divide the population into a patchwork of clans and families whose customs and costumes are older than recorded history. Though the Labor Party of Albania, the totalitarian and communist ruling party, has imposed a leaden and intermittently modern uniformity on the country, the past dies hard in Albania. You will still see farm workers in the fields in traditional dress.

Most Albanians (70%) are Moslems; the Christian remainder is split into two groups, the Catholic *Gegs* to the north and the Orthodox *Tosks* to the south. However, all religion ("the opium of the masses") is banned and the modern state is fiercely atheist.

The Albanian passion for independence is embodied in the national hero, one Skanderbeg, who fought the Turks for over 20 years in the 15th century. His modern counterpart sprang up in the person of Enver Hoxha during World War II, the leader of 70,000 guerillas against the Axis powers. A committed communist, the aging Hoxha was leader of his country until his death in 1985, and his features and sayings, emblazoned on walls, posters, even fields and hills, are still visible today.

During the '50s, the People's Socialist Republic of Albania was a forward Adriatic bastion of the Warsaw pact and thorn in the side of the Western alliance. Development of the economy was coordinated with that of the Eastern bloc. But differences between Albania and Moscow began to surface in the late '50s when Albania remained loyal to Stalinism. Albania subsequently switched allegiance to China, precipitating a total severance of relations with the Soviet Union. However, this liaison proved as unsatisfactory to Hoxha as that with the Soviet Union had done. Today, Albania is wholly non-aligned, though relations with Greece have eased and Greek tourists are now admitted. In addition, trade is increasing with both Italy and France, and Deputy Foreign Ministers from both countries have visited Albania. British links with the country were never restored after World War II; however, negotiations between the two nations were resumed in early 1986.

Discovering Albania

A modern visitor to Albania will find a country of great beauty and a society confusingly but stimulatingly idiosyncratic. A group tour is liable to find itself with a suddenly switched itinerary—the archeological site that may have been the whole object for the trip being replaced by a more ideologically acceptable cement works. Both men's and women's clothing and hair styles should be sober. But if you go expecting such things you should find it fascinating to watch a solidly communist regime working in magnificent surroundings.

Here is a list of the chief places of interest in Albania:

Apollonia. Here, near the town of Fier, a great Roman city is being excavated.

Berat. Very picturesque hill-town with an interesting medieval fortress; lower down the hill is a new town with the country's largest textile combine.

Durrës (formerly better known as Durazzo and likely to change its name to Enver Hoxha City in memory of the former leader). The country's main port. It has a magnificent beach, crowded in summer with Albanian holiday-makers, with whom it might be possible to make contact. There is an interesting Roman amphitheater, still being excavated. You can visit a large dairy farm and hear a talk on how the farm is worked.

Elbasan. Formerly a small market town, now a center of heavy industry, with an iron and steel complex, a cement factory and an oil refinery.

Gjirokastër. The chief town of southern Albania, full of highly picturesque narrow streets and ancient houses. The town is dominated by the fortress of Ali Pasha, now an armaments museum. Enver Hoxha was born here and his birthplace is now also a museum.

Korça. An important town near the Greek border; famous for its carpets. It was for nearly a century the center of Albanian culture.

Kruja. A medieval town perched on a mountain. The birthplace of Albania's national hero, Skanderbeg, it was the center of resistance against the Turks. The restored castle is now the Skanderbeg Museum.

Pogradec. A charming resort on Lake Ohrid, near the Yugoslav border, and a favorite summer resort with Albanians.

Saranda. An important port opposite the Greek island of Corfu. The coast here is exceptionally beautiful; praised by Lord Byron, it is still completely unspoiled. Excellent bathing. Nearby are the ruins of Butrint, with a Roman theater and a Baptistery with vivid mosaics.

Shkodra (formerly better known as Scutari). At one time the chief Roman Catholic stronghold of Albania, the town now contains the extraordinary Atheist Museum. Interesting market. Above the town rises the impressive ruin of the fortress of Rozafat.

Tirana. The capital, with a population of 250,000. Many of the fine, wide streets were built by the Italians before World War II. In addition to an extremely picturesque old town—and one of the finest mosques in the country—there is much that is new; a university, an interesting *Albania Today* exhibition, museums and art galleries. On Liberation Day, November 29, there is an impressive parade.

Vlora (formerly better known as Valona). Not only a major port, with an excellent bathing beach, but of great historical importance. It was here, in 1912, that Albania's independence was proclaimed.

PRACTICAL INFORMATION FOR ALBANIA

WHAT WILL IT COST. Albania can only be visited on a package tour; no individual travel is allowed. The tours include all fares and airport taxes, full-board hotel accommodation, entrance fees to archeological sites and most museums (some charge 1 lek—about 10p), the services of a tour leader from London, and the assistance of an English-speaking guide. In Britain, the chief organizers of such tours have for some years been *Regent Holidays (U.K.) Ltd.*, 13 Small Street, Bristol, BS1 1DE (tel. 0272–211711). At present this firm arranges five tours a year, each lasting 10 or 15 days. Four of the tours—those in late May, August, September and October—last 15 days and include a comprehensive bus tour of the whole country; the other tour leaves London in April and is based on Tirana, the capital; it includes a half-day visit to Kruja and a three-day excursion to the south of the country, visiting Gjirokastër, Saranda and Butrint. Other excursions can sometimes be arranged, but only if the entire party travels together. It is sometimes possible to obtain tickets to a soccer match or an evening performance of folk-singing or ballet; the average cost of such a ticket is 5 leks (about 50p). All tours are by air to Yugoslavia (Titograd or Dubrovnik) and then by bus, changing from a Yugoslav bus to an Albanian one at the frontier. Be prepared to carry your own baggage here, and at hotels. The 10-day tour costs £385 and the others £550 or £585, according to the season. Single rooms are extremely scarce and, if available, incur a supplementary charge of around £60. Be prepared to share a room; *Regent Holidays* will arrange for you to share with someone of the same sex and, when possible, of roughly the same age or occupation.

Newcomers to the field are *Swan-Hellenic Tours*, Canberra House, 47 Middlesex Street, London, E.1 7AL (tel. 01–247 0401), who offer a special-interest tour covering the whole country and lasting 17 days. This, too, is by plane to Yugoslavia, and from there by bus. The 1987 tour is due to leave on the 29th May; the all-inclusive price is £891, subject to change. No single rooms are available. Each tour is accompanied by an expert guest-lecturer.

Citizens of the U.S.A. (as well as of several other countries) *are not admitted to Albania,* nor is anyone employed as a journalist. The whole emphasis is on group tourism, and, while social contact with Albanians is not explicitly forbidden, it is not made easy, and tourists are always encouraged to remain with their group, under the ever-watchful eye of their guide. Many bars accept Western currency only, which effectively rules out Albanian customers; in addition, tourists are *not* allowed to travel on the now fairly complete rail and bus system. A new line connecting the Albanian rail network at Shkodër to the Yugoslav rail system at Titograd was expected to be opened about the time this volume went to press; it is, however, understood that it will be used for goods only, not passengers.

The unit of currency in Albania is the *lek*. The exchange rate in mid-1986 was 10 leks to the pound sterling, 8 leks to the U.S. dollar. No Albanian money may be taken in or out of the country, so take small denomination travelers' checks so as not to be left with a handful of leks at the end of your stay. It is wise to change all the money you are likely to want at once, as it is often a very time-consuming business. The lek is hardly used by tourists; all transactions of any importance are in hard currency—sterling, dollars, marks and so on. And you must be prepared to receive your change in *any* Western currency.

WHEN TO COME. Coastal regions are very hot in summer, with cool breezes; warm, humid *sirocco* wind in spring and fall. However, since two-thirds of Albania is mountainous, the towering peaks and deep valleys make for rapid and dramatic changes over a relatively short distance. Temperature sometimes soars to over 90°F. on coast.

Average maximum and minimum daily temperatures in degrees Fahrenheit for Durrës are as follows:

Jan.	Feb.	Mar.	Apr.	May	June	July	Aug.	Sept.	Oct.	Nov.	Dec.
51	53	56	63	71	77	83	82	76	68	58	53
42	43	47	55	63	70	74	72	65	58	51	46

National Holidays. Jan. 1 (New Year's Day); Jan. 2 (New Year's Observance Day); Jan. 11 (Republic Proclamation Day); May 1 (May Day); Nov. 28 (Independence Proclamation Day); Nov. 29 (Liberation Day).

VISAS. These are arranged for British tourists by *Regent Holidays* (see above); other prospective visitors should enquire from their travel agent the address of the nearest representative of the official Albanian tourist agency *Albturist*. Neither Britain nor the U.S. has diplomatic relations with Albania. For Britons, the nearest embassy for information about Albania is the Embassy of the People's Socialist Republic of Albania, 131 rue de la Pompe, Paris 16, France. The French Embassy in Tirana looks after British interests.

As only groups are permitted to enter Albania, all visas are group visas. The cost of a visa is £6.80 for U.K. subjects, £11 for Canadians, Australians and French. In Britain, *Regent Holidays* make the visa arrangements: you fill out and return their visa form with four photographs; do not send your passport.

CUSTOMS. Albanian Customs confiscate books they don't approve of; they will be returned when you leave. Do not take any books of a pornographic, political or religious nature—above all no Bibles. Cameras and photographic equipment are allowed, but make sure they are recorded on entry. Any books you buy in Albania are likely to be confiscated by the Yugoslav customs, so mail them straight home, and take brown paper, Jiffy bags, string and adhesive tape with you. Postage is inexpensive.

HOTELS. All hotels are owned by the state and operated by Albturist. They are either in main towns or fairly close to them. They are generally clean and comfortable, but often shabby and old-fashioned. In Tirana and Durrës the hotels are of a higher standard, with private bath or shower and w.c. The hotel chiefly used in the capital is the Hotel *Tirana,* about seven years old. The Hotel *Dajti,* a modernized pre-War establishment, is also sometimes pressed into service. At Durrës, the best hotel is the *Adriatik,* also with private facilities; other hotels, of a lower grade, at Durrës are the *Durrës, Kruja, Butrinti* and *Apollonia.* These have hot and cold water in the bedrooms; showers and toilets on all floors. The complex is fenced off from the general public on the long beach, but guests can sometimes contact Albanian and other tourists on the sand and in the beautiful warm sea. There is a ballroom, popular and folk dancing, bars, television, chess, souvenir shop, post office, outdoor cinema and other facilities in the high season.

Outside these main centers, hotel standards vary enormously. Often the rooms do not have their own facilities. Most of the provincial hotels were built over 25 years ago and tourists must be prepared for erratic plumbing, carpentry and electric fittings. *Never drink tap water.* For visitors prepared to put up with rather spartan accommodations, compensation will be found in the occasional very pleasant surprise; there is, for instance, a delightful tourist hotel at Pogradec, on Lake Ohrid, and the *Çajupi,* at Gjirokastër, is modern, if simple. At Saranda, on the splendid southern "riviera," there is a comfortable modern hotel on the beach near the town. Do not pitch your expectations too high and you will not be disappointed.

 FOOD AND DRINK. Typical Balkan food, such as kebabs, delicious soups, including a yogurt soup with sliced cucumbers. Soft boiled eggs for breakfast and cold omelet (better than it sounds). Fresh fish from sea or lakes. Good, light local beer; fiery *raki* (plum brandy). There are many pleasant varieties of wine and several very sweet liqueurs. Coffee is drunk in the Turkish manner, tea without milk.

SHOPPING. Carpets, filigree silver, earthenware pots and other local handicrafts can be good buys. They are priced in dollars, but any hard currency is accepted in the souvenir shops.

 PHOTOGRAPHY. Do not take pictures of docks, military establishments or military personnel. Because Albanians, particularly in the rural areas, are unused to tourists with elaborate cameras, ask their permission before you take their pictures, though they seldom object. If in doubt, ask your guide to explain before you shoot. Near resorts like Durrës and Saranda or in Tirana the populace is more sophisticated.

 MAIL AND TELEPHONES. Post-offices are open from about 8 A.M. till 10 P.M. including Sundays. The postage rate for a letter to Britain is 1 lek. Although all post to Britain goes by airmail, a letter generally takes from 10 days to two weeks. International telephone calls may be made from post-offices, though connection may take a very long time. The cost of a three-minute call (minimum) to the U.K. is 50 leks; each additional minute costs 16 leks. You can send telegrams from main post-offices and telexes from the Hotel *Dajti,* in Tirana.

HEALTH. The services of a doctor are free but prescriptions must be paid for.

ANDORRA

The tiny principality of Andorra, perched high in the Pyrenees between France and Spain (about 80 miles west of the Mediterranean), has managed to remain independent, largely because of sheer inaccessibility. But today a good tarmac road crosses Andorra from Spain to France. The impressive route from France branches off the Ax-les-Thermes—Bourg-Madame road and crosses the highest Pyrenean pass, the Envalira, at 7,897 feet.

Few countrysides are more romantic than this rugged mountain landscape, dotted with Romanesque towers. The ancient houses have jutting roofs and wooden or wrought-iron balconies. Catalan is the official language, together with French and Spanish. The Andorran national holiday, September 8, is a colorful festival honoring La Verge de Meritxell, a stern-eyed wooden figure discovered under an almond tree, miraculously blooming in the middle of winter. A visit to the new shrine of Meritxell, rebuilt after a fire in 1972, is rewarding.

If you slip into this minute country, with its deep gorges and savage mountain scenery, there are two places that are most likely to attract you—Andorra la Vella, the capital, and Les Escaldes, a spa. The visit offers a rare combination of natural beauty and strictly practical benefits, as the duty-free status of Andorra makes it a shopper's paradise —provided you hold a foreign passport you are simply waved through the customs. Though to really enjoy the beauty of the scenery you will have to leave the gross commercialism of the valley and escape higher up into the mountains. Accommodations are moderately priced and food and wine very inexpensive. One big snag is parking, as the narrow valley, hemmed in by majestic mountains on all sides, literally has not enough space to accommodate the uninterrupted influx of cars.

Andorra exerts a strong attraction for philatelists: both France and Spain maintain post offices and produce frequent changes of stamps. Between Andorran villages, postal services are free.

This small state also provides some exciting skiing slopes, at Soldeu, El Tarter, Pas de la Casa, Grau Roig, Pal, Arinsal, and Arcalis. Difficult as it is to get to these areas, some of the slopes get swamped by crowds from Barcelona at weekends. The skiing may not be as sophisticated as in some European countries, but Andorra's popularity as an international budget ski resort is growing, and centers are all well equipped.

For summer hikers there are two recommended treks (GR 7 and GR 75) across Andorra in magnificent mountain scenery provided with ample cabins and refuges.

PRACTICAL INFORMATION FOR ANDORRA

WHAT WILL IT COST. Andorran currency is French francs and Spanish pesetas; there is a tendency for francs to be more readily accepted in the north and pesetas in the south, though both are theoretically interchangeable. Prices are often lower if you pay in pesetas. Good restaurant meals cost from 1,500 ptas., moderate ones from 800 ptas. Food and drink are generally inexpensive and the tax-free shopping offers many bargains.

WHEN TO COME. High season, July-Aug.; May-June less crowded and lovely; winter sports mid-Nov., to mid-May. The climate is mild in summer, but cold at nights (remember the altitude is some 3,300 to 8,000 ft.).

Average maximum daily temperatures in degrees Fahrenheit and Centigrade:

Les Escaldes	Jan.	Feb.	Mar.	Apr.	May	June	July	Aug.	Sept.	Oct.	Nov.	Dec.
F°	43	45	54	57	63	73	79	75	72	61	50	43
C°	6	7	12	14	17	23	26	24	22	16	10	6

National Holidays. Sept. 8 (La Verge de Meritxell). Shops open throughout republic except in Meritxell itself, where festival is celebrated. **Local Holidays.** At *Canillo,* 3rd Sat. in July and following Sun. and Mon.; at *Les Escaldes,* Jul. 25–27; at *Sant Julià de Lòria,* last Sun. in July and following Mon. and Tues.; at Andorra la Vella, first Sat., Sun., Mon. in Aug.; at *Encamp* and *La Massana,* Aug. 15–17; at *Ordino,* Sept. 16, 17.

GETTING TO ANDORRA. From Spain. By bus. Twice daily service from Barcelona (Ronda Universidad 4).

By train. From Barcelona to Puigcerdà, then by bus to Seo d'Urgell and Andorra; from Madrid to Lleida (Lérida), then by bus to Seo d'Urgell and Andorra.

By plane. There is a small airport at Seo d'Urgell with daily flights to and from Barcelona; bus and taxi service to Andorra.

From France. By train. From Paris (Austerlitz) take the train to Toulouse. Here, you connect with the local service to La Tour de Carol, from where there is a bus direct to Andorra. There is a second route via Perpignan to La Tour de Carol. Buses from Hospitalet and La Tour de Carol stations also connect with Andorra.

By plane. Nearest airport is Toulouse (110 miles away).

CUSTOMS. None. French customs at Bourg-Madame and Pas de la Casa. Spanish customs at Puigcerdá and La Farga de Moles. No visas required, but if you wish to have the Andorran Coat of Arms stamped on your passport, the officials at Casa de la Vall, or the Sindicat d'Iniciativa Head Office in Andorra would be only too glad to oblige.

HOTELS AND RESTAURANTS. Andorra has some 230 hotels catering to the influx of summer tourists (book well ahead for July–Aug.) and skiers. Most hotels, except some in the ski resorts, are open year-round. In Andorra la Vella and Les Escaldes try for rooms away from the main street. As a guide, our price ranges are (E) 5,000–7,000 ptas.; (M) 3,000–4,950 ptas.; and (I) below 3,000 ptas., for two people sharing a double room (note that many hotels of a certain category will have less expensive rooms available, especially during the off-season). Cheaper full-board terms are available if you stay longer than two nights. Most hotels include a service charge in their rates though some will add a further 10% (occasionally 15%) to your bill. Restaurants usually add 10–15% to the tab; where they don't, leave 10%.

ANDORRA LA VELLA. *Andorra Palace* (E), tel. 21072. Pool. *Andorra Park* (E), tel. 20 979. Good amenities and away from the noise; pool. *Eden Roc* (E), tel. 21000. *Andorra Center* (M), tel. 24 800. Recent, moderate and comfortable in the center; pool. *President* (M), tel. 22 922. Restaurant has magnificent views. *L'Isard* (M), tel. 20 096. 55 rooms all with bath. *Florida* (I), tel. 20 105. Small; no restaurant. *Internacional* (I), tel. 21 422. Good value.

Slightly out of town at Santa Coloma is *La Roureda* (M), tel. 20 681. Pool. Open June–Sept. only.

Restaurants. *Chez Jacques* (E), tel. 20 325. Small, basically French restaurant but also serving dishes from all over the world. *Moli dels Fanals* (M), tel. 21 381. Excellent value, located in an old windmill. *Odre d'Eol* (M), La Vall 7 (tel. 23 433). Recommended.

ARINSAL. *Solana* (M), tel. 35 127. 40 rooms with bath; the best. Closed Oct.–Nov. *Palomé* (I), tel. 35 112. Good.

CANILLO. Newest is *Bonavida* (M), tel. 51 300. 40 rooms all with bath. Closed Nov. *Pelissé* (M), tel. 51 205. Fine establishment, good setting and food.

ENCAMP. *Paris* (I), tel. 31 325. Good value. Best is *Père d'Urg* (I), tel. 31 515. 65 rooms all with bath. *Rosaleda* (I), tel. 31 229; pool. *Univers* (I), tel. 31 005. 41 rooms, all with bath.

LES ESCALDES. Spa with many hotels. Two of the best are: *Valira* (E), tel. 20 565. 42 rooms all with bath; and *Roc Blanc* (E), tel. 21 486, with pool and a fine restaurant. *La Pubilla* (I), tel. 20 981. Fine value.

A little way out at Engordany is *Comtes d'Urgell* (M), tel. 20 621. 200 rooms.

Restaurants. *1900* (E), tel. 26 716. One of the best restaurants in Andorra. Small with only 8 tables. Closed July and early Aug. *El Pi* (E), tel. 21 486. The restaurant of the *Roc Blanc* hotel, consistently good standards.

GRAU ROIG. *Grau Roig* (M), tel. 51 225. 28 rooms all with bath. Open June–Sept. only.

LA MASSANA. Best is the *Rutllan* (M), tel. 35 000. 70 rooms, pool. *La Massana* (I), tel. 35 222. 50 rooms all with bath; pool.

Restaurant. *La Borda de l'Avi* (M), tel. 35 154. Good local food.

ORDINO. *Coma* (M), tel. 35 116. Recommended, with 48 large, well-equipped rooms and pool; closed Oct.–mid Dec. Also good is *Babot* (M), tel. 35 001.

PAS DE LA CASA. *Sporting* (E), tel. 55 455. With *après-ski* attractions and a good French chef. Open Dec.–Apr. only. *Central* (E–M), tel. 55 383. 52 rooms; open all year round. On the French frontier, the *Refugi dels Isards* (M), tel. 55 155, is excellent with attractive setting and good food. Open all year.

ST. JULIA DE LORIA. *Pol* (M), tel. 41 122. Highly recommended. *Sant Eloi* (M), tel. 41 100. 88 rooms; the most expensive. *Coma Bella* (M), tel. 41 220. 28 rooms in fine location about three miles out; good cuisine.

SOLDEU. *Naudi* (M), tel. 510 18. 53 rooms with bath. The small *Parador Canaro-Incles* (M), tel. 51 046, is probably best.

Restaurants. *La Borda del Rector* (M), tel. 510 30. One km out on main road. *Espiolets* (I), tel. 51 176. Open Dec.–Apr. only.

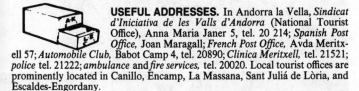

USEFUL ADDRESSES. In Andorra la Vella, *Sindicat d'Iniciativa de les Valls d'Andorra* (National Tourist Office), Anna Maria Janer 5, tel. 20 214; *Spanish Post Office,* Joan Maragall; *French Post Office,* Avda Meritx-ell 57; *Automobile Club,* Babot Camp 4, tel. 20890; *Clinica Meritxell,* tel. 21521; *police* tel. 21222; *ambulance* and *fire services,* tel. 20020. Local tourist offices are prominently located in Canillo, Encamp, La Massana, Sant Juliá de Lòria, and Escaldes-Engordany.

GETTING AROUND ANDORRA. You will need your green card for car travel. Parking in towns is very difficult, so be prepared. All main villages are linked by microbus services, very handy, but with no fixed schedules.

AUSTRIA

Austria, a pint-sized republic in the very heart of the Continent, is one of the top tourist countries of Europe. The reasons? High mountains, gorgeous scenery and a historically high-spirited population who, many say, are "the most charming people in Europe".

Austria is not a cheap country, but the Austrians are conscious of this and do everything they can to help the visitor enjoy his stay—and not feel financially stretched. It is a country proud of its reputation for hospitality. There is a new "Skiers' Best Friend" program to help visitors on the slopes, and many other official schemes to smooth the tourist's path.

Scenery and charm in solid comfort may be enough for most visitors, but Austria has much more to offer. It has one of Europe's best complexes of winter sports facilities—more than 500 places to go skiing, most of them not too crowded. You can drive down smooth roads through fairytale landscapes to villages straight out of a picture book. It is worth taking your time over a meal in one of the atmospheric country inns and then, to round off the day, heading for a musical entertainment—and they come in every guise, from the Salzburg Festival, the opera in Vienna, to a local band blasting its way through the street; wherever it is, the music will be good and the environment perfect.

Tops among the highlights of Austria is a performance by the Spanish Riding School. The fascinating combination of beautiful horses, a display of unequalled equestrian ability and romantic music, all set in a glittering baroque hall, makes it a once-in-a-lifetime event for any visitor.

PRACTICAL INFORMATION FOR AUSTRIA

WHAT WILL IT COST. Austria's low inflation rate is partly countered by the constantly rising exchange rate, and increasing prices. While not cheap, it still offers value for money. Prices directly concerned with tourism (hotels, restaurants, ski lifts, etc.), Austria's main sources of income, rise slowly, but steadily.

For deluxe restaurant meals, count on paying at least 500 Sch. per person without wine; 200 Sch. in an average restaurant; less if you take the *table d'hôte* meals (daily special menus), which are offered *only* at noon (the main meal in Austria). A bottle of wine ranges from 180–250 Sch. but the open wines are very good and cost, per ¼ liter carafe, about 30–45 Sch. The further west, the higher the price.

Take advantage of the cheaper weekly rates offered by most winter and summer resorts and several hotels in the various cities including Vienna and Salzburg. The Austrian National Tourist Office provides a list, in English, of such places and also notes where ski resort prices include ski lift expenses.

The monetary unit is the Austrian Schilling (AS), subdivided into 100 Groschen. There are *about* 18 Sch. to the dollar, and 26 Sch. to the pound sterling. Foreign currency and Austrian Schillings may be brought into Austria in unlimited quantities. Officially you must not take out more than 15,000 AS. Banknotes are being successively replaced in Austria, and the new designs and sizes can lead to confusion and even disaster, so beware!

A typical day might cost two people (schillings)

Hotel (moderate, breakfast included)	900
Lunch at restaurant (moderate)	500
Light refreshment	100
Transport and sightseeing	240
Theater (opera tickets are twice as expensive)	500
Dinner, including wine	600
Miscellaneous 10%	260
	3100

SOURCES OF INFORMATION. For advice on all aspects of travel to Austria, the Austrian National Tourist Office is invaluable. Their addresses are:

In the U.S.: 500 Fifth Ave., New York, N.Y. 10110 (tel. 212–287–8742); 3440 Wilshire Blvd., Los Angeles, Calif. 90010; 500 N. Michigan Ave., Chicago, Ill. 60611; 4800 San Felipe, Houston, TX 77056.

In Canada: 2 Bloor St. E., Suite 3330, Toronto, Ontario M4W 1A8 (tel. 416–967–3381); 1010 Sherbrooke St. W., Suite 1410, Montreal, P.Q. H3A 2R7 (tel. 514–899–3708/9).

In the U.K.: 30 St. George St., London W.1 (tel. 01–629 0461).

WHEN TO COME. Austria has two tourist seasons; one in the summer from May to September and one in the winter, for skiing, from December to April. Skiing in high altitudes lasts right through from November to June and glacier skiing all year round.

Climate. Moderate, the air clear and crisp at all times.

Average afternoon temperatures in degrees Fahrenheit and centigrade

Vienna	Jan.	Feb.	Mar.	Apr.	May	June	July	Aug.	Sept.	Oct.	Nov.	Dec.
F°	34	38	47	57	66	71	75	73	66	55	44	37
C°	1	3	8	14	19	22	24	23	19	13	7	3

SPECIAL EVENTS. *January/February,* carol singing (Sternsingers); Salzburg Mozart Week; "Fasching" (Carnival) with music and gala balls in Vienna and the Austrian provincial capitals from New Year and lasts until Ash Wednesday; in the country, "Carnival on skis"; international ski races in Kitzbühel, Badgastein, Schruns and Schladming etc.; ski jumping events in Innsbruck and Bischofshofen; long-distance and cross-country ski races in various places. *Spring:* Salzburg Easter Festival and Whitsun Concert Cycle. *May/June,* Vienna Festival; Mid-summer Day bonfires, particularly in Wachau section of Danube. *July/August,* Bregenz, Hohenems (Schubert), and Salzburg Festivals; Carinthian Summer, concerts and opera at Ossiach and Villach; Baden, Bad Ischl and Mörbisch (Neusiedler See) operetta weeks; Formula 1 automobile race for the Grand Prix of Austria on Zeltweg race course; *September,* Bruckner Festival, Linz; *November,* International Riding and Jumping Event in the Vienna Stadthalle; *December,* Christmas celebrations, mobile Christmas cribs; pre-season ski "wedel courses" in the Alpine regions; New Year's Eve events including torch-light skiing in the mountains, Strauss Concert by the Vienna Philharmonic, Kaiser Ball (Imperial Ball, tickets 2,000 Sch.) in the Vienna Hofburg etc.

National Holidays. Jan. 1 (New Year's Day); Jan. 6 (Epiphany); Apr. 17, 20 (Easter); May 1 (May Day); May 28 (Ascension); June 8 (Whit Mon.); June 18 (Corpus Christi); Aug. 15 (Assumption); Oct. 26 (National Day); Nov. 1 (All Saints); Dec. 8 (Immaculate Conception); Dec. 25, 26.

VISAS. Citizens of the United States, Great Britain, E.E.C. countries and Canada do not need visas to visit Austria. However, you must of course have a valid passport.

HEALTH CERTIFICATES. Not required for entry into Austria.

GETTING TO AUSTRIA. By Plane. The most convenient way from the States to Vienna is by ALIA (Royal Jordanian Airline), nonstop from New York on Mon., Thurs., and Fri. (returning Tues., Thurs., Sun.), or from Los Angeles via Chicago on Tues. and Sat. (returning Mon. and Fri.). Otherwise, connections can easily be made in London or a number of Continental cities such as Frankfurt, Paris or Zürich. For Salzburg, it is better to fly to London, Frankfurt or Zürich rather than Vienna; for the Alpine region of Western Austria, it is often more convenient to fly to Munich, Germany, where there are good road and rail links to the major Austrian resorts, only two hours or so from the airport. Dan Air fly from London (Gatwick) to Innsbruck three or four times weekly.

There are daily flights by Austrian Airlines DC–9 jets and British Airways Boeing 737s from London to Vienna. Flying time is under 2½ hours. Austrian Airlines, in association with BA, also flies from London to Salzburg less frequently. Tyrolean Airways operate daily flights between Innsbruck, Vienna, Graz, Zurich, and Frankfurt. Austrian Air Services also link some of the provincial capitals.

By Train. There are direct services from the Channel ports (Calais, Ostend and the Hook of Holland) to Austria. A convenient route is the "Ostend-Vienna Express" which leaves London (Victoria) at around 10.45 A.M. (one hour earlier in winter) and arrives in Vienna before 10 the next morning. Sleeping cars, couchettes and day cars from Ostend; buffet or snack bar service much of the way. For the Tirol take the "Rhein Express" from the Hook of Holland connecting with the overnight ferry from Harwich. Leaves London around 8 P.M. and arrives in Innsbruck almost 24 hours later. Dining car most of the way. From Calais the "Arlberg Express" goes via Paris and Switzerland to Austria stopping at St. Anton, Innsbruck, Kitzbühel, Salzburg, Linz and Vienna. Leaves London around 2 P.M. arriving in Innsbruck at midday the next day and Vienna at about 8 P.M. that evening. Couchettes all the way to Innsbruck. Buffet service in Austria. Light refreshments are also available in Switzerland from Basel to Buchs.

By Car. Most scenic route to Vienna, which covers almost the entire length of Austria, is from Germany or Switzerland via Bregenz, Innsbruck, Salzburg; from Innsbruck on you can drive via the autobahn or through Salzkammergut on the main road. The fastest way to reach Vienna from Germany (and beyond from Paris, Belgium, Holland and Scandinavia) is via Frankfurt, Regensburg, Passau, entering Austria at Schärding, rejoining the autobahn to Vienna at Wels. When traveling to Tirol, branch off the Munich-Salzburg autobahn; traveling to Carinthia and Styria, branch off at Salzburg.

CUSTOMS. There are two levels of duty free allowance for goods imported to Austria. Travelers coming from a European country may import 200 cigarettes or 50 cigars or 250 gr. of tobacco; 2 liters of wine and 1 liter of spirits; 1 bottle of toilet water, 50 gr. of perfume. Travelers coming from non-European countries may import 400 cigarettes or 100 cigars or 500 gr. tobacco; 2 liters of wine and one liter of spirits; 1 bottle of toilet water, 50 gr. of perfume.

HOTELS. Hotel accommodations in Austria, if you do not expect all the trimmings, are very good. By an active program of modernization the problem of the lack of baths and showers has been largely overcome. Many older inns have been adding private baths and the newer ones almost always have them. Top-category hotels are not often found in the country areas or smaller towns but the hotels there generally offer clean and comfortable rooms.

Our hotel grading system is divided into four categories. All prices are for two people in a double room. Deluxe (L) 1200–2200 schillings, Expensive (E) 750–1500, Moderate (M) 450–950, Inexpensive (I) 400–750. Prices include taxes, service charges and breakfast. Austria now operates an official rating system using from one to five stars. Usually displayed at the entrance to a hotel, five stars correspond to our (L), four to (E), three to (M) and (I). A two-star establishment may be perfectly acceptable, but have a look at the room first. Always remember that there is frequently a range of prices within the same hotel—with less attractive rooms being moderate in an expensive establishment.

Camping. Large sites with all facilities are in strategic locations around larger cities, in the vicinity of summer lake resorts, as well as in numerous other places, for instance along the Danube. Altogether about 400 camp sites. Also about 77 winter camp sites.

RESTAURANTS. Our restaurant grading system has three categories: Expensive (E) 350 Sch. and up—way up—Moderate (M) 200–350 Sch., and Inexpensive (I) 150–200 Sch. These prices are for one person and do not include wine.

Food and Drink. The specialties of Austria include such delights as: *Leberknödlsuppe,* a meat broth with liver dumplings; *Fischbeuschlsuppe,* a thick, piquant, Viennese soup made from the lungs of freshwater fish; *Gulaschsuppe,* a hot soup with Hungarian overtones, highly seasoned, full of paprika and onions; *Fogosch,* pike, *Forelle,* trout, either "blau" (boiled) or "müllerin" (fried in butter), and *Krebs,* succulent little crawfish, all from the lakes and rivers of Austria; *Wiener Schnitzel*—no need to explain. Try any kind of schnitzel, *Holsteiner, Pariser, Natur;* you won't taste such veal anywhere else in the world. Pork is beautifully prepared. Try *Schweinscarrée,* a very special cut, or that tender strip, called *Schweinsjungfrau* (pig's virgin) on the menu.

Rehrücken (venison) should be ordered with avidity and so should other game dishes, usually served with cranberries. Steaks are good; ask for it "durch" (well-done), "medium" (medium-rare) or "englisch" (rare). Austrian *Tafelspitz* (boiled beef) is delicious.

Noodles and dumplings are a national institution, and so are sweet desserts: the well known fruit *Strudel,* made here with a crust as light as gossamer; *Palatschinken,* thin dessert pancakes, rolled around a stuffing of fruit jam or nuts; *Salzburger Nockerl,* a delicious soufflé; *Torte,* rich Austrian cakes of which *Sachertorte,* created at the Sacher Hotel, is the most celebrated—chocolate cake coated with jam and iced with more chocolate. Try also *Dobosch, Linzer, Malakoff* and *Nusstorte.* Less rich is the fine-textured sponge cake called *Guglhupf,* wonderful with coffee.

Gumpoldskirchner, Grinzinger and *Nussberger* are good white wines grown in the suburbs of Vienna. The first is fruity, the other two dry. The Austrians love to make excursions into the suburbs to drink the new or *heurigen Wein* in charming taverns *(Heuriger)*.

The dry white wines of the Wachau area along the Danube, especially the selected types of *Kremser* and *Dürnsteiner,* are of very high quality, and the red wines of Vöslau and Burgenland are more than just drinkable. In fact, ordinary wine in Austria is usually good and cheap. A beneficial effect of the anti-freeze scandals of 1985 is that the wine you will be offered anywhere will now certainly be free of any additives.

SHOPPING. You may be eligible for a refund on VAT if your purchase is in a tax-free shop and is more than 1,000 Sch. Ask for details when shopping and make sure the shop itself will be handling your refund. Central clearing agents tend to charge heavily.

TELEPHONE. Major developments in the Austrian telephone system mean that numbers will be constantly changing for years to come. We make every effort to keep numbers up to date, but check on the spot if you draw a blank first go.

TIPPING. Most hotels and restaurants (among the few exceptions are smaller country inns) include service charges in their rates. However it is customary to give a 10% tip in addition.

MAIL. For the first 20 gr. (about ¾ ounce) letters cost 5 schillings inside the country and 6 schillings to Western European countries, 9 to the U.S.A. and Canada. Postcards to Austrian destinations cost 4 schillings; to the U.S., Canada and Western Europe 4 schillings. Regular-size letters (20 gr.) and postcards are forwarded within Europe automatically by airmail at no extra charge.

CLOSING HOURS. Stores open from 9 to 6; Saturdays, they close 12.30 or 1 P.M., outside major cities between 12 and 3 daily. Banking hours vary from town to town so check as necessary. They all close Saturdays. Some shops close for lunch, so best check. Most barbers and hairdressers close Mondays.

USEFUL ADDRESSES. Consulates in Vienna: *Australian,* Mattiellistr. 2–4 (tel. 52 85 80); *British,* Reisnerstr. 40 (tel. 75 61 17); *Canadian,* Dr. Karl Lueger-Ring 10 (tel. 63 36 91); *United States,* F. Schmidtplatz 2 (tel. 31 55 11). Consulates in Salzburg: *British,* Alter Markt 4 (tel. 84 81 33); *United States:* Giselakai 51 (tel. 28601).

All in Vienna: *Austrian National Tourist Office,* Margaretenstr. 1; *Austrian Travel Agency,* Opernring, opposite Opera; *Vienna Information,* Opernpassage, in subway beside the Opera; *American Express,* Kärntnerstr. 21; *Wagons Lits/ Cook,* Kärntnerring 2, also at Innsbruck, Linz, Salzburg.

Graf and Styria Information, Herrengasse 16, 8010 Graz (tel. 0316/705241–72).

Nationwide emergency first aid telephone: 144; police: 133.

GETTING AROUND AUSTRIA. By Train. Austria has an excellent railway system, most of which is now electrified. Remaining short routes and various branches are all diesel operated. The most scenic routes are along the main lines from Vienna via Salzburg and the Tirol to Switzerland and from Vienna via Kalgenfurt and Villach through Styria and Carinthia. In fact, almost all routes are scenic in one way or another. There are, in addition, a number of small narrow gauge railways such as the Zillertalbahn in the Tirol. Some of these are partially steam-driven in the tourist season. There is a runabout

"Austria Ticket" available for people up to the age of 26. It is for 2nd-class only and valid for 9 or 16 days. The Austria Ticket gives unlimited travel on all state railways and most private railways, bus routes operated by the railways or the Post Office and on Wolfgangsee steamers. In addition reduced rates apply with this ticket on Danube steamers and many mountain railways and cable cars. It costs $70 for 9 days and $105 for 16 days. If you are planning to travel at least 2,000 km. (1,240 miles) a "kilometerbank" is extremely economic. It is valid for any number of people for up to six months, on all trips over 70 km. (45 miles).

Note: There are several trains onto which you can load your car—specifically, those linking Vienna with Innsbruck and with Villach.

By Bus. Postal and local buses link up nearly every village, even those in the Alps. The service is highly efficient.

By Boat. You can travel by Danube river boats, which are large and comfortable, between Passau (on the German-Austrian border) and Vienna. The most scenic sections are those between Passau and Linz and the Wachau (Melk and Krems).

By Car. Drive to the right. Seat belts compulsory in the front seats. Gas costs about 11.30 per liter. There is a 130 kph (80 mph) speed limit on autobahns; on all other roads 100 kph (62 mph); in built-up areas 50 kph (31 mph). All roads are well maintained but most secondary roads are narrow and winding. Check the condition of mountain roads in winter before setting out. Road tunnels are kept open even if the mountain passes above are snowbound. Several mountain toll roads, notably Grossglockner and Felbertauern, scenically glorious, are congested in summer. There are the autobahns: West Autobahn (Vienna-Salzburg, Kufstein to beyond Innsbruck, and a last section from Bludenz to Bregenz); Süd Autobahn (now open from Vienna to the middle of Carinthia; and Klagenfurt-Arnoldstein on the border with Italy); Tauern Autobahn (Salzburg south through magnificent mountain scenery to Villach); parts of the last two are toll roads, the others are free. Car pilot service is available for motorists wishing to use Danube steamers between Passau and Vienna.

Car Hire. *Hertz,* Kärntnerring 17, and—for international reservations—Marxergasse 24, 1030 (tel. 73 15 96); *Avis,* Opernring 1 (also, Hilton Hotel and airport); *Inter-Rent,* Schubert Ring 7 (and airport)—all in Vienna. Branch offices in other cities. A number of firms provide you with chauffeur-driven cars, among them: *Franz Mazur,* Hasengasse 18 (and airport); *Kalal,* Rennweg 73. VAT is 20% for the first 20 days, 32% after that. It is usually cheaper, if you can, to rent a car in Germany or Switzerland and bring it over the border.

Vienna's Viewpoints

There are four ways to get a good bird's-eye view of Austria's great capital of 1,500,000 souls: (1) take one of the four-seater plane sightseeing tours at the Vienna Airport; (2) climb the 345 steps of the "Old Steffel", the south steeple of Saint Stephen's cathedral (or take the elevator to the top of the second tower if you prefer the easy way); (3) take a ride to the top of the Big Wheel (of *Third Man* fame) in the Prater; (4) go to Grinzing and take the 15-minute bus ride (no. 38a) for the view from the Kahlenberg, Cobenzl or Leopoldsberg in the Vienna Woods.

The Danube, divided by a 14-mile-long artificial island bisects Vienna's northern suburbs, dominated by the Donauturm and the highrises of the UNO City beyond. The heart of Vienna, the Innere Stadt (Inner City) is bounded by the handsome Ringstrasse (Ring), built in the 19th century on the site of the moats and ramparts of medieval Vienna. The Franz Josefs Kai, along the middle section of the Danube Canal, diverted from the main river just above Vienna and flowing through the city to rejoin the parent stream just below it, completes the Ring. About a mile beyond the Ring is the roughly parallel line of the Gürtel (Belt), which until 1890 formed the outer fortifications, or Linienwall. It was at the height of Vienna's imperial prosperity that the Ringstrasse became one of the handsomest streets in Europe, studded with such imposing buildings as the Opera House, Museums of Art and Natural History, the New Wing of the Hofburg, Parliament, the Rathaus, the

Burgtheater, the university, and the Votivkirche. Grouped round the Inner City in wedges are districts two to nine. These are enclosed by a combination of the Gürtel and the Danube, outside of which are districts ten to 23.

Vienna's weather is pleasant from spring to about halfway through the fall, but the old three-quarter time rhythm is perhaps a little more marked in winter in the glittering interiors of baroque theaters and palaces. Outstanding event of the winter season is Fasching (carnival time), which lasts from New Year's Eve until Mardi Gras. During January and February there are often as many as 10 formal balls in a single evening, the most gala being the Opernball.

The most prominent spring event is the Festival of Vienna, featuring concerts and performances in the theaters, concert houses and palaces of the city during four weeks from the second half of May. In July and August you'll hear plenty of Strauss waltzes in palace and park concerts, and these are the best months for excursions on the Danube.

Sightseeing in Vienna

One of the best ways to orientate yourself, especially if you are in a hurry, is to take a guided city bus tour. You can also take a boat tour along the Danube and the Danube Canal (see also *Practical Information*). However, the best way to explore the Inner City, that vital square mile that includes Vienna's greatest treasures of art and architecture, her leading hotels and her best shops, is on foot. All the chief buildings in Vienna have little shields attached to their façades. You can get a booklet *(Vienna from A to Z)* from the Tourist Board that lists all the numbered shields with a potted history about each building. It's an excellent system, easy to use and informative. You will also find coin-operated tape machines in most of the churches that give a description of the building in several languages.

The main artery is the three-quarter-mile of the Kärntnerstrasse-Rotenturmstrasse that runs from the Opera to the Danube Canal. Halfway down, where the street changes its name, is Saint Stephen's Cathedral, the main landmark of Vienna. Left of the cathedral is the square-like street of Graben with its famous Plague Column, and if you turn left again at the end of Graben, you proceed through the Kohlmarkt to the Michaeler Platz, where you see the main entrance to the Hofburg (Imperial Palace). All of this is an attractive pedestrian mall.

Try to see a performance of the Spanish Riding School in the beautiful baroque manège of the Hofburg. Here, under the glittering chandeliers, the famous white stallions, called Lippizaner (originally from the stud farm at Lippiza, Slovenia, but now from Piber in Styria) go through their courbettes, levades, and caprioles to the music of Mozart, Schubert and Johann Strauss. You can watch the horses training daily from 10 to midday, holidays excepted. Tickets and entrance on Josefsplatz.

In the Hofburg, historic central palace of the Austrian Empire, visit the imperial apartments of Emperor Franz Josef and Empress Elizabeth. The Schatzkammer has reopened after total renovation and now does justice to the Habsburg treasures (including the crown jewels).

The Kunsthistorisches Museum (Museum of Fine Arts) ranks as one of the most important art museums in the world. It is especially remarkable for its collection of antiquities, its huge range of paintings, from Breughel and Dürer to Titian, and the famous salt cellar of Benvenuto Cellini.

Go to Schönbrunn Palace (easy to reach by subway), designed by Fischer von Erlach to rival Versailles, for a tour of the gardens, superb view from the Gloriette, and visit to the imperial apartments. Forty-five of the palace's 1,400 rooms, sumptuously furnished in baroque and rococo style, can be visited.

The baroque Belvedere Palace, built by Lukas von Hildebrandt for Prince Eugene of Savoy, houses three museums: Medieval Austrian Art (in the Orangerie); Austrian Baroque (in the Lower Belvedere); Austrian 19th- and 20th-Century Art (in the Upper Belvedere), housing, notably, works by Klimt, Schiele, and Kokoschka.

The Albertina Collection of Graphic Arts (near the Opera) is world-renowned, and the newly-housed Gallery of the Academy of Fine Arts is equally well known for its collection of paintings by Hieronymus Bosch, Titian, Rembrandt and others. You can also visit the Herzgrüfterl der Habsburger, the small crypt in the Loretto Chapel of the Augustine Church where the hearts of the Habsburgs are enclosed in 54 urns; or the Kapuzinergruft, crypt of the House of Habsburg, containing 144 sarcophagi.

Even if your visit to Vienna is a short one, you should see the Grand Hall of the Austrian National Library at Josefsplatz 1. Built by Fischer von Erlach, it is a masterpiece of baroque architecture, possibly the most beautiful library in the world. Among other baroque monuments typical of this theatrical Austrian specialty are the restored Pestsäule (Plague Column) in the Graben; the nearby Peterskirche with its patinated copper dome; and the Karlskirche, ecclesiastical masterpiece of Fischer von Erlach.

PRACTICAL INFORMATION FOR VIENNA

 HOTELS. Unless you are motorized, and particularly if you plan to spend only a short time in Vienna, you will probably want to stay in the famous Inner City (First District) within walking distance of most museums, restaurants and the fashionable shops. From May to mid-October it is advisable to make hotel reservations well in advance (Vienna is an international congress center). If you have no reservation, consult the room information office on the Opernring, opposite the Opera, or the West or South station office, open from early morning to late night. Hotel reservations also can be made at the airport, and in summer at information offices near the West and South Autobahn approaches to Vienna. There are over 200 hotels so you should be able to find something.

Deluxe

Ambassador, Neuer Markt 5 (tel. 51 27 51 1). Modernized, but old traditions and contemporary facilities are happily combined. A favorite with diplomats, it boasts a long history of catering to important personalities.

Bristol, Kärntner Ring 1 (tel. 51 51 65 36). Opposite the Opera. 120 rooms, several plush suites. American bar and glittering *Korso* dining room. Garage.

Imperial, Kärntner Ring 16 (tel. 51 51 67 25). About 100 years old. 160 rooms have bath with heated floor, several suites have antique furnishings, though most decor is modern. Elegant restaurant and cafe with Viennese music, cozy bar.

Hilton, Am Stadtpark 1030 (tel. 75 26 52). 620 airconditioned rooms in different styles, antique and modern. Fine dining in *Prinz Eugen* restaurant; *Vindobona* wine tavern, cafe and bar are handy. Garage.

Intercontinental, Johannesgasse 28, 1030 (tel. 75 0 50). 500 airconditioned rooms, half overlooking skating rink. Several restaurants, bar, and large underground garage.

Marriott, Schubertring (tel. 51 5 18). 305 luxury rooms. Restaurants, bar and garage.

Palais Schwarzenberg, Schwarzenbergplatz 9, 1030 (tel. 78 45 15). 43 rooms with period furnishings. A quiet hotel in a wing of the baroque Schwarzenberg Palace overlooking the park. Excellent restaurant, delightful bar.

Sacher, Philharmoniker Strasse 2, 1010 (tel. 51 45 6). 120 rooms. A house of great distinction with two bars, several cafe rooms, and one of the best restaurants in town.

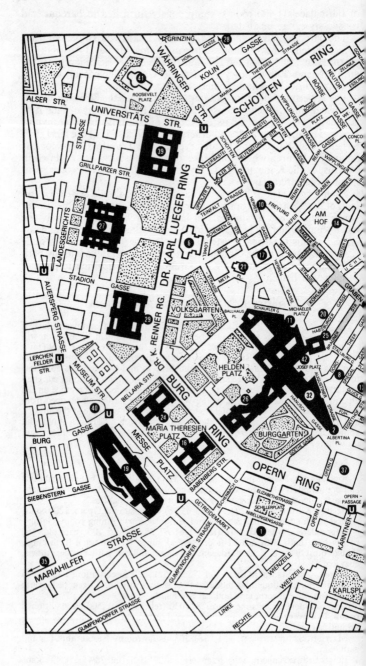

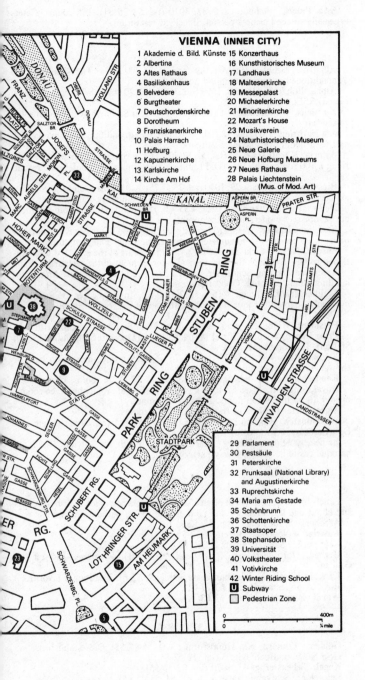

VIENNA (INNER CITY)

1 Akademie d. Bild. Künste
2 Albertina
3 Altes Rathaus
4 Basiliskenhaus
5 Belvedere
6 Burgtheater
7 Deutschordenskirche
8 Dorotheum
9 Franziskanerkirche
10 Palais Harrach
11 Hofburg
12 Kapuzinerkirche
13 Karlskirche
14 Kirche Am Hof
15 Konzerthaus
16 Kunsthistorisches Museum
17 Landhaus
18 Malteserkirche
19 Messepalast
20 Michaelerkirche
21 Minoritenkirche
22 Mozart's House
23 Musikverein
24 Naturhistorisches Museum
25 Neue Galerie
26 Neue Hofburg Museums
27 Neues Rathaus
28 Palais Liechtenstein
  (Mus. of Mod. Art)

29 Parlament
30 Pestsäule
31 Peterskirche
32 Prunksaal (National Library)
  and Augustinerkirche
33 Ruprechtskirche
34 Maria am Gestade
35 Schönbrunn
36 Schottenkirche
37 Staatsoper
38 Stephansdom
39 Universität
40 Volkstheater
41 Votivkirche
42 Winter Riding School
U Subway
  Pedestrian Zone

400m
0
0 ¼ mile

SAS Palais, Weihburggasse 32, 1010 (tel. 53 26 31). 165 rooms. Caters especially to the business person. Excellent restaurant.

Expensive

Albatros, Liechtensteinerstr. 89 (tel. 34 35 08). Near U.S. Embassy. 70 airconditioned rooms. Swimming pool, garage.

Alpha, Boltzmanngasse 8, 1090 (tel. 31 16 46). 70 rooms with bath. Located near U.S. Embassy.

Amadeus, Wildpretmarkt 5 (tel. 63 87 38). Near St. Stephen's. 29 rooms. No restaurant.

Am Parkring, Parkring 12 (tel. 52 65 24). 65 airconditioned rooms on 11th and 13th floors overlooking Stadtpark. Garage.

Astoria, Kärntnerstr. 32 (tel. 51 57 70). In the center (entrance from Führichg.). 100 rooms with bath. Old tradition, modernized facilities. Good restaurant.

Biedermeier, Landstr. 29, 1030 (tel. 75 55 75). 220 rooms. Quiet and comfortable, evoking the spirit of old Vienna. Several restaurants, garage.

De France, Schottenring 3 (tel. 34 35 40). 150 rooms. House of old tradition, but completely modernized. Restaurant, bar.

Erzherzog Rainer, Wiedner Hauptstr. 27 (tel. 65 46 46). Near Karlsplatz. 74 baths to 85 rooms; ask for quieter rooms at the back. Fine restaurant.

Europa, Neuer Markt 3 (tel. 51 59 4). In the heart of the city. 101 airconditioned rooms. Evenings there is musical entertainment in the restaurant. Cafe.

Konig von Ungarn, Schulerstr. 10 (tel. 52 65 200). Dead center. An ancient building, finely restored. Good restaurant.

Mailbergerhof, Annag. 7 (tel. 51 20 64 10). In the center. 35 rooms in modernly adapted baroque building, with a quiet courtyard. Small.

Opernring, Opernring 11 (tel. 58 75 51 8–0). 35 rooms.

President, Wallg. 23 (tel. 57 36 36). Near West Station. 77 rooms with T.V.

Prinz Eugen, Wiedner Gürtel 14 (tel. 65 17 41). Opposite Südbahnhof (South Station). 106 rooms. Modern.

Regina, Roosevelt Platz 15 (tel. 42 76 81). 129 rooms, most with bath or shower. Good restaurant.

Römischer Kaiser, Annagasse 16 (tel. 51 27 75 1). 26 rooms. Central.

Royal, Singerstr. 3 (tel. 52 46 31). Near Graben and St. Stephen's. 66 rooms, most with bath. On top floors. Italian restaurant.

Tigra, Tiefer Graben 14 (tel. 63 96 41). 42 rooms.

Westminster, Harmoniegasse 5 (tel. 34 66 04). Between Schottenring and U.S. Embassy. 75 rooms.

In nearby Klosterneuburg, **Martinschloss,** Martinstr. 34 (tel. 74 26). A baroque castle-hotel in a lovely park overlooking the Danube.

Moderate

Hotels in this category will often charge first-class prices for their best rooms and about one third less for still comfortable rooms without baths.

Arenberg, Stubenring 2 (tel. 52 52 91 0).

Austria, Wolfengasse 3 (tel. 51 52 35).

Capricorno, Schwedenplatz 3 (tel. 63 31 04).

Graben, Dorotheergasse 3, 1010 (tel. 52 15 31). 46 rooms. Just off the Graben.

Kaiserin Elisabeth, Weihburggasse 3 (tel. 51 52 6). Traditional favorite.

Ring, Am Gestade 1 (tel. 63 77 01).

Wandl, Petersplatz 9 (tel. 63 63 17).

Inexpensive

Goldenes Einhorn, Am Hundsturm 5 (tel. 55 47 55). Old-established.

Graf Stadion, Buchfeldg. 5 (tel. 42 52 84 0).

Kugel, Siebensterng. 43, 1070 (tel. 93 33 55).

Schweiger, Schikandergasse 4, 1040 (tel. 56 42 15).

Schweizerhof, Bauernmarkt 22 (tel. 63 19 31). The only one in the inner city.

Zur Wiener Staatsoper, Krugerstr. 11, 1010 (tel. 51 31 27 4). 22 rooms. Conveniently situated.

RESTAURANTS. Prices in the excellent top-class restaurants match those of equivalent hotels. Simpler establishments with a limited menu often offer outstanding value at very reasonable prices. In Austria it is always advisable to reserve a table. Ask your receptionist to do this for you.

Expensive

Altwienerhof, Herklotzgasse 6, 1150 (tel. 83 71 45). Excellent cooking along nouvelle cuisine lines; good for fish.

Drei Husaren, Weihburggasse 4, 1010 (tel. 51 21 09 2). Candlelight, antique furnishings, soft music. Superb food. Dinners only. Fills up very quickly, so reserve.

Imperial, (see hotels) (tel. 51 51 6–0). Superior Viennese and international specialties, accompanied by music. Pleasant bar. Afternoon music in the café.

Kervansaray, Mahlerstr. 9, 1010 (tel. 52 88 43). Turkish specialties from various *kebabs* to fresh Bosphorus fish, including lobster. Fish restaurant *Hummerbar* upstairs.

Korso (Hotel Bristol), Mahlerstr. 2 (tel. 51 51 6–545). Creative Austrian cuisine.

Rotisserie Prinz Eugen (Hotel Hilton), Am Stadtpark 1030 (tel. 75 26 52). One of the best restaurants in Vienna; excellent food in attractive replica surroundings.

Sacher, (see hotels) (tel. 52 33 67). A handsome setting for dining. The main restaurant sparkles as it did in the days of the Habsburgs. Alcoved, intimate dining rooms on the upper floor. Home of the *Sachertorte* chocolate cake.

Salut, Wildpretmarkt 3, 1010 (tel. 63 13 22). French cuisine in small, attractive rooms, evenings only, except for Sat. lunch.

Schubertstüberl, Schreyvogelg, 4, 1010 (tel. 63 71 87). Pleasant evening dining grill and game specialties. Garden in summer.

Steirereck, Rasumowskygasse 2, 1030 (tel. 73 31 68). On Danube Canal. One of Vienna's best restaurants; lightly cooked Austrian dishes. Closed Sat., Sun., and holidays.

Wegenstein "Weisser Schwan", Nussdorferstr. 59, 1090 (tel. 34 16 50). Renowned for its game dishes, particularly fowl and wild boar. Closed Sat.-Sun. Must reserve.

Moderate

Basteibeisl, Stubenbastei 10, 1010 (tel. 52 43 19). Genuine Viennese cuisine. Open Sun.

Eckel, Sieveringerstr. 46, 1190 (tel. 32 32 18). Not dressy, but serves some of the best all-round food. Specialties are sweet-water crayfish (in season), *Backhendl,* and delicious fluffy, hot soufflé-type desserts. Pleasant garden.

Falstaff, Währingerstr. 67, 1090 (tel. 42 27 41). Opposite the Volksoper. Large rooms and menu for after-theater dining.

Gösser Bierhaus, Wollzeile 38, 1010 (tel. 52 48 39). Large beer restaurant with simple, but good, food.

Griechenbeisl, Fleischmarkt 11, 1010 (tel. 63 19 41). Founded in the last century by Greeks, it is now very Viennese indeed, with appropriate music in the evenings.

Marhold, Fleischmarkt 9, 1010 (tel. 63 28 73). Small wood-decorated rooms on two floors of a 16th-century house. Some of the best food in this category, including game. Good wines and original Budweiser (from Bohemia) beer on tap.

Melker Stiftskeller, Schottengasse 3, 1010 (tel. 63 55 30). An outstanding cellar, serving wine from the famous monastery.

Rathauskeller, Rathausplatz 1, 1010 (tel. 42 12 19). A colossal operation in the basement of Vienna's city hall. Vaulted rooms. One of the longest, most comprehensive menus, with Schnitzel a specialty.

Zum Grünen Anker, Grünangergasse, 1010 (tel. 51 22 19 1). Excellent fresh Italian dishes, salads; remarkable Italian wines. Very good value.

Zum Weissen Rauchfangkehrer (White Chimneysweep), Rauhensteingasse 2, 1010 (tel. 52 34 71). Near Graben. A series of rooms, mostly in Tyrolean Stuben-style, 100-year-old wine bar. Excellent beef and pork dishes.

Inexpensive

Augustinerkeller, Augustinerstr. 1, 1010 (tel. 52 34 83). For atmosphere and value.

Gösser Bräu, Elisabethstrasse 3, 1010 (tel. 58 66 21 66). Large beer restaurant with simple, good food.

Paulusstube, Walfischg. 7, 1010 (tel. 51 28 13 6). Sidewalk garden in summer, music in the evening, fine bottled wines.

Stadtbeisel, Naglerg. 21, 1010 (tel. 63 33 23). Small, cozy and crowded at noon.

Stiedl's Bierklinik, Steindlgasse 4, 1010 (tel. 63 33 36).

Wienerwald, Bellariastr. 12, 1010 (tel. 93 72 79). Easy for the unadventurous visitor. One of a chain; also at Argentinierstr. 66, 1040 (tel. 65 72 34), and Annagasse 3, 1010 (tel. 52 37 66).

Zu den drei Hacken, Singerstr. 28 (tel. 52 58 95). Pleasant, friendly, neighborhood restaurant.

Zwölf-Apostelkeller, Sonnenfelsgasse 3, 1010 (tel. 52 67 77). Frequented by students, and so deep beneath the street level that some walls are covered with straw to diminish dampness. No music.

NIGHTCLUBS. Prices in Viennese nightclubs are high for what is offered and champagne is obligatory in some which have floorshows.

Café Volksgarten, in the park of the same name. There is outdoor dancing there in summer.

Casanova, Dorotheergasse 6. Has the best of the floorshows where the accent is on striptease.

Chattanooga, Graben 29. Lewd shows.

Eden-Bar, Lilengasse 2. Near St. Stephen's, this is a leading spot for dancing.

Fledermaus, Spiegelgasse 2. Has **literary** cabaret and dancing.

Maxim, Opernring 11. Has good floorshows with striptease.

Moulin Rouge, Walfischgasse 11. As the name suggests, this club specializes in striptease.

Queen Anne, Johannesgasse 12. Has professional hostesses.

Splendid Bar, Jasomirgottstrasse 3. A leading spot for dancing.

MUSIC AND THEATER. Vienna remains one of the greatest music centers in the world, supporting two superb orchestras, the *Vienna Philharmonic* and the *Vienna Symphony.* There are also innumerable chamber music and choral groups including the *Vienna Boys' Choir.* The Vienna Opera is one of the top operas in the world. The season reaches its climax in the festival in June though performances go on continuously from the beginning of September to the end of June. For details of what's on, when and where, consult the "Wochenspielplan," the weekly theater/opera poster visible all over the city. Operas and concerts are usually sold out, so to reserve seats it's best to order them through your hotel desk or one of the many ticket agencies. The world-famous *Burgtheater* retains its great reputation as one of the leading centers of German theatrical art. There is a series of other drama theaters, headed by *Akademietheater* in the Academy of Dramatic Arts. In July/August the Volksoper holds an operetta season in the Staatsoper and the Volksoper. Operettas are also performed in the newly renovated Raidmundtheater.

MUSEUMS AND GALLERIES. Vienna has a number of superb public collections. You can save money by purchasing a block of ten museum tickets at the reduced price of 70 schillings—but do enquire which museums are included. The following are worth a visit:

Albertina, Augustinerstr. 1 (tel. 52 42 32). A huge collection of the graphic arts from the Middle Ages to the present day. Open Mon., Tues., Thurs., Fri., 10–2, Wed., 10–6, Sat., Sun., 10–1.

Belvedere, Upper Belvedere, 1030, Prinz Eugen Str. 27 (tel. 78 41 58). Prince Eugen's summer palace, with works by Klimt, Schiele, Kokoschka. Open Tues. to Sat., 10–4, Sun. 9–4.

Gallery of the Academy of Fine Arts, Schillerplatz 3 (tel. 57 95 16). Select collection of European paintings. Open Tues., Thurs., Fri., 10–2, Wed., 10–1 and 3–6, Sat., Sun., 9–1.

Hofburg and Neue Hofburg (tel. 57 55 54). The great complex contains several museums—Weapons and Musical Instrument Collections, Ethnological Museum and Ephesus Museum among them. Note that the Treasury will be closed until about 1987 but some of its best pieces are on show in the Museum of Fine Arts. Open Mon. to Sat. 8.30–4.30, Sun. 9–1.

Kaisergruft (Imperial crypt), Tegetthoffstr. 2 (tel. 52 68 53). Under the Capuchin Church. Guided tours only. Open May to Sept., daily, 9.30–4, Oct. to Apr., 9.30–12.

Kunsthistorisches Museum (Museum of Fine Arts), Burg Ring 8 (tel. 93 45 41). One of Europe's greatest, with a superb collection of paintings and *objets d'art.* Open Tues. to Fri. 10–6 (Tues. and Fri. also 6–9), Sat., Sun., 9–6.

Museum of the History of Vienna, Karlsplatz, 1040 (tel. 42804). Open Tues. to Sun., 9–4.30.

Neue Galerie, Reitschulgasse 2. Fine small painting collection. Open 10–6 daily except Tues.

GETTING AROUND VIENNA. Travelers with one eye on the budget would find it advisable to get acquainted with Vienna's public transport system. There are streetcars (trams), buses, a *Stadtbahn* (City Railway), which is partly elevated, partly underground, and partly at ground level. This latter is limited in its coverage, but very practical between Schönbrunn Palace, Karlskirche, Stadtpark, Wien Mitte at the City Air Terminal, Schweden Platz and some other stops along the Danube Canal, and the Volksoper. There is also a *Schnellbahn* (Fast Railway) serving primarily the northeast and southeast suburbs, including the airport.

Tickets for buses, streetcars, subway and Stadtbahn cost 18 schillings if bought singly; 12 schillings if bought in advance in blocks of 5 at a *Tabak Trafik* (tobacco store). A three-day unlimited travel ticket can be bought in advance at a *Tabak Trafik* for 83 schillings. With a single ticket, cars and means of transport can be changed if continuing in same direction. Some streetcars have automatic ticket machines in the first car (marked by a yellow sign). They swallow 5 and 10 schilling coins, so have them handy.

Lower Austria and its Castles

Largest of the nine federal states, Lower Austria (Niederösterreich) is dotted with some 500 castles and abbeys, of which the following are outstanding: Seitenstetten, Benedictine abbey founded in 1112; Melk, one of the most beautiful baroque abbeys on the right bank of the Danube; the Renaissance castle Schallaburg near Melk; Dürnstein, ruined castle where Richard the Lionheart was imprisoned in 1193; Klosterneuburg, Augustine abbey from 12th century, just outside Vienna; Heidenreichstein, one of the most remarkable water castles; Heiligenkreuz, treasure-filled Cistercian abbey, west of Baden.

Baden, very close to Vienna, is a lively spa, whose Roman spring has been in use for 2,000 years, curing people of rheumatic and skin afflictions. South of Vienna, the resort center known as the Semmering is a favorite summer and winter weekend spot for the Viennese.

The 20-mile stretch of magnificent scenery along the Danube known as the Wachau is best seen by Danube boat. From mid-May to mid-September, there are daily steamers to take you nine hours downstream from Linz to Vienna, 17 hours upstream from Vienna to Linz. If you are going by car, take the road on the left bank between Emmersdorf (opposite Melk—cross by ferry) and the old town of Krems, founded in the 10th century, the wine capital of Austria.

PRACTICAL INFORMATION FOR LOWER AUSTRIA

BADEN. *Clubhotel* (L). *Sauerhof* (L). *Gutenbrunn* (E). *Krainerhütte* (E). *Parkhotel* (E). *Josefsplatz* (M). *Papst* (M). *Schlosshotel Oth* (M). *Helga* (I).
Restaurants. *Badener Stadtkeller* (M). Rustic atmosphere and a pleasant courtyard setting. *Krebs* (M). Near the station.

KREMS. *Parkhotel* (M). *Aufreiter* (I).
Restaurant. *Bacher* (M), over the river in Mautern. Frau Wagner, the owner, voted 1983 Cook of the Year.

MELK. *Goldener Ochs* (M). *Stadt Melk* (M).

SEMMERING. *Panhans* (E), well restored with indoor pool and sauna. *Gartenhotel Alpenheim* (M). *Park-Villa* (M). *Pension Belvedere* (M). *Daheim* (I). *Landau* (I). *Waldruhe* (I).

Miniature Burgenland

This tiny federal state is sandwiched between Lower Austria and the Hungarian border. Its principal natural curiosity is the Neusiedler Lake, whose shallow expanse of salt water expands and contracts at the caprice of the wind. Fourth largest lake in Europe, it is pleasant for summer swimming. The chief tourist attraction of Burgenland is the capital Eisenstadt, in whose church the composer, Josef Haydn, lies buried in an elaborate tomb of white marble built by his grateful patron, Prince Esterhazy. Esterhazy Palace may be visited, and the composer's home is now a museum. Bad Tatzmannsdorf, in south Burgenland, has been a health resort for hundreds of years, with treatment for heart and circulatory troubles.

PRACTICAL INFORMATION FOR BURGENLAND

BAD TATZMANNSDORF. *Kurhotel* (E). Cure facilities and a pool. *Parkhotel* (E). Cure facilities and a pool. *Sonnenhof* (M). *Zum Kastell* (M).

EISENSTADT. *Burgenland* (E), indoor pool, sauna. *Parkhotel* (M). *Eder* (I). *Haydnhof* (I).

JENNERSDORF. Restaurant. *Raffel* (M). A superb restaurant serving Pannonian cuisine. Fine wines. Worth a detour.

NEUSIEDL. *Wende* (E). *Neusiedler Csarda* (M). *Frischmann* (I). *Maut* (I).

Upper Austria

The federal state of Upper Austria (Oberösterreich) lies between Lower Austria and Salzburg. Linz, the capital, is third largest city in Austria, an important industrial center (steel, chemicals) and a busy port on the Danube. However, Linz harbors also much charm in the old town streets around the main square, in the shadows of the baroque Old Cathedral, and in the splendidly arranged Upper Austrian State Museum located in the former fortress towering over the Danube. Not far from Linz are the famous baroque abbeys of St. Florian (where composer Bruckner was organist) and Kremsmünster (founded in 777).

Most of the scenic beauty in Upper Austria is displayed in its southern part, the Salzkammergut region, a delightful summer and winter playground of lakes, streams and mountains.

Among the many charming resorts are Bad Ischl, former summer residence of Emperor Franz Josef; and, of course, St. Wolfgang on Wolfgangsee, the stage of the famous White Horse Inn operetta. There are marvelous views of the Salzkammergut region from the 5,900-foot Schafbergspitze, reached from St. Wolfgang by narrow-gauge railway, and from Feuerkogel (about 5,400 ft.), ascended by cable car from Ebensee at the southern tip of Traun Lake, not far from Bad Ischl at the northern end of Traun Lake in Gmunden, an old lake town with swans, sailboats and two lake castles.

In the eastern section of Salzkammergut is the deep Hallstätter Lake, majestically enclosed by the steep mountains that rise straight out of its depths; here is the picturesque little town of Hallstatt, known mostly for the fact that it gave its name to the prehistoric Hallstatt Period (see the museum with finds from the 11th century B.C.). From the nearby Obertraun, you can take an aerial cable car to Krippenstein, on the Dachstein Plateau, stopping off also at the middle station for a visit to the Dachstein Ice Caves whose fantastic shapes date from the Ice Age.

PRACTICAL INFORMATION FOR UPPER AUSTRIA

BAD ISCHL. *Kurhotel* (E), cure facilities, indoor pool. *Post* (E). *Grüner Baum* (M). *Zum Goldenen Schiff* (M). *Goldener Ochs* (I).

HALLSTATT. *Grüner Baum* (M), on the lakefront. Fish dishes are served in a terrace restaurant. *Seewirt* (I), with a wine tavern.

LINZ. *Hotel Schillerpark* (L), Rainerstr. 2–4 (tel. 55 40 50). 100 rooms with bath. Sauna, garage. *Tourotel* (L), Untere Donaulände 9 (tel. 27 50 75). 176 rooms, indoor pool. *Domhotel* (E), Baumbachstr. 17 (tel. 27 84 41). 53 rooms. *Novotel* (E), Wankmüllerhofstr. 39 (tel. 47 2 81). 105 rooms. *Drei Mohren* (M), Promenade 17 (tel. 27 26 26). 27 rooms, half of which have baths. *Ebelsbergerhof* (M), Wienerstr. 485 (tel. 42 1 25). 39 rooms. *Nibelungenhof* (M), Scharitzerstr. 7 (tel. 56 0 47). Most of the 37 rooms have showers. *Wolfinger* (M), Hauptplatz 19 (tel. 27 32 91). 25 rooms, 9 baths. *Pöstlingberg* (I), Pöstlingerberg 14 (tel. 23 10 43). 12 rooms.

ST. WOLFGANG. *Golfhotel* (E). *Weisses Rössl* (E). *Seehotel Cortisen* (M). *Belvedere* (I). *Wolfgangerhof* (I).

The Forests of Styria

Styria (Steiermark) is Austria's second largest federal state, an area of large, dense forests, rife with game. Some resorts, like the famous pilgrimage shrine of Mariazell visited by Pope John Paul in 1983, offer fashionable amenities for winter sports plus local flavor, at lower prices than elsewhere in Austria. Towering above the historic old town of Schladming, where the Alpine World Ski Championships was held in 1982, is Dachstein, the highest peak of Styria (almost 10,000 feet), which can be reached by cable car. Styria has the longest chair lift in the world at Tauplitz and one of the biggest ski jumps near Mitterndorf, where jumps longer than 140 yards are not uncommon. West of Mitterndorf is one of the most romantic areas of Styria, the Ausseer Land around Bad Aussee, with a string of lakes nestled among the mountains and forests; this is the Styrian section of the Salzkammergut.

The capital of Styria is Graz, a university town (second largest in Austria) with an old world atmosphere, one of the oldest museums in the world, the Joanneum; a fascinating folklore museum with Styrian folk costumes dating all the way back to the Hallstatt and Celtic periods; Schloss Eggenberg, a superb 17th-century castle, housing a unique hunting museum; and the Styrian Armory, which contains the greatest collection of ancient armor in Europe. 15 km. (nine miles) north is the open-air museum at Stübing with old farmhouses and mills.

PRACTICAL INFORMATION FOR STYRIA

ALTAUSSEE. *Tyrol* (E). *Dachstein* (M). *Kitzerhof* (M). *Zum Loser* (M).

BAD AUSSEE. *Erzherzog Johann* (E).

FROHNLEITEN. *Scholss Rabenstein* (E).

GRAZ. *Steirerhof* (L), Jakominiplatz 12 (tel. 76 3 56). 92 rooms. *Daniel* (E), Europaplatz 1 (tel. 91 10 80). 94 rooms. *Gollner* (E), Schlögelgasse 14 (72 5 21). 55 rooms all with soundproofed windows. Sauna. *Parkhotel* (E), Leonhardstr. 8 (tel. 33 5 11). 65 rooms. *Erzherzog Johann* (M), Sackstr. 3 (tel. 76 5 51). *Mariahilf* (M), Mariahilferstr. 9 (tel. 91 31 63). 50 rooms, 32 showers. *Herbst* (I), Lagerg. 12 (tel. 91 52 84). 7 rooms.

IRDNING. *Schloss Pichlarn* (L). One of Austria's finest castle hotels; offers a variety of sport.

MARIAZELL. *Mariazellerhof* (E). *Alpenhof* (M). *Drei Hasen* (M). *Feichtegger* (M). *Marienwasserfall* (I). *Erzherzog Johann* (I). *Goldenes Kreuz* (I). *Grazerhof* (I). *Grüner Kranz* (I).

RAMSAU. Situated on a most scenic plateau above Schladming. *Alpenkrone* (E). *Berghof* (M). *Laerchenhof* (M). *Matschner* (M).

SCHLADMING. *Sporthotel Royer* (L). Indoor pool. *Alte Post* (E), Hauptplatz 10 (tel. 22 57 10). In center of town, with fine restaurant. *Haus Barbara* (M). *Schladmingerhof* (M). *Planathof* (I).

TAUPLITZ ALM. *Berghotel* (M). *Sporthotel Tauplitz Alm* (M). *Hierzegger* (I).

Salzburg

Salzburg is the biggest tourist attraction of Austria after the capital city of Vienna. A baroque jewel in a perfect mountain setting on both banks of the Salzach River, the city and the surrounding countryside are dominated by the magnificent Festung Hohensalzburg, a 12th-century fortress 500 feet above the town at one end of the Mönchsberg. Accessible by cable railway or by an easy zig-zag climb, this mighty, siege-proof seat of the powerful archbishops of Salzburg is one of the most impressive sights in Europe.

Its floodlighted silhouette is familiar on summer evenings to tourists who flock to Salzburg for the annual Salzburg Music Festival, which honors the city's most famous son, Wolfgang Amadeus Mozart, from the last week in July to the end of August.

Although there are conducted tours of the castle, you can get an excellent feel for the place by wandering round it alone. Don't miss St. George's chapel, added to the ensemble in 1501. Its 16th-century 200-pipe barrel organ plays daily during the summer. Not far away from the fortress is the Nonnberg convent, founded in the 8th century.

Virtually everything in Salzburg is within a few minutes' walk of the old center of the city. The very heart of things is the handsome Residenzplatz, with its 40-foot-high fountain. The Residenz itself, a 17th-century palace of the archbishops, provides guided tours of the state rooms. From another side of the square, carillon concerts chime out at 7 and 11 A.M. and at 6 P.M. from the 35 bells in the Glockenspiel tower. Nearby is the colorful Alter Markt, with another fountain and an old chemist's shop.

The 17th-century Dom (Cathedral) on Dom Platz, was the first baroque building north of the Alps, and it remains one of the finest. Among a host of lovely city churches is the Universitätskirche (University Church), an outstanding example of the prolific Viennese architect, Fischer von Erlach, who also began the work on the lovely Mirabell Gardens. Visit the Benedictine abbey of St. Peter, begun in 847, with its Romanesque interior and Gothic cloister.

The Grosse Festspielhaus is the focus for the Salzburg Festival. Designed by Holzmeister, it holds 2,400 people, has the widest stage in the world and splendid acoustics. The guided tour of the Festival complex includes the Felsenreitchule, the winter riding academy, now used as an open-air theater; and a beautiful, small, 17th century auditorium which was once a stable, with a frescoed ceiling by Rottmayer.

Mozart's birthplace is now a museum with his clavichord, hammerklavier, family pictures and intriguing exhibits including small models of settings for his operas. The tiny house where he is reputed to have composed the *Magic Flute,* the Zauberflötenhäuschen, is also a museum. The Mozarteum music academy has two excellent concert halls and is also responsible for housing the Bibliotheca Mozartiana, a library with about 1,500 works by Mozart, another couple of thousand about him, and quantities of other books and musical works. Although the mortal remains of the immortal Mozart were buried in a common grave in Vienna, his family lies in St. Sebastian's cemetery, Linzergasse 41.

Across the river in the newer town, the Schloss Mirabell and Mirabell Gardens should not be missed, especially the lovely marble Angel Staircase, whose carved angels look more like cupids. There are often candlelit chamber music concerts here, even when the festival is not on. The north part of the Mirabell Garden is now called the Kurgarten, since it encloses the very modern Kurmittelhaus, where all kinds of cures can be taken, as well as the Kongresshaus, Salzburg's up-to-date convention hall. Try to see a performance of the famous Salzburg Marionettes in the Marionette Theater, which is headquarters for Professor Hermann Aicher, whose family has been making and exhibiting these fabulous puppets for 200 years.

About 20 minutes by car from town is 17th-century Hellbrunn palace, summer residence of the archbishops. The baroque park has marvelous fountain displays, a natural rock theater and fine sculptures. In the grounds, the Monatsschlösschen has a folklore museum.

For a splendid view over the city and the Alps, take the lift up the Mönchsberg from the Gstättengasse, climb the Kapuzinerberg and visit the Capuchin Monastery, drive up the Gaisberg, included in most sightseeing tours (sightseeing buses also take you up there) or, even better, take the daringly-constructed aerial cable car to the top of Untersberg (over 5,800 ft.), the valley station of which can be reached by bus from the city.

PRACTICAL INFORMATION FOR SALZBURG

SALZBURG FESTIVAL. This is the most celebrated festival in Europe (last week July–end Aug.), and securing tickets for its many events as well as hotel accommodations is a major problem. The demand for tickets always exceeds the supply, so get them early through your travel agent or at the official Austrian tourist office in your country. Two specialist booking agents are *Mayfair Travel Service, Inc.,* 119 W. 57th St., New York 10019 and *International Services, Ltd.,* 7 Haymarket, London SW1, who are both agents for the Association of Music

Festivals. Details also from the *Salzburger Festspiele,* Postfach 140, 5010 Salzburg (tel. 0662/425 41). The only thing you can count on in Salzburg itself is standing room for the serenade concerts and for outdoor presentations where the space is more or less unlimited.

HOTELS. It is unwise to come to Salzburg during the Festival season without hotel reservations. If you haven't time to write to individual hotels and wait for replies, try the *Landesverkehrsamt,* Mozartplatz 5, (tel. 84 15 61–2232) or the *Stadtverkehrsbüro,* Auerspergstr. 7 (tel. 71 5 11). The latter is a clearing house for placing visitors in rooms in private houses. If you are willing to accept this sort of accommodation, you can bank on clean rooms and a friendly reception. There is an information office at the station (tel. 71 7 12).

If you can't find a place to stay in Salzburg, you can do what many do—find a place nearby. If you have a car, it's fairly simple. One good spot is Fuschl. Other lake resorts where you can stay are on the Wolfgangsee and Mondsee, both serviced by buses to Salzburg, about 18 miles away. Or you can stay at Bad Gastein, which has a large number of hotels, and commute by autorail (the trip takes an hour and a half). (See subsequent regional information for hotels.)

In May, June and September, excellent months in the Salzburg region, you will have no trouble in finding accommodation in Salzburg itself. Rates during the summer season (June 1-Sept. 30) and especially during the Festival may be as much as 50 percent higher than during the rest of the year, which often makes them higher than those in Vienna. Parking is available in large municipal garages under the Mönchsberg.

Deluxe

Bristol, Makartplatz 4 (tel. 73 5 57). 90 rooms. Luxurious period furnishings. Closed Nov. through Mar.

Gastschloss Mönchstein, on the Mönchsberg (tel. 84 13 63). In a magnificent location above Salzburg, is a small exclusive castle hotel. 11 elegant suites, each with bath. Superior service; open summer only. Superb restaurant.

Goldener Hirsch, Getreidegasse 37 (tel. 84 15 11). 50 rooms in an 800-year-old house, an inn since 1564, transformed after extensive reconstruction into a charming hotel in the old Salzburg style but with modern comfort. Modern appliances ingeniously hidden; all rooms with bath; outstanding food.

Kobenzl, (tel. 21 7 76). 7 miles and 2,000 feet up Gaisberg. 36 rooms, pool, restaurant, crisp mountain air and a wonderful view over Salzburg. Open from March to September.

Österreichischer Hof, Schwarzstr. 5 (tel. 72 5 41). On bank of Salzach River near Mozarteum; 200 beds, most rooms with bath. Three restaurants with excellent cuisine; panoramic views.

Salzburg Sheraton, Auerspergstr. 4 (tel. 79 32 10). 165 rooms. Highly praised restaurant.

Expensive

Cottage, Joseph Messner Strasse 14 (tel. 24 5 71). 86 rooms and a pool.

Europa, Rainerstr. 31 (tel. 73 2 93). Next to the railroad station. Modern 15-story building spoils the city's baroque beauty. 150 rooms, most with bath or shower. Roof café and restaurant. Unique view of Salzburg and the Alps.

Fondachhof, Gaisbergstr. 46 (tel. 20 9 06). 30 rooms. Located in a large park at the foot of Gaisberg. A castle hotel with a heated pool; closed Oct. through Mar. Good restaurant.

Kasererhof, Solaristrasse 3 (tel. 21 2 65). 58 rooms, quiet location, garden restaurant.

Maria Theresien Schlössl, Morzgerstr. 87 (tel. 84 12 44). In Hellbrunn. 13 rooms, good restaurant.

Schlosshotel St. Rupert, Morzgerstr. 31 (tel. 84 32 31). 23 rooms. Near Hellbrunn Castle. Very good restaurant and bar. Open in the summer only.

Winkler, Franz Josefstr. 7 (tel. 73 5 13). 103 rooms with bath; restaurant and café.

Moderate

Auersperg, Auerspergstr. 61 (tel. 71 7 21). 51 rooms. Located between the station and Kapuzinerberg.

Bayrischer Hof, Elisabethstr. 12 (tel. 50 0 40). 50 rooms and 25 with bath. Many rooms have a view of Gaisberg. Very good restaurant.

Elefant, Sigmund-Haffner-Gasse 4 (tel. 84 33 97). 36 rooms all with shower.

Gablerbräu, Linzerg 9 (tel. 73 4 41). 40 rooms, 25 with bath.

Kasererbräu, Kaig. 33 (tel. 84 24 45). Near Mozartplatz. 25 rooms. Furnished in old Salzburg style.

Markus Sittikus, Markus-Sittikus-Str. 20 (tel. 71 1 21). 48 rooms with 27 showers. Near the main station.

Stein, Giselakai 3 (tel. 74 3 46). 60 rooms with 41 baths. Good restaurant and roof terrace.

Stieglbräu, Rainerstr. 14 (tel. 77 6 92). 50 rooms. Large restaurant divided into several sections. A garden to be taken advantage of in the summer.

Inexpensive

Alter Fuchs, Linzerg 47 (tel. 72 2 88).

Blaue Gans, Getreideg. 43 (tel. 84 13 17). 40 rooms some with showers.

Gasthof Trumerstüberl, Bergstr. 6 (tel. 74 7 76). Near station. Good value.

PENSIONS. Salzburg has a better selection of Pensions than any other city in Austria. They cover all categories and are usually well appointed.

Expensive

Dr. Wührers Haus Gastein, Ignaz Riederkai 25 (tel. 22 5 65). 13 rooms. Almost luxurious.

Fuggerhof, Eberh.-Fugger-Str. 9 (tel. 20 4 79). 13 rooms and a heated pool.

Haus Arenberg, Blumensteinstr. 8 (tel. 77 1 74). Under the Kapuziner Berg.

Haus Ingeborg, Sonnleitenweg 9 (tel. 21 7 90). 11 rooms and a heated outdoor pool.

Moderate

Am Dom, Goldg. 17 (tel. 84 27 65). 15 rooms.

Helmhof, Kirchengasse 29 (tel. 34 4 49). 18 rooms and a heated pool.

Koch, Gaisbergstr. 37 (tel. 20 4 02). 17 rooms.

Wolf, Kaigasse 7 (tel. 84 34 53 0). Reader recommended.

Inexpensive

Adlerhof, Elisabethstr. 25 (tel. 75 2 36). Near the station.

Haus Wartenberg, Riedenburgerstr. 2 (tel. 84 42 84). 23 rooms some with showers.

RESTAURANTS. Salzburg has many good restaurants though it is always wise to make reservations and check on the closing days. The hotel restaurants are all up to standard.

Expensive

Alt Salzburg, Sigmundsplatz (tel. 84 14 76). Their specialty is *Tournedos Mozart.*

Brandstätter, Liefering, Münch. Bundesstr. 69 (tel. 3 22 17). Excellent Austrian specialties in atmospheric surroundings.

Goldener Hirsch, Getreidegasse 37 (tel. 84 15 11). Fashionable restaurant with traditionally fine cuisine. In hotel of same name.

K + K, Waagplatz 2 (tel. 84 21 56). Historic wine cellar.

Österreichischer Hof, (tel. 72 54 1), in hotel of same name. Prestigious spot with excellent cooking.

Restaurant-Café Winkler, Mönchsberg 32 (tel. 84 12 15). This place has a casino as well as weekend dancing.

Sheraton, Auerspergstr. 4 (tel. 79 32 10). Highly praised.

Moderate

Brasserie "Zur Bastey," Kaigasse 7. Reader recommended. Interesting mixture of French and Austrian cuisine.

Domstuben, Goldg. 17 (tel. 84 46 81). Try their specialty, *Domstuben Geheimnis.*

Festungsrestaurant, Hohensalzburg (tel. 84 17 80). Situated high up in the fortress.

Goldene Sonne, Gstatteng. 15 (tel. 84 32 84). Fish and game specialties.
G'wurzmuhl, Leopoldskronstr. 1 (tel. 84 63 56). This place is much milder than its name; translated it means spice mill.
Schlosstube Mirabell, Mirabellplatz 4 (tel. 71 7 29). Delicious food.
Zum Mohren, Judeng. 9 (tel. 84 23 87). Cosy cellar, excellent food, friendly service.

Inexpensive

Augustinerbräu, at Mülln. Excellent beer in huge garden. Good food to take out.
Bacchus Stuben, Rudolfskai 16 (tel. 84 22 75).
Krimpelstätter, Müllner Hauptstr. 31 (tel. 32 2 74). At other end of Mönchsberg. Real local atmosphere, dishes, and beer.
Moser Weinstube, Rainerstr. 4 (tel. 74 0 80). Their specialty, Schinkenknödel, is served with south Tyrolean wines.
Sternbräu (I), Griesgasse 23 (tel. 84 21 40).

SHOPPING. Many fine stores: don't miss the *Salzburger Heimatwerk* on the Residenzplatz, a treasure trove of hand-made peasant artifacts; and world-renowned *Lanz,* Schwarzstr. 4 and Imbergstr. 5, for dirndls and trachten. Try also *Schaller,* Judengasse 6; *Fritsch,* Getreidegasse 42–44 for petit point and leather goods.

Land Salzburg, Spas and Resorts

Badgastein, in the federal state of which the city of Salzburg is the capital is Austria's outstanding spa, famous ever since its "miraculous spring" cured Duke Frederick of Styria of a gangrenous infection in the 15th century. Even without its radioactive hot springs, Badgastein would attract visitors because of its incomparable mountain setting on both sides of a rushing torrent which cascades through the center of the town. The town, together with Bad Hofgastein down the valley, and Sportgastein, up the mountain, is also a well-equipped ski resort.

Not far from here, in a northwest direction, is Zell am See, a lake resort gem and a winter sports center, with a magnificent view of the surrounding mountain ranges and deep valleys from Schmittenhöhe, reached by cable car. West of here, on the border of Tirol, are the Krimml Waterfalls, highest in Europe.

PRACTICAL INFORMATION FOR LAND SALZBURG

BADGASTEIN. *Alpenhof Bellevue* (L), reached by chair lift, it has a pool and a nightclub. *Elisabethpark* (L), a panoramic view and a fine restaurant. *Grand Hotel de l'Europe* (L), old-world magnificently renovated; therapy center; indoor pool with thermal water. *Kaiserhof* (L), in a private park, full board only. *Germania* (E), in green surroundings. *Grüner Baum* (E), in Kötschach valley about half an hour by foot from the town. *Habsburgerhof* (E), modern, on the edge of town. *Salzburgerhof* (E), located conveniently near the station. *Straubinger* (E), Emperor Franz Josef used to stay here. *Weismayr* (E), has a wine tavern and a café. *Alpenblick* (M). *Pension Haus Erlengrund* (M). *Kurhaus Schider* (I). *Moser* (I), next to waterfall. *Münchnerhof* (I), on the way to Bockstein.

BAD HOFGASTEIN. *Carinthia* (E), cure facilities and indoor pool. *Grand Parkhotel* (E), cure facilities. *Norica* (E). *Astoria* (M). *Alpina* (I). *Berglift* (I). *Haslinger* (I). *Pension Pfarrhof* (I).

KRIMML. *Gasthof Klockerhaus* (M). *Gasthof Zur Post* (I).

ZELL AM SEE. *Grand* (L). A magnificent new hotel on the lakeside. Good food. *Salzburger Hof* (E), also good food. *Sporthotel Alpin* (E). *Zum Hirschen*

(E), pretty rooms plus delicious food. *Alte Post* (M). *Tiroler Hof* (M). *Lohninghof* (I).

Grossglockner Alpine Highway

One of the thrills of Austria is driving over one of the most spectacular mountain highways in existence. You can do it by bus or private car, and this is a toll road. The road is normally open from mid-May until mid-November, but check on conditions before starting out, and don't drive it at night—fog can make it very dangerous. The road starts at Bruck, and there are a number of parking places and rest houses on the ascent. At the Edelweiss Spitze, nearly 8,500 feet up, you can sit on a terrace, sip a beer, and gaze out over a view that comprises 37 peaks higher than 10,000 feet, and 19 glaciers. At Tauerneck, the road sweeps around a curve and suddenly the Grossglockner, highest peak in Austria, bursts on your vision for the first time. The impact of this glittering snowcovered 12,461-foot giant silhouetted against the sky is thrilling. The road now turns westward, heading straight for the majestic peak, and stops at the dead end of the Franz-Josefs-Höhe, where you can have lunch on the open terrace of the Franz-Josefs-Haus (or stay overnight) nearly 8,000 feet high, with a view across the Pasterzen Glacier to the Grossglockner; the toll road descends to Heiligenblut in Carinthia. Another scenic mountain road is the Tauern Autobahn.

Carinthia, Austria's Lakeland

Carinthia (Kärnten) is the lovely southern state with lakes, rocky peaks, and a vintage history going back to the Stone Age, whose graves have yielded rich prehistoric finds. This federal state is at its best between mid-May and early October, when a fine climate, the mildest in Austria, makes it possible to swim in the emerald lakes. The most renowned is the lovely Wörthersee, with its internationally famed resorts, Velden and Pörtschach, and its outstanding landmark, almost completely surrounded by water on a small peninsula, the picturesque village of Maria Wörth, with two ancient churches. The Carinthians are also proud of their great Romanesque cathedral of Gurk, and their many castles, of which the famous Schloss Hochosterwitz is perhaps most like something out of a fairytale. The best excursion center for these two attractions is Klagenfurt, the capital of Carinthia, founded in the 13th century and capital since 1518. Another well-located excursion center is the historic town of Villach, with the nearby spa, Warmbad Villach, which has been in existence since Roman times.

PRACTICAL INFORMATION FOR CARINTHIA

FAAK AM SEE. *Inselhotel Faakersee* (M), located on small island. 40 rooms with bath. Tennis courts.

FAAKERSEE. *Karnerhof* (E). Cure facilities, fine location. *Goldene Rose* (M). *Kanz* (M). Has a pool. *Seerose* (I).

KLAGENFURT. *Dermuth* (E), Kohldorferstr. 52 (tel. 21 2 47). 51 rooms, cure facilities. *Porcia* (E), Neuer Platz 13 (tel. 51 15 90). 45 rooms. *Romantikhotel Musil* (E), 10 Oktoberstr. 14 (tel. 51 16 60). 19 cozy, period-furnished rooms, fine cuisine and renowned Konditorei. Outstanding in every respect. *Europapark* (M), Villacherstr. 222 (tel. 21 1 37). 35 rooms. *Sandwirt* (M), Pernhartg. 9 (tel. 56 2 09). 42 rooms. *Roko Hof* (I), Villacherstr. 135 (tel. 21 5 26). 70 rooms. *Waldwirt* (I), Josefi Waldweg 2 (tel. 42 6 42). 15 rooms.

MARIA WÖRTH. *Wörth* (E). With pool. *Ebner* (M). *Wulfenia* (M).

MILLSTATT. *Forelle* (E). *Postillion* (E). *Marienhof* (M). *Posthof* (M). *Seewirt* (M). *Laggerhof* (I).

PÖRTSCHACH. *Schloss Leonstain* (L). A converted castle with antique décor and candlelight dining in the courtyard. *Schloss Seefels* (L). Outdoor pool, cure facilities. *Sonnengrund* (E). *Wallerwirt* (E). *Dermuth* (M). *Osterreichischer Hof* (M). *Savoy* (M). *Gasthof Joainig* (I).

VELDEN. *Schloss Velden* (L). A converted baroque castle, antique décor in public rooms, lakeside terrace restaurant. *Seehotel Veldnerhof* (L). Garden restaurant on lake front, tennis and watersports. *Carinthia* (E). *Casino* (E). *Yacht Hotel* (E). Own beach, tennis. *Seehotel Engstler* (M). *Seehotel Europa* (M). *Wenger* (M). *Erlhof* (I). *Strandhotel* (I).

VILLACH. *Warmbaderhof* (L). Has cure facilities. *City* (E). *Parkhotel* (E). *Romantikhotel Post* (E). A 15th-century hotel in the main square; good food. *Nanky* (M). *Verena* (M).

Tirol, Home of Skiers

Across the spectacular Arlberg Pass from Vorarlberg is the best winter sports area in Austria and one of the best skiing centers in the world. This is the country of skiing masters Hannes Schneider, Toni Seelos and Toni Sailer. The region has over 200 ski schools. Going from west to east in the Tirol, the top sights are: St. Anton am Arlberg and the view from the top of Valluga above it (cable car); Wiesberg Castle and Trisanna Bridge at the entrance into the Paznaun Valley; the Silvretta group scenery at Galtür; the old Inn bridge and fort ruins at the Finstermünz Gorge on the Tirol-Swiss border; the castle of Landeck; the Fern Pass area with lakes and castle ruins; Reutte with picturesque houses and Plansee; Zugspitze; Schemenlaufen masks in the museum of Imst; the lower Ötz Valley, with the typical Tyrolean village of Ötz, and the Stuiben Waterfall near Umhausen; the upper Ötz Valley, with mountain and skiing resorts of Sölden, Hochgurgl and Obergurgl (the latter is also the highest village in Austria) and with the magnificent panorama of glaciers and mountain peaks, seen especially from the cable car trip from Sölden to Gaislachkogel (about 10,000 feet) and from the chair lift from Hochgurgl up to Wurmkogel (also about 10,000 feet); here you can also ski all year round.

The 13th-century abbey at Stams, rebuilt in baroque style; Seefeld and the view around it; the mountain scenery seen from the left side of the train when riding from Innsbruck to Seefeld and Scharnitz; Stubai and Gschnitz valleys.

The medieval streets and buildings, Mint Tower and mining museum of Hall in Tirol; Fuggerhaus, Freundsberg Castle (museum), Enzenberg Palace, the parish church, and the old streets of Schwaz; Tratzberg Castle, between Stams and Jenbach; the lake of Achensee; Mayrhofen, with the view of Zillertaler Alps from Penken (cable car) and old farmhouses in Tuxertal; Alpbach Valley; the medieval town of Rattenberg.

The castle-fortress of Kufstein, with huge outdoor organ and an interesting museum; the roundtrip of Kaisergebirge: from Kufstein to Walchsee, Kössen, St. Johann, Ellmau, Scheffau, and back. Kitzbühel, one of the top society winter resorts in the Alps.

PRACTICAL INFORMATION FOR THE TIROL

IGLS. *Schlosshotel* (L). With cure facilities and an indoor pool. *Sporthotel* (L). With cure facilities and an indoor pool. *Alpenhof* (E). *Astoria* (E). *Parkhotel*

(E). *Waldhotel* (E). *Batzenhäusl* (M). *Bonalpina* (M). *Römerhof* (M). *Sonnenhof* (M). *Gruberhof* (I). *Romedihof* (I). *Waldhof* (I).

KITZBÜHEL. *Maria Theresia* (L). *Schloss Lebenberg* (L). Pool. *Goldener Greif* (E). Established in 1274! *Hirzingerhof* (E). *Klausner* (E). *Schweizerhof* (E). *Tenne* (E), open all year. *Bruggerhof* (M). *Erika* (M). *Hahnenhof* (M). *Seebichl* (M).

ST. ANTON. *Alpenrose* (L). *Mooserkrenz* (L). *Post* (L). *St. Antonhof* (E). *Schwarzer Adler* (E). *Berghaus Maria* (M). In a good location, has excellent food. *Montjola* (M). *Nassereinerhof* (M). *Gasthof Reselehof* (I). *Goldenes Kreuz* (I).

SEEFELD. *Astoria* (L). *Klosterbräu* (L). Has pool. *Schlosshotel* (L). Has pool. *Tümmlerhof* (L). Has pool. *Alpenhotel Lamm* (E). *Alpina* (E). *Birkenhof* (E). *Eden* (E). *Kurhotel* (E). *Parkhotel* (E). *Berghof* (M). *Hochland* (M). *Royal* (M). *Stern* (M).

Innsbruck, Capital of the Tirol

Innsbruck, venue of the 1964 and 1976 Winter Olympics, is one of the most beautiful towns of its size. This 800-year-old university city is bounded on the north by the shimmering wall of the Nordkette Range of the Alps, on the south by the Tuxer Range, rising to heights of 10,000 feet. Hence, the world-famous view from Innsbruck's main street, the Maria-Theresienstrasse. The Empress Maria Theresia loved the Tirol and Innsbruck, like her ancestor Emperor Maximilian I, which accounts for the city's many beautiful buildings, especially the Roman-style Triumphal Arch, built for her in 1767; the Goldenes Dachl (Golden Roof), an ancient mansion whose ornate stone balcony is covered by a roof of heavily gilded copper shingles; the Hofburg, imperial 18th-century palace, with its wealth of paintings and elaborate furniture; the 16th-century Court Church, built as the magnificent mausoleum of Maximilian I, the kneeling emperor surrounded by 28 larger-than-life bronze statues of his ancestors and famous rulers, including King Arthur of England; and the Silver Chapel, with its beautifully executed silver altar. Don't miss a visit to the Tiroler Volkskunstmuseum (the Tyrolean Folk Art Museum), which has a complete collection of folk costumes, antique rustic furniture and delightfully furnished Tyrolean interiors. The old town has been extensively restored and repaved and is now traffic-free.

There are various fine excursions to make: you can visit sites of the 1976 Winter Olympics at Axamer Lizum and Igls, both a part of Innsbruck's winter sports area. Or take a cable railway to the Hungerburg, 2,800 feet, and thence by two-stage cable car to the Hafelekar, at 7,500 feet. The view over Innsbruck and the southern Alps is beyond praise.

PRACTICAL INFORMATION FOR INNSBRUCK

Hotels

Deluxe

Europa, Südtiroler Platz 2 (tel. 35 5 71). 122 airconditioned rooms. Excellent restaurant.

Holiday Inn, Salurnerstr. 15 (tel. 36 5 01). 194 airconditioned rooms, indoor pool.

Innsbruck, Innrain 3 (tel. 34 5 11). 60 airconditioned rooms, pool.

Expensive

Central, Am Sparkassenplatz (tel. 24 8 66). Most of the 85 rooms have baths.
Clima, Zeughausstr. 7 (tel. 28 3 61). Modern comforts, quiet, efficiently run.
Goldener Adler, Herzog Friedrich Str. 6 (tel. 26 3 34). 40 rooms.
Grauer Bär, Universitatsstr. 5 (tel. 34 5 31). Many of the 175 rooms have baths.
Maria Theresia, Maria Theresien Str. 31 (tel. 35 6 15). 84 rooms with bath.
Roter Adler, Seilerg. 4 (tel. 21 0 69). 60 rooms.
Schwarzer Adler, Kaiserjägerstr. 2 (tel. 27 1 09). 20 rooms.
Union, Adamg. 22 (tel. 23 3 13) 60 rooms.

Moderate

Greif, Leopoldstr. 3 (tel. 27 4 01). 66 rooms.
Neue Post, Maximilianstr. 15 (tel. 26 4 76). 25 rooms.
Penz, Fürstenweg 183 (tel. 30 34 07). 26 rooms.
Sailer, Adamg. 6 (tel. 20 7 74). 75 rooms and 27 baths.

Inexpensive

Binder, Dr. Glatz Str. 20 (tel. 42 2 36). 40 rooms.
Dollinger, Haller Str. 7 (tel. 37 3 51). 40 rooms.
Ölberg, Höhenstr. 52 (tel. 86 1 25). 27 rooms.
Weisses Lamm, Mariahilfstr. 12 (tel. 83 1 56). All rooms have showers.

Restaurants

Expensive

Belle Epoque, Clima Hotel, Zeughausstr. 7 (tel. 28 3 61). Elegant yet cozy atmosphere; French wines with French and international cooking.
Domstuben, Pfarrgasse 3 (tel. 33 3 53). Situated behind Golden Roof. Delightful, intimate, and sophisticated.

Moderate

Goldener Löwe, Seilerg. 8 (tel. 22 1 27).
Goethestube, in the Hotel Goldener Adler (tel. 26 3 34). Tyrolean music in the evenings.
Ottoburg, Herzog-Friedrich-Str. 1 (tel. 34 6 52). Built in 1494, it has an attractive age-old atmosphere.
Weinhaus Happ, Herzog-Friedrich-Str. 14 (tel. 22 9 80).

Inexpensive

Stiegl-Bräu, Wilhelm-Greil-Str. 25 (tel. 24 3 38).

SHOPPING. For skiing and mountain climbing equipment *Witting,* Maria-Theresien-Str. 39, *Gramshammer,* Wilhelm-Greilstr. 19, and *Schirmer,* Maria-Theresienstr. 32. For dirndls and other Tyrolean folk dress *Trachten-Konrad,* Maria-Theresien-Str. 27, and for Tyrolean handicrafts *Tiroler Heimatwerk,* Meranerstr. 2. Leather clothes at *Obholzer,* Herzog-Friedrich-Str. 32, and *Schwammenhöfer,* Burggraben 1.

Vorarlberg's Panoramic Peaks

The westernmost and smallest of Austria's nine federal states is literally before the mighty Arlberg, pierced by one of Europe's longest road tunnels. In the villages of the lovely Bregenz Forest the Vorarlbergers still wear their shiny, starched folk costumes, peculiar to this region.

Capital of Vorarlberg is Bregenz, a picturesque little town at the eastern end of the Bodensee (Lake Constance). It has a delightful annual music festival, featuring light opera and ballet on a unique water stage in the lake. The festival starts in mid-July and lasts until mid-August, and, since the 30-tier amphitheater on the shore can accommodate 6,000, this is one festival where you don't have to know the president of Austria to get seats.

A funicular from the heart of Bregenz will take you in 10 minutes to the 3,200-foot top of Pfänder Mountain and fine panoramic views. They include the old town at your feet, the 40-mile sweep of the Bodensee, the German frontier and the Bavarian town of Lindau to the right, the Rhine and Switzerland to the left. Unbeatable on a sunny day.

See the medieval town of Feldkirch and its Schattenburg Castle, the idyllic high mountain village of Gargellen, and the spectacular Flexen Pass road with Zürs and Lech. At Dornbirn, textile capital of Austria, there is the famed textile fair in August.

(Note: If planning to drive in Vorarlberg, beware the lower speedlimits.)

PRACTICAL INFORMATION FOR VORARLBERG

BEZAU. In Bregenz Forest. *Hotel Gams* (E). 35 rooms with bath. Tennis, pool; excellent cuisine.

BRAND. Highly recommended skiing resort; also indoor and outdoor tennis, pools. *Hotel Scesaplana* (E). Pool, tennis; diet restaurant.

BREGENZ. *Weisses Kreuz* (E), (tel. 22 4 88), has had complete facelift. *Bodensee Pension* (M), (tel. 22 3 00). 27 rooms, no restaurant. *Central* (M), (tel. 22 9 47). 40 rooms. *Deutschmann* (M), (tel. 31 4 74), 65 rooms, all with private showers. *Messmer* (M), (tel. 22 3 56), 27 rooms. *Schwärzler* (M) (tel. 22 4 22). 50 rooms, indoor pool. *Germania Gasthof* (I), (tel. 22 7 66). 20 rooms, 13 showers.

Restaurants. *Gasthof Zoll* (E), Arlbergstrasse 118, probably the best gourmet restaurant in Austria. *Gebhardsberg Restaurant* (E). Excellent food and a marvelous view. *Gösserbräu Stadtkeller* (M). Good food in atmospheric surroundings. *Ilge* (M). Excellent wines and imaginative cooking. Very cosy.

FELDKIRCH. *Bären* (E). 28 rooms. *Illpark* (E). 92 rooms, indoor pool. *Weisses Kreuz* (M). 38 rooms. *Büchel* (I). 45 rooms and 28 showers.

GARGELLEN. *Bachmann* (M). *Feriengut Gargellenhof* (M). *Madrisa* (M). *Alpenrose* (I). *Dörflinger* (I).

LECH. *Post* (L), popular with celebrities; has renowned food. *Arlberg* (E). *Hinterwies* (E). *Monzabon* (E). *Sonnenburg* (E). *Angela* (M). *Bergkristall* (M). *Montana* (M). *Anemone* (I). *Mallaun* (I).

SCHRUNS. *Alpenhof Messmer* (E). Has cure facilities. *Kurhotel Montafon* (E). Has cure facilities. *Löwen* (E). *Chesa Platina* (M). *Fuchsenstube* (M). *Taube Post* (I).

ZÜRS. *Zürserhof* (L). Indoor tennis; excellent cuisine. *Albona* (E). With pool. *Alpenhof* (E). With pool. *Lorünser* (E). *Flexen* (M). *Schweizerhaus* (M). *Mara* (M).

BELGIUM

Belgium covers a strip of land just under 200 miles long and 100 miles wide bordering the North Sea between France and Holland. Here over 10 million people live—making Belgium the second most densely populated country in the world.

Belgium is a divided nation, populated by two distinct peoples. The Flemish, who speak Dutch (Flemish), inhabit the northern half of the country and account for 56% of the population. The French-speaking Walloons live in the other half. The capital, Brussels, is officially designated a dual-language area.

Belgium is the most heavily industrialized country in the world, with only 5% of the working population engaged in agriculture. (Though they still manage to produce two of Europe's greatest pâtés, and any number of fine sausages.) Besides being good businessmen, the Belgians also work very hard—partly to make up for what has so long been denied them. Through the centuries, the area now covered by Belgium has become known as the "cock pit of Europe." In the course of history the Belgians have been ruled over by the Romans, the Vikings, the French, the Spanish, the Austrians, the Dutch, the English and the Germans. Many of Europe's greatest battles have been fought on Belgian soil—from Waterloo to the long slogging encounters of World War I; and in World War II this territory witnessed both the initial *Blitzkrieg* of Nazi Panzer units and Hitler's final desperate counterattack against the advancing Allies in the Ardennes—an offensive which has gone down in history as the Battle of the Bulge.

The Ardennes, in the south of the country, is a wild wooded area, with mountains rising to over 2,000 feet. In the Dutch-speaking north, on the other hand, the land is flat and heavily-cultivated, much like neighboring Holland. Here stand the medieval Flemish cities of Ghent and Bruges, with their celebrated carillons and canals—not to mention the 50 miles of sandy beaches which make up the country's northern coastline. To the north-east lies Antwerp, the country's main seaport. This is the city where Rubens lived, and is now the world's leading diamond-cutting center.

The capital, Brussels, stands plumb in the center of the country. This booming, expanding and often very expensive city is now the capital of Europe. Here the Common Market (EEC) has its headquarters, as do SHAPE (Supreme Headquarters Allied Powers Europe) and NATO. The city boasts more ambassadors than any other in the world —approximately 160. Partly as a result of this concentration of power, and partly because of the Belgians' celebrated love of good food, Brussels has become one of the most renowned gastronomic cities in the world. Nowadays the excellence of its restaurants rivals even that of Paris—with prices often exceeding even the most imaginative Parisian *addition.* Those without expense accounts beware! Yet although Belgian cuisine retains French flare, at the same time it also incorporates an element of Dutch capacity—which means that you seldom have to order so much.

Perhaps in order to work off all this good living, the Belgians are fanatical cyclists. Several of the great legendary figures of the *Tour de France* were Belgians. And despite its name, this annual race (the world's greatest and most gruelling cycling prize) usually has a stage or two running through Belgium. Another popular sport here is soccer, which is played to a high standard, as can be witnessed by the successes of the Brussels team Anderlecht in European competitions.

One other important trait characterizes the Belgian attitude to life. Because they have been ruled over by foreign masters for so many centuries, the Belgians have acquired a singularly unenthusiastic attitude towards the paying of taxes. Nowadays tax evasion to a Belgian is much the same as machismo to a South American—and no self-respecting Belgian entrepreneur is without his "private company" (with granny as managing director) registered in the nearby tax-haven of Luxembourg.

PRACTICAL INFORMATION FOR BELGIUM

WHAT WILL IT COST. Belgium enjoys a high standard of living. Consequently, as a tourist, you can expect to spend rather more than in many other European countries. Costs, of course, vary throughout the country. In Brussels itself, now regarded as the administrative capital of Europe, they can be crippling. The wooded region of the Ardennes, on the other hand, is comparatively inexpensive.

A typical day in Brussels might cost two people:

Hotel (moderate) double room	2,200	francs
Lunch at restaurant (moderate)	1,150	
Transportation (two taxis)	850	
Coffee, beer, cigarettes	420	
Theater	525	
Dinner (moderate)	1,350	
Miscellaneous 10%	620	
	7,115	

The monetary unit is the Belgium franc which is divided into 100 centimes. The money comes in coins of 25 and 50 centimes, 1, 5, 10 and 50 francs. There are 20, 50, 100, 500, 1,000 and 5,000 franc banknotes. Due to the fall of the U.S. dollar and the fluctuating exchange rates in Europe, detailed budgeting long in advance of your holiday is not advised. The exchange rate at the time of writing was about 51 francs to the U.S. dollar and 73 francs to the pound sterling. There are no restrictions on taking money in or out of Belgium.

SOURCES OF INFORMATION. For information on all aspects of travel to Belgium, the Belgian National Tourist Office is invaluable. Its addresses are:

In the U.S.: Belgian National Tourist Office, 745 Fifth Ave., N.Y., N.Y. 10022 (tel. 758–8130).

In the U.K.: Belgian National Tourist Office, 38 Dover St., London W.1 (tel. 499 5379).

LANGUAGES. Flemish (Dutch) in north and French in south Belgium are the official languages. Brussels is bi-lingual. English widely spoken and understood, especially in Flanders. German on the eastern border.

WHEN TO COME. The main tourist season runs from early May through to the end of September, with the peak period being in July and August. Belgium does not stage as many big festivals as other European countries in the peak travel months so you will not miss a great deal if you explore the country earlier or later in the year. Indeed, it might prove advantageous. The Ardennes, for instance, are quite as lovely in spring or autumn as during high summer and a good deal less crowded.

Climate. Temperatures are moderate so you need not prepare yourself for excessive heat or cold. It does drizzle frequently, however, so take a raincoat with you. Average afternoon daily temperatures in degrees Fahrenheit and centigrade:

Brussels	Jan.	Feb.	Mar.	Apr.	May	June	July	Aug.	Sept.	Oct.	Nov.	Dec.
F°	42	43	49	56	65	70	73	72	67	58	47	42
C°	6	6	9	13	18	21	23	22	19	14	8	6

SPECIAL EVENTS. *January,* parades of the Magi, especially in Flanders (on 6th). *February,* start of carnival season, best at Eupen and Malmédy, climax on Shrove Tuesday at Binche, with the procession of the Gilles. *April,* International Fair, Liege. *May.* Procession of the Holy Blood at Bruges (Ascension Day); Festival of the Cats at Ypres. Queen Elizabeth International Music Competition for young artists in Brussels; Grand Prix automobile race at Spa Francorchamps. *June,* Festival of the Lumeçon, Mons (Trinity Sunday); Carillon concerts in Bruges and Malines (through Sept.); *July,* Ommegang, an historical cavalcade in Brussels' Grand' Palace (not every year); nightly sound and light performances in front of Tournai Cathedral and at nearby Beloeil Castle; Music Festival, Bruges. *August,* Annual International Jazz Festival, Bilzen. *September.* Beer Festival, Wieze. *November,* St. Hubert Festival.

National Holidays. Jan. 1 (New Year's Day); Apr. 20 (Easter Mon.); May 1 (May Day); May 14 (Ascension); May 25 (Whit Mon.); Jul. 21; Aug. 15 (Assumption); Nov. 1 (All Saints); Nov. 11 (Armistice); Nov. 15 (King's Birthday); Dec. 25.

VISAS. Nationals of the United States, Canada, Australia, New Zealand, EEC countries and practically all other Western European countries do not require visas for entry into Belgium.

CUSTOMS. There are three levels of duty free allowance for goods imported into Belgium. Travelers coming from a European country inside the EEC may import 300 cigarettes or 75 cigars or 400gr. of tobacco; 1½ liters of spirits or 3 liters of sparkling wine or three liters of liqueur wine plus 3 liters of non-sparkling wine plus 8 liters or 10 bottles of non sparkling Luxembourg wine; 75gr. of perfume and ⅜ liter of lotion; other goods imported from EEC to value of 7,200 francs (10,000 in the case of importation from Luxembourg or the Netherlands). Goods imported from other countries to the value of 1,250 francs. Travelers coming from a country outside the EEC may import 200 cigarettes or 50 cigars or 250gr. of tobacco; 1 liter of spirits or 2 liters of fortified wine and 2 liters of non-sparkling wine and 8 liters or 10 bottles of non-sparkling Luxembourg wine; 50gr. of perfume and ¼ liter of lotion; other goods imported from the EEC to the value of 1,600 francs; goods imported from other countries to the value of 1,250 francs. Travelers coming from outside Europe may import 400 cigarettes or 100 cigars or 500gr. of tobacco; 1 liter of spirits or 2 liters of sparkling wine or 2 liters of liqueur wine and 2 liters of non-sparkling wine and 8 liters or 10 bottles of non-sparkling Luxembourg wine; 50gr. of perfume and ¼ liter bottle of eau-de-cologne; other goods imported from the EEC to the value of 1,600 francs, goods imported from other countries to the value of 1,250 francs.

GETTING TO BELGIUM. By Plane. There are many direct flights to Belgium from New York, Boston, Chicago, Dallas and Montreal in North America and from London, Manchester and Glasgow in the U.K. All these flights go to Brussels. From other European countries it is equally easy to fly to Brussels, and there is an international airport at Antwerp.

By Train and Car. Car and train ferries operate from Dover and Folkstone in the U.K. to Oostende and Zeebrugge in Belgium. There is also a car ferry from Felixstowe to Zeebrugge. Coming from the Continent, Belgium is in the middle of an extensive network of motorways and is consequently extremely simple to reach by car, and correspondingly easy to reach by train from a wide variety of European points of origin.

HOTELS. Hotel prices are all inclusive and are listed in each room. Our hotel grading system is divided into four categories. All prices are for two people in a double room. Deluxe (L) 3,700 francs upwards, Expensive (E) 2,600–3,700 francs, Moderate (M) 1,600–2,600 francs and Inexpensive (I) 1,600 francs or less. Most towns levy a small visitor's charge which comes on your hotel bill. Weekends, particularly during summer in the cities, vacant rooms are sometimes offered at half price.

CAMPING. There is no shortage of camping sites in Belgium. Information can be obtained from the *Royal Camping and Caravaning Club of Belgium,* 51 Rue de Namur, Brussels, or the *National Tourist Office,* 61 Rue Marche-aux-Herbes, 1000 Brussels.

RESTAURANTS. Belgian restaurants serve good food in lavish proportions. French fries are widely available, and chefs can never be accused of being mean in their use of cream and butter. We have graded restaurants in three categories; Expensive (E) 1,600 francs upwards (one person), Moderate (M) 850–1,600 francs, Inexpensive (I) 400–850 francs. Many restaurants feature inexpensive three-course tourist menus (from around 500 francs). *Note:* drinks are *not* included in the above rates.

Food and Drink. Try sampling some typical Belgian dishes: *Anguilles au vert* are young eels served hot or cold with a green sauce of shredded herbs, sorrel, mint, sage and verbena. They taste wonderful. *Witloof,* which is Flemish for white leaf, is endive in America, chicory in Britain. The Belgians grow it and cook it better than anyone else in the world.

The Belgians are very fond of *moules* (mussels) which are served in R months in about thirty-five different fashions and always in enormous portions.

There is a wide selection of French and German wines available everywhere. But the national drink of Belgium is beer. In fact, the Belgians rival the Germans as beer drinkers. Try *Gueuze* (bottled), which is known as *Lambic* when it's on tap. This is a wheat and barley-based beer, slightly vinous in flavor. *Kriek-Lambic* is the same thing, with a flavoring of cherries, not so grim as it sounds. *Orval,* brewed by the Trappist monks, is different, but go easy with those monastery brews: they're loaded. Visit the cellar of the tavern *Roi d'Espagne* in Brussels.

TIPPING. The Belgians are very keen on this idea. Women are liable to rattle tin boxes at the end of self-service counters and cinema usherettes to shine torches on you until you oblige. Don't be flustered into giving more than 15% (calculate and have it ready beforehand). A 16% service charge is usually included in your hotel bill, so that you needn't give any of the staff more than a token tip. Restaurants also include service charge. So do nightclubs. If they don't, you add it. Tip Brussels hatcheck girls and washroom attendants 5 frs. Taxi fares are expensive but at least the tip is included.

MAIL. Rates for airmail letters and postcards are 23 frs. to the U.S. and 14 frs. to the U.K.

CLOSING TIMES. Banks open usually from 9 to 3:30 (sometimes till 4:30). Shops must close for 24 consecutive hours once a week and they post a notice to say which day this will be; the usual opening hours are 9 to 6 or 6:30, but a number of smaller shops stay open later. For shopping centers and many supermarkets, the hours are 9 to 8.

USEFUL ADDRESSES. *U.S. Embassy,* 27 Blvd. du Regent (tel. 513 3830); *British,* 28 Rue Joseph II (tel. 219 1165); *Canadian,* 6 Rue Loxum (tel. 513 7940). *National Tourist Office,* 61 Rue Marche-aux-Herbes, 1000 (close to the Grand' Place), tel. 513–8940. *American Express,* 24 Pl. Rogier (tel. 219 0190). *Wagons Lits/Cook,* 53 Blvd. Clovis (tel. 230 5455). All in Brussels. *Emergency:* dial 900 (throughout the country).

GETTING AROUND BELGIUM. By Train. Belgium has extremely good trains that cover practically the whole country. In addition, many international expresses serve the country linking it with Paris, Amsterdam and many German cities; Oostende is also the starting and finishing point of many long distance European Expresses.

Belgian Railways have a 16-day runabout ticket—good for unlimited travel—that costs 4,420 frs. in first class and 2,940 frs. in second class. There are no reductions for children. They also have 5- and 8-day rail tickets—also good for unlimited travel—that are valid within certain specified 16-day periods, a number of which fall in the high season. These cost respectively 2,340 frs. and 3,100 frs. in first class and 1,560 frs. and 2,060 frs. in second class. There are special reductions for children and youths. A third runabout rail ticket offered by Belgian Railways is the Benelux ticket. This is valid in the Netherlands and Luxembourg, as well as Belgium, and gives 5 days' travel out of 17 in these countries. Called Benelux Tourrail, it costs 3,830 frs. in first class and 2,560 frs. in second class. It is operative from Apr. to Oct. and over Christmas and the New Year.

By Bus. There is a good network of local and regional bus services throughout Belgium. Full details are available from most rail stations and all tourist information offices.

By Car. Belgium's big motor highways are Antwerp-Liège bypass-German frontier, Brussels-Oostende, Brussels-Antwerp, the Wallonie (E 41), Brussels-Paris (E 10), Brussels-Liège (E 5), and Antwerp-Lille (E 3). There is a new ring-road to the north of Brussels, which links the motorway from Oostende to the cities of Antwerp, Liège, and Namur. There is much construction in progress, so best get the most recent road map and supplement it by up-to-date information from AAA, AA, or RAC. Many of the secondary roads are extremely good and make interesting drives.

Gasoline (petrol) prices vary, but at presstime it's 38 frs. per liter.

Car hire. If you arrive by air, you can arrange in advance for a self-drive car to pick up at the airport, and there is a similar arrangement with Belgian Rail for arrival at the chief stations. *Avis,* 145 Rue Américaine, Brussels. *Hertz,* 8 Blvd. Maurice Lemonnier, Brussels. Bicycles can be hired at railway stations.

Brussels

Brussels is a city of stark contrasts, an amalgam of steel skyscrapers and cobbled medieval streets, heartless modernization and painstaking preservation, populated by anonymous bureaucrats and unashamed *bons viveurs.* This is the capital of Europe. Here the Common Market has its headquarters, as does NATO and the Benelux Union. Yet at the heart of this busy boom town lies what, according to Victor Hugo, is the "most beautiful square in the world"—the Grand' Place. Completely surrounded by flamboyantly-decorated 17th-century guild houses, it is dominated by the Hôtel de Ville (Town Hall), which, with its 320-foot belfry, is one of the finest gothic structures in northern Europe. After you've had a beer or two in one of the many outdoor cafés in this superb *place,* you may feel ambitious enough to climb the 420 steps to the tower's summit. The view over Brussels and the green surroundings of Brabant is worth all the huffing and puffing.

Nearby on the Rue de l'Etuve is another historic sight, but on a smaller scale. This is the ancient symbol of the Rights of Man, the Manneken-Pis, the famous bronze statue of Brussels' oldest inhabitant. In the Maison du Roi, back in the Grand' Place, you can see a collection of beautifully tailored costumes which various admirers of the Manneken-Pis have bestowed upon him, including a gold-embroidered suit from Louis XV of France. On September 3, you can see the Manneken dressed in the uniform of the Welsh Guards, who liberated Brussels on this date in 1944, and on October 27, this incontinent child wears an American sailor suit in honor of United States Navy Day.

Most of the city's sights are within easy strolling distance of the central Grand' Place. Here the ancient, centuries-old city coexists, often surprisingly harmoniously, with examples of glistening modernity. In the Eglise du Finistère, you'll find a wooden statue of Our Lady of Aberdeen, whose original owner, the Bishop of Aberdeen, was a contemporary of Macbeth. Yet step outside, and at once you see the bold lines of Brussels' grand department store, Innovation, rebuilt on the site of the old fire-destroyed store. A minute's walk to the right brings you to two modern triumphs—the Philips Building (backing onto the last relic of the city's earliest fortification) and the splendid Post Office Building, opposite the Opera House (Théâtre Royal de la Monnaie), where the 1830 Revolution started and the Belgian nation was born. Had you gone to your left along Rue Neuve, an enticing shopping area, you would have arrived at Place Rogier where the Sheraton Hotel stands.

Brussels is justly famous for its shops. Try the small boutiques now in covered galleries on the ground floor of many modern buildings, through which you can walk from street to street. From the coffee shop in the Hilton, you pass out into the gardens of a Renaissance palace, past the Peter Pan statue (a gift to the children of Brussels from the children of London) and so through the one-time stables and the great courtyard to the gem-square of the Petit Sablon, with its 48 elegant bronze statues of the medieval craft guilds.

Facing you is the church of Notre Dame du Sablon, one of the city's many ecclesiastical masterpieces, the most important of which is the 13th-century Cathedral of St. Michael, with its impressive tapestries and glass and its great west window floodlit at night. On your way there from the Sablon, you will have passed the Museum of Ancient Art, a classical palace by Balat dating from 1876 (and which houses an impressive collection of Flemish masters); turning downhill from the 18th-century Place Royale, leaving on your left the Palais des Congrès.

Close on the other side of the Hilton, and the only challenge to its lofty stature, is the massive Palais de Justice. Its 19th-century architect, Poelaert, intended its dome (now the technical home of the Eurovision relays) to be a pyramid; and you will have to choose, as do the locals, whether to call it Greco-Roman or Assyro-Babylonian. It is larger than St. Peter's in Rome, dominating Brussels from the summit of the one-time Gallows Hill.

Though much of the central city (old and new) is apt to be congested, it is traversed by wide streets and surrounded by a spacious boulevard with underpasses and side lanes for local traffic. Among the open spaces, there are four parks deserving special mention. The Parc de Bruxelles stretches between the Royal Palace and the Palais de la Nation (Parliament), with the Rue Royale on one side and the Rue Ducale (residences of the US and British ambassadors) on the other. Just outside the boulevard, at the Rue Royale level, the Jardin Botanique stretches downhill towards the back of the Palace Hotel. Leaving the central area eastwards by the (one-way only) Rue Belliard, you come to the Parc Léopold; and from here an underpass brings you into the majestic Parc du Cinquantenaire, with its *gloriette* and complex of buildings which include the Musée de l'Armée and the Musée Royal d'Art et d'Histoire. Nearby, in Place Schuman, at the end of Rue de la Loi, is a huge glass building called Cité Berlaymont, seat of the European Community (EEC).

PRACTICAL INFORMATION FOR BRUSSELS

GETTING AROUND BRUSSELS. By Tram, Bus and Subway. Brussels has an extensive and comparatively inexpensive bus and tram system. It also has an adequate subway system, consisting essentially of two lines running north–south and one crosstown route. Maps of all public transport routes are available at tourist offices, as well as details of special-fare tickets. These, often combining bus and subway travel, are good value and well worth investigating. For further details, go to the *Information Center,* Rue Marche aux Herbes 61.

By Taxi. Expensive, but the blow is softened by the fact the Brussels is reputed to have the most beautiful female taxi-drivers in the world. Your tip is included in the fare. To call a taxi, ring *Taxis Verts* (Green Cabs) on 511 2244, or pick one up at one of the many stands.

By Hired Car. Again, this is expensive. The better firms run better cars, but cost more. Back-street hiring may appear less expensive, but can lead to greatly increased expenses with unreliable cars. Try *Hertz,* 8 Blvd. Lemonnier (tel. 513 2886); *Avis,* 145 Rue Americaine (tel. 538 8317); or *ABC Service Rent-a-car,* 133 Rue d'Anderlecht (tel. 513 1954).

HOTELS. Brussels has developed rapidly as the Common Market business and administrative center and it is advisable to make hotel reservations ahead. Some hotels offer reductions and vouchers for free access to the main sites (including Boitsfort racecourse) during the weekend. Most hotels are concentrated in the downtown area near the World Trade Center.

Deluxe

Amigo, 1 Rue de l'Amigo (tel. 511 5910). 183 rooms and suites in plush Empire and Directoire style, velvet upholstery, all with bath. 6th. floor terraced apartments are the ultimate. Just off the Grand' Place, behind the Hotel de Ville.

Brussels Sheraton, 3 Pl. Rogier (tel. 219 3400). The city's largest hotel (over 500 rooms) housed in modern high-rise 31 story block. Variety of restaurants, pool and disco.

Hilton International Brussels, 38 Blvd. de Waterloo (tel. 513 8877). High-rise hotel containing 373 luxury rooms and duplexes with balcony. Popular with high-flying international business community. All usual Hilton luxuries, together with English pub and a 27th-floor restaurant with great views.

Hyatt Regency, 250 Rue Royale (tel. 219 4640). 320 rooms and luxury suites. Gourmet restaurant. Most sophisticated of the modern hotels.

Royal Windsor, 5 Rue Dusquesnoy (tel. 511 4215). 285 rooms with bath, all luxuriously appointed. Excellent restaurant with international cuisine. 200 yards from Grand' Place.

Expensive

Arcade Stephanie, 91 Rue Louise (tel. 538 8060). Smallish apartment-hotel. 142 rooms and apartments (latter available for weekly to yearly hire). Near good shopping area, so back rooms are quietest.

Jolly Hotel Atlanta, 7 Blvd. Adolphe Max (tel. 217 0120). Styled after *Gone with the Wind.* Downtown hotel with 244 rooms. Handy for sights but can be a little noisy. Fine views from roof garden and restaurant.

Novotel, at Diegem, Olmenstraat (tel. 720 5830). 158 rooms, garden and outdoor heated pool. Just off Zaventem motorway.

Moderate

Albergo, 58 Ave. de la Toison d'Or (tel. 5382980). A series of old houses. 67 rooms (58 with bath). No restaurant.

Forum, 2 Ave. du Haut Point (tel. 3430100). 78 rooms, all with bath. Conference facilities.

Scheers, 132 Blvd. Adolphe Max (tel. 2177760). 62 rooms. Centrally located with inexpensive restaurant.

Inexpensive

Aux Arcades, 36 Rue des Bouchers (tel. 5112876). Near the Grand' Place in a narrow street famous for its restaurants.

Gascogne, 137 Blvd. Adolphe Max (tel. 2176962). 18 rooms. Pleasant, inexpensive restaurant. Central.

Richmond Résidence, 21 Rue de la Concorde (tel. 5124824). Quiet hotel in large house. Some rooms overlook attractive garden.

Ruche Bourse, 23 Rue des Halles (tel. 218 5887). 16 rooms, none with bath; very central, by Bourse.

 RESTAURANTS. Brussels classifies its gourmet restaurants by awarding them irises (the iris being the flower of Brussels) after review by a jury of experts. Establishments with 2, 3 and 4 irises tend to be expensive (E), but it is possible to eat well at reasonable prices at some one iris places and in newer and as yet unclassified restaurants. You can get a gourmet booklet from the tourist offices. In the moderate class (M) there is a wide choice of priced menus and these are usually displayed outside. At the inexpensive end of the market (I) there are snack bars, self-service counters and tea rooms. For a quick bite you can always find *fritures* (french fries) and waffle stalls on the street corners.

Expensive

Bon Vieux Temps, 12 Rue Marche aux Herbes (tel. 218 1546). Superb cuisine, traditional decor. Located in an alley off Marche aux Herbes.

Comme Chez Soi, Place Rouppe (tel. 5122912). Quite simply superb; has been awarded no less than 5 irises. Prices to match.

La Couronne, in the Grand' Place (tel. 5111409). Romantic dining in 17th-century decor overlooking the square. Outstanding cuisine.

L' Ecailler du Palais Royal, Rue Bodenbrook (tel. 5128751). Eternally unpretentious seafood restaurant in 16th-century guild house.

Maison du Cygne, 9 Grand' Place (tel. 5118244). One of the finest restaurants in the country.

Villa Lorraine, 75 Ave. du Vivier d' Ore (tel. 3743163). One of the rare holders of Michelin 3 stars outside France. Belgium's very best; the food defies description. In villa just outside the city.

Moderate

L' Auberge des Chapeliers, 1 Rue des Chapeliers (tel. 5137338). Specializes in Brussels cuisine. No reservations or credit cards.

Rugbyman, 8 Quai aux Briques (tel. 5125640). Seafood specialties. Handy for central sights.

BRUSSELS

1. Bourse
2. Post Office and Opera
3. St. Michel Cathedral
4. Royal Palace
5. Palace of Justice
6. Unknown Soldier
7. Manneken Pis
8. South Station
9. Sabena
10. Central Station
11. North Station
12. Royal Museum of Fine Arts
13. Hotel de Ville
14. Palais de la Nation
M. Metro Stations

0   400m

0   440yds

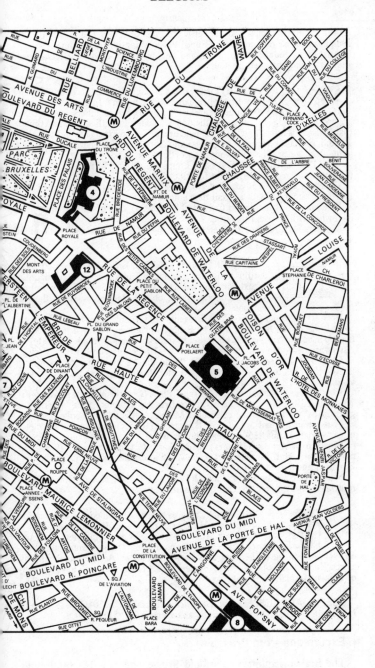

Inexpensive

Auz Armes de Bruxelles, 13 Petite Rue des Bouchers (tel. 5112118). Old restaurant on narrow street off Grand' Place. Wide ranging menu.

Aux Vieux Saint-Martin, 38 Grand Sablon (tel. 512 6476). Quick-service student restaurant open 24 hours.

NIGHTLIFE. Brussels nightlife has become markedly more sophisticated in recent years. In many cases, establishments are private clubs, but membership can be arranged at the door and costs little. Bear in mind though that Brussels is full of lonely highly-paid executives, so expensive "hostess" bars abound, especially around Ave. Louise and Gare du Nord. These tend to be clip joints in disguise. The following are worth a try:

Chez Paul au Gaity, 18 Fosse-aux-Loups (tel. 2186985). Perhaps the nudest (though not the rudest) show in town.

En Plein Ciel, 38 Blvd. Waterloo, in the Hilton hotel (tel. 5138877). A roof-top restaurant with a small dance floor.

Le Crazy, 15 Rue Captain Crespel (tel. 5118731). One of the best floorshows in town—with Parisian panache.

Mozart, 541 Chaussee d' Alsemberg (tel. 3440809). Jazz pub serving food till 4 A.M.

MUSEUMS AND SIGHTS. Brussels has over 20 major museums and innumerable minor ones, specializing in exhibits ranging from torture to tapestry. (For full details contact tourist office.) Here are some of the best spots:

Brewery Museum (Maison des Brasseurs),10 Grand' Place (Mon.–Fri. 10–5, Sat. 10–12, closed lunch 12–2). The Belgians love beer. (They drink over 120 liters per head every year.) This museum traces brewing through the centuries. Afterwards you can sample the goods in a 17th-century tavern.

Church of Notre-Dame-du-Sablon, Pl. du Petit Sablon. Superb example of late-Gothic architecture. Started in 1400 after Brussels' woman had a legendary vision.

King's House (Maison du Roi), Grand' Place (Oct. through Mar., Mon.–Fri. 10–5, closed lunch 1–2). Houses City of Brussels Museum. Fine tapestry and goldsmiths' work. Also the celebrated Manneken-Pis uniform collection.

Museum of Ancient Art, Rue de la Regence (10–5, closed Mon.). Collections of early Flemish masters, Rubens and Breughel.

Museum of Art and History, in the Parc de Cinquantaine (9.30–4.30, closed Mon.). Half its collection is shown on alternate days. Fine collection of Egyptian and Greco-Roman relics.

Museum of Modern Art, Place Royale (10–1, 2–5, closed Mon.). Newly refurbished with fine collection of modern works.

SHOPPING. Brussels has been called the shopwindow of the world. There are enough Belgian specialties to keep you broke for years. For an overall view of Belgian products, visit the permanent Design Center, at 51 Galerie Ravenstein, near the Central Station and Sabena Air Terminal. The big stores, *Au Bon Marché, Galeries Anspach,* and *A l'Innovation* all have a variety of Belgian specialties.

USEFUL ADDRESSES. *Tourist Office,* 7 Markt (tel. 050 330711). *Brussels Information Center,* 61 Rue Marche aux Herbes (tel. 513 8940).

Excursions from Brussels

The Brabant countryside around Brussels offers a delightful atmosphere of historic interest and rural calm. A good introduction is the Bois de la Cambre, a 20-minute tram ride from the heart of the city. The forest is full of smart restaurants and modest inns, and offers a perfect setting for a picnic under its centuries-old trees.

Twelve miles south, accessible by the "W" bus, is the famous field of Waterloo. The conventional tourist activity here is to climb the lion memorial. The Wellington Museum was recently installed in Wellington's old headquarters, which contains some of his furniture. Here you can reconstruct the battle with the aid of models and phase maps. It is open 9–12 and 1–6, closed Mondays in the off-season. The Battle Panorama near the Lion Monument is open all year. Hougoumont Farm is still privately owned, but you can visit the tiny, mutilated chapel where the British wounded were brought. Along the road to Charleroi, visit the farm Le Caillou, now a museum, where Napoleon spent a restless night before the battle.

Other things worth seeing near Brussels: In Anderlecht, you can visit the house where Erasmus lived; it is now a museum, and contains a library with many of his works. Genval has a pretty lake with hotels and lakeside restaurants; don't go on Sundays—too crowded. Beersel: Shakespeare and folk plays are presented outdoors here in summer at this interesting moated brick castle. Gaasbeek, a beautifully-furnished castle; don't miss it. Nivelles, a town of great historic importance, reduced almost to rubble by World War II. The one rose in the bed of thorns was the discovery of Merovingian and Carolingian remains, now being restored. Tervuren, only 20 minutes from Brussels on the Louvain road, is the site of the very authoritative African Museum (largely devoted to the Congo). It has a beautiful large park. For the sportsminded, there is a good swimming pool (Beausoleil) nearby and the links of the Ravenstein Golf Club.

PRACTICAL INFORMATION FOR THE BRUSSELS AREA

RESTAURANTS. You will probably set up your headquarters in Brussels and make an excursion or two into the Brabant countryside. If you want to eat out at a restaurant in the quiet green belt which surrounds the capital, here are some addresses in attractive spots.

BOIS DE LA CAMBRE. *Villa Lorraine* (E), 12 Ave. Lloyd-George (tel. 648 0072). One of Europe's finest, with prices to match.

GROENENDAAL. *Romeyer* (E), tel. 6570581, is outstanding. *La Père Mouillard* (M), tel. 6570410, also has a very good reputation.

NIVELLES. Historic city which is full of good eating places. Try *De la Collegiale* (M), Ave. Leon Jeuncaux (tel. 222843), opposite the park.

WATERLOO. *La Charmille* (M), tel. 3544444. Country cooking on garden terrace. Closed August.

Catholic Bastions, Malines and Louvain

To understand fully the profound Catholicism of Belgium, you should visit the picturesque old town of Malines (the Flemings call it Mechelen) and the university town of Leuven (better known abroad as Louvain, its French name).

In the tower of Malines' Saint Rombaut's cathedral (13th and 14th century) you will see and hear the most famous bells in Belgium, for this is the place where Jef Denijn revived the art of carillon. Malines is also noted for its beautiful tapestries whose fame has spread as far as the bells. You can still see the ancient art of tapestry weaving practised here with new methods and design adapted to contemporary tastes.

Louvain is dominated by its University, for over half a millenium one of the most famous in Europe. Erasmus studied here; and since the 16th century the town has been renowned for its lively student life and great breweries. (The famous Stella Artois is brewed here.) The treasures of Louvain have miraculously escaped the holocausts of two world wars. Be sure not to miss the outstanding Hôtel de Ville (Town Hall) built in 1448, one of the finest secular buildings in Belgium.

PRACTICAL INFORMATION FOR MALINES AND LOUVAIN

Hotels and Restaurants

LOUVAIN (LEUVEN). *Binnenhof* (M), 65 Maria Theresiastraat (tel. 236926). 57 rooms with bath. *La Royale* (I), 6 Martelarenplein, opposite station (tel. 221252). 23 rooms, about half with bath.

MALINES (MECHELEN). Restaurant. *Pekton* (M), 1 Van Beethovenstraat (tel. 413535). Excellent.

Antwerp—City of Rubens and Diamonds

The inhabitants of Antwerp were the original "twerps" (so-called by the English who couldn't understand the outlandish language they spoke). Owing to the importance of its harbor, Antwerp—known locally as La Métropole—has been one of the commercial centers of Europe since the days of the Romans. Nowadays, Antwerp is Belgium's second city, its main Flemish center, and its chief seaport. This is a city of historic churches, monuments, and some of Europe's finest museums. Here Van Dyck painted many of his greatest masterpieces, and Rubens established his home. Antwerp is the world's greatest diamond market and cutting center. This is found around Pelikaanstraat. Most of the big firms arrange group visits (ask at the local tourist office), and there is also an excellent diamond museum where you can watch the cutters at work. Try a steamer trip around the port—or visit the Zoo (Dierentuin), one of Europe's finest.

PRACTICAL INFORMATION FOR ANTWERP

Hotels

Deluxe

De Keyser, 66–70 De Keyserlei (tel. 2340135). 117 rooms with bath. Near the station. Cheerful, helpful service.

Holiday Inn, 66 Luitenant Lippenslaan (tel. 2359191). 180 rooms, some adapted for handicapped people.

Waldorf, 36 Belgielei (tel. 2309950). 100 rooms with bath, and apartments.

Moderate

Congress, 136–140 Planten en Moretuslei (tel. 2353000). 66 rooms, TV, minibar, and restaurants.

Theatre, 30 Arenbeigstraat (tel. 2311720). 83 rooms in old part of town, quite near to Rubens's house.

Inexpensive

Florida, 59 De Keyserlei (tel. 2318140). 38 rooms, no restaurant.
Residence Rubens, 115 Amerikalei (tel. 2383031). 25 rooms, no restaurant.

Restaurants

La Perousé (E), Steenplein (tel. 2323528). On board a ship pontoon. Highly recommended. Best restaurant in town. Superb cuisine, especially seafood.

Rooden-Hoed (M), 25 Oude Koornmarkt (tel. 2332844). An ancient restaurant which specializes in mussels and eels.

MUSEUMS. Diamond Museum (Veiligheidsmuseum), 28–30 Jezusstraat. Open daily 10–5. All about a girl's best friend; but no free samples alas.

Mayer van den Bergh Museum, 19 Lange Gasthuisstraat. Open daily 10–5, closed Mon. Sculptures, furniture, china and ancient lace as well as an important collection of paintings by Breughel the Elder, Jordaens and other heavyweights.

Open-Air Museum of Sculpture, Middelheim Park. Open daily 10–5 (later in summer). Contains works by Rodin, Maillol, Moore and many others.

Plantin-Moretus Museum, 22 Vrijdagmarkt. Open daily 10–5. An enchanting 16th-century patrician house containing, among other things, an original printing press.

Royal Museum of Fine Arts (Koninklijk), Leopold de Waelplaats. Open daily 10–5, except Mon. The most important collection in Antwerp. Rooms with the most famous paintings are specially marked.

Rubens House, 9 Rubensstraat. Open 10–5 except Mon. Rubens himself designed this opulent dwelling which was built in 1610. Paintings by the great master and pupils.

USEFUL ADDRESSES. Consulates: *American,* 64–65 Frankrijklei; *British,* 6 Van Schoonbekeplein; *Ireland,* 14 Schermerstraat, *American Express,* 87 Meir; *Wagon-Lits/Cook,* 5 Teniersplaats. *City Tourist Office,* 19 Suikerrui; also *Information Center,* Koningin Astridplein (outside front of Central Station; hotel room service).

The Belgian Coast

An unbroken belt of golden sand stretches for 40 miles along Belgium's coast from the French to the Dutch frontiers. The English Channel is less glacial here than usual because of the Gulf Stream. Given the variety of vacation attractions and the shortness of the northern summer, it is not surprising that this fringe of beaches is very popular. Broad promenades are one of their great features. They are traffic-free and provide pleasant places for walking and cycling. You can hire a bicycle or a two-seater cycle anywhere. Angling is free on all beaches and from the breakwaters and jetties at Nieuwport, Blankenberge, Oostende and from the famous mole at Zeebrugge. Each place has something special: De Haan its 18-hole golf course, Zoute its fashionable shopping street called the Rustlaan, and at Oostduinkerke you can still watch shrimp fishermen going out to sea on horseback.

Oostende is the largest resort with a fine beach which stretches the full length of the town. Most of the promenade is traffic-free as well as the shopping precincts. Parks include one along the lines of Disneyland for children. There is flat racing at the Wellington race course during July and August and trotting in the evenings under floodlights in spring and autumn.

PRACTICAL INFORMATION FOR THE BELGIAN COAST

HOTELS AND RESTAURANTS. There are over a thousand hotels and pensions, from the simplest to the most luxurious, along the coast. You should experience no difficulty in finding accommodations at short notice, except during the peak periods, July-Aug., and weekends. Prices may be up nearly 30% in full season.

KNOKKE HEIST. *La Réserve* (L), (tel. 600606). 112 rooms, heated pool. *Norfolk* (I) (tel. 610694). *Nouvel Hotel* (I) (tel. 601861).

Restaurants. *Aquillon* (E), (tel. 601274). Best in town. Booking essential. *Flots Bleus* (M), tel. 602710. Very good value.

OOSTENDE (OSTEND). *Andromeda* (L) (tel. 506811). 50 rooms. *Imperial* (M) (tel. 705481). *Ter Streep* (E) (tel. 700912). 38 rooms. *Belle-vue-Britannia* (M) (tel. 706373). On the seafront close to the Casino. **Restaurants.** *Bretonne* (E) (tel. 704222). *Prince Albert* (I) (tel. 702803).

Gastronomic weekends at Oostende consist of a specially prepared dinner by a master chef on Saturday night and breakfast at the same hotel on Sunday morning. Write or phone Oostende Casino-Kursaal (tel. 705111).

ZEEBRUGGE. *Plage* (M) (tel. 544055). 30 rooms. **Restaurant.** *Le Chalut* (M) (tel. 544115). Excellent restaurant.

Museums

OOSTENDE. Mercator Three-master Museum. A former training ship of the Belgian merchant navy with curios from 54 voyages and naval bric-a-brac. It is anchored in the inner harbor. Open daily 9–6; reduced hours in winter.

Museum of Fine Arts. Exhibits of different painting schools and a special section devoted to James Ensor. His last home is now also a museum with a documentary center, livingroom and studio. Open daily 10–12, 2–5.

Ensor House. Home of Belgium's greatest 18th-century artist. Open 10–12, 2–5; afternoons only in winter. Closed Oct.

Spas and Casinos

The Thermal Center at Oostende offers mineral baths for the treatment of rheumatism with water from a well sunk to over 1,000 feet, along with electrotherapy and other cures.

You can buy chips of 10 to 1,000 francs at the casinos of Oostende, Knokke-Heist, Blankenberge, and Middelkerke, and pray.

Flanders Art Towns

The Art Cities of Flanders is a phrase which conjures up images of Ghent, the "City of Flowers," of fabulous Ypres and medieval Bruges, the Venice of the North, contemplating its weathered beauty in the dark mirror of its calm canals. In the 15th century, these were among the proudest and richest cities of Europe, and the aura of that golden age still seems to emanate from their cloth halls, castles and cathedrals. The famous artists, the brothers Van Eyck, came from Ghent. And from Ghent University, over a century ago, Leo Hendrik Baekeland emigrated to America and there invented bakelite—the forerunner of plastics. Ypres was the "Wipers" of World War I, so called because the British Tommies found the local name impossible to pronounce.

PRACTICAL INFORMATION FOR FLANDERS ART TOWNS

Hotels and Restaurants

BRUGES (BRUGGE). *Holiday Inn* (E), 2 Boeveriestraat (tel. 81369). 128 rooms, a converted convent. *Park Hotel* (E), 5 t'zand Vrydagmarkt (tel. 333364). 37 rooms. *Au Duc de Bourgogne* (M), 12 Huidenvettersplaats (tel. 332038). 10 rooms with bath; inn-like atmosphere and a famous restaurant. *Bryghia* (M), 4 Oosterlingenplaats (tel. 338059). *Rembrandt Rubens* (I), 38 Walplaats (tel. 336439).

Restaurants. *De Snippe* (M), 52 Ezelstraat (tel. 337070). *Bakkershof* (I), Parklaan 16 (tel. 824987).

GHENT (GAND, GENT). *Holiday Inn* (E), 600 Ottergemsesteenweg (tel. 225885). 118 rooms with bath; 8 km. southeast of city center. *Europahotel* (M), 59 Gordunakaai (tel. 226071). 40 rooms with bath. *Sint Jorishof* (I), 2 Botermarkt (tel. 236791). Claims to be the oldest hotel in Europe.

Restaurant. *Horse Shoe* (E), 8 Lievekaai (tel. 235517).

YPRES. *Regina* (M), 45 Grote Markt (tel. 200165). 22 rooms; restaurant.

Museums

BRUGES. Bruges, the purest of medieval towns in Northern Europe, has several important art collections. **Groeninge Museum,** on the Dyver Canal, has masterpieces by Jan van Eyck, Memling, and Hieronymus Bosch. Open daily 10–12, 2–5.
Gruuthuse Museum, originally the palace of the lords whose name it bears today, shows lace, pottery, goldsmith's art, etc. Open daily 10–12, 1.45–5.
Memling Museum, a one-time chapter-room in St. John Hospital's precincts. A unique collection of the master's paintings is exhibited. Insist on being shown the medieval pharmacy in use until recently. Open daily 10–12, 2–5.
Museum of the Holy Blood. Contains the gold and silver reliquary made in 1617, wrought copperwork, and paintings. Open daily 9.30–11.30, 2–4.

GHENT. Fine Arts Museum in the Citadel Park. Fine collection of Breughel, Rubens, Tintoretto, Reynolds, etc. Open daily 9–12, 2–5.
Museum of Decorative Arts, former De Coninck mansion (1752). Rich collection of furniture of the period. Exhibitions of modern arts and crafts. Open daily 10–12, 1.30–5.
Folklore Museum, customs and traditions in the city of Ghent. Open daily 10–12, 1.30–5; closed Tues. Shorter hours in winter.

The Wooded Ardennes

This rolling forest region, full of fast-flowing streams and wooded glens, is a perfect vacationland. Reputedly the Forest of Arden of Shakespeare's *As You Like It,* it offers the double charm of quaint villages and towns and a beautiful landscape, still only half discovered. Whatever your budget, you will find accommodation here to suit it, from the excellent hotels of Spa and La Roche to modest, hospitable inns, manor houses transformed into youth hostels, and ideal campsites.

This is the land of Ardennes ham, smoked over sweet-smelling gorse branches, of walnut groves, fresh, hot bread, cold beer and other basic joys of life. It's difficult to imagine, but this was the site of the Battle of the Bulge. The world still remembers General McAuliffe's classic reply to the Nazi summons to surrender at Bastogne, and the citizens of that city still tend with loving care the graves of the American boys who died here.

If you're looking for wonderful scenery, food, and people, off the beaten track, try the Ardennes.

PRACTICAL INFORMATION FOR THE ARDENNES

Hotels and Restaurants

ARLON. *Arly* (M), 81 Ave. Luxembourg (tel. 215381). 27 rooms. *Hotel du Nord* (M), 2 Rue Faubourgs (tel. 212293).

BASTOGNE. *Lebrun* (I), 8 Rue Marche (tel. 211193). 26 rooms. In season their young wild boar is delicious.

HAN-SUR-LESSE. *Restaurant Hostellerie Henri IV* (M), 39 Route de Rochefort (tel. 377221). Marvellous restaurant.

LA ROCHE. *Air Pur* (E), outside town on Rte. de Houffalize (tel. 411223). Small hotel with gourmet cuisine and a magnificent panoramic view.
Restaurant. *Le Chalet* (M), (tel. 411197). Specializes in mountain game.

SPA. *Olympic* (M), 13 Ave. Amédée-Hesse (tel. 772548). 34 rooms, most with bath.

Restaurant. *Manoir de Lebioles* (E), (tel. 771020).

Spas and Casinos

The original *Spa,* and *Chaudfontaine,* close to Liège, excellent mineral springs. Both these resorts have casinos open all year. The casinos at *Dinant* and *Namur* are open all year round, also. While the former is on a more modest scale, *Namur* casino is the last word in luxury and entertainment. Its weekend gourmet dinners and dances are superb.

The Southwest—Hainaut, Sambre-Meuse

Here, in the southwest of Belgium, you are in the cradle of Walloon history. It is a proud old country, the nursery of French kings, the dowry of dynastic marriages, and for centuries the buffer between expansive France and quarrelsome Flanders. Today Hainaut is one of the most progressive parts of Belgium, a region of contrast between industry and pleasant countryside with model farms. Mons is in the center of the Borinage, where coal has been mined for over 700 years. This unscenic countryside, dotted with mine tips, saw some of the fiercest fighting in both World Wars, and it was here that the legendary "Angel of Mons" appeared in the sky in 1914.

The Carnival of Binche

The most unusual attraction of this whole area is the Carnival of Binche, a Shrove Tuesday festival which is so vigorous that it added a word to the English language: *binge.* It is a binge, too. The climax of the show is the procession and dance of the Gilles, said to stem from an Inca dance witnessed by the Spaniards after the conquest of Peru. Oranges are brought into Binche by the truckload for this annual carnival, and the crowd is pelted with these and water-inflated sheep's bladders. The costumes of the Gilles, replete with ostrich feathers and the tallest hats you ever saw, are absolutely fantastic, and so is the entire celebration. See it if you can. The museum here rates a visit.

PRACTICAL INFORMATION FOR THE SOUTHWEST

Hotels and Restaurants

BINCHE. Restaurant. *Bernard* (M), 37 Rue de Bruxelles (tel. 333775).

MONS. *Amigo* (E), near Mons at 3 chaussée Brunehault, Masnuy-St-Jean (tel. 728721). 58 rooms. *Euro Crest* (M), near Mons at 38 chaussée Bruxelles, Casteau (tel. 728741). 71 rooms. Very comfortable with a good restaurant. *Résidence Hotel* (I), 4 Rue A. Masquelier (tel. 311403). 6 rooms.
   Restaurants. *Devos* (E), 7 Rue Coupe (tel. 331335). Excellent food. *Robert* (M), 12 Boulevard Albert-Elizabeth (tel. 335908). Excellent food at a moderate price.

TOURNAI. *Prieuré* (E), (tel. 352506). Old converted monastery; 8 km. outside town at Blandain. *Aux Armes de Tournay* (M), Place de Lille 23 (tel. 226723). 20 rooms.

The Meuse Valley and Liège

What the Loire is to France, the Meuse is to Belgium. This is historic château country. Signs of the great Belgian craft of metalwork are everywhere evident, especially in Dinant (home of Adolphe Sax, who in 1846 patented the saxophone). Be sure to try the local gingerbread; it's called *couques.*

Visit the quiet town of Namur at the confluence of the Meuse and Sambre, and stopover at historic Huy. But the living symbol of Walloon independence and progress is Liège, one of the largest river ports in Europe, and also site of the first European coal mine. Don't miss the Museum of Folklore and the extraordinary puppet shows on the Rue de Féronstrée.

PRACTICAL INFORMATION FOR LIÈGE AND THE MEUSE VALLEY

Hotels and Restaurants

DINANT. *Hostellerie Thermidor* (E), 3 Rue de la Station (tel. 223135). Has the best restaurant in town. *Henrotaux* (I), 36 Av. Churchill (tel. 222766).

LIÈGE. *Ramada* (L), 100 Boulevard Sauveniere (tel. 325919). 105 rooms. *Holiday Inn* (E), 2 Esplanade de l'Europe (tel. 426020). 224 rooms. *Couronne* (M), 11 Place Guillemins (tel. 522168). 79 rooms.

Restaurants. *Chêne Madame* (E), (tel. 714127). 16 km. outside town near Neuville-en-Confroz. Superb. *Lion Dodu* (M), En Roture 11 (tel. 435769). *Chambord* (I), Rue Pont-d' Avroy 25 (tel. 237011).

NAMUR. *Sofitel* (E), 195 chaussée de Dinant, at Wepion (tel. 460811). 118 rooms with bath. Overlooks the river. *Queen Victoria* (M–I), 11 Ave. Gare (tel. 222971). 20 rooms.

Gold and silver
Greave. Circa 375 BC

BULGARIA

A country of 43,000 square miles, about the size of Tennessee, Bulgaria enjoys a close relationship with the Soviet Union, but is making great efforts to meet the needs of her considerable number of Western vacationers. Despite considerable industrialization in the postwar period, Bulgaria remains an essentially rural country. Over half the cultivated land is given over to cereal growing and vineyards in the southern valleys. Bulgaria is a major exporter of wine and its canned tomatoes and jellies are much appreciated abroad. Nor have the Bulgars wholeheartedly become city dwellers, even though more than half of them are. Even in the capital Sofia most people are not more than a generation or two from the soil.

During her troubled history, Bulgaria has known three periods of independence: the first from 681–1018, the second from 1185–1396, and the third beginning in 1879 and lasting till her occupation by the Nazis in 1941 and subsequent "liberation" by the Soviet Union in 1944. The first two were divided by a period of Byzantine rule, the second two by just about half a millenium of Turkish domination, punctuated by many uprisings whose monuments and memorials pepper the landscapes. These twin influences are reflected in many aspects of Bulgarian culture and traditions.

The Current Scene

Bulgaria, as one would imagine in an Eastern Bloc country, expects hard work and discipline from the people, but in recent years life has become noticeably more relaxed. Western pop music, a taboo in earlier times, is now heard everywhere—something of a mixed blessing! The consumer drive of the past few years, common to much of Eastern Europe, has some way to go before reaching the levels attained by

Bulgaria's more developed neighbors. But the leadership is undoubtedly making an effort not just to raise real wages but to offer people better quality and wider choice in consumer goods. Prices have remained remarkably stable in the face of adverse global trends.

PRACTICAL INFORMATION FOR BULGARIA

WHAT WILL IT COST. Package tours are available through accredited travel agents. From the US, several multi-country tours visit Bulgaria. From London, a 2-week one-center holiday costs from £195 low season, from £325 high season; a grand tour (one week coach tour, one week beach resort), £289–£480 according to hotel and season. There are increasing opportunities for sporting and other special-interest holidays; the Bulgarian National Tourist Office can advise on the latest details. Individual travel, of course, works out at a higher rate, though there are seasonal hotel reductions. Independent travelers, in any case, are well advised to make prepaid arrangements through a travel agent as far as possible, for priority is always given to those with vouchers and they will also gain from a currency bonus, advantageous hotel rates and other benefits referred to below. An excellent system of vouchers still leaves them with plenty of freedom of movement. Nevertheless, individual travelers should be prepared to exercise patience and perseverance and it is also strongly recommended that they learn the Cyrillic alphabet, if only to know that a PECTOPAHT is a restaurant, identify museums and, in general, read road signs away from main roads and tourist centers.

The monetary unit is the *lev* (plural *leva*). Banknotes circulate in denominations of 1, 2, 5, 10 and 20 leva. The leva is divided into 100 *stotinki*. Coins exist in denominations of 1, 2, 5, 10, 20, 50 stotinki and 1, 2, 5 leva.

The approximate rate of exchange is 1 lev to the US$, about 1.40 to the £ sterling. To this official rate, a bonus of 80% has been added for all tourists with prepaid services exchanging foreign currency at *Balkantourist* offices in Bulgaria. These prepaid services can be quite minimal: for example, a few nights' camping vouchers will entitle you to the currency bonus. You may bring in any amount and kind of foreign currency including travelers' checks and freely exchange it at branches of the *Bulgarian State Bank,* at *Balkantourist* hotels and offices, at the main airports and at all the frontier customs offices. *Note: the bonus is obtainable only at Balkantourist exchange offices.* The import and export of Bulgarian currency is *not* permitted. Unspent amounts of leva can be exchanged at frontiers on departure, provided that counterfoils showing the leva to have been bought with foreign currency or travelers' checks are produced.

Credit cards are accepted in larger stores, hotels, restaurants and night clubs. They can also be used in border currency formalities.

A typical day might cost two people:

Hotel (moderate) with breakfast	50	leva
Lunch without wine	20	
Dinner with wine	40	
Beer	2	
Coffee	2	
Tram (4 rides)	0.48	
Taxi (about 5 km)	1.50	
Theater	6	
Miscellaneous 10%	10	
	131.98	leva

WHEN TO COME. The Black Sea coast season lasts from May to October; July and August are the warmest and most crowded months. Inland, March and April are wet, April/May are good months for fruit blossom,

May/early June for the rose harvest, September for events and the fruit harvest, October for fall colors. The skiing season is January through March.

Climate. Very warm (but not unpleasant) in summer, 2,240 hrs. of sunshine per year in coastal areas, nearly 30% more than southern England.

Average afternoon daily temperatures in degrees Fahrenheit and centigrade:

Sofia	Jan.	Feb.	Mar.	Apr.	May	June	July	Aug.	Sept.	Oct.	Nov.	Dec.
F°	34	39	51	62	70	76	82	82	74	63	50	37
C°	1	4	11	17	21	24	28	28	23	17	10	3

SPECIAL EVENTS. *Balkantourist* can give the latest information. Otherwise, some regular festivals are: *April*, International Trade Fair, Plovdiv; *May-June*, Sofia Music Weeks, including an International Festival for Young Opera Singers every 3 years; *June-July*, Varna Summer International Festival of Music, featuring an International Ballet Festival alternate years; *June*, Golden Orpheus International Festival of Pop Songs (alternate, even-numbered years), Slunchev Bryag; Rose Festival, Kazanluk; *July*, Neptune Festivals, Black Sea resorts; *August*, International Folklore Festival, Bourgas; *September*, International Trade Fair, Plovdiv; Chamber Music Festival, Plovdiv; Bulgarian Film Festival, Varna.

National Holidays. Jan. 1; May 1 & 2 (Labor Day); May 24 (Day of Bulgarian Culture); Sept. 9 & 10 (Liberation Days); Nov. 7 (October Revolution Day).

VISAS. Tourists traveling on a package tour by charter flight or, in groups of 6 or more, by scheduled and independent transport, do not require a visa. Otherwise, nationals of almost all countries except Austria, Eastern bloc and Scandinavian countries, require visas, which may be obtained from Bulgarian embassies. The Visa Section, Bulgarian Embassy, 186–188 Queen's Gate, London SW7 5HL can supply the following visas: single transit (valid 30 hours) £6; double transit £10; tourist entry £10. Visas are not issued at border checkpoints, but are renewable in Bulgaria. It is important to retain the yellow immigration card as it is required when leaving the country.

HEALTH CERTIFICATES. Not required for entry into Bulgaria.

GETTING TO BULGARIA. By Plane. There are no direct scheduled flights from the U.S. to Bulgaria. The easiest routes, therefore, are via London, Paris or Frankfurt. *Balkan Air* (the national airline) have service linking these cities, as well as a number of other major European capitals, with Sofia. They also fly to a number of destinations in Africa and the Middle East.

By Train. There are through trains to Sofia from Munich, Vienna, Belgrade and East Berlin and from Salonika, Istanbul and Bucharest.

By Boat. New are Danube cruises all the way from Passau (Germany) or Vienna (Austria) to the Bulgarian Danube ports of Vidin and Ruse.

By Car. Three international routes cross Bulgaria: E80 London-Vienna-Sofia-Istanbul, E79/E83/E85 Thessalonika-Sofia-Bucharest-Moscow, and E87 along the Black Sea coast from Romania to Turkey. A leaflet on each of these is available from *Balkantourist*. There is a car ferry between Vidin and Kalafat in Romania across the Danube; a bridge links Ruse with Giurgiu, Romania.

Drivers will need an International Driving Permit and the International Green Card for insurance, as well as a registration certificate for their vehicle. Gasoline can be purchased only with vouchers bought with hard currency from *Shipka* offices at the border, in cities and resorts, or *Balkantourist* roadside facilities.

CUSTOMS. You may import into Bulgaria 250 gr. of tobacco; 1 liter of spirits and 2 liters of wine; 100 gr. of perfume; gifts up to the value of 50 leva. You may also import any amount of foreign currency; only the balance of this may be exported. Declare valuable items, cameras, etc., on entry.

HOTELS. Our hotel grading system has four categories: Deluxe (L), Expensive (E), Moderate (M) and Inexpensive (I). Of these about a dozen hotels in the first two categories (as specified in the hotel information for each center) are classified as *Interhotels,* which means that special care has been taken to conform to international standards. Otherwise, standards may not be as high (in terms of amenities and service) as for equivalent categories in the West; but then nor are the charges. Most of the hotels used by Western visitors are owned by *Balkantourist.* Other hotels catering for specific categories of visitor, usually in groups only, are those operated by *Shipka* (for motorists), *Orbita* (for youth), *Pirin* (for hikers) and *Cooptourist.*

Hotel rates for full board per person sharing double room with bath or shower in Sofia in the high season are $55 and up (L); $35–45 (E); $25–35 (M); $18–25 (I). Prices outside Sofia are at the lower end of these price ranges, and there are also reductions of 25%–40% out of the high season. Excellent discounts apply to children under 12 years sharing accommodations with adults.

Balkantourist also arrange holidays in self-catering accommodations. In Sofia and other main cities, you can get a room in a private home for about $8 with breakfast per person per night in the top category (lower rates and categories available). Ask for the *Rooms to Let* booklet from *Balkantourist.* Self-catering villa and apartment holidays in centers along the coast are also now packaged ex-UK.

CAMPING. There are now over 100 camping sites throughout the country, many of them near the Black Sea beaches. These are classified as "Special", I and II, and in the top two categories will have hot and cold water, showers, electricity, grocery stores and restaurants. A map showing their location is available from *Balkantourist.* Many have bungalows or cabins for hire, and one-center camping holidays are now marketed ex-UK.

RESTAURANTS. All the better hotels have restaurants which are quite expensive. Elsewhere an expensive (E) meal excluding strong drinks costs from 15–20 leva, moderate (M) 10–15 leva, inexpensive (I) 5–10 leva. You will find a lot of attractive folk-style restaurants throughout the country. A very good system of meal vouchers enables holidaymakers to eat where they wish, even if they have booked accommodations with full board. A supply of meal vouchers (the number varying according to the type of hotel at which you are booked) is issued on arrival in Bulgaria; they can be used in any *Balkantourist* restaurant in the country, which means most of them. A marked improvement in the standard of menus is still too often marred by food being served lukewarm. Smaller establishments are frequently much better than the tourist hotels. Music in most restaurants is *loud.*

Food and Drink. Bulgarians eat their one big meal in the middle of the day; supper is a snack, with wine. Bulgarian food is heavy, hearty and good, its wine light and cheap, its world-famous fruits and vegetables delicious.

Bulgarian national dishes are closely related to their Greek, Turkish and Yugoslav counterparts. You should try *tarator,* a cold yogurt soup with cucumbers, peppers, cabbage or vine leaves stuffed with meat; *gyuvech,* a hot pot of many vegetables, sometimes including meat; and also *kebapcheta,* small, tasty, strongly spiced minced meat rolls. Salads, especially *shopska,* are good. When you can get them, Bulgarian melons, apples and pears are in a class by themselves, as are the rich amber-colored *bolgar* grapes and orange-red apricots. Particularly popular is the traditional Turkish coffee, heavily sweetened, and served in small cups. *Banitsa* is a pastry eaten with fruit or cheese.

Bulgarians drink a fragrant infusion of dried lime leaves. Water, found in fountains along the road, is good anywhere. Milk bars are popular throughout the country. Bulgaria of course is the original home of yogurt—fermented sheep's milk turned thick and creamy by well-disposed bacteria, *Lactobacillus bulgaricus.* The result is good, and good for you. The real national drink is a thickish, grayish brew of fermented sesame seed, called *boza.* White wines *(bialo vino)* are of the hock type, best among them *Trakia Pinot Chardonnay* or *Songurlarski Misket;* the red ones *(tcherveno)* on the heavy side; ask for *Trakia* or *Mavroud.* Excellent fruit juices, difficult to get in hotels, should be readily available in the stores.

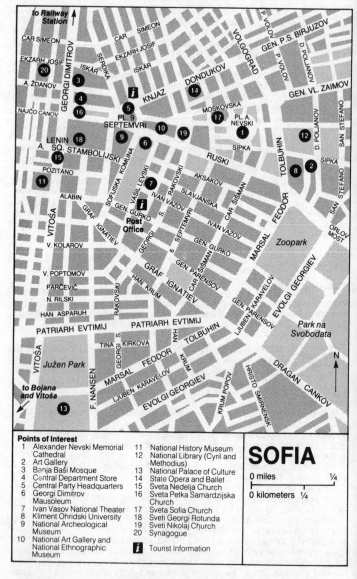

Points of Interest

1 Alexander Nevski Memorial Cathedral
2 Art Gallery
3 Banja Baši Mosque
4 Central Department Store
5 Central Party Headquarters
6 Georgi Dimitrov Mausoleum
7 Ivan Vasov National Theater
8 Kliment Ohridski University
9 National Archeological Museum
10 National Art Gallery and National Ethnographic Museum
11 National History Museum
12 National Library (Cyril and Methodius)
13 National Palace of Culture
14 State Opera and Ballet
15 Sveta Nedelja Church
16 Sveta Petka Samardzijska Church
17 Sveta Sofia Church
18 Sveti Georgi Rotunda
19 Sveti Nikolaj Church
20 Synagogue

i Tourist Information

SOFIA

0 miles   ¼

0 kilometers ¼

TIPPING. Officially discouraged, but acceptable. 10 percent is safe.

MAIL. Letters and postcards cost 45 stotinki to the UK, 55 stotinki to North America; check before mailing.

CLOSING TIMES. Generally speaking, stores keep about the same hours as their counterparts in Britain and America. Most stores open between 8 A.M. and 10 A.M. and close between 5 P.M. and 7 P.M., Monday through Friday, or 12 A.M. to 2 P.M. on Saturday. Some stores close at lunchtime for an hour or two, or even longer, staying open later in the evening.

Banks are open from 8 A.M. to 6 P.M., Monday through Saturday, but remember that only Balkantourist exchange offices give the currency bonus.

PHOTOGRAPHY. No special restrictions, except for government installations or military zones. Photographing the Black Sea coast from offshore is not recommended. Bring your own film.

USEFUL ADDRESSES. *US Embassy*, 1 Stamboliisky Blvd; *British Embassy*, 65 Tolbuhin Blvd.; *Balkantourist*, 37 Dondukov Blvd (for all accommodations other than *Interhotels*); *Balkantourist* also have offices in all main hotels; *Interhotels Central Office*, 4 Sveta Sofia St.; *Bureau of Tourist Information and Reservations*, 35 Eksarh Josif St. (near Lenin Square) and Palace of Culture (off Vitosha Blvd.); *Balkan Airlines*, 12 Narodno Sobranie Sq.; (domestic services) 10 Sofiiska komuna St.; *Rila International Railway Bureau*, 5 Gurko St; *Shipka Agency* (Union of Bulgarian Motorists), 6 Sveta Sofia St.; *Orbita Bureau for Youth International Excursions*, 45A Stamboliiski St.; *Pirin Tourist Bureau* (Union of Bulgarian Hikers), 30 Alexander Stamboliiski Blvd; *Cooptourist Tourist Bureau* (Central Cooperative Union), 33A Stamboliiski Blvd.; *Emergency* telephone 150 (motorists 146).

GETTING AROUND BULGARIA. In addition to the following guidelines, two offices in Sofia are of special interest to independent travelers as they provide a central agency for all travel reservations. Called the *Bureau of Tourist Information and Reservations* (see above).

By Plane. Balkan Air have frequent services from Sofia to Varna and Bourgas on the Black Sea Coast and limited service to one or two other towns. Booking a ticket for an internal flight can take time; best try Balkantourist first.

By Train. There are three main routes of interest. One to Bourgas via Karlovo, another to Bourgas again, but this time via Plovdiv. The third is to Varna via Pleven. Many main lines are electrified. There are no runabout tickets, but prices are low. Trains are frequently packed and it is worth ordering tickets in advance from RILA (International Railway Bureau) or the Domestic Rail Bureau. There are buffet cars on main line expresses.

By Boat. Summer hydrofoil and boat services link Black Sea resorts. There are limited hydrofoil services on the Danube, and Danube cruises sail from Germany and Austria to Vidin and Ruse.

Sofia, Capital City

With its fine situation, Bulgaria's capital city is the focal point of all major land and air routes into Bulgaria. The city sprawls on a high fertile plain in the lee of the Balkan Mountains, or Stara Planina, a high range running eastward to the Black Sea. Sofia is a fast-growing metropolis of one million, with wide, straight, fluorescent-lit, tree-shaded streets, 384 parks and grassy squares, a rash of recent architecture, and a scattering of ancient monuments and excellent museums.

The motto of ancient Sofia's coat of arms reads, "Grows, but grows not old". Modern Sofia grows, at a mushroom rate, not only in size but in stature. Some travelers still find it more provincial than other Eastern European capitals, but it is rapidly adding industrial suburbs and modern metropolitan amenities to its basic Balkan charm.

One of the most dominant features of Sofia is the glittering Alexander Nevsky Memorial Church erected to commemorate Bulgaria's liberation from the Turks in the Russo-Turkish war of 1877–78. Designed by a Russian architect, it was decorated jointly by Russian, Bulgarian and Czechoslovak artists. Excellent icons are in the crypt.

Across the square to the west is Sofia's most distinctive church, St. Sophia—from which the city took its name. This stately Byzantine basilica, with its cruciform cupola-topped structure, dates from the sixth century. A short jog south brings you to the large and pleasant Liberty Park, which offers an open-air theater, cinema and restaurant, sports stadia, tennis courts, and swimming pools.

Focal point of the city center is Lenin Square, near which the excellent new National History Museum is an absolute "must." Nearby is the restored 5th-century church of St. Georgi, a charming building that crouches in the courtyard of the Balkan Hotel. Under restoration, it houses remnants of medieval frescoes and alongside it are even earlier foundations from the Roman period.

One block east and a thousand years later, the Turks built Sofia's largest mosque, the Bouyouk. Its nine cupolas today shelter Bulgaria's archeological museum. Around the corner is Deveti Septemvri (September Ninth) Place, which does for Sofia what Red Square does for Moscow. Here the towering red star atop the semi-skyscraper of the Bulgarian Communist Party headquarters dominates the city skyline. An underpass from here takes you not only across the square, but back to the Roman period. Part of a street, foundations of walls and a variety of artifacts can be seen down there. The massive tomb of Georgi Dimitrov, Bulgaria's leading communist figure until his death in 1949, is nearby, opposite the National Art Gallery. There is a changing of the guard ceremony every hour.

Returning to Lenin Square along Dondukov Street from Communist Party headquarters, you will come to another charming little old church, sunk below ground level, and surrounded by shops and an open air café. This is Sveta Petka Samardshijska Church from the 14th century. Soaring beyond it is the other of Sofia's two mosques, Banya Bashi, and across Georgi Dimitrov Street from this is the lively central market.

From Lenin Square, Vitosha Boulevard is a lively shopping street, in due course passing the ultramodern Palace of Culture and its complex of shops and restaurants as it heads towards the mountain that dominates the capital. On the way to it you will also pass the fine, great green acres of Juzhen Park. Rising to about 7000 feet, Vitosha mountain is now a national park and natural playground for the citizens in summer and winter. It is served by chair lift and cable car. On its slopes, about 6 miles from the city center, is the beautiful little medieval church of Boyana, with 11th- to 13th-century frescoes (closed for restoration).

PRACTICAL INFORMATION FOR SOFIA

HOTELS. Note that in the case of those designated as *Interhotels,* special care has been taken to conform with international standards. See above, for rates and our grading system. It is quite common for a hotel to offer accommodations in more than one category. If you haven't booked already, go to the Interhotels Central Office, 4 Sveta Sofia St. (for Interhotels), to Balkantourist, 37 Dondukov Blvd. (for all other forms of accommodations including private), or to the Central Railway Station.

Sheraton Sofia-Balkan (L), Lenin Square. *Interhotel,* 200 rooms, four restaurants, health club, top facilities. Formerly the Grand Hotel Balkan, now completely renovated in the very heart of the city.

Vitosha-New Otani (L), 100 Anton Ivanov Boulevard (tel. 624151). 454 rooms, several suites, various restaurants (including Japanese), night club, indoor pool, saunas, sports facilities. Japanese-designed *Interhotel,* and Bulgaria's most luxurious. On south side of city, not central.

Bulgaria (E), 4 Ruski Boulevard. 72 rooms. Very central, but quiet as the street is now traffic-free. Some Moderate rooms as well. Old fashioned.

Grand Hotel Sofia (E), Narodno Sobranie Square (tel. 878821). 200 rooms, 3 suites, night club. *Interhotel,* very central. Good food and service.

Novotel Europa (E), 131 Georgi Dimitrov Boulevard (tel. 31261). 609 rooms, some suites. An *Interhotel,* and one of the French *Novotel* chain. Near railway station and not far from center.

Park-Hotel Moskva (E-M), 25 Nezabravka Street (tel. 71261). 366 rooms, 34 suites, several restaurants (including Russian), night club. *Interhotel* in parkland setting, less central.

Rodina (E), 4 Ruski Pametnik Square. Over 500 rooms and suites, several restaurants, night club, pool. Sofia's newest and largest, southwest of the center.

Hemus (M), 31 Georgi Traikov Boulevard. Over 200 rooms, suites.

Serdica (M), 1 Levski Square (tel. 443411). 140 rooms, "Old Berlin" restaurant serving German specialties. Central.

Slavyanska Beseda (M), 127 Rakovski Street (tel. 880441). 110 rooms, no restaurant. Central.

Pliska (M-I), 87 Lenin Boulevard (tel. 71281). Over 200 rooms, suites. Near Liberty Park on way to airport.

Slaviya (M-I), 2 Sofiiski Geroi Street (tel. 525551). 75 rooms. In the southwest of the city, not central.

High on the slopes of Mount Vitosha are the **Prostor** (M) and **Shtastlivetsa** (I).

RESTAURANTS. In addition to the hotel restaurants, there is a growing number of eating places serving Bulgarian and other Eastern European specialties, often in attractive folkloric surroundings.

Berlin (E), 4 V. Zaimov Boulevard. Bulgarian and German food.

Budapest (E), 145 G.S. Rakovski Street. Hungarian food and music.

Crystal (E), 10 Aksakov Street. Restaurant-tavern.

Krim (E), 2 Dobroudja Street. Russian food, summer garden.

Roubin (E), Lenin Square. Newest eating complex in city center, with elegant restaurant (and snack bar) serving Bulgarian and international foods. More moderately priced dishes also available.

Boyana (M), about 6 miles from center, near historic Boyana church. Folkloric program.

Chernata Kotka (M), about 8 miles southeast of city on E80. Folk music.

Goroublyane (M), attached to motel about 6 miles out to southeast on E80. Folk program.

Koprivshtitsa (M), 3 Vitosha Boulevard. Folk music.

Shoumako (M), 6 miles south on Simeonovo-Bistritsa road. Folk music.

Strandjata (M), 19 Lenin Square. Folk music.

Vodenicharski Mehani (M), incorporating three old mills, at foot of Mount Vitosha above Dragalevtsi district. Folkloric show.

Zlatna Ribka (M), 15 miles south on road to Borovets. Folk music.

MOTELS AND CAMPSITES. Bozhur Motel, 11 miles southeast of Sofia on E80. Restaurant.

Goroublyane Motel, about 6 miles southeast of Sofia on E80. Open all year, restaurant.

Iztok Motel, 10 miles southeast of Sofia on E80. Restaurant.

Tihiyat Kut Motel, on Mount Vitosha. Bus service from downtown area. Modern buildings with good restaurant.

Cherniya Kos campsite, between Vitosha and Lyulin mountains.

Ivaniane campsite, near Bankya spa resort. Chalets for hire.

Vrana campsite, off the E80. Best facilities.

TRANSPORTATION. Work has begun on a new metro system, but for the moment you can use trams, buses and trolleys. It's best to buy your tickets (6 stotinki each) in advance from special kiosks by the streetcar stop. The ticket must be punched in a machine after boarding the vehicle (watch how the other passengers do it). *Taxis* are inexpensive but rather scarce; quickest is to order one from your hotel or dial 142 for the central taxi service. *Balkantourist* arrange sightseeing tours of the city.

ENTERTAINMENT. Opera *(State Opera House)* is of a very high standard. Concerts are performed in the open air in summer (Liberty Park). Also excellent are classical concerts, performances by the *National Folk Ensemble,* and the *Central Puppet Theater* (14 Gurko St).

An Orthodox Church service can be a moving experience. The choir of the *Alexander Nevsky Memorial Church* is exceptional.

Foreign films at Sofia's many movie theaters are shown with their original soundtracks.

There are night clubs with floor shows at the *Vitoshi-New Otani Hotel,* the *Rodina,* the *Moskva Park Hotel,* the *Hemus* and the *Grand Hotel Sofia.* The *Novotel Europa* has a disco. The *Orient Night Club* is at 2 Stamboliiski Blvd.

The *National Palace of Culture Lyudmila Zhivkova,* along Vitosha Boulevard, includes nightclub, disco, bowling alley.

MUSEUMS. Sofia's *Archeological Museum* displays changing exhibitions of Bulgarian and foreign treasures. The *Ethnograpical Museum* shows folk art, particularly costumes, from every region of the country. This and the *National Art Gallery,* showing Bulgarian art from medieval times to the present, are housed in the former Royal Palace between 9th September Square and Moskovska Street. The Art Gallery, 6 Shipka St., shows Bulgarian and foreign art, while the crypt of *Alexander Nevsky Church* houses outstanding icons and other religious works. The recently opened *National History Museum,* 2 Vitosha Boulevard, houses many of Bulgaria's greatest treasures, including spectacular finds from recent excavations. On no account miss this.

The embalmed body of Georgi Dimitrov is on display in his great mausoleum on 9th September Square, and there is a museum devoted to the life of this revered Bulgarian leader at 66 Opulchenska Street.

Bulgaria's Highland Wonderland

Western tourists in search of new outdoor stamping grounds are now discovering the rugged, unspoiled invigorating altitudes of Bulgaria's southwestern highlands. Just off the highway leading south from Sofia to Salonika lie the Rila mountains, with the famous monastery of the same name, and Mount Moussala, highest peak in Balkans (9,596 ft.). Adjoining this range to the south is the magnificent snow country of the Pirin mountains, and to the east the beautiful untouched Rhodopes.

Rila

Shangri-la-like Rila Monastery is only 75 miles from Sofia (regular bus services). Its monastic brotherhood was founded by a holy hermit of the 10th century, Ivan Rilsky. During five centuries of Turkish domination, Rila Monastery remained a kind of oasis for Bulgarian Christian culture. Destroyed by fire on a number of occasions, most of the present buildings date from the 19th century, a notable exception being the well-preserved 14th-century Hrelio's Tower. Nevertheless, the complex is an outstanding monument to Bulgaria's National Revival architecture, art and woodcarving and its setting is superb. Nearby, *Balkantourist* run a pleasant hotel and restaurant on a panoramic site.

Borovets and Pirin

Just off the Sofia-Plovdiv highway is Borovets, the starting place for the 9,596-foot summit of Mount Moussala. At about 4,500 feet, Borovets is a well-known summer and winter mountain resort. Besides hotels and restaurants, it is well equipped for all winter sports.

South of Rila, tucked in the corner between northern Greece and eastern Yugoslavia, is the splendid upland wilderness of the Pirin mountains, part of it designated as Bulgaria's largest national park. Hunters and fishermen love its snug chalets and its 200 limpid lakes. Pirin has eagles and chamois, and the rare *balkanska zvezda* (Balkan star), a variety of Alpine edelweiss. Not far from the Greek border, the little town of Melnik has great charm and an impressive setting amid eroded sandstone cliffs.

The Rhodopes

Between Plovdiv and the Aegean sea lies the storybook land of Thrace. Its southern half belongs to Greece and is flat farmland. The Bulgarian northern half is occupied by the fabled Rhodope mountains where Orpheus is said to have been born. Archeological treasures found in the area include a Thracian tomb, and the dead city of Tamrache. The Convent of Bachkovo, near Assenovgrad, south of Plovdiv, shelters remarkable ancient frescoes and medieval manuscripts.

Many of Bulgaria's 360-odd mineral springs are to be found in the Rhodopes, which is also a skiing and mountain-climbing area, well equipped with tourist chalets. Best-known center is Pamporovo.

Plovdiv, Commercial Center

Exactly 100 miles southeast of Sofia, on the international highway to Istanbul, lies the busy city of Plovdiv, straddling the Maritsa River. For over 2,000 years, it was a commercial crossroads for caravans carrying goods between Europe, Asia and Africa. Today, it is the site of the Plovdiv International Trade Fairs, which take place annually in April and September.

Plovdiv is Bulgaria's second largest city and an important industrial center, but the past remains much in evidence in the older districts, including substantial Roman remains and charming medieval houses. These older districts clamber over hills on the north bank of the Maritsa River and are most attractive, with their twisting cobbled lanes hemmed in by 18th- and 19th-century houses in typical National Revival style. One of the hills is topped by the remains of walls from the old Thracian and subsequently Roman town. A fine Roman amphitheater has been restored.

Veliko Turnovo, Mountain Fortress

Bulgaria's turbulent history and typical art forms are strikingly summed up in the amazing city of Veliko Turnovo, midway along the Sofia–Varna highway. The city is stacked up against steep mountain slopes that hem the twisting course of the Yantra River. This setting is a natural fortress, to which Veliko Turnovo owes its role as the cradle of Bulgarian history. Indeed, during the 13th and 14th centuries, it was the capital of the country. It is today a museum city of marvelous church relics, works of art and fascinating panoramas. The oldest part, called Tsaravets, is contained within a wild loop of the river. Its substantial and partially restored ruins, including the Patriarchate and royal palace, are well worth leisurely attention.

In the environs is the impressive Preobrazhenski Monastery and a curious transplanted Albanian village, Arbanassi. About 30 miles south of Veliko Turnovo, halfway along the road to the Valley of Roses, is the busy industrial town of Gabrovo and, only a few miles from this, the delightful open-air folk museum of Etur, its old houses grouped along a mountain stream. Traditional crafts are still practiced here and their products can be bought. Gabrovo is known as Bulgaria's Manchester though its setting is a good deal more spectacular. It is well known for its jokes which provide the theme for a Festival of Humor every other year, and has a Museum of Humor and Satire.

Kazanluk, Valley of Roses

For a unique experience, go to the precise center of Bulgaria and get up before dawn on a day in May. You are in Kazanluk's Valley of Roses, sheltered between the Stara Planina on the north and the Sredna Gora Mountains to the south. The over-powering fragrance of millions upon millions of fresh pink roses reminds you that "smells are surer than sights or sounds to make your heartsrings crack". You can find out more about this rather attractive industry from the Museum of Rose Production at Kazanluk.

Kazanluk Valley is thick with archeological and artistic treasures. Fully 400 Thracian burial mounds have been discovered thus far. Kazanluk Convent contains frescos from the days of the Ottoman Empire, as well as old icons, ornamented with gold leaf and studded with precious stones. Also at Kazanluk is a beautifully preserved and decorated Thracian tomb from the 4th or 3rd century B.C. The original is not usually open to the public, but an exact replica can be visited.

In the Sredna Gora mountains a few miles south of the head of the valley, the village of Koprivshtitsa is a veritable living museum of traditional architecture, as well as a major historic site of revolutionary activity against the Turks. Tourist amenities are being developed here and it will have special appeal for walkers, painters and photographers.

PRACTICAL INFORMATION FOR THE INTERIOR

Note that in the case of those establishments designated as *Interhotels,* special care has been taken to conform to international standards. Private accommodations are available in a number of centers; check with *Balkantourist.*

BOROVETS. 4,000 feet high in the Rila Mountains. Newest is the 2,000-bed *Rila* hotel and apartment complex (E), with shops and entertainment facilities. *Bor* (M), *Moussala* (M), *Breza* (M), *Edelweis* (I). Folk restaurant in Bor Hotel. Also two holiday villages, one consisting of attractive Finnish log cabins with saunas.

PAMPOROVO. Mountain resort in the Rhodopes. Good winter skiing and splendid summer hiking. *Mourgavets* (M), 75 rooms; *Orfeus* (M), 85 rooms, folk tavern; *Perelik* (M), 230 rooms, newest and best with folk tavern, indoor pool, sports hall. Several (I)s include *Panorama,* 75 rooms, 2 miles from center, and *Prespa,* 80 rooms, recently renovated. Folk restaurants *Chevermeto* in resort center, and *Malina* by ski-lift terminal.

PLOVDIV. *Novotel Plovdiv* (E), Interhotel, 319 rooms, 9 suites, night club, indoor and outdoor pools, saunas, near fair grounds and across river from city center; *Leningrad* (E-M), 370 rooms, night club, indoor pool, modern high rise some distance from center; *Trimontium* (E-M), Interhotel, 177 rooms, 4 suites, disco, very central; *Maritsa* (M), 170 rooms, modern, near Novotel; *Bulgaria* (I), 78 rooms, central for Old Town. Attractive folk restaurants are *Pldin* (E), *Alafrangues* (M), and *Trakiyski Stan* (M). *Rhetora* is a coffee bar in a beautifully restored old house near Roman amphitheater.

RILA. *Rilets* (M), near famous monastery, in Rila mountains.

RUSE. Largest port on Danube, *Riga* (E), Interhotel, 180 rooms, 9 suites, night club; *Dunav* (M-I), Interhotel, 82 rooms, disco.

VELIKO TURNOVO. Former capital city in the mountains. *Veliko Turnovo* (E), Interhotel, 192 rooms, 9 suites, disco, pool, saunas; *Etur* and *Yantra* (M-I), the latter with stunning views across the river. Several folk restaurants, including *Bolyarska Izba*.

The Black Sea Beaches

Modern amenities punctuate a hundred-mile chain of fine sand beaches with the foothills of mountain ranges to provide an attractive backdrop.

Just about one flying hour from Sofia, or 280 miles by road, is Varna, a major industrial center and Bulgaria's main seaport with important shipyards; it has excellent museums, Roman remains and the stunning treasures in its Museum of History and Art (including gold finds from up to 3600 B.C.) especially must be seen. Varna is also the place from which to take the excursion boats up and down the coast.

North: a few miles north of Varna is the hospitable small coastal resort and spa of Drouzhba, the oldest on the Bulgarian Black Sea. It also has Bulgaria's grandest hotel, the Swedish-built Grand Hotel Varna, which is fully equipped for all kinds of balneological treatment and leisure activities. Another five miles up the coast is Zlatni Pyassatsi (Golden Sands), a two-mile-long gently sloping stretch of silky sand, 500 feet wide, the country's major resort, with very good amenities, including mineral baths. A mile or two inland lies medieval Aladja Monastery, built into the rocks.

Some miles north is Bulgaria's newest and third largest resort, the futuristic Albena, geared primarily to the young market with a varied choice of activities, skin diving, water skiing, riding, etc. Its beach, with water only knee-deep 100 meters out, is ideal for families.

Ancient Balchik, 20 miles or so up the coast, terraces down from its hillside perch to the beach. The showpiece here is the garden of an extraordinary small palace mixing Christian and Moslem elements, which was built for the last queen of Romania when Balchik was Romanian.

South: about 60 miles south of Varna, Slunchev Bryag (Sunny Beach) is Bulgaria's largest resort and very popular, with a few comparatively luxurious facilities, and good amenities for children.

Near Sunny Beach and 25 miles north of Bourgas, Nessebur is an ancient and highly historic town on a little peninsula linked to the mainland by a 1,000-foot causeway. It has a beach, but its fame is due to its incredible collection of ancient Byzantine-style churches, many displaying frescos and other items of considerable artistic value.

Pomoriye sits on a narrow rocky peninsula between the sea and a large salt lagoon. Its proudest product is mud—dark, gray, greasy mud smelling of hydrogen sulphide (like rotten eggs). Special machines dredge it up from the bottom of the lagoon and people come from all over Bulgaria to wallow in the noisome substance, which is rich in iodine compounds and reputedly good for what ails you. About 20 miles south of Bourgas, the fishing village of Sozopol is rather charming and has become a popular meeting place for artists. Still further south, the coast has good beaches and some wild and beautiful scenery, currently the focus of new tourist developments at Dyuni, with the emphasis on camping, self-catering, and sporting activities.

PRACTICAL INFORMATION FOR THE BLACK SEA BEACHES

 HOTELS. An ambitious hotel construction program has equipped most of the beach towns with comfortable modern facilities, ranging from deluxe through second class. Some hotels in Albena, Slunchev Bryag and Zlatni Pyassatsi are year round; rates are 40% less Oct. 1–May 31. Rooms in private homes are available for those interested in close contact with the local life-style.

ALBENA. *Dobroudja* (E), has excellent facilities only a short walk from the beach. *Dobrotitsa* (M), *Dorostor* (M) and *Orlov* (M) are near the beach. Restaurants with cabarets include *Arabella* (E), on board a frigate, and *Gorski Tsar* (E). *Orehite* (Walnut Trees) (M), open air, folk show; *Slavianski Kt* (M), specialty dishes, folk show; *Starobulgarski Stan* (M), game specialties, folk show.

DROUZHBA. *Grand Hotel Varna* (L), a Swedish-built Interhotel, is the best on the coast, with 296 rooms, 37 suites, night club, indoor and outdoor pools, saunas, varied sports facilities and full amenities for balneotherapeutic treatment. *Chaika* (M), 100 rooms, no restaurant; *Rubin* (I), 130 rooms, no restaurant. *Drouzhba Cottage Colony* offers self-catering accommodations. *Bulgarska Svatba* (M), *Manastirska Izba* (I) and *Mehana Chernomorets* (I) are folk restaurants.

DYUNI. New Austrian-built hotel and apartment complex with wide range of facilities, 6 miles south of Sozopol.

SLUNCHEV BRYAG (Sunny Beach). Particularly well equipped for children, the resort consists of a number of hotel complexes, each with restaurants, shops and other amenities. The following are all by or near the beach: *Bourgas* (M), 250 rooms, indoor and open-air pools; *Glarus* (M), 220 rooms; *Globus* (M), 100 rooms, probably the best, indoor pool; *Kuban* (M), 210 rooms, in resort center; *Chaika* (I), 85 rooms; *Nessebur* (I), 160 rooms. Near the resort, the cottage colonies of *Zora* and, a few miles further north, *Elenite* offer self-catering accommodations in complexes with shops and restaurants. The latter features a cultural center as well. Folk restaurants include *Bchvata* (M), *Hanska Shatra* (M), about 5 km. up in the hills, *Picnic* (M), about 13 km. north, with fire dancing and barbecue, *Vyatrna Melnitsa* (M) (above the resort), and *Churchura* (I). *Neptun* (I) and *Strandja* (I) are restaurants with taverns. *Ribarska Hiza*, by the beach, specializes in fish. *Lazur* and *Rusalka* are discos.

VARNA. Historic Black Sea port. *Tcherno More* (Black Sea) (E), is a recent Interhotel with 220 rooms, 4 suites, and night club; well sited near Marine Gardens; *Odessa* (I), overlooks Marine Gardens. In restored old Druzki St., *Starata Kushta* is one of several restaurants and bars featuring national specialties in an old-time atmosphere.

ZLATNI PYASSATSI (Golden Sands). Resort with wide range of facilities, including modern year-round spa treatment. *Ambassador* (E), 130 rooms, indoor and openair pools, medical center, recently renovated, wooded setting; *Astoria* (E), 70 rooms, night club; *International* (E), 210 rooms, indoor pool, medical center, in resort center; *Metropol* (M), 100 rooms, no restaurant but 10th floor bar with good views; *Morsko Oko* (M), 90 rooms; *Diana* (I), no restaurant, wooded setting some distance from beach. A number of folk restaurants include *Kosharata* (Sheepfold) on the outskirts of the resort, attractively set amidst the trees and with a lively folkloric show. Others, all (M), are *Mecha Poljana*, *Trifon Zarezan* and *Vodenitsata*. *Ruska Trojka* and *Tsiganski Tabor* have variety programs and *Kukeri* is a disco; all (E).

CYPRUS

Cyprus has been a divided island since 1974, when years of communal strife between the Greek-Cypriot majority and the Turkish-Cypriot minority reached a climax with the occupation of the northern part of the island by Turkish troops. Common sense—and economic sense—will probably prevail eventually and bring down the unhappy barriers, but at the time of writing northern Cyprus is still under Turkish military occupation and even intercommunal talks under UN auspices have so far failed to bring about a solution to the problem.

One might have thought that the island's troubles would have sounded the death knell for its tourist industry, but on both sides of the so-called "Attila Line" which divides the island, Cyprus is once again becoming the popular resort that it was a decade ago—aided by superb weather, beautiful scenery, friendly people and a low cost of living. Furthermore, most people the tourist is likely to come into contact with speak English.

The Greek Cypriots, whose territory—the only part of the island to be internationally recognized—is known as the Republic of Cyprus, have built a new airport near the port of Larnaca, to replace the former airport at Nicosia, which is now occupied by the United Nations Peace-keeping Force. A second airport, in the west of the island near Paphos, is now open. To the east of Nicosia, which, itself divided between Greek and Turkish Cypriots, acts as capital of both states, the Turkish Cypriots have built their own airport at Ercan. The Greek Cypriots have been fortunate in that the south coast is, perhaps, the most beautiful part of Cyprus anyway; but the Turkish Cypriots—who call their territory the Turkish Republic of Northern Cyprus—have a splendid series of sandy beaches and two of the most picturesque towns in the island. The Republic of Cyprus has the higher standard of living, and certainly a greater number of high-rises; but North Cyprus can provide every comfort too.

In the following pages we shall try to give a fair and objective picture of both parts of Cyprus.

PRACTICAL INFORMATION FOR CYPRUS

WHAT WILL IT COST. The monetary unit in the Republic of Cyprus is the Cyprus pound (C£), which is divided into 100 cents. At the time of writing (spring 1986) the exchange rate is about 60 Cyprus cents to the U.S. dollar and 80 to the pound sterling. There are notes of C£10, C£5, C£1 and 50 Cyprus cents, and coins for 20, 10, 5, 2, 1 and ½ Cyprus cents.

In the north the monetary unit is the Turkish lira (TL), which has been subject to considerable inflation; at the time of writing, there are about 600 TL to the dollar and about 850 to the pound sterling. There are notes for 10,000, 5,000, 1,000, 500, 100, 50, 20 and 10 TL, and coins for lesser sums.

There is little overall difference in the level of prices between the two parts of the island; but in the north wine, beer and spirits (which are produced locally in the south) tend to be more expensive as, for the most part, they are imported from Turkey.

A typical moderate day might cost two people (in U.S. dollars):

Hotel: double room with bath, breakfast and taxes	$40.00
Lunch at moderate restaurant or taverna, excluding drink	10.00
Dinner at good hotel or restaurant, excluding drink	15.00
Bottle of good wine in restaurant	2.00
Large bottle of beer in restaurant or bar	1.00
Coffee (Turkish) in popular café	1.00
Local transport and sightseeing	2.50
Evening's entertainment	5.00
Miscellaneous (10%)	7.50
	$84.00

WHEN TO COME. With such an equable and delightful climate the choice of when to visit this sunblessed island presents few, if any, problems. The seemingly endless summers can last from as early as March through to November, when temperatures in the lower seventies are regularly recorded. We give here the average maximum daily temperatures at Nicosia, in Fahrenheit and Centigrade:

	Jan.	Feb.	Mar.	Apr.	May	June	July	Aug.	Sep.	Oct.	Nov.	Dec.
F°	58	59	65	74	83	91	97	97	91	81	72	62
C°	14	15	18	23	28	32	36	36	32	27	22	17

VISAS. Nationals of the United States, Western Europe and the Commonwealth do not require visas for entry into either zone of Cyprus and can stay for three months. However, you must of course have a valid passport.

HEALTH CERTIFICATES. These are not required for entry into Cyprus.

GETTING TO CYPRUS. See separate sections for Republic of Cyprus and Northern Cyprus.

CUSTOMS. Customs regulations are minimal, but the export of antiques and archeological treasures is strictly forbidden.

FOOD AND DRINK. At the larger hotels in both Greek and Turkish Cyprus, food tends to be of an international type, though local dishes are often also served. But all over the island there are restaurants, small and large, which offer genuine Cypriot food, often quite mouth-watering, such as *kebab* (pieces of lamb or other meat skewered and roasted over a charcoal fire). Other favorites are *dolmas* (vegetable leaves stuffed with minced meat and rice) and *tava* (a tasty stew of meat, herbs and onions). Fresh fruit is plentiful and cheap and the *very* sweet desserts, such as *baklava*, are to be found everywhere. Cyprus produces excellent wines, spirits and beer which, however, can only be found in the south. In the north, drinks are mostly imported from the Turkish mainland, and, while also very good, tend to be more expensive than in the south. Coffee is served Turkish-style (sweet, medium-sweet or without sugar), and English tea is to be obtained everywhere.

TIPPING. A service-charge is usually made on bills, but a tip is rarely refused.

SHOPPING. Hand-made lace, and embroidery and leather goods are particularly worth buying. The usual shopping hours are from around 8 to around 1; afternoon hours vary with the season. Many shops close on Wednesday and Saturday afternoons. Throughout Cyprus the unit of weight is the *oke* (*okká*, = 2.8 lbs), divided into 400 drams; but the metric system is being gradually introduced.

GETTING AROUND CYPRUS. By car. British and international driving licenses are acceptable, or you can get a visitor's permit by presenting your national license and a passport-type photograph. In Cyprus, you drive on the *left*. The main road system is extensive and well-surfaced, but many of the roads are narrow and have sharp curves; there are service stations every few miles. You can hire a car (in both zones) from around $15 a day up; four-star fuel, at the time of writing, was around $2.50 a gallon.

By bus and taxi. Bus services link the main towns, but most visitors prefer to book a seat in a shared taxi (in the north called a *dolmush*); ask at your hotel reception desk. These run regularly, quickly and very cheaply between all the main towns and resorts. For instance, the fare from Nicosia to Larnaca (26 miles), in the south, is about $1.50 and from Nicosia to Kyrenia (16 miles), in the north, is about 50 cents.

Traveling between the two halves of Cyprus is extremely difficult, if not impossible.

The Republic of Cyprus

Nicosia, the capital, is famous for its great Venetian walls and for its splendid museum, which shows the island's history since the Neolithic age. The town is divided into two by the so-called "Green Line" and many of the more interesting ancient monuments are in the northern, Turkish, sector. (**Note:** It is at presstime impossible to cross over into the northern sector, even on foot.)

Many visitors, however, will prefer the many delightful seaside resorts. Larnaca, where your plane lands, makes an excellent center, with fine beaches close at hand. Limassol also has excellent beaches and to that it adds lively night life. Paphos, in the west of the island, is quietly beautiful and of historic interest. Ayia Napa, east of Limassol, is the latest, and perhaps most fashionable, resort. The Troödos Mountains, north of Limassol, provide shady coolness in summer; in winter they are visited for their excellent skiing facilities.

PRACTICAL INFORMATION FOR THE REPUBLIC OF CYPRUS

SOURCES OF INFORMATION. For information on all aspects of travel to the Republic of Cyprus, the Cyprus Tourist Office is an invaluable source of information. Its addresses are:
In the U.S.: 13 East 40th St., New York, N.Y. 10016.
In the U.K.: 213 Regent St., London W.1.

GETTING THERE. By plane. From North America, you fly to London, Paris, Frankfurt, Zurich, Vienna or Athens, from where there are direct flights to Larnaca and Paphos by *Cyprus Airways* (also *British Airways* in the case of London).

PUBLIC HOLIDAYS. Jan. 1 (New Year's Day); Jan. 6 (Epiphany); Mar. 2 ("Clean Monday"); Mar. 25; Apr. 1 (Eoka); Apr. 17, 19 (Easter); Jun. 27 (*Kataklysmos*—Day of the Holy Spirit); Aug. 3 (anniversary death of Pres. Makarios); Aug. 15 (Virgin Mary); Oct. 1 (Republic); Oct. 28 (National Day); Dec. 24–26 (shops open Dec. 24).

HOTELS AND RESTAURANTS. Full board at a Deluxe (L) hotel will cost about $60 a day for two; at an Expensive (E) hotel about $50; at a Moderate (M) hotel about $40; and at an Inexpensive (I) hotel around $35. These prices include double room with bath, service and taxes. The Deluxe and many Expensive hotels have full airconditioning. Hotel food is good, though sometimes unimaginative, and half-board, which will allow you once a day to follow the locals and see where they eat, is an agreeable alternative. In all major resorts there are restaurants of every category, from the fashionable fish-restaurant to the simple *taverna* (where you will often eat well for as little as C£2–C£3 a head). Here is a selection of what is available:

AYIA NAPA. *Grecian Bay* (L), (tel. 046–21301), on the beach. Pool, tennis, sauna, dancing. *Sunrise Beach* (E), at Paralimni (tel. 046–21501). Pool, tennis. *Nissi Beach* (M), also at Paralimni (tel. 046–21021), Pool, tennis, dancing.
Restaurants. There are many good fish restaurants.

LARNACA. *Sun Hall* (E), on sea front (tel. 041–53341). Good restaurant; dancing. *Four Lanterns* (M), on sea front (tel. 041–52011). Good restaurant; dancing. *Lordos Beach* (M), by the sea just outside town (tel. 041–57444). Pool, tennis, dancing.
Restaurants. *Cyprus Tavern* and *Monte Carlo,* both praised; *Venus Beach,* good fish.

LIMASSOL. *Amathus Beach* (L), on the beach 6 miles east (tel. 051–66152). Has everything that goes with five stars. *Curium Palace* (E), not on sea, but with superb pool (tel. 051–63121). *Pavemar* (M), small pleasant hotel on sea front (tel. 051–63535). Pool, dancing. *Pissouri Beach* (M), 25 miles west of town (tel. 052–214567); praised.
Restaurants. *Britannia; Scott's Steak House; Lihnari* is a first-rate taverna.

NICOSIA. *Cyprus Hilton* (L), Makarios Avenue (tel. 021–64040). All facilities; probably the island's best hotel; pool, tennis, dancing. *Churchill* (E), Achaeans Street (tel. 021–48858). Central and good value; dancing. *Philoxenia* (E), Eylenja Avenue (tel. 021–72181). Small but good; central. *Kennedy* (M), Regaena Street (tel. 021–75131). Very central; pool.
Restaurants. *Theo's; Plaka; Scorpio's,* pricey but worth it.

PAPHOS. *Paphos Beach* (E), St. Antonios Street (tel. 061–33091). Every comfort: pool, tennis, dancing. *Aloe* (M), St. Antonios Street (tel. 061–34000). Pool, dancing. Both these are near the sea. *Apollo* (M), in the town, with pool (tel. 061–33909); praised. There are many other (M) and (I) hotels.
Restaurants. There are several excellent fish restaurants.

PEDHOULAS. *Jack's* (I), (tel. 054–52350). Small, comfortable hotel in pleasant village in the Troödos Mountains.

PLATRES. *Forest Park* (E), (tel. 054–27151). Resort-style hotel in the Troödos Mountains, 1,725 ft above sea level. Pool, tennis, dancing.

MAIL. Postal rates (subject to change) are: to the U.S. and the U.K. (airmail): letters 35 Cyprus cents; postcards 30 Cyprus cents to the U.S., 25 Cyprus cents to the U.K.

USEFUL ADDRESSES. *U.S. Embassy:* near Hilton Hotel. *British High Commission:* Pallis Street. *Tourist Offices:* Nicosia, 18 Theodotou Street (tel. 43374); Larnaca, Democratias Square (tel. 54322); Limassol, Spyrou Araouzou Street (tel. 62676); Paphos, Gladstone Street (tel. 32841).

North Cyprus

The Turkish half of Nicosia is the capital of North Cyprus; in addition to the vast Venetian walls already mentioned, it contains the Selimiye Mosque, formerly the church of St. Sophia and a fine example of 13th-century Gothic architecture. Other interesting monuments include the former *Tekké* or monastery of the Whirling Dervishes, now a museum.

Of the coastal resorts, Kyrenia, situated around its picturesque semicircular yacht-filled harbor, is the chief attraction. There are excellent bathing beaches east and west of the town, which is once again attracting many foreign tourists and has a number of British residents. The ruins of the former abbey of Bellapais, a few miles out, should on no account be missed. Famagusta, North Cyprus's chief port, has fine Venetian walls and a Gothic cathedral, now a mosque. Many of its hotels lie empty and desolate in a sort of "no-man's-land" between Greek and Turkish Cypriot, but several good hotels, most of them standing on superb beaches, are once again open.

It is important to note that Turkish names—some of them the original ones—have been given to all towns and villages in North Cyprus and it is these names which you will usually find on signposts; thus Nicosia is now officially Lefkoşa, Kyrenia has become Girne and Famagusta is now Magosa. A useful map showing the new names is to be had free from travel offices.

PRACTICAL INFORMATION FOR NORTH CYPRUS

SOURCES OF INFORMATION. For information on many aspects of travel to the Turkish Republic of North Cyprus contact:
   In the U.S.: Nail Atalay, 821 UN Plaza, New York, N.Y. 10017 (tel. 212–687 2350).
   In the U.K.: Cyprus Turkish Airlines, 28 Cockspur St., London S.W.1 (tel. 839 5530).

GETTING THERE. By plane. From London, Frankfurt, Milan and Paris by *Turkish Airlines* to Istanbul or Izmir, thence by *Cyprus Turkish Airlines* to Ercan, near Nicosia. There are direct flights in the summer from London to Ercan; information from Cyprus Turkish Airlines. **By boat.** Ferries from the Turkish ports of Taşucu and Mersin to Kyrenia and Famagusta, respectively.

PUBLIC HOLIDAYS. Jan. 1 (New Year's Day); Apr. 23 (National Independence Day); May 1 (May Day); May 19 (Youth and Sports Festival); Jun. 20; Jul. 20; Aug. 30 (National Victory Day of the Army); Sept. 6; Oct. 29 (Republic Day); Nov. 15 (Declaration of Independence); Dec. 4, 5. There are also several

Moslem holidays which, being based on the lunar calendar, vary from year to year.

 HOTELS AND RESTAURANTS. All the hotels listed have private baths or showers and most have at least partial airconditioning. Full board at a Deluxe (L) hotel will cost about $50 a day for two; at an Expensive (E) hotel about $45; at a Moderate (M) hotel about $40; and at an Inexpensive (I) hotel about $35. Hotel food can be very good, though all too frequently characterless, and half-board is often preferable. Try the often excellent fish restaurants, or the *kebapçi* (where fresh grills are cooked for you over charcoal). You can eat well for as little as $3.50 and will find it difficult to spend more than $7–$8. These prices are per head and do not include drinks.

FAMAGUSTA. *Palm Beach* (L), (tel. 036–62000). On sea front near old city. Every comfort, nightclub, casino. *Park* (E), (tel. 036–65511). Pool, tennis; warmly recommended. *Salamis Bay* (E), (tel. 036–67200). Pool, tennis. These last two are on beach some six miles north of town. *Boghaz* (M), (tel. 037–12459). 16 miles north, on quiet sandy beach; good food.

  Restaurants. *La Cheminée. Kemal's Fish Restaurant.* Many others.

KYRENIA. *Celebrity* (L), (tel. 08218–751). On beach nine miles west of town, but with the hotel's own bus at guests' disposal. Casino, disco; warmly praised. *Dome* (E), on sea front in town (tel. 081–52453). Pool, casino, popular disco. "Turkish Night" every Saturday, with excellent Turkish food and Turkish dancing. *Dorana* (M), in town (tel. 081–52521). No pool, but very comfortable. *Ergenekon* (I), (tel. 081–52240). Small hotel overlooking harbor.

  Club Acapulco Village, six miles east, has well-appointed bungalows on the beach, with a restaurant, cafeteria and disco. *Ambelia Village,* inland near Bellapais, has studio-flats, pool and shop.

  Restaurants. Many around harbor, of which *Canli Balik* can be recommended; excellent fish dishes. In the town, *Kyrenia Tavern,* with English-speaking owners and a largely British clientele. *Altinkaya,* a fish restaurant five miles west, is very good; so is *Abbey,* at Bellapais four miles southeast, under British management, but with good French food and in a delightful setting.

NICOSIA. *Saray* (M), on Atatürk Square, in city center (tel. 020–71116). Comfortable, with good food and a superb view over town from ninth-floor restaurant. *Picnic* (I), (tel. 020–72122) and *Sabri's Orient* (I), (tel. 020–72161), both in suburbs.

  Restaurant. See *Saray* hotel, above.

MAIL. Rates vary with the level of inflation.

 USEFUL ADDRESSES. *Tourist Offices:* Nicosia, Mehmet Akif Avenue; Kyrenia, opposite Dome hotel; Famagusta, Fevzi Çakmak Boulevard. The *British High Commission* has an office in the Turkish sector of Nicosia.

CZECHOSLOVAKIA

At the very heart of Europe, Czechoslovakia has been the meeting place of many influences throughout her checkered history, as well as contributing enormously to the arts and the revolutionary thought of earlier centuries. Here, too, some of Europe's finest mountains unfold in increasing grandeur out of the great Danubian plains, and folkloric traditions die hard in secluded valleys.

Historically part of a loose alignment of Central European kingdoms, modern Czechoslovakia is a political union of three contrasting provinces. The Czechs, who are clever and rather serious, predominate in the western province of Bohemia, where wealthy burghers' houses still fill the narrow streets of gracious spa towns with beguiling Central European charm. In contrast, the Slavs of Slovakia are more easygoing, their landscapes characterized by virgin forests, hidden lakes and the craggy peaks of the Tatra mountain range gradually dropping down to the Danube. Moravia's gently undulating scenery, Renaissance towns and painted wooden villages link the two together.

Czechoslovakia has suffered from her geographical position in modern as well as ancient times, not least during the events leading to World War II and again, in 1968, when attempts to combine Communist ideology with democratic rights finally brought Soviet tanks rumbling into the streets of Prague. Whatever your views, it is wise to keep an open mind and respect the efforts of these intelligent and talented people to improve their lot—as indeed they have—in this sensitive corner of Europe.

Tourism here is best geared to prepaid services, which are available for independent travelers as well as groups; without these, you may run into varying degrees of bureaucratic frustration, though if you are prepared to take your chances, you may well end up with a unique experience of this rich and varied country. Enthusiasts of art, music and fine old architecture will be especially rewarded, but there are also good opportunities for all kinds of outdoor activities.

PRACTICAL INFORMATION FOR
CZECHOSLOVAKIA

WHAT WILL IT COST. Increased food prices have raised the cost of living in Czechoslovakia, but it still compares favorably with its western neighbors. Prices quoted in the following pages are based on those available in 1986, so allow for a slight increase.

Prague continues to be relatively the most expensive place, followed by the Slovak capital Bratislava, the Moravian capital, Brno, the High Tatra resorts (though these are good value for the budget-minded skier) and those in the Krkonose (Giant Mountains).

The monetary unit is the *koruna (Kcs.)*, divided into 100 *haler*. There are coins of 10, 20 and 50 halers and 1, 2 and 5 Kcs. Banknotes are in denominations of 10, 20, 50, 100, 500 and 1,000 Kcs.

The tourist exchange rate is about 11.50 Kcs. to the US$, 15.50 to the pound sterling. Note that a currency bonus was introduced in 1981 for those traveling on package tours (see below). Visitors must exchange a sum representing the value of their living expenses in Czechoslovakia at a minimum of 30 DM (approx. $10.20 or £8) per day per adult. Children from 6–14 years pay half this amount, and those under 6 are exempt. If you have booked on a prepaid tour, you will already have met this obligation and need only quote the reference number of the tour when applying for a visa. If you have a voucher for hotel accommodations or other prepaid services, or a *Cedok* currency voucher, these are also evidence that you have met the obligatory minimum expenditure. If you have no prepaid services, you will be required to make the necessary exchange on arrival in Czechoslovakia.

Foreign currency can be exchanged at any branch of the *Czechoslovak State Bank*, *Cedok* offices, most hotels, and in *Tuzex* stores in exchange for vouchers valid only in *Tuzex;* also at certain frontier customs offices. The import and export of Czechoslovak currency is *not* permitted. All exchanges should be noted on your visa as only surplus korunas from such exchanges, beyond the minimum required daily exchange rate, should be refunded to you in hard currency at your departure, but there can be communication problems.

A typical day for two people in Prague might cost:

Hotel (moderate) with breakfast	450	Kcs.
Lunch in moderate restaurant	140	
Dinner in first-class restaurant (with wine)	200	
Beer (in popular tavern)	14	
Coffee (in popular cafe)	12	
Tram, anywhere in city	2	
Taxi (about 5 km)	30	
Theater, opera, good seats	80–120	
Miscellaneous 10%	80	
	1048	Kcs.

Note: A currency bonus amounting to about 36% above the current tourist exchange rate is granted to those who have booked a *Cedok* tour (other than the Economy Tour) or spa treatment. To obtain this, you should purchase from *Cedok* prior to departure a special bonus currency voucher for the amount you require; this can only be exchanged at *Cedok* exchange offices in Prague, at any *Cedok* hotel, or at a *Balnea* hotel or sanatorium. Czech crowns thus acquired cannot be re-converted into foreign currency.

Travelers' checks and credit cards such as American Express, Diners and Eurocard may be used to exchange currency and are also accepted in better hotels and restaurants.

HOW TO GO. All foreign travel to Czechoslovakia is handled by *Cedok*, the Czechoslovak State Travel Bureau. Unlike the State Travel Offices of other East European countries, you may actually book tours to Czechoslovakia via *Cedok* as well as through the many travel agents officially accredited by them. A list of these travel agents is available from *Cedok* offices; they include many of the major agents both in the UK and the US. The tours include week-end and longer stays in Prague, one-center arrangements, coach tours of varying duration, a wide range of motoring or spa holidays, and packages based on the Prague Spring Music Festival or any number of sporting or other special-interest activities. Both *Cedok* and travel agents are also able to supply pre-paid vouchers and will be able to arrange visas (which all Western visitors for Czechoslovakia require).

As well as the many offices they have within Czechoslovakia itself, *Cedok* has a number of offices overseas. Its addresses are:

In the US: 10 East 40th St., New York, NY 10016 (tel. 212–689–9720).
In the UK: 17–18 Old Bond St., London W.1 (tel. 01–629 6058).

WHEN TO COME. Art, architecture, history, etc. can of course be enjoyed at any time, but note that some monuments, especially castles, are closed in winter. Spring and summer are generally best for sightseeing. May is an excellent time to go—for fruit blossom and for the Prague Spring Music Festival. The forests are glorious in the fall. The winter sports season is mid-December through April.

Climate. Continental: warm summers, cold winters.

Average maximum daily temperatures in degrees Fahrenheit and centigrade:

Prague	Jan.	Feb.	Mar.	Apr.	May	June	July	Aug.	Sept.	Oct.	Nov.	Dec.
F°	34	37	45	55	64	72	73	73	64	54	41	34
C°	1	3	7	13	18	22	23	23	18	12	5	1

SPECIAL EVENTS. Every five years (next in 1990), the Spartakiada is one of the world's greatest gymnastic events. *April,* Consumer Goods Fair, Brno; *April/May,* Flora Olomouc, flower show, Olomouc; *May,* Prague Spring Music Festival; Dvorak Music Festival, Pribram; Summer Theater in Castle grounds, Karlstejn and Konopiste (through August); *June,* Bratislava International Song Festival; Straznice Folk Art Festival; *July,* Vychodna Folk Art Festivals; Brno Grand Prix Motor Rally; Karlovy Vary International Film Festival (biennial); *July–August,* Bratislava Music Summer; International Festival of Dance, Telc; *September,* Znojmo Wine Festival; Engineering Trade Fair, Brno; *October,* Brno Music Festival; Bratislava International Music Festival; Pardubice Grand Steeplechase.

National Holidays. Jan. 1 (New Year's Day); Apr. 20 (Easter Mon.); May 1 (Labor Day); May 9 (Liberation); Dec. 25, 26.

HEALTH CERTIFICATES. No vaccinations are required.

GETTING TO CZECHOSLOVAKIA. By Plane. *CSA* (*Ceskoslovenske Aeroline*) maintains direct flights between New York and Montreal and Prague. There are almost daily nonstop flights from London and most major Continental cities to Prague. You usually have the choice of *CSA* or the carrier of the country you are flying from. There is a regular bus service from Ruzyne airport to town (15 km).

By Train. The most convenient route from Western Europe to Prague is from Paris (in summer this train is known as the *Zapadian Express*). The train leaves Paris late in the evening and travels via Mainz, Frankfurt, Nürnberg and Plzen and arrives in the Czech capital in the early evening of the following day, taking about 19 hours in all for the trip. It carries 1st. and 2nd. class sleepers (except on Saturdays), 2nd. class couchettes and both 1st. and 2nd. class day carriages. A buffet car operates from, and to, Frankfurt. Other trains to Prague leave from

Nürnberg and Stuttgart and from East Berlin. The best connection for Bratislava is from Vienna by bus.

By Car. Drivers will need a registration certificate for their vehicle, an International Driving Permit and the International Green Card for insurance (not compulsory but highly recommended). In difficulty contact the *Central Automobile Club* (*Ustredni Autoklub CSSR*), 29 Opletalova, Prague, tel. 22–49 –06 or 77–34–55; or *Autoturist,* Na Rybnicku 16, Prague 2, tel. 20–33–55.

It has become much easier to get "super" gasoline, but it is still wise to fill up when you can if you have a long drive ahead. Filling stations are quite often closed in the evenings. Petrol coupons reduce the price (see below).

Cedok now arrange a selection of motoring holidays ex-UK.

CUSTOMS. Personal belongings may be brought in duty-free. Also 250 cigarettes, 1 liter spirits, 2 liters wine. Jewelry and other valuable objects should be entered on your customs declarations. Foreigners are permitted to import duty free up to 600 Kcs. worth of gifts and souvenirs. Purchases up to 300 Kcs. may be exported, but note that certain items, including cut glass, porcelain and sports goods, require an export license and are subject to 100% duty. However, additional to the allowance, more valuable items purchased for officially exchanged currency, including articles from *Tuzex,* may be exported duty-free provided you have the bills.

HOTELS. Accommodations are now officially classified by the international one- to five-star system of classification. It is important to remember that most hotels have rooms in more than one category. *Cedok* runs the largest group, known as *Interhotels,* in which approximate prices per person in a double room with bath or shower and half board (bed and breakfast only in 5-star) are: 5-star, Deluxe or (L) $40–50; 4-star, Expensive or (E) $25–40; 3-star or Moderate (M) $15–35; and 2-star, Inexpensive or (I) $12–20. Prices at the higher end of the scale apply to main cities and resorts in the high season; lowest prices apply in other centers or in the low season. Accommodations in hotels operated by other groups and following a similar system of classification can be booked through *Cedok* and, as there is a shortage of accommodations in Czechoslovakia, it is wise to make advance reservations. Those without prebookings in Prague, however, should go to *Cedok's Department for Accommodation Services* at Panska 5, or *Pragotur* (for non-*Cedok* hotels), U Obecniho domu, both in city center. If you don't have prepaid vouchers for accommodations, you must be prepared to show evidence of how you obtained the Czechoslovak currency with which you wish to pay. The latter regulation is sometimes misinterpreted by hotel receptionists, who may ask you to pay in foreign currency. Private accommodations are now marketed by Cedok ex-UK, or if you haven't prebooked you can try either *Cedok* or *Pragotur,* at the above address.

Motels and Self-catering. *Cedok* run a number, generally modern, conveniently located motels, some with pools and tennis, offering half board at rather less than comparable hotel rates.

Holidays in self-catering accommodations in central Prague are now marketed by *Cedok* ex-UK. Otherwise, there are self-catering cottages or bungalows attached to many motels or autocamps.

CAMPING. The price range is $1–$1.80 per night in own tent, according to site category, plus a small charge per car or caravan. A map marking and listing all sites is available from *Cedok.*

RESTAURANTS. The cost of a main course using prepaid meal vouchers is: 5-star (L) $8.30–11.90; 4-star (E) $5.50–7.80; 3-star (M) $4.20; and 2-star (I) $3.20. Otherwise, for a full meal in restaurants estimate deluxe (L) 300 Kcs., Expensive (E) 100–200 Kcs., Moderate (M) 60–100 Kcs., and Inexpensive (I) 30–60 Kcs. You will find a wide selection of attractive restaurants, beer taverns and wine cellars in which light snacks are also available; also inexpensive self-service snack bars.

Food and Drink. A square meal starts off with a flourish of assorted cold meats—famous Prague ham, smoked tongue, Russian crab meat in mayonnaise, eggs with caviar—all garnished with plenty of pickles. As for meat, it is usually well-cooked, drowned in delicious thick gravy and accompanied by large dough *knedliky,* the Czechs' beloved dumplings. Roast pork, duck and goose all come carrying their cargo of knedliky and *zeli* or spiced red cabbage. Desserts are rich. But what is sadly lacking are fresh vegetables and salads.

Na zdravi! means "To your health!" in flawless Czech and best said to the music of two clinking mugs of *Pilsner* (Urquell) beer. *Slivovice,* a strong plum brandy, *borovicka,* a pungent gin, and *becherovka,* a herb brandy, are among the local spirits. Pleasant table wines come from Melnik and Moravia. Excellent wines (even champagne) also come from the Bratislava region.

 TIPPING. In a popular restaurant, it is usual to round up a bill by 2–3 Kcs. If in doubt, 10% is generous. Hotels and restaurants include a service charge of 10% in better places, 5% in others.

MAIL. An airmail letter to the US costs 6 Kcs., a postcard 5 Kcs.; 4 Kcs. for both to a European country. There is a 24-hour service at the main post office, Jindrisska Ulice 24, Nove Mesto, Prague.

 CLOSING TIMES. Generally, opening hours are from 9 A.M. to 6 P.M., Monday through Friday, with stores often closing for lunch and early on Saturdays. Main stores open Thursdays to 8 P.M. Food stores open early and close late. Banks open 8 A.M. to 2 P.M. Monday through Friday.

PHOTOGRAPHY. Do not photograph railway tunnels, steam locomotives, frontier areas or near barracks or military installations.

 USEFUL ADDRESSES. *US Embassy,* Mala Strana, Trziste 15; *British Embassy,* Mala Strana, Thunovska Ulice 14; *Canadian Embassy,* Mickiewiczova 6; *Cedok,* Na Prikope 18; *Cedok Accommodations Service,* Panska 5; *Prague Information Service,* Na Prikope 20; *CSA* (ticket office), Stare Mesto, Revolucni 1, and air terminal, Vltava Building, Revolucni 24; *British Airways,* Nove Mesto, Stepanska 63; *Swissair,* Stare Mesto, Parizska 11; *Balnea* (for spa treatment), Parizska 11. *Emergency* tel. 154 (motoring), 155 (medical help), 158 (police).

 GETTING AROUND CZECHOSLOVAKIA. By Plane. Regular *CSA* flights connect Prague with Banska Bystrica, Bratislava, Brno, Karlovy Vary, Kosice, Ostrava, Piestany, Poprad (for the High Tatras).

By Train. The country has a good network of trains reaching to all the main cities and towns. The principal lines are electrified. From Prague there are several fast expresses all carrying either a dining car or buffet car to other cities like Brno, Bratislava, Plzen and Kosice as well as to the spas such as Karlovy Vary and Marianske Lazne. A supplement is payable for travel on the principal expresses except where tickets have been purchased outside Czechoslovakia. There are no special tourist tickets, but costs are reasonable. On some journeys, bus travel is both cheaper and faster than by train and then seat reservations are a must.

By Car. Traffic drives on the right; usual Continental rules of the road are observed, except that a right turn is permitted on a red light (watch for arrows). There is a speed limit of 60 kph in built-up areas. Seat belts are compulsory and drinking absolutely prohibited.

You can purchase gasoline or diesel coupons entitling you to a reduction from *Cedok* in London, from *Zivnostenska Banka,* 104–106 Leadenhall St, London EC3 4AA or at border crossings. It's best to purchase them in advance to avoid tiresome waits. The saving is about 20%, unless you are entitled to the currency bonus (see p. 132), in which case it is not worth getting the coupons. Note that diesel is only available from a limited number of gasoline stations; Cedok can provide a list. The larger service stations can handle repairs, but best bring a spare parts kit.

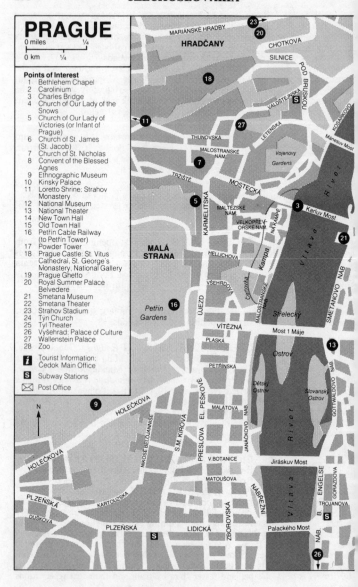

PRAGUE

0 miles ¼

0 km ¼

Points of Interest

1 Bethlehem Chapel
2 Carolinium
3 Charles Bridge
4 Church of Our Lady of the Snows
5 Church of Our Lady of Victories (or Infant of Prague)
6 Church of St. James (St. Jacob)
7 Church of St. Nicholas
8 Convent of the Blessed Agnes
9 Ethnographic Museum
10 Kinský Palace
11 Loretto Shrine; Strahov Monastery
12 National Museum
13 National Theater
14 New Town Hall
15 Old Town Hall
16 Petřín Cable Railway (to Petřín Tower)
17 Powder Tower
18 Prague Castle: St. Vitus Cathedral, St. George's Monastery, National Gallery
19 Prague Ghetto
20 Royal Summer Palace Belvedere
21 Smetana Museum
22 Smetana Theater
23 Strahov Stadium
24 Týn Church
25 Tyl Theater
26 Vyšehrad; Palace of Culture
27 Wallenstein Palace
28 Zoo

ℹ️ Tourist Information: Čedok Main Office

Ⓢ Subway Stations

✉️ Post Office

Among several new highways is the recently completed motorway from Prague via Brno to Bratislava. European roads, marked "E", are usually in good condition. Secondary roads are also good, and rougher roads off the beaten track are usually rewarded by splendid countryside. The patrols of the Automobile Club render assistance to motorists on all busy roads. For help, contact *Central Automobile Club*, 29 Opletalova, Prague, tel. 773455 or 224906; or *Autoturist*, Na Rybnicku 16, Prague 2, tel. 203355.

Cars may be hired through *Avis* and *Pragocar* at Ruzyne airport and Stepanska 42, Prague, or pre-booked through *Cedok* in all towns and resorts. Fly-and-drive is also available through *Cedok's* programme ex-London.

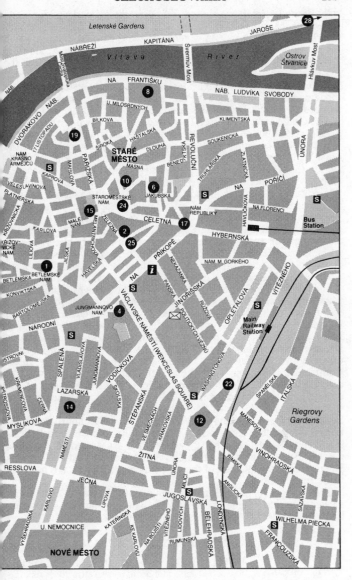

Prague

The best way to get acquainted with Prague is to start with a bird's eye view of it from the corner of Hradcanske Namesti (Castle Square). From the parapet overlooking the city you will see a magnificent panorama before you. A high point is the cupola of the baroque St. Nicholas Church. All around it, between the Castle and the Vltava River lies Mala Strana (Lesser Town) with the palaces and gardens built in the 17th and 18th centuries by the aristocracy, and the smaller but still beautiful houses constructed by burghers and artisans. To the

right of the Lesser Town are a series of interlinked parks with promenades and the ruins of a medieval wall. Below you is the 14th-century
Charles Bridge with its two watchtowers and baroque statues, which
is open to pedestrians only. Across the river are the Stare Mesto (Old
Town), the Nove Mesto (New Town) and much of modern Prague. To
the right of the Old Town, just across May 1st Bridge is the domed
neo-Renaissance National Theater, now beautifully restored, with its
modern annex; further down the embankment is Vysehrad Castle
perched on a rock and, in the same area, the fine Palace of Culture.

The Castle area, the Lesser Town and the Old Town are well worth
a visit, preferably on foot. The Hradcany (Castle) complex, once the
seat of Bohemian kings and now the residence of the president of the
republic, is over a thousand years old. It includes every kind of architecture that Prague has known, from early Romanesque (St. George's
Church) to imitation Gothic; the cathedral itself was only completed
this century. Visit the enormous Vladislav Hall where indoor jousting
tournaments were held, the Castle Gallery's spendid collection of
paintings, and the storybook Zlata Ulicka (Golden Lane). On the
righthand side of Castle Square is the National Gallery, on the left the
former Schwarzenberg Palace which is now a military-historical museum. Farther along you will come to Loretto Square with its charming
church housing the Loretto treasure of fabulous religious valuables.

From Castle Square you descend via the medieval Nerudova Street
to the Lesser Town. Notice the beautiful old house signs signifying the
trade of the original occupant. On Mala Strana Square is the 200-year
old church of St. Nicholas, a perfect baroque structure. Then take
Mostecka Street with its attractive shops and walk across Charles
Bridge, an ideal vantage point for Prague's timeless beauty. Turning
left, after about six blocks you'll come to Parizska (Paris Street), a jewel
of art nouveau architecture. On the left is the 20th-century Inter-
Continental Hotel, on the right a 13th-century synagogue with an
amazing cemetery. Continuing down Parizska, where many of the
airlines have their offices, you will come to the Staromestske Namesti,
the magnificent Old Town Square with its gothic Tyn Church. The
Square, and the enchanting 500-year old clock with its hourly presentation, is a favorite meeting place. The tastefully-reconstructed Betlem-
ska Kaple (Bethlehem Chapel) where John Huss used to preach is
nearby. Beyond the Old Town lies Vaclavske Namesti (Wenceslas
Square), commercial heart of the city, which apart from taxis has been
made traffic-free.

The foregoing is perforce only a summary of the wealth of sights an
ancient city like Prague offers. *Cedok's* half-day and day sightseeing
tours (in English) provide a more comprehensive picture.

PRACTICAL INFORMATION FOR PRAGUE

HOTELS. Prague hostelries date partly from the Empire period and a number have been attractively renovated. Unusual are the three floating botels anchored on the
Vltava River. See *Hotels* (above) for guide to rates and
grading system. All hotels listed have all or some rooms with bath or shower,
unless otherwise stated.

Alcron (L), Stepanska 40, Prague 1 (tel. 245741). 150 rooms, good restaurant,
lobby popular rendez-vous for foreigners. Central.

Esplanade (L), Washingtonova 19, Prague 1 (tel. 222552). 65 rooms, famous
Est Bar night club. Elegant, facing park near new Parliament building.

Intercontinental (L), namesti Curieovych, Prague 1 (tel. 2899). 400 rooms,
recent, three restaurants including rooftop restaurant, night club. Splendid
situation in Old Town on banks of River Vltava.

Jalta (L), Vaclavske namesti 45, Prague 1 (tel. 265541). 88 rooms, good
restaurant, popular bar. Central location on Wenceslas Square.

Parkhotel (L-E), Veletrzni 20, Prague 7 (tel. 38070). 228 rooms, modern. Not central.

Panorama (E), Milevska 7, Prague 4 (tel. 416111). 432 rooms and suites. Pool, keep-fit complex, disco, wine-cellar. High-rise, less central but near subway for easy access to center.

Pariz (E), U Obecniho Domu, Prague 1 (tel. 2312051). Over 100 rooms. Tastefully renovated in art nouveau style. Central.

Tri Pstrosi (Three Ostriches) (E), Drazickeho namesti 12, Prague 1 (tel. 536151). Its 18 rooms are the most desirable in town, magically located at Mala Strana end of Charles Bridge, in 17th-century atmospheric inn. Excellent restaurant. Reserve months ahead.

International (E-M), namesti Druzby 1, Prague 6 (tel. 320163). 375 rooms, known to some as the Russian Ritz for its architectural pretensions. Not central.

Olympik (E-M), Invalidovna, Prague 8 (tel. 828541). 314 rooms. Not central.

Europa (M), Vaclavske namesti 29, Prague 1 (tel. 263905). Over 100 rooms. Recently renovated; central.

Splendid (M), Ovenecka 33, Prague 7 (tel. 375451). 40 rooms, quiet location near Strahov Stadium and Zoo.

Zlata Husa (M), Wenceslas Square 7 (tel. 21430).

Adria (I), Vaclavske namesti 26, Prague 1 (tel. 248622). 46 rooms without bath or shower. No restaurant; central.

Opera (I), Tesnov 13, Prague 1 (tel. 2311467). 75 rooms, a few private baths. Fairly central.

BOTELS. Three botels anchored along the Vltava river are popular despite cramped quarters.

Admiral (M), Horejsi nabrezi, Prague 5 (tel. 547445). 86 rooms. Near Mala Strana (Lesser Town).

Albatros (M), Nabrezi L. Svobody, Prague 1 (tel. 2316996). 82 rooms. Near Old Town.

Racek (M), U Dvorecke louky, Prague 4 (tel. 426051). 86 rooms. Out of city center.

MOTELS. Club Motel (E), at Pruhonice (tel. 723241). 10 km south of city. 92 rooms, well-designed, fun restaurant-club.

Konopiste (E) (tel. Benesov 2748). 44 km south of Prague, near chateau of same name. 40 rooms, autocamp. Nearby, in castle grounds, **Myslivna** (M), 32 rooms, attractive.

Stop (M), Plzenska 103, Prague 5 (tel. 523251). 120 rooms. On road to Plzen.

 RESTAURANTS. Your choice is of typically Czech cooking, international cuisine or foreign specialties. Taverns are divided into better class *vinarny* (serving wine) and more earthy *hospody* (serving beer).

Restaurants are generally open from 11.30 A.M. to midnight. Reservations are advisable. Many are closed weekends or Mondays. There is an all-night snack bar in **Slovansky-Dom** at na Prikope 22.

Chalupa (E), in the Club Motel Prague, 10 km south of town (tel. 723241). Farmhouse atmosphere and country cooking.

Lobkovicka vinarna, Vlasska 17 (tel. 530185). Wine restaurant in Lesser Town with good atmosphere and service.

Opera Grill (E), Divadelni 24, Old Town (tel. 265508). One of the best in town, elegant decor with antique Meissen candelabra, French cuisine.

U Labuti (E), Hradcanske nam. 11, Castle area (tel. 539476). Exclusive dining in tastefully remodeled stables.

U Mecenase (E), Malostranske nam. 10, Lesser Town (tel. 533881). Medieval inn, elegant especially in the back room.

Espreso Kajetanka (M). Just under the castle ramparts, gorgeous view.

Klasterni (M), Narodni Trida 8, Old Town (tel. 294863). Good wine restaurant in former Ursuline convent, for lunch or after-theater snack.

Rotisserie (M), Mikulanska 6, Old Town (tel. 206826). Excellent kitchen, always crowded for lunch.

U Lorety (M), Loretanske nam. 8, Castle area (tel. 536025). Next to the baroque church of the same name with its carillon bells, an agreeable spot.

U **Zlate Ulicky Grill Bar** (M), U Daliborky 8. In the Castle grounds. Food served with care.

Valdstejnska Hospoda (M), Valdstejnske nam., Lesser Town (tel. 536195). Pleasant; good food (international or Czech).

Vikarka (M), Hrad Vikarska 6, Prague (tel. 536910). Very popular, may be crowded.

U **Medvidku** (I), Na Perstyne 7, Old Town (tel. 246114). South Bohemian food in a jolly atmosphere.

U **Pastyrky** (I), Belehradska 12, Prague 4 (tel. 434093). Slovak setting, simple and good.

TAVERNS, BARS AND WINE CELLARS. U Zlate Konvice (E), Melantrichova 20, Old Town (tel. 262128). Unusual underground Gothic labyrinth with tables set among huge wine barrels. Generous portions, but cold food only.

U **Fleku** (M), Kremencova 11, New Town (tel. 293937). Most famous of all Prague's beer taverns, brewing its own 13° caramel-dark beer. Several rooms and entertainment, garden, convivial atmosphere.

U **Kalicha** (M), Na Bojisti 12, Prague 2 (tel. 296017). Associated with the Good Soldier Svejk. Czech food.

U **Maliru** (M), Maltezske nam. 11 (tel. 531883). 16th century, in lovely old part of town. Relaxed, Bohemian atmosphere.

U **Rudolfa II** (M), Maislova 3, Old Town (tel. 2312643). Very small, intimate, excellent food.

U **Tomase** (M), Letenska 12, Lesser Town (tel. 536262). Founded by Augustinian monks in 14th century. Serves super 12° dark ale in ancient-style rooms; plain honest food.

U **Zelene Zaby** (M), U Radnice 8, Old Town (tel. 262815). Medieval home of a legendary hangman, popular with the young arty set. Cold snacks are overpriced.

U **Zlateho Jelena** (M), Celetna 11, Old Town (tel. 268595). A restored ancient wine cellar.

U **Bonaparta** (I), Nerudova 29, Lesser Town. Packed with young people.

U **Pinkasu** (I), Jungmanovo nam. 15, Prague 1 (tel. 261804). Popular beer tavern.

U **zlateho tygra** (I), Husova 17, Prague 1 (tel. 265219). Good beer tavern.

TRANSPORTATION. Tickets costing 1 Kcs. are valid for all forms of the city's public transport system; note that each piece of luggage also requires a ticket. Tickets must be bought in advance (you might as well get several) from newsstands, tobacco shops, and some stores and hotels.

By Subway/Underground. Prague's sleek modern network is easy to use and provides the simplest and fastest means of transport. Most new maps of Prague mark the routes.

By Tram/Bus. Tickets should be punched in a machine after boarding the vehicle (watch how others do it). Broadly speaking, trams serve the city center, buses the suburbs and both feed the growing subway network.

By Boat. In summer there are regular trips of varying duration on the Vltava river.

By Taxi. These are marked with a broken white line. Charges are reasonable but taxis can be hard to get.

NIGHTLIFE. Western-style nightlife is not one of Prague's specialties. You can enjoy dinner dancing at the better hotels' restaurants. Some night bars with music and, in some cases, cabaret, are: the *Night Club* at the Intercontinental Hotel, *Est Bar* in the Hotel Esplanade, *Jalta Club* in Hotel Jalta, *Embassy Bar, Park-Club*, the Georgian atmosphere of *Gruzia*, na Prikope 29, and the *Lucerna Bar*, Stepanska 61, near Wenceslas Square. All (E). Others include the *Alhambra*, recently renovated and now a top night club; *Variete Praha*, an entertainments center with a more moderate night club; and the *International Hotel*, which puts on special programs, especially in the season. There are quite a few discos nowadays, including on the three botels listed under *Hotels* (see above).

ENTERTAINMENT. A monthly program of events is available from the Prague Information Service. Book well ahead (through *Cedok,* hotels or box offices), especially during the *Prague Spring Music Festival* (mid May/early June), one of the great events of the European calendar.

Czech opera is outstanding. The *National Theater* (*Narodni Divadlo*) has been magnificently restored, and now it is the turn of the *Tyl Theater* (Zelezna 11, near Old Town Square), which should reopen in 1987. Also notable is the superbly restored *Smetana Theater* (Vitezneho unoro 8, near the National Museum). Remember that the Czechs dress up on such occasions.

The *Laterna Magika* (Narodni 40), an extravaganza combining live actors, mime and advanced cine techniques, is very popular with foreign visitors. This is scheduled to move to the new section of the National Theater. The *Theater on the Balustrade* (*Divadlo Na Zabradli,* Anenske nam. 5) is the home of the famous Black Theater (shadow ballet) and where the mime Fialka and the chanson singer Hegerova perform.

Puppet theater is an art form at the *Spejbl & Hurvinek Theater* (Rimska 45).

Some regular concert venues include the *House of Artists* (*Dum Umelcu*), *Smetanovo Sin,* the *National Museum, Strahov Library,* and various historic palaces. There are regular Mozart concerts at the *villa Bertramka,* marvellous organ recitals in churches such as *St. Jacobs* (Old Town), *U Krizovniku* (near Charles Bridge) and *St. Nicholas* (Lesser Town), and rousing military bands in the *Castle gardens.*

MUSEUMS. There is a large number of good ones, generally open from 9 or 10 to 4 or 5, closed Mondays. Among the best are:

Amerika, Ke Karlovu 20, New Town. Baroque former summer palace, now Dvorak museum.

Bertramka, Mozartova 169. Delightful villa in which Mozart stayed when visiting Prague, now housing Mozart Museum.

Convent of the Blessed Agnes, Anezska ulice, Old Town. Built in the 13th century and recently restored to display 19th-century Czech art.

Jewish Museum. Spread over several buildings in the former ghetto in Old Town, including an old synagogue, ancient cemetery and many Jewish artifacts, and reflecting the Nazi murder of nearly 80,000 Jews in World War II.

National Gallery, Sternberg Palace, Hradcanske nam. 15. Near the castle, with superb collection of woodcuts and carvings; also many paintings by Dürer, Breughel, French Impressionists and others.

National Museum. A landmark dominating Vaclavske nam. (Wenceslas Sq.), built in the 1880s, with historical, archeological and numismatic exhibits and famous mineralogical collection.

St. George's Monastery. Ideal setting in Prague castle for national collection of old Czech art.

Strahov Library, Strahovske nadvori 132. Beautifully-preserved ancient manuscripts, including Bibles from all over the world, but viewing of magnificent rooms restricted to prevent damage.

SHOPPING. *Tuzex,* a government chain selling export items for hard currency, often at lower prices than local currency shops, has several specialist shops in the city center, including *Moser,* Na Prikope 12, for Bohemian glass and porcelain, Rytirska 14 for antiques, and Stepanska 23 or Lazarska 1 for clothes and leather products. *Tuzex* information center is at Rytirska 19, Prague 1. *Tuzex* vouchers make a very welcome gift to your Czech hosts or friends.

There are many excellent local currency shops selling antiques, jewelry, glass and porcelain, folk art, objets d'art, paintings and prints. Records are particularly good and inexpensive. Folk art and handicrafts can be purchased at *UVA,* Na Prikope 25, and at other shops run by Czech craftsmen (list from *Prague Information Service,* Na Prikope 20).

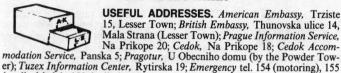

Environs of Prague

You should take advantage of several interesting one-day excursions and visit the castles of Zbraslav, Karlstejn and Krivoklat, the chateaus of Konopiste and Veltrusy and the towns Lidice and Nelahozeves. Zbraslav, once a Cistercian monastery, now a graceful 18th-century castle, houses the National Gallery's excellent collection of 19th- and 20th-century Czech sculpture. Karlstejn, a massive old fortress, was built as a safety deposit vault for the Bohemian crown jewels in the 14th century by Charles IV. Alas, its most important feature—the stunning gem-encrusted Chapel of the Holy Rood—has been closed indefinitely after being vandalized and restored. Krivoklat is a pure Gothic castle from the 13th century in a magnificent woodland setting. The mainly 19th-century chateau of Konopiste was the hunting residence of Austrian Crown Prince Ferdinand, whose assassination in 1914 had such cataclysmic results. Surrounded by forests, it contains an overwhelming collection of hunt trophies and arms. Veltrusy is a baroque chateau situated in a park, noteworthy for its remarkable rococo furnishings and collection of oriental porcelain. Nearby is Nelahozeves, the birthplace of Dvorak, now a museum. Lidice is the village that was razed to the ground by the Nazis in retaliation for the assassination of Heydrich. A new village has been built, and the former is now only a peaceful meadow with a monument and flowers.

The Four Corners of Bohemia

West: You will want to see the three famous spas in this region, Karlovy Vary (Carlsbad), Marianske Lazne (Marienbad) and Frantiskovy Lazne. Karlovy Vary has attracted Europe's crowned heads and ailing bodies for ages. The oldest and largest of the spas, its sulphurous waters taste so awful, they must be good for you! Just outside town are the world-famous Moser crystal works and arrangements can be made to visit the factory and watch the glass being made. Purchases may be made on the spot. Also worthwhile is a visit to the Brezova porcelain factory which has an interesting museum. Karlovy Vary plays host on even years to an International Film Festival. And, it has a challenging 18-hole golf course, as does Marianske Lazne, 30 km. (18 miles) away. This is the youngest and prettiest of the spas, admired by Britain's Edward VII, Beethoven, Goethe and others. Its waters are only mildly salty. Frantiskovy Lazne dates its mineral spring back to the 11th century and is chiefly known for its nearby peat bogs. But the place that really revolutionized medical science is Jachymov, north of Karlovy Vary, from which two rail cars of local pitchblende (uranium ore) were sent by the then Austrian government to a certain M. and Mme. Curie to assist with their research. From this, in 1898, they isolated two miracle elements: polonium and radium. The now-exhausted silver mines of Jachymov (once known as Joachimsthal) also made it the original home of the famous Maria Theresa "thalers," from which the American dollar derives its name. In the Chod region farther to the southwest is the preserved town of Domazlice with arcaded houses in

Renaissance and baroque styles. Slav Chods were traditional guardians of Bohemia's frontiers; their villages are ethnically interesting.

South: South of Prague, the Vltava river soon forms a chain of lovely lakes which offer many recreation facilities. South Bohemia is scenically a beautiful region of lakes and woods, and has many points of interest. The old part of Tabor was the seat of the 14th-century Hussite movement. Ceske Budejovice has a beautiful square and the Budvar brewery. Nearby is Hluboka Castle, a carefully maintained mini replica of Windsor Castle with a remarkable collection of Gothic wood carvings. Cesky Krumlov is a gem of a medieval town, currently undergoing major restoration, and has an historic open-air theater. Then there are the castles Rozmberk (13th century), Orlik (19th century) and Zvikov (13th century), the latter two reached by boat.

East. Near to Prague is Kutna Hora; it was here that silver deposits were discovered in the 13th century which helped finance the splendor of medieval Bohemian kings; the fine building of Vlassky Dvur, once housing the Royal Mint, is well worth visiting. The distinctively domed St. Barbara Cathedral is also a sight to see, and for those who fancy the macabre, the church in Sedlec contains a famous ossuary entirely lined with human skulls. Hradec Kralove, old and new, may be seen on the way to Litomysl, an ancient town dating from the 10th century whose claim to fame is a Renaissance chateau opposite which the composer Smetana was born. The Eagle Mts. (Orlicke Hory) running along the Polish border, are unspoiled, have clearly marked trails, and are ideal for camping.

North: The Giant Mts. (Krkonose) are one of the most popular holiday areas in the country and are best visited in winter. Spindleruv Mlyn and Pec pod Snezkou are picturesque ski resorts and the wooded hills are dotted with fairytale cottages out of Hansel and Gretel. A pilgrimage to Terezin can be a moving experience. The town's 18th-century fortress was turned into a concentration camp by the Nazis and the cemetery at the entrance bears mute witness to the many who perished here. Not far away is the summer resort of Stare Splavy on Lake Macha (Machovo Jezero) in a lovely woodland setting under the eye of Bezdez Castle, a fantastic 11th-century ruin. Unfortunately, the place is utterly overcrowded in summer. The castle restaurant in Melnik, overlooking the confluence of the Vltava and Labe rivers, is a good place for a lunch of fresh trout and local white wine. Novy Bor is the center of the unique painted glassmaking industry. Farther in the northeast, rock climbing is popular in the Jizersky Mts.

PRACTICAL INFORMATION FOR BOHEMIA

Good hotels outside Prague are to be found mainly at the better spas and ski resorts. When possible, choose one with at least an (M) rating. All hotels have restaurants unless otherwise stated, and all, except those in (I) category, have all or some rooms with bath or shower.

Most towns and resorts have a *Cedok* office. The principal ones of the region are: *Ceske Budejovice* Hroznova 21; *Hradec Kralove* Leninova trida 63; *Karlovy Vary* Trziste 23; *Kladno* nam. Revoluce 4/5; *Liberec* Revolucni 66; *Mlada Boleslav* trida Lidovych milici; *Plzen* Presovska 10; *Trutnov* Gottwaldovo nam. 120/21; *Usti nad Labem* Hrncirska 9/3.

CESKE BUDEJOVICE. *Gomel* (E), 180 rooms, new, wine cellar. A short walk from main square. *Zvon* (E), 50 rooms, some (I).

CESKY KRUMLOV. *Krumlov* (M), 32 rooms, on the lovely Old Town square; *Ruze* (M), 16 rooms in attractively restored old building in Old Town, snack bar only; *Vysehrad* (M), 48 rooms, fine views on edge of Old Town.

HLUBOKA. *Park* (M), 54 rooms, some (I). Lakeside situation.

KARLOVY VARY. *Moskva-Pupp* (L-M), 160 rooms, renovated, grand old-style spa hotel where the action is; *Parkhotel* (M), 110 rooms, also central location; latest, but only for those following treatment and their companions, is *Thermal* (E). *Motel* (E) has 40 rooms. *Alice,* modern, and *Central* are (M).

MARIANSKE LAZNE. *Golf* (L), just outside town opposite golf course, recently renovated and one of the best in the country, with excellent restaurant. *Palace Praha* (E), 37 rooms. *Corso* (M) and *Excelsior* (M) are both good value and central. *Esplanade* (M).

PEC POD SNEZKOU. *Horizont* (M), modern, 126 rooms with good facilities, and nearby *Kovarna* (M) restaurant and disco.

PLZEN (Pilsen). *Ural* (E), 84 rooms, modern; *Continental* (M), 53 rooms; *Slovan* (M-I), 115 rooms. Home of arguably the world's best beer: try it at two taverns outside the Pilsner Urquell brewery on the eastern outskirts.

SPINLERUV MLYN. *Montana* (E), 66 rooms, modern, good facilities on resort outskirts; *Savoy* (E-M), 58 rooms, more traditional and in center of resort; *Praha* (M), newly renovated; *Alpsky* (I), 20 rooms, traditional style in Sv. Petr above resort. Very modern and in fine mountain setting by source of Labe (Elbe) river is *Labska Bouda* (M), 69 rooms.

Moravia

Moravia is the rich little agricultural and industrial region sand-wiched between Bohemia and Slovakia, offering sightseers a variety of wooded highlands, subterranean Karst grottoes, painted villages, re-nowned vineyards, folk art, and castles.

Brno, its capital, is a busy modern industrial city with beautiful parks and vestiges of the past, situated on an open plain. Grim Spilberk Castle, which dominates the city's skyline, has an infamous history as a political prison. The Moravian Museum in the Dietrichstein palace has a folk-art wing where elaborate embroidered costumes, laces, folk pottery and shepherd woodcarvings give an impressive idea of how rural Moravians have traditionally spent their long winter evenings.

A short drive north of Brno are famous grottoes, the most impressive probably being those of Punkva combined with the Macocha abyss; the visit includes a boat trip along an underground river. Further to the northwest is the magnificent 13th-century Pernstejn Castle, a center of resistance against the Habsburgs, and most famous of Moravia's cas-tles. Only a few miles east of Brno is the Napoleonic battlefield of Slavkov (Austerlitz) with various monuments and museums, the best being in the baroque chateau of the town of Slavkov. Further east still, in the Moravia valley, are some of the most notable finds from the days of the Great Moravian Empire of the 9th century, especially near Mikulcice, a few miles from Hodonin, where excavations are still in progress. Also in this region is Straznice, where one of Czechos-lovakia's most famous folk festivals takes place at the end of June.

In southern Moravia, the medieval core of Telc, near the Bohemian border, is well worth a detour. Znojmo, down towards the Austrian border, stages wine festivals.

PRACTICAL INFORMATION FOR MORAVIA

Regional hotels are heavily booked in summer. All hotels have restaurants unless otherwise stated. All except those in (I) category have all or some rooms with bath or shower.

Main *Cedok* offices in Moravia are: *Brno* Divadelni 3; *Gottwaldov* Kvitkova 80; *Olomouc* nam. Miru 2; *Ostrava* Dimitrovova 9.

BRNO. *Continental* (E), Leninova 20 (tel. 58616). 230 rooms. *International* (E), Husova 16 (tel. 26411). Large, modern, central. *Voronez* (E), Krizkovskeho 47 (tel. 3135). 380 rooms and suites, night club, pool, sauna; next to exhibition grounds. Next door is *Voronez 2* (M), 110 rooms. Modern. *Metropol* (M-I), Dornych 5 (tel. 337111). 55 rooms, near rail station. *Slovan* (M), Lidicka 23 (tel. 56735). 110 rooms.

Restaurants. *U Kralovny Elisky* (E), wine cellar in former cloister with fireplace grill. *Hradni Vinarna* (M), wine restaurant in Castle Spilberk, good atmosphere, folk band. *M Club* (M), small, pleasant, with cellar, between Cathedral and market place. *Myslivna* (M), in outskirts, good views of city.

OLOMOUC. University town. *Flora,* (M), 170 rooms, new; *Narodni Dum* (M), 65 rooms, some (I).

OSTRAVA. *Imperial* (E-M), 125 rooms; *Palace* (M-I), over 200 rooms.

TELC. Beautiful little town with arcaded streets. *Cerny Orel* (M-I), 26 rooms.

ZNOJMO. *Druzba* (M), 69 rooms; *Dukla* (M), 110 rooms.

Slovakia

Easternmost and most mountainous region of Czechoslovakia, Slovakia can claim to be the Switzerland of Central Europe, not only because it is similar in size, population and geography, but because like Switzerland, it is really three "countries" in one. Southwestern Slovakia is the vast bountiful monotonous plain of the Danube river, bordering on Hungary and rising northward to the Carpathian foothills. Its food, architecture, music and folkways recall the influence of centuries of Hungarian rule.

Bratislava, capital of Slovakia, is the region's main city. This major river port, which dates from Roman times, became an important trading center in the Middle Ages, and is still developing. The river and the town are dominated by the castle on its hill, destroyed in a disastrous fire in 1811, and recently reconstructed. Maria Theresa liked to stay here, and many of the noble houses in the old part of town were built by the high-ranking families attracted here by her presence. Much restoration work is in progress. Bratislava's other great landmark is the elegant modern bridge which very soon leads into Austria. There is a remarkably fine view of the Danube, the city and the surrounding countryside from the restaurant atop a pylon high above the bridge.

Central Slovakia's main city, Banska Bystrica, was the cradle of the 1944 Slovak uprising against the Nazi occupiers. Since the early Middle Ages, the Low Tatras, High Tatras and Slovak Ore Mountains have been a storehouse of mineral treasure. Today its ancient mining towns form a chain of medieval museum sites, alongside thoroughly modern and industrialized communities.

Eastern Slovakia includes along its northern rim one of the most exciting natural wonderlands in Europe—the High Tatra Mountain National Park. The main ridge of this imposing Carpathian arc is more than ten miles wide and 16 miles long, with side spurs forming the beautiful Tatra valleys and lakes. The region, snow-topped the year round, is alive with whistling marmot, rare chamois, eagle and bear, and has several good resorts. Gateway to this area is the town of Poprad. The best-known resorts here are Tatranska Lomnica with its fine Museum of the Tatra National Park and cable cars running to the summit of the stupendously scenic Lomnicky Stit (8,645 ft.), Smokovec with very satisfactory skiing runs, and Strbske Pleso on the edge of a lake at 4,400 feet.

South and east of the mountains, the rolling countryside is dotted with exquisite little Gothic and Renaissance towns of which Levoca and Kezmarok are outstanding examples. Beautiful old wooden churches are also a feature of eastern Slovakia—Bardejov and Presov are good bases from which to visit these.

A 100-foot geyser can be seen at Herlany near the town of Kosice; the local Cedok office should give you its eruption "schedule."

PRACTICAL INFORMATION FOR SLOVAKIA

The winter sports season in Slovakia is from December to the end of April, but mountain resorts are open all summer and offer a variety of outdoor recreation. Spas may be visited all the year, the high season being May to September. The main cities are linked with Prague by air and rail. *Cedok* bus tours or your own car are best for getting about. The Liberty Highway *(Cesta Svobody)* connects all the resorts in the High Tatra National Park *(TANAP)*.

The *Cedok* office in Bratislava is at Sturova ulice 13; other main branches are: *Banska Bystrica* nam. V.I. Lenina 4; *Kosice* Rooseveltova 1; *Nitra* Leninova tr. 72; *Piestany* Pavlovova 38; *Stary Smokovec* Stary Smokovec 22; *Zilina* Hodzova 9.

Mountain and spa hotels are very comfortable, with good cuisine and central heating in winter. Most offer sports facilities (tennis, golf, swimming, skiing, etc.) and reduce rates during off-season. All have restaurants unless otherwise stated. All except those in (I) category have all or some rooms with bath or shower, unless otherwise stated.

BANSKA BYSTRICA. *Lux* (M), 150 rooms, most recent; *Narodny Dom* (M), 42 rooms; *Urpin* (M-I), 45 rooms, no restaurant. *Ulanka Motel* (M), 30 rooms, new and attractive, 6 km. out of town to the northwest.

BARDEJOV. *Dukla* (I), 37 rooms, a few (M); *Mineral* (M), 70 rooms, in peaceful Bardejov spa about 6 km. away.

BRATISLAVA. *Devin* (L), Riecna 4 (tel. 330851). 92 rooms, good facilities, by Danube. *Kyev* (E), Rajska c. 2 (tel. 56341). 212 rooms, modern, comfortable. *Bratislava* (M), Urxova ul. (tel. 293524). 344 rooms, in new Ruzinov district. *Juniorhotel Sputnik* (M), Drienova 14 (tel. 293651), 100 rooms, wine cellar, sports complex, new, by lake, on outskirts of town. *Krym* (M-I), Safarikovo nam. 6 (tel. 55471). 49 rooms, central, near Danube. *Tatra* (M-I), nam. 1 maja 7 (tel. 51464). 81 rooms, less central. *Palace* (M-I), Postova ul. 1 (tel. 333656). 69 rooms, central. *Motel Zlate Piesky* (M), (tel. 65170). 40 rooms, summer only. On outskirts of town, with pool, camping facilities.

Restaurants. Bratislava has numerous wine-cellar restaurants, including the *Hradna vinaren* (Castle Wine Cellar) in the Bratislava castle complex. Among others are *Velki Frantiskani,* Diebrovo nam.; *Klastorna vinaren,* Pugacevova, in 300-year-old monastery; *Pod Bastou* and *Rybarsky Cech. Slovenska Restauracia* is one of the best for Slovak specialties. In the main square of Slovak National Uprising is *Polom,* an attractive new complex of coffee houses and small restaurants (open air and indoor). The *rotating café* atop the TV tower and the *Bystrica* perched on a pylon above Slovak bridge both offer outstanding views. *Koliba Expo,* farther out, has gypsy music in a lovely setting. All are (M).

KOSICE. *Slovan* (E), 212 rooms, good facilities, central. *Imperial* (M), 48 rooms, central.

PIESTANY. Famed spa. *Magnolia* (E), 123 rooms. *Eden* (M), 53 rooms.

POPRAD. Gateway to High Tatras. *Europa* (M), 73 rooms without bath or shower, near rail station; old-fashioned, over-priced. *Gerlach* (M), 120 rooms, modern. *Zimny Stadion* (M), 15 rooms.

PRESOV. *Dukla* (M), 90 rooms, a few with bath or shower, near main square. *Saris* (M), 110 rooms, new, a short distance from the attractive main square.

SMOKOVEC. Three resorts in one, linked together on the lower slopes of the High Tatras. Main center for shops and information is **Stary Smokovec,** with the plush *Grand* (E), the first major hotel, built in 1904. *Udernik* (M), modern, 34 rooms without bath or shower. **Novy Smokovec:** *Park* (M), 96 rooms, modern, one of the best for value. *Tokajik* (M), 13 rooms. *Bystrina* (I), 44 rooms with shower, snack bar. In **Horny Smokovec:** *Bellevue* (E), 110 rooms, modern, pool, comfortable but insufficient elevators. Next door is *Sport* (M), modern, 66 rooms without shower.

At Hrebienok, reached by funicular, several chalets with good, simple accommodation and restaurants.

STRBSKE PLESO. Scene of many international ski championships, with three major triangular-shaped hotels scattered about the forested slopes. *Patria* (E), 157 rooms, is the newest, with attractive paved garden in foyer. *FIS* (M), 50 rooms, faces the ski jumps. *Panorama* (M), 80 rooms.

TATRANSKA LOMNICA. *Grandhotel Praha* (E), 50 rooms, traditional style, next to cable car station. *Motel Eurocamp* FICC (M), splendid camp site with chalets for hire, shops, restaurant and fabulous view of the High Tatras. *Slovan* (M), 180 rooms.

Restaurant: *Zbojnicka koliba* (M), excellent food, with Slovak folk band.

DENMARK

The Danes have always been known as "the Latins of Scandinavia," quite different from their Swedish and Norwegian brothers, not to mention the phlegmatic Germans on their other border. As the nation which abolished its laws against pornography in the late 1960s, Denmark had the last laugh on a horrified Anglo-Saxon world when consumption of dirty books and blue films took a nosedive. But the Danes are not all beer-and-skittles, as it were, for despite their easy-going attitude towards life in general and sex in particular, they are a tough lot, devoted to hard work and the idea of progress. They're just lucky enough to be able to enjoy life with as much zest as they put into their pursuit of thrift and cleanliness.

As for tourist highlights, it can all be summed up in one long sentence: Denmark is a kind of miniaturized Scandinavia—Danish to be sure, but crammed with beautiful little villages, blessed with good food, midsummer sun and fresh air, and a people eager to greet the knowledgeable visitor, especially if he speaks English and comes armed with a smile.

The Country and the People

Denmark, like Norway and Sweden, started decades ahead of the rest of the world in social legislation. The citizens of this progressive monarchy have social security from the cradle to the grave. There are no real slums, and social injustice is at a minimum. "The last place in Europe", wrote Negley Farson, "where sanity survives". He meant of course: "The only place where sanity has as yet occurred".

As for efficiency, though Denmark's soil is among Europe's most infertile, she has for generations been a leading food exporter. Today the agricultural labor force is declining steadily, but production still

148

rises, despite frantic efforts to curtail it because of marketing difficulties. Danish farming cooperatives have much to do with this superefficiency. The mere fact of dealing with a cooperative gives a man a say in its running: he may even become its president. So farmers and produce dealers or suppliers do not fall out. Denmark, however, is no longer primarily an agricultural country. Today she exports more industrial than farm products, even though she possesses no natural source of power and no raw materials whatsoever, except china clay.

Educational standards are high. You can't, for instance, be a humble cop unless you speak a second language well enough to take evidence in it. Almost everyone speaks good English.

Finally, if there's one sound that typifies Denmark, it's laughter. Danes seem incapable of conversing without endless jokes and wisecracks. Something will have gone sadly astray if you don't thoroughly enjoy your contacts with this friendly and hospitable people, wherever you go and whatever the time of year.

PRACTICAL INFORMATION FOR DENMARK

WHAT WILL IT COST. The rate of inflation in Denmark is not high, and should not rise above about 5% in 1987. Hotel prices are considerably lower outside Copenhagen and North Zealand, though they are rising in the North Sea coastal resorts. The best areas, cost-wise, are probably still Funen and Jutland. A stay in a country inn is another good bet for the budget traveler. It provides the ideal chance of meeting the Danes, and rooms will be clean and comfortable; however, there are often no private bathrooms. In recent years Denmark has entered the self-catering field in a big way and it is a highly popular form of holiday among the Danes themselves. Apart from the obvious financial savings, it is a wonderful way to see the country.

The monetary unit in Denmark is the krone (kr.), which divides into 100 øre. The smallest coin is 5 øre, so all prices are rounded to a multiple of 5. If you wish to export more than 50,000 kr. you must be able to show that you brought the money *in,* or that you exchanged foreign currency or travelers' checks for the amount in Denmark. At presstime, the exchange rate for the krone was 9 kr. to the U.S. dollar, and 12.50 kr. to the pound sterling.

A typical day in Copenhagen might cost two people:

Hotel (Moderate) double room	700 kr.
Breakfast	80
Lunch at popular restaurant	135
Transportation (bus, taxi)	105
Coffee (in cafeteria)	25
Theater	140
Dinner (incl. wine or beer)	300
Miscellaneous 10%	150
	1,635 kr.

SOURCES OF INFORMATION. For information on all aspects of travel in Denmark, the Danish Tourist Board is invaluable. Their addresses are:

In the US. 655 Third Ave., New York, N.Y. 10017.
In Canada. P.O. Box 115, Station "N", Toronto, Ontario, M8V 3S4.
In the UK. 169 Regent St., London, W.1.

WHEN TO COME. Most visitors come to Denmark during the months of July and August, but the wiser minority choses May, June or September, when there is more comfort. While summer congestion in hotels is terrific, the season for Copenhagen and indeed for big hotels throughout the country now lasts virtually the year round.

Climate. Temperatures in general are moderate rather than extreme. However, evenings tend to be cool so come prepared.

Average maximum daily temperatures in degrees Fahrenheit and Centigrade:

Copen-hagen	Jan.	Feb.	Mar.	Apr.	May	June	July	Aug.	Sept.	Oct.	Nov.	Dec.
F°	36	36	41	50	61	66	72	70	65	54	43	39
C°	2	2	5	10	16	19	22	21	17	12	6	4

SPECIAL EVENTS. *April,* Numus Festival—the biggest "new music" celebration in Scandinavia—in Århus (to May). *May,* the Tivoli Gardens open (to September). *June,* Frederikssund's Viking Festival from mid-June to first week in July. The Sorø Organ Festival starts (every Wednesday to September). *July,* American celebrations on the 4th in Rebild Park, Aalborg. Copenhagen Jazz Festival. Hans Christian Andersen openair play in Odense. Roskilde Festival, the biggest in north Europe for jazz, rock and folk music. *August,* Lumière Festival at Koldinghus Castle in Kolding. *September,* Århus Festival Week during the second week. The Royal Theater opens with ballet, opera and classical drama. The Royal Guards start marching through the city at noon to relieve the sentries at Amalienborg Palace, coinciding with the return to the town of the Queen.

National Holidays. Jan. 1 (New Year's Day); Apr. 17–19 (Easter); Apr. 25 (Common Prayer); May 8 (Ascension); May 19 (Whitsun); Jun. 5 (Constitution) —shops closed from noon; Dec. 25, 26.

VISAS. Nationals of the United States, Canada, Australia, New Zealand, EEC countries and practically all other European countries do not require visas for entry into Denmark. However, you must have a valid passport, or in the case of travelers from the U.K., a British Visitor's Passport.

HEALTH CERTIFICATES. Not required for entry into Denmark.

GETTING TO DENMARK. By Plane. There are direct or through plane flights from the following North American cities to Copenhagen—New York, Boston, Detroit, Chicago, Los Angeles, Minneapolis, Seattle. And there are services from most other European capitals, either non-stop or through flights. From the U.K., in addition to London, there are flights from Aberdeen, Glasgow, Newcastle, Leeds, Manchester, Birmingham and Dublin. Also, *Air UK* fly from Humberside, Norwich and London to Esbjerg. *SAS* also fly from London to Århus, and *Maersk Air* from Southend (near London) to Billund in central Jutland.

By Train. There are three basic routes from London. The first is using the short sea-crossing from Dover to Ostend and then by the *Nord Express* which carries day carriages, sleeping cars and (from Aachen) 2nd class couchettes; leaves London in the morning and arrives in Copenhagen just under 24 hours later. Buffet car or refreshment service part of the way.

The second route is via Harwich to the Hook of Holland. With this you leave London (Liverpool St.) at about 9.40 A.M. and travel to Harwich for the crossing to the Hook. Here you board the *Nord-West Express* which goes via Rotterdam, Bremen, Hamburg and Puttgarden for the crossing to Rødby, thence to Copenhagen arriving there within 23 hours of leaving London. Day carriages and 2nd class couchettes from the Hook to Copenhagen. Refreshment service part way.

The third route is to use the *DFDS* car ferry service from Harwich. With this you leave London (Liverpool St.) in the mid-afternoon, departing from

Harwich at 4.30 P.M., reaching Esbjerg about 1.30 P.M. the next day where there is a direct fast train to Copenhagen, reached just after 7 P.M.

And there is also a service by DFDS from Newcastle-upon-Tyne to Esbjerg with train connection to Copenhagen taking about 26 hours in all. Does not operate all year. Always check.

By Sea. *DFDS Seaways* operates drive on/off car ferries to Esbjerg from Harwich (daily year-round). From Newcastle (three times weekly in summer).

By Car. All car routes from Continental starting-points converge at Hamburg. From here the motorist has two choices: he can travel either north via Flensburg into Jutland or via Lübeck to Puttgarden and then by ferry to Rødbyhavn, shortest sea crossing and quickest route to Copenhagen. A ferry links Gelting (near Flensburg) to Fåborg on Funen. Another ferry-crossing is from Travemünde (nr. Lübeck) to Gedser. In summer, best reserve in advance for ferry space at any main rail station in Germany. Reservations are free.

 CUSTOMS. The import of duty-free goods varies according to residence country and way of entry into Denmark, so check before your trip for full details. Allowances at presstime were as follows. Travelers who are resident in Europe and coming from a European country outside the EEC may bring in 200 cigarettes or 50 cigars or 250gr. of tobacco; 1 liter of spirits or 2 liters of alcoholic beverage up to 22% proof; 2 liters of table wine; 50 gr. of perfume and 0.25 liter of toilet water; other goods to the value of 375 kr. Travelers resident in Europe and coming from an EEC country may bring in 300 cigarettes or 75 cigars or 400gr. tobacco; 1.5 liters of spirits or 3 liters of alcoholic beverage up to 22% proof; 75gr. of perfume and 0.375 liter of toilet water; other goods to the value of 2,300 kr. Travelers resident outside Europe may bring in 400 cigarettes or 100 cigars or 500gr. of tobacco; other regulations as above on entry from EEC or other countries.

 HOTELS. In Copenhagen the high season runs from May through October, in the seaside resorts and provincial towns from mid-June to August 20. Off-season hotel prices are lower in Copenhagen but this is not the general practice elsewhere, although some seaside resorts and new hotels may offer reductions. Your best bet is to avoid peak-period travel and to ask for the off-season rates. In Copenhagen, as a rule, breakfast is included in the room price unless indicated, but some hotels will ask you to take half- or full-pension rates during the high season.

Best among the less-expensive hotels are the unlicensed Mission accommodations. These always offer better facilities than their modest price would indicate. Most serve beer and wine, but no spirits. The budget hotel area in Copenhagen is near the Central Station, around Colbjørnsensgade-Helgolandsgade. The Danish Tourist Board can supply a useful gazetteer listing hotels, inns (called *kros* in Denmark), motels, holiday centers and pensions.

The hotels listed in this chapter are graded by price in one of three categories. All prices are for 2 people in a double room with bath/shower. In Copenhagen: Expensive (E) 900 kr. and up, Moderate (M) 550–900 kr., Inexpensive (I) 345–550 kr. In the provinces, (E) 500 kr. and up, (M) 350–500 kr., (I) 200–350 kr.

CAMPING. Denmark claims—with justification—to have the best camp sites in Europe, if not in the world. A comprehensive leaflet giving details of more than 500 sites is available from the Danish Tourist Board. Visitors should bring an International Camping Carnet, otherwise a visitor's camping pass can be purchased at the first site. Overnight stays in cars and trailers parked outside camp sites are not permitted in Denmark without prior permission of the landowner. Camping in parks and parking lots is not permitted either. Unauthorized parking in dunes and on beaches results in on-the-spot fines for offenders. Further details from Campingradet, Skjoldsgade 10, DK–2100 Copenhagen. General camping information from Dansk Camping Union, 74D Gammel Kongevej, Copenhagen (tel. 01–210600).

RESTAURANTS. We have categorized our restaurant listings for Denmark under 3 headings—Expensive (E), with a likely price range of 160 kr. and up, Moderate (M), 80–160 kr. and Inexpensive (I) 60–80 kr. Remember to check the menu posted outside a restaurant. Standards of restaurant food are very high in Denmark, and if you don't feel like a full meal, there are plenty of delicious snacks on offer.

Food and Drink. The normal Danish breakfast or *Morgen complet* consists of coffee or tea and an assortment of breads, cheeses, cold meats, salami, jams and marvelous Danish pastries. Danish coffee is delicious.

The famous Danish cold table is served at many restaurants at midday and is always good value for money. Selections can be made from a variety of hot and cold meats and fish, shellfish, salads, sauces and specialty hot dishes. *Smørrebrød* are open sandwiches that have become almost an art form, with a delicious selection of imaginative fillings. These are on offer throughout the day in many restaurants and cafés, and can also be taken away from special Smørrebrød shops.

There are many varieties of Danish beer made by a score of breweries: those from the *Carlsberg* and *Tuborg* firms (both in Copenhagen) are world-famous. Most popular is pilsner, a light beer, but there is also lager, a darker beer. (What is "lager" in Britain is "pilsner" in Denmark.)

The other national drink of Scandinavia is Akvavit, popularly known as *snaps:* neither an aperitif, cocktail nor liqueur, it is meant to be drunk with food, preferably with a beer chaser. Akvavit is served icy cold and should never be sipped or left to get warm. Knock it back and damn the consequences. Remember that snaps goes with cold food, particularly herrings and cheese, not hot.

TIPPING. Hotels and restaurants quote fully inclusive prices; you should tip only for special personal help. Washroom attendants get 1 kr. Taxi fares include the tip, so don't tip extra. Don't tip movie or theater ushers or in barbershops.

MAIL. Surface letters are 3.80 kr. for 20 grams to the U.S.; airmail is now the same price for 20 grams; postcards 3 kr. Letters to the U.K. and rest of Europe cost 3.80 kr. and go airmail automatically. Letters and postcards within Denmark and Scandinavia cost 2.80 kr.

CLOSING TIMES. Shops are open from 9 to 5.30 P.M., with the exception of Friday when they stay open to 7 or 8. A few are also open Thursday to 7. Saturday they close between noon and 2 P.M. Post offices open from 10 to 5 or 9 to 5.30. Bank hours are 9.30 to 4 weekdays (Thursday to 6 P.M.), but closed Saturday; hours vary outside Copenhagen.

USEFUL ADDRESSES. *American Embassy,* Dag Hammarskjölds Allé 24; *British Embassy,* Kastelsvej 36 –40; *Canadian Embassy,* Kristen Bernikowsgade 1; *Danish Tourist Board,* H.C. Andersens Boulevard 22 (opposite the City Hall). All in Copenhagen.

GETTING AROUND DENMARK. By Plane. Although a small country Denmark has an internal air service operated by *SAS* and two private companies. These link Copenhagen with Århus, Aalborg, Billund, Esbjerg, Karup, Skrydstrup, Sønderborg, and Thisted (in Jutland), Odense (in Funen) and Rønne on the Baltic island of Bornholm.

By Train. Long distance trains are either *Inter-City* (shown as IC in timetables) and have modern stock, or *Lyntog* (literally translated as Lightning Train, shown as 'L' in timetables) express-diesel-railcar units with limited accommodation. Both have 1st and 2nd class carriages and most have either refreshment or buffet car service. Reservation is advisable—obligatory on services using the *Great Belt* (Nyborg to Korsør) ferry services. Trains are clean and kept in excellent repair. Weekend travel is dense and reservations are essential on long distance trains then. Copenhagen's suburban services are partially electrified and more electrification is underway. Various special fares apply.

Denmark is also a partner along with Norway, Sweden and Finland in the Scandinavian Railpass, giving unlimited rail travel throughout all four countries, a 50% reduction on ferries between Denmark and Sweden, Denmark and Norway, and Sweden and Finland. The pass can also be used on certain ferries within Denmark. Valid for 21 days, the approximate cost is $220 first class, $147 second class. It can be purchased at any railway station in Scandinavia. Inquire about other seasonal special rail offers.

By Bus. Denmark has an excellent network of local buses linking towns and villages and well-integrated with train services.

By Car. Drive on the right. There is a general town speed limit of 50km/hr (30mph); outside towns the maximum is 80km/hr (50mph), on motorways 100km/hr (60mph). Seat belts are compulsory. Penalties for drinking and driving are severe. Third party (green card) insurance is obligatory for U.S. registration vehicles. The cost of gasoline at presstime is around 6 kr. per liter.

The excellent roads and the countryside make Denmark an ideal country for touring by car. Bridges, connecting many of the islands, are toll-free; fares on automobile ferries are moderately priced.

Car Hire. *Hertz,* Hammerichsgade 1; *Avis,* Kampmannsgade 1; *Auto–Pitzner,* Trommesalen 4. All Copenhagen and all at airport. *Budget Rent a Car,* Vester Farimagsgade 3.

Copenhagen, Happy Capital

The center of Danish fun is Copenhagen, biggest and liveliest of the Scandinavian capitals and by almost unanimous agreement one of the happiest cities of Europe. More than a million Danes, a quarter of the country's population, live and let live here. The city, on the island of Zealand, is just as flat as the sea that embraces it, as flat as the rest of Denmark, which averages only 98 feet above sea level. (This is why every second inhabitant has a bicycle.)

When is the best time to come? Denmark is lovely in summer, autumn and spring. The circus comes to Copenhagen in April. May marks the liberation from the bonds of the long northern winter. That incomparable pleasure garden of Tivoli throws wide its gates in Copenhagen, and the "season" has begun. The amusement park, Bakken—in existence for more than 300 years, it's the oldest in the world—opens in the Klampenborg Forest, and Denmark begins to rock like the yachts between Elsinore and Copenhagen, warming up for that June water carnival known as the Round Zealand Race, the world's biggest sea yacht race. The Royal Danish Ballet concludes the Copenhagen season in May, and June comes to a climax on June 23 with Midsummer Eve, a night of outdoor dancing, singing, feasting, bonfires and fireworks, transforming the whole nation into one big carnival. Try to celebrate this night along the Sound. You'll never forget the unreal summer twilight, streaked with rockets, edged with a thousand fires along the shores of the Kattegat.

With the end of June, everyone in Copenhagen goes to the country, and everyone in the country comes to Copenhagen, a most inconvenient arrangement, since it fills all the hotels at the height of the tourist season. This is the period of long, sun-flooded days and short, balmy nights in Denmark. Make your reservations early. The Danes will do the rest.

Sightseeing In Copenhagen

A good place to orient yourself is in the Rådhusplads or Town Hall Square. The huge red brick town hall was built in 1905, and from here there is access to the 350-foot-high tower with its fine view of the city

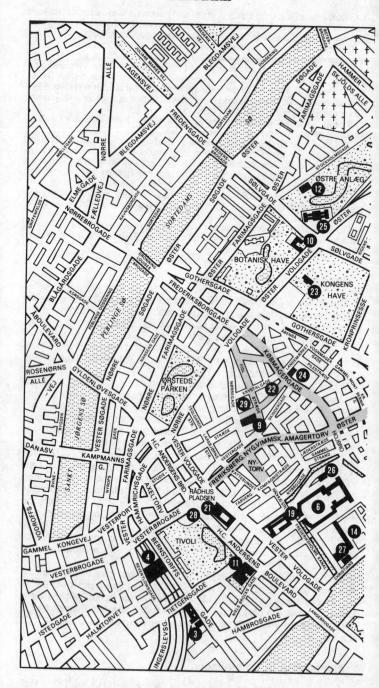

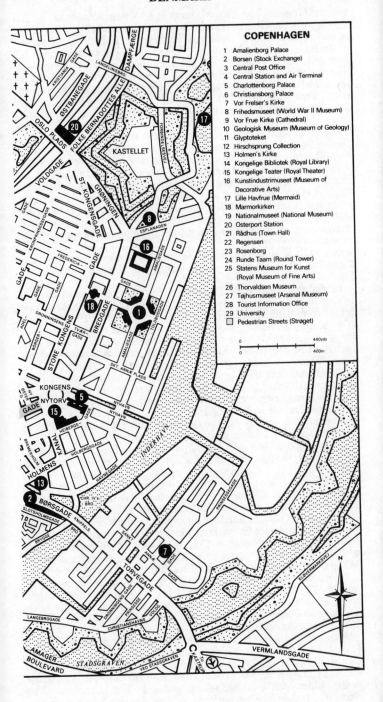

COPENHAGEN

1 Amalienborg Palace
2 Borsen (Stock Exchange)
3 Central Post Office
4 Central Station and Air Terminal
5 Charlottenborg Palace
6 Christiansborg Palace
7 Vor Frelser's Kirke
8 Frihedsmuseet (World War II Museum)
9 Vor Frue Kirke (Cathedral)
10 Geologisk Museum (Museum of Geology)
11 Glyptoteket
12 Hirschsprung Collection
13 Holmen's Kirke
14 Kongelige Bibliotek (Royal Library)
15 Kongelige Teater (Royal Theater)
16 Kunstindustrimuseet (Museum of
   Decorative Arts)
17 Lille Havfrue (Mermaid)
18 Marmorkirken
19 Nationalmuseet (National Museum)
20 Osterport Station
21 Rådhus (Town Hall)
22 Regensen
23 Rosenborg
24 Runde Taarn (Round Tower)
25 Statens Museum for Kunst
   (Royal Museum of Fine Arts)
26 Thorvaldsen Museum
27 Tøjhusmuseet (Arsenal Museum)
28 Tourist Information Office
29 University
□ Pedestrian Streets (Strøget)

0   440yds
0   400m

and countryside. The City Museum is at Vesterbrogade 59. Behind Tivoli, visit the Glyptotek, a gallery with a remarkable collection of sculpture magnificently displayed. From the Town Hall Square a series of streets, collectively known as "Strøget", run eastwards (Strøget is a pedestrians-only area from 11 A.M. each day). South of Gammeltorv Square a short walk will bring you to the Frederiksholm Canal and the splendid National Museum with its exhibits of Stone and Bronze age relics, Viking camps and ships, and all the fascinating panoply of old Scandinavian life, handsomely re-created. The museum sells interesting silver and bronze replicas of certain of the exhibits. Directly across the bridge from the National Museum is Christiansborg Palace, seat of the Danish Folketing (parliament). Nearby, set in an idyllic garden, is the Royal Library with a great collection including the earliest records of Viking expeditions to America and Greenland. On the side of the Library is Tøjhuset, Copenhagen's arms museum with outstanding displays of weapons, armor and uniforms. Flanking the Library on the other side is the red-brick Børsen, oldest stock exchange in the world still partly used for its original purpose, and a splendid example of Renaissance architecture (no admittance). Opposite the quays of this island, Slotsholmen, the flower vendors tie up their boats and sell their wares. Still on Slotsholmen, but on the inland side of Christiansborg Palace, is Thorvaldsen Museum, containing the famous sculptor's tomb and works.

Behind and north of the Thorvaldsen Museum you recross the canal by the Højbro, or High Bridge. You will see the Knippelsbro drawbridge from here and the green and gold spire of Vor Frelsers Kirke (Our Saviour's Church); the view from the tower is worth the climb up the gilded spiral staircase which winds around it. Four blocks from here is the Round Tower which Christian IV, warrior-architect-scholar king of Denmark, built as an astronomical observatory. Peter the Great of Russia mounted its internal spiral ramp in a horse-drawn carriage; you'll probably have to do it on foot. If you stroll up the Købmagergade —Store Kannikestraede to Nørregade—from here you'll come to the University and the Vor Frue Kirke, Our Lady's Church, the cathedral of Copenhagen with its marble statues of Christ and the Apostles by Thorvaldsen. The church was restored in 1977–1979.

At the opposite end of Strøget from the Town Hall Square is Kongens Nytorv, the southern side of which is flanked by the Royal Theater, home of Copenhagen's opera, classical theater and internationally-famed ballet. Even closer to the square is the Dutch baroque building of Charlottenborg, which has housed the Danish Academy of Fine Arts since 1754. The Nyhavn Canal, which runs up to Kongens Nytorv, is lined with picturesque 18th-century buildings and former sailors' cafés converted into gourmet restaurants. Attractions in this "newer" part of Copenhagen are: Amalienborg Square with its four immense rococo palaces including the residence of Queen Margrethe II and Prince Henrik where the guard is changed every day at noon, the Museum of Decorative Arts, and—definitely not to be missed—the Langelinie Promenade, where foreign navies moor their ships, all of Copenhagen strolls on Sunday afternoon, and the Little Mermaid of Hans Christian Andersen gazes across to Burmeister and Wain's vast shipyards.

An excursion you are sure to enjoy in Copenhagen is that to the Rosenborg Palace, a museum containing a dazzling display of all the Danish crown jewels together with fine furniture and other personal effects of Danish monarchs since the time of Christian IV, whose pearl-studded saddle is one of the palace's chief attractions. This charming, rather liveable museum still belongs to the royal family. Opposite it are 25 acres of botanical gardens at the north end of which is the Statens Museum for Kunst, the National Art Gallery, very fancy with a liveried doorman and first rate collection, not only of Danish art, but of Rembrandt, Cranach, Rubens, Dürer, the French Impressionists, and Matisse.

Sorgenfri, on Copenhagen's northwest outskirts and well-served by electric trains, is the site of the open air museum known as Frilandsmuseet. Here in a park covering 40 acres is a collection of reconstructed Danish farms, windmills and country houses.

PRACTICAL INFORMATION FOR COPENHAGEN

 GETTING AROUND COPENHAGEN. By bus and train. A joint zone fare system covers all buses and trains in Copenhagen. A 1-hour ticket valid for three zones costs 12 kr. A "yellow card" valid for 9 1-hour rides in three zones costs 50 kr. Cancel the card when entering the bus or train. 2 cancellations entitle you to a 1½-hour ride within 6 zones and 3 cancellations entitle you to a 2-hour ride within the entire zone system. You can change from bus to train and vice versa within the zone and time limit. This system is in operation in an area extending from the south of Køge, the west of Roskilde, and covering these towns as well as Hillerød, Elsinore and Copenhagen.

The new *Copenhagen Card* gives unlimited bus and rail travel in the city; free entry to many museums and places of interest; and 50% off certain boat/hydrofoil trips to and from Sweden. Of 1-, 2-, and 3-days' duration, it costs 70, 120, and 150 kr. respectively, and is widely available in Copenhagen and elsewhere; check with Tourist Office for details.

 HOTELS. Hotels in Copenhagen are almost always full during the summer season; so get a reservation. If you find yourself without a place to stay, go to the billeting bureau in the Airport or Central Station (Kiosk P.).

Expensive

Hotel d'Angleterre, Kongens Nytorv 34 (tel. 01–120095). 139 rooms. Ranks first among the older Copenhagen hotels. Aristocratic, spacious, with excellent food and service. Recently renovated.

Imperial, Vester Farimagsgade 9 (tel. 01–128000). 163 rooms. Excellent restaurant and bar. Central. Facilities include a 250-car garage.

Nyhavn 71, Nyhavn 71 (tel. 01–118585). Charmingly converted former storehouse, overlooking canal and harbor. Gourmet food. One of the Romantic hotel group.

Royal, Hammerichsgade 1 (tel. 01–141412). 273 rooms and suites in a skyscraper. Panoramic lounge on the top floor.

Scandinavia, Amager Blvd. 70 (tel. 01–112324). 550 rooms. Rooftop restaurant, indoor pool, sauna. Facing old city moats.

Sheraton Copenhagen, Vester Søgade 6 (tel. 01–143535). 474 rooms, all with airconditioning and TV. Central; restaurant overlooks lakes.

Moderate

Alexandra, H.C. Andersens Blvd. 8 (tel. 01–142200). 65 rooms. Close to Town Hall Square. Quiet and modest. Open Mar. 1 to Dec. 1.

Astoria, Banegaardsplads 4 (tel. 01–141419). 91 rooms, all with bath. Near Tivoli and Central Station. Restaurant, garage.

Codan, Sankt Annoe Plads 21 (tel. 01–133400). 134 rooms, all with bath. Guests use the restaurant of the adjacent Copenhagen Admiral which has a connecting corridor. Good, quiet, comfortable rooms.

Copenhagen Admiral, Tolbodgade 24 (tel. 01–118282). 366 rooms, with Wiinblad decorations and modern Danish design, in 18th-century former granary. Intact Pomeranian pine beams.

Danhotel, Kastrup Airport (tel. 01–511400). 272 rooms with bath or shower. Various room categories. Restaurant, 300-car service garage.

Marina, at Vedbaek, north of Copenhagen (tel. 02–891711). 106 rooms with bath; also apartments. Sauna, garage. Near beach and station.

Neptun, Sankt Annae Plads 18 (tel. 01–138900). Just off Nyhavn area. Small bar; breakfast included in the price.

Opera, Tordenskjoldsgade 15 (tel. 01–121519). 66 rooms, all with bath. Restaurant, bar.

Park, Jarmers Plads 3 (tel. 01–133000). 71 rooms, 50 with bath. Limited facilities. 5 minutes' walk from Town Hall Square.

SAS Globetrotter, Engvej 171, near Kastrup Airport (tel. 01–551433). 156 rooms, all with bath. Restaurant, sauna.

Savoy, Vesterbrogade 34 (tel. 01–214073). Renovated and modernized. Ideal situation near Tivoli, station and airport bus terminal. Member of the Best Western group. Restaurant open for breakfast only.

3 Falke, Falkoner Allé 9 (tel. 01–198001). 162 rooms, all with shower and TV. Situated in the charming Frederiksberg section, it's part of a complex.

Inexpensive

Esplanaden, Bredgade 78 (tel. 01–132175). 50 rooms. Limited facilities but near bus and underground. Overlooking Langelinie.

Hotel Danmark, Vester Voldgade 89 (tel. 01–114806). 49 rooms, all with bath. No restaurant.

Østerport, Oslo Plads 5, opposite Østerport Station (tel. 01–112266). 74 rooms, 52 with bath. Open Jan. 3-Dec. 22.

Skovriderkroen, Strandvejen 235 (tel. 01–626340). 21 rooms, in various categories. Breakfast extra. In wonderful surroundings at edge of Charlotten-lund wood. Near the beach.

Skovshoved Hotel, Strandvejen 267 (tel. 01–640028). 20 rooms, all with bath. Situated in charming, old-fashioned fisherman's village. Gourmet restaurant. Good bus connections to central Copenhagen.

Weber, Vesterbrogade 11 (tel. 01–311432). 76 rooms, most with bath. Modest but spacious and comfortable. Centrally located.

 RESTAURANTS. Many hotel dining rooms serve good food. Amongst the best are the Royal, Nyhavn 71, Copenhagen Admiral, Hotel d'Angleterre and the Imperial. Below is a selection of recommended restaurants from among more than 2,000 in Copenhagen.

Expensive

l'Alsace, Pistolstraede/Ny Østergade 9 (tel. 01–145743). French restaurant in charming old area. Mainly fish with some other specialties. Closed Sunday.

Den Sorte Ravn, Nyhavn 14 (tel. 01–131233). French/Danish cuisine served in 18th-century house. Menu varies with seasonal produce. Specialties include fresh local fish garnished with crayfish or clams.

Els, Store Strandstraede 3 (tel. 01–141341). Just off Nyhavn. Menu changes daily. Gourmet food made from fresh produce. Moderately priced lunch "plates" of Danish specialties. Enchanting 1853 decor.

Fiskekaelderen, Ved Stranden 18 (tel. 01–122011). Menu includes two meat dishes, otherwise lobster, salmon, turbot and sole with delicious sauces. Specialties of the day displayed on a blackboard. Closed Sunday lunch.

Gilleleje, Nyhavn 10 (tel. 01–125858). Decorated with fascinating antiques from old spice-trading, sailing-ship days. Interesting spices used in some of the recipes. Closed Sunday.

Kong Hans Kaelder, Vingardsstraede 6 (tel. 01–116868). Real luxury and highest-quality gourmet food. Closed for lunch, Sunday and all of July.

Langelinie Pavillonen, Langelinie (tel. 01–121214). Near Little Mermaid. Good for lunch, tea or dinner, with dancing most evenings. Superb views of the harbor. International menu.

Pakhuskaelderen, Nyhavn 71 (tel. 01–118585). In the basement of the hotel. Best cold table lunch in town. International menu in the evenings. Restored old warehouse.

St. Gertruds Kloster, Hauser Plads 32 (tel. 01–146630). Medieval atmosphere, cloister arches, antique church art, illuminated by 1,200 candelabra. Open from 4 P.M. daily. Sophisticated restaurant which also makes children welcome with special dishes on the menu.

Moderate

Bof & Ost, Grabrodretorv 13 (tel. 01–119911). Basement restaurant in charming area. Closed Sunday.

Cafe Royal, Hammerichsgade (tel. 01–141412). In Royal Hotel. Open 6.30 A.M. to midnight. Light meals and snacks.

Cafe Victor, Ny Østergade 3 (tel. 01–133613). Open 10 A.M. to 2 P.M. Very smart, international atmosphere.

Hereford Beefstouw. Two branches in Copenhagen: large one at Vesterbrogade 3 (tel. 01–127441); and smaller, intimate one at Abenra 8 (tel. 01–119190). Open 11.30 A.M. to 2 P.M. and 5–9 P.M. Closed Saturday and Sunday lunch. Best steaks in town, cooked to specific order.

Ida Davidson, Store Kongensgade 70 (tel. 01–113655). Traditional Danish lunch dishes and the very best open sandwiches. Lunch only, closed weekends.

La Tour, Jarmers Plads 3 (tel. 01–130001). Lebanese buffet with hot and cold dishes. Other Middle Eastern specialties.

Peder Oxe, Grabrodretorv 11 (tel. 01–110077). Renowned for salad table and steaks. Charming area.

Inexpensive

Amagertorv 8. Restaurant in Royal Copenhagen Porcelain Shop. Also tearoom with delicious array of pastries. Open during shopping hours, closed Sunday.

Cafe Asbaek, Ny Adelgade 8. Restaurant in modern art gallery. Open 11 A.M. to 6 P.M., Saturday to 4 P.M. Closed Sunday.

Cafe Nikolaj, Nikolaj Plads. In disused Nikolaj Church. Open 12 P.M. to 12 A.M., except Sunday and Monday. Good Danish atmosphere.

Cafe Smukke Marie, Knabrostraede 19. Specialty buckwheat pancakes with various fillings. Open Monday to Friday 1 P.M. to midnight, weekends 4 P.M. to midnight.

Chico's Cantina, Borgergade 2. Informal Mexican restaurant. Very popular; best to go early or late. Open noon to 3 P.M. and 5 P.M. to midnight.

Green Kitchen, Larsbjørnstraede 10. Vegetarian restaurant. Open noon to 10 P.M. Closed Sunday.

Krasnapolsky, Vestergade 10. Popular modern café. Light dishes, seasonal ingredients. Cultural events and art exhibitions.

Peppes Pizza, Gothersgade 101, Radhuspladsen 57, and Falkoner Alle 17 (also branch in Aalborg). Excellent choice of freshly made pizzas. Open noon to midnight, Friday and Saturday to 3 A.M.

 NIGHTLIFE. There's plenty of it. All night membership clubs are now things of the past. About 35 restaurants are allowed to stay open until 5 A.M. (ask your hotel porter to see the newspaper). If you are still reluctant to go home, the first morning restaurants are open at this hour to serve you a nice early breakfast and another drink. For shows, see the *Ekstrabladet* newspaper ads.

Annabels, Lille Kongensgade 16. With the *Tordenskjold* (see below), the most talked-of disco in town.

Den røde Pimpernel, H.C. Andersens Blvd. 7, in the city center. Always crowded. Closed Sunday.

Drachmann's Kro, Allégade 7–9. An ancient, atmospheric tavern recommended for quiet dining in authentic surroundings.

Faergekroen, Tivoli Gardens. For drinking and singing. Always crowded.

Foyer Scenen, Magstraede 14. Dancing to traditional jazz. Fri. and Sat. only.

Kakadu Bar, Colbjørsensgade 6. For men in search of wine, women and song.

Lorry Landsbyen, Allégade 7–9. Roofed beer-garden restaurant with nonstop music, singers and variety artists; family cabaret. Closed Sun./Mon.

Montmartre, Nørregade 41. Top jazz artists are the main attraction.

Slukefter, Tivoli Gardens. Beer and jazz, often with top artists.

Taverna, Tivoli Gardens. Teenager-oriented. Dancing.

Tordenskjold, Lille Kongensgade 4. *The* disco of the moment, together with *Annabels* (see above).

De tre Musketerer, Nikolaj Plads 25. For traditional jazz enthusiasts. Closed Sunday.

Vin og Ølgod, Skindergade 45. German beerhouse atmosphere, with communal singing and dancing to 2 A.M. Closed Sunday.

Vise Vers Huset, Tivoli Gardens. Presents contemporary folk singing.

Wonder Bar, Studiestraede 69. Mainly patronized by single men looking for a good drink, a good woman, and a good time.

MUSEUMS. Botanical Garden, Gothersgade 128. Includes all Danish plants, also foreign mountain plants and a palm house with tropical and subtropical specimens.

Ny Carlsberg Glyptotek, Dantes Plads. Egyptian, Greek, Etruscan, Roman art. French Impressionists and 19th-century Danish art. Winter garden.

Frihedsmuseet, Churchillparken. Museum of Danish Resistance 1940–45.

Hirschsprungske Samling, Stockholmsgade 20. A collection of 19th-century Danish paintings and arts, situated in a public park.

Kastellet, Langelinie. 300-year-old military fortifications.

Københavns Bymuseum, Vesterbrogade 59. 800 years of the city's past recorded in pictures and other mementos. Includes Kierkegaard curios.

Kunstindustrimuseet, Bredgade 68. Museum of Decorative Art, both European and Oriental, in rococo building. Changing special exhibitions.

Nationalmuseet, Frederiksholms Kanal 12. From the Ice Age to the Vikings, from the Vikings to the 20th century.

Rosenborg Slot, Øster Voldgade 4A. Renaissance castle built by Charles IV. Royal exhibits, crown jewels, costumes.

Rundetårn, Købmagergade. A 120-ft.-high round tower, built in 1642 as an observatory. A long spiral walkway leads to the top.

Statens Museum for Kunst, Sølvgade. Art and sculpture from Denmark, plus varied collection of European paintings.

Thorvaldsen Museum, Slotsholmen. Sculptor Bertel Thorvaldsen's work.

Zoologisk Múseum, Universitetsparken 15. A modern exhibition of animal life. Includes dioramas with animal noises and working models.

 SHOPPING. Many shops display a "Tax-free for Tourists" sign and will give details of refunds. Department stores: *Illums,* Østergade 52, and *Magasin du Nord,* Kongens Nytorv, are the biggest, with a huge selection. *Illums Bolighus,* Amagertorv 10, also called the Center of Modern Design, has a superb display of the very best of Scandinavian goods and clothes. *Georg Jensen,* 40 Østergade, has a permanent display of tables set with silver flatware, holloware and other items, and also has a fascinating small museum of original Jensen pieces. *Haandarbejdets Fremme* (Danish Handicraft Guild), Vimmelskaftet 13, has a huge selection of handmade items, embroidery, clothing, etc., while *Den Permanente,* Vesterbrogade 8, has the best of Danish design on show in the form of furniture, glass, jewelry, small gift items, clothing and souvenirs. *Royal Copenhagen Porcelain* and *Bing & Grøndahl,* at Amarertorv 4 and 6 respectively, have a large selection of Copenhagen porcelain, while *Holmegaard Glassware* is at Østergade 15.

Dyrehaven, Bellevue and Zealand

Dyrehaven, the Deer Park near Klampenborg (less than half an hour by electric train from the capital) is the Copenhageners' favorite place to spend a few hours in the country. If you go by car, remember you are not allowed to motor within the park. Here nearly 2,000 deer wander freely about. There's a golf course, a summer fun-fair (mid-Apr. to Aug. 15) and several year-round restaurants in this beautiful 3,500 acre haven of forests, paths and ponds. Near the entrance to the park is the Bellevue bathing beach. If you travel to the Klampenborg station, or to any other by electric train (S-train), remember you have to cancel your ticket in the machine at the platform entrance.

After Copenhagen, Zealand is the part of Denmark most visited, and the classic tour is up the coast to Elsinore and Kronborg Castle, down to Frederiksborg Castle, back to Copenhagen.

The coastal road between Copenhagen and Elsinore takes you along the so-called Danish Riviera, and offers lovely views of both the Danish and Swedish coast along the Sound. The fine, recently-built Louisiana Museum at Humlebaek, devoted to modern art, is well worth visiting on the way; there is a good restaurant, too. Chamber music concerts are given here in summer.

Elsinore (Helsingør) is one of Denmark's oldest towns. Its medieval church of St. Mary and attached Carmelite monastery attest to its importance in the early 15th century; they are both architectural treasures. Kronborg Castle, popularly known as Hamlet's "Castle of Elsinore" was actually built by Frederick II between 1574 and 1585, about 600 years after Prince Hamlet lived, and is quite unlike the sort of castle we visualize as the setting of Shakespeare's play. Visit this central courtyard first, then the inner and outer ramparts, the splendid 200-foot-long banqueting hall and the gloomy dungeons where the brooding figure of Holger the Dane waits to unsheathe his sword in the hour of Denmark's danger. Remember to see the chapel, too. The castle occupies a magnificent position overlooking the Sound, with Sweden only a few miles away. Elsinore also houses a Technical Museum.

The beautiful Renaissance-style castle of Frederiksborg is at Hillerød. Built by Christian IV between 1602 and 1620, it was gutted by fire in 1859 and has been fully restored with money from the Carlsberg brewery and private subscriptions. It is Denmark's National Historic Museum. The kings of Denmark used to be crowned here; these days they're not crowned at all. The castle is handsomely situated on a lake, and you will enjoy strolling through the adjacent chapel.

Fredensborg, just six miles from its twin city, Hillerød, has two claims to fame; its palace and its inn. The palace, built between 1719 and 1726, is still a royal residence and has the charm of a place that is lived in. It can be visited when the royal family is not there in July. The park is open to the public at all times.

At Odsherred in the most northwesterly part of Zealand, Mary Queen of Scots' impetuous lover, the Earl of Bothwell, lies buried at Faarevejle Church. Not far away is Dragsholm Castle where he died in 1578, completely insane.

At Trelleborg off the main road from Copenhagen to Korsør there's a famous, thousand-year-old Viking fortress, partly reconstructed to show the elaborate style of military construction.

At Roskilde, the red brick cathedral is the burial place of Denmark's kings and queens, and has 38 royal tombs. The Viking Ship Museum has restored Viking ships from about A.D. 1000 found in Roskilde Fjord.

Southern Zealand and the Southern Isles

Southern Zealand abounds in interesting towns with half-timbered houses and enough castles to make it one of Denmark's château regions. Gavnø is among the castles open to the public. Near Køge is Vallø Castle, with fine gardens open to the public.

For idyllic natural beauty it would be hard to beat the southerly island of Møn, with its white cliffs towering 400 feet up from the blue sea in fantastic shapes and its forests of beech.

PRACTICAL INFORMATION FOR ZEALAND

ELSINORE. *Marienlyst* (E), tel. 02–211801. 213 rooms. Gambling casino, pool, sauna. Fashionable. *Hotel Hamlet* (I), Bramsstraede 5, tel. 02–210591. 46 rooms.

FREDENSBORG. *Store Kro* (E), tel. 02–280047. 49 rooms, all with bath. Unrivaled food. Garden. Open Jan. 11 to Dec. 28.

HORNBAEK. *Trouville* (E), tel. 02–202200. 50 rooms, all with bath. Sauna, pool, garden. Fashionable.

KØGE. *Hvide Hus* (E), tel. 03–653690. 118 rooms. Sauna, garden.

NAESTVED. *Mogenstrup Kro* (M), just outside Naestved, tel. 03–761130. 49 rooms. Sauna, pool, garden. Excellent food.

ROSKILDE. *BP Motel* (M), on Highway A1, tel. 02–354385. 29 rooms. *Prindsen* (M), tel. 02–358010. 41 rooms. Has a good restaurant. *Risø* (M), tel. 02–356800. *Lindenborg Kro* (M), just outside Roskilde, tel. 02–402111. 14 rooms in renovated old-fashioned country inn. Fine food.

Funen and the Central Islands

Funen (Fyn), second largest of Denmark's 500 islands, is the garden of Denmark. Its capital is Odense, birthplace of Hans Christian Andersen, a journey of three hours by train from Copenhagen.

Odense's 13th-century Cathedral of St. Knud is one of the finest gothic buildings in Denmark. But the chief tourist attractions are the mementos of the great Hans Christian Andersen: the museum on Hans Jensensstraede presumably on the spot where he was born, and the house where he lived between the ages of 2 and 14, another museum which you may visit at Munkemøllestraede 3.

South Funen contains fine woods and hill scenery and the lovely old towns of Svendborg and Fåborg. Among the numerous old manors and castles, Egeskov is outstanding. The five superb gardens are open to the public, together with an excellent museum of old cars, planes and motorcycles, housed in the estate's former barn.

AErøskøbing, on AErø island (ferry from Svendborg), is the best-preserved and loveliest of all Denmark's ancient small towns. From Svendborg, you can also drive to the islands of Taasinge and Langeland.

Jutland and Neighboring Islands

Jutland is the only part of Denmark attached to the continent of Europe. A spit of sand, where you can stand with one foot in the waves of the Skagerrak and the other in the Kattegat, forms its northern tip. From here a magnificent sandy beach, backed mainly by dunes but sometimes by limestone cliffs, stretches for some 250 miles down the west coast, all the way to Esbjerg and the lovely island of Fanø opposite it. Løkken, Blokhus and a number of smaller resorts are dotted along this stretch of coast, where thousands of Danish families spend their holidays in small wooden chalets.

The region's eastern half is much hillier and often attractive. Rold Forest (Rold Skov) and the Rebild Hills National Park, 15 miles south of Aalborg, are lovely in both summer and winter. If you're here on the 4th of July, you'll think you're in America because tens of thousands of Danes and Danish-Americans gather on the Rebild Hills to celebrate America's Independence Day with speeches and other festivities in the National Park, purchased by Danish Americans in 1911.

Ebeltoft, the Mols Hills and the broad bay on which Århus, Denmark's second largest city, stands are justly renowned for their scenery. So is the Silkeborg region, with its innumerable lakes fed by the River Guden and its hills, which include Himmelbjerget, Denmark's highest.

Many of Jutland's towns and villages are especially appealing. Skagen, near the northernmost tip, is a holiday resort, fishing village and artists' colony rolled into one.

Aalborg, the most important town of north Jutland, has a harmonious combination of old and new. Sights here include the magnificent Jens Bang's House, St. Botolph cathedral from ca. 1500, the early 16th-century Aalborghus Castle, and the early 15th-century Monastery of the Holy Ghost, and last but not least the North Jutland

Museum of Art, with works by outstanding contemporary Danish and foreign artists.

Århus, an attractive large town, boasts the oldest Danish university after Copenhagen's, as well as a thriving port and a good deal of heavy industry. The 13th-century cathedral, old city center and Den gamle By (the Old Town) open-air museum are especially worth visiting. The latter consists of authentic medieval town houses collected from all parts of the country and re-erected. The most recent attraction is Musikhuset (for concerts, theater, exhibitions, etc.).

Ebeltoft, 30 miles from Århus, possesses fine medieval streets (like Ribe, Møgeltønder and other Jutland towns) and an excellent beach as well. Silkeborg and Skanderborg, 30 and 15 miles from Århus, are your bases for seeing the Lake District. Vejle is a small industrial town and major holiday center at the head of a deep, picturesque fjord.

Randers has its Tourist Information Office in the ancient House of the Holy Ghost, where storks nest all year. Many visitors are invited to become members of Randers Stork Society. Nearby, Mariager is an idyllic village where roses grow around many of the ancient houses. Ribe is Denmark's oldest town and has numerous medieval houses and an 800-year-old cathedral.

Billund, home of Legoland, has a 10-acre amusement park and a museum of antique dolls. (Closed October 1 to April 30, but indoor attractions open all year.) Sønderborg on the island of Als is a favorite yachting center.

Bornholm

Bornholm (accent on the second syllable), Denmark's outlying Baltic island, 100 miles due east of Copenhagen but only 22 from the Swedish coast, is unique not only in Denmark but also in Europe. Its dimensions are 225 square miles, with 93 miles of coast. The scenery ranges from white sand in the south to sheer cliffs in the north.

The wooden Paradisbakkerne (Paradise Hills) in the east, the Almindingen region in the island's center, the cliffs at Helligdommen, and the gaunt ruins of Hammershus fortress are all well worth visiting.

Herring fishing is an ancient occupation and the coast is dotted with tiny, pocket-handkerchief-sized harbors, of which Tejn is the minutest. Neksø, Svaneke, Gudhjem (where you can buy freshly-smoked herrings that you drink rather than eat), Allinge, Sandvig and Hasle are all picturesque. Rønne, the capital, has well-preserved medieval streets.

Bornholm possesses four of Denmark's seven surviving round churches. Located at Nyker, Nylars, Østerlars and Olsker, all were built in the 12th century for defense as well as worship.

PRACTICAL INFORMATION FOR FUNEN, JUTLAND, AND BORNHOLM

AALBORG. *Hvide Hus* (E), Vesterbro 2 (tel. 08–138400). 198 rooms. Sauna, pool. *Limfjordshotellet* (E), Ved Stranden 14–16 (tel. 08–164333). 85 rooms. *Phønix* (E), Vesterbro 77 (tel. 08–120011). 150 rooms. Sauna, garden, garage. *Central* (M), Vesterbro 38 (tel. 08–126933). 70 rooms. *Scheelsminde* (M), Scheelsminde-vej 35 (tel. 08–183233). 56 rooms, all with bath.

Restaurants. *Bondestuen* (E), Vingaardsgade 5 (tel. 08–138776). *Brigaderen* (E), Vesterbro 73 (tel. 08–120011). *Duus Vinkjaelder* (E), Osteraagade 9 (tel. 08–125056). Old, intimate wine cellar. *Faklen* (E), Jomfru Ane Gade 21 (tel. 08–137030). British style; exclusive. *Gaslight* (E), Jomfru Ane Gade 23 (tel. 08–137377). Disco open till 3 A.M. *Spisehuset Kniv og Gaffel* (E), Maren Turisgade 10 (tel. 08–166972).

Den lille Kro (M), Kastetvej 118 (tel. 08–136169). *Fyrtøjet* (M), Jomfru Ane Gade 19 (tel. 08–137377). *Limfjorden* (M), Østeraagade 18 (tel. 08–124252). *Stygge Krumpen* (M), Vesteraa 1 (tel. 08–121212). Old-fashioned cooking. *Gla-*

shuset (I), Bispensgade 18 (tel. 08–139177). Cafeteria. *Rio Bravo* (I), Østeraagade 27 (tel. 08–139450). Western saloon.

ÅRHUS. *Atlantic* (E), Europlads (tel. 06–131111). 102 rooms. Garage. *Marselis* (E), Strandvejen 25 (tel. 06–144411). 100 rooms. *Royal* (E), Store Torv 4 (tel. 06–120011). Among the most exclusive hotels in Århus, recently renovated. 130 rooms. Garage. *Missionshotellet Ansgar* (M), Banegårdspladsen 14 (tel. 06–124122). 180 rooms. Centrally located. *Park Hotel* (I), Sdr. Alle 3 (tel. 06–123231). 14 rooms. B&B only.

Restaurants. *De fire Årstider* (E), Åboulevarden 47 (tel. 06–199696). Nouvelle cuisine. *Gl. Åbyhøj* (E), Bakke Allé 1 (tel. 06–157733). Traditional French menu; recommended. *Maritza* (E), Frederiksgade (tel. 06–122588). Nightclub. First class French food. *Tordenskjold* (E), Store Torv 4 (tel. 06–139577). Disco. *Børsen* (M), Mindebrogade 2 (tel. 06–122229). Excellent food at reasonable prices. *Café Casablanca* (M), Rosensgade 12 (tel. 06–138222). Small French style café with light snacks. *Europa* (M), Europaplads (tel. 06–123215). Traditional Danish food. *Jacob's Bar B.Q.* (M), Vestergade 3 (tel. 06–122042). *Kroen i Krogen* (M), Banegårdsplads 4 (tel. 06–122401). Danish food. *Raadhuus Kafeen* (M), Sønderallé 3 (tel. 06–123774). Cosy place, Danish food. *Pizzeria Napoli* (I), Vestergade 36 (tel. 06–121776).

EBELTOFT. *Hvide Hus* (M), tel. 06–341466. 52 rooms, all with bath. Sauna, pool. *Vaegtergården* (M), tel. 06–362211. 26 rooms. Garden.
Restaurant. *Mellem Jyder* (M), housed in an old, half-timbered building. Lopsided floors, rustic furniture, genuine antiques.

ESBJERG. *Britannia* (M), tel. 05–130111. 79 rooms, all with bath. Garden. *Esbjerg* (I), tel. 05–128188. 45 rooms.

FANO. *Sonderho Kro* (E), tel. 05–164009. On Fano island, reached by car ferry from Esbjerg (approximately 15 minutes). Idyllic inn in a village of thatched medieval cottages near beach. Superb interior decor; luxury bedrooms, individually decorated. Gourmet restaurant. Sophisticated retreat.

ODENSE. *Grand* (M), Jernbanegade 18 (tel. 09–117171). 150 rooms. *Hotel H.C. Andersen* (E), Claus Bergsgade 7 (tel. 09–147800). 148 rooms. Opened summer 1981, of the Hvide Hus chain. Sauna. *Motel Odense* (M), Hunderupgade 2 (tel. 09–114213). 46 rooms. Highly rated. A converted farmhouse on Highway A1. *Frederik VIs Kro* (M), Rugårdsvej 590 (tel. 09–941313). 48 rooms, all with bath. Suburban, good as a base for excursions. *Missionshotellet Ansgar* (I), Østre Stationsvej 32, (tel. 09–119693). 48 rooms.

Restaurants. *Skoven* (E), Hunderup Skov, Laessøegade 215 (tel. 09–114300). In forest; Danish food. *Under Lindetraeet* (E), Ramsherred 2 (tel. 09–129286). Danish and French menu. *A Hereford Beefstouw* (M), Vestergade 13 (tel. 09–120222). Mostly beef and salads. *Den gamle Kro* (M), Overgade 23 (tel. 09–121433). Cosy and old-fashioned. *Den grimme Aelling* (M), Hans Jensens Straede (tel. 09–115025). *Franck-A* (M), Jernbanegade 4 (tel. 09–122757). *Klods Hans* (M), Vindegade 76 (tel. 09–135600). Pub-like. *Sortebro Kro* (M), Den Fynske Landsby (tel. 09–132826). Old-fashioned inn.

RANDERS. *Hotel Randers* (E), tel. 06–423422. Original decor, beautifully maintained, with antiques, elegant atmosphere, excellent service, very good food. In town center. Highly recommended; one of Denmark's best.

RIBE. *Dagmar* (E), tel. 05–420033. 42 rooms. 16th-century building, with sloping floors, antiques and a memorable, fascinating atmosphere. In town center. Very good restaurant.

RØNNE. *Griffen* (E), tel. 03–955111. 142 rooms, all with bath. Sauna, pool. Sea view. *Ryttergården* (M), tel. 03–951913. 119 rooms, all with bath. Open May 1 to Oct. 1. Seaside hotel.

SILKEBORG. *Dania* (M), tel. 06–820111. 48 rooms, most with bath. Garden; garage.

SKAGEN. *Klithotellerne* (E), tel. 08–441322. Apartment hotel. In great demand so it is best to book. *Skagen* (E), tel. 08–442233. 47 rooms. Modern. Open Jan. 1 to Dec. 23.

SKANDERBORG. *Skanderborghus* (M), tel. 06–520955. 50 rooms, most with bath. *Landsbykroen* (M), Nørre Vissing (tel. 06–943716). Small country inn. Open Jan. 10-Dec. 20.

SIBELIUS

FINLAND

Finland has long been famous for sunlit nights, patriotism, design and architecture, Sibelius, and saunas. It's also famous, among discerning visitors these days, for being among the first of European nations to promote tourism on the basis of ecological conservation. There's certainly plenty of natural beauty worth conserving, for a very high proportion of Finland's surface is covered by lakes and forests, rising gently to low ridges or, in the north, higher bare-topped fells from which the views are infinite. The Finns have learned how to make the most of their marvelous horizons during their short but often brilliant summers, and the crisp white winters. There are excellent accommodations and fine sports facilities. And in the towns—even quite modest ones—there's sophisticated cultural and other entertainment, good eating—and, of course, plenty of evidence of the imaginative architecture for which Finland has become a byword.

There are about 4¾ million Finns. They are basically reserved (which is probably why some of them drink so much), but will go to endless trouble if approached for help. Their attractive-sounding language is related to Hungarian or Estonian (Swedish is a second official language), but happily English is quite widely spoken.

The light of freedom burns fiercely in this country, which was ruled for seven centuries by the Swedes, for one by the Russians, and which has only been independent since 1917. Since the Second World War, Finland has maintained its independence in face of its sensitive geographical situation, and is careful about its neutrality. It is a member of the United Nations, the Nordic Council, and the free trade area of Western Europe as well as having free trade agreements with the EEC (Common Market), Eastern Europe and the U.S.S.R.

PRACTICAL INFORMATION FOR FINLAND

 WHAT WILL IT COST. The hotel and restaurant price categories given under the respective headings and based on 1986 figures, will act as a guide. However, it is estimated that prices will increase by about 10% in 1987. Generally speaking, accommodation and restaurant prices in the capital, Helsinki, are about 20% higher than in the provinces, where costs don't vary much as there are no large resorts and rarely low standards. One point to note, though, is that double rooms cost very much less per person than singles.

The monetary unit in Finland is the markka (Fmk.), which breaks down into 100 penni. At presstime, there were about 5.3 Fmk. to the U.S. dollar and 7.90 Fmk. to the pound sterling.

A typical day in Helsinki might cost two people:

Hotel (moderate) double room with tax and service	350 Fmk.
Lunch at restaurant (moderate) with coffee	80
Transportation (taxi for 5 km.)	30
Coffee in a popular café	8
Beer in a popular café	18
Theater (middle range)	100
Dinner (moderate) with coffee	120
Miscellaneous 10%	70
	776 Fmk.

SOURCES OF INFORMATION. For information on all aspects of travel to Finland, contact the Finnish National Tourist Office. Its addresses are:
In the U.S.: 655 Third Ave., New York, N.Y. 10017 (tel. 212–949–2333).
In the U.K.: 66 Haymarket, London S.W.1 (tel. 01–839 4048).

 WHEN TO COME. From mid-June to mid-August is the warmest period, with daylight up to 24 hours long. Spring is fresh and green; fall, from early September in the far north, produces fabulous coloring. There's good skiing conditions throughout the winter, and this activity reaches its peak in March, when the days are long and often sunny. Helsinki can be at its best in May.

Climate. There is permanent snow in southern and central Finland from early December to mid or late April; in the Far North, early November to mid-May.

Average maximum daily temperatures in degrees Fahrenheit and centigrade:

Helsinki	Jan.	Feb.	Mar.	Apr.	May	June	July	Aug.	Sept.	Oct.	Nov.	Dec.
F°	27	27	32	43	57	66	72	68	59	46	37	30
C°	−3	−3	0	6	14	19	22	20	15	8	3	−1

 SPECIAL EVENTS. Salpausselka Int'l. Winter Games at Lahti, early March; Ounasvaara Int'l. Winter Games at Rovaniemi, late March. *Vapunaatto* (Walpurgis Night) on *April* 30 is a nation-wide welcome to the return of spring with an emphasis on students' festivities followed by Vappu (*May Day* or Labor Day) celebrations. Midsummer Eve is celebrated during the weekend closest to *June* 24, festivities throughout the country; Vaasa Summer, Kuopio Dance and Music Festival, Naantali Music Festival, in *June*;; Jyväskylä Arts Festival (with a different theme each year) begins end of June; Savonlinna Opera Festival, Pori Jazz Festival, Kuhmo Chamber Music Festival and Kaustinen Folk Music Festival are in *July;* Turku Music Festival, Lahti Organ Festival and Tampere Theater Summer, in *August.* The Helsinki Festival, offering two weeks of music and drama of all kinds, begins late August.

National Holidays. Jan. 1 (New Year's Day); Jan. 10 (Epiphany); Apr. 17, 20 (Easter); Apr. 30 (May Day Eve); May 1 (May Day); May 23 (Ascension); Jun. 6, 7 (Whitsun); Jun. 19, 20 (Midsummer's Eve and Midsummer's Day); Oct. 31 (All Saints); Dec. 6 (Independence); Dec. 24–26.

 VISAS. Nationals of the United States, Canada, Australia, New Zealand, EEC countries and practically all other European countries do not require visas for entry into Finland. However, you must have a valid passport.

HEALTH CERTIFICATES. Not required for entry into Finland from any country.

 GETTING TO FINLAND. By Plane. From North America, only *Finnair* flies direct (from New York, Montreal, Seattle and Los Angeles). Finnair and reciprocal flag carriers maintain regular flights between Helsinki, London and many major European cities. Flying time from Britain or central Europe is about three hours.

By Train. There are no through trains between Western Europe and Finland as the railway gauge is different, being the "broad" gauge as in the U.S.S.R. (with which there is a daily through train from Leningrad and a sleeping car service to and from Moscow). In the far north there are linking services via Haparanda (in Sweden) with Tornio (in Finland) by changing trains. From Western Europe the best train-ferry route is by rail to Stockholm and then by ferry to Turku, thence train to Helsinki or direct by ferry to the Finnish capital. From London via the Hook of Holland, Copenhagen and Stockholm route to Helsinki takes 2 days.

By Car. Numerous car ferries link Denmark, north Germany and especially Sweden with Finland. Routes also lead to northern Finland from Sweden and Norway, also from Helsinki to Leningrad.

 CUSTOMS. All travelers entering the country may bring in noncommercial goods up to 1,000 Fmk., which may include foodstuffs up to 15kg. inclusive of 5kg. of edible fats; however, not more than 2.5kg. of butter. Also, 200 cigarettes or 250gr. of other tobacco products (double for residents of non-European countries), and, for travelers 20 years and over, 1 liter of spirits, 2 liters beer and 1 liter of other mild alcoholic drinks.

 **HOTELS.** A free list of all hotels in Finland is available from the Finnish Tourist Board and this gives considerable detail of the amenities offered by each, as well as indicating those providing full board. There is no official hotel grading system in Finland, however, and often little difference in the amenities offered by Deluxe and Expensive (see below) establishments. The following, then, is an indication of price range rather than of standards which, generally speaking, are very high. A flexible Finncheck hotel check system operates in many hotels in three price categories all over Finland.

Our hotel grading system is divided into four categories. All prices are for 2 people in a double room: Deluxe (L), 580–700 Fmk., Expensive (E) 400–580 Fmk., Moderate (M) 250–400 Fmk., and Inexpensive (I) 150–250 Fmk. In the provinces, (L) is 450–550 Fmk., (E) 300–450 Fmk., (M) 180–300 Fmk., and (I) 120–180 Fmk.

CAMPING. The best way to enjoy Finland's wealth of lake-and-forest scenery is to get out into it. There are camping areas near most cities and throughout the countryside open to all. About 350 camping sites have been established in Finland by various organizations and, as the Finn has an eye for beauty, most have choice locations on the shores of lake, river or sea. Generally, free camping is not allowed without the landowner's permission, and fires are forbidden.

A free list of camp sites is available from Finnish Tourist Board offices and most of them are marked on the excellent Suomen Tiekartta (Finnish Road Map) and Autoilijan Tiekartta (Motorist's Road Map), available from bookshops or the Automobile and Touring Club in Helsinki.

 RESTAURANTS. Taking account of Finland's cost of living and high standards, you can get a good meal at a reasonable price, especially if you stick to *table d'hôte* menus served between fixed times, which are usually fairly early, particularly in more moderate establishments. About 200 restaurants and cafés (list available from Finnish Tourist Board) offer the special Finland Menu featuring traditional dishes at fixed and reasonable prices. The number of pleasant snack bars has increased enormously in recent years. The number and range of restaurants specializing in food from different parts of the world has also increased greatly. What is more, the food is always attractively served.

In the restaurant listings later in this chapter, we have used three price categories; in each case, the price is for one person, eating *table d'hôte*. Expensive (E) covers the 75–130 Fmk. range, Moderate (M) 45–75 Fmk., and Inexpensive (I) 20–45 Fmk.

Food and Drink. You will meet Swedish *smörgaasbord,* with Finnish variations, in many restaurants, and as Finns are solid eaters, no one will be surprised if you return for two or three helpings. Finland also has some unusual dishes of her own—reindeer tongue, for instance (*poronkieltä*). You might also try the provincial *kalakukko,* a mixture of fish and pork baked in a round rye dough, *lihapullia,* meat balls, *Karelian hotpot,* beef, mutton and pork cooked together, and *Karjalan piirakka,* a rice-filled pasty. The season for crayfish, a great delicacy, begins about 20th July and lasts several weeks.

Three especially good Finnish liqueurs are *Mesimarja* (Arctic Bramble), *Lakka* (Cloudberry) and *Polar* (Cranberry). Imported spirits (very expensive) and wine (relatively reasonable) are marginally lower priced if bottled in Finland. Finnish vodka is particularly good, and she has some excellent beers.

 TIPPING. The hotel service charge of 15% takes care of everything. 5 Fmk. fee per bag to railway porters (when you can find them); usually 3 Fmk. to bellhops or restaurant doormen. The 14% service charge in restaurants and nightclubs (15% weekends and holidays) is sufficient. Taxi drivers, ushers, washroom attendants, barbers, and beauty salon attendants are not tipped. A general guideline is that you can tip for good service, but it is not expected.

MAIL. Up to 20 grams, letters airmail to the U.K. are 2.20 Fmk.; to the U.S. and Canada 2.70 Fmk. Postcards airmail to all three, 2.20 Fmk.

 CLOSING TIMES. Shops open from 8.30 or 9 in the morning to 5 or 6 P.M. on weekdays (can be later Monday and Friday); Saturday they close at 1 or 2 P.M. In the subway by Helsinki rail station, shops of all kinds remain open until 10 P.M. including Sundays. Banks open Monday through Friday between 9.30 A.M. and 4 P.M.; Saturdays they are closed all day. Additional exchange facilities exist at Helsinki station and airport seven days a week.

 USEFUL ADDRESSES. *American Embassy,* I. Puistotie 14A. *British Embassy,* Uudenmaankatu 16–20. *Canadian Embassy,* Pohjoisesplanadi 25b. *City Tourist Office,* Pohjoisesplanadi 19. All in Helsinki.

 GETTING AROUND FINLAND. By Plane. Finland has an elaborate service of internal flights operated by *Finnair.* Helsinki is connected with most of the large towns and there are also cross-country flights linking several of these. Fares are among the lowest in Europe with special rates, such as the Finnair Holiday Ticket offering unlimited travel within Finland for 15 days, and reductions for those aged 12–23, over 65, and family groups.

By Train. Although it is sparsely populated, Finland has a very good and extensive railway system reaching all main centers of the country. Standards of comfort and cleanliness are high. Most trains have 1st and 2nd class, a few 2nd class only. There is a small supplement for travel on main expresses. Reductions apply to groups of a minimum of three persons, and special rates also apply to children and to those over 65 holding a card available at modest cost from any rail station in Finland.

Tickets which combine rail, bus and ferry travel (and in some cases air travel as well) are available in Finland, with advanced planning, giving a small discount. There are car-carrying trains to and from Lapland from Helsinki, Turku and Tampere. A *Finnrailpass* gives unlimited travel for eight, 15 and 22 days costing in 1st class respectively $99, $138 and $180, or, in 2nd class, $66, $92 and $120. No reductions for children. *Inter-Rail* and *Eurail* passes are valid on Finnish railways and offer some reductions on Baltic sea crossings. Finland is also a partner in the *Scandinavian Railpass* (see under Denmark).

By Boat. A number of the lakes have ferry and pleasure boats on them in summer (in winter they are frozen over). You can have a short ride or go for a "cruise" of several days. On Lake Päijänne there is a hydrofoil service from Lahti to Jyväskylä taking three hours—the ordinary steamer takes nearly nine hours. Boats are for hire (including flotilla sailing) on some of the many lakes and also around the coast. There is a ferry system both at Helsinki and at Turku. From the latter there are regular services to the Åland Islands.

By Bus. Bus travel plays a leading role in Finland with an extensive network, linked in many cases to the railway system. In the far north (Lapland), and in parts of the eastern area close to the Soviet border, it is the only means of public transport. Costs are slightly lower than by rail.

By Car. The main road network is excellent, except for a few roughish sections in the far north. Some secondary roads may be temporarily closed during the spring thaw. Gasoline costs 3.60–3.67 Fmk. per liter.

Car Hire. *Helsinki* firms include: *Avis,* Fredrikinkatu 36; *Hertz,* Hotel Intercontinental, 46–48 Mannerheimintie; *Europcar Car Rental,* Mariankatu 24; *InterRent,* Hitsaajankatu 7B. Self-drive cars are available in most main centers, and there are advantageous fly-drive schemes, such as the one operated by Finnair/Hertz.

Exploring Helsinki

The heart of Helsinki is the gracious Senate Square, designed in the 1820s and '30s by the German-born architect, Carl Ludvig Engel, and his Finnish partner Johan Albrekt Ehrenström. Between them, they replanned the town which had been devastated by fire in 1808 and which now became Finland's capital (formerly Turku). Here stand the cathedral, the State Council Building, and the University Library (Engel's masterpiece), a group of majestic buildings composed in a pure classic style which certainly presaged the well-known work of such later Finnish architects as Eliel Saarinen and Alvar Aalto. Engel also designed the Town Hall in the Market Square, down by the South Harbor. The colorful market flourishes here in the morning whatever the season and, in summer, from 3.30–8 P.M., along the waterfront and around the fountain of Havis Amanda, the sea maiden who represents Helsinki rising from the waves. It's a splendidly lively place with its stalls of flowers, fruit, vegetables, fish fresh and still flipping from the sea, and quite a few traditional handicrafts. That building along the edge of the square, facing the sea and patrolled by a sentry in field gray, is the President's Palace. Behind the Town Hall you will see once again the silhouette of Helsinki's most famous landmark, the cathedral, just a few steps away in Senate Square. The broad avenue and gardens of Esplanadikatu lead west from the market; many of the excellent shops along here are open on Sundays in summer.

For further orientation, you might try the Hotel Torni for lunch at the top of the tower. Get a table by the window and survey the town while you eat. You will recognize the cathedral, the massive railway station designed by Saarinen, the Stadium Tower and the broad street running through the city center, Mannerheimintie, named after Finland's great hero, Marshal Mannerheim.

After lunch, here are some of the sights you should examine at closer quarters—the richly decorated Orthodox Uspenski Cathedral with its gleaming "onions" towering above the rocky island of Katajanokka, east of the President's Palace; the Sederholm House in the Great Square, built in 1757, the oldest house in this modern town; the impressive red granite Eduskunta or Parliament House, with its peristyle of 55-foot columns and its lavishly-decorated interior; the National Museum, with ethnographical exhibits illustrating Finland's history; the Ateneum Art Gallery and its collections of work by Wäinö Aaltonen and the other leading sculptors and painters of Finland; the National Theater in the huge square before the railway station, and the station itself, which, with its strong, massive lines and 155-foot-high granite tower, is one of Eliel Saarinen's most widely-known buildings. One of Helsinki's latest shopping precincts, Kaivopiha (off Mannerheimintie), is an attractive oasis in the center, linked to the railway station and the city's new metro network.

Other good examples of Finland's famous modern architecture include the magnificent Finlandia Concert Hall and Congress Center, designed by Alvar Aalto, near the National Museum; the City Theater, Eläintarhantie; the busy shopping complex of the City Center opposite the railway station; the extraordinary Dipoli Hall at the engineers' suburb of Otaniemi, and the whole of the satellite town of Tapiola. One of Europe's most unusual churches is that of Taivallahti, built into the living rock in Töölö, one of the older residential districts of the city.

Three highly recommended outdoor attractions are the Botanical Gardens and their Water Tower, if you want another splendid panorama; Linnanmäki, close to the water tower, Helsinki's permanent amusement park; and the Open Air Museum of Seurasaari.

You will also enjoy the island fortress of Suomenlinna, currently being developed as a cultural and recreational center. Begun in 1748 this "Gibraltar of the North" was never taken by assault. The surrounding parks and gardens are lovely in spring and summer, and there's an excellent restaurant, Walhalla, in one of the forts. Good bathing facilities and sandy beach here too. There is a frequent ferry service from the South Harbor marketplace. The Zoo, on another island, can be reached by ferry from the North Harbor or by footbridge from Mustikkamaa island, accessible by road.

PRACTICAL INFORMATION FOR HELSINKI

GETTING AROUND HELSINKI. The **Helsinki Card,** valid 1 day (50 Fmk.), 2 days (75 Fmk.) or 3 days (90 Fmk.), from the Helsinki Tourist Office and many other outlets, entitles you to unlimited travel on city public transport, free entry to many museums, reductions on sightseeing tours and in many hotels, shops, restaurants, etc.

By Subway. The first section of Helsinki's splendid subway has now opened. It goes from the main rail station east to Itäkeskus (same fares and transfers as bus/tram system).

By Tram/Bus. A ride costs 5.50 Fmk (small reduction for 10-ride tickets) and allows transfers within a one hour period. A tourist ticket valid for 24 hours and giving unlimited travel is available from the Helsinki Tourist Office or public transport ticket offices. It costs 35 Fmk. It is not available on board the vehicles. The 3T tram, with commentary in several languages in summer, follows a figure-eight circuit right round the city center.

By Boat. Regular ferries link the South and North Harbors with island sights, and there are sightseeing excursions by boat throughout summer.

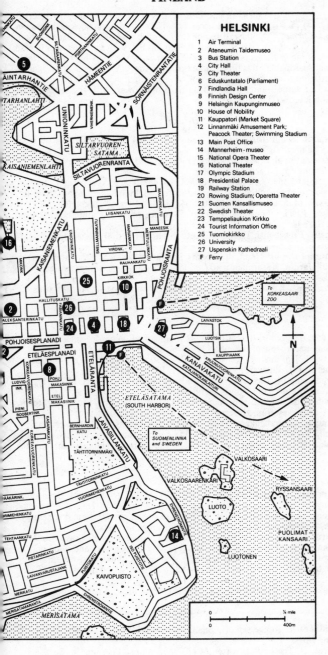

HELSINKI

1 Air Terminal
2 Ateneumin Taidemuseo
3 Bus Station
4 City Hall
5 City Theater
6 Eduskuntatalo (Parliament)
7 Findlandia Hall
8 Finnish Design Center
9 Helsingin Kaupunginmuseo
10 House of Nobility
11 Kauppatori (Market Square)
12 Linnanmäki Amusement Park;
   Peacock Theater; Swimming Stadium
13 Main Post Office
14 Mannerheim - museo
15 National Opera Theater
16 National Theater
17 Olympic Stadium
18 Presidential Palace
19 Railway Station
20 Rowing Stadium; Operetta Theater
21 Suomen Kansallismuseo
22 Swedish Theater
23 Temppeliaukion Kirkko
24 Tourist Information Office
25 Tuomiokirkko
26 University
27 Uspenskin Kathedraali
F Ferry

HOTELS. During the peak summer months reservations are necessary. The central room booking bureau in the rail station (in summer, weekdays 9–9, Sat. 9–7, Sun. 10–6; in winter, Mon. to Fri. 9–6) can assist you in case of need. Summer hotels (student hostels the rest of the year) offer comfortable rooms at reasonable rates (open June through Aug.). Most hotels have saunas, and restaurants are licensed unless otherwise stated. All establishments listed have all or some rooms with private bath or shower, with the exception of boarding houses (I).

Deluxe

Hesperia, Mannerheimintie 50 (tel. 43101). 384 rooms, a short stroll from the city center. Nightclub and pool.

Inter-Continental, Mannerheimintie 46 (tel. 441331). 555 rooms, nightclub, pool. Again, not far from the center.

Kalastajatorppa, Kalastajatorpantie 1 (tel. 488011). 235 rooms at a gorgeous shore-side location, but away from the center. Nightclub, pool, sports facilities.

Marski, Mannerheimintie 10 (tel. 641717). 164 rooms, nightclub. Central.

Palace, Eteläranta 10 (tel. 171114). 58 rooms offering a stunning view over South Harbor.

Ramada Presidentti, E. Rautatiekatu 4 (tel. 6911). 500 rooms, disco, nightclub, pool.

Rantasipi Airport Hotel, 300 rooms, is right by the airport. Nightclub, pool.

Rivoli Jardin, Kasarmikatu 40 (tel. 177880). 53 rooms, winter garden. New, central, with particularly well equipped rooms.

Seurahuone, Kaivokatu 12 (tel. 170441). 114 rooms; very centrally situated. Its *Café Socis* is a favorite turn-of-century style rendezvous. Nightclub.

Expensive

Garden, Tapiontori (tel. 461711). 82 rooms, pool, in garden suburb of Tapiola, some miles west of the city.

Helsinki, Hallituskatu 12 (tel. 171401). 130 rooms, disco. Very central.

Klaus Kurki, Bulevardi 2 (tel. 602322). 135 rooms, central.

Korpilampi, 14 miles west of city in lovely forest setting (tel. 8558431). 161 rooms, night club, pool, sports facilities.

Merihotelli Cumulus, Hakaniemenranta 4 (tel. 711455). 87 rooms, nightclub, pool. A little way from the city center.

Olympia, L. Brahenkatu 2 (tel. 750801). 100 rooms, pool. Not central.

Torni, Yrjönkatu 26 (tel. 644611). 158 rooms, varied restaurants, central.

Vaakuna, Asema-aukio 2 (tel. 171811). 290 rooms, nightclub; near rail station.

Moderate

Academica, Hietaniemenkatu 14 (tel. 440171). 115 rooms, pool. Open summer only.

Aurora, Helsinginkatu 50 (tel. 717400). 75 rooms, pool, beer and wine only.

Finn, Kalevankatu 3B (tel. 640904). 28 rooms, no restaurant.

Haaga, Nuijamiestentie 10 (tel. 578311). 110 rooms, pool. Less central.

Helka, P. Rautatiekatu 23 (tel. 440581). 152 rooms, beer and wine only.

Hospiz, Vuorikatu 17B (tel. 170481). 166 rooms, unlicensed restaurant.

Marttahotelli, Uudenmaankatu 24 (tel. 646211). 44 rooms, unlicensed restaurant.

Ursula, Paasivuorenkatu 1 (tel. 750311). 46 rooms, no restaurant.

Inexpensive

Asuntohotelli Kongressikoti, Snellmaninkatu 15 (tel. 174839). 10 rooms, boarding house.

Clairet, It. Teatterikuja 3 (tel. 669707). 15 rooms, boarding house.

Erottajanpuisto, Uudenmaankatu 9 (tel. 642169). 15 rooms, boarding house.

Lönnrot, Lönnrotinkatu 16 (tel. 605590). 26 rooms, boarding house.

Omapohja, It. Teatterikuja 3 (tel. 666211). 14 rooms, boarding house.

Private Hotel Borg, Cygnaeuskatu 16 (tel. 499990). 4 rooms, boarding house.

Regina, Puistokatu 9 (tel. 656937). 6 rooms, boarding house.

Satakuntatalo, Lapinrinne (tel. 6940311). 64 rooms; summer only.

RESTAURANTS. You will meet Swedish smörgasbord, with Finnish variations, as well as various national dishes, international cuisine and specialties from most parts of the world. Note that *table d'hôte* meals served between fixed hours work out much more cheaply than eating à la carte. Several English-style pubs also serve food, and there are many cafes and snack bars. All restaurants included here are licensed unless otherwise stated.

Expensive

Adlon, Fabianinkatu 14 (tel. 664611). Fine cuisine, cabaret.

Finnish Cuisine, Sibeliuksenkatu 2 (tel. 493591). Finnish specialties prepared in traditional way.

Kaivohuone, Kaivopuisto (tel. 177881). Picturesque location looking out to South Harbor. Cabaret.

Kalastajatorppa (Fisherman's Cottage), Kalastajatorpantie 1 (tel. 488100). An old favorite in a lovely setting, adjoining the modern hotel of the same name. Cabaret. Not central.

Karl König, Mikonkatu 4 (tel. 171271). First-class food in subdued, sophisticated setting below ground.

Mestaritalli, Toivo Kuulan puisto (tel. 440274). Formerly stables, now an elegant restaurant in a seashore park. Not central.

Motti, Töölöntorinkatu 2 (tel. 494418).

Punainen Hattu, Keskuskatu 7 (tel. 639527). Intimate atmosphere.

Walhalla, on the island of Suomenlinna (tel. 668552). A few minutes by ferry from South Harbor. Authentic 18th-century fortress atmosphere. Open summer only.

Moderate

El Greco, Eteläesplanadi 22 (tel. 607565). Greek food.

Happy Days, Pohjoisesplanadi 2 (tel. 624023). Next to the Swedish Theater. A selection of several restaurants at different price levels.

Kappeli, in the Esplanade gardens near South Harbor (tel. 179242). Several sections, including openair summer restaurant.

Perho, Mechelininkatu 7 (tel. 493481). Run by Helsinki Hotel and Restaurant College. Good value. Recently renovated.

Säkkipilli, Kalevankatu 2 (tel. 605607). Cozy English atmosphere.

Savoy, Eteläesplanadi 14 (tel. 176571). Favorite business lunch place.

Troikka, Caloniuksenkatu 3 (tel. 445229). One of a chain of three small eating places specializing in excellent Russian food.

Tullinpuomi, Mannerheimintie 118 (tel. 412058). Cabaret.

Välskärin Kellari, Hallistuskatu 3 (tel. 174395). Intimate cellar atmosphere in Helsinki's "Whitehall" district.

Wellamo, Vyökatu 9 (tel. 663139). Small, intimate, rustic atmosphere, good food if you like garlic.

Inexpensive

Chez Marius, Mikonkatu 1 (tel. 669697). Good-value French cooking. Beer and wine only.

Davy's, Fredrikinkatu 22 (tel. 651939). Excellent pizzas, rustic style. Beer and wine only.

Eliel, in the railway station. Genuine art nouveau style. Self-service.

Groovy, Ruoholahdenkatu 4 (tel. 6945118). Good jazz restaurant.

Kellarikrouvi, P. Makasiininkatu 6 (tel. 655198). Cozy wine-cellar atmosphere.

Rivoli, Albertinkatu 38 (tel. 643455). Italian food, good for quick lunch.

 ENTERTAINMENT. Free publications such as *Helsinki This Week* and *Helsinki Today* are good sources of information about what's on and where. The solid façade of the old-established *National Theater* is a dominant feature of the railway station square. Here plays are given in Finnish, whereas at *Svenska Teatern* or the *Swedish Theater,* a familiar landmark where the Esplanade meets Mannerheimintie, performances are in Swedish. There are also the ultra-modern *City Theater,* Eläintarhantie, near Töölönlahti Bay, and the splendid Aalto-designed *Finlandia Hall,* Concert and Congress Center, on Mannerheimintie. The *National Opera* is in Bulevardi.

Though the theaters are closed in summer, they are replaced by summer theaters of various kinds in charming island or park settings.

Musical performances are also held in a number of attractive settings in summer, such as organ recitals on Sunday evenings in the *Lutheran Cathedral,* concerts in *Temppeliaukio Church* and the *House of Nobility,* and open-air concerts of various kinds in *several parks.*

In the many *cinemas* all films are shown in their original language.

Linnanmäki amusement park is Helsinki's Tivoli, with the Peacock Theater, side shows, Monorail sightseeing train, open-air dancing, etc. in summer (closed Mon.).

The *Helsinki Festival* for two weeks at the end of August and beginning of September is a major event, combining all kinds of cultural events.

MUSEUMS. Most close for one or more days each week, usually including Mondays. The following are some of the more important sights.

Ateneum Art Gallery, Kaivokatu 2–4. Foreign and Finnish paintings and sculptures.

Burgher's House, Kristianinkatu 12. Oldest surviving wooden house (1817) in Helsinki, furnished in 1860s style.

Cathedral, Senaatintori. C.L. Engel's fine neoclassical building, completed 1852.

Gallen Kallela Museum, Leppävaara, Tarvaspää, reached by tram No. 4 to Munkkiniemi, then a pleasant 2 km. walk. The home and works of one of Finland's greatest painters in charming surroundings.

Helsinki City Museum, Karamzininkatu 2, off Mannerheimintie. Illustrates the history of the city.

Korkeasaari Zoo, reached by ferry from North Harbor, or by footbridge from Mustikkamaa island, which is accessible by road.

National Museum, Mannerheimintie 34. Three sections; prehistoric, historic, ethnographic.

Seurasaari. On an island linked by causeway to the city. A fine collection of old farms and manor buildings from various parts of the country.

Sinebrychoff Art Museum, Bulevardi 40. Collection of old masters, especially Dutch and Flemish.

Suomenlinna, frequent ferry service from South Harbor. Fortifications on series of islands, currently being restored and developed into a multipurpose center; Nordic Arts Center, museums, etc.

Temppeliaukio Church, Lutherinkatu 3. Beautiful modern church carved out of the living rock.

 SHOPPING. *Important:* Purchases made at shops displaying "tax-free for tourists" signs entitle you to a tax refund of approximately 11% when leaving Finland. You'll need your passport with you to claim. Finland's largest department store is *Stockmann's,* on Aleksanterinkatu. See also the *Finnish Design Center,* Kasarmikatu 19. *Hakaniemi Market Hall,* Hämeentie, with 50 shops above the covered food market, is varied and fun. There are many attractive boutiques in new shopping precincts such as *Kaivopiha* off Mannerheimintie and linked to the railway station; and *Kiseleff Bazar* on the corner of Aleksanterinkatu and Unioninkatu where 40 different shops sell traditional Finnish handicrafts. Famous establishments include: *Aarikka,* Bulevardi 7 or Pohjoisesplanadi 25; *Poppana,* Liisankatu 19; *Neovius,* City Center. Especially for fabrics and fashion: *Marimekko,* Pohjoisesplanadi 31 and Keskuskatu 3; *Metsovaara,* Pohjoisesplanadi 23; *Vuokko,* Pohjoisesplanadi 25 and Fabianinkatu 12; (in fine wool) *Arola,* Kalevankatu 4. *Kalevala koru,* Unioninkatu 25, has beautiful traditional jewelry and textiles. And you'll find everything for the sauna at the *Sauna Shop,* Mannerheimintie 22–24.

Note. The shops in the subway by Helsinki railway station are open every evening until 10. Most shops in Explanadikatu are open Sundays.

By Lake and Seashore

Ainola, the home of Sibelius, and Hvitträsk, the lakeside former studio and residence of three leading Finnish architects, both in beautiful settings, are among the excursion destinations near the capital.

Another, Porvoo (Borga), is on the coast east of Helsinki, three hours by boat or one hour by bus. This is one of the oldest towns in Finland, its narrow winding streets contrasting with more rational gridiron pattern of the capital. The Hotel Aulanko, in the midst of a superb national park at Hämeenlinna, is one of the show places of Finland, 1¼ hours by train from Helsinki. There's a lake for swimming. Notable sights in the vicinity include the town of Hämeenlinna, birthplace of Sibelius and site of a castle which dates from 1249. See also the Hattula Church, built of stone about 1250, with remarkable medieval frescos.

West of Helsinki is the pretty town of Tammisaari (Ekenäs), and further on the sailing and seaside resort of Hanko. The islands of the archipelago around Helsinki are easily accessible by boat in summer.

Three other main centers are Lahti (1½ hours by rail), Jyväskylä (1 hour by air) and Savonlinna (1 hour by air), all on major lake systems with good sports facilities. Any of these makes an excellent center from which to explore the forest-and-lake-scapes that are the great features of central and eastern Finland. You can use a combination of lake boats, bus or rail and travel for days without ever doubling back on your tracks. Dotted about these peaceful landscapes are small communities, many of them offering fine examples of modern architecture or some church, castle or manor house surviving from a bygone age. In particular, Savonlinna on Lake Saimaa has a glorious old castle; Jyväskylä has become an important center for holiday villages of luxury log cabins in the heart of wild forestland. Yachts can be rented in a number of places and there are water sports in plenty. Every place has a tourist office that will be able to advise you.

The rest of Finland, including "industrial" cities like Turku and Tampere, is more of the same—a magnificent stretch of unspoiled fen and forest, interlaced with waterways and dotted by more than 60,000 beautiful lakes. Tampere's famous sights include Scandinavia's first planetarium, a fine aquarium, the world's first open-air theater with revolving auditorium, many old churches in the surrounding countryside, and a wide choice of lake excursions. Turku has an old castle, ancient cathedral, and is the gateway to thousands of islands on which there are many possibilities to rent cottages.

PRACTICAL INFORMATION FOR THE REGIONS

HOTELS AND RESTAURANTS. Unless otherwise stated, all the hotels listed below have licensed restaurants on the premises; and all or some of the rooms have private baths or showers. An explanation of the price grading system employed is given at the start of the chapter under the heading, *Hotels.* (I) restaurants are licensed for wine and beer only.

HÄMEENLINNA. *Rantasipi Aulanko* (L–E), set in a beautiful national park nearby. 216 rooms, night club, pool, sports facilities. *Cumulus* (E), 57 rooms, pool. *Vouti* (E), 41 rooms.

HYVINKÄÄ. *Rantasipi Hyvinkää* (E–M), 190 rooms, night club, pool, sports facilities.

JYVÄSKYLÄ. *Rantasipi Laajavuori* (L), 176 rooms, night club, pool, sports facilities. Set in hotel/sports complex just outside town. *Cumulus* (E), 200 rooms, pool. *Jyväshovi* (E), 120 rooms, pool. *Milton* (M), 35 rooms. *Rentukka* (M), 136 rooms, disco, summer only. *Amis* (I), 93 rooms without shower. Cafeteria only.

    Restaurants. *Katinhäntä* (E), *Priimus* (M), *Kantakrouvi* (M), *Katrilli* (M–I), *Pikantti* (I).

KALAJOKI. *Rantakalla* (E), 35 rooms, sports facilities. *Kalajoki* (E–M), 35 rooms, disco, sports facilities.

KOLI. *Koli* (E), 42 rooms, pool, superb hilltop location. *Loma Koli* (M), 51 rooms, sports facilities.

KUOPIO. *Atlas* (L–E), 40 rooms. *Cumulus* (E), 134 rooms, night club, pool. *Kuopio* (E), 24 rooms. *Puijonsarvi* (E), 61 rooms, night club. *Rauhalahti* (E), 126 rooms, pool, sports facilities. *Kalla* (M), 37 rooms. *Savonia* (M), 46 rooms. *Kaupunginhotelli* (I).
Restaurants. *Peräniemen Kasino* (E), *Puijon Torni* (E), *Kummeli* (M), *Sampo* (M), *Lekkeri* (I).

LAHTI. *Seurahuone* (L), 119 rooms, night club, pool. *Musta Kissa* (E), 72 rooms, disco. *Tallukka* (E), 144 rooms, night club, pool. *Lahti* (M), 85 rooms. *Messilä* (M), 36 rooms, pool, sports facilities in old manor. *Mukkula Summer Hotel* (M), 80 rooms, sports facilities. Open summer only.
Restaurants. *Rosso* (E), *Alexander* (M), *El Toro* (M), *Ravuri* (M), *Oululainen* (I), *Torvi* (I).

LAPPEENRANTA. *Cumulus* (E), 95 rooms, pool; *Lappeenranta* (E), 40 rooms, disco, sports facilities. *Patria* (E), 66 rooms; *Viikinkihovi* (E), 28 rooms, pool. *Karelia-Park* (M), 73 rooms, open summer only. *Rotelli* (I), 20 rooms, unlicensed restaurant, pool.
Restaurants. *Casa Nostra* (E), *Kerhomestarit* (E), *Kolme Lyhtyä* (M), *Willikissa* (M), *Repsikka* (I).

PORVOO. *Haikko Manor Hotel* (L), 180 rooms, night club, pool, sports facilities, health treatment. A beautiful, converted old manor house in lovely grounds on the seashore. *Seurahovi* (E), 32 rooms. Situated in town.

SAVONLINNA. *Casino* (L–E), 79 rooms, night club, disco, pool, sports and keep-fit facilities. *Tott* (E), 48 rooms, night club. *Malakias* (M), 220 rooms, cafeteria only. *Vuorilinna* (M), 150 rooms, sports facilities; open in summer only.
Restaurants. *Kasino* (E), summer only, *Linnantupa* (M), in castle, *Majakka* (M), *Olavila* (M), *Savo* (M), *Musta Pässi* (I), *Restaurant Ship Hopeasalmi* (I), *Savo* (I).

TAMPERE. *Rosendahl* (L), Pyynikintie 13 (tel. 112233), 213 rooms, night club, pool, sports facilities. *Cumulus* (E), Koskikatu 5 (tel. 35500). 230 rooms, pool. *Grand Hotel Tammer* (E), Satakunnankatu 13 (tel. 25380). 90 rooms, night club. *Tampere* (E), Hämeenkatu 1 (tel. 21980). 260 rooms, pool. *Victoria* (E), Itsenäisyydenkatu 1 (tel. 30640). 100 rooms, disco, pool. *Domus* (M–I), Pellervonkatu 9 (tel. 550000). 200 rooms, disco, pool; open summer only. *Rasti* (I), Itsenäisyydenkatu 1 (tel. 30640). 94 rooms without bath or shower; disco; open summer only.
Restaurants. *Aleksi* (E), Aleksanterinkatu 20; *Laterna* (E), Puutarhakatu 11; *Nasinneula* (E), Särkänniemi; *Sorsapuiston Grilli* (E), Sorsapuisto 1; *Hällä-Pub* (M), Hämeenkatu 25; *Kaijakka* (M), Laukontori 12; *Kaupunginkellari* (M), Hallituskatu 19; *Kultainen Ilves* (M), Hämeenkatu 5; *Merirosvo* (M), Särkkäniemi; *Ohranjyvä* (M), Nasilinnankatu 15; *Antika* (I), Väinölänkatu 1; *Hermanni* (I), Insinöörinkatu 23; *Kantarelli* (I), Kalevanpuistotie 16; *Tavastia* (I), Hämeenkatu 18.

TURKU. *Hamburger Börs* (L), Kauppiaskatu 6 (tel. 511211). 160 rooms, night club, pool. *Marina Palace* (L), Linnankatu 32 (tel. 336300). 182 rooms, night club, pool; lovely river-side location. *Henrik* (E), Yliopistonkatu 29A (tel. 20921). 87 rooms, unlicensed restaurant. *Rantasipi Ikituuri* (E), Pispalantie 7 (tel. 376111). 150 rooms, night club, pool. *Rantasipi Ruissalo* (E), (tel. 306222). 136 rooms, pool, sports facilities. In lovely park setting 3 miles out of town. *Domus Aboensis* (M), Piispankatu 10 (tel. 29470). 76 rooms, cafeteria only,

summer only. *Rantasipi Ikituuri Summer Hotel* (M), Pispalantie 7 (tel. 376111).
600 rooms, night club, disco, pool; open summer only.

Restaurants. *Brahen Kellari* (E), Puolalankatu 1; *Pinella* (E), Porthanin
puisto; *Le Pirate* (E-M), Läntinen Rantakatu; *Haarikka* (M), Eerikinkatu 19;
Hämeenportii (M), Hämeenkatu 7; *Jarrita* (M), Martinkatu 1; *Kantakrouvi* (M),
Humalistonkatu 18; *Hiivari* (I), Rauhankatu 10; *Nättinummi* (I), Ekmaninkatu
4; *Tammio* (I), Konstantsankatu 4.

Finnish Lapland

This northernmost province of the country extends from just a bit
south of the Arctic Circle to almost the edge of the Arctic Ocean.
Rovaniemi, Finnish Lapland's administrative center almost on the
Arctic Circle, is a thriving modern town with excellent accommodation
and facilities, accessible by air or railroad. Air services continue as far
as Ivalo; otherwise, local public transport is by bus, reaching to the
remotest corners. Amenities throughout the province continue to expand rapidly, with well-equipped centers such as Saariselkä and Pyhä-
tunturi and, a little to the south, Rukatunturi, all in wild and lovely
landscapes. A fishing paradise in summer and ski paradise in winter,
it is becoming one of the offbeat tourist goals par excellence. In the
extreme north of the province, you can see the midnight sun for two
months; in winter the sun is invisible for the same period. True seekers
of the wilderness will find marked paths through some of the loneliest
landscapes. There is one about 90 km. long linking the lone fell-side
hotel of Pallastunturi and the typical Lapland community of Enontekiö
across the fells. Wilderness huts (unattended log cabins) along such
marked paths offer shelter and simple overnight accommodation,
though you will need a sleeping bag. This is ideal camping country, too,
and there are quite a few official camp sites. In summer, mosquito
repellent is a *must!* The early fall colors are simply stunning; and in
winter the magical Northern Lights and lively reindeer round-ups are
unforgettable experiences.

There are endless opportunities for swimming in the region. For
salmon fishing, one of the best waters is the Teno River between Finland and Norway. Boat trips with Lapp guides are arranged into the
wilderness near Inari, an attractive community on the shores of the
huge island-studded lake of the same name. Just off the main road, near
Vuotso, you can try your hand at gold washing at Tankavaara
. . . for a nominal fee.

An invaluable source of information is *Lapland Travel,* Koskikatu
1, 96200 Rovaniemi, who specialize in all types of travel in Lapland.

PRACTICAL INFORMATION FOR LAPLAND

HOTELS AND RESTAURANTS. Unless otherwise
stated, all listed hotels also have licensed restaurants and
all or some rooms with private bath or shower. Details
of the price grading system are given at the start of the
chapter in the general section on Finland, under the *Hotels* heading.

ENONTEKIO. *Hetta Tourist Hotel* (E), 39 rooms, sports facilities. Lakeside
location.

INARI. *Tourist Hotel* (M). 22 rooms without bath or shower. Lovely riverside
location.

IVALO. *Ivalo* (E), 62 rooms, pool, new. *Ivalo Tourist Hotel* (M), 38 rooms
without bath or shower. Both beside the river.

KILPISJÄRVI. *Tourist Hotel* (E), 39 rooms. Fine setting.

ROVANIEMI. *City-Hotelli* (E), 66 rooms, sports facilities. *Ounasvaara* (E), 39 rooms, lovely hilltop location. *Polar* (E), 53 rooms, nightclub, pool. *Lapinportii* (E–M), 19 rooms, pool. *Rantasipi Pohjanhovi* (E–M), 214 rooms, disco, pool. *Domus Arctica* (M), 130 rooms, beer and wine only, open summer only. *Rovaniemi Ammattikoulun Kesähotelli* (I), 36 rooms, unlicensed restaurant, open summer only.

Restaurants. *Hartsuherra* (E), *Lappia* (E), *Oppipoika* (E), *Lapinpoika* (M), *Haarikka* (I), *Iisakki* (I), *Pisto* (I).

RUKATUNTURI. *Rantasipi Rukahovi* (E), 80 rooms, pool, in wild fell district to the north. *Kuusamo* (E–M), 112 rooms, night club, disco, pool, sports facilities.

SAARISELKÄ. Hiking Center, near the Arctic Highway south of Ivalo: an expanding wilderness center with sports facilities and accommodations in all categories, including *Laanihovi,* 20 rooms, *Lapin Maja,* 60 rooms, *Riekonkieppi,* 103 rooms, and *Saariselän Retkeilykeskus,* 35 rooms, all (E–M).

FRANCE

"Is France the same as ever?" Returning to France after being absent for a while, the visitor wants to know if he'll find the qualities which lured him there before. First-timers, if they've done their homework, will know what France should offer . . . and, for both, it's the same thing.

Well, the answer is "yes" *and* "no": affirmative because France still has charm as no one else has it; style as no one else *can* have it; and beauty, as no one but the French can make it. These assets were never more appreciated than they are today.

But the negative side is soon visible when the visitor spots the ugly skyscrapers which have already ruined the Paris skyline, or finds his favorite bistrot replaced by a flashy "drugstore". Not content with having torn up some of Paris' lovely chestnut-tree-lined squares to build underground garages, recent governments and the City of Paris allowed the construction of such controversial architecture as the 56-story Tour Montparnasse, sticking up over the skyline like an overlarge cigar box, and the cement-and-steel Centre Georges Pompidou, looking rather like an oil refinery.

Surrounded by larger and uglier technological monstrosities, by the pollution of our cities and by the noise of scientific development, man needs the positive Gallic qualities more than ever. The French have managed to hang on to these intangible qualities, keeping much from the past, but also transforming some of the ugliness of today by their skill in applying standards of good taste. What do the French drugstore and the Pierre Cardin blazer have that the originals lacked? Well, you come back to charm, beauty and style.

Despite their good taste, the French are all anarchists, said Jean Cocteau, but they are conservative anarchists. This Gallic paradox helps to explain the most interesting and the most complex people in

181

Europe. In no other country will you find more respect and veneration for tradition and the glories of the past, still physically manifest everywhere in France, though successive governments seem to have decided to sacrifice some of the country's beauty in an effort to streamline the nation's infrastructure.

From the time when it was known as Gaul, France has been a pivotal state in the affairs of Europe. Its territory violated constantly by invading armies, and torn by civil war, plagues and revolution, France seemed always to alternate between unbearable chaos in her public life and magnificent esthetic order in her private pursuits. Up to and including World War II, the Americans and the British could say (and frequently did, with some contempt) that one never quite knew where one stood with the French. And even after 1945, it seemed for a while that this not-quite-noble tradition would continue.

After a period of postwar instability, France grew increasingly prosperous and stable under Presidents de Gaulle and Pompidou, in spite of major unrest in 1968. It managed to avoid the worst effects of worldwide recession under President Valéry Giscard d'Estaing. Then in the 1981 presidential elections François Mitterrand, the Socialist Party leader, won a surprise victory, giving the Left its first taste of power since prewar days. However, Mitterrand's presidency has been by no means entirely happy, and has been marked by a considerable falling away of popularity and significant economic decline.

The Country and the People

The French passion for individual liberty explains why so many expatriates have found their spiritual home in this country, and especially in that overgrown village of Paris, where in bistrots and student restaurants, in elegant cafés and bourgeois salons, the eternal discussions of art and life go on, constantly recharging that incandescent glow of the intellect that illuminates the City of Light. Even if your stay in France is limited to a few days, you will be conscious of an endless babble of animated discussion, guaranteed to make the most verbal English-speaker feel almost taciturn by comparison. So brush up on your French if you want to enjoy the full flavor of this country. But you'll have a good time in France even if your French is not quite as good as you might wish. Which leads us to that most difficult of rumors—the one that says the French are inhospitable, and sometimes even nasty, to the traveler (particularly, it is alleged, if he can't speak good French). To begin with, when it is true, it's almost always a Parisian who's the villain—out in the country, you'll find genuine hospitality the order of the day.

The Parisian is an odd bird, a mockingbird almost, for that's his favorite sport, indoors and out, mocking people all around him. He doesn't particularly dislike Americans or the British—he more or less doesn't like anybody, and it's the lack of his ability to communicate with you that tends to make you think he's being brusque, or even rude. Away from Paris, especially in country districts, people are generally friendly and helpful.

Tourist Highlights

From the Alps to the Pyrenees, from the trout-filled torrents of the Vosges to the placid Lake of Annecy, from the windswept Breton coast to the sun-drenched Riviera, there is almost every kind of scenery that exists. Wherever possible, this scenery has been cultivated, tempered by the hand of man. The land seems to have been molded and trimmed with an unerring instinct for proportion, and this celebrated sense of

Gallic measure is visible in some of the most impressive cities, châteaux and cathedrals in Europe.

PRACTICAL INFORMATION FOR FRANCE

WHAT WILL IT COST. With inflation in France still around the 7–8% mark, costs for 1987 are difficult to estimate; but the good news for U.S. travelers is that the franc remains relatively weak against the U.S. dollar, making what is basically an expensive country look rather less so. With sensible timing and budgeting, a stay in France may prove no more expensive than in some neighboring countries.

Prices are generally highest in high season (July–Aug.), and, in ski and Mediterranean resorts, at Easter and Christmas. Off-season, they can be 30–40% lower. However, remember that many small resort hotels, and some in major resorts too, are closed out of season.

Generally speaking, it is safe to say that prices in large provincial cities (Bordeaux, Marseille, Toulouse, etc.) are 20–30% lower than in Paris; in rural areas, from 40–60% less. Fashionable resorts (Cannes, Nice, St. Tropez, Megève) are as expensive as Paris or even more expensive.

A typical day in Paris might cost two people:

Hotel (moderate) double room with bath and breakfast	Frs.	380
Lunch at restaurant (moderate)		300
Transportation (public transport)		40
Two coffees in chic café		20
Two beers in local café		16
Theater, 2 middle-price seats		220
Dinner, moderate restaurant		360
Miscellaneous 10%		131
	Frs.	1,467

Money. Exchange rates with the franc are so volatile, advance predictions are almost impossible. At this writing, there are approx. 7 francs to the U.S. dollar, 10 to the pound sterling. There are, incidentally, 100 centimes to the franc.

Some stores give the VAT discount (usually 18.6%, but can be up to 33%) on purchases with dollar or other foreign currency to persons residing outside France. If you are resident in a Common Market country this exemption applies only to goods worth a minimum of 1,030 francs *per item;* residents of other countries benefit on items worth *a total of* 400 francs and upwards. The store must fill out a form in quadruplicate, giving three copies to the tourist, who gives two to customs on leaving. Be warned, however, that this procedure is complicated, and you must make sure you leave plenty of time at the airport or border point to fulfill the necessary formalities. Also, you may well find that what you save on VAT is swallowed up by customs duty back home!

SOURCES OF INFORMATION. For information on all aspects of travel to France, the French Government Tourist Office is invaluable. Their addresses are:

In the U.S.: 610 Fifth Ave., New York, NY 10200 (tel. 212-757-1125); 9401 Wilshire Blvd., Suite 314, Beverly Hills, CA 90212 (tel. 213-272-2661).

In the U.K.: 178 Piccadilly, London W.1 (tel. 01-491 7622).

WHEN TO COME. Main tourist season: Easter to Sept. 30, high season July–Aug. On the Riviera, the winter is no longer smart, but Easter is popular; summer is the biggest season. Winter sports season is from Dec. through Mar., with Jan. the budget month: Christmas, Feb. half-term holidays and Easter are sky-high. Height of the Paris season is May and June, but Easter and Sept. are also popular.

184 FRANCE

Climate. Varies considerably between north and south regions.

Average afternoon daily temperatures in degrees Fahrenheit and centigrade:

Paris	Jan.	Feb.	Mar.	Apr.	May	June	July	Aug.	Sept.	Oct.	Nov.	Dec.
F°	42	45	52	60	67	73	76	75	69	59	49	43
C°	6	7	11	16	19	23	24	24	21	15	9	6
Nice												
F°	56	56	59	64	69	76	81	81	77	70	62	58
C°	13	13	15	18	21	24	27	27	25	21	17	14

SPECIAL EVENTS. *January,* Monte Carlo Rally. *February,* Lemon Festival in Menton, Mimosa Carnival in La Napoule, Festival of Saint Bernadette (18th), Lourdes. *March,* mid-Lent celebrations in various cities, Carnival and Battle of Flowers in Nice (Feb. or March). *April,* Provençal Easter festivities in Vence; Bullfights in Roman arena, Arles; Prix du Président de la Republique, Longchamp; Basque folklore and Easter festival, Biarritz. *May,* Joan of Arc celebrations in Orléans and Rouen; Bordeaux Festival of Music, Ballet and Theater; Int'l Film Festival, Cannes; religious Festival and Fair of the Gypsies at Saintes Maries-de-la-Mer. *June,* Air show, Paris; 24-hour automobile race, Le Mans; Festival du Marais, Paris; Prix de Diane, Chantilly; Gascony Festival, Auch; Music Festival, Strasbourg, Festival at Angers. *July,* beginning of fountain displays and Son et Lumière programs in châteaux throughout the country (through Sept.); Bastille Day (14th), Music Festival, Aix-en-Provence; great Celtic Festival, Quimper in Brittany. *August,* Heures Musicales, Mont St.-Michel; Casals Festival, Prades; Napoleon's Birthday celebrations, Corsica. *October,* Auto Show, Paris (held every two years now; even-numbered years only); grape-picking festivals in wine-growing regions; International Dance Festival, Paris. *November,* Les Trois Glorieuses, 3 days of celebrating in honor of Burgundy wine, with processions, meeting of the Knights of Tastevin, wine auction in the Hôtel Dieu in Beaune. *December,* special midnight masses on Christmas Eve with cribs (and real shepherds and sheep in parts of Provence) throughout the country.

National Holidays. Jan. 1 (New Year's Day); Apr. 20 (Easter Mon.); May 1 (Labor Day); May 8 (anniversary end World War II); May 28 (Ascension); Jun. 8 (Whit Mon.); Jul. 14 (Bastille Day); Aug. 15 (Assumption); Nov. 1 (All Saints); Nov. 11 (Armistice); Dec. 25.

VISAS. Not required for nationals of the United States, Canada, United Kingdom and most countries of the British Commonwealth for a stay of less than three months. If that period is about to expire and you wish to stay longer, go to the Préfecture de Police, and apply for a *carte de séjour.* The préfecture in Paris is located on the Ile de la Cité, near Notre-Dame.

HEALTH CERTIFICATES. Not required for entry into France.

GETTING TO FRANCE. By Plane from the U.S. There are excellent direct or through-flight services from the U.S.A. and Canada to Paris including from New York, Washington, Chicago, San Francisco, Los Angeles, Miami, Houston, Montreal and Toronto. There are also non-stop flights between New York and Nice.

By Plane from the U.K. There are many flights from London (Heathrow and Gatwick), Birmingham, Manchester, Cardiff, Bristol, Glasgow and Norwich, in addition to services from London to many provincial cities including Lyon, Marseilles, Nice, Bordeaux, Biarritz, Strasbourg, Toulouse, Montpellier, Perpignan, Nantes, Dinard, Tarbes and Lille. Some of these operate in summer only, but dates vary so check with your travel agent. And also from the U.K. there are flights from Southampton to Cherbourg, Dinard and La Baule, from Southend to Calais and Gatwick to Le Touquet.

By Train. There are boat trains from London (Victoria) to both Dover and Folkestone for Calais and Boulogne, the sea crossing taking about 1¼ to 1½ hours; on the service from Newhaven to Dieppe the crossing is about 3½ to 4 hours. The Hovercraft (*Hoverspeed* service) from Dover to both Calais and Boulogne takes 35 to 40 minutes. With all of these there is a boat train service, although not linking with every sailing or Hovercraft flight. Over-all traveling time from central London to central Paris by rail and sea (both ferry and Hovercraft) is between six and eight hours. At the time of writing (Easter '85), plans for a reorganization of cross-Channel services were afoot which, if carried out, will affect foot passengers traveling by train. Full details from travel agents.

By Bus. There are excellent express bus services from London (Victoria Coach Station) to Paris (Coach Station, place Stalingrad), operated by Supabus. Daily daytime and overnight services run throughout the year via Dover and Calais or Boulogne: the daytime service leaves London at 9 A.M., reaching Paris at 9 P.M.; the overnight services leaves at 9 A.M. and reaches Paris at 7.15 A.M. Full details from *Supabus,* 172 Buckingham Palace Rd., London S.W.1.

By Car. See *Planning Your Trip* section, page 27.

CUSTOMS. Everything obviously for personal use, not for resale, comes in duty free. Americans may bring 400 cigarettes, 100 cigars or 500 grams of pipe tobacco duty free. British: 300 cigarettes, or 75 cigars or 400 grams of tobacco. You may bring in 2 cameras of different makes duty free (if used), 10 rolls of film, a movie camera and ten reels of film.

You can bring in as many French francs and foreign bills as you wish, and can take out 5000 francs both in francs and foreign exchange without declaration.

There are no take-out restrictions on travelers checks or letters of credit obtained outside France. All currency declared upon entry can be taken out.

HOTELS. France has many comfortable hotels in all price categories. They are required by law to post the price of each room on its wall and cannot legally charge more than that rate, which is fixed by the government. This is not true of deluxe hotels, where prices are not subject to government control. In some hotels, the posted prices do not include the service charge or taxes, which together can increase your hotel bill about 25%. The letters TTC mean *toutes taxes comprises* (i.e. inclusive of all forms of tax).

Cost of Hotel Room for Two (including breakfast, taxes and service) in francs

	Super-deluxe	Luxury (L)	Expensive (E)	Moderate (M)	Inex-pensive (I)
Paris	1000–1800	650–950	400–650	250–400	100–250
Major resort	—	700–1800	500–700	300–500	200–300
Major provincial city	—	600–1000	400–600	250–400	100–250
Budget resort	—	—	—	175–300	100–175

Relais et Châteaux. This is a chain of châteaux, inns and manor houses covering the whole of France (around 150 members), with an emphasis on regional character. Each hotel thus has a distinct atmosphere of its own, which makes for a very pleasant stay, where the accent is on relaxation, peaceful surroundings and fine cuisine. Hotels range from the luxurious (including the Ritz in Paris and the fabulous Oustau de Baumanière in Provence) to far more modest establishments. A booklet listing all member hotels is obtainable from *Relais et Châteaux,* 10 pl. de la Concorde, 75008 Paris.

Logis de France. The Fédération Nationale des Logis de France is a highly meritorious organization that has undertaken to raise the standards of smaller and less expensive hotels. The Fédération insists upon minimum standards of comfort in all hotels on its lists, such as running hot and cold water in every room, and the establishments are pledged not to raise prices filed with the Fédération and printed in its booklets during the year. The food in the *logis* is regional cooking, simple but abundant and well prepared. For regional booklets, write to the *Fédération Nationale des Logis de France,* 25 rue Jean Mermoz,

75008 Paris, stating which region interests you. You also can buy the booklets from major department stores in Paris.

Gîtes ruraux. The Fédération Nationale des Gîtes Ruraux de France lists fairly inexpensive furnished rooms, apartments or small houses in rural areas of the country that can be rented by the month, or for a fortnight or a week. They must conform to minimum standards of comfort and agreed price. There are also various specialized holidays connected with the rental of a *gîte*, such as for skiers, riders, etc. Write—well ahead of time—to the *Fédération Nationale des Gîtes Ruraux de France,* 34 rue Godot de Mauroy, 75009 Paris, indicating what region interests you, or to the French Government Tourist Office in London, which runs a special reservation service.

Many smaller tourist offices near tourist centers keep a card index of local residents willing to take in guests on a bed-and-breakfast basis.

RESTAURANTS. French cooking is world famous and the high standards of this country mean that you can get a reasonably good meal far more often than elsewhere. But beware of the recent plethora of fast-food outfits.

Breakfast at your hotel may not be included in the room-rate quoted: make sure, when you reserve, to clarify this point. Where breakfast is not included, and depending on the class of hotel and what you eat, it will cost 18 to 80 frs. An American breakfast will cost much more than a French *café complet* or *thé complet* (coffee or tea with rolls and butter).

Restaurant Prices (including service and wine) per person in francs

	Expensive (E)	Moderate (M)	Inexpensive (I)
Paris	250–650	150–250	80–150
Major resort	350–650	200–300	100–200
Major provincial city	250–350	150–250	50–150
Budget resort	100–250	120–180	70–120

Food and Drink. There is almost complete unanimity of opinion that French food is the best in the Western world. The vegetables, cheese, butter and fruit you eat in French restaurants are usually fresh; they were bought at the local wholesale market that morning, although with the mushrooming of cafeterias and quick eateries, quality is no longer always perfect, as it was a few years ago. Stick to the old-fashioned *bistrot* to find simple, delicious cooking.

Traditional *haute cuisine* is now complemented by what is called *la nouvelle cuisine française,* or "new" French cooking. This relies less on rich sauces than on the fresh flavor of natural ingredients, often combined in unorthodox ways. It is much less fattening than traditional cooking: in fact one version calls itself *cuisine minceur* ('slimmers' cooking'). In the hands of a talented chef it is a delightful gastronomic experience, but the publicity surrounding it has inevitably led some restaurateurs to overdo it—and to overcharge. We believe that it has come to stay, but recommend that you should be cautious before entering a *nouvelle cuisine* restaurant: stick to our recommendations or to those from local people; be prepared to pay high prices (inevitable with the use of ultra-fresh ingredients and last-minute preparation); avoid the more outlandish combinations; be prepared for very lightly cooked (or even raw) fish and shellfish; don't be surprised if the portions are small.

Generally speaking, you can get better value for money in the provinces, where the main dish, even in a modest restaurant, is cooked for you while you are eating the *hors d'oeuvre.* You also get better value if you stick to the fixed-price menu (known in French simply as a *menu,* whereas what we call "the menu" is *la carte*). Even expensive restaurants nowadays usually offer one or more *menus,* sometimes with wine and/or service included. In our restaurant listings we grade them according to the *à la carte* prices, but you'll often find that an expensive restaurant can work out at moderate rates if you choose the least expensive *menu.*

A meal without wine is like a day without sun, say the French, who are the world's greatest producers and greatest consumers of wine; the subtlety and quality of French wines do not have their equal elsewhere.

The best-known wines come from Burgundy and the Bordeaux region (clarets). But those from Alsace, the Loire Valley and the Rhône Valley can also be excellent. A popular and inexpensive red wine, excellent with red meat and most cheeses, is *Beaujolais.* For a reasonable dry white wine, good with seafood and white meat, try *Muscadet, Champagne Nature* (non-sparkling) or *Chablis.*

 TIPPING. The practice of adding 12 or 15 percent service charge to the bill is common in restaurants, hotels and cafés all over France. When added, there is no obligation to leave anything additional, but, in effect, most people leave a little "extra something" (from one to five francs, depending on the size of the bill). If the wine steward *(sommelier)* has been particularly helpful, you may wish to give upwards of 5 francs extra. Tip bellboys almost everywhere. In the international luxury hotels in Paris, the bellhops expect at least 3–5 francs for each service. Tip the doorman 3–5 francs for getting you a cab. On leaving, tip chambermaids around 10 frs. a day. Two francs to hatcheck girls and washroom attendants, 2–5 francs per person to theater ushers, 5–10 frs. if in very expensive seats; 2–3 frs. to cinema ushers; 15% of the fare to cabdrivers; 15% to barbers and beauticians. Rail or airport porters: the official minimum is around 8–10 frs. per bag (look for the porters badge), but use your judgment.

 MAIL. If you are staying at a large hotel, it is simplest to hand your mail to the porter. Stamps may be purchased at tobacconist's counters in cafés as well as in post offices. Rates in early 1986 were: letters to U.K. 2.50 fr., postcards 1.80 frs.; letters to U.S., airmail, 3.65 frs. for 5 grams, with 65 centimes extra per 5 grams thereafter. Air letters cost 3.50 frs. to all destinations. Rates are liable to have risen since the time of writing so check locally.

 CLOSING TIMES. Ordinary shops open around 9–9.30 and close at 7, but food shops normally start at 7.30 or 8 and don't close until 7.30 or 8 in the evening. They close for lunch between 12.30–1 and 3.30 or 4. Some elegant boutiques in Paris, and virtually all provincial stores, close from 12 or 12.30–2. The capital's department stores stay open Mon. through Sat., opening some time between 9 and 9:45 and closing at 6:30 or 7, though Trois Quartiers closes on Mondays in July and August. Some of the big stores stay open until 9 or 10 P.M. one night a week (usually Wednesday). Most of Paris's "drugstores" (which sell everything from newspapers to prepared salads and take-away hot dishes) are open until 2 A.M. And Sunday isn't a problem: bakeries and other food shops can be found open all over the country, usually mornings only, and so can open-air markets as well as newspaper shops and tobacconists. Except in Paris, banks usually close about 12–2 (and even in Paris the exchange counter may well close for at least an hour at lunchtime); in provincial towns they are often open Sat. but closed Mon. Hairdressers and barbers are usually shut Mon. In some cities most stores, and some services, such as dry cleaners, close Mon. morning, or all day Mon.

 GETTING AROUND FRANCE. By Plane. *Air Inter,* the associate company of *Air France,* operates an intensive network of routes within France. Many of these radiate from Paris but there are also cross-country air links such as between Nice and Toulouse, Lille and Bordeaux, Lyon and Biarritz, etc. On the busiest routes (e.g. Paris to Nice) Air Inter and Air France now use the splendid A300 "Airbus". In addition to these (which also operate from Paris, Lyon, Marseille, and Nice to Corsica) there are a number of smaller airlines offering good services to smaller cities, towns and resorts.

By Train. France has an excellent railway system (known as the SNCF), with all main lines electrified. It now operates the TGV or High-Speed Train service —a pioneering venture rapidly dubbed "the train of the century." Journey time to Lyon from Paris is down to 2 hrs (instead of 4 hrs). You don't even have to pay extra, except at peak times. Other cities served include Dijon, Macon, St. Etienne, Chambéry, Grenoble, Geneva, Montpellier and Marseille. A new high speed line is being built to serve Brittany and the southwest of France.

However, ordinary trains are also excellent, and the SNCF has an enviable time-keeping reputation. Whenever possible, choose a *Train Corail:* these modern, streamlined trains have airconditioning, self-closing doors, airplane-type seats, and most daytime trains have a Grill Express (cafeteria) service too. Trans-Europ-Express trains are first-class only and for travel on these trains extra is charged, as it is for some particularly fast trains in both first and second classes. Apart from suburban and some local country services, all trains carry first and second class carriages.

Sleeping cars are operated by the *Wagons Lits Company* on behalf of French Railways, couchette cars are railway operated. Dining, buffet and refreshment services are either Wagons Lits operated or franchised out to other companies. Light refreshments are available on many trains.

Rail tickets purchased and used in France *must* be date-stamped before boarding the train. *The inspector in the train will impose a fine if you fail to obey this regulation.* All stations have bright orange machines at the entrance to platforms. Put your ticket in, move it slightly to the left and wait till you hear a click. If you put it in upside down, the machine will light up with the words *Tournez votre ticket* or "Turn your ticket round." You can break your journey as often as you like, but if you make an overnight stop, you *must* have your ticket stamped again when you board your next train.

Much of the best of French scenery can be seen from the train—such as the main line (both the old and the new routes) from Paris through Burgundy to Lyon and down the Rhône valley to the Riviera and along that fabled coast. There are also panoramic rail cars with "double decker" sections for scenic viewing on routes in southeast France and on some cross-country lines as well.

Basic fares in France are on a kilometrage basis. Travel over 1500 kilometres (about 930 miles) and you get 20% reduction in the fare for two single journeys. But for extensive rail travel we certainly recommend the runabout *France Vacances Special* ticket. It gives free travel on all French railways on any 9 or 16 days in any one month period. Costs for 1987 are expected to be approximately (for 9 and 16 days respectively): 1,288 frs. (child 660 frs.) in 2nd class and 1,800 frs. (child 960 frs.) in 1st class, and 1,560 frs. (child 860 frs.) in 2nd class and 2,300 frs. (child 1,200 frs.) in 1st class. Gives unlimited travel on all French Railways services with special concession on Paris Transport, plus reduced rates for car hire made through the railway (for 1st. class ticket holders only).

In addition to these there are also *Family Fares* in France for individual journeys (single or return) where two or more of the same family travel together; *Couple fares* for couples traveling together; and *Elderly Persons fares* for women over 60 and men over 62. In each case you need a special pass (*carte*), for which you must provide a passport-sized photo. The Family pass is free and entitles everyone in the family after the first person to a 50% reduction. The Couple pass is also free and entitles one of the two to a 50% reduction. The Elderly Persons pass (*Carte Vermeille*) costs around 70 francs but is available for those traveling alone; it too gives a 50% reduction. UK senior citizens' rail passes also entitle you to these reductions, but you must have a Rail Europe Senior card. All reductions apply in both first and second class, *but only during the SNCF's* "blue" *periods.* Ask at any station for the red-white-and-blue calendar.

By Boat. Holidays on the canals and rivers of France have become increasingly popular in the last few years. We can only give a few pointers here and advise you to contact a good travel agent for full details of these. Some are "cruises" with full or half board, such as on the Marne or the Canal du Midi; others are by boat or motor cruiser rental. The canals of Brittany, Burgundy, the Canal du Midi and its extensions and the Camargue (Rhône delta) are the most popular areas.

By Car. Drive on the right hand side; green card is not obligatory but recommended. Super gasoline (*super*) costs around 6 frs. per liter. It's best to fill up in towns as prices are often higher in country districts. Ordinary petrol is *essence,* but we advise you to stick to the superior grade. On the motorways (roads labeled 'A') there is a speed limit of 80 m.p.h. (130 km/h); 68 m.p.h. (110 km/h) on specially-marked fast roads and approach roads to motorways; on all other roads 50 m.p.h. (90 km/h) and in built-up areas it is 31 or 37 m.p.h. (50 or 60 km/h). There are lower maximum speed limits in rain: check locally. *Safety belts are obligatory at all times,* as is a black-and-white tag identifying country of origin and a red warning triangle. In some *départements* horns may be sounded only in moments of dire need. Children under 12 may not travel in the front passenger seat. On the whole it is advisable to do your homework on French motoring regulations before setting out.

Parking. Increasingly difficult in towns. Discs for *zones bleues* are valid for all towns using this system. They're obtainable free from tourist offices, tobacco kiosks, police stations, customs offices, garages and hotels . . . so get yourself a supply. All sizeable towns have paying garages. Maps indicating them are available from tourist offices. In Paris, as well as major provincial towns, carry a supply of 1 franc and 50 centime pieces for the parking meters.

Car hire. Available in all principal cities by Avis, Hertz, etc. For central reservations for major car-hire companies call the following numbers (English-speakers available): *Avis* (1) 46–09–92–12; *Citer* (1) 43–41–45–45; *Europcar* 30–43–82–82; *Hertz* (1) 47–88–51–51; *Inter-Rent* (1) 42–85–32–03; *Mattei* (1) 43–46–11–50. Many other smaller firms can be found, but on the whole it's advisable to stick to these major companies, especially in Corsica, where the winding roads often are too risky for the rattletraps provided at temptingly low rates by the local firms.

By Bus. The French division of *Supabus* have a fairly extensive network mainly from Paris to the south, to the Channel coast, into Belgium, southeast into Switzerland and east to Germany. Travel on these can be on a "seat only" basis or as an inclusive tour with accommodation and some meals included. In addition there are other privately owned buses operating scheduled services. And the SNCF has rail-motorcoach tours from two days to a week in the more scenic or tourist parts of the country. Add to this the coach tours operated by French companies and international travel organizations like *Thomas Cook* and *American Express.* Most cities have goodish local bus routes with Paris having a really comprehensive one. But buses normally stop running about 8.30 or 9 P.M. and few run on Sundays. Fewer country bus services operate in summer school holidays (late June–early Sept.), though there are local sightseeing excursions April through Sept.

Paris

Paris is a city of vast, noble perspectives and intimate streets, parks and squares. This combination is one of the secrets of its perennial charm. For the first-time visitor with only a few days at his disposal, one of the half-day sightseeing tours organized by a reputable travel agency, such as Cook's or American Express, is recommended. After that, the best way to know this city is on foot with a *Plan de Paris par Arrondissement,* which shows every boulevard, street and *place,* supplemented by good *métro,* express *métro* (RER) and bus maps. It can be bought from bookstores, newspaper kiosks, drugstores, souvenir shops, etc., but bear in mind that streets are listed alphabetically under their full name (so the rue Jacques-Offenbach is under J, not under O).

Here are some of the outstanding places and monuments which you should see, not including the museums and parks we have listed:

The Champs-Elysées Area

The Place Charles de Gaulle, formerly the Etoile, the great circle at the western end of the Champs-Elysées, which is one of 12 avenues radiating like rays of light from the star. In the center is the colossal Arc de Triomphe (164 feet high), more than twice the size of the Arch of Constantine in Rome. Planned by Napoleon to honor his victorious army, it contains some magnificent sculpture, most notably "The Marseillaise" by Rude. A perpetual flame to France's Unknown Soldier burns under the arch. Take the elevator to the top for a splendid view of Paris.

At the other end of the Champs-Elysées is the Place de la Concorde. There is nothing in its present harmonious proportions to suggest that it was once the notorious Place de la Guillotine, splashed with the blood of Louis XVI, Marie Antoinette, Lavoisier and 1,340 other victims of the French Revolution. In the center of the Place is the Obelisk of Luxor, a 200-ton stone needle from Egypt, erected here in 1836 during the reign of Louis-Philippe and over 3,000 years old.

Facing the Tuileries Gardens (with your back to the Champs-Elysées), you have a long vista, framed by the winged horses of Coysevox, down through the little Arc de Triomphe du Carrousel to the Louvre. On your left, the Rue Royale, leading to the classic Church of the Madeleine, is framed by two 18th-century buildings designed by Gabriel. The one on the right is the French Navy Ministry. Its western twin houses the Automobile Club of France and the Hôtel Crillon. The vista toward the Seine is equally impressive, leading the eye across the Pont de la Concorde to the Palais Bourbon, home of the National Assembly.

The Place de la Concorde is further embellished by two splendid bronze fountains and eight rather formidable stone females symbolizing the cities of Nantes, Brest, Rouen, Lille, Strasbourg, Lyon, Marseille and Bordeaux. Even if you have only one night in Paris, don't miss seeing this square illuminated.

Iles de la Cité and St.-Louis

The best approach to the Ile de la Cité, that tiny island where Paris began as a Gallo-Roman village named Lutetia, is by the Pont Neuf, the capital's oldest bridge, completed in 1604. At the statue of Henri IV, turn left into the charming Place Dauphine, walk around the massive Palais de Justice and into the court where that Gothic jewel known as the Sainte Chapelle stands. Built by Louis IX to house the true crown of thorns and other holy relics, the chapel was consecrated in 1248. A marvel of stone lacework and ancient stained glass, this soaring chapel is one of the most impressive things in Paris.

A short walk from here will bring you to Paris' grand cathedral, Notre Dame de Paris. Begun in 1163, completed in 1345, badly damaged during the revolution, restored by Viollet-le-Duc in the 19th century, Notre Dame is one of the most beautifully proportioned of cathedrals, large enough to accommodate 9,000 persons. If your heart and legs are sturdy, climb to the top of the tower for a fuller appreciation of the architectural detail of the cathedral as well as for a view of the heart of Paris.

Don't miss a walk through the cathedral garden and across the bridge to the Ile St.-Louis, whose historic houses and picturesque quais have changed little since the 17th century. From here, you have romantic views of the Seine and the apse of Notre Dame, and it is just a step over to the Rive Gauche, the Left (or South) Bank, and the Latin Quarter, so called because the students of the Sorbonne spoke and heard lectures in Latin during the Middle Ages.

The Left Bank (south of the Seine)

St.-Germain-des-Prés, onetime citadel of Paris' intellectual life, is now invaded by foreigners and provincials who think they are rubbing shoulders with the intelligentsia on the terraces of the Café de Flore and the Deux-Magots. The area is still stuffed with expensive antique shops, avant-garde art galleries and bookstores, but the artists and writers who used to enliven the cafés and bars have migrated to less expensive haunts. However, this old and romantic neighborhood has many permanent charms. Don't fail to notice the massive Romanesque bell tower of St.-Germain-des-Prés, dating from the beginning of the 11th century, one of the oldest *clochers* in France. The quiet streets in the immediate vicinity are worth a ramble, especially the enchanting little Place Fürstemberg, with its catalpa trees and old lamps, a stamp-size remnant of the aristocratic glory of the Faubourg St.-Germain.

A short distance away is the busy blvd. St.-Michel, heart of the student quarter. Deeper into the Left Bank you'll find the famous Rue

Mouffetard market—visit either in the morning or after 4 P.M.—a riot of marvelously arranged foodstalls and the raucous cries of the vendors.

Further west, but still on the Left Bank, is *the* symbol of Paris, the Eiffel Tower. M. Eiffel's celebrated *tour*, 1,000 feet high and still the fourth-tallest edifice in the world, was inaugurated on June 10, 1889, by Edward VII of England, then Prince of Wales. During the World War II occupation of Paris, the Germans thought of requisitioning its 12,000 sections of metal and 2,5000,000 rivets, but they thought better of it, perhaps because so many Germans, like good tourists, enjoyed climbing it. It will cost you a few francs by elevator to the first level, more if you go higher. The trip to the top is highly recommended on a clear day.

Even a short visit to Paris would be incomplete without a visit to Mansart's masterpiece of Jesuit architecture, the Church of the Invalides, with its golden dome, the most beautiful in Paris, under which, in a sarcophagus of red porphyry, lie the mortal remains of Napoleon Bonaparte. While you are in the neighborhood, you may want to take a look at one of the city's outstanding attractions in the way of modern architecture, the UNESCO building on place de Fontenoy; you can visit the building with the help of a plan and a special cassette recorder you hold up to your ear (available in English).

The Right Bank (north of the Seine)

There are several places on the Right Bank that you must not miss. One is the Palais-Royal, which Richelieu built opposite the Louvre. You can enter the palace garden from the rue Montpensier or the rue de Beaujolais, and you will be delighted by its arcaded shops and its oasis-like tranquility in the heart of bustling, modern Paris.

Nearby is Paris's splendid opera house, generally referred to simply as "the Opéra", a 19th-century building majestically set off by the huge square in front of it. In these democratic days you no longer have to attend a performance of the opera or ballet to see the gilded, grandiose, marble interior of this immense baroque palace and Marc Chagall's famous ceiling, painted in 1964—a visit to the Opéra Museum will be open sesame for you.

To the east, in the heart of the ancient Marais district, is the lovely place des Vosges, all of whose houses were built of rose-colored brick under the direction of Henri IV in the early 17th century. Once the center of fashion, royal tournaments and brilliant fêtes, this nobly-proportioned square is a good starting-point for a fascinating walk through this historic district. One of the outstanding annual attractions is the Festival du Marais, held in June and July, where you can combine enjoyment of the architectural beauty of this neighborhood with high-class modern and classical ballet, theater and music.

The Les Halles/Beaubourg district, once the home of the famous central market, is now one of the most-visited areas of Paris. This is mainly as a result of the amazing Centre National d'Art et de Culture Georges Pompidou (often referred to as the Centre Beaubourg), opened in 1977 and a definite "must." Be prepared for a shock when you see the outside, with pipes and escalators visible in their naked glory. The Center, which attracted over six million visitors in its first year, is the most-visited building in Europe at the moment, both because of its novelty and because it houses the National Museum of Modern Art (formerly in the avenue Wilson), a very popular library, an acoustical research center, and all sorts of special exhibits. Don't miss the splendid view from the fifth floor. The streets around the Center are now full of delightful boutiques, an interesting mixture of the "in"—and the way out! The famous "hole" that resulted from the banishment of the market to the suburbs near Orly Airport has at long last been filled, or at least part of it has, with a very stylish shopping and entertainment center in glass and concrete known as "the Forum." Opened in 1979, it is well worth a visit, both for its smart boutiques and as an example of how the French deal with urban planning. The whole scheme, which includes an aquarium and a children's garden, should be completed by 1986. However, this area has attracted quite a lot of undesirables, so keep a tight hold on your purse or wallet.

The last "must" on your Right Bank itinerary is the Basilica of the Sacré Coeur, which dominates all of Paris from the heights of Montmartre. This and the nearby place du Tertre are among the most popular tourist attractions of the city. The ascent into the dome of Sacré Coeur will give you several vertiginous eyefuls of the huge interior of this church, and you will be rewarded for your dizzying climb by a 30-mile view over Paris and its environs from the top. As for the place du Tertre and adjacent narrow streets, they're full of painters and pseudo-painters, all aching to paint or sketch your portrait.

PRACTICAL INFORMATION FOR PARIS

 HOTELS. There are hundreds of hotels in Paris, many of them good, though it is always advisable to reserve well ahead, especially at the times when major shows (the air show in June, the auto show in October, the ready-to-wear collections in March and October) attract many visitors to Paris. Also, the small Left Bank hotels tend to be fully booked in the summer months. We can list only a small sample here, classified as Super-deluxe (extremely expensive, among the world's best-known hotels), Luxurious (L), Expensive (E), Moderate (M), and Inexpensive (I). The official grading is in terms of stars, based partly on price and partly on such details as whether rooms have telephones, and the number of bathrooms; roughly speaking, the hotels we refer to as Inexpensive are graded with one or two stars; Moderate have three stars; and Expensive have three or four stars. But prices and facilities vary considerably within each category.

The great majority of hotels nowadays quote a price that includes all taxes, but just to make sure, check the price posted up in the room (this is compulsory, except in super-deluxe hotels). The letters *ttc (toutes taxes comprises)* mean that there'll be nothing extra to pay.

You should expect to pay at least 1,000 frs. per night for a double room with bathroom in a Super-deluxe hotel, around 650–950 frs. in a Luxury hotel, 400–650 frs. in an Expensive hotel, 250–400 frs in a Moderate hotel and 100–250 frs. in an Inexpensive hotel. These figures do not include breakfast, which will range upwards from about 20 frs. per person for a Continental breakfast (coffee or tea, plus croissant, rolls and jelly). Top rates in a Super-deluxe hotel may be as much as 80–90 frs. Avoid the temptation to add fruit juice, eggs or cereal if you're interested in keeping extras to a minimum on your final bill. Until recently breakfast has normally been served in your room, but increasingly the modern hotels are charging extra for this service and encourage you to come down to a breakfast room or restaurant; the smaller and older hotels still generally serve it in your room.

The (M) and (I) hotel categories include many hotels that have been recently modernized, and many hotels in these categories now have attractive, functional little bathrooms. However, the demand for hotel rooms in Paris in recent years has been such that many hoteliers have been reluctant to close for much-needed redecoration and some rooms are becoming shabby. In all but the very inexpensive examples in our list, you will normally find someone who speaks at least a little English. On the whole Left Bank hotels are smaller and less formal, but often more picturesque than their Right Bank counterparts.

In the following list we give the super-deluxe hotels first, grouped together, since if you're able to stay in this category it'll be the hotel rather than the district that you go for. All the other hotels are grouped according to district.

Super-deluxe

Bristol, 112 fbg St-Honoré, 8e (tel. 42–66–91–45). One of the most elegant in Paris and the most expensive; it is close to the British Embassy and the Elysée Palace. Rooms and suites are luxurious. Extremely chic clientele: British, German and American diplomats; distinguished foreigners. 205 rooms. Good restaurant.

Crillon, 10 pl. de la Concorde, 8e (tel. 42–65–24–24). In a grandiose location with views across to the National Assembly building on the far side of the Seine. 206 rooms and suites. Excellent cuisine. Along with the George V, this is the headquarters for wealthy Americans in Paris.

George V, 31 av. George V, 8e (tel. 47–23–54–00), off the Champs-Elysées, 292 rooms and suites, some furnished with antiques, as are the reception halls. Modern art displays in restaurant. Fashionable, and often used by rich Arab businessmen.

Grand, 2 rue Scribe, 9e (tel. 42–68–12–13). With 583 rooms, it is the largest in the area. Cheerful bars, salons and boutiques.

Intercontinental-Paris, 3 rue de Castiglione, 1er (tel. 42–60–37–80). Superb comfort. An assortment of pleasant restaurants, cafeterias and grill-rooms, with particularly attractive flower-filled patio for summer meals. 500 rooms.

La Pérouse, 40 rue La Pérouse, 16e (tel. 45–00–83–47). 36 ultra-comfortable rooms and suites, very attractively furnished. Good restaurant called *L'Astrolabe.* Near the Etoile and very well run (belongs to Swiss Nova Park Group).

Meurice, 228 rue de Rivoli, 1er (tel. 42–60–38–60). Halfway between the Ritz and the Crillon, it was once known as the hotel of kings, because so many of them stopped here. Kings are scarcer now, but it is still one of the top-notchers. 221 rooms (air-conditioned), *Copper Bar* grill and small bar. Much of the hotel is now air-conditioned. Belongs to British Grand Metropolitan Group.

Plaza-Athénée, 25 av. Montaigne, 8e (tel. 47–23–78–33). Just far enough off the Champs-Elysées to escape the noise and the glitter. Very elegant. Its *Régence* restaurant is where you'll see some of the prettiest girls in town at lunch, and the *Relais-Plaza* is just right for an expensive after-theater supper. Or try the smart snackbar for a single main dish. Pianist in bar from around 9 P.M. till the early hours. 218 soundproofed rooms and suites.

Prince de Galles, 33 av. George V, 8e (tel. 47–23–55–11). 160 rooms, restaurant. Friendly, attractive.

Raphaël, 17 av. Kléber, 16e (tel. 45–02–16–00). Old-fashioned, but a favorite in spite of its rather out-of-the-way location near the Bois de Boulogne. 87 rooms. Much frequented by movie stars, whose privacy it very effectively protects. Comfortable and very quite; all rooms have balcony.

Ritz, 15 pl. Vendôme, 1er (tel. 42–60–38–30). 163 rooms and magnificent suites, set in a 17th-century square midway between the Opéra and the Tuileries Gardens. Owned by the same Egyptian family that purchased London's Harrods, this stately spot has undergone a facelift, yet has lost none of its old-world charm and legendary service. The *Espadon* and *Vendôme* restaurants are now presided over by topflight chefs, and the two small and select bars and pretty courtyard garden are great attractions.

Near the Tuileries and the Louvre

Louvre-Concorde (L), pl. André-Malraux, 1er (tel. 42–61–56–01). 219 rooms, 209 with bath. Just by Comédie-Française and the Palais-Royal.

Régina-Paris (L), 2 pl. des Pyramides, 1er (tel. 42–60–31–10). 126 rooms, all but 2 with bath. Facing Tuileries.

Duminy (E), 3 rue du Mont-Thabor, 1er (tel. 42–60–32–80). 79 rooms, all with bath or shower.

Madeleine-Palace (E), 8 rue Cambon, 1er (tel. 42–60–37–82). 104 rooms, all with bath or shower. On quiet street, has popular bar-restaurant.

Mayfair (E), 3 rue Rouget-de-l'Isle, 1er (tel. 42–60–38–14). 53 rooms, all with bath or shower. On quiet side street off the rue de Rivoli.

Normandy (E), 7 rue de l'Echelle, 1er (tel. 42–60–30–21). 138 rooms, 123 with bath. Comfortable.

Continent (M), 30 rue du Mont-Thabor, 1er (tel. 42–60–75–32). 28 rooms, most with bath or shower.

Family (M), 35 rue Cambon, 1er (tel. 42–61–54–84). 25 rooms, most with bath or shower. Has long-established clientele. Friendly.

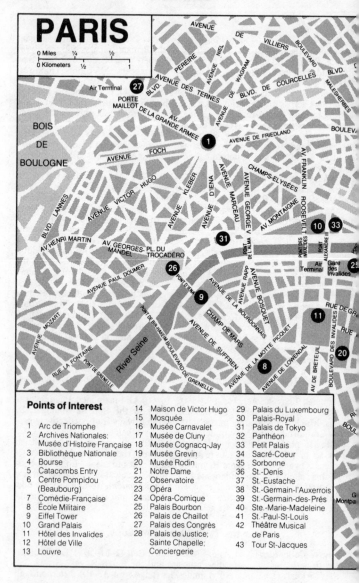

PARIS

0 Miles ¼ ½
0 Kilometers ½ 1

Points of Interest

1 Arc de Triomphe
2 Archives Nationales:
  Musée d'Histoire Française
3 Bibliothèque Nationale
4 Bourse
5 Catacombs Entry
6 Centre Pompidou
  (Beaubourg)
7 Comédie-Française
8 École Militaire
9 Eiffel Tower
10 Grand Palais
11 Hôtel des Invalides
12 Hôtel de Ville
13 Louvre
14 Maison de Victor Hugo
15 Mosquée
16 Musée Carnavalet
17 Musée de Cluny
18 Musée Cognacq-Jay
19 Musée Grevin
20 Musée Rodin
21 Notre Dame
22 Observatoire
23 Opéra
24 Opéra-Comique
25 Palais Bourbon
26 Palais de Chaillot
27 Palais des Congrès
28 Palais de Justice;
  Sainte Chapelle;
  Conciergerie
29 Palais du Luxembourg
30 Palais-Royal
31 Palais de Tokyo
32 Panthéon
33 Petit Palais
34 Sacré-Coeur
35 Sorbonne
36 St.-Denis
37 St.-Eustache
38 St.-Germain-l'Auxerrois
39 St.-Germain-des-Prés
40 Ste.-Marie-Madeleine
41 St.-Paul-St-Louis
42 Théâtre Musical
  de Paris
43 Tour St-Jacques

Londres Stockholm (M), 13 rue St-Roch, 1er (tel. 42–60–15–62). 28 rooms, all but 2 with bath or shower.

Ducs d'Anjou (I), 1 rue Ste-Opportune, 1er (tel. 42–36–92–24). 38 rooms, all but 5 with bath or shower. In a tiny street close to Les Halles.

Near the Madeleine and the Opéra

Edouard-VII (L), 39 av. de l'Opéra, 2e (tel. 42–61–59–90). 100 rooms, all but 6 with bath. Close to the Opéra.

Westminster (L), 13 rue de la Paix, 2e (tel. 42–61–57–46). 102 rooms, all with bath. Has very good restaurant.

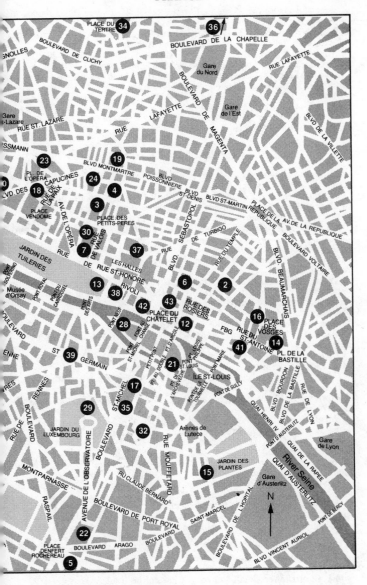

Burgundy (E), 8 rue Duphot, 1er (tel. 42–60–34–12). 92 rooms, all with bath, just off the pl. de la Madeleine.

Opéra d'Antin l'Horset (E), 18 rue d'Antin, 2e (tel. 47–42–13–01). 60 rooms, 52 with shower. Well-located for Opéra and department stores.

Royal Médoc (E), 14 rue Geoffroy-Marie, 9e (tel. 47–70–37–33). 41 rooms, all with bath. Very comfortable. Close to Folies Bergère.

Choiseul-Opéra (M), 1 rue Daunou, 2e (tel. 42–61–70–41). 43 rooms, all with bath or shower. On the same street as the celebrated Harry's Bar.

Cusset (M), 95 rue de Richelieu, 2e (tel. 42–97–48–90). 115 rooms, most with bath.

Etats-Unis Opéra (M), 16 rue d'Antin, 2e (tel. 47–42–43–25). 52 rooms, all with bath. Just by the Opéra.

Excelsior-Opéra (M), 5 rue La Fayette, 9e (tel. 48–74–99–30). 53 rooms, all with bath. Behind Opéra.

London Palace (M), 32 blvd des Italiens, 9e (tel. 48–24–54–64). 49 rooms, 47 with bath. Offers reductions in July and August.

Madeleine Plaza (M), 33 pl. de la Madeleine, 8e (tel. 42–65–20–63). 52 rooms, all but 4 with bath. Just by the Madeleine church.

Queen Mary (M), 9 rue de Greffulhe, 8e (tel. 42–66–40–50). 36 rooms, all with bath. Between Madeleine and the big stores.

Tronchet (M), 22 rue Tronchet, 8e (tel. 47–42–26–14). 32 rooms, all but 5 with bath or shower. Near Madeleine.

Newton (I), 11 bis rue de l'Arcade, 8e (tel. 42–65–32–13). 29 rooms, 17 with bath. Close to the Madeleine.

Near the Champs-Elysées

Château-Frontenac (L), 54 rue Pierre-Charon, 8e (tel. 47–23–55–85). 103 rooms with bath. Inviting restaurant.

Lancaster (L), 7 rue de Berri, 8e (tel. 43–59–90–43). 67 rooms, all with bath or shower. Charmingly furnished rooms, the nicest overlooking a courtyard. Quiet, popular with movie stars who like staying incognito.

Napoléon (L), 40 av. de Friedland, 8e (tel. 47–66–02–02). Elegant restaurant, pleasant bar; the sort of charm missing from newer hotels.

San Régis (L), 12 rue Jean-Goujon, 8e (tel. 43–59–41–90). 43 rooms, all with bath or shower. Quite close to Champs-Elysées, but comparatively quiet. Must reserve well ahead.

Trémoille (L), 14 rue de la Trémoille, 8e (tel. 47–23–34–20). 112 rooms with bath. Same management as Plaza-Athénée. Popular with top models, good service and attractive period furnishings.

Vernet (L), 25 rue Vernet, 8e (tel. 47–23–43–10). 63 rooms, all with bath or shower. Very close to the Etoile and the Champs-Elysées.

Windsor (L), 14 rue Beaujon, 8e (tel. 45–63–04–04). 135 rooms with bath. Belongs to the Frantel chain. Quiet, smart but not showy. Good restaurant.

Atala (E), 10 rue de Chateaubriand, 8e (tel. 45–62–01–62). 49 rooms with bath. Close to the Etoile.

Celtic (E), 6 rue Balzac, 8e (tel. 45–63–28–34). 80 rooms with bath. Restaurant, bar. Frequented by businessmen.

Powers (E), 52 rue François 1er, 8e (tel. 47–23–91–05). 57 rooms, 56 with bath. Pleasant atmosphere.

Royal-Alma (E), 35 rue Jean-Goujon, 8e (tel. 42–25–83–30). 84 rooms, all with bath or shower. Close to the Seine.

Schweizerhof (E), 11 rue Balzac, 8e (tel. 45–63–54–22). 20 rooms, all with bath or shower. Tiny.

Angleterre-Champs-Elysées (M), 91 rue La Boëtie, 8e (tel. 43–59–35–45). 40 rooms, all but 4 with bath or shower.

Arc-Elysée (M), 45 rue de Washington, 8e (tel. 45–63–69–33). 26 rooms, all with bath or shower. Good value.

Arromanches (M), 6 rue Chateaubriand, 8e (tel. 45–63–74–24). 27 rooms, all with bath or shower.

Céramic (M), 34 av. de Wagram, 8e (tel. 42–27–20–30). 59 rooms, 44 with bath or shower. Good value, a favorite with businessmen.

Chambiges (M), 8 rue Chambiges, 8e (tel. 47–23–80–49). 30 rooms, 22 with bath or shower. Pleasant little hotel close to the Seine.

Mayflower (M), 3 rue Chateaubriand, 8e (tel. 45–62–57–46). 24 rooms, all with bath or shower. Small and cozy. Close to the Etoile.

Résidence Lord Byron (M), 5 rue de Chateaubriand, 8e (tel. 43–59–89–98). 26 rooms with bath. Pleasant small hotel close to the Etoile.

Royal (M), 33 av. de Friedland, 8e (tel. 43–59–08–14). 57 rooms, all with bath or shower. Has restaurant and bar; friendly service. Some rooms are (E).

Champs-Elysées (I), 2 rue d'Artois, 8e (tel. 43–59–11–42). 40 rooms, 19 with bath or shower.

Ile Saint-Louis

Deux-Iles (E), 59 rue St-Louis-en-l'Ile (tel. 43–26–13–35). 17 rooms, all with bath and shower. Attractive small hotel in a 17th-century house, with bar and sitting-room in the old cellars.

Lutèce (E), 65 rue St-Louis-en-l'Ile, 4e (tel. 43–26–23–52). 23 rooms, all with bath or shower. Another small and delightful hotel, peaceful and with some rooms arranged as duplexes.

Saint-Louis (M), 75 rue-St-Louis-en-l'Ile, 4e (tel. 46–34–04–80). 25 rooms, 17 of them with bath or shower. Attractive rooms on five floors (the top floor has marvelous view, but there's no elevator), with good modern bathrooms.

Near Notre Dame

Colbert (E), 7 rue de l'Hôtel Colbert, 5e (tel. 43–25–85–65). 40 rooms, all with bath or shower. 18th-century building by the Seine with attractive, smallish rooms.

Esmeralda (M), 4 rue St.-Julien-le-Pauvre, 5e (tel. 43–54–19–20). 19 rooms, all but 3 with bath or shower. A 17th-century building this time, just by the pretty sq. Viviani, again with smallish rooms, but pleasantly furnished.

Latin Quarter

Collège de France (M), 7 rue Thénard, 5e (tel. 43–26–78–36), 29 rooms, all with bath or shower. In quiet side street; good value.

Grand Hôtel Suez (M), 31 blvd St.-Michel, 5e (tel. 46–34–08–02). 50 rooms, all with bath or shower.

Avenir (I), 52 rue Gay-Lussac, 5e (tel. 43–54–76–60). 47 rooms, only 6 with bath or shower. A modest budget hotel. On six floors but no elevator.

Nevers-Luxembourg (I), 3 rue Abbé-de-l'Epée, 5e (tel. 43–26–81–83). 29 rooms, all but 4 without bath or shower. Attractively decorated, yet very inexpensive.

Saint-Jacques (I), 35 rue des Ecoles, 5e (tel. 43–26–82–53). 39 rooms, 15 of them with bath or shower.

Sorbonne (I), 6 rue Victor-Cousin, 5e (tel. 43–54–58–08). 37 rooms, 22 of them with bath or shower. Another modest budget hotel in this student area.

Saint-Germain-des-Prés

L'Hôtel Guy-Louis-Duboucheron (L), 13 rue des Beaux-Arts, 6e (tel. 43–25–27–22). 27 rooms furnished with antiques, including Mistinguett's mirror-lined bed. Attractive, very chic, very expensive. Restaurant.

Lutétia-Concorde (L), 45 blvd Raspail, 6e (tel. 45–44–38–10), near Bon-Marché department store. 295 rooms with bath or shower; restaurant, bar. Pleasant atmosphere, good traditional service.

Pont-Royal (L), 7 rue Montalembert, 7e (tel. 45–44–38–27). 80 rooms, all but 6 with bath or shower, some of them rather cramped, but pleasant atmosphere. Attractive bar is popular with publishers. Restaurant.

Abbaye Saint-Germain (E), 10 rue Cassette, 6e (tel. 45–44–38–11). 45 rooms, all with bath or shower. Quiet and attractive hotel in former monastery.

Angleterre (E), 44 rue Jacob, 6e (tel. 42–60–34–72). 31 rooms, all with bath or shower. Once the home of the British ambassador, and Hemingway used to live here too. Excellent service, traditional; highly recommended.

Cayré (E), 4 blvd Raspail, 6e (tel. 45–44–38–88). 131 rooms, all with bath or shower. Quiet, popular with writers.

Relais Christine (E), 3 rue Christine, 6e (tel. 43–26–71–80). 51 rooms, all with bath. A 16th-century convent lately converted into a charming and comfortable hotel in a quiet street in the heart of Saint-Germain-des-Prés.

Université (E), 22 rue de l'Université, 7e (tel. 42–61–09–39). 28 rooms, all with bath or shower. In small converted mansion; attractive decor. Some (M) singles available.

Fleurie (M), 32 rue St. Grégoire-de-Tours, 6e (tel. 43–29–59–81). 30 rooms, all with bath or shower. Just off blvd. St.-Germain.

Madison (M), 143 blvd St-Germain, 6e (tel. 43–29–72–50). 57 rooms, all with bath or shower. Set back from the boulevard slightly, in tiny square facing the church; front rooms have delightful view, but are rather noisy; popular with publishers.

Marronniers (M), 21 rue Jacob, 6e (tel. 43–25–30–60). 37 rooms, all with bath or shower. Quiet, with lovely garden. Light lunches served in bar or garden.

Odéon (M), 3 rue de l'Odéon, 6e (tel. 43–25–90–67). 34 rooms, all with bath. Apparently this mansion once belonged to Madame de Pompadour.

Pas-de-Calais (M), 59 rue des Sts-Pères, 6e (tel. 45–48–78–74). 41 rooms, all with bath or shower. Has been here since the early 19th century and is still popular. Built around a tiny courtyard, but try to get a room away from the street.

Principautés-Unies (M), 42 rue de Vaugirard, 6e (tel. 46–34–44–90). 29 rooms, 25 with bath or shower. Recently redecorated, some suites with mini-kitchen. Friendly.

Quai Voltaire (M), 19 qu. Voltaire, 7e (tel. 42–61–50–91). 33 rooms, 26 with bath or shower. Overlooking the Seine, but rooms in front are noisy.

Saints-Pères (M), 65 rue des Sts-Pères, 6e (tel. 45–44–50–00). 35 rooms, 33 with bath or shower. An old favorite. Has one or two (E) rooms, too.

Scandinavie (M), 27 rue de Tournon, 6e (tel. 43–29–67–20). 22 rooms, all with bath. Attractive mansion with fine Louis XIII furniture, close to Luxembourg Garden. Must reserve well ahead.

Welcome (M), 66 rue de Seine, 6e (tel. 46–34–24–80). 30 rooms, all with bath or shower. Quiet and well-decorated. Under same management as the Marroniers.

Avenir (I), 65 rue Madame, 6e (tel. 45–48–84–54). 35 rooms, 12 with bath or shower. Well-run hotel, with a glimpse of the Luxembourg Gardens from some rooms, quiet.

Studio (I), 4 rue du Vieux Colombier, 6e (tel. 45–48–31–81). 34 well-renovated rooms with bath. In heart of St.-Germain-des-Près.

Vieux Paris (I), 9 rue Gît-le-Coeur, 6e (tel. 43–54–41–66). 21 rooms, 14 with bath or shower. In picturesque sidestreet near the Seine and the place Saint-Michel.

Montparnasse

Montparnasse-Park-Hotel (L), 19 rue Commandant-Mouchotte, 14e (tel. 43–20–15–51). 952 rooms, all with bath. Large, rather impersonal hotel near the Tour Montparnasse, with restaurants, bars, shops. Wonderful view from top floors. Now run by Swiss Nova Park group.

PLM-Saint-Jacques (L), 17 blvd St-Jacques, 14e (tel. 45–89–89–80). 797 rooms, all with bath. Not on the usual tourist track, convenient for Orly airport (airport bus even stops here). Like its sister hotel, the Méridien at the Porte Maillot, it has a variety of restaurants and bars to suit all tastes and purses. Offers reduced rates to businessmen who apply for a special *carte d'affaires.*

Littré (E), 9 rue Littré, 6e (tel. 45–44–38–68). 110 rooms, all with bath or shower. Same management as the Victoria-Palace; popular with publishers.

Victoria-Palace (E), 6 rue Blaise-Desgoffe, 6e (tel. 45–44–38–16). 113 rooms, all with bath or shower. In a tiny side street, well run, good service. Same management as Littré.

Aiglon (M), 232 blvd Raspail, 14e (tel. 43–20–82–42). 50 rooms, all with bath or shower. Central but quiet.

Residence Elysées-Maubourg (E), 35 blvd Latour-Maubourg, 7e (tel. 45–56–10–78). 30 rooms, all with bath. Nicely modernized and decorated, with old-world style but modern amenities; opened 1984.

Orléans Palace (M), 185 blvd Brune, 14e (tel. 45–39–68–50). 92 rooms, all with bath or shower. Near Cité Universitaire.

Rennes-Montparnasse (M), 151 rue de Rennes, 6e (tel. 45–48–97–38). 38 rooms, 23 with bath or shower.

Royal (M), 212 blvd Raspail, 14e (tel. 43–20–69–20). 48 rooms, all with bath or shower. Close to Coupole and Montparnasse restaurants and movies.

Timhôtel Montparnasse (M), 22 rue de l'Arrivée, 14e (tel. 45–48–96–92). 33 rooms, 31 with bath or shower. By Montparnasse station; another of the new group of well-run, attractive small hotels; pleasant service.

Bréa (I), 14 rue Bréa, 6e (tel. 43–54–76–21). 26 rooms, all but 3 without bath or shower. Very low prices.

Delambre (I), 35 rue Delambre, 14e (tel. 43–20–66–31). 36 rooms, 34 with bath or shower. Close to Tour Montparnasse.

Parc Montsouris (I), 4 rue du Parc, 14e (tel. 45–89–09–72). 22 rooms, only 12 with bath or shower. A bit off the beaten track unless you need to be near the Cité Universitaire, but close to the attractive Parc Montsouris. Very low prices.

Near Les Invalides and the Eiffel Tower

Hilton International Paris (L), 18 av. de Suffren, 15e (tel. 42–73–92–00). 480 rooms, all with bath and balcony. Has rooftop restaurant and another restaurant, plus coffee shop, boutiques, hairdresser, bank. No extra charge for children who sleep in their parents' room.

Nikko (L), 61 quai de Grenelle, 15e (tel. 45–75–62–62). 778 rooms all with bath. Owned by Japan Air Lines, overlooking the Seine to the west of the Eiffel Tower. Mixture of Japanese and French décor; has Japanese restaurant too (and a French one). Pool, sauna, shops, the lot.

Bourgogne et Montana (E), 3 rue de Bourgogne, 7e (tel. 45–51–20–22). 35 rooms, all with bath. Just by the Chambre des Députés. Restaurant.

Saxe-Résidence (E), 9 villa de Saxe, 7e (tel. 47–83–98–28). 52 rooms, all with bath or shower. In quiet cul-de-sac near the Ecole Militaire.

Suède (E), 31 rue Vaneau, 7e (tel. 47–05–00–08). 41 rooms, all but 4 with bath or shower. Attractive, has pretty inner courtyard.

Suffren la Tour (E), 20 rue Jean-Rey, 15e (tel. 45–78–61–08). 407 rooms, all with bath. Just by the Eiffel Tower, with restaurant and garden.

Bourdonnais (M), 111 av. de la Bourdonnais, 7e (tel. 47–05–45–42). 60 rooms, all with bath or shower. Quiet, cheerful bar. Restaurant.

Pavillon (M), 54 rue St-Dominique, 7e (tel. 45–51–42–87). 19 rooms, all but 2 with bath or shower. Good value.

Ségur (M), 34 blvd Garibaldi, 15e (tel. 43–06–01–85). 34 rooms, all with bath or shower. Near the Ecole Militaire.

Varenne (M), 44 rue de Bourgogne, 7e (tel. 45–51–45–55). 24 rooms, all with bath or shower. A converted mansion, peaceful and friendly, with a pretty little patio.

Empereur (I), 2 rue Chevert, 7e (tel. 45–55–88–02). 40 rooms, 23 with bath or shower. Close, as its name suggests, to Napoleon's tomb in the Invalides.

Palais Bourbon (I), 49 rue de Bourgogne, 7e (tel. 47–05–29–26). 34 rooms, all but 8 with bath or shower. Small but pleasant rooms, good for visiting Les Invalides and the Rodin Museum.

Pretty (I), 8 rue Amélie, 7e (tel. 47–05–46–21). 57 rooms, only 6 with bath or shower. Close to Eiffel Tower and Les Invalides.

Near the Gare du Nord and Gare de l'Est

Diamond (M), 73 rue de Dunkerque, 9e (tel. 42–81–15–00). 52 rooms, 40 with bath or shower.

Londres et Anvers (M), 133 blvd Magenta, 10e (tel. 42–85–28–26). 43 rooms, 13 with bath or shower.

Europe (I), 98 blvd Magenta, 10e (tel. 46–07–25–82). 36 rooms, all but 12 with bath or shower.

Near the Gare de Lyon

Modern Hôtel Lyon (M), 3 rue Parrot, 12e (tel. 43–43–41–52). 53 rooms, all with bath or shower. Quiet, popular with businessmen.

Paris-Lyon-Palace (M), 11 rue de Lyon, 12e (tel. 43–07–29–49). 128 rooms, all with bath or shower. Restaurant.

Terminus-Lyon (M), 19 blvd Diderot, 12e (tel. 43–43–24–03). 61 rooms, all but 1 with bath or shower.

Near the Town Terminal for Roissy/Charles-de-Gaulle Airport

Concorde-Lafayette (L), 3 pl. du Général-Koenig, 17e (tel. 47–58–12–84). 1000 rooms, all with bath. Vast complex with conference rooms, secretaries, restaurants for all tastes and most pocketbooks. Rather impersonal, but functional.

Méridien (L), 81 blvd Gouvion-St-Cyr, 17e (tel. 47–58–12–30). 1027 rooms, all with bath. Efficient American-style hotel, with 4 restaurants, including a reasonably priced help-yourself buffet, bar with jazz, boutiques.

Splendid Etoile (E), 1 bis av. Carnot, 17e (tel. 47–66–41–41). 57 rooms, all with bath or shower. Pleasant furnishings. Also convenient for the Etoile.

Near the Airports

ORLY. Hilton (E) (tel. 46–87–33–88). 379 rooms, all soundproofed and airconditioned, *Louisiane* restaurant (M), coffee shop.

Motel PLM (M) (tel. 46–87–23–37). 200 rooms, restaurant (I).

Frantel Orly (E) (tel. 46–87–36–36). 206 rooms, all with bath. At nearby Rungis.

Holiday Inn (E) (tel. 46–87–26–66). 171 rooms, all with bath. At nearby Rungis.

ROISSY/CHARLES-DE-GAULLE. Holiday Inn (E), 54 rue de Paris (tel. 49–88–00–22). 250 rooms, restaurant, sports facilities, free bus service to airport.

Sofitel (E) (tel. 48–62–23–23). 352 rooms, restaurant, discothèque, at airport.

Arcade (M) (tel. 48–62–49–49). 356 rooms, all with bath. Functional, conveniently close to Roissy Rail terminus, free bus service to airport.

 RESTAURANTS. Paris has literally thousands of restaurants and the average quality at all price ranges is a great deal higher than in any other of the world's capitals. We can only list a small number here, chosen both for their excellence within their category and for their convenience in terms of being near districts you're likely to be visiting. Remember that all restaurants in France except the really deluxe ones are compelled by law to have a priced menu visible outside, so you need never have an unpleasant surprise when the bill arrives. For an explanation of the "new cuisine", see our Restaurant heading at the beginning of this chapter. Hotel restaurants are not included. Do please note that telephone numbers change very frequently in France. Numbers were correct at our presstime, but may have changed since.

The Gastronomic Temples

First of all, here is a short list of truly outstanding restaurants, for which you must naturally reserve ahead of time. These aren't places to slip into if you happen to be in the area—they deserve a special journey, not to mention a specially fat pocketbook! All are (E).

Faugeron, 52 rue de Longchamp, 16e (tel. 47–04–24–53). Closed weekends and August (but open Sat. evening from October to around Easter). Again *nouvelle cuisine*, served in very pretty setting with elegant atmosphere. Serves good-value (M) *menu* at lunchtime.

Lucas-Carton–Alain Senderens, 9 pl. de la Madeleine, 8e (tel. 42–65–22–90). Following the closure of his celebrated restaurant L'Archestrate, Alain Senderens has set up shop in the old established Lucas Carton. For a sensational combination of *nouvelle cuisine* at its subtle best, magnificent *art nouveau* decor and luxurious turn-of-the-century atmosphere, this place is unbeatable.

Robuchon, 32 rue de Longchamp, 16e (tel. 45–53–02–13). Closed weekends and July. Near the Trocadéro and not far from the Arc de Triomphe; long-fashionable restaurant (formerly *Jamin*) run by exceptionally inventive chef, who produces some of the best *nouvelle cuisine* in Paris.

Taillevent, 15 rue Lamennais, 8e (tel. 45–61–12–90). Closed weekends and August. Superb *nouvelle cuisine* and magnificent wines in a very elegant setting close to the Arc de Triomphe.

Tour d'Argent, 15 quai de Tournelle, 5e (tel. 43–54–23–31). Closed Mon. A world-famous restaurant that is worth the expense for the décor, the superb wines and not least the cuisine, which is classical *haute cuisine* at its best. At lunchtime during the week you can even enjoy a fixed-price meal at considerably less than the usual sky-high prices.

Near Notre Dame

Le Grand Véfour (E), 17 rue de Beaujolais, 1er (tel. 42–96–56–27). Closed weekends and August. This time-honored restaurant near the Palais Royal, once presided over by the legendary chef Raymond Oliver, has now been bought by Jean Taittinger, head of the world-famous Concorde hotels, and is back on form as one of Paris's greatest restaurants, with a mixture of classical and modern cuisine. The fabulous décor (it's officially listed as a historic monument) has been restored.

Auberge des Deux Signes (M), 46 rue Galande, 5e (tel. 43–25–46–56). Closed Sun. Wonderful medieval setting overlooking Notre Dame serves as a delightful background (along with classical music) to an interesting mixture of hearty Auvergnat fare and *nouvelle cuisine* dishes.

La Bûcherie (M), 41 rue de la Bûcherie, 5e (tel. 43–54–78–06). Closed July. Open to 1 A.M. Log fires, classical music, relaxed atmosphere. Good new cooking at almost reasonable prices. Portions can be small, though. On the Left Bank side of the river opposite Notre Dame.

La Colombe (M), 4 rue de la Colombe, 4e (tel. 46–33–37–08). Closed Sun., Mon for lunch, most of February, part of Aug., open till midnight. Openair dining beneath a vine trellis in a little street close to Notre Dame.

Au Gourmet de l'Ile (I), 42 rue St-Louis-en-l'Ile, 4e (tel. 43–26–79–27). Closed Mon., Thurs. and August. Good value, crowded, friendly, on the Ile St-Louis.

La Brasserie de l'Ile (I), 55 quai de Bourbon, 4e. No telephone reservations. Closed Weds. and Aug. Crowded, cheerful brasserie on the Ile St-Louis, with lively waiters who keep smiling in spite of the crush. Traditional Alsatian dishes and good fruity wines. No advance reservations, so get there early.

Chez Paul (I), 15 pl. Dauphine, 1er (tel. 43–54–21–48). Closed Mon. and Tues. Attractive bistrot in the charming little square behind the law courts and the Sainte-Chapelle, genuine marble counter and straightforward home cooking.

Near the Louvre, the Palais-Royal and the Tuileries

Le Bistro d'Hubert (E), 36 pl. du Marché-St-Honoré, 1er (tel. 42–60–03–00). Closed Sun. and Mon. Good new cuisine, with good-value *menus* at lunchtime.

Le Mercure Galant (E), 15 rue des Petits-Champs, 1er (tel. 42–97–53–85). Closed Sat. for lunch and Sun. Fashionable, with turn-of-century decor. Good mixture of new and traditional cuisine. Good-value dinner *menu*.

Pierre Traiteur (E), 10 rue de Richelieu, 1er (tel. 42–96–09–17). Closed weekends and Aug. Small, friendly restaurant behind the Comédie-Française, with traditional dishes plus a few *nouvelle cuisine* specialties. Always crowded.

L'Absinthe (M), 24 pl. du Marché-St.-Honoré, 1er (tel. 42–61–03–32). Closed Sat. for lunch and Sun. Smart little restaurant near the pl. Vendôme with attractive decor and mostly new cuisine.

La Ferme Irlandaise (M), 30 pl. du Marché-St.-Honoré, 1er (tel. 42–60–02–99). Irish specialties, but with a Gallic touch (the chef is French). Fashionable.

Ruc'Univers (M), 159 rue St.-Honoré, 1er (tel. 42–60–31–57). Diagonally opposite the Comédie Française and close to the Opéra and many theaters, so good for a late supper after a show as it's open till 1 A.M. Typically Parisian old-style restaurant, spacious and comfortable. Excellent oysters.

Faure (I), 40 rue de Mont-Thabor, 1er (tel. 42–60–74–28). Closed Sun. and Aug. Near the Tuileries Gardens and the pl. de la Concorde, a good place for a home-style lunch or "farmhouse dinner." Lunchtime trade includes models from the nearby fashion houses.

Le Soufflé (I), 36 rue du Mont-Thabor, 1er (tel. 42–60–27–19). Closed Sun. Specializes, as its name suggests, in soufflés of all kinds, both sweet and savory.

Near the Madeleine and the Opéra

Maxim's (E), 3 rue Royale, 8e (tel. 42–65–27–94). Closed Sun., open to 1 A.M. Turn-of-the-century décor, chic atmosphere, world-famous. Classical cuisine with many imaginative touches. Now owned by couturier Pierre Cardin.

Le Grand Café (M), 4 blvd des Capucines, 9e (tel. 47–42–75–77). Excellent seafood restaurant close to the Opéra, very typical of traditional Paris with its aproned waiters and splendid display of shellfish outside. Open day and night.

Julien (M), 16 rue du fbg Saint-Denis, 10e (tel. 47–70–12–06). Closed Sun. and July. Fashionable art nouveau décor and interesting food, so very popular (must reserve and even then you'll probably have to wait for your table). Fashionable clientele, especially in the evenings, when it stays open to 1.30 A.M.

Le Petit Coin de la Bourse (M), 16 rue Feydeau, 2e (tel. 45–08–00–08). Well-run, very Parisian atmosphere.

Au Petit Riche (M), 25 rue Le Peletier, 9e (tel. 47–70–68–68). Late 19th-century decor, traditional home-style dishes.

Saintongeais (M), 62 rue du faubourg Montmartre, 9e (tel. 42–80–39–92). Closed Sat. for lunch, Sun. all day, and Aug. Good for fish.

L'Amanguier (I), 110 rue de Richelieu, 2e (tel. 42–96–37–39). Delightful green-and-white restaurant near the Bourse, summery atmosphere with parasols and garden chairs. Short but imaginative menu.

Le Bistro de la Gare (I), 38 blvd des Italiens, 9e, no reservations. A short menu with newish cuisine, superb desserts, turn-of-the-century décor. Crowded, open late.

Chartier (I), 7 rue du Faubourg-Montmartre, 9e. Turn-of-the-century decor and ludicrously low prices.

Near the Champs-Elysées

Le Bernardin (E), 18 rue Troyon, 17e (tel. 43–80–36–22). Closed Sun., Mon. and Aug. Run by a young Breton brother and sister. Spacious, elegant. Delicious new cuisine fish, but rather small portions.

Chiberta (E), 3 rue Arsène-Houssaye, 8e (tel. 45–63–77–90). Closed weekends Feb. and Aug. Owner and chef are passionate exponents of the *nouvelle cuisine*. Results sometimes unexpected, mostly delicious. One of Paris's best, so go if you can afford it.

Lamazère (E), 23 rue de Ponthieu, 8e (tel. 43–59–66–66). Closed Sun. and Aug. Chic and expensive, with particularly good dishes from southwest France, cooked in the new style, including splendid cassoulet.

Laurent (E), 41 av. Gabriel, 8e (tel. 43–59–14–49). Closed Sat. for lunch and Sun. all day. Open to midnight in summer months. Fashionable restaurant overlooking the gardens running down the Champs-Elysées to the Concorde. Splendid *hors d'oeuvres* trolley, fine wine list, rather grand atmosphere.

Le Lord Gourmand (E), 9 rue Lord-Byron, 8e (tel. 45–59–07–27). Closed weekends and Aug. and Christmas period. In a quiet side street off the Champs-Elysées. The still-lifes of game and fish on the walls seem to spring to life as you contemplate your food! Basically "new" cuisine.

Ramponneau (E), 21 av. Marceau, 16e (tel. 47–20–59–51). Closed Aug. Quiet and distinguished. Good, carefully prepared home-style cooking. Openair tables pleasant for an unhurried lunch. Good shellfish too.

Alsace (M), 39 av. des Champs-Elysées, 8e (tel. 43–59–44–24). Open day and night year-round. Always busy, well run. Good Alsatian specialties (the Alsace region's tourist office is next door), plus excellent seafood.

Chez Edgard (M), 4 rue Marbeuf, 8e (tel. 47–20–51–15). Closed Sun., open to 1 A.M. Always crowded, popular with after-theater crowd. Good straightforward cooking, with some modish dishes too.

Fouquet's (M), 99 av. des Champs-Elysées, 8e (tel. 47–23–70–60). Open to midnight daily. Not gastronomically exciting but the food is basically good in this eternal landmark. A place to be seen.

Au Vieux Berlin (M), 32 av. George-V, 8e (tel. 47–20–88–96). Well-known German restaurant with good sauerkraut and game in season.

L'Assiette au Boeuf (I), 123 av. des Champs-Elysées, 8e (no telephone reservations). Open to 1 A.M. The same set menu as in the other restaurants of the same name. Fashionable decor.

Bar des Théâtres (I), 6 av. Montaigne, 8e. In the heart of couture and theater land. Basic bistrot-type cooking.

Fermette-Marbeuf (I), 5 rue Marbeuf, 8e (tel. 47–20–63–53). Open daily, year-round. Marvelous art nouveau decor in rear dining room was discovered during redecoration; front room is now decorated in same style. Food's good, too.

L'Hippopotamus (I), 6 av. Franklin-Roosevelt, 8e (no telephone reservations). Open to 1 A.M. One of a menagerie of four beasts, known for their good meat, low prices and cheerful atmosphere. Not a gastronomic experience, but fun.

Near the Bois de Boulogne

La Grande Cascade (E), tel. 45–06–33–51. In the Bois de Boulogne, 16e. Closed mid-Dec. to mid-Jan. Attractive leafy setting near the famous Longchamp racecourse, with the refreshing sound of the nearby waterfall that gives it its name. Built like a spacious garden pavilion, it seems to belong to a more leisurely era (which probably explains why the service can be very slow). Now serves *nouvelle cuisine,* but also a good place for a delicious ice cream after the races or a stroll in the Bois. Much used for society weddings, so excellent for people-watching.

Pré Catalan (E), route de Suresnes, Bois de Boulogne, 16e (tel. 45–24–55–28). Closed Sun. eve., Mon. and Feb. Run by Gaston Lenôtre, France's most famous pastry cook, who's turned it into one of Paris's best and most sought-after restaurants. Lovely decor. Rather grand.

Le Vieux Galion (E), 10 allée du Bord-de-l'Eau, 16e (tel. 45–06–26–10). A huge galleon moored opposite the Longchamp racecourse and just right for openair dining in summer (though it's open in winter too), with a view over the Seine. Generous helpings, elegant diners.

Brasserie Stella (I), 133 av. Victor-Hugo, 16e (tel. 47–27–60–54). Closed Aug. Chic and lively, frequented by the well-heeled inhabitants of this fashionable residential part of Paris. Good basic cooking, a bit cramped. Open to 2 A.M.

Near Les Invalides and the Eiffel Tower

Chez les Anges (E), 54 blvd de Latour-Maubourg, 7e (tel. 47–05–89–86). Closed Sun. for dinner, Mon. and most of Aug. Spacious and comfortable restaurant near the Invalides with a judicious mix of classical and new dishes.

Divellec (E), 107 rue de l'Université (tel. 45–51–91–96). Closed Sun., Mon., and Aug. Opened in 1984 and already one of Paris's greatest eating places, specializing in mouthwateringly fresh fish.

Ile de France (E), port Debilly (opposite 32 av. de New-York), 16e (tel. 47–23–60–21). Closed weekends. A barge-restaurant moored opposite the Eiffel Tower and bearing a distinct resemblance to a Mississippi paddle steamer. You can eat well here too *(nouvelle cuisine)* as well as admiring the delightful view.

Jules Verne (E), on 2nd floor of Eiffel Tower, 7e (tel. 45–55–20–04). It's good to be able to report that the Eiffel Tower has a restaurant worthy of it, but you may have trouble getting a table as it's very popular. Marvelous views, attractive décor, good food.

Quai d'Orsay (M), 49 quai d'Orsay, 7e (tel. 45–51–58–58). Closed Sun. and August. This pleasant spot has long been fashionable, but it may have changed hands by the time you read this.

La Fontaine de Mars (I), 129 rue Saint-Dominique, 7e (tel. 47–05–46–44). Closed Sat. for dinner, Sun. and Aug. Typically French little restaurant near the Eiffel Tower, plain and very popular with local residents in this chic area. Straightforward home cooking, tables outside in summer. Friendly service.

Thoumieux (I), 79 rue Saint-Dominique, 7e (tel. 47–05–49–75). Closed Mon. and mid-July to mid-Aug. Typically French home cooking in typically French bistrot.

Saint-Germain-des-Prés

Allard (M), 41 rue St.-André-des-Arts, 6e (tel. 43–26–48–23). Closed weekends and Aug. One of the most authentic bistro-type restaurants in Paris, pleasantly set in a narrow street close to the pl. St.-Michel. Classical cooking.

Caleche (M), 8 rue de Lille, 7e (tel. 42–60–24–76). Good home-style cooking in pleasant ambiance.

Au Charbon de Bois (M), 16 rue du Dragon, 6e (tel. 45–48–57–04). Closed Sun., Mon. lunch and Aug. Specializes in charcoal-grilled dishes.

Ferme Saint-Simon (M), 6 rue Saint-Simon, 7e (tel. 45–48–35–74). Closed Sat. for lunch and Sun. and most of Aug. Chef used to be assistant to the great Gaston Lenôtre, and his decorative wife is a well-known T.V. announcer, but diners come here for the food. New cuisine at its lightest and best.

Lipp (M), 151 blvd. St.-Germain, 6e (tel. 45–48–53–91). Closed Mon. and July. A Paris institution, still the favorite haunt of politicians, writers and cine-folk. Fair home-style cooking of the *brasserie* type and reasonably priced.

Restaurant des Saints-Pères (M), 175 blvd. St.-Germain, 6e (tel. 45–48–56–85). Closed Wed., Thurs. and mid-Aug. to mid-Sept. Old-style Parisian atmosphere, from the way the food's arranged to the bentwood hatstand.

Tan Dinh (M), 60 rue de Verneuil, 6e. Vietnamese version of *nouvelle cuisine* served with fine French wines.

Vagénende (M), 142 blvd. St.-Germain, 6e (tel. 43–26–68–18). Open to 2 A.M. Charming turn-of-the-century decor and a readers' favorite. Good game in season.

Aux Charpentiers (I), 10 rue Mabillon, 6e (tel. 43–26–30–05). Closed Sun. Typically Parisian bistro, unpretentious and delightful. Once the H.Q. of the Carpenters' Guild—with photos to prove it. Food is plain but good. Open to midnight.

La Petite Chaise (I), 36 rue de Grenelle, 7e (tel. 42–22–13–35). Charming, slightly shabby, traditional, always full—not surprisingly as it's excellent value. Has been going since the late 17th century and may well be the oldest restaurant in Paris.

Petit Saint-Benoît (I), 4 rue Saint-Benoît, 6e (no telephone reservations). Closed weekends. One of Paris's few remaining genuine bistrots, and always busy. Simple home cooking and lots of atmosphere; highly recommended.

Polidor (I), 41 rue Monsieur-le-Prince, 6e (tel. 43–26–95–34). Closed Sun., Mon. and Aug. Old-established genuinely Parisian bistro with literary associations—Gide and Valéry among others. Good home cooking in generous portions. Attracts a youngish set and a lot of foreigners. Exceptional value.

Le Procope (I), 13 rue de l'Ancienne Comédie, 6e (tel. 43–26–99–20). Closed July, open to 1.30 A.M. Large, crowded bustling café-restaurant with a famous past. Voltaire and Balzac knew it as a coffee house.

Montparnasse

La Closerie des Lilas (E), 171 blvd. du Montparnasse, 6e (tel. 43–26–70–50). Some people find it overrated, but this is still a very popular spot in Paris, especially with writers, artists and actors, and is always crowded to 1 A.M. Lovely openair terrace (M) is as delightful as it was in the thirties. The food is good, if unoriginal, but the atmosphere is what counts.

Le Duc (E), 243 blvd. Raspail, 14e (tel. 43–22–59–59). Closed weekends and Mon. Probably Paris's finest seafood restaurant firmly anchored in the 'new' cuisine.

La Coupole (M), 102 blvd. Montparnasse, 14e (tel. 43–20–14–20). Closed Aug., open to 2 A.M. The whole of Paris and their guests seem to meet for lunch or supper at this famous and longstanding *brasserie* that looks like an arty rail station. Fun people, sound classical cooking.

Lous Landès (M), 157 av. du Maine, 14e (tel. 45–43–08–04). Closed Sun., Mon. for lunch. Excellent cooking from the Bordeaux region, with tables outside in summer.

Le Bistro de la Gare (I), 59 blvd. Montparnasse, 6e (no telephone reservations). Close to the monster tower. Short, imaginative menu, with superb desserts. Served in huge room with turn-of-the-century decor. Always crowded, but fine value and rather smart.

Hippopotamus (I), 12 av. du Maine, 14e (tel. 42–22–36–75). Yet another hippo from the same zoo as its namesake. Very good value.

Latin Quarter

Le Coupe-Chou (M), 11 rue Lanneau, 5e (tel. 46–33–68–69). Closed Sun. for lunch. Open to 1 A.M. Fashionable, attractive spot in old house. Cooking can be uneven, but you're bound to enjoy eating here—handy for late dining.

Dodin Bouffant (M), 25 rue Frédéric-Sauton, 5e (tel. 43–25–25–14). Closed weekends and Aug. and over Christmas and New Year. Very fashionable. Inspired new cuisine, and fine reasonably-priced wines.

Le Mange-Tout (M), 30 rue Lacépède, 6e (tel. 45–35–53–93). Interesting, inventive cooking in plain modern surroundings. Dishes from the southwest. Always crowded. Closed Sun., Mon. lunch and Aug.

Moissonnier (M), 28 rue des Fossés-St.-Bernard, 5e (tel. 43–29–87–65). Closed Sun. for dinner, Mon. and Aug. Excellent rich cuisine from the Lyon region.

Au Pactole (M), 44 blvd. St.-Germain, 5e (tel. 46–33–31–31). Careful cooking blends new and classical cuisine. Discreet atmosphere. Good value lunchtime menu.

Villars-Palace (M), 8 rue Descartes, 5e (tel. 43–26–39–08). Closed Sat. for lunch. Mostly fish. Chic, with inventive cuisine—one of the best in the Latin Quarter.

Le Balzar (I), 49 rue des Ecoles, 5e (tel. 43–54–13–67). Closed Tues. and Aug. Open to 12.30 A.M. Very typical Parisian bistrot, with aproned waiters, *banquettes,* mirrors and traditional home-style cooking.

Les Halles and Beaubourg

Escargot Montorgueil (E), 38 rue Montorgueil, 1er (tel. 42–36–83–51). Opened in the 1830s and still going strong, with delightful decor and smart clientele.

Au Quai des Ormes (E), 72 quai de L'Hôtel-de-Ville, 4e (tel. 42–74–72–22). Closed weekends and Aug. Attractive setting beside the Seine and close to the city hall; beautifully served *nouvelle cuisine;* discreet, chic ambiance.

Baumann-Baltard (M), 9 rue Coquillière, 1er (tel. 42–36–22–00). Open year-round in what was once a butcher's shop near Les Halles. Excellent Alsace wines and specialties (best known for *choucroute*), good value. Open till 2 A.M.

Louis XIV (M), 1 bis pl. des Victoires, 1er (tel. 42–61–39–44). Closed week-ends and August. Lyonnaise cuisine, bistrot atmosphere, in pretty 17th-century square.

Pharamond (M), 24 rue de la Grande-Truanderie, 1er (tel. 42–33–06–72). Closed Sun., Mon. for lunch and July. In the heart of Les Halles, traditional cooking (with tripe as specialty) served in turn-of-the-century decor.

Pied de Cochon (M), 6 rue Coquillière, 1er (tel. 42–36–11–75). Open day and night year round. You can still enjoy the pig's trotters and onion soup that made this picturesque spot famous, even though the food market has vanished.

Le Tourtour (M), 20 rue Quincampoix, 4e (tel. 48–87–82–48). Open to 1 A.M. Fashionable, crowded, attractive restaurant, very close to the Pompidou/Beau-bourg Center. Good value.

Bistro de la Gare (I), 30 rue St-Denis, 1er (tel. 42–60–84–92). Cheerful, bustling, good-value *menus,* open to 1 A.M.

The Marais

Bofinger (M), 5 rue de la Bastille, 4e (tel. 42–72–87–82). Open to 1 A.M. Turn-of-the-century decor, brasserie-style cuisine, a bit overpriced, but attrac-tive.

Coconnas (M), 2 pl. des Vosges, 4e (tel. 42–78–58–16). Closed Mon. and Tues. and Christmas and New Year period. Attractive decor and setting in this lovely square.

Guirlande de Julie (M), 25 pl. des Vosges, 3e (tel. 48–87–94–07). Closed Mon., Tues., and Feb. Very pretty, garden-like decor, rather smart, good newish cuisine, pleasant atmosphere.

Montmartre

Clodenis (M), 57 rue Caulaincourt, 18e (tel. 46–06–20–26). Closed Sun. and Mon. Inventive cooking here, a real gastronome's delight. Trendy turn-of-the-century decor. Some tables outside.

La Crémaillière 1900 (M), 15 pl. du Tertre, 18e (tel. 46–06–58–59). Closed Mon. and Tues. from Nov. to Easter. Pianist, Mucha posters and delightful tiny garden. Food adequate, but atmosphere the thing. Remember that the pl. du Tertre is very crowded in summer.

Le Tournant de la Butte (I), 46 rue Caulaincourt, 18e (tel. 46–06–39–86). Closed Mon. and Sept. Good fixed-price *menu,* cheerful atmosphere. Crowded, even though this isn't the touristy part of Montmartre.

GETTING AROUND PARIS. Buy a *Plan de Paris* at any newsstand; it is one of the best city guides in exis-tence with alphabetical street directory and clear maps of all 20 *arrondissements,* Métro (subway), RER and bus lines. The quickest way to get about in Paris is by Métro. Every station has a big map showing all the lines and stations, and you can make as many transfers (*correspondances*) as you want to on a single ticket. Certain times of day are "classless periods," when everyone may use both first- and second-class seats, whatever tickets they hold. First-class carriages still operate during the morning and evening rush hours, however. Check exact times once you're in Paris. Most economical way of traveling is to buy a *carnet* (10 tickets) for 26.50 francs (second-class). Hold on to your ticket; an inspector may ask to see it. The labyrinth of Paris bus lines also touches nearly every point of interest in the city, and there are obvious advantages to staying above ground and watching Paris go by. Your *carnet* of Métro tickets is valid on the buses, though they work out to be more expensive this way, because for longer trips you'll need two tickets.

The RER (regional express subway) is fully integrated with the Métro, its fast and modern trains whisking you out to the suburbs at great speed, and also cutting traveling time within Paris dramatically. There are clear maps in all Métro and RER stations. Ordinary Métro tickets are valid for the RER within city limits. If you're going outside you'll need to buy a special ticket from one of the slot machines. The RER has now been extended to the Gare du Nord, a boon for travelers arriving at that major rail terminal. The Métro is gradually being extended to various points north, east and west.

You may have heard that there have been a number of muggings and other attacks in the Métro. In fact the chances of being molested, even if you traveled on the Métro every day for thirty years, are, say the police and transport authorities, very slim. But it's wise to be cautious, especially at night, and keep well clear of groups of youths. Also, make sure you always carry your passport, as police are using spot checks of identity papers to discourage loiterers and troublemakers—with considerable success.

The latest bargain is the *Formule 1* pass, good for unlimited travel on the Métro, R.E.R. and buses within the city limits in one 24-hour period. A second, more expensive, version is good for unlimited travel into the suburbs as well as central Paris. Another bargain is the *"Paris Sesame"* ticket issued by the Paris Public Transportation System (RATP). Valid for two, four, or seven consecutive days, it entitles you to unlimited travel on the Métro or RER (first class), as well as all RATP buslines in Paris and environs. You may buy the tourist ticket from the RATP Tourist Service, 53 bis quai des Grands Augustins, 6e, or at their excursion bureau at 20 pl. de la Madeleine, 8e (on the right side of the church when you are facing the facade), in any of more than 50 Métro or RER stations (look for the list posted up on Métro platforms), at the six main rail stations and at the rail terminal at Roissy-Charles-de-Gaulle airport; at the Banque Nationale de Paris, 6 blvd. des Italiens, 9e, or the Crédit Commercial de France, 115 av. des Champs-Elysées, 8e. Tourist tickets can also be bought in SNCF offices in Chicago, Los Angeles, Miami, New York and San Francisco. In the U.K., they are available from Barclay's Bank, Oceanic House, 1 Cockspur St., London S.W.1.

DISABLED VISITORS. There is an excellent booklet, *Access in Paris,* available in England from Access, 39 Bradley Gardens, West Ealing, London W.13, and brimful of useful advice. Free, but a donation to cover postage would be appreciated.

NIGHTLIFE. Nightspots are expensive by London standards (all but the very top London ones, that is), though not by those of New York. The topnotch clubs may not let you in unless you're with a regular or a celebrity.

The Chic Spots

L'Apocalypse, 40 rue du Colisée, 8e (tel. 42–25–11–68). Popular with the affluent jet set.

L'Atmosphere, 45 rue François-Ier, 8e (tel. 47–20–49–37). Very expensive, very exclusive, frequented by the wealthy-playboy-beautiful-people-celebrity set.

Castel's, 15 rue Princesse, 6e (tel. 43–26–90–22). Extremely chic and certainly the hardest to get into, unless you happen to be a friend, or a friend of a friend, of the great Jean Castel, king of Paris's night life. On three floors and very plush, with good food too, mostly enjoyed by a very young and trendy set.

Elysées-Matignon, 2 av. Matignon, 8e (tel. 43–59–81–10). Ultra-fashionable with showbiz crowd.

Le Garage, 41 rue Washington, 8e (tel. 42–25–53–20). Dazzling strobe lighting, rather flashy decor.

Keur Samba, 79 rue La Boétie, 8e (tel. 43–59–03–10). Long-standing, open very late, popular with the hardened night owls.

Palace, 8 rue de fbg. Montmartre, 9e (tel. 42–70–44–37). Is terribly "in", though not exactly chic. Live music and disco, strobe lighting, audiences in wayout gear.

Regine's, 49 rue de Ponthieu, 8e (tel. 43–59–21–60). Extremely luxurious and expensive, difficult to get in. Excellent orchestra, good food.

The Show's the Thing

Alcazar de Paris, 62 rue Mazarine, 6e (tel. 43–29–02–20). Dinner and witty floorshow. Not as chic as it once was, but still a good place for a great evening out.

Don Camilo, 10 rue des Sts.-Pères, 7e (tel. 42–60–20–31). Good dinner and show at reasonable price. Comfortable and not too frenetic. Attracts some big names.

Folies-Bergère, 32 rue Richer, 9e (tel. 32–46–77–11). The best-known name and it deserves its reputation. Extravagant sets, showy costumes, elaborate sound effects.

Lido, 116 bis av. des Champs-Elysées, 8e (tel. 45–63–11–61). A large lavish production; many American acts; dancing between shows; champagne theoretically obligatory, but you can always ask for the overpriced whiskey. You can also dine expensively.

Moulin-Rouge, pl. Blanche, 9e (tel. 46–06–00–19). On the edge of Montmartre and still cashing in on the most famous name in Montmartre's nightlife, thanks to Toulouse Lautrec and a whole string of famous artists.

Paradis Latin, 28 rue du Cardinal Lemoine, 5e (tel. 43–25–28–28). The most crowded show in town. Dinner around 8, show around 10.

Raspoutine, 58 rue Bassano, 8e (tel. 47–20–04–31). Russian in the grand style, with red velvet, mirrors, the lot. A bit old-fashioned, but marvelously luxurious. Stays open to at least 4 A.M.

Les Girls

Crazy Horse Saloon, 12 av. George V, 8e (tel. 47–23–32–32). The oldest, and best, striptease establishment in town.

Milliardaire, 68 rue Pierre Charon, 8e (tel. 42–25–25–17). Striptease on a big scale. Not as stylish as the Crazy Horse, but still good.

MUSEUMS. Paris has well over 100 museums, many of them with good modern presentation of exhibits, though a few still seem a bit old-fashioned. State-owned museums close Tues., as in the rest of the country, but those owned by the City of Paris close on Mon. Many museums are closed on public holidays (check with *Pariscope* or *L'Officiel des Spectacles* for that week), but virtually all of them are open on Sun., when you get in half-price or even free. Children, students, teachers, men over 65 and women over 60 can usually get in half-price at all times. Everyone over 62 is now admitted free to all City of Paris museums at all times. Sun. is inevitably a bit too crowded for comfort, so avoid it if you can. But remember that the French rarely skip lunch, and as most museums nowadays are open all day, 12.30 to 2 is always a good time for peaceful browsing both in the week and at weekends. In the following selected list the *museums are open every day except Tues. unless otherwise stated.* Opening times are sometimes changed without warning, so we advise you to check when you arrive, especially if you are planning a lunchtime or late afternoon visit.

Affiche et publicité, 18 rue de Paradis, 10e, 12–6. Closed Mon. and Tues. Attractive premises in what used to be a china showroom. Posters and other advertising material.

Archeological Crypt, pl. du Parvis de Notre-Dame, 4e, 10–5 daily. Medieval and later exhibits revealed during excavations beneath the square in front of Notre Dame.

Arts Africains et Océaniens, 293 av. Daumesnil, 12e, 9.45–12, 1.30–5.15; closed Tues. African (including North African) art and civilization, plus the arts of the South Seas and a tropical aquarium.

Arts Décoratifs, 107 rue de Rivoli, 1er, 12–6. In the opposite wing of the Louvre Palace from the Louvre Museum proper, this deals with interior decoration and furniture, including an excellent medieval collection. Extensive redecoration and reorganization have made this an exceptionally pleasant museum.

Archives Nationales and History of France Museum, 60 rue des Francs-Bourgeois, 3e, 2–5. Documents and other exhibits relating to the history of France.

Art Moderne de la Ville de Paris, 11 av. du Président-Wilson, 16e, 10–5.30, except Mon.; open Wed. to 8.30. 20th-century painting, sculpture, engravings, etc., plus temporary exhibits and a special children's museum. (City of Paris museum.)

Arts et Traditions Populaires, 6 rte du Mahatma-Gandhi, Bois de Boulogne, 16e (Sablons entrance); 10–5.15; closed Tues. An astounding variety of objects related to rural activities in pre-industrial environments. Interesting audiovisual presentation makes this a particularly good place to take children, who will be able to press knobs and push buttons to their hearts' content. Also a research lab., library and photo lab.

Balzac's House, 47 rue Raynouard, 16e, 10–5.40, closed Mon. (City of Paris museum.) Charming house where the great writer lived, with authentic furniture, plus many fascinating exhibits.

Bricard, Musée de la Serrure, 1 rue de la Perle, 3e, 10–12, 2–5, closed Sun., Mon. and holidays. Locks and locksmiths through the ages, displayed in a beautifully restored 17th-century mansion in the Marais.

Carnavalet, 23 rue de Sévigné, 3e, 10–5.40, except Mon. Costumes through the ages, china, history of Paris. Mementoes of Mme de Sévigné; 17th–18th-century French furniture. (City of Paris museum.)

Centre National d'Art et de Culture Georges Pompidou (usually known as the **Beaubourg Center,** or just **Beaubourg**), rue St-Martin, 4e, 12–10; Sat. and Sun. 10–10. Houses the National Museum of Modern Art plus industrial design, vast library with large microfilm and colored slide section; theater, experimental music, children's workshop. This very lively and always crowded arts complex has some excellent temporary exhibits and is full of interesting things for those who aren't put off by the sneers of dyed-in-the-wool Parisians who don't care for the futuristic architecture.

Cernuschi, 111 blvd. Malesherbes, 8e, 10–5.40, closed Mon. and hols. Devoted to Chinese art. (City of Paris museum.)

Cluny, 6 pl. Paul-Painlevé, off rue des Ecoles, 5e, 9.45–12.30, 2–5.15, except Tues. Medieval museum in a delightful 15th-century abbey, with remains of Roman baths. Also 17th-century Jewish tombstones and monuments found in the area (you have to ask to see these). Don't miss the 'La Dame à la Licorne' tapestries or the recently discovered fragments of sculptures removed from Notre-Dame during the Revolution.

Cognacq-Jay, 25 blvd. des Capucines, 2e. 10–5.40, closed Mon. Finely furnished 18th-century mansion.

Delacroix's studio, pl. de Fürstemberg, 6e, 9.45–5.15. In a charming old square, the painter's studio has been preserved as he left it.

Fashion and Costume, palais Galliéra, 10 av. Pierre-ler-de-Serbie, 16e, 10–5.40, closed Mon. Covers 18th, 19th and 20th centuries. (City of Paris musuem).

Grand Palais, av. du General-Eisenhower, 8e, 10–8, Weds. 10–10; closed Tues. Splendid glass-domed 19th-century building housing excellent temporary exhibits, often devoted to a single painter (e.g. Monet, Turner).

Histoire Naturelle, 57 rue Cuvier, Jardin des Plantes, 5e, 1.30–4.50. Botanical, entomological, zoological and paleontological exhibits. Menagerie open 9–5 (7 in summer).

Holography, Forum des Halles, 3e, 11–7, Sun. and public hols. 1–7. Includes an incredibly realistic metro carriage.

Invalides and Musée de l'Armée, Esplanade des Invalides, 7e, daily 10–5. Napoleon's tomb, military museum, weapons, armor, battle flags. *Son-et-Lumière* show, 'The Return of the Ashes', twice nightly in English in summer.

Jeu de Paume, Tuileries Garden, pl. de la Concorde, 1er, 9.45–5.15 except Tues. Houses a famous collection of Impressionists.

Louvre. The most famous, of course, open 9.45–5.15 (6.30 for some sections). All sections normally open Mon. and Wed.; on other days some may be closed (call 42–60–39–26 to check if you particularly want to visit one department). The world's largest museum, in the world's largest palace. Main departments are: Greek and Roman; Oriental; Egyptian; sculpture; paintings and drawings; furniture and art objects from the Middle Ages to the 19th century. And, of course, the Mona Lisa (now behind a rather reflective glass frame), and the

Venus de Milo. Frequent lecture tours in English between 10 and 4 daily, except Tues. and Sun. Huge selection of books, posters, cards and copies of exhibits for sale on ground floor. Snackbar in Pavillon Mollien.

Marine, Palais de Chaillot, pl. du Trocadéro, 16e, 10–6. Ship models and seafaring objects.

Marmottan, 2 rue Louis-Boilly, 16e, 10–6, closed Mon. Includes magnificent collection of Monet's works.

Montmartre, 12 rue Cortot, 18e, closed Mon., 2.30–5.30, Sun. 11–5.30. Exhibits associated with Montmartre painters such as Toulouse-Lautrec, plus some of their works.

Musée de l'Homme, Palais de Chaillot, pl du Trocadéro, 16e, 9.45–5.15. Fine anthropological museum, with modern presentation. Documentaries daily.

Musée Picasso, Hotel Salé, 5 rue de Thorigny, 3e, 10–5.15 daily, Weds. 10–10; closed Tues. Magnificent new museum (opened '85) containing "Picasso's Picassos," works he refused to part with. The building is almost equally interesting, and very beautiful.

Notre-Dame de Paris, 10 rue du Cloître Notre-Dame, 4e, 2.30–6, Weds. and weekends only (except public holidays). The cathedral treasure, gold plate, embroidery.

Opéra, pl. de l'Opéra, 9e, 10–5, closed Sun. and holidays. History of the opera and theatrical costumes.

Orangerie des Tuileries, pl. de la Concorde, 1er. 9.45–5.15; closed Tues. Private collection of Impressionists and modern paintings, now state-owned, plus Monet's *Waterlilies* in a specially designed room in the basement (which cannot be viewed between 12 and 2).

Orsay, quai Anatole-France, 7e. Check whether this new museum of 19th-century art (and a bit of 20th-century too) has opened at the time of your visit—opening is scheduled for November 1986.

Palais de la Découverte, 1 av. Franklin-Roosevelt, 8e, 10–6, daily except Mon. Scientific, mechanical, technical exhibits, working models. Several demonstrations daily; planetarium.

Panthéon, pl. du Panthéon, 5e, 10–12, 2–4. Formerly the church of Ste-Geneviève, now the burial place for great men—Voltaire, Rousseau, Victor Hugo, etc.

Petit Palais, av. Winston-Churchill, 8e, across the street from the Grand Palais, 10–5.40, closed Mon. Permanent collections of French painting and art objects, with regular important temporary shows. (City of Paris museum.)

Rodin, 77 rue de Varenne, 7e, 10–4.30 (5.45 in high summer). An old house set in a garden, both filled with Rodin's sculptures.

Victor Hugo's House, 6 pl. des Vosges, 4e, 10–5.40, closed Mon. Exhibits connected with the writer and artworks by him. (City of Paris museum.)

Close to Paris

Cé ramique de Sèvres, 4 Grande-Rue, 92410 Sèvres, 9.30–12, 1.30–5.15. Devoted to the famous Sèvres porcelain. The nearby factory can be visited on first and third Thurs. in the month at 1.30 and 3 (go to the museum entrance). Closed Aug. No children under 14.

Ecouen. Museum of the Renaissance. This newish museum is in the Château d'Ecouen, which is set in attractive grounds nearly 20 km (12 miles) north of Paris; 9.45–12.30, 2–5.15. Tapestries, furniture, bronzes, etc., dating from the Renaissance period.

Fontainebleau. 10.45–12.30, 2–5 or 6. Guided tours Sat. at about 3 P.M.

Malmaison. 10–12.30, 1.30–5.30. Exhibits connected with Napoleon and Josephine, in the château where they lived.

St-Germain-en-Laye, National Antiquities Museum, 10–12, 2–5, closed Mon., Tues., and Fri. mornings. Archeological exhibits.

Sceaux. Musée de l'Ile de France, 10–6 daily. Paintings and other exhibits connected with the Ile de France.

Musée de Versailles in the Château de Versailles. Royal apartments, chapel, Galerie des Glaces, queen's bedroom, 9.45–5.30; Grand Trianon, 9.45–5; Petit Trianon, Tues.–Fri. only, 2–5. Guided visits at frequent intervals. Everything closed Mon. and public hols. Fountains play 1st and 3rd Sun. every month from May through Sept, between 4 and 5 P.M. Magnificent *fêtes de nuit* (fireworks, floodlighting, fountains) in July and Sept. (must reserve ahead).

OTHER SIGHTS. The famous Paris sightseeing boats, **Bateaux-Mouches**, have trips on the Seine every half hour in season (Palm Sunday to early November) between 10 and 12 A.M., 2 to 6:30 (or 7 if weather is fine) and 9–10.30 P.M. (11 if fine). The "cruise" lasts about 1¼ hrs. and costs about 22 francs (half-price for children). Out-of-season trips start at 11, 2.30, and 4 (more frequently in good weather). You can have lunch on board (1 P.M., daily except Monday in season, weekends only out of season) or dinner (8.30 P.M. approximately; daily, except Mon., in season, Fri. and Sat. only in winter; no children under 12). Starting point is the Right Bank end of the Pont de l'Alma. The **Bateaux Vedettes-Tour Eiffel**, using smaller (82-seat) boats of the kind so popular in Amsterdam, sail from the Right Bank end of the Pont d'Iéna and the Quai Montebello (Rive Gauche) every 30 mins. from 9 A.M. to 5 P.M. out of season, every 20 mins. from 9 A.M. to 11 P.M. between May 1 and Oct. 15. Lasts about 1 hr. and costs 20 francs (half price for children). Evening cruises at 9 out of season and 9.30 and 10.30 between May 1 and Oct. 15, for 25 fr. (half price for children). There's a taped commentary in French, English, and German. The **Vedettes Pont-Neuf** leave from Square du Vert Galant, near Notre Dame, at 10.30, 11.15 and 12 A.M., then every half-hour between 1.30 and 6 P.M. (5 P.M. in winter). From May to mid-Oct. there are evening trips at 9, 9.30 and 10 P.M. Around 20 frs.; taped commentary in five languages. 'Cruises' further afield are sometimes organized and are very memorable. Check locally.

The Ile de la Cité flower market, open daily except Sun. morning (when it becomes a bird market and doesn't open till 9 A.M.), from 8 A.M. to 7.30 P.M., (6 in winter), is lovely to look at. There's another flower market by the Madeleine church (Tues., Weds., Fri., Sat. and the day before all public holidays).

Caveau des Echansons (Wine Museum), rue des Eaux, 16e. Splendid vaulted cellars dating from the 13th and 14th centuries where you can taste wine and learn about wine production and tasting. 2–6 P.M. Closed Mon.

If you're in Paris around Bastille Day (July 14), look out for posters advertising openair dancing venues (generally these local hops are held on the evening of the 13th) and the splendid firework display organized by the City of Paris (location varies from year to year).

To visit the famous sewers of Paris, be at the pl. de la Résistance, 7e, at the Rive Gauche end of the Pont de l'Alma, Mon., Wed., and last Sat. in the month (except public holidays and the day before and after public holidays), between 2–5 P.M. *Don't wear slippery shoes.*

Another unusual excursion is to the Gallo-Roman Catacombs under the Left Bank. 2 pl. Denfert-Rochereau, 14e, Tues.-Fri. 2–4 P.M.; Sat. and Sun. 9–11 and 2–4. *Bring your own torch.*

BEST PARKS AND GARDENS. The parks and gardens of Paris are varied and beautiful, whether they are the large rambling wooded variety or the formally laid-out open spaces in the center of the city. Most are enclosed and are shut at dusk. These are the most important:

Bois de Boulogne (Métro: Porte d'Auteuil, Porte Dauphine, Sablons or Porte Maillot). Not enclosed, it is always open. It contains 7 lakes, a waterfall, the Longchamp and Auteuil racetracks, the Roland-Garros tennis stadium, a polo field, a children's zoo (the Jardin d'Acclimatation), a campsite, Bagatelle Park (Métro: Pont de Neuilly), which exhibits spring flowers, roses (June) and water lilies, and a Shakespeare Garden. (*Unaccompanied women should be cautious in the Bois at all times, and everyone should avoid it at night.*)

Jardin des Plantes, 57 rue Cuvier, 5e, near the Austerlitz rail station (Métro: Gare d'Austerlitz). Botanical gardens with special exhibits of pharmaceutical plants, an Alpine garden, greenhouses, a small menagerie, and Natural History Museum.

Bois de Vincennes (Métro: Porte Dorée). On the eastern edge of Paris. Contains a racetrack, three lakes (boats for hire on Lac Daumesnil), and Vincennes Zoo, largest in Paris.

Parc Monceau, on blvd. de Courcelles (Métro: Monceau), is quiet, charming, frequented mostly by the residents of the well-to-do-quarter about it and their children.

Luxembourg Garden, famous throughout the world. On the Left Bank, off blvd. St.-Michel (Métro: Luxembourg), it encloses the Palais du Luxembourg and the now disused Petit Luxembourg.

Jardin des Tuileries, in the heart of Paris (Métro: Concorde, Tuileries). Designed by Le Nôtre, it is particularly notable for its trees and pools, its formal gardens embellished with statues, its continuation between the two wings of the Louvre, and above all for the magnificent vista that sweeps all the way from the Louvre through the Tuileries to the Arc de Triomphe, though, alas, the vista is somewhat spoiled by the Défense skyscrapers in the background.

 SHOPPING. Although the goods for which Paris has long been famous—fashion, jewelry, glass and china, food and drink—now tend to be expensive, if you're careful you can still buy something memorable for a reasonable sum. Anyway, window shopping is one of the joys of Paris, as the displays are stylish and infinitely varied.

The major department stores are *Galeries Lafayette* and *Printemps,* more or less side by side on the boulevard Haussmann, near the Opéra and the Madeleine. Their downmarket counterparts are near the Hôtel-de-Ville (*Bazar de l'Hôtel-de-Ville, Samaritaine*). Inexpensive chain stores, good for up-to-the-minute accessories, children's clothes and attractive stationery, are found all over the city: look for the names *Monoprix* and *Prisunic.* But you'll probably find it more enjoyable to head for the little boutiques, selling everything from food to fashion.

Paris shopping divides conveniently into areas. *Fashion* is best in St.-Germain-des-Prés (chic, stylish), Les Halles (avant-garde), Passy (classy), Faubourg St.-Honoré (expensive couture outfits). For *prints* and *books* make for St.-Germain-des-Prés and the quais of the Seine. For *china* and *glass* the mecca is the rue de Paradis near the Gare de l'Est (10th *arrondissement*), where all the major showrooms are. Mouthwatering displays of *food and drink* will tempt you on almost every street in this food-loving capital, but the best-known shops are on the place de la Madeleine. For *antiques* and *junk* you'll want to go to the famous flea markets near the Porte de Clignancourt, the Louvre des Antiquaires in the place du Palais-Royal, and the smart little shops in St.-Germain-des-Prés. The rue de Rivoli (the Tuileries end) is the place for *souvenirs, silk scarves* and *costume jewelry.* The big (and very expensive) jewelers are all on or around the nearby place Vendôme. For *copies of works of art* you've admired, the best bet is the Louvre (ground floor). Lastly, you probably won't be able to resist the temptation of buying a little flask of *perfume* for yourself or to take back to friends and family: we recommend that you head for the department stores, where a huge selection is available, rather than the little *parfumiers.*

 USEFUL ADDRESSES. *Embassies:* U.S.A., 2 av. Gabriel, 8e; British, 35 fbg. St.-Honoré, 8e; *American Express,* 11 rue Scribe, 9e; *Wagons-Lits Cook,* 2 pl. de la Madeleine, 8e.

Information Office, Paris official tourist office, 127 av. des Champs Elysées, 8e, tel. 723–61–72, open weekdays and Sat. 9 A.M. – 10 P.M. (8 in winter); Sun. 9–8 (6 in winter): for information on other parts of France, as well as Paris, reservations in Paris hotels (not more than 5 days ahead, though). For run-down in English on week's cultural and other activities call 720–88–98. Branch offices at the major rail stations, at the Invalides air terminal and the Palais des Congrès (upstairs from the air terminal for Roissy/Charles-de-Gaulle), but these are not open Sun. or public holidays. The City of Paris also has an information bureau at 29 rue de Rivoli, 1er, open 8:45 A.M. to 6:30 P.M., closed Sun. and public holidays.

American Hospital, 63 blvd. Victor-Hugo, 92200 Neuilly-sur-Seine, tel: 47–47–53–00; *British Hospital,* 48 rue de Villiers, 92300 Levallois-Perret, tel: 47–48–13–12.

Ile de France

The Ile de France is the ancient heartland of France, a beautiful region of gray stone villages, silver poplars and magnificent châteaux, all bathed in a luminous haze that fascinated Renoir, Monet, Sisley and other great painters who captured this landscape on canvas. The average tourist visits the Ile de France on one or more day-long excursions from Paris. There are excellent guided tours in luxury buses to Versailles, Chantilly, Compiègne, Fontainebleau and Chartres. Or you can rent a small car in Paris for a day and be the master of your own fate on the road. All these places can also be reached by rail.

Versailles

Don't try to visit all of this vast royal domain in a single day. The main château, with its fabulous gardens, created over a period of 50 years by Louis XIV, is the secular climax of French architecture. Regular tours of the palace include the huge gilded reception rooms, the king's bedchamber (now sumptuously redecorated and furnished), the royal chapel (designed by Mansart), the celebrated Galerie des Glaces (Hall of Mirrors), where the Treaty of Versailles ending World War I was signed in 1919, the *petits appartements* where the king and queen actually lived and the glittering little opera house, built by Gabriel for Louis XV. The palace gardens, designed by Le Nôtre, with their lawns, flowerbeds, fountains and ornamental canal, are the last word in formal French gardening.

While at Versailles you will also want to see the Grand Trianon, built by Mansart for Louis XIV in 1687, completely furnished in the most elegant Empire (Napoleon I) style. The Petit Trianon was commissioned by Louis XV and built by Gabriel, designer of the place de la Concorde in Paris. This little palace was a favorite of the ill-starred Marie-Antoinette, who preferred it to the overwhelming and overcrowded atmosphere of the main château. Nearby is her model village, *le petit hameau,* where she and her companions played at being shepherdesses among flocks of perfumed sheep.

Rambouillet, Breteuil, Port Royal and Chartres

Rambouillet, the 14th-century château of Catherine de Médicis and Henri IV, an official residence for the President of France, can be visited except when the flag flying from the château turret indicates that the president is in residence (call (3) 483–02–49 to check, especially during the shooting season). The beautiful grounds are also open to the public.

Not far from Rambouillet is the château de Breteuil, which has been owned and lived in by the same family since it was built in the early 17th century. The life-size wax figures in period dress in many of the rooms (including King Edward VII of England and the novelist Marcel Proust) bring the château's past to life in a particularly attractive way. The young Marquis de Breteuil and his wife have won an award for their dynamism in restoring the château and organizing all sorts of concerts, plays and other events to attract visitors. As with many English stately homes, you'll probably find the owners greeting visitors in person.

Also nearby are the ruins of the Jansenist abbey of Port-Royal-des-Champs, where the great 17th-century dramatist Jean Racine received much of his education, with a museum a short walk away.

The spires of Chartres cathedral are visible from miles away, seeming to rise out of the wheatfields of the Beauce plain. All the descriptive prose and poetry which have been lavished on this cathedral can only begin to suggest the glory of its sculpture and stained glass and the strange sense of the numinous which the whole imparts even to non-believers. Recently, some of the famous stained glass windows have been restored, and although at first experts claimed that the glowing "Chartres blue" had been destroyed during cleaning, it is now generally agreed that the windows are as fine as when they were first made. Notre

Dame de Chartres was built after a fire in 1194 had destroyed most of the former church, except the lying-in shirt of the Virgin, whose preservation from the flames was considered miraculous.

Maintenon and Malmaison

The château of Maintenon, with its Renaissance façade and gardens designed by Le Nôtre, is still furnished as it was in the days of Madame de Maintenon, the amazing woman who started out as the governess of Louis XIV's children by Madame de Montespan, replaced the latter as the favorite of the king, and finally became his morganatic wife.

Other attractions west of Paris are Mansart's masterful château of Maisons at Maisons-Laffitte; the little river town of Bougival on the Seine, a great favorite of the Impressionist painters; and Malmaison, the authentically-furnished small château where Napoleon spent his happiest years with Josephine, and where Josephine spent her remaining years after their divorce. A short walk from Malmaison is the château of Bois-Préau, bought by Josephine in 1809 and now used as a sort of annex to Malmaison, housing many relics of the imperial family, including Napoleon's famous triangular hat. Bois-Préau was bought in 1920 by the former American consul in Paris, Edward Tuck, and his wife, and bequeathed to the French nation in his will. Also near here are Marly-le-Roi, where a royal château once stood—only the grounds are left now—and Saint-Germain-en-Laye, an attractive town with a Renaissance château built by François I and subsequently lived in by Mary, Queen of Scots, and James II. The château now houses the Museum of National Antiquities, with an excellent prehistory collection.

Fontainebleau

A popular excursion south of Paris is to the forest and château of Fontainebleau. On the way, you pass through the village of Barbizon, immortalized in the paintings of Corot, Millet and Daumier. The forest of Fontainebleau is typically and delightfully French, wild and romantic, yet thoroughly mapped and classified so that every path is recorded on Touring Club maps.

The château was begun by Louis VII in the 12th century, then was transformed into a magnificent Renaissance palace by François I, who imported Primaticcio and Rosso from Italy to supervise the army of decorators employed to make the place suitable for his mistress, the Duchesse d'Etampes. The king installed Benvenuto Cellini here and bought Leonardo da Vinci's famous *Mona Lisa* to hang in one of the rooms. François's successor, Henri II, ornamented the palace with his initial interlaced with D for Diane de Poitiers, his mistress. The gardens were designed by Le Nôtre under Louis XIV, who did some remodeling of the palace according to his own classical tastes. After that, Fontainebleau declined to the status of a royal hunting lodge. Napoleon rehabilitated the palace, used it as a prison for Pope Pius VII, lived here himself for a while, first with Josephine and then with his second wife, Marie Louise of Austria.

North of Fontainebleau, just outside of Melun, is the château of Vaux-le-Vicomte, built for the young Louis XIV's minister of finance, Fouquet. When the château was finished in 1661, Fouquet gave a banquet for his king which was so sumptuous that Louis XIV, wild with rage at being outshone, imprisoned Fouquet, commandeered his artists, confiscated his wealth and proceeded to build Versailles.

A short distance southeast of Fontainebleau by way of Montigny lies the ancient walled town of Provins. Famous for rose growing since the time of the Crusades, it introduced the red rose of Provins into the arms of the House of Lancaster in the 13th century. The old ramparts still enclose orchards and winding streets as they did in the Middle Ages.

Battlefields and Champagne

East of Paris lie the World War I battlefields of the Marne, Meaux with its 13th-century cathedral, Château-Thierry with its ancient castle built by Charles Martel in 720 and the 16th-century mansion (open to visitors) where La Fontaine was born, and Reims, capital of Champagne.

Reims cathedral, begun in 1211, is one of the triumphs of Gothic architecture and sculpture. Here, in 1429, Joan of Arc arranged the consecration of Charles VII. Reims's other famous contribution to civilization dates from 1665, when Dom Pérignon, a monk from nearby Epernay, conceived the brilliant idea of adding sugar, and consequently effervescence, to the excellent white wine produced on the chalky slopes of Champagne. The secret formula was standardized in 1836, since which time Reims has been the capital of Champagne in every sense of the word. A visit to one of the great wine cellars will show you the process involved in producing these sparkling wines and allow you to sample some, too. The SNCF occasionally runs day trips from Paris which include a visit to a champagne cellar.

North of Paris: Senlis, Compiègne, Beauvais, Chantilly

Excursions north and northeast of Paris include the delightful town of Senlis, only 31 miles from the capital. Its Gothic cathedral is older than Notre Dame and Chartres. Fragments of the Gallo-Roman walls are still standing, and the ancient streets and alleys invite exploration. In odd-numbered years many of the city's private gardens are opened to the public for a weekend in October and cultural events of all kinds are staged. Don't miss visiting Senlis then if you can. It also has a museum of hunting.

Majestic oak and beech forests lead to historic Compiègne, where the Armistice that ended World War I was signed (you can visit a replica of the famous railway car in which this historic event took place, in a clearing in the forest). Here you should see Louis XV's impressive château; the Vehicle Museum; the 16th-century Hôtel de Ville built by Louis XII; the Musée des Figurines Historiques, with its 85,000 lead, tin and wooden soldiers from Vercingetorix to De Gaulle; the 12th-century tower from which Joan of Arc is said to have set out before being captured by the Burgundian armies.

On the northern edge of Paris, and reachable by Métro or, very pleasantly, by barge, is St.-Denis, whose basilica is the necropolis of the kings of France. Further north are the château of Ecouen, now housing the interesting Museum of the Renaissance; and the two tourist "musts" of this area—Beauvais and Chantilly. In the unfinished cathedral of Beauvais, Gothic architecture reached its most audacious heights. Chantilly is famous for lace, cream, horseraces, a forest and a romantic château, built on two islands in the middle of a small lake. The château houses the Musée Condé, whose treasures include a collection of miniatures by Fouquet and the fabulous 15th-century illuminated manuscript, the *Très Riches Heures du Duc de Berry*. In the grounds, designed by the ubiquitous Le Nôtre, visit the charming Maison de Sylvie, and don't fail to see the magnificent 18th-century stables, built to house 240 horses. Chantilly's annual moment of glory comes in early June, with a week of special events. The SNCF has combined rail and entrance ticket. Nearby Royaumont Abbey, founded by Louis IX in the early 13th century, is now a cultural center staging excellent concerts and art exhibits. As with many châteaux in the Ile-de-France area, Royaumont's concert calendar is particularly full during the annual Ile-de-France Festival, held in May, June and July. Write to Festival de l'Ile de France, 15 av. Montaigne, 75008 Paris, for program.

PRACTICAL INFORMATION FOR ILE DE FRANCE

Note that it is advisable to reserve a table in all restaurants, especially for Sunday lunch.

BARBIZON (36 miles). *Bas-Bréau* (L), tel. 60–66–40–05, attractive gardens, excellent food.

Restaurants. *Grand Veneur* (E), tel. 60–66–40–44, classical cuisine, handsome, on Fontainebleau road. *Relais* (M), tel. 60–66–40–28. Traditional dishes.

BEAUVAIS (45 miles). Best is *Chenal* (M), tel. 44–45–03–55; no restaurant. Then *Mercure* (M), on the Paris road, tel. 44–02–03–36, with pool and restaurant.

Restaurants. *Côtelette* (M), tel. 44–45–04–42; *Marignan* (I), tel. 44–48–15–15; and *Crémaillière* (M), tel. 44–45–03–13.

BOUGIVAL (11 miles). *Château de la Jonchère* (E), tel. 39–18–57–03, an 18th-century château set in grounds and converted in 1984 into an ultramodern hotel with good restaurant (M). *Forest Hill* (M), tel. 918–17–16, modern building overlooking the Seine, with pool and restaurant.

Restaurants. *Camélia* (E), tel. 39–69–03–02, one of the country's best-known restaurants for *nouvelle cuisine;* very chic. *Coq Hardy* (E), tel. 39–69–01–43, very pricey, delightful, good newish cuisine, tables outside in summer.

CHANTILLY (30 miles). *Campanile* (M), tel. 44–57–39–24, quiet, modern, and comfortable, on outskirts. In **Lys-Chantilly** (4½ miles south), try *Hostellerie du Lys* (M), tel. 44–21–26–19, quiet, set in garden, with terrace for summer meals.

Restaurants. *Tipperary* (E), tel. 44–57–00–48, good-value *menus* in the week. *Quatre-Saisons* (M), tel. 44–57–04–65, an offshoot of a well-known Danish restaurant in Paris; mixture of French and Danish cuisine. *Relais Condé* (M), tel. 44–57–05–75, in a converted chapel. *Capitainerie du Château* (I), tel. 44–57–15–89. Help-yourself buffet, nonstop from 10.30 to 6.30.

CHARTRES (55 miles). *Grand Monarque* (M), tel. 37–21–00–72, very comfortable, with good restaurant (M). Belongs to Mapotel group.

Restaurants. Best is well-known *Henri IV* (E), tel. 37–36–01–55, with both classical and "new" dishes. *Vieille Maison* (M), tel. 37–34–10–67, is excellent. *Buisson Ardent* (M), tel. 37–34–04–66. Attractive old house, serves *nouvelle cuisine,* with fine-value fixed-price meals.

COMPIÈGNE (51 miles). *Harley* (M), tel. 44–23–01–50, no restaurant. *Hôtel de France et Rôtisserie du Chat qui tourne* (M), tel. 44–40–02–74, has good restaurant. *Nord* (I), tel. 44–83–22–30. By station; rôtisserie for straight-forward meals.

Restaurants. *Hostellerie du Royal-Lieu* (E), tel. 44–42–20–10–24, on edge of forest. Has a few rooms. *Bonne Idée* (M), tel. 44–42–84–09, in the forest, small, with good restaurant.

DREUX (51 miles). **Restaurant.** *Auberge du Gué des Grues* (M), tel. 37–43–50–25, 2½ miles away at **Montreuil,** successful mixture of classical and new cooking, overlooking fields and river.

FONTAINEBLEAU (41 miles). *Aigle Noir* (E), tel. 64–22–32–65, good restaurant (E) with excellent nouvelle cuisine. Belongs to Mapotel group. *Novotel*

(M), tel. 64–22–48–25, 6 miles northeast at Ury. Has pool and restaurant. *Toulouse* (I), tel. 64–22–22–73. Small and cozy in town center; no restaurant.

Restaurants. Best is *Beauharnais* (E), in Aigle Noir hotel. *Filet de Sole* (M), tel. 64–22–25–05, close to palace. *Dauphin* (I), reader-recommended. Good-value meals. *Ile-de-France* (I), charming Chinese restaurant in a typically French provincial house; also has rooms.

IVRY-LA-BATAILLE (50 miles). **Restaurant.** *Moulin d'Ivry* (E), tel. 32–36–44–50, long a favorite with Parisians, no longer has rooms after renovation but is delightful restaurant in an old mill on the banks of the Eure river.

LAON (86 miles). Best is *Angleterre* (M), tel. 23–23–04–62; then *Bannière de France* (I), tel. 23–23–21–44, with good (M) restaurant.

Restaurants. *Chateaubriand* (M), tel. 23–23–40–79, quite elegant; and 4 miles south of N2 at **Etouvelles,** *Bon Acceuil* inn (I), tel. 23–23–07–43.

MAISONS-LAFITTE (13 miles). **Restaurants.** Attractive *Vieille Fontaine* (E), tel. 39–62–01–78, one of France's finest—*nouvelle cuisine*—and worth the high prices. *Tastevin* (M), tel. 39–62–11–67, more "new" cooking, by a former Maxim's chef. *Laffitte* (M), tel. 39–62–01–53, has a good-value *menu*.

PROVINS (52 miles). *Fontaine* (I), tel. 64–00–00–10, central. Good restaurant with mostly Burgundian dishes.

Restaurants. *Vieux Remparts* (M), tel. 64–00–02–89, excellent traditional cuisine served in old beamed dining room in the Ville Haute. *Médiéval* (I), tel. 64–00–01–19, with garden.

RAMBOUILLET (32 miles). *Saint-Charles* (M), tel. 34–83–06–34, on edge of park, no restaurant.

Restaurant. *Poste* (M), tel. 34–83–03–01, is good value.

REIMS (89 miles). *Boyer-Les Crayères* (L), 64 blvd. Henri-Vasnier (tel. 26–82–80–80). Marvelous late 19th-century château in town center, yet with large grounds, run by famous chef Gérard Boyer, so restaurant is fabulous. *Frantel* (E), tel. 26–88–53–54, with good restaurant. *Novotel* (M), tel. 26–08–11–61, and *Mercure* (M), tel. 26–05–00–08, both outside town. *Paix* (M), tel. 26–40–04–08, good restaurant. *Bristol* (I), tel. 26–40–52–25, without restaurant.

Restaurants. Best restaurant, with inventive "new cuisine, is *Boyer* (E), in hotel (see above). *Florence* (E), tel. 26–47–12–70, and *Foch* (M), tel. 26–47–48–22, both in former distinguished private houses, are also good.

ST.-GERMAIN-EN-LAYE (14 miles). *Forestière* (E), tel. 39–73–36–60; also contains the best restaurant in town, the *Cazaudehore* (E). *Pavillon Henri IV* (E), tel. 34–51–62–62. A grand mansion on the edge of Grande Terrasse, with wonderful views of Paris and the Seine Valley.

Restaurants. *Cazaudehore* (E), in Forestière hotel, best for classical cuisine. *Pavillon Croix de Noailles* (E), tel. 39–62–53–46, converted 18th-century hunting lodge; light and modern cuisine. *Pavillon Henri-IV* (E), in hotel, serves classical cuisine in grand dining room. *7 rue des Coches* (M), tel. 39–73–66–40, rather elegant, inventive cuisine. *Petite Auberge* (M), tel. 34–51–03–99. Home-style cooking, good value.

SENLIS (31 miles). *Hostellerie Porte-Bellon* (I), tel. 44–53–03–05. Close to town center and bus station; with restaurant. 4 miles away at **Fontaine-Chaalis,** *Auberge Fontaine* (I), has just 7 attractive rooms in a peaceful setting on the edge of the forest; pleasant restaurant (M).

Restaurants. Nearby *Rôtisserie Formanoir* (M), tel. 44–53–04–39, in one of Senlis's oldest buildings, is delightful. *Bistrot de Formanoir* (I), tel. 44–53–04–39. On second floor of Rôtisserie and excellent value.

VERSAILLES (14 miles). *Trianon Palace* (L), tel. 39–50–34–12, compares with the best in Paris and also has good restaurant. *Versailles* (M), tel. 39–50–64

–65. Modern, near château, and *Richaud* (I), tel. 39–50–10–42, small, comfortable, has no restaurant.

Restaurants. *Trois Marches* (E), tel. 39–50–13–21, now in beautiful building opposite the palace, is best restaurant—one of the best in the Paris area, with prices to match. *Boule d'Or* (M), tel. 39–50–22–97, boasts of being the "oldest inn in Versailles" and dates from 1696. *Potager du Roy* (I), tel. 39–50–35–34, run by the same excellent chef as the Trois Marches and very good value.

Normandy

Spending just one night away from Paris, you can easily see the Invasion Coast of Normandy, the famous Bayeux Tapestry depicting the Norman Invasion of England in 1066, and that marvel of French architecture, Mont-St.-Michel. This sea-surrounded mass of granite, rising 400 feet, was begun in 709. The "Marvel", or great monastery that crowns it, was built during the 13th century, and the fortifications added 200 years later to withstand attacks from the English. You approach this tiny island by a causeway, and enter a medieval village of 250 inhabitants by three massive stone gates. The guided tours during the summer are apt to be too large. Try to arrange to have a private English-speaking guide, provided by the official guide service. It is worth every extra franc for the intimate, detailed and leisurely tour. *Be careful, however:* Don't wander around on the acres of inviting-looking sand that surround Mont-St.-Michel at low tide. There are many quicksands, and the tide rushes in a rate of 210 feet a minute.

The Norman coast has also been swept by the great tides of history, most recently in the D-Day invasion of 1944. In the coastal town of Arromanches, you can see the landings and history of the invasion recapitulated in a diorama. The remains of Mulberry, the great artificial port built by the British, and the American landing beaches of Omaha and Utah are moving reminders of World War II battles. In the impressive American cemetery at St.-Laurent, the columns of white crosses will stir silent memories.

Nearby in Bayeux, miraculously undamaged, with its fine Norman Gothic cathedral affording a splendid view from its high central tower. An 18th-century seminary near the cathedral now houses the famous embroidered sampler, 235 feet long and 20 inches wide made in 1077 to depict, in 58 colorful scenes, the conquest of England by William the Conqueror in 1066.

The old city of Caen was virtually flattened (three-quarters of it was destroyed) in 1944 but has been extensively restored, so that it is now an attractive mixture of good modern buildings and brilliantly restored architectural masterpieces such as the Gothic and Renaissance church of Saint-Pierre. The famous abbey churches built by William the Conqueror and Queen Mathilde (the Abbaye aux Hommes and Abbaye aux Dames) miraculously survived the bombing, while William's castle is seen to much better advantage now than before the bombs fell, because restoration work has removed the buildings hemming it in. The area around the citadel has two interesting museums: the modern Fine Arts Museum, with fine paintings and engravings and well-designed special exhibits, and the little Musée de Normandie, a folklore museum devoted to Norman life and customs.

Even the briefest tour of Normandy should include a visit to Rouen, packed with lovely churches and old half-timbered houses, as well as poignant reminders of Joan of Arc, who was burned alive here on May 30, 1431. A dazzling modern church and memorial dedicated to Joan, who is France's patron saint, can now be visited in the centuries-old market place where she was burnt at the stake. This blend of old and new is the hallmark of this lively city, with modern hotels, apartment blocks and shopping precincts contrasting with its ancient center, where the city's finest buildings have been restored after wartime bombing. Don't miss the Gothic cathedral, the nearby church of St.-Maclou, with its extraordinary five-gabled façade, and the abbey church of St.-Ouen.

Close to the busy pedestrians-only rue du Gros-Horloge you'll find the early Renaissance law courts and, a new discovery, the earliest surviving Jewish building in France. And two museums are well worth a visit: the Fine Arts, with wonderful ceramics and painting collections, and the Secq-des-Tournelles, with probably the world's finest display of wrought iron.

On the southeastern edge of Normandy you can visit the house lived in by the Impressionist painter Claude Monet at Giverny near Vernon in the Epte river valley, together with his wonderful gardens and the famous lily pond that features in so many of his paintings. The house, studio and other buildings have been restored, thanks to generous donations from both sides of the Atlantic (including $250,000 from former U.S. ambassador to Britain Walter Annenberg). Giverny is easily reached from Paris by train (alight at Vernon), coach or car.

PRACTICAL INFORMATION FOR NORMANDY

AVRANCHES. *Auberge St.-Michel* (M), tel. 33–58–01–91, good food. *Croix d'Or* (M), tel. 33–58–04–88, also with restaurant.

BAGNOLES-DE-L'ORNE. *Bois Joli* (E), tel. 33–37–92–77, attractive, good restaurant. *Christol et Dante* (I), tel. 33–37–80–31. Quiet, with restaurant.

BAYEUX. *Lion d'Or* (M), tel. 31–92–06–90, peaceful, good service, is comfortable. Good restaurant with good-value fixed-price meals.

CAEN. Pleasantest is *Relais des Gourmets* (M), 15 rue de Geôle (tel. 31–86–06–01). Very comfortable, overlooking castle, good restaurant. Nearby *Moderne* (M), 116 blvd. Général-Leclerc (tel. 31–86–04–23). Functional, convenient, with restaurant. *Univers* (I), 12 quai Vendeuvre, tel. 31–85–46–14. Central but no restaurant.

Restaurants. *Bourride* (E), tel. 31–93–50–76, charming old building, very modern cuisine, with good-value *menus*. *Dauphin* (M), 29 rue Gémare (tel. 31–86–22–26). Mixture of new and classical dishes. *Relais des Gourmets* (M), in hotel, well run; classical cuisine. *Chalut* (I), 3 rue Vaucelles, tel. 31–82–01–06. Not far from the station.

Six miles away toward the coast at **Bénouville,** is the excellent and attractive *Manoir d'Hastings* (E), tel. 31–73–38–66, with imaginative food in a 17th-century setting.

CAUDEBEC-EN-CAUX. *Manoir de Rétival* (E), tel. 35–96–11–22, is a pleasant quiet hotel, but has no restaurant. *Marine* (M), tel. 35–96–20–11, a fine hotel-restaurant. Good value.

CHERBOURG. *Mercure* (M), Gare Maritime, tel. 33–44–01–11, handsome, comfortable, close to new car ferry terminal. *Louvre* (I), 2 rue Henri-Dunant, tel. 33–53–02–28. Friendly atmosphere; close to beach.

Restaurant. *Plouc* (M), 59 rue Blé, tel. 33–53–67–64. Good fish dishes.

DEAUVILLE. *Normandy* (L), tel. 31–88–09–21, and *Royal* (L), tel. 31–88–16–41, very much in the grand style. *PLM* (E), tel. 31–88–62–62, by new marina, all modern facilities. *Marie-Anne* (M), tel. 31–88–35–32. Converted private house, no garden. *Patio* (I), tel. 31–88–25–07. Pleasant rooms, no restaurant. *Résidence* (I), tel. 31–88–07–50, near racecourse, no restaurant.

Restaurants. *Ambassadeurs* (E), tel. 31–88–29–55. In the casino. *Chez Camillo* (M), tel. 31–88–79–79. Good classic cuisine. *Filoché* (M), tel. 31–88–82–52. Traditional cuisine. *Yearling* (I), tel. 31–88–33–37. Not far from racecourse.

DIEPPE. *Présidence* (E), tel. 35–84–31–31, is best; *Univers* (E), tel. 35–84–12 –55, pleasant but a bit old-fashioned; *Windsor* (M), tel. 35–84–15–23. All three are comfortable and overlook the sea.
  Restaurants. *Marmite Dieppoise* (M), tel. 35–84–24–26. Old favorite with British visitors. *Sully* (I), tel. 35–84–23–13. Attractive quayside restaurant. *Port* (I), tel. 35–84–36–64. Quayside restaurant with good fish cooked in the classic manner.
  4 miles south near **Offanville** on road to Rouen, *Bucherie* (M), has marvelous fish.

ETRETAT. *Dormy House* (E), tel. 35–27–07–88, attractive location near golf links, views of beach and cliffs, quiet, with restaurant. *Angleterre* (I), tel. 35–27– 01–65, small, with restaurant. *Escale* (E), tel. 35–27–03–69, small and central, with good-value restaurant. *Welcome* (I), tel. 35–27–00–89, small, with restaurant.
  Restaurant. *Escale* (I), in hotel, good value.

FECAMP. *Angleterre* (M), tel. 35–28–01–60, comfortable, close to beach, no restaurant.
  Restaurants. First-rate regional cuisine at *Auberge de la Rouge* (M), a mile south of town on D925, tel. 35–28–07–59. *Escalier* (M), tel. 35–28–26–79. Overlooks harbor. Good fresh fish.

LE HAVRE. *Bordeaux* (E), 147 rue Louis Brindeau (tel. 35–22–69–44). Modern, no restaurant, close to the marina. Newest is *Mercure* (E), Chaussée Angoulême in World Trade Center (tel. 35–21–23–45). Every modern amenity. *Marly* (M), 121 rue de Paris (tel. 35–41–72–48). Convenient for cross-Channel ferries; no restaurant. *Monaco* (M), 16 rue de Paris, tel. 35–42–21–01, with good restaurant.
  Restaurants. *Manche* (M), 18 blvd. Albert-ler (tel. 35–41–20–13); lovely harbor views, *nouvelle cuisine*, good *menus*. *Monaco* (M), 16 rue Paris, tel. 35–42–21–01. Not far from car ferry terminal. Good for fish. *Nice Havrais* (M), tel. 35–46–14–59, on the edge of town at Sainte-Adresse, elegant, rather grand cuisine.

HONFLEUR. *Lechat* (M), tel. 31–89–23–85, close to harbor. Good hotel-restaurant is *Ferme St.-Siméon* (E), tel. 31–89–23–61, rich Norman food, very attractive, smart, essential to reserve. *Cheval Blanc* (M), quai des Passagers, tel. 31–89–13–49, a bit old-fashioned but nice harbor views.
  Restaurants. *Absinthe* (M), tel. 31–89–39–00. Mixture of traditional and nouvelle cuisine. Good service. *Ancrage* (M), tel. 31–89–00–70, just by the harbor, good seafood platters. *Vieux Honfleur* (M), tel. 31–89–15–31, good fish dishes in picturesque old building overlooking harbor. *Gars Normand* (I), also by harbor, busy and bustling. Several cafés round the harbor serve seafood all day, not just at mealtimes.

MONT-ST.-MICHEL. *Mère Poulard* (E), tel. 33–60–14–01, with its famous restaurant. *St.-Aubert* (M), tel. 33–60–08–74. Modern hotel with large, well-decorated rooms. No restaurant.

PONT-AUDEMER. Restaurants. Colorful and famous *Auberge du Vieux Puits* (M), tel. 32–41–01–48. Has a few (I) rooms. Good Norman cuisine. Nearby at **Campigny,** delightful *Petit Coq aux Champs* (E), tel. 32–41–04–19. Has a few (E) rooms. *Frégate* (M), tel. 32–41–12–03, has good seafood.

ROUEN. *Dieppe* (E), pl. Bernard-Tissot (tel. 35–71–96–00). Convenient for station, very comfortable. Good grill room. *Frantel* (E), rue Croix-de-Fer, tel. 35–98–06–98, modern, but in heart of old town; good restaurant. *Cathédrale*

(M), 12 rue St.-Romain (tel. 35–71–57–95). Old-fashioned but charming, in old town; no restaurant.

Restaurants. *Bertrand Warin* (E), 7 rue de la Pie (tel. 35–89–26–69). In old mansion next to Corneille's house; attractive and chic. *Couronne* (E), 31 pl. de Vieux-Marché (tel. 35–71–40–90). Said to be France's oldest inn. For more inventive cuisine, try *P'tits Parapluies* (E), 46 rue Bourg-l'Abbé (tel. 35–88–55–26). In attractive old house. *Beffroy* (M), 15 rue Beffroy (tel. 35–71–55–27). Attractive. *Nouvelle cuisine. Maison Dufour* (M), tel. 35–71–90–62. Genuine Norman atmosphere, good fish. *Vieux-Marché* (I), 2 pl. du Vieux-Marché (tel. 35–71–59–09). Bistrot-type.

TROUVILLE. *Sablettes* (I), tel. 31–88–10–66. Small, no restaurant.

Restaurants. *Galatée* (M), right on the beach, tel. 31–88–15–04. Deliciously fresh seafood in definitely nautical ambience. *Vapeurs* (M), tel. 35–88–15–24. Lively brasserie overlooking harbor. Good choice of fish. *Maison Normande* (I), also has rooms.

Brittany

When you have gone as far west as Mont-St.-Michel, you are at the border of one of France's most unusual provinces, Brittany. A little way beyond Mont-St.-Michel is the marvelous walled town of the corsairs, St.-Malo, jutting out into the English Channel. Just west of it, by ferry across the estuary of the Rance, is Dinard, a delightful resort town beloved by the English since 1826, full of imposing 19th-century Gothic villas rising from the rocky shore.

Brittany is a region of infinite variety and particular charm. The Bretons are of Celtic, rather than Latin, stock, and in many places, particularly the remote villages of Lower Brittany, they speak Breton, a language related to Welsh and Cornish. Brittany offers a living tradition of folklore expressed in the costumes of the women and in the great religious festivals known as *Pardons*. There are colorful fishing villages, remains of a pre-Christian Druidic religion such as the megaliths of Carnac and the dolmens of Locmariaquer; superb châteaux, and churches with characteristically Breton stone calvaries in their churchyards.

The holiday-seeker will be delighted with the fine sandy beaches and the lively social life at such resorts as Dinard, Concarneau and Perros-Guirec. Smaller and more modestly-priced resorts are Bénodet, Pornichet, Roscoff, Carnac-Plage, and Île de Bréhat. The tidal estuaries of the Emerald Coast are excellent havens for yachtsmen. In contrast are wild and spectacular Cap Frehel, and stormy Pointe du Raz. To the delight of local people and conservationists, the nuclear power station planned for this wild area has been axed by President Mitterrand.

PRACTICAL INFORMATION FOR BRITTANY

Note. Many hotels are closed from Oct. through Mar., when the weather is poor.

BÉNODET. *Gwell-Kaër* (E), tel. 98–57–04–38 and *Kastel Moor* (M), tel. 98–57–05–01 and its twin *Ker-Moor*, tel. 98–57–04–48, with pool and tennis courts, very close to beach.

Restaurant. *Jeanne d'Arc* (M), 3½ miles away, outside town at **Saint-Marine**, tel. 98–56–32–70, has excellent seafood.

BREST. *Sofitel-Océania* (E), tel. 98–80–66–66. Modern, airconditioned, good restaurant. *Continental* (M), tel. 98–80–50–40. Well-placed for station and harbor, old-fashioned but comfortable. *Voyageurs* (M), tel. 98–80–25–73, 15 av. Clémenceau. Good restaurant.

Restaurant. *Frère Jacques* (M), 15 rue de Lyon (tel. 98–44–38–65). Has local specialties seen through the eyes of a new cuisine chef.

CARNAC. Best hotel is *Diana* (E), tel. 97–52–05–38, at Carnac-Plage. *Tal Ar Mor* (E), tel. 97–52–16–66, belongs to the Novotel chain. *Alignements* (M), tel. 97–52–06–30, in town, with (I) restaurant.

Restaurant. *Lann Roz* (E), tel. 97–52–10–48, delicious food and a few rooms.

CONCARNEAU. *Ty Chupen Gwenn* (M), tel. 98–97–01–43, and *Sables Blancs* (I), tel. 98–97–01–39, in town. At **Cabellou-Plage**, *Belle Etoile* (E), tel. 98–97–05–73, with good restaurant.

Restaurants. Best is *Galion* (E), tel. 98–97–30–16, in the "Ville Close." *Coquille* (M), tel. 98–97–08–52. On the harbor, good fish.

DINAN. *Avaugour* (E), tel. 96–39–07–49, comfortable and attractive, with excellent restaurant (M). *Remparts* (I), tel. 96–39–16–10, popular with readers for its hospitable atmosphere and friendliness to English-speaking visitors; no restaurant.

Restaurants. *Caravelle* (E), tel. 96–39–00–11, is another good restaurant. For classical dishes try *Mère Pourcel* (M), tel. 96–39–03–80, in a 15th-century building.

DINARD. *Grand* (E), tel. 99–46–10–28, nice views, close to marina. Good restaurant. *Vieux Manoir* (M), tel. 99–46–14–69, in the center but quiet, no restaurant.

Restaurants. *Dunes* (M), tel. 99–46–12–72, spacious, good value; also a hotel. *Altair* (I), tel. 99–46–13–58, good value, pleasant atmosphere. Also a hotel.

PERROS-GUIREC. *Grand Hôtel de Trestraou* (M), tel. 96–23–24–05, close to beach. *Printania* (M), tel. 96–23–21–00, lovely views, also near beach. Both have restaurant. *Morgane* (I), tel. 96–23–22–80, friendly, with pool and restaurant.

Restaurants. *Rochers* (E), 3½ miles away at **Ploumanach**, tel. 96–23–23–02, also has a few rooms. *Homard Bleu* (E), tel. 96–23–24–55, beside Trestraou beach.

PONT-AVEN. Restaurants. *Moulin Rosmadec* (E), tel. 98–06–00–22, in an old mill. Lots of atmosphere. Essential to reserve. *Taupinière* 98–06–03–12, friendly; good food.

QUIBERON. *Sofitel-Thalassa* (L), tel. 97–50–20–00, attached to saltwater treatment center; handsome, with very good restaurant. *Beau-Rivage* (M), tel. 97–50–08–39, good views, restaurant. *Hoche* (I), tel. 97–50–07–73, pleasant, good value, with restaurant.

Restaurants. *Ker-Noyal* (M), 97–50–08–41, also hotel. *Pêcheurs* (I), tel. 97–50 –12–75, good value, bistrot-type, at Port Maria.

RENNES. *Frantel* (E), 1 rue Cap-Maignan (tel. 99–31–54–54). Central, modern; goodish restaurant. *Novotel* (E), av. du Canada (tel. 99–50–61–32). Away from center, with pool. *Du Guesclin* (M), 5 pl. Gare (tel. 99–31–47–47). Traditional hotel near station. *Angelina* (I), 1 quai Lamennais (tel. 99–79–29–66). Close to old part of city. No restaurant.

Restaurants. *Corsaire* (M), 52 rue d'Antrain (tel. 99–36–33–69). Mainly seafood, good classical cuisine. *Escu de Runfao* (E), 5 rue Chapitre (tel. 99–79–13–10). Attractive, in old town, very good cuisine, popular with readers. *Ti-Koz* (M), 3 rue St.-Guillaume (tel. 99–79–33–89). Near cathedral, classical cooking.

ROSCOFF. *Gulf-Stream* (M), small, tel. 98–69–73–19, modern, friendly, right by sea. Has good restaurant too.

ST. MALO. *Central* (M), 6 Grande Rue (tel. 99–40–87–70). Inside walls. Comfortable, modernized rooms, good restaurant. *Elisabeth* (M), 2 rue Cordiers (tel. 99–56–24–98). In 16th-century building inside walls, no restaurant. At

St.-Servan, on road to Dol, *Valmarin* (E), 7 rue Jean-XXIII (tel. 99–81–94–76). 18th-century house set in lovely garden. Large, comfortable rooms; no restaurant.

   Restaurants. *Duchesse Anne* (M), tel. 99–40–85–33, smart, excellent seafood. *Atre* (I), tel. 99–81–68–39, modest little spot right by the sea at nearby **Saint-Servan.**

Burgundy

An easy day's drive southeast of Paris will lead you through the famous vineyards, the undulating countryside and the stone villages of Burgundy, one of the gastronomic centers of Europe's most gastronomic country, with more than a hundred well-preserved châteaux, many still family-inhabited, which are open to the public.

At Dijon, capital of the province, wine quite literally flows in the Barenzai fountain during the September wine festival, and during the annual November Gastronomic Fair gourmets can sniff, sip and sample all sorts of French regional foods. Dijon, the ancient capital of the dukes of Burgundy, is one of the most complete cities in France from an artistic and intellectual point of view; the Ducal Palace, the first-rate Museum of Fine Arts, with a new and excitingly arranged modern section, and the 14th-century Chartreuse of Champmol are among the outstanding sights here.

Even if you aren't lucky enough to be in Burgundy during a wine festival, don't miss the fascinating wine district, a treat for both palate and eye. At Gevrey-Chambertin you may taste the famous Chambertin wine, prized above all wines by Napoleon. Clos-Vougeot's 16th-century Renaissance château rises in the midst of the vineyards planted by the monks of the Abbey of Cîteaux, whose ruins may be visited on this wine tour.

Nuits-St.-Georges has been producing superb wines since Roman times. Stop here for a look and a sip before proceeding south to Beaune, capital of the great region known as the Côte de Beaune (including the famous vineyards of Pommard and Volnay) and chief wine center of Burgundy. Here, in the skillfully restored 15th-century Hôtel des Ducs de Bourgogne, is a Wine Museum, tracing the entire history of wine-making and the step-by-step process by which the sunshine of France is captured in bottles. There is one other "must" in Beaune: the celebrated Hôtel-Dieu or Hospice de Beaune, which received patients from its opening in 1450 right down to 1975. In its museum there is medieval and surgical equipment that will cure any romantic historical notions. But the chief attraction of the Hospice is the priceless polyptych of *The Last Judgment* by Roger Van der Weyden.

But even if there were not a drop of wine in Burgundy, this province, rich in history, art, and tradition, would be worth an extended visit. The remarkable Treasure of Vix, in the museum of Châtillon-sur-Seine, includes objects that decorated the tomb of a Celtic princess buried more than 2,500 years ago. At Vézelay, Autun, and Cluny you will find magnificent examples of Romanesque architecture. Vézelay and its splendid church of the Madeleine is especially recommended, as is medieval Tournus.

PRACTICAL INFORMATION FOR BURGUNDY

   AUTUN. Napoleon is alleged to have stayed in the 17th-century building now housing *St.-Louis* (M), tel. 85–52–21–03, pleasant restaurant.

   AUXERRE. *Maxime* (M), tel. 86–52–14–19. *Parc des Maréchaux* (M), tel. 86–51–43–77. 19th-century mansion; no restaurant.
   Restaurant. *Grilladerie* (I), tel. 86–52–32–80, good value.

AVALLON. *Poste* (E), tel. 86–34–06–12, back on form after a bad patch; elegant décor and good restaurant serving classical cuisine and exceptional wines.

BEAUNE. *Cep* (E), 27 rue Maufoux (tel. 80–22–35–48). Small, charming, in attractive 17th-century building, no restaurant. *Poste* (E), 1 blvd. Clemenceau (tel. 80–22–08–11). Very comfortable, good service, airconditioned and sound-proofed rooms; good restaurant. *Motel PLM* (M), tel. 80–21–46–12, on A6 motorway, with restaurant nearby.

Restaurants. Apart from hotel restaurants, try *Auberge St.-Vincent* (M), pl. de la Halle (tel. 80–22–42–34). For delicious cooking. *Chez Maxime* (M), 3 pl. Madeleine (tel. 80–22–17–82). Is more modest but has excellent fare. *Raisin de Bourgogne* (M), 164 route Dijon, tel. 80–24–69–48. Good value menus. *Ecusson* (I), pl. Malmédy, tel. 80–22–83–08. Good value and friendly welcome; garden for summer meals.

BOUILLAND. Delightful *Vieux Moulin* (M) is a lovely place to stop off for a few days in peaceful countryside, or merely enjoy an excellent meal at a reasonable price.

DIJON. *Cloche* (E), 14 pl. Darcy (tel. 80–30–12–32). Old-established, city-center hotel; closed at presstime but should be back in 1986 as Dijon's grandest establishment, with good cellar restaurant, outdoor meals in summer. *Frantel* (E), 22 blvd. de la Marne (tel. 80–72–31–13). Central, with pool and good restaurant. *Chapeau Rouge* (E), 5 rue Michelet (tel. 80–30–28–10). Central, good classical restaurant. *Europe* (M), 4 rue Audra (tel. 80–30–78–08). No restaurant. *Nord* (I), pl. Darcy, tel. 80–30–58–58, traditional, good restaurant. *Terminus* (I), 22 av. Maréchal-Foch (tel. 80–43–53–78). Near station, with restaurant.

5 miles south, at **Marsannay:** *Novotel* (M), tel. 80–52–14–22, modern, with pool.

Restaurants. *Chouette* (M), 1 rue de la Chouette (tel. 80–30–18–10). In attractive old street. *Pré aux Clercs et Trois Faisans* (M), 13 pl. de la Libération (tel. 80–67–11–33). Smart, good classical cuisine. *Rallye* (M), 39 rue Chabot-Charny (tel. 80–67–11–55). Good value. *Thibert* (M), 23 rue Crébillon (tel. 80–30–52–34). Fine *nouvelle cuisine.* Good value. *Toison d'Or Les Oenophiles* (M), 18 rue Ste-Anne (tel. 80–30–73–52). Marvelous range of Burgundies, good newish cuisine and very attractive decor. *Vinarium* (M), 23 pl. Bossuet (tel. 80–30–36–23). Attractive, good regional cooking served in 13th-century crypt. At **Marsannay,** *Gourmets* (M), (tel. 80–52–16–32), pleasant atmosphere, mostly traditional cuisine.

GEVREY-CHAMBERTIN. *Rôtisserie du Chambertin* (M), tel. 80–34–33–20. One of the best restaurants in Burgundy (and in France), with superb wines, as you'd expect. Must reserve. *Millésimes* (M), tel. 80–51–84–24, family run, with meals served in an attractive cellar decorated with winemaking paraphernalia; elegant yet friendly atmosphere.

MÂCON. *Frantel* (M), tel. 85–38–28–06, with good restaurant. *Rocher de Cancale* (M), tel. 85–38–07–50. Good fish dishes; river views.

Restaurant. *Auberge Bressane* (M), tel. 85–38–07–42, mixture of refined specialties and fish dishes.

SAULIEU. *Côte d'Or* (E), tel. 80–64–07–66, with famous restaurant (E), new cuisine, one of France's best. *Poste* (M), tel. 80–64–05–67, no restaurant.

Restaurant. *Borne Imperiale* (M), 80–64–19–76, good classical cooking.

TOURNUS. *Sauvage* (M), tel. 85–51–14–45, friendly member of Mapotel group, with garden and restaurant. *Motel Clos-Mouron* (I), tel. 85–51–23–86, a genuine motel close to town center; modern and functional, but friendly service too. *Paix* (I), tel. 85–51–01–85. Logis de France with restaurant.

Restaurant. *Greuze* (M), tel. 85–51–13–52, excellent classical cuisine, very attractive. Famous wine list.

VÉZELAY. *Poste et Lion d'Or* (E), tel. 86–33–21–23, good classical restaurant. At **Saint-Père**, 1½ miles away, is an excellent restaurant, *Espérance* (E), tel. 86–33–20–45, with interesting "new" dishes. Must reserve. Also has rooms (M).

Lyon and the Rhône Area

Busy bustling Lyon, France's second-biggest town after Paris, is surprisingly little known to foreign tourists, who tend to pass through on their way down south, maybe stopping off for a gastronomic meal (at astronomic prices, more than likely, but undoubtedly worth it) in the heartland of French *haute cuisine*. Because of its very size, Lyon doesn't perhaps have the immediate appeal of many of France's fine towns, but it's certainly worth visiting the fascinating Vieux Lyon, the "old city", which contains one of the most beautiful groups of medieval and Renaissance buildings in France. Try to visit the medieval village of Pérouges, unchanged through the centuries.

Valence is attractively situated on the Rhône (the Maison des Têtes and the cathedral are certainly worth a visit), while Montélimar (world-famous for its nougat) is a good starting-point for many delightful excursions in the lavender-filled region stretching towards the Alps: Grignan has an interesting château where Madame de Sévigné used to stay; Nyons is a particularly pleasant small town. On the other side of the Rhône (and the *autoroute*) the Ardèche has much to offer.

Alas! we have no space here to do justice to this little-known region of France, but we hope that we've whetted your appetite and that the few hotels and restaurants we give below will enable you to branch out on your own.

PRACTICAL INFORMATION FOR LYON AND THE RHÔNE AREA

BOURG-EN-BRESSE. Small *Logis de Brou* (M), tel. 74–22–11–55, no restaurant, but modern and comfortable.

Restaurant. Just outside the town limits at Brou, opposite cathedral, *Auberge Bressane* (M), tel. 74–22–22–68, fine regional cooking.

LYON. *Concorde* (E), 11 rue Grô Lée (tel. 78–42–56–21). Comfortable, traditional hotel with restaurant. *Sofitel* (E), 20 quai Gailleton (tel. 78–42–72–50). Overlooking the Rhône, with superb terrace restaurant (M). *Frantel* (E), 129 rue Servient (tel. 78–62–94–12). On top of tower block, with good restaurant (E). *PLM Terminus* (E), 12 cours de Verdun (tel. 78–37–58–11). *Royal* (M), 20 pl. Bellecour (tel. 78–37–57–31). Very central, with restaurant. Belongs to Mapotel group.

Bristol (M), 28 cours de Verdun (tel. 78–37–56–55). Well run, a bit old-fashioned, close to Perrache station, no restaurant.

Moderne (I), 15 rue Dubois (tel. 78–42–21–83). No restaurant; near St.-Nizier church; central. *Normandie* (I), 3 rue Bélier (tel. 78–37–31–36). A good bet for budgeteers; again, near station.

At Lyon-Satolas Airport: *Méridien* (E), tel. 78–71–91–61. At the smaller Bron Airport: *Novotel* (M), tel. 78–26–97–48.

On northern outskirts, at the "Porte de Lyon" complex, at **Dardilly**, at junction of A6 and N6, *Holiday Inn* (M), tel. 78–35–70–20, *Mercure* (M), tel. 78–35–28–05, and *Novotel* (M), tel. 78–35–13–41. All have pools and restaurants.

Restaurants. Lyon has so many fine restaurants, we can only give a very brief selection here. *Mère Brazier* (E), 12 rue Royale (tel. 78–28–15–49). Serves classical cuisine at its best, good-value *menu*.

But traditional Lyon has several excellent *nouvelle cuisine* restaurants too, such as *Henry* (E), 27 rue de la Martinière (tel. 78–28–26–08), and *Léon de Lyon* (E), 1 rue Pléney (tel. 78–28–11–33). Other "new" restaurants are: *Nandron* (E), 26 quai Jean-Moulin (tel. 78–42–10–26), charming; *Vettard* (E), 7 pl. Bellecour (tel. 78–42–07–59); *Tour Rose* (E), 16 rue du Boeuf (tel. 78–37–25–90), in the Old Town. *Orsi* (E), 3 pl. Kléber (tel. 78–89–57–68), with excellent-value (M) *menu* and pretty setting. A relative newcomer is *Léonard Vanotti* (M), 2 rue Stella, tel. 78–37–43–76, inventive cuisine, good value.

Bonne Auberge (M), 48 av. Félix-Faure (tel. 78–60–00–57), bustling, good regional dishes. *Chevallier* (M), 40 rue du Sergent-Blandan (tel. 78–28–19–83), good for regional specialties, good value *menus*. *Tante Alice* (I), 22 rue Remparts-d'Aisnay (tel. 78–37–49–83), a typical provincial restaurant with good service. *Bistrot de Lyon* (I), 64 rue Mercière (tel. 78–37–00–62). Rather smart, plenty of atmosphere, and good newish cuisine too, at very reasonable prices.

Outside town—at **Charbonnières-les-Bains,** 5 miles west via N7, *Gigandon* (M), tel. 78–87–15–51, very good value. At **Collonges-au-Mont-d'Or,** 5½ miles north via N51, *Paul Bocuse au Pont de Collonges* (E), tel. 78–22–01–40, owned and run by world-famous chef Paul Bocuse, so food is superb. Opulent décor, a place to remember. 12 miles away at **Mionnay** is another "must," *Alain Chapel* (E), tel. 78–91–82–02, which also has a few rooms (book well ahead).

MONTÉLIMAR. *Parc Chabaud* (E), tel. 75–01–65–66, quiet, attractive, with garden. *Relais de l'Empereur* (E), tel. 75–01–29–00, with garden and good restaurant. *Printemps* (M), tel. 75–01–32–63, small and peaceful, with restaurant open evening only. At **Malataverne,** 5½ miles away via D144, *Domaine du Colomber* (M), tel. 75–51–65–86, has 11 rooms set in marvelous position in lovely countryside. Pool and pleasant restaurant.

Restaurant. Grillon (M), tel. 75–01–79–02, nice atmosphere, mostly regional cuisine.

NYONS. *Alizés* (M), tel. 75–26–08–11, *Caravelle* (M), tel. 75–26–07–44, both without restaurant. At Aubres, 2½ miles away, is the small and peaceful *Auberge du Vieux Village* (M), tel. 75–26–12–89, with a nice view, pool and restaurant. Has some (E) rooms too.

PÉROUGES. *Ostellerie Vieux Pérouges* (E), tel. 74–61–00–88, an enchanting 13th-century hostelry in a medieval village. The setting alone makes it worth a visit. Restaurant (M) has local specialties. Also serves famous teatime specialties (with cider).

ROANNE. Restaurant. *Troisgros* (E), tel. 77–71–66–97, one of France's very best for *nouvelle cuisine,* even though several members of the famous Troisgros family have died tragically young; also a small Relais et Châteaux hotel (E), with very comfortable rooms.

TAIN L'HERMITAGE. *Commerce* (M), tel. 75–08–65–00, small, good place for a night or a lunch in the good-value restaurant (M).

VALENCE. *Hôtel 2000* (M), tel. 75–43–73–01, no restaurant, and *Novotel* (M), tel. 75–42–20–15, just outside town, are best.

Restaurant. Pic (E), tel. 75–44–15–32, with *nouvelle cuisine,* is really marvelous; also has 5 rooms for which you must reserve months ahead.

VIENNE. *Résidence de la Pyramide* (M), tel. 74–53–16–46, a comfortable small hotel near the world-famous restaurant. At **Pont-Evêque,** 2 miles east, *Midi* (I), tel. 74–85–90–11. Set in lovely garden, friendly service; no restaurant.

Restaurant. Pyramide (E), tel. 74–53–01–96, one of the world's greats under the famous chef Fernand Point, is now run by his widow, with mostly excellent classical cuisine.

VONNAS. *Georges Blanc* (E), tel. 74–50–00–10, a famous restaurant between Mâcon and Bourg, is also a small, delightful hotel, with airconditioning and heated pool. "New" cuisine, with local specialties. Reserve rooms well ahead.

The Châteaux of the Loire Valley

The valley watered by the broad and shallow Loire is one of the most beautiful areas of France. It was here in the 15th and 16th centuries that the kings of France chose to build their fabulous *châteaux d'agrément,* or pleasure castles, and these are the chief attractions of a region rich in history. The best known of the châteaux, Amboise, Azay-le-Rideau, Blois, Chambord and Chenonceau, date from the Renaissance and reflect the luxury and elegance of that period. But many were built as defensive fortresses in the Middle Ages, and you will see the stern necessities of feudal life in the massive walls of Châteaudun, Chinon, Langeais and Loches. To round out the picture, you should visit one of the later "classical" châteaux of the 17th or 18th century—Cheverny, for example, or Valençay. Before scheduling your visit to the château country, inquire about the dates of its *son et lumière* (sound and light) performances. A good way of seeing the châteaux in all their splendor is to take a circuit in a small plane (information from tourist office in Blois or Tours).

If your time is very limited, you can get an excellent idea of the château country from the "five Ch's"—Chambord, a royal palace built by François I in the midst of a hunting preserve as big as the whole city of Paris; Chenonceau, the lovely castle built across the Cher River and given by Henri II to his mistress, Diane de Poitiers; Chaumont, the rather forbidding-looking castle to which Henri II's widow sent Diane when the king died; Chinon, the fortified château where Joan of Arc performed her first miracle in 1429 by recognizing the Dauphin the disguise among 300 of his courtiers; and Cheverny, a sumptuously furnished 17th-century château, still inhabited by a descendant of the original owners, but open to the public.

Aside from the châteaux, there are other major architectural attractions in this region. They are the abbey of St.-Benoît-sur-Loire, dating from the year 1000, one of the great achievement of Romanesque art; the Cothic cathedral of Bourges, one of the most beautiful in France, with its five sculptured portals, its high vaulted roof and magnificent stained glass windows; and the Abbey of Fontevrault, which once housed a community of 5,000 monks and nuns, where you can visit the curious, domed octagonal tower, one of the few remaining medieval kitchens in Europe. In the abbey church, in a pure Romanesque nave of white stone, unmarred by Gothic or baroque additions, is the necropolis of the Plantagenet sovereigns—Eleanor of Aquitaine and her second husband, Henry II of England; their famous son, Richard Coeur de Lion, and their daughter-in-law, Isabelle of Angoulême, wife of England's King John. Their tombs lie side by side in the empty nave, surmounted by their polychrome statues. Good concerts are held in the abbey.

Lovers of religious music should try to visit the lovely Benedictine abbey of Solesmes to the north of this region, where Gregorian plainchant is still sung at Sunday masses.

PRACTICAL INFORMATION FOR THE LOIRE VALLEY

AMBOISE. *France et Cheval Blanc* (I), quai Général-de-Gaulle (tel. 47–57–02–44). Close to river; good value, with appetizing food. At **Chargé,** a mile from Amboise, *Château de Pray* (M), tel. 47–57–23–67, quiet, a converted 12th-century château with formal gardens.

Restaurants. *Lion d'Or* (M), tel. 47–57–00–23, and *Mail* (M), tel. 47–57–60–39, are pleasant little restaurants with a few rooms. *Crêperie dans un jardin* (I), in grounds of Clos Lucé manor house.

ANGERS. *Concorde* (E), tel. 41–87–37–20, modern. *Anjou* (M), tel. 41–88–24–82, central, pleasant restaurant. Just by station. *Croix de Guerre* (I), tel. 41–88–66–59, central, no restaurant.

Restaurants. *Logis* (M), 17 rue St.-Laud (tel. 41–87–44–15). Specializes in seafood. *Toussaint* (M), tel. 41–87–46–20, has local specialties, deliciously cooked in new style. Good value. *Amandier* (I), 7 rue Cordelle, tel. 41–88–22–78, a welcome find just off Anger's central square; friendly little place with excellent-value cuisine and attractive décor.

BEAUGENCY. *Ecu de Bretagne* (I), tel. 38–44–67–60, with good regional dishes in restaurant (M). Two miles away at **Tavers** is *Tonnellerie* (M), tel. 38–44–68–15, with pool, pretty grounds and good restaurant (M).

LES BEZARDS. *Auberge des Templiers* (E), tel. 38–31–80–01, comfortable, elegant, with pool and tennis. In the Relais et Châteaux group. Excellent restaurant too.

BLOIS. *Anne de Bretagne* (M), 31 av. Jean Laigret (tel. 54–78–05–38). Between station and château; no restaurant. Pleasantly atmospheric is little *Hostellerie Loire* (M), 8 rue Maréchal-de-Lattre-de-Tassigny (tel. 54–74–26–60), on the Paris-Tours road below the castle, with river view and good restaurant. *Novotel* (M), tel. 54–78–33–57, outside town.
Restaurants. *Péniche* (M), tel. 54–74–37–23, is more unusual: a converted barge moored on the Loire; good service, newish cuisine.

BOURGES. *Monitel* (I), tel. 48–50–23–62, and *Olympia* (I), tel. 48–70–49–84. Neither has restaurant.
Restaurant. *Jacques Coeur* (E), tel. 48–70–12–72, very good classical cooking, served in medieval setting.

CHAMBORD. *St.-Michel* (M), tel. 54–20–31–31, comfortable, opposite château, with restaurant.

CHAUMONT. *Château* (M), 2 rue Maréchal-de-Lattre-de Tassigny (tel. 54–20–98–04). Well-run; close to château; (I) restaurant.

CHENONCEAUX. *Bon Laboureur et Château* (M), tel. 47–29–90–02, delightful, opposite château, good restaurant. Rooms overlooking the street can be noisy.
Restaurants. *Bon Laboureur* (M), in hotel. *Château de Chissay* (I), 2½ miles east via N76 (tel. 54–32–32–01). Pleasant atmosphere; good food.

CHINON. *Boule d'Or* (M), tel. 47–93–03–13, river view, restaurant. *Gargantua* (M), tel. 47–93–04–71, central, near château, housed in 15th-century former residence of Baillis. *France* (I), tel. 47–93–33–91, small, close to château and river, no restaurant.
3½ miles south, *Château de Marçay* (E), tel. 47–93–03–47, in 15th-century building with pool, tennis courts, good restaurant. Relais et Châteaux member.
Restaurants. *Plaiser Gourmand* (M), tel. 47–93–20–46. Inventive cuisine; delicious local wines. *Sainte-Maxime* (M), generous helpings, nice atmosphere.

COUR-CHEVERNY. *Saint-Hubert* (I), tel. 54–79–96–60, with restaurant.

MONTBAZON. *Château d'Artigny* (E), tel. 47–26–24–24, good restaurant (though some readers have found it overpriced), rooms furnished with period pieces; pool, musical weekends and golfing holidays. *Domaine de la Tortinière* (E), tel. 47–26–00–67, attractive small inn with regional cooking.

ORLÉANS. Most modern is *Sofitel* (E), 44 quai Barentin (tel. 38–62–17–39). Pool and goodish restaurant (M), near the river. *Auberge Montespan* (M), tel. 38–88–12–07. 1¼ miles along the Blois road. *Orléans* (M), 6 rue Adolphe Crespin (tel. 38–53–35–34), no restaurant.
Restaurants. *Crémaillère* (E), 34 rue Notre-Dame-de-Recouvrance (tel. 38–53–49–17), has *nouvelle cuisine*. *Antiquaires* (M), 2 rue au Lin, tel. 38–53–52–35, chic; good classical cuisine. *Bigorneau* (M), 54 rue Turcies (tel. 38–53–52–35), specializes in fish. *Poutrière* (M), 8 rue de la Brèche (tel. 38–66–02–30), nouvelle

cuisine. *Etoile d'Or* (I), 25 pl. du Vieux-Marché (tel. 38–53–49–20), also has a few rooms. All are closed Aug.

SAUMUR. *Gare* (M), 16 av. David d'Angers, tel. 41–67–34–24. Good value restaurant. *Roi René* (M), 94 av. de Gaulle, tel. 41–67–45–30, reader-recommended for comfort and service.

At **Chênehutte-les-Tuffeaux**, 5 miles away, is the delightful hotel *Prieuré* (E), tel. 41–50–15–31, in converted priory set in wooded grounds. Breathtaking views of Loire. Good restaurant with newish cuisine.

Restaurants. *Auberge St-Pierre* (I), pl. St-Pierre (tel. 41–51–26–25), good value, popular with French families. *Gambetta* (I), 12 rue Gambetta (tel. 41–51–11–13), excellent for classical regional dishes.

SOLESMES. *Grand Hôtel de Solesmes* (M), tel. 43–95–45–10, well-planned, modern rooms just opposite the abbey; good restaurant too, plus friendly service.

TOURS. *Bordeaux* (E), 3 pl. Maréchal-Leclerc (tel. 47–05–40–32), very central, with good restaurant. *Univers* (E), 3 blvd. Heurteloup (tel. 47–05–37–12), central, elaborately furnished, good restaurant. *Châteaux de la Loire* (M), 12 rue Gambetta (tel. 47–05–10–05). Small and friendly; no restaurant. *Grand* (M), 9 pl. Maréchal-Leclerc (tel. 47–05–35–31). Spacious; no restaurant. *Colbert* (I), 78 rue Colbert (tel. 47–66–61–56). Near cathedral; small and friendly but no restaurant.

Restaurants. *Poivrière* (M), 13 rue du Change (tel. 47–20–85–41). In Old Town, rather chic. *Tuffeaux* (M), 19 rue Lavoisier (tel. 47–47–19–89), near cathedral. *Bidoche* (I), 18 rue Longue-Echelle (tel. 47–64–44–09). In heart of Old Town, with generous hors d'oeuvre selection and good grilled meat. *Rûche* (I), 105 rue Colbert (tel. 47–66–69–83). Charming atmosphere, good value, near the cathedral.

Provence

The southern stretch of the Rhône Valley, known as Provence (from *Provincia Romana*), will offer you some of the most perfect monuments of classical and medieval heritage under the Mediterranean sun. July is the month for the great music and drama festivals, staged amid such magnificent surroundings as the amphitheater at Nîmes, the Palace of the Popes at Avignon, and the great Roman theater at Orange. The most famous of these summer offerings are the music festival at Aix-en-Provence and the Avignon drama festival.

The outstanding antiquities of Provence include Orange's splendidly preserved Roman theater (seating 10,000) and its Triumphal Arch of Tiberius (49 B.C.); and Nîmes, a treasure house of Roman antiquities with its harmonious Maison Carrée, its vast arena and Roman baths. Nearby is the superb, three-tiered Roman aqueduct, the Pont du Gard.

Arles is one of the most fascinating of Provençal towns. You can see bullfights in its arena and stroll down the Alyscamps, a pagan burial ground. At St.-Rémy-de-Provence are some of the most interesting excavations in the Mediterranean area. So far, two ancient cities have been unearthed—a Gallo-Greek city dating from the second century B.C. and, at Les Antiques, the Gallo-Roman city of Glanum. The Roman remains at Vaison-la-Romaine are almost as complete as those of Pompeii, though less extensive.

Among the masterpieces of post-classical times, you should not miss the superb Romanesque church of St.-Trophime in Arles with its 12th-century cloister, filled with remarkable statuary; and the machicolated battlements of Avignon and the huge Palace of the Popes, dominating the town with its massive splendor. East of Avignon is the Fontaine de Vaucluse, where Petrarch retired at the age of 33. See also the impressive Carthusian monastery of Villeneuve-lès-Avignon across the river, and St.-Bernard's Abbey of Sénanque, one of the finest Cistercian abbeys in France.

Finally, before swinging down to Marseille and the Riviera, you should not miss Aix-en-Provence, a lovely city which has somehow kept its classical calm despite the growth of its suburbs. The famous Cours Mirabeau, a magnificent avenue lined with shady plane trees, is the Champs-Elysées of Aix. Visit the Fine Arts Museum, in rue du Quatre Septembre near the 17th-century Fountain of the Dolphins. Nearby is the studio of Paul Cézanne, one of Aix's greatest citizens. Lovingly restored by American admirers of the artist, the *atelier* is exactly as it was when Cézanne worked there. See also the cathedral of St.-Sauveur, dating from the fifth of the 16th centuries, and the famous collection of Beauvais tapestries in the adjacent museum.

PRACTICAL INFORMATION FOR PROVENCE

AIX-EN-PROVENCE. *Paul Cézanne* (E), 40 av. Victor-Hugo (tel. 42–26–34–73). Very attractive, near station; no restaurant. *Roy René* (E), 14 blvd. Roi-René (tel. 42–26–03–01). Central and very comfortable, with fairly good restaurant. *Nègre-Coste* (M), 33 cours Mirabeau (tel. 42–27–74–22). 18th-century building; no restaurant. *Caravelle* (I), 29 blvd. Roi-René (tel. 42–62–53–05). Well-run; no restaurant.

Restaurants. Best is *Caves Henri IV* (E), 32 rue Espariat (tel. 42–27–86–39). Offers inventive variants on local dishes. Good value. *Abbaye Cordeliers* (M), 21 rue Lieutard (tel. 42–27–29–47). 14th-century cloister, serving newish cuisine. *Arbaud* (M), 19 cours Mirabeau (tel. 42–26–66–88). Elegant. For morning coffee, light lunches, teas, and more elaborate dinners. *Jardin* (I), 7 av. Victor-Hugo (tel. 42–26–07–04). Friendly; good value.

ARLES. *Jules César* (E), tel. 90–93–43–20, delightful 17th-century building, once a monastery, good restaurant. *D'Arlatan* (M), tel. 90–93–56–66, very comfortable and well-furnished; good value; no restaurant. *Forum* (M), tel. 90–93–48–95, with pool, no restaurant. *Calendal* (I), pl. Pomme (tel. 90–96–11–89). Small, family hotel; no restaurant. *Saint-Trophime* (I), tel. 90–96–88–38, particularly helpful and friendly management, no restaurant.

Restaurants. *Balance* (I), tel. 90–93–55–76, modest little place serving local dishes. *Grillon* (I), tiny café opposite the arena, good for light meals. *Agneau sur le Toit* (I), tel. 90–49–67–28. Regional fare.

AVIGNON. Best is *Europe* (E), 12 pl. Crillon (tel. 90–82–66–92), charming. Restaurant serves dinners only. *Bristol Terminus* (M), 44 cours Jean-Jaurès (tel. 90–86–21–21), central, restaurant. *Cité des Papes* (M), 1 rue Jean-Vilar (tel. 90–86–22–45), modern, near Palais des Papes, no restaurant. Outside town on N7 road: *Novotel* (M), tel. 90–87–62–36, and *Mercure* (M), tel. 90–88–91–10. Both have pools. On A7, *Sofitel* (E), 90–31–16–43. Good restaurant.

Restaurants. For good *nouvelle cuisine: Brunel* (E), 46 rue de la Balance (tel. 90–85–24–83) and *Vernet* (M), 58 rue Joseph-Vernet (tel. 90–86–64–53). *Hiély-Lucullus* (E), 5 rue de la République (tel. 90–86–17–07), excellent mixture of classical and new cuisine, good value. *Fourchette* (I), 7 rue Racine (tel. 90–82–56–01), amazing value.

A couple of miles west, at **Angles,** *Ermitage Meissonnier* (M), tel. 90–25–41–68, excellent and inventive cuisine at reasonable prices. Is also a comfortable hotel.

LES BAUX. Elegant *Oustau de Baumanière* (E), tel. 90–97–33–07, delightful, with excellent restaurant; pool. *Cabro d'Or* (E), tel. 90–97–33–21, charming, with good restaurant. *Hostellerie de la Reine Jeanne* (I), tel. 90–97–32–06, in village, is peaceful.

NÎMES. *Imperator* (E), quai de la Fontaine (tel. 66–21–90–30). Central, lovely garden, good restaurant with regional specialties. *Cheval Blanc et Arènes* (M), 1 pl. Arènes (tel. 66–67–20–30). Opposite Roman arena; with restaurant. *Louvre* (M), 2 sq. de la Couronne (tel. 66–67–22–75). Lovely 17th-century building, near arena, goodish restaurant. *Milan* (I), 17 av. Fenchères (tel. 66–29 –29–90). By station; no restaurant.

NOVES. *Auberge de Noves* (E), tel. 90–94–19–21, peaceful and elegant, in beautiful setting. Excellent 'new' dishes in restaurant. Pool.

ST.-REMY-DE-PROVENCE. *Château des Alpilles* (E), tel. 90–92–03–33, friendly, family-run hotel with pretty garden; a good place to stay or to enjoy an alfresco meal. *Château de Roussan* (E), tel. 90–92–11–63, attractive, no restaurant, pool, a mile away on Tarascon road. Also good: *Hostellerie du Vallon de Valrugues* (E), tel. 90–92–04–40, beautiful. *Antiques* (M), tel. 90–92–03–02. Both have pool, as has modern *Van Gogh* (M), tel. 90–92–14–02, no restaurant. *Arts* (I), tel. 90–92–08–50, small and comfortable.

VILLENEUVE-LÈS-AVIGNON. *Prieuré* (E), tel. 90–25–18–20, exceptionally pleasant and attractive, good restaurant, pool. *Magnaneraie* (M), tel. 90–25–11–11, with pool. Has pleasant restaurant. *Atelier* (I), tel. 90–25–01–84, in 16th-century building, no restaurant.

The Riviera

From Marseille east to Menton and the Italian border stretches one of the most famous coastlines in the world, the French Riviera. From St.-Raphaël to the frontier, this coast is protected by the Alpes Maritimes, and the countriside is a riot of exotic vegetation—orange, eucalyptus, lemon, olive and pink laurel fill the air with their perfume, while palms and cactus lend a tropical atmosphere to the scenery. This is the sun-kissed Côte d'Azur, along which are strung the famous resorts of the St. Tropez, Port Grimaud, Cannes, Antibes, Nice and Menton. It is best to come here out-of-season, since July, and most particularly August, are horribly crowded. There is always something going on on the Côte d'Azur: horseracing, automobile rallies, fashion shows, concerts, ballets and folk festivals. The most famous event of the year is the 2-week Nice Carnival in February or March. With the opening of Nice's Palais des Congrès in 1983 the Riviera acquired a new cultural center too.

Unfortunately, the natural beauties of this coastline are becoming more difficult to find every year as gigantic marinas and building developments cover the sea-fronts with a wall of cement and sea and beaches grow more polluted. However, you can still discover patches of extraordinary beauty and secluded coves.

In Marseille, one of the world's most colorful big ports, you should see the celebrated Canebière, the main drag, lined with luxury shops and enormous cafés; the Museum of Fine Arts; the Roman Docks Museum; Le Corbusier's La Cité Radieuse; the Vieux Port and, up the hill from it, the nicely restored Cours Julien area; and the Château d'If, from which Dumas' Count of Monte Cristo made his escape. See the *calanques,* cobalt blue miniature fiords of Cassis, and take one of the fascinating guided tours through a perfume factory at Grasse.

Aside from the Mediterranean beaches, you should plan several visits to the nearby villages, ancient towns fortified against the Saracens —Vence, St. Paul-de-Vence, Ramatuelle, Grimaud, Eze, Cagnes and Gourdon, all of which offer magnificent views. They can be reached by bus from the main centers.

You might expect to find the best beaches near the popular resorts of Cannes, Nice, Monte Carlo and Menton. Actually, except for Cannes, these beaches are rather poor. At Cannes, the once-narrow sandy beach is being widened yearly with sand brought from Fréjus, and it is now quite a respectable size. Nice is also growing a sandy beach. From Nice to the Italian border, the beaches are of gravel or shingle. Between Cannes and St.-Raphaël is the magnificent Corniche, which, although beautiful, has few swim spots.

The best beaches are located along the more than 60 miles of coast from St.-Maxime to Hyères—at Cavalaire, Le Lavandou, St.-Clair, Cavalière, Pampelone; these range from tiny jewel-like crescent beaches to dazzling ones that sweep for over 3 miles along the sea. Off-season, they are all clean, fine, white-sand beaches that slope gently into the sea. From July 15-Aug. 31, when hordes sweep down, they become dirty and disagreeable.

PRACTICAL INFORMATION FOR THE RIVIERA

ANTIBES. *Bleu Marine* (M), tel. 93–74–84–84. Good views; no restaurant. *Mas Djoliba* (M), tel. 93–34–02–48, with huge garden. 2 miles north on N7, *Tananarive* (M), tel. 93–33–30–00, pool, good restaurant. On the road to Grasse, and rather hard to find, *Novotel Sophia-Antipolis* (M), tel. 93–33–38–00, secluded in a pine forest, with pool and snackbar.

Restaurants. *Bonne Auberge* (E), one of the Riviera's top eating spots. Lovely Provençal dining room and terrace. 3 miles north via N7 at La Brague. Must reserve, tel. 93–33–36–65.

Auberge Provençale (M), very attractive, rather smart. *Vieux Murs* (M), chic. *Cameo* (I), very popular, on main square. Also has rooms. *Oursin* (I), good value.

BANDOL. *PLM Ile-Rousse* (E), tel. 94–29–46–86; good restaurant and pool. *Ker Mocotte* (M), tel. 94–29–46–53. Converted seaside villa. Private beach; restaurant. *Provençal* (M), tel. 94–29–52–11. On **Bendor Island:** *Delos Palais* (E), tel. 94–29–42–33, very comfortable, with pool.

Restaurants. *Auberge du Port* (E). *Réserve* (M). Also has rooms. *Grotte Provençale* (I).

BEAULIEU-SUR-MER. *Métropole* (L), tel. 93–01–00–08, vast terrace overlooking sea, pool. *Réserve* (L), tel. 93–01–00–01, extremely luxurious interior, wonderful views, famous restaurant. *Don Grégorio* (E), tel. 93–01–12–15. Modern, comfortable; on main street; pool, no restaurant. *Frisia* (M), tel. 93–01–01–04, with fine view. *Comté de Nice* (I), tel. 93–01–19–70. No restaurant.

Restaurants. *Métropole* (L), tel. 93–01–00–08. *Réserve* (L), tel. 93–07–00–01. Both in hotels. *La Pignatelle* (I), tel. 93–01–03–37, serves local dishes.

CAGNES. *Cagnard* (E), tel. 93–20–73–21, Provençal atmosphere. Lovely views and good restaurant too.

Restaurants. At Haut-de-Cagnes, *Josyjo* (M), a cheerful bistro. *Auberge du Port* (M), at **Cros-de-Cagnes,** cozy atmosphere, better-than-home cooking. Also has a few rooms.

CANNES. Magnificently set along the famous boulevard de la Croisette, overlooking the sea—*Carlton* (L), at no. 58 (tel. 93–68–91–68); *Grand* (L), at no. 45 (tel. 93–38–15–45); *Majestic* (L) (tel. 93–68–91–00), at no. 6; *Martinez-Concorde* (L), at no. 73 (tel. 93–68–91–91). All have expensive restaurants and private beaches or pools.

Frantel Beach (L), 13 rue du Canada (tel. 93–38–22–32), a stone's throw from the Croisette and very comfortable; pool, but no restaurant. *Gray d'Albion* (L), 6 rue Etats-Unis (tel. 93–48–54–54), opened in the early '80s and the last word in luxury, with airconditioning throughout, private beach, and an excellent restaurant. *Montfleury-Intercontinental* (L), 25 av. Beausejour (tel. 93–68–91–50), above town with a splendid view and its own pool. *Sofitel Méditerranée* (L), 2 blvd. Jean-Hibert (tel. 93–99–22–75), just by the old harbor.

Modern *Century* (M), 133 rue d'Antibes (tel. 93–99–37–64), very central. *France* (M), 85 rue d'Antibes (tel. 93–39–23–34), is a good bet. *Molière* (M), 5 rue Molière (tel. 93–38–16–16), pleasant garden, reasonable. None of these has restaurant.

Restaurants. *Croquant* (E), 18 blvd. Jean-Hibert (tel. 93–39–39–79), with very good-value *menus,* specializes in dishes from southwest France (open evenings only). *Poêle d'Or* (E), 23 rue des Etats-Unis (tel. 93–39–77–65), for good classical cuisine. *Rescator* (E), 7 rue Maréchal-Joffre (tel. 93–39–44–57), fine *nouvelle cuisine*. Best in town is *Royal Gray* (E), in Gray d'Albion hotel, very chic, marvelous newish cuisine, superb wines, and reasonably priced *menus* for such a luxury spot.

Félix (M), 64 blvd. de la Croisette (tel. 93–94–00–61), is as chic as ever. *Festival* (M), 52 blvd. de la Croisette (tel. 93–38–04–81), very popular and chic; mostly seafood. *Pompon Rouge* (M), 4 rue Emile-Négrin, no telephone, cheerful, home-style cooking. *Mal Assis* (I), 15 quai Saint-Pierre (tel. 93–39–13–38), by harbor, has amazingly inexpensive *menus*.

CAP D'ANTIBES. *Cap* (L), tel. 93–61–39–01. Lovely setting in huge grounds overlooking sea. Luxurious rooms and famous *Eden Roc* restaurant. *Gardiole* (M), tel. 93–61–35–03, comfortable.

Restaurant. *Cabestan* (E), tel. 93–61–77–70, delicious seafood, good *menus*.

CASSIS. *Liautaud* (M), tel. 42–01–75–37, small. *Roches Blanches* (M), tel. 42–01–09–30, has own beach, lovely site, quiet. Both have restaurants. *Grand Jardin* (I), tel. 42–01–70–10, small and attractive, with friendly atmosphere, just by harbor. No restaurant.

Restaurants. *Presqu'île* (E), tel. 42–01–03–77, lovely setting, good *nouvelle cuisine*. *Chez Gilbert* (M), by harbor.

CAVALAIRE. Best is *Calanque* (M), tel. 94–64–04–27, with lovely view and pool. *Raymond* (M), tel. 94–64–07–32, good restaurant.

CAVALIÈRE. *Club* (L), tel. 94–05–80–14, on the beach, excellent cuisine. *Moriaz* (M), tel. 94–05–80–01. *Surplage* (M), tel. 94–05–84–19, indoor pool, restaurant, view.

LA CIOTAT. *Ciotel* (E), tel. 42–83–90–30, is 3 miles east. *Lavandes* (M), tel. 42–08–42–80, *Rotonde* (I), tel. 42–08–67–50, neither has restaurant.

EZE-BORD-DE-MER. *Cap Estel* (E), tel. 93–01–50–44, on peninsula, with private beach and pool; generally very comfortable. *Cap Roux* (M), tel. 93–01–51–23, with kitchenettes.

EZE-VILLAGE. Restaurants. Famous *Chèvre d'Or* (E), also has 10 luxurious rooms, tel. 93–41–12–12. *Nid d'Aigle* (M), tel. 93–41–19–08. Provincial fare.

FRÉJUS. *Residences du Colombier* (M), tel. 94–51–45–92, 1½ miles out on the road to Bagnols, with attractive Provençal-style bungalows. *Oasis* (M), tel. 94–51–50–44, on the beach.

GRASSE. *Panorama* (M), tel. 93–36–80–80. Well-run and friendly; rooms overlooking garden. *Bellevue* (I), tel. 93–36–01–96, with restaurant.

Restaurants. *Chez Pierre* (I), tel. 93–36–12–99, pleasantly unpretentious. *Petite Auberge* (I), tel. 93–36–20–34, 3 miles away on Nice road. Also has a few rooms.

GRIMAUD. *Boulangerie* (M), tel. 94–43–23–16, small, quiet, with pool.

HYÈRES. At Hyères-Plage, *Pins d'Argent* (M), tel. 94–57–63–60, convenient for the airport. 8 miles south, *Provençal* (E), tel. 94–58–20–09, on **Presqu'Ile de Giens.** Charming atmosphere, excellent food, pool.

Restaurants. *Roy Gourmet* (M), tel. 94–65–02–11. Small and elegant; interesting menu. *Tison d'Or* (M), tel. 94–65–01–37, specializes in Burgundian dishes.

ILE DE PORQUEROLLES. *Mas du Langoustier* (M), tel. 94–58–30–09. Good restaurant. *Ste.-Anne* (I), tel. 94–58–30–04, full board only.

Restaurant. *Arche de Noé* (I), with a few rooms.

JUAN-LES-PINS. *Belles-Rives* (L), tel. 93–61–02–79, lovely views, private beach. *Juana* (L), tel. 93–61–20–37, with fine restaurant, new cooking. *Beausé-jour* (E), tel. 93–61–07–82, small and comfortable, with garden and pool. *Pré-Catalan* (M), tel. 93–61–05–11, peaceful, with little garden. *Régence* (M), tel. 93–61–09–39, half-board only in summer, close to beach. *Eden* (I), tel. 93–61–05 –20.

Restaurants. Best is *Terrasse* (E), in Juana hotel. *Perroquet* (I) good. *Régence* (I), in hotel, good value.

LE LAVANDOU. *Beau Rivage* (M), tel. 94–71–11–09, overlooking beach. *Calanque* (M), tel. 94–71–05–96, good food, pretty spot. A mile away at **Saint-Clair** is *Orangeraie* (M), tel. 94–71–04–25, modern, same management as Vieux Port restaurant. No restaurant. Also at St-Clair, attractive *Belle-Vue* (M), tel. 94–71–01–06, small, nice atmosphere, very attractive, with pleasant restaurant.

Restaurants. *Bouée* (M), tel. 94–71–11–88, mostly Norman dishes. *Vieux Port* (M), tel. 94–71–00–21, by harbor.

MARSEILLE. *Petit Nice* (E), corniche Kennedy (tel. 91–52–14–39), close to Vieux Port, overlooking sea, excellent restaurant (*nouvelle cuisine*). *Sofitel* (L), 36 blvd. Charles Livon (tel. 91–52–90–19), just by Vieux Port, very comfortable, again has good *nouvelle cuisine* restaurant.

Concorde Palm Beach (E), 2 promenade de la Plage (tel. 91–76–20–00), on Corniche overlooking sea. *Frantel* (E), rue Neuve-St.-Martin (tel. 91–91–91–29), with excellent restaurant, very central.

Bompard (M), 2 rue des Flots-Bleus (tel. 91–52–10–93), quiet, close to Corniche, no restaurant. *Esterel* (M), 124 rue de Paradis (tel. 91–37–13–90), small, good value. No restaurant. *Genève* (M), 3 bis rue Reine-Elisabeth (tel. 91–90–51 –42), central. No restaurant.

Restaurants. *Maurice Brun* (E), 18 quai Rive-Neuve (tel. 91–33–35–38), an old favorite that keeps up the same excellent standards of regional cuisine every year. *Michel-Les-Catalans* (E), 6 rue des Catalans (tel. 91–52–64–22), famous for bouillabaisse and other fish dishes.

Ferme (M), 23 rue Sainte (tel. 91–33–21–12), good for *nouvelle cuisine. Max Caizergues* (M), 11 rue Gustave-Ricard (tel. 91–33–58–07), excellent classical cuisine with some "nouvelle" touches. *Miramar* (M), 12 quai du Port (tel. 91–91–10–40), by Vieux Port, excellent fish. *Pescadou* (M), 19 pl. Castellane (tel. 91–78–36–01), good for fish, but closed July and Aug.

Tire-Bouchon (M), 11 cours Julien (tel. 91–42–49–03), bistrot-type cuisine. Many other nice little spots in the up-and-coming Cours Julien.

MENTON. *Napoléon* (E), tel. 93–35–89–50. *Europ'Hôtel* (M), tel. 93–35–59–92. *Méditerranée* (M), tel. 93–28–25–25. Modern and central; marvelous views; no restaurant.

Restaurants. *Santons* (E), tel. 93–35–94–10. Good value, high quality. *Nautic* (I), tel. 93–35–78–74. Good meals.

MOUGINS. *Moulin de Mougins* (L), tel. 93–75–78–24, a few delightful rooms attached to one of France's best-known restaurants (E). *Mas Candille* (E), tel. 93–90–00–85. Comfortable; good "new" regional fare. *Clos des Boyères* (M), tel 93–90–01–58. Peaceful; lovely gardens.

Restaurants. *Amandier* (M), tel. 93–90–00–91, under same management as the Moulin, delightful. *Bistrot* (I), tel. 93–75–78–34, very good value, chic. *Feu Follet* (I), tel. 93–90–15–78, lovely for outdoor dining in typically Provençal square.

LA NAPOULE. *Ermitage du Riou* (L), tel. 93–49–95–56, with pool, close to beach, attractive Mediterranean architecture. *Calanque* (M), tel. 93–49–95–11, nice view; closed Oct.–March. Small *Corniche d'Or* (I), tel. 93–49–92–51, no restaurant.

Restaurant. *Oasis* (E), fine new cuisine, one of France's best, must reserve, tel. 93–49–95–52.

NICE. World-famous *Negresco* (L), 37 promenade des Anglais (tel. 93–88–39 –51), is officially listed as a "historic monument", but it has been modernized and is wonderfully comfortable, with excellent restaurant too.

Hyatt-Regency (L), 223 promenade des Anglais (tel. 93–83–91–51), has all modern conveniences and, unusually, doesn't charge for children under 18 sharing their parents' rooms. Modern *Méridien* (L), 1 promenade des Anglais (tel. 93–82–25–25), comfortable but a bit impersonal.

Frantel (E), 28 av. Notre-Dame (tel. 93–80–30–24), large modern hotel in center of town with very comfortable rooms, pool on roof with lovely views and restaurant. *Plaza* (E), 12 av. de Verdun (tel. 93–87–80–41), has a magnificent rooftop terrace overlooking the bay. *Sofitel-Splendid* (E), 50 blvd. Victor-Hugo (tel. 93–88–69–54), with pool, sauna and sun terrace. *Westminster-Concorde* (E), 27 promenade des Anglais (tel. 93–88–29–44), good service.

Continental Masséna (M), 58 rue Gioffredo (tel. 93–85–49–25), modern, very central. Has some (E) rooms. *Novotel* (M), tel. 93–31–61–15, 5 miles beyond airport, convenient if you are motorized; pool. *La Pérouse* (E), 11 quai Rauba Capeu (tel. 93–62–34–63), good for visiting the old town, the castle and harbor, is an old favorite. *Windsor* (M), 12 rue Dalpozzo (tel. 93–88–59–35), older, with pool.

Flots d'Azur (I), 101 promenade des Anglais (tel. 93–86–51–25), in a convert-ed villa. *Petit Palais* (I), 10 av. Bieckert (tel. 93–62–19–11). Central, with restau-rant. *Radio* (I), 6 rue Miron (tel. 93–62–10–65), central but quiet, friendly management.

Restaurants. Best is *Chantecler* (E) in Negresco hotel. Outstanding *nouvelle cuisine*. Also in the Negresco is the *Rotonde* (M), misleadingly called a "coffee shop", has good home-style cooking in magnificent art nouveau setting. *Ane Rouge* (E), 7 quai Deux-Emmanuel (tel. 93–89–49–63), an old favorite over-looking the harbor and appropriately serving excellent fish, cooked mostly in classical style. Classical cuisine too at another old favorite, *Poularde (Chez Lucullus)* (M), 9 rue Gustave-Deloye (tel. 93–85–22–90). *Barale* (M), 39 rue Beaumont (tel. 93–89–17–94). Very popular; genuine Niçois dishes. *Bistrot de la Promenade* (M), 7 promenade des Anglais (tel. 93–81–63–48), under new management and now one of Nice's best; modernized versions of regional dishes and good-value *menus.*

In the Old Town, charming and fashionable spots include: *Mérenda,* 4 rue de la Terrasse, no phone; *Safari* (M), 1 cours Saleya (tel. 93–80–18–44), popular with Nice's bright young things, has local specialties and is just by attractive flower market; *Madrague* (M), 13 cours Saleya (tel. 93–85–61–91), an old favorite for fish dishes.

A bit far out, but in a lovely setting overlooking the bay, *Coco Beach* (E), 2 av. J.-Lorrain (tel. 93–89–39–26), chic, for seafood.

RAMATUELLE. *Baou* (E), tel. 94–79–20–48, comfortable, modern but Pro-vençal decor, overlooking village.

ROQUEBRUNE-CAP MARTIN. *Vistaëro* (E), tel. 93–35–01–50, stunning view of coast, on Grande Corniche about 2 miles southwest. Attractively located *Alexandra* (M), tel. 93–35–65–45, and *Victoria* (M), 93–35–65–90, are less expensive, as is the *Westminster* (I), tel. 93–35–00–68.

Restaurants. *Roquebrune* (E); *Vistaëro* (E), in hotel; *Hippocampe* (M); *Luci-oles* (M), all with lovely view.

STE. MAXIME. *Résidence Brutus* (M), tel. 94–96–13–55. *Calidianus* (M), tel. 94–96–23–21, peaceful, with little Provençal-style bungalows and pool, no res-taurant. At **Plan-de-la-Tour**, about 7 miles up in the hills, is a charming, tiny, quiet hotel, *Ponte Romano* (E), tel. 94–43–70–56, good food. *Golf Hôtel* (E), tel. 94–96–06–09, at **Beauvallon**, 2½ miles west, is quiet, with many sporting facilities.

Restaurants. *Gruppi* (M), small, excellent. *La Réserve* (M), mostly regional cuisine. *Sans Souci* (M), close to harbor, good value.

ST.-JEAN-CAP-FERRAT. *Grand Hôtel du Cap Ferrat* (L), blvd. Général-de-Gaulle (tel. 93–01–04–54), isolated, exclusive, very good view, with pool and good restaurant. *Voile d'Or* (L), overlooking harbor, tel. 93–01–13–13. Chic. *Brise Marine* (M), av. Jean-Mermoz (tel. 93–01–30–73), in converted Provençal villa. *Clair Logis* (M), allée des Brises (tel. 93–01–31–01). No restaurant. *Panoramic* (M), av. Albert-ler (tel. 93–01–06–62).

Restaurants. *Hirondelles* (E), tel. 93–01–30–25. Overlooks port. *Voile d'Or* (E), in hotel, with magnificent view. *Petit Trianon* (M), tel. 93–01–31–68, highly recommended.

ST.-PAUL-DE-VENCE. Overlooking the village is the elegant *Mas d'Artigny* (L), tel. 93–32–84–54; bungalows each have mini-pool, superb views. *Colombe d'Or* (E), tel. 93–32–80–02, gorgeous setting, good food. *Orangers* (M), tel. 93–32–80–95, attractive, no restaurant.

Restaurants. *Aubergo dou Sóuleu* (M). One mile via D7 is *Oliviers* (E), good cuisine and nice garden.

ST.-RAPHAËL. *Beau Séjour* (M), tel. 94–95–03–75, sea views. At **Valescure** about 1 mile north, *Mapotel Golf* (E), tel. 94–52–01–57, quiet, view; near to 18-hole golf course. *Potinière* (M), tel. 94–95–21–43, 3 miles away at **Boulouris,** peaceful, close to sea, attractive restaurant and pool.

Restaurant. *Voile d'Or* (E), tel. 94–95–17–04, delicious food and lovely view.

ST. TROPEZ. *Byblos* (L), tel. 94–97–00–04, exotic with excellent restaurant, nightclub. *Mandarine* (L), tel. 94–97–21–00, modern, pool. *Ponche* (E), tel. 94–97–09–29, chic. *Residence de la Pinède* (E), tel. 94–97–04–21, on the beach. *Résidence des Lices* (E), tel. 94–97–28–28, with pool and quiet garden, is comfortable.

2½ miles west is the attractive *Mas de Chastelas* (E), tel. 94–56–09–11, pool, restaurant. At **Tahiti Beach,** *Figuière* (E), tel. 94–97–18–21, peaceful, with pool and tennis court.

Restaurants. *Leï Mouscardins* (E), tel. 94–97–01–53, seafood. *Chez Fuchs* (E), tel. 94–97–01–25. Long-established and still popular. *Escale* (M), on the port. *Rascasse* (M), tel. 94–97–04–47. Modest and good value with an (I) menu.

SANARY. *Grand Hôtel des Bains* (M), tel. 94–74–13–47, comfortable, good value. *Primavéra* (I), tel. 94–74–00–36, comfortable. *Tour* (I), tel. 94–74–10–10.

TOULON. *Frantel Tour Blanche* (E), blvd. Amiral-Vence (tel. 94–24–41–57), modern, peaceful, with pool. *Grand* (E), 4 pl. de la Liberté (tel. 94–22–59–50), with view over bay, no restaurant. *Résidence* (I), 18 rue Gimelli (tel. 94–92–92–81), small and central, no restaurant; convenient for harbor.

Restaurants. Best is *Lutrin* (E), 8 littoral Frédéric-Mistral (tel. 94–42–43–43), smart. Also good are *Dauphin* (M), 21 bis rue Jean-Jaurès (tel. 94–93–12–07), and *Madeleine* (M), 7 rue Tombades (tel. 94–92–67–85) with good value fixed-price meals.

TOURTOUR. *Bastide de Tourtour* (L), tel. 94–70–57–30, in pinewood, with pool. *Auberge St.-Pierre* (M), tel. 94–70–57–17, has pool, good restaurant.

Restaurant. *Chênes Verts* (E), tel. 94–70–55–06, a mile away, good *nouvelle cuisine.*

VENCE. *Château St.-Martin* (L), tel. 93–58–02–02, with pool shaded by olive trees, fine restaurant. *Floréal* (M), tel. 93–58–64–40. Well-run hotel on road to Grasse. No restaurant.

Restaurants. *Auberge des Templiers* (M), very popular. *Portiques* (M), delicious cuisine. *Farigoule* (I), excellent value.

VILLEFRANCHE-SUR-MER. *Versailles* (E), tel. 93–80–89–56, very comfortable. *Welcome* (E), tel. 93–55–27–27, at port. *Provençal* (M), tel. 93–80–71–42. *Flore* (I), tel. 93–56–80–29. Good views over harbor; pleasant restaurant.

Restaurants. *Campanette* (M), tel. 93–01–79–98, in picturesque street in Old Town. *Mère Germaine* (M), tel. 93–01–71–39, also on waterfront. *St.-Pierre* (M), tel. 93–55–27–27. Pleasant waterfront restaurant; attractive.

The French Alps

Along the southeastern border of France rises a mighty barrier of mountains that provides some of the most spectacular scenery in Europe—the French Alps, soaring to their climax in Europe's highest peak, Mont Blanc, stabbing 15,781 snowy feet into the air. Its chief divisions, north to south, are the Mont Blanc region; Savoie, lying along the Italian border; Dauphiné, of which Grenoble is the capital; the Hautes Alpes, centered about Briançon; and the Aples-de-Haute-Provence and Alps Maritimes, which slope down to the palms and bougainvillaea of the Côte d'Azur. The region is equally attractive in summer and winter. Chamonix, for example, oldest of French winter resorts, is a summer mountain climbing center for mountaineers who come to scale Mont Blanc.

In addition to scenery and resort centers, there are many other points of interest—the abbey of Hautecombe, the burial place of the princes of the House of Savoie, and remains of Roman baths at Aix-les-Bains; the castle of the dukes of Savoie at Chambéry, and nearby Les Charmettes, the country residence of philosopher Jean-Jacques Rousseau and his patron, Madame de Warens; the secluded monastery of the Grande Chartreuse, original home of the world-famed liqueur; the 17th-century château of Vizille, a residence of the president of the French Republic; the Lake of Laffrey, where Napoleon, returning from exile in Elba in 1814, was joined by the royal troops sent to arrest him; Grenoble, with its 16th-century law courts, outstanding art museum, and museum devoted to novelist Stendhal; the 13th–16th-century château of Menthon-St.-Bernard; the city of Briançon, with ramparts by Vauban and a statue of France by famed sculptor Antoine Bourdelle, and nearby Château-Queyras, with its medieval watertower and fortifications; the modern (1950) church at Assy, designed by Novarina and decorated with paintings and sculptures by Matisse, Léger, Bonnard, Rouault, Braque and others; the Romanesque cathedral at Embrun; picturesque villages, such as Pont-en-Royans, Queyras, Bourget, Colmars, Tout, Flumet and Conflans; the 13th–15th-century Château Bayard, near Pontcharra, birthplace of the Chevalier Bayard, the knight "without fear and without reproach"; the impressive cathedral of St.-Pierre at Moutiers, with its rich treasure of medieval ivories and enameled ware; the medieval watchtower of Crest, dominating the Drôme Valley; the curious and fortified little stronghold of Mont-Dauphin.

Rivaling the other Alpine wonders are such engineering achievements as the 287-mile Route Napoléon-Route des Alpes which transports the motorist from Cannes via Grenoble to St.-Julien, and the 416-mile Route des Grandes Alpes from Nice to Evian; the dam of La Girotte, built under the glacier; the 7½-mile-long Mont Blanc tunnel connecting France and Italy; the dam of Tignes, highest in Europe; the cablecar of l'Aiguille de Midi and of Serre-Chevalier, the longest in Europe (almost two miles).

PRACTICAL INFORMATION FOR THE ALPS

AIX-LES-BAINS. *Iles Britanniques* (E), tel. 79–61–03–77, by spa center, lovely gardens. *Bristol* (M), tel. 79–35–08–14, close to casino, with restaurant. *International Rivollier* (M), tel. 79–35–21–00, with classical cuisine restaurant. *Soleil Couchant* (M), tel. 79–35–05–83. At **Grand Port**, 2 miles north, *Lille* (E), tel. 79–35–04–22, by lake, has good restaurant, again with classical cuisine.

ANNECY. Charming *Trésoms et Fôret* (E), tel. 50–51–43–84, wonderful view, quiet, with restaurant. *Carlton* (M), tel. 50–45–47–75, near station. *Splendid* (M), tel. 50–45–20–00, opposite casino. *Crystal* (I), tel. 50–57–33–90, near station. None has restaurant. *Ibis* (I), rue de la Gare (tel. 50–54–43–21); modern, convenient for station, with adequate restaurant.

At **Albigny**, 1 mile east on D909 is *Faisan Doré* (M), tel. 50–23–02–46, with restaurant.

On road to Aix-les-Bains: *Mercure* (M), tel. 50–51–03–47; pool and views.

Restaurants. *Amandier* (M), tel. 50–51–74–50, pleasing mixture of local and southwestern cuisine. *Belvédère* (M), tel. 50–45–04–90, good *nouvelle cuisine*, also a small and modest hotel. *Salino* (M), tel. 50–23–07–90, elegant, just outside town at **Annecy-le-vieux**, with lovely views, good sound cuisine.

Pavillon Ermitage (M), tel. 50–60–11–09, at **Chavoires**, about 2 miles east via D509; food good, flower gardens running down to lake.

CHAMBÉRY. *Grand Hôtel Ducs de Savoie* (E), tel. 79–69–54–54, by station, with pleasant restaurant. *Novotel* (M), tel. 79–69–21–27, 1½ miles north.

Restaurants. *Roubatcheff* (E), tel. 79–33–24–91, offers classical dishes, while the cuisine is "new" style at the little *Vanoise* (M), tel. 79–69–02–78.

EVIAN. *Royal* (E), tel. 50–75–14–00, near funicular, traditional "grand hotel." *Verniaz* (E), tel. 50–75–04–90, at **Verniaz**, exclusive, isolated, excellent cuisine. A charming Relais and Châteaux hotel. *Prés Fleuris* (E), tel. 50–75–29–14, at nearby **St.-Paul**, with stunning views and grounds and an excellent restaurant. *Plage* (M), tel. 50–75–29–50, near beach. *Cygnes* (I), tel. 50–75–01–01, 1 mile west on lake, nice view.

Restaurants. *Bourgogne* (E), has a few rooms. *Chez Lapierre* (E), in casino. *La Verniaz* (E), see above.

GRENOBLE. *Mercure* (L), 1 av. d'Innsbruck (tel. 76–09–54–27), modern, comfortable, away from town center, near conference center. *Park* (E), 10 pl. Paul-Mistral (tel. 76–87–29–11), particularly pleasant atmosphere, well-furnished, close to city center and opposite park, with grill room (M).

Angleterre (M), 5 pl. Victor-Hugo (tel. 76–87–37–21), very central, no restaurant. *Gallia* (M), 7 blvd. Maréchal-Joffre (tel. 76–87–39–21), central, no restaurant. *Alpotel* (M), 12 blvd. Maréchal Joffre (tel. 76–87–88–41), very comfortable, central, with restaurant. *Novotel* (M), tel. 76–50–81–44, 7½ miles away via motorway to Lyon. *Terminus* (M), 10 pl. de la Gare (tel. 76–87–24–33), convenient for station, well-run, good value.

Alpes (I), 45 av. Félix-Viallet (tel. 76–87–00–71), modern, near station and river. *Paris-Nice* (I), 61 blvd. J.-Vallier (tel. 76–96–36–18), away from center but very reasonable for a big city.

Restaurants. *Auberge Bressane* (M), 38 ter. rue Beaublache (tel. 76–87–64–29), fine classical cuisine. *Poularde Bressane* (E), 12 pl. Paul-Mistral (tel. 76–87–08–90), for *nouvelle cuisine.A Ma Table* (M), 92 cours Jean-Jaurès (tel. 76–96–77–04), tiny and friendly, newish cuisine.

Outside town: *Escale* (E), 8 miles away at **Varces**, delicious *nouvelle cuisine*, plus a few rooms (M). *Chavant* (E), 4½ miles south at **Bresson**, friendly, classical dishes; lovely garden; also has a few attractive rooms (E).

TALLOIRES. **Hotel-restaurants.** *Abbaye* (L), tel. 50–67–40–88, with terrace and lake view, good classical dishes. *Cottage* (E), tel. 50–60–71–10, lovely views and good restaurant. Both these are beautifully quiet, as is the more modest *Beau Site* (M), tel. 50–60–71–04, with private beach.

Restaurant. *Auberge du Père-Bise* (L), tel. 50–60–72–01, very expensive, but one of the best restaurants in the country for classical cuisine, in a charming setting beside the Lac d'Annecy. Is also a very comfortable hotel.

Alsace and Lorraine

Nancy, capital of Lorraine, is one of the most charming cities in France, owing its harmonious beauty to Stanislas Leczinsky, the ex-king of Poland, father-in-law of Louis XV. The place Stanislas, with its wrought-iron gates and railings and its fountains, is one of the loveliest and most perfectly-proportioned squares in the world. The place de la Carrière, reached through Stanislas's Arc de Triomphe, is its close rival with its trees and elegant 18th-century houses.

A delightful detour along D164 between Contrexéville (a Vosges spa) and Void will take you through Joan of Arc country, almost unchanged since the Maid of Orléans was born here in Domrémy in 1411. You may visit her birthplace and the garden where she first heard the voices at the age of 13.

Strasbourg, capital of Alsace, with its carved, half-timbered houses, its little bridges and its glorious red stone cathedral is worth more than a casual stop. It is now the home of the European Parliament. Take a drive along the Wine Road at the foot of the Vosges Mountains. Its vineyards produce the delectable Alsatian wines.

Don't miss Ribeauville, with its ruined castles and storks nesting on the roofs, and stop at Riquewihr so that you can explore on foot the medieval walls, ancient houses and old courtyards of this tiny village in the center of vineyards. Not much farther south is Colmar, with its painted and carved houses and its "Venetian Quarter" crisscrossed by the Lauch River. One of the loveliest towns in Alsace, Colmar is famous for its Unterlinden Museum, with its priceless *Descent from the Cross* by Grünewald and its collection of paintings, sculpture and Alsatian earthenware.

PRACTICAL INFORMATION FOR ALSACE AND LORRAINE

AMMERSCHWIHR. *Aux Armes de France* (E), tel. 89–47–10–12, has only 8 rooms but is best known for its excellent restaurant with nouvelle and classical cuisine (E).

COLMAR. *Terminus-Bristol* (E), 7 pl. de la Gare (tel. 89–23–59–59), opposite station, has very good *nouvelle cuisine* restaurant (E). *Fecht* (M), 1 rue Fecht (tel. 89–41–34–98). Close to old town; pleasant terrace, restaurant and beer cellar. *Novotel* (M), at airport, tel. 89–41–94–14.

Restaurants. Best is *Schillinger* (E), 16 rue Stanislas (tel. 89–41–43–17), which now serves excellent *nouvelle cuisine; good-value menus. Nouvelle cuisine,* with good-value fixed-price *menus,* also at both *Au Fer Rouge* (M), 52 Grande-Rue (tel. 89–41–37–24), and *Rendez-vous de Chasse* (E), in Terminus Bristol Hotel. *Maison des Têtes* (M), 19 rue Têtes (tel. 89–24–43–43). 17th-century building; plenty of color.

ILLHAEUSERN. Restaurant. *Auberge de l'Ill* (E), tel. 89–71–83–23, one of France's greatest, beautifully sited on the banks of the river Ill. Good value.

METZ. *Frantel* (E), 29 pl. St.-Thiébault (tel. 87–37–17–69), modern, central, goodish restaurant. *Sofitel* (E), pl. des Paraiges (tel. 87–74–57–27), modern, comfortable, central, pool, good restaurant (M) (*nouvelle cuisine*). Older, attractive *Royal-Concorde* (M), 23 av. Foch (tel. 87–66–81–11), convenient for station, with restaurant.

Cécil (I), 14 rue Pasteur (tel. 87–66–66–13), near station, no restaurant. *Foch* (I), 8 av. Foch (tel. 87–75–56–42), modest, pleasant, no restaurant.

Restaurants. Apart from *Rabelais* (M), in Sofitel hotel, try *Dinanderie* (M), 2 rue de Paris (tel. 87–30–14–40), inventive "new" dishes. *Ville de Lyon* (M), 7 rue Piques (tel. 87–36–07–01), good value, but closed Aug.

MULHOUSE. Modern *Frantel* (M), 4 pl. Charles-de-Gaule (tel. 89–46–01–23), near station, good restaurant. *Sofitel* (E), northeast of town at Sausheim, on N422A road (tel. 89–44–75–75), modern, with pool and restaurant. *Novotel* (M), also at Sausheim, rue de l'Ile Napoléon (tel. 89–44 –44 –44).

Bourse (M), 14 rue de la Bourse (tel. 89–56–18–44), central, no restaurant. *Bristol* (M), 18 av. de Colmar (tel. 89–42–12–31), has some (I) rooms, no restaurant.

Restaurants. *Alsace* (M), in Frantel hotel, good newish cuisine. *Guillaume Tell* (M), 1 rue Guillaume-Tell (tel. 89–45–21–58), attractive half-timbered building, Alsatian specialties.

Relais de la Tour (M), 3 blvd. de l'Europe (tel. 89–45–12–14), rotates on 31st floor of huge tower, reasonably good food, magnificent panoramic view. *Wir* (M), 1 porte de Bâle (tel. 89–56–13–22), good, mixture of classical and more modern cuisine.

At **Steinbrunn-le-Bas**, 5 miles away, is the excellent *Moulin de Kaegy* (M), tel. 89–81–30–34, with "new" cuisine in 16th-century building. Good-value menus.

NANCY. *Frantel* (E), 11 rue Raymond-Poincaré (tel. 83–35–61–01), with good *nouvelle cuisine* restaurant (M). *Grand Hôtel Concorde* (E), 2 pl. Stanislas (tel. 83–35–03–01), lovely building in beautiful setting, very comfortable. *Astoria* (M), 3 rue de l'Armée-Patton (tel. 83–40–31–24), quiet yet near station. No restaurant. *Europe* (M), 5 rue Carmes (tel. 83–35–32–10). Convenient for sightseeing; no restaurant.

Restaurants. *Capucin Gourmand* (E), 31 rue Gambetta (tel. 83–35–26–98), excellent *nouvelle cuisine*. *Gastrolâtre* (M), 39 rue des Maréchaux (tel. 83–35–07–97), also for *nouvelle cuisine Gentilhommière* (M), 29 rue des Maréchaux (tel. 83–32–26–44), elegant, classical cuisine served in the house where Victor Hugo's father was born.

RIQUEWIHR. *Riquewihr* (M), tel. 89–47–83–13, attractive modern hotel on outskirts, overlooking vineyards; quiet, no restaurant.

Restaurant. *Auberge du Schoenenbourg* (M), tel. 89–47–92–28, a friendly inn with some interesting dishes.

STRASBOURG. *Hilton* (E), av. Herrenschmidt (tel. 88–37–10–10), comfortable and central. Good restaurant. *Holiday Inn* (E), 20 pl. de Bordeaux (tel. 88–35–70–00), close to conference center, modern, comfortable. *Sofitel* (E), pl. St.-Pierre-le-Jeune (tel. 88–32–99–30), very central and comfortable, goodish restaurant. *Bristol* (M), 4 pl. de la Gare (tel. 88–32–00–83), near station, excellent restaurant (M). *France* (M), 20 rue du Jeu-des-Enfants (tel. 88–32–37–12), nice views over old town, no restaurant. *Monopole-Métropole* (M), 16 rue Kuhn (tel. 88–32–11–94), close to station, reasonably priced for the high level of comfort, no restaurant.

Gutenberg (I), 31 rue des Serruriers (tel. 88–32–17–15), period furniture (18th-century), no restaurant. *Saint-Christophe* (I), 2 pl. de la Gare (tel. 88–22–30–30), covenient for station and town center; quiet, pleasant atmosphere; no restaurant.

Restaurants. *Buerehiesel* (E), 4 parc de l'Orangerie (tel. 88–61–62–24), delightful atmosphere, subtle "new" dishes. *Crocodile* (E), 10 rue de l'Outre (tel. 88–32–13–02), best in town, mixture of classical, regional and *nouvelle* cuisine, excellent service. *Kammerzell* (E), 16 pl. de la Cathédrale (tel. 88–32–42–14), generous helpings of classical and *nouvelle cuisine* served in picturesque old house beside cathedral.

Maison des Tanneurs (M), 42 rue du Bain aux Plantes (tel. 88–32–79–70), in another picturesque old building, classical cuisine. *Zimmer-Sengel* (M), 8 rue du Temple-Neuf (tel. 88–32–35–01), interesting "new" cuisine.

Strissel (I), 5 pl. de la Grande-Boucherie (tel. 88–32–14–73), picturesque *winstub* with typically Alsatian dishes.

At **Marlenheim**, 12½ miles north, *Cerf* (M), 30 rue Général-de-Gaulle (tel. (tel. 88–87–73–73). Good for local dishes and seafood; also has some rooms (I).

Languedoc and Roussillon

This sun-soaked region of southern France stretches from the Camargue westwards to the Spanish border beyond Perpignan, with attractive inland areas varying from the eastern Pyrenees—with several good ski resorts—to the wild uplands of the Cévennes. One of its main attractions is its blend of ancient and modern: its wealth of Romanesque churches and Cathar castles, ever-present reminders of its rich historical past, contrast strangely with the futuristic new seaside resorts that have transformed the coast into a lively holiday playground.

The new resorts are well equipped for every leisure activity and range from surrealist La Grande-Motte, with colorful apartment blocks in a variety of shapes and sizes, to pleasant little Gruissan, which manages to combine a small yacht marina with a picturesque fishing village mirrored in a sleepy saltwater lagoon. Cap d'Agde, famous for its nudist center, has pastel-washed houses and a cleverly maintained fishing village atmosphere. Further down the coast towards Spain are the twin resorts of Port Leucate (with another nudish colony) and Port Barcarès, plus St-Cyprien, with a country club and golf course.

Travel inland and you come to sleppy, timeless villages with acres of vines and fruit trees, and beyond them, the rugged Cévennes Mountains. Close to the coast is elegant Montpellier, the capital of the region, with good museums, pleasant parks and gardens and a lively atmosphere thanks to its importance as a university center. A very different town is majestic Carcassonne, the largest medieval fortress in Europe and a breathtaking sight with its impressive ring of towers and battlements. Narbonne, once a bustling Roman city and one of the Western Mediteranean's major ports, is now a charming and peaceful little inland town with a fine cathedral and museums. And near the Spanish border you'll enjoy visiting lively Perpignan, the capital of Roussillon, once the capital of the kingdom of Majorca and still with a distinctly Spanish feel about it.

PRACTICAL INFORMATION FOR LANGUEDOC AND ROUSSILLON

CAP D'AGDE. Pleasant *St.-Clair* (E), tel. 67–26–36–44, with pool is good value. *Matago* (M), tel. 67–26–00–05. Pool and restaurant; some rooms have kitchenettes.

Restaurants. *Brasero* (M), tel. 67–26–24–75, good for fish dishes. At nearby Agde, excellent *Tamarissière* (E), serving *nouvelle cuisine,* also has rooms (M).

CARCASSONNE. *Cité* (E), tel. 68–25–03–34, very comfortable, is inside the walled towns and therefore quiet. So is friendly *Donjon* (M), tel. 68–71–08–80. No restaurant. *Aragon* (M), tel. 68–47–16–31, pleasant, no restaurant.

In the Ville Basse, *Logis de Trencavel* (M), tel. 68–71–09–53, has good (M) restaurant. Attractive *Montségur* (M), tel. 68–25–31–41, is delightfully furnished.

Restaurants. *Auberge du Pont-Levis* (M), just outside the walls, has good-value grills downstairs, regional dishes upstairs. *Languedoc* (M), tel. 68–25–22–17. In hotel Montségur; family-run place with excellent regional dishes. *Crémade* (I), is conveniently close to St-Nazaire basilica.

COLLIOURE. *Frégate* (M), tel. 68–82–06–05, with good restaurant. *Hostellerie des Templiers* (M), tel. 68–82–05–58, crammed with paintings, geraniums and atmosphere, plus good fish in the restaurant. *Madeloc* (M), tel. 68–82–07–56, and *Villa Basque* (M), tel. 68–82–04–82, are comfortable, but don't have restaurants.

Restaurants. *Balette* (M), with lovely terrace perched high above the harbor on the road to Port-Vendres. *Bodéga* (M), lots of local color and good regional cuisine. *Frégate* (M) (in hotel) for good regional dishes and good-value *menus*. *Puits* (I) is in small street behind the pretty harbor.

LA GRANDE MOTTE. *Frantel* (E), tel. 67–56–90–81, one of the resort's surrealist buildings, is very comfortable and has good restaurant, but is low on atmosphere. *Méditerranée* (M), tel. 67–56–53–38, quiet. Has pool but no restaurant, and the same applies to *Europe* (M), tel. 67–56–62–60, near harbor.

Restaurants. *Amirauté* (E), excellent fish dishes cooked in *nouvelle cuisine* style; elegant decor. *Estrambord* (M), good value, mostly fish. *Ponant* (M), in Frantel hotel.

GRUISSAN. *Corail* (I), tel. 68–49–04–06, beside harbor; friendly, with restaurant.
Restaurant. *Chébek* (M), by new marina, good for fish dishes.

MONTPELLIER. *Demeure des Brousses* (E), route de Vauguières (tel. 67–65–77–66), 1½ miles from center, delightful 18th-century buildings set in huge grounds, with good restaurant next door called *Le Mas* (E), tel. 67–65–52–27. *Métropole* (E), 3 rue Clos-René (tel. 67–58–11–22), also very comfortable, but the prices are lower and furnishings delightful; good restaurant, with garden. *Sofitel* (E), allée Jules-Milhaud (tel. 67–54–04–04), modern, very comfortable, with good restaurant. *Parc* (I), 8 rue A-Bégé (tel. 67–41–16–49), a bit out of the way, quiet; no restaurant. *Arceaux* (I), 33 blvd. les Arceaux (tel. 67–92–61–76), close to Peyrou Gardens, no restaurant.
Restaurants. *Réserve Rimbaud* (E), 820 av. de St-Maur (tel. 67–72–52–53), both "new" and classical fare, perfect for a summer lunch out of doors. *Chandelier* (M), 3 rue Leenhart (tel. 67–92–61–62), chic, good for *nouvelle cuisine*. *Isadora* (M), 6 rue du Petit-Scel (tel. 67–66–25–23), delightful setting in 12th-century cellar in Old Town, yet with twenties décor; mostly fish. *Olivier* (M), 12 rue Aristide Olivier (tel. 67–92–86–28), nice atmosphere, convenient for station. *Nice* (I), 14 rue Bousairolles (tel. 67–58–42–54), an old favorite. Also has rooms.

NARBONNE. *Languedoc* (M), 22 blvd. Gambetta (tel. 68–65–14–74), with good value restaurant. *Résidence* (M), 6 rue du 1er-Mai (tel. 68–32–19–41), attractive, central, no restaurant. *Régent* (I), 15 rue Suffren (tel. 68–32–02–41), a bit away from center but pleasantly quiet; no restaurant.
A couple of miles away, on the road to Perpignan, *Novotel* (M), tel. 68–41–59–52, with pool, quiet.
At **Narbonne-Plage**, 9½ miles away by the sea, *Caravelle* (I), tel. 68–49–80–38, friendly, with restaurant.

PERPIGNAN. *Loge* (M), pl. de la Loge (tel. 68–35–54–84), central, comfortable, no restaurant. *Park* (M), 18 blvd. Jean-Bourrat (tel. 68–35–14–14), pleasant setting opposite park, good restaurant. *Christina* (I), 50 cours Lassus (tel. 68–35–24–61), small, friendly. *Pyrénées* (I), 122 av. L.-Torcatis (tel. 68–61–19–66), by river, a bit away from center.
Restaurants. *Festin de Pierre* (E), 7 rue du Théâtre (tel. 68–51–28–74), reader-recommended for excellent food and service; must reserve. *Apéro* (M), 40 rue de la Fusterie (tel. 68–51–21–14), good value, attractive decor, *nouvelle cuisine*. *François Villon* (M), 1 rue du Four-St-Jean (tel. 68–51–18–43), regional dishes served in converted monastery. *Relais St-Jean* (I), 1 cité Bartissol (tel. 68–51–22–25), just by cathedral.

PORT-BARCARÈS. *PLM Lydia Playa* (M), tel. 68–86–25–25, comfortable, pool, tennis courts. *Front-de-Mer* (I), tel. 68–86–13–84, central.

SAINT-CYPRIEN. *Mas d'Huston* (E), tel. 68–21–01–71, comfortable atmosphere, by golf-course. *Glycines* (M), tel. 68–21–00–11, pleasant restaurant.

SÈTE. *Grand* (M), tel. 67–74–71–77, more central, with good traditional restaurant. *Mapotel Impérial* (M), tel. 67–53–28–32, just outside town, lovely views, no restaurant.
Restaurants beside the harbor—*Chalut* (M), *Palangrotte* (M), *Rascasse* (I), all specializing in beautifully fresh seafood.

The Southwest

Beyond Carcassone stretch the Pyrenees, rugged mountains of great natural beauty forming the frontier with Spain. Skiing is good here in winter, with pleasant family-type resorts not attempting to compete with the glamor of the Alpine centers.

Busy Toulouse, on the northern edge, still has many attractive and elegant buildings in spite of its recent mushroom growth of industries and housing estates. Lourdes is naturally a major center of religious pilgrimages, and has been since the 14-year-old Bernadette Soubirous saw her first vision of the Virgin Mary. Sophisticated Pau is a good center for excursions into the Pyrenees.

On the western edge of the Pyrenees lies the Basque country, where in spite of recent political troubles many colorful customs and costumes survive. The Atlantic coast has resorts to suit all tastes and pocketbooks, ranging from elegant Biarritz and picturesque St-Jean-de-Luz to tiny family resorts further north offering long sandy beaches and water sports galore. Further north still is flourishing Bordeaux, center of the wine trade since the time of the Romans. Excursions into the surrounding vineyards, punctuated by wine tastings, are easily arranged.

Inland from Bordeaux lie the old rural provinces and regions of the Limousin and the Périgord, the Rouergue and Quercy, and the beautiful river valleys of the Dordogne and the Lot. All these are ideal territory for those who love picturesque villages, Romanesque churches and lonely castles perched high on sheer cliffs, prehistoric remains and a peaceful way of life away from the stresses and strains of urban living. Don't expect to find four-star hotels here, but you will find country inns, family hotels, and excellent restaurants specializing in regional dishes.

PRACTICAL INFORMATION FOR THE SOUTHWEST

BIARRITZ. *Palais* (L), 1 av. de l'Impératrice (tel. 59–24–09–40), supremely elegant and comfortable; pool and good restaurant (E). *Plaza* (E), tel. 59–24–74–00, near beach, well run. *Eurotel* (E), tel. 59–24–32–33, recent, comfortable; some rooms have self-catering facilities. *Mirador* (M), tel. 59–24–13–81, with good restaurant. *Edouard-VII* (I), tel. 59–24–07–20, small, with restaurant.

BORDEAUX. *Frantel* (E), 5 rue Lateulade (tel. 56–90–92–37), central, modern, well run, good *nouvelle cuisine* restaurant. *Grand Hotel de Bordeaux* (E), pl. de la Comédie, tel. 56–90–93–44, comfortable and well-modernized, but small rooms in this long-established hotel in the heart of Bordeaux; rooms overlooking street are noisy. No restaurant, but cafe-bar serves light meals.

At Exhibit Center:*Aquitania* (E), tel. 56–50–83–80; *Sofitel* (E), tel. 56–50–90–14; *Novotel* (M), tel. 56–50–99–70; all modern, with pools and restaurants. *Arcade* (M), 60 rue P. Le-Roy (tel. 56–90–92–40), opposite main station, with restaurant. *Etche Ona* (I), 11 rue Mautrec (tel. 56–44–36–49), small and central, with restaurant.

Restaurants. *Chez Philippe* (E), 1 pl. du Parlement (tel. 56–81–83–15), very good fish. *Christian Clément* (E), 58 rue du Pas-St.-Georges (tel. 56–81–01–39), excellent *nouvelle cuisine,* good-value *menu.* *Clavel* (E), 44 rue Charles-Domercq (tel. 56–92–91–52), excellent *nouvelle cuisine.* *Dubern* (E), 42 allées de Tourny (tel. 56–48–03–44), classical cuisine. *Ramet* (E), 7 pl. Jean-Jaurès (tel. 56–44–12–51), tiny, with inventive new-style cuisine. *Bistrot de Clavel* (M), less expensive annex of Clavel (see above). *Tulpina* (M), 6 rue Porte de la Monnaie (tel. 56–91–56–37), regional fare, charming atmosphere; take-out next door. *Ombrière* (I), pl. du Parlement, tel. 56–44–82–69, rather chic clientele; pleasant if unexciting cuisine, good for outdoor meals in attractive square in old town.

CAHORS. *France* (M), tel. 65–35–16–76, central, comfortable, no restaurant.

Restaurant. *Taverne* (M), tel. 65–35–28–66, excellent, good value, for regional dishes.

LIMOGES. Best is *Frantel* (E), tel. 55–34–65–30, central, every modern comfort, plus good *nouvelle cuisine* restaurant. *Jeanne d'Arc* (M), tel. 55–77–67–77, convenient for station, no restaurant.

Restaurants. *Petits Ventres* (M), tel. 55–33–34–02, attractive 15th-century building, regional dishes, good value *menu.* *Versailles* (M), tel. 55–34–13–39, good value.

LOURDES. *Gallia et Londres* (E), tel. 62–94–10–20, very comfortable, pleasant gardens. *Christina* (M), tel. 62–94–26–11, nice views. *Mapotel de la Grotte* (E), tel. 62–94–58–87, very close to Grotto. *Aquitaine* (I), tel. 62–94–20–31, close to Grotto, with restaurant.

PAU. *Continental* (M), tel. 59–27–69–31, central, good restaurant. *Ronceveaux* (M), tel. 59–27–08–44, small and friendly, restaurant.

Restaurants. *Pierre* (E), tel. 59–27–76–86, excellent regional dishes. *Patrick Jourdan* (M), tel. 59–27–68–70, for elaborate versions of local recipes. Good (E) *menu.*

PÉRIGUEUX. *Domino* (M), tel. 53–08–25–80, central, with restaurant. *Régina* (I), tel. 53–08–40–44, convenient for station, no restaurant. 4 miles south at **Antonne,** *Ecluse* (M), tel. 53–06–00–04, a peaceful inn.

Restaurants. *Flambée* (M), tel. 53–53–23–06, well-known for its excellent *foie gras. Léon* (M), tel. 53–53–41–93, good *nouvelle cuisine. Oison* (M), tel. 53–09–84–02, popular with the upper crust of Périgueux; mostly *nouvelle cuisine. Marcel* (I), tel. 53–53–13–43, good value.

SARLAT. *Madeleine* (M), tel. 53–59–12–40, attractive, good regional cuisine in restaurant. *St.-Albert et Salamandre* (I), tel. 53–59–01–09, also has good restaurant.

Just outside town, a couple of attractive little hotels that are very typical of the Dordogne: *Hoirie* (M), tel. 53–59–05–62, to the south, very peaceful, no restaurant; and *Hostellerie de Meysset* (M), tel. 53–59–08–29, to the northwest at **Argentouleau,** also very peaceful, but this one has a good restaurant.

TOULOUSE. *Frantel-Wilson* (E), 7 rue Labéda (tel. 61–21–21–75), central, very comfortable, no restaurant. *Grand Hôtel de l'Opéra* (E), pl. du Capitole, tel. 61–21–82–66, delightful spot in which to treat yourself—prices are high; right in center of Toulouse, elegant, quiet rooms, attractive courtyard-garden, pool, excellent restaurant. *Caravelle* (M), 62 rue Raymond-IV (tel. 61–62–70–65), close to main station, modern, no restaurant. *Concorde* (M), 16 blvd. Bonrepos (tel. 61–62–48–60), convenient for main station, low prices for degree of comfort; pool. *Ours Blanc* (I), 2 rue Victor-Hugo (tel. 61–21–62–40), very central.

Sofitel (E), tel. 61–71–11–25, is at airport, and *Novotel* (M), tel. 61–49–34–10, is close by. Both have pool.

Restaurants. *Darroze* (E), 19 rue Castellane, tel. 61–62–34–70, deliciously inventive versions of regional dishes, good-value *menus. Frégate* (E), 1 rue d'Austerlitz (tel. 61–21–59–61), Languedoc dishes. *Séville* (M), 45 rue des Tourneurs (tel. 61–21–37–97), now has inventive, newish cuisine. *Bistrot Van-Gogh* (M), 21 pl. Saint-Georges, no telephone reservations; light, interesting cuisine, lively atmosphere. Several other good spots in this square in central Toulouse. *Vanel* (M), 22 rue Maurice Fontvieille (tel. 61–21–51–82), superb regional dishes cooked in *nouvelle cuisine* style.

Cassoulet (I), 40 rue Peyrolières (tel. 61–21–18–99), serves local specialties.

Corsica

The Mediterranean island of Corsica has been a *département* of metropolitan France for over two centuries. The Corsicans, a handsome, olive-skinned, hot-blooded people, have been famous throughout a long history for brigandage, vendettas, and taking to the brush or *maquis* as outlaws whenever the laws of the land displeased them.

In the capital, Ajaccio, you can visit Napoleon's birthplace and the Napoleonic room in the Hôtel de Ville. Corte, high in the center of the island, is the ancient capital and lies on the main road between Ajaccio and Bastia, the second largest port and town. Sartène is ancient, perched in the mountains on the Ajaccio-Bonifacio road, and should be explored. Bonifacio, on the extreme southern tip of the island, is a fascinating medieval fortress town. The beaches of Corsica vary from long wide bays to tiny crescents, but most have fine sand. Ajaccio has both varieties; Ile Rousse, Calvi, Cargèse, Sagone, Propriano and Porto Vecchio have excellent beaches, while the smaller coves are at Porto, Saint-Florent and around Cap Corse.

PRACTICAL INFORMATION FOR CORSICA

AJACCIO. *Etrangers* (M), 2 rue Rossi (tel. 95–21–01–26). Try for a room in the delightful villa annex. *Albion* (M), 15 av. Général-Leclerc (tel. 95–21–66–70), central, close to beach, comfortable, no restaurant. *Fesch* (M), 7 rue Fesch (tel. 95–21–50–52) in old town (some rooms are noisy), is airconditioned, with regional decor, no restaurant. Recent *San Carlu* (M), blvd. Casanova (tel. 95–21–13–84).

At **Ajaccio-Sanguinaires** and by beach: modern *Dolce Vita* (E), tel. 95–52–00–93; *Cala di Sole* (M), tel. 95–21–39–14; and *Eden Roc* (M), tel. 95–52–01–47. All with outdoor pools and sea views.

At airport: *Campo dell'Oro* (E), tel. 95–22–32–41.

Restaurants. *Palmiers* (M), 3 pl. Foch (tel. 95–21–02–45), by harbor. *U Scalone* (M), 2 rue du Rio-de-Rome (tel. 95–21–50–05), cheerful spot in a converted cellar, serving dishes typical of the Lyon region on the mainland. *Pardi* (I), 60 rue Fesch (tel. 95–21–43–08), with good local specialties. *St.-Hubert* (I), rue Colonel-Colonna-d'Ornano (tel. 95–23–23–78), good range of fixed-price meals; pleasant atmosphere, airconditioned.

BASTIA. *Bonaparte* (M), tel. 95–34–07–10, modern.

Some people prefer to stay a little way out. *Ostella* (M), 2½ miles south on Ajaccio road (tel. 95–33–51–05). Modern. At **Pietranera,** 2 miles north of Bastia, *Alivi* (M), tel. 95–31–61–85. *Pietracap* (M), tel. 95–31–64–63, pool, no restaurant.

Sablettes (M), tel. 95–33–26–13, at **Miomo,** 3½ miles north, small, well situated and with good cuisine. Has motel annex.

Restaurants. Make for the excellent *Chez Assunta* (M), if you want to try some genuine Corsican dishes. *Taverne* (M), good value for local specialties.

BONIFACIO. *Solemare* (E), tel. 95–73–01–06, own pool. Both near harbor. *Etrangers* (I), tel. 95–73–01–09, is in town.

CALVI. *Grand* (E), tel. 95–65–09–74, no restaurant. *Résidence des Aloës* (I), tel. 95–65–01–46. Modern, slightly away from center, nice views. *Kalliste* (M), tel. 95–65–09–81, quiet.

Restaurants. *Ile de Beauté* (E), quai Landry (tel. 95–65–00–46), well sited overlooking harbor, rather chic. Serves excellent fish and good regional wines. *U'Spuntino* (M), tel. 95–65–07–06, lovely country setting on road to Bonifacio. Genuine regional dishes, must reserve.

PORTO. *Flots Bleus* (M), tel. 95–26–11–26, overlooking sea, modern and comfortable. *Bella Vista* (I), tel. 95–26–11–08. Lovely views; no restaurant. *Capo d'Orto* (I), tel. 95–26–11–14. Sea-views, and good-value restaurant.

At **Piana,** 7½ miles southwest, *Capo Rosso* (M), tel. 95–26–12–35. Glorious setting with sea vistas; restaurant specializing in fish.

Restaurant. *Soleil Couchant* (I), tel. 95–26–10–12, overlooking sea, a few rooms.

EAST GERMANY (G.D.R.)

The festivities in 1987 marking Berlin's 750 years may be sufficient inducement to draw many tourists to the German Democratic Republic (G.D.R., or East Germany) this year. Equipped with visas, marks and curiosity about this interesting but relatively unknown country, many will venture beyond East Berlin and find the effort well worth while. The country is scenically and culturally rich, and slowly such landmarks as the Berlin cathedral and the old Leipzig market are being put back into shape. The art galleries and museums hold world treasures; the theaters, opera houses, and concert halls match or surpass their equivalents in the West. Indeed, the country's Communist government has purposefully set out to create a favorable image, a feature alas more evident for the tourist in the monumental buildings and restorations than in the willingness of the people to welcome strangers of any sort. But after all, these are the descendants of the Prussians, such leaders as Frederick the Great and Bismarck having set the tone for whole empires. The East Germans today are a generally dour folk, particularly in urban areas. The leadership has committed the country to the destiny of the Soviet Union for decades to come. At the same time, East Germany's schizophrenic relationship with West Germany continues to have a leavening influence. The effort to achieve economic independence has placed East Germany firmly among the world's leading industrialized nations. There are surprisingly few products that this small country of only 16 million does not turn out.

But such progress has its price, and the visitor will experience this in the form of red tape and formalities from the moment he or she requests a visa application form. Nevertheless, there are compensations to a visit to the GDR, and officials are genuinely trying to upgrade the country's touristic appeal as well as its facilities.

PRACTICAL INFORMATION FOR EAST GERMANY

$P£ **WHAT WILL IT COST.** East Germany, particularly in comparison to Western countries, is definitely in the budget bracket. However, you will find that you will probably be obliged to remain either in the major cities or more important tourist centers, which tend to be more expensive than other, less frequented spots. Bear in mind that visitors must change convertible currency equivalent to M 25 per person per day. Children between 6 and 15 must change currency equivalent to M 7.50 per day. These minimum amounts are not reconvertible and must be spent in East Germany. You may bring into East Germany as much foreign currency as you want, but it must be declared on arrival. Failure to do so will mean that none of it may be re-exported. No East Germany currency can be either imported or exported.

The monetary unit of East Germany is the Mark (M), which is divided into 100 pfennigs. There are banknotes of 100, 50, 20, 10 and 5 marks and coins of 20, 10, 5, 2 and 1 mark and 50, 20, 10 and 1 pfennig. The exchange rate for the East German mark is the same as that for the West German deutschemark; at the time of writing, M 2.45 to the U.S. dollar and M 3.53 to the pound sterling. These rates will certainly change throughout 1987.

A typical day might cost two people:

	Marks
Hotel (moderate) double room with bath and breakfast	70
Lunch at restaurant (moderate)	25
Transportation (taxi)	2.20
Coffees and pastries in café	8.80
Liter beer	7
Museum	2
Theater (moderate seats)	25
Dinner at restaurant (moderate)	35
Miscellaneous 10%	14
	M189

 HOW TO GO. Despite the fact that visa requirements for the GDR have been very much simplified, it is nonetheless highly advisable to book trips through a travel agent authorized by the *Reisebüro der DDR*, the official East German travel authorities. A considerable number of package tours are available, many of them inexpensive and all of them reducing the amount of red tape otherwise so frequently experienced in East Germany.

Among the authorized agents are: *Koch*, 206 East 86th St., New York, NY 10028 (tel. 212–535–8600); *Maupintours*, 1515 St. Andrews Dr., Lawrence, KS 66046 (tel. 800–255–4266); *Security Travel*, 1631 Washington Plaza, Reston, VA 22090 (tel. 703–471–1900); *Travelworld*, 6922 Hollywood Blvd., Los Angeles, CA (tel. 213–461–7715).

In the U.K., *Berolina Travel Ltd.*, 20 Conduit Street, London W.1 (tel. 629–1664), the representative in Britain for the Reisebüro der DDR, will make reservations. Lists of British agents dealing with East Germany can be obtained there.

However, if you decide to travel independently to East Germany, the procedure is as follows. You must still go to one of the officially-approved travel agencies, who will forward your request for a visa, together with a request for hotel vouchers (which you must buy before entering East Germany) to the Reisebüro der DDR. This process takes 6 to 8 weeks and there is a fee of $25 ($30 for "express handling"). The GDR consulates in the U.K. and U.S. will not assist with visas or travel information; you will find that the consulate in the U.S. (1717 Massachusetts Ave. N.W., Washington, D.C. 20036) will simply refer you to a travel agent in your area, and the U.K. embassy (34 Belgrave Sq., London, S.W.1) will head you directly toward Berolina Travel.

If you wish to visit East Berlin from West Berlin, daily pass cards (good for a 24 hour visit, but which can be extended to cover a stay of up to one week once in the GDR) are available at border points, as are transit visas for stays of up to 72 hours. In both cases, accommodations must be booked and paid for.

WHEN TO COME. The main tourist season runs from late April to early October when of course the weather is best and most events of tourist interest occur. The advantages of off-season travel are outweighed by the fact that prices are low even in high season, and the winter weather is grim.

Climate. Normally settled in the summer; extremely cold in the winter.

Average afternoon daily temperatures in degrees Fahrenheit and centigrade:

Berlin	Jan.	Feb.	Mar.	Apr.	May	June	July	Aug.	Sept.	Oct.	Nov.	Dec.
F°	35	38	46	55	65	70	74	72	66	55	43	37
C°	2	3	8	13	18	21	23	22	19	13	6	3

SPECIAL EVENTS. The *Leipzig Trade Fair* is held in the first week of Mar. *and* Sept. All accommodations during this period are preempted for business visitors. Weimar holds a *Shakespeare Festival* in Apr.; in July the Hanseatic cities of Rostock and Stralsund stage a week of festivities, the *Ostseewoche;* Sept./Oct. sees the *Berlin Music and Drama Festival.* These months are liable to be altered occasionally and dates must be checked when booking.

National Holidays. Jan. 1 (New Year's Day); Apr. 17 (Good Fri.); May 1 (Labor Day); June 8 (Whit Mon.); Oct. 7 (Republic); Dec. 25, 26.

HEALTH CERTIFICATES. Not required for entry into the German Democratic Republic from any country.

GETTING TO EAST GERMANY. By Plane. *Pan American* and *British Airways* fly into West Berlin's airport, from which you can cross into East Berlin. Direct flights to East Berlin's Schönefeld Airport via *Interflug,* GDR airline, from Amsterdam, Brussels, Copenhagen, Stockholm, Rome, and Vienna; *KLM* also flies to Schönefeld from Amsterdam, and *Austrian Airlines* direct from Vienna. The airport is about 15 miles from Berlin center, 40 mins. by bus, 30 mins. by the *S-Bahn* city train. A shuttle bus links the terminal with the rail station. For transit travelers, a coach service runs twice hourly, at 15 and 45 mins. past the hour, from Schönefeld to the Radio Tower Central Bus Station in West Berlin and to West Berlin's Tempelhof S-Bahn station and back. Fare: DM 7.00.

By Train. There are through-coaches to East Berlin from Paris, Oostende, Hook of Holland, Basel, and from all large West German cities. Trains are frequent, fast, and comfortable. Western rail frontier points are at Herrnburg, Schwanheide, Oebisfelde, Marienborn, Gerstungen, Probstzella, Gutenfuerst, West Berlin, and at Sassnitz (from Trelleborg, Sweden) and Warnemünde (from Gedser, Denmark). There are several road and rail crossing-points from Poland and Czechoslovakia. At all of these, entry and transit visas can be obtained. Alternatively, you may be given a pass and instructed to collect your visa at your first destination point. The Reisebüro will fix this for you.

By Car. Other than the points of entry from West Berlin into East Germany, there are currently ten highway borders (West German highway numbers/West German town/East German town): B104/Lübeck-Schlutup/Selmsdorf; A24/ Gudow/Zarrentin; B5/Lauenburg/Horst; B71/Bergen (Dumme)/Salzwedel; A2/Helmstedt/Marienborn; B247/Duderstadt/Worbis; Herleshausen/Wartha; B19/Eussenhausen/Meiningen; B4/Rottenbach/Eisfeld; A9/Rudolphstein/Hirschberg. Your travel agent or automobile club will be able to give you up-to-the-minute details on crossing points and other tips on road travel in the G.D.R. Highways are well marked, but a detailed road map will be useful if you plan to wander off of the main routes. Tolls are collected in the form of a road use tax (see *Getting Around East Germany* below). Green cards are required as evidence of insurance coverage.

CUSTOMS. Customs officials are very meticulous. You may import into East Germany any amount of tobacco, spirits or wine. Spare parts for cars may be imported only with permission. You may import gifts to the value of M 200 duty free per person for visits of up to 5 days. If you plan to visit for more than 5 days, you may bring gifts to the value of M 100 duty free for each day of your stay. Note that the value of goods is based on their sales price in the GDR, not necessariy what you paid for them. Note also that some books, all Western newspapers, tape and video cassettes, and medicines beyond those for immediate personal use are not allowed to be brought in. When you leave the country, duties may be charged on goods you take out, beyond the value of M 20 per person per day's stay in the GDR for up to 5 days, or M 100 for a longer stay. For regulations governing the import and export of money, see *What Will it Cost* above.

HOTELS. Visitors to East Germany are effectively obliged to stay in hotels belonging to the government-run Interhotel chain. These include all the major hotels in all cities and other tourist centers. Privately-run hotels are small, rather tatty and liable to sudden and unexplained closures. Of the Interhotels, those in major cities such as the Metropol and Palast in Berlin, Merkur in Leipzig and Bellevue in Dresden are up to the best international standards. Most of the others suffer the same uninviting uniformity. However, they are clean, fairly comfortable and reasonably efficient. GDR travel officials will try to book you into one of the best hotels; you may have to press hard if you prefer a more moderate price category.

Our hotel grading system is divided into four categories. All prices are per person. Deluxe (L) M 100, Expensive (E) M 90–100, Moderate (M) M 70–90, Inexpensive (I) M 40–70.

CAMPING. There are over 30 Intercamp sites in East Germany, most with good facilities. They are open from May 1 to Sept. 30. You must, however, book your camp-site before arriving in East Germany (details from East German Tourist Office). You will be issued with vouchers which you must surrender on entering the country in exchange for marks. This apparently rather complicated system exists merely to ensure that camps are not overbooked (and to keep an eye on who is booking them).

RESTAURANTS. East German restaurants, other than those in major hotels, do not enjoy much in the way of variety or sophistication. However, more restaurants and cafés are being privately run, with an improvement in quality, variety and service. Outside major towns and cities, you are unlikely to find anything much more elaborate than a bar or café. Food everywhere is generally plentiful and the ingredients the best the country has to offer even if the final result is a little nondescript. The better restaurants are in hotels and those listed as inexpensive are either cafés or bars.

Our restaurant grading system is divided into three categories. Expensive (E) M 30–40, Moderate (M) M 20–30, Inexpensive (I) M 10–20. These prices are for one person.

Food and Drink. Dishes on East German menus in cities are heavily influenced by Eastern European cuisine. Explanations are usually given in several languages, including English, and generally speaking regional specialties manage to make themselves known.

Just outside Berlin, in the haven and tranquility of Spreewald (the Spree woods) and their "streets" of waterways (much of this district has no roads, so boats are the only means of transport), freshwater fish specialties abound, as well as the familiar sausages peculiar to every spot of Germany, East or West. Good ones to try are *Spreewälder Wurstplatte mit Meerrettich* and *Quark mit Leinöl* (various types of sausage with horseradish and cream cheese). *Fisch in Spreewaldsosse* (fish in season with a local sauce) or *Aal mit Gurkensalat* (eel and cucumber salad) number among the best fish dishes. There are seafood restaurants throughout East Germany, many of them called *Gastmahl des Meeres*.

Wines and spirits tend to come from eastern rather than western climes, and Bulgarian wines and Polish and Russian vodkas are worth sampling. A local throat-scorcher, found around the Harz Mountains, is *Schierker Feuerstein*.

 TIPPING. Officially abolished, but accepted in hotels and restaurants. Tip in West German deutschemarks if possible, otherwise US dollars and coins. Tips in local currency will rarely improve service.

 MAIL. Prices are the same as in West Germany. (See next chapter). If you mail cards and letters from one of the large hotels, they may ask for West German currency in payment of the stamps.

 CLOSING TIMES. Variable. Stores are mostly open from 9–6 outside Berlin, 10–7 (8 on Thurs.) in Berlin. Only departmental and larger stores open Sat. morning. Banks open from 8 to midday, Mon.-Fri., and from 2:30 P.M. to 5:30 P.M., Mon. and Thurs., closed Sat.

 **USEFUL ADDRESSES.** American Embassy in East Berlin is Neustadtische Kirchstr. 4–5 (tel. 220–2741). The British Embassy is located at 108 Berlin, Unter den Linden 32/34 (tel. 220–2431). Reisebüro der DDR: Generaldirektion, Alexanderplatz 5, East Berlin (tel. 215–4402); Kreuzstr. 4, Dresden (tel. 44001); Sachsenplatz 1, Leipzig (tel. 79590); Friedrich-Ebert-Str. 115/corner Yorckstr., Potsdam (tel. 4221).

 GETTING AROUND EAST GERMANY. The country is relatively small so there are virtually no internal flights. Trains are the preferred means of travel and services are frequent and cheap. Highways are constantly being improved, but roads other than major routes are often in poor condition.

By Train. There are three types of trains—Express, the fastest, shown as "Ex" in timetables, fast, shown as "D", and semi-fast, shown as "E". All have varying degrees of supplementary fare. Local trains do not. But rail travel in the German Democratic Republic is not expensive. Most long and medium distance trains have both 1st. and 2nd. class and many have either dining or buffet cars, though these are available only unpredictably. Meals are not expensive but it is rare to get a choice. There are also 1st. and 2nd. class sleeping cars and 2nd. class couchettes. The Berlin underground (U-Bahn) costs 20 pfennigs per trip, the suburban railway (S-Bahn) costs 25 to 85 pfennigs per trip. As rail travel is popular, trains are usually very full.

By Car. There are nearly 1,000 miles of motorway and nearly 7,000 miles of secondary roads in East Germany. Routes are well marked, but detailed maps are useful. Traffic regulations are strictly enforced, from parking rules to speed limits, for which radar traps have been cleverly contrived. Drivers would do well to get a copy of the rules in English before attempting to motor in the GDR, as the policy levy fines (in West German currency, for foreigners) for the slightest offense. Drinking and driving is strictly forbidden and fines are heavy for violators. Speed limits on the Autobahn are 63 m.p.h. (100 km), on other roads 55 m.p.h. (80 km), and in towns 30 m.p.h. (50 km). Gasoline (petrol) is available at either *Minol* or *Intertank* filling stations. Both chains sell regular and premium grades by the liter. Minol stations supply gasoline for either GDR marks (you may be asked to show your currency exchange receipt) or coupons, which may be bought at a discount at the border. Otherwise, the Intertank stations sell gasoline at reduced prices for West German deutschemarks. Foreign cars pay a tongue-twisting *Strassenbenutzungsgebühr*, (Road Users' Tax or road toll) M 5.00, 15.00, 20.00, or 25.00 for up to 200km, 300km, 400km, or 500km, respectively. Tolls are to be paid in foreign currency. *Minol* denotes motorway filling stations and *Mitropa* service stations, sometimes with motels.

Car Hire. Cars are Lada 2101 and 2103, Fiat 1315, Volvo 264 and Fiat 132, and are bookable through official tourist agencies or your local travel agent. They can be collected at one place and left at another and can be used for excursions into Czechoslovakia and Poland. They cost from $14 daily or $72.95 weekly, plus 11 cents per km. to $40 daily or $202 weekly plus 40 cents per km.

East Berlin and Potsdam

The massive Brandenburg Gate at the west end of Unter den Linden marks what was once a major axis of the city before the famous wall went up, literally overnight, in 1961. Crossings are now more generally made at the Friedrichstrasse S-Bahn station or the Friedrichstrasse–Zimmerstrasse ("Checkpoint Charlie" on the West Berlin side). The stretch of the Friedrichstrasse leading up to Unter den Linden has undergone extensive renovation and restoration for Berlin's 750th birthday party and now offers attractive shops, a new hotel (see below), and a number of restaurants and cafés, all making the entrance to the eastern part of the city far more attractive than previously.

But the restored Brandenburg Gate is a good starting point for a walk down Unter den Linden, with its reflections of past glories, plus some interesting shops and cafés. Humboldt University and the Museum of German History on the left are housed in glorious buildings; the State Opera on the right is justly famous. At the Marx-Engels bridge over the Spree canal, the choice is difficult. Turn left toward the outstanding collection of museums (Bode, Pergamon, National Gallery) or right down the canal for a surprisingly charming assortment of narrow streets, canal bridges, and finally the Fischer-Insel and the Märkisches Museum portraying the history of the city. The restored cathedral and St. Hedwig's cathedral are both worth a visit. Unattractive as it may be, the television mast (with revolving restaurant, what else?) draws like a magnet. The tourist office at the base of the tower offers city maps and information.

Theater, opera and music in Berlin are outstanding, although some productions are given unmistakably Marxist overtones! The opera house has been completely restored and refurbished (Unter den Linden 7); opera and musicals can also be found at the Komische Oper (Behrenstrasse 55–57) and the MetropolTheater (Friedrichstrasse 101–102). Tickets for concerts and opera are ridiculously cheap by Western standards, but may be hard to get. Given West German deutschemarks, the hotel concierge may achieve the impossible.

Potsdam, a smallish settlement, became a flourishing town in 1660 when the Prince Elector Friedrich Wilhelm decided to build his castle there. His successors, kings of Prussia, of whom Frederick the Great is the best known, embellished Potsdam in the manner of Versailles, and left many a gem of baroque architecture. Of the numerous palaces in Potsdam the finest is Sans souci, built by Knobelsdorff in 1745. The Cecilienhof, the 20th-century palace where the Potsdam Agreement was signed in 1945, is also interesting. Day trips to Potsdam from Berlin can be arranged.

PRACTICAL INFORMATION FOR EAST BERLIN AND POTSDAM

GETTING AROUND EAST BERLIN. There is a day tourist ticket offering unlimited travel on all public transport in East Berlin for M 2. This is available from the tourist office at Alexanderplatz 5. The metro is fairly extensive and maps are available from the Alexanderplatz city railway station and from the tourist office.

Hotels and Restaurants

EAST BERLIN. *Palasthotel* (L), Karl-Liebknechtstr. (tel. 2410). The most luxurious of all East Berlin hotels; with every facility. Close to the Palace of the Republic; the French restaurant is good. The new *Grand Hotel* (E), on the Friedrichstrasse, should be open by 1987, with full facilities to the best international standards and prices to match, for its 300 rooms. But its restaurants and shops should be more moderately priced. *Metropol* (E), Friederichstr. 150/153 (tel. 22040). Indoor pool, solarium, sauna; service agency on the 11th floor where you can book hotels in other cities in the GDR. *Stadt Berlin* (M), Alexanderplatz (tel. 2190). All rooms with private facilities. Travel agency, shops, bank, sauna, and hairdresser. *Unter den Linden* (M), Unter den Linden 14 (tel. 2200311). Comfortable; good location. Restaurant, theater and nightclub reservations. *Newa* (M), Invalidenstrasse 115 (tel. 282–5461). Not as grand as the hotels mentioned above but restaurant and service are good. *Berolina* (M), Karl-Marx Allee (tel. 210–9541). Medium-sized hotel with many facilities. *Minerva* (I), Clara Zetkinstr. 41 (tel. 207–1247). *Berliner Hof* (I), Friederichstr. 113a (tel. 282–7478).

Restaurants. *Die Möwe* (M), Hermann-Matern-Str. 18 (tel. 282–5741). On the first floor, beautiful decor. The building is a historical landmark. *Ermeler Haus* (M), Märkisches Ufer 10 (tel. 279–4036). A stately restaurant in 16th-century house, a former haunt of Western diplomats; wine restaurant on the second floor, cafe on the ground floor. *Ganymed* (M), Schiffbauerdamm 5 (tel. 282–9540). Good central location, friendly service; reservations a must. *Haus Budapest* (I), Karl-Marx Allee 91 (tel. 436–2189). Almost as good as the Hungarian original; folk music helps put you in the mood, as do the superb Hungarian wines. *Historische Weinstube* (M), Poststr. 23 (tel. 212–4122). Situated on ground floor of merchant's house; small, so reservations essential. Cozy atmosphere. *Ratskeller* (I), Rathausstr. 14 (tel. 212–5301). Historic setting in the basement of the red brick town hall. *Lindencorso* (M), Unter den Linden 17 (tel. 220–2461). Complex of wine tavern, concert cafe and the Havanna Bar. *Zum Goldbroiler* (M), Rathausstr. 5 (tel. 212–3290). Situated in the town hall passage; good for chicken dishes. Right next door is *Cafe Rendezvous* for that coffee break. *Telecafé* T. V. Tower (tel. 210–4232). The view is much better than the food, but it's still worth the trip up. 207 meters high! *Sofia* (M), Leipzigerstr. 46 (tel. 229–1831), Bulgarian dishes; the wine restaurant has a Bulgarian (what else) band. *Zenner* (I), Alt-Treptow 14–17, Puschkin Allee (tel. 272–7211). A great view of the Spree river from the terrace. One of Berlin's oldest and largest beergardens; plus cafe on the first floor. *Zur Letzten Instanz* (I), Waisenstr. 16 (tel. 212–5528). Historical restaurant that dates back to 1525; good atmosphere and food.

POTSDAM. *Interhotel Stadt Potsdam* (M), Lange Brücke (tel. 4631). 17-story hotel, all rooms with private facilities; excellent value. *Cecilienhof* (I), Neuer Garten (tel. 23141). Extremely good value though short on facilities in some rooms; quiet.

Restaurants. *Cafe Rendezvous* (M), Friedrich-Ebert-Str. 114. A very nice concert-cafe. *Klosterkeller* (M), Friedrich-Ebert-Str. 94. Central. *Kulturhaus Hans Marchwitza* (M), Am Alten Markt. Choice of restaurant proper, wine restaurant, bar with dancing. *Weinbergterrassen* (M), Gregor Mendel Str. 19. Wine pub, bar, and restaurant with dancing.

Museums

EAST BERLIN. Altes Museum, Marx-Engels Platz. Exhibitions from the National Gallery, including works by East German artists; print room, collection of sketches and prints. Open Wed. to Sun. 9–6.

    Arts and Crafts Museum, Köpenick Palace. European arts and crafts spanning four centuries; special exhibitions. Open Wed. to Sat. 9–5, Sun. 10–6.

    Bodemuseum, Am Kupfergraben. Egyptian department, early Christian and Byzantine collections, Italian Masters. Open Wed. to Sun. 9–6.

    Märkisches Museum, Am Köllnischen Park 5. Everything you always wanted to know about Berlin's history, art and theater. Wed. to Sat. 9–5, Sun. 9–6.

    Museum of German History, Unter den Linden. German history from 1789 to the present. Open Tues. to Fri. 9–6, Sat. and Sun. 9–4.

    Museum of Natural History, Invalidenstr. 43. Paleontological, mineralogical and zoological departments. Open Tue. to Sun. 9–5.

    National Gallery, Bodestr. 19th- and 20th-century paintings and sculptures, plus special exhibitions. Open Wed. to Sun. 9–6.

    Pergamon Museum, Am Kupfergraben. Its name derives from its most famous treasure, the Pergamon Altar (180 B.C.). This alone is sufficient to draw thousands of tourists to East Berlin, but just as impressive is the Babylonian Processional Way in the Asia Minor department. Also: Egyptian Museum, Early Christian–Byzantine and East Asian collections, sculptures from 12th–18th centuries. Open Wed. to Sun. 9–6. Pergamon Altar also Mon., Tues.

Leipzig, Trade Center

As a center of the printing and book trade as well as of the European fur trade, Leipzig acquired world renown soon after the Napoleonic wars. Richard Wagner was born here and was moulded by a long-established musical tradition which boasts such names as the Gewandhaus Orchestra, founded in 1781, and now housed in a modern concert hall built to replace the old Gewandhaus badly damaged during the war. Astride great trade routes, Leipzig became an important market town in the early Middle Ages. The twice yearly Trade Fair has now been bringing together exhibitors and buyers for more than half a century. Little is left of old Leipzig: the Renaissance Town Hall, some baroque buildings in the inner city, and in Gohlis, the poet Schiller's house and a charming rococo palace, the Gohliser Schlösschen, can be visited. The Thomaskirche, where for years Bach was in charge of music, is a point of pilgrimage for many. Of recent vintage are the Opera House in Karl Marx Platz, and the sports stadium. Leipzig has an International Bach festival every year, and the University in Schillerstrasse has the largest Egyptian collection in Europe.

    Halle, birthplace of Handel, is only 22 miles from Leipzig. There is an annual Handel Festival here. Visit his monument and museum as well as the Luther University and church where Luther preached.

PRACTICAL INFORMATION FOR LEIPZIG AND HALLE

HALLE. *Interhotel Stadt Halle* (M), Thälmannplatz (tel. 38041). Good restaurant, pleasant terrace and cafe.

LEIPZIG. *Hotel Merkur* (L), Gerberstr. (tel. 7990). The most prominent (and expensive) hotel in town with sauna, indoor pool, solarium. *Astoria* (M), Platz der Republik 2 (tel. 71710). Good restaurant; but across from the rail station, so noisy. *Hotel am Ring* (M), Karl-Marx-Platz (tel. 79520). A viable alternative to more expensive Merkur. *Stadt Leipzig* (M), Richard Wagnerstr. 1 (tel. 228–814). Facilities are adequate and the service is helpful.

    Restaurants. *Auerbachs Keller* (I), Grimmaischestr. 2 (tel. 209131). Immortalized in Goethe's *Faust;* one of the country's most famous restaurants. Has been in existence over 450 years. Reservations a must. *Burgkeller* (M), Nasch-markt 1. Romanian dishes. *Stadt Kiev* (I), Am Markt. Good cheap food.

Dresden

The city enjoys a particularly attractive location on the Elbe river. Although Dresden can be visited in one day by special sightseeing bus from Berlin that runs once a week, the trip is long and the city is really worth more than a passing acquaintance, offering a treasure trove of 18th-century architecture, much of it lovingly restored. The most out-standing buildings are the Zwinger Palace, the Hofkirche and the National Gallery, which has an excellent collection of paintings. The picture gallery in the Semper building of the Zwinger Palace complex houses 12 Rembrandts, 16 Rubens, and 5 Tintorettos in addition to its most famous masterpiece, Raphael's *Sistine Madonna.* The rebuilt Semper Oper, the Dresden opera house which saw the premieres of many Richard Strauss operas, has itself become a point of pilgrimage for many since its reopening in 1985. Tickets are all but impossible to get, so if you plan to include Dresden in your itinerary, ask the Reisebü-ro der DDR to arrange tickets well in advance.

A short trip down-river brings us to the city of Meissen, famed for its porcelain. Its castle and late-Gothic cathedral (an excellent Cranach in the latter) are vivid reminders of the town's ancient history. A few miles inland, the baroque Moritzburg Castle houses a fine museum. Upstream by river boat, you can enjoy the mountains rising steeply from both banks of the meandering Elbe. The most impressive of all hills is the Lilienstein, opposite the fortress-town of Königstein.

PRACTICAL INFORMATION FOR DRESDEN

Hotels and Restaurants

Bellevue (E), Köpkestr. (tel. 53927). Dresden's newest hotel, opened in 1985, and cleverly incorporating an old town house into its complex. Every facility, including fitness center and sauna, a host of restaurants and cafés. *Astoria* (M), Ernst-Thälmann Platz 1 (tel. 44171). 88 rooms, simple but comfortable. Located near the zoo, slightly less central. *Interhotel Newa* (M), Pragerstr. (tel. 496–7112). The city's next best hotel after the Bellevue, with a good restaurant which, however, is not open to non-residents. *Interhotel Prager Strasse* (M), Prager Str. (tel. 48560). Consists of two hotels, the "Königstein" and "Lilien-stein," near the main rail station; all rooms with private baths. *Gewandhaus* (I), Ringstr. 1 (tel. 496–286). Some rooms with bath. *Parkhotel Weisser Hirsch* (I), Bautzner Landstr. 7 (tel. 36851). On the outskirts in pleasant surroundings.

Restaurants. *Buri-Buri* (E), a Polynesian restaurant, *Canaletto,* and *Elbter-rassen,* both (E), and *Wackerbarths Keller* (E), a wine restaurant, all in Hotel Bellevue. *Café Pöppelmann* (M), Grosse Meissner G. 15. Baroque atmosphere in a restored old city house adjacent to the Bellevue. *Café Prag* (M), Am Altmarkt. Central, very popular. *International* (M), Pragerstr. 15. Pleasant atmosphere, food quite good. *Luisenhof* (M), Bergbahnstr. 8. Great location overlooking city; access by cable car. *Ratskeller* (M), Dr. Külz Ring. In base-ment of the town hall; excellent variety. *Sekundogenitur* (M), Brühlsche Ter-rasse. Wine restaurant and café with view of the Elbe; terrace dining in fine weather. *Szeged* (M), Ernst Thälmannstr. 6. Popular Hungarian restaurant; on first floor. *Aberlausitzer Töppl* (I), Strasse der Befreiung. Dresden specialties, and a great dark beer. *Kügelgen Haus* (I), Strasse der Befreiung 13. Choice of Neustädter Grill, coffee bar, restaurant proper, and basement bierkeller.

Museums

Albertinum, Brühlsche Terrasse. Houses the Picture Gallery of New Mas-ters, plus the famous Green Vault, and the numismatic and sculpture collec-tions. Open Tues. to Sun. 9–5.

Brühlsche Terrasse. Remains of the city fortifications dating from 16th century. Transformed into a private amusement garden in 1738, opened to public 1814. Adorned by the sculptures and monuments of famous artists.

Jägerhof, Köpkestr. 1. Renaissance building dating from 16th century, of which only west wing of main building and three turrets have survived. Used as Museum of Folk Art since renovation in 1913.

Schloss Pillnitz. Hillside and riverside palaces on the Elbe, home of Museum of Arts and Crafts. The Schloss is a harmonious blend of baroque and Chinese/oriental architecture. Open Tues. to Sun. 9–5.

Zwinger Palace, Julian Grimm Allee/Theater Platz. Dresden's most famous building, rebuilt after its total destruction. Includes Picture Gallery (Old Masters), Historical Museum, Porcelain Collection, and mathematical and physical sciences salon. Open Tues. to Sun. 9–5 (allow plenty of time for a visit).

Other Places of Interest

At the two extremities of the Thüringer Wald lie two historic cities: Eisenach and Saalfeld. The former is dominated by the Wartburg, mentioned in many a German legend. It served as a refuge to Martin Luther during the stormy days of the Reformation, and Bach was born in this city in 1685. Further east, Erfurt, untouched by events, remains one of the finest German cities with its Cathedral and the church of St. Severin, its matchless Gothic and German Renaissance houses, and its bridge, with 33 houses built on it. Only a few miles away, Weimar retains the atmosphere of the old residential town of German princes. Lucas Cranach lived and worked here. Its greatest period came at the turn of the 18th century when it became the capital of humanist literature and philosophy.

Situated on the Elbe, Wittenberg recalls the life and work of Luther. At the gates of the Palace Church, cast in bronze, are his 95 Articles posted there in 1517 challenging the spiritual leadership of Rome. The church itself houses a unique altarpiece with paintings by Cranach. Also on the Elbe, Dessau, with its Bauhaus, became between the two world wars the cornerstone of modern art and architecture.

The Harz is the best known of mountain districts in central Germany. Delightful surroundings help to enhance the medieval character of Wernigerode, dominated by a feudal castle. The thousand-year-old Quedlinburg is now a dreamy little town, with its half-timbered houses, winding lanes and its outsize cathedral.

PRACTICAL INFORMATION FOR THE REST OF EAST GERMANY

EISENACH. *Hotel Sadt Eisenach* (M), Luisenstr. 11–13 (tel. 3682); and *Parkhotel* (M), Wartburg Allee 2 (tel. 5291). Both simple but comfortable; not all rooms with private bathroom, etc.

ERFURT. *Erfurter Hof* (M), Am Bahnhofsvorplatz 1–2 (tel. 51151). Very central; with restaurant, café, nightclub, gift shop. *Hotel Kosmos* (M), Juri Gagarinring 126/127 (tel. 5510). Modern, with most facilities.

KARL-MARX STADT. *Hotel Kongress* (E), Karl Marx Allee (tel. 6830). All rooms with private facilities. Good restaurant, café, nightclub. *Hotel Moskau* (E), Strasse der Nationen 56 (tel. 60311). Similar to Kongress but not so large or ultramodern.

LUTHERSTADT-WITTENBERG. *Goldener Adler* (M), Marktstr. 7 (tel. 2053). Evokes a little of the past; no private facilities.

WEIMAR. *Hotel Elephant* (M), Markt 19 (tel. 61471). Central but quiet. Goethe, Wagner, and Bach have all lived here, for the building dates from 1696, though considerably modernized. Excellent restaurant.

WEST GERMANY (F.R.G.)

Richly endowed with natural assets and a people capable of hard work, sacrifice and endurance, Germany is one of the wealthiest and technologically most advanced nations in Europe. True, the exigencies of the current international situation have been eroding the rich rewards of "the German Miracle", but they can in no way lessen that vast achievement. The changing climate is marked by a growing disenchantment with over-optimistic government and an increase in unemployment, resulting in a hardening of prejudices against the huge colony of foreign workers who helped bring about the country's current affluence. The Deutschmark, however, remains one of the most stable monetary units in the world. And a member of the European Common Market, Germany wields enormous political influence through sheer economic capability, financial contributions and aid to backward and underdeveloped countries.

There are still two Germanys—"West Germany", officially entitled the Federal Republic of Germany, and "East Germany", the German Democratic Republic, still ruled by a Communist one-party government and one of the Soviet Union's most solid satellites. The constant ebb and flow of East/West entente is reflected nowhere more vividly than in the changing balance of relationships between the two parts of sundered Germany.

Germany has had the reputation for being an expensive country to visit, and, while this reputation is not entirely undeserved, a low rate of inflation combined with a reasonably favorable exchange rate against the dollar, the still-low transatlantic air fares and the many advantageous offers that your travel agent can tell you about, should bring the problem of budgeting your trip into more manageable proportions. Certainly, Germany has a wide enough variety of possibilities to suit any and every pocketbook, and, you can be sure, in Germany you will get value for money.

Along with such traditional strongholds of tourism as the Bavarian Alps, the Romantic Road, the Black Forest, the castled Rhine and Neckar rivers and medieval Franconia, Germany also possesses an incomparable chain of glittering cities where sophisticated modern living vies with historic fascination. Many of these maintain opera, ballet and drama companies which are among the most interesting in the world. Supported largely out of civic funds and often housed in beautifully designed performing-arts centers, these companies can afford to experiment on a scale not possible for their commercially-oriented brethren. We can heartily recommend a visit to a performance of one of these companies. If your lack of German worries you, then try for opera or ballet, although many major cities have English-speaking theaters.

Don't deny yourself the pleasures of visiting one of the great, historic cities, or swanning down the popular Rhine, but balance out those parts of your holiday with visits to other, less frequented areas—North Germany, perhaps, or the quiet, forested stretches of East Bavaria. One of the very best ways to do this is to take advantage of the many cheap rail tickets that Germany offers to its visitors. The rail network in Germany is extensive and excellently maintained, so you can expect to reach even the most remote areas easily and at low cost.

German hotels and restaurants stress comfort and efficient service. A large number of reconstructed and newly-built hostelries offer everything from moderately priced to super-deluxe accommodation. A special attraction, much sought after by foreign visitors, is the castle or manor hotel, once the haunt of medieval knights and seat of nobility or minor royalty, where the romantically-inclined guest may dream himself back into ages long past.

PRACTICAL INFORMATION FOR WEST GERMANY

WHAT WILL IT COST. Germany has one of the world's lowest inflation rates—approximately 2.3%—and it is not expected to rise much above that in 1987. However, that is not to say that Germany is an inexpensive country to visit, indeed the better known tourist destinations, health spas and all the larger cities are generally very expensive. But needless to say, if you visit one of the lesser-known resorts or towns, your vacation costs will run to considerably less than in one of the major tourist centers or cities. Try, for instance, the Harz mountains in Lower Saxony for summer and particularly reasonable winter sports holidays; the Eifel mountain region of the Rhineland-Palatinate; the Swabian Mountains and Forest (Schwäbische Alb and Wald) in Baden-Württemberg, with their marvelous caves, rocks, castles, endless woods and some 7,000 miles of marked hiking routes; or the romantic Black Forest itself. The Allgäu in southwestern Germany has charming resorts like Kleinwalsertal, while East Bavaria in particular (Oberpfalz and Bayerischer Wald—Upper Palatinate and Bavarian Forest) offers excellent quality at very reasonable rates. In all these areas there are many new and comfortable vacation apartments and bungalows; 2–4-room flats accommodating up to six people. Prices vary according to location, season and facilities, but run from 200 to 350 marks per week for a small studio apartment for two, to 600 to 1,000 marks for a deluxe chalet for five or more.

Special all-inclusive rates are offered almost everywhere, but particularly attractive are the off-season (*Nachsaison*) or better "edge-of-high-season" (*Zwischensaison*) reductions which can be up to 20%. Special weekend rates are a popular feature throughout Germany, including many large cities, such as Munich. Even exclusive Baden-Baden offers special out-of-season bargains, often including such extras as reductions in Casino admission. Several hotels in the Black Forest have joined forces to relieve the usual monotony of full-board terms: a guest staying in any one of these hostelries is free to alternate his meals at any of the other member-hotels. For a full list of all such special offers, write or visit the nearest branch of the German Tourist Department (*Fremdenverkehrsamt*).

The German monetary unit is the mark (DM), which is divided into 100 pfennigs. Coins are issued in denominations of 1-, 2-, and 5-mark pieces, 1-, 2-, 5-, 10-, and 50-pfennig pieces, and there are also 5-, 10-, 20-, 50-, and 100-mark notes.

At the time of writing, the exchange rate for the mark was 2.40 to the dollar and 3.40 to the pound sterling.

A typical day outside a major city might cost two people:

	DM
Hotel (moderate) double room with bath and breakfast	90
Lunch at restaurant (moderate)	35
Transportation (1 tram, 1 taxi)	25
Coffee and pastries	15
2 beers	6
Theater (good seats)	50
Dinner (3-course) at restaurant (moderate) including wine	70
Miscellaneous 10%	27
	DM 318

SOURCES OF INFORMATION. For advice on all aspects of travel in West Germany, the German National Tourist Board can be extremely helpful. Their addresses are:

In the U.S.: 747 Third Ave., New York, N.Y. 10017 (tel. 212–308–3300); 444 S. Flower St., Los Angeles, CA 90017 (tel. 213–688–7332).

In Canada: 2 Fundy, P.O. Box 417, Place Bonaventure, Montreal, P.Q. H5A 1B8 (tel. 514–878–9885).

In the U.K.: 61 Conduit St., London W.1 (tel. 01-743 2600).

WHEN TO COME. The main tourist season in Germany runs from May to late October when the majority of the folk festivals take place and the weather is at its best. However, there is also a secondary season in the Bavarian Alps for winter sports. This runs from late December to late March.

Climate. Delightful and normally settled in the summer months although regionally variable; it can be pretty cold in winter, however.

Average afternoon daily temperatures in degrees Fahrenheit and centigrade:

Munich	Jan.	Feb.	Mar.	Apr.	May	June	July	Aug.	Sept.	Oct.	Nov.	Dec.
F°	33	37	45	54	63	69	72	71	64	53	42	36
C°	1	3	7	12	17	21	22	22	18	12	6	2

SPECIAL EVENTS. From Dec. 31 through Ash Wednesday is Carnival (*Fasching* in German), particularly celebrated in Munich, Cologne, Düsseldorf, Mainz, Augsburg and Aachen. International ski events at Garmisch-Partenkirchen, Jan. Leaders in the long list of annual musical and theatrical events are the *Wiesbaden International Festival* and Stuttgart summer theater and ballet week in May, the *Munich Opera Festival,* mid-July to mid-Aug., and the *Wagner Festival* in Bayreuth, late July through late Aug. *Munich Oktoberfest* (beer festival over two weeks beginning the third Sat. in Sept.) is world-known. *Christkindl Markt,* Christmas markets all over Germany, especially Munich, Regensburg and Nuremburg, Dec. There are numerous folklore events and trade fairs year-round; for full details enquire at any German Tourist Office.

National Holidays. Jan. 1 (New Year's Day); Apr. 17, 19, 20 (Easter); May 1 (Labor Day); May 28 (Ascension); Jun. 8 (Whit Mon.); Jun. 17 (German Unity Day); Nov. 1 (All Saints); Nov. 18 (Day of Prayer and Repentance); Dec. 24 (half-day closing), 25, 26; Dec. 31 (half-day closing).

VISAS. Nationals of the United States, Canada, Australia, New Zealand, EEC countries and practically all other European countries do not require visas for entry into Germany. However, you must of course have a valid passport.

GETTING TO GERMANY. By Plane. The principal airport for transatlantic flights is Frankfurt to and from which there are direct flights or through plane flights connecting with Boston, New York, Washington, Philadelphia, Chicago, San Francisco, St. Louis, Los Angeles, Miami, Houston, Anchorage, Montreal and Toronto. *TWA* also operate a direct daily flight from New York to Munich. Other German cities served are Hamburg, Munich, Cologne/Bonn and Stuttgart. Airlines on the trans-Atlantic route are *Lufthansa*, *TWA*, *PanAm* and *Air Florida*. There is an extensive network of flights from most European capitals to various German cities, including Frankfurt, Hamburg, Hannover, Cologne/Bonn, Düsseldorf, Berlin, Munich, Nuremburg, Saarbrücken, Stuttgart and Bremen.

By Train. The two main routes are from London (Victoria) via Dover and Ostend, and thence via Aachen and Cologne; and from London (Liverpool Street) via Harwich and the Hook of Holland to the Rhine valley, Düsseldorf, Hamburg and Berlin. Connecting boat trains operate from London for both the day time and night time crossing between Harwich and the Hook. Sample— leave London by the *Night Continental* train or the day *Britannia Express* (dep. approx. 7.40 P.M. or 9.40 A.M.) for Harwich and then cross to the Hook arriving there at 6.15 A.M. or 7 P.M. The *Britannia Express* is a through train leaving the Hook at 7.55 P.M., reaching Cologne at 11.30 P.M., and continuing directly to Munich where it arrives at 6.50 the next morning with a connection for Innsbruck, Austria. The *Night Continental* will arrive at the Hook in time to take the Rhein Express at 7.16 A.M., which reaches Cologne at 10.48 A.M. and continues via Bonn, Mainz, Darmstadt, Heidelberg, Karlsruhe, and Freiburg to Basle, Switzerland.

By Ferry. There are direct ferry sailings from England (Harwich) to Hamburg by *Prins Ferries* taking 16 to 20 hours for the crossing. There are linking boat trains from London (Liverpool St.) for these sailings. There are excellent train connections from Hamburg to most parts of Germany.

CUSTOMS. There are three levels of duty free allowance for goods imported into Germany. Travelers coming from a European country outside the EEC may bring in 200 cigarettes or 50 cigars or 250gr. of tobacco; 1 liter of spirits more than 22% proof or 2 liters of spirits less than 22% proof and 2 liters of wine; 50gr. of perfume; other goods to the value of DM 100. Travelers coming from an EEC country may bring in 300 cigarettes or 75 cigars or 400gr. of tobacco; 5 liters of wine and 1.5 liters of spirits more than 22% proof or 3 liters of spirits or sparkling wine up to 22% proof; 75gr. of perfume and 25cl. of toilet water; other goods to the value of DM 460. Travelers coming from outside Europe may bring in 400 cigarettes or 100 cigars or 500gr. of tobacco; spirits and perfume limits are the same as those for non EEC countries; other goods to the value of DM100.

HOTELS. In the last 15 years hotel rates have increased dramatically, but quality and amenities have also improved. Most costly is Hamburg, then Düsseldorf, Frankfurt and Munich. Cheapest are Stuttgart and Berlin. However, even the most modest accommodations are both clean and comfortable. There are any number of good, middle range hotels throughout the country, which are as friendly as they are reliable. And at the top end of the scale, deluxe hotels in Germany are comparable to the very finest anywhere in the world, and may offer reduced weekend rates upon inquiry.

Our hotel grading system is divided into four categories. Deluxe (L) DM 200 and up, Expensive (E) DM 150–250, Moderate (M) DM 90–150 and Inexpensive (I) DM 60–100. All prices are for two people in a double room.

There is a fascinating chain of country hotels called the *Romantik Hotels* dotted throughout Germany. None is less than 100 years old and many have been owned by the same families for just as long. Apart from their rich historical connections—some date back to the Middle Ages—they all offer first class personal service, excellent cuisine, and a high degree of comfort. Though a bit pricey, they afford a marvellous means of seeing the country.

MOTELS. Autobahn Hotels *(Rasthäuser)* usually represent a combination of a restaurant, café, service station, and offer a number of hotel rooms. Sometimes they are similar to motels, sometimes not. It is strictly forbidden to make a U-turn on the autobahns, so be on the lookout to select a hotel located on your lane of the autobahn; special underpasses, however, are frequently sited. There are no charges for children under 12; baby beds also available.

A folder, *Autobahn Service,* showing the entire motorway system and all facilities available en route, is available in English from filling stations and road houses, or from the frontier crossing points.

CAMPING. The *German Camping Club,* Mandelsstr. 28, Munich 23, publishes each year a guide of the camping sites in Germany at DM19.80 for non-members, DM 10 for members (1986 prices), the German National Tourist Office issues a folder, *Camping in Germany* and the German Automobile Association (ADAC) has a useful map showing campsites near autobahn exits. There are also about 500 winter camping sites and their number is increasing.

Every weekend in high season VHF services of several regional broadcasting authorities give out details of available pitches on camp sites. Timings can be seen on motorways and are also listed in the Autobahn Service brochure.

SPAS AND BEAUTY FARMS. Taking the waters in Germany has been popular since Roman times, whether for healing the body or merely beautifying it. Germany has 250 officially registered spas and health resorts and some 50 beauty farms. (If the name of a place includes the word *Bad,* then it's a good sign that it's a spa and prices are going to be high.) Today they constitute a major tourist attraction.

There are four main groups of spas and health resorts. The mineral and moorland spas, where treatments are based on natural warm-water springs; those by the sea (on the North Sea and Baltic coasts); hydropathic spas, which use an invigorating process developed in the 19th century; and climatic health resorts, which depend upon their climates—usually mountainous—for their health giving properties.

A full spa treatment under medical supervision normally lasts from 3 to 4 weeks and costs from DM 700 to DM 1,200. A booklet on German spas is available from the German National Tourist Office in most major cities.

 RESTAURANTS. We grade the restaurants in our Practical Information sections as Expensive (E), Moderate (M) and Inexpensive (I). Naturally, the variation of prices within each category will be marked from region to region and from town to town. The approximate range (for a main course) is—(E) DM30–45 and up; (M) DM15–30; (I) DM7.50–20. We stress that this is only an approximation. Cheaper table d'hôte menus, costing between DM10.50 and DM32.00 are normally available at lunchtimes. You could, however, pay well over these rates in Frankfurt and under them in a small country town. These rates are for one person and do not include wine.

Except for a few very expensive ones, restaurants display their menu outside next to the entrance, including at lunchtime the day's special, and, of course, the prices, so you can shop around until you find the place which suits you.

Service charges are included in all restaurant prices. Menus and wine lists automatically quote prices *inclusive* of taxes and service charges.

Food and Drink. German food leans unmistakably towards the rich and the fulsome. Germans love sausages, pork, veal and game. Butter is used in most dishes and starch is practically the national dish—potatoes in the north, bread dumplings *Knödel* or *Spätzle* (a kind of noodle) in the south. (In the smaller

Bavarian inns, anything that *can* be served with dumplings *is* served with dumplings.) In short, German food is delicious and plentiful.

When in Rome . . . The south Germans are very fond of dipping into a little *Brotzeit* (a snack of bread—of which there are countless varieties—sausage and beer). Follow suit and you'll find that this is the moment to sample those tempting regional sausages. Frankfurters, for example, of which the American version is no more than a facsimile; Regensburger, a heavily-spiced pork sausage; Weisswurst, a white sausage made of veal, calves' brains and splean and seasoned with fresh herbs; Bratwurst, the grilled pork sausage of Nürnberg after which the famous *Bratwurststube* restaurants all over Germany are named.

Other outstanding German specialties: *Falscher Hase,* a delicious meatloaf, *Schweinebraten* or *Schweinshax'n* (roast pork or roast knuckle of pork), *Eisbein mit Sauerkraut* (boiled leg of pork served with pickled cabbage), *Sauerbraten* (a joint of beef marinated in herbs and wine, then roasted) and, of course, *Schnitzel,* pork, beef or veal escalopes fried in batter or served plain. The gamut of mouth-watering sweets includes: *Käsekuchen,* delicious cheesecake, *Schwarz-wälder Kirschtorte,* a Black Forest cherry cake liberally soaked in *Kirschwasser* cherry Schnaps, spicy *Apfelkuchen* (apple tart) or, in southern Germany, juicy plum tart known as *Zwetschgen-Datschi* and *Lebkuchen* (gingerbread).

The beer is good. In Bavaria, say *helles* if you want light, *dunkles* if you want dark beer. Try the beer brewed from wheat, *Weissbier.*

Germany produces a lot of wine, some of it of superlative quality. Generally speaking, you will probably be happy with the house wine in most restaurants, or with one of those earthenware pitchers of cold Mosel that are usually available. These are refreshing and inexpensive. From the southernmost end of the Rhine wine region, a number of fruity white wines are produced. The best include *Forst, Deidesheim, Wachenheim, Ruppertsberge* and *Schwarzer Herrgott.*

The Rhine Hesse region, beginning at Worms, produces the world-famous *Liebfraumilch,* though this may disappoint you since the Milk of Our Lady does not come from any one particular vineyard so the name by itself is no guarantee of quality. But a little further north you will find two very fine wines indeed, the best of this region: *Niersteiner* and *Oppenheimer.* Other top wines in this region are *Nackenheimer* and *Bodenheimer.* The Nahe valley produces the smooth white *Monzinger, Kreuznacher* and *Huffelsheimer.*

TIPPING. The service charges on hotel bills suffice, but if for any reason you wish to tip (the porter who brings in your bags might be one example), quite small amounts are acceptable. Whether you tip the hotel concierge depends on whether he has given you any special service. Although restaurant bills include 10% for service, it is customary, as is also the case with taxi drivers, to round up the price to the next half-mark or full mark, but not more than 5%. Station porters (available only in resorts and small towns) get 2 marks for one bag, 1 mark for each additional bag; add 40–50 pfennigs as a tip. Chambermaids get 1 mark per night's stay, 5 marks a week, but only in deluxe hotels. No need to tip doormen, except 1 mark for calling a cab, theater ushers, or barmen.

MAIL. Current rates for airmail letters up to 20 grams: to the U.S. DM 1.40; to the U.K. 100 pfennigs; within Germany 80 pfennigs. Postcards are 60 pfennigs. These prices are liable to change before 1987.

CLOSING TIMES. In general, shops are open from 8.30 or 9 to 6 or 6.30 and close Sat. afternoons, except for the first Sat. in each month. Hairdressers close Mon. Banks: 8.30–1 and 2.30 to 4, Mon.-Fri.; Thurs. until 5.30.

USEFUL ADDRESSES. The *United States Embassy:* 52 Bonn-Bad Godesberg, Mehlemer Ave, Bonn 2. Consulate-General offices: Bremen, Düsseldorf, Frankfurt, Hamburg, Munich and Stuttgart. *Canadian Consulate-General:* Esplanade 41–7, 2000 Hamburg 36 (consulates in West Berlin, Stuttgart and Düsseldorf). *British Embassy:* Friedrich-Ebert Allee 77, 5300 Bonn 2, with Consulate-General offices in Berlin, Hamburg, Düsseldorf, Frankfurt, Munich, Stuttgart, Hannover and Bremerhaven. *Australian Consulate-General:* Neuerwall 39, 2000 Hamburg 36. Also consulate offices at Berlin, Bonn and Cologne. *New Zealand Embassy:* Bundeskanzlerplatz 902, 5300 Bonn 2.

GETTING AROUND GERMANY. By Plane. *Lufthansa* operate an extensive network of air services in Germany, all by jets including the Airbus on the more heavily trafficked routes. But the German national airline is still not allowed to operate into West Berlin. Services to that city from various cities in West Germany, including Hamburg, Frankfurt, Cologne/Bonn and Munich, are operated by *PanAm* and *British Airways,* the latter operating some flights on behalf of *Air France.* Lufthansa also offer American-style weekend reductions (*Städtetours*) to major cities within Germany, as well as a special reduced rate on selected inland flights called "Flieg und Spar," which are about 40% cheaper. A round-trip ticket must be booked.

Frankfurt International airport has excellent links to all parts of the country, with thirty trains daily serving the airport. In addition, a special, reduced-rate "Rail and Fly" ticket, available to passengers holding a valid round-trip plane ticket, allows you to travel by train between Frankfurt airport and all the other principal airports in the country. All surcharges and subway transfers are included in the price of DM 70 (2nd class) and DM 100 (1st class).

By Train. With one of the best railway networks in Europe, West Germany offers the very latest in rail travel. In addition to the Inter-City (IC) fast, modern two-class express train network, are the Fern Express (FD) trains, replacing most of the former TEE (Trans-Europe-Express) routes and intended to provide direct connections between major industrial and residential areas of Germany and regions of major tourist/recreation interest. There is a supplement for travel by all *IC* trains. There are also very many slightly slower (but still both fast and frequent) services known as *Schnellzuge* and shown as *D* in timetables.

Most long distance trains carry some form of restaurant service; either full dining car (on all FDs and many ICs), buffet cars, grill cars or refreshment services. These, along with the sleeping cars, are operated by the *DSG* company, a subsidiary of the German Federal Railways, generally known as DB (*Deutsche Bundesbahn*). International sleepers are sometimes operated by *Wagons Lits,* or by *Mitropa* from East Germany. The Amsterdam–(Hook-of-Holland)–Cologne –Basle express *Rheingold* remains a TEE and has instituted a club car in the 1st class section. On the Hamburg–Munich–Berchtesgaden IC line, you will find the first traveling playground for 4–11 year-olds. Furthermore, the *Rheingold* has a special compartment which leaves the express route at Mannheim and winds its way through the picturesque Neckar Valley.

Germany has one of the best runabout rail tickets in Europe given the vast scale of their network and the modest price charged for unlimited travel. Holders of these tickets also get reduced rail travel to West Berlin, free travel on certain *Europabus* routes and reduced rate travel on all *KD Rhine* vessels. The ticket is the *DB Tourist Card.* Issued for both 9 and 16 days, it costs respectively in 1st class $340 and $475, and in 2nd class $255 and $350. There are half fares for children aged 4 to 12 inclusive.

By Bus. *Europabus* have a number of long distance services in Germany running from Travemünde (near Lübeck) in the far north of the country right down to Austria and with connecting routes to Belgium and France in the west and to Poland in the east. Several are of particular interest to the tourist such as the Romantic Road from Wiesbaden to Munich.

River Trips. The rivers Rhine and Mosel are served by a number of regular boats operated by the *Köln-Düsseldorfer* line, usually referred to as the KD line. From the end of March to the end of October they sail between Cologne and Mainz, with some additional services to Frankfurt. In addition, one-week Rhine cruises can be booked with KD which include flight from London to Rotterdam or Amsterdam (with transfer to Nijmegan, the embarkation point), plus all meals, sightseeing trips, a night in Basle and flight home from Basle or return rail trip on the T.E.E. *Rheingold Express.* There is also a four-day cruise between Rotterdam and Basle, calling at Düsseldorf, Cologne, Koblenz, Heidelberg, Speyer and Strasbourg. In addition, wine seminars, art, and history cruises are offered. On the Mosel, KD operate between Koblenz and Trier, with a new service extending to Cologne. On both rivers, there are fast and local services and all boats have dining facilities. However, only the cruise ships that sail to and from the Netherlands have overnight accommodations. All the boats sail daily, though the frequency of departures varies. Other shipping lines operate passenger services and excursions.

By Car. Traversing the country and still being extended, the German super-highways (*Autobahnen*) are the most important road network in Europe. Other roads are first class, with a 100-kph speed limit. There is no speed limit on autobahns but a maximum of 130 kph is recommended. Seat belts are compulsory. Autobahn Service, a folder with maps of the entire network, is available at all autobahn gas stations and inns (English editions from Lufthansa and National Tourist Offices). Entrance formalities are simple and international insurance cards no longer required. Gasoline (petrol) prices are competitive in Germany and at time of writing vary from DM 1.20 to DM 1.40 though it can be more expensive on the autobahns. Prices are not expected to rise in 1987. The Automobile Club of Germany has introduced a system of patrol cars (yellow) to help motorists on autobahns: orange-colored emergency telephones are situated at frequent intervals; emergency calls by foreign tourists are taken by Radio Hessen—dial 0611/1551 and Bavarian Radio's third program (*Bayern 3*); call 089–59001. Children under 12 must sit in the back.

Car Hire. Self-drive cars may be ordered at the ticket windows of 130 major railroad stations and on TEE and Inter-City trains. Another railroad service is the *Autoreisezug* system by which a passenger's car is transported on the same train—usually overnight. All the larger Western German towns have drive-yourself car hire service such as *Autourist, Selbstfahrer Union* or *Metro Rent-a-Car. Hertz* and *Avis* have offices in major cities, *Auto Sixt* and *Autohansa* in Munich, Frankfurt and Hamburg.

Average car rental costs: from DM 95 (for a simple Volkswagen, such as a Golf) to DM 165 (Mercedes 190E) per day with unlimited mileage, or if you prefer to pay the mileage separately, around DM 30 less per day plus an additional 90 pfennigs to DM 1.18 for each kilometer. This is better value only if you require the hire car for very short distances. Weekly rates are lower, for example DM 475 for a VW Golf and DM 825 for a Mercedes 190E.

Frankfurt

Frankfurt on the Main lies at the crossroads of the major routes of the world and is the city most tourists reach first. It is a pleasant—not too attractive—city, and it has always been a center of trade and of German liberalism. Famous for its role in international finance—it is the domicile of the Central Bank of Germany and of more than 350 other national and international banks—it has also been renowned for its trade fairs since the Middle Ages. The city continues this tradition with an annual international fair in March, a second one at the end of August, and the greatest book fair in the world in September/October.

Charlemagne took up residence in this city in 794, and Frankfurt became the place of election and coronation of the Holy Roman emperors. Johann Gutenberg, inventor of printing, set up shop here in 1454; 100 years later, Frankfurt was Europe's most important printing center. Goethe was born here in 1749, and this great liberal city, to its everlasting honor, opposed the Nazis.

The chief tourist attractions of the Altstadt (Old Town) in Alt Sachsenhausen are Goethe's house, carefully and lovingly restored after its destruction in World War II; what is left of the 13th- to 16th-century Karmeliterkloster; the 13th-century Romanesque Loenhardskirche (don't miss the wonderful old doors inside), the Steinernes Haus (now reserved for art exhibitions), the Saalhof, once the palace of Frederick Barbarossa, and the famous Frankfürter Börse (Stock Exchange).

On no account should you miss the Römerberg, a marvelous medieval square, which was a scene of gay rejoicing during the coronations of the Holy Roman emperors of the German nation. Its name derives from the Römer, a group of three Gothic buildings located here. This structure, for centuries the symbol of Frankfurt (and also housing the Town Hall for 550 years), was remarkably well rebuilt after the last war. The emperors' coronation hall is among the rooms which can be visited. Also preserved are the Gothic church of St. Nicholas (Nikolaikirche) (with modern clock-orchestra) and the 15th-century Cathedral of St. Bartholomew, with its beautiful carved pews and murals. Across from the cathedral (Dom) is the restored Cloth Hall (Leinwandhaus) built in 1399.

PRACTICAL INFORMATION FOR FRANKFURT

Hotels

Deluxe

Canadian Pacific Frankfurt Plaza, Hamburgerallee 2 (tel. 770721). Vast modern hotel complex, 1200 beds, with three restaurants and nightclub.

Frankfurt Intercontinental, Wilhelm-Leuschner-Str. 43 (tel. 230561). 1500 beds. Located by the river Main; in the top deluxe class. Private suites, penthouse supper club with panoramic view, ballroom and banquet hall; the *Dell' Arte* restaurant is also excellent.

Frankfurt Sheraton, Frankfurt airport (tel. 69770). 3 restaurants, several bars, disco, indoor pool. Connected directly to arrivals hall.

Gravenbruch-Kempinski, Neu Isenberg 2, (tel. 06102–5050). South of the city. Has fine restaurant, indoor pool. Prices between new and old buildings vary considerably. Near airport.

Steigenberger Frankfurter Hof, Am Kaiserplatz (tel. 20251). Vast and glittering with a particularly high degree of comfort and service. With grill room, first-class French restaurant, and *Frankfurter Stubb* tavern.

Expensive

Crest Hotel, Isenburger Schneise 40, Niederrad (tel. 67840). Very quiet and comfortable if a little remotely situated in the suburb of Niederrad.

Frankfurt Savoy, Wiesenhüttenstr. 42 (tel. 230511). Has *Le Tourbillon* bar, Savoy Grill, a disco, sauna.

Hessischer Hof, Friedrich-Ebert-Anlage 40 (tel. 75400). Near the fair grounds. Former townhouse of the Hessen Royal Family.

Holiday Inn City Tower, Mailänderstr. 1 (tel. 68020). 190 rooms. In old quarter of Sachsenhausen in pedestrians only street, so quiet; fine view.

Novotel, Philipp-Helfmann-Str. 10 (tel. 06196–42812). Near airport.

Parkhotel, Wiesenhuttenplatz 28–38 (tel. 26970). Very comfortable hotel with old-style charm, though the rooms in the older section are a little noisy.

Savigny, Savignystr. 14–16 (tel. 75330). 85 rooms. Modern, elegant with good atmosphere. Not far from station.

Steigenberger Airport Hotel, by airport (tel. 69851). 350 rooms with color TV; quiet. Rooftop pool.

Moderate

Admiral, Hölderlinstr. 25 (tel. 448021). Near the zoo.

Ebel, Taunusstr. 26 (tel. 230756). Breakfast only; near the main station.

Schwille, Grosse Bockenheimer Str. 50 (tel. 283054). Near the rail station.

Westfälinger Hof, Düsseldorfer Str. 10 (tel. 234748).

Zentrum, Rossmarkt 7 (tel. 295291). Small.

Inexpensive

Maingau, Schifferstr. 38 (tel. 617001). Quiet, though near the main station.

Vera, Mainzer Landstr. 118 (tel. 745023). Breakfast only.

Württemberger Hof, Karlstr. 14 (tel. 233106). Garni; hot meals until 2.30 in the morning.

Restaurants

Expensive

Bistrot 77, Ziegelhüttenweg 1–3 (tel. 614040) in Sachsenhausen. Highly recommended French restaurant with imaginative dishes.

Brückenkeller, Schützenstr. 6 (tel. 284238). In an old cellar reeking of medieval atmosphere. Excels in vintage wines; splendid food. Music.

Da Bruno, Elbestr. 15 (tel. 233416). *The* Italian establishment in town.

Erno's Bistro, Liebigstr. 15 (tel. 721997). Has won lavish praise from gourmets. Setting modest; prices anything but. Reservations a must.

Frankfurter Stubb, Hotel Frankfurter Hof, Kaiserplatz 17 (tel. 20251).

Heyland's Weinstuben, Kaiserhofstr. 7 (tel. 284840). Game and fish specialties in this venerable establishment with its maze of small bars and quiet nooks.

Dell' Arte, Frankfurt Intercontinental, Wilhelm-Leuschner-Str. 43 (tel. 230561). Among Frankfurt's grander spots.

Rheinpfalz Weinstuben, Theaterplatz (tel. 233870). Good vintage wines with the delicious *Zwiebelkuchen* (onion tarts) to accompany them.

Moderate

Alt Frankfurt, Berlinerstr. 10 (tel. 281064). Romantic, old-style locale; has a beer fountain. Specialty is roast suckling pig.

Altanchen, Gr. Ritter Str. 112. Local specialties amid Sachsenhausen bustle.

Atschel, Wallstr. in Alt Sachsenhausen. Typical Frankfurt tavern serving local specialties and *Ebbelwoi* (strong cider) from own cellar.

Dippegucker, Eschenheimer Anlage 40 (tel. 551965). Delicious crisp salads are a house specialty. Rustic and reasonable. Busy at lunchtime.

Henninger Turm, in Sachsenhausen across the river (tel. 6063600). Two rotating restaurants about 400 ft. up in a brewery tower.

Jawne, Friedrichstr. (tel. 728618). Kosher restaurant next to the West End Synagogue. Open noon–3, Fri. 6.30–8 P.M., closed Mon.

Maredo, Bockenheimer Str. 24 (tel. 288054). American steaks a trademark.

St. Hubertus, Gartenstr. 175 (tel. 637266). Game predominates here.

Inexpensive

Intercity, in main rail station (tel. 231956). Good value.

Sudpfanne, Escherscheimer Landstr. 20 (tel. 552122).

Zum Anker, Grusonstr. 9 (tel. 439027). Plates heaped with sausages.

 NIGHTLIFE. In Kaiserstr., Moselstr., Munchner Str., and the vicinity of the main station, there are many night spots showing uninhibited striptease and crowded with dance hostesses. The jazz scene is one of the busiest in Europe and a visit to one of the cellars such as **Schlachthof** on Deutscherrnufer is a must. Most of the more elegant night spots are in the larger hotels, but two convivial starting points are *Jimmy's Bar,* Friedrich Ebert Anlage 40, and *Fidelio,* Bockenheimer Landstr. 1. For those who want something lively, but need a guiding hand, there is an organized cabaret tour which departs from the south side of the railway station. Lasting four hours, the price of DM 90 includes two drinks and a red hot show.

 MUSEUMS. Over the past years, Frankfurt has gradually been assembling its most important museums in new buildings along the banks of the Main, known as Museums Ufer.

Museum of Applied Art, Schaumainkai 15. Furniture, porcelain, glass, silver, textiles, handwritten scrolls. Tues. through Sun. 10–5.

Deutsches Architekturmuseum, Schaumainkai 43. The history of man's settlement and housing development from the Stone Age to present-day urban planning. Tues. through Sun., 10–5; Wed. to 8 P.M.

Deutsches Filmmuseum, Schaumainkai 41. Latest addition to the collection of Main Bank museums. The only one of its kind in Germany, presenting exhibits of everything associated with movies and movie-making.

Goethe's House and Museum, Grosser Hirschgraben 23. Daily 9–6, Sun. 10–1.

Heinrich-Hoffmann Museum (known as Struwwelpeter Museum), Schubertstr. 20. Dedicated to the creator of the famous children's book hero, Struwwelpeter. Tues. through Sun. 10–5.

Historical Museum and Children's Museum, Saalgasse 19. Exhibits from the Middle Ages to the 19th century. Children's Museum in same building. Tues. and Thurs. through Sun. 10–5, Wed. 10–8, closed Mon.

Liebieghaus, Schaumainkai 71. Fine sculpture collection of Egyptian, Greek, Roman, German and Italian works, among others. Tues. and Thurs. through Sun. 10–4, Wed. 10–8, closed Mon.

Prehistoric and Archaeological Museum, Justinianstr. Local antiquities and ancient handicrafts. Tues. and Thurs.–Sun. 10–5, Wed. 10–8, closed Mon.

Senckenberg Natural History Museum, Senckenberganlage 25. Largest of its kind in Germany. Daily 9–4.

Städel Art Institute, Schaumainkai 63. Important collection of Europe's leading painters, ancient and modern. Daily 10–4, Sun. 10–1.

 SHOPPING. Any excursion into the pedestrian shopping precincts will bring you to the *Hauptwache* at the heart of the city and the center of public transport. You can shop here both above and below ground level. To the east of the Hauptwache is the largest pedestrian zone called the *Zeil,* which is lined with fine department and furniture stores. A right turn down Neue Kräme or Hasengasse will find you at the indoor market, *Kleinmarkthalle,* which overflows with stalls selling fresh fruits, vegetables and the like. Schillerstrasse offers many elegant boutiques, while Goethestrasse has perfumeries and jewellers. The center of Frankfurt's famous fur trade lies in the area around the main station. Great leathergoods bargains can be had along the Kaiserstr. and boutiques in Goethestr. There is a Saturday flea market in Alt Sachsenhausen, along the banks of the Main between the Alte Brücke and Untermain Brücke bridges.

USEFUL ADDRESSES. *Consulates:* U.S.A., Siesmayerstr. 21; British, Bockenheimer Landstr. 51. *American Express,* Steinweg 5. *Wagons-Lits/Cook,* Kaiserstr. 11. *Frankfurt Tourist Office,* B-level, Hauptwache Passage. Room reservations: tel. 231055.

Hesse—Spa Country

This is a land of storied castles and healing springs. Bad Homburg, only 12 miles from Frankfurt, has 11 therapeutic springs already famous in Roman times. More recently Dwight D. Eisenhower declared his affection for Bad Homburg; the place has never lost its vogue. The state apartments of Bad Homburg's schloss can be visited on conducted tours. Other sights are the 13th-century Weisser Turm, the castle gate, the lower bridge and the Church of the Redeemer; while the elegant casino and schloss concerts supply entertainment.

But the most famous attraction of Bad Homburg is four and a half miles away at Saalburg, where you will the best preserved Roman fort in Europe. Bad Homburg is but one stop in Hesse's "international promenade of spas" stretching from Wiesbaden to Bad Wildungen.

From Marburg to Kassel

A visit to the castle and university town of Marburg is fascinating for the lover of folklore. Old customs and traditions have survived here. If you're in this area in summertime, see the folk plays, concerts and festivals in the park of the castle. Also not to be missed: St. Elizabeth's Gothic Cathedral, one of the oldest in Germany. Among the interesting old towns en route from Marburg to Kassel are Winterberg, a well-known health resort; Korbach, with its ancient church of St. Kilian and its medieval buildings; Waldeck, whose castle overlooks the Edersee; the cathedral town of Fritzlar; and Schotten, equally notable for its mountain road races and its gems of baroque architecture. The country around here looks like a setting for Grimm's fairy tales, as a visit to the Brothers Grimm Museum in Schloss Bellevue will confirm.

Kassel, industrial capital of Hesse-Nassau, has a museum which houses one of Germany's finest art collections, the Staatliche Kunstsammlung in Wilhelmshöhe Palace.

PRACTICAL INFORMATION FOR HESSE

BAD HERSFELD. *Am Kurpark* (E), tel. 1640. New in 1985 in the Cure Park section. Restaurant, café with terrace, beer and wine tavern. Romantik Hotel *Zum Stern* (M), Lingplatz 11 (tel. 06621–72007). Former lodging house of Benedictine monastery dating from 15th century. Indoor pool and restaurant.

Parkhotel Rose (M), Am Kurpark 9 (tel. 14454). First-class comfort, modern yet rustic style. *Wildes Wässerchen* (M), Meisebacherstr. 31 (tel. 5055). Good restaurant.

BAD HOMBURG. *Kurhaushotel Maritim* (E), Ludwigstr. (tel. 28051). Elegant, with indoor pool, restaurant, wine-tavern, and cafe. *Geheimrat Trapp* (M), Kaiser-Friedrich-Promenade (tel. 26047). Medicinal baths to go with its other facilities. *Hartwald-Hotel* (M), Philosophenweg 31 (tel. 25016). Quiet. *Haus Baur* (M), Gymnasiumstr. 14 (tel. 22612). Breakfast only. *Taunus* (I), Louisenstr. (tel. 22315).

Restaurants. *Casino* (E), at the casino (tel. 20041). Serves fine French food. *Table* (E), Kaiser-Friedrich-Promenade 85 (tel. 24425). High standard French cuisine. Open 6.30–10.30. *Darmstädter Hof* (M), Frankfurter Landstr. 77 (tel. 41347). Good-value à la carte menu with steaks from the grill. Rustic surroundings. *Hamburger Hof* (M), in hotel of same name (tel. 41040). Hearty home cooking. *Landgrafen* (M), at the Castle (tel. 21530). Panoramic view across the Taunus. Excellent wines.

For fresh trout in rural surroundings, try *Forellengut Taunus* in the middle of the forest at Oberursel 4 (tel. 35119). Open Mar.–Oct., 11.15–6; in winter, Sat. and Sun. only.

BAD NAUHEIM. *Am Hochwald* (E), Carl-Oelemann-Weg 3 (tel. 3480). Quietly located with restaurant, bar and sauna. *Parkhotel am Kurhaus* (E), at the Cure Park (tel. 3030). New, but continuing the tradition of the former Hilberts Parkhotel. Quiet and modern, with 2 restaurants, beer and wine taverns. *Gaudes* (M), Hauptstr. 6 (tel. 2508). Small hotel-restaurant. *Grünewald* (M), Terrassenstr. 10 (tel. 2230). Breakfast only; small, but particularly comfortable and attractive. Non-smokers only.

FULDA. *Romantik Hotel Goldener Karpfen* (E), Simplicius Platz 1–5 (tel. 70044). Atmospheric with style. Good restaurant. *Bachmühle* (M), Künzeller Str. 133 (tel. 77800). Highly recommended. Good restaurant. Quiet. *Lenz* (M), Leipzigerstr 122 (tel. 77067). Has sauna, solarium and fitness room. *Kurfürst* (M), Schlosstr. 2 (tel. 70001). *Hessicher Hof* (I), Nikolausstr. 22 (tel. 77289).

Restaurants. *Hauptwache* (M), Bonifatiusplatz 2 (tel. 75153). Hot food from 10 A.M. to 1 P.M. Closed Wed. *Orangerie-Diana-Keller* (M), in the Hotel Maritim at the Schlossgarten, Pauluspromenade 2 (tel. 73121). *Alte Post am Dom* (M), Wilhelmstr. 2 (tel. 72373).

KASSEL. *Schlosshotel Wilhelmshöhe* (E), Schlosspark 2 (tel. 30880). Palatial castle hotel in the park-on-the-hill at Wilhelmshöhe. *Excelsior* (M), Erzbergerstr. 2 (tel. 102984). *Gasthaus Elfbuchen* (M), in the Habichtswald forest (tel. 37416). Particularly quietly located near the Hercules Monument; taxis transport guests up to the hotel which is not otherwise approachable by private car. Restaurant; ponies for hire. *Holiday Inn* (E), 10 miles out at the Autobahn exit at Kassel-East (tel. 52151). Indoor pool and fitness center along with the other usual Holiday Inn facilities. *Dorint-Hotel Reiss* (E), Werner-Hilpertstr. 24 (tel. 78830). In city center. Has notable restaurant, *Alt-Cassel. Im Rosengarten* (M), Burgfeldstr. 16 (tel. 36094). Particularly comfortable with good service; breakfast only.

Restaurants. *Landhaus-Meister-Silberdistel* (E), Fuldatalstr. 140 (tel. 875050). Rustic but modern restaurant with daily specialties in French style. 7-course gourmet set menu for about DM 100. *Henkel* (M), in main rail station. Hot food till 11 P.M. *Ratskeller* (M), Obere Königsstr. (tel. 15928). Ye-olde-worlde-style, good value.

KRONBERG. *Schlosshotel* (L), Hainstr. 25 (tel. 7011). Converted baronial mansion; antique furniture, golf course and first class restaurant.

MARBURG. *Europäischer Hof* (M), Elisabethstr. 12 (tel. 64044). Breakfast only. *Dammühle* (M), tel. 23007, on the banks of the river Lahn in the quiet suburb of Wehrshausen in old mill house; garden terrace, fine restaurant. *Waldecker Hof* (M), Bahnhofstr. 23 (tel. 67087).

Restaurants. *Alt-Weidenhausen* (E), Weidenhauserstr. 72 (tel. 25728). In the historical old town in the center of the city; cosy and rather rustic. *Gasthaus Zur Sonne* (I), Markt 14 (tel. 25314). In a half-timbered house that dates from 1600; colorful, and also has a few rooms. Both open until 11 P.M.

SABABURG. *Burghotel Sababurg* (M), about 10 miles north of Kassel, near Hofgeismar (tel. 1052). The legendary castle of the Sleeping Beauty.

TRENDELBURG. *Burghotel Trendelburg* (E), near Hofgeismar (tel. 1021). 13th-century building; dining by candlelight or on the ramparts.

Westphalia

This province between the Weser and the Rhine is synonymous throughout the civilized work with ham. It is full of oak forests and these have provided Westphalia's pigs with luscious acorns.

But this country's attractions are not limited to the table. The regions of Sauerland, Siegerland, Wittgensteineland, Münsterland and Teutoberg Forest, with their numerous nature parks, forests, lakes and hills exert a wide appeal to all travelers: from the Youth Hostels of the Münsterland, the center of castled Altena and the stalactite caves of Attendorn to the Stone, Bronze and Iron Age relics of the Lippisches Landmuseum of Detmold.

Münster and Dortmund

The regional capital of Münster, seat of Westphalia University, is interesting for its many old buildings and as a center for excursions to such places as Freckenhorst, with its Romanesque church; Burgsteinfurt, with its important moated castle; Coesfeld, a Hanseatic city with its old walls and gates still standing; and Nordkirchen, with its impressive ensemble of baroque castles.

Dortmund, on the other hand, takes pride in modern achievements rather than in those of the past. Here is a booming city, typical of the resurgent industrial Ruhr, the empire of coal and steel which is "the forge of Germany". Take a look here at the ultramodern Westfalenhalle, largest sports arena in Western Europe. As a brewing center, Dortmund comes second in the world only to Milwaukee.

PRACTICAL INFORMATION FOR WESTPHALIA

DORTMUND. *Romantik Hotel Lennhof* (E), Menglinghäuser Str. 20 in Barop suburb (tel. 75726). Half-timbered house dating from 1395. *Römischer Kaiser* (E), Olpe 2 (corner of Kleppingstr.) (tel. 54321). Has fine restaurant and cafe. *Parkhotel Westfalenhalle* (E), Strobelallee 41 (tel. 1204230). *Novotel* (M), Brennaborstr. in Oespel suburb (tel. 65485). 104 rooms, indoor pool.
Restaurants. *Hövelpforte* (E), Hoher Wall 5 (tel. 142803). Atmospheric. *Krone* (M), Markt 10 (tel. 527548). Has terrace and cafe. *Turmrestaurant* (M), on top of the TV Tower in the Westfalenpark. Rotates and, needless to say, has fine view. *Zum Treppchen* (M), Hörder Burgstr. 3 (tel. 431442). In suburb of Hörde. Regional specialties in traditional surroundings. Reservations recommended. *Zum Alten Markt* (I), Markt 3 (tel. 572217). Wholesome food in a colorful setting.

MÜNSTER. *Waldhotel Krautkrämer* (E), about 3 miles south of the city on Lake Hiltrupersee (tel. 02501–8050). Swimming pool, sauna, solarium, fitness center and tennis; excellent restaurant and an interesting collection of antique dolls. *Conti* (M), Berliner Platz 2 (tel. 40444). Breakfast only; near the main station. *Horstmann* (M), Windhorststr. 12 (tel. 47077). Breakfast only. *Kaiserhof* (M), Bahnhofstr. 14 (tel. 40059). Close to station. *Schloss Wilkinghege* (M), Steinfurterstr. 374 (tel. 213045). A castle hotel just a little out of town; has quiet and comfortable annexe, *Gästehaus,* as well as golf course and a good restaurant. *Überwasserhof* (M), Überwasserstr. 3 (tel. 40630). Breakfast only. *Schloss Hohenfeld* (I), Dingbänger Weg 400 (tel. 02534–7031). A castle hotel in the suburb of Roxel, just out of town.

Restaurants. *Kleines Restaurant im Oerschen Hof* (M), Königstr. 42 (tel. 42061). Fine food and nostalgic decor. *Stuhlmacher* (M), Prinzipalmarkt 6 (tel. 44877). *Altes Gasthaus Leve* (I), Alter Steinweg 37 (tel. 45595). Over 350 years old. *Pinkus Müller* (I), Kreuzstr. 4 (tel. 45151). Local specialties and "Alt Bier."

SOEST. *Im Wilden Mann* (E), Am Markt 11 (tel. 2595). A Romantik Hotel in the center of town. Delightful half-timbered house with an original beer parlor and elegant restaurant that specializes in game and fish dishes as well as traditional Westphalian recipes. Reservations are essential.

The Northern Rhineland

The A, B, C and D of Northern Rhineland cities are Aachen, Bonn, Cologne and Düsseldorf. We could add a capital E for Essen, the largest city of the region. But despite its ninth-century Münster Church and other treasures, industrial Essen is not recommended for tourists.

Aachen

Aachen is another stein of beer. This spa (among the hottest springs in northwest Europe) is steeped in history. It was Charlemagne's capital, and 32 of the Holy Roman emperors were crowned here, either in the emperor's cathedral, begun in the ninth century, or in the Coronation Hall of the Rathaus. In the cathedral, you will see the marble chair of Charlemagne, and what remains of his body lies near the main altar. The cathedral's other great treasure is the Shrine of Mary, an intricately sculptured gold and silver reliquary, finished in 1237, possibly the finest medieval reliquary in Germany. The lofty Gothic choir, whose walls are virtually all glass, is a masterpiece of 14th-century architecture.

Bonn

Bonn, gateway to the romantic Rhine Valley, is more than 2,000 years old. Beethoven was born in this city in 1770, at Bonngasse 20, now a museum, and Schumann spent his last years in Sebastianstr. 182. The Beethoven-Halle is an important center of musical life. Among Bonn's other attractions are the baroque Jesu Church, the 13th-century Remigius Church, the 18th-century Poppelsdorf Castle, and the Alte Zoll, a mighty bastion overlooking the Rhine, with a magnificent view of the Siebengebirge. The Drachenfels, with its romantic castle ruins celebrated by Lord Byron, is one of Europe's most frequently visited mountains. From the Alte Zoll, follow the attractive promenade along the Rhine to the Bundeshaus, the German equivalent of the Capitol or Houses of Parliament, for Bonn is presently the West German capital. The official residence of the Federal President is at Villa Hammerschmidt in the Adenauerallee.

Cologne

Cologne, first city of the Rhineland, was almost wiped out by aerial bombardment in the war. But the great cathedral still stands, and much else remains of cultural interest.

The cathedral, nearly 500 feet long, is one of the largest Gothic churches in the world and one of the most beautiful. Don't miss the reliquary of the Three Magi, a masterpiece of medieval goldsmith's art, nor the altar's center panel, painted by Stefan Lochner, the greatest native artist of Cologne.

The Romanesque basilica of St. Pantaleon also survived the bombing, and in the rebuilt church of St. Ursula is the famous Golden Room, full of relics and treasures which are quite literally fabulous. Still another Romanesque monument is the extraordinary church of St. Gereon, with its ten-sided nave. The 15th-century Gürzenich, built for dancing and feasting in the Middle Ages, still serves the same purpose today, especially at carnival time.

But Cologne does not live on the glory of past monuments. The vitality of this city can be measured by the tremendous modern buildings that are replacing the lost medieval ones—the Opera House, the Chamber of Commerce building, the new Philharmonic Hall, the Wallraf-Richartz/Museum Ludwig visual arts center opened in September 1986, and the Gerling skyscraper, the most modern radio building in Europe.

Düsseldorf

Düsseldorf, administrative center of the most industrialized area of Germany, is called "the desk of the Ruhr district". It is also an important cultural center; Heine, Brahms, Schumann and Goethe all lived here. The last is honored by the Goethe Museum, containing more than 20,000 manuscripts, drawings, first editions and other memorabilia. In the Municipal Art Museum are outstanding collections of paintings, sculpture, medieval arts and crafts, and 2,000 years of ceramics.

PRACTICAL INFORMATION FOR NORTHERN RHINELAND

AACHEN. *Steigenberger Parkhotel Quellenhof* (L), Monheimsallee 52 (tel. 152081). 5 minutes' walk from Aachen's city promenade; indoor pool with thermal baths. Kneipp cures and sauna. *Novotel* (E), Europaplatz (tel. 164091). Centrally located with good public transport connections. Romantik Hotel *Altes Brauhaus Burgkeller* (M), Steinweg 22-A in the Stolberg suburb, 7 miles from city center (tel. 27272). *Drei Könige* (M), Büchel 5/corner Markt (tel. 48393). Centrally located and very good value. With an old, rustic restaurant. *Trawigo* (M), Julicherstr. 91a (tel. 153051). Has bowling and billiards; restaurant only does evening meal.

Restaurants. *Gala* (E), Monheimsallee 44 (tel. 23713). In the casino and very expensive indeed. *Gut Schwarzenbruch* (E), in the suburb of Stolberg (tel. 02402 –22275). 8 miles out of town, but with first-class cuisine and particularly attractive period decor. *Ratskeller* (E), corner of Markt and Kramerstr 2 (tel. 35001). *Elisenbrunnen* (M), Friedrich-Wilhelm-Platz (tel. 21383).

BAD GODESBURG. *Godesburg* (E), tel. 316071. Small hotel attached to medieval Godesburg castle; fairly modern itself, however. *Drachenfels* (M), Siegfriedstr. 28 (tel. 343067). Good value. *Park Hotel* (M), Am Kurpark 1 (tel. 363081). Breakfast only. *Rheinhotel Dreesen* (M), Rheinstr. 45 (tel. 364001). Bar, indoor seawater pool, Rhine-terrace and concerts and dancing in the summer. *Rheinland* (M), Rheinallee 17 (tel. 353087). *Zum Adler* (M), Koblenzer Str. 60 (tel. 364071). Excellent restaurant. *Bungertshof* (I), on the opposite bank of the Rhine at Königswinter (tel. 02223–21429). *Rheingold* (I), Drachenfelsstr. 36 (tel. 02223–23048). Also at Königswinter.

Restaurants. *Haus Maternus* (E), Loebestr. 3 (tel. 362851). Exceptionally well decorated with high-quality cuisine. *Mövenpick* (E), Ahrstr. 45 (tel. 379170). Several bars and international specialties. *Wirtshaus Sankt Michael* (E), Brunnenallee 26 (tel. 364765). One of Germany's most famous and best restaurants. Outstanding cuisine at really quite reasonable prices.

BONN. *Königshof* (L), Adenauerallee 9–11 (tel. 26010). Also apartments. Excellent restaurant with particularly good wines; quiet and with fine view.

Steigenberger Bonn (L), Bundeskanzlerplatz (tel. 20191). In the top five floors of the Bonn Center building. Ultramodern. Very fine restaurant on the 18th floor. *Beethoven* (M), Rheingasse 26 (tel. 631411). Near the landing stage. *Bergischer Hof* (M), Münsterplatz 23 (tel. 633441). *Eden* (M), Am Hofgarten 6 (tel. 224077). *Esplanade Sternhotel* (M), Markt 8 (tel. 654455).

Restaurants. *Am Tulpenfeld* (M), Heussallee 2 (tel. 219081). In hotel of same name. Fine food; exceptionally good value. *Im Bären* (M), Acherstr. 1 (tel. 636200). *Im Stiefel* (M), Bonngasse 30 (tel. 634806). *Weinhaus Jacobs* (M), Friedrichstr. 18 (tel. 637353). Colorful spot. *Weinhaus Zum Kapellchen* (M), Brüdergasse 12 (tel. 651052). Gourmet cuisine; very good value.

COLOGNE. *Excelsior Hotel Ernst* (L), Domplatz (tel. 2701). Long established fine French restaurant and grill room. *Dom Hotel* (L), Domkloster 2a (tel. 233751). Near the Cathedral and also has an excellent French restaurant. *Ascot* (E), Hohenzollernring 95 (tel. 521076). New in 1985; modern, centrally-located hotel. Ground-floor bistro and fitness center in basement. *Intercontinental* (L), Helenenstr. 14 (tel. 2280). Rooftop dining and dancing; indoor pool. *Inter-City Hotel IBIS* (E), Hauptbahnhof (tel. 132051). At station square with view of cathedral. *Novotel-Köln* (E), Horbeller Str. 1 (tel. 16081). In Marsdorf section. First class hotel in Novotel chain. All rooms with bath, colour TV, radio etc. Restaurant open from 6.00 A.M. to midnight. *Bremer* (M), Dürenerstr. 225 (tel. 405013). In the suburb of Lindenthal. *Consul* (M), Belfortstr. 9 (tel. 731051). Indoor pool, sauna, solarium; good restaurant. *Holiday Inn* (M), Waldstr. 255 (tel. 02203–5610). Out by the airport in the suburb of Porz. *Kommerz* (M), Breslauerplatz (tel. 124086). New, very centrally located; all rooms with shower, W.C., T.V. and telephone. Sauna. *Weinbauhotel-Kunibert der Fiese* (M), Am Bollwerk 1 (tel. 235808). Sited between the Franken Tower and Mauthgasse; has a fine view. *Regent* (M), Melatengurtel 15 (tel. 54991). In west suburb of Braunsfeld; fine rooftop restaurant. *Stapelhäuschen* (M), Fischmarkt 1 (tel. 212193). Small, old inn with good wine tavern. Convenient location around the corner from Rhine steamers' landing stage. *Berg* (I), Brandenburger Str. 6 (tel. 121124). Centrally located near the main station. *Rossner* (I), Jakordenstr. (tel. 122703). Breakfast only.

Restaurants. *Bastei* (E), on the Rhine banks in Konrad-Adenauer-Ufer 80 (tel. 122825). Panoramic view over the river through floor to ceiling windows. *Chez Alex* (E), Muhlengasse 1 (tel. 230560). First class French cuisine. *Goldener Pflug* (E), Olpener Str. 421 in the suburb of Merheim (tel. 895509). One of the finest restaurants in town, and indeed in Germany. Elegant and very expensive, but good value. Reservations recommended. *Restaurant Bado (La Poele d'Or)* (E), Komödienstr. 52 (tel. 134100). Rated among the very finest restaurants in Germany; luxurious furnishings. *Alt-Köln Am Dom* (M), Trankg. 7 (tel. 134471). Old tavern. *Zum Roten Ochsen* (M), Thurnmarkt 7 (tel. 235642). Rustic decor. Typical old-Cologne taverns (*Altkölsche Weetschafte*) with scrubbed tabletops and cosy rooms, serving local specialties, include: *Brauhaus Sion* (I), Am Hof 20 (tel. 214203). *Früh am Dom* (I), Am Hof 12 (tel. 212621); with garden. *Früh am Veedel* (I), Chodwigplatz 28 (tel. 314470). *Haus Töller* (I), Weyerstr. 96 (tel. 214086). Furnished in traditional local style. *Mohr Baedorf* (I), Neumarkt 43 (tel. 216065). With terrace. *Pfäffgen* (I), Friesenstr. 64. Dixieland jazz and home-brewed "Kölsch" beer.

DÜSSELDORF. *Breidenbacher Hof* (L), Heinrich Heine Allee 36 (tel. 8601). A hotel with a long-standing reputation for service. *Hilton-International* (L), Georg-Glockstr. (tel. 434963). Situated between Kennedy Dam and the Rhine; a modern hotel with very fine restaurant, *San Francisco. Inter-Continental* (L), Karl-Arnold-Platz 5 (tel. 45530). Heated pool, sauna, solarium, golf course, fitness center and Restaurant *Rotisserie. Steigenberger Park Hotel* (L), Corneliusplatz 1 (tel. 8651). Has infrared heated terrace, unusual even by German standards! *Ramada* (E), Am Seestern 16 (tel. 591047). In suburb of Oberkassel. *Ramada Renaissance* (E), Nördlicher Zubringer 6 (tel. 62160). Superbly equipped; international restaurant, café, and English bar. *Esplanade* (E), Furstenplatz 17 (tel. 375010). *Terminus* (E), Am Wehrhahn 81 (tel. 350591). Breakfast only. *Schnellenburg* (M), Rotterdamerstr. 120 (tel. 434133) near the airport. Built on the ruins of a medieval castle. Local style with modern interiors and all first class facilities. *Uebechs* (M), Leopoldstr. 3 (tel. 360566). Has well-known restaurant. *Komet* (I), Bismarckstr. 93 (tel. 357917). Central.

Restaurants. *Frickhöfer* (E), Stromstr. 47 (tel. 393931). In the suburb of Oberkassel; outstanding cuisine. *Im Schiffchen* (E), Kaiserswerther Markt 9 (tel. 401050). In Kaiserswerth suburb; excellent French menu. *M + F* (Müllers + Fest) (E), Königsalle 14 (tel. 326001). Good cooking and attentive service. KD restaurant on ground floor, with terrace. *Orangerie* (E), Bilkerstr. 30 (tel. 373733). Small, with period furniture and extremely good food. Recommended. *Robert's Restaurant* (E), Oberkasseler Str. 100 (tel. 575672). In Oberkassel; internationally renowned. *Frankenheim* (I), Wielandstr. 12–16 (tel. 351447). Hearty local specialties. *Im Füchschen* (I), Ratinger Str. 28 (tel. 84062). Typical brewery tavern with home cooking. *Zum Schiffchen* (I), Hafenstr. 5 (tel. 132421). On the edge of the old town, and full of local color. *Zum Schlüssel* (I), Bolkerstr. 43 (tel. 326155). Good, inexpensive tavern.

The Upper Rhineland

Above Cologne, the Rhine becomes typical of romantic Germany. The Cologne-Düsseldorf (KD) Rhine Steamer Company operates clean, comfortable ships between Cologne and Mainz, the most interesting stretch of the river, between banks landscaped with romantically turreted castles, precipitous vineyards and Gothic cathedrals. Take a look at the ruined castle of the Drachenfels on the dizzy heights overlooking Königswinter, or visit the vineyards said to have been planted by Charlemagne. Upstream, count on from 13 to 16 hours for this trip, depending on whether or not you take an express steamer. Downstream, it will take 8½ or 9. You can buy a combined train-steamer ticket, enabling you to switch from one to the other.

A shorter trip, one in which most of the attractions of the Rhine are concentrated, is the voyage from Koblenz to Mainz. Koblenz, in the shadow of the famous Ehrenbreitstein Fortress (you can reach it by chairlift), is the gateway to the most romantic section of the Rhine and the Mosel, at whose confluence the city stands. It is studded with such Romanesque churches as St. Castor's (9th century), Liebfrauenkirche (12th century) and St. Florin's (12th century with Gothic additions).

Trier

Just a step from the Luxembourg frontier at the confluence of the Saar, Ruwer and Mosel rivers, is Trier, the oldest city in Germany. In 1984 it celebrated its 2000th anniversary. This was the northern capital of the Roman Empire. The pride of Trier is the Porta Nigra, the massive northern gate to the Roman Empire, which compares favorably with the finest architectural accomplishments of the Romans. The Provincial Museum contains much Roman work, and the City Library has remarkable illuminated manuscripts.

East of Koblenz

Just east of Koblenz is the internationally-known spa of Bad Ems, pleasantly laid out along both banks of the Lahn River; for 20 years (1867–1887), it was the spot Kaiser Wilhelm chose for his yearly cure.

From Koblenz onward, all the settlements are jewels, and if you want a quiet vacation, you can choose almost any of the riverside towns at random. One such town is Rüdesheim, center of Rhine wine production. The wine museum, the many wine cellars, the beautifully-designed old houses with their half-timbered walls and quaint gables and turrets, give this town a very special charm.

Bingen, on the other side of the Rhine, is another tourist center, an important pilgrimage goal at the end of August when the town's deliverance from the Black Plague is celebrated annually in the Festival of St. Rochus. From Bingen, one enters the Palatinate at the "town of roses and nightingales", Bad Kreuznach, with picturesque 15th-century houses built on its bridge.

PRACTICAL INFORMATION FOR THE UPPER RHINELAND

BAD EMS. *M.C.I.-Hotel Staatliches Kurhaus* (E), Römerstr. 1 (tel. 3016). Solarium, thermal baths, sauna and all the other accoutrements of an excellent spa hotel. *Parkhotel* (M), Malbergstr. 7 (tel. 2058). Panoramic view. *Russischer Hof* (M), Römerstr. 23 (tel. 4462). Czar Nicholas II stayed here, hence the name. *Berghotel-Café Wintersberg* (I), Braubacher Str. (tel. 4282). In quiet forest high above town. Panoramic view. Also apartments; sauna, solarium.
Restaurants. *Kursaal* (M), Romerstr. 8 (tel. 2818). *Altes Weinhaus* (I), Silberaustr. 18 (tel. 4960). Game specialties and *zwiebelkuchen.* First class wines.

BAD KREUZNACH. *Steigenberger-Hotel-Kurhaus* (L), tel. 2061. Particularly comfortable establishment; quiet, with bowling, billiards, café and restaurant. *Caravelle* (E), in Oranien Park (tel. 2495). Restaurant, pool, sauna, medicinal baths. *Der Quellenhof* (M), Nachtigallenweg 2 (tel. 2191). Quiet, with solarium, medicinal baths, fitness center, pool, sauna and restaurant. *Rosenhof,* Salinenstr. 139 (tel. 28753). Wine tavern. Breakfast only.

BINGEN. *Weinstube Schinderhannes* (E), tel. 3021. In the little suburb of Bingerbruck. *Römerhof* (M), Rupertsberg 10 (tel. 32248). Also in Bingerbruck. *Starkenburger Hof* (M), Rheinkai 1 (tel. 14341). Faces the river.

BOPPARD. *Bellevue* (E), Rheinallee 41 (tel. 1020). All modern comforts; riverside bathing lawn; pool. Very fine *Pfeffermühle* (E) restaurant. *Klostergut Jakobsberg* (E), tel. 3061. 207 beds. Sited in a former monastery founded by Frederick Barbarossa, and overlooking the Rhine. All imaginable facilities, including a wedding chapel and helicopter landing pad! *Adams* (I), P. J. Kreuzbergstr. 15 (tel. 2556). Easy access to town center on foot. Pleasant view.

KOBLENZ. *Kleiner Riesen* (M), Rheinanlangen 18 (tel. 32077). On the banks of the river and with fine view. *Hohenstaufen* (I), Emil-Schullerstr. 41 (tel. 35051). *Höhmann,* Bahnhofsplatz 5 (tel. 35011). Breakfast only; near the station. *Pfälzer Hof-Continental* (I), Bahnhofsplatz 1 (tel. 33073). Good restaurant.

OBERWESEL. "Castle-Hotel" *Auf Schönberg* (E), tel. 8198. A 1,000 year old castle-fortress above the Rhine; only 10 rooms, though with delightful period furnishings, so book ahead. Excellent restaurant. Open Mar.-Nov. *Römerkrug* (I), tel. 8174. Near the Market Place in old half-timbered house with 500 year old wine cellar; good food but reservations essential as only 7 rooms. *Pension-Restaurant Winzerhaus* (I), Rheingoldstr. 8 (tel. 1366). In the Urbar section opposite the Lorelei on a hill above the Rhine. Good restaurant.
Restaurant. *Gutsschänke Weintorkel* (M), Koblenzer Str. 89 (tel. 8123). Rustic cosy wine-tavern.

TRIER. *Dorint Hotel Porta Nigra* (L), Porta Nigra Platz 1 (tel. 27010). 175 beds. Sauna, solarium; choice of three restaurants. *Holiday Inn* (E), An der Mosel (tel. 23091). Close to station. *Kessler* (E), Brückenstr. 23 (tel. 73561). Garni. *Am Hügel* (M), Bernhardstr. 14 (tel. 33066). *Petrisberg* (M), Sickingenstr. 11 (tel. 41181). Breakfast only. *Haag* (I), Stockplatz 1 (tel. 72366). Breakfast only. Wine tasting.
Restaurants. *Domstein* (M), Hauptmarkt 5 (tel. 74490). Roman wine cellar with 2000-year-old recipes. *Zum Krokodil* (I), Justizplatz (tel. 73107).

Wiesbaden—Taunus

The Taunus is outdoor country, a region of pine forests, wooded hills and valleys, bounded on the west by the Rhine and on the south by the Main, and belonging to the state of Hesse. One of the loveliest regions of Germany, it is a paradise for nature lovers, and has many spas, including Wiesbaden.

One of the leading watering places of the world, Wiesbaden has long been internationally renowned, a favorite with everybody from royalty downwards. The international May Festival presents opera companies, ballet groups and theatrical groups from all over Europe. This brilliant activity is centered about the famous *Brunnenkolonnade* (Spring Colonnade). Golf and tennis tournaments and horse racing are the order of the day at the height of this Wiesbaden season, and the roulette wheels never stop turning in the casino. If you want the sophisticated and wordly life of a leading spa, this is for you. If not, the surrounding countryside could not be more attractive for in addition to its spas, Wiesbaden lies at the gateway to the famous Rheingau region. This idyllic district of castles, monasteries and undulating vineyards along the north bank of the Rhine is renowned for its wines. Stop off at the Drosselgasse in Rüdesheim for a glass of *Rheingauer Riesling,* one of the most famous white wines in the world.

Mainz, Worms and Mannheim

Across the Rhine from Wiesbaden is Mainz, capital of the Rhineland Palatinate, an ancient city, dominated by the great tower of its thousand-year-old Romanesque cathedral. The inner town here was much damaged in the war, but is still fascinating, with its narrow winding streets and gabled houses. It was here that Gutenberg was born and died, and here that he invented the process of printing with movable type. A monument, a university and a museum honor him.

Further down the Rhine, Worms is known for the edict issued there in 1521 against Luther. Its 12th-century Romanesque cathedral is one of the finest in Germany.

Where the Neckar River flows into the Rhine is the city of Mannheim, long a German cultural center. Its baroque buildings reflect the splendor of the period when this was the residence of the Prince Electors of the Palatinate. Note especially the Rathaus, the Jesuit church, and the Water Tower. Speyer's cathedral, started in 1030, is the largest Romanesque church in Europe. Here, too, is the start of the 200-mile Castle Road *(Burgenstrasse),* via Heidelberg and Heilbronn to Nürnberg with more than 30 fortified castles, palaces, and historical places.

PRACTICAL INFORMATION FOR MAINZ AND TAUNUS

MAINZ. *Hilton* (L), Rheinstr. 68 (tel. 2450). All the usual amenities; situated on the banks of the river. *Mainzer Hof* (E), Kaiserstr. 98 (tel. 233771). Modern and with a fine view from the roof garden restaurant. *Hammer* (M), Bahnhofsplatz 6 (tel. 611061). Near the station; breakfast only. *Mira* (I), Bonifaziusstr. 4 (tel. 613087). Breakfast only.

Restaurants. *Rats- und Zunftstuben Heilig Geist* (M), Rentengasse 2 (tel. 225757). Parts date back to Roman times, with present-day sections in vaulted Gothic style. Very popular, so reservations a must. *Walderdorff* (M), Karmeliterplatz 4 (tel. 22515). Excellent value. *Weinhaus Schreiner* (M), Rheinstr. 38 (tel. 225720). Rheingau and Riesling wines in historic atmosphere. Regional dishes.

MANNHEIM. (Hotels are filled during March, May, and September, so book far in advance for these times.) The city center is divided quadratically into sections and the streets are referred to by numbers and letters from A1 to U6. *Maritim Parkhotel* (E), Friedrichsplatz 2 (tel. 45071). Near Kunsthalle and National Theater. *Steigenberger Hotel Mannheimer Hof* (E), Augusta-Anlage 4 (tel. 45021). Courtyard with sun-terrace, bowling; celler restaurant *Holzkistal* in rustic style. *Augusta* (M), Corner August-Anlage (tel. 408001). Comfortable restaurant with good food. *Holiday Inn* (M), in the new city center at Kunststr.

(tel. 10710). Offers motorists indoor pool, two restaurants and a bar as well as the usual Holiday Inn comforts. *Holländer Hof* (M), U1/11–12, near Kurpfalz Bridge (tel. 16095). Breakfast only. *Wartburg* (M), F4/4–11 at the Market Place (tel. 28991). *Basler Hof* (I), Tattersallstr. 27 (tel. 28816). Near the station; breakfast only.

Restaurants. *L'Epi d'Or* (E), H7,3 (tel. 14397). First class French cuisine. *Da Gianni* (E), R7/34 (tel. 20326). Italian food in elegant surroundings. Also local specialties. Closed three weeks in July. *Kopenhagen* (M), Friedrichsring 4 (tel. 14870). Near the water tower and good value. *Rhein-Café* (I), overlooking the Rhine.

RÜDESHEIM. *Jagdschloss Niederwald* (E), tel. 1004. Castle hotel in the forested national park of Rheingau-Untertaunus located above the town; reached by cable car. *Parkhotel Deutscher Hof* (E), Rheinstr. 21 (tel. 3016). *Rüdesheimer Hof* (E), Geisenheimerstr. 1 (tel. 2011). Elegant restaurant and with rustic Bauernstuben tavern. *Rheinstein* (M), Rheinstr. 20 (tel. 2004). Romantik Hotel *Schwan* (M), tel. 3001. In Oestrich, 5 miles east of Rüdesheim; dates back to 1628 and even has its own vineyard. *Lindenwirt* (I), Drosselgasse (tel. 1031). Has bar, courtyard terrace and rustic tavern-restaurant.

Restaurants. *Aussichtsrestaurant-Rheinblick* (E), at the Niederwald Monument. *Bergkeller* (M), Oberstr. *Krone* (M), Rheinufer 10 in Assmannshausen (tel. 2036). Historic inn with spacious interiors. Extensive wine list and good food.

One of Germany's top attractions is the double row of wine houses (*Weinhäuser*) in the Drosselgasse, *the* place for merry wine drinking. Of the Weinhäusers, the *Drosselhof, Bei Hannelore,* and *Zum Engel* are the best.

SPEYER. *Goldener Engel* (M), Mühlturmstr. 27 (tel. 76732). *Luxhof* (M), tel. 06205–32333. On the opposite side of the Rhine in Hockenheim. Small inn with delicious food and also offering very good fishing and hunting. *Trutzpfaff* (M), Webergasse 5 (tel. 78399). 8 rooms with bath; quiet. Restaurant.

WIESBADEN. *Nassauer Hof* (L), Kaiser-Friedrich-Platz 3–4 (tel. 39681). Extremely comfortable. *Schwarzer Bock* (L), Kranzplatz 12 (tel. 3821). Also very much in the deluxe range. *Aukamm* (E), Aukamm Allee 31, approach from Parkstr., (tel. 56841). Has a fine view. *Forum* (E), Abraham-Lincolnstr. 17 (tel. 778811). Café, rotisserie, pool and sauna. *Rose* (E), Kranzplatz 8–9 (tel. 39591). Thermal pool, sauna, solarium. *Am Kochbrunnen* (M), Taunusstr. 15 (tel. 522001). Historic building; breakfast only. *Bären* (M), Bärenstr. 3 (tel. 301021). Thermal pool. *Central* (M), Bahnhofstr. 65 (tel. 372021). Centrally located near the main station. *Hansa* (I), corner of Bahnhofstr and Rheinstr (tel. 39955). Largest of the inexpensive hotels and near the station. *Pension Kranig* (I), Rheingaustr. 146 in Biebrich suburb (tel. 61657).

Restaurants. Both the *Nassauer Hof* and *Schwarzer Bock* Hotels (see above) have excellent restaurants: *Ente vom Lehel* and *Le Capricorne* respectively; both (E). *Alte Münze* (E), Kranzplatz 5 (tel. 524833). *Kurhaus Restaurant* (E), Kurhaus on J.F. Kennedy Platz (tel. 526937). Daily dancing and music. *Mövenpick* (M), Sonnenburgerstr. 2 (tel. 524005). Has a variety of specialties in its two bars, *Orangerie* and *La Chesa.*

WORMS. *Domhotel* (E), Obermarkt. 10 (tel. 6913). *Kriemhilde* (M), Hofgasse 2 (tel. 6278). *Central* (I), Kämmererstr. 5 (tel. 6457). Breakfast only. *Hüttl* (I), Peterstr. 5 (tel. 87874). Opposite town hall with a view of the cathedral. Very pleasant, small hotel with notably good breakfasts.

Restaurant. *Rôtisserie Dubs* (E), Kirchstr. 6 (tel. 06242–2023). First-rate food; excellent service, in the Rheindürkheim suburb. Reservations recommended.

Southwestern Germany

South of the Main, and east of the Rhine, and sharing a frontier with France and Switzerland, lies a region that looks as though it had come out of a story book. It includes the valley of the Neckar, the Swabian

Mountains, the Black Forest, Lake Constance and the Allgäu, and that perfectly-named section, *Die Romantische Strasse,* the Romantic Road.

The Neckar River, flowing northward between the heights of the Black Forest and the Swabian Mountains, waters a fascinating land that includes the Odenwald, where you may see the very well from which Siegfried was drinking when he was killed by Hagen's spear, and the *Bergstrasse,* the Mountain Road, where fruit trees bloom in March and tobacco is grown, thanks to a freakishly warm climate.

Heidelberg

The jewel of the Neckar is Heidelberg, with town, castle and wooded hills rising above the river. The ideal time for a visit is June through August, when the castle, one of Europe's most flourishing ruins, provides a superb backdrop for the Heidelberg Drama Festival and the open-air concerts. The castle is best reached by a cable railway, which will also take you to Königstuhl, 2,000 feet high, with a splendid panorama of the Neckar Valley.

A close runner up to the castle is Germany's oldest university, forever immortalized (or embalmed in sugar, perhaps) in *The Student Prince.* It is as delightful as any operetta, with its student inns, student prison (the university did its own disciplining, and no joking about it), and the narrow streets of the old town. This is an enchanting city to walk around in. Don't forget the old bridge, the Church of the Holy Ghost, the Jesuit Church, and the matchless Altar of the Twelve Apostles, an extraordinary example of 16th-century wood carving in the Kurpfälzisches Museum.

There are a variety of boat trips available from Heidelberg on some of the loveliest stretches of the Neckar and Rhine rivers, to Koblenz or Rüdesheim, for example, or to Neckargemünd or Eberach.

PRACTICAL INFORMATION FOR HEIDELBERG AND HEILBRONN

HEIDELBERG. *Europäische Hof* (L), Friedrich-Ebert-Anlage 1a (tel. 27101). Stylish and comfortable, with good restaurant and rustic *Kürfursten-stube. Parkhotel Atlantic-Schlosshotel* (E), Schloss-Wolfsbrunnenweg 23 (tel. 24545). *Holiday Inn* (M), tel. 06227–62051. Good stop for motorists in Walldorf, in Roter Str., and also in Viernheim (tel. 06204–5036). *Romantik Hotel Zum Ritter* (M), Hauptstr. 178 (tel. 20203). In a 16th-century inn. *Hackteufel* (I), Steingasse 7 (tel. 25589). *Monpti* (I), Friedrich-Ebert-Anlage 57 (tel. 23483). Breakfast only.

Restaurants. *Altdeutsche Stuben* (M), Untere Neckarstr. 54. In Hotel Schönberger Hof. *Gaudeamus igitur* (M), Hirschg. 3 (tel. 49921). In Hotel Hirschgasse. Offers first-rate cuisine at good value. Of "Student Prince" fame. *Roter Ochsen* (I), Hauptstr. 217 (tel. 20977). Historical students' tavern.

HEILBRONN. *Insel* (E), Friedrich-Ebert-Brücke (tel. 88931). *Kronprinz* (M), Bahnhofstr. 29 (tel. 83941). *Beck* (I), Bahnhofstr. 31 (tel. 81589).

Restaurants. *Wirtshaus am Götzenturm* (E), Allerheiligenstr. 1 (tel. 80534). Noted historic restaurant with high class cuisine. *Ratskeller* (M), in the town hall (tel. 84628). *Harmonie* (M), Allee 28 (tel. 86890). Large wine tavern near the gardens.

Castle Hotels

Burg Hirschhorn (M), tel. 06272–1373; *Burg Hornberg* (M), tel. 06261–4064; *Schloss Hochhausen* (M), tel. 06261–3142; *Schloss Neuberg* (M), tel. 06261–7330; all in the Neckar Valley. *Götzenburg* (M), tel. 07943–2222. At Jagtshausen in Jagst Valley.

The Swabian Mountains

If you are looking for something away from it all, the Swabian Mountains are an answer to your prayer. Here, you will find marvelous caves, rocks, castles, endless woods and 7,000 miles of well-marked hiking trails. The farmers, shut up in their mountain villages, dress in somber black. This is Protestant country, and the people are less outgoing than the Catholics (to the south on Lake Constance) and the easy-going Rhinelanders. Nevertheless, you can be sure of a welcome, a comfortable bed and a good solid meal in any mountain Gasthof.

Stuttgart

In contrast to the primitive charms of this countryside is the great city of Stuttgart, capital of the State of Baden-Württemberg and the largest and one of the most beautiful cities of southwestern Germany. Home of Zeiss-Ikon, Bosch, Daimler-Benz and Porsche products, to name but a few, it is the economic center of the region and ranks second among the most productive exporting cities of the Federal Republic. It is also the home of over 200 book publishers and a wealth of museums and art galleries. The face of the city itself is a model of a modern city landscaping and a lesson for town planners. Stuttgart is actually a garden city with only 25 per cent of its area built over, and instead of endless rows of houses, one finds spacious parks, market gardens, vineyards, fields and hills.

Apart from its reputation as the greenest city in West Germany it is also one of the most therapeutic, with 19 natural mineral springs.

Nearby Ludwigsburg boasts the largest baroque castle in Germany, with a children's fairytale garden in its grounds and open-air theater festival in summer. To the north, Schwäbisch Hall is the most romantic town in the Swabian Mountains.

Ulm

Another important city of the southwest is Ulm. Its 14th-century Gothic cathedral is the highest church tower in the world. The cathedral is one of the most beautiful in Germany; its 15th-century carved choir stalls by Jörg Syrlin are outstanding. The old city walls of Ulm are still standing, with their gates and towers.

Other interesting places in this area are: Donaueschingen, at the source of the Danube River, with the Duke Fürstenberg Palace housing an important art museum with major works by Grünewald, Holbein and Cranach; Beuron, with the famous baroque Benedictine abbey, which has fostered arts and choral singing since 1077; Sigmaringen and its impressive castle of the princes of Hohenzollern, with a fine museum and painting gallery; Hohenzollern Castle, the original seat of this great German aristocratic family which, among others, produced Kaiser Wilhelm, on a high elevation commanding the surrounding area near the town of Hechingen; Reutlingen, a former imperial town with some very fine Gothic architecture; the area around Erpfingen, a speleologist's paradise, with its fantastic stalactite caverns (there were 70 at the last count), and finally Tübingen. This famous university town on the Neckar possesses many fine buildings—the Gothic Collegiate Church, the massive Pfalzgrafen Castle, and the 15th-century Rathaus.

PRACTICAL INFORMATION FOR THE SWABIAN MOUNTAINS

STUTTGART. *Novotel* (E), Korntalerstr. 207 (tel. 801065). In Stammheim section. Modern, with usual Novotel standards. *Am Schlossgarten* (L), Schillerstr. 23 (tel. 299911). Has very good restaurant and tavern apart from the usual deluxe comforts. *Steigenberger Hotel Graf Zeppelin* (L), Arnulf-Klett-Platz 7, (tel. 299881). High degree of comfort with first class service; grill room and excellent *Stuble* restaurant. *Stuttgart International* (L), Plieningerstr. 100 (tel. 72021). Very modern with garden terrace, tavern bar and restaurant; near the Autobahn so good for motorists. *Airport Hotel Mövenpick* (E), at the airport (tel. 79070). Modern, convention hotel. Swiss specialty restaurant. *Parkhotel* (E), Villastr. 21 (tel. 280161). Has attractive garden terrace. *Royal* (E), Sophienstr. 35 (tel. 625050). *Waldhotel Schatten* (E), Gewant Schatten 2 (tel. 681051). In suburb of Vaihingen-Büsnau, 15 min. from city center. All rooms with bath; Swabian specialty restaurant.

Astoria (M), Hospitalstr. 29 (tel. 223321). *Intercity-Hotel* (M), Arnulf-Klett-Platz (tel. 299801). Near the main station. *Wartburg* (M), Langestr. 49 (tel. 221991). *Espenlaub* (I), Charlottenstr. 27 (tel. 240022). *Hotel-Gasthof Bäckerschmide* (I), Schurwaldstr. 44 (tel. 466035).

Restaurants. *Alte Post* (E), Friedrichstr. 43 (tel. 293079). High class cuisine that is particularly good value; atmospheric. *Alte Simpl* (E), Hohenheimerstr. 64 (tel. 240821). Atmospheric and traditional. Gourmet menu. *Hirsch-Weinstube* (E), Maierstr. 3 (tel. 711375). First class food featuring Swabian specialties. *Öxle's Löwen* (E), Veitstr. 2 (tel. 53226). The renowned chef, Martin Öxle, has relocated his rustic but elegant gourmet restaurant in the Mülhausen suburb. Reservations essential. *Scheffelstuben* (E), Haussmannstr. 5 (tel. 234042). Also first class. Reservations recommended.

Bäcka-Metzger (M), Aachenerstr. 20 (tel. 544108). Traditional Swabian wine tavern in the suburb of Cannstatt; typical Swabian hospitality and atmosphere and a wide selection of Württemberg wines direct from the barrel as well as wines from their own vineyard. *Bäckerschmide* (M), Schurwaldstr. 44 (tel. 466035). With own wine cellar. *Börse* (M), Heustr. 1 (tel. 292698). Good-value; first-class Swabian food in cosy surroundings. *Ratskeller* (M), Marktplatz 1 (tel. 244951). Old-world atmosphere in the center of town. *Weinstube Hasen* (M), Innsbruckerstr. 5 (tel. 322070). Recommended.

TÜBINGEN. *Krone* (E), Uhlandstr. 1 (tel. 31036). Excellent restaurant. *Am Bad* (M), Rottenburgerstr. (tel. 73071). *Hospiz* (M), Neckarhalde 2 (tel. 26003).

Restaurants. *Landgasthof Rosenau* (E), tel. 66466. Near the Botanical Gardens. *Waldhorn* (M), tel. 61270. Recommended; in the suburb of Bebenhausen. *Zur Forelle* (M), Kronenstr. 8 (tel. 22938). Student wine tavern, and good fish and game restaurant. *Zum Hirsch* (M), tel. 61281. Also in Bebenhausen.

ULM. *Mövenpick Hotel* (E), Silcherstr. 40 in Neu-Ulm (tel. 80110). Large, modern and first-class, with well-known restaurant. Pool, sauna, solarium, etc. *Intercity-Hotel* (M), Bahnhofsplatz 1 (tel. 61221). Near the station; bar, bowling, conference rooms; access to the station from hotel lobby. *Neutor-Hospiz* (M), Neuer Graben 23 (tel. 15160). *Stern* (M), Sterngasse 17 (tel. 63091).

Restaurants. *Weinstube Pflugmerzler* (E), Pfluggasse 6 (tel. 68061). Antique furnishings and good value for money. *Kornhauskeller* (M), Hafeng. 19 (tel. 68503). Swabian specialties. *Zur Forelle* (M), Fischergasse 25 (tel. 63924). Rustic tavern; fish specialties and international cuisine; exceptionally good value.

The Black Forest

The Black Forest (Schwarzwald) is one of those magic names that evoke a feeling of romance. Its dark evergreens, which give it that "black" look, rise from a forest floor so free of underbrush that it looks as though it has been swept. These conifers clothe the hills and mountains east of the Rhine, starting at the Swiss frontier and extending north to Karlsruhe. It is not an unbroken forest. There are green valleys, open meadows, postcard towns, and farmhouses with steep thatched roofs. In this region, old traditions still live, and you may see colorful local dress on festive occasions and on Sundays. The Open-Air Museum at Gurach has many interesting exhibits of country life in bygone days.

Walks and drives, either by car or carriage and pair, or organized cycling tours, through the charming little resorts of the Black Forest are most rewarding. Typical is Freudenstadt, which claims to have more hours of sunshine during the year than any other German resort. It lies in beautiful country, surrounded by 100 miles of well-tended paths designed for the pleasures of walking in the Black Forest. Another recommended resort is Triberg, with its waterfalls and delightful swimming pool in the midst of the evergreen hills. Don't miss the remarkable clock museum at Furtwangen.

Baden-Baden

If the Black Forest conjures up an image of picturesque peasant life, its chief spa, Baden-Baden, evokes all the worldly luxury of a bygone day. But Baden-Baden, for all its memories of 19th-century glory, is very up to date. Among the ailments it undertakes to treat with its healing springs are "diseases due to the strain of modern civilization". This delightful spa has owed its fame since Roman times to radioactive chloride hot springs. You may drink their waters, recline in them, take mud baths made of them, or even inhale them in vapor form. Then, when you feel a little stronger, you can play roulette and baccara at the casino or participate, actively or as spectator, in the countless activities arranged here for your pleasure. Remember, though, that you may still save money and have a good time by staying in a nearby village. For example, Hügelsheim, just off the autobahn and minutes by car from Baden-Baden, is enchanting.

Freiburg

Freiburg im Breisgau, capital and largest city of the Black Forest, is an old university and cathedral town. The cathedral, begun about 1200, has a 370-foot steeple of open stone lacework which has been called the most beautiful Gothic tower of its type. The cathedral itself is a remarkable treasure house of painting, wood carving and 13th- to 16th-century stained glass windows. A colorful open-air market carries on its busy trade on the cathedral square in front of the Kaufhaus, a beautiful example of a medieval merchants' hall. Do not miss the two other fascinating squares in this attractive city—the Rathaus Square, with its old and new city halls (one medieval, the other Renaissance), and the Oberlinden, surrounded by medieval burgher houses, and the towering 13th-century Swabian Gate.

PRACTICAL INFORMATION FOR THE BLACK FOREST

BADEN-BADEN. *Brenners Parkhotel* (L), Schillerstr. (tel. 3530). Internationally famous and extremely luxurious; near the casino and has indoor pool, sauna, solarium, beauty-farm, bridge-salon, garden terrace, park and excellent *Schwarzwaldgrill* restaurant. *Steigenberger-Badhotel Badischer Hof* (L), Langestr. 47 (tel. 22827). Those rooms with bathroom have thermal water. Includes apartments. *Steigenberger-Hotel Europäischer Hof* (L), Kaiserallee 2 (tel. 23561). Opposite the pump room and Kurhaus. *Golfhotel* (E), Fremersbergstr. 113 (tel. 23691). In outskirts and with indoor and outdoor pools. *Holiday Inn Sporthotel* (E), Falkenstr. 2 (tel. 33011). With a fine restaurant. *Quisiana* (E), Bismarckstr. 21 (tel. 3446). With apartments; particularly quiet and comfortable. *Atlantic* (M), Lichtentaler Allee (tel. 24111). Quiet with friendly atmosphere; breakfast only. *Badhotel Holland* (M), Sofienstr. 14 (tel. 25595). Garden terrace, solarium and bowling; breakfast only. *Tannenhof* (M), Hans-von-Bredowstr. 20 (tel. 271181). Quiet with fine view and excellent restaurant. *Waldhotel Der Selighof* (M), at golf course, (tel. 07221–23385). Indoor and outdoor pools. *Bad-Hotel Zum Hirsch* (M), Hirschstr. 1 (tel. 23896). Atmospheric; has own thermal bath. *Reichert* (M), Sofienstr. 4 (tel. 24191). Indoor pool, sauna. *Am Markt* (I), Marktplatz 18 (tel. 23896). Has own thermal bath.

Restaurants. *Kurhaus-Restaurants* in Kaiserallee 1: the *Mirabell* (E), tel. 29611, is particularly good value; the *Boulevard-Terrasse,* tel. 22717, has wine tavern and dance bar. *Stahlbad* (E), am Augustaplatz (tel. 24569). Fine food served around the clock in local-style surroundings. *Weinstube Schloss Neuweier* (E), Mauerbergstr. (tel. 07223–57944). Romantic setting in moated castle of same name. Gourmet food. *Zum Alde Gott* (E), Weinstr. 10 (tel. 07223–5513). Nouvelle cuisine and Baden specialties in rustic elegance. *Sinner Eck* (M), Luisenstr. 2 (tel. 22836). Bohemian specialties. *Prager Stube* (M), Gernsbacherstr. 31 (tel. 26492). More Bohemian specialties. *Das Süsse Löchel* (M), Sofienstr. 27. In Hotel Quellenhof. Particularly praiseworthy and good value.

FREIBURG. *Colombi* (E), Rotteckring 16 (tel. 31415). Has restaurant, wine tavern and bar. *Panorama Hotel am Jägerhäusle* (E), Wintererstr. 89 (tel. 551011). Modern; indoor pool. *Novotel* (E), Karlsplatz (tel. 31295). *City* (M), Wasserstr. 2 (tel. 31766). Breakfast only. *Kühler Krug* (M), Torplatz 1 (tel. 29103). In the suburb of Günterstal. Has fine restaurant specializing in fish and game. *Rappen* (M), Münsterplatz 13 (tel. 31353). *Victoria* (M), Eisenbahnstr. 54 (tel. 33211). Near the station. *Zum Roten Bären* (M), Oberlinden 12 (tel. 36969). A Ring hotel, dating back to 1311. Good restaurant.

Restaurants. *Eichhalde* (E), Stadtstr. 91 (tel. 54817). In the suburb of Herden; particularly fine cuisine; excellent value. *Ratskeller* (E), Münsterplatz (tel. 26941). In the restored Kornhaus. *Weinstube zur Traube* (E), Schusterstr. (tel. 32190). Old furnishings and excellent food and wines. *Dattler* (M), near the end-station of the Schlossberg cable car (tel. 31729). *Greifenegg-Schlössle* (M), also up on the Schlossberg (tel. 32728). Both have magnificent views. *Zähringer Burg* (M), Reutebachgasse 19 (tel. 54041). In the suburb of Zähringen; recommended. *Bier und Speck* (M), Münsterplatz 18 (tel. 34367).

FREUDENSTADT. *Waldhorn Post* (E), tel. 07085–711. The hotel is halfway between Freudenstadt and Wilbad at Enzklösterle and dates back to 1145; tennis courts, indoor swimming pool, sauna and delightful period-furnished restaurant; game dishes a specialty. At Nagold, roughly 30 miles east of Enzklösterle, is the Romantik Hotel *Post* (M), tel. 07452–4048. Established in 1696, it has been run by the same family since 1773.

Lake Constance (Bodensee)

Lake Constance (or the Bodensee, as the Germans call it) is shared by three countries. Most of its northeast shoreline is German; most of its southwest bank is Swiss; Austria has a toehold at its eastern end. However, the inhabitants of all its shores speak the same German dialects, and blood relations frequently link them across the borders. Konstanz (Constance), its chief resort city, is a frontier anomaly, a German town on the Swiss side of the lake, completely surrounded by Swiss territory except where it fronts on the water, across from the land to which it belongs. Konstanz is a delightful summer vacation spot, due partly to the singularly mild climate of the whole Bodensee region, as a result of which the bathing season lasts from spring to late fall. The city is also blessed with a fine cathedral, a 14th-century Council Hall, a Renaissance Rathaus, good hotels and facilities for all water sports.

Among the jewels that line the German shore of the Bodensee, Meersburg is outstanding. It is a marvellous old town with a 7th-century castle, charming houses and a number of colorful taverns— only appropriate to this ancient center of wine growing. Ferry boats ply between here and Konstanz, directly across the lake. Lindau, built on an island in the lake, is another Bodensee gem; a stage set of narrow streets and old buildings.

Don't fail to visit another island in the lake, that of Mainau—the island of flowers. Throughout the season, a staff of over 300 ensure that the island is a multi-colored carpet of petals: beginning in the spring, with a magnificent show of orchids and the transformation of the former Grand Duke of Baden's palace grounds into a vast field of tulips, through June and July when lilies and irises predominate and into the spectacular roses and dahlias of late summer and fall.

PRACTICAL INFORMATION FOR LAKE CONSTANCE

KONSTANZ. *Steigenberger Insel* (E), Auf der Insel 1 (tel. 25011). Former monastery on small island with rustic restaurant, *Dominikaner Stube. Bayerischer Hof* (M), Rosengartenstr 30 (tel. 22075). Breakfast only. *Buchner Hof* (M), Buchner Str. 6 (tel. 51035). A little outside the town center. Quiet and comfortable; breakfast only. *Seeblick* (M), Neuhauserstr. 14 (tel. 54018). Quiet location. *Bodan* (I), Furstenbergstr. 2 (tel. 78002). Garni. *Dom-Hotel St. Johann* (I), Brückeng. 1 (tel. 22750). Dates from 10th century; noted restaurant.

Restaurants. *Siber* (E), Seestr. 25 (tel. 63044). New in 1984. Fine French and regional cuisine; elegant art nouveau decor; terrace. *Casino* (M), tel. 63615. On first floor of the casino; also has the rustic *Tessiner-Stube* and a dance bar. *Graf Zeppelin* (M), St. Stefansplatz 15 (tel. 23780). *Konzil* (M), Hafenstr. 2 (tel. 21221). In old Council Hall. *Stefanskeller* (M), Am Stefansplatz 41 (tel. 23566). Historic wine tavern with good food in antique surroundings.

LINDAU. *Bad Schachen* (L), at the nearby spa (tel. 5011). Quiet with an institute for physiotherapy, indoor and outdoor pools, solarium, fitness center, boating and tennis; fine and elegant restaurant. *Bayerischer Hof* (L), Seepromenade (tel. 5055). Also has outdoor pool; closed in the winter. *Zum Stift* (M), Stiftsplatz 1 (tel. 5516). Outside beer garden.

Restaurants. *Spielbank* (E), in casino (tel. 5200). *Zum Lieben Augustin* (E), Augustin-Arkaden, Seepromenade (tel. 5055). *Weinstube Frey* (M), Maximilianstr. 15 (tel. 5278). Building dates from 1560.

MAINAU ISLAND. Restaurants. *Schwedenschenke* (M), the Swedish Inn (tel. 31362); the heart of Mainau catering. *Torkelkeller* (M), with huge wine barrel for post-flower-gazing refreshment.

MEERSBURG. *Villa Bellevue* (E), Am Rosenhang 5 (tel. 9770). On the hill above the lake and with marvellous views. *Drei Stuben* (M), Winzerg (tel. 6019). 16th-century half-timbered building; fine restaurant. *Strandhotel Wilder Mann* (M), Bismarckplatz 2 (tel. 9011). Closed in winter; café with music and dancing. *Zum Schiff* (M), Bismarckplatz 5 (tel. 6025). Lakeside terrace and good food.

Restaurants (which in Meersburg means mostly wine taverns): *Zum Becher* (M), Hollgasse 4 (tel. 9009). Oldest wine tavern in Meersburg, with outstanding food. *Ratskeller* (I), tel. 9004. Vaulted town hall cellar. *Winzertrinkstube* (I), tel. 6484. Wines from the local wine growers' cooperative. *Burgkeller* (M), tel. 6028. With garden and music.

ÜBERLINGEN. *Romantik Hotel Hecht* (M), Münsterstr. 9 (tel. 07551–63333). A meeting place for gourmets the world over.

The Romantic Road

The Romantic Road (*Die Romantische Strasse*) is much more than just a road from Füssen to Würzburg. It provides the concentrated essence of picture-book Germany, a progression through a continuous and unbroken pageant of marvels. Starting at Füssen in Bavaria on the Austrian border, you proceed through the Allgäu Alps. Your only problem is going to be how long you would like to stay where; each town on this route is more enchanting than the one before it. (Special buses—Europabus Routes EB190/190A—travel up and down the road, and by all means use them—they're inexpensive and convenient.)

Just a few miles from Füssen, you will find lofty Neuschwanstein, facing Hohenschwangau on a nearby hill, another royal castle. Neuschwanstein, built by Bavaria's eccentric King Ludwig II, has to be seen to be believed, and even then you may wonder if this pinnacled castle perched on a mountain peak is real. If you have a chance to hear one of the summer Wagner concerts in this setting, don't miss it.

Following the Lech River, you will pass through Schongau, Landsberg, one of the finest medieval cities in southern Bavaria with its matchless Bayertor (Bavarian) Gothic gate, then right through the Rote Tor (Red Gate) into the spectacular metropolis of the Romantic Road, Augsburg, the capital of Bavarian Swabia which celebrated its 2000th anniversary in 1985. The tower, bridge, ramparts, and moat of this castled city, against whose massive background Germany's finest open-air opera season takes place in July and August, will give you a foretaste of Landsberg's architectural riches. Don't miss the cathedral, begun in 995, which has the oldest stained glass windows in the world (11th-century), altar paintings by Holbein (who was born here), and an early 11th-century bronze door. See St. Ulrich's Church, the only church with two towers and two religions, Catholic *and* Protestant, embodying in stone the spirit of the Religious Place of Augsburg, achieved in 1555. Stroll down Maximilianstrasse, Germany's finest Renaissance street.

Continuing north through Bavarian Swabia, the Romantic Road follows a chain of medieval cities—Donauwörth, on the Danube; Harburg, with its castle and its splendid Gobelin tapestries; Nördlingen, "the living medieval city", where the night watch's call still echoes through the narrow streets as it has for centuries, and Dinkelsbühl, its walls still standing, complete with bastions, gates, towers, and a moat. In July, however, it celebrates its escape from destruction during the Thirty Years' War with the *Kinderzeche* (Children's Tribute), a festival of sword dances, guild dances and historic pageants (tickets may be booked in advance from the Tourist Office). Rothenburg, a walled city on the Tauber, is another must stop on the Romantic Road. Its towers and gates are intact, its ancient fountains brilliant with scarlet geraniums. It holds *its* festival of salvation at Whitsun, commemorating its salvation with a play in the Rathaus called *Der Meistertrunk,* "The Master Drink", in honor of a burgomaster who saved the city by a prodigious feat of quaffing. Another link in the golden chain is Bad Mergentheim, with its great castle of the Teutonic Knights.

Würzburg is the terminus of the Romantic Road, an old university town on the River Main which was the site of a bishopric as early as 741. Here you are in the center of the Franconian wine growing region, scene of a riotous wine festival each September. Its chief ornament is the baroque residence castle of the prince-bishops, built by the master architect Balthasar Neumann. Here, with a background of Tiepolo frescos, an annual Mozart Festival is held in June, July or August. Open-air concerts are given in the castle garden, and the Marienberg, mighty fortress of the prince-bishops, is illuminated during the Main Festival of August. Riemenschneider, the great wood carver, was mayor of this town. We recommend a visit to the nearby Schlosspark Veitshöchheim, a most remarkable rococo garden.

PRACTICAL INFORMATION FOR THE ROMANTIC ROAD

AUGSBURG. *Steigenberger-Drei-Mohren* (L), Maximilianstr. 40 (tel. 510031). Opened in 1723 and quite definitely one of Germany's truly historic hotels; Russian Czars and German Emperors have been guests, as well as Mozart and Goethe. *Holiday Inn* (E), Imhofstr. 12 (tel. 577087). Next to the Kongresshalle; tallest hotel tower in Europe. *Alpenhof* (M), Donauwörtherstr. 233 (tel. 413051). With motel. *Gästhaus Iris* (M), Gartenstr. 4 (tel. 510981).

Quiet location; breakfast only. *Post* (M), Fuggerstr. 7 (tel. 36044). *Riegele* (M), Viktoriastr. 4 (tel. 39039). *Thalia* (I), Obstmarkt 5 (tel. 313037). In the old fruit market.

Restaurants. *Welser-Küche* (E), in old patrician Stiermann House. Original medieval recipes in a 16th-century atmosphere. Advance reservations essential on 08231–4049. *Fuggerkeller* (M), Maximilianstr. 38 (tel. 516250). In the historic Fuggerhaus. *Ratskeller* (M), tel. 517848. In the town hall. *Sieben-Schwaben-Stuben* (M), Burgermeister-Fischerstr. 12 (tel. 510272). Rustic-style decor; good Swabian food.

BAD MERGENTHEIM. *Kurhotel Victoria* (E), Poststr. 2 (tel. 7036). Most rooms with bath; rooftop pool. Full cure facilities. *Am Markt* (M), tel. 6101. Garni. *Petershof* (I), Wachbacherstr. 14 (tel. 2336). *Steinmeyer* (I), Wolfgangstr. 2 (tel. 7220). *Zum Wilden Mann* (I), Reichengasse 6 (tel. 7638).

DINKELSBÜHL. *Deutsches Haus* (M), Weinmarkt 3 (tel. 2346). Half-timbered 15th-century building; best-known hotel in town, with good moderately priced *Altdeutsches* Restaurant; frescos, coats of arms, serves delightful local specialties and Franconian wines. *Goldene Rose* (M), Marktplatz 4 (tel. 831). Has *Ratskeller* tavern (tel. 2622). *Goldener Hirsch* (I), Weinmarkt 6 (tel. 2347). An unpretentious small hostelry with good food. Fresh fish from own waters.

NÖRDLINGEN. *Hotel am Ring* (M), tel. 4028. Near the station. *Schützenhof* (M), Kaiserwiese 2 (tel. 3940). Good local specialties in restaurant. *Sonne* (M), Marktplatz 3 (tel. 5067). Established in 1477. *Zum Goldenen Lamm* (I), Schäflesmarkt 3 (tel. 4206). Historic inn.

ROTHENBURG OB DER TAUBER. *Eisenhut* (L), Herrengasse 3 (tel. 2041). Located in four 12th-century patrician houses. Excellent restaurant and cellar. *Goldener Hirsch* (E), Untere Schmiedgasse 16 (tel. 2051). Outstanding view and dining room. *Adam* (M), Burggasse 29 (tel. 2364). Small and quiet with good view. *Arktiv-Hotel Bären* (M), Hofbronneng 7 (tel. 6033). With indoor pool. *Markusturm* (M), Rödergasse 1 (tel. 2370). Romantik Hotel; fine restaurant. *Tilman Riemenschneider* (M), Georgengasse 11 (tel. 5061). Good restaurant. *Pension Herrnmühle* (I), Taubertalweg 54 (tel. 2176). Quiet and small pension; also has some holiday apartments. *Pension Then* (I), Johannitergasse 8A (tel. 5177). Extremely good value; near station.

Restaurants. *Baumeisterhaus* (M), Obere Schmiedgasse 3 (tel. 3404). In 16th-century building. Good food and wines. *Goldene Rose* (I), Spitalgasse 28 (tel. 4638). Good but crowded.

WÜRZBURG. *Rebstock* (E), Neubaustr. 7 (tel. 50075). In neo-Baroque building; wine tavern. *Franziskaner* (M), Franziskanerplatz 2 (tel. 50360). *Russ* (M), Augustinerstr. (tel. 50016). With good restaurant; garage. *Schloss Steinberg* (M), tel. 93061. On hill with famous vineyard; pool; dancing and wine-tasting.

Restaurants. *Bürgerspital-Weinstuben* (M), Theaterstr. (tel. 13861). Wines from their own vineyards in atmospheric surroundings; light snacks only. *Hemmerlein* (M), Balth.-Neumann-Promenade, (tel. 52744). Opposite Hofgarten; grill-specialties from their own farm, fish from their own waters; terrace and beer garden. *Ratskeller Würzburg* (M), Langgasse 1 (tel. 31021). Their Ratsbierstuben tavern serves particularly fine wines and Würzburg beer from the barrel.

Bavaria, Holiday Land

This extensive territory, holiday land for Germany and much of Europe, was for centuries an important nation in its own right. Upper Bavaria (Oberbayern or Südbayern) is in the south, Lower Bavaria (Niederbayern or Ostbayern) is in the middle and towards the east, and Franconia is in the north. Upper Bavaria is called "Upper" because it is a mountain region, and Lower Bavaria is called "Lower" because it consists of undulating small hills interspersed with plains.

Franconia takes up most of northern Bavaria. It is dotted with medieval cities like Bamberg and Coburg and with old fortress towns like Kronach, but its chief attractions for the tourist, in addition to Würzburg, are Bayreuth and Nuremberg (Nürnberg).

Bayreuth

Bayreuth is world-famous for its Richard Wagner Festival in July and August, so popular now that it is advisable to book accommodations and buy tickets through your travel agent many months in advance. If you should arrive without reservations, however, the local tourist office can arrange for you to be put up in private homes. The Wagner productions still under the direction of the great man's family are the last word in modern stage technique, so different from the traditional productions that they scandalize the old guard, forgetful perhaps of the scandals Wagner himself caused with his bold innovations. If you are one of those who find Wagner a little on the long-winded side, go to Bayreuth in June for the Franconian Baroque Festival—ballets and concerts of the 18th century, given in the perfect setting of the Margraves' Opera House, which was built in 1745.

Nürnberg

Nürnberg (Nuremberg in English) was the home of Mastersinger Hans Sachs, of Tannhäuser and Albrecht Dürer. Renowned for its industry, the intellectual achievements of many of its citizens and for its high-roofed, half-timbered medieval dwellings and imposing public buildings, Nürnberg became a kind of prototype of German glory. Hitler's exploitation of this glory to exacerbate the nationalism he represented brought tragedy to this great city. But Nürnberg has survived both Hitler and his war. It's amazing how painstakingly the old buildings of the city have been reconstructed after the devastating air raids during World War II. If you're here in the summer, try to plan it for a weekend, when the old buildings are floodlit. And wander through "Alt Nürnberg" in the Handwerkerhof, where you can watch basketmakers, blacksmiths, bakers and other craftsmen at work.

Here are the other things you shouldn't miss: the riverside view from the Maxbrücke; the Kaiserburg (Imperial Castle), restored to its pre-war glory, with apartments open to the public; St. Sebald's Church (13th century) with the *Sebaldusgrab,* a masterpiece of bronze and silverwork by Peter Vischer and his sons; the Altstadt Museum (Fembohaus), the only surviving medieval patrician house; the restored 14th-century Gothic Frauenkirche, with its fine porch and statuary by Adam Kraft; the Albrecht Dürer House, an effective rebuilding of the destroyed original; St. Lawrence's Church, largest and most beautiful in the city (Gothic), with famous rose window, wood carving (the *Angelic Salutation* by Veit Stoss) and stone Tabernacle, with statues by Adam Kraft.

Finally, pay a visit to the Germanic National Museum. One of the finest in the nation, it presents a complete view of all German art up to the 18th century, including the applied arts. It has a fascinating collection of toys and dolls' houses, a link with the present, for Nürnberg today, as it has been for centuries, is the toy capital of Germany. The annual national Toy Trade Fair is held here in March. But if you really want to indulge in an orgy of toy shopping, come here for the Christ Kindl Markt in December.

PRACTICAL INFORMATION FOR BAVARIA AND FRANCONIA

BAMBERG. *Bamberger Hof-Bellevue* (E), Schönleinsplatz 4 (tel. 22216). *National* (E), Luitpoldstr. 37 (tel. 24112). Garni. *Weinhaus Messerschmitt* (M),

Lange Str. 41 (tel. 26471). Romantik Hotel that has been in the same family since 1832. Restaurant serving game and fish is excellent; also café with garden terrace. Only 18 beds, so reservations are essential. *Altenburgblick* (I), Panzerleite 59 (tel. 54023). Delightful hotel-pension; breakfast only. *Café Bug-Lieb* (I), Regnitz Ufer 23 (tel. 56078). 23 beds; on the banks of the Regnitz.

Restaurants. *Böttingerhaus* (E), Judenstr. 4 (tel. 54074). Best restaurant in town, located on the first floor of a baroque house. Elegant; first-class wines. *Brauerei-Ausschank, Schlenkerla* (I), Dominikanerstr. 6 (tel. 56060). Old-style tavern serving local specialties accompanied by *Rauchbier*, a smokey-flavored dark ale. *Steinernes Haus* (I), Lange Str. 8 (tel. 22049). Local fish specialties including fresh carp from their own waters. *Würzburger Weinstube* (I), Zinkenwörth 6 (tel. 22667). Franconian specialties.

BAYREUTH. *Bayerischer Hof* (E), Bahnhofstr. 14 (tel. 22081). Full of style and atmosphere and with particularly good service; roof garden, sauna and solarium. *Am Hofgarten* (M), Lisztstr. 6 (tel. 69006). Garni. Quietly situated near the Hofgarten, the palace gardens of the Neues Schloss. *Goldener Hirsch* (M), Bahnhofstr. 13 (tel. 23046). Near the main station. *Königshof* (M), Bahnhofstr. 23 (tel. 24094). Also near the station. *Gasthof Zum Edlen Hirschen* (I), Richard-Wagnerstr. 77 (tel. 64120).

Restaurants. *Annecy* (E), Gabelsberger Str. 11 (tel. 26279). French bistro in art nouveau style with nouvelle cuisine and good wines. *Wolffenzacher* (M), Badstr. 1 (tel. 64552). *Die Eule* (I), Kirchgasse 8 (tel. 64346). Artist's tavern. *Mohrenstube* (I), Mittelstr. 2 (tel. 27604). Wine tavern.

NÜRNBERG. *Carlton* (L), Eilgutstr. 13 (tel. 203535). *Grand-Hotel* (L), Bahnhofstr. (tel. 203621). Excellent restaurant, plus the expected deluxe comforts. *Am Sterntor* (E), Tafelhofstr. 8 (tel. 203101). *Merkur* (E), Pillenreutherstr. 1 (tel. 440291). *Burghotel* (M), Lammsgasse 3 (tel. 204414). Very central, with indoor pool and sauna. Breakfast only. Book at the "Grosses Haus" rather than the pleasant, but not so centrally located annex. *Deutscher Hof* (M), Frauentorgraben 29 (tel. 203821). Modern hotel with good-value restaurant and friendly service. *Grüner Bräu* (I), Augustinerstr. 2 (tel. 226451). *Haus Vosteen* (I), Lindenaststr. 12 (tel. 533325). Breakfast only.

Restaurants. *Goldenes Posthorn* (E), an der Sebalduskirche (tel. 225153). Once frequented by the likes of Dürer and Sachs; historic and atmospheric. *Romantik Restaurant Rottner* (E), Winterstr. 15 in the Grossreuth suburb (tel. 612032). A real tip, though not easy to find. Excellent Franconian specialties in old half-timbered house. *Zum Waffenschmied* (E), Obere Schmiedgasse 22 (tel. 225859). Excellent food; recommended. *Heilig-Geist-Spital* (M), Spitalgasse 12 (tel. 221761). Offers more than 100 wines from all over Germany. *Nassauer Keller* (M), Karolinenstr. 2 (tel. 225967). For atmosphere, fine food and wines and music; deep in the 13th-century cellar of the Nassau Haus. *Bratwurst-Häusle* (I), Rathausplatz 1 (tel. 227695). Great for Nürnberg sausages—a splendid local specialty—and local color. *Bratwurstküche* (I), im Handwerkerhof (tel. 227625). More colorful local atmosphere.

Munich, Capital of Bavaria

Dating from 1158, Munich is an old city, an industrial city (beer capital of the world), an intellectual city, and a fun-loving city. The place is vibrant all the time. The lid is really off at carnival time; Fasching, the Bavarians call it, and they celebrate it from New Year's Eve until Mardi Gras. As Mardi Gras approaches, you will meet more and more costumed refugees from masquerade balls in the city streets, and on Shrove Tuesday itself—*Faschingsdienstag* in German—shops close early and revelry reigns. Make reservations well in advance.

July and August, the height of the tourist season, are the months for the festivals of the Bavarian State Opera and Theater. The last two weeks in September are devoted to the famed Oktoberfest, a country fair in the big city. The big breweries erect tremendous beer tents on the fair grounds (*Messegelände*). Bavarian brass bands are everywhere;

you drink beer from 1-liter (just over a quart) mugs which is the only measure allowed and appropriately called *Mass* (measure).

The city also contains some truly worthwhile museums, among them the Alte Pinakothek, the Neue Pinakothek, the Deutsches Museum and the Bavarian National Museum. After a visit to one of the above, you might wish to stop at one of the local beer gardens for a real taste of Munich, before continuing your exploration of the city's sights.

Some places to visit are the Residenz, now largely restored with the original furniture; the Hofgarten, palace park north of the Residenz, famous for its flowerbeds; the famed beer palace, the Hofbräuhaus, where you can have just one more liter of fabulous Munich beer; the Peterskirche, reconstructed (climb the tower if a white disk is posted on the north side of the platform; it means the view is clear all the way to the Alps; a red disk means visibility limited to Munich); the famous Frauenkirche, Munich's much-photographed cathedral; the Asamkirche, a little rococo gem in the Sendlingerstr; and the parlor of Munich, the pedestrian zone in the Marienplatz where you'll find the mighty town hall (Rathaus) and the famous Glockenspiel.

One final attraction is Schloss Nymphenburg, far out in the northwest part of the city. Summer residence of the kings of Bavaria, Schloss Nymphenburg is an exceptionally harmonious baroque palace. Its showpiece is the great Festsaal, where concerts are given in the summer, and the Royal Coach Museum. Ludwig I's "Gallery of Beauties" is worth a passing glance, too, with its portraits of 24 ladies who took the king's eye, including the notorious Lola Montez. If you like porcelain, don't overlook the Residenzmuseum in the northern wing of the Schloss, or the showrooms of the famous Nymphenburger Porzellan Manufaktur, which are also here. The park around Schloss Nymphenburg is even more beautiful than the palace.

PRACTICAL INFORMATION FOR MUNICH

HOW TO GET AROUND. Munich's public transport system (MVV) is a combined network of trains, trams, subways, and buses. Tickets are uniform for all types of transport. All tickets must be cancelled in one of the blue cancelling machines bearing a large black E on a yellow background *before* starting your ride; tickets are checked regularly, and anyone found with an uncancelled ticket can be fined DM 40 or more. If you intend to use a lot of public transportation, you would do best to purchase a 24-hour unlimited travel ticket costing DM 6.50 covering the inner city; DM 12 for the suburban S-Bahn network as well.

Hotels

Deluxe

Bayerischerhof, Promenadeplatz 6 (tel. 21200). Traditional elegance, particularly in the Montgelas annex; heated rooftop swimming pool.

Continental, Max-Joseph-Str. 5 (tel. 557971). Over 200 beds and suites. Elegant, antique furnishings. Fine food in well-known *Conti-Grill.*

Der Königshof, Karlsplatz 25 (tel. 558412). Centrally located between the station and the pedestrian shopping zone; terrace restaurant.

Sheraton, Arabellastr. 6 (tel. 924011). In the suburb of Bogenhausen; marvelous view and all the expected comforts.

Vier Jahreszeiten Kempinski, Maximilianstr. 17 (tel. 228821). Palatial is the only word; service also magnificent, excellent *Walterspiel* restaurant.

Expensive

Admiral (E), Kohlstr. 9 (tel. 226641). New in 1983. Located near Deutsches Museum in quiet side street. Garni.

Arabella, Arabellastr. (tel. 92321). In the suburb of Bogenhausen; sauna, solarium and rooftop pool with marvellous view.

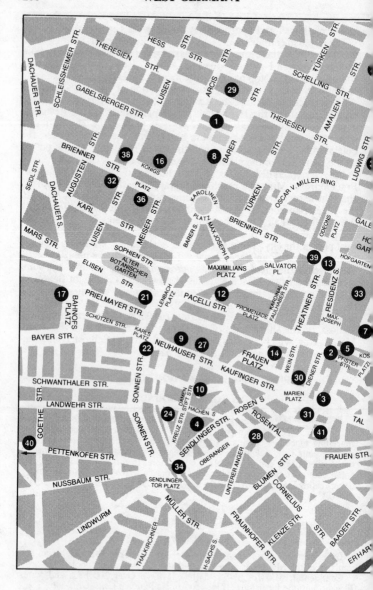

Audi, Landwehrstr. 33 (tel. 596067). New in 1986.

Deutscher Kaiser, Arnulfstr. 2 (tel. 558321). Has terrace bar on the 3rd. floor, and restaurant and café with panoramic view (naturally) on the 15th floor.

Eden-Hotel-Wolff, Arnulfstr. 4 (tel. 558281). 214 rooms with bath.

Europe, Erzgiessereistr. 15 (tel. 186055). New in 1985. On edge of city center with good subway connections.

Excelsior, Schutzenstr 11 (tel. 557906). Very comfortable.

Munich Hilton, Am Tucherpark 7 (tel. 340051). Quietly situated between the English Garden and Isar near the Tivoli Bridge; rooftop restaurant, pool.

Holiday Inn, Leopoldstr. 194 (tel. 340971). Good disco, nightclub.

Holiday-Inn International, Schleissheimerstr. 188 (tel. 309010). Near the Olympic Park, and well located for Nürnberg autobahn.

MUNICH

0 Miles · ¼
0 Kilometers · ¼

ENGLISCHER GARTEN

Points of Interest

1 Alte Pinakothek
2 Alter Hof
3 Altes Rathaus
4 Asamkirche
5 Bayerisches Hauptmünzamt (State Mint)
6 Bayerisches Nationalmuseum
7 Bayerisches Nationaltheater
8 Bayerisches Staatsarchiv
9 Bügersaal Kirche
10 Damenstiftskirche
11 Deutsches Museum
12 Dreifaltigkeitskirche
13 Feldherrnhalle and Preysing Palais
14 Frauenkirche
15 Gasteig Kulturzentrum
16 Glyptothek
17 Hauptbahnhof
18 Haus der Kunst
19 Hofbräuhaus
20 Isartor
21 Justizpalast
22 Karlstor
23 Kleine Komödie am Max II Denkmal
24 Kreuzkirche
25 Ludwigskirche
26 Maximilianeum
27 Michaelskirche
28 Münchner Stadtmuseum
29 Neue Pinakothek
30 Neues Rathaus
31 Peterskirche
32 Propyläen
33 Residenz
34 Sendlinger Tor
35 Siegestor
36 Staatliche Antikensammlungen
37 Staatsbibliothek
38 Stadtische Galerie
39 Theatinerkirche
40 Theresienwiese
41 Viktualienmarkt
42 Universität

Novotel, Rudolf-Vogel-Bogen 3 (tel. 638000). New in 1985. In Neu-Perlach suburb with good S-Bahn connection to city center.

Preysing, Preysingstr. 1 (tel. 481011). Near Deutsches Museum. One of Munich's most respected hotels. Garni, but first-class cellar restaurant in house.

Prinzregent, Ismaningerstr. 42–44 (tel. 4702081). Central.

Residence, Artur-Kutscher-Platz 4 (tel. 399041). Indoor pool, terrace.

Moderate

Adria, Liebigstr. 8a (tel. 293081). Quietly located in easy walking distance of Maximilianstr. and public transport to center. Breakfast only.

Biederstein, Keferstr. 18 (tel. 395072). Peaceful location near the Kleinhesseloher Lake in the English Garden. Antique furnishings, modern façade.

Brack, Lindwurmstr. 153 (tel. 771052). Breakfast only.
Bräupfanne, Oberföhringerstr. 107a (tel. 951095). In Oberföhringer suburb. Modern building in traditional Bavarian style. Good restaurant.
Bundesbahnhotel, in main station (tel. 558571). Has self-service cafeteria with fine Italian specialties among the round-the-clock restaurants.
Gästehaus Englischer Garten, Liebergesellstr. 8 (tel. 392034). Quiet, ivy-clad house on edge of English Garden.
Munich Penta Hotel, Hochstr. 3 (tel. 4485555). In the suburb of Haidhausen; largest hotel in Munich, 600 rooms in two different price categories. Restaurants, cocktail lounge, *Münchner-Kindl* tavern, rooftop pool and many shops.
Senator, Martin-Greifstr. 11 (tel. 530468). Fully modernized; breakfast only.
Senefelder, Senefelderstr. 4 (tel. 592877). Small, breakfast only.
Tourotel, Domagkstr. 26 (tel. 340011). Quiet with indoor pool and solarium.

Inexpensive

Braunauer Hof, Frauenstr. 40 (tel. 223613). Excellent restaurant, too.
Pension Beck, Thierschstr. 36 (tel. 225768). Central.
Pension Steinberger, Ohmstr. 9 (tel. 331011).

Restaurants

Expensive

Die Aubergine, Maximilian's Platz 5, entrance in Max-Josefstr. (tel. 598171). Munich's finest and most expensive five-star restaurant serving the highest quality French cuisine. Reservations essential.
Bouillabaisse, Falkenturmstr. 10 (tel. 297909). Opposite the Opera, cosy surroundings on two floors with cellar wine-tavern.
La Cave, Maximilianstr. 25 (tel. 223029). Elegant; mostly French cuisine.
Le Gourmet, Ligsalzstr. 46 (tel. 503597). Next to the Fairgrounds; particularly comfortable with attractive antique furniture. Excellent food.
Haxnbauer, Münzstr. 5 (tel. 221922). Pork and veal shank roasted over an open fire and other delicious Munich specialties on offer in this characteristic and atmospheric spot.
Käferschänke, Schumannstr. (tel. 41681). On the corner of Prinzregentstr, you can find practically every culinary specialty in the plush surroundings of this restaurant over the famous delicatessen of the same name.
Königshof, Karlsplatz 25 (tel. 558412). Elegant, traditionally fine restaurant, plush decor and good view over the city centre.
Maximilianstube, Maximilianstr. 27 (tel. 229044). Italian specialties in a luxurious atmosphere; an after-the-theater favorite.
La Mer, Schraudolphstr. 24 (tel. 284535). French cuisine in a comfortable and atmospheric location.
La Piazzetta, Briennerstr. 20 (tel. 282999). Italian rosticceria with spacious dining restaurant, serving first rate food.
Preysing Keller, Innere Wiener Str. 6 (tel. 481015). Topnotch establishment in 300-year-old vaulted cellar.
Sabitzer, Reitmorstr. 21 (tel. 298584). Fine nouvelle cuisine in baroque surroundings. Superb desserts. Reservations essential.
Tai-Tung, Stück Villa, corner Prinzregenten—Ismaningerstr (tel. 471100). Best Chinese food in town; excellent service.
Tantris, Johann-Fichtestr. 7 (tel. 362061). High-class French food. Reservations essential.

Moderate

Asia, Einsteinstr. 133 (tel. 472124). Good Chinese food; best to book.
Bei Mario, Luisenstr. 47 (tel. 521519). Good-quality pizzeria/restaurant.
Csarda Piroschka, Prinzregentenstr. 1 (tel. 295425). In the Haus der Kunst. Hungarian specialties and gypsy music.
Franziskaner, Perusastr. 5 (tel. 225002). Off Theatinerstr. Can be crowded.
Halali, Schonfeldstr. (tel. 285909). Small restaurant with long tradition. Bavarian and international cuisine. Reservations recommended.
Hofbräuhaus, Platzl 9 (tel. 221676). Probably the most famous beer restaurant in Munich; beer hall on the ground floor, restaurant one flight up.
Neuner, Herzogspitalsr, 8 (tel. 2603954). Old wine tavern; music.
Nürnberger Bratwurstglöckl, Frauenplatz (tel. 295264). At the Frauenkirche; rustic and full of atmosphere.

Straubinger Hof, Blumenstr. 5 (tel. 2608097). Typical Munich specialties in rustic surroundings. Beer-garden restaurant in summer.

Inexpensive

Berni's Nudelbrett, Petersplatz 8 (tel. 264469). Opposite St. Peter's Church near the Market. Mainly Italian fare, with plenty of pasta. Very good value.

Hackerkeller, Theresienhöhe 4 (tel. 507004). Characteristic beer cellar.

Il Mulino, Görresstr. 1 (tel. 523335). Crowded; Italian food.

Pschorr Keller, Theresienhöhe 7 (tel. 501088). Good beer drinking spot.

NIGHTLIFE. Folklore variety shows are headed by *Platzl* on the tiny square of the same name. Yodeling and *Schuhplattler* dances are regular features of these shows. Variety shows filled with striptease: *Maxim,* Färbergraben 33. Primarily striptease: *Intermezzo,* Maximilianplatz 16; *Lola Montez,* Am Platzl 1. *Blauer Engel,* Wolfgangstr. 11, in Haidhausen, has striptease plus "frivolous" films.

Aquarius in The Holiday Inn at Leopoldstr. 200 is an underwater nightclub built into a steel tank; plan to pay at least twice as much for a drink here. *Nightclub* in Hotel Bayerischer Hof; *St. James Club,* Briennerstr. 10; *P. 1* in Haus der Kunst. If you wish to dance, are past school-age and not looking for pro-company: *Ball der einsamen Herzen* (Ball of Lonely Hearts), Klenzestr. 71. *Fregatte,* Josephspitalstr. 14, caters to all ages and features live groups, as does *Lenbach Palast* at Lenbach Palast Sq. For *intime* drinking: *King's Corner Club* in Hotel Königshof. *Boccaccio,* Briennerstr. and *Zaraz,* Maximilianstr. 34 belong to Munich's newest nightclubs/discos.

In Schwabing, the artists' and students' area, there are many additional night spots, some of considerable originality in atmosphere and décor. You may try *Gaslight Club,* Ainmillerstr. 10; *Arena,* Occamstr. 8; *Der brave Schwejk,* Neureutherstr. 15; *Charly M,* Maximiliansplatz 5. Live music, jazz and rock at *Kaffee Giesing* (tel. 6920579), *Rigan Club,* Apian Str. 7 (tel. 3087171), and *Max Emanuel,* Adalbert Str. 33 (tel. 2715158).

MUSEUMS. Alte Pinakothek, Barer Str. 27. A superb selection of European art of the 14th–18th centuries. Daily 9–4.30, Tues. and Thurs. also 7–9 P.M.; closed Mon.

Bavarian National Museum, Prinzregentenstr. 3. Arts and crafts, plus the world's largest nativity crib collection. Tues. through Fri. 9–4.30, Sat. and Sun. 10–4.30; closed Mon.

BMW Museum, Petuelring 130, opposite Olympia Park. An exciting treatment of the history and future of Bavaria's auto industry. Daily 9–5.

Deutsches Museum, Museum Island (near Ludwigsbrücke). Contains a planetarium and scientific exhibits from alchemy to zymurgy. Daily 9–5.

Glyptotheck und Antikensammlung, Königsplatz 1 and 3. Greek, Roman and Etruscan handiwork. Tues., Wed., Fri. and Sun. 10–4.30, Thurs. 12–8.30; closed Mon. and Sat.

Münchner Stadtmuseum, St. Jakob's Platz 1. Exhibits of Munich life-style from 1700 through 1900; beer-brewing museum. Daily 9–4.30, closed Mon.

Neue Pinakothek, Barer Str. 29. European art and sculpture of the 19th century. Worth it. Daily 9–4.30, Tues. 7–9 P.M.

Residenzmuseum, Max-Joseph-Platz 3. Staterooms and princely suites in Renaissance, Rococo and neo-Classical styles. Important treasury and a fine coin collection. Tues. through Sat. 10–4.30, Sun. 10–1; closed Mon.

Schackgalerie, Prinzregentenstr. 9. Works by German masters of the 18th and 19th centuries. Daily 9–4.30; closed Mon.

State Collection of Modern Art, in *Haus der Kunst,* Prinzregentenstr. 1. Daily 9–4.30, Thurs. 7–9 P.M.; closed Mon.

SHOPPING. Munich is generally considered Germany's most varied shopping town. It is also its art center. Schwabing has many art galleries where you are advised to browse. The Türkenstr. in the center of Schwabing is one of the best streets for finding old prints, books and other objets d'art. *Antiques:* About a dozen antique shops in the *Kunst-Block* at Ottostr. 6; also at *Bierstorfer* and *Wimmer,* Residenzstr. 25 and Briennerstr. respectively as well as at *Kunstring,* Briennerstr. 4, which is tops for antique porcelain. *Bavarian folklore fashions and dirndls* at *Dirndl-Ecke* on Platzl near Hofbräuhaus and *Wallach,* Residenzstr. 3. *Beer steins: Mory,* in the Rathaus, is the best. Bavarian handicrafts from *Ludwig Beck's* gift boutique, attached to department store of same name opposite the Rathaus. Interesting antique market in Haidhausen, Kirchstr. Open Sat. mornings.

USEFUL ADDRESSES. *American Express,* Promenadeplatz 3; *Cook's,* Lenbachplatz 3; local tourist information in the central front-section of main station, and at airport. *U.S. Consulate,* Königinstr. 5; *British Consulate,* Amalienstr. 62. *Avis,* Nymphenburgerstr. 59; *Auto Sixt,* Seitzstr. 11; *Hertz,* Nymphenburgerstr. 1; all have desks at airport.

The Bavarian Alps

South of Munich lie the Bavarian Alps, those beautiful snow-clad mountains separating Germany from Austria, and providing one of the world's great winter and summer playgrounds. This is a skier's paradise in winter and spring, and a hiker's in summer and fall.

Garmisch-Partenkirchen, the number one winter sports center of Germany, has registered facilities for more than 5,000 visitors. Here you can depend on an unbeatable combination of snow and sun from the beginning of December—on the Zugspitz plateau as early as October—to the middle of May. All the man-made facilities are here too— the stadia, the jumps, bobsled run, rinks, the ski lifts. In summer there are miles of well-marked hiking routes.

The number one excursion from Garmisch is by mountain railway and aerial cable cars to the summit of the Zugspitze, 9,722 feet high. Choose a very clear bright day for this, and you will see all the way to the central Alps of Switzerland.

Other Bavarian centers less popular than Garmisch are equally attractive. Try Mittenwald, famous for its manufacture of violins and for the supermodern aerial cable car, which takes you straight up over the vertical mountain walls to an elevation of 7,350 feet on the ridge of the Karwendel Range. Mittenwald prides itself on its slopes, easy ones for novices, and hard ones to challenge the skill of the experts. For a less expensive skiing vacation try Reit im Winkl, close to the Austrian border. It's a tiny place, reputed to receive the heaviest snowfalls in Bavaria; recommended for beginners.

Bad Reichenhall, on the Austrian frontier, is equally desirable in winter and summer, an important spa with luxurious hotels, a casino, and all the comforts of a smart watering place. South of this spa is the chief tourist attraction of the eastern Bavarian Alps—Berchtesgaden. However cracked he may have been on other subjects, Hitler had a good eye for scenery. One look at the grandiose landscape here is enough to make you understand why he chose to establish his eagle's nest here. Berchtesgaden has 14 ski and mountain huts, ski schools, skating and curling rinks, everything except a bobsled run.

Eastern or Lower Bavaria (Niederbayern) is something of an unknown quantity to many visitors to Germany. In fact, its winter sports facilities are growing all the time and—from cross-country to downhill —have something to offer all grades of skiers. There are at least two dozen quiet and simple towns offering inexpensive accommodations and numerous sports' facilities. The most important winter sports centers are in Bayerisch Eisenstein, Bodenmais and St. Englmar, the latter being the highest village in the Bayerischer Wald at 3,000 feet.

Oberammergau

You certainly shouldn't skip Oberammergau, even if it is not the time of the famous Passion Play, given in fulfilment of a 300-year-old vow to present it every decade (years ending in zero) if the Black Plague were ended. However, exceptionally, a 350th anniversary performance was given in 1984. If you cannot see the play, you can still see the remarkable theater where it is given and the principal actors carrying on their daily occupations in this woodcarving center of Bavaria. The town itself is a rewarding place to visit, with its attractive old houses and church, peaceful against the background of the towering Alps.

You can take the bus trip from here to visit Schloss Linderhof, one of King Ludwig II's most extravagant palaces.

PRACTICAL INFORMATION FOR THE BAVARIAN ALPS

BAD REICHENHALL. *Steigenberger Axelmannstein* (L), Salzburger Str. 4 (tel. 4001). Attractively furnished traditional hotel in quiet location; cure facilities and good restaurant. *Luisenbad* (E), Ludwigstr. 33 (tel. 5081). Very comfortable cure hotel with indoor pool, sauna, solarium, fitness room, elegant restaurant and rustic tavern. *Panorama* (E), Baderstr. 3 (tel. 61001). Quiet location and fine view; indoor pool, sauna, solarium, fitness room and garden terrace. *Bayerischer Hof* (M), Bahnhofsplatz 14 (tel. 5084). Near the main station; modern apartment-hotel, bar, terrace, roof garden with cafe, three restaurants, nightclub, sauna and bowling. *Salzburgerhof* (M), Mozartstr. 7 (tel. 2062). Quiet. *Hansi* (I), Rinckstr. 3 (tel. 3108). Small.

BERCHTESGADEN. *Fischer* (E), Königsseerstr. 51 (tel. 4044). Near the station; pool, sauna, solarium and terrace. *Geiger* (E), Stang Gass (tel. 5055). Borders on the luxurious with even more comfortable adjoining guest house; indoor pool, heated outdoor pool, massage, fitness center and elegant restaurant in traditional style. *Alpenhotel Denninglehen* (M), in Oberau section, nestling in the mountainside at about 3,000 ft. (tel. 08652–5085). Alpine-style comfort; pool, sauna, restaurant, and beauty farm. *Grüner Baum* (M), in Schönau (tel. 08652–2467). Good restaurant. *Krone* (M), Am Rad 5 1/3 (tel. 2881). Quiet with attractive view and garden terrace. *Post* (M), Weihnachtsschützenstr. 3 (tel. 5067). Near the Kurhaus with adjoining annexe and restaurant.

GARMISCH-PARTENKIRCHEN. *Alpina* (E), Alpspitzstr. 12 (tel. 55031). Indoor and outdoor pools, sauna. *Bernrieder Hof* (E), Von Müller Str. 12 (tel. 71071). Full of atmosphere with every comfort. Garni. *Grand-Hotel Sonnenbichl* (E), Burgstr. 97 (tel. 52052). Splendid view; owned by Sultan of Oman. *Holiday Inn* (E), Mittenwalderstr. 2 (tel. 7561). 117 luxurious rooms. Restaurant, bars and nightclub. *Posthotel Partenkirchen* (E), Ludwigstr. 49 (tel. 51067). Comfortable and elegant hotel full of atmosphere; wine tavern with dancing, and fine Alte Posthalterei restaurant with particularly good-value food. *Silence Hotel Obermühle* (E), Mühlstr. 24 (tel. 59051). Traditional hotel 5 mins. from town center in own park; has good restaurant, plus indoor pool and sauna.

Bellevue (M), Riesserseestr. 9 (tel. 58008). Garni. *Garmischer Hof* (M), Bahnhofstr. 53 (tel. 51091). Near the station. Garni. *Partenkirchener Hof* (M), Bahnhofstr. 15 (tel. 58025). Near station with very fine restaurant. *Reindl's Drei Mohren* (M), Ludwigstr. 65 (tel. 2075). Restaurant. *Romantik Hotel Clausings Posthotel* (M), Marienplatz 12 (tel. 58071). Baroque chalet; outstanding restaurant. *Roter Hahn* (M), Bahnhofstr. 44 (tel. 54065). Indoor pool; breakfast only. *Schneefernhaus* (M), on the Zugspitze (tel. 58011). The highest hotel in Germany at all of 8,700 ft. *Wittelsbach* (M), Von-Brugstr. 24 (tel. 53096). Indoor pool, sauna and terrace. Fantastic view. *Gästehaus Kornmüller* (E), Höllentalstr. 36 (tel. 3557). Guesthouse in local style three minutes by car from center. Also apartments.

MITTENWALD. *Rieger* (E), Dekan-Karl-Platz 28 (tel. 5071). Indoor pool and cure facilities. *Wetterstein* (E), Dekan-Karl-Platz 1 (tel. 5058). Also with indoor pool and cure facilities. *Alpenhotel Erdt* (M), Albert-Schott-Str. 7 (tel. 2001). Also apartments. Pleasant hotel with particularly good food. Terrace. *Alpenrose* (M), Obermarkt 1 (tel. 5055). In 13th-century house with tavern-restaurant on 1st floor and *Josefikeller* bar with music at night. *Jagdhaus Drachenburg* (M), tel. 1249. Beautiful view; restaurant with Bavarian specialties. *Post* (M), Obermarkt 9 (tel. 1094). Centrally located; cure facilities.

OBERAMMERGAU. *Alois Lang* (E), St. Lukas Str. 15 (tel. 4141). Quiet location with panoramic view, garden terrace, sauna and solarium. *Alte Post* (M), Dorfstr. 19 (tel. 6691). Garden restaurant and Ludwig-Thomas-Stube tavern; very Bavarian. *Böld* (M), König Ludwig Str. 10 (tel. 4470). All amenities and recommended restaurant. Located right at start of famous König-Ludwig Lauf cross-country ski-track. *Wolf* (M), Dorfstr. 1 (tel. 6971). Indoor pool. *Gasthof zur Rose* (I), Dedlerstr. 9 (tel. 4706). Bavarian specialties restaurant.

REIT IM WINKL. *Steinbacher Hof* (E), Steinbachweg 10 (tel. 08640–8410). Located on hill in Blindau section; fine view, quiet. Ski lift, sauna, pool, medicinal baths. In Winklmoosalm (3,800 ft., 7 miles southeast): *Alpengasthof Augustiner* (M), tel. 08640–8235 and *Alpengasthof Winkelmoosalm* (M), tel. 1097. Near ski lifts. *Haus Lorey* (M), Blindauerstr. 8 (tel. 8731). New 1983. Apartment hotel; indoor pool. *Unterwirt* (M), Kirchplatz 2 (tel. 8811). Comfortable, central hotel with indoor pool, sauna and solarium and pleasant restaurant. *Zur Post* (M), tel. 1024. Central.

Regensburg and Passau

Regensburg is an old city on the Danube, founded by the Celts about 30 B.C. It is the best center for exploring that unspoiled region of forested mountains along the border of Bohemia—the Bavarian Forest, or Bayerischer Wald. In Regensburg, see the 12th-century Steinerne Brücke (Stone Bridge); St. Peter's Cathedral, "the finest Gothic church in Bavaria" (though currently under partial renovation); the Porta Praetoria, third-century gate of Celto-Roman Radasbona (whence Ratisbon); the 12th-century Romanesque Schottenkirche St. Jakob, famous for its north portal, on which Christian and pagan sculpture are curiously intermixed, and the Old Chapel, parts of which date from the year 1,000. There are open-air operas and operettas in summer, presented in Dörnberg Park by Regensburg's excellent municipal theater, and you should try to hear the boys' choir of the cathedral, famous throughout Germany.

Passau, known to the Romans, who founded it, as Castra Batava, lies at the meeting point of the Danube and the Inn and the smaller Ilz. The city sits on a rocky promontory with wooded heights rising around it. As a result both of this dramatic location and its many beautifully-preserved historic old buildings, Passau ranks today among Germany's loveliest cities. In the 8th century the city was established as a Bishopric by Pope Gregory III, and under the Prince-Bishops, as they later became, the city has enjoyed both prosperity and significance.

The principal treasure of Passau is the dominating and magnificent 15th-century Cathedral of St. Stephan, situated at the highest point of the town. It contains the largest church organ in the world—17,000 pipes and 208 stops. You can hear it every day at noon throughout the summer. A later architectural gem is the baroque New Residence Palace of the Prince-Bishops. Don't miss its beautiful rococo interiors. The Palace is in Residenzplatz, which also contains many fine old patrician houses. On the opposite bank of the Danube, which you cross by Luitpold Bridge, is the Veste Oberhaus, a great fortress started in the early 13th century by the Prince-Bishops and continually added to almost to the present day. And among the city's other architectural splendors are the marvelous Gothic Rathaus, the Old Residence of the Prince-Bishops—now the Law Courts—and the former Niedernburg

Abbey, which today is a school. From Passau, there are many interesting bus excursions to be made into the Bayerischer Wald, as well as delightful motorboat trips.

PRACTICAL INFORMATION FOR REGENSBURG AND PASSAU

PASSAU. *Altstadt-Hotel* (M), Bräugasse 27 (tel. 33451). Near the Danube and the town hall; café. *Schloss Ort* (M), am Dreiflusseck (tel. 34072). At the meeting point of Passau's three rivers; terrace with good view across the Inn. *Hotel-Pension Abrahammhof* (I), Innstr. 167 (tel. 6788). Just out of town; terrace garden on the Inn. *Dreiflüssehof* (I), Danzigerstr. 42 (tel. 51018). Rustic comfort and good-value food.

Restaurants. *Heilig-Geist-Stiftsschenke* (M), Heiliggeistgasse 4 (tel. 2607). Historic wine tavern founded in 1358; very atmospheric and with garden. *Ratskeller* (M), Rathausplatz (tel. 34686).

REGENSBURG. *Avia* (E), Frankenstr. 1 (tel. 42093). Across the river; fine restaurant. *Park Hotel Maximilian* (E), Maximilianstr. 28 (tel. 561011). Fully renovated. *Bischofshof* (M), Krauterermarkt 3 (tel. 59086). Near the cathedral and with a cosy restaurant. *Karmeliten* (M), Dachauplatz 1 (tel. 562256). With bar and restaurant, though evenings only. *Weidenhof* (I), Maximilianstr. 23 (tel. 561826). Breakfast only.

Restaurants. *Historisches Eck "Zur Stritzelbäckerin"* (M), Watmarkt 6 (tel. 52966). You are received through a mighty vaulted door decorated with a huge door knocker; atmospheric, as one might imagine. *Historische Wurstkuche* (I), Thundorferstr. 3 near Stone Bridge (tel. 561810). Over 800 years of tradition. *Kneitinger Garten* (I), Müllerstr. 1 (tel. 52455). Nostalgic beer tavern.

Hamburg, Northern City

Hamburg is Germany's biggest city after Berlin, and was once the leading port of Europe. It is penetrated by the River Elbe and threaded with canals, and hence, inevitably, is called The Venice of the North. If you see any real resemblance to Venice here, you've had one too many steins of beer. But this is not to disparage this ancient bastion of the Hanseatic League. She has charms of her own, and her size and vitality make Venice look like a tranquil toy city by comparison.

Hamburg's long cohabitation with the water is responsible for one of its outstanding characteristics. Where there's sailors, there's girls, to put it crudely, and Hamburg has the most roaring night life in Germany. It is concentrated in the St. Pauli Reeperbahn quarter, the Ankerplatz der Freude. That phrase means The Anchorage of Joy.

The energy that's concentrated on stripping at night is devoted to shipping by day. Every half hour in summer, and twice daily in winter, a boat leaves the St. Pauli wharf for a tour of Hamburg's bustling harbor. Don't miss this exciting trip, nor the famous Altona Fish Market, if you are an early riser (Sundays from 6–10 A.M.).

Sightseeing tours by bus are also recommended. Of course, you will see more and be freer to wander if you use choose walking. Here is a special suggestion: stroll to the Deichstrassenfleet on one of those days when the typical luminous fog of the city is hovering above the high and narrow old houses, whose reflections in the water are shrouded in the mist. There you will have a glimpse of old Hamburg as it was in Hanseatic days.

Here are some of the other sights of Hamburg: the Kunsthalle, (16th- to 20th-century art); the view in both directions from the Lombards-brücke; the Stadtpark (Municipal Park), one of the finest in Europe; the celebrated Planten un Blomen, a world-famous permanent display of the gardeners' craft at its best; the Musikhalle, number one concert hall, continuing the tradition of one of the city's most famous native sons, Johannes Brahms; Staatsoper (State Opera), founded as a theater in 1678, and boasting such notable premieres as *Lohengrin* and *Rigoletto;* the newly reopened Deutsches Schauspielhaus on Kirchenallee, the biggest theater in the Federal Republic; the Hamburg Historical Museum (old ship models); and the Altonaer Museum (historical folkdress, toy collection, and other historical items of the area).

There's the 110-foot Bismarck Monument, and just east of it, St. Michael's Church, whose greenish cupola is accessible by an elevator. Try it for a good view over the town. Hard by St. Michael's (site of lunchtime organ concerts), in little streets that have hardly changed since the Middle Ages, you will find the Krameramtswohnungen, built for the widows of municipal officials in medieval times. Go east along the Michaelstrasse and explore the Fleete, a fascinating labyrinth of narrow canals and quaint streets. The grand climax of any tour in this area is the Renaissance Rathaus, with its tall clock tower. If you visit only one building in Hamburg, this should be it—for its fine festival hall, vaulted ceilings, elaborate doorways and other remarkable decorative features. The whole building is supported by 4,000 piles driven deep into the marshy ground.

PRACTICAL INFORMATION FOR HAMBURG

Hotels

Deluxe

Atlantic, An der Alster 72 (tel. 248001). On lakeshore but still central; has indoor pool, sauna, solarium, fitness room and 2 restaurants; the *Atlantic Grill* and a late-night spot, open to 2 A.M. with music.

Ramada Renaissance, Grosse Bleichen (tel. 349180) Very pleasant. *Noblesse* restaurant.

Vier Jahreszeiten, Neuer Jungerstieg 9 (tel. 34941). Also on lakeshore and with fine view; 3 restaurants, one open to 2 P.M. with dancing and cabaret.

Expensive

Ambassador, Heidenkampsweg 34 (tel. 234041). Pool and restaurant.

Hamburg-Plaza, Marseillerstr. 2 (tel. 351035). Heated pool, 2 excellent restaurants and bars.

Intercontinental, Fontenay 10 (tel. 414150). Large, with several restaurants including the very fine rooftop restaurant *Fontenay;* pool, sauna, solarium.

Prem, An der Alster 9 (tel. 241727). Has a splendid view.

Moderate

Apart-Hotel Panorama, Billstedter Hauptstr. 36 (tel. 731736). The suburb of Billstadt; with indoor pool and some apartments.

Baseler Hospiz, Esplanade 11 (tel. 341921). Special rates for groups.

Behrman, Elbchaussee 528 (tel. 863673). Near the station. Good value.

Berlin, Borgfelderstr. 1 (tel. 251640). Excellent restaurant.

Falck, Kielerstr. 333 (tel. 5402061). A traditional-style hotel.

Graf Moltke, Steindamm 1 (tel. 2801154). Near the station.

Motel Hamburg, Hoheluftehaussee 119 (tel. 473067).

Oper, Drebahn (tel. 341656). Near the opera; parking.

Wappen von Hamburg, St. Pauli Landungsbrücken. This "typical" Hamburg hotel is a ship docked at St. Pauli in winter, offering overnight accommodations in single- to three-bed cabins.

Inexpensive

Auto-Hotel Am Hafen, Spielbudenplatz 11 (tel. 316631).

Forsthaus, Reinbekerweg 77 (tel. 7213084). Small and quiet; in the southern suburb of Bergedorf.

Gasthaus zum Wattkorn, Tangstedter Landstr. 230 (tel. 5203797). Small inn/café with 13 rooms. Garden with wild-bird enclosure and pond.

Wedina, Gurlittstr. 23 (tel. 243011). Pool and sauna; breakfast only.

Restaurants

Expensive

Atlantic Grill, Atlantic Hotel, Alster 72 (tel. 248001). First class.

La Bonne Auberge Zum Goldenen Stern, Alsterdorferstr. 303 (tel. 512410). Cozy restaurant with round-the-clock service. In Alsterdorf suburb.

Fischereihafen-Restaurant Carl Voss, Grosse Elbstr. 143 (tel. 3898218). Elegant Hanseatic atmosphere and a wonderful view across the harbor; fish specialties of the highest quality.

Haerlin, Hotel Vier Jahreszeiten, Neuer Jungerstieg (tel. 34941). Excellent; some of the finest eating in town. Also Jahreszeiten Grill.

Le Canard, Martinistr. 11 (tel. 4604830) in Eppendorf suburb. Highly recommended French cuisine at realistic prices; good value.

Süllberg, on Süllberg hill overlooking the Elbe (tel. 861686). Fine food.

Moderate

Am Michel, Englische Planke 8 (tel. 365541). Fish and mussels in an old Hamburg atmosphere.

Bavaria-Blick, Bernhard-Nochtstr. 99 (tel. 314800). Splendid view.

Fischerhaus, St. Pauli fish market (tel. 314053). Delicious fresh fish.

Fischkajüte, Brücke 5, at the St. Pauli landing stages (tel. 314162). Germany's oldest fried fish restaurant.

Landungsbrücken-Restaurant, at the pier (tel. 314527). Fish everywhere.

Mövenpick, Grosse Bleichen 36 (tel. 351635). Three differently priced restaurants: *Café des Artistes, Backstube* and *Weinkeller.*

Old Commercial Room, Englische Planke 10 (tel. 366319). Don't be confused by the English name—Hamburg specialties, plus a variety of beer.

Ratsweinkeller, Gr. Johannisstr. 2 (tel. 364153). In the Rathaus cellar; has a beautifully vaulted ceiling and sailing ship motifs dotted around the walls.

Schiffer-Börse, Kirchenallee 46 (tel. 245240). Opposite the main station; typical old Hamburg tavern with maritime decor and fish specialties.

Überseebrücke, at ferry boat pier (tel. 313333). The port bustles in the background of this characteristically good fish restaurant.

Vierlander Kate im Altonaer Museum, Museumstr. 23 (tel. 3807483). Good, wholesome regional dishes in the rustic atmosphere of an authentically reconstructed Lower-Saxony farm building.

NIGHTLIFE. Nightclubs being subject to high mortality and swift changes of pace, it is pretty impractical to give individual recommendations, but in Hamburg it isn't necessary to try. All you have to do is to go to St. Pauli, say a little before 10 P.M., find the Reeperbahn (get off at the St. Pauli station on the underground, or take a taxi) and look around. The best idea, however, is to join in one of the organized night tours of St. Pauli and the Reeperbahn run by the Hamburg Tourist Office. These depart daily at 8.00 P.M. from the square in front of the Main Station (Hachmannplatz) and include a ferry-trip across the Alster Lake, a city-by-night bus sightseeing tour, supper and a visit to one or two nightclubs, rounding off with a sex show at the famous *Colibri.* There are plenty of places that go in for girls wearing as little clothing as the law allows (the law in Hamburg is liberal) and most of them are located in the street properly and remarkably named Grosse Freiheit (Great Freedom).

SHOPPING. The shops along the Jungfernstieg, Grosse Bleichen, Neuer Wall and Dammtorstrasse are gorgeous. So are the picturesque bordering streets like Arkaden and Colonnaden. Mönckebergstrasse and its side streets are crowded with less expensive stores. Maritime *objets d'art* are found around Rödingsmarkt.

USEFUL ADDRESSES. *Consulates:* U.S.A., Alsterufer 27; British, Harvestehuder Weg 8A. *American Express,* An der Alster 30, *Wagons-Lits/Cook,* Ballindamm 39.

Bremen, Germany's Oldest Port

Forty miles up the Weser is Bremen, Germany's oldest, and today her second, port (Hamburg is the first), a great center of world trade since the days when, with Hamburg and Lübeck, it was one of the Big Three of the Hanseatic League. Since World War II, the port of Bremen has surpassed its highest prewar traffic volume by 75 per cent.

Servicemen who remember Bremen as a staging area are familiar with St. Peter's Cathedral, with its lead-crusted crypt and mummies in open coffins; with the famous Rathaus, a colorful building with its Renaissance façade of rose-colored brick and its sidewalk arcade, and with the Schütting Guild House of the merchants, to say nothing of Bremen's trademark, the Roland Monument, whose huge medieval knights have been in the marketplace since 1404.

Hannover

Hannover is a big industrial city with a long cultural tradition. Badly damaged during the war, its monuments are now largely restored. The 17th-century Leine castle looks as good as it ever did now. The Opera House, considered the most beautiful in Germany, was recently extensively renovated and reopened in all its former splendor at the end of 1985. Even more interesting, however, are the modern buildings such as the Funkhaus am Maschsee, the 15-story Continental-Verwaltungs-gebäude, and the Anzeiger skyscraper, which has a fine view of the city from its ninth-floor restaurant. More impressive than anything in Hannover is the Guelph Herrenhausen Castle just outside, celebrated for its beautiful baroque garden.

Among Hannover's special attractions are two zoos (one supplies animals to zoos all over the world); the Landesmuseum (Rembrandt, Rubens, Van Dyck and modern paintings); the Kestner Museum, showing arts and crafts of all times and countries (wonderful Egyptian collection) and the Maschsee, city lake for swimming, sculling, canoeing and motorboat regattas. Each spring, Hannover is host to the famed International Industries Fair.

West of Hannover is the town of Hamelin (Hameln), worth a visit just for its wonderful Weser Renaissance houses. Among the palatial timbered homes, you will see the house which is supposed to have been the residence of the famous Pied Piper.

Lüneburg and the Lüneburger Heide

Lüneburg in Lower Saxony is a Hanseatic city that rose to fame principally as a salt producing center, though the origins of the city can be traced back more than 1,000 years. For the visitor, however, Lüneburg's chief attraction is its marvellous and intricate medieval brick architecture—to some extent the city is almost a living museum to brick building. The 14th-century church of St. John and the church of St. Nicholas are both magnificent examples, but Lüneburg's finest medieval brick building—tantamount to saying the world's finest—is undoubtably the 13th–15th-century Rathaus. The city also contains a number of splendid half-timbered buildings.

Lüneburg stands on the northern edge of Germany's largest area of heathland—the Lüneburger Heide (Heath). It is a mysterious and rather desolate area of flatlands and undulating hills; tracts of heath proper, dotted with old juniper shrubs of bizarre shape, wild flowers and flocks of sheep, alternating with rich farmlands and forests.

The heath boasts a number of relatively inexpensive vacation resorts such as Bendestorf, Hanstedt, Jesteburg, Scheverdingen and Walstrode. But in addition to these old towns and pretty villages, the heath has a landmark of a considerably more sober nature. This is the memorial to the victims of the Bergen-Belsen Concentration Camp, standing in solitude in a clearing about 4 miles southeast of Bergen, roughly 30 miles north of Hannover.

The third-largest city in Lower Saxony is Osnabrück, a lively town with a thousand-year-old cathedral. It was here in 1660 that George I of England was born, German founder of the dynasty that still rules Britain. Also worth visiting is the late Gothic town hall with its treasury and the baroque university building, former residence of the Prince Bishops.

PRACTICAL INFORMATION FOR BREMEN, HANNOVER AND LÜNEBURG

BREMEN. *Parkhotel* (L), Bürger Park (tel. 34080). In delightful setting; very quiet and offering a high degree of comfort; good restaurant; bar and heated garden terrace. *Canadian Pacific Bremen Plaza* (E), Hillmannplatz 20 (tel. 17670). New in 1985. Modern hotel with all comforts. Two restaurants. *Columbus* (E), Bahnhofsplatz 5 (tel. 314161). Opposite the station. *Crest* (E), August Bebel Allee 4 (tel. 23870). In the suburbs. *Zur Post* (E), Bahnhofsplatz 11 (tel. 30590). Near the station; indoor pool, sauna, solarium, fitness room. *Munte am Stadtwald* (M), Zur Munte 2 (tel. 212063). Pool, sauna and restaurant. *Überseehotel* (M), Am Markt (tel. 320197). Breakfast only; near the Rathaus. *Bölts am Park* (I), Slevogtstr. 23 (tel. 341348). Quiet.

Restaurants. *Le Bistro* (E), Sögerstr. 54 (tel. 314749). In the back room of a delicatessen; highly recommended gourmet food. Booking a must. *Das Kleine Lokal* (E), Besselstr. 40 (tel. 71929). First-class food and wines. Book ahead. *Rolf Diehl* (E), H. H.-Meier-Alle 2 (tel. 213213). First class cuisine though pretty expensive; all in all, it's worth it. *Alt-Bremer Brauhaus* (M), Katharinenstr. 32 (tel. 320404). Its 24 rooms are decorated with different motifs from 18th- and 19th-century Bremen. *Alte Gilde* (M), Ansgaritorstr. 24 (tel. 311712). Located in a deep vaulted cellar of Gewerbehaus. *Deutsches Haus* and *Haus am Markt* (M), Am Markt 1 (tel. 321048). 3 in 1; the elegant *Ratsstuben* is on the 2nd. floor, the *Marktstuben* and *Hangeboden* are on the 1st. floor and the rustic *Seefahrtsstuben zum Jonas,* in all its nautical glory, is on the ground floor; good view from upstairs. *Flett* (M), Böttcherstr. 3 (tel. 320995). In Haus St. Petrus; rustic and recommended. *Ratskeller* (M), Am Markt (tel. 320936). In business since 1408; wine, atmosphere and tradition in profusion. *Hotel-Restaurant Deutsches House* (M), Findorffstr. 3, in Worpswede suburb (tel. 4792–1205). Picturesque; rustic interiors. Restaurant has fine selection of game and local specialties.

HANNOVER. *Hannover Intercontinental* (L), Friedrichswall 11 (tel. 16911). Casino; has *Prinz-Taverne* gourmet restaurant and bar; all in all, a very classy spot. *Grand-Hotel-Mussmann* (E), Ernst-August-Platz 7 (tel. 327971). In city center opposite rail station and airport terminal. Sound-proofed windows keep rooms quiet. *Holiday Inn* (E), by airport (tel. 0511–730171). In the suburb of Langenhagen. *Kastens Hotel Luisenhof* (E), Luisenstr. 2 (tel. 16151). Dating back to 1856. Next to opera and near station; quiet. *Maritim Hotel Hannover* (E), Hildesheimer Str. 34 (tel. 16531). New, central. *Central-Hotel-Kaiserhof* (M), Ernst-August-Platz 4 (tel. 327811). *Grünewald* (M), Grünewaldstr. 28 (tel. 695041). Breakfast only. *Georgenhof* (I), Herrenhauser Kirchweg 20 (tel. 712244). In the outskirts with excellent restaurant.

Restaurants. *Schuh's Restaurant* (E), in Hotel Schweizerhof. Opened in 1984 and now one of the leading eating houses. *Wichmann* (E), Hildesheimerstr. 230 (tel. 831671). *Witten's Hop* (E), Gernsstr. 4 (tel. 648844). In Bothfeld suburb. Fine cuisine in converted farmhouse. *Wein-Wolf* (M), Rathenaustr. 2 (tel. 320788). Good traditional wine tavern. *Alte Mühle* (I), tel. 05139–6768. Good value in rustic surroundings; in the suburb of Kirchrode. *Fey's Weinstuben* (I), Sophienstr. 6 (tel. 325973). Jolly, inexpensive wine tavern.

LÜNEBURG. *Residenz* (E), Munstermannskamp 10 (tel. 45047) near the Kupark. Has *Schnecke* restaurant. *Seminaris* (E), Soltauer Str. 3 (tel. 2081). Has fitness room and bowling. *Wellenkamp* (M), Am Sande 9 (tel. 43026). Particularly good restaurant. *Zum Heidkrug* (M), Am Berge 5 (tel. 31249). A Romantik Hotel in a late-Gothic building that dates back to 1455 and where the beer has been brewed and sold since 1561. Only 14 beds, so reservations essential. *Bremer Hof* (I), Lünerstr. 13 (tel. 36077). Has a very quiet guest house just a few minutes' walk away.

Restaurants. *Ratskeller* (M), Am Markt 1 (tel. 31757). In the old town hall; antique furniture and historic atmosphere. *Zur Krone* (M), Heiligengeiststr. 41 (tel. 208200). In historic building that dates back to 1485; atmospheric.

LÜNEBURGER HEIDE. (Listed throughout the area from north to south.) Jesteburg: *Heidschnucke* (E), Zum Auetal 14 (tel. 04183–3481). Very comfortable and quiet with especially attractive period furnishings; excellent restaurant serving local specialty of roast moorland lamb *(Heidschnucke)*. Hanstedt: *Landhaus-Augustenhöh* (M), Am Steinberg 77 (tel. 04184–323). Breakfast only. Egestorf: *Hof Sudermühlen* (M), tel. 04175–1441. Bispingen-Niederhaverbeck: *Pension Haus Heidetal* (I), tel. 05198–743. Can only be reached by horse-drawn wagon. Schneverdingen: *Pension Hof Tütsberg* (I), tel. 05199–241. Bergen: *Kohlmann* (I), Lukenstr. 6 (tel. 05051–3014).

OSNABRÜCK. *Hohenzollern* (E), Heinr.-Heinestr. 17 (tel. 27292). At the main station; has good restaurant. *Hotel Dom* (M), Kleine Domsfreiheit 5 (tel. 21554). *Himmelreich* (M), Zum Himmelreich 11 (tel. 51700). In Nahne suburb. Quiet with picturesque outlook; indoor pool. *Kulmbacher Hof* (M), Schlosswall 67 (tel. 27844). Terrace, bowling; evening meals in the *Kulmbacher Cellar*. *Parkhotel* (M), Am Heger Holz (tel. 46083). A few miles west of town; pool, sauna, terrace and bowling.

Restaurants. *Chez Didier* (M), Buersche Str. 2 (tel. 2331). Bistro-restaurant with French regional specialties in boulevard-café style. Closed 15 Jul.–2 Aug. *Niedersachsenhof* (M), Nordstr. 109 (tel. 77535). In Schinkel section. Antique furnishings and garden restaurant. *Ratskeller* (M), Markt 30 (tel. 23388). In the Rathaus (town hall).

Schleswig-Holstein

Queen of the Hansa, Lübeck is one of Germany's most exciting old cities, a short drive by autobahn north from Hamburg into Schleswig-Holstein. It owed its dominant position in the Hanseatic League to its favorable location on the Trave River, where it empties into the Baltic. The old harbor buildings and docks still indicate the ancient prosperity of this former Imperial Free City, and so do the handsome buildings in the center of town. Most spectacular of these is the City Hall, a masterpiece of Lübeck brickwork, retaining the black glazed tiles characteristic of this region. See also the impressive Marienkirche (St. Mary's church), the cathedral, dating from 1173, with its Romanesque interior and Gothic façade; the striking Holstentor, fortified gateway of the medieval city; the 700-year-old Holy Ghost Hospital, oldest almshouse in Germany; and Buddenbrooks House, in the Mengstrasse.

Fourteen miles from Lübeck is Travemünde, most popular of all Baltic beach resorts, and very lively the whole year round, thanks to its luxurious casino overlooking the beach. In addition to roulette and baccara, the casino provides a restaurant, café, dancing and nightclub. This is the first of a whole string of sandy dune beaches backed by thick pine woods, characteristic of the Baltic coast.

PRACTICAL INFORMATION FOR SCHLESWIG-HOLSTEIN

LÜBECK. *Lysia-Mövenpick* (E), Beim Holsentorplatz (tel. 15040). On the Wall promontory, with restaurant and dance-bar; modern. *Autel-Auto-Hotel* (M), near Lohmüle autobahn exit (tel. 43881). Indoor and outdoor pools; breakfast only. *International* (M), at station (tel. 81144). With pool and sauna. *Jensen* (M), An der Obertrave 4 (tel. 71646). At the Holstentor gate.

Restaurants. *Schabbelhaus* (E), Mengstr. 48 (tel. 72011). Garden in summer for outdoor dining. *Haus der Schiffergesellschaft* (M), Breitestr. 2 (tel. 76776). Very good food and drink in an historic and characteristic medieval building that dates back to 1535; recommended. *Lübecker Hanse* (M), Kolk 3 (tel. 78052). Dine in the style of the old Lübeck gentry.

TRAVEMÜNDE. *Maritim-Strandhotel* (L), on the promenade (tel. 4001). Large, with thermal baths, solarium, fitness room, bowling. *Deutscher Kaiser* (M), Vorderreihe 52 (tel. 5028). In the old town. Terrace and bowling. *Strandhaus Becker* (M), Strandpromenade 7 (tel. 75035). On the seafront with fine view; café and restaurant.

In addition to roulette, the *Casino* (tel. 811) has a nightclub, a restaurant and a delightful terrace.

Berlin—City of Contrasts

For an exciting sense of history in the making and a striking contrast between two systems of life, you should include Berlin in your German itinerary. The best and easiest way to approach Berlin is by air, landing at Tegel Airport. You can fly in regularly by Pan American, British Airways or Air France from Hamburg, Frankfurt, Munich, Düsseldorf, Bremen, Hannover, Cologne, Saarbrücken, Stuttgart or Nuremberg, and many German travel agencies offer special reduced rates for week-end flights.

If you drive or go by train, you will need a transit visa from the German Democratic Republic, otherwise known as East Germany. This can be obtained at an interzonal border check point. The so-called Peoples' Police of East Germany have been known to cause great difficulties and complications for petty—or even nonexistent—reasons and extricating oneself from these complications can easily turn out to be difficult and time-consuming, which is why most tourists fly.

Transit visas are issued at the following border crossing points: Helmstedt-Marienborn (rail/road); Rudolphstein-Hirschberg (road); Lanenburg-Horst (road); Ludwigstadt-Probstzella (rail); Bebra-Gerstungen (rail); Buchen-Schwanheide (rail); Herleshausen-Wartha (road); Hof-Gutenfürst (rail); Gudow-Zarrentin (road); Warnemünde and Sassnitz ferry landings. These, incidentally, are only some of the routes American and British tourists may use. You will be charged a very high fee and you must see that your exit point is indicated correctly—if you don't say anything, your return transit visa is issued for the same border checkpoint as your entry.

East and West Berlin are a third the size of Luxembourg, and a third of Berlin consists of water, trees and fields. It has large woods, lakes and much agricultural land and a number of independent villages, besides the huge industrial compounds and the pulsating center of the western sector—the Kurfürstendamm, which by itself has tended to give Berlin the reputation of being one large den of conspicuous nightclubs and bars. In addition to the forests of Grünwald, Duppel, Spandau and Tegel, there are large areas of unspoilt countryside under the protection of national trusts with over 450 miles of foot-paths and bicycle tracks throughout the state. Among the numerous lakes dotted all over the city's environs, Wannsee is the most appealing. A number of cruise ships operate on the Wannsee, Havelsee, and the river Spree.

Returning to the city itself, a sightseeing tour of West Berlin should begin in its most famous shopping street, the Kurfürstendamm *(Kudamm),* the heart of the city by day and night. Along its 2-mile stretch and in the neighboring side-streets, you will find over 1,100 shops, boutiques, department stores, and antique galleries—something indeed for every taste. After dark, the Ku-damm is transformed into the throbbing heart of Berlin nightlife. This is theaterland: the Kömodie on Kurfürstendamm itself, the Schiller Theater nearby and the Opera just a block away, as well as a row of private theaters, among which the Schaubühne, relocated and renovated in 1981, is generally considered the most innovative in Germany.

Other highpoints of West Berlin are: the Zoo (Zoologischer Garten), one of the best in Europe with its new Aquarium in Budpaesterstr, both in the Tiergarten district; the Siegesäule or Victory Column (commemorates the Franco-Prussian war) on the square called Grosser Stern, and from the 210 ft top of which you will have a sweeping view of Berlin; Schloss Charlottenburg, the former summer residence of the Prussian kings; the English Garden, opened by Anthony Eden (hence known to Berliners as The Garden of Eden), which is in the vast stretch of Parkland called Tiergarten, in the suburb of the same name; east of the English Garden is Schloss Bellevue, the restored official residence of the President of West Germany, open to the public in summer months. Beyond it to the southeast is the concert hall of the Berlin Philharmonic Orchestra (Philharmonie) and the New National Gallery containing Berlin's new *Staatsbibliothek,* the largest archive of its kind in the world. The Hansa Viertel, a district around the Tiergarten of delightfully painted, fancifully-balconied apartment houses, includes the work of leading architects from a dozen nations; the Reichtagsgeb-äude (Government Building) at the Platz der Republik in Tiergarten, built between 1884 and 1894 and reconstructed after the war. A little further east, at the end of the Strasse 17 Juni, and on the border of the eastern sector is the famous Brandenburg Gate (*Brandenburger Tor*), once the Triumphal Arch of the German capital. Here also is the infamous Wall, built of concrete and running for 28 miles across the city. Rathaus Schönberg at John F. Kennedy Platz, is the seat of Berlin's House of Representatives and Senate. It has a replica of the Liberty Bell on top of its 215 ft. tower which rings out at noon every day. Deutschlandhalle on Messedamm at Charlottenburg is Germany's largest sports and entertainment hall, seating over 11,000 people. Finally, there is the nearby Messegelände or Fair Grounds, a whole city of exhibition buildings grouped around the 490 ft. Funkturm radio tower. An elevator takes you to the top for an extensive view.

Historical Milestones

The history of the city on the River Spree dates back to 1237. In 1470 Berlin became the seat of government of the Brandenburg Prince-Electors, the Kurfürsten (hence the name of Berlin's most famous street). In the 17th century under Prince Frederick-William the Great Elector, Berlin began to prosper. By the time of his death in 1688 the population had risen to over 20,000. From 1701 the Kings of Prussia took up residence here, and by the end of the reign of Frederick II (the Great), Prussia was a major power.

Capital of the German Empire since 1871, her fortunes were tied to those of Germany as a whole. However, in November 1918 the Empire disintegrated and the Reichstag proclaimed the foundation of the Republic.

At the end of World War II Berlin was divided into four sectors under the control of a four-power Kommandatura, each sector reflecting the policies and viewpoint of the nation that administered it. However, in June 1948 the Soviet General walked out of the Kommandatura and the Berlin blockade was begun. West Berlin lay isolated deep inside Soviet-occupied Germany. The only means of getting supplies into the city was by the air, and a memorial commemorat-

ing the great airlift of June 24, 1948 to October 6, 1949 can be seen at
the Platz der Luftbrücke in front of Tempelhof Airport. 31 American
and 39 British airmen lost their lives flying in food and medicine.

PRACTICAL INFORMATION FOR BERLIN

HOW TO GET AROUND. Public transport is efficient
and frequent, single fares costing DM 2.00 within the
city limits. Tourists are advised to purchase a multiple
ticket good for 5 rides on any bus or underground train;
costs DM 8.50 and valid for two hours' travel in one direction. Unlimited travel
tickets, good for all forms of public transport (including ferries), are valid for
2 or 4 consecutive days, cost DM 15 and DM 30 respectively, and are available
from the underground station at Kleistpark or the Zoo.

Hotels

Deluxe

Ambassador, Bayreutherstr. 42 (tel. 240101). 120 rooms, all with bath; pool,
sauna, grill-restaurant and *Conti Fischstuben*. Breakfast buffet.

Bristol-Hotel-Kempinski, Kurfürstendamm 27 (tel. 881091). 360 rooms, all
with bath; some suites; luxurious. Good restaurant; indoor pool with bar.

Excelsior, Hardenbergstr. 14 (tel. 31991). 603 beds. Breakfast buffet.

Intercontinental, Budapesterstr. 2 (tel. 26020). 1150 beds and 70 apartments.
Pool, sauna, solarium. *Zum Hugenotten* for extra-fine food. Breakfast buffet.

Penta, Nürnberger Str. 65 (tel. 240011). 850 beds, all with bath; pool, sauna,
fitness rooms, cinema. Breakfast buffet.

Steigenberger-Berlin, Los Angeles Platz 1 (tel. 21080). 600 beds, 11 apartments; indoor pool and sauna. First class *Park* restaurant and Berliner Stube.
Breakfast buffet.

Expensive

Berlin, Kurfürstenstr. 62 (tel. 269291). Large and modern with noted *Berlin
Grill* restaurant. Breakfast buffet.

Crest Motor Hotel, Güntzelstr. 14 (tel. 870241). Near Kurfürstendamm; has
a number of apartments. Breakfast buffet.

Ibis, Messedamm 10 (tel. 302011). All rooms with bath or shower; has roof
garden café-restaurant *Bellevue* with dancing in the evening.

Novotel, Ohmstr. 4–6 (tel. 381061). Near the airport.

Palace in Europa Center, Budapesterstr. (tel. 262011). 200 rooms, all with
bath; 2 elegant restaurants and a good bar.

President, An der Urania 16 (tel. 2138061). All rooms with bath or shower;
roof garden. Near to Ka-De-We department store.

Schweizer Hof, Budapesterstr. 21 (tel. 26961). 370 airconditioned rooms
with bath or shower; grill restaurant, pool and fitness room.

Seehof, Lietzensee Ufer 11 (tel. 321051). Overlooks the Lietzensee, with
restaurant and lakeside cafe terrace and indoor pool. Breakfast buffet.

Moderate

Astoria, Fasanenstr. 2 (tel. 3124067). Near zoo; breakfast only; garage.

Börse, Kurfürstendamm 34 (tel. 883021). Has good *Black Angus* restaurant.

Bremen, Bleibtreustr. 25 (tel. 8814076). Small and comfortable.

Frühling am Zoo, Kurfürstendamm 17 (tel. 8818083). Near the zoo.

Hamburg, Landgrafenstr. 4 (tel. 269161). 240 rooms on 11 floors, all soundproofed and all with bath; restaurant and bar. Breakfast buffet.

Schloss-Hotel Gerhaus, Brahnsstr. 4–10 (tel. 8262081). Quiet location, extremely attractive hotel. Good value.

Sylter Hof, Kurfürstenstr. 116 (tel. 21200). 130 rooms with bath; restaurant.

Inexpensive

Alster, Eisenacherstr. 10 (tel. 246952). Breakfast pension in Schöneberg.

Central, Kurfürstendamm 66 (tel. 8816343). 60 beds.

Derby, Wielandstr. 18 (Uhlandstr. subway) (tel. 32434).

Engelberger, Mommsenstr. 6 (Uhlandstr. subway) (tel. 8815536).

Pension Havelhaus, Imchenallee 35. On the banks of the River Havel, with own bathing beach and boats for hire. Quiet. Restaurant next door.

Stephanie, Bleibtreustr. 38 (tel. 8818073). Garni. 40 rooms, half with bath. Near zoo.

Restaurants

Expensive

Anselmo, Damaschkestr. 17 (tel. 3233094). Italian specialties.

Berlin-Grill, Hotel Berlin, Kurfürstendamm 62 (tel. 240101). Excellent.

Ritz, Rankestr. 26 (tel. 247520). Generally considered Berlin's finest restaurant. Small and elegant with excellent service and with dishes from Arabia, China, Japan, Korea, India and Russia. Good value.

Rockendorf's Restaurant, Düsterhauptstr. 1 (tel. 4023099). Highly recommended for excellent good-value food. Reservations essential.

Moderate

Alt-Berliner-Bier-Salon, Kurfürstendamm 225. North German specialties in Empire-style building. Very good value. Dancing in the evening. In summer on Sundays from 11 A.M. early-morning concert.

Alte Fritz, Lindenstr. 77. Berlin's oldest inn, where King Frederick II of Prussia once stayed. Offers homely cooking in two large, palatial halls. Beer and coffee garden has room for 3,000 guests.

Berliner Kindl Bräu, Bismarckstr. 66 and many others. One of the chain that features beer and Eisbein. Full meals at fixed prices are also good.

Blockhaus Nikolskoe, Nikolskoerweg (tel. 8052914). In a charming sylvan location a long, long taxi ride from downtown Berlin. Worth it though.

Funkturm-Restaurant, Messedamm 11 (tel. 30382996). In the high radio tower at the fairgrounds; excellent food and a marvellous panoramic view.

Hardtke, Meinekestr. 27 (tel. 8818726). A typical Berlin atmosphere and huge portions along with home made *wurst*.

I-Punkt Berlin, Europa Center (tel. 2611014). High up on the 20th-floor; several sections, dancing and fine view.

Kopenhagen, Kurfürstendamm 203–4 (tel. 8819827). Danish food and beers on the terrace.

Le Paris, Kurfürstendamm 211 (tel. 8834848). French cuisine and wines upstairs with dancing; good location overlooking the Ku-damm.

Ratskeller Schmargendorf, Berkaer Platz 1 (tel. 8262307). Wine cellar and wine garden; Berlin specialties as well as French cuisine.

Ristorante Bacco, Marburgerstr. 5 (tel. 2118687). Italian food. Very good value in atmospheric surroundings.

Silberterrasse im Ka-De-We, Tauentzienstr. 21. On 5th floor of the world-famous store. Good value.

Zlata Praha, Meinekestr. 4 (tel. 8819750). Bohemian specialties and famous Pilsner Urquell beer.

Inexpensive

Alter Krug, Konigin-Luisestr. 52, in Dahlem (tel. 8325089). With attractive terrace for outdoor eating.

Essen & Trinken, Leibnitzstr. 35 (near Kantstr.) (tel. 3128335). Open Mon. to Sat. 10 A.M. to 11 P.M. As the name implies ("eating and drinking"), honest and simple Berlin cooking at honest and simple prices.

Kardell, Gervinnsstr. 24 (tel. 3241066). In the hotel of the same name.

Tante Anna, Joachim Friedrich Str. 45 (near Ku' damm) (tel. 8926524). Open daily 6 P.M. to 2 A.M. Regional German specialties.

Weissbierstube im Berlin Museum, Lindenstr. 14 (tel. 2514015) in Kreuzberg. Large cold buffet, Berlin-style, for museum visitors.

Zum Ambrosius, Einemstrasse 14 (at Lützowplatz) (tel. 2612993). Hearty German home-cooking at good-value prices.

NIGHTCLUBS. Berlin's nightlife has always been famous, not to say notorious. There are a number of small places of no particular distinction, almost indistinguishable from one another—small smoke-filled rooms, minute bars, barmaids with plunging necklines, three-piece bands—but the specialty of Berlin is huge entertainment places. Here are some of the best:

Chez Nous, Marburgerstr. 14. Empire-style plush with drag show and cabaret beginning at 10.30 P.M.; 2 shows a night.

Chez Romy Haag, Welserstr. 24 (tel. 3236006). Revue with non-stop strip. Reservations recommended.

La Vie en Rose, Waitzstr. 22. Revue theater; spectacular shows.

New Eden, Kurfürstendamm 71. 2 dance bands and a midnight show. **Big Eden** (popular with the young), Kurfurstendamm 202.

Rififi, Fuggerstr. 34. One of the spiciest strip joints in Berlin.

Scotch Club 13, Marburgerstr. 15. Good striptease; reasonably-priced.

Separé Centrum, Kantstr. 162. Striptease German style; very expensive.

 MUSEUMS. Some of Berlin's most important museums are contained in a huge complex called the **Dahlems Museums,** located between Arnimallee and Lansstr. Open daily except Monday, 9–5. Housed in the Dahlems are:

Ethnology Museum, Lansstr. 8. Five sections representing the five continents. Noted especially for its Aztec collection and Asian artifacts.

Gemäldegalerie, Arnimallee 23. Marvelous collection of paintings from the 13th through 18th centuries, including such artists as Rembrandt, Rubens and a slew of others from Giotto to the Impressionists. Also contains a lovely Graphics Collection *(Kupferstichkabinett)* with sketches by the Old Masters, as well as a Sculpture Collection; also in the complex are the **Museum of East Asian and Islamic Art,** Lansstr. 8; **Museum of Indian Art,** Lansstr. 8; and the **German Folklore Museum,** Im Winkel 6.

In addition are the **State Museums of Prussian Cultural Possessions,** located at Schloss Charlottenburg which also houses the **Museum for Prehistoric and Early History** (West Wing); **Antiquities Museum,** Schlossstr. 1; **Museum of Applied Arts** (East Wing), with European handiwork from early Middle Ages to the present; the **Library of Art History;** and the **Egyptian Museum,** opposite the Schloss, containing the celebrated bust of Queen Nefertete.

Musical Instrument Collection, Bundesallee 1–12 in Wilmersdorf.

Motor Museum, near Schloss Charlottenburg. Interesting collection of old automobiles.

New National Gallery, Potsdamerstr. 50, in a building designed by Mies van der Rohe. Excellent collection of works by Picasso, Braque, Chagall, Munch.

On the edge of the Tiergarten at Kemperplatz a new cultural center is in the process of being built. Other museum buildings are planned for the entire collections of the **Foundation of Prussian Cultural Possessions,** at present housed in Schloss Charlottenburg.

In 1985 the new **Kunstgewerbemuseum,** Mattäikirchplatz 10, was opened; it houses a marvelous collection of European arts and crafts from the Middle Ages.

 SHOPPING. Berliners have made their beloved Kudamm (Kurfürstendamm) a sparkling show-window of the West. Other important shopping areas are to be found around the Wittenbergplatz (where you will find Europe's biggest department store, *Ka-De-We*), Tauentzien, Europa-Center, Bleibtreustr., and the area between the Ku-damm and Savignyplatz. Many shops remain open until 11 P.M.

Don't forget the secondhand or "junk" shops *(Trödelmärkte)* famous to Berlin, found in the Kreuzberg area around the Bergmannstr., in Neukölln and the particularly popular market at the U-Bahn station Nollendorfplatz.

USEFUL ADDRESSES. *Consulates:* U.S.A., Clay-Allee 170, Dahlem (tel. 8324087); Gt. Britain, Uhlandstr. 7–8 (tel. 3095292/3/4). *Tourist information:* Berlin Tourist Information Office, Europa Center, Charlottenburg (tel. 7823031); Pavillon am Zoo, Hardenbergstr. 20 (tel. 317094); Pavillon in Tegel Airport (tel. 41013145). *American Express,* Kurfürstendamm 11. *Wagons-Lits/Cook,* Kurfürstendamm 42. Reservations and information about special offers and package deals in Berlin hotels from *Kurfürstendamm Reiseburo,* Kurfürstendamm 63, 1000 Berlin 15 (tel. 030–883041).

GIBRALTAR

The outline of the great Rock of Gibraltar is known to millions all over the world, even if they have never seen it. This tiny British Crown Colony, usually called simply "Gib", is just under 2¾ square miles in area. Much of that is sheer rock. Although a well-known landmark in classical times, it acquired its present name (more or less) in the eighth century, when it was captured by a Moorish chief called Tariq, giving it the title "Gebel Tariq"—the rock of Tariq. Captured by Spain in 1462, it was held by that country until taken, in 1704, by Sir George Rooke, when it became a British possession under the Treaty of Utrecht.

Gibraltar has been a British naval base and dockyard ever since. After the battle of Trafalgar on 25th October 1805 *HMS Victory* anchored for repairs before returning home. Nelson's body was aboard and some of the wounded were put ashore. Those who died are buried in the Trafalgar Cemetery, a peaceful and rather charming spot.

Gibraltar has an airfield and a large harbor much frequented by cruise liners. The opening of the frontier with Spain in February 1985 has made Gibraltar an ideal holiday center. It is within easy reach of Tangier, while southern Spain is but a ten-minute walk away. Excursions to Tangier, Jerez, Ronda, Malaga, and the Costa del Sol can be easily fitted into a day's outing, returning to the Rock in time for dinner. This strategic hub has many attractions in its own right, however. It is rich in history, heritage and bird life, and offers spectacular views of two continents. Shopping is varied and nothing is much more than a 15-minute walk from your hotel. Two marinas and good ship-repair facilities cater for an expanding demand in yachting.

The inhabitants are a mixture of English, Scottish, Irish, Welsh, Spanish, Maltese, even 18th-century Genoese—plus a sprinkling of other nationalities, some dating back three centuries. Proximity to

Spain has made the Gibraltarians bilingual, though English is the official language, which makes shopping easy. If you get lost, ask a policeman. (He would look quite at home in London with his "bobby's" helmet.) And when you want to escape from the town, go around to the east side of the Rock and Catalan Bay which, despite its name, was founded by Italian settlers. Today it is a small fishing village with a beach just over a mile away, or a 20p bus ride.

A curious, cinnamon colored, tailless ape has inhabited the mountain for centuries and there is an old belief that if the apes leave Gibraltar so will the British. The apes have always been pets of the Army and a corporal of the local regiment feeds them religiously once a day at their den. They are popular with visitors but remember that they are loose and, although well fed, very mischievous.

PRACTICAL INFORMATION FOR GIBRALTAR

WHAT WILL IT COST. Costs in Gibraltar need not be prohibitive—running at about 15% less than their equivalents in Britain. Tax is minimal, so shopping costs are among the lowest in Europe. Taxis are reasonably priced: by law, they should always display a pink tariff card.

Gibraltar's currency is issued in the same denominations as British money. In fact, British pounds sterling can be used there.

A typical day might cost two people:

Hotel, moderate, with breakfast	£35
Lunch, moderate restaurant	10
Transport	1.50
Coffee	.50
Evening entertainment	5
Dinner, moderate restaurant	14
Miscellaneous 10%	6
	£72.00

SOURCES OF INFORMATION. For advice on all aspects of travel to Gibraltar, the Gibraltar Tourist Board is very helpful. Its address in the U.K. is Arundel Great Court, 179 Strand, London W.C.2 (tel. 836 0777).

WHEN TO COME. The climate is temperate all year round, with warm summers and cool winters. It can be rainy between September and May, but it is basically dry June through August. Frosts are extremely rare.

Average afternoon daily temperatures Fahrenheit and Centigrade.

	Jan.	Feb.	Mar.	Apr.	May	June	July	Aug.	Sep.	Oct.	Nov.	Dec.
F°	60	62	65	69	73	79	83	84	80	74	67	62
C°	16	17	18	21	23	26	28	29	27	23	19	17

SPECIAL EVENTS. A favorite attraction is the regular Tuesday morning Changing of the Guard Ceremony and there are special parades on Commonwealth Day and the Queen's Birthday.

National Holidays. Jan. 1 (New Year's Day); Mar. 10 (Commonwealth Day); Apr. 17, 19 (Easter); May 1 (May Day Bank Holiday); May 26 (Spring Bank Holiday); June 16 (Queen Elizabeth's official birthday); Aug. 25 (August Bank Holiday); Dec. 25, 26.

GETTING TO GIBRALTAR. By Plane. Currently *British Airways* and *Air Europe,* in conjunction with *G.B. Air,* operate four flights a week from London Gatwick. Both operate the latest Boeing 737 jets on the route, taking about 2½ to 2¾ hours for the non-stop flight. In addition there are frequent charter flights from the U.K. in conjunction with package holidays, details of which are available from all good travel agents.

By Land. Since February 1985 the frontier with Spain has been open 24 hours a day, so you can now drive or walk into Gibraltar. However, remember that you are crossing an international frontier and thus require a passport, also a green card if driving.

North Africa Trips. *G.B. Air* also operate a twice daily service to Tangier in Morocco, the flight taking only 20 minutes. In the summer months you can go to Tangier or Algeciras daily by air, car ferry or hydrofoil. In the winter by air or ferry 5 days a week, and by hydrofoil 4 days per week. *Note:* these services vary frequently so you would be advised to check the latest schedules with your travel agent.

CUSTOMS. Import allowances are—200 cigarettes or 100 cigarillos or 250 gr. of tobacco; 1 liter of spirits, or 2 liters of fortified wine, or 2 liters of table wine; 50 gr. of perfume and .25 liter of toilet water. Also articles to the value of £28.

HOTELS AND RESTAURANTS. The Rock is not over-blessed with hotels, and accommodation is tight in summer. However, winter visitors will find things easier. Our hotel grading system is divided into three categories. Expensive (E) £40 and up, Moderate (M) £30–40, Inexpensive (I) £20–30. All prices are for 2 people in a double room.

There is quite a good selection of restaurants varying from small, select ones through the hotel restaurants, down to fast food. Chinese, Indian, Spanish, Italian, French and even the English tearoom can be found. For a more comprehensive listing than we give below, get a copy of the "Eating Out" guide from the Tourist Office.

Our restaurant grading system is as follows—Expensive (E) £7 and up; Moderate (M), £4–£7; Inexpensive (I), £4 and below. All prices per person.

Hotels

Caleta Palace (E), tel. 76501. 200 rooms with bath or shower, most with balcony, telephone. Restaurant, bars, disco, pool, boutique. On the cliff overhanging the picturesque village of Catalan Bay.

Holiday Inn (E), tel. 70500. 123 rooms with bath, TV. Pool, sauna, nightclub. Near Main Street.

The Rock (E), tel. 73000. Most rooms with private bath, telephone, balcony. Good restaurant, disco, pool, garage. Overlooks the bay.

Both Worlds (M), tel. 76191. 62 studio units with bedsit, bath and balcony; also 61 apartments, all with weekly maid service and seaview. Central restaurant, supermarket for do-it-yourself families. Baby-sitting. Situated at Sandy Bay, with safe, sandy beach.

Bristol (I), tel. 76800. 56 rooms, many with bath or shower. Sauna, pool.

Montarik (I), tel. 77065. 71 rooms with bath or shower, telephone. Bar, sun terrace with superb view of the sea and the sunsets. Central.

Restaurants

Casino Royal (E), Europa Road (tel. 76666). Luxurious surroundings.

Cornwall's Club (E), Cornwall's Passage (tel. 72011). Gourmet food.

Spinning Wheel (E), tel. 76091. Continental cuisine.

Lotus House (M), 292 Main St. (tel. 75153). Chinese cooking; butterfly prawns a specialty.

The English Eating House (M), 13 Market Lane (tel. 77313). Steak and kidney pie, etc.

Village Inn (M), Catalan Bay (tel. 75158). Specialty swordfish.

Winstons (M), 4 Cornwall's Parade (tel. 77655). Openair terrace.

NIGHTLIFE. Prominent in the night (and day) entertainment of Gibraltar is the casino, which opens at 9 in the morning. The same complex also features a restaurant, nightclub, disco and—in summer—a roof restaurant, situated in a Japanese-style garden. Discos are *Penelope* at the north end of Main Street, *Pigalle* at the casino, *Romanos* in Ocean Heights, and *Chimney Corner* in Fish Market Rd.

MUSEUMS. Gibraltar Museum, Bomb House Lane (tel. 74289). Tells the Rock's story from prehistoric times through the Great Siege of 1779–1783 and the battle of Trafalgar up to the present day. Open Mon. to Fri. 10–1 and 3–6, Sat. 10–1.

Moorish Castle, situated high on the Rock (tel. 71566). Built by the Moors during their conquest of the Iberian Peninsula. Tableaux are on show.

St. Michael's Cave, halfway to the Rock summit (tel. 73130). A natural cave 1000 ft. above sea-level with a fantastic display of stalactites and stalagmites. Musical shows and other performances are often given. Also used as a conference center.

Upper Galleries. Tunnels cut out of the sheer rock over 1000 meters deep with gun embrasures from a previous era are now displayed with tableaux so lifelike that the tourist moves stealthily. During World War II army engineers excavated some 40 km. of tunneling even deeper into the rock. Obey directions and do not get lost!

GETTING AROUND GIBRALTAR. Taxis carry a pink tariff card which you can ask to see. Fares are around £1 a mile, or longer trips by arrangement. There is a bus service, but as Gibraltar is so small, it is easy to walk almost everywhere. There are walking, fishing, and cruising tours on offer, details of which can be obtained from the Tourist Office.

Car Hire. Self-drive car hire in Gibraltar is among the cheapest in the world and cars can be taken into Spain and Portugal. Try: *Avis,* tel. 77867; *Budget Rent-a-Car,* tel. 77438; *Exchange,* tel. 71101; *Hertz,* tel. 71101.

SHOPPING. Shopping has always been a big attraction in Gibraltar, not least because of the many duty free goods. In Main Street you can find silks, carvings, radios, cameras, leatherwork, watches and many other bargains.

MAIL. Postage rates at presstime were, to the U.S. and Canada, 21p for the first 10 grams and 14p for each additional 10 grams; to the U.K. and Europe in general, 20p for the first 20 grams and 7p for each additional 10 grams.

CLOSING TIMES. Business hours in Gibraltar are from 9 in the morning through to 7 at night, Monday to Friday. Most banks are open Monday to Friday 9–3.30; a number also reopen on Fri. from 4.30–6. Post offices close Sat., Sun., and public holidays.

USEFUL ADDRESSES. *Gibraltar Tourist Office,* Cathedral Square (tel. 76400). *Gibraltar Information Center,* The Piazza, Main Street (tel. 75555).

Car Hire. *M.H. Bland* are agents for *Avis* and *Hertz.* Cars hired in Gibraltar can be taken across to Morocco. It is less costly to hire a car in Gibraltar than in Morocco.

GREAT BRITAIN

Britain has several exceptional bonuses for the visitor. For a start, if you come from an English-speaking country there's no language barrier. Then there's that long and colorful history that remains so much in evidence wherever you go. The British are also a tolerant and hospitable people; and if you come from the United States or the Commonwealth you might even have distant relatives still living here—or at least there might be a spot from which your forebears set out to seek a new life. There's another plus for the visitor. Britain is still reasonably inexpensive where holidays are concerned, particularly with regard to good-quality shopping. However, don't expect everything to be cheap. Hotels and restaurants can be expensive, especially in London. And there is enough to see in the capital to occupy one for a month. But it is very easy to get outside London on a weekend or even a day trip to the seaside resort of Brighton, or Oxford or Cambridge, or by the new high-speed train, to Bath or York, or any of a hundred other destinations.

If you do manage to wander away from London to enjoy the delights of the countryside, be prepared for a marked change in two things. Hotels will be at one and the same time less ritzy and more friendly, and prices a good bit lower. As to the hotels, if you are lucky enough to find yourself in an oak-beamed bedroom, with a lumpy mattress, pipes that gurgle in the night, a defective heating system and an owl in the tree by the window that hoots dolefully all night long, just tell yourself that it's atmosphere! But, be warned: find out where the bathroom is *before* you go to bed. After London prices, country hotels and restaurants will seem veritable bargains.

The Englishman's home is his castle, yet he is very proud of his heritage. This means that visitors to Great Britain now have access to literally hundreds of stately homes and castles, many of them still

308

occupied by their aristocratic owners and containing more art treasures than some metropolitan museums. Just how long this state of affairs can continue is anyone's guess. The crippling burden of estate duty is rapidly forcing the owners of stately homes into bankruptcy. Some— such as the Greville family who had owned Warwick Castle, one of Britain's most splendid, for centuries—have turned their backs on generations of tradition and sold out, lock, stock and Grecian urn. Warwick Castle is now owned by the firm that runs Madame Tussaud's in London.

Britain has become much more tourist conscious in the last few years. Many cities—York is a leading example—have gone out of their way to make it easy and interesting to visit them. They have dynamic, well-informed tourist offices, ever ready to help the passing guest.

But it is still true that if you want to get to know the historic Britain and its way of life, then you should turn to the quieter country towns and to the rich depths of the countryside itself. In this other world, people are fighting a steadily losing battle with bureaucracy—with the planners who change ancient regional names for meaningless modern ones, with civil servants who close rail and bus lines with no regard for present or future need, with all the mechanics of a staggering economy that pays more attention to the needs of the cities, where the votes are, than to the needs of the rural backwaters that have so little voice in affairs of state. But it is still possible to see in ancient brick and hand-hewn timber, in cottage garden or stately park, along the banks of a well-kept canal or willow-hung river, the environment created over slow millennia as a rich natural habitat for that sadly endangered species, the Briton.

PRACTICAL INFORMATION FOR GREAT BRITAIN

WHAT WILL IT COST. With the British economy in its present uncertain state, financial crystal-gazing at press time is a chancy occupation. However, it looks as if the inflation rate in 1987 is likely to be around 5%. This will leave unchanged the gulf that is fixed between the relative costs of visiting London and visiting the rest of the country. It costs, on average, one third less to visit outside London, where hotel and restaurant costs have been forced up by a combination of excessive local taxes, labor rates and a dash of greed. Anyone visiting London would be very well advised to shop around for a hotel—and there are many still at reasonable prices—and case a restaurant before going in, to be sure that the menu lies within the scope of his pocket. For years we have been urging our readers to share their time between London and other parts of Britain, and never has the advice been more solidly based than today. Quite apart from the levelling effect on costs, there is so much to be seen outside London that will balance a visitor's impression of the country.

A typical day *outside* London might cost two people:

Hotel (moderate), double room with bath and breakfast	£36.00
Lunch at restaurant (pub)	6.00
Transportation	7.50
Coffee and pastry	2.00
Drink at a pub	1.80
Dinner (moderate inc. wine)	26.00
Miscellaneous	8.00
	£87.30

For a comparable day in London, add *at least* 10%

Money. The monetary unit is the pound sterling, approximately $1.45 at the current rate of exchange, though this is liable to fluctuate considerably.

There are banknotes of £50, £20, £10 and £5. The £ is divided into 100 New Pence and there are cupro-nickel coins value £1, 50p, 20p, 10p, and 5p; bronze coins value 2 and 1p. All are clearly marked "New Pence" and the 50p and 20p ones are seven-sided. The old "florin", or two shilling piece, is still in use and is the equivalent of 10p.

There is a 15% Value Added Tax (a form of purchase tax). This is added to everything in sight, including meals. If you are shopping for goods to take home, do enquire about the "Over-the-Counter" export scheme, whereby you can claim the tax back. Many stores operate it.

SOURCES OF INFORMATION.

For information on all aspects of travel to Britain, the British Tourist Authority is an endlessly useful organization. Their addresses are:

In the U.S.: 40 West 57th St., New York, NY 10019; 612 South Flower St., Los Angeles, CA 90017; Suite 210, Cedar Maple Plaza, 2305 Cedar Springs Rd., Dallas, TX 75201.

In Canada: 94 Cumberland St., Suite 600, Toronto, Ontario, M5R 3N3; 409 Granville St., Suite 451, Vancouver, B.C. V6C 1T2.

WHEN TO COME. The traditional tourist season runs from Easter to mid-October, though of recent years parts of the winter, especially in December, are almost as busy. The spring is the time to see the countryside at its most freshly beautiful, while the colors of fall can be strikingly lovely. In September and October, the northern moorlands and Scottish highlands are at their colorful best. June is a good month to visit Wales and the Lake District. July and August are the months when most British take their vacations, that is when accommodation in most resorts is at a premium, and when the ferries to the Continent can be booked solid. Theater and other entertainments are, by and large, year-round, but most theaters are closed on Sundays.

Climate. Rarely too hot; cooler air in the north. Often showery. (Always take warm and thoroughly waterproof clothes, to Scotland especially.)

Average afternoon daily temperatures in degrees Fahrenheit and centigrade:

London	Jan.	Feb.	Mar.	Apr.	May	June	July	Aug.	Sept.	Oct.	Nov.	Dec.
F°	43	45	49	55	62	68	71	70	65	56	49	45
C°	6	7	9	13	17	20	22	21	18	13	9	7
Edinburgh												
F°	43	43	47	50	55	62	65	64	60	53	47	44
C°	6	6	8	10	13	13	17	18	16	12	8	7

SPECIAL EVENTS. *January,* International Boat Show, London; *February,* Cruft's Dog Show, London; *March,* Ideal Home Exhibition; Oxford and Cambridge Boat Race; Grand National Steeplechase (sometimes early April) at Liverpool. *April,* beginning of the season at the Royal Shakespeare Theater, Stratford-upon-Avon (through Dec.); Pitlochry Festival (through Sept.), Scotland. *May,* Royal Horse Show at Windsor; Chelsea Flower Show; International Festival of Music, Bath; Chichester Drama Festival (through Sept.). *June,* Glyndebourne Opera Season (through Aug.); The Oaks and Derby horse races at Epsom; Trooping the Colour, celebrating the Queen's birthday; Royal Ascot Race Meeting (third week in June); Open Tennis Championships at Wimbledon; Antique Dealers' Fair, London; Aldeburgh Festival. *July,* Royal Regatta at Henley-on-Thames, Festival of Contemporary Music in Cheltenham; International Eisteddfod, Wales; British Open Golf Championship; Albert Hall Promenade Concerts (through Sept.). *August,* Edinburgh Festival; Cowes Week, Isle of Wight. *September,* Highland gathering in Braemar, Scotland, and similar events at about the same time in many of the towns and villages. Three Choirs Festival (Hereford, Gloucester or Worcester).

November, The Lord Mayor's Show, London; London to Brighton Antique Car Rally.

National Holidays. Jan. 1; April 17, 20* (Easter); May 4; May 25 (Spring Bank Holiday); August 31* (Summer Bank Holiday); Dec. 25, 26. * Not in Scotland.

VISAS. Not required for entry into Britain by American citizens, nationals of the British Commonwealth and most European and South American countries.

HEALTH CERTIFICATES. Not required for entry to Britain.

There are extremely rigid controls on the importation of animals into Britain, caused by the rapid spread of rabies on the Continent. If you are likely to be taking animals into Britain (from the Continent or elsewhere), make sure you have checked on the quarantine (*always* 6 months) and other regulations.

GETTING TO BRITAIN. By Plane. No country in the world is served by as many airlines from as many countries as the United Kingdom, and London remains unquestionably the aerial crossroads of the globe. Wherever you happen to live in the New World, you will not have to travel far to catch a plane to London, thanks to a startling number of routes recently awarded to airlines for new services between the two countries. New York has the largest number of airlines, flying direct to London, but *B.A., T.W.A., Pan Am, Delta,* and others, share services from most large cities, with the addition of *Air Canada* from the Canadian capitals. It can be significantly less expensive to fly to London via Ireland (Dublin or Shannon). For further details, see *Planning Your Trip,* page 23.

By Ship. Cunard's *QE2* now provides the only regularly scheduled passenger liner service between North America and Europe—New York-Cherbourg-Southampton—this is only from mid-April to just before Christmas. For details of this service, and the possibilities of passenger-carrying cargo ships, see *Planning Your Trip,* page 25.

CUSTOMS. There are two levels of duty free allowance for people entering the U.K.; one, for goods bought outside the EEC or for goods bought in a duty free shop within the EEC; two, for goods bought in an EEC country but not in a duty free shop.

In the first category you may import duty free: 200 cigarettes or 100 cigarillos or 50 cigars or 250 grammes of tobacco (*Note* if you live outside Europe, these allowances are doubled); plus one liter of alcoholic drinks over 22% vol. (38.8% proof) or two liters of alcoholic drinks not over 22% vol. or fortified or sparkling wine; plus two liters of still table wine; plus 50 grammes of perfume; plus nine fluid ounces of toilet water; plus other goods to the value of £28.

In the second category you may import duty free: 300 cigarettes or 150 cigarillos or 75 cigars or 400 grammes of tobacco; plus 1½ liters of alcoholic drinks over 22% vol. (38.8% proof) or three liters of alcoholic drinks not over 22% vol. or fortified or sparkling wine; plus four liters of still table wine; plus 75 grammes of perfume; plus 13 fluid ounces of toilet water; plus other goods to the value of £163 (*Note* though it is not classified as an alcoholic drink by EEC countries for Customs' purposes and is thus considered part of the "other goods" allowance, you may not import more than 50 liters of beer).

In addition, no animals or pets of any kind may be brought into the U.K. The penalties for doing so are severe and are strictly enforced.

HOTELS. Our selection of hotels in Britain follows the simple grading system—(L) for Luxury establishments, (E) for Expensive ones, (M) for Moderate and (I) for Inexpensive. The price range for these categories is as follows: in London—(L) over £110 (in some cases a long way over), (E) £85–£110, (M) £50–£85, (I) under £50 (more usually around £30–£40); outside London—(L) over £85, (E) £65–£85, (M) £30–£65, (I) under £30. All these prices are for two people in a double room. As in most countries today, a single room costs more than half the price of a double.

Always try and make your reservations in advance for hotels and other forms of accommodation; it is far better to be safe than sorry, particularly during the summer months and at Easter. When you book, remember to stipulate numbers of double, single, twins or suites required, and number of persons; date of arrival and approximate time; number of nights and date of departure. In smaller country hotels it's wise also to request those meals that you will require. Remember also that breakfast is often *not* included in hotel rates, particularly in London—so bear this in mind when comparing prices.

Confirm rates before making that final booking, and don't be afraid to request hotel brochures to assist your decision. Many hotels have "good" and "bad" sides; when apparently similar accommodation bears different rates, it is therefore worth inquiring why. You can easily be kept awake by passing traffic or moaning plumbing for the sake of a small saving, and you may decide that it is better to pay slightly more, particularly in older hotels.

Tourist Accommodation Service. If you are having problems finding overnight accommodation in a particular town or country area during your visit, you could try the Bed Booking Service operated by the Tourist Boards at many of their local Tourist Information Centers. The service is available to personal callers only, and a complete list of centers throughout Great Britain is available from the British Tourist Authority, Thames Tower, Blacks Road, Hammersmith, London W.6 9EL. The London Visitor and Convention Bureau helps visitors to locate and book accommodations in a wide price range at over 800 hotels and guest houses within a 20-mile radius of central London. For advance bookings of two nights or more please write to the bureau at 26 Grosvenor Gardens, London S.W.1W ODU, at least four weeks before your arrival date: please specify dates, area and type of room required, number in party, and the price range per person. Reservations on arrival are handled at offices at the Heathrow Central Underground Station, Heathrow Airport, and at the Tourist Information Center at Victoria Railway Station. A returnable deposit must be paid when making a reservation (this is deducted from your hotel bill); a small, nonreturnable booking fee is also charged.

PENSIONS, GUEST HOUSES AND BED AND BREAKFAST. The French call it a "pension" and such romantic tones tend to uplift the simple English "guest house". By either name, these are budget accommodation houses, generally small, and almost always family run. They are often without private bathrooms and dining facilities, other than for breakfast. Certain guest houses are known as bed & breakfast establishments—tending toward fewer facilities and lower prices. Generally speaking, these establishments provide really excellent value for money.

MOTELS. The budget motel concept with minimal services has never really proved itself in Britain. British motels tend, therefore, to provide similar services to their hotel counterparts, and no true motel chain of any size really exists. One smallish group of quality, however, is *Mercury Motor Inns*. Half of their motels are in excellent locations in Scotland.

 RESTAURANTS. We have adopted the simple grading system, (E) for Expensive, (M) for Moderate and (I) for Inexpensive. The price range within these categories is: in London—(E) £50–£75 (and way up, possibly exceeding £100), (M) £25–£50, (I) below £25 and as low as £12 but not with wine; outside London—(E) £35–£60 (not often more than this), (M) £20–£35, (I) under £20. These prices are for a meal for two, including a bottle of wine.

The range of restaurants in Britain has expanded alarmingly in the last few years; "alarmingly" because standards of cooking and service have not always kept pace with the pretensions of the menus. London, especially, has seen a rapid growth of "smart" establishments, which do not justify the prices they charge. We suggest that you either follow our recommendations (we carry many more establishments in our *Guide to Great Britain*, of course), or invest in a copy of *The Good Food Guide*, which, while a very quirky compilation, does contain some detailed descriptions of restaurants selected by many discerning food fans.

Scattered around London, and throughout the country too, there are restaurants with an exceptionally high standard. They mostly fall into the expensive range, but do offer a dining treat. We have included several of them in our listings here. The thing to remember nowadays is that the cost of the meal can be almost doubled by the price of the wine.

If you are desperately homesick, you will be glad to know that *McDonald's* are now well established here. *Burger King,* though not as well established, offers good value.

The pub is a good bet for lunchtime drinks. Most pubs serve both hot and cold food at lunchtime, but the standard is not always very high. They are, however, usually cheap. You can have a very filling meal without drinks for as little as £2.00.

Food and Drink. The vast influx of immigrants from Britain's former colonies has profoundly influenced the range of food available to the public. Almost all towns now have an Indian restaurant (flavorsome, spicy cuisine) and a Chinese restaurant, both of which offer good-quality food at low prices. Perhaps spurred by holidays on the Continent, the British public is now much more adventurous in its eating habits, with the result that restaurants with exotic antecedents, Lebanese, Spanish or Turkish, can be found in even the most unlikely places, joining the longer-established favorites from France, Italy, Greece and Germany. That's the good news, the bad is that standards and prices vary wildly.

The traditional British dishes can still be found—game soup, various meat pies, potted shrimps (though these are increasingly difficult to obtain), Yorkshire pudding, syllabub and trifle. Regional specialties are still excellent, with both Scotland and Wales providing delicious dishes from excellent produce such as Scotch beef and Welsh lamb. The baking in Scotland is especially fine.

Many traditional British staples are disappearing. But when one ingredient fades from view, another takes its place, and the variety of styles of cooking now available ensures that even if the traditional fare is hard to find, a good meal is not.

Drink in Britain generally means beer, thanks to unbelievably high taxes on spirits, though wine is becoming increasingly popular. There's bitter, brown ale, light ale and stout, but when in doubt we recommend lager, which is closer to the German idea of a beer. The locals tend to prefer "real ale," which is drawn from the barrel with traditional hand pumps. Unlike lager, and to the amusement of most visitors, it is served tepid (to bring out the flavor more).

 HISTORIC BUILDINGS AND GARDENS. Opening days and admission charges for houses, etc., are liable to change from season to season, especially as many are still privately owned and occupied. We therefore list only approximate days and times. The British Travel Center, Lower Regent Street, London S.W.1, or the National Tourist Information Center, Victoria Station Forecourt (tel. 730 3488, Mon.–Fri., 9–5.30) can confirm the current times and charges if you are in doubt.

In our regional chapters we are able to list only a few of the outstanding stately homes, castles, and other properties that may be visited. An extremely useful publication, giving opening times and admission fees of over 500 houses and gardens open to the public, is *Historic Houses, Castles and Gardens in Great Britain and Ireland,* published by British Leisure Publications, Windsor Court, East Grinstead House, East Grinstead, West Sussex and available at bookshops throughout Britain (they also publish a similarly excellent guide to museums). Equally comprehensive is the guide *Stately Homes, Museums, Castles and Gardens,* published by the Automobile Association, Fanum House, Basingstoke, Hants. Entrance fees to the houses range from around 80p to £2.50, but are usually around £1.80.

Many homes belong to the National Trust, a privately funded organization, founded to help preserve the national heritage. (We denote these in our lists with the letters NT.) An annual membership (£14.50) entitles you to visit free over 150 historic properties; for information write *The National Trust,* 42 Queen Anne's Gate, London SW1. Or, for Scotland only, *The National Trust for Scotland,* 5 Charlotte Sq., Edinburgh 2. Further information about gardens can be obtained from: *National Gardens Scheme,* 57 Lower Belgrave St., London SW1, and *Scotland's Gardens Scheme,* 26 Castle Ter., Edinburgh 1. The National Gardens Scheme publish a valuable guide to 1,700 visitable gardens.

TIPPING. Some restaurants and most hotels add a service charge to the bill, usually 12½ to 15%. If hotels do not add a service charge, divide this proportion among those giving you service. Bellboys and doormen calling you a cab are tipped separately. Tip taxi drivers about 10% with a 20p minimum, hairdressers about £1, cloakroom attendant 10p. Railroad porters get about 25p per bag, though they may not be available. Be prepared to help yourself to a baggage trolley and "do it yourself".

MAIL. The postage rates at time of writing are: *Inland,* letters and postcards not over 60 grams, 12p (slow), 17p (fast); to *Europe,* letters and postcards 22p, first 20 grams; to the *U.S. and Canada,* airmail, postcards 26p, letters 31p for the first 10 grams. (These rates may be increased in 1987.)

CLOSING TIMES. Shops do not usually close for lunch, except in small country towns or villages, and are open from 9 to 5.30. They close at about 1 P.M. on one weekday ("early closing day") which is variable according to district (usually Wednesday or Thursday). Most shops in central London stay open all day, 6 days a week, with one late evening, usually Wednesday or Thursday, till 7.30 or 8.

Banks are open from 9.30 to 3.30, Monday to Friday, most are closed Saturday and all on Sunday, with slight variations in Scotland.

USEFUL ADDRESSES. *British Travel Center,* Lower Regent Street, London S.W.1, *Information Center,* Victoria Station. The *London Visitor & Convention Bureau* (tel. 730 3488) has Tourist Information Centers at Selfridges and Harrods, and at Victoria Station and Heathrow Underground.

U.S. Embassy, 24–31 Grosvenor Square, London W.1 (tel. 499 9000).

Canadian High Commission, Canada House, Trafalgar Square, S.W.1 (tel. 629 9492).

American Express has offices in London (Haymarket) and at 25 Smallbrook Ringway, Birmingham; India Buildings, Water Street, Liverpool; Queens Way, Southampton; 139 Princes Street, in Edinburgh; 115 Hope Street, Glasgow.

Thomas Cook has offices in London and all major cities.

Royal Automobile Club, Pall Mall, London S.W.1 (tel. 839 7050).

For *emergency calls* throughout the country (fire, ambulance, police) dial 999.

GETTING AROUND BRITAIN. By Plane. For flights within the U.K.—which in fact range from the Shetland Islands in the far north to the helicopter service from Penzance to the Scilly Isles—the main airlines are *British Airways, British Caledonian, Air U.K., British Midland Airways, Brymon Airways,* and *Dan Air.* The network is more extensive than is generally realized. The trunk routes from London (Heathrow) to Glasgow, Edinburgh, Manchester and Belfast are operated by a British Airways "Shuttle" with no advance booking. British Caledonian also fly on the Glasgow and Edinburgh routes from Gatwick while British Midland operates another Heathrow to Glasgow and Edinburgh service.

Through flights from London (either Heathrow or Gatwick or both) go to Glasgow, Edinburgh, Aberdeen, Inverness, Manchester, Newcastle, Leeds/Bradford, Teesside, Liverpool, Belfast, Birmingham, Isle of Man, Jersey and Guernsey (in the Channel Islands). In addition there are excellent links via Aberdeen and Inverness to both the Orkney and Shetland islands and via Glasgow to the Outer Hebrides.

Because of the extent of fast trains it is often quicker to go by rail to cities like Birmingham or Manchester or even Newcastle than to fly.

By Train. There is a very extensive railway network throughout England, Scotland and Wales—even if large areas now have no trains at all. Several main lines (e.g. London to Birmingham, Manchester, Liverpool and Glasgow) are electrified. Diesel High Speed Trains—InterCity 125—operate over many other routes such as to Newcastle, Edinburgh and Aberdeen and also to Bristol,

Devon, Cornwall and South Wales traveling for long distances at 125 m.p.h. In spite of a series of cut-backs in the rail network over the last 25 years (and more possibly to come), the trains do reach many comparatively remote areas.

Only the up-graded, first-class "Pullman" carriages, used on certain designated trains linking London (Euston) with Manchester and Liverpool, require additional surcharges. In all other British Railways trains only standard fares (first and second class) are charged. All High Speed Trains, and most on the London to Glasgow, Manchester and Liverpool services, are fully airconditioned as are the sleeping cars.

A wide variety of restaurant, buffet and grill cars are carried on most expresses with light refreshments available on others. Sleeping cars are both first and second class. The former have one passenger per sleeper compartments, 2nd class two people. There are no couchettes on British Rail.

Various discount tickets are available, many offering substantial savings. In addition, fares vary from region to region (those for the area around London, for example, are regulated quite differently than those applying to the rest of the country). The best advice is to consult a British Rail Travel Center (located in most larger cities; several in London). They will provide up-to-the-minute information and many useful brochures, etc. Given the complexity of some fares, and the less-than-helpful attitude of some ticket clerks, take the opportunity to study the best bargains going at leisure.

For information on the unlimited runabout ticket, BritRail Pass, see *Planning Your Trip* section, page 42. But please note that this pass cannot be purchased inside the U.K. It must be obtained abroad.

British Rail also operate "package tours" of one- or two-week duration, under the trade name *Golden Rail Holidays.* These offer hotel accommodation with rail travel at advantageous prices. Full details from Travel Center or travel agents. In addition B.R. also have short (one or two day) *Stardust* holidays, with hotel, sightseeing, etc. included.

All this information applies to England, Scotland and Wales. In Northern Ireland they have their own railway organization. There are railway services from Belfast to Londonderry and also south to the Republic of Ireland (including Dublin). They issue runabout tickets in conjunction with bus travel within the Province.

By Car. You drive on the *left.* Your local license is valid. Speed limit in cities and outskirts is 30–50 m.p.h., clearly designated. Maximum speed is 70 m.p.h. All the Continental road signs apply in Britain, though in country areas some old-fashioned ones appear still. Gasoline averages £1.90 (at time of writing) an Imperial gallon. The Imperial gallon is larger than the American: four of the former equal five of the latter. Prices vary slightly according to regions and firms.

Car Hire. There are many London car hire firms, among them *Avis, Kennings, Hertz* and *Godfrey Davis Europcar.* All have various pick-up points throughout London. Godfrey Davis will arrange to have a self-drive car waiting for you at a railway station or at an airport. All you do is order it when you buy your ticket at a major terminus. Similar arrangements can be made through most firms to have cars waiting at port or airfield of entry.

By Bus. Britain has always had excellent bus and coach services, and in recent years these have been improved immeasurably in speed, comfort, and frequency, especially on the long-distance routes. Deregulation of bus services has meant freer competition and a massive increase in the number and variety of routes. The National Bus Company (in England and Wales) and Scottish Omnibuses—both currently state-owned—provide first-class services. In fact the "Rapide" intercity services of the National Bus Company are particularly good, on some routes nearly as swift as the train and very much less expensive. At the same time, the newer vehicles operated both by the state and the ever-increasing number of private operators are also to be recommended; many boast full air-conditioning, videos, and food.

For details of services, contact the *National Bus Company,* Victoria Coach Station, Buckingham Palace Rd., London S.W.l. In Scotland, contact *Scottish Omnibuses,* Buchanan Bus Station, Killermont St., Glasgow G2 3NP. For private operators, contact travel agents or the local Yellow Pages.

Please note that in England and Wales the word "coach" is used for long distance bus services. In Scotland "bus" is used to cover all types.

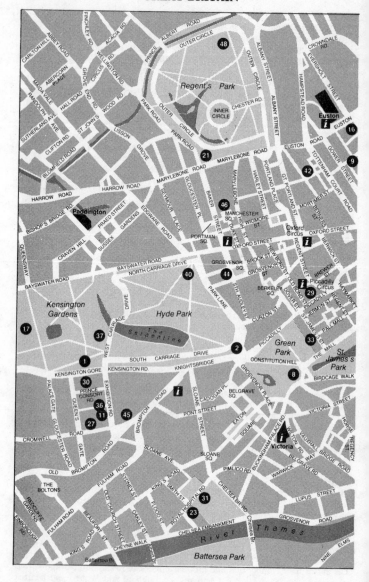

The English Tourist Board offers a television holiday information service on British Telecom's Prestel system. Tourtel, as it is called, is to be found on Prestel pages 222/2.

London

London is one of the most fascinating cities in the world, a conglomeration of villages that has brought 7 million souls together in a vast metropolis, more than you could explore in several decades, much less in a few days. Discovering London for the first time (or the tenth) is an exciting business, and a pleasant one. The London policeman or

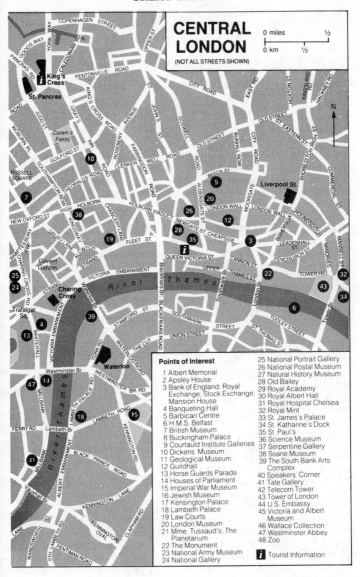

CENTRAL LONDON
(NOT ALL STREETS SHOWN)

0 miles ½
0 km ½

Points of Interest

1 Albert Memorial
2 Apsley House
3 Bank of England; Royal Exchange; Stock Exchange; Mansion House
4 Banqueting Hall
5 Barbican Centre
6 H.M.S. Belfast
7 British Museum
8 Buckingham Palace
9 Courtauld Institute Galleries
10 Dickens Museum
11 Geological Museum
12 Guildhall
13 Horse Guards Parade
14 Houses of Parliament
15 Imperial War Museum
16 Jewish Museum
17 Kensington Palace
18 Lambeth Palace
19 Law Courts
20 London Museum
21 Mme. Tussaud's; The Planetarium
22 The Monument
23 National Army Museum
24 National Gallery
25 National Portrait Gallery
26 National Postal Museum
27 Natural History Museum
28 Old Bailey
29 Royal Academy
30 Royal Albert Hall
31 Royal Hospital Chelsea
32 Royal Mint
33 St. James's Palace
34 St. Katharine's Dock
35 St. Paul's
36 Science Museum
37 Serpentine Gallery
38 Soane Museum
39 The South Bank Arts Complex
40 Speakers' Corner
41 Tate Gallery
42 Telecom Tower
43 Tower of London
44 U.S. Embassy
45 Victoria and Albert Museum
46 Wallace Collection
47 Westminster Abbey
48 Zoo

i Tourist Information

"bobby" is famed for his courtesy and patience, even under the stress and strain of London traffic. People in the street, however busy, will usually go out of their way to help you if you lose your way.

Let's get a few orientation spots and neighborhoods identified before proceeding. Piccadilly Circus, ablaze with lights and recently completely refurbished, is the Times Square of London. Eastward, along Coventry Street, you'll come to Leicester Square, now a pedestrian precinct, surrounded by a good selection of movie theaters. You'd never think that it was once a residential area, housing such eminent Englishmen as Hogarth, Swift and Reynolds, to say nothing of French aristocrats fleeing the terrors of revolution. In the center of the square stands William Shakespeare, unperturbed by the welter of cinemas, restaurants, and pubs that have sprung up since Londoners crossed the Thames to see his plays at the Globe nearly four centuries ago.

Going away from Piccadilly Circus in the other direction is Piccadilly itself. Starting with shops and hotels (Simpson's for clothes, Fortnum and Mason's for food, Hatchard's for books), Wren's Church of St. James, renovated after the blitz, you will come to the Royal Academy, on the righthand side, home of many prestigious art exhibitions.

Running up beside the Academy is the Burlington Arcade, a fascinating covered arcade of luxury shops. A little further on, *Old* Bond Street, created from a muddy country lane by Sir Thomas Bond in 1686, leads out of Piccadilly to join *New* Bond Street, built in 1700. Here the upper class built country houses to escape the smoke and noise of Westminster and the City. Tailors, milliners and glovers followed. The aristocrats eventually moved farther west, but the tradesmen remained in what is, consequently, one of the most famous shopping streets in the world.

Leading off Piccadilly to the left is St. James's Street, a special world of gentlemen's clubs and shops. Don't miss the William IV street lamps in Little St. James's Street and the great houses bordering St. James's Park, a perfect place for strolling on a spring or summer day. At one end of the park is Buckingham Palace. With the wide sweep of the square in front of it (dominated by a statue of and an elaborate memorial to Queen Victoria) this symbol of the continuing tradition of British monarchy is a notable exception to the rule that Londoners do not know how to set their monuments and public buildings off to the maximum advantage.

Houses of Parliament and Westminster Abbey

At the other end of St. James's Park from Buckingham Palace lies Westminster. This was the first important settlement to appear beyond the walls of the ancient City of London. It encompasses not only the Abbey but also Whitehall, administrative center of Britain, whose most famous address is No. 10 Downing Street, home and office of the Prime Minister.

Westminster Abbey, founded in 1050 on an earlier church site, is where all but two of England's kings and queens have been crowned since Saxon Harold in 1066. The core of the Abbey as we know it today is Edward the Confessor's Chapel, around which, in the 13th century, Henry III built a series of chapels. Many kings and queens of England are buried here. In addition there are buried in the Abbey poets from Chaucer to Kipling; statesmen like Disraeli, Palmerston, Gladstone and Robert Peel; scientists like Newton and Darwin. Don't miss the Henry VII Chapel, a gem of Tudor architecture, and the Coronation Chair of Edward I, enclosing the celebrated Stone of Scone. Outside the Abbey, the old atmosphere has been preserved in the cloisters, which date from the 14th century, and from which you have the best views of the exterior of the Abbey itself. See also the adjoining Church of St. Margaret with its east window, the oldest in London, a gift from Ferdinand and Isabella of Spain.

Across the Parliament Square from the Abbey are the imposing Houses of Parliament, built between 1840 and 1860 in the late Gothic-Tudor style. Practically all that remains of the medieval palace of Westminster is Westminster Hall, which dates from 1097. The magnificent hammerbeam roof was added in Richard II's reign. The House of Commons, destroyed by German bombs in 1941, was restored and reopened in 1950. The 320-foot-high Clock Tower of Westminster Palace incorporates the most popular landmark in London, Big Ben, named after the portly Sir Benjamin Hall, Commissioner of Works when the tower was erected. For millions all over the world, the chimes of Big Ben speak with the very voice of Britain, and the Palace of Westminster is a democratic symbol of the triumph of popular government after a protracted struggle with divine-right autocracy. For an amusing and instructive insight into the workings of the British parliamentary system, you are recommended to visit the Strangers' Gallery in the Commons (or the House of Lords). In busy times, tickets can be had from the American Embassy—though you will need to give several days' notice. The Lords is easier to get into than the Commons.

Whitehall is the wide avenue that runs from Parliament Square to Trafalgar Square, and is lined with the buildings of Britain's government. The Cenotaph, commemorating the dead of two wars, stands in the middle of the road. Downing Street, where you will find the Prime Minister's official residence, leads off to the left. Higher up on the right is the Banqueting Hall, the only surviving remnant of the vast Palace of Whitehall. It was here that King Charles I was beheaded in 1649. His statue stands at the top of Whitehall, where it joins Trafalgar Square.

Trafalgar Square

Trafalgar Square, commemorating Nelson's defeat of the French fleet at the Battle of Trafalgar in 1805, is dominated by a statue of that naval hero, three times life-size, atop a column 185 feet high. There are as many pigeons here as there are in St. Mark's Square in Venice, and they're just as photogenic and even more dirty. They roost along the cornices of the National Gallery, St. Martin's-in-the-Fields, and South Africa House. Trafalgar Square is a popular spot for political meetings and celebrations.

The National Gallery, on the north side, houses one of the world's great art collections, while tucked into its righthand side, opposite the beautiful church of St. Martin's in the Fields, is the National Portrait Gallery, rich in pictures and sculptures of thousands of Britain's men and women, famous and less well known. For an insight into the British spirit, the National Portrait Gallery is unbeatable.

Then comes St. Martin's Lane, where on the right you will see the Coliseum, home of the English National Opera. Opposite here is a series of alleyways with secondhand book shops.

A little further on, and to the west, lies Soho, full of restaurants, pâtisseries, delicatessens and a rather sleazy atmosphere with sex shops and porno movie houses. By exactly the same orientation which links Times Square and Broadway in New York, this is the heart of London's theaterland, with some 20 theaters all within a very few blocks.

The Strand and Covent Garden

The Strand, once a thin line of houses linking the City and Royal Westminster, leads off from Trafalgar Square at Charing Cross Station. The first part is dominated by the Coutts Bank building, rebuilt behind most of the original facade. If you turn up Southampton Street, on the lefthand side, you will come to Covent Garden, once the fruit and vegetable market for London, and now refurbished as a trendy shopping precinct. The *My Fair Lady* church of St. Paul's stands to one side of the market buildings and Covent Garden Opera House on another. It is a neighborhood that repays the hours spent wandering around its narrow streets. Crafts shops and wine bars rub shoulders with up-market boutiques and long-established perfumeries. The area is renowned for its colorful street performers.

Drop in at Somerset House, home of the Inland Revenue and the Probate Registry, where, for a modest fee, you see the last will and testament of such well-known Englishmen as Shakespeare and Milton. This is also the place where many American visitors start to trace their British ancestry. You can't miss the Law Courts, at the Fleet Street end of the Strand, an overpowering edifice in latter-day Gothic style, but you'll find more of human interest at the Magistrates' Court in Bow Street, whose doors are immediately opposite the entrance to the Royal Opera House. Slightly to the east are the Inns of Court, Gray's and Lincoln's, havens of peace where you can rest in the sun surrounded by superb architecture.

The City and St. Paul's Cathedral

The City, underneath which lies the original Roman London, can be entered from the west at Temple Bar in the Strand. A little further along you enter Fleet Street, headquarters of many of Britain's newspapers. Journalists are a thirsty lot, and you'll find the taverns of Fleet Street are worth a visit. Try El Vino's for sherry; The Cock, if you want to hobnob with lawyers from the nearby Inns of Court; above all, Ye Olde Cheshire Cheese, rebuilt in 1667 after the Great Fire, and as much a part of the London scene today as it was then, even if it has become a very touristy spot. Nearby, in Wine Office Court, you'll find the house in which Oliver Goldsmith lived and wrote *The Vicar of Wakefield* and, in Gough Square, where Johnson lived and prepared his celebrated Dictionary. Up Ludgate Hill is St. Paul's Cathedral, surrounded by modern office blocks that have risen from the ashes of the most bomb-devastated area in the City. The narrow streets and Cheapside, Cornhill, and Leadenhall Street, are somber with great banking houses, insurance companies, shipping offices, the Stock Exchange, the Bank of England, the Royal Exchange and Lloyds. This whole area was devastated during the worst of the bombing in the early '40s, and there are whole streets of rather undistinguished modern office blocks. London missed a great opportunity for imaginative planning when this rebuilding was carried out.

St. Paul's Cathedral was completed in 1711 when its architect, Christopher Wren, was nearly 90. This ambitious baroque structure (365 feet high, 515 feet long, with a nave 125 feet wide) is crowded with memorials. See the effigy of the poet John Donne, once Dean of the cathedral, in the south choir aisle. The tombs of Nelson and Christopher Wren are in the crypt, the latter's adorned with a proud and laconic epitaph: *Lector, si monumentum requiris, circumspice* (Reader, if you seek his monument, look about you).

Just north of St. Paul's, in the vast Barbican complex, is the attractive modern Museum of London, which illustrates 2,000 years of history, and the new Barbican Centre, housing a concert hall and the London home of the Royal Shakespeare Company.

The Tower of London and Greenwich

Started about 1078 under William the Conqueror, the White Tower, or central keep of the Tower of London, is one of the oldest buildings in the capital. Once used as a palace, this fortress-like Norman building became a prison, its history one of imprisonment, execution and murder. Among the scores of famous people who were beheaded in the Tower were Sir Thomas More, two of Henry VIII's wives (Anne Boleyn and Catherine Howard) and that versatile favorite of Queen Elizabeth I, the Earl of Essex. Elizabeth herself was imprisoned here in the Bell Tower by Mary Queen of Scots, and Sir Walter Raleigh spent 13 years in the Tower, working on his *History of the World*. The axe which severed so many distinguished heads from their bodies can still be seen but you will probably prefer the dazzling splendor of the Crown Jewels and the Yeomen Warders of the Tower, (the "Beefeaters"), resplendent in their Tudor-style uniforms. The renovation of St. Katherine's dock has provided a new focus for tourists in this area.

We recommend the veranda of The Prospect of Whitby, a fascinating pub in Wapping High Street, if you really want to absorb the atmosphere of London's waterfront, or the Mayflower, near Rotherhithe Underground Station, or the Waterman's Arms, Glengarnock Avenue, E.14. A trip down the river to Greenwich can be a highlight of your visit to London. Boats ply up and down from Westminster, the Tower of London and other piers. Greenwich is the home of the National Maritime Museum, the Royal Naval College, the Old Royal Observatory, the *Cutty Sark,* last of England's great clipper ships, and *Gipsy Moth IV,* in which Sir Francis Chichester sailed solo around the world in 1967.

Bloomsbury and Oxford Street

Bloomsbury is London's student quarter, dominated by the white pile of the University of London administrative building on Malet Street. It is a district of neat squares—Russell, Bedford, Woburn and Bloomsbury, the last and oldest having been planned by the Earl of Southampton in 1661. Disraeli lived in Bloomsbury as a youth; Virginia Woolf reigned here in the twenties.

The focal point is the British Museum. This vast museum is one of the world's truly great collections, all the more exciting to visit since the adoption of stunning new display techniques has revivified the rich treasures from all over the world.

The district's busiest thoroughfare is Tottenham Court Road, one of London's main arteries. It must have been more interesting in the 17th century when it was a country lane, notorious for gaming, prizefighting and general hellraising. Running from east to west, at right angles, is Oxford Street, with its great department stores, Selfridges, John Lewis, Marks & Spencer and C&A, and its multitude of jeans marts and budget caverns. Once past the junction of Oxford Circus and you will be passing along the top edge of Mayfair (south of Oxford Street), the heartland of London's rich. Here are more attractive squares: Grosvenor Square, the site of the American Embassy; Berkeley Square, once a distinguished residential center, which still has some fine buildings, now almost all containing offices. This is a neighborhood of attractive small shops, wealthy houses and apartment blocks, discreet gaming clubs and, along the edge facing Hyde Park, a clutch of grand hotels, the Dorchester, the Grosvenor, Inn on the Park and the Inter-Continental. Two of the grandest of the lot, Claridges and the Connaught, are safe in the very center of Mayfair.

Hyde Park and Kensington Gardens

Hyde Park (and its continuation, Kensington Gardens), with its acres of grass, fine trees and flowers, will help you relax, as it has done for generations of Londoners. You can ride along Rotten Row, swim or row in the Serpentine, have a meal in the café overlooking the lake. Best time to see the famous Speakers' Corner in action is Sunday afternoon, just inside the gates at Marble Arch. Virtually no subject is sacrosanct here. Only treason and obscenity are illegal. You'll hear everything from incendiary appeals for revolution to earnest pleas for vegetarianism.

We have already mentioned St. James's Park. Taken together with the wide expanse of Green Park, the three parks, St. James's, Green and Hyde, form a chain of trees, grass and lakes, which provides relaxation right across the center of London.

By turning north from Oxford Street at Oxford Circus, passing the B.B.C. and following Portland Place you come to Regent's Park. Here are the rose-filled delights of Queen Mary's Gardens, the Openair Theater and the Zoo, with its huge collection of animals and the attractively designed houses in which they live.

Kensington, Chelsea and the South Bank

Kensington, officially known as the Royal Borough, is one of the capital's most distinguished residential districts, site of Kensington Palace (on the western edge of Kensington Gardens), a royal residence occupied by Princess Margaret and the Prince and Princess of Wales. Don't miss delightful Edwardes Square, one of London's loveliest, developed around 1802 by a Frenchman named Changier; not surprisingly, it has an excellent pub. You'll enjoy strolling along the quiet streets and terraces on either side of High Street and prowling among the antique shops, some of the best in the country, on Church Street.

The area below Hyde Park, called South Kensington, is the site of one of the world's first arts complexes. Conceived by the Prince Consort, Victoria's husband, it contains the Albert Hall (home of the world-famous Promenade Concerts), the Science Museum, the Museum of Natural History, the Geological Museum with its magnificent gemstone collection and, above all, the Victoria and Albert Museum, with its vast collections of furniture, jewelry, medieval art, armor, musical instruments, costumes and much, much more.

Chelsea is the most central of the riverside suburbs and was once the artists' quarter of London. The scene along Chelsea Embankment is no longer as tranquil as it was when painted by Turner, but there are pleasant little streets throughout the area which appear not to have changed for decades. Cheyne Row and Walk constitute one of the most attractive groups of houses in London. Carlyle, Leigh Hunt, George Eliot and Dante Gabriel Rossetti were among the distinguished residents of Cheyne Row. See the Chelsea Hospital, built for old or disabled soldiers; a fine example of Sir Christopher Wren's secular style. (The famous Chelsea Flower Show is held in the grounds in May.) Look for antique shops and boutiques along King's Road, the principal thoroughfare. The best time to be there is on Saturdays, about lunchtime.

On the other side of the river, there is a fine walk to be taken from Lambeth Palace (London home of the Archbishop of Canterbury) eastwards. Walk past County Hall (once London's local government H.Q.), the South Bank complex of the Royal Festival Hall, the Hayward Gallery and the National Film Theater, until, passing under Waterloo Bridge, you reach the modern National Theater. If you then climb onto Waterloo Bridge, you will have one of the finest views of London.

PRACTICAL INFORMATION FOR LONDON

HOTELS. London's hotels may no longer be the most expensive in Europe, but they are still very pricey. And they can vary considerably in price for virtually the same standard of accommodations. So it's worth shopping around. Needless to say, make sure you know exactly what your room will cost before you check in. In common with most other European countries, British hotels are obliged to display a tariff on the reception desk. Study it carefully.

Remember also that rates in June, July and August can be 30% higher than in slacker seasons.

The general custom is for rates to be quoted for both bed and breakfast. But more and more London hotels, especially the top-class ones, have begun to give rates for room only. Again, check if this applies in your case.

If you haven't booked your hotel before you arrive, the following organizations can help you find a room: *Hotel Bookings International,* Kingsgate House, Kingsgate Place, London NW6 (328 1790); *Hotel Reservation Center* (828 2425), and the *London Visitor and Convention Bureau,* both at Victoria Station, SW1. The latter cannot make bookings over the telephone.

After the words of warning, a small measure of cheer. London's hotels, especially in the lower-priced range, can still represent good value for money. Hoteliers have become very conscious of the "over priced" image and are keen to dispel it. Similarly the B.T.A. is trying hard to promote good value hotels. And if you are prepared to face the price tags in the higher ranges, you'll find the more famous hotels are still as gracious and comfortable as ever.

Our grading system is as follows: Deluxe, over £110, sometimes way over; Expensive, £85 to £110; Moderate £50 to £85; Inexpensive, under £50, usually around £30 to £40. These prices are for two people in a double room, VAT included.

Deluxe

Athenaeum, 116 Piccadilly, W.1 (tel. 499 3464). Really excellent modern hotel with a strong dash of originality and managerial flair. Rooms are first class and well-positioned at the "right end" of Piccadilly, near the Park.

Berkeley, Wilton Place, S.W.1 (tel. 235 6000). Impeccable decor, service and dining facilities. One of the last of the modern greats. *Le Perroquet* restaurant is more relaxed than the main *Berkeley Restaurant,* but both are sophisticated tops.

Blakes, 33 Roland Gardens, S.W.7 (tel. 370 6701). Something out of the ordinary. Attractive, sometimes zany decor. Friendly atmosphere.

Britannia, Grosvenor Sq., W.1 (tel. 629 9400). Top marks for a modern hotel facade blending unobtrusively with Grosvenor Sq. Inside, restrained decor and comfort. Central location with friendly service.

Browns, Dover St., W.1 (tel. 493 6020). Very British, very Victorian, discreet favorite with visiting businessmen.

Churchill, 30 Portman Sq., W.1 (tel. 486 5800). Large regency style lobby and splendidly comfortable bedrooms. Excellent management; ideal for Oxford Street shopping.

Claridge's, Brook St., W.1 (tel. 629 8860). A living legend. Where visiting royalty and heads of state stay. But don't be discouraged if you're a mere citizen—the staff are friendly and not in the least condescending, while the rooms are luxurious.

Connaught, Carlos Pl., W.1 (tel. 499 7070). With only 90 superb rooms and a world-wide reputation, here is true quiet luxury. One of the best hotel bases for touring London. Their famous kitchen is splendidly dominated by Michel Bourdin, one of the world's best chefs.

Dorchester, Park Lane, W.1 (tel. 629 8888). The traditional luxury standards are still intact at this bastion of good living with the famous *Terrace Restaurant* still justifying its high reputation.

Grosvenor House, Park Lane, W.1 (tel. 499 6363). Completely renovated as well-appointed conference hotel without a trace of former Grosvenor style. Individual guests can feel "uncared for". Excellent amenities.

Hilton, Park Lane, W.1 (tel. 493 8000). Not the best of the chain, but keeps the Hilton flag flying. Fine views and plenty of variety in bars and restaurants.

Hyatt Carlton Tower, Cadogan Pl., S.W.1 (tel. 235 5411). Convenient for town and Chelsea. Elegant accommodation suited particularly to guests who like a touch of Bohemia nearby.

Hyde Park, Knightsbridge, S.W.1 (tel. 235 2000). Facing Knightsbridge for shopping and backing onto Hyde Park for relaxation (try for a room at the back with a park view). Solidly sumptuous, with marble and chandeliers.

Inn on the Park, Hamilton Pl., Park Lane, W.1 (tel. 499 0888). An opulent interior, eminent situation and high standards. The rooms are all beautifully furnished and ultra-comfortable. Excellent, if pricey, restaurants.

Inter-Continental, Hyde Park Corner, W.1 (tel. 409 3131). Cool and modern with flawless rooms and service—fantastic views straight over Hyde Park Corner. *Le Soufflé* is elegant but highly priced.

London Marriott Hotel, Grosvenor Sq., W.1 (tel. 493 1232). The latest addition to London's luxury hotels, with every amenity and comfort, extensively refurbished in 1984. In the heart of Mayfair, by the U.S. Embassy.

Mayfair, Stratton St., W.1 (tel. 629 7777). Animated lobby reflects the Mayfair bustle outside. Comfortable rooms; very popular.

Montcalm Hotel, Great Cumberland Place, W.1 (tel. 402 4288). Encased in an elegant Georgian crescent and centrally placed. An extremely civilized house, admirably suited to those of sybaritic tastes.

New Piccadilly, Piccadilly, W.1 (tel. 734 8000). Recently received a multimillion pound refurbishment and superb new health and leisure complex. In heart of West End.

Park Lane Hotel, Piccadilly, W.1 (tel. 449 6321). Pleasing hotel with spacious lounge and rooms. Victoriana throughout.

Ritz, Piccadilly, W.1 (tel. 493 8181). César Ritz' elegant landmark provides sumptuous decor and fine service. New ownership has refurbished many of the rooms to their former splendor. Casino may shock earlier devotees.

Savoy, Strand, W.C.2 (tel. 836 4343). Synonymous with old-fashioned luxury, yet pleasurable also for those small corners of happy informality. The recent slimming-down in room numbers to 200 has not affected the standards at all. All restaurants magnificent.

Stafford, 16 St. James's Place, S.W.1 (tel. 493 0111). In a secluded courtyard complete with gaslights, yet only five minutes from Piccadilly. Excellent choice for small-hotel fans; attentive service, pleasing decor.

Expensive

Basil Street Hotel, 8 Basil Street, S.W.3 (tel. 581 3311). Ideal for the well-heeled single woman. Close to Harrod's and Knightsbridge shopping.

Cadogan, 75 Sloane St., S.W.1 (tel. 235 7141). This rejuvenated hotel has original Adam-style ceilings in the bar where Lillie Langtry once lived, before it became a hotel, that is! Bedroom standards and amenities are variable.

Capital, 24 Basil St., S.W.3 (tel. 589 5171). Small, tasteful and near Harrods. Excellent personal service and décor. Book well ahead. Highly recommended.

Cavendish, Jermyn St., S.W.1 (tel. 930 2111). Centrally located for St. James's shopping and theaters; functional hotel, in spite of its Edwardian *Duchess of Duke Street* memories. 24-hour coffee shop.

Clifton Ford, Welbeck St., W.1 (tel. 486 6600). Pedigree situation. Popular with tours and business visitors.

Cumberland, Marble Arch, W.1 (tel. 262 1234). Large (over 900 rooms), centrally located and good value, if rather anonymous.

Dukes, 35 St. James's Pl., S.W.1 (tel. 491 4840). Quietly, but centrally located in a small backwater reeking of old London. An excellent choice, for those who relish small-scale, sedate accommodation backed by friendly service.

Gloucester, 4 Harrington Gdns., S.W.7 (tel. 373 6030). Modern hotel in a well-appointed fashion. British cuisine in *The Master Carver*.

Goring, 15 Beeston Pl., S.W.1 (tel. 834 8211). The Goring family provide personal and friendly service in this modernized Edwardian hotel.

Holiday Inn Swiss Cottage, 128 King Henry's Rd., N.W.3 (tel. 722 7711). Well appointed and handy for North London, but a fair bit from the center. Also at **Chelsea** (tel. 235 4377) and **Marble Arch,** George St., W.1 (tel. 723 1277). Both reliable and well managed; indoor pools.

Lowndes Thistle, 21 Lowndes St., S.W.1 (tel. 235 6020). Deep in the residential heart of Knightsbridge. Adam decor, picturesque people.

Royal Garden, Kensington High St., W.8 (tel. 937 8000). Crisp modern hotel convenient for this shopping street, some rooms with stunning views of the Park.

Royal Lancaster, Lancaster Ter., W.2 (tel. 262 6737). Excellent views from a well-decorated hotel with everything for an enjoyable stay.

St. George's, Langham Pl., W.1 (tel. 580 0111). Close to the BBC and handy for shopping. Try for one of the higher rooms—the views are really something!

Selfridge, Orchard St., W.1 (tel. 408 2080). Attached to the famous store for obvious shopping expedition possibilities. Modern and attractively conceived with well-fitted bedrooms and willing staff.

Tower Thistle, St. Katharine's Way, E.1 (tel. 481 2575). A vast modern hotel by St. Katharine's Dock and the Tower of London overlooking Tower Bridge. Five minutes from the nearest tube, but handy for the City.

Waldorf, Aldwych, W.C.2 (tel. 836 2400). Midway between theaterland and the city with a blended atmosphere of both, plus a touch of Edwardiana.

Westbury, New Bond St, W.1 (tel. 629 7755). A bit past its prime, but friendly and comfortable, particularly the restaurant. The bar's the coolest place in London on a hot summer's day.

The White House, Albany St., N.W.1 (tel. 387 1200). A large hotel with a solid reputation for comfort. Good value.

Moderate

Bedford, 83 Southampton Row, W.C.1 (tel. 636 7822). Functionally efficient and close to the British Museum.

Bloomsbury Crest, Coram St., W.C.1 (tel. 837 1200). Businesslike, good value for their small bedrooms and reasonable location.

Charing Cross, Strand, W.C.2 (tel. 839 7282). Gaunt exterior but a friendly heart, beside theaterland with excellent restaurant and interesting architectural features preserved. Rooms are comfortable.

Coburg, 129 Bayswater Rd., W.2 (tel. 229 3654). Most rooms with bath; solidly traditional. Close by Kensington Gardens and busy Queensway.

Colonnade Hotel, 2 Warrington Crescent, W.9 (tel. 289 2167). Four poster beds in some rooms, plus pleasant garden for barbecues.

Durrants Hotel, George St., W.1 (tel. 935 8131). Family owned, Regency-style hotel behind the Wallace Collection. 86 rooms of variable decor. Friendly service and a quiet bar.

Ebury Court, 26 Ebury St., S.W.1 (tel. 730 8147). Considerable genteel charm and courteous, friendly staff. Good restaurant and elegant Belgravia location. Book ahead.

Grand, 126 Southampton Row, W.C.1 (tel. 405 2006).

Great Western Royal, Praed St., Paddington, W.2 (tel. 723 8064). Huge bedrooms and lofty ceilings remain in this imposing, and well-modernized Victorian hotel, joined to Paddington Station.

Kensington Close, Wrights Lane, W.8 (tel. 937 8170). Facilities include two squash courts and swimming pool.

London Embassy, 150 Bayswater Rd, W.2 (tel. 229 1212). Handy for Kensington Gardens, town and the colorful Queensway scene.

Londoner, Welbeck St., W.1 (tel. 935 4442). Well-placed small hotel within strolling distance of shops, pubs, and quiet residential London.

London International, 147 Cromwell Rd., S.W.5 (tel. 370 4200). Modern tower block hotel; not the most elegant location, but handy for South Kensington museums.

London Tara, Wrights Lane, W.8 (tel. 937 1115). Good value accommodation on 13 stories—factory style but competently run. Just off Kensington High Street.

Mornington Lancaster, 12 Lancaster Gate, W.2 (tel. 262 7361). Convenient, English/Swedish style.

Mount Royal, Bryanston St., W.1 (tel. 629 8040). Big and central, beside Marble Arch; reasonable rooms and good value *Carvery.*

Pastoria, St. Martin's St, Leicester Sq., W.C.2 (tel. 930 8641). A small, relaxed establishment off Leicester Square, with well-kept bedrooms at reasonable prices for a prime location.

Portobello Hotel, 22 Stanley Gdns., W.11 (tel. 727 2777). An unconventional and enjoyable small hotel; potted palms and military furniture in "antique land".

Regent Palace, 12 Sherwood St., W.1 (tel. 734 7000). Still one of the biggest hotels and one of the only ones where no room has a private bathroom. Bang on Piccadilly Circus though, to make up for the lack of creature comforts.

Royal Court, Sloane Sq., S.W.1 (tel. 730 9191). Well-located and highly convenient for Chelsea sorties. Most rooms have bath.

Royal Horseguards, 2 Whitehall Court, S.W.1 (tel. 839 3400). Variable room standards and functional public areas in a good 'historical' situation for touring town.

Royal Trafalgar, Whitcomb St., W.C.2 (tel. 930 4477). Very handy for Nelson's column and almost everywhere else.

Rubens, Buckingham Palace Rd., S.W.1 (tel. 834 6600). Near Buckingham Palace and Victoria Station; comfortable. Most rooms with bath.

St. James, Buckingham Gate, S.W.1 (tel. 834 2360). Most rooms with bath; refurbished hotel set in interesting little streets.

Strand Palace, Strand, W.C.2 (tel. 836 8080). Comfortable and good value, without frills and fuss.

Westmoreland Hotel, 18 Lodge Rd., St. John's Wood, N.W.8 (tel. 722 7722). Overlooking Lord's cricket ground and popular with our readers for its friendly staff, good rooms, and value for money *Carvery Restaurant.*

Whites, Lancaster Gate, W.2 (tel. 262 2711). Elegant building with views over Hyde Park, but the interior is mixed in styles and age.

Wilbraham, Wilbraham Place, S.W.1 (tel. 730 8296). Small and intimate, with a delightful old-fashioned air. Close to Sloane Square. Recommended.

Inexpensive

Alison House, 82 Ebury St., S.W.1 (tel. 730 9529).

Arlanda, 17 Longridge Rd., S.W.5 (tel. 370 5220).

Colin House Hotel, 104 Ebury St., S.W.1 (tel. 730 8031).

Eden House, 111 Old Church St., S.W.3 (tel. 352 3403).

Elizabeth, 37 Eccleston Sq., S.W.1 (tel. 828 6812).

George, 58 Cartwright Gdns., W.C.1 (tel. 387 1528).

Manor Court, 35 Courtfield Gdns., S.W.5 (tel. 373 8585).

Montague, Montague St., W.C.1 (tel. 637 1001).

Princes Lodge, 8 Prince of Wales Terr., W.8 (tel. 937 6306).

Sumner Hotel, 11 Sumner Pl., S.W.7 (tel. 589 9854).

Willet House, 32 Sloane Gdns., S.W.1 (tel. 730 0634).

London Heathrow

Heathrow (L), Bath Rd., Hounslow (tel. 897 6363). Luxury hotel actually within the airport borders and filled with every jet-age facility; getting known for good eating.

Ariel (M), Harlington Corner, Bath Rd., Hayes (tel. 759 2552). Unusual circular hotel with well-maintained bedrooms for an overnight airport stopover.

Excelsior (M), Bath Rd., West Drayton (tel. 759 6611). Located at the north entrance to airport, with a businesslike atmosphere for stopovers.

Heathrow Penta (M), Bath Rd., Hounslow (tel. 897 6363).

Holiday Inn (M), Stockley Rd., West Drayton (tel. 08954 45555).

Post House Hotel (M), Sipson Rd., West Drayton (tel. 759 2323). Comfortable rooms, good food.

Sheraton Heathrow (E), West Drayton (tel. 759 2424). Quite adequate for the one-night stopover. Still, downstairs can be good for drinks and dining, prior to catching the next flight out.

Sheraton Skyline (E), Bath Rd., Hayes (tel. 759 2535). The really bright airport spot with lovely bedrooms and lively entertainment.

Skyway (M), Bath Rd., Hayes (tel. 759 6311). Modern. 445 rooms.

 RESTAURANTS. The listing below of London eating places is, of course, just a selection of the enormous range available. We feel that they are all reliable and will offer a rewarding dining experience. The London tourist boom brought on a rash of quasi-smart restaurants that charge grossly inflated prices for mediocre food at tables set much too close together. Even the oldest establishments have had to increase their rates, forced into an ever-rising spiral by high rents and taxes. But most restaurants post their menus outside, so that the wary passerby can check before committing himself. Unless you are traveling on an expense account, we strongly suggest you look before you eat.

There are still some serious defects to eating in London. The main one is that it is difficult to do so on Sunday or late at night. You should always check if a restaurant is open on Sundays; it could save you a wasted journey.

Another point to remember is that not all restaurants accept credit cards. One kindly owner remarked, when asked if he accepted plastic money, "No. We take only cash, checks and hostages."

A new law obliges all UK restaurants to display their prices, including VAT, outside their establishments. Not all restaurants conform to this sensible piece of consumer legislation. But most do display their prices, and if you are on a very tight budget, it's wise to read them carefully. Look for the hidden extras such as service, cover and minimum charge which are usually at the bottom of the menu and make sure the menu inside is the same. Lunch is usually cheaper than dinner, sometimes considerably.

Our simple grading system is as follows: Expensive, £50–£75 and up (!); Moderate, £25–£50; Inexpensive, under £25. These ranges are for two people, with a bottle of wine. But bear in mind that wine can double the cost of the food—so go very canny with the wine list.

Expensive

Athenaeum Hotel Restaurant, 116 Piccadilly, W.1 (tel. 499 3464). Reliable, with excellent wine list.

Belvedere, Holland Park (behind Commonwealth Institute), W.8 (tel. 602 1238). Very pretty decor and views, though best in summer. Excellent service, fine food.

Berkeley Hotel Restaurant, Wilton Place, S.W.1 (tel. 235 6000). Superb classical cuisine perfectly served by friendly and professional staff in elegant surroundings. *Le Perroquet,* in the same hotel, offers popular lunchtime buffet, and an evening change of mood to serious dining and music.

Bill Bentley's Oyster Bar, 239 Baker St., N.W.1 (tel. 935 3130). Classic seafood hangout.

Capital Hotel Restaurant, 22–24 Basil St., S.W.3 (tel. 589 5171). It's wise to book and wiser to take the food seriously here. Dedication to the highest standards becomes instantly apparent to both palate and the eye.

Claridges Restaurant, Brook St., W.1 (tel. 629 8860). Best restaurant in the celebrated hotel. Elegant mirrored dining room, highly sophisticated ambiance. Classic haute cuisine with superb wine list. Prices can be astronomical.

Connaught Hotel Restaurant, Carlos Place, W.1 (tel. 499 7070). One of London's most enduring gastronomic temples, and, befitting its status, it has more than a touch of hierarchical tradition. The range of dishes is vast and their wine selection extremely good value. But don't forget this is in the very expensive category.

L'Etoile, 30 Charlotte St., W.1 (tel. 636 7189). Small and sophisticated French restaurant with the true taste of Paris. Generally very good to know.

Le Gavroche, 43 Upper Brook St., W.1 (tel. 408 0881). London's number one gastronomic paradise, run by the celebrated Albert Roux. Here food reigns supreme in formally elegant surroundings, the whole conforming to the most time-honored tenets of classical French cuisine and service. Priced at the *very* top of the range.

Hyde Park Hotel, Cavalry Room, 66 Knightsbridge, S.W.1 (tel. 235 2000). A hold-over from the palmy days of Edwardian London with its marble and plush well-maintained. Popular lunchtime buffet.

Inigo Jones, 14 Garrick St., W.C.2 (tel. 836 6456). Close to gaslights and the Bow Street Runners' narrow street, this Covent Garden venue offers original bare brick and stained glass decor and an original, well-cooked menu. A fine spot for a reasonable lunch or an expensive dinner.

Intercontinental Hotel, Le Soufflé, 1 Hamilton Place, Hyde Park Corner, W.1 (tel. 409 3131). '20s décor is a backcloth here to first-class food, expertly served, but a bit overpriced. Despite the name, there are many dishes to surpass their soufflés.

Interlude de Tabaillau, 7 Bow St., W.C.2 (tel. 379 6473). *Prix fixe* excellence immediately beside Covent Garden Opera House. Superb French cuisine in distinctly chic surroundings.

Keats, 3 Downshire Hill, N.W.3 (tel. 435 3544). Superb French food includes their special 12-course gourmet dinners, on set dates by reservation only. Wise to book on ordinary days, too.

Langan's Brasserie, Stratton St., W.1 (tel. 493 6437). Trendy lunches or after-theater dining when the '30s' mood, background jazz and celebrities complement good food and fast service. Must book.

Locket's, Marsham Court, Marsham St., S.W.1 (tel. 834 9552). Close to the House of Commons; traditional English cooking. Long popular as a haunt for M.P.s.

Ma Cuisine, 113 Walton St., S.W.3 (tel. 584 7585). Currently among London's most popular for excellent cooking, especially lunch. Book well in advance.

Maxim's, Panton St., Haymarket, W.C.2 (tel. 839 4809). London version of the famous Paris restaurant. Sumptuous, elegant decor. 200-seat dining room with dance floor. Classic French cuisine.

Mirabelle, 56 Curzon St., W.1 (tel. 499 4636). This is *the* place for a celebration—followed by bankruptcy. 50s atmosphere, great wines.

Pomegranates, 94 Grosvenor Rd., S.W.1 (tel. 828 6560). An international culinary extravaganza. The food ranges from Scandinavian to Chinese.

La Tante Claire, 68 Royal Hospital Rd., S.W.3 (tel. 352 6045). Forget the decor and the crowded tables; this is the temple of *cuisine minceur* and similar chic food. Book ahead.

Thomas de Quincey, 36 Tavistock St., W.C.2 (tel. 240 3972). Particularly good for fish. Handy before or after Covent Garden Opera.

Trader Vic, Hilton Hotel, Park Lane, W.1 (tel. 493 7586). Still one of London's best spots for a touch of the exotic at those difficult hours between 6 and 8 P.M.; they continue into the small hours, of course. Menu large and variable.

Waltons, 121 Walton St., S.W.3 (tel. 584 0204). One of the small band of new top-rate restaurants. Service superb, food consistent, but expensive.

Wheelers, 12A Duke of York St., S.W.1 (tel. 930 2460), 19 Old Compton St., W.1 and others including **Braganza,** 56 Frith St., W.1 (tel. 437 5412) and **Alcove,** 17 Kensington High St., W.8 (tel. 937 1443). An excellent, long established seafood chain with interesting atmosphere.

Moderate

Ajimura, 51–53 Shelton St., W.C.2 (tel. 240 0178). Certainly not elegant, but simple, excellent Japanese food at very reasonable prices. The *tonkatsu* is especially good.

Le Café des Amis du Vin, 12 Hanover Place, W.C.2 (tel. 379 3444). French cuisine just around the corner from the Royal Opera House. Upstairs is best, with intimate atmosphere.

Ark, 35 Kensington High St., W.8 (tel. 937 4294). Unbeatable for excellent value and really good cooking. Small, crowded and very much better than places charging twice the price. Wise to book. Closed Sunday lunch.

Ashoka Tandoori, 181 Fulham Rd., S.W.3 (tel. 352 3301). Varied Tandoori cooking with intriguing decor. A long established favorite.

Bali, 101 Edgware Rd., W.2 (tel. 723 3303). Upstairs for a quick lunch of Indonesian and regional dishes. Downstairs for the set 12-course dinner, with exotic palm-tree background; taped music and good service.

Baron of Beef, Gutter Lane, Gresham St., E.C.2 (tel. 606 9415). A popular lunchtime venue for traditional English fare. Closed weekends.

Le Bistingo, a popular bistro chain. All the branches have plenty of atmosphere and the food is always reasonable. Branches at: 5 Trebeck St., Shepherd Market, W.1 (tel. 499 3292); 7 Kensington High St., W.8 (tel. 937 0932); 56 Old Brompton Rd., S.W.7 (tel. 589 1929); 57 Old Compton St., W.1 (tel. 437 0784); 117 Queensway, W.2 (tel. 727 0743); 235 Kings Rd., S.W.3 (tel. 352 2350).

Blooms, 90 Whitechapel High St., E.1 (tel. 377 1120). Jewish restaurant particularly popular for that East End Sunday excursion, but excellent anytime. Enormous portions, reasonable service; takeaway also.

Bombay Brasserie, Courtfield Close, Courtfield Rd., S.W.7 (tel. 370 4040). New departure in Indian restaurants; old Colonial club atmosphere with wicker chairs and ceiling fans. Excellent buffet lunch, but be sure to book. Near South Kensington museums.

Brasserie du Coin, 54 Lambs Conduit St., W.C.1 (tel. 405 1717). Genuine French brasserie with friendly atmosphere. Off High Holborn.

Bubbs, 329 Central Market, E.C.1 (tel. 236 2435). Characteristic French restaurant, well praised for food and wine. Next to Smithfield meat market.

Café Pelican, 45 St. Martin's Lane, W.C.2 (tel. 379 0309). Large French brasserie-type spot, deep in theaterland and open until very late.

Carlo's Place, 855 Fulham Rd., S.W.6 (tel. 736 4507). Extrovert surroundings in this small friendly restaurant of bright tablecloths and cuckoo-covered walls. Book early; well recommended.

Le Chef, 41 Connaught St., W.2 (tel. 262 5945). Small, maybe even too intimate, but unpretentious and very French (they even close in August—very Parisian!). Book in advance.

Chez Gerrard, 8 Charlotte St., W.1 (tel. 636 4975). Simple, good-value and wholesome French steak house north of Oxford St. Sensibly restricted menu and convivial atmosphere.

Chez Moi, 3 Addison Ave., W.11 (tel. 603 8267). Relaxed restaurant with quiet lighting and French cuisine. Lunch not served.

Chez Solange, 35 Cranbourn St., W.C.2 (tel. 836 0542). Satisfactory basic French cooking and character.

Chez Victor, 45 Wardour St., W.1 (tel. 437 6523). Solitary survivor of Soho's once-numerous authentic French restaurants. Some may find it shabby, but for those with a taste for simple and delicious French food in unpretentious surroundings, Chez Victor is a delight. Try their tripe, or brains.

Chuen Chang Ku, 17 Wardour St., W.1 (tel. 734 3281). Excellent Cantonese style at very reasonable prices.

Como Lario, 22 Holbein Pl., S.W.1 (tel. 730 2954). All the family works to run a very happy restaurant, with a particularly good *zabaglione*.

La Croisette, 168 Ifield Rd., S.W.10 (tel. 373 3694). Genuinely French cuisine, with much of the fish flown in from France.

Didier, 5 Warwick Place, W.9 (tel. 286 7484). Small, discreet and welcoming French restaurant in Little Venice with the accent on home cooking; a visit here is always a pleasure.

Dolphin Square Restaurant, Chichester St., S.W.1 (tel. 828 3207). Intimate spot with palm trees and piano. Classic international cuisine.

Drakes, 2a Pond Place, Fulham Rd., S.W.3 (tel. 584 4555). Atmospheric cellar with wine-bottle decor. Well recommended for high standards verging on excellence. Always enjoyable for both food and service.

The English House, 3 Milner St., S.W.3 (tel. 584 3002). 18th-century English court and country cooking, in quiet Chelsea house.

Flounders, 19 Tavistock St., W.C.2 (tel. 836 3925). Attractive Covent Garden seafood haunt, with imaginative dishes.

Frederick's, Camden Passage, N.1 (tel. 359 2888). An imaginative menu served beneath high ceilings with a lovely conservatory too.

Gay Hussar, 2 Greek St., W.1 (tel. 437 0973). A long-standing favorite; Hungarian cooking at reasonable prices. Book well in advance.

Gennaro's, 44 Dean St., W.1 (tel. 437 3950). Extensive Italian range at this old favorite.

Greenhouse, 27a Hays Mews, W.1 (tel. 499 3331). Airy setting for interesting range of dishes in this smart restaurant.

Hungry Horse, 196 Fulham Rd., S.W.10 (tel. 352 7757). Stands out in an area of small interesting restaurants. Friendly service and well-prepared traditional English dishes make this busy basement the place for a relaxed, enjoyable meal.

India of Mayfair, 52 Hertford St., W.1 (tel. 629 1786). Western-style decor with subtle, freshly prepared Indian cooking.

Joe Allen's, 13 Exeter St., W.C.2 (tel. 836 0651). Not so much the food as the people, piano, and theatrical flavor of this basement haunt. Particularly good late night.

Kerzenstuberl, 9 St Christopher's Pl., W.1 (tel. 486 8103). Appetizing Austrian home cooking. Good value and good fun.

Luigi's, 15 Tavistock St., W.C.2 (tel. 240 1795). Very attractive restaurant with excellent Italian food in a competitive district.

Magno's Brasserie, 65A Long Acre, W.C.2 (tel. 836 6077). Excellent French locale in Covent Garden area.

Manzi's, 1 Leicester St., W.C.2 (tel. 734 0224). A happy fish spot; value is good and the helpings generous. Always crowded to the gunwales, so be sure to book.

Ménage à Trois, 14 Beauchamp Pl., S.W.3 (tel. 589 4252). Princess Diana has been known to drop in. Menu includes intricate, filling starters and sumptuous puddings.

Mon Plaisir, 21 Monmouth St., W.C.2 (tel. 836 7243). A bustling French bistro in the heart of theaterland. Must book. Closed Sun.

Monsieur Thompson's, 29 Kensington Park Rd., W.11 (tel. 727 9957). Excellent seasonal cooking in attractive decor.

Neal Street Restaurant, 26 Neal St., W.C.2 (tel. 836 8368). Prized spot for business lunch or dinner. Trendy but cool Conran decor. High in this price range.

La Provence, 8 May's Court, W.C.1 (tel. 836 9180). Friendly spot with excellent French cooking right beside the Coliseum—very handy for pre- and post-theater eating.

Rules, 35 Maiden Lane, W.C.2 (tel. 836 5314). Nearly 200 years of serving classic English food. Must book.

St. Moritz Restaurant, 161 Wardour St., W.1 (tel. 734 3324). Close by Oxford Street for genuine Swiss food at reasonable prices.

San Frediano, 62 Fulham Rd., S.W.3 (tel. 584 8375). Some of the people who used to go up West in white tie and tails are around here now in levis. Basic Italian, good and fast service.

Sheekey's, 29 St. Martin's Court, W.C.2 (tel. 240 2565). Traditional haunt for good pre-theater fish meals of large proportions.

South of the Border, 8 Joan St., S.E.1 (tel. 928 6374). Convenient for the National Theater to dine among the bricks and rafters in this converted factory.

Surprise, 12 Great Marlborough St., W.1 (tel. 434 2666). Imaginative, New York style eating house with emphasis on American food. Ideally placed just behind Liberty's for shoppers and theater-goers.

Sweetings, 39 Victoria St., E.C.4 (tel. 248 3062). Old-fashioned fish restaurant, much frequented by city gents at lunchtime.

Throgmorton Restaurant, 27 Throgmorton St., E.C.2 (tel. 588 5165). Beside the Stock Exchange; excellent value for traditional English beef, pies and fish. A city institution.

Trattoria Il Carretto, 20 Hillgate St., W.8 (tel. 229 9988). Candlelit restaurant with music and good steaks.

Upper Crust in Belgravia, 9 William St., S.W.1 (tel. 235 8444). Traditional English dishes such as kedgeree, pies and plum pudding.

Viceroy of India, 3 Glentworth St., N.W.1 (tel. 486 3401). Something special in the way of Indian restaurants. Imaginative elegance in the decor, subtly spiced food, discreet service.

Wild Thyme, 96 Felsham Rd., S.W.15 (tel. 789 3323). Here is a tiny place with enthusiastic food and friendly service, just south of Putney Bridge.

Inexpensive

London has many thousands of budget eating places, which often do better than their expensive relations. We can only list a few, so please use your nose and your judgement for the others. Remember that meat is expensive whether you're a housewife or a restaurateur, so you'll get far better value with concocted dishes rather than steak.

Brasserie des Amis, 27 Basil St., S.W.3 (tel. 584 9012). French food in light and airy restaurant; good atmosphere.

Byblos, 262 Kensington High St., W.8 (tel. 603 4422). Lebanese food genuinely prepared and priced.

Caravan Serai, 50 Paddington St., W.1 (tel. 935 1208). Afghan specialties; comfortable and modern.

Chicago Pizza Pie Factory, 17 Hanover Sq., W.1 (tel. 629 2669). Hectic and crowded, purveying the deep-dish pizza species to enthusiastic customers.

Columbina, 4–5 Duke of York St., S.W.1 (tel. 930 8279). Reasonable prices for good standard Italian fare.

Costas Grill, 12 Hillgate St., W.8 (tel. 229 3794). Excellent fresh fish in Greek Cypriot spot.

Geales, 2 Farmer St., W.8 (tel. 727 7969). Best fish-and-chip dining in west London. Friendly, authentic; limited wines.

Hard Rock Café, 150 Old Park Lane, W.1 (tel. 629 0382). A loud-rocking favorite with burgers and juke box. Unfortunately, you must always stand in line.

Joy King Lau, 3 Leicester Sq., W.C.2 (tel. 437 1132). Authentic Cantonese—full of Chinese at lunchtime and early evening.

Justin de Blank, 54 Duke St., W.1 (tel. 629 3174). Delicious food, mainly salads.

Kettners, 29 Romilly St., W.1 (tel. 437 6437). Swishest pizza joint in town. Excellent value amidst elegant decor.

Khyber, 56 Westbourne Grove, W.2 (tel. 727 4385). Excellent Indian food in cool setting. Friendly service. Wise to book.

Luba's Bistro, 6 Yeomans Row, S.W.3 (tel. 589 2950). Russian Bistrovitch with a long-established reputation for good portions. No license—so bring your own bottle. Cramped but fun.

Monsoon, 3 Westbourne Grove, W.2 (tel. 727 8156). Cool interior, excellent inexpensive Indian food. Highly recommended.

Paesana, 30 Uxbridge St., W.8 (tel. 229 4332). 'Padrone Toni' provides excellent Italian food with finesse at extraordinarily reasonable prices.

Pooh Corner, 246 Battersea Park Rd., S.W.11 (tel. 228 9609). Wide range of well-cooked food; bistro ambiance.

Poons, 4 Leicester St., W.C.2 (tel. 437 1528). Authentic chinatown restaurant for cooking rather than comfort. The expensive branch in King St., WC2 (tel. 240 1743) has the reverse order of priorities.

Porters, 17 Henrietta St., W.C.2 (tel. 836 6466). Pies and other goodies with wrap-around sound. Run by Viscount Newport. Open Sun.

Spaghetti House, 74 Duke St., W.1 (tel. 629 6097); 216 High Holborn, W.C.1 (tel. 405 5215). Chain of pasta houses, excellent value for money.

Tent, 15 Eccleston St., S.W.1 (tel. 730 6922). There isn't actually a tent here, but what you will find is good, solid value.

Tuttons, 11 Russell St., W.C.2 (tel. 836 1167). Popular, chic and trendy eating house opposite the restored Covent Garden Market, somewhat overpriced. You'll pay a bit extra for peace and quiet in the basement.

Wine Bars

Wine bars, scattered all over central London, provide a slightly raffish way of having a bite to eat and a glass or two of wine—in neither case at budget rates—in crowded, often noisy, surroundings. Recommended for atmosphere and for the chance to taste good vintages, but not always easy on the pocket.

Archduke, Arch 153, Concert Hall Approach, South Bank, S.E.1 (tel. 928 9370). Attractive decor, good food. Handy for after Festival Hall concerts or a visit to the National Theater.

Brahms and Liszt, 19 Russell St., W.C.2 (tel. 240 3661). Very good value food supported by funky decor, very loud music. The odd name is Cockney rhyming slang for . . . well, drunk.

Cork and Bottle, 44 Cranbourn St., W.C.2 (tel. 734 6592). A welcome civilized downstairs oasis amid the tawdriness of Leicester Sq. Renowned for its imaginative hot dishes and salads. Excellent wines.

Crusting Pipe, 27 The Market, Covent Garden, W.C.2 (tel. 836 1415). Good spot to refresh yourself after a visit to the new market at Covent Garden. On the expensive side.

Downs, 5 Downs St., W.1 (tel. 491 3810). Top-drawer bar for huge portions and excellent wines, especially from the Loire. Convenient for Park Lane and Mayfair.

Fino's Wine Cellar, 123 Mount St., W.1 (tel. 492 1640). The discreet Mayfair address conceals a vaulted cellar for candlelit dining. Good also as a friendly meeting spot. Also at 37 Duke St., W1 (tel. 935 9459). Quieter and more relaxed.

El Vino's, 47 Fleet St., E.C.4 (tel. 353 6786). Famous watering-hole for journalists, lawyers and press barons—a discriminating and expert clientele. They now serve women at the bar, a state of affairs brought about only by frequent court cases.

Jimmy's Wine Bar, Kensington Church St., W.8 (tel. 937 9988). This converted section of the barracks becomes more enjoyable as the evening lengthens, particularly when guitar music is featured. Can be noisy.

Mother Bunch's Wine House, Arches F & G, Old Seacoal Lane, E.C.4 (tel. 236 5317). Worth the search underneath the arches for the Victorian charm plus good wines. Service can be erratic. Book for a lunchtime table.

192, 192 Kensington Park Rd., W.11 (tel. 229 0482). The new fun spot. Bar upstairs, good restaurant downstairs.

Whittington's Wine Bar, 21 College Hill, E.C.4 (tel. 248 5855). Vaulted cellar reputed to have been owned by Dick Whittington. Buffet food at the bar or you can lunch in their small restaurant. No food in the evening.

Pubs

The pub is a unique British institution. And, like many British institutions, it is both admirable and rather eccentric. The first quirk that strikes many visitors is how frequently pubs are closed. The dreaded licensing hours in London are from 11 to 3 and from 5.30 or 6 to 11 and, on Sundays, from 12 to 2 and from 7 to 10.30.

A point to remember is the unusual system of drink measurements. Those for spirits are self-explanatory—though Americans may find the measures small

—but beer comes in two "sizes"; pints and half pints. If you're feeling curious about British beer, but nothing more, have a half. If you feel more than curiosity, have a pint.

While on the subject of beer, one healthy feature of London pub life is the return of real ale. Over the last few years, there has been an increasing reaction against the insipid offerings of the big brewers (who own most London pubs). As a result, the smaller brewers, who produce stronger and more traditional beer, have grown in popularity and more and more good beer has become available. But it can be strong, so be careful.

You will also find that many pubs provide reasonable lunches; sandwiches, steak-and-kidney pie, shepherds pie and other English staples. If you are looking for a quick budget meal, these can be a very good idea.

A final point to bear in mind is that children under fourteen are not allowed in pubs. If they go in, they will certainly be asked to leave. Those under 18 may not order, or consume, alcohol. Pubs with gardens sometimes allow children into these.

 GETTING AROUND LONDON. Early Warning: The London transport system, like that in many major cities, has to cope with uncomfortable rush-hour periods, a situation exacerbated by the influx of 13 million-plus visitors annually. Tubes and buses can become very packed, so try to travel out of the peak rush hours when the stoical Londoners are going to and from work.

By Bus. London is served by fleets of single-deck and double-decker buses, and bus travel is easy and cheaper than the tube. Route numbers and maps are listed on signs at bus stops and as the bus arrives, quickly check the bus's destination window to make sure you're going in the right direction. A bus map is available at Underground ticket offices. This is a slow and often crowded method of getting around London, but you will see a lot of the town, especially from the top deck.

By Underground. Colloquially known as the "tube", London's underground train system is a good deal more comfortable than the New York subway, except of course during rush hours, when trains on some routes become sardine cans on wheels. By the way, a "subway" in Britain is a pedestrian tunnel.

Underground routes cover all inner London, and you'll often find it's the quickest way to get about. The various lines are clearly marked in stations, and easy-to-understand maps of the system are found along platforms and within carriages. Ticket offices also supply handy pocket maps free on request.

You buy your ticket at the station before starting your journey. Fares are calculated on a zonal basis, with a flat fare of 50p for all journeys within the central zone and 60p for all journeys from the second zone into the inner zone (prices may increase by 1987). All stations display prominent charts giving details of fares. Tickets are sold in ticket offices at all stations and at automatic machines, for which you will need 10, 20, 50p and £1 coins. Cheap day returns and one-day *Travelcards* (both available after 10 A.M.) can save money, as can weekly or monthly Travelcards (passport photo required) for buses and Underground trains. The *London Explorer* (also available from Britrail offices in North America and Europe) gives unlimited travel on London buses and trains including Underground and Airbus services between London and Heathrow, for 1, 3, 4 or 7 days. The *Capitalcard,* another money-saving ticket, is available for weekly or longer periods. You can buy these tickets from any London Regional Transport Travel Information Center or Underground station.

By Train. If you want to visit suburbs not served by the underground (and many, like Kew and Richmond, are), try the electric services of *British Rail.* To places like Croydon (10 miles in 15 minutes), Ilford (7 miles in 12 minutes), Woolwich (9 miles in 13 minutes), this is the quickest way. For round trip, ask for "return ticket", or for the cheaper "day-return" if you're coming back on the same day out of rush hours.

By Taxi. These unmistakable vehicles, with square bodies and the driver in a separate forward compartment, are liberally scattered throughout the streets of central and west London. If their flags are up, or a "for hire" sign is lighted on the top, just hail them.

London's distinctive black cabs are generally easy to find (except when you really want one in a hurry!), and drivers are both reliable and polite. If the orange light above the driver is illuminated, simply put out your arm and he'll stop for you. Fares start at £1 and there are additional charges for luggage and for rides after six and at weekends. Fares may be increased for 1987. Tip the driver 10% (although this is really at your discretion), but never less than about 20p.

By Car. Driving in London is not recommended for tourists. It is a very, very, big city, and whereas in New York, for example, there is some logic in the street planning, in London there is none. To make matters worse, the confusing street configuration is made almost incomprehensible by an extensive one-way system. Drivers who get lost and think to retrieve the situation by returning to base through a series of left-hand turns invariably find themselves somewhere else.

For those who must drive in London, however, the speed limit is 30 m.p.h. in the royal parks as it is theoretically in all streets, unless you see the large 40 m.p.h. signs—and small repeater signs attached to lamp posts—found only in the suburbs. Pedestrians have total priority on "zebra" crossings. These have black and white stripes between two striped beacon poles topped with orange globes (that flash at night) and have zig-zag road markings on both sides. It is an offense to park within the zig-zag area on either side, or overtake another vehicle on the approach side. On other crossings pedestrians must give way to traffic, but do take precedence over that turning left at controlled crossings, if they have the nerve.

The red, yellow and green traffic lights sometimes have arrow-style filter lights directing left- or right-hand turns, so do not get into the turn lane if you mean to go straight on (if you can catch a glimpse of the road markings in time). The use of horns is prohibited in all built-up areas between 11.30 P.M. and 7 A.M. You can park at night in 30 m.p.h. limit zones provided that you are within 25 yards of a lit street lamp, but not within 15 yds of a road junction. To park on a bus route, side (parking) lights must be shown—but you'll probably be arrested for obstruction or have the car towed away. In the day time it is safest to believe that you can park nowhere but at a meter or in a carpark.

Car hire. Among the leading firms in the London area supplying both chauffeur-driven and self-drive cars are: *Avis Rent-a-Car,* Hilton Hotel, W1; *Hertz Rent-a-Car,* 200 Buckingham Palace Rd, SW1, or 29–35 Edgware Rd, W2; *Godfrey Davis,* Wilton Rd, SW1. Or, you can contact *Car Hire Center International;* it has contacts in all the main hire centers in Britain; 23 Swallow St, Piccadilly, London W1 (tel. 734 7661).

By River Boat. In recent years, the River Thames has come back into its own as a transport highway. Boats operate from Easter to the end of Oct., upstream to Kew, Richmond and Hampton Court, and all year round downstream to the Tower, Greenwich and the Thames Barrier. You can join them at Tower Pier, Charing Cross Pier or Westminster Pier. Special cruises offer interesting alternatives: floodlit trips along the Thames by night; evening cruises with dinner and/or live entertainment; disco cruises. For details, call the River Boat Information service on 730 4812.

 NIGHTLIFE. In London, nightclubs usually put more emphasis on cuisine than elsewhere. They are really clubs, and most people join them for the exclusive atmosphere, for the floor shows, and for an opportunity to dance way into the small hours. To join a nightclub, telephone the secretary, then take your passport along to be shown at the door. Most Americans will be made temporary members for a nominal subscription fee right on the spot. Commonwealth or foreign visitors resident in London will have to join normally, and annual subscriptions vary from £5 to £25. Establishments requiring membership are indicated by "sub" after the name.

Nightclubs come—and they go—so we list only a few well-established ones, together with some good dinner-dance spots. Evening dress is optional in most, desirable in a few. The average expenditure for two could well hit £100, though a few places would be no more than half of that. Average will be around £40. At some clubs there's a special low-price dinner-dance arrangement available before midnight. Since the licensing law amendments came into force, clubs have far more freedom in serving hours—but the law is still complicated so you'll have to check as you go. Alcohol is generally not served after 2 A.M.

For the latest "in" spots, consult *City Limits, Time Out,* or the daily and Sunday papers.

Nightclubs and Dinner-Dance

As several of these are "in" spots, you may find it impossible to get in. Always phone in advance to see what the state of war is. Most of these places are incredibly expensive.

Barbarella's, 428 Fulham Road, S.W.6 (tel. 385 9434). One of the few discos where you can also eat in reasonable comfort, and hear each other talk. Suitable for all ages.

La Bussola, 42 St Martin's Lane, W.C.2 (tel. 240 1148). Convenient and elegant for a post-theater dinner-dance but prices require caution.

Dorchester Terrace Restaurant, Park Lane, W.1 (tel. 629 8888). An exceedingly good choice for that 'certain' evening, where you want to enjoy the food as well as the company.

Hilton Hotel Roof Restaurant, 22 Park Lane, W.1 (tel. 493 8000). Cooking is surprisingly consistent, and of course the view sets the mood from this top-of-the-hotel nightspot.

Hippodrome, Hippodrome Corner, Leicester Sq., W.C.2 (tel. 437 4311). The very latest thing in nightspots. Reputed to have cost around £3 million for the original conversion this is a spectacular way of spending the evening. As this is strictly a jeunesse joint and style is vital if you want to get in, it is perhaps not a spot for the older, staider visitor—but if you can win through Checkpoint Charlie then the laser shows and general concept spawned by nightlife boss Peter Stringfellow may well make your trip. Live music and disco most nights to 3 in the morning.

Raymond's Revuebar, Brewer St., W.1 (tel. 734 1593). Two shows nightly of super-sexy striptease; the only one we can list as good value for money. Not for the puritanical.

Royal Roof Restaurant, Royal Garden Hotel, Kensington High St, W.8 (tel. 937 8000). Terrific view from this 10th-story nightspot with dance band music and an ambitious menu.

Samantha's, 3 Burlington St., W.1 (tel. 734 6249). Long established popular disco.

Savoy Hotel Restaurant, Strand, W.C.2 (tel. 836 4343). This granddaddy of all London's nightspots comes into its own for a special dinner out with dancing.

Stringfellow's, 16–19 Upper St. Martin's Lane, W.C.2 (tel. 240 5534). Up-market, classy nightspot.

Tiddy Dols, 55 Shepherd's Market, W.1 (tel. 499 2357/8). British food, 18th-century setting, great wines, live entertainment 7–11, disco 11–2. Great evening for very reasonable cost.

ENTERTAINMENT. Theaters. London has about 50 theaters staging plays and musicals all the year round. West End productions maintain a very high standard, and many Broadway shows are put on with top casts from Britain and America. Most theaters have a matinee twice a week, and an evening performance beginning between 7.30 and 8. Prices for seats vary widely; unreserved gallery seats *can* be had for about £3.50 but you may have to wait in line for hours. The reserved seat list usually starts with upper circle at £3.50, then dress circle (reminiscent of the days when theater-goers all wore tuxedos for the better seats) at £5.00 up and stalls from £7.00. Top prices are around £15.00.

Of the alternative theaters, the *Royal Court,* in Sloane Square, puts on variable productions. But one of London's most interesting experiments is at the *Riverside Studios,* in Hammersmith. Originally TV studios, this art center has achieved wide acclaim, not only for its theater productions, but for film, opera and other events. If you're interested in off-beat theater, which can be fun and is cheap, as well as a whole range of entertainment, including pub shows, get *Time Out,* or *City Limits,* weekly. Most theaters have at least one bar. In some theaters you can reserve your intermission drink before the performance starts.

London's theaters have so far weathered the economic chills of the early '80s with surprising success. Though some still prefer safe productions with big names to draw the crowds or tried and trusted old favorites, others remain highly innovative and imaginative. Not for nothing is London known as the theater capital of the world. Try the National Theater on the South Bank or the

Royal Shakespeare Company at their new London home in the Barbican Center and you'll see why.

A really excellent bargain in theater tickets can be found in the Leicester Square ticket booth, which sells tickets for 45 London theaters at half price, plus 75p. service charge, on the day of performance (subject to availability). Open Mon.–Sat. 12–2 for matinees, 2.30–6.30 for evening performances.

Opera and Ballet. The *Royal Opera House*, Covent Garden, W.C.2 (tel. 240 1066), and The English National Opera at the *Coliseum* (tel. 836 3161), are the two major opera houses, with international stars at Covent Garden—and at international prices—and with native talent singing in English at the Coliseum. Ballet is regularly staged at Covent Garden (Royal Ballet) and there are seasons of visiting companies at the Coliseum. Ballet and opera is also staged by visiting companies at *Sadler's Wells Theater*, Rosebery Ave., E.C.1 (tel. 278 8916).

Concerts. The *Royal Festival Hall* complex (with its three auditoria) has the lion's share of music performances. On the South Bank near Waterloo Station, (Box office 928 3191, information 928 3002). The *Barbican Hall* in the modern Barbican Center in the City has daily concerts (tel. 628 8795).

The *Albert Hall*, Kensington, S.W.7 (tel. 589 8212) houses the annual Promenade Concerts, which have to be experienced to be believed. *St. John's*, Smith Sq., S.W.1 (tel. 222 1061), is a delightfully converted church, now a concert hall. The *Wigmore Hall*, 36 Wigmore St., W.1 (tel. 935 2141) is a small auditorium, famous for debuts and chamber work.

Jazz. Top of the jazz scene in London is *Ronnie Scott's Club*, 47 Frith St., W.1 (tel. 439 0747). This is the place for international jazz at its very best. Some pubs also feature jazz, such as the *Bull's Head*, Barnes Bridge, S.W.13, though this is a bit out of the center. Also popular is the *100 Club*, 100 Oxford St., W.1 (tel. 636 0933), with Chinese food and jazz personalities.

 PLACES OF INTEREST. London is one of the two or three most important centers of western civilization, and many of its museums are incomparable in their scope, variety, and imaginative presentation. Museums are open daily including Bank Holidays, except where otherwise stated. The best museums are open Sunday afternoons but, be warned, some museums are liable to close in full or part one day a week to save costs. At press time, for example, the Victoria and Albert Museum is closed on Fridays. In most, entry is free; in some, there is a small charge.

We also include in this section details of such focal points as the Abbey and Buckingham Palace.

Battle of Britain Museum, Aerodrome Road, Hendon N.W.9 (near Colindale Tube, Northern Line). New museum commemorating the dark days of 1940, sited on an old RAF airfield. Replica of bombed London street, period planes, RAF fighter control room, etc. Mon.–Sat. 10–6, Sun., 2–6.

British Museum, Great Russell St., W.C.1. The single most important institution of its kind in the world. Among the various departments are prints and drawings; coins and medals; Egyptian and Assyrian antiquities; Greek, Roman, British, Medieval, Oriental antiquities; and library. Lecture tour begins at 3 daily, except Sundays from the main entrance hall. Try to find time to take in some of the excellent modern display techniques which have injected new life, e.g., the Parthenon Frieze. Also features excellent traveling exhibitions. Weekdays, 10–5, Sun. 2:30–6.

British Museum/Museum of Mankind, Burlington Gardens, W.1 (behind Royal Academy). Exhibits of life and culture throughout the world, excitingly displayed. Same times as British Museum.

Buckingham Palace, The Mall, S.W.1. With its surrounding parks, the official royal residence is appropriately majestic and beautifully situated. Best approached down the Mall from Trafalgar Square. The statue of Queen Victoria in front provides a good vantage point for Changing of the Guard. Not open to the public. (See Queen's Gallery below).

Cabinet War Rooms, Clive Steps, King Charles St., S.W.1 (930 6961, 735 8922). Churchill's wartime bunker; fascinating glimpse of wartime London. Daily 10–5.50, closed Mon.

The Commonwealth Institute, Kensington High St., W.8. Open daily, 10–5:30. Sun. 2–5. Modern exhibition hall with permanent displays for all Commonwealth countries. Films, restaurant.

Courtauld Institute Gallery, Woburn Square, W.C.1. Outstanding collection of French Impressionists, varying modern collection. Daily 10–5, Sun. 2–5.

Covent Garden Market, The Piazza, Covent Garden, W.C.2. Beautifully restored 19th-century building, former home of London's vegetable market. Now has some of London's trendiest shops and great buskers.

Dickens' House, 48 Doughty St., W.C.1. Weekdays 10–5; closed Sundays and Bank Holidays. Occupied by the author from 1837 to 1839. On display are portraits, letters, first editions, furniture, and autographs.

Geological Museum, Exhibition Road, S.W.7. Collections of gemstones and exhibitions of basic earth science and geology. Also has good free film shows for children. Daily 10–6, Sun. 2:30–6.

Guildhall, King Street, Cheapside, E.C.2. The 15th-century council hall of the City, scene of civic functions. It has a library, open daily, 9:30–5, closed Sun. and 3 or 4 days before and after any special function. Also the Museum of the Worshipful Company of Clockmakers. Closed Sat, Sun.

Hayward Gallery, South Bank, S.E.1. Exhibitions with emphasis on ethnic and feminist art. Combine a visit here with a concert at the Royal Festival Hall or a play at the National Theatre. Mon.–Wed. 10–8, Thurs.–Sat. 10–6, Sun. 12–6. Varied admission charge.

H.M.S. Belfast, Symon's Wharf, Vine St., E.C.1 (ferry across from Tower of London). Magnificent WW II cruiser. Daily in summer, 11–5.20, winter 11–4.

Historic Ships Collection, St Katharine's Dock, E.C.3. Daily 10–5. Splendid, and growing, collection of historic sailing ships.

Houses of Parliament, Westminster, S.W.1. *House of Commons* sits from 2.30 onwards from Mon–Thurs., from 9.30 A.M. on Fri. To hear debates in the Strangers' Gallery, join the queue or apply to Admission Order Office in St. Stephen's Hall (but foreign visitors are advised to apply to their embassies or high commissioners in London). For a view of Parliament at its best, try to go on Tuesdays or Thursdays for Prime Minister's Question Time. *House of Lords* (to hear debates in Strangers' Gallery apply as for House of Commons) sits from 2:30 onwards, Mon–Wed; from 3 P.M. Thurs. and from 11 A.M. Fri.

ICA Gallery (Institute of Contemporary Art), Nash House, Carlton House Terrace, S.W.1. The latest "happenings" in art and art forms. Tues.–Sun., 12–9.

Imperial War Museum, Lambeth Road, S.E.1. Comprehensive collection of the Commonwealth during two world wars, including an art collection and a library of films, photographs, and books. Daily 10–5:50, Sun. 2–5:50; closed on Public Holidays. Public film shows Sat. and Sun. at 3.

Jewish Museum, Woburn House, Upper Woburn Place, W.C.1. Jewish antiquities. Tues.–Thurs. (and Fri. in summer) 10–4, Sun. (and Fri. in winter) 10–12.45.

Dr. Johnson's House, 17 Gough Square, E.C.4. Open daily May–Sept. 11–5:30, Oct.–April 11–5. Closed Sundays and Bank Holidays. Home of the great lexicographer from 1748–59.

Keats' House and Museum, Keats Grove, N.W.3. The home of the poet during the most creative years of his brief life. Daily 10–1, 2–6, Sun. 2–5.

Kensington Palace State Apartments, Kensington Gardens, W.8. The official residence of the Royal Family before Buckingham Palace. Paintings, furniture, and *objets d'art* from Royal Collections, plus Court Dress Collection. Daily 9–5, Sunday 1–5.

Kenwood House, Hampstead Lane, N.W.3. Fine paintings, Adam decoration amid rural Hampstead Heath scenery. Daily 10–5; April–Sept. 10–7.

Law Courts, Strand, W.C.2. The legal enclave called the Temple at the entrance to Fleet Street comprises the Inns of Courts or Courts of Law. The whole area forming the Law Courts across the Middle Temple and down to the Thames is worth visiting on a tranquil afternoon. The public is admitted to the galleries; sessions are 10:30–1, 2–4, Mon. to Fri., except during Law Vacations.

London Dungeon, Tooley St., SE1. Authentic exhibitions of the Great Plague, Tyburn and other gruesome aspects of Britain's history. Ideal for horror movie addicts of all ages, but not for the squeamish. Daily 10–5:45; Oct.–March 10–4:30.

London Transport Museum, Covent Garden, WC2. Relics from London Transport's better days. Daily 10–6.

Madame Tussaud's, Marylebone Road, NW1. World's most famous wax-works. Open daily 10–5.30. Often overcrowded.

Monument, near King William St., EC3. Commemorates the Great Fire of 1666, which broke out in Pudding Lane 202 ft. from the monument—its height. The upper gallery is open Apr.–Sept. Mon.–Sat. 9–5.40, Sun. 2–5.40. Oct.–Mar. Mon.–Sat. 9–4, closed Sun.

Museum of London. This museum in the prestigious Barbican is devoted to 2,000 years of history of this unique city. From Roman times to the present day this attractive museum traces London and the Londoners, using the latest techniques of display and lighting to create an unforgettable experience. Open Tues. to Sat. 10–6, Sun. 2–6.

National Army Museum, Royal Hospital Road, SW3. The story of the British Army from Tudor times up to 1914. Open daily 10–5:30, Sun. 2–5:30.

National Gallery, on Trafalgar Square, WC2. Open weekdays 10–6, Sun. 2–6. Collection of Italian, Dutch, Flemish, Spanish, German, and French painting up to 1900, plus British painters from Hogarth to Turner; in effect there is at least one masterpiece by every major European painter of the last 600 years.

National Maritime Museum, Romney Road, Greenwich, SE10. Open Mon.–Sat. 10–6 (10–5 in winter). Sun. 2–5:30 (2–5 in winter). Superlative collection of ship models, navigational instruments, charts, uniforms, medals, portraits, and paintings of naval scenes. First class throughout. Train: Cannon Street, Charing Cross or Waterloo to Greenwich (change at London Bridge). Buses: 188; 53 for observatory.

National Portrait Gallery, at St. Martin's Place, Trafalgar Square, WC2. Paintings, drawings, busts of famous British men and women from Tudors to the present. Same hours as National Gallery except closes at 5, Mon.–Fri.

Natural History Museum, Cromwell Rd., S.W.7. Animals, plants, minerals, fossils (nearly 15,000,000 specimens). Daily 10–6, Sun 2:30–6.

Photographers' Gallery, 8 Great Newport Street, W.C.2. Exhibits of contemporary photography, with books and prints on sale. Open Tues.–Sat. 11–7.

Planetarium, Marylebone Road, N.W.1. Next to Madame Tussaud's. Study of night sky with explanatory talks and displays from 11–4.30 daily. The *Laserium* show is a dazzling performance with laser beams. Shows every evening except Mon. Ring 486 2242 for details.

Public Record Office Museum, Chancery Lane, W.C.2. 1987 plans still to be finalized at press time—check with London Visitor & Convention Bureau for latest.

Queen's Gallery, adjoining Buckingham Palace. Selection of paintings and other masterpieces from the Royal Collection. Weekdays (exc. Mon.) 11–5, Sun. 2–5.

Royal Academy, on Piccadilly. The temple of traditional art. Mounts some of the largest exhibitions, especially of prestigious crowd-pleasers. Open 10–6 daily.

Royal Exchange, Ironmonger Lane, E.C.2. Originally built in 1564, present building from 1844. An active exchange once more, permission is required to visit.

Royal Hospital, Chelsea, S.W.3. Charming home for old soldiers ("pensioners"), founded by Charles II and designed by Wren. Open weekdays, 10–12 and 2–4.

St. Paul's Cathedral, E.C.4. The masterpiece of Sir Christopher Wren, built after the Great Fire of London. Contains memorial chapel to the American forces in Britain. Tours of the Cathedral take place daily (except Sun.) at 11, 11.30, and 2. Open daily. Check times for Crypt and Upper Dome.

Science Museum, Exhibition Road, S.W.7. Illustrates the development of most branches of science. Originals of famous locomotives, aircraft and cars. Many working displays; children's gallery: daily 10–6; Sun. 2:30–6.

Serpentine Gallery, Kensington Gardens, W.2. Regular exhibitions of contemporary art. Open, during exhibitions, Mar.–Oct. 10–6, Nov.–Feb. 10–4.

Sir John Soane's Museum, 13 Lincoln's Inn Fields, W.C.2. Collection of antiquities and works of art. Open Tues.–Sat., 10–5.

Tate Gallery, Millbank, S.W.1. The nation's foremost collection of modern art; plus excellent collection of British paintings, especially Turner, Blake, and the pre-Raphaelites. Daily 10–5.30, Sun. 2–5.30.

Tower of London, Tower Hill, E.C.3. Outstanding collection of armor, uniforms, historic relics; and Crown Jewels in the Jewel House. The entire complex is highly atmospheric and traditional. Price of admission depends on the time of year. Daily, Mar.–Oct. 9.30–5, Sun. 2–5; Nov.–Feb., weekdays 9.30–4 (closed Sun.). The Tower gets very crowded, so try to avoid midday and weekend visits.

Tower Bridge, beside the Tower. Walkway open 10–5.45 in summer, 10–4 in winter; 7 days a week.

Victoria and Albert Museum, Cromwell Road, S.W.7. Displays fine and applied arts of all countries and styles, British, European, and Oriental; a magnificent collection. Sunday lectures. Cafeteria. Daily 10–5:30, Sun. 2:30–5:30. Closed Fri.

Wallace Collection, in Hertford House, Manchester Square, W.1. Exceptionally fine paintings together with sculpture, furniture, china, armor, and work in gold. Daily 10–5, Sun. 2–5.

Wellington Museum (Apsley House), Hyde Park Corner, W.1. The London home of the famous duke, containing uniforms, decorations, trophies, and some paintings. Tues.–Thurs. and Sat. 10–6, Sun. 2:30–6.

Westminster Abbey, Parliament Square, S.W.1. Open daily 8–6 all year. Closes for Sunday services. Admission free. Royal Chapels open weekdays, 9–4:45, last tickets at 4. Wed. 6–8 free. Sat. 9–2, 3:45–5:45, last tickets 5. Closed all day Sun.

Westminster Cathedral, Ashley Place, S.W.1. Most important Roman Catholic church in England. Daily 7 A.M.–8P.M. View London from 270-ft. tower, open 10.30–7.30 (Apr.–Oct.).

Zoo, situated in Regent's Park, N.W.1, the huge London Zoo contains one of the world's largest collections of animals, reptiles, and birds. Children's Zoo shows farm animals and offers pony and donkey rides. Open daily from 9–6 in summer, 10 to dusk in winter. Sundays and Bank Holidays closes 7 P.M. Closed on Christmas Day. Admission adults £2.65 (£3.20 in summer), children £1.30 and £1.60.

PUBLIC SPECTACLES. *Changing of the Guard,* London's leading colorful ritual takes place at Buckingham Palace daily at 11:30, May–July, every other day at 11.30 Aug.–Apr. The *Life Guards* ceremony is at the Horse Guards, Whitehall, every morning at 11 (Sun. 10). Either ceremony may be cancelled without notice.

PARKS. London's great parks (*Hyde Park, Kensington Gardens, Regent's Park, Green Park, St. James's Park* in the center, and *Battersea Park* and *Hampstead Heath* further out) are more than just wide green oases in the middle of a concrete desert. They are places where you can go boating, picnicking, riding, play tennis, listen to a military band, and more.

Other parks well worth a visit are *Greenwich* (where the world's central time is taken from the former Royal Observatory), *Holland Park* (Kensington), with remains of an Elizabethan mansion, now a youth hostel, and open air concerts, *Blackheath, Kew Gardens* (botanical), with magnificent, extensive grounds, and *Richmond.* Richmond is easily accessible by bus or underground, and it still has the atmosphere of a medieval forest or heath—with herds of wild deer.

SHOPPING. Shopping in London easily divides itself into interesting areas. For the visitor who just wants to windowshop for a few hours, getting the taste of what London has to offer, the answer is to aim for one of these areas and wander around letting fancy be the guide.

The premier shopping goal has to be the neighborhood of **Bond Street.** With South Molton Street at the top, the Burlington Arcade along the south side, and all the roads that lead off, this forms a chic focus, full of international shops and smaller local ones, but almost all elegant and excitingly stocked. For paintings, carpets, linens and clothes, this is the first place to head for.

Piccadilly itself, and the Jermyn Street area to the south, are ideal for the window-shopper, especially in the older streets, where specialist outfitters have snuggled behind ancient bow windows for countless decades.

Then must come **Knightsbridge** where Harrods is but one part of the lure. Old Brompton Road, Beauchamp Place, the top end of Sloane Street, all spread out a wealth of shops from the central point like courtiers round a monarch. This area tends to specialize in whatever is the latest "in" thing, with Harvey Nichols giving Harrods an up-market run for its money.

For an exhausting brush with the brash, **Oxford Street** is the place. Endless jean shops attract the down-market shoppers, but there's still Marks & Spencers and C&A where quality and value are excellent.

If you are interested in books, then you should head for the **Charing Cross Road**, and the small courts leading from it to St. Martin's Lane. This is the area for both secondhand volumes and new ones. Foyle's, though not necessarily the best, claims to be the largest bookshop in the world.

The latest arrival on London's shopping scene is the born-again **Covent Garden Market**. The great central building, once the home of wholesale green-grocers and an integral part of picturesque London, has been lovingly restored and now houses a shopping mall featuring a mixture of the very best of British craftmanship and trendy boutiques. Craftwork is the place for lovely pottery from many of Britain's leading potters; the Dollshouse has dollhouses (what else!) of every shape and period, and Pollock's features fascinating toy theaters; stalls sell jewelry and other small items which would make an excellent gift to take home. Relax in one of the small restaurants with a glass of beer or wine. All the streets for blocks round about are bursting with trendy craftwork and imported goodies. On a sunny day, this is a very rewarding area for a long stroll.

If you are after the tops in atmosphere, and also relish the chance of finding something special hidden in a mountain of trash—then you should visit one of London's many street markets. Here are a few of the most colorful.

Bermondsey, one of London's most extensive. Hundreds of booths and stalls, with a wealth of junk from the attics of England. A special stamping-ground for dealers. Take the 15 or 25 bus to Aldgate, then the 42 over Tower Bridge to Bermondsey Square. But get there early. The market can start as early as 4 in the morning and runs till about midday *on Fridays only*.

Camden Lock (Dingwalls Market), (Tube or buses 24, 29, 68, 134 and others to Camden Town). Antiques and crafts market. Open Saturday and Sunday, 9–6.

Camden Passage, Islington (Tube or buses 19, 38, to "The Angel"). Openair antique market on Saturdays and Wednesdays. Fascinating antique shops in Camden Passage and Pierrepont Arcade, particularly for silverware. Stick to Association of British Antique Dealers members here. Shops open daily, 10:30–5:30; market Wednesday and Saturday.

Leadenhall Market, E.C.3. A Victorian covered arcade with food and plants; lashings of atmosphere. Monday to Friday, 9–5. Tube to Bank station.

Leather Lane, Holborn E.C.1. A blend of traditional fruit, vegetable and crockery stalls with new-fangled wares like spare Hi-Fi parts. Monday to Friday, 11–3.

Petticoat Lane, in Middlesex St., E.1. Open on Sunday mornings (9–2) only, for pets, clothes, fabrics and curios of all descriptions. (Watch your wallets!).

Portobello Market, Portobello Road, W.11. (Take 52 bus or tube to Ladbroke Grove or Notting Hill Gate.) Best day is Saturday, from 9 A.M. to 6 P.M. for all kinds of curios, silverware, antiques, etc. Several dealers with shops in other parts of London have booths here. No bargains and sometimes can be a trap for tourists but gets less expensive the farther north you go. Closed Sun.

Smithfield, E.C.1. London's main meat market and one of the biggest in the world. Best days are Mondays and Thursdays. Tube to Farringdon or Barbican.

Day Trips from London

Rural calm and places of historic interest are within easy reach of London. If you are not driving yourself, check the schedule of the Green Line, and also the "London Country Buses", whose excellent bus service extends to about a 30-mile radius from London. London's electric suburban train services are convenient, but often very grubby.

Especially recommended in the western environs of London are the following—Richmond, with its famous view of the Thames from Richmond Hill, and the enchanting 2,350-acre Richmond Park, full of flowering shrubs and freely-wandering deer.

Hampton Court, red brick Tudor palace residence of rumbustious English monarch Henry VIII, reputedly haunted (of course!), and surrounded by courtyards, gardens, fountains and deerpark; and you can puzzle your way through the celebrated Maze.

Windsor Castle, the base of whose Round Tower was built in the 12th century by Henry II, has long been one of the chief residences of English sovereigns. Don't miss its beautiful St. George's Chapel. Begun by Edward IV and finished in 1516, it ranks next to Westminster Abbey as a royal mausoleum (Henry VIII and George VI, among others, are buried here). See also the adjoining reception rooms with their Gobelin tapestries, the Rubens room, the Van Dyck room, and the royal library, whose collection includes drawings by Leonardo da Vinci and 87 portraits by Holbein. In the town of Windsor itself, you can see houses formerly inhabited by Jane Seymour, third wife of Henry VIII and mother of Edward VI, and Nell Gwynne, the Restoration actress who became the mistress of Charles II. The delightful Theater Royal opposite the castle is the home of a talented repertory company. A short walk across the river from Windsor Castle is world-renowned Eton College, most famous of English public schools.

Guildford, 40 minutes south by rail from Waterloo station, has a Norman castle, modern cathedral, and a steep cobbled main street plunging down between 17th-century shops and inns to the winding River Wey and the excellent Yvonne Arnaud Theatre.

Epsom also lies to the south, and should not be missed, especially if you can come at the beginning of June, when the Derby is run. This famous affair is one of England's noisiest and most boisterous picnics, guaranteed to change your ideas about the quiet and reserved English. The hats and costumes are always spectacular. Yes, this is also the birthplace of Epsom Salts, discovered here in 1618 in the mineral springs that made Epsom a fashionable 18th-century spa.

Visit Sevenoaks in Kent and nearby Knole Park for a clear, indelible impression of old England. Another must in Kent, Winston Churchill's former home, Chartwell, is open to the public.

Harrow, to the north of London, was founded in 1572 and granted a charter by Queen Elizabeth I. It is one of England's most famous schools, numbering Byron, Robert Peel and Winston Churchill among its alumni.

St. Albans, the ancient Roman city of Verulamium, 20 miles north of London, offers unusually interesting Roman remains and many ancient buildings. See the Verulamium Museum, the handsome Norman cathedral (which claims to have the longest nave in the world, after Winchester Cathedral), and the 15th-century clock tower. Also in St. Albans are several good antique shops.

PRACTICAL INFORMATION FOR THE ENVIRONS OF LONDON

TRANSPORT. Traveling around the environs of London is really very easy. As it is one vast commuter belt, there are plenty of trains running at frequent intervals. If you can; avoid traveling in the rush hours.

An alternative way of seeing some of this lovely countryside is to take the Green Line Coach—good value, especially if you have plenty of time. A drawback is that they can hold only just so many people.

The London telephone number for Green Line coaches and other London Regional Transport enquiries is 222 1234. This number is often busy. You may be able to get the information you want from High Street travel agents, the British Travel Center in Lower Regent Street, the National Information Center at Victoria Station, or from the London Regional Transport Information Centers at Victoria, Oxford Circus, Piccadilly Circus, St. James's Park, King's Cross, Euston and Heathrow Underground stations.

HOTELS AND RESTAURANTS. Here are some selected hotels and restaurants in the most attractive towns within easy reach of London by rail, bus, or car, which may appeal to those who prefer a quieter atmosphere or to visit the metropolis on a daily basis. Hotels are mainly Moderate and all have sufficient bathrooms available where there are no rooms with bath.

ASCOT (Berks). *Berystede Hotel* (E), tel. 23311; 90 rooms, all with bath or shower. Victorian turreted building set in wooded grounds.

BRAY (Berks). *Waterside Inn* (E), tel. Maidenhead 20691. Perhaps the finest restaurant in the land, overlooking weeping willows and river jetty. Run by chef Michel Roux. Superb cuisine, prices to match.

EGHAM (Surrey). *Great Fosters* (E), tel. 33822; 44 rooms with bath, 16th-century house, former royal hunting lodge with beautiful formal gardens, once the home of Anne Boleyn; try the stately bedrooms. Runnymede meadow nearby; also John Kennedy and Commonwealth Air Forces Memorials.

HAMPTON COURT (Gtr. London). *Bastians Restaurant* (M), tel. 01–977 6074. Faces the Lion Gate entrance to the Palace. Intriguing decor and excellent cuisine with some original house specialties. *Etoile Bistro* (I), 41 Bridge Road, Hampton Court (tel. 01–979 2309). Excellent value bistro-type restaurant; home cooking at its best and friendly service.

KEW (Surrey). *Le Provence* (I), tel. 01–940 6777. Offers excellent value with French cooking beside Kew station. Bring your own bottle. Reader recommended. Dinner only (lunch served Sat.) and you must book.

MARLOW (Bucks). *Compleat Angler* (L), tel. 4444; 46 rooms with bath. Gracious hotel in an active riverside setting. Excellent for rooms and service.

REIGATE (Surrey). *Bridge House* (M), tel. 44821; 30 rooms with bath. Spectacular views from well-equipped rooms on Reigate Hill; large restaurant and dancing.

RICHMOND-UPON-THAMES (Gtr. London). *Gate* (M), tel. 01–940 0061; 52 rooms with bath. Well-placed hotel for hill-top views and riverside walks. Friendly service. *Lichfields* (M), tel. 01–940 5236. Friendly spot specializing in good French food, with wide range of wines.

ST. ALBANS (Herts). *St. Michael's Manor* (M), tel. 64444; 26 rooms, 13 with bath, 9 with shower. Extremely well-run in the manor-hotel tradition plus a certain style that brings many guests back. *Sopwell House* (M), Tel. 64477; 27 rooms, most with bath. Delightful situation in wide grounds. *Aspelia* (M), tel. 66067. Elegant Greek restaurant, which offers good value and a view of the Cathedral.

TAPLOW (Berks). *Cliveden* (L), tel. 06286–68561; 27 rooms with bath. One of England's great stately houses, converted into an hotel where guests enjoy the lifestyle of a country mansion. Promises to be exceptional—and expensive.

TUNBRIDGE WELLS (Kent). *Spa* (E), tel. 20331; 70 rooms with bath. Impressive 18th-century house in large gardens. Comfortable hotel with good restaurant. *Thackeray's House* (E), tel. 37558. Excellent restaurant with imaginative dishes.

WEYBRIDGE (Surrey). *Ship Thistle* (L), tel. 48364; 39 rooms with bath. Tastefully furnished town center hotel.

WINDSOR (Berks). *Oakley Court* (E), Windsor Rd., tel. Maidenhead 74141; 90 rooms with bath. Victorian Gothic mansion near Windsor; excellent reputation. *Don Peppino* (M), tel. 60081. Pleasant Italian restaurant with views of Windsor Castle. Good wine list.

Historic Houses

BEDFORDSHIRE. Luton Hoo. Home of the Wernher family. Adam exterior, famous jewel and art collection. Open Apr.–Oct., Mon., Wed., Thurs., Sat., Good Friday 11–5.45. Sun. 2.45–5.45. Gardens open until 6.

Woburn Abbey, Woburn. Ancestral home of the Duke of Bedford (even if he does actually live in a Paris apartment for tax purposes!). 18th-century treasure house, with deer park. House stands in 3,000-acre park, now part of Woburn Wild Animal Kingdom, reputedly the biggest drive-thru game reserve in Europe. Open daily Apr.–Oct., 11–5.45 (to 6.15 Sun.). Grounds open and close one hour earlier.

BERKSHIRE. Windsor Castle, Windsor. Royal residence. The world's largest inhabited castle. The Queen owns one of the greatest collections of treasures in the world, and part of the Aladdin's cave is housed here at Windsor. Open daily except when the Royal Family is in residence. Times vary according to the time of year. Also, Royal Windsor Safari Park, 3 miles southwest of Windsor. A drive-in zoo, featuring lion and cheetah reserves among its many attractions. Open all year daily 10–5.30, or dusk.

GREATER LONDON. Chiswick House, Burlington Lane, Chiswick, W4. Lovely Palladian villa designed by the Earl of Burlington in 1725. Open daily mid-Mar.–mid-Oct. 9.30–6.30; mid-Oct.–mid-Mar., Wed.–Sun. 9.30–4.

Ham House, Richmond. Beautifully furnished 17th-century house; excellent portrait gallery. Open daily year round (except Mon.) 11–5.

Hampton Court Palace, Hampton Court. Former residence of Cardinal Wolsey, Henry VIII and William III; fantastic maze in the famous gardens. Open daily year round, 9.30–6, Sun. 11–6; winter 9.30–5, Sun. 2–5.

Hogarth's House, Hogarth Lane, Chiswick. Copies of the artist's paintings in what was his country house for 15 years. Open weekdays 11–6 (winter 11–4, closed Tues), Sun 2–6, winter 2–4.

Kew Palace, Kew. A Dutch-style building erected in 1631 and situated in the celebrated Kew Gardens. Open daily 11–5.30 Apr.–Oct. Gardens open all year 10–4 or 8 depending on season.

Syon House, Isleworth. Home of the Duke of Northumberland; Adam interior and furnishings and Capability Brown landscape. Open Easter–Sept., daily (except Fri. and Sat.) 12–5. Also **Syon Park Gardens,** open daily.

KENT. Chartwell, Westerham. Former home of Sir Winston Churchill. Open Apr.–Oct., Tues.–Thurs. 12–5, Sat., Sun., Bank Holiday Mon., 11–5; also Mar. and Nov., Sat., Sun., Wed., 11–4. Gets very crowded. (NT)

The Thames Country and the Cotswolds

The Thames rises in the picturesque Cotswold Hills in Gloucestershire. During its 200-mile course to the sea it passes through seven counties and some of England's finest rural scenery.

Highlights of the Thames Country include the enchanting villages of the Cotswolds, a rural world of golden stone cottages and meticulous gardens—Old England, apparently untouched by the ravages of the 20th century. Perhaps the finest example of them all is the village of Lacock at the southwestern edge of the Cotswolds. When you step into this village you're transported back more than 200 years.

Gloucester is a historically important town with some quaint streets and gabled and timbered houses among modern development. Its chief glory, and one of the glories of England, is Gloucester Cathedral, erected in the 11th century on the foundations of a seventh-century abbey, and with a beautiful gothic tower added in the 15th century. Don't miss the crypt and the splendid fan vaulting in the cloister.

Oxford, whose earliest colleges, University, Balliol and Merton, were founded in 1249, 1263 and 1264 respectively, is probably the most famous university in the English-speaking world. You can spend a delightful day here, wandering down the splendid High Street, flanked by the façades of a score of colleges, then among the buildings, quadrangles, spires and bridges of this ancient university. Entry charges are now made in some Oxford colleges, but these are only nominal. The most rewarding colleges from the tourist point of view are St. John's, All Souls and Magdalen. The last, pronounced "Maudlin", has the most beautiful gardens of all. See also the handsome garden of New College, surrounded by part of the old city wall, and its chapel with 14th-century stained glass windows; the superb 13th-century chapel of Merton College; the famous Bodleian Library, the Ashmolean Museum, oldest in the country.

PRACTICAL INFORMATION FOR THE THAMES COUNTRY AND THE COTSWOLDS

 TRIPPING UP THE THAMES. Apart from the river buses that operate in the London area, steamers serve the upper and lower Thames throughout the summer. *Salters Steamers* run services from mid-May to mid-September. Their vessels do return trips between the following points: Oxford-Abingdon; Reading-Henley; Marlow-Windsor; Staines-Windsor. Teas and light refreshments can be obtained on board. There are bus connections. For further information you should contact *Salter Bros. Ltd.*, Folly Bridge, Oxford (tel. 0865–243421 or 07535–63832).

HOTELS AND RESTAURANTS

ABINGDON (Oxon). *Upper Reaches* (E), tel. 22311; 26 rooms with bath, ancient converted abbey buildings.

BROADWAY (Heref. and Worcs.). *Lygon Arms* (L), tel. 852255; 61 rooms with bath. 600-year-old inn, complete with fourposter beds. Hugely popular so booking essential. *Dormy House* (E), tel. 852711; 50 rooms with bath. A tastefully renovated 17th-century Cotswold farmhouse; comfortable and relaxed, with fine food. *Hunter's Lodge* restaurant (E), tel. 853247; excellent cooking and long wine list.

BURFORD (Oxon). *Bay Tree* (M), tel. 3137; 24 rooms, all with bath. Tudor house, good food. History also surrounds the *Cotswold Gateway* (M), tel. 2148; 14 rooms, 3 with bath, this is indeed aptly named. Tiny *Inn For All Seasons* (M), tel. Windrush 324; 9 rooms with bath (at The Barringtons, 3 miles west). Delightful stone inn, hospitable hosts and good food. *Winter's Tale* (M-E), tel. 3176; 9 rooms, 5 with bath. Homely spot with good food.

CHELTENHAM (Glos.). *The Greenway* (L), tel. 862352; 12 rooms with bath. Old manor house, now a charming, stylish hotel 2½ miles out of town. *Hotel De La Bere* (E), tel. 37771; 34 rooms, 32 with bath. A modernized mellow 15th-century mansion with excellent sporting facilities.

La Ciboulette (E), tel. 573449. Varied range of French dishes with delicious sauces. Best value at lunchtime. *Queens Hotel* (E), tel. 514724; 77 rooms with bath. Colonnaded 19th-century hotel in front of Imperial Gardens. Regency decor.

CHIPPING CAMPDEN (Glos). *King's Arms* (M), tel. 840256. 17th-century and Georgian house with 14 rooms, 2 with bath. Excellent restaurant.

CHIPPING NORTON (Oxon). *White Hart* (M), tel. 2572; 22 rooms, 6 with bath, good overnight stop on way west.

CIRENCESTER (Glos). *King's Head* (M), tel. 3322; 70 rooms with bath. Friendly staff and an interesting menu.

GLOUCESTER (Glos.). *Crest* (E), tel. 63311. 100 rooms with bath. Modern. 24 rooms, 11 with bath, 8 with shower. *Tara* (E), tel. 67412; 22 rooms, 15 with bath. Lies just 3 miles out of town at Upton St Leonards.
Peebys (M), tel. 25636. Traditional English food. Close to city center.

GREAT MILTON (Oxon). *Le Manoir Aux Quat' Saisons* (E), tel. 8881. Outstanding French restaurant in manor near Oxford. Also offers accommodations.

LACOCK (Wilts). *Sign of the Angel* (E), tel. 230. Restaurant, historic half-timbered inn with period decor. Intimate spot with superb, small dining room and authentic atmosphere. Also has several delightful old bedrooms with modern facilities (M).

MAIDENHEAD (Berks). *Fredrick's Hotel* (E), tel. 35934; 34 rooms with bath or shower. High standards of accommodations and superb dining.

OXFORD (Oxon). *Linton Lodge* (E), tel. 53461; 72 rooms with bath. Well-converted Edwardian town house. The Gothic style *Randolph* (E), tel. 247481; 109 rooms with bath. *Oxford Moat House* (M), tel. 59933; 156 rooms with bath. Modern hotel on outskirts with good views across town. Numerous smaller hotels and guest houses include *River* (M), tel. 243475; 17 rooms, 6 with bath, 5 with shower.
Saraceno (E), tel. 249171. Excellent Italian dishes. *La Sorbonne* (E), tel. 241320, is consistently good for both food and wine. *La Salle à Manger* (M), tel. 62587. Informal French cooking at its best.
Interesting pubs include *Turf Tavern* (described in Hardy's *Jude the Obscure*) and *Welsh Pony*, popular with students. *Emperor's Wine Bar* (I), tel. 732642, is crowded and bustling; morning coffees and good meals too.

UPPER SLAUGHTER (Glos.). *Lords of the Manor Hotel and Restaurant* (M-E), tel. Cotswold 20243; 15 rooms with bath. Mellowed 17th-century house off the well-beaten Cotswold track. Good rooms with views. Local ingredients are competently prepared in their restaurant, and the service is friendly. Ideal touring base. Wise to book.

WESTON-ON-THE-GREEN (Oxon). *Weston Manor* (E), tel. Bletchington 50621; 23 rooms with bath (two 4-poster beds). Extensive gardens and sumptuous accommodation (one room even boasts a ghost); restaurant renowned for décor and cuisine.

WOODSTOCK (Oxon). *The Bear* (E), tel. 811511; 44 rooms, 37 with bath. Fine Cotswold-stone inn with lively bars and a good restaurant. A favorite haunt for romantic weekenders. Booking imperative. *Feathers* (E), tel. 812281; 15 rooms with bath. Charming, welcoming hotel. *Luis* (M), tel. 811017, offers an intriguing menu with good value set meals. Closed Mon.

Historic Houses

OXFORDSHIRE. Blenheim Palace, Woodstock. Birthplace of Sir Winston Churchill (who is buried nearby at Bladon). Built by Vanbrugh for Duke of Marlborough in 1705. Magnificent planned gardens by Capability Brown. Open mid-Mar.–Oct., daily 11–6. Charity cricket 25 May.
Chastleton House, Moreton-in-Marsh. Built 1603; the box garden is said to be the oldest in England. Open Good Fri.–end Sept., Fri.–Sun. and Bank Holiday Mon. 2–5.

GLOUCESTERSHIRE. Hidcote Manor Garden, near Chipping Campden. Outstanding English garden. Open Easter–end Oct., daily except Tues. and Fri. 11–8 (NT).

Snowshill Manor, near Broadway. An important collection of musical instruments, clocks and toys, interesting for children. Open Apr. and Oct., Sat., Sun., Bank Holiday Mon., 11–1, 2–5; May–end Sept., Wed., Thurs., Fri., Sat., Sun., Bank Holiday Mon., 11–1, 2–6 or sunset if earlier. (NT)

Sudeley Castle, near Winchcombe. Dates from the 12th century and contains tomb of Queen Katherine Parr. Largest private collection of toys in Europe. Open Apr.–Oct., daily 12–5. Grounds open from 11. Falconry displays May–Aug., Sun., Tues., Wed., Thurs.

Southern England

All around the coasts of Kent, Sussex and Hampshire, resort towns stretch along beaches and bays, their hotels and guest houses cheek-by-jowl. The busy season here is summer, though an increasing number of hotels now stay open almost all year.

The gentle, orderly landscape of southeast England is packed from end to end with castles, country houses, cathedrals and historic highspots by the score. And none of them are more than a couple of hours from London.

Down in the apple-blossom county of Kent, the chief tourist magnet is Canterbury, with its historic religious associations and magnificent Gothic cathedral. It was here that the Archbishop of Canterbury, Thomas à Becket, was murdered on orders of King Henry II in the 12th century, and here that the Canterbury Pilgrims came to seek the holy blissful martyr. Not far from Canterbury is the first English Christian Church, St. Martin's, where the Christian wife of the Saxon King Ethelbert worshipped in the sixth century. See also Chiddingstone and Chilham, "the prettiest villages in Kent". And remember to book hotel reservations way in advance for Canterbury—in July and August every good inn is full to the rafters.

In East and West Sussex are Rye, of the cobbled streets, timbered dwellings and oak-paneled Mermaid Inn; historic Hastings and nearby Battle (the Normans called it Senlac), where William the Conqueror defeated Harold in 1066 and changed the whole course of English history. Hastings Castle, and Bodiam, not far away, are both ruined, but Bodiam nevertheless provides you with a moated, curtain-walled fortress without equal in England. Popular summer coastal spots are Bexhill-on-Sea, Eastbourne and the dizzy chalk cliffs of Beachy Head, where begin the South Downs and the charming villages of Sussex like Alfriston and West Dean. In the ancient and romantic town of Lewes, see the handsome Elizabethan "Anne of Cleves House", and Bull House, home of Thomas Paine, author of *The Rights of Man*.

Brighton is the brightest and most sophisticated of the south coast resorts where you certainly should visit the Royal Pavilion, one of Britain's most exotic and eccentric buildings. Try also to include Chichester on your itinerary. Its cathedral is a "sermon in stone"; its ancient market cross one of the most impressive things in Sussex. In summer the Festival Theater provides some excellent drama. A couple of miles out of town is Fishbourne Palace, the excavated remains of the Romano-British palace. Well worth a visit.

Highlights of Hampshire include Winchester, the ancient capital of Alfred the Great. The steep and narrow High Street is flanked by some of the oldest houses in England, and the Great Hall, all that remains of the castle, has in it what is traditionally supposed to be King Arthur's Round Table. Winchester's huge cathedral, where Alfred and other English kings were crowned, has a handsome baptismal font (Norman) and some interesting Gothic tombs of the 15th-century bishops. See also Winchester's public school, the oldest in England, opened in 1382. Don't miss its chapel and the ancient cloisters.

Along the coast are Portsmouth, steeped in maritime heritage and site of the *Victory,* Nelson's flagship, and the Tudor warship, the *Mary Rose,* Southampton and fascinating old Lymington where there is a lively antiques street market on Saturdays and from where ferries run to the Isle of Wight. Bournemouth, in Dorset, is one of England's best seaside resorts and an ideal base from which to explore the New Forest, once the hunting preserve of the Norman kings and still roamed by wild deer and ponies.

The rounded hills of Wiltshire form a breezy plateau called Salisbury Plain, south of which lies Salisbury, the county town, dominated by the 404-foot stone spire of its cathedral, frequently painted by Constable, who was not alone in thinking it the most glorious spire in Christendom. Inside the cathedral, see the lancet windows, the 14th-century wrought iron clock, and the tombs of Englishmen who died in the crusades and at the great victory of Agincourt in 1415. And don't miss the octagonal chapter house. Close to Salisbury is Wilton House, splendid home of the Earls of Pembroke, with an incomparable art collection including 16 Van Dycks in the double-cube room, where Eisenhower and staff planned the invasion of Normandy. On Salisbury Plain stands Britain's most famous prehistoric circle, Stonehenge, whose impressive monoliths may date as far back as 2,000 years before Christ. Closer to our own times are the 18th-century landscape gardens of Stourhead, owned by the National Trust.

PRACTICAL INFORMATION FOR SOUTHERN ENGLAND

HOTELS AND RESTAURANTS. Holiday hotels often quote all-inclusive rates for a week's stay, a plan that works out a good deal cheaper than taking a room and meals by day. But the overseas visitor probably hasn't time or doesn't care to spend more than a day or so in each part of the country, so we've listed a selection of hotels at popular centers where you can put up for the night pretty comfortably. And if you are not stopping overnight, most of the larger hotels and all inns serve meals.

BOURNEMOUTH (Dorset). *Carlton* (L), tel. 22011; 56 rooms with bath. Justly treasured by its many devotees as a hotel-home away from home. *Royal Bath* (E), tel. 25555; 135 rooms with bath. Much more impressive inside, with enjoyable Buttery restaurant, new library and casino. Both have heated pools and good views. *Ladbroke New Normandie* (M), tel. 22246, is a reasonably-priced alternative.

Trattoria San Marco (M), tel. 21132. Small family restaurant with good range of Italian specialties.

BRIGHTON (E. Sussex). *Grand* (E), tel. 21188; 166 rooms with bath. Very stylish, opulent seafront hotel, also very comfortable. *Old Ship* (M), tel. 29001; 152 rooms, most with bath. Steeped in history, with a friendly staff.

Dining in Brighton is lively with *Wheeler's Sheridan Tavern* (E), tel. 28372; beside the well-known 'Lanes' area, full of seafood restaurants.

CANTERBURY (Kent). *Chaucer* (M), tel. 464427; 47 rooms, 41 with bath. Pleasant and efficient with good restaurant. *Slatters* (M), tel. 463271; 30 rooms, 23 with bath. For dinner, try the *Falstaff Inn* (M), tel. 462138; or several miles out, at Pett Bottom, visit the *Duck Inn* (E), tel. 830354; fine country restaurant. Also recommended, especially for its buffet lunches, is the *George & Dragon Inn* (M), tel. 710661, at Fordwich (3 miles).

CHICHESTER (W. Sussex). *Chichester Lodge* (M), tel. 786351; 43 rooms with bath. A good series of French and English platters is available at *Christophers of Chichester* restaurant (M), tel. 788724.

CHIDDINGSTONE (Kent). *Castle Inn* (E), tel. 870247. Excellent English cooking in restaurant in historic village; also a pub.

CHILHAM (Kent). *Woolpack Inn* (M), tel. 0227 730208; 14 rooms, 11 with bath. 15th-century hostelry in historic village.

EASTBOURNE (E. Sussex). *Grand* (E), tel. 22611; 178 rooms with bath. The essence of Eastbourne elegance with fine cuisine and all amenities. *Queen's* (M), Marine Parade, tel. 22822. 108 rooms with bath. Impressive, late Victorian, facing the sea.
    At *Jevington* (7 miles), the *Hungry Monk* (M), tel. Polegate 2178, serves carefully considered food and excellent wine. You must book and arrive on time, but it's well worthwhile.

EAST GRINSTEAD (W. Sussex). *Gravetye Manor* (L), tel. Sharpthorne 810567; 14 rooms with bath. This stone Elizabethan mansion offers superb vistas in every direction; wonderful surroundings for a stroll before or after dinner. Excellent restaurant with French and Austrian specialties: do book first (a *Relais de Campagne* hotel). *Felbridge* (M), tel. 26992; 50 rooms with bath. Has a popular pool and adjacent health club; restaurant.

FOLKESTONE (Kent). *Burlington* (M), tel. 55301; 56 rooms with bath. Good sea views. *Clifton* (M), tel. 41231; 62 rooms, 36 with bath.
    Paul's (M), tel. 59697. French cuisine, chic atmosphere.

HASTINGS & ST LEONARDS (E. Sussex). *Beauport Park* (M), tel. 51222; 23 rooms with bath. Roomy, comfortable, in extensive grounds; 3 miles north.

HIGH HALDEN (Kent). *Hookstead House Restaurant* (E), tel. 522. Noteworthy food and ambience in old manor house near Ashford. Also some accommodations.

LEWES (E. Sussex). *Shelley's Hotel* (E), tel. 472361; 21 rooms, 9 with bath, 12 with shower, and *White Hart* (M), tel. 474676, 32 rooms, 13 with bath. Both for vintage atmosphere and overnighting after Glyndebourne.
    Kenwards (M), tel. 472343; English dishes served in historic building.

MIDHURST (W. Sussex). *Angel* (M), tel. 2421; 18 rooms, 8 with bath. 16th-cent. spot; charming atmosphere. *Spread Eagle Hotel* (M), tel. 2211; 29 rooms, 25 with bath, splendid black-and-white timbered showplace building, comfortable, with good food and 'authentic' beer.

PORTSMOUTH (Hants). *Holiday Inn* (E), tel. 383151; 170 rooms with bath. *Portsmouth Crest* (E), tel. 827651; 170 rooms with bath. *Pendragon* (M), tel. 823201; 58 rooms, 37 with bath.

RYE (E. Sussex). *Mermaid* (M), tel. 223065; 30 rooms, 27 with bath or shower. Ancient lovely building, bursting with history. *George* (M), tel. 222114; 20 rooms with bath or shower; almost as evocative.
    Flushing Inn (M), tel. 223292, for reliable food (closed Tues. and dinner Mon.).

SALISBURY (Wilts.). *Rose and Crown* (M), tel. 27908; 27 rooms, all with bath. Combines idyllic views with low-beamed atmosphere. *Red Lion* (M), tel. 23334; 52 rooms, 40 with bath. A 16th-century coaching inn.

WINCHESTER (Hants). *Lainston House*, Sparsholt (L), tel. 63588. 17th-century house in 63 acres of grounds. 32 rooms with bath. *Wessex* (E), 61611; 94 rooms with bath. Modern and very comfortable beside the cathedral. *Old Chesil Rectory* (M), tel. 53177, offers good French food in a 15th-century rectory.

Historic Houses and Museums

HAMPSHIRE. Jane Austen's House, Chawton. Home of the famous 19th-century writer. Open daily Apr.–Oct.; Wed.–Sun. in Nov., Dec., Mar.; Sat. and Sun. in Jan. and Feb.; all 11–4.30.

Broadlands, Romsey. Former home of Lord Palmerston and Earl Mountbatten. Adam interior and Capability Brown park and gardens close to the River Test. Open daily 10–6 (closed Mon. except in Aug., Sept. and Bank holidays). Where Charles and Diana spent the first night of their honeymoon.

National Motor Museum, Palace House, Beaulieu. One of the world's finest collections of historic cars, attached to 13th-century Abbey. Open daily, 10–6, 10–5 in winter.

KENT. Dover Castle, Dover. Keep built by Henry II in 1180–6. Open all year, mid-March–mid-Oct., weekdays 9.30–6.30, rest of year 9.30–4. Open Sun., Apr. to Sept. 9.30–4, winter 2–4.

Hever Castle, near Edenbridge. Home of Henry VIII's second wife, Anne Boleyn. Splendid gardens. Open daily Easter–early Nov. Gardens 11–6, castle from 12 noon.

Ightham Mote, near Ightham. Medieval moated manor house. Recently donated to the National Trust by its American owner. Open Easter through Oct., Mon., Wed., Fri. and Sun. 11–5. (NT)

Knole, Sevenoaks. Home of Lord Sackville. Built in 1456. Open Easter through Oct., Wed.–Sat. and Bank Holiday Mon., 11–5; Sun. 2–5. (NT)

Leeds Castle, near Maidstone. One of the most outwardly impressive castles in Britain, standing in a lake. Open Easter through Oct., daily 11–5; winter, Sat. and Sun. only, 12–4.

Penshurst Place, Tunbridge Wells. Dating from 1340, one of England's great houses, home of poet Sir Philip Sidney. Now the residence of the Rt Hon. Viscount de L'Isle. Has a unique toy museum. Open Apr.–Oct., daily (except Mon.), 12.30–6. Also open Bank Holiday Mon.

Sissinghurst Castle, Tudor house with the famous gardens of V. Sackville-West and Sir Harold Nicolson; a gardener's joy. Open Apr.–mid-Oct., Tues.–Fri., 1–6.30, Sat., Sun., and Good Fri. 10–6.30. (NT).

SUSSEX (EAST AND WEST). Arundel Castle. Home of the Duke of Norfolk. Norman castle rebuilt in the 18th century and altered at the end of the 19th century. Open Apr.–Oct. Sun.–Fri., 1–5, plus all Bank Holidays. Nearby is a *Wildfowl Trust,* open daily year round 9.30–5.30, or dusk.

Batemans, near Burwash. Built 1634. Delightful home of Rudyard Kipling from 1902–36. Open Easter through Oct., Sat. to Wed. 11–6; open Good Fri. (NT)

Firle Place, near Lewes. Has important collection of pictures and many items of particular interest to visitors from the USA. Open June–Sept., Wed., Thurs. and Sun. from 2.15 (last admission 5); also Easter and Bank Holiday Suns. and Mons.

Lamb House, Rye. English home of the American author Henry James. Open April–Oct., Wed. and Sat. only, 2–6. (NT)

Michelham Priory, near Hailsham. Tudor farmhouse, originally an Augustinian Priory. Surrounded by medieval moat. Extra attractions—cream teas, craft shop and working watermill. Open Easter–Oct., daily 11–5.30.

Petworth House, Petworth. Palatial mansion rebuilt in 1696 by the 6th Duke of Somerset. Fine collection of paintings. Open Apr.–Oct., Wed., Thurs., Sat., Sun. and Bank Holiday Mon. 2–6; deer park daily 9–dusk. (NT)

Royal Pavilion, Brighton. A dazzling and exotic folly built in 1787 and transformed by John Nash for the Prince Regent in the early 19th-century. A 'must' sight. Open daily, 10–5; June–Sept. 10–6.30.

Weald and Downland Open Air Museum, Singleton. A fascinating collection of historic buildings saved from destruction and re-erected on a magnificent

40-acre site; woodland nature trail. Open Apr.–Oct., daily 11–5; Nov.–Mar., Wed. and Sun. 11–4.

WILTSHIRE. Avebury Manor, near Marlborough. Romantic Elizabethan house and gardens ringed by giant prehistoric stone circle and earthworks. Open Apr.–Sept., Mon.–Sat. 11.30–6.30, Sun. 1–6.30; also weekends in winter, 1.30–5.

Lacock Abbey, near Chippenham. 13th-century abbey, converted 1540. Later Georgian 'gothick' additions. In one of the most beautiful villages in England. Open Apr.–Oct., Wed.–Mon., 2–6. (NT)

Longleat House, near Warminster. Home of Marquess of Bath. Built 1566–80, superb Renaissance building, lavishly decorated. One of the great houses of the world. Also lions and children's zoo. Open all year, daily 10–6, Easter–Sept., rest of year 10–4.

Stourhead, Stourton, near Mere. 18th-century house with gorgeous gardens. House open May through Sept., daily (except Fri.) and Apr. and Oct., Sat.–Wed., 2–6 (or sunset). Gardens: all year, daily, 8–7 (or sunset, if earlier). (NT)

Wilton House, Salisbury. Partly the work of Inigo Jones. Art treasures, exhibition of 7,000 model soldiers. Ancient lawns and cedars of Lebanon. Open Apr.–Oct., Tues.–Sat., and Bank Holiday Mon., 11–6, Sun., 1–6.

GLYNDEBOURNE FESTIVAL OPERA is held during summer in a fine, but small, auditorium set in beautiful grounds of a private estate near Lewes, Sussex. During the long interval, the audience picnics, or dines in the excellent restaurants. For tickets to Glyndebourne's Opera, apply well in advance to any ticket agency (Keith Prowse, for example) or through your travel agent. Wear evening dress if possible. Take a train from Victoria (most opera-goers ride down to Lewes Station mid-afternoon: buses meet suitable trains). An expensive outing. Reckon on about £65–80 for two.

The Isle of Wight

The Isle of Wight, opposite Southampton Harbor, has a stretch of coast known as the Undercliff, facing south along the channel. Here, there are palm trees and subtropical vegetation, accounting for the popularity of such resorts as Ventnor, Sandown and Shanklin. At the mouth of the Medina River lies Cowes, scene during the first week in August of the annual Cowes Regatta, one of the greatest yachting events in the world.

PRACTICAL INFORMATION FOR THE ISLE OF WIGHT

HOW TO GET THERE. There are four main routes to the island: Lymington to Yarmouth via *Sealink* car/passenger ferry; Portsmouth to Fishbourne via *Sealink* car ferry; Southampton to Cowes via *Red Funnel* car ferry or passenger-only hydrofoil; Portsmouth to Ryde Pier via *Sealink* passenger ferry. If you are taking your car to the Isle of Wight during the summer months advance booking is vital.

Hotels and Restaurants

COWES. *Holmwood* (E), tel. 292508; 19 rooms, 7 with bath, 7 with shower. Reserve for Cowes Week. Fine views over the Solent.

FRESHWATER. *Farringford* (M), tel. 752500; 68 rooms with bath. Once Tennyson's home; 200-year-old stone mansion. Good sea fishing and golf nearby.

RYDE. Popular resort with sandy beaches overlooking the Solent. *Yelf's* (M), tel. 64062; 21 rooms, all with bath.

SHANKLIN. Sea fishing and golf available. *Cliff Tops* (M), tel. 863262; 102 rooms, 80 with bath. Modern comfortable hotel with good views. *Luccombe Hall* (M), tel. 862719; 32 rooms, 25 with bath. Overlooking the bay.

VENTNOR. *Peacock Vane* (E), tel. 852019, is in a country house hotel at Bonchurch. Highly praised cuisine. *Winterbourne* (M), tel. 852535; 19 rooms with bath. Where Charles Dickens wrote *David Copperfield;* he thought it the prettiest place he ever saw.

The Southwest

Dorset remains one of the last truly unspoiled corners of the old rural England of popular imagination, full of mellow stone manor houses, thatched cottages, cider apple orchards and winding country lanes, leading from one steep little valley to the next. This is the "Wessex" of Thomas Hardy's pastoral novels. In Dorchester, the county town, there is a special room of Hardy relics in the museum, along with other relics of the town's Roman origins, and Hardy's birthplace at Higher Bockhampton, only three miles away, is open to visitors. Dorchester is an excellent center for visiting Dorset's sightseeing highspots, which include the giant Iron Age ramparts of Maiden Castle; the unique Swannery at Abbotsbury; Sherborne, with its ancient Abbey Church and two castles (one formerly the home of Sir Walter Raleigh); the dramatic Purbeck Coast around Lulworth Cove and, guarding a gap in the Purbeck Hills, the ruins of Corfe Castle.

Camelot-haunted Somerset offers the spectacular natural attractions of Cheddar Gorge and Wookey Hole Cave, the windswept Exmoor Hills piled against the Devon border, and the man-made charms of her towns. Glastonbury is one of the most ancient places in Britain, a cradle of early Christian faith and the traditional burial-place of King Arthur. Wells is a charming old cathedral city with a village atmosphere. At its heart stands the West Country's loveliest cathedral. Dunster is an old market town with a 17th-century Yarn Market, a wide main street lined with old shops and houses, and a magnificent castle, lived in by the Luttrell family since 1376.

In Avon is Bath, a spectacular and infinitely elegant city of Georgian streets, crescents and squares. The city was founded by the Romans, however, and their famous Baths rank among the most striking Roman relics in Britain. Claverton Manor, two miles from Bath, houses a fascinating American Museum. Underlining the classical appeal of Bath is a summer festival with a strong emphasis on 18th-century music and drama.

Devon has not one, but two, holiday coasts, completely different in character. The rugged north coast faces the Atlantic, with surfing beaches around Woolacombe, towering cliffs at Ilfracombe, the leading north Devon seaside town, and thickly-wooded hills plunging into the sea around picturesque Lynton and Lynmouth. One of the most-visited spots on this coast is Clovelly, whose cobbled main street is so steep that it can be explored only on foot.

The south Devon coast is more gentle, almost Mediterranean in appearance, with rich red sandstone cliffs framing the intensely blue waters of Torbay. Torquay is perhaps the best-known of all the West Country resorts, and together with the neighboring seaside towns of Paignton and Brixham, is comprehensively promoting itself as a three-in-one resort under the name of Torbay. Farther west is the little port of Dartmouth, which figures in the story of the voyage of the *Mayflower.* Another port with *Mayflower* associations is the proud city of Plymouth, also famed for its links with Sir Francis Drake. Between the north and south coasts lie the high and empty hills of Dartmoor, crowned by gaunt granite outcrops known as "tors", and roamed by shaggy wild ponies. And to the east of Dartmoor, at the head of the Exe estuary, is the historic city of Exeter, complete with Elizabethan guildhall and great medieval cathedral.

Cornwall is the sharp end of the rocky wedge that is the West Country peninsula. The principal center on the Atlantic coast is Newquay, England's surfing capital, while Falmouth, its gardens bristling with palm trees, is the main resort on the Channel coast. From either one, you can visit all the regular Cornish haunts—St. Michael's Mount; the ruins of King Arthur's clifftop castle at Tintagel; the shark-angling port of Looe; St. Ives, part fishing port, part holiday resort and artist colony; and of course, the tumbled granite cliffs of Land's End, westernmost point of mainland England. Steamers and helicopters leave Penzance for the Isles of Scilly, for a day trip or longer stay.

PRACTICAL INFORMATION FOR THE SOUTHWEST

Hotels and Restaurants

BATH (Avon). *Kings Circus* (L), tel. 28288; 6 rooms with bath. Charming, unusual little hotel in immaculately restored town house. *Royal Crescent* (L), tel. 319090; 35 rooms with bath; in an elegant crescent, a luxurious hotel for sybarites. *Francis Hotel* (E), tel. 24257; 90 rooms with bath. Superb 18th-century spot in historic square. *Priory* (E), tel. 331922; 21 rooms with bath. Personally run, own pool and just outside town. *Lansdown Grove* (M), tel. 315891; 41 rooms, 38 with bath. Interesting views; quality restaurant.

Restaurants. *The Hole in the Wall* (E), tel. 25242, maintains consistently high standards; also has accommodations. *Moon and Sixpence* (M), tel. 60962. Stylish wine bar cum restaurant in delightful courtyard setting. *Woods* (M), tel. 314812. Interestingly varied menu. Try tea and scones—and the spring waters—in the *Pump Room* (I), tel. 66728, an historic setting with string quartet.

BRISTOL (Avon). *Dragonara* (E), tel. 20044; 210 rooms with bath. Squash and sauna, dancing most nights. *Grand* (E), tel. 291645; 180 rooms with bath. *Holiday Inn* (E), tel. 294281; 284 rooms with bath, heated pool and sauna. *Unicorn* (E), tel. 28055; 191 rooms with bath, overlooking the harbor.

Harveys Restaurant (E), tel. 277665. Long-standing reputation in ancient wine cellar. *Les Semailles* (E), tel. 686456, in the northern suburbs. *Rajdoot Restaurant* (M), tel. 28033. Good Indian food at reasonable prices.

DARTMOUTH (Devon). *Royal Castle* (M), tel. 2397; 20 rooms, 16 with bath, 4 with shower. 17th-century coaching inn, centrally sited on the quay.

DORCHESTER (Dorset). *Antelope* (M), tel. 3001; 22 rooms, 5 with bath. Former coaching inn with memories of the infamous Judge Jeffreys.

EVERSHOT (Dorset). *Summer Lodge* (M), tel. 424; 9 rooms with bath. Cosy, immaculate little hotel with excellent restaurant.

EXETER (Devon). *Buckerell Lodge* (M), tel. 52451; 54 rooms, all with bath. House dates back to the 12th-century. *Exeter Moat House* (M), tel. Topsham 5441; 44 rooms with bath.

FALMOUTH (Cornw.). *Greenbank* (M), tel. 312440; 40 rooms with bath. Overlooks the harbor with own landing stage. *Hotel St. Michael's* (M), tel. 312707; 75 rooms with bath or shower. Stands among superb gardens by beach, with sweeping views.

GLASTONBURY (Som.). *George and Pilgrim* (M), tel. 31146, 12 rooms, most with bath, has old-world charm and a few four poster beds. *No. 3* (E), tel. 32129 is a good small restaurant. Lunch only on Sun. Closed Mon.

HONITON (Devon). *Deer Park* (M), tel. 2064; 31 rooms, 27 with bath, at Weston, 2½ miles west of town; 200 years old, standing in wide grounds; trout fishing.

Home Farm Hotel (M), Wilmington, near Honiton, tel. Wilmington 278; 14 rooms, 7 with bath. Small, partially thatched, originally 17th-century farmhouse. Walks and golf, sea close by. Booking essential. Closed Jan. and Feb.

ISLES OF SCILLY (Cornw.). *Hotel Godolphin* (M); 31 rooms, 25 with bath. Excellent and popular holiday hotel run by Mumford family. Half pension only. Booking essential.

LYME REGIS (Dorset). *Alexandra* (M), tel. 2010; 26 rooms, 19 with bath. *Royal Lion* (M), tel. 2768; 19 rooms, 10 with bath. *Tudor House* (M), tel. 2472; 17 rooms, 4 with bath. Close to the sea; architecturally interesting. Closed mid-Oct. to mid-Mar.

LYNTON & LYNMOUTH (Devon). *Tors* at Lynmouth (M), tel. Lynton 53236; 39 rooms, 32 with bath. In spacious grounds with extensive sea views, heated pool. Closed Nov.–Feb.

Shelley's Cottage at Lynmouth (M), tel. Lynton 53219; 15 rooms. Overlooks the sea. Shelley wrote part of his *Queen Mab* here in 1812; closed Nov. to Feb.

PENZANCE (Cornw.). *The Abbey* (M), tel. 66906; 6 rooms with bath. Unconventional, stylish hotel, more like a private house. *Queens* (M), tel. 62371; 71 rooms with bath or shower. Views over Mounts Bay. *Yacht Inn* (I), tel. 62787; 8 rooms. Overlooks the sea, sauna.

PLYMOUTH (Devon). *Holiday Inn* (E), tel. 662866; 222 rooms with bath. One of the finest of the chain in the country; heated pool, sauna, dancing on Sat. *Mayflower Post House* (M-E), tel. 662828; 104 rooms with bath, heated pool. *Chez Nous* (E), tel. 266793. Informal restaurant with seafood specialties.

ST. IVES (Cornw.). *Tregenna Castle* (E), tel. 795254; 80 rooms, 59 with bath. British Transport hotel southeast of town; vast grounds and splendid sea views; excellent cuisine and impressive wine list. *Garrack* (M), tel. 796199; 21 rooms, 13 with bath. Quiet spot for a relaxed holiday.

TRURO (Cornw.). *Brookdale* (M), tel. 73513; 39 rooms, 23 with bath. Multi-national cuisine.

WELLS (Som.). *Swan* (M), tel. 78877; 32 rooms with bath or shower. Attractive old hotel beside cathedral. *White Hart* (M), tel. 72056; 14 rooms, 7 with bath. Opposite cathedral; good food and ambience.

Historic Houses and Museums

AVON. Claverton Manor, near Bath, contains one of the few American museums in Britain. Open late Mar.–Oct., daily 2–5 (except Mon.).

Clevedon Court, near Clevedon. 14th-century manor house with 18th-century gardens. Open Apr.–end Sept., Wed., Thurs., Sun. and Bank Holiday Mon., 2.30–5.30 (NT).

CORNWALL. Barbara Hepworth Museum, St Ives. The former home, studio and workshops of the famous sculptor. Open Mon.–Sat. 10–5.30 (to 4.30 in winter). Sun. 2–6 in summer.

Cotehele, Calstock. Fortified Elizabethan manor house on river Tamar where there is a mill workshop, shipping museum and reconstructed Tamar barge. Open Apr.–Oct., daily (except Fri.), 11–6. Garden open in winter to dusk (NT).

Godolphin House, Helston. Tudor house once belonging to Earls of Godolphin. Open May and June, Thurs., 2–5; July, Aug., Sept., Tues., Thurs., 2–5.

Lanhydrock, near Bodmin. 17th-century mansion in beautiful wooden valley and gardens. Apr.–Oct. 11–6. Gardens open in winter to dusk (NT).

St. Michael's Mount, Penzance. Home of Lord St. Levan. Open all year, Apr. and May, Mon.–Wed., and Fri.; June through Oct., Mon.–Fri., 10.30–4.45 (restricted tours in winter). (NT)

DEVON. Buckland Abbey, Tavistock. 13th-century Cistercian monastery, later home of Sir Francis Drake. Open Easter–Sept., Mon.–Sat., Bank Holidays, 11–6, Sun. 2–6. Winter, Wed., Sat., Sun., 2–5. (NT)

Powderham Castle, near Exeter. Medieval castle, home of Earl of Devon. Open late May–Sept., daily (except Fri. and Sat.), 2–5.30.

Tiverton Museum, Tiverton. One of the best and most wide-ranging folk museums in the West Country. Open Mon.–Sat. 10.30–4.30.

DORSET. Athelhampton, near Puddletown. Splendid stone-built medieval house with enchanting gardens. Open Apr.–early Oct., Wed., Thurs., Sun., Bank Holidays, 2–6; also Mon. and Tues. in Aug.

Corfe Castle. Historic 10th-century ruin in village of the same name. Open 10–6 daily, Winter, Sat. and Sun. 12–4.

SOMERSET. Barrington Court, near Ilminster. Beautiful 16th-century Tudor mansion and gardens. Open Apr. through Sept., Wed. 2–5 (House), Sun.–Wed. 2–5.30 (Gardens), (NT).

Montacute House, Yeovil. Elizabethan house. Permanent collection of paintings (in Long Gallery) from National Portrait Gallery. Open Apr.–Oct., daily (except Tues.), 12.30–6 (NT).

East Anglia

This was the name of the ninth-century Saxon kingdom on the east coast of England. Today it refers to the counties of Essex, Suffolk, Norfolk, Cambridgeshire and Lincolnshire, all within the area bounded by the Thames, the Wash and the North Sea, and east of the railroad line from London to Doncaster. Time is said to have had less effect upon Norfolk than anywhere else in the British Isles, and though Suffolk is already becoming an overspill for London, the area is still largely agricultural. The Norfolk Broads (over a hundred square miles of rivers and lakes) are a unique sailing and cabin-cruising holiday playground which is unfortunately currently threatened by serious water pollution problems. The translucent light is ideal for painters— East Anglia produced Gainsborough and Constable. If you are not traveling by car, a good network of buses covers the area, taking you through delightful villages on the way.

Dominating the flat, far-spreading East Anglian farms and fenlands are three ancient cathedral cities—Ely, Norwich and Lincoln. Ely was the last stronghold of the Saxons under Hereward the Wake, who defied the Normans until 1072. Norwich not only has a fine Norman cathedral, but also 30 other medieval churches and an outstanding collection of paintings in the city's old Castle Keep, mainly of the Norwich School. Lincoln's triple-towered cathedral is one of the supreme architectural glories of Britain; it also contains one of the original drafts of *Magna Carta.*

Other historic East Anglian towns are Colchester, renowned for its oysters, roses and Roman treasures; Bury St. Edmunds, which has an interesting cathedral, market square and abbey ruins; and Ipswich, county town of Suffolk, where you should seek out the Christchurch Mansion, a museum of folk art and antiques.

But in between the big cities, lying like tight little islands in a sea of cornfields and meadows, are the small towns and villages in which you will capture the true feel of East Anglia. Places like Lavenham and Long Melford, with their timbered inns and handsome churches; Kersey, where you drive through a watersplash in the main street; the

Essex village of Finchingfield, dreaming around its duckpond and village green; and the little coastal town of Aldeburgh, which stages a famous music festival, founded by Benjamin Britten, each year in June, the high point of a year-round program of concert series.

Seventeen miles south of Ely is Cambridge, seat of the great university. Most tourists find it more charming than Oxford, which, as they say, "is a university in a town" whereas "Cambridge is a town in a university." You can't miss King's College Chapel, one of the greatest examples of ecclesiastical architecture in existence. See Trinity College gateway and Great Court, and stroll along the "Backs," the lawns and gardens which extend behind the colleges to the River Cam. See also St. John's College (1511), one of the most beautiful; Magdalene, with its 17th-century library given by Samuel Pepys; Jesus College, in the 12th-century Benedictine abbey of St. Radegund, and Christ's College (1436), with its beautiful gardens and associations with John Milton.

PRACTICAL INFORMATION FOR EAST ANGLIA

Hotels and Restaurants

ALDEBURGH (Suffolk). *Brudenell* (M), tel. 2071; 47 rooms with bath. *Wentworth* (M), tel. 2312, 33 rooms, 20 with bath. *Uplands* (M), tel. 2420; 19 rooms, 7 with bath. An 18th-century house. At **Snape Maltings**. *Plough and Sail* (I), tel. 413. For real ale, cider, and local game in the restaurant.

BURY ST. EDMUNDS (Suffolk). *Angel* (M), tel. 3926; 43 rooms, 38 with bath. Faces the Abbey gardens; good English dining. *Suffolk* (M), tel. 3995; 41 rooms, 13 with bath, is friendly.

CAMBRIDGE (Cambs.). Excellent bedrooms at the well-established *Garden House* (E), tel. 63421; 117 rooms with bath. *Blue Boar* (M), tel. 63121; 48 rooms, 11 with bath, pleasant and central. *University Arms* (M), tel. 351241; 114 rooms, all with bath. Well-run centrally located hotel. The *Fort St. George* (I), tel. 354327, is a good pub. Agreeable meals and facilities for children.
Panos (M), tel. 212958. Friendly spot serving Greek and French specialties. *Peking* (M), tel. 354755. Excellent Chinese cuisine. *Xanadu* (M), tel. 311678. Interesting Continental and vegetarian cooking in former private club.

DEDHAM (Essex). *Maison Talbooth* (L), tel. 0206 322367; 10 rooms with bath. A truly individual hotel in the country house tradition of hospitality and friendship. Their *Le Talbooth* (E), restaurant, tel. 0206 323150, offers superb flavors, subtly spun in an ancient weaver's cottage. (A member of the *Relais de Campagne*.) *Dedham Vale* (E), tel. 0206 322273; 6 rooms, all with bath, has friendly resident owners and fine food.

ELY (Cambs.). *The Lamb* (M), tel. 3574; 32 rooms. A superb old Georgian coaching inn well worth a visit.
Try the *Old Fire Engine House* (M), tel. 2582, for traditional fare.

FELIXSTOWE (Suffolk). *Orwell Moat House* (M), tel. 5511; 62 rooms, 53 with bath. Attractive grounds; excellent value.

IPSWICH (Suffolk). *Post House* (M), tel. 212313; 118 rooms with bath. *Belstead Brook* (E), tel. 684241; 33 rooms with bath.

KING'S LYNN (Norfolk). *Duke's Head* (M), tel. 774996; 72 rooms with bath. Has excellent restaurant; fine old building on main square.

LAVENHAM (Suffolk). *Swan* (M), tel. 247477; 42 rooms with bath. An atmospheric Elizabethan inn.

NEWMARKET (Suffolk). *Rutland Arms* (M), tel. 664251; 49 rooms, 41 with bath. *Bedford Lodge Hotel* (M), tel. 663175; 14 rooms, 8 with bath. A favorite with the racing fraternity.

Just outside at Six Mile Bottom is *Swynford Paddock Hotel and Restaurant* (L), tel. 063870 234; 15 rooms with bath. A must for horse fanciers, situated in an actual stud with visits to stables and Jockey Club nearby.

NORWICH (Norfolk). *Maid's Head,* (M), tel. 628821; 80 rooms, 69 with bath, 11 with shower, where Elizabeth I once slept. *Nelson* (M), tel. 628612; 122 rooms with bath, celebrates the county hero. *Norwich* (M), tel. 410431; 102 rooms with bath. Excellent amenities and friendly host.

Marco's (E), tel. 624044, for Italian dining.

Shipdham Place (M), near Thetford, tel. 0362 820303. 17th-century rectory run by Justin and Melanie de Blank. 6 rooms all with bath. Excellent restaurant. Feb. and weekdays Jan.

WOODBRIDGE (Suffolk). *Seckford Hall* (M), tel. 5678; 24 rooms, 22 with bath. Blends original Tudor with modern comfort and personal service. Beautiful grounds.

Historic Houses and Museums

CAMBRIDGESHIRE. Anglesey Abbey, near Cambridge. Elizabethan manor house incorporating 13th-century monastic undercroft and 100-acre gardens. May–Oct., Wed.–Sun., Bank Holidays, 1.30–5.30; also Sat., Sun. and Bank Holiday Mon. in Apr. (NT)

ESSEX. Audley End House, near Saffron Walden. Jacobean mansion in original condition and setting. Open Apr.–Sept., daily (except Mon.), 1–5.30. Open Bank Holiday Mon.

St. Osyth's Priory, St. Osyth. Perhaps the finest monastic remains in Britain, the Priory was an Augustinian abbey for 400 years—until the monasteries were dissolved by Henry VIII. Also contains art collection. Open Easter, May–Sept., daily, 10–5.

NORFOLK. Castle Museum, Norwich. Archeology, natural history and fine paintings of the Norwich school. Open weekdays, 10–5, Sun., 2–5.

Castle Rising, near King's Lynn. Superb Norman castle with Roman ditches. Open mid-Mar.–mid-Oct., daily 9.30–6.30; winter until 4; opens Sun., Apr.–Sept., at 9.30, otherwise at 2.

Holkham Hall, Wells. Palladian mansion. Open June–Sept., Sun., Mon., Thurs., also Wed. in July and Aug., 1.30–5. June–Sept., Sun., 2–5.

Sainsbury Centre for Visual Arts, Norwich. Permanent collection of ethnographic, modern and pre-Columbian, ancient and medieval design. Also houses the University of East Anglia's art collection. Open daily (except Mon.), 2–5.

Sandringham House, Sandringham. Home of H.M. the Queen. House and gardens open Apr.–Sept., Mon.–Thurs. 11–4.45, Sun. 12–4.45, except when Royal Family is in residence.

SUFFOLK. Ickworth House, near Bury St Edmunds. Late Regency. Open May–Sept., daily (except Mon. and Thurs) and Bank Holiday Mon, 1.30–5.30 (NT).

Melford Hall, Long Melford. Tudor mansion with Regency interiors. Open Apr. through Sept., Wed., Thurs., Sun., Bank Holiday Mon. 2–6.

Somerleyton Hall, near Lowestoft. Tudor mansion, rebuilt in 1846. 12 acres of grounds with maze and miniature railway. Open Apr. through Sept., Sun., Thurs., Bank Holidays, also Tues., Wed. in July and Aug. 2–5.30.

The Midlands and Shakespeare Country

The tourist center for any exploration of the English Midland shires is Stratford-upon-Avon in Warwickshire, the very heart of England. The town is a shrine, and you will feel very close to Shakespeare when you see his birthplace in Henley Street, his baptismal record in Holy Trinity Church, his grave with its mysterious epitaph which has stimulated such flights of speculation, Anne Hathaway's Cottage at nearby Shottery, and, of course, the riverside theater home of the Royal Shakespeare Company. But even without these Shakespearian links, the town of Stratford would attract visitors with the charm of its half-timbered houses and its strong connections with America—Harvard House in High Street, built in 1596 by the grandfather of John Harvard (who bequeathed half his estate and a library to the college that bears his name) and the *Red Horse Inn,* where Washington Irving worked on his *Sketch Book.*

In addition to these historic houses, here are some of the places to watch for in your exploration of the Midlands—Warwick Castle, now owned by Tussaud's, the waxworks people, and a superb example of an English castle; Kenilworth, the romantic, ruined castle immortalized by Walter Scott, not far from Warwick; Leamington Spa, a pleasant watering place on a tributary of the Avon, famous for its mineral springs since the Middle Ages; Sherwood Forest, north of Nottingham, heart of the Robin Hood country; Nottingham Castle, built on a rock honeycombed by caves; Eastwood, the birthplace of D.H. Lawrence; Derbyshire's idyllic wooded limestone dales and historic houses, notably medieval Haddon Hall, Elizabethan Hardwick Hall and 18th-century Chatsworth, the "Palace of the Peak".

Also: Lichfield, with its cathedral, whose three spires are called the "Ladies of the Vale", and the house where the celebrated Dr. Johnson was born in 1709, now a museum. Shrewsbury, with its great wealth of magpie-colored houses, dominated by its red sandstone castle. For fans of A. E. Housman, there is the Shropshire town of Ludlow, with its black-and-white houses and great castle, and "Clunton, Clunbury, Clungunford and Clun, the quietest places under the sun".

The city of Worcester, with its ancient buildings and cathedral, still embracing part of the monastery founded in the seventh century by monks from the Yorkshire Abbey of Whitby. Malvern, renowned for its 11th-century Norman priory church and its fine views over tranquil, low-lying countryside.

Hereford, a lovely old shire town still sleeping beside the River Wye. Its magnificent cathedral contains the *Mappa Mundi,* one of the oldest maps of the world in existence. Hereford is the heart of that beautiful area between the Malvern Hills and the uplands of the Welsh Border, with its rich farmlands and matchless black-and-white villages, one of which, Hay on Wye (just inside Wales), is a center for the book trade and houses the world's largest second-hand bookshop.

PRACTICAL INFORMATION FOR THE MIDLANDS

Hotels and Restaurants

BIRMINGHAM (W. Midlands). *Albany* (E), Smallbrook, Queensway, tel. 021–643 8171; 254 rooms, all with bath. International cuisine, sports/leisure club, multi-story adjacent car-park. *Metropole & Warwick* (E), National Exhibition Center hotel, tel. 021–780 4242; 700 rooms, all with bath; 13 miles outside the city—Shakespeare country easily accessible from here. *Grand* (M), tel. 021–236 7951, facing the Cathedral; 188 rooms with bath; international cuisine. *Holiday Inn* (M), Broad St., tel. 021–643 2766; 304 rooms, all with bath. Motorists' hotel with heated pool and sauna.

Two good restaurants are *La Cappanna* (M), Hurst St., tel. 021–622 2287, excellent standard Italian fare, closed Sun.; and *Lorenzo's* (M), Park St, tel. 021–643 0541, friendly Italian restaurant for a reasonable lunch, closed Sun.

COVENTRY (W. Midlands). *De Vere* (E), tel. 51851; 215 rooms with bath. Central and up-to-date. *Leofric* (M), tel. 21371; 90 rooms with bath. Modern, popular with local people
Chase Crest (M), tel. 303398; 68 rooms with bath. Refurbished, popular hotel on London road A423 (5 miles).

DERBY (Derbys.). *Midland* (M) (a British Transport hotel), tel. 45894; 63 rooms, 39 with bath. *Pennine* (M), tel. 41741; 100 rooms, 56 with bath, 44 with shower.

GREAT MALVERN (Heref. and Worcs.). *Abbey* (M), tel. 3325; 107 rooms, 86 with bath, 21 with shower. Ivy-clad hotel beside the medieval abbey gateway. *Cottage in the Wood* (M), tel. 06845 3487; 20 rooms with bath. Highly recommended. Attractive views, good dining room and pleasant service. *Walmer Lodge* (M), tel. 4139; 9 rooms, 4 with bath, 3 with shower. Comfortable, friendly; good food.

HEREFORD (Heref. and Worcs.). *Effy's* (M), tel. 59754. Imaginative, interesting cooking. Closed Sun. *Green Dragon* (M), tel. 272506; 88 rooms with bath. A reliable establishment near the Cathedral.

LEAMINGTON SPA (Warwicks.). *Manor House* (M), tel. 23251; 53 rooms, most with bath. Delightful gardens down to river.

LEDBURY (Heref. and Worcs.). *Hope End* (M), tel. 3613; 7 rooms with bath. Delightful country hotel with reputable restaurant.

LEICESTER (Leics.). *Post House* (M), tel. 896688; 179 rooms with bath (3 miles out). *Holiday Inn* (M), tel. 531161; 190 rooms with bath, heated pool.

LINCOLN (Lincs.). *White Hart* (E), tel. 26222; 68 rooms, 52 with bath. Hotel with an air of history. Friendly staff and good, local food. Must book. *Wig and Mitre* (I), tel. 35190; low beams and homespun decor are an excellent background to this pub's magnificent bar meals and wines.

LUDLOW (Salop). *Feathers* (E), tel. 5261; 35 rooms, all with bath. Famous historic hotel, Elizabethan architecture at its best.

NOTTINGHAM (Notts.). *Albany* (E), tel. 470131; 160 rooms with bath. Good Carvery restaurant. *Post House* (M), tel. 397800, 106 rooms, is consistent. *La Grenouille* (M), tel. 411088, is strong on the 'Bistrophere'.

OAKHAM (Leics.). *Hambledon Hall* (L), tel. 56991; 15 rooms with bath. Beautifully appointed mansion with splendid restaurant.

ROSS ON WYE (Heref. and Worcs.). *Pengethley Hotel* (E), tel. 098987 211; 20 rooms, all with bath. Georgian house in peaceful countryside with excellent food.

SHREWSBURY (Salop). *Lion* (M), tel. 53107; 60 rooms, all with bath.
Try the *Penny Farthing* restaurant (M), tel. 56119. Consistently good dining in cottage atmosphere.

STRATFORD-UPON-AVON (Warwicks.). *Ettington Park* (L), tel. 740740; 49 rooms with bath. Lavishly restored Victorian mansion near Stratford; now a leading hotel with fine restaurant. *Alveston Manor* (E), tel. 204581; 116 rooms with bath. A 16th-cent. manor house with great atmosphere. *Billesley Manor* (E), tel. Alcester 763737. 28 rooms with bath. 16th-century, with antique furniture and oak panelling. Restaurant specializing in English country cooking and French *nouvelle cuisine*. *Moat House International* (E), tel. 67511; 253 rooms with bath. Modern luxury, plus a super location right by the river and looking over at the theater. *Shakespeare* (E), tel. 294771; 66 rooms with bath. Older than the Bard himself, with friendly bars. *Welcombe* (E), tel. 295252; 84 rooms with bath. Newly decorated. Good base. *Falcon* (M), tel. 20577; 73 rooms with bath. Half Elizabethan, half modern. Very central. *Stratford House* (M), tel. 68288; 9 rooms, 7 with bath. Friendly little Georgian town house close to theater.

Good restaurants are surprisingly scarce. There are lots of 'eateries', but try *Hill's* (E), 3 Greenhill St., tel. 293563, for imaginative cooking. The *Dirty Duck* is good for an after-dinner drink and also pre- and post-theater pub meals.

Nearby **Wilmcote** (4 miles) is well worth the drive for lunch at the *Swan House* (I), tel. Stratford-upon-Avon 67030; 11 rooms, 3 with bath.

WARWICK (Warwicks.). *Woolpack* (M), tel. 496191; 29 rooms, 16 with bath or shower. Atmosphere and history. *Lord Leycester* (M), tel. 491481; 47 rooms with bath or shower. Both hotels tend to be dominated by coach parties in the high season.

WORCESTER (Heref. and Worcs.). *Giffard* (M), tel. 27155; 104 rooms, all with bath. Good view of the cathedral from the dining room. Or riverside views from the simpler *Diglis* (M), tel. 353518; 15 rooms, 4 with shower.

Historic Houses and Museums

HEREFORD AND WORCESTER. Croft Castle, near Leominster. Continuously inhabited by the Croft family for 900 years, mentioned in Domesday. Open May.–Sept., Wed.–Sun. Bank Holiday Mons., 2–6; April and Oct., Sat., Sun., and Bank Holidays, 2–5. (NT)

Dyson Perrins Museum of Worcester Porcelain, Worcester. Best collection of old Worcester in the world. Open Mon.–Fri., 9.30–5; also Apr.–Sept., Sat.

LEICESTERSHIRE. Belvoir Castle near Grantham. Present building is stupendous Victorian Gothic. Seat of the Dukes of Rutland since Tudor times. Special events such as medieval jousting on Sundays. Open late Mar.–Oct., Tues.–Thurs. and Sat., 12–6, Sun. 12–7; also Bank Holiday Mon. 11–7 and Sun. in Oct., 2–6.

Bosworth Battlefield. Site of famous 1485 battle, with imaginative new visitor center. Open Easter–Oct., Mon.–Sat. 2–5.30, Sun. and Bank Holidays 1–6.

LINCOLNSHIRE. Tattershall Castle, near Woodhall Spa. One of the finest brick fortified houses; 100-ft.-high keep remains. Marvelous Fenland views from the top. Open Easter–end Oct., daily 11–6.30; winter 12–6 or sunset; Sun. 1–6.30. (NT)

NORTHAMPTONSHIRE. Althorp, Northampton, 16th–18th-century home of the Spencers. Open daily all year, 1.30–5.30 (June–Aug. and Bank Holidays 11–5.30).

Burghley House, near Stamford. Elizabethan mansion of the Marquess of Exeter. Open Apr.–Oct., daily 11–5. Annual horse trials in the fall.

Rockingham Castle, near Kettering. Medieval and Elizabethan house. Open Easter–Sept., Thurs., Sun., Bank Holiday Mon. and Tues.; Tues. in Aug., 2–6.

Sulgrave Manor, near Banbury. Home of George Washington's ancestors. Feb.–Dec., daily except Wed., 10.30–1, 2–5.30 (to 4 in Jan.).

NOTTINGHAMSHIRE. Newstead Abbey, north of Nottingham. Byron relics in 12th-century priory. Open Easter–Sept., daily 1.45–6. Garden daily all year, 10–dusk.

Wollaton Hall Natural History Museum, Nottingham. Elizabethan mansion with insect gallery, geological collection and fine gardens. Open Apr.–Sept., Mon.–Sat. 10–7, Sun. 2–5; Oct.–Mar. 10–dusk, Sun. 1.30–4.30.

SHROPSHIRE. Ironbridge Gorge Museum, Telford. This fascinating museum, mainly open-air and including the famous bridge built in 1779, is a must for anyone interested in the early history of the industrial revolution. Open daily from 10.

Stokesay Castle, Craven Arms, 13th-century moated manor house. Open Apr.–Sept., daily (except Tues.) 10–6; early Mar. and Oct. 10–5.

Weston Park, nr. Shifnal, Staffs. Built in 1671, one of the finest examples of Restoration architecture. Extensive gardens designed by Capability Brown. Open Apr., May and Sept., weekends and Bank Holidays only; June–Aug., daily 11–7 (last admission 5). Parties at any time, by arrangement.

 THE SHAKESPEARE BIRTHPLACE TRUST PROPERTIES. Inclusive ticket admitting you to all five properties costs around £4. Each of these properties can be visited for between £1 and £1.50. **Shakespeare's Birthplace,** Henley St. Open Apr.–Oct. Mon.–Sat. 9–6, Sun. 10–6 (to 5 in Oct.); Nov.–Mar. Mon.–Sat. as Birthplace, except closed Sun. in winter. Sun. 1.30–4.30. **Anne Hathaway's Cottage,** Shottery. Open same times as for Shakespeare's Birthplace. **Hall's Croft,** Old Town. Open Apr.–Oct. 9–6, Sun. 2–6; Nov.–Mar. 9–4 (closed Sun.). **New Place,** Chapel St. Open same times as Hall's Croft. **Mary Arden's House,** Wilmcote. Open same times as Hall's Croft.

Seats for performances at *The Royal Shakespeare Theatre* on the banks of the Avon can be reserved in advance at any office of *Keith Prowse,* London, or at the box office at Stratford (tel. 0789 295623). Reservable seats cost about £5 to £15. For details of "Shakespeare Stopover" packages call 0789–295333; and for "Guide Friday," a local tour operator with some tours starting in London, call 0789–294466.

The North, Scenic and Historic

The long ridge of hills running through northern England from the Scottish border to the Midlands shires is known as the Pennine Chain. English schoolchildren learn to speak of it as "the backbone of England". Here you will find a varied countryside, ranging in interest from the wild Yorkshire moorlands immortalized in *Wuthering Heights* to the medieval walled cities of York and Chester, the bustling industrial hives of Manchester and Liverpool, and the romantic ruins of Fountains Abbey, near Ripon.

Richmond Castle, with its perfect Norman keep, is one of the noblest medieval fortifications in the land; York Minster, the biggest medieval cathedral in England (badly damaged by fire in fall 1984)—and York itself is full of attractive historic buildings; Durham cathedral; Whitby, one of the glories of the Yorkshire coast, with the gaunt ruins of Whitby Abbey lowering over the North Sea, and the grand headlands of the Northumberland coast, crowned with ancient castles like Dunstanburgh and Bamburgh which overlook some of the finest sandy beaches in Britain. The early Christian shrine of Holy Island, accessible by low-tide causeway, also lies along this wild coast.

A mecca for American visitors lies between Durham and Newcastle. It is the little village of Washington, with the ancestral home of George Washington, Washington Old Hall, a 17th-century manor house (parts of which go back to 1183).

Chester was founded by the Romans in A.D. 70 as a military camp (*castra,* which became Chester). It is completely encircled by its medieval walls, and a walk around those walls will bring you closer to the Middle Ages than anything we can think of unless it's a shopping expedition in the city's medieval Rows, arcaded, timber-framed two-story shops, unique in England. But avoid office-hours if you just want to sightsee, as the place is seriously crowded with traffic.

PRACTICAL INFORMATION FOR THE NORTH
Hotels and Restaurants

BERWICK-UPON-TWEED (Northumb.). *King's Arms* (M), tel. 307454; 36 rooms, all with bath or shower. Good touring center (Holy Island a few miles south). *Turret House* (M), tel. 7344; 11 rooms, 6 with bath. Small but good.

BLANCHLAND (Northumb.). *Lord Crewe Arms* (M), tel. 251; 8 rooms, 6 with bath; 7 more rooms with bath in annex. In one of the loveliest villages in England, this delightful hotel has been converted from the remains of the 13th-century Blanchland Abbey.

BRADFORD (West Yorks.). *Stakis Norfolk Gardens* (M), tel. 734734; 125 rooms with bath, sauna, disco. *Cottage Restaurant* (M), tel. 832752.

CARLISLE (Cumbria). *Carlisle Crest* (M), tel. 31201; 160 rooms with bath. Modern hotel at junction A7/M6. *Central,* (M), tel. 20256; 83 rooms, 21 with bath.
At **Brampton,** *Farlam Hall* (L), tel. 06976 234; 13 rooms in attractive 17th-century manor house with own grounds and interesting restaurant.

CHESTER (Ches.). *Grosvenor* (L), tel. 24024; 100 rooms, all with bath. Splendid Victorian place with excellent food and comfortable amenities. Wise to book. *Mollington Banastre* (E), tel. 851471; 72 rooms with bath. Expertly run in extensive grounds. *Queens* (M), tel. 28341; 91 rooms, all with bath. Victorian hotel handy for station and city center.
Pippa's In Town (M), tel. 313721, is a pleasant French restaurant. Children welcome. *The Bear and Billet* (I), tel. 21272, is a lovely old pub serving excellent bar snacks including Dee salmon in season.

DURHAM (Durham). *Ramside Hall* (M), tel. 65282; 11 rooms, 5 with bath. Old country house set in its own park. *Royal County* (M), tel. 66821; 122 rooms with bath. Pleasant modernized coaching inn, sauna and restaurant. *Squire Trelawny* (M), tel. 720613. Good choice of dishes.

HARROGATE (N. Yorks.). *Majestic* (E), tel. 68972; 160 rooms, all with bath (Trust House Forte). *Old Swan* (E), tel. 500055; 143 rooms, all with bath, wide grounds, tennis. *Oliver Restaurant* (M), tel. 68600. Attractive spot near conference center, serving good range of continental specialties.

LEEDS (W. Yorks.). *Dragonara* (E), tel. 442000; 234 rooms, 204 with bath, 30 with shower. Modern and businesslike, cabaret twice a week. *Merrion* (M), tel. 439191; 120 rooms with bath; and *Metropole* (M), tel. 450841; 113 rooms, 76 with bath; both modern and dependable.
Gardini's Terrazza (E), tel. 432880. Smart Italian restaurant worth a visit for its interesting menu.

LIVERPOOL (Merseys.). *Britannia Adelphi* (M), tel. 051–709 7200; 350 rooms, 320 with bath or shower. One of England's famous hotels, well recommended, but choose your room carefully; restaurant is suave and famous. *Holiday Inn* (M), tel. 051–709 0181; 258 rooms with bath, heated pool and sauna.

MANCHESTER (Gtr. Manchester). *Midland* (E), tel. 061–236 3333; 302 rooms, 274 with bath (British Transport), one of *the* hotels in Britain, with an air of peaceful elegance, sauna; French restaurant. *Piccadilly* (E), tel. 061–236 8414; 250 rooms with bath. An efficient skyscraper hotel, with wonderful views from famous restaurant. Book early for all Manchester hotels.
Sam's Chop House (M), tel. 061–834 1526; dinner not served; for solid sensible fare. *Yang Sung* (M), tel. 061–236 2200. Popular basement restaurant serving excellent Cantonese food. Can be crowded.

NANTWICH (Cheshire). *Rookery Hall* (E), tel. 626866; 11 rooms, all with bath; tranquil grounds, magnificent food and antiques.

NEWCASTLE-UPON-TYNE (Tyne and Wear). *Gosforth Park Thistle* (E), tel. 091–236 4111; 178 rooms with bath. In parkland north of city center. *Osborne* (M), tel. 091–281 4778; 25 rooms, 1 with bath, 9 with shower.
For a superb meal, try *Michelangelo* (M), King. St. (tel. 614415).

SCARBOROUGH (North Yorks.). Hotels match the old-world elegance of this magnificent seaside town. *Holbeck Hall* (E), tel. 374374; 30 rooms, all with bath, is truly gracious. *Royal* (M), tel. 364333; 137 rooms, 102 with bath, 30 with shower, is really grand. Eat at the *Lanterna Ristorante* (M), tel. 363616, for serious Italiano among crowded tables.

SHEFFIELD (S. Yorks.). *Grosvenor House* (E), tel. 20041; 103 rooms with bath. *Hallam Tower* (M), tel. 686031; 135 rooms with bath. Both are Trust House Forte. *Royal Victoria* (M), tel. 78822; 64 rooms, 37 with bath (British Transport).
At the *Crucible Theatre,* tel. 760621, there is, apart from excellent stage productions, a worthwhile restaurant (closed on Sun.).

YORK (North Yorks.). *Middlethorpe Hall* (L), tel. 641241; 30 rooms with bath. Restored historic mansion overlooking York racecourse. *Judges Lodging* (E), tel. 38733; 13 rooms with bath. Delightful Georgian town house. *Viking* (E), tel. 59822; 187 rooms with bath. *Chase* (M), tel. 707171; 80 rooms, 63 with bath. Friendly, well-appointed hotel. *Giovanni's* (M), tel. 23539; good Italian restaurant (closed Mon.).

Historic Houses and Museums

DERBYSHIRE. Chatsworth, near Bakewell. Magnificent 17th-century home of the Dukes of Devonshire. House and garden open April–Oct., daily 11:30–4:30, farmyard open daily, Apr.–Sept. 10.30–4.30.
Haddon Hall, Bakewell. Medieval home of Duke of Rutland. Open Apr.–Sept., Tues.–Sat., 11–6. Closed Sun. in July.
Hardwick Hall, near Chesterfield. Splendid Elizabethan house built by "Bess of Hardwick." Open Apr.–Oct., Wed., Thurs., Sat., Sun., Bank Holiday Mon., 1–5:30 or sunset. Garden open daily in season, 12–5.30. (NT)
Kedleston Hall, Derby. Splendid Robert Adam house in 500 acre park. Open Easter; Sun. end Apr.–Sept., 2–6; most Bank Holidays Mon.–Tues. 1–5.30.

DURHAM AND TYNE AND WEAR. Bowes Museum, Barnard Castle, Co. Durham. Imposing Victorian "chateau"; fabulous collection of Spanish pictures, many fine objets d'art. Open all year 10–5.30 (Sun. 2–5), to 4 or 5 in winter.
Washington Old Hall, near Sunderland. Jacobean manor house, with portions of 12th-century house of the Washington family. Open May–Sept., daily except Fri., 11–5; Easter weekend, Wed., Sat. and Sun. in Apr. and Oct. (NT)

GREATER MANCHESTER. Manchester City Art Gallery, Mosley St., Manchester 2. English and French paintings. Fine collections of Stubbs, pre-Raphaelites, Henry Moore. Open weekdays 10–6, Sun. 2–6.
Museum of Science and Industry, Liverpool Rd. Large new museum at world's oldest passenger rail station. Open daily 10.30–5. Exciting Air and Space Museum opposite.

HUMBERSIDE. Burton Agnes Hall, near Bridlington. Fine Elizabethan house with collection of antique furniture. Impressionist and modern paintings. Open Easter, Apr. through Oct., daily 11–5.
Sledmere House, Driffield. Grand Georgian house with furniture, paintings, fine library, gardens by Capability Brown. Outstandingly beautiful interior. Open May–Sept., daily (except Mon. and Fri.) 1.30–5.30, also Easter weekend, Bank Holidays and Suns. in Apr. and Oct.

NORTHUMBERLAND. Alnwick Castle, Alnwick, 12th-century home of the Duke of Northumberland. Medieval fortifications. Open May–early Oct., daily (except Sat.), 1–5 (last adm. 4.30).

Lindisfarne Castle, Holy Island. Romantic 16th-century castle on lovely island accessible by low-tide causeway. Open May–Sept., daily (except Fri.) 11–5; also Easter week, Wed., Sat. and Sun. in Apr., weekends in Oct. (NT)

YORKSHIRE (NORTH, SOUTH AND WEST). Castle Howard, near York. Palatial 18th-century house by Sir John Vanbrugh for the 3rd Earl of Carlisle, with pictures, furniture, costume galleries. Open Easter–Oct., daily from 11.

Harewood House, near Leeds, 18th-century home of the Earls of Harewood, with Chippendale furniture. Exotic bird garden in grounds. Open Apr.–Oct., daily from 11. Limited opening Nov., Feb. and Mar.

Jorvik Viking Centre, York. Viking York memorably brought to life. Open Apr.–Oct., daily 9–7. Also the outstanding **York Castle Museum,** open Apr.–Sept., daily 9.30–6.30 (Sun. 10–6.30); winter 9.30–5.

HADRIAN'S WALL. The Northumbria Tourist Board, 9 Osborne Terrace, Jesmond, Newcastle, can supply publications on the wall. Be sure to visit the excavations at Vindolanda, the Roman army settlement west of Hexham, about 30 miles from Newcastle, and the magnificent Housesteads fort. The trip along the length of the Wall makes a fascinating experience for those interested in modern archeology.

The Lake District

The famous English Lake District, in the county of Cumbria, still has the peace which attracted Wordsworth, although its roads are now heavily congested on summer weekends. The entire area, with its hills and calm lakes, is preserved as a National Park, and it has been consecrated in the dreams of the poets. Wordsworth spent 60 years here. Gray found the region enchanting, and so did Coleridge, De Quincey, Shelly, Keats, Scott, Carlyle and Tennyson. So if you are looking for a few days or weeks of Wordsworthian wandering among hills, vales and somnolent villages, you can count on enough tranquility in which to recollect a whole lifetime of emotion. If you are carless and don't especially hanker to go about on foot as Wordsworth did, the National Bus Company (National Travel) obligingly services the main towns and outlying villages of the Lake District, and steamers run on Lake Windermere and Ullswater during the summer months.

PRACTICAL INFORMATION FOR THE LAKE DISTRICT

Hotels and Restaurants

AMBLESIDE. *Rothay Manor* (E), tel. 33605; 16 rooms with bath. Lovely spot with superb restaurant and warm hospitality. Must book. *Kirkstone Foot Country House* (M), tel. 32232; 14 rooms, 12 with bath. Beautiful 17th-century building with excellent restaurant. *Langdales* (M), tel. 09667 253; 20 rooms, 16 with bath, well situated at Chapel Stile for hearty walkers with hearty appetites.

COCKERMOUTH. *Trout* (M), tel. 823591; 16 rooms, 15 with bath or shower. Comfortable rooms and good food. *Wordsworth* (M), tel. 822757; 18 rooms, 4 with bath. An old inn beside the River Cocker.

CONISTON. Beautifully situated *Sun* (M), tel. 41248; 10 rooms. Wonderful view of mountain scenery in all directions.

GRASMERE. *Michael's Nook* (L), tel. 496; 10 rooms, all with bath. A highly individualistic establishment of great charm; a competent restaurant. *Swan* (M), tel. 551; 41 rooms, 25 with bath, was visited by Sir Walter Scott and Words-worth. *White Moss House* (M), tel. 295; 6 rooms with bath; superb cooking.

KENDAL. *Woolpack* (M), tel. 23852; 58 rooms, all with bath or shower. So called because its bar was once a wool trade auction room.

KESWICK. *Underscar* (L), tel. 72469; 18 rooms with bath or shower. Attrac-tive Italianate country house in own grounds. *Derwentwater* (M), tel. 72538; 42 rooms, 34 with bath. *Red House* (M), tel. 72211; 23 rooms, 16 with bath. Lovely mountain views. *Royal Oak* (M), tel. 72965; 43 rooms, 22 with bath.

POOLEY BRIDGE. *Sharrow Bay* (L), (1¾ miles S) tel. 301; 12 rooms, 7 with bath, annex has 17 rooms, 15 with bath. Justly-acquired outstanding reputation for cooking. Well-appointed bedrooms. *Leeming on Ullswater* (E), tel. 444; 24 rooms. Immaculate Georgian manor house with gardens leading down to lake.

WINDERMERE. *Belsfield* (E), tel. 2448; 66 rooms, 30 with bath, 16 with shower. Imposing 19th-century building overlooking the lake at Bowness ferry. Heated pool. *Langdale Chase* (E), tel. 0966 32201; 35 rooms, 31 with bath, beautifully furnished country house. John Tovey's *Miller Howe* (E), tel. 2536; 13 rooms, all with bath, represents an expert combination of comfort and superbly original cooking. Staying here is an experience. *Old England* (E), tel. 2444; 84 rooms with bath, comfortable and right by the waterside. *Linthwaite* (M), tel. 3688; 11 rooms, all with bath. Good little hotel. *The Porthole* (M), tel. 2793; serves excellent Continental food.

Historic Houses and Museums

Dove Cottage, Grasmere. The early home of Wordsworth (1799–1808) and Thomas de Quincey. Open Easter–Sept., weekdays 9.30–5.30, Sun. 11–5.30. Mar. and Oct., weekdays 10–4.30, Sun. 11–4.30.
Levens Hall, near Kendal. Elizabethan house with lovely gardens full of topiary work. Open Easter–Sept., Sun.–Thurs., 11–5.
Rydal Mount, Ambleside. Wordsworth's home from 1813 till his death in 1850. Much memorabilia; interesting small garden designed by the poet. Open Mar.–Oct., daily 10–5.30; winter 10–12.30, 2–4.
Sizergh Castle, near Kendal. With notable gardens, especially Rock Garden. Open Easter–Oct., Sun., Mon., Wed., Thurs., 2–5.45; gardens open 12.30–5.45. (NT)

Wales, Land of Poets and Singers

Wales is a remote and romantic region of Great Britain, the place in whose mountain fastnesses the Britons sought refuge from conquer-ing Romans, Saxons and Normans. Here they preserve their sense of Celtic individuality and their own language. There is an active Home Rule movement as well as a National Theater and Orchestra. The Welsh National Opera, based in Cardiff, is now regarded as one of the best in Britain. Aberystwyth, on the west coast, is the seat of the National Library of Wales. The Prince of Wales, Prince Charles, car-ries on a link with the royal family forged nearly 700 years ago.

The capital, Cardiff, is a cosmopolitan seaport and university city, and an administration center with an architecturally magnificent Civic Center and the large National Museum of Wales. It is dominated by the imposing castle. Nearby are the ruins of Tintern Abbey, which inspired Wordsworth's famous poem, and the beautiful Wye Valley. The west and north are mountainous, though very different in charac-ter; the west is open hill sheep-farming country, apart from the beauti-ful coast, while the north is more rugged. Its high points, in addition to stunning Caernarfon Castle, are Conwy (Conway) Castle, Harlech Castle high above Tremadog Bay, the woods and waterfalls of Betwys-y-Coed in Snowdonia National Park, Snowdon itself, the highest mountain in England and Wales, Bodnant Gardens, one of the great gardens of the world, and Llandudno, most popular of Welsh seaside resorts.

Southwest Wales is an area of beautiful secluded beaches, white-washed houses and golden sands, perfect for a beach holiday. Its attractions include St. David's Cathedral; the rugged Pembrokeshire Coast National Park; Tenby, one of the prettiest little coast resorts in Britain; and the area around Laugharne, immortalized by Dylan Thomas in *Under Milk Wood*.

Wales's most important cultural event is the National Eisteddfod, a poetry and music festival presided over by white-robed Druids. It is a kind of tournament of song, with the best poets and singers of Wales participating. But the sites vary, so consult your travel agent or write to the Wales Tourist Board, Brunel House, Fitzalan Road, Cardiff, for detailed information about this and the colorful International Eisteddfod, held each summer at Llangollen.

PRACTICAL INFORMATION FOR WALES

Hotels and Restaurants

ABERYSTWYTH (Dyfed). *Conrah* (M), tel. 617941; 22 rooms, 19 with bath. Beautiful setting in extensive grounds south of town.

BONTDDU (Gwynedd). *Bontddu Hall* (M), tel. 661; 24 rooms, most with bath. Relaxing hotel with superb views across lovely Mawddach Estuary.

CARDIFF (S. Glamorgan). *Angel* (E), tel. 32633; 93 rooms, 82 with bath, has stylish public rooms. *Park* (M), tel. 383471; 108 rooms, all with bath, has a friendly set of staff. *Post House* (M), tel. 731212; 150 rooms with bath, good of its type. 5 miles from center, off A48 road.
Restaurants: *Gibsons* (M), tel. 41264; *Harvesters* (M), tel. 32616.

CRICCIETH (Gwynedd). Beautifully situated *Bron Eifion* (M), tel. 2385; 19 rooms with bath or shower, is well recommended. *Parciau Mawr* (M), tel. 2368; 7 rooms, 2 with bath, and 6 rooms in annex.

HARLECH (Gwynedd). *Maes-y-Neuadd* (M), tel. 780200; 14 rooms, most with bath. In secluded hillside setting at Talsarnau north of Harlech. Good food.

HAVERFORDWEST (Dyfed). *Wolfscastle* (M), tel. 043787 225; 15 rooms with bath or shower. Centrally located for touring Pembrokeshire. Reputable restaurant.

LLANBERIS (Gwynedd). *Y Bistro* (M), tel. 871278. Award-winning restaurant with Welsh specialties.

LLANDDERFEL (Gwynedd). *Pale Hall* (E), tel. 285. 17 rooms with bath. Lavishly restored Victorian mansion.

LLANDRILLO (Clwyd). *Tyddyn Llan* (M), tel. 264; 6 rooms, 4 with bath. Small, immaculate country house hotel near Corwen. Worth seeking out.

LLANDUDNO (Gwynedd). *Bodysgallen Hall* (E), tel. 84466; 28 rooms with bath. Plush hotel in its own grounds. An historic building, tastefully renovated —probably the best hotel in Wales. *St. Tudno* (M), tel. 74411; 21 rooms, 19 with bath. Charming seafront hotel with "Alice in Wonderland" connections.

LLANRWST (Gwynedd). *Meadowsweet* (M), tel. 640732. 10 rooms with bath or shower. Small, well run. Tasty French cuisine; good value.

LLANGAMMARCH WELLS (Powys). *Lake Hotel* (M), tel. 202; 26 rooms with bath or shower. Gracious old-world style. Good country sporting facilities in away-from-it-all location.

MONMOUTH (Gwent). *Beaufort Arms* (M), tel. 2411; 26 rooms, 3 with bath. 18th-century inn with old coaching courtyard. *King's Head* (M), tel. 2177; 28 rooms with bath or shower. Historic inn overlooking main square.

PEMBROKE (Dyfed). *Old King's Arms* (M), tel. 683611; 21 rooms all with bath. Their restaurant is well recommended. Standard cuisine, no highs or lows.

PENRHYNDEUDRAETH (Gwynedd). *Portmeirion* (E), tel. 770228. Hotel in this famous Italianate village is under restoration after a disastrous fire a few years back; guests stay in village cottages and flats, a unique experience.

ST DAVID'S (Dyfed). *St. Non's* (M), tel. 720239; 20 rooms with bath. Friendly, good value, good food. *Warpool Court* (M), tel. 720300; 25 rooms with bath. Splendidly situated with a fine restaurant to add to the enjoyment.

SWANSEA (W. Glamorgan). *Dragon* (M), tel. 51074; 118 rooms with bath. *Drangway Restaurant* (M), tel. 461397. Successfully combines Welsh and French gastronomic traditions. Wise to book.

TENBY (Dyfed). *Fourcroft* (M), tel. 2516; 38 rooms, all with bath. Cliffside hotel overlooking bay.

TRECASTLE (Powys). *Castle* (M), tel. 354; 6 rooms, 2 with bath. Old coaching inn with tastefully appointed bedrooms.

Historic Houses and Museums

CLWYD. Chirk Castle, near Wrexham. Marcher fortress, built 1310 and exterior unaltered, inhabited continuously for 660 years. Open Apr. through Sept., Sun., Tues.–Thurs., Bank Holidays, 12–5; also weekends in Oct. (NT)

GWENT. Big Pit Mining Museum, Blaenafon. Underground tours of authentic coal mine in Welsh Valleys. Open mid-Mar.–Nov., daily from 10.
    Chepstow Castle, Chepstow. First stone-built castle in Britain. Open mid-Mar.–mid-Oct., daily 9.30–6.30; winter, Mon.–Sat. 9.30–4, Sun. 2–4.

GWYNEDD. Bodnant Garden, Tal-y-Cafn. Begun in 1875, one of the finest gardens in Britain. Magnificent rhododendrons. Mar.–Oct., daily, 10–5. (NT)
    Caernarfon Castle, 13th-century, and **Conwy Castle** were two of Edward I's fortresses for subduing the Welsh. Both are open all year. Both open as Chepstow Castle, Gwent.
    Harlech Castle, Harlech. 13th-century, famous in song (*Men of Harlech*). Same opening times as Caernarfon and Conwy.

POWYS. Powis Castle, Welshpool. Dates from 13th century and has beautiful gardens. Open Apr.–Sept., Wed.–Sun. 1–6; also Tues. July–Aug. (NT)

SOUTH GLAMORGAN. Cardiff Castle, Cardiff. Begun in the 11th century, richly-decorated interior. Open May–Sept., daily 10–6; winter 10–4.

Scotland

The Scots have a personality and a national tradition which is very much their own and, in places, vastly different from that of England. You will sense it the moment you cross the Tweed, even before you see your first Scotsman in a kilt or hear the first stirring sound of the pipes. It's in the language and in the very special welcome which Scotsmen accord to Americans (or anybody else who's had a brush or two with the English in the past). The important fact is that the Scots, politically united for three centuries now with the English, have not lost any of their individuality and national character. And Scottish Nationalism has become an important political force. Although there are no border formalities and no basic change in language, when you have crossed the Tweed, you have entered a different country.

Edinburgh is one of Europe's great and beautiful cities, "the Athens of the North". Only the most stolid visitor to Scotland's capital could fail to respond to the broad, handsome sweep of Princes Street and its gardens, beyond which is the thrilling vista of Castle Rock, dominated by the ramparts of historic Edinburgh Castle.

Of Edinburgh's many monuments, two are worth the special attention of even the hurried tourist—Edinburgh Castle and Palace of Holyroodhouse. The first, commanding a splendid view of the city and the Firth of Forth, is steeped in Scottish history. In the heart of the castle, there is a magnificent display of the ancient regalia of Scotland—crown, scepter, sword of state and other treasures of the Scottish people. Holyroodhouse is rich in memories of the turbulent life of Mary Queen of Scots, not least the room in which Lord Darnley, husband of Mary, is said to have murdered her favorite, Rizzio. The palace is still occasionally used as a residence by members of the royal family when they visit Scotland.

Among recommended excursions by car or bus are the following: Abbotsford, the elaborate medieval-style home built by Sir Walter Scott; Dryburgh Abbey, where Scott is buried; Dirleton and Tantallon castles; the romantic ruins of Melrose Abbey, where lies the heart of Robert the Bruce; ten-centuries-old Traquair House; Linlithgow Palace, birthplace of Mary Queen of Scots; and historic Stirling Castle.

Glasgow boasts that it is the friendliest city in Scotland, but even that formidable reputation will probably not be enough to lure the average tourist to this bustling industrial city. Nevertheless, it has its moments —a fine cathedral; one of the best art museums (Rembrandt, Rubens, Corot, Turner, Whistler); the trip down the Clyde Estuary to the place where the Atlantic rolls in to die, some impressive Victorian domestic architecture, a famous Necropolis and the Botanical Gardens. Artistically, Glasgow has a rich life, with the Scottish National Opera and Ballet, and the Citizens Theater.

Most visitors prefer to avoid industrial Glasgow and concentrate on the romantic beauty of the Scottish Highlands and the historic houses and castles of Scotland. For anyone with a taste for the wilder aspects of landscape, the Inner and Outer Hebrides, the Orkneys and Shetlands, remote islands of unspoiled loveliness, can give a great deal of pleasure, but they need plenty of time to be explored properly.

Although we use the new regional names for Scotland—Borders, Tayside and so on—these bureaucratic vacuities have never really been accepted by the Scots, who prefer to use the age-old names of their fathers. You will, therefore, find both the old and the new in use.

PRACTICAL INFORMATION FOR SCOTLAND

Edinburgh

 HOTELS. There are hundreds of hotels and boarding houses in and around Edinburgh, so that only a very small selection can be given here. You may book accommodation at the *Tourist Information Center,* Waverley Market (tel. 031–557 2727).

Caledonian (L), tel. 031–225 2433; 254 rooms, all with bath or shower. Traditional hotel at west end of Princes Street.

Carlton Highland (E), tel. 031–556 7277; 207 rooms with bath. Close to Princes Street.

North British (E), tel. 031–556 2414; 193 rooms, 171 with bath. Above the rail station, old and ornate, slightly faded, but excellent service. Very central.

Post House (E), tel. 031–334 8221; 208 rooms, all with bath. Modern hotel close by zoo with views over city.

Prestonfield House (E), tel. 031–667 8055; 5 rooms. Beautiful old house, mainly famous as a restaurant with great atmosphere but also a hotel. A little bit out of the way.

Roxburghe (E), tel. 031–225 3921; 76 rooms, 64 with bath, 12 with shower. On lovely Charlotte Square, small, attractive, fair restaurant.

Albany (M), tel. 031–556 0397; 22 rooms, all with bath or shower. Comfortable, with excellent, friendly staff. Good basement restaurant.

Braid Hills (M), tel. 031–447 8888; 68 rooms, 47 with bath, 21 with shower. Large family hotel; comfortable and with adequate restaurant.

Crest (M), tel. 031–332 2442; 120 rooms, 60 with bath, 60 with shower. One mile from center, comfortable and well-serviced.

RESTAURANTS. Chumley's (E), tel. 031–225 3106. Interesting combinations, often with such local goodies as venison.

Howtowdie (E), 27 Stafford Street, tel. 031–225 6291. Traditional dishes, interesting decor.

Lune Town (M), 38 William Street, tel. 031–225 9388. Good Chinese cooking.

Maridor's (M), 39a Albany Street, tel. 031–556 0397. Swiss, French, German specialties. Also quick snacks and bar lunches.

Ristorante Cosmo (M), 58A North Castle Street, tel. 031–226 6743. Italian restaurant renowned for its fish dishes. Good Italian wines.

Verandah Tandoori (M), 17 Dairy Street, tel. 031–337 5828. Stylish Indian restaurant, recommended.

Chez Julie (I), 110 Raeburn Place, tel. 031–332 2827. Pleasant bistro-type restaurant.

Henderson's (I), 94 Hanover Street, tel. 031–225 3400. Established salad table and wine cellar, much favored by students.

MUSEUMS, GALLERIES AND GARDENS. Canongate Tolbooth, 163 Canongate. Highland dress, tartans. Open weekdays 10–5 (10–6, June–Sept.).

Craft Centre, Acheson House, Canongate. Weekdays and Sat. 10–5.

City Art Centre, 1–4 Market Street, works by late 19th and 20th century artists, mostly Scottish, frequent exhibitions. Weekdays 10–5, June–Sept., 10–6.

Edinburgh Castle, ancient fortress. Open 9.30–5, Sun., 12.30–4.

Huntly House (City Museum), Canongate. Old-fashioned Scots kitchen. Weekdays, 10–5, Oct.–May; 10–6 June–Sept.

John Knox's House, High St. 15th-century religious objects. Mon.–Sat. 10–5.

Lady Stair's House, Lawnmarket. Relics of Burns, Scott and R. L. Stevenson. Weekdays, 10–5 Oct.–May, 10–6 June–Sept.

Museum of Childhood, Hyndford's Close, High St. Oct.–May, weekdays 10–5; June–Sept. 10–6. Games, toys and dress.

National Gallery of Scotland, The Mound. Weekdays 10–5, Sun. 2–5.

National Museum (formerly National Museum of Antiquities of Scotland), Queen Street (east end). Celtic and Roman finds. Weekdays 10–5, Sun. 2–5.

National Museum (formerly Royal Scottish Museum), Chambers St. Archeology, technology, ethnography, decorative arts. Outstanding scale models in Technology Department. Mon.–Sat., 10–5, Sun. 2–5.

Palace of Holyroodhouse. Dating from James IV, it is the official residence of royal family in Scotland. Relics of Mary, Queen of Scots. Oct.–Mar., weekdays 9.30–3.45, closed Sun; Mar.–Oct., weekdays 9.30–5.15, Sun 11–4.30 (except during royal visits, usually late May and early June).

Royal Botanic Garden, Inverleith Row, open 9–1 hour before sunset, Sun. 11–1 hour before sunset; winter, 10 to dusk.

Scottish National Gallery of Modern Art, Inverleith House. 20th-century paintings and sculpture. Weekdays 10–5, Sun. 2–5 (winter, 7 to dusk).

Scottish National Portrait Gallery, Queen St. (east end). Weekdays 10–5, Sun. 2–5.

THE EDINBURGH FESTIVAL. The Festival takes place each year during August. For a detailed program write to the Festival Office, 21 Market St, Edinburgh 1. Details regarding the *Film Festival,* which is concurrent, can be had from the Director, Edinburgh International Film Festival, Edinburgh Film Centre, 88 Lothian Road, Edinburgh. *Tattoo* bookings and enquiries should be addressed to the Tattoo Office, 22 Market Street, Edinburgh EH1 1QB. The *Festival Fringe,* an offshoot of the Festival itself, has a huge program of theater, music, poetry, dance and exhibitions. Details from Festival Fringe Society, Royal Mile Centre, High St, Edinburgh EH1 1RB.

THE REST OF SCOTLAND

Hotels and Restaurants

ABERDEEN (Grampian). *Holiday Inn Bucksburn* (E), tel. 713911; 99 rooms. Close to the airport on A947. *Ardoe House* (M), tel. 867555. 21 rooms. Pleasant and comfortable. *Stakis Treetops* (M), tel. 33377; 94 rooms, 86 with bath. Luxurious, with glamorous *Gershwin's* restaurant. Try the food at *Atlantis* (M), tel. 591403—seafood, naturally.

ARRAN, ISLE OF (Strathclyde). *Douglas Arms* (M), in Brodick, tel. Brodick 2155; 26 rooms, 12 with bath. Modern, comfortable, with food of good standard, sauna.
  Kinloch (M), at **Blackwaterfoot,** tel. Shiskine 286; 49 rooms with bath.

AUCHTERARDER (Tayside). *Gleneagles* (L), tel. 2231; 254 rooms with bath. One of the most famous hotels in the land, stands among endless golf courses and gardens with wonderful view, heated pool, tennis, squash, sauna.

AVIEMORE (Highland). *Badenoch Hotel* (M), tel. 810261; 81 rooms, 61 with bath. Functional, folk music once a week. *Coylumbridge* (M), tel. 810661; 173 rooms, with bath; on A951. Tennis, close to Loch Marich for yachting and skiing on slopes above; English and French food. *Strathspey* (M), tel. 810681; 90 rooms.
  Post House (M), tel. 810771; 103 rooms with bath, in Sports Centre, lively and modern with high-quality bedrooms, sauna.

BALLATER (Grampian). *Tullich Lodge* (E), tel. 55406; 10 rooms with bath, good decor, fishing and restaurant. *Invercauld Arms* (M), tel. 55417; 24 rooms. Owners friendly and welcoming. Reader recommended.

BANCHORY (Grampian). *Banchory Lodge* (E), tel. 2625; 27 rooms, 23 with bath. Georgian house in own grounds with salmon river.

BRAEMAR (Grampian). *Fife Arms* (M), tel. 644; 90 rooms, 42 with bath. Can be noisy in season.

CALLANDER (Central). *Roman Camp* (M), tel. 30003; 11 rooms, most with bath. An old hunting lodge with fabulous gardens bordering river; food consistently good.

DUNBLANE (Central). *Cromlix House* (L), tel. 822125; 14 rooms, 13 with bath, 1 with shower. Superb hotel in own estate; excellent restaurant.

DUNDEE (Tayside). *Angus* (M), tel. 26874; 58 rooms with bath. Modern, comfortable, and well-run. *Invercarse* (M), tel. 69231; 27 rooms, all with bath. In grounds overlooking the River Tay, fishing.

DUNKELD (Tayside). *Dunkeld House* (E), tel. 771; 31 rooms, 26 with bath. A really charming and friendly place in wide grounds by River Tay

FORT WILLIAM (Highland). *Inverlochy Castle* (L), tel. 2177; 16 rooms with bath. Ranks indisputably among the greatest in the U.K., superbly run in setting of antique furniture and carpets; personal service well beyond average; first-class restaurant.

GATEHOUSE OF FLEET (Dumfries & Galloway). *Murray Arms* (M), tel. 207; 19 rooms, 14 with bath. Good game fishing, some Scottish dishes, strong associations with Robert Burns.

GLAMIS (Tayside). *Strathmore Arms* (M), tel. 248. Village pub converted into a smart restaurant by two of the Queen's relatives. Excellent food.

GLASGOW (Strathclyde). *Albany* (E), tel. 041 248 2656; 258 rooms with bath, modern comfortable rooms, international cuisine, excellent diversity of bars. *Holiday Inn* (E), tel. 041 226 5577. 297 rooms, comfortable and convenient. *Hospitality Inn* (E), tel. 041 332 3311; 316 rooms with bath. Scotland's largest hotel. *Stakis Grosvenor* (E), tel. 041 339 8811; 94 rooms with bath. Imposing, traditional building impressively modernized.
Fountain Restaurant (M), 2 Woodside Crescent, tel. 041 332 6396; serves French cuisine in intimate surroundings. *Loon Fung* (M), 417 Sauchiehall Street, tel. 041 332 1240, is good for Cantonese food.

INVERNESS (Highland). *Culloden House* (L), tel. 790461; 20 rooms with bath. Splendid and luxurious 18th-century mansion beside Culloden battlefield. Excellent restaurant combining Scottish and French influences. Staff are unfailingly helpful. Booking recommended.
Station Hotel (M), tel. 231926; 65 rooms, 52 with bath. Victorian and extremely comfortable. Ambitious restaurant achieves high standards; friendly staff. Book ahead, particularly in summer.

KENTALLEN (Highland). *Ardsheal House* (E), tel. Duror 227; 13 rooms, 9 with bath or shower. American-run hotel in 18th-century mansion, with views over Loch Linnhe. Highly recommended.

KYLE OF LOCHALSH (Highland). *Lochalsh* (M-E), tel. 4202; 45 rooms, 28 with bath. Offers beautiful views of the Isle of Skye across the Loch from the front rooms; their kitchen does wonderful things with lamb and local produce.

NAIRN (Highland). *Golf View* (M), tel. 52301; 55 rooms, all with bath or shower. Heated pool, tennis, sauna, popular restaurant.

OBAN (Strathclyde). *Alexander* (M), tel. 62381; 56 rooms, 47 with bath. Victorian seafront hotel with views over bay.

PEEBLES (Border). *Peebles Hydro* (M), tel. 20602; 139 rooms, all with bath. In huge grounds bordering River Tweed; heated pool, sauna, squash and every other amenity, sports or social. *Tontine* (M), tel. 20892; 37 rooms with bath, also has excellent game fishing.

PERTH (Tayside). *Balcraig House* (E), tel. 51123; 10 rooms with bath. Tasteful, stylish country house hotel with reputable restaurant.

PITLOCHRY (Tayside). *Hydro* (M), tel. 2666; 62 rooms with bath. In own grounds above the town and somewhat old-fashioned; tennis. *Green Park* (M), tel. 2537; 38 rooms, 28 with bath. Overlooking Loch Faskally, good touring base.

ST. ANDREWS (Fife). *Old Course* (L), tel. 74371; 148 rooms with bath. Alongside 17th hole of famous golf course, views of the bay. *Rusacks* (E), tel. 74321; 50 rooms with bath. Golfers' rendezvous for 100 years. Golf holiday packages available.

SKYE, ISLE OF (Highland). At Portree, *Royal* (M), tel. Portree 2525; 25 rooms, 17 with bath. Wonderful views over sea to hills beyond. At Skeabost Bridge, *Skeabost House* (M), tel. Skeabost Bridge 202; 27 rooms, 18 with bath. Beautifully decorated bedrooms, largest log fire imaginable in lounge; excellent.

STORNOWAY (Isle of Lewis). *Caberfeidh Hotel* (M), tel. 2604; 36 rooms with bath. Simple and adequate.

TARBERT (Strathclyde). *Stonefield Castle* (M-E), tel. 207; 34 rooms with bath. Lovely castle in miraculous surroundings; with dancing, fishing, boating.

TURNBERRY (Strathclyde). *Turnberry* (L), tel. 202; 130 rooms with bath. One of the finest hotels in Scotland with two world-famous golf courses, tennis, heated pool and fine views over Firth of Clyde.

Historic Houses and Museums

BORDERS. Abbotsford House, Melrose, was the home of the 19th-century writer Sir Walter Scott. Open late-Mar.–Oct., weekdays, 10–5, Sun., 2–5.

Mellerstain, Gordon. Outstanding Adam house; lovely interior and views. Easter, May to Sept., daily (except Sat.), 12.30–4.30.

Traquair House, Innerleithen. Reputed to be the oldest inhabited house in Scotland, unaltered from 1664. Associated with Mary, Queen of Scots and the Jacobite risings. Treasures date from 12th century and include embroideries, glass, manuscripts, silver and pictures. Open Easter–Aug. daily 10.30–5, Oct. daily 1.30–5.30.

Linlithgow Palace, Linlithgow. Birthplace of Mary, Queen of Scots. Open all year, 9.30–4, later in summer, and Sun afternoon.

FIFE. Culross Palace, Culross. Well-restored 16th- and 17th-century buildings, fine painted ceilings and terraced gardens. Open all year, weekdays 9.30–7, Sun. 2–7 (winter, 9.30–4 and 2–4).

GRAMPIAN. Balmoral Castle, near Ballater. H.M. the Queen's Highland home. Grounds only, open May–July, daily 10–5 (except Sun.), except when royal family is in residence.

Crathes Castle, Banchory. 16th-century Jacobean castle with painted ceilings. Gardens date from 1702. Castle open Easter and May–Sept., Mon.–Sat. 11–5.15, Sun. 2–5.15. Gardens open all year daily 9.30 to dusk. (NT)

Pitmedden, Udny. Reconstructed 17th-century garden. Museum of farming life. Gardens open daily, 9.30–sunset. Museum, May–Sept., daily, 11–6.

HIGHLAND. Cawdor Castle. nr. Inverness. 14th-century keep forms part of a massive fortress. Splendid grounds. Open May–Sept., daily, 10–5.

Dunvegan Castle, Isle of Skye, dates from 13th century and continuously inhabited by chiefs of Clan MacLeod. Open Easter–mid.-Oct., Mon.–Sat., 2–5, mid-May–Sept. 10.30–5.

Inverewe, Poolewe, Wester Ross. Unique garden of the late Osgood Mackenzie, with rare and sub-tropical specimens. Open all year, daily 9.30 to sunset.

LOTHIAN. Hopetoun House, South Queensferry. Fine example of 18th-century Adam architecture. Deer parks and grounds laid out on Versailles pattern. Open May–Sept., daily 11–5.30.

The House of the Binns, near Linlithgow. Historic house with fine 17th-century plaster ceilings. Open Easter, May–Sept., daily 2–5.30 (park, 10–7). Closed Fri.

STRATHCLYDE. Brodick Castle, Isle of Arran. Seat of Dukes of Hamilton. Magnificent gardens, furniture, art. Castle open Apr., Mon., Wed. and Sat. 1–5, May through Sept., daily 1–5. Gardens open all year, 10 to sunset. (NT)

Burns' Cottage, Alloway, near Ayr. Birthplace of Burns, Scotland's national poet. Also has a museum. Open June–Aug., Mon.–Sat. 9–7, Sun. 10–7; Apr., May, Sept., Oct., Mon.–Sat., 10–5, Sun. 2–5; winter, 10–4 (closed Sun.).

The Burrell Collection, Pollock Country Park, Glasgow. Magnificent collection of objets d'art, textiles, ceramics, etc. given by Sir William and Lady Burrell. Open Mon.–Sat. 10–5, Sun. 2–5.

Culzean Castle, Maybole. Designed by Adam in the 18th century. Beautiful gardens laid out in 1783. Open Apr–Sept., daily, 10–6. (NT)

Glasgow Art Gallery and Museum, Kelvingrove Park. Fine collection of paintings, sculpture, costumes, etc. Open daily 10–5, Sun. 2–5.

Glasgow Botanic Gardens, Great Western Rd., 40 acres or gardens, glasshouses, plus Kibble Palace collection of tree ferns and temperate flora. Open Oct.–Mar., daily 7–4.15; Apr.–Sept., daily 7–dusk.

TAYSIDE. Blair Castle, Blair Atholl. Built in 1269, home of the Duke of Atholl. Jacobite relics, splendid selection of antique toys, firearms, tapestries, etc. Open Easter–mid. Oct., Mon.–Sat. 10–5, Sun. 2–5.

Glamis Castle, near Kirriemuir. Partly 14th-century, seat of Earls of Strathmore and present Queen Mother's childhood home. Grounds laid out by Capability Brown. Open Easter, May–Oct., daily (except Sat.), 1–5.

Museum of Scottish Tartans, Drummond St., Comrie. Open Nov.–Easter, Mon.–Fri., 11–3, Sat. 10–1, Easter–Oct. Mon.–Sat. 10–5, Sun. 2–5.

Scone Palace, near Perth. Home of the Earl of Mansfield. Many treasures to be seen in state rooms. Rebuilt in 1803, incorporating parts of old palace originally built on site from Pictish times. Open Easter–mid-Oct., Mon.–Sat. 10–5.30, Sun. 2–5.30. July and Aug. 11–5.30.

The Channel Islands and the Isle of Man

The Channel Islands of Jersey and Guernsey are the warmest places in Britain. From April to October, day temperatures usually exceed 60 degrees; sharp frosts are rare, though the islands can be windy. The archipelago of which Jersey and Guernsey are the chief islands is an admirable blend of France and Britain. It lies closer to the French than the British coast. St. Helier, capital of Jersey, and St. Peter Port, the Guernsey capital, are full of quaint streets and good hotels. The food here is better cooked than in most English resorts; you'll be delighted with this touch of France on British soil. And don't miss a boat trip to Alderney and the tiny, traffic-free islands of Sark and Herm.

The Isle of Man is in the Irish Sea. Though interesting for its Norse relics (it was once a Viking colony), Man is apt to be overcrowded in summer by hordes of tourists from the great English Midland cities. But despite the noise (including international motorcycle races) and overcrowding on the main beaches, there are still some secluded coves and solitary glens within access of the main centers. One form of amusement for which the Isle of Man has long been famous is the casinos, where anyone can enjoy the classic games for low stakes.

PRACTICAL INFORMATION FOR THE CHANNEL ISLANDS AND THE ISLE OF MAN

The Channel Islands

GETTING THERE. *Sealink–British Ferries* operate frequent passenger and car ferry services from Weymouth and Portsmouth to Jersey and Guernsey in summer (taking between about 6 and 9 hours), as well as a restricted service in winter. A fast train service from London (Waterloo) connects with all sailings. *Channel Island Ferries* operate year-round services to the islands from Portsmouth, and *Torbay Seaways* run a car/passenger ferry twice a week from Torquay. Hydrofoils operate between the islands, and also to France.

British Airways and *Air UK* operate several daily flights from London to Jersey; Air UK also flies to Guernsey. Flying time is about one hour. There are also daily services from Southampton Airport (about 40 mins) operated by Air UK. *British Caledonian* also operate from Gatwick (under 1 hour) to Jersey. In all, the islands are well served by air links from around 30 provincial airports (from Aberdeen to Plymouth) operated by a variety of carriers, including *British Midland, Jersey European Airways* and *Brymon.* There is also an intensive inter-island air service.

HOTELS AND RESTAURANTS. Channel Island hotels are mostly attractive and often have a strong French flavor. Most of them quote favorable weekly, all-inclusive rates, but you must book well ahead for the summer season.

ALDERNEY. *Chez André* (M), tel. 2777; 14 rooms, 7 with bath.

GUERNSEY. St. Martins. *Bella Luce* (M), tel. 38764. 31 rooms, 27 with bath, 4 with shower. *St. Margaret's Lodge* (M), tel. 35757; 42 rooms with shower.
St. Peter Port. *Old Government House* (M), tel. 24921; 75 rooms, all with bath. Exactly what its name implies, with impressive views and atmosphere. *La Frégate* (M), tel. 24624; 13 rooms with bath, but especially notable for an excellent restaurant; specialties, of course, French. More super seafood at *Le Nautique* restaurant (M), tel. 21714.

JERSEY. Bouley Bay. *Water's Edge* (M), tel. Jersey 62777; 56 rooms all with bath. Exactly what it says—ideal for a sea holiday.
Corbière. *Sea Crest* (M), tel. Jersey 42687; 7 rooms all with bath. Especially notable for restaurant.
Gorey. *Old Court House* (M), tel. Jersey 54444; 58 rooms with bath. Excellent spot as hotel, but good food as well.
St. Brelade's Bay. *Atlantic* (E), tel. Jersey 44101; 46 rooms with bath; splendid setting. *L'Horizon* (E), tel. Jersey 43101; 103 rooms, all with bath. Right on beach, attracting smart clientele. With *Star Grill* restaurant for excellent fish dishes. *St. Brelade's Bay* (M), tel. 43281; 80 rooms, all with bath, in pleasant gardens. *Château Valeuse* (M), tel. Jersey 43476; 26 rooms, 23 with bath or shower. This time there is an Italian tang.
St. Helier. *Beaufort* (M), tel. Jersey 32471; 50 rooms with bath, bright and pleasing. *Pomme d'Or* (M), tel. Jersey 78644; 151 rooms, all with bath. **Restaurant:** *Mauro's* (M), tel. Jersey 20147; seafoods French and Italian style.
St. Saviour. *Longueville Manor* (E), tel. 25501; 35 rooms, all with bath. Secluded hotel in own grounds. Good food.

SARK. *Petit Champ* (M), tel. 2046; 16 rooms, 11 with bath. *Aval du Creux* (M), tel. 2036; 10 rooms, 5 with bath or shower. *Dixcart* (M), tel. 2015; 25 rooms; all three are normally only full board. All, also, are secluded and really tranquil on this idyllic island. *Petit Champ* and *Aval du Creux* have fine restaurants.

Isle of Man

GETTING THERE. By steamer (drive-on/drive-off car ferry service) operated by the *Isle of Man Steam Packet Company* from their main port of Heysham (accessible from the South of England by the M1/M6 Motorway) to Douglas—crossing time just under 4 hours. Regular, though less frequent services also operate from Liverpool, Fleetwood and Stranraer (Scotland), Belfast (N. Ireland) and Dublin (S. Ireland).
Manx Airlines have daily services in the main season to the island from London (Heathrow), Liverpool, Manchester, Blackpool, Glasgow, Belfast and Dublin; also weekend services from Birmingham, Leeds, Newcastle-upon-Tyne and Edinburgh. Flying time from London is just over an hour. *JEA* have regular services from Blackpool, Dublin and Glasgow, and seasonal services from Newcastle, Edinburgh, and Leeds.

HOTELS AND RESTAURANTS. The Isle of Man is seasonal and most of the hotels and guest houses close by the last week of September though the larger hotels in each resort stay open with limited accommodation during the winter. The island's Tourist Board is located at 13 Victoria St., Douglas (tel. 74323). If you arrive without accommodation, make use of the free bed booking service, available throughout the year from the Board's information bureau in Victoria St.

CASTLETOWN. *Golf Links* (M), tel. 822201; 75 rooms, 46 with bath or shower. Surrounded by the sea—and the golf course. Pleasant accommodation is complemented by well-cooked food and friendly service; tennis, heated pool.

DOUGLAS. Largest resort on the island. Plenty of entertainment and good center for exploring. *Sefton Hotel* (M), tel. 26011; 80 rooms with bath or shower. Modern *Palace* (M), tel. 4521, 138 rooms, all with bath, pool, and the only public casino in Britain. Good food at *Boncomptie's* (M), tel. 75626. Continental cuisine. Also many other excellent restaurants.

PEEL. *The Lively Lobster* (M), tel. 2789. Specializes in fish and makes full use of the local seafood.

GREECE

Breathtaking natural beauty combines with an unsurpassed variety of archeological treasures in making Greece one of the most appealing areas of contemporary tourism. Sun, sand and sea; ruins of fortresses, castles, palaces, temples and churches, from neolothic caves and villages through the millenia of Minoan, Mycenaean, archaic, classical, Hellenistic, Roman and Byzantine civilizations; you name them, Greece has them. Yet the birthplace of Western culture has not escaped its modern adverse effects, particularly those felt so acutely during the height of the travel season as the number of annual visitors approaches two thirds of the population. The concrete highrises that disgrace so much of the Western Mediterranean shores in Greece are concentrated in a relatively few sites, albeit once the loveliest, although dreary modernity is spreading along the 106,000 miles of coastline and the some 2,000 surrounding islands.

Greece has always drawn lovers of art, history or mythology and she will continue to do so. But Greece has also become one of Europe's leading centers for nautical sports of all kinds, beside remaining ideal for plain sunbathing and swimming, except near the big towns where air and sea are badly polluted.

After having invented some—and having tried all possible and several impossible—forms of government in 4,000 years of historical surfeit, Greece in 1985 re-elected a socialist government. It is frequently at odds with its EEC and NATO partners, loosening the traditional ties with the West.

The nearly ten million present-day Greeks call themselves Hellenes, their country *Elliniki Dimokratia,* the Hellenic Republic. Dotted with cypress groves, oleander and olive trees, the nation's 51,123 square miles (about the size of New York State) are cut by rugged mountain chains, often plunging sheer into the sea. The Pindus Range, running from north to south, touches on the fabled peaks of Mount Olympus, home of the Gods, and Mount Parnassus, favorite haunt of Apollo and the Muses. From the quarries of Mount Pentelicon came the gleaming marble of the Acropolis and now the facing of huge apartment blocks.

Even longer is Greece's connection with shipping. Dominant in the Mediterranean for 2,500 years, Greeks now own one of the world's largest tonnage, about 40 million, and the Greek flag flies over the fourth biggest merchant fleet, some 32 million tons. Membership of the European Economic Community has favored export of olives, grapes, figs, currants (whose name derives from Corinth) and, most important, the best tobacco in Europe. Beautiful rugs and other handwoven textiles are still made from the wool of their flocks, but the colorful regional costumes are now only to be seen at folkloric events organized by the National Tourist Organization.

PRACTICAL INFORMATION FOR GREECE

WHAT IT WILL COST. Devaluation has failed to keep pace with increasing inflation; hotel prices are still fairly reasonable, but meals are expensive for the quality offered. There are no regional price differences, variations within the categories depending on the location and the frills: swimming pool, sauna, conference facilities, etc. Off-season rates are 15–20% lower from Apr. 15 to May 31 and Sept. 15 to Oct. 31, up to 40% in the few seaside hotels that stay open Nov. 1 to Apr. 15, excluding Christmas and Easter holidays. A word of warning: seaside taverns, despite their deceptively simple appearances, often have high official classification, charging accordingly. Check the category, always prominently indicated, and follow the Greek habit of choosing your fish in the kitchen, having it weighed and priced.

An *ouzo* costs from 50–120 dr., a bottle of beer 60–150 dr., a bottle of local wine 180–750, half a liter of retsina 80–120 dr., Turkish, now called Greek, coffee 60–130 dr.

Money. Monetary unit is the *drachme.* Rate of exchange at presstime: app. 155 drachmes to the dollar; 215 to the pound sterling. **This is subject to change.** There are coins of 1, 2, 5, 10, 20, and 50 dr. and notes of 50, 100, 1,000, and 5,000 dr.

You may bring in unlimited amounts of foreign currency, but sums in excess of $500 must be declared for re-export. Only 3,000 dr. may be imported or exported.

Cost of a moderate day in high season for two (drachmes):

Hotel with breakfast, tax and service charges	4,200
Lunch in a seaside or tourist restaurant, with one bottle of wine	3,500
Dinner (set menu) at hotel, local aperitif, one bottle of wine	2,600
Light refreshment	600
Transport and sightseeing	1,400
Evening entertainment	1,800
Miscellaneous (10% for contingencies)	1,400
	15,500

SOURCES OF INFORMATION. For information on all aspects of travel in Greece, the Greek National Tourist Organization is invaluable. Their addresses are:

In the U.S.: 645 Fifth Avenue, Olympic Tower, New York, N.Y. 10022 (tel. 212–421–5777); 611 West 6th St., Los Angeles, CA 90017 (tel. 213–626–6696); 168 North Michigan Ave., Chicago, IL 60601 (tel. 312–782–1084); Building 31, State St., Boston, MA 02109 (tel. 617–227–7366).

In Canada: 1233 de la Montagne, Montreal, P.Q. H3G 1Z2 (tel. 871–1532); 80 Bloor St. West, Suite 1403, Toronto, Ont. M5S 2V1 (tel. 968–2220).

In the U.K.: 195 Regent St., London W.1 (tel. 01–734 5997).

 WHEN TO COME. Greece is radiant with sunshine from April to October. It rains sporadically throughout the winter, which is mild near the sea, though very cold inland. June, July and August are hot but not humid; the air is translucent, except near Athens and Thessaloniki, both of which are badly polluted.

Average afternoon daily temperatures in degrees Fahrenheit and centigrade:

Athens	Jan.	Feb.	Mar.	Apr.	May	June	July	Aug.	Sept.	Oct.	Nov.	Dec.
F°	54	55	60	67	77	85	90	90	83	74	64	57
C°	12	13	16	19	25	29	32	32	28	23	18	14

 SPECIAL EVENTS. Performances by renowned foreign orchestras and theater groups in late June are the curtain raiser to Greece's main cultural manifestation, the *International Athens Festival,* which lasts well into September, alternating nightly concerts, opera and ballets with classical Greek tragedies and comedies in the ancient Herodes Atticus open-air theater on the slopes of the Acropolis; this is the cheapest international festival, the most expensive ticket being about 2,500 dr. The *Epidaurus Festival* presents ancient drama every weekend from early July through August, while a week or two of the same classical fare is the norm through the summer in antique theaters all over the country.

Greek Folkdances from May to September on the Philopappos Hill opposite the Acropolis, where the pageant of the *Sound and Light* spectacle is presented from April through October as well as on the islands of Corfu and Rhodes.

The *International Fair of Thessaloniki* is held in the first fortnight of September in the capital of northern Greece. This event is accompanied by a *Song Festival* and followed first by a *Greek Film Festival* and in October by the *Demetria,* a *Byzantine Art Festival* dating back to the 13th century.

From July to early September a *Wine Festival* is held at Daphni, 7 miles from Athens, but it may be transferred to a village in the vineyards just north of Athens. A similar festival takes place at Alexandroupoli (Northern Greece) from early July to mid-August.

In February, *Carnival* is celebrated everywhere, culminating in a parade with floats on the last carnival Sunday (usually early March) in Patra.

Most famous of many Holy Day celebrations is that of the *Epitaph* on Good Friday with impressive Greek Orthodox processions.

National Holidays. Jan. 1 (New Year's Day); Jan. 6 (Epiphany); Mar. 2 (Lent Monday); Mar. 25 (Greek Revolution Memorial Day); Apr. 19 (Easter); May 1 (May Day); Jun. 7 (Pentecost); Aug. 15 (Assumption); Oct. 28 (Oxi); Dec. 25, 26.

VISAS. Not required. Nationals of the US and most American countries have to apply for a residence permit after a stay of two months; British subjects and Europeans, after three months.

HEALTH CERTIFICATE. Not required for entry into Greece.

 GETTING TO GREECE. By Plane—From North America. There are trans-Atlantic flights by *Olympic Airways* (the Greek national airline) and *TWA* from New York to Athens and also by Olympic from Montreal. Olympic also flies to most European capitals from Athens.

From the U.K. From London *Olympic* and *British Airways* operate non-stop flights to Athens, Corfu, Iraklio (Crete), Rhodes and Thessaloniki.

By Train. There are through trains from Dortmund, Munich and Salzburg to both Thessaloniki and Athens with 2nd class couchettes all the way and also 1st and 2nd class sleeping cars on certain trains. From Munich the total journey is about 42 hours. Connecting trains from Paris and Ostend link with these services at either Munich, Salzburg or Zagreb. Dining car part of the way only.

There are car-carrying sleeper trains from Brussels and Boulogne to Milan, and from Brussels to Ljubljana in Yugoslavia.

By Boat. There is an extensive summer network of ferries linking Italy with Greece, a substantial number—especially the short route ones—running all the year round. Venice, Ancona, Brindisi and Bari are the Italian ports, with Corfu, Igoumenitsa and Patra being the main Greek ports.

The shortest routes are from Brindisi to Corfu (about 9 hours) and Patra (14 hours) the latter with bus connection to Athens.

By Car. London to Athens, the fastest route via Ostend-Cologne-Munich-Salzburg-Vienna-Budapest-Belgrade is about 1,850 miles. Same from Paris via Basel-Innsbruck-Ljubljana-Belgrade.

 CUSTOMS. Two hundred cigarettes or 50 cigars or one quarter lb. smoking tobacco and one bottle of liquor duty free. No duty on articles for personal use. Your car, camping and sport equipment, typewriter, etc. are registered in your passport upon entry to prevent sale within the country.

 HOTELS. Greek hotels and restaurants are categorized as L, A, B, C and D, but this is likely to change. Several, officially listed as L, failed to measure up; along with the best A's they equal our own grading of Expensive (E). The B's are the equal of our Moderate (M), the C's and a few outstanding D's our Inexpensive (I).

All L and E, most M, even some I listed are airconditioned. All listed have been constructed or completely renovated subsequent to 1965, with private baths or showers, but few I's have their own restaurant. All prices in the table below are for high season and include 15% service charges, taxes, airconditioning in the top categories, and heating (but not breakfast).

Hotel prices (drachmes)

Category	(L)	(E)	(M)	(I)
Single	14,000–25,000	5,500–9,000	3,000–5,000	1,500–2,800
Double	16,000–30,000	6,500–12,000	3,500–6,000	1,800–3,200

 RESTAURANTS. By far the most economical meals are the set hotel menus at the lower end of the indicated E to I range (below). Except in a few, only a few, luxury establishments, hotel food is of the international-dreary variety which calls itself, wrongly, French. Most beach resorts, unfortunately, insist on half board. The simple fish taverns on the coast and islands *can* be excellent, but could be three times the cost of the hotel menu.

Meal prices per person (drachmes)

	(L)	(E)	(M)	(I)
Breakfast	500–1,000	300–500	250–400	200–280
Lunch/Dinner	3,000–6,000	1,800–3,500	1,000–2,000	600–950

Food and Drink. A great specialty of the Greek cuisine is stuffed vine leaves, piquantly seasoned rice, meat and onions. The Greeks call it *dolmades,* and it's very good. More familiar to Anglo-Saxon palates is *moussaka,* a meat and eggplant combination. Try *kalamarakia,* fried baby squid or *garides tiganites,* fried shrimps. *Youvetsi* is lamb with noodles. *Souvlakia* is Greek for shishkebab. Also recommended: *youvarlakia,* tiny meat balls sautéed in butter and served with a lemon sauce; *oktapodi,* octopus cooked in a wine and onion sauce; *barbounia,* grilled mullet, and *kedonia,* little Greek clams on the half shell; but all seafood is expensive. Pies are great favorites, *spinakopitta,* spinach and goatcheese pie, is the most original, but even plain *tyropitta,* goatcheese pie, is very tasty. The whole gamut of *baclava, kadaif* and similar honey-and-nut pastries is excessively sweet.

The best table wine is Porto Carras, white, rosé (*kokineli*) and red, followed by the three varieties of *Cellar.* Also drinkable are the white *Amalia, Elisar* and *Santa Helena,* as well as the red *Mirabello, Petit Chateau* and the rougher *Naoussa;* sweet dessert wines are *Mavrodaphni* and *Samos.* Since ancient times, the Greeks have been adding resin to their wines, and the resulting mixture is called *retsina.* Try it if you must, though more likely than not, you'll return to *aretsinato,* meaning no resin. The best-known of Greek contributions to tippling is *ouzo,* the national aperitif. It has a faint overtone of licorice while its country cousin is *tsipouro,* stronger and cruder. Greek beers are refreshing light lagers, but soft drinks are often too sweet, as are the prettily colored liqueurs.

TIPPING. Hotels add 15% service charge, but a little extra is expected. Restaurants and nightclubs also add 15%, rising to 20% round Christmas and Easter. Round off the charge on the taxi meter to the next 50 dr.; an extra 30 dr. is charged per bag for luggage put in the boot. Porters charge according to a fixed scale, usually 50 dr. a bag; hatcheck girls 50 dr., cinema and theater ushers 10–20 dr.

MAIL. Airmail letter within Europe, 35 dr. for 20 grams; postcards 27 dr. To the U.S. and Canada: 40 dr.; postcards 32 dr.

CLOSING TIMES. The GNTO supplies a list of banks which remain open afternoons, Saturdays, and Sundays. Business hours vary from season to season and from district to district; thus, Athens summer hours are:

banks	8 A.M. to 2.30 P.M. (Mon.–Fri.)
travel agencies	9 A.M. to 1.30 P.M. and 4.30 to 7.30 P.M. (closed Sat. afternoons)
restaurants	noon to 3.30 P.M. and 7.30 P.M. to midnight
cafés	8 A.M. to well after midnight
nightclubs.	9 P.M. to 5 A.M.
cinemas	5 P.M. to midnight (open-air, 8 to midnight.)

PLACE AND STREET NAMES are given in Greek and Latin characters, according to the modern Greek pronunciation, so that Piraeus becomes Pireas. *Odós* (street) is omitted, but not *Leofóros* (avenue) or *Platia* (square), while the name is in the possessive case; thus Stadium Street becomes simply Stadiou.

USEFUL ADDRESSES. *Consulates: U.S.* Vassilissis Sophias 91; *British* Ploutarhou 1; *Canadian* Ioannou Genadiou 4. *Tourist Police,* Ermou 15; *Emergency first aid* tel. 166. *American Express,* Syntagma Square 2; *National Tourist Information Office,* tel. 322 2545; *Wagons Lits/Cook,* Karageorgi Servias 2. All in Athens.

GETTING AROUND GREECE. By Plane. *Olympic Airways* maintain a remarkably extensive network of internal air routes between Athens and most of the bigger towns and islands. Within a group of islands the smaller are connected by helicopter to the largest. Thessaloniki is linked with the main islands. Between Athens and Thessaloniki there are about eight flights a day, more at peak holiday times.

By Train. Although Greece does not have a very big railway system, it does have one main route from Athens north to Thessaloniki. There it splits, one section continuing into Yugoslavia, another to Bulgaria and the third east to Turkey and Istanbul. There is also a secondary line from Thessaloniki west and then north into Yugoslavia. This is a standard gauge line, diesel operated. The fastest trains between Athens and Thessaloniki take about 6 hours, for the 320 miles.

Greece also has another railway system operating from Athens and Piraeus to the Peloponese peninsula via Corinth and on a circular route to Patra and Kalamata back to Corinth. This is a narrow gauge line (there are plans to standardise it) and picturesque. It is slow, but in many ways very pleasant, with dining or refreshment facilities on most trains. All trains carry first and second class.

Greek Railways have a "Runabout" ticket giving unlimited travel on both its systems, standard gauge and narrow gauge as well as on the extensive network of express buses. This is issued for 2nd class travel only however; with no reductions for children. Available from within Greece only.

By Bus. Greek Railways and several private companies operate long and medium distance bus services in Greece. These are moderately priced and always very popular. Reservations are essential. Full information on these, with timetables, is available at tourist information offices. Departures are on time, arrivals less likely to be so. Except to out-of-the-way villages, buses are fairly comfortable but tend to be overcrowded.

By Boat. The boat and ferry network is both extensive and complicated with schedules constantly changing, although on the trunk route—e.g. Piraeus to Crete or Rhodes or Patra to Corfu—they are reliable. In addition many ferries link the various islands with each other. All ferries carry cars and pre-booking for these, except in the quieter winter weeks, is absolutely essential. Details from travel agents or the various shipping and ferry offices in Athens and Piraeus. Always double-check departure times.

By Car. You drive on the right side of the road. International driving license and green card required. Frontier points are Gevgelija (Yugoslavia) to Evzoni Bitola (Yug.) to Niki; Kulata (Bulgaria) to Promahonas; Kastanea and Kipi-Ipsala Bridge (from Turkey). Major points are open night and day. Daily connection by car-ferry boats between Bari and Brindisi (Italy) and Corfu, Igoumenitsa and Patra from April to October. The Automobile & Touring Club of Greece (ELPA), Athens Tower, 2 Mesogion, Athens, tel. 779 1615, is most helpful to foreign tourists. The AAA is at Syntagma Square, Athens.

Car Hire: *Hellascars,* 7 Stadiou; *Hertz,* 12 Syngrou Ave., and 71 Vassilissis Sofias; *Avis,* 48 Amalias Ave., Athens; all have branches in the bigger towns.

Athens

The origins of Athens are lost in the mists of mythology, in which dim time the Phoenician Kekrops founded a city on the great rock near the sea, later to become the Acropolis. Both the sea god Poseidon and the goddess of wisdom Athena contended for the patronage of Kekropia, with Athena winning the prize. Though Athens rarely knew peace in almost 2,800 years of recorded history, it achieved the first, and by no means least, flowering of European civilization.

The serpent-king Erechtheus was perhaps not strictly historical, but his descendant Codrus was certainly overthrown by an aristocratic oligarchy in the 7th century B.C. Though Solon, one of the Seven Wise Men of Antiquity, tried in the following century to alleviate social tensions, he was no more successful than most reformers and in a typical Greek paradox it needed a tyrant to impose the Solonian constitution. But tyrants in those happier days were mainly benevolent rulers supported by the emerging middle class of merchants and artisans against the great landowners. And it was under Pisistratus that Athens became a major power in Greece, to assume leadership in the national struggle with the Persians. A politician of genius, Themistocles, and a brilliant general, Kimon, prepared Athens for its Golden Age in the 5th century B.C. when Pericles presided over the construction of the Erechtheion, the Parthenon and the Propylaea on the Acropolis. The great dramatists Aeschylus, Sophocles and Euripides; the comedian Aristophanes; the sculptors Phidias and Myron; the historians Herodotus, Thucydides and Xenophon; and, above all, the philosophers Socrates and Plato firmly established a cultural predominance that was to last almost till the end of antiquity.

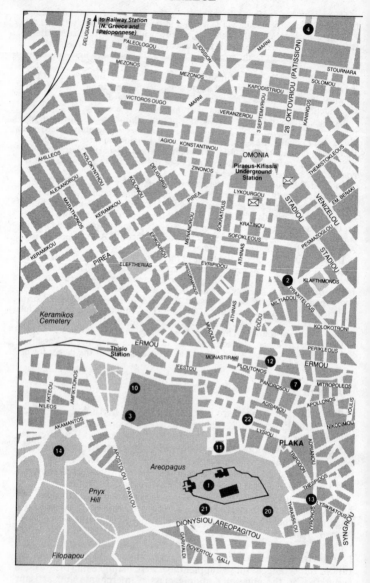

The sack of Athens by the Goths under Alaric at the end of the 4th century A.D. left Athens moldering into total insignificance, despite the shortlived Frankish Duchy under Florentine bankers, who gave way to the Turks in 1455. In 1834, when it became the capital of the newly founded Greek kingdom, its population together with its port, Piraeus, was under 10,000; today it contains over 4,000,000 inhabitants.

The Old City clusters at the foot of the famous, flat-topped hill known as the Acropolis. The new city sprawls over the Attic plain from the sea to the mountains for some 150 square miles, intersected by wide boulevards and squares, lined with high new buildings constructed of the same Pentelic marble as the ancient Parthenon.

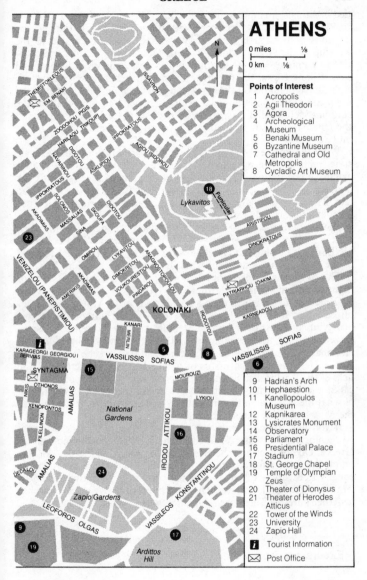

ATHENS

0 miles   ⅛
0 km   ⅛

Points of Interest

1. Acropolis
2. Agii Theodori
3. Agora
4. Archeological Museum
5. Benaki Museum
6. Byzantine Museum
7. Cathedral and Old Metropolis
8. Cycladic Art Museum

9. Hadrian's Arch
10. Hephaestion
11. Kanellopoulos Museum
12. Kapnikarea
13. Lysicrates Monument
14. Observatory
15. Parliament
16. Presidential Palace
17. Stadium
18. St. George Chapel
19. Temple of Olympian Zeus
20. Theater of Dionysus
21. Theater of Herodes Atticus
22. Tower of the Winds
23. University
24. Zapio Hall

ℹ️ Tourist Information
✉️ Post Office

But the chief point of interest in Athens remains the Acropolis round which all the ancient monuments are clustered, so that sightseeing is concentrated in a fairly limited area. Approached by Dionysiou Areopagitou Ave., the first among the antique miscellanea to the right is Pisistratus' theater of Dionysus, scheduled for partial reconstruction. The larger theater of Herodes Atticus is the scene of the annual Athens Festival of Music and Drama. The Sacred Way winds up through the five momumental gates of the Propylaea, the magnificent gateway to the Upper City. To the right stands the graceful temple of Nike Apteros (Wingless Victory), commemorating the victories over the Persians in the 5th century B.C., when the goddess of victory seemed to have settled in Athens, no more in need of wings. The whole of the now barren rocky plateau was once crowded with statues, right up to the majestic columns of the Parthenon, the Virgin's Chamber dedicated to the worship of the virgin goddess Athena. Designed by Ictinus and decorated by Phidias with 92 sculptured metopes, 2 superb pediments and a 523ft-long frieze, the rectangle of the Parthenon is surrounded by eight fluted columns on the short and seventeen on the long sides; the uniqueness lies in the absence of any straight line—the shaft of the columns inclines slightly inward, all horizontal levels are oblique, and the entablature rises gradually to a point three inches higher in the middle.

What the Parthenon is to the Doric, the Erechtheion is to the Ionic style, matchless once again for sheer elegance and refinement after extensive restoration. The replacement by casts of the Caryatids, six maidens in long draperies supporting the southern portico came too late. The faces of the originals in the Acropolis museum are leprous from sulphurous rain.

Having withstood 2,500 years of wars and occupations, the sacred rock is today threatened by a more insidious enemy, air pollution. UNESCO is helping the Greek government to preserve what remains of the "shrine to the moment when European art was born".

The Acropolis is open from 7:30 A.M. to sunset, from 9 P.M. to midnight on full moon nights. Admission 150 dr.

Other highlights which even a one-day visitor to Athens should not miss are the Monument of Lysicrates, the Arch of Hadrian, the Temple of Olympian Zeus, the Olympic Stadium and the Theseion, best-preserved of all the temples dominating the Agora, focal point of ancient Athenian community life, a kind of combination market place and civic center. Here the impressive Stoa of Attalos was reconstructed with the help of the Rockefeller Foundation by the American School of Classical Studies in Athens. This impressive building gives an excellent idea of what life was like in the ancient city-state of Athens. It also houses the Museum of the Agora Excavations.

If you have time for only one museum, it should be the National Archeological Museum. Its collections are the most important in Greece. Do not overlook the Byzantine Museum and the Benaki Museum, the former for its unique collection of icons, the latter for an equally rich variety of Greek regional costumes, Byzantine and Moslem *objets d'art* and weapons. The most interesting Byzantine churches in Athens are St. Theodore, Kapnikarea and Aghios Eleftherios.

Excursions from Athens

These may be taken in one of the many comfortable coaches that operate regularly from Athens. Largest of the companies are *American Express,* Syntagma Sq., *Chat,* and *Hellas,* 4 and 7 Stadiou. Their English-speaking guides all sound as though they had gone to graduate school in archeology, and we recommend seeing the sights with them.

Among the shorter excursions well worth taking are: Mount Parnis, 19 miles, altitude 3,281 feet, with lovely alpine scenery; Marathon Lake, 19 miles; Marathon Mound, 24 miles, with collective tomb of the Athenian soldiers killed in the great victory over the Persians in 490 B.C.; and Sounion, 44 miles, with the Temple of Poseidon on a hill overlooking the Aegean Sea.

PRACTICAL INFORMATION FOR ATHENS

 HOTELS. Of strictly utilitarian sameness, hotels in both Moderate and Inexpensive catagories all offer the expected modern comforts, but lack any individual features, location constituting their only distinction.

Deluxe

Athenaeum Intercontinental, somewhat off-center at Syngrou Ave. 89 (tel. 922 5950). With 600 rooms, Athens' largest; nightclub, pool, shopping center.

Athens Hilton, Vassilissis Sofias Av. 46 (tel. 722 0201). Typical of the chain, with a pool, restaurants and nightclub on the roof terrace.

Caravel, Vassileos Alexandrou Av. 2 (tel. 729 0721). Pool. Across the road from the Hilton.

Grande Bretagne, on Syntagma Square (tel. 323 0251). Distinguished and very central. Excellent restaurants.

Holiday Inn, Mihalakopoulou (tel. 724 8322). Not far from the Hilton. Disco, nightclub, pool.

Ledra Marriott, Syngrou Ave. 115 (tel. 952 5211). Away from center, but outstanding with excellent restaurant and all the expected comforts; pool.

NJV Meridien, on Syntagma Square (tel. 325 5301). Representing the French chain, complete with brasserie.

Expensive

Ariane and **Embassy,** Timoleontos Vassou 22 and 15 (tel. 646 6361 and 642 1152). Furnished apartments, behind the U.S. Embassy.

Athens Chandris, Syngrou Av. 385 (tel. 941 4824). Pool, roofgarden. Far from center; near, but not on, the sea.

Delice, Vassileos Alexandrou 3 (tel. 723 8311).

Divani Zafolia Palace, Parthenonos 19 (tel. 922 2945). Pool; near Plaka.

Electra, Ermou 5 (tel. 322 3222). Very central.

Electra Palace, Nikodimou 18 (tel. 324 1401). Small pool; close to Plaka.

Esperia Palace, Stadiou 22 (tel. 323 8001). Least expensive; close to Syntagma Square.

Golden Age and **Riva,** Mihalakopoulou 57 and 114 (tel. 724 0861 and 770 6611). Near the Hilton.

King Minos, Pireos 1 (tel. 523 111). Overlooks noisy Omonia Square.

Olympic Palace, Filellinon 16 (tel. 323 7611). With nightclub.

Parthenon, Makri 6 (tel. 923 4596). Near the Acropolis.

President, Kifissias Av. 43 (tel. 692 4600). Some way out. Pool.

St. George Lycabettus, Kleomenous 2 (tel. 729 0710). Commands a splendid view from the slopes of the Lycabettus hill.

Moderate

Near Omonia Square—Athens Center, Sofokleous 22 (tel. 524 8511). 136 rooms, roofgarden.

Candia, Deliyanni 40 (tel. 524 6112). 142 rooms, pool, roofgarden.

Dorian Inn, Pireos 15 (tel. 523 9782). 146 rooms, pool, roofgarden.

Eretria, Halkokondyli 12 (tel. 363 5311). 63 rooms, fairly quiet.

Grand, Veranzerou 10 (tel. 522 2010). 99 rooms, above average food.

Ionis, Kalkokondyli 41 (tel. 523 2311). 102 rooms, one of the newest.

Marathon, Karolou 23 (tel. 523 1865). 93 rooms, no restaurant.

Titania, Venizelou Av. 52 (tel. 360 9611). 398 rooms, roofgarden.

Beyond Omonia Square—Anastasia, Platia Viktorias 7 (tel. 883 4511). 61 rooms; in residential district.

Crystal, Achilleos 4 (tel. 523 1083). 84 rooms, slightly cheaper.

Oscar, Samou 25 (tel. 883 4215). 124 rooms, disco, roofgarden; near railway station.

Plaza, Acharnon 78 (tel. 822 5111). 126 rooms, roofgarden.

Stanley, Odysseos 1 (tel. 524 1611). 395 rooms, pool, roofgarden.

Xenophon, Acharnon 340 (tel. 202 0310). 186 rooms, roofgarden.

Closer to Syntagma Square—Aphrodite, Apollonos 21 (tel. 323 4357). 84 rooms, no restaurant, slightly cheaper.

Arethusa, Mitropoleos 6 (tel. 322 9431). 87 rooms, roofgarden.
Athens Gate, Syngrou Av. 10 (tel. 923 8302). 106 rooms; close to Acropolis.
Lycabette, Valaoritou 6 (tel. 363 3514). 39 rooms; in quiet pedestrian zone.
Minerva, Stadiou 3 (tel. 323 0915). 47 rooms; on top floors of office block.
Omiros, Apollonos 15 (tel. 323 5486). 37 rooms; roofgarden.
Pan, Mitropoleos 11 (tel. 323 7816). 48 rooms; near the Plaka district.

Beyond Syntagma Square—Christina, Petmeza 15 (tel. 921 5353). 93 rooms, quiet.
Damon, Syngrou Av. 142 (tel. 923 2171). 96 rooms; roofgarden.
Sirene, Lagoumitzi 15 (tel. 922 9310). 103 rooms, roofgarden, pool.

Beyond the U.S. Embassy—Alexandros, Timoleontos Vassou 8 (tel. 644 1511). 96 rooms; close to the Lycabettus hill.
Athinais, Vassilissis Sofias Av. 99 (tel. 643 1133). 84 rooms; close to the embassy.
Ilissia, Mihalakopoulou 25 (tel. 724 4051). 69 rooms, pleasant restaurant, behind the Hilton.

Inexpensive

Near Omonia—Alkistis, Platia Theatrou 18 (tel. 321 9811). 120 rooms, roofgarden.
Aristides, Sokratous 50 (tel. 522 3940). 90 rooms, no restaurant.
Aristoteles, Acharnon 15 (tel. 522 0509). 60 rooms.
Asty, Pireos 2 (tel. 523 0424). 128 rooms.
Attalos, Athinas 29 (tel. 321 2801). Most of the 80 rooms with showers, roofgarden.
Balaska, Liossion 45 (tel. 883 5211). 83 rooms, airconditioned, roofgarden.
Capri, Psaromilingou 6 (tel. 325 2091). 44 rooms, airconditioned, roofgarden.
Iniochos, Veranzerou 26 (tel. 523 0811). 134 rooms, airconditioned.
Odeon, Pireos 42 (tel. 523 9206). 56 rooms.
Omonia, Platia Omonias 4 (tel. 523 7210). 260 rooms, large bar overlooking the busy square.

Near Syntagma—Amazon, Pendelis 7 (tel. 323 4002). 36 rooms, near the Plaka district.
Hermes, Apollonos 19 (tel. 323 5514). 45 rooms, roofgarden.

At Piraeus

Overlooking the Saronic Gulf—Cavo D'Oro (M), Vassileos Pavlou Av. 19 (tel. 411 3742). 74 rooms, airconditioned, disco, roofgarden.
Arion (I), Vassileos Pavlou Av. 109 (tel. 412 1425). 36 rooms, no restaurant.
Leriotis (I), Akti Themistokleous 294 (tel. 451 6640). 45 rooms, quiet for a longer stay, no restaurant.

Near the main harbor—Homeridion (M), Trikoupi 32 (tel. 451 9932). 59 rooms, airconditioned, disco, roofgarden.
Park (M), Kolokotroni 103 (tel. 452 4611). 80 rooms, airconditioned, disco, roofgarden.
Savoy (M), Vassileos Konstantinou 93 (tel. 413 1102). 71 rooms, airconditioned.
Anemoni (I), Evripidou 65 (tel. 411 1768). 45 rooms, no restaurant.
Anita (I), Notara 25 (tel. 412 1024). 26 rooms, no restaurant, very close to the port.
Atlantis (I), Notara 138 (tel. 452 6871). 54 rooms, no restaurant.

Beach Resorts

The southeast coast of Attica, from Faliro to Sounio, is studded with hotels authorized to charge half board. Distances from Athens in miles, in brackets.

Anavissos (31). *Alexander Beach* (E); *Apollo Beach,* the large *Eden Beach, Kalypso Motel* (M); *Silver Beach* (I).

Glifada (11). Near airport. *Astir Beach,* deluxe prices, but not airconditioned, bungalows and nightclub. *Atrium, Congo Palace, Golden Sun, Oasis, Palace, Palmyra* (E); *Emmantina, Fenix, Four Seasons, Gripsholm, London, Niki, Regina Maris, Sea View* (M); all airconditioned. *Adonis, Avra,* airconditioned *Beau Rivage, Glyfada, Oceanis, Perla, Rial* (I).

Kalamaki (8). Very near airport. *Albatross, Saronis, Tropical, Venus* (M); *Attica, Blue Sea, Galaxy, Hellenikon* (I).

Kavouri (14). *Pine Hill, Sunrise* (M).

Lagonissi (25). *Xenia Lagonissi* (E), hotel and bungalows on private beach, nightclub. *Var* (M), not on beach.

Paleo Faliro (5). Polluted Sea. *Avra, Coral,* airconditioned *Poseidon* (M); *Ephi* (I).

Saronida (27). *Saronic Gate* (E). *Delfinia* (M).

Sounio (44). *Aegeon; Belvedere Park* and *Sounion Beach* (E), bungalows; the large *Surf Beach* (M), disco, pool, tennis.

Varkiza (19). *Apollonia* (E); *Glaros, Varkiza* (M); *Holiday* (I).

Voula (13). None airconditioned. *Voula Beach* (E); *Castello Beach* (M); *Noufara, Orion, Palma, Rondo* (I).

Vouliagmeni (16). *Astir Palace* (L), 3 hotels and bungalows, indoor and outdoor pools, private beach. *Armonia* (E). *Greek Coast, Margi House, Paradise, Strand* (M); all airconditioned.

Mount Parnis

Mont Parnes (L) (tel. 246 9111). 106 rooms, casino, nightclub, pool. On the highest of the mountains around Athens (22 miles from the city), reached by road or cable car.

 RESTAURANTS. Of the dining rooms of the (L) hotels, the Hilton's *Supper Club* and St. George Lycabettus' *Grand Salon* command outstanding views, while the Ledra Marriot offers the most original choice. The *Brasserie des Arts* of the Meridien on Syntagma Square is as French as one can expect.

Expensive

The greatest concentration is in the town center near Syntagma Square and around the Hilton, but **Dionyssos,** Rovertou Galli 43 (tel. 923 3182), enhances meals by the view over the Acropolis opposite.

Right in the center, **Floca's** and **Zonar's,** both Venizelou Ave. 9 (tel. 323 0069 and 323 0336), are the leading café restaurants. Both ideal for watching the passing crowd.

Nearby **G.B. Corner,** (tel. 323 0251), in the Grande Bretagne Hotel, is outstanding for the price. **Corfu,** Kriezotou 6 off Syntagma Square (tel. 361 3011), excellent for business lunches, efficient service.

Stage Door, Voukourestiou 4 (tel. 361 2801), small, good for steaks.

All near the Hilton are—**Mike's Saloon,** Vassileos Alexandrou 5 (tel. 729 1689). **Othello's,** Mihalakopoulou 45 (tel. 729 1481), specialty Beef Stroganoff. **Papakia** (Duckling), Iridanou 5 (tel. 721 2421), naturally concentrating on duck, in a pleasant old house with patio; and from Oct. to May, for piano music, **Riva,** Mihalakopoulou 114 (tel. 770 6611); **Flame Steak House,** Chatziyanni Mexi 9 (tel. 723 8540), and **Steak Room,** Aeginitou 6 (tel. 721 7445), both specialize in grills.

Bajazzo, Ploutarhou 35 (tel. 729 1420). An attractive new spot, run by an Austrian patron/chef. Imaginative food and chic decor. In a street up above Kolonakis.

In the cool Kifissia Suburb you can select trout from the pond at the **Belle Hélène,** Platia Politias (tel. 801 4776); **Blue Pine,** Tsaldari 37 (tel. 801 2969), also recommended.

Foreign cooking—Constantinopolitan at the pretentious **Gerofinikas,** Pindarou 10 (tel. 362 2719).

American at the **Saloon,** Alkmanos 36 (tel. 724 2208), and **Stage Coach,** Loukianou 6 (tel. 724 3955).

French at **Escargot,** Ventiri 9 (tel. 723 0349); **L'Abreuvoir,** Xenokratous 51 (tel. 722 9061); **Je Reviens,** Xenokratous 49 (tel. 721 1174); **La Bohème,** Pratinou 80 (tel. 723 3546).

Italian at **Al Convento,** Anapiron Polemou 4 (tel. 723 0163).

Chinese at **China,** Evfroniou 72 (tel. 723 3200).

At all these establishments it is advisable to make reservations during the summer season, but not in the fish restaurants or lower categories.

For seafood you have a wide choice all along the coast from Piraeus to Vouliagmeni. In the picturesque boat harbor of Mikrolímano, a string of excellent fish restaurants, **Aglamair,** the most touristy and expensive, **Kanaris, Miaoulis,** line the waterfront. Further along **Marides** and **Soupies** at Kalamaki, **Antonopoulos** and **Psaropoulos** at Glifada and **Petros** at Varkiza are the pick of the bunch.

Moderate

Delphi, Nikis 13 off Syntagma Square; busy, but worth it.

Dionysos, a second one, on top of Mount Lykabettas with panoramic views, reached by cog railway from near Kolonaki Square.

Diros, Xenofondos 10–12, a couple of blocks from Syntagma. New and solid place; expert with tourists.

Ideal, Venizelou 46, exceptionally large menu.

Jimmy's Cooking, Loukianou 36, limited but worthwhile choice.

Remezzo, Haritos 6, off Kolonaki Square. Dining area, lounge and bar; nightly after 8.

Among the bewildering variety of *tavernas* in the maze of the old Plaka district, a pedestrian zone at the foot of the Acropolis, the **Epta Adelfia, Kastro, Mostrou. Old Rock** and especially **Palaia Athena** are really nightclubs with Greek food and floorshows. Opening earlier and content with orchestras are the **Arias, Bacchus** and **Kalokerinos.**

More genuinely Greek, with only the traditional three guitarists are **Fandis, Geros tou Morea, Vlachou, Xynou.**

Inexpensive

American Coffee Shop, Nikis 1; **Meteora,** Xenofontos 5; **Syntrivani,** Filellinon 5, with garden, all off Syntagma Square.

Bretannia, Omonia Square; fried eggs at sunrise, yogurt with honey in the small hours.

 GETTING AROUND ATHENS. None of the 15,000 yellow taxis ever has their sign illuminated to indicate emptiness in the rush hours, which seem to stretch longer and longer, or when it rains. Drivers appear to have arrived in town simultaneously with the tourists, judging by their ignorance of any but the main streets, which, to add to the confusion, are renamed more frequently than seems justifiable. A show of authority might even get you to your destination by a less round-about route. Fare from the airport or Piraeus harbor to the town center about 500 dr.

Buses, and the more comfortable yellow trolleybuses, run until midnight; at rush hours they are dangerously overcrowded and one has literally to fight one's way through a seething, gesticulating crowd in order to board the vehicle. All suburbs and beaches of the southern coast are connected with buses from the center of the city. An electric service connects Omonia Square via Monastiraki and the Theseion with Piraeus; and via the northern suburbs with the resort of Kifissia.

There are conducted motor coach tours of the city by day and night, organized by *American Express,* Syntagma Square, *CHAT,* Stadiou 4, *Key Tours,* Ermou 2, among others.

NIGHTLIFE. The indigenous tavernas, bouzoukia, tourist and regular tavernas are as varied as the Western-style nightspots, cabarets, discos, and disco-restaurants. All those listed are expensive, by Greek standards anyway. Few tourists trying the music and dancing of the extremely noisy bouzoukia orchestras, a clanging oriental mandoline, come back for more. The largest are on Syngrou Ave.: *Athina,* 165; *Diogenes,* 255; *Regina,* 40. Tourist tavernas with floor shows are concentrated in the Plaka quarter below the Acropolis: try *Dionyssos,* Lysiou 7, *Mostrou,* Mnisikleous 22, or *Palia Athena,* Flessa 4. In the same neighborhood are several much cheaper and simpler tavernas, usually with an "orchestra" of three guitarists. As well as the nightclubs in the international hotel chains, cabarets boast equally international programs, though with vague local color: *Coronet,* Venizelou 4; *Maxim,* Othonos 6, Syntagma. The most fashionable disco-restaurants are: *Athinea,* Venizelou 6, and *Papagayo,* Patriarhou Ioakim 37; both conveniently central. The discos *Make Up,* Venizelou 10, and *Disco 14,* Kolonaki Sq. 14, are similarly central.

MUSEUMS. Opening hours: Winter (Oct. 15-March 15) 9 A.M.–3:30 P.M.; Summer, 8 A.M.–1 P.M., 3–6 P.M. Most closed on Tuesdays. Liable to change. Archeological sites are open from 7.30 A.M. in the summer to sunset. In winter, they open at 8 or 9 A.M. The Acropolis is also open at night at full moon.

The Acropolis Museum, full of rare objects found on the Acropolis. Among the main exhibits are the Caryatids of the Erechtheion, brought indoors to save them from further pollution.

Byzantine Museum, Vassilissis Sofias Ave. 22, in attractive 19th-century building with modern additions. Huge collection of icons, and some lovely embroidery, especially the 14th-century *Epitaphios of Thessaloniki.*

Benaki Museum, Koumbari 1, open 8.30 to 2. Large and varied collection, largely from private sources, from ancient sculpture, through Byzantine pieces, Ottoman ceramics and Chinese jade to modern pictures. Stunning collection of Greek national costumes.

Museum of Greek Folk Art, Kydathineon 17, large exhibit of traditional folk art, a wonderful collection of Rhodian pottery, clerical robes, costumes and embroideries.

The Keramikos Museum, Ermou 148, has finds from the ancient cemetery.

The Kanellopoulos Museum, small, excellent, and overlooked, at junction of Theorias and Panos Streets, behind Acropolis. Traditional arts, Byzantine jewelry, icons etc. Worth a visit.

National Archeological Museum, 28 Oktovriou 44, one good reason for visiting Athens. Staggering collection of treasures beginning with Schliemann's finds from Mycenae. Exhibits not always well labeled, but they speak for themselves. This is a must for anyone wanting to get oriented to Greek classical art and history, before setting off on a tour of sites elsewhere in Greece.

National Gallery, Vassileos Konstantinou 50, opposite the Hilton, contains some El Grecos, but mainly 19th-century paintings.

Stoa of Attalos Museum at the ancient Agora shows finds of the American School of Classical Studies, worth visiting while seeing the Agora itself.

Delphi

Less than 100 miles northwest of Athens is one of the most impressive sights in Greece—Delphi—where the famous Delphic Oracle once foretold the destiny of men. When you see these extensive ruins 2,000 feet above the Bay of Itea, you will realize why it was regarded with religious awe by the ancient Greeks. In the lee of windswept Mount Parnassus, this is one of the most beautiful spots in Europe, the silver-green Sea of Olives extending to the blue gulf far below the Temple of

Apollo, the Treasuries along the Sacred Way, the Theater, the Stadium, the Temples of Athena excavated on the steep slopes by the French Archeological School, beginning in 1892. Among the masterpieces of sculpture in the museum, covering a millenium from the archaic to the late Roman periods, are the famous bronze Charioteer and a marble Antinous. The sacred Castalian spring flows as pure and cold as when pilgrims to the Delphic Oracle had to undergo ablution thousands of years ago.

After passing uninteresting Thebes and Levadia, where a medieval fortress towers above the springs of Lethe (Oblivion) and Mnemosyne (Remembrance), the road enters the splendid mountain scenery of the Parnassus shortly before the fateful crossroads where Oedipus fulfilled the dreadful prophecy of the Sphinx by killing his own father. A sideroad leads the few miles to Osios Loukas, an 11th-century Byzantine monastery with beautiful mosaics in a peaceful setting.

PRACTICAL INFORMATION FOR DELPHI

HOTELS. *Amalia, Vouzas, Xenia,* all (E); *Castalia, Europa, King Iniohos,* all (M); *Hermes, Leto, Parnassos, Phaeton, Pythia, Stadion,* all (I).

Restaurants. Except for the *Challet Maniati* (M) and *Taverna Asteras* (I), meals on the terraces overlooking the olive groves in the gorge below are more memorable for the view than the food.

The Peloponnese

Shortly after the last houses of the sprawling Athenian conglomeration on the way to the Peloponnese, the 6th-century monastery of Daphni, rebuilt some seven hundred years later by Cistercian monks as the burial place of Athens' Frankish dukes, contains superb mosaics. Facing the island of Salamis across the narrow straits where Xerxes' Persian fleet was decisively defeated in 480 B.C., the ruins of Eleusis, site of antiquity's most important mystery celebrations since times immemorial, are badly polluted by the surrounding factories.

Old Corinth, 58 miles by the motorway and across the Corinth Canal, was a Roman town founded by Julius Caesar on the site of the destroyed Greek city, of which only the sixth-century B.C. temple of Apollo remains. You can drive up to the huge Crusader castle of Acro-Corinth, once crowned by a sanctuary to Aphrodite, with a thousand sacred prostitutes earning their dowry while working for the goddess.

Even if you are not in Greece for the annual Epidauros Festival in summer, you should visit Epidaurus, only 18 miles from Nafplio, another shrine of ancient Greece, the sanctuary of Aesculapius, God of Healing. See the foundations of the temples and hospitals, but especially the incomparable open-air theater, whose acoustics you can test yourself. You can actually hear a stage whisper from the top row of this theater which still seats 14,000 spectators at the summer festival.

Mycenae, 80 miles from Athens, was a fortified town, destroyed in 468 B.C. and totally forgotten until 1874, when the German archaeologist Schliemann unearthed this fabulous stronghold of the 13th-century B.C. Achaean kings. This was the seat of the doomed house of Atreus, of Agamemnon and his wife, the vengeful Clytemnestra, sister of Helen of Troy. When Schliemann uncovered the six shaft graves of the royal circle he felt sure that among these were the tombs of Agamemnon and Clytemnestra. The gold masks and crowns, the daggers, jewelry and other treasures found in the tombs of Mycenae are now in the National Archaeological Museum in Athens. The astounding beehive tombs cut into the hills outside the reconstructed walls, the Lion

Gate and castle ruins crowning their barren hill are the shell of the first great civilization of continental Europe. Further south, beyond Argos, Europe's oldest continuously inhabited town, and the cyclopean ramparts of Tiryns, Nafplio is a beautifully situated, picturesque little town protected by huge Venetian fortifications.

Matching Delphi's majestic grandeur with idyllic serenity, Olympia lies 200 miles southwest of Athens, by the motorway via Patra, capital of the Peloponnese. The first Olympic Games were held in 776 B.C. and were celebrated quadrennially until 393 A.D. Excavations are still uncovering statues and votive offerings among the olive groves and pine trees surrounding the Olympic stadium, the imposing ruins of the temples of Zeus and Hera in the sacred precinct. Outstanding among the two museum's many treasures is one of the most perfect pieces of sculpture in existence—the *Hermes of Praxiteles.*

PRACTICAL INFORMATION FOR THE PELOPONNESE

MYCENAE. *Agamemnon, Petite Planète,* small (I).

NAFPLIO. *Xenia's Palace* (L), hotel and bungalow above town with splendid views.
Amalia (E), in spacious grounds 2 miles out; by the sea. *Amphytrion, Xenia* (M). *Alkyon, Dioskouri, Galini, Nafplia, Park* and *Rex,* comfortable (I).

OLYMPIA. Best is the *Amalia; Spap* overlooks the ruins. Both (E).
Antonios, Apollo, Neda, Neon Olympia, airconditioned *Olympic Village* and *Xenia* are all (M). *Ilis, Kronion* (I).
Miramare Olympia Beach (E), hotel, bungalow and villa complex with pool, sports facilities, on a sandy beach 18 miles from Olympia.

PATRA. *Astir* (E), tel. 27 6311, 120 rooms; *Moreas* (E), tel. 42 4541, 105 rooms, not airconditioned, but comfortable; *Galaxy* (M), tel. 27 8815, 53 airconditioned rooms; *Mediterranee* (I), tel. 27 9602, 96 rooms; off-center and closer to the beach is *Delfini* (I), 71 rooms, pool; both airconditioned, with restaurants.
On neighboring beaches—*Averof Grand, Kyllini Golden Beach,* (E). *Achaia Beach, Alexander Beach, Kalogria Beach,* (M). *Rion Beach,* (I).

North of Athens

On the western confines of the Thessalian plain, Greece's granary, rises a forest of gigantic rock needles to 1,820 ft., crowned by improbable 14th-century monasteries. Visitors used to be hauled up in nets, but in the 1920s, stairs were hollowed out of the sheer cliff face. One of Europe's unique sites, Meteora is easily accessible by road from Kalambaka, two miles away.

Thessaloniki, Greece's second city, is a large modern town containing some outstanding Byzantine churches, most famous being St. George's, originally the mausoleum of the Roman Emperor Galerius, whose Triumphal Arch (A.D. 303) still stands.

The lovely beaches along the three prongs of the mountainous Halkidiki peninsula to the east have become the playground of northern Greece, with a large choice of modern hotels. On Mount Athos, the Eastern prong, some seven hundred Orthodox monks still live the secluded life of the Middle Ages in imposing monasteries, the oldest dating back to 963. Women are not permitted to visit this living vestige of medieval piety and seclusion; men without a permit can go only during the day.

The astounding gold treasures which have come to light since 1978 at Vergina in the burial mound of 4th-century B.C. Macedonian kings—

most likely including the tomb of Philip II, father of Alexander the Great—are the pride of the Archeological Museum.

PRACTICAL INFORMATION FOR NORTH OF ATHENS

HALKIDIKI. Remote and spacious, managed by Grand Metropolitan Hotels of London, the huge selfcontained resort complex of *Porto Carras* includes *Meliton Beach* (L), *Sithonia Beach* (E), and *Village Inn* (M), casino, golf course, yacht marina.

All (E) are—*Athos Palace, Eagle's Palace, Kassandra Palace, Mendi, Pallini Beach, Robinson Club Phocea.*

All (M) are—*Alexander Beach, Ammon Zeus, Gerakina Beach, Mount Athos, Sermili, Strand, Xenia Ouranopolis* and *Xenia Paliouri.*

Both (I)—*Kallithea, Kouvraki.*

KALAMBAKA. *Motel Divani,* (E). *Xenia,* (M). *Galaxias, Olympia, Rex,* (I).

THESSALONIKI. *Macedonia Palace* (L), with pool; on the seafront.

Both (E) are—*Capitol, Electra Palace.*

All (M) are—*Astor,* large *Capsis, City, El Greco, Metropolitan, Olympia, Queen Olga, Rotonda, Victoria.*

All (I), airconditioned in Thessaloniki's rather noisy center are—*Amalia, Esperia, Park, Pella.*

In the hills of Panorama, commanding an enchanting view over the town and the Thermaïc Gulf, both (E), are—*Nefeli, Panorama.*

At Agia Triada, 13 miles across the Gulf are *Sun Beach* (M); and *Galaxy* (I).

Restaurants. The seafront boulevard, Vassileos Konstantinou, is lined with restaurants and cafes. *Stratis* (M) is famed for *mídia tiganitá* (fried mussels). Good but expensive seafood in the fish restaurants of the Aretsou suburb.

The Isles of Greece

Rhodes, less than an hour by air from Athens, is like a splendid outdoor museum of ancient Greek, Roman and Crusader history. Among the chief sights is the medieval city of the Knights Hospitalers of St. John of Jerusalem, still girdled by impressive walls. See also the acropolis of the ancient town of Lindos, with its temple of Athena overlooking the blue Aegean. Rhodes has taken first place as a tourist resort and a large choice of excellent modern hotels is available.

Corfu is just as beautiful. It lies in the Ionian Sea, less than an hour by air from Athens. The civilized formality of Venetian life still lingers on, despite the intensive tourist development.

Mykonos is a perfect place for swimming and exploring in the Aegean Sea. Marked by the numerous windmills rising above gleaming white houses in stunning contrast to the blue sea, it is a sophisticated mundane contrast to the ruins of Apollo's sanctuary on nearby Delos.

Crete is a paradise for the amateur archeologist who does not consider it infra dig. to relax on fine sandy beaches. Forty-five minutes south of Athens by air, this large island was the seat of the great Minoan civilization, whose fascinating remains, including the stupendous Palace of Knossos, are one of the most impressive sights in the entire Mediterranean area. The more beautifully sited Palace of Festos near the south coast is 36 miles south of the largest town, Iraklio, which is still surrounded by the Venetian ramparts that withstood a 24-year Turkish siege. The less imposing ruins of Malia dominate the loveliest north coast beach.

Hios, Kos, Lesbos and **Samos** are becoming increasingly popular. Kos, the birthplace of Hippocrates, Father of Medicine, rivals neighboring Rhodes in variety of sites, and was endowed with an Olympic Health Center in 1984. Wooded Lesbos, where burning Sappho loved and wrote, and mountainous Samos close to Turkey abound in antiquities and scenic beauties.

The islands of the Saronic Gulf, off the mainland shores, are more easily visited than any others. In summer the frequent daily ferryboats to **Egina,** and hydrofoils to **Poros, Idra** and **Spetses** are supplemented by one-day cruises.

PRACTICAL INFORMATION FOR THE ISLANDS

CORFU. In the lovely town are—the *Corfu Palace* (L).
All (M) are—*Arion, Astron, King Alkinoos, Marina, Olympic.*
All (I) are—*Arcadion, Atlantis, Bretagne, Ionion.*
Elsewhere in the island, on or near the beaches are the following. The *Corfu Hilton,* one of the few island hotels to justify an (L); the others tend to be good (E)s: *Astir Palace,* the former royal residence *Castello, Eva Palace, Ilios, Miramare Beach, Poseidon Beach, Val Tour Kerkyra.*
All (E) are *Aghios Gordios, Akrotiri, Ariti, Corfu Chandris* and *Dassia Chandris, Corcyra Beach, Corfu Divani Palace, Delfinia, Elaea Beach, Ermones, Grand Glyfada, Kerkyra Golf, Kontokali Palace, Nissaki, Regency, Robinson Club, San Stefano, Yaliskari Palace.*
All (M)—*Aeolus Beach, Akti, Emerald, Ipsos Beach, Irinna, Messoghi, Oceanis, Paleokastritsa, Potamaki, Roda Beach.*

CRETE. Agia Galini, fishing village on the unspoilt south coast: *Acropolis, Areti, Astoria, Candia, Dedalos,* all (I).
Ierapetra. Both (E): *Ferma Beach, Petra Mare. Atlantis* (I).
All other places listed are on the much more developed north coast.
Agios Nikolaos. All (L)—*Istron Bay, Minos Beach, Minos Palace, Mirabello Village.* Both (E)—*Hermes, Mirabello.* Both (M)—*Ariadne Beach, Coral.* All (I)—*Akratos, Creta, Cronos, Du Lac, Rea.* 4 miles out of town, *Astir Palace Elounda, Elounda Beach, Elounda Mare,* all (L). *Elounda Marmin* (E).
Hania. Both (E)—*Kydon, Panorama.* All (M)—*Doma, Porto Veneziano, Samaria, Xenia.* All (I)—*Canea, Creta, Diktyna, Lucia,* and the bungalows of *Aptera Beach.*
Iraklio. All (E)—*Astoria, Atlantis, Galaxy.* All (M)—*Castron, Esperia, Mediterranean, Petra.* All comfortable (I)s—*Castello, Daedalos, Domenico, El Greco, Galini, Heraklion, Olympic, Park.*
On nearby beaches. All (E) are—*Agapi Beach, Arina Sands, Capsis Beach, Creta Beach, Knossos Beach, Minoa Palace.* Both (M)—*Amnissos, Motel Xenia.*
Limenas Hersonissou. (L)—*Creta Maris.* All (E)—*Belvedere, Candia Beach, Lyttos, Marina, Nora* (M). Both (I)—*Albatros, Glaros.*
Linoperamata. Both (E)—*Apollonia Beach, Zeus Beach.*
Maleme. *Crete Chandris* (M).
Malia. All (E)—*Ikaros Village, Kernos Beach, Sirens' Beach. Malia Beach* (M). *Grammatikaki* (I).
Rethymno. All (E) on nearby beaches—*El Greco, Kalypso Village, Rithymna.* All (M) are—*Brascos, Ideon, Joan, Orion.* All (I) are—*Astali, Bali Beach, Golden Beach.*
Sitia. *Kappa Club* (E). *Maresol* (M). *Itanos* (I).
Stalida. *Anthoussa Beach* (E). *Blue Sea* (M). *Iliotropion* (I).

EGINA (AEGINA). Both (M)—*Danae, Nafsika.* All (I) are—*Areti, Avra, Klonos, Pharos.*
4 miles from town: *Aegina Maris, Moondy Bay,* both (M).
On the beach of Agia Marina: *Apollo, Argo* (M). *Akti, Aphaea, Galini, Marina,* all (I).

IDRA. All (M) and rather unsatisfactory are—*Hydroussa, Miramare, Miranda.* Better try *Porto Hydra* or *Kappa Club,* both (E), on the mainland opposite.

KOS. *Hippocrates Palace* (L), Dr. C. Barnard's Olympic Health Center. All (E) are—*Atlantis, Carlos Village, Caravia Beach, Continental Palace, Dimitra Beach, Norida Beach, Oceanis, Ramira Beach, Sun Palace.* All (M)—*Agios*

Konstantinos, Alexandra, Kos, Theoxenia. All (I) are—*Elli, Elma, Koulias, Messoghios, Milva, Oscar, Veroniki.*

MYKONOS. *Cavo Tagou, Leto* (E). All (M) are—*Despotiko, Kouneni, Petassos, Rhenia, Rohari, Theoxenia.* Both (I)—*Manto, Zannis.* In the hills is the excellent *Ano Mera* (E). Beach hotels are: *Aphrodite, Alkistis,* both (M); *Manoulas Beach, Mykonos Beach* and *Paralos Beach,* all (I).

Beaches: there are several popular ones near town but they're crowded. Better to go a distance, by bus, to lovely *Psarrou,* by boat to *Ilia, Paradise* and *Super Paradise* beaches (the last two for nude sunbathing); or right across the island by bus to beautiful *Kalafatis* beach.

MYTILENE (Lesbos). All (M) are—*Blue Sea, Katia Beach, Xenia. Lesvion* (I).

At **Mithymna,** on a pebbly beach below a picturesque village, are the *Alkeos, Delphinia* and *Molyvos,* all (M).

POROS. All (M)—on pine-fringed beaches are *Neon Aegli, Pavlou, Poros* and, largest, *Sirene,* pool and disco. On the village waterfront above openair restaurants more remarkable for their situation than their food are *Latsi* and *Saron,* both (M). *Angyra, Chryssi Avgi,* both (I), are on nearby beaches.

At **Galatas** on the mainland opposite—*Stella Maris* (M); *Galatia* (I).

RHODES. Quality and quantity of accommodations are among the best in Greece.

Out of town the *Rodos Palace* (L) groups chalets round a hotel, but only the *Electra Palace, Golden Beach* and *Miramare Beach* bungalows, all (E), are directly on the sea.

Just across the road to the airport along the west coast are *Olympic Palace* (L); *Avra Beach, Bel Air, Dionyssos,* the huge *Metropolitan, Oceanis, Rhodos Bay,* all (E); *Leto, Solemar,* both (M).

On the east coast *Apollo Beach, Blue Sea, Colossos Beach, Eden Roc, Faliraki Beach* are (E).

In town the leader is the *Grand Hotel* (L), which houses the casino. Attractive (E)s are—*Belvedere, Blue Sky, Cairo Palace, Chevaliers Palace, Ibiscus, Imperial, Kamiros, Mediterranean, Park, Regina, Siravast, Sunwing.*

Among the numerous (M)s you'll find the *Acandia, Alexia, Amphitryon, Angela, Athina, Delfini, Despo, Esperia, Europa, Konstantinos, Manousos, Phoenix, Plaza.*

The larger (I)s are—*Achillion, Africa, Als, Aphrodite, Arion,* airconditioned *Caracas, Carina, El Greco, Marie, Semiramis.*

SAMOS. In town: *Aeolis, Samos Bay,* airconditioned *Xenia* (M); *Samos, Sun Waves* (I). On its own beach near the pretty village of **Pythagorio:** *Doryssa Bay,* pool, minigolf, tennis (E). In the village: *Phito* (M), bungalows. *Glikoriza Beach, Ilios, Polyxeni, Pythagoras* (I). At **Karlovassi:** *Aegeon, Merope* (M).

SPETSES. Both (E) are—*Kastelli, Spetsae.* All (M) are—*Ilios, Possidonion, Roumanis.* All (I) are—*Faros, Myrtoon, Star.*

At **Kosta** on the mainland opposite—*Cap D'Or* and *Lido,* both (M).

At **Porto Heli** on the Peloponnese close by—*Cosmos, Hinitsa Beach, Porto Heli,* all (E). All (M) are—*Apollo Beach, Galaxi, Giouli, La Cité,* and *Ververoda Holiday Resort.*

HOLLAND

"God made the world," say the citizens of Holland, "but the Dutch made the Netherlands." Nearly half of this democratic monarchy's 15,450 square miles has been reclaimed from the sea, and the doughty inhabitants have been working for generations to keep it from slipping back. Hence the special look of the Dutch landscape. Dikes are everywhere, holding out the waters, and picturesque windmills, along with a far more important network of ingenious pumps, are ceaselessly engaged in keeping the land dry or carefully irrigating it. In addition to the encroaching flood, the Dutch have had bouts with the Romans, Franks, Burgundians, Austrians, Spanish, English, French and Germans, all of whom at one time or another have conquered the Netherlands, but none of whom has ever been able to hold it. Indeed, the Dutch story has been one of constant struggle against nature and neighbor alike. A struggle which the Dutch not only survived but during which they managed to build a great colonial empire and simultaneously establish a distinctive and influential artistic tradition.

Perhaps because of this tempestuous history, the Dutch are a serious and hardworking people, though lacking nothing in humor. They have their paradoxical side too. While maintaining traditions keenly, they also have a strongly rebellious streak, particularly in regard to authority imposed from above or outside. Though individual liberties are thus jealously guarded, a number of social problems, chiefly youthful rebellion and chronic drug abuse, have arisen. Amsterdam for example is one of Europe's most picturesque cities—and its capital of graffiti. Similarly, while one of the world's leading industrial nations, and correspondingly prosperous, the country is also preoccupied with the problems of housing and employing a rapidly expanding population of immigrants from her former Indonesian colonies in an increasingly competitive world beset with economic problems.

Despite a high density of population, you certainly won't be conscious of any overpopulation problem as you travel through the green countryside, spacious and flat, laced with blue canals and tree-bordered roads. The biggest slopes are those leading up to the canal bridges; the tallest objects are the church spires (visible for miles) and many multi-storied modern apartment blocks, offices and factories. You will find cozy villages tucked away behind streamlined motorways, and noisy, overcrowded cities. The Dutch, though not especially gregarious, are far from dour. Their ideal of social behavior is to be at one and the same time *deftig* (dignified, respectable and decorous) and *gezellig* (cozy, comfortable, and enjoying oneself).

PRACTICAL INFORMATION FOR HOLLAND

WHAT WILL IT COST. Holland is a prosperous country with a high standard of living so the basic minimum you can expect to have to pay is a little higher than in some other European countries. As in all countries, some areas are more expensive than others so outside major tourist centers your holiday costs can be kept relatively low. Full board at Scheveningen during the high season will necessarily run higher than equivalent accommodations at one of the family resorts higher up the coast (or down in Zeeland). Similarly, a week in Amsterdam will be more expensive than seven days touring the smaller provincial towns. There are a number of package tours offered, one real bargain being the VVV's "The Amsterdam Way," a 1–3 day low-cost, inclusive program with lots of free extras. Bear in mind that as distances in Holland are never great, traveling costs can be kept correspondingly modest.

The monetary unit is the guilder *(gulden)* or florin, written as fl 1 (or Hfl 1 in banks) or *f* 1. It is divided into 100 cents. Notes are in denominations of 1,000, 100, 50, 25, 10 and 5 guilders. Coins are 2.5 guilders, 1 guilder, 25, 10 and 5 cents.

At the time of writing, the exchange rate for the guilder was fl 2.77 to the U.S. dollar and fl 4.00 to the pound sterling.

A typical day outside Amsterdam might cost two people:

Hotel (Moderate) double room with shower and breakfast	fl 120
Snack lunch at restaurant (Moderate)	25
Coffee and pastry	10
Half day city tour	70
Theater (good seats)	60
Dinner (tourist menu) including wine	60
Miscellaneous, including local travel	22
	fl 367

SOURCES OF INFORMATION. The Netherlands Board of Tourism (NBT) is an excellent source of information on all aspects of travel to Holland. Their addresses are:

In the U.S.: 355 Lexington Ave., New York, NY 10017 (tel. 212–223–8141); 605 Market St., Suite 401, San Francisco, CA 94105 (tel. 415–543–6772); 36 South Warbash Ave., Suite 600, Chicago, IL 60603 (tel. 312–236–3636).

In Canada: 25, Adelaide St. East, Suite 710, Toronto M5Z 1Y2 (tel. 416–363–1577).

In the U.K.: 25–28 Buckingham Gate, London S.W.1 (tel. 01–630 0451).

WHEN TO COME. The main tourist season in Holland runs from mid-April to mid-October the peak naturally falling in July and August at the height of the summer when the weather is most likely to be at its best. The famous bulbfields normally bloom from early April to mid-May. June is a good time to visit; facilities are less busy and the weather often excellent.

Climate. Summers are good, but beware sudden rains and cold winds, particularly by the sea. Winters are intermittently cold and wet, but with many bright, clear days.

Average afternoon temperatures in degrees Fahrenheit and centigrade:

Amster-dam	Jan.	Feb.	Mar.	Apr.	May	June	July	Aug.	Sept.	Oct.	Nov.	Dec.
F°	41	41	46	52	60	65	69	68	64	56	47	41
C°	4	5	8	11	16	18	21	20	18	13	8	5

SPECIAL EVENTS. *Late March,* opening of annual Keukenhof Flower Exhibition at Lisse in the heart of the bulb fields (to mid-May). *Mid-March to mid-April,* various bulb field shows and flower processions. *April,* cheese markets on Thursdays at Gouda and Purmerend, Friday at Alkmaar (June through September). Queen Beatrix's birthday celebrated throughout the country (Apr. 30). *June,* cheese market at Purmerend (through September). Annual Holland Festival of concerts, opera and ballet in all major Dutch cities. *July,* about 15 windmills in action every Saturday afternoon at Kinderdijk near Rotterdam (through August). *September,* opening of the Dutch Parliament by the Queen at the Hague (3rd. Tuesday). Throughout the summer, folk markets are held in many older towns, usually on Saturdays. *November,* three Saturdays before December 5 Santa Claus (St. Nicholas) arrives with processions etc. in most Dutch towns.

National Holidays. Jan. 1 (New Year's Day); Apr. 19, 20 (Easter); Apr. 30 (Queen's birthday) (shops open unless falls on Sun.); May 5 (Liberation) (shops open unless Sun.); May 28 (Ascension); Jun. 7 (Whit Mon.); Dec. 25, 26.

VISAS. Nationals of the United States, Canada, Australia, New Zealand, EEC countries and practically all other European countries do not require visas for visits up to three months. However, you must of course have a valid passport.

HEALTH CERTIFICATES. Not required for entry.

GETTING TO HOLLAND. By Plane. From North America there are direct flights to Amsterdam's Schiphol Airport from many major cities. From England there are direct flights to Amsterdam, Eindhoven, Maastricht, and Rotterdam from London, Heathrow or Gatwick, and most large cities. Schiphol Airport is connected to all European countries and to major cities throughout the world on the national carrier *KLM* and other flag carriers.

By Train. The most convenient way from the U.K. is to use the Harwich to the Hoek van Holland ferry service. With this there are two basic services, the one with a day time crossing, the other overnight. With the daytime route the boat train the *Day Continental* leaves London (Liverpool Street) at 9.40 A.M. and travels to Harwich for the ferry crossing. At the Hoek there are several train connections, the most convenient of which has you in Rotterdam by 7.50 P.M. and in Den Haag some 15 minutes later, reaching Amsterdam at 8.55 P.M. The overnight service leaves Liverpool Street at 7.40 P.M. for the overnight crossing to the Hoek from Harwich. With this service you are in Rotterdam by 7.34 A.M., Den Haag at 8.07 A.M. and Amsterdam at 9 A.M.

From other parts of Western Europe there are many trains connecting Holland with Belgium, Germany and France—and beyond. By fast expresses, including intercity services, it takes only 2¾ to 3 hours from Brussels to Amsterdam, and 5 to 6½ hours from Paris or Frankfurt.

By Bus. The cheapest connection between London and Amsterdam is by bus/ship. One is operated by the Grey Green Bus Co. in London and Budget Bus in Holland. Daily and nightly services taking about 12 hours between city centres.

By Car. Drive-on/off ferries from Harwich to the Hoek van Holland (day and night boats), Sheerness to Vlissingen (twice daily), Great Yarmouth to

Scheveningen (twice daily). International travel by self-drive car is easy and convenient between all key points in Europe.

CUSTOMS. There are three levels of duty free allowance for goods imported to Holland. Travelers coming from a European country outside the EEC may bring in 200 cigarettes or 50 cigars or 100 cigarillos or 250gr. of tobacco; 1 liter of spirits more than 22% proof or 2 liters of spirits less than 22% proof and 2 liters of wine; 50gr. of perfume; other goods to the value of fl 110. Travelers coming from an EEC country may bring in, provided they were *not* purchased in a duty-free shop, 300 cigarettes or 75 cigars or 400gr. of tobacco; 3 liters of wine and 1.5 liters of spirits more than 22% proof or 3 liters of spirits or sparkling wine up to 22% proof; 75gr. of perfume and 37.5cl. of toilet water; other goods to the value of fl. 500. Travelers coming from outside Europe may bring in 400 cigarettes or 100 cigars or 500gr. of tobacco; wines, spirits and perfume limits are the same as those for non EEC countries; other goods to the value of fl 500.

HOTELS. Dutch hotels are generally spotlessly clean no matter how modest their comfort, and service is normally courteous and efficient. English is spoken or understood by desk clerks almost everywhere. In major Dutch cities one can choose between the luxurious international chain hotels, older but just as luxurious traditional hotels or out of center motels (convenient for car travelers as city center parking is increasingly difficult). There is also a wide selection of moderate and inexpensive hotels, most of which are relatively small. In the provinces the range of accommodations is more limited, but also less expensive. Particularly delightful are the inexpensive, often family-run hotels in smaller cities. These are generally centrally located and offer charming atmosphere. Most have good, if modest dining facilities. VVV offices in some towns have lists of boarding houses and private homes taking in paying guests.

Our hotel grading system is divided into four categories. All prices are for 2 people in a double room. In major cities: Deluxe (L) fl 300 and up, Expensive (E) fl 175–300, Moderate (M) fl 90–175, Inexpensive (I) fl 50–90. Prices are 10–20% less in the E–M range in outlying areas.

A very useful booklet is published by the NBT, the official Dutch tourist organization. It lists every city and town of importance and nearly all Dutch hotels and their prices. Local VVV information offices are usually able to help you find a hotel room upon arrival for a small charge.

CAMPING. Holland is a splendid country for camping, though only in the summer! There are over 2,500 camp sites. Information from NTKC, Daendelstraat 11, Den Haag, from NBT offices abroad, or from VVV offices. Rates are government controlled.

There are over 50 youth hostels throughout Holland offering mainly dormitory facilities. Those in main towns are quite large, but are usually full during high season. To use them one must be a member of the International Youth Hostels Federation. Rates range from fl 15–20, including breakfast. Further information from NJHC, Prof. Tulpplein 4, 1018GX, Amsterdam; or any NBT or VVV office.

RESTAURANTS. These are usually classified from four to one star, which generally corresponds with our rating of Expensive (E) fl 75–100, Moderate (M) fl 40–75, Inexpensive (I) less than fl 15–30. These prices are for one person and do not include drinks. Over 700 restaurants offer special tourist menus, which at around fl 19 per person, provide honest and ample three-course meals. All Dutch restaurants include 15% service and tax on the bill.

Food and Drink. Of the many earthly pleasures the Dutchman enjoys, eating probably heads the list, with the appetite sharpened by the national institution of the *borreltje,* a little nip of gin at five o'clock usually taken with a little snack like the tasty *bitter-ballen*—fried meat balls. You'd better take something to stimulate your appetite in this hearty land. Your breakfast, replete with several varieties of bread, cheese, cooked ham or meat, possibly a boiled egg, butter, jam and steaming coffee or tea, is a far and welcome cry from the usual Continental *petit déjeuner.* It will hold you until the Dutch ritual of eleven o'clock coffee, just as the *Koffietafel,* a "light" lunch of bread, cold cuts and cheese, or particularly an *uitsmijter,* slices of bread topped with cold meat or ham and fried eggs, will fend off starvation until dinner, which is usually eaten around 6 P.M.

Typical Dutch dishes appear in season (mostly in winter). Some of the best Dutch specialties are: *Erwtensoep,* a rich and delicious thick pea soup with bits of sausage or pig's knuckles, a meal in itself, but served only from October to March as is *Hutspot,* a meat, carrot and potato stew. *Haring* is particularly popular, especially the "new herring" caught between May and September and served brined, garnished with onions; *Rodekool met Rolpens,* red cabbage and rolled spiced meat with sliced apple. Other specialties include *Pannekoeken* and *Flensjes,* pancakes, in various varieties, shapes and sizes, all of them delectable and often eaten in special pancake restaurants. *Koeken* and *Koekjes,* cakes and cookies, usually on the sweet and rich side.

As for cheeses, the two famous classifications are *Gouda* and *Edam,* both mild in comparison with French and Italian cheeses. Try the spicier *Leidse* cheese with cumin or *Friese* cheese with cloves for a change. Seafood is abundant and well-prepared; most shellfish is rather expensive, except for the delicious mussels from the province of Zeeland.

If run-of-the-mill Dutch fare begins to pall, try an Indonesian restaurant (the best are in Amsterdam and Den Haag) where the specialties of Holland's former colony are served. The chief dish here is *rijsttafel,* a heaping bowl of perfectly steamed rice together with 20 or more side dishes like *saté babi,* bite-size morsels of pork skewered on a wooden spit and cooked in a mouthwatering sauce. The best beverage to accompany an Indonesian *rijsttafel* is beer, of which there are several excellent varieties, both Dutch and foreign.

The indigenous Dutch short drink is *jenever* (gin), a potent and warming spirit. It comes in many varieties depending on the spices used, but most popular are the *jonge* (young) and the *oude* (old). Neither has the remotest similarity to dry gin, being both sweeter and oilier. Jenever is drunk neat and chilled (it's not a good mixer). Dutch liqueurs are good.

TIPPING. Hotel prices now include a 15% service charge and VAT, as do most restaurant checks, and nightclub charges. Tip porters or bellhops fl 1 per bag or per service, especially if it is personal, while the doorman expects a similar sum for calling a cab. Taxi fares generally include 15% service charge (when indicated on meter), but it is usual to give the driver any small change. Hairdressers' and barbers' prices usually include service. Rail stations and airports have fixed porterage charges of fl 1 per piece.

MAIL AND PHONES. Current rates for airmail letters to the U.S. are fl 1.15, to the rest of Europe 70 cents; postcards are 50 cents to Europe, 65 cents to the U.S. Aerogramme letters are 90 cents to any destination.

Direct dial international calls can be made from post offices, from most coin operated public phones or from any hotel. Hotels may, however, add a service charge for overseas calls.

CLOSING TIMES. Shops are open in general from 8:30 or 9 A.M. to 5.30 or 6 P.M. weekdays, but some close for lunch. Do not plan to shop on *Mondays:* department stores and most shops, especially in shopping precincts (Den Haag, Amsterdam, Rotterdam) do not open till 1 P.M. and many others close on Wednesday afternoons. Late night shopping is usually till 9 P.M. Thursday and Friday, but varies locally.

Banks open from 9 to 4, most closed Saturdays. Only central post offices in the large cities are open on Saturday until noon. GWK Bureau de Change usually open 7 days a week in major rail stations and tourist centers.

USEFUL ADDRESSES. *American Embassy* and *U.S. Information Service,* Lange Voorhout 102 (tel. 184140); *British Embassy,* Lange Voorhout 10 (tel. 645800); *Canadian Embassy,* Sophialaan 7 (tel. 614111); all Den Haag, for which the telephone prefix is 070. *American Consulates,* Museumplein 19, Amsterdam (tel. 020–790321); Baan 50, Rotterdam (tel. 010–4117560). *British Consulate,* Konigslaan 44, Amsterdam (tel. 020–764343).

American Express, Amsterdam, Damrak 66 (tel. 020–262042); Den Haag, Venestraat 20 (tel. 070–469515); Rotterdam, Meent 92 (tel. 010–4330390) and Meent 19–21 (tel. 010–4116200); Den Haag, Buitenhof 46.

National Tourist Office (NBT), Vlietweg 15, 2266KA Leidschendam, tel. 070–705705, (head office). Local information offices (VVV) in all major cities and tourist centers (usually in or close to rail stations).

GETTING AROUND HOLLAND. By Train and Bus. Holland has an excellent railway system—fast, frequent, clean and comfortable trains operate throughout the country. All lines are now electrified. An intensive service operates from Amsterdam to Rotterdam over two routes, one via Den Haag and the other via Gouda, taking between an hour and 75 minutes for the run. All trains carry 1st and 2nd class in the Netherlands, and many have refreshment, buffet or dining car services. Be careful however when traveling by train. Very often these are made up of two basic sections dividing en route; make sure you are in the right section.

Best value over the Netherlands network (usually known by its initials NS) is given by a 1, 3 or 7 day unlimited travel ticket called *Rail Rover;* truly excellent value (no reductions for children). The 7-day ticket costs fl 108.50. Offered in conjunction with the Rail Rover is the *Link Rover,* which for a small fee entitles the purchaser to unlimited travel on all public transport within the major cities.

In addition, there are many one day excursion fares and sightseeing tours to major attractions, as well as tickets issued for both rail and local bus travel. A one-day "travel-anywhere" bus ticket covering all urban bus/tram networks costs fl 20. And when families travel together in the Netherlands there are also substantial reductions. Ask at railway information bureaux or VVV offices.

By Car. Drive on the right. Cars—and bicycles—coming from the right have right of way. When turning left at a crossing, leave the pylon or policeman on his pedestal to your *right.* Holland has a comprehensive motorway system—and a comprehensive and frequently confusing series of one-way systems which can take a fair bit of figuring out. Nationals of EEC countries do not need a green card showing proof of third party insurance; nationals from all other countries do. Gasoline (petrol)—*benzine* in Dutch—costs around fl 1.90 per liter. Experienced uniformed mechanics of the *Wegenwacht* patrol highways in yellow cars and will help with breakdowns etc. The main driving problems in most cities are the narrow streets, throngs of cyclists and, of course, parking.

Car Hire. Renting a self-drive car in Holland is relatively inexpensive. One of the small European or mini cars will cost from fl 49 a day in season to include, usually, the first 100 km, with extra mileage at 40 cents per kilometer and with the renter paying for the fuel. The rates will be proportionately higher for bigger cars. You will be asked to show your domestic driver's license at the time the car is delivered to you and to pay a deposit in advance and additionally fl 13 per day to waive your liability (usually the first 1,000 guilders) in case of accident. A "drop charge" may also apply, although this charge is sometimes not made if the car is hired for 14 days or longer. All charges are subject to a 19% VAT.

Avis-Holland, Keizersgracht 485, Amsterdam (tel. 020–262201) and airports. *Hertz,* Overtoom 333, Schiphol and Rotterdam airports (tel. 020–122441). *Europcar,* Overtoom 51, Amsterdam and at Schiphol and Rotterdam airports (tel. 020–184595). There are a number of local Dutch hire companies such as *InterRent,* Amstelveensweg 294, Amsterdam (tel. 020–730477).

Amsterdam, Cosmopolitan City

Despite, or perhaps because of, more than 700 years of eventful history, Amsterdam is one of the most dynamic and youthful of European cities, as well as being one of the Continent's key cultural and tourist destinations. Built on a latticework of concentric canals bordered by delightful houses, the city is just made for sightseeing. One almost gets the impression that Amsterdam is a museum in itself, so packed is it with monuments, museums, statues and fine architecture.

One word of caution: the city authorities have a relaxed attitude toward many issues, drugs in particular. Visitors should steer well clear of the area around the Central Station at night. That apart, you are as safe here as in any European capital.

The city has many "musts." Start by taking a trip on a glass-roofed boat along the canals (many leave from in front of the station). Then, on foot, explore the area around the stately Royal Palace on Damsquare and the Tower of Tears, from which Hendrik Hudson set sail on the voyage that led to the discovery of New York. A stroll around the older parts of the town is richly rewarding. Walk down the Joordan, a charming network of narrow streets between Rozengracht and Westerstraat. Visit the attic church of the Amstelkring Museum; the Begijnhof Almshouse, with memories of the Pilgrim Fathers; and the Mint Tower. "Must" museums include the Rijksmuseum and nearby Rijksmuseum Vincent Van Gogh.

PRACTICAL INFORMATION FOR AMSTERDAM

HOW TO GET AROUND. By Bus, Tram and Metro. A zonal fare system is used. Tickets are purchased from automatic dispensers on the metro; from the driver on trams and buses. The best bet is to buy "strippenkaart" tickets which are good for several journeys or, even better, tickets for unlimited travel over one, two, three, or four days. Costs are fl 8, 10.75, 13.20 and 15.60 respectively.

By Taxi. These are expensive (flagfall varies from fl 3–4, and thereafter fl 2–4 per km.). They are not usually hailed on the street but from ranks near stations and at other key points.

On Foot. Amsterdam is a small, congested city of narrow streets, ideal conditions for exploring on foot. The VVV issue useful leaflets for walking tours of the city center.

HOTELS. The city is well supplied with hotels both large and small, new and old. The central district hotels are all within walking distance of the major places of interest. But those in south Amsterdam are recommended in preference, if only to avoid the area around the Central Station. In high season (Easter and the period July–September), accommodations are tight; book ahead. The VVV office opposite the Central Station can usually help find a room for a small fee. Many older and smaller hotels do not always have bath or shower in the rooms; a room with these facilities is more expensive. Note that most hotels have rooms in more than one price range, so specify at the time of booking. Many older hotels have steep stairs and usually no elevator. The telephone prefix for all Amsterdam numbers is 020, if calling from outside the city.

Deluxe

Amstel, Prof Tulpplein 1 (tel. 226060). 116 rooms and the most expensive hotel in town. Excellent facilities, including river view from bar and outstanding *La Rive* restaurant. Ask for river view when booking.

Amsterdam Hilton, Apollolaan 138 (tel. 780780). 276 rooms with bath or shower. *The Terrace* restaurant is good for sophisticated dining; also has the *Half Moon Bar* and an excellent Japanese restaurant.

Amsterdam Marriott, Stadhouderskade 19–21 (tel. 835151). 400 rooms, all amenities. Front rooms with good views, rear rooms quieter.

Amsterdam Sonesta, Kattengat 1 (tel. 212223). A luxurious combination of old and new, with excellent *Rib Room* restaurant and coffee shop. Many interesting features, including a converted church/conference hall. 380 rooms, all with bath.

De l'Europe, Nieuwe Doelenstraat 2 (tel. 234836). Small and very pleasant; not all rooms have baths. Canalside location. Excellent restaurant and bar.

Okura Inter-Continental, Ferd. Bolstraat 175 (tel. 787111). 402 rooms including some Japanese-style, but the Japanese flavor is noticeable in all parts of the hotel, not least in the excellent Japanese restaurant. There is also a French roof-top restaurant, *Ciel Bleu.*

Expensive

American, Leidsekade 97 (tel. 245322). 184 rooms. Next door to the City Theater and only a few minutes from the center of town. Attractive interior.

Arthur Frommer, Norderstraat 46 (tel. 220328). 90 quiet rooms. Comfortable.

Grand Hotel Krasnapolsky, Dam 9 (tel. 554911). 325 rooms; very central, with three good restaurants, including an excellent Japanese.

Novotel Amsterdam, Europaboulevard 10 (tel. 5411123). 600 rooms and good facilities. Close to train connection for airport.

Pulitzer, Prinsengracht 315–31 (tel. 228333). 176 interesting rooms, each in a different style. The hotel itself is a row of attractive medieval houses, but rather out of center.

Sheraton Schipol, Kruisweg 495 (tel. 02503–15851). 252 beds. Easy access to the airport.

Moderate

Ambassade, Herengracht 341 (tel. 262333). 27 rooms; good value, delightful location.

Het Canal House, Keizersgracht 148 (tel. 225182). 14 rooms, all with bath or shower. Extremely attractively furnished. American-run; good value.

Estherea, Singel 305 (tel. 245146). 60 renovated rooms.

Poort van Cleve, Nieuwe Zijds Voorburwal 178 (tel. 244860). 110 rooms with bath or shower. Excellent restaurant.

Rembrandt Crest, Herengracht 255 (tel. 221727). 110 rooms; in restored row of patrician houses.

Sander, Jac. Obrechtstraat 69 (tel. 722495). Family atmosphere and excellent restaurant.

Trianon, J. W. Brouwerstraat 3 (tel. 733918). 60 rooms. Next to the Concertgebouw and Rijksmuseum.

Inexpensive

Cok Budget Hotel, Koniginneweg 30 (tel. 728095). 60 rooms with bath.

Paap, Keizersgracht 37 (tel. 249600). 41 beds, some rooms with bath.

Wiechmann, Prinsengracht 328 (tel. 263321). 72 beds, 13 rooms with bath. American-owned and very friendly. Handy for the Central Station.

 RESTAURANTS. The Dutch eat early; many restaurants close by 10.30. Service tends to be formal and unhurried. If all you want is a light lunch and an opportunity to sit down, try one of the sidewalk cafés, snack bars or *broodjeswinkels,* which sell soft buns stuffed with anything you like: smoked eel, eggs, ham, crab, cheese, and other tempting fillers. For budget meals, remember to look for the Tourist Menu sign—three courses for around fl 19.

The city of course has many excellent "international" restaurants, but for a characteristic and atmospheric meal try one of the Brown Cafes. The name of these Amsterdam institutions—more like a British pub than a Continental cafe—derives from their being painted only rarely, though they are in every other sense colorful and well worth visiting. For the better-class restaurants one should book ahead. Note that not all accept credit cards.

Expensive

Bali, Leidsestraat 95 (tel. 227878). Fast for a day before you come here! The *saté* and *rijsttafel* are delicious.

De Boerderij, Korte Leidsedwarsstraat 69 (tel. 236929). The atmospheric interior of this converted farm house and good cooking make it a definite favorite. Strongly recommended.

Dikker & Thys, Prinsengracht 444 (tel. 267721). Popular after-theater place with haute cuisine.

D'Viff Vlieghen, Spuistraat 294 (tel. 248369). A tourist mecca though it's the decor rather than the food or service which is the real attraction.

Moderate

Adrian, Reguliersdwarsstraat 21 (tel. 239582). French cuisine and good wines in an old and attractive house.

Bodega Keyzer, van Baerlestraat 96 (tel. 711411). Near the Concertgebouw and the museum quarter. Good atmosphere.

Dorrius, Nieuwe Zijds Voorburgwal 336 (tel. 235245). Another business-men's haunt (closed Sun.), where the emphasis is on serious eating. Possibly the best authentic Dutch cooking in town.

Fong Lie, P. C. Hooftstraat 80 (tel. 716404). Probably the best Chinese food in the city. Prawn, fish and chicken specialties. Closed Mon.

De Groene Lanteerne, Haarlemmerstraat 43 (tel. 241952). Three floors high and only five feet wide, this is the narrowest restaurant in the country and probably in Europe as well. Closed Tues.

De Oesterbar, Leidseplein 10 (tel. 232988). Famous seafood restaurant on the lively Leidseplein.

Die Port van Cleve, N.Z. Voorburgwal 178 (tel. 125511). Next to Main Post Office, with lots of old Dutch character and cuisine.

Restaurant Speciaal, Leliestraat 89 (tel. 249706). Excellent Indonesian fare.

Sluizer, Utrechtsestraat 45 (tel. 263557). Very popular with the student/arty crowd and consequently very lively. Seafood specialties.

Inexpensive

Amsterdam positively overflows with good inexpensive restaurants, many grouped in one area; Leidseplein and the surrounding streets. Round here you'll find diverse international styles and reasonable prices, and all in an animated and lively area. Individual recommendations are largely impossible, but browsing will pay dividends.

 NIGHTLIFE. Amsterdam has a wide variety of night-clubs, bars and cabarets, and now has places even sur-passing the "hot spots" of cities like Hamburg, although none has the elegance of Paris. The most bizarre sexy haunts are not over-publicized, but any hotel porter or good barman will supply the information. Apart from the special (and very expensive) "live" shows in the areas around Rembrandtsplein, Leidseplein and Thorbeckeplein, there is plenty of respectable though earthy entertainment and near-honkytonk spots, some open until 2 or 4 A.M.; though names or locations, or both, change from year to year. Stay well clear of the area around the Central Station at night.

Except at weekends, very few of the nightclubs make an admission charge, although the more lively ones sometimes ask for a "club membership" fee of 15 guilders or more. Moreover, drinks are normally not exorbitant in price. The following are worth a try:

De Amstel Taverne, Halvemaansteeg, close to Rembrandtplein. Lively and pleasant bar with music.

Bell's Club, Amsterdamseweg 497. A little out of the center and comes to life only in the small hours. Popular with Dutch high fliers.

Boston Club, Sonesta Hotel, Kattengat 1. Trendy.

Louis Seize, Reguliersdwarsstraat 88. Strip shows and cabaret.

MUSEUMS. If you're a real culture-vulture, the *Museumcard*, available from VVV, covers entry fees to dozens of top museums nationwide and is valid for a year. Costs fl 7.50 (under 25), fl 20 (over 25), or fl 12.50 (senior citizens). Among the city's 50 or so museums, the following are of particular importance.

Amsterdams Historisch Museum, Kalverstraat 92. Housed in renovated orphanage; interesting audiovisual show. Open Tues.–Sat. 10 to 5, Sun. 1 to 5. Closed Mon. (fl 3.50).

Anne Frank Huis, Prinsengracht 263. Tragic and moving attic hideaway of the eloquent young diarist. Open Tues.–Sat. 10 to 5, Sun. 1 to 5. Closed Mon. (fl 4.50).

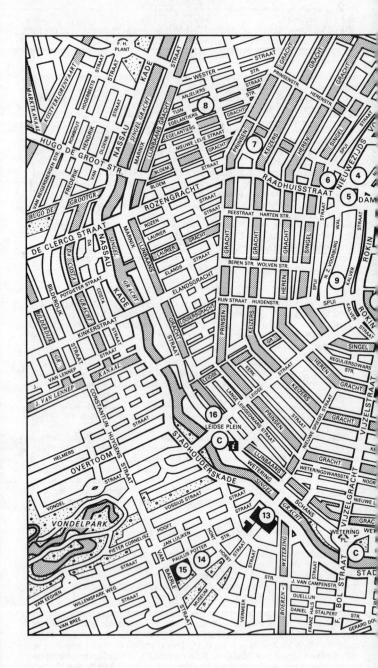

AMSTERDAM

1 Central Station
2 St. Nicolaaskerk
3 Oude Kerk (Old Church)
4 Nieuwe Kerk (New Church)
5 Koninklijk Paleis (Royal Palace)
6 Main Post Office
7 Anne Frank Huis
8 Joordan District
9 Amsterdam Historisch Museum
10 Zuiderkerk (South Church)
11 Museum het Rembrandthuis
12 Zoological Gardens
13 Rijksmuseum
14 Rijksmuseum Vincent Van Gogh
15 Stedelijk Museum (Municipal Museum)
16 Stadsschouwburg (Theater)
ⓒ Canal Trips - starting points
𝒊 VVV Tourist Information Offices

SCALE

0   440yds
0   400m

Museum Het Rembrandthuis, Jodenbreestraat 4–6. The great man's house for over 20 years; fascinating. Open Mon.–Fri. 10–5, Sun. and holidays 1–4 (fl 2.50).

Nederlands Scheepvaart Museum, Kattenburgerplein 1. Fine coverage of the nation's maritime past. Open Tues.–Sat. 10 to 5, Sun. 1 to 5. Closed Mon. (fl 5).

Rijksmuseum, Stadhouderskade 42. Unrivaled collection of Dutch painting from 15th to 19th centuries. Key works by Rembrandt, Vermeer, Hals, Ruysdael etc. Open Tues.–Sat. 10 to 5, Sun. 1 to 5. Closed Mon. (fl 6.50).

Rijksmuseum Vincent van Gogh, Paulus Potterstraat 7. Marvelous collection of pictures (over 200) and drawings. Open Tues.–Sat. 10 to 5, Sun. 1 to 5. Closed Mon. (fl 6.50).

Stedelijk Museum, Paulus Potterstraat 13. Next door to the Van Gogh museum. Excellent gallery of modern art; works by van Gogh, Mondrian, Chagall, Kandinsky and many others. Open daily 11–5 (fl 5).

SHOPPING. Amsterdam is an excellent shopping center, and, being so compact, is tailor made for browsing. The main shopping streets in the center are around Nieuwendijk and Kalverstraat. They are mostly all closed to traffic. Visits to the city's many markets are something of a must. The best are the Singel flower market, the flea market on Waterlooplein and the book markets opposite the University—all open Mon.–Sat. 10 to 4. For antiques, try the Nieuwmarkt—Sun., May to Sept. only. The adjacent side streets also contain many interesting antique shops. Finally, take in a visit to one of the diamond-cutting houses. Amsterdam is the diamond-cutting capital of the world and, even if you can't afford to buy any of the jewels, all the leading firms give guided tours. Details from the VVV.

Excursions from Amsterdam

There are many delightful destinations in the Amsterdam area which can be visited using the capital as a tour base. Distances are small, travel inexpensive and easy, so one need not take an organized tour. Covered conveniently from Amsterdam are these towns in North Holland:

Monnickendam, 13km. (8 miles) northeast of Amsterdam takes you back through history. The late Gothic church, dating from the 15th century, the Town Hall, built as a private house in 1746, and the gabled houses in the Kerkstraat dating from the 17th and 18th centuries, are all charming. Six km. further takes you to Volendam, a centuries-old fishing village with a rich history. Some older inhabitants still wear national costume with a sense of pride and tradition, not just to please the tourists. Beyond Volendam, on the local road, is Edam. Stroll along the Dam, formerly a lock, with sluice gates; admire the old Town Hall (1737), the Great, or St. Niklaas, Church and, on the other side of the Begijnhof, the home of the ancient Beguine nuns. Edam's cheese is world famous and at the market you can visit the weighing house with its scales and cheeses.

Next on the touring plan should be the Westfrisian towns of Hoorn, Enkhuizen and Medemblik, all of which had their golden age in the 16th and 17th centuries when they were powerful Zuidersee ports with wide colonial trade links. Enkhuizen is the best preserved and is still a fishing port; its fish auctions are fascinating. The Pepperhouse, the only remaining warehouse of the Dutch East India Company, now houses the Zuidersee Museum. Medemblik is less spectacular, but offers remains of the Radboud castle (1288). Hoorn, a well preserved 17th-century commercial town, has a Folk Market every Wednesday from mid-June to mid-August. Also worth visiting is the Westfrisian Museum with, among other exhibits, a remarkable collection of silver utensils.

Alkmaar, with its fine old buildings, more than repays a strolling visit. Its popular Cheese Market is held on Friday mornings, mid-April to mid-September. Purmerend offers another weekly cheese market, Thursdays, mid-June to mid-August, which many consider the most authentic and interesting.

Heading south from Amsterdam you come almost immediately to Haarlemmermeer Polder, once a large lake which regularly flooded Haarlem and even Amsterdam. In 1836 the whole area was flooded badly and it was decided to drain the lake to settle the problem for ever. The Haarlemsee now is a huge polder divided into sections. One, in the northwest, carries the asphalt of Schiphol Airport. Haarlem is the capital of the province and has preserved its historical and artistic appearance. In the heart of the town is the country's oldest center of Dutch art, the Grote Markt with its City Hall, part of which dates back to 1350. Towering over this is the late Gothic Grote-church, St. Bavo-kerk. Everywhere you are surrounded by picturesque houses. Along the Spaarne you will find the Teylers Museum Haarlem, with 200 years of history and the oldest museum in Holland. Among other treasures it houses a truly superb collection of over 1,000 drawings by such masters as Michelangelo, Titian, Leonardo da Vinci, and Raphael. The 900-year-old city is also home to the Frans Hals Museum, boasting a fine collection by Hals and other masters of the Haarlem School.

Along the whole North Sea coast and its islands are endless lines of sand dunes and some fine beaches, providing an ideal, if windy, location for various resorts. All have facilities for a range of water sports. Fishing facilities are good in Ijmuiden while Zandvoort offers motor racing, the Kennemerduinen sand dunes and beach and a casino. Lisse, about 18 km. (11 miles) south of Haarlem is noted for its Keukenhof Garden. From the end of March to the end of May the estate has an openair flower show, unique in the world.

PRACTICAL INFORMATION FOR THE AMSTERDAM AREA

ALKMAAR. *Comfort Inn* (M), Arcadialaan 2 (tel. 072–120744). 92 rooms. Lower rates Jan.-Mar.
Restaurant. *'t Guiden Vlies,* Koorstraat 20 (tel. 072–112451).

BENNEBROEK. Restaurant. *De Oude Geleerde Man* (M), Rijksstraatweg 51 (tel. 02502–6990). Fine spot right in the middle of the bulb growing area.

ENKHUIZEN. *Die Port Van Cleve* (M), Dijk 74 (tel. 02280–12510). 20 rooms. **Restaurant.** *Markenwaard,* Dijk 62.

HAARLEM. *Lion d' Or* (E), Kruisweg 34 (tel. 023–321750). 40 rooms. *Die Raeckse* (M), Raaks 1–3 (tel. 023–326629). 33 rooms.

HOORN. *Petit Noord* (M), Kleine Noord 55 (tel. 02290–12750). 39 rooms.
Restaurant. *De Waag* (M), Roode Steen 8 (tel. 02290–15195). Historic restaurant in 17th-century building.

LAGE VUURSCHE. *Kastanjehof* (M), Kloosterlaan 1 (tel. 02156–248). Right in the middle of one of the most beautiful forests in Holland; also has one of the best restaurants in the area.

LISSE. *De Nachtegaal van Lisse* (E), Heereweg 10 (tel. 02521–14447). 165 rooms. *De Duif* (M), Westerdreef 17 (tel. 02521–10076). 30 rooms; lower rates Jan.–Mar.

MEDEMBLIK. *Het Wappen van Medemblik* (M), Oosterhaven 1 (tel. 02274–3844). 28 rooms; lower rates Oct.–Mar.

Restaurant. *Twee Schouwtjes* (M), Oosterhaven 27. Fine restaurant in 17th-century building.

MONNICKENDAM. *De Waegh* (M), Haven (tel. 02995–1241). *Gouwzee* (I), Jachthaven 1 (tel. 02995–3751). 17 rooms.
Restaurant. *de Posthoorn* (E), Noordeinde 41 (tel. 02995–1471). Decorated in the "Dutch Granny" manner; on the IJsselmeer.

OUDERKERKA/D AMSTEL. Restaurant. *De Paardenburg* (E), Amstelzijde 55 (tel. 02963–1210). In small, picturesque village only 15 miles from Amsterdam.

PURMEREND. *Waterland* (I), Herengracht 1 (tel. 02920–23981). 11 rooms.

VOLENDAM. *Van Diepen* (M), Haven 35 (tel. 02993–63705).
Restaurant. *V. D. Hogen* (I), Haven 106 (tel. 02993–63775). Fish specialties; and a lovely view over the colorful and busy harbor.

ZANDVOORT. *Bouwes* (E), Badhuisplein 7 (tel. 02507–15041). 60 rooms. *Astoria* (I), C. A. Gerkestraat 155 (tel. 02507–14550).

South Holland

43 km. (27 miles) south of Amsterdam is Den Haag, abroad known as The Hague. It is the capital of the Province of South Holland and political and diplomatic center of the Netherlands. Den Haag is also the Royal residence, and Queen Beatrix still lives here. As well as the Dutch Parliament, Den Haag is also home to a number of important international institutions, the most significant of which is the European Court of Human Rights. Architecturally, the city is distinguished by the spacious mansions of the many wealthy Dutch colonialists who retired here, attracted by its elegance and ample green spaces. It is also important culturally, not least for its 15 major museums.

Originally, Den Haag was the site of a hunting lodge built by Count Willem II around 1248. Today the heart of the city is the medieval fortress of the Binnenhof, or Inner Court, which has a splendid Knights' Hall, the Ridderzaal. This is the scene of the State opening of Parliament, a ceremony performed by Queen Beatrix on the third Tuesday of September. Next to the Binnenhof is the lovely Mauritshuis, a marvelous Renaissance building dating from 1633 and now housing the Royal art collection. Its highlights include works by Holbein the Younger, Cranach, Rembrandt and Rubens as well as a number of superb Vermeers.

Among the other pleasures of this sophisticated city are walks through the Lange and Korte Voorhout, lined with splendid patrician houses, and down the Grote Marktstraat. The Gemeentemuseum has an excellent collection of modern art with works by van Gogh, Picasso, Monet, Dufy and Mondrian among many others. The Mesdag Museum has a representative collection of 19th-century pictures, particularly of the Barbizon and Den Haag schools.

The most popular tourist attraction here is the miniature city of Madurodam, open from end-March to mid-October. It contains remarkable models of characteristic Dutch towns and villages, industries and transportation, all lovingly reproduced on a scale of 1:25.

Adjacent to Den Haag is the new port of Scheveningen. It's been a fishing village since the 14th century, but came to life only in the last century when it developed as a popular summer resort for the rich. Today it is one of the busiest and most popular seaside destinations in the country, claiming, among its many amenities, a famous Casino.

Rotterdam

Some 14 km. (9 miles) south of Den Haag is Rotterdam, straddling the mouths of the Rhine and the Maas—the largest port in the world. To some extent it owes its current maritime pre-eminence to its almost total obliteration in World War II when German bombing in 1940 and Allied bombing in 1943 combined to leave its historic center in ruins. After the war, the city authorities determined to transform Rotterdam into a model of modern city planning, as indeed they did. The War Memorial in front of the Town Hall and the *Destroyed City* sculpture are eloquent witnesses to the losses Rotterdam has sustained. However, the Laurenskerk, a splendid Gothic cathedral, was spared the planners' dreams and was instead lovingly restored, stone by stone, in the '50s.

The city has a rich and proud heritage as a center of learning and the arts. The University is named after Rotterdam's most famous son, the Humanist philosopher Erasmus (there's a statue of the wise man in front of the Cathedral). And the Boymans-van-Beuningen museum has works by the brothers van Eyck, the Brueghels, Bosch, Hals, Rembrandt and Rubens. Its modern collections are equally good. Other fine museums, both chronicling Rotterdam's history, are the Historisch Museum De Dubbelde Palmboom, and the Maritiem Museum de Buffel on board an iron warship of 1868.

Among the city's modern attractions are the Euromast near the Maas tunnel with a superb view from its 300-foot high terrace, while at Pernis, just across the Mass, the largest oil refinery in Europe glowers over an array of supertankers.

Delft, Leiden and Gouda

Equidistant between Den Haag and Rotterdam—7 km. (4½ miles) —lies the lovely city of Delft. Once a Royal capital, it has long been famous for its distinctive and beautiful Blue Delft china. A good part of the center has survived from the city's heyday in the 17th century and is a delight for the modern traveler. The Market Square is known as the most beautiful in South Holland. But also visit the Nieuw Kerk, a late Gothic church built in the 15th century. Here lies Willem the Silent, the founder of the Netherlands. Beneath his monumental tomb is the family crypt of the Dutch Royal family. More memories of Willem are found in the venerable Prinsenhof, where he lived and was assassinated. The Paul Tetar van Elven Museum, a former artist's house, has a reconstructed studio of the period of Delft's greatest painters, Vermeer and de Hoogh.

Northwest of Delft is Leiden, site of one of Europe's greatest Universities. The town is also something of a pilgrimage center for New Englanders. The Pieterskerk here was for 10 years before their epic voyage to the New World the church of the Pilgrim Fathers. The historic heart of Leiden is rivaled only by Amsterdam in terms of importance and beauty and amply repays strolling and browsing. Be sure to visit the Lakenhal which, among its many masterpieces, houses Lucas van Leyden's famous triptych.

Gouda, to the southwest of Leiden, is justly famous for its Thursday morning (June–August) cheese market and should be more so for its superb 15th-century Town Hall and the wonderful stained glass in the Sint Janskerk. Nearby on the Lek River is the quiet village of Schoonhoven, a silver center, with its fine Goud Zilver en Klokkemuseum, and Kinderdijk, which has a greater concentration of windmills than any other town in the world. At Oudewater you can be weighed to discover whether you are a witch, and be presented with a certificate (assuming you aren't).

PRACTICAL INFORMATION FOR SOUTH HOLLAND

DELFT. *De Ark* (E), Koornmarkt 65 (tel. 015–140552). *'t Raethuis* (M), Markt 38 (tel. 015–125115).
Restaurants. *Le Chevalier* (E), Oude Delft 125 (tel. 015–124621). Excellent if pricey. *Prinskelder* (E), Schoolstaat 11 (tel. 015–121860). In the old Prinsenhof museum.

DEN HAAG AND SCHEVENINGEN. *Steigenberger Kurhaus* (L), Gevers Deynootplein 30 (tel. 070–520052). 260 rooms, all with bath. Right on the beach at Scheveningen with casino, nightclubs, restaurants and shops. *Des Indes* (E), Lange Voorhout 56 (tel. 070–469553). 77 rooms, all with bath. Excellent location and stylish interior; good restaurant. *Europa Crest* (E), Zwolsestraat 2 (tel. 070–512651). 300 rooms, most with bath. Close to the beach at Scheveningen and with moderate restaurant. *Grand Hotel Central* (E), Lange Poten 6 (tel. 070–469414). 137 rooms, all with bath. Centrally located in Den Haag. *Parkhotel de Zalm* (E), Molenstraat 53 (tel. 070–624371).
Corona (M), Buitenhof 41 (tel. 070–637930). Overlooks Den Haag's central square; old Dutch cafe downstairs. *Esquire* (M), Van Aerssenstraat 59, (tel. 070–522341). 12 rooms. *Hoornwick Motel* (M), J. Thyssenweg 2 (tel. 070–903130). 82 rooms with bath or shower. Snackbar and restaurant make this a popular stopping off point. *Hotel Petit* (M), Groot Hertoginnelaan 42 (tel. 070–465500). *Savion* (M), Prinsestraat 86 (tel. 070–462560). Small and comfortable.
Restaurants. *La Coquille* (E), Gevers Deynootplein 30 (tel. 070–520052). In Kurhaushotel; French style. *Boerderij De Hoogwerf* (E), Zijdelaan 20. 17th-century farmhouse; international menu. *House of Lords* (E), Hofstraat 4 (tel. 070–644771). In the Grand Hotel Central; formal. *Royal* (E), Lange Voorhout (tel. 070–600772). Best French cooking in town; expensive. *Saur* (E), Lange Voorhout 51 (tel. 070–463344); for good seafood. *Hof van Brederode* (M), Grote Halsstraat 3 (tel. 070–646455). In cellar of 16th-century building; interior more interesting than food.
Bali (M), Badhuisweg 1 (tel. 070–551014). For a memorable, and gigantic, Indonesian meal. *'t Goude Hooft* (M), Groenmarkt 13 (tel. 070–469713). Old Dutch atmosphere; near Grote Kerk. *Het Groene Geveltje* (M), Molenstraat 25a (tel. 070–602368). Vast selection. *Meer en Bosch* (M), Heliotrooplaan 5 (tel. 070–257748). Converted farm house in wooded surroundings; cozy bar, good food. *Raden Mas* (M), Gav. Deynootplein 125 (tel. 070–545432), serves good Indonesian food, as does *Tempat Senang* (M), Laan van Meerdervoort 6 (tel. 070–636787).
Garoeda (I), Kneuterdijk 18a (tel. 070–465319). Central; good spot for morning coffee.

GOUDA. *De Zalm* (M), Markt 34 (tel. 01820–12344). 22 rooms with bath.
Restaurants. *Mallemolen* (E), Oosthaven 72 (tel. 01820–15430). Traditional Dutch food in a traditional setting. *Julien* (M), Hoge Gouwe 23 (tel. 01820–23338). Reasonable value.

LEIDEN. *Holiday Inn* (E), Haase Schouweg 10 (tel. 071–769310). 185 rooms, all with bath. Numerous facilities; good restaurant.
Restaurant. *Oudt Leyden* (M), Steenstraat 51 (tel. 071–133144). Two restaurants in one: delicious *pannekoeken* (pancakes) on blue Delft plate—which you can buy—in one; in the other, an excellent though expensive rotisserie.

ROTTERDAM. *Rotterdam Hilton* (L), Weena 10 (tel. 010–4144044). 250 rooms, all with bath. Several restaurants (Le Jardin the best), disco and usual Hilton amenities. *Parkhotel* (E), Westersingel 70 (tel. 010–4363611). 150 rooms with bath. *Rijnhotel Rotterdam* (E), Schouwburgplein 1 (tel. 010–4333800). 140 rooms with bath or shower. Good restaurant; snackbar and sauna.
Commerce (M), Henegouwerplein 56 (tel. 010–4774564).

Savoy (M), Hoogstraat 81 (tel. 010–4139280). 100 rooms with bath or shower; lower rates Jan. to Mar. *Skyway Hotel and Motel* (M), Vliegveldweg 61 (tel. 010–4158000). 100 soundproofed rooms, all with bath.

Holland (I), Provenierssingel 7 (tel. 010–4653100). 24 rooms; modest, but good value.

Restaurants. *Coq d' Or* (E), Vollenhovenstraat 25 (tel. 101–4366405). Snacks on the ground floor; candlelit dining upstairs; recommended. *In Den Rust Wat* (E), Honingerdijk 96 (tel. 010–4134110). In charming, old-style cottage. *Old Dutch* (E), Rochussenstraat 20 (tel. 010–4360242). One of the best in town.

Beef Eater Steakhouse (M), Stationsplein 45 (tel. 010–4119551). One of a group of restaurants right by the station/air terminal; this one's a pub restaurant, English-style. *Chalet Suisse* (M), Kievitslaan 31 (tel. 010–4365062). Good value; near the park. *Euromast* (M), Parkhaven 20 (tel. 010–4364811). The snack bar near the top is reasonable, the grill excellent though expensive.

Bali (I), Diergaardesingel 96 (tel. 010–4145548). Indonesian food at reasonable prices. *Kiang Nan* (I), Lijnbaam 35 (tel. 010–4110662). Chinese.

Utrecht—City and Province

Utrecht is 36 km. (22 miles) to the northeast of Rotterdam and is the capital of the Province of the same name. The city today is noted for a number of important industrial fairs, but there is also much of interest, principally historical, here. You might start by climbing the 465 steps to the top of the Dom Tower, a campanile standing some distance from the splendid Gothic cathedral and a part of which was destroyed in a great storm in 1674. The view is superb, particularly in April and May when the apple, cherry and pear blossom is at its peak. The cathedral, or Domkerk, also has a series of famous bells (seven dating from 1506 and the wonderful 50-bell carillon from 1663). The best place to hear them is in the cloister between the new cathedral and the University. Museums here include the National Museum van Speelklok tot Pierement, with musical items from clocks and boxes to street organs; the Rijksmuseum het Catharijneconvent, a superb collection of religious history; and the Universiteitsmuseum.

Outside the city, the little medieval town of Amersfoort is worth a visit, 21 km. (12 miles) northeast of Utrecht, as is the castle of de Haar, 8km. (5 miles) out of the city.

PRACTICAL INFORMATION FOR UTRECHT

AMERSFOORT. *Berghotel* (E), Utrechtsweg 225 (tel. 033–620444). 50 rooms; full facilities. *Het Witte Huis Hotel* (M), Birkstraat (tel. 033–17147). 35 rooms; comfortable.

S' GRAVENLAND. *De Drie Dorpen* (I), Cannenburgerweg 51 (tel. 035–61187). 35 rooms; modest but comfortable. **Restaurant.** *'t Swaentje* (E), Noordereinde 339 (tel. 035–62106). Close to Utrecht and one of the more famous restaurants in the country.

RHOON. Restaurant. *Kasteel Rhoon* (E), Dorpsdijk 63 (tel. 01890–8896). Beautifully-renovated castle close to Rotterdam.

UTRECHT. *Des Pays Bas* (E), Janskerkhof 10 (tel. 030–333321). 75 beds, some rooms with bath. *Holiday Inn* (E), Jaarbeursplein 24 (tel. 030–91055). 235 rooms, close to Industries Fair complex; many facilities. *Hotel Hes* (M), Maliestraat 2 (tel. 030–316424). 19 rooms. *Smits* (M), Vredenburg 14 (tel. 030–331232). 39 rooms.

Restaurants. *Hoog Brabant* (M), Radoudkwartier 23 (tel. 030–331525). Surprisingly good. *Kromme Elleboog* (M), Lange Nieuweienstraat 71 (tel. 030–319716). Good. *Victor Conseal* (I), Neude-Utrecht. For Dutch-style pancakes.

ZEIST. *Figi* (E), Het Rond. 3 (tel. 03404–17211). 40 rooms; good facilities. *t' Kerkebosch* (M), Arnhemse Bovenweg 31 (tel. 03404–14734). 28 rooms; with restaurant.

Zeeland, North Brabant and Gelderland

Zeeland, the southwestern Province of Holland, has for centuries been in the forefront of the country's fight against the encroaching sea. Today, the battle has largely been won following the completion some years ago of the massive Delta Project, a 25-year construction project to close up most of the sea arms along the coast. The Delta Expo in Stellendam, open from Easter to the end of October, gives much background information on this huge and fascinating enterprise. The capital of Zeeland is Middelburg. It endured much destruction in the war, but its former glories have since been beautifully restored.

Away to the northeast of Zeeland is the Province of North Brabant. Its capital 's Hertogenbosch is famous for its magnificent late-Gothic cathedral, decorated with a series of extraordinary carvings. The painter Hieronymus Bosch was born here in 1450; he took his name from the town and there's a statue of him in the market square. In the neighborhood of 's Hertogenbosch lies the little village of Drunen, where you will find Lips Autotron, home of 400 vintage cars and motorcycles. In Oisterwijk, near Tilburg, you can meet Snow White and the Seven Dwarfs or peep into Sleeping Beauty's castle in the large amusement park of De Efteling. Also worth a visit is Eindhoven to the southwest of 's Hertogenbosch. This is the home of the giant Philips company, one of the world's largest electrical firms. Go see the Evoluon here, an exhibition devoted to scientific achievements. To the northwest is Breda whose castle, dating from 1527, houses the Royal Military Academy. There is also a fine 15th-century cathedral regarded as one of the best examples of Gothic-Brabantine style.

North of 's Hertogenbosch and North Brabant is the Province of Gelderland. Its capital is Arnhem, perhaps best known for the gallant but doomed action fought here by the Allies in 1944. Today Arnhem's attractions include not only its battlefields, which have become something of a pilgrimage center, but its modern city center, nearby Safari Park and magnificent 75-acre openair museum with traditional farms, windmills, thatched cottages, medieval crafts, costumes and so on. Nearby in the Hoge Veluwe National Park is the Kröller-Müller Museum at Otterlo. It is one of the most important collections of pictures by van Gogh in the world. Finally, the castle of Het Loo near the village of Apeldoorn, is eminently visitable. It was built by William III, later King of England, for his wife Mary at the end of the 16th century. It is now restored to show the life-style of the ruling House of Orange. A museum in the stables houses royal memorabilia, including cars and carriages.

Limburg

Limburg, the southernmost Province of Holland, has a polyglot character to match its checkered history and proximity to Germany in the east and Belgium to the west. Many different cultures have left their mark here and the countryside boasts Roman remains, medieval castles and Gothic cathedrals. Even the landscapes are more varied than in other parts of the country. The capital is Maastricht, one of the oldest cities in Holland. With the single exception of Amsterdam, the city has the finest array of 17th- and 18th-century houses in all Holland. Maastricht's two churches, St. Janskerk and the Onze Lieve Vrouwebasiliek, are among the most beautiful in the country.

PRACTICAL INFORMATION FOR ZEELAND, NORTH BRABANT, GELDERLAND AND LIMBURG

ARNHEM. *Groot Warnsborn* (E), Bakenbergseweg 277 (tel. 085–455751). With good restaurant. *Rijnhotel* (E), Onderlangs 10 (tel. 085–434642). 26 rooms, all with bath; faces the river. *Haarhuis* (M), Stationsplein 1 (tel. 085–427441). 99 rooms; close to the station. *Postiljon Motel* (M), Europaweg 25 (tel. 085–453741). 40 rooms.
Restaurant. *de Steenen Tafel* (E), Weg achter het Bosch 1 (tel. 085–435313).

BREDA. *Motel Breda* (E), Roscam 20 (tel. 076–222177). 115 rooms; just off the motorway outside town. *Hotel de Klok* (I), Grote Markt 24 (tel. 076–134082). Close to the church; delightful and small family run spot with modest restaurant.

DRUNEN. *Hotel Royal* (I), Raadhuisplein 13 (tel. 04163–72381). 15 rooms.
Restaurant. *de Duinrand* (M), Steegerf 2 (tel. 078–144929). Grill restaurant.

EINDHOVEN. *Grand Hotel de Cocagne* (E), Vestdijk 47 (tel. 040–444755). 205 rooms, all with bath or shower; very comfortable. *Holiday Inn Eindhoven* (E), Montgomerylaan 1 (tel. 040–433222). 200 rooms, most with bath; usual Holiday Inn comforts. *Motel Eindhoven* (M), Aalsterweg 322 (tel. 040–116033). 180 rooms; modern.

's HERTOGENBOSCH. *Central* (E), Loeffplein 98 (tel. 073–125151). 76 rooms. *Eurohotel* (M), Hinthamerstraat 63 (tel. 073–137777). 42 rooms with bath.
Restaurants. *De Pettelarr* (E), Pettelaarseschaus 1 (tel. 073–137351). Excellent international cuisine. *Raadskelder* (E), Markt 1a. Historic restaurant in 16th-century building.

MAASTRICHT. *Hotel Maastricht* (E), De Ruiterij 1 (tel. 043–54171). 135 rooms with bath; on the Maas with fine view. *Beaumont* (M), Stationstraat (tel. 043–54433). 68 rooms. *Grand Hotel de l'Empereur* (M), Stationstraat 2 (tel. 043–13838). 48 rooms.

MIDDELBURG. *Hotel Du Commerce* (E), Loskade 1 (tel. 01180–36051). *De Nieuwe Doelen* (M), Loskade 3–7 (tel. 01180–12121). 20 rooms, with bath or shower.

Drenthe, Groningen, Friesland and Overijssel

The four Provinces of Drenthe, Groningen, Friesland and Overijssel make up the northeast corner of Holland. The Ijssel valley is a delightful part of the country, inspiration of many a landscape painter. During the middle ages, the towns of Kampen, Deventer and Zwolle here were of major importance. It still offers Renaissance buildings and gateways, like the lovely Sassenport in Zwolle, and, in Kampen, the church of St. Nicholas with its stunning choir.

Drenthe is an area that should really be explored by bicycle. It is a land of great natural beauty with woods alternating with green fields and moors dotted with hundreds of small lakes, flocks of sheep and picturesque villages. Some of the best spots to explore are the Hunebedden (prehistoric graves)—best done by bicycle.

Groningen is steeped in history and culture, and full of surprises. The Province is dominated by the city of the same name; it makes an ideal excursion base. In the north, Uithuizen has a notable castle, Menkemaborg, with period furnishings and gardens, while over to the east is Heiligerlee. Ter Apel features a medieval convent; Zoutkamp has shrimping and a fish auction; in Leens the Ommelander Museum of

Agriculture is housed in a fortified manor house; Appingedam is particularly picturesque with a church dating from 1255 and a Town Hall from 1630; Delfzijl is a fast growing port and ocean terminal; and Loppersum has a large medieval church with vault paintings and a massive 14th-century tower.

Friesland Province offers plenty to explore. It is inhabited by a fiercely independent people, proud of their separate history, language and traditions. This is the area in which Rembrandt found his wife Saskia, and where Pieter Stuyvesant, the man who founded New York, was born. Its borders contain the Wadden Islands, the unique birdland of Western Europe; a very extensive lake district; large woods and moors; old towns and charming villages; and, from the viewpoint of recreation, the most varied choice of all Holland.

PRACTICAL INFORMATION FOR DRENTHE, GRONINGEN, FRIESLAND AND OVERIJSSEL

APPINGEDAM. *Hotel Langoed Ekenstein* (M), Alberdaweg 70 (tel. 05960–28528). 30 rooms; 19th-century mansion.

ASSEN. *Overcingel* (M), Stationsplein 10 (tel. 05920–11333). 32 rooms, most with bath; opposite the rail station and with good restaurant.
Restaurant. *Bistro La Belle Epoque* (M), Markt 6 (tel. 05920–15818).

BEETSTERZWAAG. *Lauswolt* (E), van Harinxmaweg 10 (tel. 05126–1245). 24 rooms; fine old building in spacious grounds.

GASSELTE. *'t Gasselterveld* (M), Bosweg. 2 (tel. 05999–4435). 48 rooms.
Restaurant. *de Wiemel* (M), Gieterweg (tel. 05999–4725). In former farmhouse.

GRONINGEN. *Crest* (E), Donderslaan 156 (tel. 050–252040). 60 rooms. *De Doelen* (M), Grote Markt 36 (tel. 050–127041). 39 rooms, very central.

HAREN. *Postiljon* (E), Emmalaan 33 (tel. 050–347041). 100 modern rooms.
Restaurant. *Herberg de Rietschans* (M), Meerweg 221 (tel. 05907–1365). Close to Groningen by the lake of Paterswolde.

KAMPEN. *De Stadsherberg* (M), Ijsselkade 48 (tel. 05202–12645). 20 rooms.

LEEUWARDEN. *Eurohotel* (M), Europaplein 19 (tel. 058–131113). 60 rooms. *Oranje Hotel* (M), Stationsweg 4 (tel. 058–126241). 80 rooms, good facilities.

ROODKERK. Restaurant. *de Trochreed* (M), Bosweg 25 (tel. 05103–2266). In beautiful rural setting.

HUNGARY

Hungary—officially the Hungarian People's Republic—is a small, mostly flat, land; but there are several sizable ranges of hills, chiefly in the north and west of the country. The highest peak reaches 3,300 feet. One of the country's most striking features is the Great Plain (Nagyalföld) stretching east from the Danube to the foothills of the Carpathians in the Soviet Union, to the mountains of Transylvania in Romania, and south to the Fruška Gora range in Yugoslavia. Traversed by the River Tisza, it is a vast granary and the historic habitat of Hungary's great horsemen, still visible cracking their long whips and driving their herds across the landscape of the Hortobágy, a corner of the Great Plain equally famous for the mirages that develop over its horizons on hot summer days.

Lake Balaton, the largest unbroken stretch of inland water in central Europe, offers splendid summertime facilities, while the beauty of the Danube near Visegrád, the gaiety of the capital Budapest, superb cuisine and good wines, and the hospitality of the people can be enjoyed the year round. Roughly the size of Ireland or Indiana (35,919 square miles), and with a population of nearly 11 million, Hungary has over 15 million visitors a year.

Budapest is the largest and brightest of all Communist capitals with smart (and sometimes privately owned) shops and a way of life that is the envy of neighboring nations. Restaurants and cafés stay open late into the night serving fine wine, excellent pastries and strong coffee to a clientele that loves gossip, political satire and style in all things.

A Bit of History

A thousand years ago, a fiery nomad chieftain named Árpád led his warlike Magyar tribes from the region of the river Dnieper into the flat

413

fertile Danube plain. The Magyars, unlike their Slav neighbors, were fighters, not farmers, and sent out raiding parties into Germany, Italy and as far as southern France. All Europe trembled before these "Asiatic hordes". A later chieftain, Stephen (who became Hungary's patron saint) was converted to Christianity and the reformed ogres became stout sentinels of Christian Europe. From the 17th century Hungary was a Habsburg vassal state, despite all efforts by the national hero Prince Rákóczy, until after World War I.

After a brief communist regime under Béla Kun in 1919 the country was governed for twenty-five years by Nicolas Horthy as a kingdom without a king. In 1947 the communists took over but—with a regime unswervingly loyal to Moscow—Hungary has nevertheless developed the most liberal atmosphere within the Soviet orbit.

PRACTICAL INFORMATION FOR HUNGARY

WHAT WILL IT COST. Foreign travel to Hungary is handled by *IBUSZ*, the state tourist agency. *IBUSZ* represents the best hotels in Hungary, runs everything for tourists and has branch offices in major hotels and the more important cities throughout Hungary. In most Western countries, *IBUSZ* is represented by accredited travel agents who take care of all arrangements, including visa, hotel accommodations and payment.

Traveling as an individual, your stay in Hungary should cost you between $50 and $80 a day for comfortable accommodations with private bath and three meals; these are your basic expenses. Traveling as a member of a group, count on saving about 25%. For a typical day's expenses, see below.

The *Hungarian Equestrian Federation* in conjunction with *IBUSZ* offers riding tours. A 10-day tour for skilled riders starts at $600; horseback holidays at studfarms and riding clubs start at $50 per day, with accommodations and tuition.

The monetary unit is the *forint* (Ft.), divided into 100 *fillér*. There are coins of 5, 10, 20 and 50 fillérs and 1, 2, 5 and 10 forints; banknotes circulate in denominations of 20, 50, 100, 500 and 1000 forints.

A typical day might cost two people:

Hotel (moderate)—with bath and breakfast	2,800	Ft.
Lunch with beer	600	
Dinner with wine	800	
Beer in a bar	80	
Coffee	40	
Bus or metro	10	
Taxi (about 3 km)	70	
Theater (moderate seats)	120	
Miscellaneous 10%	430	
	4,950	Ft.

At the time of going to press, the exchange rate for tourists is approximately 47 forints to the US$, 70 Ft. to the £ sterling. All rates are subject to change.

You may bring in any amount and kind of foreign currency including travelers checks, and freely exchange it at all offices of *IBUSZ*, the state tourist agency, banks, rail and air terminals, and railway dining cars. You should declare your foreign currency and travelers checks on entering the country. The import and export of Hungarian currency is strictly limited to 100 forints *in coin;* no Hungarian banknotes may be taken in or out of the country. As it is very difficult to change forints back to a Western currency, you should take great care not to change too many dollars or pounds.

The usual credit cards are widely accepted.

WHEN TO COME. The best time is May through September, though July and August can be hot and busy. Spring is delightful, and fall can be rewarding, with many events to enjoy. The winter sports season is from late November through early March.

Climate. Continental: summers (June-August) very warm; winters cold, with snow and frost.

Average maximum daily temperatures in degrees Fahrenheit and centigrade:

Budapest	Jan.	Feb.	Mar.	Apr.	May	June	July	Aug.	Sept.	Oct.	Nov.	Dec.
F°	34	39	50	63	72	79	82	81	73	61	46	39
C°	1	4	10	17	22	26	28	27	23	16	8	4

SPECIAL EVENTS. *February,* Gypsy Festival, Budapest; *March,* Spring Festival Week, Budapest; *May,* International Trade Fair, Budapest; *May-June,* Film Festival, Miskolc; *July,* Bartók Choral Festival, Debrecen; Chamber Music Festival, Veszprem; Film Week, Siófok; *August,* Ethnic Folk Festival, Keszthely; National Flower Festival, Debrecen; Summer Music Festival, Békéscsaba; Horse Show, Bugac puszta; *September,* International Trade Fair, Budapest; Budapest Musical Weeks; *October,* Limestone Cave Concerts, Aggtelek.

National Holidays. Jan. 1 (New Year's Day); Apr. 4 (Liberation); Apr. 20 (Easter Mon.); May 1 (Labor Day); Aug 20 (St. Stephen's and Constitution Day); Nov. 7 (anniversary of Russian Revolution); Dec. 25, 26.

VISAS. It is advisable to obtain a visa beforehand from a Hungarian embassy or *IBUSZ* representative. The completed application form must be accompanied by two recent photographs. The fee is $10 or £7, and the visa is valid for up to 30 days. Travelers by air or private car can obtain visas on arrival at airports or border points, but not those traveling by bus, train or hydrofoil.

HEALTH CERTIFICATES. No vaccinations are required to enter Hungary from any country.

GETTING TO HUNGARY. By Plane. From North America to Britain or the Continent and then a connecting flight to Budapest. *Malév Hungarian Airlines* and reciprocal flag carriers link the capital with most major cities in Eastern and Western Europe.

By Train. There are two through trains from Western Europe to Budapest. The first, the *Orient Express* (a mere shadow, however, of its former greatness), goes from Paris nightly, departing from the Gare de l'Est about 11.15 P.M. and traveling via Strasbourg, Munich, Salzburg and Vienna. It reaches the Hungarian capital about 8.40 P.M. the next day. Sleeping cars on certain days, 2nd. class couchettes every day. Some sleeping cars only go to Salzburg. Through 1st. and 2nd. class carriages always from Paris to Budapest. The train goes on to Bucharest. Buffet and restaurant car part of the way.

The other through train is the *Wiener Walzer* which leaves Basel in Switzerland nightly at around 8 P.M. It travels via Zurich, Innsbruck, Salzburg and Vienna gets into Budapest about 2.30 P.M. the next day. Sleeping cars from Basel to Vienna, also 2nd. class couchettes, 1st. and 2nd. class carriages all the way. Refreshment and buffet services part of the way. It also goes through to Rumania in the summer. From Britain the best route is via Dover and Ostend, taking the *Ostend-Vienna Express* (sleeping cars, 2nd. class couchettes and day cars) to Vienna, and there changing to the *Wiener Walzer* (which waits on the other side of the platform).

By Bus. There are regular bus services to Budapest and other points in Hungary from Vienna and other towns in countries adjoining Hungary.

By Boat. A hydrofoil service runs on the Danube from early April to mid-October daily except Sunday, Vienna-Budapest and return. Travel time about 5 hours one way. Danube cruises from Vienna to the Black Sea call at Budapest.

By Car. Budapest is on routes E5 from Germany and Austria to Yugoslavia, E15 from Czechoslovakia to Romania and the Black Sea, and E96 to Yugoslavia and the Adriatic. Motorists require an international driving license and green international insurance card. Visas are issued at border crossings.

 CUSTOMS. Personal belongings and 250 cigarettes or 40 cigars or 200 gr. tobacco and one liter of spirits and two liters of wine and 250 gr. of perfume may be brought in duty-free. Valuable gifts for people in Hungary should be declared. Gifts of a non-commercial nature which have been bought with hard currency (or legally exchanged forints) may be freely exported, as may goods bought at the *Intertourist* or *Konsumtourist* stores, but you must keep bills or receipts for any such purchases to produce at customs. You may only take out of the country enough food for three days.

 HOTELS. Hungarian hotels are officially classified by stars, from 5-star down to 1-star. These grades correspond closely to our grading system in the lists that follow of Deluxe (L) for 5-star, Expensive (E) for 4-star, Moderate (M) for 3- and the better 2-star, and Inexpensive (I) for the cheaper 2-star and 1-star. 1-star hotels usually consist of the simpler motels, tourist hostels, and small inns; they are unlikely to have many rooms with bath. Under our rating, Deluxe prices range from $75 upwards, Expensive from $50 to $75, Moderate from $35 to $50, and Inexpensive from $25 to $35. *All these prices are for a double room with breakfast.* In Budapest and some Lake Balaton resorts prices may sometimes be higher and, correspondingly, in small towns they are likely to be lower. At hotels on Lake Balaton full board is usually compulsory. The larger and cheaper (M) and the (I) hotels are often full of sometimes noisy "groups." There are now also a number of privately run guest houses in Budapest and main tourist resorts, generally comfortable and with a "family" atmosphere. Details from *Tourinform* (see under *Useful Addresses* for Budapest).

Accommodations in private houses are available in Budapest and in all major resorts and are inexpensive (around $10 to $15 for a comfortable double room, with use of the bathroom but without breakfast). There are around 100 camping sites, three in Budapest, others around Lake Balaton and in other frequented parts of the country. Camping is forbidden except in the officially designated areas. Bungalows (wooden chalets) and other self-catering accommodations can be rented in Budapest and at Lake Balaton at reasonable rents.

 RESTAURANTS. Hungary has many excellent restaurants, mostly state-owned. In the inexpensive range are self-service restaurants *(önkiszolgáló étterem)*, snack bars *(bisztró* or *étel-bár)* and buffets *(büfé)*. But even quite high-class restaurants often provide a modest but tasty and substantial fixed-price meal known as a *menü* for between 40 and 100 Ft. At the top of the scale, a gourmet meal at a famous establishment would cost at least 500 Ft. For a moderate meal reckon on spending about 350–400 Ft. A bottle of wine costs from 100 Ft. upwards, a carafe around 40–50 Ft.

Note that only top-grade restaurants have menus in English, so make quite sure what you are ordering and, to avoid a possible unpleasant surprise, what it will cost.

There are many small cafés or coffee bars *(eszpresszó)* and excellent pastry shops *(cukrászda)*.

Food and Drink. One of the few original cuisines in Europe, Hungarian cooking is too often identified with paprika only. True, dishes flavored with this piquant spice are very popular. But roasts, vegetables and desserts are often superb, too.

Paprika dishes come in a great variety—from mild to burning hot. Incidentally, the six "basic" dishes are called *gulyás* (a soup with cubed beef or pork and diced potatoes, spiced with sweet red paprika); *pörkölt* (outside Hungary called goulash) can be made from veal, pork, beef or chicken; it's a stew in which onions play a bigger role; *paprikás* (sauce of onions, sour cream and red pepper) used for fish and poultry dishes; *tokány* (stew with black pepper flavoring); *rostélyos* (round steak potted in paprika sauce), and *halászlé* (fish soup—Hungary's answer to *bouillabaisse*), which can be fiery indeed!

In the dessert department, Hungary's classic is *rétes* (strudel to you). Crisp and flaky it comes filled with cherries, apple, nuts, almonds, poppy-seed or cottage cheese and, believe it or not, peppered cabbage (eaten as a savory).

Wine-tasting is a prime tourist activity. Vintners and wine co-operatives welcome visitors to their cellars for sampling and discussion. Budafok, on the southern outskirts of Budapest, is a town of wine-cellars with miles of passages tunneling into the hillside. One of its casks, built in 1850, held nearly 26,500 gallons.

Tokay wine comes from the hillside of Tokaj, in northeastern Hungary. The most famous variety is the *Tokaj Aszu,* a sweet syrupy nectar. *Szamorodni* is a much drier wine of the same vintage.

Fine wines also come from the volcanic slopes on the northern shore of Lake Balaton and the hillsides near Pécs. Don't leave Hungary without tasting "Bull's Blood" *(bikavér)* from the sunny region of Eger. Apricot brandy, *barack* (pronounced "borotsk"), has been distilled for centuries on the great plain between the Danube and Tisza rivers, particularly in the city of Kecskemét. Other fruit brandies are plum brandy *(szilvapálinka)* and cherry brandy *(cseresznyepálinka).*

TIPPING. Tips are generally expected, in addition to any service charge. Hotel porters, waiters and barber shops should not be given less than 10%. Taxi drivers receive about 15 to 20 percent of the fare.

MAIL. An airmail letter to the US (5g) costs 10 Ft., an airmail postcard 7 Ft. An airmail letter to Western Europe (including the UK) costs 9 Ft., an airmail postcard 6 Ft. However, surface mail to Western Europe is almost as fast as airmail and costs 8 Ft. for a letter and 5 Ft. for a postcard.

Public **telephones** are operated by a 2 Ft. coin. If placing a long-distance call from your hotel, check the surcharge beforehand.

CLOSING TIMES. Most stores open between 8 A.M. and 10 A.M. and close at 6 P.M. On Saturdays they close between 1 P.M. and 3 P.M. Banks: Monday to Friday, 9 to 1; offices: Monday to Friday, 8 to 5.

PHOTOGRAPHY. Do not photograph military installations or railways.

USEFUL ADDRESSES. *US Embassy,* Szabadság Tér 12, Budapest V (tel. 124–224); *British Embassy,* Harmincad Utca 6, Budapest V (tel. 171–430); *Canadian Embassy,* Budakeszi Út 55/d, Budapest II (tel. 165–858). *KEOKH* (Aliens' Police), Népköztársaság Útja 93, Budapest VI; *IBUSZ* main office, Tanács Körút 3/c (near Astoria Metro stop) (tel. 423–140). The *IBUSZ* branch at Petöfi Tér 3 (behind the Intercontinental Hotel) is very helpful in finding accommodations of all kinds; multilingual staff, open day and night; personal applications only. Other travel organizations are: *Budapest Tourist,* Roosevelt Tér 5–7, Budapest V (tel. 186–003) and *Express Student Travel,* Szabadság Tér 16, Budapest V (tel. 317–777). *MALÉV* (the Hungarian airline), Váci Utca, Budapest V; *British Airways,* Apáczai Csere János Utca 5 (behind Intercontinental Hotel); *PanAm,* in Intercontinental Hotel.

GETTING AROUND HUNGARY. By Train. The Hungarian Railway System radiates mainly from Budapest and most trunk routes are electrified. Indeed, the entire network is perhaps the best in Eastern Europe. For the average visitor, the line from and to Austria, the line southeast to Yugoslavia and the line to Lake Balaton are of considerable scenic interest. All trains carry 1st. and 2nd. class and many have either dining, buffet or refreshment services. As rail travel is comparatively inexpensive the trains are usually full. Where possible, and especially on longer distance routes, make reservations (they are compulsory on the crack expresses). Budapest has a good network of local trains and also an excellent Underground (Metro), one line of which is the oldest on the European continent. A useful runaround ticket, giving unlimited travel on the State Railways, is available outside Hungary. For 10-, 20-, or 30-day passes, the cost for 1st. class is £46.70, £69.80 and £93.20, respectively, while 2nd. class runs £31.30, £46.70 and £62.10; apply to *Danube Travel*, 6 Conduit St., London, W.1. These prices are subject to change.

By Bus. There is an extensive bus network, often linked with rail services. The frequency, however, is not as high as in some Western countries. Fares are low; buses are often full.

By Car. Drive on the right; Continental rules of the road observed, plus right turn permitted in front of red light. City transport has priority. Speed limits are 60 kph in town, 80 kph on main roads and 100 kph on highways. The state roads are identified by a one-digit number: thus Highway No. 1 runs from Budapest toward Vienna; highways 2–7 radiate out from Budapest, in a clockwise direction. There are three motorways, distinguished by the letter "M". M1 reaches the neighborhood of Györ on the way to Vienna; M3 connects Budapest with eastern Hungary; and M7 provides a fast means of reaching Lake Balaton. All are being improved and extended. An excellent road map showing camp sites is available through IBUSZ or its agents.

Car Hire. Cars can be hired through IBUSZ offices and hotels with prepaid vouchers, otherwise a deposit of $150 is required. *Avis* is at the airport and 8 Martinelli Ter, Budapest V. in the Inner City.

Budapest

The city is divided by the Danube into two sections: Buda and Pest. Buda dominates the scene with its many rounded hills and bluffs rising from the curved arms of the Danube. Pest is east of the river, flat, commercial and in parts completely rebuilt since the forties. The lovely Margaret Island (Margitsziget) is a 112-acre park. Budapest has 526 parks and green spots, totalling some 1500 acres. It has a wonderful zoo, 123 mineral hot springs, Roman ruins, a 100,000-fan sports stadium, and the second subway (Metro) in the world (after London), built in 1896.

For a first, wonderful look at Budapest, go to the Buda side, climb the Gellért Hill from Gellért Square, and see the panorama of all the Danube bridges, Parliament and Pest to the south, Buda Castle and the blue mountains to the north.

Gellért Hill is crowned by a stone fort built in 1851, and topped by a towering memorial to the liberation of Budapest by Soviet troops in 1944–45. During the 14-week winter siege, 33,000 buildings were totally destroyed, and every bridge between Buda and Pest demolished. Restoration work is still not entirely completed.

Two other hillocks rise up from the Danube on the Buda side—Castle Hill (Várhegy) and the Hill of Roses (Rózsadomb). Behind these scenic summits curves a range of higher hills, of which the loftiest is the conical Jánoshegy, 1,435 feet in height, and topped by a lookout tower. The hills are easily reached from Buda by a cogwheel railway (terminus at Városmajor). A chair-lift runs to János Hill from the Zugligeti Út.

Before leaving the Buda side, ramble around Castle Hill (Várhegy) with its many Gothic landmarks. This oldest section of the city suffered the most damage during the Second World War. Bombardments destroyed a great deal of Renaissance and baroque architecture, revealing many older walls and arches, some medieval. The postwar governments rebuilt much of the district following its original town plan. The rebuilt former Royal Palace, now a museum and cultural center, covers the southern end of Castle Hill. Farther north is the Fishermen's Bastion, a round Romanesque lookout tower and wall built in the last century; in front of the Bastion stands the beautiful and historic 13th-century Matthias (or Coronation) Church, in which the last two kings of Hungary were crowned—Francis Joseph in 1867 and Charles in 1916.

From the Matthias Church, walk down to the Danube; here, going north, runs Buda's main street, Fö Utca, which contains several interesting buildings, among them the baroque Church of St. Anna. A few hundred yards beyond this is one of the city's beauty spots, the tomb of Gül Baba, a 16th-century Turkish poet.

Margaret Island and Pest

Back on the embankment, a few steps beyond Bem József Tér, you come to the Margit Híd (Margaret Bridge) which connects Buda and Pest with lovely boat-shaped Margaret Island, or Margitsziget. Seven centuries have passed since a young princess named Margaret retired to a nunnery here, but it is only recently that she was canonized by the Church, and is revered as Budapest's patron saint. The island is also notable for its roses, sports facilities and a Japanese rock garden.

When the Budapest Opera House and theaters close for the summer, their companies stage operas, operettas, plays and ballets in the open air theater on Margaret Island. Just beyond are the ruins of Saint Margaret's cloister and a Gothic chapel.

Across the handsome chain bridge (Lánchid)—built over 130 years ago by a British engineer, Adam Clark—lies flat, bustling Pest. This modern part of the city has no hills to slow down its development. Nucleus of old Pest is the Belváros, or Inner City, included within the irregular semicircle of the Inner Körút (Boulevard). The stretch of riverside running south is known as the Corso (now a pedestrian precinct) whose outdoor cafés are crowded in fine weather. Halfway along the Corso stands the Vigadó, a concert hall built in a striking Romantic style in the middle of the last century. It was badly damaged in World War II, but is now again the venue for great musical events. The south end of the Corso broadens out into Március 15 Tér, on which stands the 12th-century Belvárosi Templom, the oldest church in Pest. Just off the square stands a slightly sunken building, the Százéves (Hundred Year Old) restaurant. A wide arched passage leads under the nearby Central University to Váci Utca, one of the main shopping streets and a pedestrian precinct. Many good cafés and restaurants, such as the Mátyás Pince, make this section the heart of old Pest.

Beyond the Inner City, Pest's main thoroughfare curves down from the Margaret Bridge all the way to the Petöfi Bridge. Within its sweep lie most of the city's main buildings, including the neo-Gothic Parliament House. Budapest's grandest boulevard, the Nepköztársaság útja, runs for 1½ miles out from the Inner City to the Hösök Tere (Heroes' Square), at the entrance to the city park; under it runs the original Underground line.

Városliget Park has a lake used for boating in summer, skating in winter. On an islet are replicas of several medieval buildings. In the north corner of the park is the only zoo in Europe where hippopotami give birth to calves in captivity, due, it seems, to the natural hot mineral spring which feeds their pool.

Adjoining the city park is the Vidám Park, Budapest's Coney Island, complete with scenic railway, dodgems, a rollercoaster and, close by, a circus.

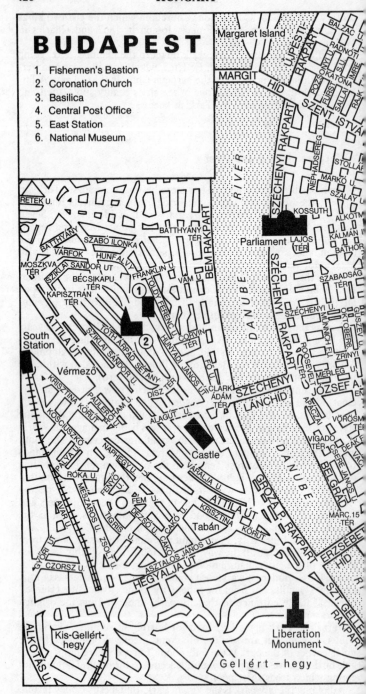

BUDAPEST

1. Fishermen's Bastion
2. Coronation Church
3. Basilica
4. Central Post Office
5. East Station
6. National Museum

Margaret Island

MARGIT

Parliament

South Station

Castle

Tabán

Kis-Gellért-hegy

Liberation Monument

Gellért – hegy

RIVER

DANUBE

Vérmező

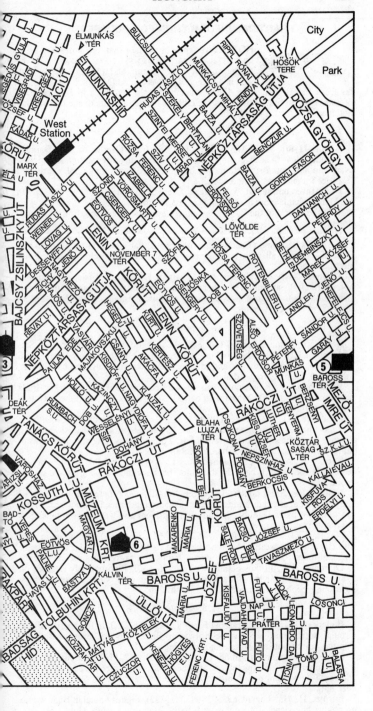

PRACTICAL INFORMATION FOR BUDAPEST

HOTELS. In spite of the fact that new hotels are being opened each year, Budapest is very crowded in the spring, summer and autumn, and it is advisable to book well in advance. There is a good (M) hotel, the *Aero,* not far from the airport. *Note:* the Roman numerals, e.g. VII., in Budapest addresses, refer to the "district" of the city. In the restaurants of the top-ranking hotels guests should be suitably dressed.

Deluxe

Atrium-Hyatt, V., Roosevelt Tér 2 (tel. 383–000). Overlooking the Danube. 357 rooms, all with bath, color TV and mini-bar. Fully airconditioned and with every modern comfort: restaurants, bars, covered swimming-pool, sauna and facilities for business conferences.

Duna-Intercontinental, V., Apáczai Csere János Utca 4 (tel. 175–122). On the Danube bank, close to shopping center. 349 rooms, all with bath and all with view of the river and the Castle. Several restaurants, night-club. Fully airconditioned.

Hilton, I., Hess András Tér 1–3 (tel. 853–500). Finely situated next to the Fishermen's Bastion on Castle Hill, with spectacular view over the Danube and Pest. 323 rooms, all with bath; several restaurants, night-club, casino. Fully airconditioned.

Thermal, XIII., Margitsziget (tel. 111–000). On Margaret Island. Luxurious hotel with all the amenities of a thermal spa; hot springs, curative treatment and swimming-pool. 216 rooms with bath, restaurant, night-club. Direct bus to Marx Tér, near city center.

Expensive

Béke, VI., Lenin Körút 97 (tel. 323–300). Traditional hotel near West Station, completely refurbished and modernized, with airconditioning throughout. 238 rooms, all with bath, TV and minibar. Several restaurants and bars. Swimming pool, sauna, garage, dancing.

Buda-Penta, I., Krisztina Körút 41–43 (tel. 250–060). New hotel in Buda near South Station. 400 rooms with bath. Public rooms airconditioned. Restaurants, nightclub, swimming pool, and sauna.

Flamenco, XI., Tass Vezér Utca 7 (tel. 252–250). 360 rooms, all with bath, TV and minibar. New hotel in the Buda green belt, run by Spanish interests; Spanish specialties in restaurant and bar. Public rooms airconditioned. Swimming pool, sauna, tennis courts, nightclub.

Forum, V., Apáczai Csere János Utca 12–14 (tel. 178–088). On the Danube bank, 408 rooms with bath. Restaurants, bars, swimming pool, sauna, underground garage. Fully airconditioned.

Gellért, XI., Szent Gellért Tér 1 (tel. 460–700). 235 rooms, all with bath or shower. Partial airconditioning. Thermal swimming-baths. Outdoor terrace restaurant. Overlooks Danube. Splendidly traditional and warmly recommended; excellent food.

Novotel, XII., Alkotás Utca 63–67 (tel. 869–588). New hotel on main road into city from the west. 324 rooms with fine views, all with bath. Public rooms airconditioned. Swimming pool, sauna, tennis courts, restaurants, and bars.

Olympia, XII., Eötvös Sétany 40 (tel. 166–450). Picturesquely situated on Szabadság Hill, near the Buda woods. 172 rooms with bath, restaurant, bars, swimming pool, sauna, tennis courts; nightclub.

Moderate

Budapest, II., Szilágyi Erzsébet Fasor 47 (tel. 153–230). In the heart of Buda; circular hotel opposite cog-wheel railway to Buda Hills. 280 rooms with bath. Popular restaurant and wine-cellar; dancing.

Erzsébet, V., Károlyi Mihály Utca 11–15 (tel. 382–111). Famous old hotel in the Inner City, completely refurbished and modernized. 123 rooms with shower, TV and mini-bar. Public rooms airconditioned. Restaurant and popular beer-hall.

Európa, II., Hárshegyi Utca 5–7 (tel. 387–122). 13-story hotel in Buda woods area with fine views. 160 rooms with bath. Restaurant, night-club.

Hungária, VII., Rákóczi Út 90 (tel. 229–050). Enlarged and completely refurbished and modernized hotel opposite East Station. 540 rooms, all doubles and most singles with bath or shower and all with TV and mini-bar. Several restaurants and bars. Sauna; garage.

Rege, II., Pálos Utca 2 (tel. 387–311). New hotel in the Buda Hills. 77 double rooms with bath. Restaurant, bar; swimming-pool, sauna.

Stadion, XIV., Ifjúság Utca 1–3 (tel. 631–830). In eastern part of city, near sports complex and metro (subway) station. 379 rooms with bath. Restaurant, swimming-pool, sauna.

Taverna, V., Váci Utca 20 (tel. 180–846). New hotel in Inner City pedestrian zone. 224 rooms, all with bath or shower, radio and mini-bar. Restaurant, grill-room and beer-hall. Sauna.

Volga, XIII., Dózsa György Utca 16 (tel. 290–200). Away from city center, but with good metro (subway) connections. 313 rooms with bath, all of them with two or more beds; very popular with groups. Restaurants, bars, juke-boxes and other amusements.

Inexpensive

Citadella, XI., Gellérthegy (tel. 665–794). In the former fortress, with fine views over the city. Its 20 rooms each contain from 2 to 4 beds and have hot and cold running water, while there are showers in the corridors; popular and inexpensive restaurant. The hotel is primarily a hostel for young people.

Expo, X., Dobi István Utca 10 (tel. 153–230). Some way out of town and adjoining the Trade Fair grounds. 160 rooms with bath; restaurants. Every facility for businessmen.

Park, VIII., Baross Tér 10 (tel. 130–420). Opposite East Station. 174 rooms, many with bath or shower; restaurant. Very popular with groups.

Vörös Csillag, XII., Rege Utca 21 (tel. 166–404). Alpine-style hotel on Széchenyi Hill, with fine views. 41 rooms, some with bath. Restaurant, swimming-pool. There are bungalows in the wooded grounds.

Wien, XI., Budaörsi Út 88–90 (tel. 665–400). On southwestern outskirts, near junction of Vienna and Lake Balaton motorways. 110 double rooms, many with bath. Restaurant. Car-repair shop and garage with filling-station.

CAMPING. Sites at Hárshegy, in the Buda Hills, and at Római Fürdö and Csillaghegy, north of the city and near the Danube. Book through the Budapest Tourist Agency, Roosevelt Tér 5, Budapest V.

RESTAURANTS. There are more than 2,000 restaurants and taverns in Budapest. Our selection is classified as expensive (E), moderate (M) and inexpensive (I). Expect to pay more for dinner than lunch as there is often an orchestra playing in the evening.

Alabárdos (E), I. Országház Utca 4 (tel. 160–828). On Castle Hill; perhaps *the* restaurant of Budapest. Small and intimate; dinner only. Must book.

Fortuna (E), I. Hess András Tér 4 (tel. 160–270). Opposite the Matthias Church, in the Castle district. Good food and wine and lively orchestra.

Gundel (E), XIV., Állatkerti Út (tel. 221–002). Famous old restaurant in the City Park. Terrace dining; dancing.

Hungária (E), VII., Lenin Körú 9–11 (tel. 223–859). Splendid *art nouveau* café-restaurant, food can be variable.

Kárpátia (E), V., Károly Mihály Utca 4 (tel. 173–503). Outdoor terrace and garden.

Mátyás Pince (E), V., Március Tér 15 (tel. 180–608). Excellent. Features one of Hungary's most famous gypsy orchestras. Booking essential.

Régi Országház (E), I., Országház Utca 17 (tel. 160–225). Very old inn on Castle Hill; famous for its wines. Evening music.

Apostolok (M), V., Kígyó Utca 4–6 (tel. 183–704). Tasty cold dishes in the evening; excellent beer.

Arany Szarvas (M), I., Szarvas Tér 1 (tel. 351–305). Famous for its game and venison. Evenings only.

Fehér Galamb (M), I., Szentháromság Utca 9 (tel. 160–809). Specialty: meats roasted on the grill. Evenings.

Dunakorzó (M), V., Vigadó Tér 3 (tel. 186–435). On the Danube Bank; marvelous view.

Opera (M), VI., Népköztársaság Útja 44 (tel. 328–586). In theater district. Italian specialties. Gypsy music.

Pest-Buda (M), I., Fortuna Utca 3 (tel. 360–768). Charming. Open evenings only; old-time music.

Sipos Halászkert (M), III, Fö Tér 6 (tel. 88–745). Very popular fish restaurant, gypsy music.

Tabáni Kakas (M), I., Attila Út 27 (tel. 352–159). Delightful small restaurant specialising in poultry (try the goose). Evenings only.

Vigadó (M), V., Vigadó Tér (tel. 176–222). Elegant beer-hall in the Vigadó Concert Hall.

Bástya (I), VII., Rákóczi Út 29 (tel. 130–477). Popular, on city's main shopping street.

Lucullus (I), Lenin Körút 7 (tel. 420–398). Very simple, but with good food.

Szeged (I), XI., Bartók Béla Út 1 (tel. 251–268). On the Danube. Traditional fish restaurant; gypsy music in the evenings.

There are numerous foreign-style restaurants, with music in the evenings: **Bajkál** (Russian), at corner of Semmelweis Utca and Kossuth Lajos Utca, in the Inner City; **Bukarest** (Romanian), Bartók Béla Út, beyond the Hotel Gellért, in Buda; **Havanna** (Latin-American), József Körút 46; **Karczma Polska-Kis Royal** (Polish), Márvány Utca, near the South Station; **Szecsuan** (Chinese), Roosevelt Ter 5; **Szófia** (Bulgarian), Kossuth Lajos Tér, behind the Parliament. All are (M) or (I), except the Szecsuan, which is (E).

PASTRY SHOPS, CAFÉS AND SNACK BARS. *Gerbeaud,* Vörösmarty Square, in Inner City. Long famous, has crystal chandeliers and is usually crowded. Seats in the open. Excellent tea, coffee and pastries. *Ruszwurm,* on Castle Hill, Szentháromság Tér. Oldest pastry shop, a bakery since the 16th century. *Anna* and *Muskátli,* two pleasant cafés in Váci Utca, in the Inner City pedestrian precinct, with seats in the open. There are cafés (*eszpresszó*) in almost every busy street, as well as countless snack bars (*ételbar* or *bisztró*) and self-service restaurants (*önkiszolgáló étterem*).

 TRANSPORTATION. Public transport makes sightseeing cheap and painless, though it is sensible to avoid rush hours (7–9, 4–6). All tickets must be bought in advance from tobacconists or special kiosks and must be cancelled in a special machine in each bus, tram or trolleybus and at the entrance of each Metro station. Tickets for buses cost 3 Ft.; for trams, trolleybus and the Metro 2 Ft. Line 1 of the Metro, known as the old subway (it was opened in 1896, but has been modernised) runs from Vörösmarty Tér, in the heart of the business district, out to the City Park and beyond. Line 2 connects the East Station with the Inner City, dives under the Danube and terminates at the South Station. Line 3 runs from the southern suburbs to Deák Square (Deák Tér, where all three lines cross) and northwards to the West Station and beyond. The celebrated *cog-wheel railway* to the Buda Hills leaves opposite the Hotel Budapest. *Taxis* are plentiful and inexpensive (tip around 20%).

 NIGHTLIFE. The best floorshows are at the *Moulin Rouge,* VI., Nagymezö Utca 17, and *Maxim's,* at the Emke hotel. The *Troubadour* at the Hilton and the *Starlight* at the Intercontinental are sedate, with no floor show. For dancing, try the *Old Firenze,* a charming spot in Buda (I., Táncsics Mihály Utca 25), or the *Hungária,* VI., Lenin Körút 9–11. The *Casanova,* on the Danube bank in Buda (I., Batthyány Tér 4) is in a picturesque old baroque house. Far less sedate is the *Pipacs,* in the Inner City of Pest (V., Aranykéz Utca 5) and the crowded *Funko Disco* at the *Éden* (I., Széna Tér 7). The choice is enormous and you would do well to ask a friend—or, if you're young, find a Hungarian student.

 ENTERTAINMENT. Budapest has a rich musical life, with several world famous string quartets, chamber and symphony orchestras. Concerts are held at the *Erkel Theater* (VIII, Köztársaság Tér 30) and the *Academy of Music* (Liszt Ferenc Tér 8). Excellent church music is to be heard at the *Matthias* or *Coronation Church* on Castle Hill. Opera is performed at the *State*

Opera House on Népköztársaság Útja and the Erkel Theater. Dress is almost always informal.

There are 25 permanent theaters in Budapest. In summer open-air performances are given, notably on Margaret Island.

Hungarian films can be outstanding. Cinemas also show foreign films, usually dubbed.

For details of all events, consult the monthly *Programme,* in English, French, and German; it is available free at your hotel.

 MUSEUMS. All are closed Mondays. Admission is usually free Saturdays. **Budapest History Museum,** in the former Royal Palace in Buda. An impressive exhibition of the 1,000-year-old history of the city.

Fine Arts Museum, Hösök Tere, at the entrance to the City Park. The largest collection of painting and sculpture in Hungary; particularly rich in Flemish, Dutch and Spanish old masters; also an Egyptian exhibition.

Folklore Center, Fehérvári Út 47. Open in the summer only. Performances of folk music and dancing.

Gastronomy Exhibition, Fortuna Utca 4, on Castle Hill. Illustrates aspects of Hungarian cookery with many original menus and utensils.

Museum of Applied Arts, Üllöi Út 33. A building in true Hungarian style; its chief collections are of ceramics and of the goldsmith's art.

National Gallery, in the former Royal Palace in Buda. A fine and representative display of Hungarian painting and sculpture from the 14th century to the present day.

National Museum, Múzeum Körút 14–16. Itself a piece of flawless classical architecture. Large and impressive historical collections including Beethoven's piano. The Hungarian regalia, notably the Holy crown of St. Stephen, are on show in the Hall of Honor.

Stamp Museum, Hársfa Utca 37. Contains an example of every Hungarian stamp ever issued. (Open on Sunday, Wednesday and Saturday only.)

 THERMAL SPRINGS. In the sea around Budapest there are over 100 mineral springs, many naturally hot. Try *Palatinus Bath* on Margitsziget Island or the *Gellert Medicinal Bath;* prices are reasonable. *Széchényi Medicinal Bath* at City Park offers very hot (163–169 deg. F) baths, various treatments, nude sunbaths (the sexes are segregated).

 SHOPPING. Main shopping area is Váci Utca, in Pest's Inner City, and its side streets. Here you will find, among much else, exquisite *Herend* porcelain, cut glass, fine peasant embroidery and needlework, homespun cloth, carpets, charming carved wood objects and, of course, dolls in national dress. Prices are fixed, no bargaining. In the *Intertourist* and *Konsumtourist* shops, where the choice is perhaps wider, you must pay in foreign currency; elsewhere Hungarian money is accepted. Other excellent buys are records of classical and folk music—pop, too! If you want to see how the locals shop, visit either the *Central Market (Vásárcsarnok)* in Tolbuhin Körút, or one of the large department stores, for instance the *Corvin Nagyáruház,* in Rákóczi Út, or the newest and largest of them all, the *Metro-Skála,* in Marx Square, opposite the West Station.

USEFUL ADDRESS. *Main Post Office,* Petöfi Sándor Utca, Budapest V., with *Tourinform* (Tourist Information Office) one floor up.

Exploring the Danube Bend

An all-day excursion trip up the Danube by hydrofoil, steamer or coach, from Budapest to Szentendre (steamer or coach only), Visegrád, and Esztergom, travels through a thousand years of history. Upstream is the photogenic town of Szentendre, which has hardly changed in the last 150 years. Its old streets lined with baroque and rococo houses have attracted many Hungarian artists. Farther north is Visegrád, where the medieval kings of Hungary held court, with splendid remains of their palace.

Still farther upstream we come to Esztergom. This ancient town was once Charlemagne's eastern border fortress. Later it was the birthplace of Saint Stephen, and for over seven centuries has been the seat of Hungary's Roman Catholic primate. Its massive domed basilica is visible for many miles across the country. In the primate's palace is the Christian Museum, rich in early Hungarian and Italian paintings and Gobelin tapestries.

Balaton, the Landlocked Riviera

Two hours or less from Budapest, by car or train, lies a family-style paradise named Lake Balaton. Here the sun shines an average of 2,000 hours per year, the beaches are sandy, the water tempers the summer heat, the bass bite on any bait, and, on the southern shore, children can wade out for hundreds of feet in the shallow water, which sparkles with bracing carbonic gas as well as sunlight. Both shores of the 50-mile-long "Hungarian Sea" (slightly larger than Lake Geneva) form one continuous summer resort; winegrowing, fishing and running the attractive hotels keep the local inhabitants busy. Siófok is the most popular resort.

A storybook thumb of land, the Tihany Peninsula, all but cuts Lake Balaton in two. Its two or three-mile area is a national park, riddled with extinct geyser craters surrounding a tiny lakelet. Aromatic lavender fields clothe its volcanic hills, rare birds nest by the lake, and nature lovers can count 800 different kinds of butterfly. Tihany is also the site of one of Hungary's oldest pieces of architecture—an 11th-century monastery crypt. Just north lies Balatonfüred, oldest watering place on the lake. Here the mineral hot springs, prototype of the legendary "fountain of youth", are particularly reputed for cardiac sufferers, and the Balatonfüred State Hospital for Heart Diseases is world-famous.

Among indoor sports, along the Balaton's north shore winetasting is an odds-on favorite, best practiced in the cool cellars of Badacsony, a hillside village on volcanic soil, famed for its bottled grape. At Hévíz, near the far end of Lake Balaton, is a large lake of water whose mineral springs run warm even in winter.

Kis-Balaton is a large marshland area. Here, 3,700 acres have been set aside as a nature reserve, where many kinds of wild fowl are being saved from extinction. (Special permission is needed to enter the reserve.)

Lake Velence, only 30 miles southwest of Budapest, lies on the route to Balaton and offers a mini-version of the latter's aquatic and natural attractions; of special appeal to anglers and bird watchers.

PRACTICAL INFORMATION FOR BUDAPEST ENVIRONS AND LAKE BALATON

BALATONALMÁDI. *Auróra* (M), tel. 38–090; 240 double rooms, all with bath, restaurant; swimming-pool; tennis nearby. Large camping-site.
Restaurants. *Vadvirág* (M), tel. 38–436; *Hattyú* (M), tel. 38–007.

BALATONFÖLDVÁR. *Neptun* (M), tel. 40–388; new, with every comfort, 210 double rooms, all with bath; swimming-pool. *Express* (I), tel. 40–313; no private baths. *Motel* (I) with restaurant.
Restaurants. *Flekken* (M); *Kukorica Csárda* (M), tel. 40–387; *Keringö Csárda* (M), tel. 40–266, popular night-spot.

BALATONFÜRED. *Annabella* (M), tel. 40–110; picturesquely situated on lake shore; 384 double rooms with bath and balcony; private beach and tennis nearby. *Marina* (M), tel. 40–810; also on lake, well run, 374 double rooms with bath, private beach. Both hotels have swimming-pools and good restaurants. *Margaréta* (M), tel. 40–810; self-catering apartment house, with the use of all the amenities of the *Marina*. *Arany Csillag* (I), tel. 40–323; in town center; 102 single and double rooms, none with bath. *Motel,* bungalows to let and first-class camping-site, all on lake shore.

Restaurants. *Balaton, Yacht Club* and *Halászkert* (fish a specialty), all (M). Excellent pastry-shop (*Kedves*).

DOBOGÓKÖ. *Nimród* (M), tel. 336–508; in forest behind Buda Hills. 79 double rooms with bath; restaurant; swimming-pool, sauna, tennis-court.

ESZTERGOM. *Fürdö* (I), tel. 147; spa hotel, 88 rooms, many doubles with bath, garden restaurant.

HÉVÍZ, famous spa for disorders of the nervous system. *Thermal* (E), tel. 11–190. 203 rooms, restaurant, casino. *Aqua* (M); 231 rooms with bath; restaurant. *Gyöngyvirág* (I), tel. 12–937; 16 rooms without bath.

KESZTHELY. *Helikon* (M), tel. 11–330; 240 double rooms with bath, on lakeside, restaurant; swimming-pool; tennis-courts nearby. *Amazon* and *Motel* (both (I)), on lakeside; neither has rooms with bath.

Restaurants. *Debrecen, Béke.*

RÁCKEVE, on Csepel island, some 25 miles south of Budapest. New resort complex with motel and camping-site. Apply Tourist Office, Ráckeve, tel. 10–639.

SIÓFOK. *Európa* (M), tel. 11–400; *Balaton* (M), tel. 10–655; *Hungária* (M), tel. 10–677; *Lidó* (M), tel. 10–633; four almost identical hotels close together on lakeside, each with 137 double rooms with bath; central restaurant. *Napfény* (I), also near lake, tel. 10–675; 57 double rooms with bath, restaurant a few yards away. *Vénusz* (M), tel. 10–660; 58 doubles with bath, away from lake, restaurant nearby. *Motel* (M) is next door. *Touring* (I), tel. 10–684; in western suburb.

Restaurants. Among the many we single out the *Fogas* and the *Matróz,* each with garden. The *Borharapó* (M) has local wines.

SZENTENDRE. *Danubius* (I), tel. 93–77; simple but attractive hotel on Danube bank north of town; 50 double rooms, no private baths. *Party* (I); new, on Danube bank; 16 doubles, no private bath. Also guesthouse, tourist hostel, and camp site.

Restaurants. *Arany Sárkány,* good, *Görög Kancsó* and many others, all (M) to (I).

TIHANY. *Tihany Club Hotel* (E), tel. 44–170; 330 double rooms with bath; part of a large new "club complex"; adjoining is the *Tihany Holiday Village* with 161 luxurious bungalows, lido, indoor pool and tennis, gym, restaurants, nightclub. *Kis Tihany* (M), very comfortable, completely rebuilt and refurbished.

Restaurants. Among the numerous popular eating-spots are the *Fogas* (M) and the *Sport* (dancing). Very popular is the *Révcsárda,* an old inn on the opposite shore (a few minutes in the ferry), with gypsy music and good food (M).

VISEGRÁD. *Silvánus* (M), tel. 136–063; attractively located on hill top in wooded region of the Danube Bend. 70 double rooms with bath. Good restaurant.

The Northeast

If at all possible time should be found for a visit to the vast beech forests of the Bükk and Mátra hills, home to big and small game. Time seems to have forgotten this remote corner, with its endless limestone caverns rich in traces of prehistoric man. The Aggtelek Caverns to the north of Bükk, near the Czechoslovak border, are a 14-mile chain of weirdly beautiful vaults and chambers and Europe's largest stalactite cave system. Orchestral concerts are held in one called "Concert Hall" with unique acoustics.

Mezökövesd, main town of Matyó Land, is a living museum; folk costumes are still sometimes worn on Sundays. Matyó House in the middle of town is a cooperative workshop, where the local folk art is preserved and developed on a cottage industry basis.

Eger and Tokaj are two of Hungary's chief wine-producing centers. Eger is a historic and artistic treasure, one of the loveliest baroque towns in Hungary.

Eastern Far West

Longhorn cattle, fast range ponies, cowboys in broadbrimmed hats —Hungary's Far West lies 100 miles due east of Budapest. Its quarter million acres of tree-less rangeland is called the Hortobágy Puszta. Actually, the puszta is more of a marsh (like the French Camargue) than a prairie, and is the country's first national park. There are various historical inns where you can eat or stay over and the horse shows are very entertaining.

Debrecen is the main town in this area and is famous for its August Flower Festival. It is the chief center of Protestantism in Hungary.

Another fascinating and less-known puszta region is Bugac, part of the Kiskunság National Park 80 miles southeast of Budapest, where sand dunes alternate with marshes and various types of forest, and a chain of small lakes yields rich bird life.

Western Hungary

Two outstanding towns in western Hungary are Pécs, near the Yugoslav border, with a magnificent Romanesque cathedral and many relics of the Turkish occupation, and Sopron, near the Austrian frontier, perhaps the most picturesque town in the country. A few miles away stands the great Esterházy palace at Fertöd, the "Hungarian Versailles", where Haydn lived and where concerts of his music are held in the summer. Other places in the area well worth a visit are Szombathely, with its many fine baroque buildings, and Köszeg, a fascinating small medieval town; it was here that a few hundred Hungarian troops halted the advance of the vast Turkish army on Vienna. Veszprém is a picturesque town built on five hills.

PRACTICAL INFORMATION FOR THE REGIONS

DEBRECEN. *Arany Bika* (M), tel. 16–777; one of Hungary's famous hotels; 270 rooms, many with bath. Good restaurant. *Debrecen* (M), tel. 16–550; 81 double rooms, some with bath. *Fönix*, tel. 13–950; and *Sport*, tel. 16–792; both (I).

Restaurants. *Hungária, Szabadság,* both (M).

EGER. *Eger I* and *Eger II, Park,* all (M) and adjoining one another (tel. 13–323 applies to all). The two *Eger* hotels are sternly modern, the *Park* traditionally elegant. All have restaurants and all have some rooms with private bath. *Unicornis* (I), tel. 12–886, a few rooms with bath. All are near swimming-pools and thermal baths. Also two tourist hotels and camping-site.

Restaurants. *Vadászkürt* (M), game, *Kazamata* (M), *Vörös Rák* (M) and others.

FERTÖD. *Kastély Szálló* (Castle Hotel), a simple tourist hostel (I), adjoining castle, tel. 9341; 18 rooms with 70 beds. *Haydn* restaurant (I) close by.

GYÖNGYÖS. *Mátra* (M), tel. 12–057; 55 rooms with bath. There is comfortable accommodation of all kinds at the village of **Mátrafüred,** 5 miles away in the Mátra Hills.

Restaurants. *Kékes, Szabadság,* both (M).

GYÖR. *Rába* (M), tel. 15–533; 195 rooms, many doubles with bath, restaurant.

Restaurants. *Vaskakas, Hungária, Park,* all (M) and many others.

HORTOBÁGY. In the center of the national park is the country's oldest inn, the *Csárda* (I), tel. 17; primarily a restaurant, it has 6 rooms, each with 2 or more beds. The *Fogadó* (I), has 10 double rooms.

KECSKEMÉT. *Arany Homok* (I), tel. 20–011; 103 doubles, some with bath, restaurant, garage.

Restaurant. *Hirös* (M).

KÖSZEG. *Irottkö* (M), tel. 333, some rooms with bath or shower; and *Strucc* (I), tel. 281; both in town center, the latter a historic inn. *Panorama* (M), tel. 280; on hills outside town, with view.

MISKOLC. *Arany Csillag* (I), tel. 35–114; 43 rooms, some doubles with bath. *Avas* (I), tel. 37–931; 63 rooms, some doubles with bath. *Pannónia* (I), tel. 16–434; 43 rooms, some doubles with bath. In spa suburb of Tapolca, two (M) hotels: *Juno,* tel. 14–891, 108 doubles, all with bath, good restaurant; and *Park,* 60 doubles, half with shower, restaurant and tennis-court.

Restaurants. *Kisvadász,* in Tapolca suburb (M), *Bortanya, Polonia, Belvárosi, Béke* (all (M) to (I)), in town center.

PÉCS. *Pannónia* (M), tel. 13–322; 118 doubles, all with bath. *Hunyor* (I), new; 51 doubles with bath. *Nádor* (I), tel. 11–477; 63 rooms, some doubles with bath. Both these are in town center. *Dömörkapu* (I), tel. 15–987; 24 rooms, no private baths; tourist-hostel and camping-site adjacent, on the hills above the town.

Restaurants. *Rózsakert, Elefánt,* both (M), are among the many.

SÁROSPATAK. *Bodrog* (M); 50 rooms, the doubles with bath. Restaurant.

SIKLÓS. *Tenkes* (M–I), tel. 6. Beautiful 13th-century castle, 20 miles south of Pécs. 17 rooms, some doubles with bath. Restaurant.

SOPRON. *Lövér* (M), tel. 12–308, in wooded southern outskirts. 203 rooms with bath; restaurant. *Palatinus* (M), tel. 11–395. 32 rooms, some with bath. *Sopron* (M), new; 114 doubles with bath. Swimming-pool, sauna, tennis-courts. *Pannónia* (I), tel. 12–180. 42 double rooms, some with bath. The last three are in the town center.

Restaurants. *Gambrinus* (M), in town center; *Fenyves* (M), on hills above town.

SZEGED. *Hungária* (M), tel. 10–855; 138 double rooms with bath. *Royal* (I), tel. 12–911, 110 rooms, many doubles with bath. *Tisza* (I), tel. 12–466; 82 rooms, some with bath. *Motel* and camping-site on river bank.

Restaurants. *Hági* (M), famous old house, *Szeged* (M), and *Halászcsárda* (M), fish-restaurant.

SZÉKESFEHERVÁR. *Alba Regia* (M), tel. 13–484; 104 double rooms, all with bath. *Velence* (I), tel. 11–262; 63 rooms, some doubles with bath. Both are in town center, the *Alba Regia* near historic ruins.
Restaurants. *Ósfehérvár* (M), good; *Arany Szarvas* (M), *Szabadság* (M).

SZEKSZÁRD. *Gemenc* (M), tel. 11–722; 86 doubles with bath, restaurant, nightclub. *Garay* (I), tel. 12–177; 22 rooms, some doubles with bath. Camping-site.
Restaurant. *Kispipa* (M).

SZOLNOK. *Pelikán* (M), tel. 11–283; 60 doubles with bath and 36 singles with shower. *Touring* (M), tel. 13–056; 36 doubles with bath. *Tisza* (M), tel. 12–222; 28 rooms, some doubles with bath. Tourist-hostel, camp-site.
Restaurants. *Béke, Múzeum, Halászcsárda* (fish), all (M).

SZOMBATHELY. *Claudius* (E), tel. 13–760; modern and good, on shore of small lake, 110 double rooms with bath. *Isis* (I), tel. 14–990; 72 rooms, some with bath, in town center. Tourist-hostel, camping-site.
Restaurants. *Gyöngyös* (M), and *Pelikán* (M), in town; *Tóvendeglö* (M), on shore of lake.

TATA. *Diana* (E), tel. 715; in converted castle 3 miles out, 9 doubles with bath; near State Riding School, with excellent opportunities for riding; tennis-courts. *Diana Touring* annexe is (I); some private baths.

TOKAJ. *Tokaj* (I), tel. 62–741; 41 rooms, some with bath. Camping-site. Excellent taverns and restaurants, including *Rákóczi* cellar wine shop.

VESZPRÉM. *Veszprém* (M), modern, tel. 12–345; 96 double rooms, many with bath, restaurant. Tourist-hostel at University during summer vacation.
Restaurants. *Bakony, Vadásztanya,* both (M); *In Vino Veritas,* wine-bar.

Thingvellir

ICELAND

Perched far out in mid-North Atlantic, Iceland has remained comparatively little known, despite the loyal band of naturalists and openair enthusiasts who return to her regularly. But things are undoubtedly changing as the news gets around that here modern comforts and primeval landscapes really can go hand-in-hand, and that you don't have to rough it to enjoy even the wildest scenery. If you do like the openair life, whether as a walker, photographer, rock-hound, bird-watcher, botanist or simply an enthusiast of fantastic natural beauty, then you'll be in your element.

Iceland's temperamental climate often supplies all four seasons in one day, but usually it's not as cold as its name leads you to expect. Also contrary to her name, Iceland is gloriously colorful, with black lava, red sulfur, blue hot springs, gray and white rivers with falls catching multi-colored rainbows, and lusciously-green valleys (unlike Greenland, which *is* ice). In addition, there are few more fascinatingly-rugged places in the Northern Hemisphere.

The first settlers in Iceland were probably Irish monks who left few traces. It was the Norsemen from Norway who truly got to grips with her, from about 870 A.D. (before going on to discover North America), until the Danes by various means made her into a Danish "colony" some centuries later. There was a long, tough period in which Icelanders had to wrestle with famine, epidemic, volcanic eruptions, earthquakes *and* unsympathetic government from far away. After a gradual improvement in her affairs, she became self-governing in 1918, though still part of the Danish kingdom, and in 1944 finally declared her independence. The present Head of State is Vigdís Finnbogadóttir, the only woman president in Europe.

Fishing and farming continue to dominate the national economy, but increasing and imaginative use is being made of the one great asset Iceland is not short of: energy.

PRACTICAL INFORMATION FOR ICELAND

WHAT WILL IT COST. Iceland's horrific rate of inflation is fortunately amply compensated by regular reviews of her rates of exchange; so it's wise not to change money until you need to. At presstime, the exchange rate was 42.5 króna (Ikr.) to the U.S. dollar and 60 Ikr. to the pound sterling. There are 100 aurar to the Ikr.

The cost of accommodations in Reykjavik is considerably greater than elsewhere, up to twice as much in some places. Particularly good value, however, is the chain of 14 Edda Hotels operated by the Iceland Tourist Bureau. Most hotels accommodate for free children up to 12 years sharing with parents. Some hotels offer group rates for meals.

A typical day might cost two people:

Hotel (moderate) double room with breakfast	3000	Ikr.
Lunch, moderate, with coffee	400	
Public transport plus taxi (5 km)	350	
Coffee in popular café	50	
Dinner, moderate	1300	
Good cinema seats	200	
Miscellaneous 10%	200	
	5500	Ikr.

SOURCES OF INFORMATION. The Iceland Tourist Information Bureau can supply much helpful information on all aspects of travel to Iceland. Their addresses are:

In the U.S.: 610b Fifth Ave., Rockefeller Center, New York, NY 10017 (tel. 212–967–8888); 908 17th St. N.W., Washington, D.C. 20036 (tel. 800–223–5500).

In the U.K.: 73 Grosvenor St., London W.1 (tel. 01–499 9971).

WHEN TO COME. Mid-June to the beginning of September is the best time to visit. In June and July there is perpetual daylight and in early autumn the colorful Northern Lights (Aurora Borealis) begin to appear. Iceland has modest winter sports facilities, mainly centered near Akureyri. The island has a surprisingly mild climate in winter, thanks to the Gulf Stream.

Average afternoon temperatures in degrees Fahrenheit and centigrade:

Reyk-javik	Jan.	Feb.	Mar.	Apr.	May	June	July	Aug.	Sept.	Oct.	Nov.	Dec.
F°	36	37	39	43	40	55	58	57	51	44	39	38
C°	2	3	4	6	10	13	14	14	11	7	4	3

NATIONAL HOLIDAYS. Jan. 1 (New Year's Day); Apr. 16 (Maundy Thursday); April 17, 19, 20 (Easter); Apr. 23 (First Day of Summer); May 1 (Labor Day); May 28 (Ascension Day); June 7 (Whitsun); June 17 (National Day); Aug. 3 (Bank Holiday); Dec. 25, 26 (Christmas); Dec. 31 (New Year's Eve).

VISAS. Visas are not needed by citizens of the U.S., U.K. or Canada. No vaccination certificates are required.

GETTING TO ICELAND. By Air. *Icelandair,* the country's national airline, fly from New York, Chicago, Baltimore, Orlando and Detroit to Keflavik, the international airport for Iceland. Frequencies vary according to season. They also fly from London, Glasgow, Oslo, Copenhagen, Frankfurt, Stockholm, Gothenburg and Luxembourg to Keflavik.

By Sea. There are no regular passenger services from the USA or Canada to Iceland. From Europe, the *Smyril Line* operate a car ferry service from Hanstholm (in Jutland), Bergen and Lerwick (in the Shetland Islands) via the Faroe Islands to Seydisfjordur in Iceland. Sailings operate only between June 4 and September 3.

CUSTOMS. The import of 200 cigarettes or 250 gr. of tobacco, 1 liter of alcohol and 1 liter of wine is allowed, or 12 cans of beer instead of wine. Note that you can buy duty-free liquor and tobacco at Keflavik Airport on arrival as well as departure.

HOTELS. The Edda Hotel chain mostly comprises modern boarding schools adapted into summer accommodations; these give excellent value. Many have swimming pools and sauna. Guesthouses, private homes, and farmhouse accommodation may prove a little less expensive.

We have graded the hotels listed in this chapter into one of three categories. In every case the price is for 2 people in a double room with bath or shower—excluding breakfast. These grades are Expensive (E) 3,000–4,000 Ikr., Moderate (M) 2,500–3,000 Ikr., and Inexpensive (I) 950–2,000 Ikr. Breakfast normally adds about another 280 Ikr. per person to the bill.

RESTAURANTS. Meals are expensive, but tourist menus are becoming more widely available and bring costs down. Service and a hefty sales tax will be included in the final bill (the latter pushing up prices by about 25%).

We have graded restaurants as Expensive (E) 900–1,500 Ikr., Moderate (M) 650–900 Ikr., and Inexpensive (I) 400–650 Ikr. These prices are per person and do not include alcohol.

Food and Drink. Restaurants in the main centers offer international cuisine with *à la carte* dishes to suit all tastes. A good selection of wine and spirits is available, but the beers are of a low alcoholic content and leave much to be desired tastewise. Iceland has, however, a few specialties of its own—*hangikjöt* (smoked lamb), *hardfiskur* (dried fish), *graflax,* raw pickled salmon (a national dish), and *skyr* (curds). Icelandic *sild* (herring), especially in hors d'oeuvre, is delicious.

For refreshment, there's a potent variant of aquavit, *brennivin,* which derives its kick from the placid potato.

TIPPING. Hotels and restaurants will add an all-inclusive service charge to the bill and extra tipping is therefore not expected and may be resented. Taxi drivers, hairdressers and washroom attendants are not tipped.

MAIL. Rates for postcards are 10 Ikr. for Europe, 12 Ikr for the U.S.; for letters, 12 Ikr. for Europe, 20 Ikr. for the U.S. These prices may well increase during 1987.

CLOSING TIMES. Shops are open on weekdays from 9 A.M. to 6 P.M. except on Saturdays from 9 A.M. to noon. Some stay open until 8 or 9 P.M. on Friday. Candy stores and flower shops are open until 11 P.M. daily. Many shops are closed on Saturdays during the summer months. Banks are open for business weekdays 9.15 A.M. to 4 P.M., and Thursday till 5 or 6 P.M. Saturday closed. Offices are open 9 A.M. to 5 P.M. on weekdays, but most offices are closed on Saturdays.

USEFUL ADDRESSES. Embassies. U.S. 21 Laufásvegur (tel. 29100); British, 49 Laufásvegur (tel. 15883); both in Reykjavik. Tourist information: Laugavegur 3 (tel. 27488); and at the Information Tower on Laekjartorg (tel. 10044); Tourist Bureau: 6 Reykjanesbraut, (tel. 25855), Reykjavik. Branch offices at Akureyri and at Keflavik Airport Terminal.

Travel agents. *American Express International Banking Corporation,* Keflavik Airport. *Snocat Tours to Vatnajökull,* Adalstraeti 54, Akureyri (tel. 12777). There are several travel agencies in Reykjavik: *Útsýn,* Austurstraeti 17 (tel. 26611) (American Express representative); *Samvinn-travel,* Austurstraeti 12 (tel. 27077); *Iceland Safari Tours,* Austurstraeti 9 (tel. 13499); *G. Jónasson Ltd.* (Highland Tours), Borgartún 34 (tel. 83222); *Reykjavik Excursions,* Gimli, Laekjargata 3 (tel. 23025), free pick-up service from hotels.

Central Post Office. Reykjavík, on the corner of Austurstraeti and Posthússtraeti; weekdays 9–5, Saturday 9–12 A.M. Branch P.O. Bus Terminal Hringbraut, open daily. Stamps are available at candy stores and some hotels.

GETTING AROUND ICELAND. By Plane and Bus. *Icelandair* (tel. 29555/26622) has domestic flights and connections with 50 towns and villages, and serves about a dozen domestic airports. There are no railways, but a comprehensive network of bus services reaches to all communities and, though the roads may often seem rough, they take you through superb scenery. Good buys if you want to explore extensively are the special holiday ticket (Omnibus Passport) valid for unlimited travel by scheduled bus services, and the Full Circle Passport valid for a circular trip around Iceland without time limit. There are also advantageous air rover and air/bus rover tickets.

By Car. Apart from the asphalt roads through and around the towns, the only other long stretches of highway are those from the capital to Keflavik and Selfoss. However, every year short stretches of the main Iceland ring road are improved. Outside of this, motoring is, to say the least, a hazardous exercise, often along lava track or dirt and gravel surfaces. Service stations and garages are few and far between. You drive on the right.

An international driving license is required for Iceland, but if you don't have one you can apply for a permit from the local police.

Car Hire. *Icelandair Car Rental* in Reykjavik, and *Akureyri Car Hire* (Höldur S.F.) in Reykjavik and Akureyri. Also, *ALP Car Rental,* Hladbrekka 2, Kópavogi (tel. 91–42837), and *Geysir,* Borgartún 24, Reykjavik (tel. 11015). *Icelandair Car Rental* offer 10% discounts between September 1 and June 21.

Reykjavik

The Icelandic capital is often called "the Capital of the North" because of its location, roughly midway between New York and Moscow. It has several good museums and art galleries, especially if you are interested in the fascinating culture of the early settlers and the sagas which they contributed to the world's literature, or if you like modern art and sculpture at which the Icelanders excel. But a day or two will be enough for most people to do the city sights.

The most important buildings are the Parliament, the Cathedral, National Library, National Theater, University, Navigation School, and the Hallgrims Church from whose tower there are fine views over the city and surroundings. The church dominates the rocky plateau above the harbor, along with a statue of Leif Erikson, presented to the people of Iceland by the United States on the one thousandth anniversary of the Althing, the Icelandic Parliament, in 1930. Right in town, Lake Tjörnin is a delightful oasis for strollers and bird-spotters.

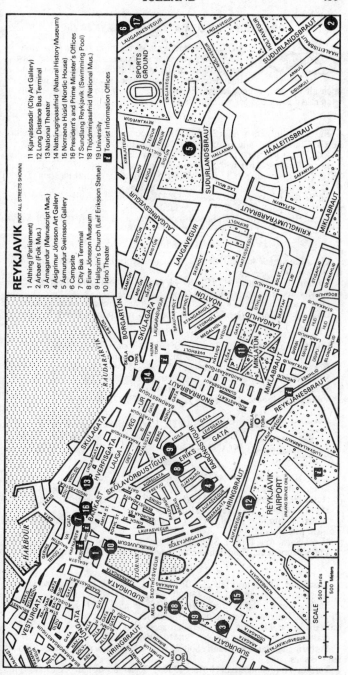

REYKJAVIK (NOT ALL STREETS SHOWN)

1 Althing (Parliament)
2 Árbaer (Folk Mus.)
3 Árnagardur (Manuscript Mus.)
4 Ásgrimur Jónsson Art Gallery
5 Ásmundur Sveinsson Gallery
6 Campsite
7 City Bus Terminal
8 Einar Jónsson Museum
9 Hallgrim's Church (Leif Eriksson Statue)
10 Idnó Theater
11 Kjarvalsstadir (City Art Gallery)
12 Long Distance Bus Terminal
13 National Theater
14 Náttúrugripasafnid (Natural History Museum)
15 Norraena Húsid (Nordic House)
16 President's and Prime Minister's Offices
17 Sundlaug Reykjavik (Swimming Pool)
18 Thjodminjasafnid (National Mus.)
19 University
ℹ Tourist Information Offices

PRACTICAL INFORMATION FOR REYKJAVIK

 HOTELS. Standards of accommodations are high in Reykjavik, but then so too are the prices. Breakfast is not included in the overall quoted price, but state tax is included; there is no service charge. Most hotels are open all the year round, except Edda Hotels which are boarding schools in winter. An extra bed for an adult is approx. $7.

Expensive

Borg, Pósthusstraeti 11 (tel. 11440). 46 rooms, in one of the city's older hotels. Comfortable and central, with cosy restaurant.

Esja, Sudurlandsbraut 2 (tel. 82200). 133 rooms, in the new business center of town. Penthouse bar with tremendous views.

Holt, Bergstadastraeti 37 (tel. 25700). 52 rooms, in central location. Something of a showpiece for Icelandic arts. Gourmet restaurant.

Loftleidir, Reykjavik Airport (tel. 22322). 218 rooms in Iceland's largest and most sophisticated hotel. Conference facilities.

Saga, Hagatorg (tel. 29900). 106 rooms, near Reykjavik Airport but within strolling distance of the town center. Rooftop grill.

Moderate

City, Ránargata 4a (tel. 18650). 31 rooms, central. Group rates for lunch/dinner available.

Gardur, Hringbraut (tel. 15918). 44 rooms without bath. Belongs to the university and is open in summer only.

Hof, Raudarárstigur 18 (tel. 28866). 52 rooms. Home-like atmosphere.

Ódinsvé, Ódinstorg (tel. 25224). 20 rooms, 2 restaurants. Centrally located.

Inexpensive

Guesthouse, Brautarholt 22 (tel. 20986). 24 rooms. Open summer only.

Guesthouse, Snorrabraut 52 (tel. 16522). 18 rooms.

Royal Inn Guesthouse, Laugavegur 11 (tel. 24513). 11 rooms. Open all year.

Salvation Army Guesthouse, Kirkjustraeti 2 (tel. 13203). 24 rooms.

Stadur, Skipholt 27 (tel. 26210). 23 rooms.

Viking Guesthouse, Ránargata 12 (tel. 19367). 11 rooms.

 RESTAURANTS. Reykjavik has a small but attractive choice of restaurants that cater to all pockets. Remember that tax and service will be included in the bill.

Expensive

Alex, Hlemmtorg (tel. 24631). Superior spot.

Arnarhóll, Hverfisgata 8–10 (tel. 18833). Seafood dishes a specialty.

Hotel Holt, Bergstadastraeti 37 (tel. 25700). Excellent gourmet restaurant.

Hotel Loftleidir. Excellent cold table.

Naust, Vesturgötu 8 (tel. 17759). Top-class restaurant with an attractive nautical atmosphere.

Hotel Saga, (tel. 25090). Superior food with beautiful view.

Vid Sjàvarsíduna, Hamarshusinu Tryggvagata (tel. 15520). French cuisine.

Moderate

Braudbaer, Ódinstorg (tel. 25090). International and Icelandic specialties.

Krákan, Laugavegur 22 (tel. 13628). Long-time favorite.

Laekjarbrekka, Bankastraeti 2 (tel. 14430). In a restored timberhouse in old Reykjavik. Icelandic meat and fish specialties, including smoked lamb with mustard sauce. Morning and afternoon snacks.

Náttúran, Laugavegur 20b (tel. 28410). Vegetarian.

Potturinn og Pannan, Brautarholt 22 (tel. 11690). American salads, fish and lamb dishes.

Torfan, Amtmannsstigur 1 (tel. 13303). Icelandic dishes. Charming olde worlde atmosphere.

Inexpensive

Duus-Hús, Fischersund 4 (tel. 14446). Restaurant and wine bar; popular.

Hornid Restaurant, Hafnarstraeti 15 (tel. 20366). Icelandic seafood, pizza, expresso coffee.

El Sombrero, Laugaveg 73 (tel. 23866). Pizzas and Spanish food.

Kaffivagninn, Grandagardi 10 (tel. 15932) Bustling site on the fish wharf.

Kokk-Húsid, Laekjargötu 8 (tel. 10340). Central; reasonably priced.

Lauga-ás, Laugarásveg 1 (tel. 31620). Popular dishes at sensible prices.

ENTERTAINMENT. Leading drama theaters are the *National Theater* and the *Idnó Theater*. These are closed during July and August.

Operas: Performances only during the winter months. The Icelandic Symphonic Orchestra gives concerts every other Thurs., Oct.–Apr. in Háskólabíó. *Light Nights* (Tjarnarbíó at Tjarnargata), is a multimedia show depicting Icelandic culture through the ages; there are performances from June to Aug. on Thurs., Fri., Sat., and Sun. at 9 P.M. *Film Studio Osvaldur Knudsen* by Hotel Holt, shows Icelandic nature and volcano films daily (except Sun) 8 P.M., Thurs. and Sat. 6 P.M.

For dancing, try *Broadway*, the *Hotel Borg*, *Hollywood*, the *Hotel Saga*, *Kreml*, *Leikhúskjallarinn*, *Upp og Nidur*, and the *Restaurant Naust*.

MUSEUMS. Most are open daily from 1.30–4.30 P.M. Closed Mondays. *'Arbaer*, on the outskirts of town, is a charming collection illustrating Iceland's past way of life, housed in an old farmhouse. *Ásgrimur Jónsson's Gallery*, *Ásmundur Sveinsson's Gallery*, *The Living Art Museum* and *Einar Jónsson Museum* display the works of well-known Icelandic artists and famous Icelandic sculptors. The *National Art Gallery*, Hringbraut, and *Reykjavik Art Gallery*, Miklatún, are more extensive exhibitions. The *National Museum*, Hringbraut, has historic and ethnographic sections. The *Nordic House* near the University is an interesting cultural center.

SHOPPING. Reykjavik has many excellent bookshops. Ceramics, gold and silver items, inspired by the Icelandic scenery, are most attractive. And, of course, knitted Icelandic woollen sweaters are world-famous. Foodstores have specially-packed samples of Icelandic food to take home or send abroad; the smoked salmon, herring and shrimps are the best in the world. The Iceland Tourist Bureau's souvenir shop near their head office in Reykjavik stocks many Icelandic items and warrants a visit.

Exploring Iceland

One of the most popular day trips out of Reykjavik is called the Golden Circle, and takes in the spectacular waterfalls of Gullfoss (the Golden Falls), Geysir (a seething area of erupting hot springs) and Thingvellir, the lava arena in which the ancient Viking parliament met for centuries.

The wealth and variety of volcanoes and hot springs are among Iceland's top attractions. In addition to their sheer fascination, much of all this geothermal activity has been harnessed and put to excellent use, providing heating and hot water for entire communities, and power for industrial enterprises. A favorite destination of short sightseeing trips from Reykjavik is the hot spring town of Hveragerdi, where huge greenhouses are heated by natural thermal waters. Tomatoes, other vegetables, and flowers are grown in commercial quantities, and you can even enjoy the strange sight of bananas and other tropical plants flourishing in the shadow of the Arctic Circle. Hveragerdi is also famed for its many geysirs, as well as a vegetarian health resort where you get accommodation, meals and medically-supervised physiotherapy. In fact, swimming year-round in outdoor pools heated by natural thermal water is pretty well a national sport and available in most parts of the country.

Mývatn, Vatnajökull, and the Westmann Islands

In the north, the Mývatn area is famed for its abundant wild life, its purple-hued boiling sulfur springs, the wild lunar landscape of Dimmuborgir, and the natural underground hot pools where tradition demands you swim naked (separate pools for the sexes). Also in this part of the country are Dettifoss, Europe's biggest waterfall, and Godafoss, the breathtakingly beautiful "waterfall of the Gods." Mývatn, combined with Akureyri (Iceland's second largest town, with a population of 14,000), can be visited on a day trip from Reykjavik, but it would be much better to allow longer.

The magnificent area around Vatnajökull—Europe's greatest ice cap —offers more incredible scenery. Providing you are properly equipped and accompanied by someone with local knowledge, you can walk on some of the tongues of its many glaciers. In fact, whenever walking in the difficult terrain of Iceland, you should tell the local people where you are going *and* take their advice. The Skaftafell National Park, beneath Vatnajökull's highest peaks, is a beautiful green oasis that is now easily accessible by road. The Grand Circle tours of Iceland (made possible by a new road completed only a few years ago) include this area on a 10-day itinerary.

The Westmann Islands, off Iceland's south coast, can be visited on a day trip by air, though a longer stay is worth while. Although it is some years since the spectacular eruption of Holy Mountain (Helgafell), the effects of nature's violence can be seen in the new hillsides of lava formed over what were once the Westmann Islanders' homes on the island of Heimaey. But these sturdy folk have dug out many houses and built a great number of new ones, and it is truly impressive to witness what has been accomplished out of the devastation. The "new" volcanically-created island of Surtsey can be seen from the air on the same trip, as well as a view of Mount Hekla.

The Uninhabited Interior

Finally, the overland tours across the uninhabited interior of Iceland, escorted by experienced guides, are unique. You don't have to be young and hearty or tremendously energetic to enjoy these, but you do need to be an outdoor enthusiast and prepared to camp. Transport is in specially constructed buses, and tents and all necessary equipment are provided; you are usually expected to be in charge of your tent during the trip, but meals are prepared for you. Since this kind of tour tends to attract those who are interested in birds or flowers or geology, it's usually a fine meeting ground for like-minded souls of all ages and many nationalities. Overnights may be spent near a small community or in the heart of a rugged and uninhabited nowhere, perhaps on the edge of a lava field or beneath some craggy white glacier. One thing is certain: it all adds up to an unforgettable experience.

These then are some of the distinctive features of Iceland, a country of contradictions and natural wonders that weave a subtle spell all its own. It's a spell that captures nearly all who have once stood on Iceland's gray shores and felt the rock beneath them tremble with the subterranean forces of an unseen world.

PRACTICAL INFORMATION FOR THE REGIONS

HOTELS AND RESTAURANTS. Particularly good value is the chain of Edda Hotels that are operated by Iceland Tourist Bureau. Mostly, these are modern boarding schools that have been adapted into summer hotels. Many have swimming pools and sauna. In country districts, restaurants are usually limited to those in hotels, though some gas stations have limited diners.

The North

AKUREYRI. *K.E.A.* (E), tel. 96–22200. 51 rooms with bath/shower. *Vardborg* (M), tel. 96–22600. 24 rooms. *Edda* (I), 68 rooms without bath; open summer only.

BLÖNDUÓS. *Edda* (M), tel. 95–4126. 30 rooms with bath/shower.

HÚNAVELLIR. *Edda Svínavatn* (M), tel. 95–4370. 23 rooms. Swimming pool and sauna.

HÚSAVIK. *Húsavik* (M), tel. 96–41220. 34 rooms with bath/shower.

MÝVATN. *Reykjahlíd* (M), 12 rooms without bath; summer only. *Reynihlíd* (M), tel. 96–44170. 44 rooms. Swimming pool. U.S. astronauts were trained in the surrounding lunar-like landscape.

SAUDARKRÓKUR. *Maelifell* (M), tel. 95–5265. 7 rooms.

SIGLUFJÖRDUR. *Höfn* (I), tel. 95–71514. 14 rooms without bath.

SKAGAFJÖRDUR. *Varmahlid* (I), tel. 95–6170. 17 rooms, without bath.

The East

BREIDDALSVÍK. *Edda Stadarborg* (I), tel. 97–5683. 9 rooms without bath.

EGILSTADIR. *Valaskjálf* (M), tel. 97–1500. 24 rooms with bath/shower. *Egilstadir* (I). 15 rooms with bath; open summer only.

EIDAR. *Edda* (I), tel. 97–3803. 60 rooms without bath; summer only.

HALLORMSSTADIR. *Edda* (I), tel. 97–1683. 22 rooms without bath; summer only.

HORNAFJÖRDUR. *Höfn* (M), tel. 97–8240. 40 rooms. *Edda* (I), tel. 97–8470. *Nesjaskóli* (I), 30 rooms without bath, summer only.

NESKAUPSTADUR. *Egilsbúd* (I), tel. 97–7321. 5 rooms without bath.

The South

FLÚDIR. *Summerhotel/Motel Flúdir* (M), tel. 99–6630. 27 rooms.

GRINDAVIK. *Bláa Lónid* (M), tel. 92–8650. 10 rooms. Special facilities for psoriasis sufferers, who can bathe in the Blue Lagoon. Transport from Keflavik airport available.

HVERAGERDI. *Ljósbrá* (I), tel. 99–4588. 7 rooms without bath.

HVOLSVÖLLUR. *Hvolsvöllur* (M), tel. 99–8187. 20 rooms.

KIRKJUBAEJARKLAUSTUR. *Edda* (M), tel. 99–7626. 32 rooms with bath/shower.

LAUGARVATN. *New Edda* (M) tel. 99–6154. 27 rooms; open summer only. *Edda* (I). 88 rooms with bath/shower, summer only.

SKÁLHOLT. *Guesthouse Skálholt* (M), tel. 99–6870. 10 rooms with bath/shower; summer only.

SELFOSS. *Thóristún* (M), tel. 99–1633. 17 rooms.

SKÓGAR. *Edda* (I), tel. 99–8870. 34 rooms without bath; summer only.

THINGVELLIR. *Valhöll* (M), tel. 99–4080. 37 rooms; summer only.

WESTMANN ISLANDS. *Hótel Gestgjafinn* (M), tel. 98–2577. 14 rooms with bath/shower. *Guesthouse Heimir* (I), tel. 98–1515. 22 rooms without bath.

The West

AKRANES. *Akranes* (I), tel. 93–2020. 11 rooms without bath.

BORGARNES. *Hótel Borgarnes* (M), tel. 93–7119. 35 rooms with bath/shower.

BORGARFJÖRDUR. *Hótel Bifröst* (M), tel. 93–5000. 31 rooms.

REYKHOLT. *Edda* (I), tel. 93–5260. 64 rooms without bath; open summer only. Swimming pool.

SNAEFELLSNES. *Búdir* (I), tel. 93–8111. 20 rooms without bath; summer only.

STYKKISHÓLMUR. *Stykkishólmur* (M), tel. 93–8330. 26 rooms

KRÓKSFJÖRDUR. *Edda Bjarkalundur* (I), tel. 93–4762. 12 rooms without bath.

ÍSAFJÖRDUR. *Ísafjördur* (E), tel. 94–4111. 31 rooms with bath. *Mánakaffi* (I), 15 rooms without bath. *Salvation Army Hostel* (I), 17 rooms without bath.

VATNSFJÖRDUR. *Edda* (I), tel. 94–2011. *Flókalundur*, 14 rooms without bath; summer only.

IRELAND

Ireland, the most westerly country in Europe, has retained a distinct character of its own across the centuries. It is a small island of only 32,595 square miles, but contains a wide variety of memorable scenery. The northeastern corner of the island, Northern Ireland remains a part of the United Kingdom, while the Republic, Eire, has been independent since 1921. The "troubles" which feature so prominently in international news bulletins are confined to localized areas in the north and should by no means deter the visitor. Both Northern Ireland and the Republic offer a genuinely friendly welcome to tourists, and Ireland's location makes it a popular and practical first stop for American visitors to Europe.

Ireland is an active member of the European Economic Community, and Dublin a thriving modern city with an excellent selection of hotels and restaurants. Theater tickets are modestly priced and easy to obtain, even at the famous Abbey where the talents of John Millington Synge, W.B. Yeats and Sean O'Casey flourished. Trinity College, Dublin Castle and the magnificent public buildings and elegant squares of Georgian Dublin have all been restored, and the elegance of 18th-century Dublin has emerged again after decades of neglect.

The population of the Republic is only three and a half million, and over a million people live in the Dublin area. As a result the rest of the country has escaped urban blight. Its 1,970 miles of coastline are among the most unspoilt and beautiful in Europe. Tourist facilities, however, are very well developed, while prices remain remarkably reasonable. The dollar and the British pound enjoy a very favorable rate of exchange.

The pace of life in rural Ireland is slow, making the country an ideal place to relax. Anglers and golfers will find excellent, uncrowded facilities. Race-goers have a selection of meetings all over the country throughout the year. Most of the roads are narrow and twisting, but almost devoid of other traffic, which makes touring by car a special pleasure. Irish bars are friendly, sociable places where the conversation is as important as the drink, and sightseeing tips will readily be passed on. Between the romantic lakes and mountains of Killarney, the eerie limestone landscape of the Burren, the lush Wicklow Hills, the historic castles of the Shannon region, the rugged beauty of Connemara and the fabled "Yeats country" in Sligo, there are destinations to suit every taste.

PRACTICAL INFORMATION FOR IRELAND

WHAT IT WILL COST. Prices in Ireland are rising, like everywhere else, but in 1987 it should be possible to live well for IR£45 per person per day, and better still if you buy one of the packages offered by U.S. and British tour operators. Stay in guesthouses and farmhouses as well as hotels to get the flavor of Ireland. IR£20 will get you a bed in a good hotel in Dublin, but if you are traveling with a family try for a family room which can sleep three for a price usually only about twice the single rate. Breakfast is not included in hotel prices in some places, but costs about IR£5 for a hearty meal; guesthouse rates are about half. In the country hotels are about IR£12, while farmhouses and guesthouses (including breakfast) run about IR£9. There is usually a reduced rate for a three-night stay. A two-week package with open hotel vouchers, good at any of 18 hotels around the country, is available at around U.S. $800.

Get the *Guide to Hotels & Guesthouses* (published by the Irish Tourist Board, IR£1) and *Farmhouses, Town and Country Homes* if you want to sample farmhouses and home life (also published by the Irish Tourist Board, 50p). Both give maximum prices to provide a check on spending. Each tourist region publishes a list of self-catering accommodations and cottages suitable for families. A good bet if you are making a stay for a week or more.

Approximate expenses for two people on an average day in a provincial city. Add about 10–15% for Dublin.

Hotel (inexpensive) with breakfast	IR£29.00
Lunch	10.00
Dinner	20.00
Transport (2 taxis, 2 buses)	9.00
Theater	7.00
Coffee	1.00
Beer	3.00
Whiskey	3.00
Miscellaneous 10%	8.20
	IR£90.20

Irish currency is in the same denominations as British, but Ireland joined the European Monetary System with most other European Economic Community countries in 1979 and the Irish pound (punt, pronounced "poont," in Ireland) is no longer directly linked to the British pound sterling. There is likely to be some variance in the rates of exchange between Ireland and the United Kingdom (which includes Northern Ireland). This is likely to favor the visitor. Change U.K. pounds (sterling) at a bank when you get to Ireland: change Irish pounds before you leave. Certain hotels and some shops will accept sterling, but banks give the best rate. The rate of exchange at press time was IR£.90p to the dollar and IR£1.10 to the pound sterling.

SOURCES OF INFORMATION. For information on all aspects of travel in Ireland, the Irish Tourist Board is invaluable. Their addresses are:

In the U.S.: 681 Market St., San Francisco, CA 94105; tel. 415–781–5688.
757 Third Ave., New York, NY 10017; tel. 212–418–0800. 230 N. Michigan
Avenue, Chicago, IL 60601; tel. 312–726–9356.

In Canada: 10 King St. E., Toronto, Ontario M5C 1C3; tel. 416–364–1301.

In the U.K.: 150 New Bond St., London W1Y OAQ; tel. 01–629 7292.

WHEN TO COME. The main tourist season in Ireland
runs from June to the end of September. However, the
attractions of Ireland are not so dependent on the weather as in other countries and thus one can visit at almost
any time. Though in all seasons one must be prepared for wet weather.

Climate. Winters are mild though wet, and summers can be warm, but again
beware of sudden showers.

Average afternoon temperatures in degrees Fahrenheit and centigrade:

Dublin	Jan.	Feb.	Mar.	Apr.	May	June	July	Aug.	Sept.	Oct.	Nov.	Dec.
F°	47	47	51	54	59	65	67	67	63	57	51	47
C°	8	8	11	12	15	18	19	19	17	14	11	8

SPECIAL EVENTS. *January,* horseracing in eight centers. *February,* Holiday and Leisure Fair, Dublin; inter-
national rugby match, Dublin. *March,* Feis Ceoil (music
festival) in Dublin finds the stars of tomorrow—John
McCormack was one; international rugby match against Scotland; St. Patrick's
Day, celebrated with spectacular parade through the streets of Dublin, Gaelic
football, national dog show. *April,* Irish Grand National at Fairyhouse, Co.
Meath. *May,* Dublin Spring Show and Sale of country's finest cattle; Maytime
Festival, Dundalk. *June,* Irish Derby, Curragh; Writers' Week, Listowel, Co.
Kerry; International Sea Angling Festival, Westport, Co. Mayo. *July,* Dublin
Flower Show; Irish Open Golf championship, Dublin. *August,* Dublin Horse
Show Week; Antique Dealers' Fair, Dublin; Puck Fair, Killorglin, County
Kerry. *September,* International Festival of Light Opera, Waterford; Oyster
Festival, Galway. *October,* Dublin Theater Festival; Wexford Festival Opera;
Great October Fair, Ballinasloe, County Galway, reputedly the world's oldest
horse fair. *November,* Cork International Jazz Festival. *December,* Dublin
Grand Opera.

Bank and Public Holidays. Jan. 1; Mar. 17 (St. Patrick's Day); Apr. 17
(Good Friday); Apr. 20 (Easter Monday); May 25; Aug. 3; Oct. 26; Dec. 25–26
(Christmas Day and St. Stephen's Day). If you're planning a visit at Easter
remember that theaters and cinemas are closed for the last three days of the
preceding week.

VISAS. Arrivals from North America and Western Europe require only a
valid passport.

HEALTH CERTIFICATES. Not required for entry from any country.

GETTING TO IRELAND. By Air. Currently *Aer Lingus,* the Irish airline, flies non-stop from New York and
Boston to Shannon and Dublin. Other carriers flying
directly to Shannon are *Northwest Orient* from Boston
and *Transamerica* from the West Coast. Dublin has excellent air links by *Aer
Lingus* and national carriers of other countries with London (Heathrow and
Gatwick), Paris, Brussels, Amsterdam, Rome, Zurich, Dusseldorf and Copenhagen among others. From the U.K. there are flights also from many provincial
airports including Birmingham, Manchester, Liverpool, Cardiff, Newcastle,
Glasgow, Bristol and Edinburgh. There are also flights from London to both
Shannon and Cork and also to the latter from Cardiff and Bristol.

By Sea. There are daily ferries with drive-on/off car facilities between Fish-
guard and Rosslare, Holyhead and Dun Laoghaire, with connecting boat trains
for non-motorized passengers from London (5 hours) and in Ireland to Dublin,
Waterford, Mallow (change for Killarney) and Cork. At the time of writing

(Easter '86) it looks as if ferry services on other routes will be dropped. Irish Continental Line operates car ferry service between Le Havre and Cherbourg (France) to Rosslare (20 hrs.); Brittany Ferries operates from Roscoff (France) to Cork.

CUSTOMS. Visitors arriving are permitted to bring in the following free of duty: 200 cigarettes (or approximately 9 ozs. of tobacco), 1 liter bottle of spirits, 2 liter bottles of wine, and other dutiable goods to the value of IR£31. If you buy goods in any of the EEC countries and pay duty or tax on them at the time of purchase, keep the receipts to show the Customs on arrival, if they ask, to ensure no additional duty is charged.

HOTELS. At the peak of the season, between June and September, pressure on accommodations is heavy, so book well ahead. This can be done through *International Reservations Service,* 70–48 Austin St, Forest Hills, Long Island, NY or through the *Tourist Information Office* at the port of entry.

Our hotel grading system is divided into four categories. All prices are for 2 people in a double room. Deluxe (L) IR£50 and up, Expensive (E) IR£40–50, Moderate (M) IR£30–40, Inexpensive (I) around IR£30.

The Irish Tourist Board publishes an official *Guide to Hotels and Guesthouses* (IR£1) and also *Farmhouses, Town and Country Homes* (50p) covering approved accommodations in private homes. They also publish *Accommodation and Restaurant Guide for Disabled Persons* (30p). All available from the Irish Tourist Board and local information offices.

CAMPING. Ireland is a beautiful country for camping or caravanning, though under canvas one must be prepared for wet weather. There are many caravan sites where camping is also allowed, and a friendly farmer is never far away (though do ask first!).

RESTAURANTS. In most places in Ireland, the top hotels have excellent dining rooms that rate high in cuisine, wine cellars, decor and service. These are classified using our rating system of Expensive (E) IR£18 up, Moderate (M) IR£8–18, Inexpensive (I) under IR£8. Prices are for one person. Irish food is good, inexpensive, and served in ample portions. Look for places advertising "Special Value Tourist Menus" which are approved by the Irish Tourist Board and cost either IR£5 or under, or IR£7 or under, for a three-course meal. Many bars serve inexpensive food at lunchtime.

Food and Drink. The food is familiar to British and American visitors, with heavy reliance in menus on beef, lamb, and plenty of fresh fish from stream and sea. Dublin Bay prawns are fine, especially with a spicy sauce; and the mussels from the Wexford coast are superb—try *moules mariniere* when you see them on the menu, and oysters with Guinness is a combination no mere mortal could surpass. Typical Irish dishes include corned beef and carrots, boiled bacon and cabbage, Irish stew, crubeens (pig's feet), colcannon (potatoes and cabbage cooked together in a mix), soufflé flavored with seaweed, and soda bread, but you'll have to enquire for them.

Ireland has been distilling a well-known spirit for about eight hundred years, calling it *Uisge Beatha* and pronouncing it, more or less, as "whisgeh" (water) "baha" (life). The Irish whiskey of today has a distinctive smoothness and a flavor totally different from that of Scotch whisky—note the difference in spelling, too. Another favorite Irish drink is Guinness stout, available on tap or in bottles in every pub in Ireland, and—particularly around Cork—Murphy's stout. But if you like a lighter brew there are several lager beers on the market. And of course, Irish coffee—i.e. a jigger of whiskey added to hot black coffee with sugar and topped with thick whipped cream.

TIPPING. The standard tip in Ireland is 12½%. Most hotels include this service charge on the bill: guesthouses don't. In more elegant establishments, an extra tip is expected. It's common practice to tip porters, car-park attendants, taxi drivers, barbers, and waiters or waitresses—but not the staff behind the bar.

MAIL AND TELEPHONES. Airmail rates to Canada, United States and Commonwealth are 44p for the first 10 grams, airletters 37p and postcards 26p. Letters to Britain and Continental Europe cost 26p, postcards 22p. Rates may change in 1987.

Telephone Codes. For calls to the U.S. and Canada, dial 161 followed by the area code. All country codes are in an early page of the Telephone Directory.

CLOSING TIMES. Shops and stores are open from 9 to 5.30 daily. (Early closing Wednesday, Thursday or Saturday depending on locality.) Banks: 10–12.30 and 1.30–3, with late opening to 5 P.M. on a selected weekday in most towns. Closed Saturdays and Sundays.

Licensing Hours. On weekdays in summer, from 10.30 A.M. to 11.30 P.M.; closing at 11 P.M. the rest of the year; there's an hour shutdown from 2.30 to 3.30 P.M. in Dublin, Waterford, Limerick and Cork. Sunday hours are 12.30 to 2 P.M. and from 4 to 10 P.M. Licensed hotels are open all hours to residents.

USEFUL ADDRESSES. *United States Embassy,* 42 Elgin Road. *Canadian Embassy,* 65 St. Stephen's Green. *British Embassy,* 33 Merrion Road. *Irish Tourist Office,* 14 Upper O'Connell Street. *American Express,* 116 Grafton Street. *Thomas Cook,* 118 Grafton Street. *C.I.E.,* 35 Lower Abbey Street. *Automobile Association,* 23 Suffolk Street. All in Dublin.

GETTING AROUND IRELAND. By Train and Bus. We have put these two together as in the Republic of Ireland they are very closely linked, being owned and operated by the same state corporation—*Coras Iompair Eireann,* or C.I.E., as it is usually known. The railway network, although much cut back in the past 25 years, is still quite extensive with the main routes radiating from Dublin to Cork, Galway, Limerick (and on to Tralee and Killarney) and both to Westport and Sligo as well as the line north to Belfast. All trains are diesel with the main expresses now having very comfortable airconditioned stock. There are two classes on many but by no means all trains—Super Standard (1st. in effect) and Standard (2nd.). Buffet cars are carried on main expresses. There are no sleeping cars or couchettes in Ireland. Speeds are not high by contemporary standards. Dublin, however, now has a modern commuter train—the DART—running south from Howth through the city to Bray on the Wicklow coast, with various stops en route.

The C.I.E. bus system is remarkably wide spread even if the frequency of services in the remoter areas is not great. But the routes do go all over the country and are often linked into rail services.

For the keen independent traveler, the 15 day "Rambler" ticket gives unlimited travel by train and bus, and is excellent value at IR£73. It can be purchased from any main city bus terminal or railway station booking office. A "rail only" ticket is available for about IR£12 less, but as the bus system is far more extensive than the railway, we strongly recommend the former. Day return and four-day return rail tickets are also available at low rates.

In addition, C.I.E. operate excellent inclusive holidays from one day to 10 days touring by rail or bus or both. These include accommodations and main meals. Costs range from around IR£185 for a 4-day tour, to IR£360 for a 10-day tour in July/August.

By Car. One of the most rewarding ways to explore this country. Keep to the left is the rule of the road. Petrol costs about 61p per liter, or about IR£2.95 per Imperial or Irish gallon (5 of which equal 6 U.S. gallons). Third party insurance compulsory. Maximum speed is 55 mph.

Car Hire. Among the many agencies in Dublin are *Hertz,* Leeson Street Bridge; *Cahill's,* 36 Annesley Pl.; *Kenning Car Hire* (Ireland) Ltd., 42/43 Westland Row; *Avis,* 1 Hanover Street E.; *Murray's Europcar,* Baggot St. Bridge. Cars for hire at Cork, Shannon and Dublin Airports.

Dublin

Dublin is the capital of Ireland and one of the most charming cities of Europe, situated as it is on the banks of the Liffey, and still redolent in parts of the dignity of the 18th century. It is a shopper's and sportsman's paradise (there are 30 golf courses in the immediate vicinity), and if you can schedule your trip to include the world-famous Dublin Horse Show in August, you will be seeing the capital at its liveliest. Dublin doesn't suffer extremes of climate, so low-priced fall-through-spring special interest vacations and tours are a good buy.

Statue-filled O'Connell Street makes a good beginning for a walking tour around town. We recommend visiting Trinity College, though the popularity of its library is so great that you may have to stand in line to view its superb collection of manuscripts including the world-famous Book of Kells, dating from the eighth century, perhaps the most beautiful illuminated manuscript in existence. Dublin's noblest public buildings are the 18th-century Parliament House (now the Bank of Ireland) and the Custom House, located on the north bank of the River Liffey, and designed by the great architect, James Gandon, in 1791. Another Gandon masterpiece is the restored Four Courts on the northern quays. Dublin Castle, dating from 1208, has magnificent state apartments and a famous heraldic museum, the only one of its kind in the world; for a modest fee its trained staff will trace your family tree for noble ancestors.

St. Patrick's Cathedral was founded in 1130. Jonathan Swift was dean here for 32 years, and you can see the pulpit from which he preached (1713 to 1745) and the great satirist's tomb with the bitter epitaph he composed himself. Next door to St. Patrick's is Marsh's Library, founded in the early 1700s and with books dating back to 1472. Another cathedral you should not miss is Christ Church, begun by King Sitric the Dane in 1038. Its nave is considered the finest example of Gothic architecture in Ireland. For an experience on the macabre side, the vaults of Saint Michan's church have on display a number of bodies that have been there in a perfect state of preservation for centuries. For a glimpse of some of Dublin's most beautiful 18th-century mansions, go to Merrion Square where Oscar Wilde, Daniel O'Connell, the Duke of Wellington and the writer George Moore once lived. In the same area, visit the the National Gallery where a fine collection of paintings and sculpture is well displayed. Leinster House, once the home of Dukes of Leinster and now the seat of the Dail and Senate (Congress/Parliament) is close by.

Horse enthusiasts will also want to visit the farm of Ireland's National Stud, nursery of some of racing's most famous horses, in Tully, County Kildare. For a complete list of all racing events and information about such great Gaelic games as hurling and Gaelic football, write to the Irish Tourist Board. (See *Useful Addresses, Practical Information* section.) They can also supply information on hunting, golfing and fishing holidays in a land which has few rivals in them.

PRACTICAL INFORMATION FOR DUBLIN

HOTELS. It's as well to make your reservations in advance if you're coming to Dublin during the high season. If you can't find accommodations, the Tourist Information Office will be able to help.

Deluxe

Berkeley Court, Lansdowne Rd. (tel. 01–601711). Built in 1978 it has 200 rooms with bath. Spacious and rather ornate. Excellent dining room and food to match. Coffee bar is good and moderately priced.

Bloom's, Anglesea St. (tel. 01–715288). 84 rooms with bath, in city center. *Bloom's Bar* is a popular spot, and the *Blazes Boylan* Coffee Shop rates high.

Jury's, in Ballsbridge (tel. 01–605000). 314 rooms with bath. New complex includes aperitif bar and two restaurants, plus revamped coffee shop. *Dubliner Bar* is popular.

Shelbourne, St. Stephen's Green (tel. 01–766471). 166 rooms, all with bath. Trusthouse Forte flagship in Ireland. Has a quiet dignity and maintains an excellent reputation. Dining room deservedly held in great esteem.

Westbury, off Grafton St. (tel. 01–791122). 75 rooms with bath. Dublin's newest hotel, with elegant *Russell Room* restaurant, *Sandbank Bar* for seafood, plus a coffee shop.

Expensive

Ashling, Parkgate St. (tel. 01–772324). 42 rooms with bath. Close to rail terminal (Heuston Station) for south and west.

Burlington, Upper Leeson St. (tel. 01–605222). 420 rooms with bath. Indoor pool. Conference center. Good restaurant and coffee shop.

Buswell's, Molesworth St. (tel. 01–764013). 68 rooms with bath. Comfortable and large, if somewhat faded. Very central location.

Dublin International, Dublin Airport (tel. 01–379211). 180 rooms with bath. Convenient and quieter than most airport hotels.

Royal Dublin, O'Connell St. (tel. 01–749351). 110 rooms with bath. Good central location.

Sachs, Morehampton Rd. (tel. 680995). 20 rooms with bath. With fashionable restaurant and bar.

Moderate

Clarence, Wellington Quay (tel. 01–776178). 70 rooms, half with bath. Very good food and old-fashioned charm. Centrally located.

Gresham, O'Connell St. (tel. 01–746881). 179 rooms with bath. Coffee shop and bistro-style restaurant. Excellent central location.

Marine, Sutton Cross (tel. 01–322613). 27 rooms with bath.

Montrose, Stillorgan Rd. (tel. 01–693311). 190 rooms, most with bath. Close to University and TV/radio studios.

Power's, Kildare St. (tel. 01–605244). 30 rooms, half with bath.

Skylon, Upper Drumcondra Rd. (tel. 01–379121). 88 rooms with bath.

Tara Tower, Merrion Rd. (tel. 01–694666). On the south side of the city. 84 rooms with bath. Front rooms have a fine view of Dublin Bay.

Inexpensive

Northbrook, Northbrook Rd. (tel. 01–688951). 12 rooms, some with bath.
Ormond, Ormond Quay (tel. 01–721811). 70 rooms, half with bath.

Guesthouses

Ariel, 52 Lansdowne Rd. (tel. 01–685512). 16 rooms with bath. Good restaurant (M) open to non-residents is new.

Egan's, Iona Park (tel. 01–303611). 23 rooms with bath.

Mount Herbert, Herbert Rd. (tel. 01–684321). 88 rooms, 77 with bath. South side of city near US Embassy.

The Maples Iona Rd. (tel. 01–303049). 20 rooms with bath. On the airport side of town.

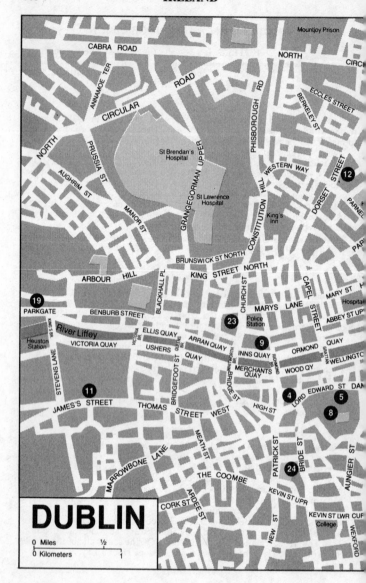

DUBLIN

| 0 Miles | ½ |
| 0 Kilometers | 1 |

RESTAURANTS. Irish food is good, inexpensive, and served in ample portions. Fine grills and thick steaks are famous. Game is plentiful in this sportsman's heaven. Menus will feature all the fish—salmon, trout, lobster— you can eat plus game birds such as wild duck, snipe, plover, pheasant and partridge in season. Dublin's top hotels have excellent dining rooms that rate high in cuisine, wine cellars, décor, and service (see hotels, above).

Phone numbers are given for spots where it's advisable to book.

Points of Interest

1. Abbey Theater
2. Bank of Ireland
3. Central Bus Station
4. Christ Church Cathedral
5. City Hall
6. Civic Museum
7. Custom House
8. Dublin Castle
9. Four Courts
10. General Post Office (GPO)
11. Guinness' Brewery
12. Hugh Lane Gallery of Modern Art
13. Leinster House
14. Mansion House
15. National Gallery
16. National Library
17. National Museum
18. Natural History Museum
19. Phoenix Park
20. Royal Irish Academy
21. Royal Irish Academy of Music
22. St. Mary's Catholic Pro-Cathedral
23. St. Michan's
24. St. Patrick's Cathedral
25. St. Theresa's
26. Trinity College
27. University College
    (National Concert Hall)

i Tourist Information Office

Expensive

The Abbot of Monkstown, Monkstown Crescent (tel. 01–805174). Situated among a group of excellent restaurants near the sea on the south side of the city. See Dalkey and Don Laoghaire below.

Ernie's, Mulberry Gardens, Donnybrook, on the edge of town (tel. 01–693300). Owner-chef Ernie Evans is one of the best.

Gallery 22, 22 St. Stephen's Green (tel. 01–686169). Delightful decor with open fire. Specializes in roast meat and poultry.

King Sitric, Howth (north side of Dublin Bay) (tel. 01–325235). Very good for fresh fish and game in season.

Le Coq Hardi, Pembroke Rd. (tel. 01–689070). A top *chef-patron.*
Lord Edward, Christchurch Place (tel. 01–752557). Fine for fish; reserve.
Patrick Guilbaud Restaurant, 46 James's Place, just off Lower Baggot St.
(tel. 01–764192). Skilled chef-patron specializes in French cuisine.
Tandoori Rooms Restaurant, Lower Leeson St. (tel. 01–762286). Imaginative
Indian and European dishes.

Moderate

Berni Inn, Nassau St. A group of restaurants in one building.
Casper and Giumbini's, Wicklow St., off Grafton St. Bright and busy.
Dobbin's Wine Bistro, Stephen's Lane (tel. 01–764670). Good basic Conti-
nental dishes. Central, but not too easy to find so phone first.
George's Bistro, 29 South Frederick St. (tel. 01–603177). Close to Trinity
College. Piano bar.
Kilkenny Design Center, Nassau St., just beside Trinity College. Good for
a light lunch.
Unicorn, Merrion Court, near St. Stephen's Green. Pleasant food with an
Italian accent.

Inexpensive

Bewley's Cafes, Grafton St., South Great George's St. and Westmoreland St.
Captain America's Cookhouse, Grafton St. Mexican and American dishes.
Full bar license.
Granary, East Essex St. Over a pub, great at lunch time.
Murph's, 99 Lower Baggot St., 21 Bachelor's Walk and 18 Suffolk St.
National Gallery, Merrion Sq. Convenient self-service spot when viewing the
famous collection.
Peacock, Abbey St. The foyer of the pocket Peacock Theater under the
Abbey Theater is a great gathering place at lunch-time for light meals.
Rick's Cafe Americain, Westmoreland St. Lively and central.

NIGHTLIFE. Dublin does not have nightclubs in the
international sense. There are mostly local discos, of
which there are several. However, there is a very animated bar scene, some with live music and folk singing.
There is also a strong theatrical tradition that brings out the best of the Irish
culture both past and present.

NIGHTSPOTS. Annabel's, behind the Burlington Hotel, Mespil Rd., is a
popular late evening spot.
Bailey, Duke St. Famous Dublin landmark; today, very much a student's
pub.
Braemor Rooms at the County Club, Churchtown, just out of town, provides
mixed traditional Irish and modern entertainment, plus dinner.
Burlington, Mespil Rd. Another hotel that offers a meal and Irish cabaret.
Davy Byrne's, Duke St. Small and unusual, with literary associations; long-
standing favorite.
Doheny and Nesbitt's in Baggot St. is a good place for talk.
Jules, Baggot St. Nightclub for eating and dancing.
Jury's Hotel, Ballsbridge. Nightly Irish cabaret during tourist season.
Kitty O'Shea's bar at Grand Canal Bridge, Shelbourne Rd. Very much an
"in" spot.
Mulligan's, Townsend St. Typically Irish and very popular.
Scruffy Murphy's, off Lower Mount St. Where you'll find the literati and
people in the arts.

THEATERS. Abbey Theatre, Abbey St. Best place for traditional Irish cul-
ture. *The Peacock,* under the Abbey building, is also worth a visit for new plays
and good revivals.
Gaiety, South King St. Grand Opera. Musical comedy and drama.
Gate, Parnell Sq. Modern drama and Irish plays.
Olympia, Dame St. Similar to the Gaiety but with occasional vaudeville.

MUSEUMS AND GALLERIES. Dublin has a number of fine museums and
galleries; admission is mostly free.

Chester Beatty Library, Shrewsbury Rd. Excellent collection of oriental and medieval manuscripts, including the oldest manuscript of the New Testament. Open Mon. 2–5.30, Tues.–Fri. 10–1, 2.30–5.30.

Dublin Civic Museum, South William St. Fine museum of interesting pieces of Dublin history in a former courthouse. Open 10–6, Sun. 11–2; closed Mon.

Heraldic Museum, Dublin Castle. Part of the Genealogical Office where family histories may be traced. Open Mon.–Fri. 9.30–1 and 2.15–4.30, Sat. 10–12.30. Has been closed for structural work, so check.

Hugh Lane Gallery of Modern Art, Parnell Square. Open weekdays 10–6, Sun. 11–2. Closed Mon.

Joyce Museum, Sandycove. Has a collection of material associated with writer James Joyce who once lived in this Martello Tower. Open daily in summer, 11–4.

Marsh's Library (beside St Patrick's Cathedral). Founded in 1707 and still holds its collection. Open Mon., Wed.–Fri. 2–4, Sat. 10.30–12.30.

National Gallery, Merrion Square. Open Mon.–Fri. 10–5, Sat. 10–1, Sun. 2–5. Latenight viewing Thurs.

National Museum of Irish Antiquities, Kildare St. See famous gold ornaments of the 8th and 9th centuries. Open Tues.–Fri. 10–5, Sun. 2–5; closed Mon.

National Portrait Gallery, Malahide Castle. Guided tours (about IR£1). Open Mon.–Fri. 10–5, Sat. 10–1, Sun. 2–5.

National Wax Museum, Parnell Sq. Open Mon.–Fri. 10–6.30, Sun. 1–6. Adults IR£2.50, children IR£1.

Trinity College Library. Exhibits include the famous Book of Kells. Open weekdays 10–4, Feb.–Oct.; 10–3 Nov.–Jan.; Sat. 10–1 mid-July–mid-Sept.

 SHOPPING. Among the bargains are Irish handwoven tweeds, including the white tweeds known as *bawneen*. The price is more or less the same everywhere and very reasonable; and look at the hand knits, in traditional design.

Switzer's on Grafton Street, *Kevin & Howlin* in Nassau Street, and the *Irish Cottage Industries* in Dawson Street all have extensive stocks. Tweed hats for men are stylish and David Hanna's designs have an international reputation.

If you really want to explore the tweed possibilities, you should visit Connemara and Donegal where the wool is washed, dyed and teazed. If you are in the West try *Mairtin Standun* at Spiddal, near Galway, for a wide choice of excellent tweeds at reasonable prices. The *Avoca Handweavers* at Avoca, Co. Wicklow, and *Cleo* on Kildare St., Dublin, are also good for tweeds.

Sybil Connolly at 71 Merrion Square has an international reputation with her imaginative use of tweeds for every occasion. Also worth visiting are *Raymond Kenna,* 56 Merrion Sq., *Ib Jorgensen,* 24 Fitzwilliam Sq. and *Mary O'Donnell,* 43 Dawson St.; also *Thomas Wolfangel,* 99 Lower Baggot St., and *Rufina,* Merrion Row, *Michael Mortell,* 1 Cope St., is another well-respected designer, and at Enniskerry (12 miles south of Dublin), *Donald and Mary Davies* are the people to meet for stylish clothes.

Paul Costelloe, at 42 Drury St., is another who has achieved international status for his designs.

Other excellent buys in Ireland are Waterford glass, Belleek china and Peterson pipes—and, to go with the pipe, a blackthorn walking stick, perhaps from *Johnston Ltd.,* Wicklow St. For a gun or a rod, try *Garnetts & Keegan's,* 31 Parliament St.; *Fred Smyth* at the *Royal Dublin Golf Club,* has an international reputation for making golf clubs. Irish pewter is another unusual souvenir; you can get a tankard with your family crest at the mill in Timolin, Co. Kildare, 40 miles from Dublin.

Irish jewelry is unusual and attractive; see *Rionore,* 38 Molesworth St. Old Irish silver is a good buy at auctions or antique shops in the Grafton Street area. The *Kilkenny Shop* has a fine display of Irish crafts in the Setanta Center on Nassau St., beside Trinity College.

Environs of Dublin

Not to be missed are: Howth Castle, a 16th-century baronial mansion in a setting of azaleas and rhododendrons; Malahide Castle, where a sensational discovery of important Boswell manuscripts was made in

1950; a trip from Drogheda along the Boyne Valley, where Irish history goes back 5,000 years to the days when all roads led to Tara; Slane, where St. Patrick, celebrating the Christian rites of Easter, kindled, in defiance of the Druid religion, the fire "that would burn forever and consume Tara"; Brugh na Bóinne, the pre-Christian burying ground of Tara's kings, and the fascinating primitive cairns and tombs near Dowth and Knowth; the impressive church, abbey, and castle ruins, like an outdoor museum, at Trim, Co. Meath; Kells, in whose eighth century abbey the Book of Kells was written—see also the perfect round tower, St. Columbcille's House, and the Kells collection of high crosses. The beautifully-sculptured high crosses at Monasterboice are worth a special trip. Sportsmen will be interested in Navan, a fox-hunting center, and the National Stud in Tully, County Kildare. South of Dublin, visitors can see Torca Cottage on Dalkey Hill, where Bernard Shaw lived for many years, and may be admitted for a small fee to Powerscourt Demesne to see the formal gardens and the 3,400-acre park. Finally, there are the great religious ruins of Glendalough, 30 miles south of Dublin by way of picturesque Sally Gap. The round tower and tiny barrel-vaulted Church of St. Kevin still survive.

PRACTICAL INFORMATION FOR COUNTY DUBLIN AND WICKLOW

BLESSINGTON (County Wicklow). *Downshire House* (I), tel. 045–65199. 25 rooms with bath, near the famous Russborough House with its art collection. *Glenview* (M), tel. 01–862896, 23 rooms with bath, fabulous views from excellent restaurant.

DALKEY (County Dublin). **Restaurants.** Eight miles from Dublin city center, six or more restaurants in a tiny townlet, most notable being *Nieve's,* Castle St. (tel. 01–856156). All are (E) but worth the expedition.

DUN LAOGHAIRE (County Dublin). *Pierre* (M), Sea Front (tel. 01–800291). 32 rooms most with bath, in this sailing town. *Royal Marine* (M), Sea Front (tel. 01–801911). 115 rooms most with bath.
   Restaurants. *Creole* (E), Adelaide St. (tel. 01–806706). *Digby's* (E), Sea Front (tel. 01–804600). *na Mara* (E), Sea Front (tel. 01–806767). This restaurant is in the top bracket for fish.

HOWTH (County Dublin). *Deer Park Hotel* (E), tel. 01–322624. 35 rooms, 29 with bath. Situated in a small fishing port on the north side of Dublin Bay. Golf. *Howth Lodge* (I), tel. 01–390288. 14 rooms with bath. For restaurant, see *King Sitric* (E), Dublin.

GLENDALOUGH (County Wicklow). *The Royal* (M), 13 rooms with bath.

KILLINEY (County Dublin). *The Court* (E), tel. 01–851622. 32 rooms with bath, well-located and lively. *Fitzpatrick's Castle* (E), tel. 01–851533. 48 rooms with bath, a heated swimming pool. Very elegant.

KILTERNAN (County Dublin). *Dublin Sport Hotel* (E), tel. 01–893631. 52 rooms with bath, in the foothills of the Dublin mountains. Has major sports complex, artificial ski slope and professional tennis coaching center.

MALAHIDE (County Dublin). *Grand* (M), tel. 01–450633. 48 rooms half with bath. In a little coastal village 9 miles north of Dublin, another sailing center, with golf and horseback riding.
   Restaurant. *Johnny's* (E), James's Terrace (tel. 01–450314).

RATHNEW (County Wicklow). *Hunter's Hotel* (M), tel. 0404–4106. 18 rooms, 10 with bath. One of Ireland's oldest coaching inns. Excellent food fresh from the sea and the garden.

Southeast Vacationland

Southeast of Dublin is the beguiling scenery of the Vale of Avoca and Tom Moore's country. Near the "Meeting of the Waters" you can sit under the same tree in whose shade the poet dreamed lyrics while looking over his beloved countryside. The town of Avoca itself is the place to see and buy the Avoca handwoven tweeds.

Wexford was a Danish settlement for two centuries, subsequently a walled stronghold of the Anglo-Norman conquerors. See the Westgate Tower, part of the old fortifications, the ruins of 12th-century Selskar Abbey, the Bull Ring where the Normans baited bulls, and Johnstown Castle, now an agricultural college. Wexford County was John F. Kennedy's ancestral home. To commemorate this, the Kennedy Memorial Park has been opened in the mountains nearby; it is a forest park where trees from all over the world have been planted for beauty and research. Even if you are not interested in trees it's worth a visit for the magnificent views of the coast and countryside. The Wexford Festival of Opera (late October) is a major international cultural event. For information and bookings write early in the year to Wexford Festival Office at the Theatre Royal, Wexford. There is a statue to John Barry, founder of the American Navy, who came from hereabouts, on the quays and a maritime museum in a lightship.

Waterford brings to mind the dazzling cut glass that has carried this city's name to the homes and banquet halls of the world. Nearly ruined by a 19th-century British excise tax, the glass industry has been revived and Waterford glass is again available. The factory may be visited to see craftsmen at work, Monday through Friday. Check with the local tourist office for tour times (free). See the great fortress, Reginald's Tower, erected in 1003, now a museum, the city walls dating back to the Danish invasion, and the 18th-century City Hall. Eight miles from Waterford is Tramore, a popular beach resort with swimming, fishing, golf, and, as the high point of interest, horse racing, especially in August.

PRACTICAL INFORMATION FOR THE SOUTHEAST

GOREY. *Marlfield House* (L), tel. 055–21124. 12 rooms with bath and excellent food. One of the top small hotels in the country with a Victorian-style conservatory for dining.

ROSSLARE. *Casey's Cedars* (M), tel. 053–32124. 35 rooms with bath. *Golf* (M), tel. 053–32179. 25 rooms, 13 with bath. *Great Southern* (E), tel. 053–33233. 100 rooms with bath, updated in 1981. *Hotel Rosslare* (M), tel. 053–33110. 25 rooms, most with bath. *Kelly's* (M), tel. 053–32114. 97 rooms, 87 with bath, overlooking the strand (beach) and has a high reputation for food. *Rosslare Beach Villas* form a new self-catering holiday complex right on the beach. Contact Peter and Noreen Fox at Rosslare.

WATERFORD. *Ardree* (E), tel. 051–32111. 100 rooms with bath. *Granville* (E), tel. 051–55111. 50 rooms with bath. *Tower* (M), tel. 061–75801. 81 rooms with bath. Attractively refurbished. *Dooley's* (I), tel. 051–73531. 40 rooms, most with bath; a comfortable, family-run hotel.

WEXFORD. *Bargy Castle* (E), Tomhaggard (tel. 053–35203). A 12th-century castle with modern comforts. *Talbot* (E), tel. 053–22566. 104 rooms with bath. Indoor heated pool; excellent food. *White's* (M), tel. 053–22311. 55 rooms, most with bath. *Ferrycarrig* (I), Ferrycarrig Bridge on town outskirts (tel. 053–22999). 40 rooms with bath.
  Restaurants. *Captain White's* (E), North Main St. (tel. 053–22311). Seafood and quality steaks. *Farmer's Kitchen* (M), on the road to Rosslare ferryport. Pub

lunches as well as good à la carte. *Galley* (M), at New Ross (tel. 051–21723). Cruise the quiet scenic waters of the "sister rivers"—the Barrow, Nore and Suir—whilst enjoying your lunch or dinner. (April through October.)

Cork City and County

The City of Cork, on the River Lee, is Ireland's third largest city (after Dublin and Belfast). It is a city of proud people, with a long history of spirit, and one which has supplied a number of patriots to the Irish independence movement of the past.

Cork people are reputed to be the most talkative in Ireland—and that's saying a lot! But they have a lilt to their voices that is a pleasure to hear, and maybe they caught the talkative reputation from kissing the Blarney Stone at nearby Blarney Castle; it is reputed to give the gift of eloquence to all who kiss it.

The city has the finest choirs in the country and the International Choral and Folk Dancing Festival in the spring attracts groups from many countries who provide lots of informal entertainment.

Cork is also the home of the state-sponsored Irish Ballet Company; if a performance is scheduled it will be worth a visit. And to round off the ebullient entertainment interests of the Corkonians, the International Jazz Festival, only a few years old, has built into an event which attracts the top people in the jazz world in November.

Cork is served by regular air services to Britain and the Continent. By train it's less than three hours from Dublin.

A new national wildlife park has been established on Fota Island, a few miles southeast of the city. Fota House has the finest private collection of Irish landscape paintings of the 18th and 19th centuries; a must for art buffs.

The country behind the City of Cork is backed by mountain ranges, but in between there is some of the richest agricultural land in the country. The coastline is indented with bays and harbors, some of them—Kinsale is the best known—are outstanding for deep-sea fishing.

Kinsale also has several excellent restaurants and hosts an annual gourmet festival in October. To the west, near Skibbereen, lies the charming coastal village of Castletownshend, home of Edith Somerville, co-author of the "Irish R.M." stories, which has remained almost unchanged since her death in 1949. The drive across Bantry Bay to Glengarrif provides spectacular views. Hire a rowning boat from Glengarrif to visit Garnish Island with its unusual Italian Gardens.

PRACTICAL INFORMATION FOR CORK REGION

BLARNEY. *Blarney* (M), tel. 028–85281. 76 rooms with bath. Special facilities for disabled guests and has menus and room plans in Braille.

CORK. *Arbutus Lodge* (E), Montenotte (tel. 021–501237). 20 rooms with bath, and with one of Ireland's outstanding restaurants. *Imperial* (E), South Mall (tel. 021–23304). The most traditional of Cork's hotels with 80 rooms with bath. *Jury's* (E), Western Rd. (tel. 021–26651). 188 rooms with bath. considerably developed in 1980 with a lounge and dancing area, indoor/outdoor pool and two restaurants—the *Fastnet* is upmarket and the *Glandore* is for fast service. *Silver Springs* (E), Tivoli, on the edge of town (tel. 021–507533). 72 rooms with bath. *Country Club* (M), Montenotte (tel. 021–502922). 47 rooms, most with bath. *Grand Parade* (M), Grand Parade (tel. 021–24391). 21 rooms with bath. *Metropole* (M), MacCurtain St. (tel. 021–508122). 121 rooms, most with bath. *Victoria* (M), Cook St. (tel. 021–509166). 30 rooms with bath; central. *Corrigans* (I), MacCurtain St. (tel. 021–501620). 20 rooms. *Moore's* (I), Morrison's Island (tel. 021–227361). 38 rooms, most with bath.

Restaurants. *Ballymaloe House* (E), Shanagarry (tel. 021–652531). Worth going out of town to enjoy a great meal. *Lovett's* (E), Churchyard Lane (tel. 021–294909). *Ashbourne House* (M), Glounthaune (tel. 021–821230). *Glassialleys* (M), Drawbridge St. (tel. 021–22305). Prettily decorated wine bar. *Jacques* (M), in Phoenix Street is well run by two enthusiastic sisters who know their cooking. *Oyster Tavern* (M), Market Lane (tel. 021–272716). Old-established favorite for seafood and game.

GLENGARRIF. *Casey's* (I), tel. 027–63010. 20 rooms, some with bath. *Eccles* (I), tel. 027–63003. 25 rooms with bath. *Golf Links* (I), tel. 027–63009. 16 rooms. *Mountain View* (I), tel. 027–63103. 20 rooms, some with bath.
Restaurant. *The Wooden Shoe* (M).

GOUGANE BARRA. *Gougane Barra* (I), tel. Ballingeary 69. 34 rooms, half with bath. If you want real peace this is the place.

INNISHANNON. *Innishannon* (I), tel. 027–75121. 13 rooms with bath in a lovely riverside location, excellent food.

KINSALE. *Acton's* (M), tel. 021–72135. 58 rooms most with bath in this top sea angling spot on the south coast, also popular with cruising yachtsmen. *Trident* (I), tel. 021–72135. 40 rooms with bath. *Blue Haven* (I), tel. 021–72209. 12 rooms and a deservedly high reputation for food.
Restaurants. *Man Friday* (E), tel. 021–72260. *The Vintage* (E), tel. 021–72443. *Cottage Loft* (M), tel. 021–72803. *Le Toucan* (M), Market Square. *Max's Wine Bar* (I).

MALLOW. *Longueville House* (E), tel. 022–27306. 20 rooms with bath. Georgian mansion in 500-acre wooded estate.

SKIBBEREEN. *West Cork Hotel* (M), tel. 028–21277. 42 rooms with bath. Family run, excellent food.
Restaurant. *Mill House* (E), Rineen (tel. 028–36299).

Killarney and the Ring of Kerry

Killarney deserves all of its fame in song and story, and so does the whole Kingdom of Kerry, with its romantic glens, towering peaks, majestic seacoast and constantly-changing colors. It's been said more than once that Kerry is the best that Ireland has to offer, and when you see it, you won't be surprised that visitors flock from all over the world to see this magnificent southwestern tip of Ireland. Since you can't do Killarney's famous lakes by car we recommend slowing down here and seeing them from one of the slow-moving horse-drawn jaunting cars, a trademark of Killarney. Don't miss the Muckross Estate and Muckross Abbey, under whose spell Tennyson wrote, "The splendor falls on castle walls . . . " and travel the famous Ring of Kerry, the complete circuit around the peninsula between the Kenmare River and Dingle Bay, one of Europe's greatest scenic drives. "Irish Nights," an entertainment of ballads, dancing and old tales, are regular events: ask at your hotel for the location. Accommodation is tight in summer, so contact your travel agent early. (Fall and spring are good times to visit, too.) Best headquarters for seeing Killarney's lakes and the spectacular coastline of Kerry are Killarney, Kenmare, Parknasilla, Glenbeigh.

PRACTICAL INFORMATION FOR KERRY

CAHERDANIEL. *Derrynane* (M), tel. 066–5136. 51 rooms with bath. Good, off the beaten base for tourism.

CARAGH LAKE. *Caragh Lodge* (M), tel. 066–69115. A famous guesthouse, 10 rooms with bath, where the real anglers meet.

DINGLE. *Sceilig* (M), tel. 066–51144. 79 rooms with bath. Great location.
Restaurant. *Doyle's Seafood Bar* (M), tel. 066–51174. An outstanding spot.

KENMARE. *Park* (L), tel. 064–41200. 50 rooms with bath; is the refurbished and updated Great Southern. *Kenmare Bay* (I), tel. 064–41300. 100 rooms with bath. *The Wander Inn* (I), tel. 064–41038. 14 rooms, 2 with bath.
Restaurants. *The Park Hotel* (E) is outstanding for its food. *The Purple Heather* (E), tel. 064–41016. Maintains its reputation. *Remy's House* (M), Main St. (tel. 41589), has a top-notch French chef and 5 bedrooms.

KILLARNEY. *Dunloe Castle* (E), tel. 064–4411. 140 rooms with bath, a few miles out of town but ideally located—German operated. *Europe* (E), tel. 064–31900. 168 rooms with bath, indoor pool and conference center. Again out of town. *Great Southern* (E), tel. 064–31262. 180 rooms with bath, conference center and indoor pool. *Aghadoe Heights* (M), tel. 064–31766. 46 rooms with bath, magnificent view over lakes. *Castlerosse* (M), tel. 064–31144. 40 rooms with bath. *Killarney Ryan* (M), tel. 064–31555. 168 rooms with bath. *Three Lakes* (M), tel. 064–31479. 70 rooms with bath. *Torc Great Southern* (M), tel. 064–31611. 96 rooms with bath. *Arbutus* (I), tel. 064–31037. 31 rooms most with bath. *Dromhall* (I), tel. 064–31894. 58 rooms most with bath. *Gleneagle* (I), tel. 064–31870. 74 rooms with bath. *International* (I), tel. 064–31816. 88 rooms with bath. *Lake* (I), tel. 065–31035. 55 rooms, 44 with bath.
Restaurants. *Dingles* (M), New St. *Foley's* (M), High St. Peat fires, seafood and steaks. *Gaby's Seafood* (M), High St. (tel. 064–32519). *Linden House* (M), New Rd. (tel. 064–31379). *The Whaler* (M), Brewery Lane.

PARKNASILLA. *Great Southern* (L), tel. 064–45122. 60 rooms with bath. Heated pool. In a beautiful setting on Kenmare Bay with facilities for cruising and fishing in the bay. Truly outstanding food.

SNEEM. Restaurant. *Stone House Inn* (M). In an attractive little village which is worth a halt.

TRALEE. *Ballyroe Country Club* (M), tel. 066–26796. 16 rooms with bath. *Brandon* (M), tel. 066–21311. 162 rooms with bath. *Earl of Desmond* (M), tel. 066–21299. 52 rooms with bath.

VALENTIA ISLAND. *Valentia Heights* (I), tel. 0667–6138. 8 rooms, 6 with bath. Guesthouse. The island is an away-from-it-all spot reached by a bridge.

WATERVILLE. *Waterville Lake* (L), tel. 0667–41333. 20 rooms with bath. *Butler Arms* (M), tel. 0667–4144. 37 rooms, most with bath. *Waterville Beach* (M), tel. 0667–2353. 40 rooms with bath. *Bay View* (I), tel. 0667–4122. 24 rooms, some with bath.
Restaurants. *Huntsman* (M), tel. 0667–4124, specializes in seafood, as does *Smuggler's* (M), tel. 0667–4330.

The Shannon Region

Embracing a wide area, the Shannon region stretches from Kerry Head at the mouth of the Shannon estuary, inland to Limerick and part of Tipperary and north along the spectacular Clare coast with the Cliffs of Moher rising straight out of the Atlantic. The area has a natural gateway through Shannon airport, which has direct links from the U.S. and to Britain and Continental Europe—and also an outsize in duty free shops. If you've been touring in Kerry and want to cut out a lot of mileage and driving through Limerick City, take a ferry from Tarbert to Killimer (14 minutes). It's in County Clare that you'll hear and see some of the finest performers of Irish traditional music and dancing.

Despite its historic associations, Limerick City has comparatively few attractions, but see the Treaty Stone—the symbol of a long-gone broken promise; the 13th-century King John's Castle, and St. Mary's Cathedral which dates back to the 9th century—the tower reputedly once housed the legendary "Bells of St. Mary's". The city is also where the infamous dancer Lola Montez, one-time mistress of King Ludwig of Bavaria, was born; and, more importantly, the birthplace of the actress Ada Rehan, once the pride of the Broadway theater.

Visit nearby Adare, one of the most attractive villages in the country. Currahchase is closeby; this one-time 700-acre estate of the poet Sir Aubrey de Vere (1814–1902) has recently been opened as a national forest park and is well worth a visit. It has a camping site.

A few miles up the Shannon at Killaloe is where the river begins to interest the tourist who wants to cruise up through the lakes and up the longest river in Britain or Ireland.

Eastward lies the Golden Vale of Tipperary, the heart of Ireland's dairy land and the breeding place of many fine racehorses.

Closer to Shannon there is Bunratty Castle with its lively medieval banquets; a reconstructed and operating folk village; a lake-dwelling of centuries ago; and relics from neolithic times to the present day. Pause a while. In County Clare there is the Burren, a seeming limestone desert but full of plants from both the Arctic and the Mediterranean, strange tombs, monuments and caves. It is a place of excitement, beauty and mystery. An interpretative center adds to the interest.

PRACTICAL INFORMATION FOR THE SHANNON REGION

BALLYVAUGHAN. *Gregan's Castle* (M), tel. 065–77005. 16 rooms, most with bath. A good location to explore the Burren.

BUNRATTY. *Fitzpatrick's Shannon Shamrock* (E), tel. 061–61177. 100 rooms with bath.
Restaurant. *McCloskey's Bunratty House Restaurant* (M) is excellent. (*Durty Nellie's Pub* is worth a visit.)

ENNIS. *Old Ground* (E), tel. 065–28127. 63 rooms with bath. Is the nearest town to Shannon airport and hotel is elegant and restful. *West County* (M), tel. 065–28421. 110 rooms with bath.

LAHINCH. *Vaughan's Aberdeen Arms* (M), tel. 065–81100. 48 rooms, all with bath. An outstanding hotel with kindly, concerned service and good food.

LIMERICK. *Cruise's Royal* (M), tel. 061–44977. 80 rooms, 55 with bath. *Jury's* (E), tel. 061–55266. 96 rooms with bath. *Limerick Inn* (E), tel. 061–51544. 133 rooms with bath. *Limerick Ryan* (M), tel. 061–53922. 184 rooms with bath. *The New Greenhills* (M), tel. 061–53033. 55 rooms with bath. Extensively refurbished in 1982. *Parkway* (M), tel. 061–47599. 93 rooms with bath. *Two Mile Inn* (M), tel. 061–53122. 47 rooms with bath. *Woodfield House* (I), tel. 061–53023. 25 rooms, 18 with bath.
Restaurants. *Galleon Grill* (M), O'Connell Street (tel. 061–48358). Has traditional style grill, and a bistro in the basement. *Jury's Hotel* has a Coffee Dock (M), and a Piano Bar (I) which specializes in cold plates. *The New Greenhills Hotel* operates its new restaurant 17 hours a day from 7.30 A.M. *The Granary Tavern* (M), on Charlotte Quay, is a tavern embracing both a singing bar and a good restaurant. *Mortells* (I), Roches St. Irish music can also be heard at *The Olde Tom,* Thomas St.

SHANNON. *Dromoland Castle* (L), tel. 061–71144. 67 rooms with bath and considerable elegance in a 16th century castle at Newmarket-on-Fergus (8 miles). *Clare Inn* (E), tel. 061–71161. 121 rooms with bath. *Shannon International* (E), tel. 061–611222. 118 rooms with bath, across the road from the airport terminal. It is now owned by the airport authority and has recently been updated and developed.

Galway and the West

Galway, main city of the west of Ireland, is an ancient seaport whose waterfront was frequented by Spanish grandees and traders. Little of old Galway remains today, but there is still a hint of the Iberian influence in some of the buildings. The salmon fishing in the River Corrib is unsurpassed. In early summer you can stand at the Weir Bridge and watch thousands of these fish in the clear water as they leap and teem through the narrow access to the inland lakes. Lynch's "Castle" in Shop Street, now a bank, is an example of a 16th-century fortified house. In Eyre Square stands the statue of Padraic O'Conaire, greatest of Irish storytellers. Today Galway is a university city with major research departments on the Atlantic seaboard for the study of oceanography and marine life. The Druid, one of Ireland's leading theater companies, started life in a Galway pub and has now built its own theater in a warehouse.

Galway is also the center from which one visits the fascinating Aran Islands—Inishmore, Inishmaan and Inisheere. The mode of life on these islands, 30 miles off the coast, epitomizes man's unremitting struggle against nature in the most dramatic and primitive terms. The strikingly handsome men of Aran wear knitted tams, fanciful woolen sweaters, heel-less rawhide slippers called *pampootie,* white *bawneen coats,* and a really colorful woolen *crios* (waistband). During summer, boats leave Galway at least three times a week for the islands, and it's possible to visit the main island for several hours and pick up the boat on its return trip. An air ferry operates to Inishmore and Inishmaan; check locally for schedules. There are no hotels on the isles, but there are three guesthouses.

The city is a good base from which to explore the beauties of Connemara. In the north of the region is Knock, the site of an Apparition of the Virgin a century ago and now a major shrine of pilgrimage.

Early in September there is an Oyster Festival at Galway to inaugurate the new season. This is a lively festival, with oysters from Clarenbridge and stout.

Many people have found relaxation at places like Achill in County Mayo, an island reached by bridge, and Cong, between Lough Mask, and Lough Corrib, where the lonely, lovely countryside has a soothing effect. While in the vicinity, see Westport House (Westport), a well-preserved and still lived-in Georgian mansion, now a museum of antiques and paintings; it's the family home of the Marquess of Sligo. A zoo park is located in the grounds.

PRACTICAL INFORMATION FOR THE WEST

ACHILL ISLAND. The island is reached by a bridge and provides a lively life in its hotels and uncrowded beaches. *Ostan Gob a Choire (Achill Sound Hotel)* (I), tel. 098–45245. 36 rooms with bath. *Achill Head* (I), tel. 098–43131. 24 rooms. *Atlantic* (I), tel. 098–43113. 10 rooms, 2 with bath. *Slievemore* (I), tel. 098–43224. 18 rooms.

BALLINA. *Downhill* (E), tel. 096–21033. 54 rooms with bath and heated indoor pool. *Belleek Castle* (M), tel. 096–22061. 16 rooms with bath and a restaurant worth traveling to.

BALLYNAHINCH. *Ballynahinch Castle* (L), tel. Clifden 135. 20 rooms with bath. Elegance and good living in wonderful location.

CARRAROE. *Hotel Carraroe* (M), tel. 091–75116. 24 rooms, most with bath. In the heart of Connemara. Lots to do and see. Some self-catering cottages.

CASHEL BAY. *Cashel House* (M), tel. 095–21252. 29 rooms, most with bath. Splendid location and excellent food.

CASTLEBAR. *Breaffy House* (M), tel. 094–22033. 40 rooms with bath.

CONG. *Ashford Castle* (L), tel. 094–65281. 77 rooms with bath. In magnificent estate, and with great fishing.

GALWAY. *Ardilaun House* (M), tel. 091–21433. 73 rooms with bath. *Corrib Great Southern* (M), tel. 091–64041. 115 rooms with bath. *Flannery's* (I), tel. 091–5511. 98 rooms with bath. *Galway Ryan* (M), tel. 091–63181. 96 rooms with bath. *Great Southern* (L), tel. 091–64041. 120 rooms with bath. *Imperial* (I), tel. 091–68409. 65 rooms, most with bath.
Restaurants. *The Fishery* (E), Ballyconneely, tel. Ballyconneely 31. In converted 18th-century fishermen's cottages. *Paddy Burke's* Oyster Inn (M), Clarinbridge, tel. 091–86107. *The Silver Teal* (M), tel. 091–85109. *The Gallows Bar* (I), Prospect Hill (tel. 091–62440). Log fire and intimate atmosphere.

OUGHTERARD. *Connemara Gateway* (M), tel. 091–82328. 48 rooms with bath. Good location as a touring base. *Currarevagh House* (I), tel. 091–82312. 15 rooms, most with bath. Excellent food.

RENVYLE. *Renvyle House* (M), tel. Renvyle 3. 69 rooms most with bath. One of the best, lively.

WESPORT. *Wesport* (M), tel. 098–25122. 49 rooms with bath. *Westport Ryan* (M), tel. 098–25811. 56 rooms with bath. *Clew Bay* (I), tel. 098–25438. 32 rooms, 23 with bath.
Restaurants. *Ardmore* (M), tel. 098–25994. On the quay, as is *Chalet Swiss Restaurant* (M), tel. 098–25874. Run by chef-proprietor, Heinz Haechler.

Sligo and the Northwest

Sligo is the gateway to Ireland's scenic northwest. Hereabouts are the places and lakes immortalized by William Butler Yeats, who is buried, where he chose, in lonely Drumcliff churchyard, in the shadow "of Ben Bulben's head". Sligo Town, with its seaside resorts and championship golf courses, is the main center. See Sligo Abbey founded in 1252; St. John's Church, dating from 1635; Glencar Lough, a lake with waterfalls, rivaling Killarney for beauty; the ancient Celtic Cross by the roadside at Drumcliff near the grave of Yeats, whose work is studied at annual Yeats International Summer School sessions in Sligo.

Tucked up in the northwestern corner of Ireland is mountain-ringed Donegal, Ultima Thule, "the world's end". Now that highways span the windswept moors and highlands, it is easy to reach this dramatically scenic area. Be sure to visit the 25,000-acre Glenveagh National Park with its castle, herds of deer, and spectacular gardens. Also of note is Derek Hill's internationally-famous art collection and museum which should be open, but best check locally. A good spot to buy handloomed tweeds is McNutt's in Downings, or Magee's in Donegal town. County Donegal is also a great place for cottage-living for the get-away-from-it-all vacation. There are rental cottages in many scenic areas.

Leitrim is a county neglected by visitors, but it's the place where the River Shannon starts to attract inland waterway holidaymakers and fishermen. The principal town, Carrick-on-Shannon, is the base for river-cruise boat operators.

PRACTICAL INFORMATION FOR THE NORTHWEST

BUNBEG. *Gweedore* (M), tel. 075–31177. 30 rooms with bath, in a beautiful area of Country Donegal (seasonal, mid-April to September).
Restaurant. *Mooney's* (M), tel. 075–31147. Old-style décor with a heart-warming open peat fire.

CARRIGART. *Carrigart* (M), tel. 074–55114. 56 rooms, most with bath. Is first rate for relaxation and good talk.

DONEGAL. *Abbey* (M), tel. 073–21014. 40 rooms, some with bath. *Hyland Central* (M), tel. 073–21027. 49 rooms with bath.

DUNFANAGHY. *Arnold's* (I), tel. 074–36208. 40 rooms, most with bath.

DUNGLOE. *Ostan na Rossan* (*Hotel of the Rosses*) (I), tel. 075–21088. 50 rooms with bath.

RATHMULLAN. *Rathmullan House* (M), tel. 074–58188. 21 rooms, 16 with bath. Country residence with outstanding food.

ROSAPENNA. *Rosapenna Golf* (M), tel. 074–55301. 40 rooms with bath. On the Rosguil Peninsular and, as the name suggests, a good golf spot.

ROSSES POINT. *Yeats Country Ryan* (M), tel. 071–77211. 79 rooms with bath. Another famed spot for golfers.
Restaurant. *The Moorings* (E), tel. 071–77112. On the sea front.

ROSSNOWLAGH. *Sand House* (E), tel. 072–51777. 40 rooms with bath. Overlooks wide beach and Donegal Bay. Fine family-run hotel.

SLIGO. *Sligo Park* (M), tel. 071–60291. 60 rooms with bath. *Silver Swan* (I), tel. 071–3232. 24 rooms, 16 with bath. *The Southern* (I), tel. 071–2101. 52 rooms, 38 with bath.
Restaurant. *The Italian Warehouse* (I), tel. 071–62978. Located in town center and specializing in homemade Italian fare.

The Inland Counties

Geographically, Ireland is shaped rather like a dish, a rim of mountains and hills near the coast and a central plain which may lack the dramatic scenery of Donegal, Kerry and the West but provides plenty of interest. The vast peatlands (bogs) of the Midlands provide much of the fuel used in Ireland. The traveler will also find some excellent hotels and restaurants along the way.

For the angler in search of the coarser varieties of fish, Cavan and Monaghan have hundreds of lakes and all you need is a rod and a can of bait. Robert Trent Jones designed the golf course in the grounds of Glaslough House in County Monaghan.

Westmeath is noted mainly for its hunting country, but Tullynally Castle near Mullingar is a must. It's the family home of the Earls of Longford and is open to visitors in summer, when there's usually a member of the family around to talk entertainingly about the wonderful collection of antiques gathered by their ancestors. To the south, in Offaly, Cloghan Castle at Banagher (built in 1120) is one of the oldest inhabited buildings in Ireland. The gardens of the Earl of Rosse's estate at Birr Castle are famous, and so were the giant telescopes of his forebears, parts of which can still be seen.

Down in the South, in Tipperary, there is the spectacular Rock of Cashel topped by age-old buildings and homes of kings; and in the shadow of the Knockmealdown Mountains lies the village of Ballyporeen from which President Ronald Reagan's great-grandfather emigrated to the United States; the nearest town is Cahir.

PRACTICAL INFORMATION FOR INLAND COUNTIES

BALLYMASCANLON. *Ballymascanlon* (E), tel. 042–71124. 36 rooms with bath. Not really in an inland county, but worth visiting if traveling North.

CAHIR. *Keane's Cahir House Hotel* (M), tel. 052–41207. Well-located on main road. *Kilcoran Lodge* (M), tel. 052–41288. 18 rooms, 9 with bath.

CASHEL. *Cashel Palace* (E), tel. 062–61411. 20 rooms with bath. Has excellent restaurant. *Dundrum House* (M), tel. 062–71116. 30 rooms with bath, and a high reputation for food. *Rectory House* (M), tel. 062–71115. 10 rooms, most with bath. *Grant's Castle* (I), tel. 062–61044. 12 rooms, 2 with bath.

CASTLEDERMOT. *Kilea Castle* (M), tel. 0503–45156. 53 rooms with bath. Attractive location about 30 miles from Dublin.

MAYNOOTH. *Moyglare Manor* (E), tel. 01–286351. 11 rooms with bath. A converted Georgian manor.

NAAS. *Curryhills House* (M), tel. 045–68336. An elegantly converted farmhouse.

NAVAN. Restaurant. *Dunderry Lodge* (E), tel. 045–31671. A few miles outside of town, 28 miles from Dublin. Housed in converted barns; good food.

THURLES. *Hayes* (M), tel. 0504–22122. 37 rooms, 22 with bath. Has been updated and refurbished. Deservedly good reputation for food.

VIRGINIA. *The Park* (M), tel. 049–47235. 30 rooms, most with bath. Based on old farm estate house. Overlooks Lough Ramor and is on a golf course.

NORTHERN IRELAND

Northern Ireland—sometimes referred to as Ulster, although it embraces only six of the nine counties of the ancient province of Ulster (hence it is sometimes called The Six Counties)—occupies the northeast corner of the Emerald Isle and offers some of the most interesting scenic, coastal, sporting and historic attractions of the entire island. The population is just over 1,500,000.

Politically, it is still part of the United Kingdom, being hived-off from the rest of Ireland in 1920 and given its own Parliament (suspended in 1972) but still sending members of Parliament to the House of Commons in London. Northern Ireland, as a constituency of the United Kingdom, also sends three members to the European Parliament.

The complexities of the political and religious differences of the people of the area—a situation compounded by the Anglo-Irish Accord signed in late 1985—should not concern short-stay visitors, and the internal problems do not diminish the warmth of regard and welcome for overseas visitors. The people have a wry sense of humor and their voices have a harder accent than the lilt of the far south, and they are hard workers whether in the industries, some of which (like shipbuilding) have suffered from the recession, or on the farms.

Culturally, the people of Northern Ireland are closely linked with Scotland; but they are Irish and proud of it, no matter what their forbears or political links may be. St. Patrick, Ireland's patron, landed (A.D. 432) in what is now Northern Ireland and his reputed burial place is at Downpatrick in County Down.

Many Ulstermen made an important contribution to the foundation of the United States. One of them, Charles Thomson, wrote out the Declaration of Independence in his office as Secretary of the Continental Congress; and no fewer than ten U.S. Presidents have been of Ulster stock. The Northern Ireland Tourist Board has prepared an American Heritage Trail to help U.S. visitors trace their ancestral background.

Scenically, Northern Ireland has much to offer from the Mountains of Mourne in the south of County Down, which has many attractive fishing villages, to around the coast and the Giant's Causeway, 38,000 strange basalt columns which are, if you ignore legends, the spill-over of an ancient volcano. Architecturally, Belfast is not a very attractive capital city, but the damaged Grand Opera House has now been restored to its former ornate Edwardian splendor and is worth seeing; the nearby brick façade of the Royal Belfast Academical Institution dates back to 1810 and is an excellent example of its period.

Queen's University (founded 1849) is one of the Province's two universities. The other is the Ulster University, based at Coleraine, which links several top-level educational institutions with a high standard of faculties, both technological and academic. If you visit in the fall Queen's has a fine Arts Festival which attracts many international personalities in the performing arts. The Ulster Museum in Belfast's Botanic Gardens is worth a visit, and there you will see some of the treasures recovered from ships of the Spanish Armada (1588) which were wrecked off the Irish coast; there are more at Magee College in Londonderry. Incidentally, you may also hear Londonderry referred to as Derry—they are the same place.

A "must see" is the Ulster Folk and Transport Museum at Cultra, Co. Down, where the past has been brought to the present in a 176-acre park. A church, a school and a row of industrial workers' homes are among the transplants to ensure a living record of days gone by. Castle Ward, on the shore of Strangford Lough in the same county, is one of Northern Ireland's several notable "great houses." Architecturally, it is something of a joke: one façade is in the classical Palladian style; the other, in what is described as "Strawberry Hill Gothic," is reputedly the result of a husband and wife agreeing to differ on what face the house should present to the world.

There are nine famous glens (valleys) in County Antrim, every one with its own special beauty as it leads up from the sea. Lough Neagh is the largest lake (153 square miles) in Ireland or Britain. Just off the coast is Rathlin Island where Guglielmo Marconi (1874–1937) established his first off-shore radio station linking with Ballycastle on the mainland. If you are here in August visit the Auld Lammas Fair at Ballycastle, a survival of a festival that dates back to the earliest days of the country. In the little village of Bushmills is a distillery that claims to be the home of the world's oldest whiskey; naturally it bears the name of the village. Join a conducted tour of the distillery and finish in a visitor center which features much craft work from the village.

What is generally referred to as West Ulster embraces the North's wonderful Lakeland—Upper and Lower Lough Erne linked by the River Erne on which stands the town of Enniskillen. The Loughs provide a vast and uncrowded waterway for inland cruising: Lusty Beg,

Killadea and the new marina at Castle Archdale Forest Park are the main centers for cruiser hire. There is a wildlife reserve in the same area at Castle Caldwell.

Fermanagh lace, made in some of the villages, is one of the best souvenirs you can find; another is Belleek pottery made in the Border village of the same name.

For the golfer Royal Portrush and Royal County Down are the most famous of Northern Ireland's many courses. The annual "Ulster Classic" international coarse angling competition takes place on the Erne Waterway in County Fermanagh in May.

PRACTICAL INFORMATION FOR NORTHERN IRELAND

 GETTING TO NORTHERN IRELAND. By Air. Belfast is linked to Shannon in Ireland and to London, Birmingham, Manchester, Liverpool, East Midlands, Glasgow, Isle of Man, Aberdeen and Edinburgh by several airlines. From North America there are charter flights linking New York with Belfast in the summer months. There are also a number of charters from Toronto; check with *Wardair* and *Worldways*. There's a direct Dutch-operated service to Amsterdam (Holland) but for other Continental destinations route through Dublin, Manchester or London.

By Sea: Car ferries operate between Liverpool and Belfast, Stranraer-Larne, Cairnryan-Larne.

By Rail. From the Republic of Ireland, Dublin (Connolly Station).

By Road. From the Republic of Ireland. Use Approved Roads only and stop at Customs posts and checkpoints.

Car Hire. Belfast: *Avis,* 69 Great Victoria St.; *Hertz Rent-a-Car,* Airport Rd.; *Budget Rent-a-Car,* 511 Lisburn Rd.; *Godfrey Davis Europcar,* 52 Linenhall St.

CURRENCY AND MAIL. As in Britain.

PUBLIC HOLIDAYS. (Bank Holidays). Jan. 1; Mar. 17 (St. Patrick's Day); Apr. 17 (Good Friday); Apr. 20 (Easter Monday); May 4; July 13 (Orangemen's Day or "The Twelfth"—a day for parades of the Orange Order); Aug. 31; Dec. 25–26.

Hotels in Belfast

Deluxe

Conway, Dunmurry (tel. 612101). 78 rooms with bath. On the fringe of the city.

Culloden, Bangor Rd. (tel. 175223). 80 rooms with bath.

Belfast Forum (formerly **Europa**), Great Victoria St. (tel. 245161). 100 rooms with bath. Owned by the Grand Metropolitan Group.

Expensive

Drumkeen (tel. 645321). 26 rooms with bath.

Greenan Lodge, Dunmurry (tel. 628234). 13 rooms with bath. Recently remodeled and refurbished, notable restaurant, and *Pickwick Bar* has character.

Stormont, tel. 658621. 51 rooms with bath, plus 8 self-catering apartments.

Moderate

Ambassador, Antrim Rd. (tel. 781016). 10 rooms with bath; restaurant specializes in Cantonese food.

Glenmachan Tower, Glenmachan Rd. (tel. 768810). Small, 9 rooms with bath, but 6 with lounge en suite. Good restaurant.

Le Mon House, Castlereagh (tel. 123631). 30 rooms with bath.

Wellington Park (tel. 661232). 48 rooms with bath.

Restaurants in Belfast

Most restaurants close early, around 10.30 P.M.

Moderate

Belmont Court, 45 Park Avenue.
Carlton, Wellington Place, Royal Avenue.
Ciro's Trattoria, Great Victoria St. Lively and bright, with an Italian setting, good food and service.
Manor House, 47 Donegall Pass. Exotic Chinese.
Old Vic and Theatre Lounge. Maintains its period character.
Tramps Bistro, 50 Dublin Rd.

Inexpensive

Coffee House in the *Robinson and Cleaver* department store.
Skandia, Callender Street and Howard Street.
Truffles, Donegall Square West, a bistro spot.
Ulster Museum Cafe in the museum at Stranmillis.
University Cafe, University Road.
The Crown Bar (opposite the Forum) is a first-class example of 19th-century pub architecture and familiar to film buffs from Carol Reed's *Odd Man Out.*

THEATERS. The *Grand Opera House* has been reconstructed in all its 19th-century exuberance and stages drama, ballet, opera, and concerts. *Lyric* in Ridgeway St., Stranmillis, Belfast, is a lively theater which encourages new Irish writers and has a high standard.

 USEFUL ADDRESSES. *Northern Ireland Tourist Board,* River House, 48 High St, Belfast, BT1 2DS; *U.S. Consulate-General,* Queen's House, Queen St., Belfast 1; *Canadian Counsulate-General,* Canada House, North St., Belfast; *American Express,* 9 North St, Belfast 1; *Thomas Cook Ltd,* 11 Donegall Place, Belfast.

PRACTICAL INFORMATION FOR THE REGIONS

Phone numbers of hotels and restaurants should be requested by prefixing the number with the name of the town, except Belfast where dialling is direct.

BALLYCASTLE (Co. Antrim). *Antrim Arms* (I), tel. 62284. 16 rooms, 1 with bath. Small seaside resort close to the Nine Glens of Antrim.

BANGOR (Co. Down). Ulster's top sailing center, 13 miles from Belfast. *The Sands* (E), tel. 473696. 11 rooms, 10 with bath. *Ballyholme* (M), tel. 472807. 26 rooms, some with bath. *O'Hara's Royal* (M), tel. 473866. 32 rooms with bath.

CRAIGAVON (Co. Armagh). *Silverwood* (E), tel. 0762–2772. 28 rooms with bath.

CRAWFORDSBURN (Co. Down). *The Old Inn* (E), tel. 0247–853255. 28 rooms, 15 with bath. Excellent for food. In a seaside village.

DONAGHADEE (Co. Down). *Copelands* (I), tel. 888189. 14 rooms with bath. Attractive fishing port.

ENNISKILLEN (Co. Fermanagh). *Killyhevlin* (E), tel. 0365–23481. 33 rooms, most with bath. *Fort Lodge* (I), tel. 0365–3275. 12 rooms, 8 with bath. *Manor House* (I), tel. 03656–21561. 15 rooms, most with bath.

GIANT'S CAUSEWAY (Co. Antrim). *Causeway Hotel* (I), tel. 02657–31226. 13 rooms with bath. It is worth a visit to see the astonishing geometric shapes of the basalt rocks and hear the tale of how they once formed a road for the giants. A visitor's center tells the story of the Causeway from its geological origins on to the myths and legends of later centuries.

LARNE (Co. Antrim). *Maghermorne House* (M), tel. 0574–7944. 23 rooms with bath. Touring center for the Glens of Antrim.

LONDONDERRY. Also known as Derry. See Derry's Walls (built 1614–1618), the only complete fortifications of any city in Ireland or Britain, and thought to be the last built in Europe. 75 miles from Belfast and a gateway to County Donegal (Irish Republic) across the River Foyle. *Everglades* (E), tel. 0504–46722. 38 rooms with bath. *Broomhill House* (M), tel. 0504–44854. 21 rooms, 5 with bath. *White Horse Inn* (M), tel. 0504–860606. 44 rooms with bath. Good restaurant. If the *Field Day Theater* is playing, go and see it; Brian Friel *(Philadelphia, Here I Come* and *Translations)* presents his new work here. Also visit the Orchard Gallery, Orchard St.

MAGHERA (Co. Londonderry). *Glenburn House* (I), tel. 0648–42203. Small country guesthouse close to the Sperrin Mountains. Pleasant coffee shop.

NEWCASTLE (Co. Down). *Slieve Donard* (M), tel. 03967–23681. 110 rooms with bath. A top golfing spot, and center for trips to the Mountains of Mourne.

NEWTOWN ABBEY (Co. Antrim). *Chimney Corner* (M), tel. 0231–44925. 63 rooms with bath. *Edenmore* (M), tel. 0231–62531. 44 rooms with bath.

NEWTOWNARDS (Co. Down). *Strangford Arms* (E), Church St. (tel. 0247–814141). 36 rooms with bath. Restaurant and attractive bar. Beside the scenic Strangford Lough and 20 minutes from Belfast city center.

OMAGH. (Co. Tyrone). *Royal Arms* (I), tel. 0662–3262. 19 rooms, most with bath. *Silverbirch* (I), tel. 0662–2520. 32 rooms, most with bath. *Silverbirch* (M), tel. 2520. 24 rooms, 20 with bath. Close to the Ulster-American Folk Park.

PORTRUSH (Co. Antrim). Famous for its championship golf course. *Northern Counties* (I), tel. 0265–823755. 94 rooms, 30 with bath. *Skerrybhan* (I), tel. 0265–822328. 52 rooms, some with bath.
Restaurant. *Dionysis Greek Taverna* (M), Eglinton St. Something different.

PORTSTEWART (Co. Londonderry). *Carrig-na-Cule* (M), tel. 026583–2016. 33 rooms, 10 with bath. *Edgewater* (M), tel. 026583–3314. 30 rooms with bath.
Restaurant. *Galvey Lodge* (M), Station Rd. Lobster and game in season.

WARRENPOINT (Co. Down). *Osborne* (I), tel. 06937–73521. 16 rooms with bath.

WHITEHEAD (Co. Antrim). *Dolphin* (I), tel. 09603–72481. 19 rooms, 6 with bath. On the scenic coastal road north from Belfast.

Houses, Gardens and Museums

Historic houses, except where indicated, are open daily (except Tues.) April through September 2 to 6 P.M. Admission fees may be up in 1987.

CO. ANTRIM. Arthur House, near Cullbackey. Once the home of President Chester A. Beatty's grandfather.
Causeway Coast Lion Park, Benvarden. Easter to June, Sat. and Sun. 11–7; June to Oct. 11–7 daily. Admission 50p.
Lisburn Museum. New (1981), relating the history of the area.
Shane's Castle Railway and Nature Reserve, beside Lough Neagh (tel. Antrim 3380). Phone for bookings.

CO. ARMAGH. Astronomy Center, Armagh. Shows daily in July and August, also every Sat. through rest of year, at 3. Admission 40p.

CO. DOWN. The Argory, near Moy. This is an 1820 neoclassical house with 300 acres of woodlands and forest walks. A new (1981) acquisition of the National Trust. Admission 80p.

Castleward, 2 miles from Strangford. Classical and Gothic mansion—an odd but impressive mixture. Open year round, dawn to dusk. Admission £1.

Mount Stewart House, 4 miles from Newtownards. Eighteenth-century house associated with the famous Lord Castlereagh. The gardens, designed by the 7th Marchioness of Londonderry, feature the Temple of the Winds, an 18th-century replica of an Athenian temple. Admission £1; temple, 35p.

Rowallane Gardens, Saintfield. Famous for the display of rare plants and shrubs. Open 9–6 weekdays, 2–6 Sat. and Sun. Admission 50p.

Ulster Folk Museum, Cultra. A "must see" to learn something of life in the long ago in these parts. Open weekdays 11–7, Sun. 2–7; closes 2 hours earlier Oct. to Apr. Admission 50p.

FERMANAGH AND TYRONE. Castlecoole, half a mile from Enniskillen. A neoclassical 18th-century house designed by James Wyatt (1746–1813).

Gray's Printing Press, Strabane. Here John Dunlap, printer of America's Declaration of Independence, learned his trade. Open daily except Thurs. 9–6, Sun. 2–6. Admission 40p.

Ulster-American Folk Park, Camphill, 3 miles from Omagh. Stresses Ulster's many links with North America. Open Sept. to Apr. daily 10.30–4.30; May to Aug., Mon.–Sat. 10.30–6.30. Admission £1.25.

Wilson House, Dergalt, 2 miles from Strabane. Home of President Woodrow Wilson's grandfather.

CO. LONDONDERRY. Mussenden Temple, 2 miles from Downhill. Built in 1783 by the Earl Bishop of Derry to honor his "very great friend", a Mrs Mussenden. Admission 60p.

Springhill, Moneymore. A 17th-century manor house with a fine costume museum. Admission 75p.

ITALY

For the past 2,000 years, more foreigners have been exploring Italy than any other European country. Why? Not just because she is a pace setter in the field of fashion, design and the cinema, not to mention being the birth place of *la dolce vita*. Those are only recent manifestations. The reason for her age-old fascination lies more in the fact that she has been at the very basis of our Western way of life, creating incredible works of art, century after century, producing some of the greatest thinkers, writers, politicians and saints. And the traces of their lives and works still exist in the great buildings and lovely countryside.

The whole of Italy is one vast attraction, but since we must select a target area, we'd advise the triangle of her most-visited cities—Rome, Florence and Venice—for first-time visitors, with side trips, time permitting, to Siena and Pompeii. Art lovers should also visit Naples and Milan. For natural beauty see Sorrento, the Amalfi coast, Capri and Ischia, or the lake region, and, for wild mountain scenery, the Dolomites. Sea and scenery are fine in Sardinia. For winter sports in an elegant setting, try Cortina d'Ampezzo.

For the religious faithful, a trip to Italy can concentrate on visits to the Vatican, to Assisi, Loreto and Turin, among other sites of pilgrimage. For a combination of art, history, religion and vibrant humanity, it's Rome!

The natural splendor of this sunflooded peninsula, flanked by the Tyrrhenian and the Adriatic, and stretching 700 miles from the Alps and flower-bordered lakes of the north to the cobalt seas and golden beaches of Sicily, is good enough reason to come. But that is just a happy accident of geography. More important is the fact that this varied landscape is almost everywhere punctuated by the works of men, and the men of this peninsula seem always to have had the instincts and skills of creative artisans.

The People

The Italian people, inheritors of the beauty that surrounds them in such profusion, have that old, conservative respect for technical competence which comes to them from a long background in which craftsmen were artists yet in which artists remained craftsmen. And their reactions, both negative and positive, are apt to be vocal, violent, as direct as a child's. They do not bottle up their resentment; they just explode.

You will always know where you stand with the Italians. Their approach to you as a tourist will be refreshingly direct. They will be curious about you in a simple friendly way because their chief interest is in human personality. Less intellectual, less closed, more accessible and far more sentimental than the French, they will put themselves out for you in all sorts of ways.

PRACTICAL INFORMATION FOR ITALY

WHAT WILL IT COST. Generally speaking, costs in Italy are not especially high though the country is certainly no longer a budget destination—an annual inflation rate of about 10% has meant that prices have kept consistently on the move. You can fight this upward trend, however, by keeping your stay in major tourist centers down to a minimum and giving some time to the smaller cities and towns in more inexpensive areas such as the South Tyrol, Umbria, Tuscany, and southern Italy. Venice, Milan and northern cities are more expensive than, say, Rome and Florence. Except in luxury restaurants, dining out is relatively reasonable throughout Italy and downright cheap in small towns everywhere and in southern Italy in particular. The usually favorable exchange rate for dollars and sterling helps you stretch your travel budget a long way.

Money can be changed in Italy not only at banks, travel agencies, and hotels, but, in effect, by anyone. That is to say, you may pay any bill or make any purchase in your own currency as well as in lire. To avoid misunderstandings, be sure to check the exchange rate you are getting, it will be more favorable in banks and at exchange and American Express offices, less so in hotels, restaurants and shops.

A typical day might cost two people:

Hotel (moderate) double room with bath and breakfast	Lire 140,000
Lunch at a snack bar or *tavola calda*	25,000
Transportation, four tram rides and one taxi	12,000
Tours, entrance fees, tips	25,000
2 coffees	1,500
2 beers	4,000
Dinner (moderate restaurant) including wine	80,000
Miscellaneous 10%	28,000
	Lire 315,500

The exchange rate varies these days. As we go to press, the rate is around 1,610 to the U.S. dollar and around 2,300 to the pound sterling.

Air fares are relatively high within Italy. It's cheaper to travel by train and generally more convenient, except for long hauls such as Milan–Rome or Rome–Palermo.

SOURCES OF INFORMATION. For information on all aspects of travel to Italy, the Italian Government (ENIT) Travel Office is invaluable. Their addresses are:

In the U.S.: 630 Fifth Ave., New York, NY 10111 (tel. 212–245–4822); 500 N. Michigan Ave., Chicago, IL 60611; 360 Post St., San Francisco, CA 94108.

In Canada: 3 Place Ville Marie, Montreal, P.Q. H3B 2E3 (tel. 416–392–6206).

In the U.K.: 1 Princes St., London W.1 (tel. 01–408–1254).

WHEN TO COME. Main tourist season is from beginning of May to end of September. Secondary seasons: December to March for winter sports in the Dolomites; February to March in sunny Sicily. Seasoned travelers prefer Florence in May, Venice in September, Rome in April and May or in October. *Don't* travel in Italy in August if you can avoid it. Throngs of Italian vacationers crowd transport and resorts, and most big-city restaurants and shops close down.

Climate. July and August temperatures can soar into the 90's in Rome, Venice, Florence and Naples. Winters are rainy, not very cold.

Average afternoon temperatures in degrees Fahrenheit and centigrade:

Rome	Jan.	Feb.	Mar.	Apr.	May	June	July	Aug.	Sept.	Oct.	Nov.	Dec.
F°	54	56	62	68	74	82	88	88	83	73	63	56
C°	12	13	17	20	23	28	31	31	28	23	17	13
Milan												
F°	40	47	56	66	72	80	84	82	76	64	51	42
C°	4	8	13	19	22	27	29	28	24	18	11	6

SPECIAL EVENTS. *January,* Greek Catholic Epiphany rites at Piana degli Albanesi, near Palermo. *February,* pre-Lenten carnivals, particularly those of Viareggio and Venice (sometimes in March); Almond Blossom Festival at Agrigento; the Saint Agatha Festival at Catania; the Flower Show at San Remo. *March,* nationwide mid-Lent festivals, and popular feasts, usually on St. Joseph's Day, the 19th; Florence's Scoppio del Carro on Easter Sunday. *April,* International Handicrafts Fair, Florence; "Spring in Merano" automobile rally; International Horse Competition, Rome. *May,* Feast of S. Efisio in Cagliari; Festa dei Ceri, Gubbio; Sardinian Costume Cavalcade at Sassari; Maggio Musicale, Florence; Italian haute couture week, Florence. *June,* Tournament of the Bridge, Pisa; Festival of the Two Worlds, Spoleto; International festival of Drama, Venice. *July,* the Palio, Siena (repeated in August); the Feast of the Redeemer, Venice; International Ballet Festival, Nervi. *August,* Palio della Contrade, medieval horse races, Siena; Tournament of the Quintana, Ascoli Piceno; opening of the International Film Festival, Venice; Feast of the Redeemer, Nuoro (Sardinia). *September,* The Joust of the Saracen, Arezzo; Historic Regatta, Venice; Joust of the Quintana, Foligno. *October,* celebrations in honor of Columbus, Genoa; Festival of Tyrolean brass bands, Merano. *November,* Feast of the Madonna della Salute, Venice; International Automobile Show, Turin. *December,* traditional Christmas celebrations throughout the country; opera season opens at La Scala, Milan and other major opera houses (through April).

National Holidays. Jan. 1 (New Year's Day); Jan. 6 (Epiphany); Apr. 20 (Easter Mon.); Apr. 25 (Liberation); May 1 (May Day); Aug. 15 (Assumption); Nov. 1 (All Saints); Dec. 8 (Immaculate Conception); Dec. 25, 26.

VISAS. Nationals of the United States, Canada, Australia, New Zealand, EEC countries and practically all other European countries do not require visas for entry into Italy. However, you must of course have a valid passport.

HEALTH CERTIFICATES. Not required for entry into Italy.

GETTING TO ITALY. By Plane. From North America, there are direct or through flights from New York, Boston, Chicago, Los Angeles, Toronto and Montreal to Rome and mostly also to Milan. And both Rome and Milan have excellent services from many European capitals as well as some of the more important European provincial cities. From the U.K., there are flights from London (mainly Heathrow but some also from Gatwick) to Rome, Milan, Turin, Venice, Bologna, Pisa, Genoa, Naples, Catania and Palermo.

By Train. There are excellent and frequent fast train services linking Italy with her neighbors France, Switzerland, Austria and, to a lesser extent, Yugoslavia. There are through expresses from cities as diverse as Copenhagen, Cologne, Amsterdam, Paris, Vienna and Zurich to Rome, calling en route at various other Italian cities. From London to Italy the most convenient trains are the Calais-Basel express which has through 1st. and 2nd. class couchettes and day coaches from Calais to Milan. Departure from London is about 2.00 P.M., and arrival at Milan about 22 hours later. Buffet car part of the way. There is also the Calais-Venice express which, from May to September, has through sleeping cars (1st. and 2nd. class), 2nd class couchettes and 1st. and 2nd. day cars from Calais to Venice. These also operate over the Christmas, New Year and Easter holidays. Departure 2.00 P.M. from London, arrival at Milan at midday, at Verona at 3 P.M. and Venice at 4.45 P.M. Refreshments part of the way. The luxurious Orient Express operates between London and Venice.

The best train to Rome from Paris is the *Palatino* which leaves Paris (Gare de Lyon) at about 7.00 P.M. and travels via Switzerland, Genoa, Pisa and Leghorn, arriving in Rome around 10.15 A.M. Carries 1st. and 2nd. sleeping cars and 2nd. class couchettes to all cities. No day cars on through service. Buffet car in France and also between Genoa and Rome.

By Bus. *Supabus* have through express services in summer from June to mid-July and from mid-August to mid-September from Brussels, via Milan, to Rimini and Cattolica. They operate once a week. Advance reservation is obligatory. There are also several other independent bus services some of which go through to Yugoslavia and Greece. The *Supabus* consortium operate two bus routes from London to Italy: one to Milan, where it splits with one section going on to Venice via Verona, and the other continuing to Rome via Bologna, and Florence; the other route goes to Brindisi in southeast Italy (for the ferry to Greece), traveling via Turin, Florence, and Rome. Journey times are about 26 hours to Milan, 34 to Rome.

By Car. Starting from England, the first hurdle is the Channel crossing. Car ferry services to the Continent increase yearly to keep pace with the growing number of carborne tourists, but only a few of them concern people making their way to Italy. There are the routes from Dover or Folkestone to Calais or Boulogne, by ship or Hovercraft; from Newhaven to Dieppe, and Southampton to Le Havre. It is conceivable that someone wishing to make a night crossing would go Dover-Dunkirk, which costs the same as the shorter routes, takes longer, but provides door to door motorway (toll) travel. All ferries now have drive on/off loading.

From the French channel ports, you have a choice between the fast motorways through France or the slower, but more scenic main roads. In either case, however, roads to Italy are reliable and good.

CUSTOMS. Travelers arriving in Italy from an EEC country are allowed, duty-free, a total of 300 cigarettes (*or* 150 cigarillos *or* 75 cigars), 1½ liters of alcoholic spirits *or* 3 liters of sparkling wine, *plus* 3 liters of still wine, 90 cc. of perfume if duty and taxes have already been paid on them at the time of purchase. Travelers carrying goods from outside the EEC or goods that were purchased in duty-free shops or on aircraft are allowed 400 cigarettes and cigars or tobacco not exceeding 500 grams, 0.75 liter of spirits, 2 liters of still wine. Officially 10 rolls of still camera film and 10 reels of movie film may be brought in duty-free. Not more than 400,000 lire in Italian banknotes may be taken into or out of Italy.

HOTELS. Our hotel grading system is divided into four categories. All prices are for two people in a double room. Deluxe (L) 300,000–600,000 lire, Expensive (E) 150,000–250,000 lire, Moderate (M) 100,000–150,000 lire, and Inexpensive (I) 75,000 lire down. The letter P preceeding the hotel category in our listings means the establishment is a pension; generally speaking, an (E) pension is equivalent in price to an (M) hotel and so on. All deluxe hotels and most moderate hotels have baths in all rooms.

Bear in mind that hotel charges in Rome, Milan and above all Venice are higher than in most other cities and that outside cities and the major tourist resorts prices are lower. Service charges and taxes are usually included in the rates quoted, but double check this when you book. Some hotels charge supplements for heating in winter or airconditioning in summer, even though airconditioning may be turned off in the early morning hours as an energy conservation measure. Rates are posted in rooms. Breakfasts are pricey.

CAMPING. There are about 1,700 campsites well-distributed throughout Italy, many with bungalows, many open all year. Apply to the *Federazione Italiano del Campeggio,* Casella postale 649, 50100 Florence, for an international camping carnet and for the *Guida Camping Italia,* with multilingual text.

RESTAURANTS. One of Italy's boasts is that in almost all its restaurants, from the ultra-chic to the most unpretentious, you'll find food that is good and often excellent. A *ristorante* can be anything from deluxe to just another *trattoria,* generally a rather simple, family-run place where the emphasis is on wholesome, appetizing food. At *rosticcerie* or a *tavola calda* you can get snacks or dinners at the counter. In tourist cities, restaurants offer a limited-choice, fixed-price *menu turistico,* inclusive of cover and service charges which would otherwise increase your check by 15 to 20 percent; quality and quantity vary. Where we list restaurants (E), (M), or (I), this indicates Expensive, Moderate or Inexpensive (averaging 70,000 lire and up, 45,000 and 30,000 per person respectively for a full meal). Fish is generally expensive, as are truffled dishes (*con tartufi,* or *tartufato*). Items marked "S.Q." are priced by weight. It's wise to reserve for the evening meal; your hotel porter will call for you. Most restaurants close one day a week.

Food and Drink. Italian cuisine, truly distinctive and generally recognized as one of the world's best, is complex and colorful. You're likely to find it more subtle and delicate here than in Italian restaurants abroad. There are a few basic differences between northern and southern Italian cooking, while central Italian food generally combines the best features of both. For example, *polenta,* a cornmeal mush, and *risotto* are more popular than pasta in the North. Similarly, while butter is widely used in the North, olive oil predominates in the South.

Pasta is the staple southern Italian dish and relies heavily on tomatoes as a seasoning. Regional variations include *pesto,* Genoa's famous sauce of garlic, oil and fresh basil.

The main meal, either lunch or dinner, consists of several courses and may start with an *antipasto.* One summertime delicacy is *melone* (melon) or *fichi* (fresh figs) with *prosciutto* (spicy ham). Next is the first course, which may be a *minestra* (soup), such as *minestrone* or *tortellini in brodo* (pasta in broth), or *asciutta,* either risotto or pasta. The main course, either *pesce* (fish) or *carne* (meat) comes next. Ready-to-serve dishes are the *piatti del giorno* (dish of the day); they usually include some local specialties and are well worth ordering. Although good beef is hard to come by in Italy, Florentine steaks are tender and tasty. The Italians work wonders with veal, pork, chicken and lamb. Look for *bocconcini di vitello, osso buco, pollo alla diavola, pollo alla cacciatora* and *abbacchio.* Fish specialties include *triglia alla livornese* (mullet in tomato sauce), *baccala alla vicentina* (salt cod in butter sauce), and *pesce spada* (swordfish).

Vegetables, salads and fruit are fresh from the market. Order *melanzane* (eggplant), *peperoni* (sweet peppers) or, for a light lunch, *insalata caprese,* a colorful dish of ripe tomatoes and mozzarella, garnished with basil.

Pizza is probably Italy's most successful culinary export. The commonest type is *pizza alla napoletana,* with tomatoes, mozzarella, anchovies and oregano. *Pizza margherita* has more cheese and no anchovies. *Pizza ai funghi* (with mushrooms) or *alla capricciosa* (with prosciutto, egg, and olives) are variations. Similar dishes to order at a *pizzeria* are *crostini* (a kind of mozzarella toast) and *calzone* (an envelope of dough baked around a stuffing of prosciutto and mozzarella). Pizza can substitute for pasta as a first course.

Italian cheeses are excellent; ask for the local cheese, which may be a *caciotta* (firm and mild), *pecorino* (hard, sharp), or *provolone* (hard, either sharp or mild). *Gorgonzola, mozzarella* and *parmigiano* need no introduction.

Italy's wines are as varied as her cuisine. Try local wines wherever you go. Generally speaking the best reds come from the North, among them Barbera, Grignolino, Barolo and Valpolicella. Sparkling red Lambrusco is a perfect accompaniment to a heavy meal *alla bolognese.* Among the whites, Soave is famous, but you should try two other whites from the Veneto region, Tokai and Prosecco. Chianti is Central Italy's best-known wine, but there are also the dry white Orvieto, fruity golden Frascati or Velletri, and the reds and whites of Umbria. Calabria produces heady Cirò reds and whites, while Sicily offers Corvo di Salaparuta reds and whites, and Regaleali white. Some Italian spumantes are worthy alternatives to champagne. Along with an overwhelming variety of aperitifs and sweet liqueurs, Italy is known for *grappa,* an *aquavit.*

SECURITY. It goes without saying that in the country that perfected purse snatching you must at all times keep your passport and any money you have on you in a secure place; leave what you can in the hotel safe. Wear shoulder bags and cameras bandolier fashion. Beware of pickpockets in railway stations, in trains and on buses. If you think you might doze off on the train, secure your valuables first. Avoid offers of food or drink. Whenever you pay for something— ticket, meal or souvenir—always check your change carefully.

TIPPING. Charges for service are included in all hotel bills and restaurant checks. In general, tip chambermaids 1,000 lire per day (3,000–4,000 per week), bellboys 1,000–2,000 lire. Give room service waiters from 1,000 lire, and the doorman who calls a cab 500 lire. Figure on 15 percent for the concierge if he has provided extra services. Checkroom attendants and theater ushers expect 500–1,000 lire, washroom attendants 200–300 lire. A service charge is included on restaurant bills, but add another 5 percent for the waiter in cities and resorts. Taxi drivers expect a few hundred lire extra. Railway porters charge a fixed rate for each piece of luggage. If your suitcases are unusually heavy, or if you keep your porter waiting for longer than normal, an additional 1,000 lire will be appreciated. Service station attendants are tipped a few hundred lire if they do more than fill the tank of your car. Guides should be tipped about 1,000 lire per person, more if very good.

MAIL. Air mail to the U.S. is 850 lire for lightweight paper and envelope, to England 600 lire. Postcards are 600 and 350 lire respectively, but pay letter rate if you write more than a few words. You can buy stamps only at tobacco shops and post offices. Check postal rates—a rise is due.

CLOSING TIMES. In Rome, Naples and the south, shops are usually open from 9 to 1, closed from 1 to 4.30, then open again from 4.30 to 8. In the northern cities, this siesta is either not observed or considerably abbreviated. At all events, there will be individual variations in this individualistic land of *dolce far niente.* Banking hours are from 8.30 to 1.30 mornings, 3 to 4. Banks are closed on Saturdays. Exchange (*cambio*) offices, however, have store hours. Museum hours vary greatly, and it's best to check locally. All are open at least in the morning; some close Monday. Vatican Museums close Sundays and religious holidays. Rome shops close Saturday afternoons from June through Sept., Monday mornings in other months. Churches keep their own mysterious hours and are a law unto themselves.

USEFUL ADDRESSES. Embassies: *American,* Via Vittorio Veneto 119, Rome; *British,* Via XX Settembre 80A, Rome; *Canadian,* Via Zara; *Irish,* Via del Pozzetto 108; *Australian,* Via Alessandria 215.

Emergency phone number for police, fire, or ambulance: 113.

The addresses of *Wagons-Lits/Cook* are: Via Buoncompagni 25, Rome; Piazza Strozzi 14, Florence; Piazzetta dei Leoncini 289, Venice; Via Porta degli Archi 12, Genoa; Via Depretis 126, Naples; Viale XX Settembre 45, Catania; Piazza San Carlo 132, Turin; Corso Nuvoloni 19, San Remo.

The most widespread national organization for all branches of touring is the CIT *(Compagnia Italiana Turismo)* which also has excellent interpreter service at every branch.

GETTING AROUND ITALY. By Plane. Italian mainland cities are linked by air with each other and with Sicily and Sardinia. Services are operated by *Alitalia, ATI,* and *Alisarda.* Bookings for all domestic flights can be made at any travel agency.

By Train. The state owned *Ferrovie delle Stato,* usually known by its initials FS, extends all over the country and into Sicily which is linked by train ferries across the Straits of Messina. There are also railway services in Sardinia. All main lines and many minor ones are electrified. The principal expresses are among the best in Europe—fast, comfortable and reliable. There are three types of long and medium distance trains—Rapido (Rap in timetables), Express (Espresso) and Fast (Diretto). A supplement is payable for travel in all Rapidos which, incidentally, may not be used for very short journeys. It is essential for Rapidos and advisable at all times to make seat reservations in advance at stations or travel agencies.

Although much new rolling stock has been introduced in recent years, there are still quite a number of older carriages in operation. Sleeping cars and dining and buffet cars are operated by *Wagons-Lits* but the couchettes services are operated by the railway itself.

Italian trains are generally very busy, especially at holiday periods. In 2nd. class they are usually very crowded. Choose compact bags for easy overhead storage. Porters are scarce, luggage carts non-existent.

Pride of the Italian system is the new *Direttissima* (it means very fast) line between Florence and Rome; a masterpiece of engineering which has taken many years and vast capital expenditure to construct. Years behind in construction, it won't be completed for another year or so. It has already reduced the traveling time between the two cities and helped relieve the very congested older route.

For the independent traveler anxious to see a lot we recommend the *Travel at Will* ticket which gives unlimited travel on all FS trains including TEE and Rapidos (with first class tickets) without additional charge. This is also valid on ferries between Reggio di Calabria and Messina in Italy. Issued for 8, 15, 21 and 30 days, the cost in 1st. class is $100, $140, $175, and $200 respectively. 2nd. class tickets cost $75, $85, $110, and $130 respectively. Children under 12 travel at half fare; those under four travel free.

By Bus. There is a good network of bus services, details of which are in a timetable published by ANAC, Piazza Esquilino 29, Rome (tel. 06–463383). For example: regular, year-round service between Rome or Florence and Siena; May–Oct. Rome to Assisi; Jul.–Aug. Rome to Naples, Pompeii and Amalfi. CIAT also operate a variety of inclusive tours by motor coach.

By Car. Drive on the right side of the road; that's the rule, even if the Italians show a preference for the middle (one of the reasons why automobile insurance is compulsory in Italy). Gasoline (petrol) costs about 1,300 lire per liter for super. Petrol discount coupons are again available to tourists, along with autostrada toll discounts. Apply at ACI frontier offices or from AA/RAC and Barclays Bank. Passport and car log book required. Except on autostrada, gas stations close at lunchtime and take turns closing Sat. afternoons, Sun.

It is compulsory to exhibit a red warning triangle at a reasonable distance from your car should you stop—a useful precaution on narrow and winding roads. The triangle will be lent you at Italian frontier posts against a small deposit which will be refunded when leaving the country. *ACI* offers emergency breakdown service. Throughout Italy, dial 116 for quick towing and/or repairs, charge-controlled by ACI. Carry your own club card or obtain international carnet.

The Italian Automobile Club has built a chain of wayside motels or *autostelli,* in effect, small second-class hotels for motorists. Beginning in central Italy, they are strategically located along highways south along both coasts to Sicily. For a complete list, write to Motels, Via Marsala 8, Rome. Rates vary from about 40,000–60,000 lire for a double room with bath. The AGIP motels are consistently clean and functional, with rates up to 100,000 lire.

There are several motorways crossing Italy, most scenic of which is the *Autostrada del Sole* joining Milan and Reggio Calabria; others link Turin-Venice, Rome-Civitavecchia, Milan-Genoa, Florence-Pisa, Naples-Bari, Milan-Como—still growing. These are all toll roads so your ticket must be kept and given up when quitting the autostrada. The speed limit throughout Italy varies according to the engine capacity of the car. Get the Italian Tourist Office's invaluable *Traveler's Handbook* to discover what the individual limits are. Autostrada costs are also variable—but you will find that they are also listed in the handbook.

Car Hire. In most large cities and resorts you'll find a branch of *Avis* or *Hertz*, with either self-driven cars or chauffeur service, and with pick-up points at railroad stations and airports. (Reservations through travel agents or directly.) Alitalia and Avis offer a Jet-Drive combination: car included in ticket price; seven-day, two-adult minimum.

Rome, the Eternal

Popes, Vandals, the Borgias and Napoleon, Garibaldi, Michelangelo and Mussolini, and of course the Ancient Romans themselves, all have left their physical and spiritual mark on Rome, but though she keeps the glory of an ancient day about her, she remains a wellspring of creative energy; in short, she really *is* the Eternal City.

You might as well begin your search for Rome in the Piazza Venezia. You can't avoid the huge white Victor Emmanuel Monument, known to the Italians as the Altare della Patria (the Country's Altar). The unknown soldier is buried here, and all official ceremonies take place in this square. Behind it stands the Church of Ara Coeli and Michelangelo's stairs lead you to the Campidoglio, Rome's City Hall. Behind the Campidoglio lie Rome's greatest archeological treasures, the ruins of the Imperial Fora and the Roman Forum.

Highly recommended from here is the half mile walk down the Via dei Fori Imperiali to the most stupendous monument of ancient Rome —the Colosseum. See it at dawn, at sunset, or at night with the spotlights illuminating the old stone. And walk to the top for an impression of the real size of this stadium, which used to seat 50,000.

Outside the Colosseum, you'll pass the Arch of Constantine, hidden by scaffolding while experts study anti-pollution measures. The Baths of Caracalla, grandest of Rome's ruined public baths, are nearby, as are the ruined imperial palaces of the Palatine and Celian hills.

The Highlights

Here are some other sights of Rome you should try to fit in even if your time is limited: the Campidoglio, with its views and the Capitoline Museums; the Piazza del Quirinale, with the Quirinale Palace, residence of the Italian president, and the fine fountain of Castor and Pollux; the Porta Pia, a huge gateway designed by Michelangelo; Piazza Navona, much as it was in the 17th century, and Bernini's great Fountain of the Rivers; the Church of Sant'Agnese fuori le Mura, with its maze of third-century catacombs, a refuge of the early Christians; the Fountain of Trevi, where a coin tossed into the huge basin guarantees your return to toss another one; the bustling Piazza Barberini, with its Fountain of the Triton, designed by Bernini in 1640; the macabre

Church of the Capuchin Monks (Santa Maria della Concezione), with its subterranean chapels full of skeletons, after which sobering experience you may look with a jaded eye on the nearby Via Veneto. Once a great cosmopolitan boulevard, it has lost a lot of its luster in recent years, but its sidewalk cafés still come to life on pleasant evenings. As a tonic antidote to this, we recommend a stroll through the Trastevere region, where you will find "the Romans of Rome", blunt, uninhibited, sharp-eyed, hawk-nosed, friendly, sincere, often beautiful and seldom varnished. They mix with American and English bohemian types in the atmospheric Piazza di Santa Maria.

You will, of course, want to explore the Piazza di Spagna, with its lovely Bernini fountain and the famous Spanish steps which ascend past Babington's tea room and the house in which Keats died to the Church of Trinitá dei Monti. Nearby is the Pincio, Rome's original public gardens, and the enchanting Villa Borghese park, with its fountains, glades, statues and museums. If you're lucky, the Galleria Borghese museum will have been reopened by 1987 with its fine art works again on view. The sculpture collection on the ground floor boasts some stunning works by Bernini, and Canova's nude of Pauline Borghese, Napoleon's sister, reclining so enticingly on her couch. The Villa Giulia Etruscan museum is outstanding.

Two major antiquities demand your attention before proceeding to St. Peter's and the Vatican. They are the Castel Sant'Angelo, built by the Emperor Hadrian in 135, a most impressive castle from whose terrace you will have all Rome at your feet; and the Pantheon, rebuilt by Hadrian as a pagan temple, the best-preserved monument of Roman antiquity.

If you have time, visit some of Rome's magnificent churches: the Gesù, Sant'Ignazio and the splendid Santa Maria Maggiore. In San Pietro in Vincoli you'll find Michelangelo's famous statue of Moses.

The Vatican City

Since the Lateran Accord of 1929 the Vatican City has been an independent and sovereign state. When you step into the great square before St. Peter's, you are on Vatican territory, though, of course, you can enter the basilica, the Borgia apartments, the Sistine Chapel, and the museums without formalities. A bus runs from the Information Office on the left of St. Peter's, through the Vatican gardens to the museums. Shorts, miniskirts and bare shoulders are taboo in the Vatican (and in churches generally).

San Pietro in Vaticano, better known as St. Peter's (it is not a cathedral), is the largest church in the world and a fitting climax to Rome, no matter what your religion. The enormous Piazza San Pietro, which took Bernini 10 years to build, has held as many as 400,000 people within the confines of its quadruple colonnade; it is one of the world's most beautiful squares. The church had its beginnings about 326, when the Emperor Constantine built a basilica here over the tomb of St. Peter, but it was not until 1626 that St. Peter's stood as we know it today, a masterpiece of Renaissance architecture and art. Bramante, Raphael, Michelangelo, Maderno and Antonio Sangallo were all busy beautifying this church at the time of their deaths. Note the mosaic by Giotto in the portico, Michelangelo's *Pietà* in the first chapel, the reliquary of St. Peter's Chair by Bernini and the Confessional Altar marking the burial place of St. Peter. Visit the Treasury and then take the elevator to the roof of the basilica. From here the incomparable dome soars for another 308 feet, and you can clearly view the Piazza and the approach. From the roof a short stairway leads to a gallery with a breathtaking view of the interior. The climb from here to the lantern

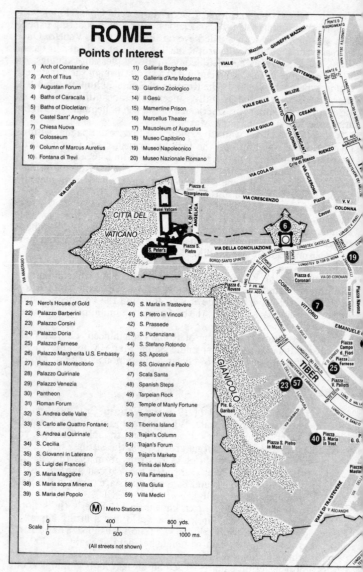

ROME
Points of Interest

1) Arch of Constantine
2) Arch of Titus
3) Augustan Forum
4) Baths of Caracalla
5) Baths of Diocletian
6) Castel Sant' Angelo
7) Chiesa Nuova
8) Colosseum
9) Column of Marcus Aurelius
10) Fontana di Trevi
11) Galleria Borghese
12) Galleria d'Arte Moderna
13) Giardino Zoologico
14) Il Gesù
15) Mamertine Prison
16) Marcellus Theater
17) Mausoleum of Augustus
18) Museo Capitolino
19) Museo Napoleonico
20) Museo Nazionale Romano

21) Nero's House of Gold
22) Palazzo Barberini
23) Palazzo Corsini
24) Palazzo Doria
25) Palazzo Farnese
26) Palazzo Margherita U.S. Embassy
27) Palazzo di Montecitorio
28) Palazzo Quirinale
29) Palazzo Venezia
30) Pantheon
31) Roman Forum
32) S. Andrea delle Valle
33) S. Carlo alle Quattro Fontane;
    S. Andrea al Quirinale
34) S. Cecilia
35) S. Giovanni in Laterano
36) S. Luigi dei Francesi
37) S. Maria Maggiore
38) S. Maria sopra Minerva
39) S. Maria del Popolo
40) S. Maria in Trastevere
41) S. Pietro in Vincoli
42) S. Prassede
43) S. Pudenziana
44) S. Stefano Rotondo
45) SS. Apostoli
46) SS. Giovanni e Paolo
47) Scala Santa
48) Spanish Steps
49) Tarpeian Rock
50) Temple of Manly Fortune
51) Temple of Vesta
52) Tiberina Island
53) Trajan's Column
54) Trajan's Forum
55) Trajan's Markets
56) Trinità dei Monti
57) Villa Farnesina
58) Villa Giulia
59) Villa Medici

Ⓜ Metro Stations

Scale
0   400   800 yds.
0   500   1000 ms.

(All streets not shown)

is claustrophobic and very taxing. Save the Vatican Grottos for last; their exit is outside the basilica.

PRACTICAL INFORMATION FOR ROME

GETTING AROUND ROME. By bus. The city's extensive ATAC bus network would be an ideal way to get around if it wasn't usually overcrowded and so frequently blocked by traffic. Avoid the rush hours: 8 to 9, 1 to

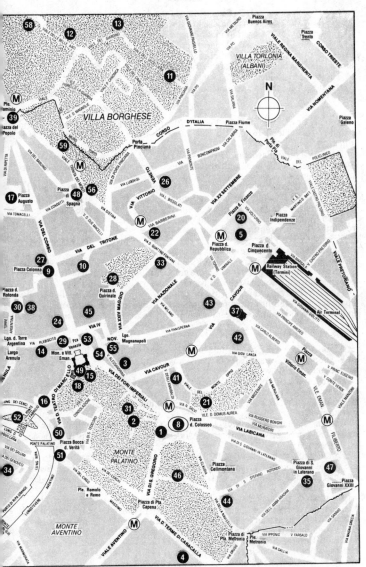

2, 7 to 8. The ATAC booth in front of Termini station provides information, sells a transport map, touts an inexpensive sightseeing tour, and offers weekly tourist tickets. Fares about 600 lire, buy tickets before you get on the bus.

By metro. The metro has two lines, the fast new Line A and the slower Line B. They connect at Termini station and provide fast transportation to many points of interest. Fares about 600 lire. Have exact change for ticket machines, or buy books of tickets at tobacconists or newsstands.

By taxi. Taxis wait at stands or are called by phone; extra charges for night service, luggage, Sundays and holidays. Use Yellow cabs only.

Tourist information. *EPT*, Via Parigi 5 (tel. 463748).

HOTELS. Rome is an all-year-round city, well provided with hotels, but it's always a good idea to make a reservation in advance. To get a clear picture of total costs, ask for quotations of the inclusive rate. As for the top-level hotels in the Italian capital, they are all excellent. All better hotels are airconditioned but systems may be turned off at night.

The *EPT*, the official tourist office, operates a hotel information service at Termini railway station, Fiumicino airport, and at autostrada exits to Rome.

Deluxe

Ambasciatori, Via Vittorio Veneto 70 (tel. 473831). Quieter, smaller and elegant. An Italhotel; bright, spacious rooms, some facing Via Veneto and U.S. Embassy.

Bernini, Piazza Barberini 23 (tel. 463051). Posh modern hotel in one of the busiest squares of Rome, with the famous Triton fountain. Attractively furnished, spotless rooms.

Cavalieri Hilton, Via Cadolo (tel. 3151). Splendid panoramic views and *La Pergola* restaurant-nightclub on the roof terrace. 400 rooms and suites on 11 floors, two more restaurants, pool, tennis in 7-acre park outside center.

Eden, Via Ludovisi 49 (tel. 480551). Near the Via Veneto; with very fine rooftop bar, restaurant; central but quiet.

Excelsior, Via Vittorio Veneto 125 (tel. 4708). It's bustling, palatial and very comfortable; *La Cupola* restaurant and pleasant bar.

Grand, Via Vittorio Emanuele Orlando 3 (tel. 4709). A big place, like the Excelsior, catering in general to a more conservative, solid clientele. It's Rome's most elegant and expensive. Grill room; *Rallye* restaurant.

Hassler, Piazza Trinità dei Monti 6 (tel. 6792651). Scenic location above Spanish Steps; well-furnished rooms, generally good service. Spectacular view, indifferent food in penthouse restaurant. Highly recommended. No credit cards.

Expensive

Atlante, Via Vitelleschi 34 (tel. 6544738). Near St. Peter's, it has attractive, well-equipped rooms and panoramic rooftop restaurant. Free pickup from the airport on request.

Boston, Via Lombardia (tel. 4751592). This hotel has the blessing of a quiet location that's a few steps from the Via Veneto and a few more to the main shopping district. It's nicely decorated and quite comfortable, with a good restaurant.

Colonna Palace, Piazza Montecitorio (tel. 6781341). Very central, near Parliament and popular with politicians. Modern comforts in attractive old palace. No restaurant.

Flora, Via Veneto (tel. 497821). The décor is rather dated, but the bedrooms are ample and comfortable, and many have a view of the Villa Borghese. Service retains the old-world attentiveness that's becoming a lost art in more modern, anonymous hotels.

Forum, Via Tor dei Conti (tel. 6792446). A Renaissance palace near Piazza Venezia, converted into a fine hotel and furnished in lovely textures of wood and velvet. Rooms aren't large, but they're quiet and elegant. The indoor-outdoor rooftop dining terrace has a fantastic view of the Roman Forum.

Giulio Cesare, Via degli Scipioni 287 (tel. 310244). Just out of the mainstream, but within walking distance of some sights, handy to metro. Elegant, well-run. Lavish buffet breakfast, reasonable rates.

Hotel De La Ville, Via Sistina (tel. 6798941). Once the 'in' place to stay, it still provides very pleasant lodgings in an excellent location cheek by jowl with the deluxe Hassler. There's a lovely garden, too. It's owned by the British Grand Metropolitan Group.

Inghilterra, Via Bocca di Leone (tel. 672161). Garni. In the heart of the shopping district, a stone's throw from the Spanish Steps. The atmosphere and charm of a posh private club. The bar is a popular rendezvous.

Jolly, Corso d'Italia (tel. 8495). Just a few steps from the top of the Via Veneto, and on the edge of the Villa Borghese. A strikingly-modern burnished glass-and-steel building. The rooms looking out onto the umbrella pines in the park are worth the extra charge; all are completely soundproofed, with the modern, functional furnishings typical of the Jolly chain.

Londra e Cargill, Piazza Sallustio (tel. 473871). Occupies a thoroughly-renovated palazzo on an interesting piazza about five minutes' walk from the

Via Veneto. The interiors are elegantly modern; rooms are good-size and attractively decorated.

Lord Byron, Via de Notaris (tel. 3609541). A small hotel that shuns groups. The relaxed, intimate atmosphere of a private villa. It's near the National Gallery of Modern Art, on the edge of the Villa Borghese and the Parioli district, a bit out of the way, but in delightful surroundings. Le Jardin restaurant is a luxurious haven of classic cuisine. A member of the Relais et Chateaux hotels. Book well in advance.

Plaza, Via del Corso (tel. 672101). A big old hotel with various types of rooms. On the busiest shopping street in the center of town and handy to everything.

Quirinale, Via Nazionale (tel. 479901). There's a feeling of restrained luxury in this hotel on the very central Via Nazionale. The rooms are welcoming and the lovely garden courtyard is a delightful oasis. The hotel has its own private entrance to the Rome Opera House next door.

Raphael, Largo Febo (tel. 6569051). This smallest, ivy-clad hotel is on a tiny piazza a few steps from Piazza Navona in the center of Old Rome. It's a favorite with top-level politicians (the Senate's nearby). Rooms are rather small but comfortable, and there's a roof garden.

Regina Carlton, Via Veneto (tel. 4758841). The usual advantages of a convenient location together with tastefully-cheerful décor and attentive service make this a good choice.

Moderate

Arcangelo, Via Boezio 15 (tel. 311098). Garni. Welcoming and well-kept small hotel near St. Peter's.

Britannia, Via Napoli 64 (tel. 465785). Garni. A small, attractive hotel a block from the Rome Opera House in the better part of the Termini Station area.

Carriage, Via delle Carrozze (tel. 6795166). Garni. Quite small but very well located in the main shopping district near the Piazza di Spagna.

Columbus, Via della Conciliazione (tel. 6564874). A large, well-furnished hotel in a handsome 15th-century palace just down the street from St Peter's. Room standards and prices vary.

Esperia, Via Nazionale 22 (tel. 487245). Garni. This good-size hotel is on one of the city's main thoroughfares and is handy to everything.

Fontana, Piazza di Trevi 96 (tel. 6786113). At Trevi Fountain. Small, well furnished, with roof garden.

Gregoriana, Via Gregoriana (tel. 6794269). Garni. There are only 19 rooms in this delightful hotel on an interesting street of high-fashion *ateliers* near the Spanish Steps. Book well in advance.

Internazionale, Via Sistina 79 (tel. 6793047). Garni. Another smallish hotel on a famous street near Santi Trinità dei Monti. Rooms are well-furnished and the atmosphere is pleasant. Book ahead.

Locarno, Via della Penna 22 (tel. 3610841). Central, near Piazza del Popolo; solid, older, comfortable hotel.

La Residenza, Via Emilia 22 (tel. 6799592). Garni. A very comfortable small hotel in a former town house with a garden, only a block away from the Via Veneto.

Siena, Via Sant'Andrea delle Fratte 33 (tel. 6796121). Very central, near Spanish Steps; small, no restaurant.

Inexpensive

Aventino, Via San Domenico 10 (tel. 572831). Garni. Like staying in a private villa in one of Rome's quietest, prettiest districts, on the Aventine Hill. The Forum is within walking distance; buses and the Metro are nearby.

Dinesen, Via Porta Pinciana 18 (tel. 4751524). Near the Via Veneto; spotless.

Portoghesi, Via dei Portoghesi (tel. 6564231). Central, picturesque location in Old Rome; comfort and atmosphere. No restaurant.

Sicilia Daria, Via Sicilia 24 (tel. 493841). Garni. Comfortable pension occupying part of a palazzo near the Via Veneto.

 RESTAURANTS. There are a very great many deluxe restaurants in Rome where they can serve any specialty, Italian or international, with a fine flourish of silver and linen and a whopping *conto* (check) at the end. But if it's true Roman and/or family-style cuisine you want, then try the *trattorias* (from the Latin word *tractare,* meaning "to treat"), smallish and unassuming, where your bill will run about 30,000 lire for a full meal with a carafe of wine. Fixed-price tourist menus may be scanty and unimaginative. All restaurants close one day a week; many close for mid-August vacation.

Expensive

Alberto Ciarla, Piazza San Cosimato 40 (tel. 588668). Evenings only. Closed Sunday. In Trastevere, seafood restaurant *par excellence.*

Al Vicario, Via Uffizi del Vicario 31 (tel. 6791152). Closed Sunday and August. In this eminently-comfortable and tasteful locale, you may find the food a disappointment; stay with the classic dishes.

George's, Via Marche 7 (tel. 484575). Closed Sunday and August. Considered by some a bit passé, it's still a fine restaurant with one of the best wine lists in Rome and a delightful summer garden.

Hostaria dell'Orso, Via dei Soldati 25 (tel. 6564250). Dinner only. Closed Sundays and in August. Handsome décor, so-so food, very expensive.

Le Jardin, in the Lord Byron Hotel, Via de Notaris 5 (tel. 3609541). A select menu of beautifully-prepared dishes in an elegant atmosphere.

Papa Giovanni, Via dei Sediari (tel. 6565308). Tiny and excellent.

Passetto, Via Zanardelli 14 (tel. 659937). Near Piazza Navona; a classic place for excellent food and courteous service.

Rallye, in Grand Hotel, Via V. Orlando (tel. 4709). Outstanding.

Ranieri, Via Mario dei Fiori 26 (tel. 6791592). Closed Sunday and two weeks in August. Founded more than a century ago by Queen Victoria's chef, it hasn't changed a bit since then. The food is Italian-international but you go mainly for the atmosphere.

Sabatini, Piazza Santa Maria in Trastevere 13 (tel. 582026). Beautiful setting, outdoor tables in summer, Roman cuisine, popular with tourists.

El Toulà, Via della Lupa (tel. 6781196). Closed Sunday and August. Absolutely tops for ambience, cuisine and service, another jewel in the exclusive chain created by Alfredo Beltrame, whose chefs exalt and elaborate on the themes of *alta cucina italiana.*

Moderate

Alfredo alla Scrofa, Via della Scrofa 104 (tel. 6540163). The best of Rome's three Alfredos.

Angelino, Tor Margana 37 (tel. 6783328). Near the Piazza Venezia; a favorite of the self-styled *intellighentsia;* with outside tables on pretty piazza.

Archimede, Via Santa Chiara 31 (tel. 655216). Closed Sunday. Near the Pantheon; classic Roman dining.

Barroccio, Via dei Pastini (tel. 6793797). Near the Pantheon; has something of a Tuscan accent.

Il Buco, Via Sant'Ignazio 8 (tel. 6793298). Recommended for its fine Tuscan steaks.

La Carbonara, Campo dei Fiori 23 (tel. 656483). On historic piazza in Old Rome. Good Roman food.

Giovanni, Via Marche 19 (tel. 493576). Two blocks behind the Excelsior hotel and excellent.

Grappolo d'Oro, Piazza della Cancelleria 80. Excellent Roman specialties at reasonable prices.

La Maiella, Piazza Sant'Apollinare (tel. 6564174). Closed Sunday. Fine country-style cooking.

Al Moro, Vicolo delle Bollette (tel. 6783495). Near the Trevi fountain and popular; best to reserve.

La Rampa, off Piazza di Spagna (tel. 6782621). Behind the American Express office; fine pastas at moderate prices.

Regno di Re Ferdinando, Via Banchi Nuovi 8 (tel. 6541167). In Old Rome, inconspicuous entrance, Neapolitan tavern.

Tana del Grillo, Salita del Grillo 6 (tel. 6798705). Closed Sunday. Near the Forum; fine food in a *simpatico* atmosphere.

Vecchia Roma, Piazza Campitelli (tel. 6565451). Near the Piazza Venezia. Closed Wednesday. A somewhat pricey favorite.

Inexpensive

Buca di Ripetta, Via Ripetta 36 (tel. 6789578). Closed Friday. A tiny restaurant a few steps from the Piazza del Popolo. It's very popular; get there early.

Da Catena Ai Due Scalini, Via G. B. Morgagni (tel. 363819). Closed Sunday and August. Near the Policlinico and University. A typical Roman eating-place.

Da Enzo, Vicolo Scavolino 72 (tel. 6790974). Closed Sunday. Near Trevi Fountain, popular for hearty food; low prices.

Otello alla Concordia, Via della Croce 81 (tel. 6791178). Closed Sunday. There's nothing more refreshing than lunch in the vine-shaded courtyard of this old favorite in the center of the shopping district.

Pierluigi, Piazza Ricci (tel. 6561302). Off Via Monserrato in Old Rome. Cordial atmosphere, good Roman dishes.

La Pentola, Piazza Firenze 20 (tel. 6542607). Closed Saturday and July 15 to August 15. Politicians from the nearby Chamber of Deputies (Montecitorio) flock here for the day's special. Order the sherbet for dessert.

Polese, Piazza Sforza Cesarini 40 (tel. 6561709). Near Chiesa Nuova; straightforward cuisine, outdoor tables in summer.

Spaghetteria, Via Arno 38 (tel. 855535). Closed Monday and August. In the Salario district and a favorite with night owls, but popular at all times for garlic bread, more than 30 kinds of spaghetti, and low, low prices.

Vecchia Roma da Severino, Via Monserrato 96 (tel. 6569383). Closed Monday. Near Piazza Farnese, family-run and fine.

 ENTERTAINMENT. One of Rome's nicest places for dancing is the *Cabalà,* atop the *Hostaria dell'Orso.* More contemporary in atmosphere and action is the *Jackie-O,* Via Buoncompagni, very much *in* with celebrities and such. The cellar of the *Ulpia* is usually thronged with a lively after-dinner crowd, while the *Open Gate,* Via San Nicolo, just off Via Bissolati, is a glittering, *art deco* restaurant-piano bar with a solid, moneyed clientele. Among the discos, *Cage aux Folles,* Via Gregoriana, near Spanish Steps, and *Veleno,* Via Sardegna, attract a young crowd; *Easy Going,* Via delle Purificazione, is a gay disco; *Piper,* Via Tagliamento, is vast and frenetic. For a full-fledged nightclub with floor show, *Paradise,* Via Mario dei Fiori 95. Usually the last to close for the night, *Club 84,* Via Emilia 84, is always lively. As nightclubs everywhere are ephemeral and many close during the summer, *ask your hotel porter.*

Organized Rome-By-Night tours are dreary, expensive affairs. Better to arrange with a taxi driver to show you some of the piazzas and monuments, then have him drop you off at a nightclub or disco of *your* choice.

Opera fans will find the opera house at Via Viminale; performances in the winter only. Tickets go on sale only two days before performances but can be ordered by mail. In summer there are open-air operas, concerts and ballets. Concerts of classical music abound throughout the year; many are held in churches. There's plenty of pop music and jazz, too. Ask your hotel porter, EPT office, or buy *This Week in Rome* bulletin at newsstands.

 MUSEUMS. Part of Rome's enormous artistic heritage is on view in its monuments and museums. Monuments such as the Forum, the Colosseum and the Pantheon are generally open from 9 A.M. until one hour before sunset. Others, such as Castel Sant'Angelo, are open until 2 P.M. only. Museum hours vary, but generally are from 9 A.M. to 2 P.M. Most monuments and museums close Monday, city-run museums Tuesday but open some afternoons and evenings. The majority are free one day a week. Always check with Rome EPT office or your hotel porter.

Gabinetto Nazionale delle Stampe, Via della Lungara 230. An important collection of prints from 15th to 19th centuries, housed in handsome Villa della Farnesina (decorated by Raphael).

Galleria Borghese, Villa Borghese. Canova's famous statue of Pauline Borghese, lots of Berninis and magnificent paintings. May still be closed.

Galleria Colonna, Via della Pilotta 17. The Colonna family collection, on view in their magnificent palace. Saturday only.

Galleria Doria Pamphili, Piazza Collegio Romano 1A. Art treasures of a patrician family. Open Tues., Fri., Sat., Sun. 10 to 1.

Galleria Nazionale dell'Arte Antica (in two locations). Palazzo Barberini, Via Quattro Fontane. Houses a rich collection of 13th- to 16th-century paintings. Palazzo Corsini, Via della Lungara. Contains the 17th- and 18th-century sections.

Galleria Nazionale di Arte Moderna, Viale delle Belle Arti. An important collection of modern painting and sculpture. Many sections closed for renovation.

Keats and Shelley Memorial House, Piazza di Spagna. In the house where Keats lived, a collection of memorabilia.

Museo Baracco, Corso Vittorio 168. A fine collection of ancient sculptures.

Musei Capitolini, Piazza del Campidoglio. Twin museums that share an impressive collection of Greek and Roman antiquities.

Museo di Palazzo Venezia, Piazza Venezia 3. Captivating collection of Renaissance arts and crafts in 15th-century palace.

Museo Nazionale di Arte Orientale, Via Merulana 248. Objects from the Middle and Far East.

Museo Nazionale Romano, Via delle Terme di Diocleziano (Piazza Repubblica). In a monastery adapted from the Baths of Diocletian, a vast collection of antiquities. Currently being renovated and rearranged.

Museo Nazionale di Villa Giulia, Villa Borghese. Beautifully displays one of the world's great Etruscan collections.

Museo di Palazzo Venezia, Piazza Venezia. In a 15th-century palace; Renaissance arts and crafts.

Musei Vaticani, Viale Vaticano. Represents one of the most important collections of art of all ages that can be seen in the world today. The entrance fee includes admission to the Sistine Chapel, Michelangelo's masterpiece. The Vatican museums are closed on Sundays and religious holidays, but remain open on the last Sunday of the month, when admission is free. Winter hours are 9 A.M. to 2 P.M. Holy Week and July to Sept., 9 to 4.

Quirinale, Via Venti Settembre. Official residence of the president of Italy. Apply for entrance permission at Via Dataria 96.

SHOPPING. Start from the American Express on Piazza di Spagna, roam around the square, then head down the famous Via Condotti, exploring the irresistible Via Borgognona, Via Frattina and Via della Vite. You'll be fascinated by the sumptuous and expensive array of fine leather goods, jewels, fashions, silver and gift items all along the way.

For less extravagant shopping, the Via Tritone, Via del Corso, Via Ottaviano and Via Cola di Rienzo generally offer good buys. Antique fanciers will find gallery after gallery of tempting stuff on the Via del Babuino, leading from the Piazza di Spagna to the Piazza del Popolo, and on the Via Coronari.

Rosaries, medals and other religious mementos abound in the shops around the Vatican, on Piazza San Pietro and Via Porta Angelica.

For small gifts, look for charming old prints at the Piazza Fontanella Borghese, or in little shops around the Piazza di Spagna or behind the Pantheon.

Lazio and the Environs of Rome

All major tourist agencies in Rome feature bus tours through both the environs of Rome and the Lazio area. Recommended itineraries include the Appian Way, ancient Rome's "Queen of Roads", built over 2,000 years ago by Appius Claudius and literally walled with ancient monuments and Roman tombs; the Castelli Romani (Roman Castles); a day's trip to Albano, Frascati, Castel Gandolfo, Rocca di Papa and other fascinating towns of the Alban Hills.

Also suggested: Ostia Antica, port of ancient Rome, fascinating excavations of a once-flourishing city. (Nearby, modern Ostia is an unattractive and overcrowded beach suburb of the Eternal City.) Tivoli, with its ruins of Hadrian's sumptuous villa, and the fabulous Villa d'Este, with its indescribably lovely gardens, its beautiful fountains floodlit in summer; Anzio and Cassino, both completely rebuilt after the ravages of war; medieval Viterbo, and Tarquinia, famous for its medieval monuments, museum and the Etruscan Necropolis.

The shoreline of Lazio is a broad stretch of fine sand beach, dotted with resorts, all overcrowded in summer months. Such resorts as Santa Marinella, Terracina, Sperlonga, Gaeta and Formia attracted the ancient Romans, too. A 40-mile superhighway speeds motorists to the northern beaches and the Etruscan treasures of Cerveteri and Tarquinia. The island of Ponza, 30 miles off the coast, overflows in summer but is pleasant off-season (hydrofoil from Anzio April-September; car ferry from Formia year-round).

PRACTICAL INFORMATION FOR LAZIO

Don't schedule excursions outside Rome for Sundays, when the traffic is heavy and the restaurants crowded. Avoid beach resorts in July and August.

ANZIO. Beach resort. *Dei Cesari* (M), tel. 9848000. Bright, functional resort-type hotel with pool; on the beach. *Golfo* (M), tel. 930118. Large and modern; well equipped. *Lido Garda* (M), tel. 9845389. Modest but comfortable old hotel. **Restaurants.** *Da Alceste* (E), Piazza Sant'Antonio, tel. 9846744. Typical and good. *Romolo* (M), on the port, tel. 9844079. Fish specialties, some pricey.

CASTEL GANDOLFO. Restaurants. *Cacciatori* (M), tel. 9320993. Veranda with lake view. *Pagnanelli* (M), tel. 9360004. Good food and view.

CIVITAVECCHIA. Rome's port. *Sunbay Park* (E), tel. 22801. In Baia del Sole; smart and on beach with tennis, pools, nightclub and marina. *Mediterraneo* (M), tel. 23156. Plain but comfortable; nearly all of its 67 rooms with bath. **Restaurants.** *Villa dei Principi* (E), tel. 21220. Seaside veranda. *Cambusa* (M), tel. 23164. *Trattoria del Gobbo* (M), tel. 23163, both at port.

FIUGGI. Important spa. *Palazzo della Fonte* (L), tel. 55681. Posh, large and comfortable with thermal pool. *Silva Splendid* (E), tel. 55791. Very good. *Vallombrosa Majestic* (E), tel. 55531. Similarly good. *Imperiale* (M), tel. 55055. **Restaurant.** *Tre Abruzzi* (M), tel. 55945. In town.

FORMIA. Beach resort. *Castello Miramare* (E), at Pagnano, tel. 24238. Peaceful, tiny. *Miramare* (E), tel. 267181. Resort style, on sea. *Caposele* (M), tel. 21925. Attractive and modern with pool, beach and marina. **Restaurants.** *Da Italo* (M), tel. 21529. *Sirio* (M), tel. 21917.

FRASCATI. Restaurants. *Cacciani* (M), tel. 9420378. Classic and good. *Da Blasi* (M), Piazza del Mercato. On the road to Colonna is *Richelieu* (M), tel. 9485293, fine food. *Spartaco* (M), tel. 942031. Very good.

GAETA. Beach resort. *Le Rocce* (M), tel. 460606. On beach outside town. *Summit* (M), tel. 463087. Similar location, resort style. Both seasonal. **Restaurants.** *Salute* (M), tel. 460050. On port. *Sciamm* (M), tel. 465216. Good trattoria. *Taverna del Marinaio* (M), tel. 461342. Near port.

GROTTAFERRATA. Restaurants. *Castagneto* (M), tel. 9468289. On Montecompatri road. *Spuntino* (M), tel. 9459366. In town. *Squarciarelli* (M), tel. 9549580. Classic, popular. *Tuscolo* (M), tel. 9459325. Garden setting, good food.

MARINO. Restaurant. *Quattro Mori* (M). Hearty local specialties and heady wines.

NETTUNO. Beach resort and site of U.S. war cemetery. *Scacciapensieri* (M), tel. 9802428. On private beach with pool.

OSTIA. Restaurants. In Ostia Lido, *Negri* (M), tel. 5622295. Seafood. *Santa Barbara* (M), tel. 5601327. Seafood specialties, some pricey. At Ostia Antica archeological site are *Monumento* (M), tel. 5650021, and *Sbarco di Enea* (M), tel. 5650034. Good lunch stops.

PONZA. Island resort. *Chiaia di Luna* (E), tel. 80113. Bungalows overlooking the island's best beach with pool. *Bellavista* (M), tel. 80036. On beach.
Restaurants. *Aragosta, Ippocampo, Kambusa,* all (M).

SABAUDIA. Site of the popular Baia d'Argento resort colony. *Le Dune* (M), tel. 55551. Smart and modern, with pool, beach and tennis.
Restaurant. *Saporetti* (M), tel. 536024. Seasonal.

SAN FELICE CIRCEO. Elegant beach resort. *Maga Circe* (E), tel. 528014. With tennis and swimming pool. *Punta Rossa* (M), tel. 528069. White-washed bungalows in park; pool and beach.

SPERLONGA. Old town with fine beaches. *La Playa* (M), tel. 54106. On the beachfront with pool and balconied rooms. *Parkhotel Fiorelle* (M), tel. 54092. On the beach.

TARQUINIA. Site of Etruscan treasures. *Tarconte* (M), tel. 61272. Excellent for its category and recommended for location, service and restaurant.
Restaurants. *Giudizi* (M). Near the museum. *Solengo* (M). Fine restaurant of the Hotel Tarconte.

TERRACINA. Medieval town; beach resort. *L'Approdo* (M), tel. 727671. Modern; 40 rooms overlooking the sea and private beach.
Restaurants. *Hostaria Porto Salvo* (E), tel. 76251. On the sea. *La Capannina* (M), tel. 737339. Good seafood.

TIVOLI. Restaurants. *Cinque Statue* (M), tel. 20366. At Villa Gregoriana, good food in attractive setting. *Eden Sirene* (M), tel. 21352. Terrace with lovely view.

VITERBO. Restaurants. *Ciro* (M), tel. 34722. In medieval quarter, good food. *Aquilante* (E), tel. 31701. At La Quercia; best in the area; reserve ahead. *Grottino* (M). Good moderate trattoria. At Bagnaia are *Biscetti* (M), tel. 28252, also good, and *Checcarello* (M), tel. 28255, on piazza.

Piedmont and the Valle d'Aosta

Piedmont—the region of Turin and the Valle d'Aosta in the northwest corner of Italy—is a land of spectacular natural beauty with medieval villages in close proximity to Europe's highest mountains—Mont Blanc, Monte Rosa, the Gran Paradiso, and the Cervino, which last is Italian for the Matterhorn. The mountain valleys of Piedmont provide some of the finest skiing in the world. Your best bets as far as winter resorts are concerned are Sestriere, Courmayeur, Breuil-Cervina, Gressoney, Bardonecchia, Limone Piemonte, and Saint Vincent, where there is also a year-round casino. But remember that all these towns double as summer resorts for tourists in search of cool restful holidays as well as for those more ambitious characters who want to climb mountains.

Turin, Capital of Piedmont

Turin is an Italian city with a French accent. The Piedmontese are very proud of its beauty, calling it *La Parigi d'Italia,* the Paris of Italy. It is situated on the left bank of the Po on level ground and is dramatically encircled by the Alps. The city is characterized by its wide streets, its many beautiful squares and its fine buildings. The Via Roma, a handsome shopping street, connects three striking squares, the Piazza Carlo Felice, the Piazza San Carlo and the Piazza Castello. The Piazza San Carlo, with its two churches of Santa Cristina and San Carlo, is considered by some to be the best square in Italy after St. Mark's in Venice.

Things to see in Turin—the Castello or Palazzo Madama, housing the civic museum of ancient art; the Royal Palace with its sumptuously-furnished interiors and Royal Armory, one of the most important collections of armor in Europe; the Palazzo Carignano, a masterpiece of baroque architecture; the Egyptian museum and the Galleria Sabauda's fine paintings; and the bizarre Mole Antonelliana, built as a synagogue in 1863. Just outside Turin, the palace of Stupinigi is a baroque marvel, inside and out.

Along the left bank of the river Po, you'll see the Parco del Valentino and the 17th-century Castello del Valentino, thoroughly French in style. Farther along, close to the river's edge, is the medieval village and castle built for the Turin Exposition of 1884. A visit to this village with its furnished houses, stores and shops is fascinating.

Automobile-conscious Turin (the big Fiat works are nearby) boasts a fascinating automobile museum on the Corso Unita d'Italia, with gleaming ranks of shining antique roadsters.

Finally, don't miss Turin's unique relic of the Holy Shroud in the 15th-century white marble cathedral in the Piazza San Giovanni. In the monumental chapel is the urn containing one of the most precious relics of Christendom, the shroud in which Jesus Christ is said to have been wrapped when he was taken from the cross and which is believed to be marked with the imprint of his body.

PRACTICAL INFORMATION FOR PIEDMONT

HOTELS AND RESTAURANTS. Reserve well in advance, as Turin has a full calendar of trade fairs, art shows, Easter events for children and a folklore festival from June 23–26. Special package weekends are convenient. Hotels in the Piedmont winter and summer resorts are generally open between December 20-March 31, and from June 15 to September 30. Some also reopen for the Easter holidays. Be sure to check on these dates. Valle d'Aosta area hotels offer special bargains off season, mid-January–mid-April, September–late December.

AOSTA. Good ski facilities at nearby Conca di Pila. *Valle d'Aosta* (E), tel. 41845. 102 rooms, all with bath; part of Rank chain. *Ambassador* (M), tel. 42230. On outskirts, good.
Restaurants. *Brasserie Valdotaine* (E), tel. 32076. Rather elegant, very good. *Cavallo Bianco* (E), tel. 2214. One of Italy's best. *La Croisée* (M), tel. 2441.

BARDONECCHIA. Resort town. *Riki* (E), tel. 9353. 76 rooms, all with bath; modern, rather elegant hotel with pool. *De Geneys-Splendid* (M), tel. 99001. Comfortable, old hotel.

BREUIL-CERVINA. *Cristallo* (E), tel. 948121. Overlooks town; sunny and elegant. *Eurotel Cieloalto* (E), tel. 948755. Residence-type hotel; pool and disco. *Breuil* (M), tel. 94537. In village, cosy. *Hermitage* (M), tel. 948998. Smallish, very good. *Petit Palais* (M), tel. 949371. Near lifts, rustic. *Bucaneve* (I), tel. 94119. *Les Neiges d'Antan* (I), tel. 948775. Delightful place just outside town; fine restaurant.

COGNE. Winter and summer resort. *Miramonti* (M), tel. 74017. Small, comfortable. *Bellevue* (M), tel. 74022. Has chalet annex (E).
Restaurants. *Lou Ressignon* (M), tel. 74034. *Notre Maison* (M), tel. 74104.

COURMAYEUR. Most important winter and summer resort in the Valle d'Aosta, below Mont Blanc. *Palace Bron* (E), tel. 842545. Above town, posh. *Pavillon* (E), tel. 842420. Lively and attractive, with indoor pool. *Royal* (E), tel.

843621. Modern; informal yet elegant. *Cresta Duc* (M), tel. 842585. Pleasant, well-furnished. *Bouton d'Or* (M), tel. 842380. Small; very good.

Restaurants. *Al Camin* (E), tel. 841497. At Entrèves, *Maison de Filippo* (M), tel. 89968. A must.

GRESSONEY. Important winter sports resort, and summer resort, in the Valle d'Aosta; the more fashionable Gressoney La Trinité is about 800 ft. higher than Gressoney St. Jean. *Busca-Thedy* (M), tel. 356136. Most rooms with bath; tennis and garage. *Residence* (M), tel. 356148. Fine views. *Stadel* (I), tel. 355225. Lots of atmosphere and comfort. *Villa Tedaldi* (PM), tel. 355123. Tiny pension just above St. Jean; comfortable and friendly.

LIMONE PIEMONTE. Principal winter and summer resort in southern Piedmont. *Principe* (M), tel. 92389. Quiet and comfortable. *Tripoli* (M), tel. 92397. Terrace; many rooms with bath.

SAINT VINCENT. Popular spa resort. *Billia* (L), tel. 3446. Elegant modern comforts in Victorian hostelry. *Elena* (M), tel. 2140.

Restaurant. *Batezar* (E), tel. 3164. Outstanding.

SESTRIERE. Top winter sports and summer resort. *Grand Hotel Sestriere* (E), tel. 76476. Large, all comforts. *Cristallo* (E), similar. *Savoy Edelweiss* (M), tel. 7040. Refurbished, comfortable. *Miramonti* (I), tel. 7048. Pleasant, friendly atmosphere.

TURIN. *Principe di Piemonte* (L), Via P. Gobetti 15 (tel. 532153). One of Italy's leading hotels; airconditioned elegance throughout. *Ambasciatori* (E), Corso Vittorio Emanuele (tel. 5752). Airconditioned. *City* (E), Via Juvarra (tel. 540546). Modern and elegant. *Palace Hotel Turin* (E), Via Sacchi 8 (tel. 515511). A fine establishment. Central, quiet and very comfortable. Handy for the station. *Villa Sassi* (E), Strada Traforo del Pino (tel. 890556). Sumptuous villa in park just across Po. *Alexandra* (M), Lungo Dora Napoli 14 (tel. 858327). Walking distance from center; modern, good. *Genio* (M), Corso Vittorio Emanuele (tel. 6505771). At station. *Victoria* (M), Via Nino Costa 4 (tel. 553710). Central, comfortable.

Restaurants. *Cambio* (E), Piazza Carignano (tel. 546690). Turin's most famous; belle époque decor, classic cuisine, excellent *fonduta*. *Gatto Nero* (E), Turati 14 (tel. 590414). *Ferrero* (E), Corso Vittorio Emanuele 54 (tel. 547225). *Rendezvous* (E), Corso Vittorio Emanuele 38 (tel. 539990). International cuisine. *Tiffany* (E), Piazza Solferino 16 (tel. 540538). Elegant and very good. *Vecchia Lanterna* (E), Corso Umberto 21 (tel. 537047). Good atmosphere, pianist in evenings; local and Venetian specialties. *Villa Sassi* (E), Strada Traforo Pino 47 (tel. 890556). On hillside 2 miles from the center of town; enchanting antique-furnished villa restaurant with gardens; very expensive.

Just below these leaders are half a dozen others which are very good, but about a third cheaper: *Bue Rosso* (M), Corso Casale 10 (tel. 830753); *Capannina* (M), Via Donati 1 (tel. 545405); *Ciacolon* (M), Viale Venticinque Aprile 11 (tel. 630782). Local cuisine; *Al Ghibellin Fuggiasco* (M), Via Tunisi 50 (tel. 390750). Attractive place with Tuscan cuisine. *Ostu Bacu* (M), Corso Vercelli 226 (tel. 264579); *Tre Galline* (M), Via Bellezia 37 (tel. 546833); *Vecchia Puglia* (M), Via Principe Eugenio 17 (tel. 538802). Even more reasonable are *Antica Trattoria Parigi* (M), Corso Rosselli 83 (tel. 592593); *Cesare*, Via Carlo Alberto 3 (tel. 511407); *Da Giuseppe* (M), Via San Massimo 34 (tel. 876090); *Da Mauro* (M), Via Maria Vittoria 21 (tel. 8397811); *Da Roberto* (M), Via Lagrange 22 (tel. 544545).

 SHOPPING. The Balon flea market (at Porta Palazzo on Saturdays) is fun but junky; at the Crocetta open-air market (at the Church of the Crocetta, Tuesday, Saturday), you'll find first-quality goods at one-third off. If you like lace, you'll find an incredible variety (9,000 types, they claim) at the *Fabbrica Pizzi* (lace factory), Cascine Vica at Rivoli. Factory prices; open to the public on Tuesday, Thursday, Saturday.

Lombardy

The fabulous Lombardy area of Italy stretches south from the Alps to the river Po. It takes its name from the Lombards who pounced on the lush fields of the Po in the sixth century and were eventually defeated by Charlemagne, who was crowned with their famous iron crown. The region's recorded history dates back 3,000 years to the Etruscans and includes domination by Rome, the Huns, the Goths, the Spanish, the Austrians—and Mussolini, which last the Milanesi strung up by his heels.

Milan

Milan, capital of Lombardy, is a sprawling industrial city and a great art center, the commercial capital of Italy. Its center is the Piazza del Duomo, with its great cathedral; the second largest church in the world and the biggest Gothic building in Italy. As elaborate as a wedding cake, the exterior of this edifice is decorated with 2,245 marble statues and 135 marble spires. The 15th- and 16th-century stained-glass windows illuminate the five great aisles and huge pillars of the church with a dim and moving light. The effect is magnificent and should not be missed. Walk or take the elevator to the terraces of the cathedral from where you'll have wonderful views of Milan, the Lombardy Plain and the distant Alps seen through a filigree of spires and statues.

From the Piazza del Duomo you can enter the celebrated Galleria Vittorio Emanuele, with its roof of glass, cafés, restaurants, bars, bookstores, souvenir shops; in short, everything necessary to make it the traditional smart gathering place that it is. A stroll through this fabulous gallery will bring you into the Piazza della Scala, with its world-famous Teatro della Scala. The opera season runs from December to June here with concerts and ballet in the spring and autumn. Tickets are a problem, especially for the opera performances, which are invariably sold out well in advance. Ask your travel agent's advice about getting them. Most of the big hotels in Milan will assign a porter to stand in what passes for a line at La Scala in order to procure tickets. Don't attempt to do this yourself. It's an exhausting, frustrating, time-consuming experience. There's too much else to see in Milan.

For example—the Palazzo di Brera with its superb collection, one of the greatest in Italy; the Castello Sforzesco, designed in 1450 by Filarete, with Michelangelo's moving *Rondanini Pietà;* the 17th-century Palazzo dell' Ambrosiana, with its gallery including works of Botticelli, Titian, Raphael and 1,750 notes and drawings by Leonardo da Vinci; San Satiro church, rebuilt by Bramante in 1480, a masterpiece of Renaissance design and perspective which makes the rather small interior seem vast; San Lorenzo Maggiore with its fourth-century mosaics and Roman columns; Sant' Ambrogio, Milan's greatest medieval monument (and founded even earlier, in 386).

Finally, a pilgrimage to one of the most famous paintings in the world—Leonardo da Vinci's *Last Supper,* still glowing faintly with glory, after centuries of abuse from damp weather and war, from the wall of the refectory of Santa Maria delle Grazie on the Corso Magenta. The painstaking task of restoring this masterpiece is underway; you may find parts of it hidden from view.

Modern Milan thrusts upward in some of Italy's largest, most striking skyscrapers *(grattacieli),* and burrows underground with the city's ultra-modern subway.

Environs of Milan

Suggested excursions by car or bus from Milan include visits to the Certosa di Pavia, one of the world's greatest monasteries, a complete masterpiece of Lombard Renaissance architecture; to Cremona, famous for its Stradivarius and Guarnerius violins and for its splendid Piazza del Comune, which, with its 12th-century Duomo, is one of the most impressive squares in Italy; to Mantua, the birthplace of Vergil, with the Gonzaga castle, containing Mantegna's stupendous frescos; and to Brescia, whose marble Renaissance *Loggia* palace and 11th-century Rotonda cathedral are worth a visit, to say nothing of its Roman and Christian Museum. Bergamo Alta, the older, upper part of Bergamo, is steeped in authentic medieval atmosphere. Its fine monuments include the Colleoni Chapel, tomb of the great *condottiere* whose statue is in Venice.

PRACTICAL INFORMATION FOR MILAN

 HOTELS. Best book well ahead for hotels in Milan, especially during April when the International Trade Fair crowds city hotels to bursting point. You'll find that many of the newer moderate-range hotels tend to have pint sized rooms, though often with bath or shower, and serve breakfast only. Some hotels close in August. Room rates average 15 percent above general guidelines.

Deluxe

Excelsior Gallia, Piazza Duca d'Aosta 9 (tel. 6277). Elegant and comfortable hotel handy to the railway station; fully airconditioned, classic decor, good service.

Grand Hotel et de Milan, Via Manzoni 29 (tel. 870757). Traditional Milanese style; central.

Milan Hilton, Via Galvani 12 (tel. 6983). On top of the Alitalia air terminal near the station. Airconditioning throughout and the usual Hilton comforts.

Palace, Piazza della Repubblica 20 (tel. 6336). Quiet though centrally located; with roof garden and smart *Casanova* grill room.

Principe e Savoia, Piazza della Repubblica 17 (tel. 6230). Very central and very popular; many rooms furnished with fine period pieces.

Expensive

Carlton Senato, Via Senato 5 (tel. 798583). Central, in smart shopping district; bright, modern.

De la Ville, Via Hoepli 6 (tel. 867651). Central and elegant.

Diana Majestic, Viale Piave 42 (tel. 202122). Handsome, medium-sized hotel in art deco style with garden.

Duomo, Via S. Raffaele 1 (tel. 8833). Duplex suites and airconditioning.

Galileo, Corso Europa 9 (tel. 7743). Central, comfortable, good atmosphere.

Marino alla Scala, Piazza della Scala 5 (tel. 867831). Central, airconditioned and nicely furnished.

Plaza, Piazza Diaz (tel. 8058452). Central, tasteful decor, airconditioning.

Splendido, Via Andrea Doria 4 (tel. 2050). Large, modern and efficient.

Windsor, Via Galilei 2 (tel. 6346). Modern and reasonable.

Moderate

Canada, Via Lentasio 15 (tel. 8052527). Small, modern, fairly central.

Gran Duca di York, Via Moneta 1A (tel. 874863). Central, small, pleasant.

Lancaster, Via Sangiorgio 16 (tel. 3453811). Pleasant, near Sempione park and public transport.

Lord Internazionale, Via Spadari 11 (tel. 862420). Good value.

Madison, Via Gasparotto 8 (tel. 6085991). At main station.

Manzoni, Via Santo Spirito 20 (tel. 705697). Central but quiet.

Inexpensive

Numerous inexpensive hotels fill Milan, though you will be hard put to find one with a private bath in your room.

Adler, Via Ricordi 10 (tel. 221441). Handy for Metro, bus; good.

Bolzano, Via Boscovich 21 (tel. 665037). Near station, friendly.

Città Studi, Via Saldini 24 (tel. 744666). Just outside center and handy for public transport; pleasant and comfortable.

London, Via Rovello 3 (tel. 872988). Central, simple.

RESTAURANTS. All expensive are: **Alfio Cavour,** Via Senato 31 (tel. 700633). Classic, excellent.

Biffi Scala, Piazza della Scala (tel. 876332). Suppers only, very smart clientele.

El Brellin, Vicolo Lavandai at Naviglio Grande (tel. 8351351). Pricey.

Giannino's, Via A Sciesa 8 (tel. 5452948). It's one of the best-known in Milan and one of Italy's best. Very good but *very* expensive.

Gran San Bernardo, Via Borgese 14 (tel. 389000). Popular with newspapermen and actors; book ahead; expensive.

Marchesi, Via Bonsevin de la Riva (tel. 741246). Exquisite and very expensive cuisine; considered Milan's best restaurant. Book ahead.

Momus, Via Fiori Chiari 8 (tel. 8056227). Smart, booking necessary.

La Nôs, Via Amedi 2 (tel. 898759). Excellent, reservations a must.

Savini, tel. 8058343. A Milanese institution; superb food and sensational ice cream; in the Galeria; must book.

Scaletta, Piazzale Stazione Genova (tel. 8350290). Book a week ahead for *Marchesi's* top rival. Superb food.

El Toulà, Piazza Ferrari 6 (tel. 870302). Very chic and expensive.

On the less expensive side, there are many fine restaurants in Milan. To mention just a few, all (M): **Aurora,** Via Savona 23 (tel. 8354978). Old-style atmosphere. **Brasera Meneghin,** Via Circo 10 (tel. 808108). Typical trattoria. **Charleston,** Piazza del Liberty 8 (tel. 798631). Busy and good. **Fulvio,** Via Durini 26 (tel. 790823). Near San Babila. **Matarel,** Via Mantegazza 2 (tel. 654204). **Mercante,** Piazza Mercanti 17 (tel. 8052198). Seafood specialties. **Pesa,** Viale Pasubio 10 (tel. 665741). Turn-of-century décor. **Porta Rossa,** Via Vittor Pisani (tel. 652912). Unpretentious trattoria. **Quattro Toscani,** Via Plinio 33 (tel. 639886). Tuscan cuisine. **Solferino,** Via Castelfidardo 2 (tel. 639886). In Brera district. **Torre di Pisa,** Via Mercato 26 (tel. 874877). **Toscanino,** Piazza Erculea 9 (tel. 873589). Tuscan food, summer garden.

Budgeters can eat well and fairly cheaply at the snack bars in the Galleria or at the *Peck* shops on Via Hugo and Via Cantù, or at the many trattorias along the Corso Garibaldi.

 MUSEUMS. Although world-famous as an industrial center, Milan has a surprisingly large number of excellent museums. Check with concierge or at local tourist offices for hours. Among the best—

Castle of the Sforzas, Piazza Castello, with Museum of Ancient Art, painting and sculpture gallery, with a Michelangelo *Pietà,* and armory.

Church of Santa Maria delle Grazie, Corso Magenta, Leonardo da Vinci's *Last Supper* (Cenacolo Vinciano).

Pinacoteca Ambrosiana, Piazza Pio XI, contains famous Leonardo da Vinci manuscripts, as well as paintings by great masters.

Pinacoteca di Brera, Via Brera, notable 15th and 16th-century frescos of Lombard school, paintings by Mantegna, Raphael and Bronzino, among others. One of the world's great collections. Recent modern art annex.

Poldi-Pezzoli Museum, Via Manzoni 12, picture gallery, paintings by Botticelli, Tiepolo and others, 15th–18th-century Murano glass, 15th-century Persian carpets.

Portinari Chapel, Church of Sant'Eustorgio, Corso di Porta Ticinese, frescos depicting the life and death of St. Peter Martyr, by Foppa.

Scala Theater Museum, Piazza della Scala.

SHOPPING. This is the center of the silk area so you will find the best selections of Italian fabrics: lavish brocades, upholstery materials, lovely dress fabrics. In contrast, a vast assortment of just plain silk is on view at Milan's flea market on Via Calatafimi every Saturday.

Take a look around the most famous department store in Italy, *Rinascente* on the Piazza del Duomo, full of fashion merchandise, utilitarian articles, and an inviting assortment of gifts.

Walk down Via Montenapoleone, one of the world's most elegant shopping streets; you'll see the ultra-chic boutiques of *Mila Schön, Valentino* and *Roberta di Camerino* interspersed with those of top French designers. The *Vergottini,* lively family of famous hairdressers, are here too. *Fiorucci's* big shop on Via Torino is an exhilarating experience.

The Lakes

The lake regions of Lombardy—famed for the beauties of Como, Garda, Maggiore and Lugano—lie at the foot of the Alps. Lake Garda, ten miles wide, stretches for 32 miles through groves of olive, lemon and orange trees at the foot of mountains often covered with snow. A complete tour of it by car or bus is recommended, or take a lake steamer for a restful, tranquil cruise through this lovely scenery.

Lake Como, bordered by delightful towns like Como, Bellagio and Colico, lies placidly in a setting of lush green foliage, brilliant flowers and beautiful villas. Take the lake steamer and get off anywhere your fancy dictates—there'll be another one along in an hour or so—and proceed by foot along the roads and lanes that wind through the gardens on the banks. The mountain air is perfumed with a thousand flowers as it is at Lake Lugano.

Perhaps the most brilliant gem in this crown of Northern Italy is Lake Maggiore, a two-mile-wide watery ribbon connecting the plain of Lombardy with the Alps of Switzerland 40 miles away. The loveliest of the many cruise possibilities here is from Stresa to Arona and Baveno. The climax of the cruise is Isola Bella, ten terraces of gardens forming a setting for the 17th-century Palazzo Borromeo. The view from here is one of the scenic wonders of the world.

PRACTICAL INFORMATION FOR THE LAKE REGION

HOTELS AND RESTAURANTS. The lake-resort hotels are open only from spring to late fall, though hotels in towns such as Bergamo and Mantua are open all year round of course. It is advisable to check before making your plans and be sure to reserve early. If you take full board at a lake hotel, you can often have a picnic lunch packed for you. Rates at most (E) hotels are lower than general guidelines, lowest in spring and fall. Many hotels are on lakeside road; expect some noise in front rooms.

BAVENO. Resort on Lake Maggiore. *Splendido* (E), tel. 24583. Heated pool, tennis courts and extensive lakeside grounds along with private beach. *Simplon* (M), tel. 24112. Private beach, pool, park and tennis.

Restaurants. *Romagna* (M-E) has pleasant lakeside terrace for outdoor dining. At nearby Feriolo, *La Serenella* (M).

BELLAGIO. Lake Como resort. *Grant Hotel Villa Serbelloni* (L), tel. 950216. Magnificent hotel; elegant furnishings, tennis and pool. *Belvedere* (M), tel. 950410. Terrace restaurant and pool among the facilities. *Du Lac* (M), tel. 950320. Opposite steamer landing; comfortable with restaurant with panoramic view.

BERGAMO. *Excelsior San Marco* (E), Piazza Repubblica 6 (tel. 232132). Splendid hotel; airconditioned. *Moderno* (E), Viale Giovanni XXIII (tel. 233033).

Central with attractive rooms and a sidewalk café. *Arli* (M), Largo Porta Nuova 12 (tel. 222014). Near the station, comfortable and well-equipped but without restaurant. *Moro* (M), Porta Nuova 6 (tel. 242946). Excellent restaurant. *Agnello d'Oro* (I), Via Gombito 22 (tel. 249883). In the heart of picturesque Bergamo Alta.

Restaurants. *Pergola* (E), Borgo Canale 62 (tel. 256335), in Bergamo Alta. Small, excellent. *Taverna dei Colleoni* (E), Piazza Vecchia 7 (tel. 232596). Historic ambiance, fine food. *Tino Fontana* (E), Piazza Repubblica 6 (tel. 215321). In San Marco hotel, large, fine. *Vittorio* (E), Via Papa Giovanni 21 (tel. 218060). Very good, especially for fish. *Gourmet* (M), Via San Vigilio 1 (tel. 256110). Lovely setting. *Moro* (M), Largo Porta Nuova 6 (tel. 218074). A classic.

BRESCIA. Important art city near Lake Garda. *Vittoria* (E), Via Dieci Giornate 20 (tel. 52125). Central and modernized. *Master* (M), Via Apollonio 72 (tel. 294121). Just outside the center with pleasant rooms and cool garden. *Europa* (I), Piazza Ospedale 7 (tel. 300355). Good value.

Restaurants. *Augustus* (M), Via Laura Cereto 8 (tel. 292130). Excellent cuisine. *La Sosta* (M), Via S. Martino 20 (tel. 295603). Atmosphere, good food.

CERNOBBIO. Lake Como resort. *Villa d'Este* (L), tel. 511471. One of Italy's, and for that matter the world's, great hotels and correspondingly expensive. Its 171 rooms are arranged in a Renaissance villa. Has swimming pool, nightclub and piano bar. Conference trade dims appeal.

COMO. *Barchetta-Excelsior* (E), tel. 266531. Comfortable and with fine food. *Metropole e Suisse* (E), tel. 269444. Best in town. *Villa Flori* (E), tel. 557642. On the Cernobbio road; recommended. *Como* (M), tel. 266173. *Tre Re* (M), tel. 265374. Central; unpretentious, friendly.

Restaurants. *Barchetta* (E), hotel restaurant (see above) and *Celestino* (M), Lungo Lario Trento (tel. 263470) are both very good. *Gesumin* (E), Via Cinque Giorante (tel. 266030). Tiny, family-run, excellent; booking essential. *Angela* (M), Via Foscolo (tel. 263460). *Faro* (M), Via Luini (tel. 269596). *Perlasca* (M), tel. 260142. Lakeside dining, fine food, well served. *Pizzi* (M), Via Geno 12 (tel. 266100). Good medium-range restaurant.

CREMONA. Violin city and art town. *Astoria* (M), Via Bordigallo 19 (tel. 22467). Quiet modern comforts behind an ancient facade. *Continental* (M), Piazzale Libertà 27 (tel. 434141). Best in town.

Restaurants. *Ceresole* (M), Via Ceresole 4 (tel. 23322). Popular, good. *Cerri* (M), Piazza Giovanni XXIII 3 (tel. 22796). Family-run trattoria, homey local specialties.

DESENZANO DEL GARDA. Summer resort on Lake Garda. *Park* (M), tel. 9143494. Central, modern, on lake with garden. *Villa Rosa* (M), tel. 9141974. Lakeside garden. *Vittorio* (I), tel. 9141504. Clean, quiet.

Restaurants. *Esplanade* (E), Via Lario (tel. 9143361). Classic cuisine. *Molino* (M), Piazza Matteotti (tel. 9141340).

GARDONE RIVIERA. On Lake Garda. *Fasano* (E), tel. 21051. Classic lakeshore hotel with good service, pool and private beach. *Grand* (E), tel. 20261. Equally good hotel with similar facilities. *Villa del Sogno* (M), tel. 20228. Small, on lake. *Monte Baldo* (M), tel. 20951. Lake view and garden.

Restaurants. *Casino* (M), tel. 20387. *La Stalla* (M), tel. 21038.

ISOLA DEI PESCATORI. Restaurant. *Verbano* (M), tel. 30408. Graces the little island on which it resides; peaceful and picturesque surroundings reached by boat from Stresa.

MANTUA. *San Lorenzo* (E), Piazza Concordia (tel. 327044). Smallish and elegant with splendid view from the terrace. *Apollo* (M), Piazza Leoni (tel. 350522). *Dante* (M), Via Corrado (tel. 326425). *Mantegna* (M), Via Filzi (tel. 350315). Central, small.

Restaurants. *Cigno* (M), Piazza d'Arco (tel. 327101). A 13th-century inn with lots of paintings and excellent local dishes. *Da Baffo* (M), Borgo Virgiliana (tel. 370313). Best to go in a group for the rustic fare and home-made bread; 3 miles from town. *Al Ducale* (M), Piazza Sordello (tel. 324447). Small, family-run. *Romani* (M), Piazza delle Erbe 13 (tel. 323627). Good trattoria. *Garibaldini* (M), Via S. Longino 7 (tel. 329237). A local classic.

MENAGGIO. Popular Lake Como resort. *Victoria* (E), tel. 32003. Large lakeside hotel; quiet and traditional. *Bellavista* (M), tel. 32136. Modern hotel on the lakeside.

PAVIA. *Ariston* (M), Via Scopoli (tel. 34334). An adequate overnight stop in the middle of town.
Restaurants. *Bixio* (E), Via Strada Nuova 81 (tel. 25343). Good food, atmosphere. *Giulio* (M), Via Guffanti 19 (tel. 26304). For tasty risotto and local specialties. At **Certosa,** *Chalet* (M), tel. 92115. *Vecchio Mulino* (M), tel. 925894. Good.

SIRMIONE. Popular Lake Garda resort. *Sirmione* (E), tel. 916331. Very comfortable hotel on the lake. *Villa Cortine Palace* (E), tel. 916021. Old villa on hillside with modern annex; park and pool. *Continental* (M), tel. 916031. Good medium range hotel. *Olivi* (M), tel. 916110. Reasonable.
Restaurants. *Sirmione* (E). Hotel restaurant a cut above average. *Antica Taverna del Marinaio* (E), tel. 916056. Lakeside terrace, classic menu. At Lugana Vecchia, *Vecchia Lugana* (E), tel. 919012. Exceptional.

STRESA. Major summer resort on Lake Maggiore. *Grand Hôtel et des Iles Borromées* (L), tel. 30431. Most famous of Stresa's many fine hotels; on the lake with tennis, golf and a private beach. *Villa Aminta* (E), tel. 32444. On lake; top comfort and service, pool, gardens. *La Palma* (E), tel. 30266. Large and modern and very comfortable; pool. *Regina Palace* (E), tel. 30171. Traditional hotel on the lake with tennis and garage. *Speranza Hotel du Lac* (M), tel. 31178. Attractive medium-range hotel overlooking lake. *Royal* (M), tel. 30471. Good, reasonably priced establishment.
Restaurants. *Emiliano* (E), tel. 31396. Best in town by a long way. *Grand Hôtel et des Iles Borromées* (E), tel. 30431. Expensive and sophisticated dining. *La Barchetta* (M), tel. 30305. Good eating. *Luina* (M), tel. 30285.

TREMEZZO. Lake Como resort. *Grand Hotel Tremezzo* (E), tel. 40446. 100 rooms with bath; all front rooms with balcony and panoramic view; beach, bar and dancing. Also has less expensive annex. *Bazzoni* (M), tel. 40403. 140 rooms, all with shower; modern, attractive decor and restaurant with panoramic view of the lake.
Restaurants. *Grand Hotel Tremezzo* (E), tel. 40446. Best in town though expensive. *Al Velu* (E), tel. 40510. At Rogaro. Fine food.

Venice

Venice is eternally preoccupied with the contemplation of its own beauty. Founded on marshes, it rose to dominate the Adriatic and hold the gorgeous East in fee. At the height of her power in the 16th century, Venice was a wealthy city-republic glorying in fêtes and pageants, reveling in the splendor of her painting, sculpture and architecture. Those days of glory are gone, but her art survives, and the grace and refinement of Venice remain in all the cities of the Venetian area— Verona, Vicenza, Padua, Treviso and Belluno. A visit to any of these is enough to fill the soul, but if your time is limited, let it be Venice alone.

Incredibly crowded with tourists during the hot and humid summer months, Venice is much more welcoming in early spring and late fall, though many also plump for December to March when prices are lower and the city's atmosphere has an especially haunting quality. Throughout the year, the famous International Biennial Exhibition sponsors events in all arts. In August, there's a night fête on the Grand Canal and café-orchestra music every evening in Piazza San Marco. "Musical Autumn" begins in September with a regatta on the Grand Canal, and the illustrious La Fenice theater, where *Rigoletto* and *Traviata* were first performed, is the scene of distinguished musical events. (The regular opera season here is from December to March.) On the third Sunday in July, the Feast of the Redeemer is celebrated, and Venetians and visitors flock across the Giudecca Canal to the Church of the Redeemer, built to commemorate the end of a devastating plague, for a day of worship and feasting, ending in glorious fireworks. Carnival time in Venice (the week before Lent) sweeps up Venetians and visitors alike in wild and captivating celebrations and masquerades.

Arrival in Venice is a thrill. If you come by train, you walk down the station steps right to the Grand Canal. If you fly, you land at Marco Polo airport, and the motorboat that takes you to Venice gives you a view from the lagoon of its pink and gilded palaces. If you drive, you park in the Piazzale Roma garage, on the Tronchetto parking island, or at the newer, cheaper terminals of Fusina or San Giuliano on the mainland (closed in winter), proceeding to the center by vaporetto.

Discovering Venice

You could spend a year exploring this city and its environs. For a short visit (two or three days) concentrate on the Piazza San Marco, the Grand Canal and environs, and the lagoon islands of Murano, Burano and Torcello.

A gondola (or vaporetto) picked up at the San Marco station will take you on the leisurely two-mile tour of Venice's 'main street', the S-shaped Grand Canal, which winds through four centuries of Gothic-Renaissance palaces. There are at least 200 of them, and your gondolier will point out the outstanding ones.

On foot you will explore the Piazza San Marco, the heart and soul of Venice, a regal square bordered on three sides by arcades, on the fourth by the great Basilica of St. Mark, one of the world's most magnificent churches. The interior, faced with marble and gold mosaic, is incredibly rich. Qualified English-speaking guides are available to point out the plethora of treasures in detail. If you prefer to do it alone, don't miss the Vault of Paradise with Titian's *Last Judgment* and the Pala d'Oro, a 10th-century altarpiece of gold and enamel, studded with precious gems. Take the stairway to the outer terrace for a view of the replicas of the four magnificent horses of gilded copper; a third-century (B.C.) Greek work, which once adorned the Hippodrome of Constantinople, they were installed here in 1207. The originals can be seen in the Basilica's museum.

The Palazzo Ducale, the Doges' Palace, next to the Basilica, a fantasy of pink and white marble with its immense rooms and Scala dei Giganti (Stairway of the Giants) is one of the treasure houses of the world. Visits with English-speaking guides are recommended. The tour ends on a somber note with a visit to the gloomy cells of the Pozzi Prison. On the east side of the palace is the celebrated Bridge of Sighs. Try to time your visit for a sunny day, as the Palace's interior is dimly lit.

Other Highlights

Before going to the Lido or the outer islands, here are a few other highlights of Venice proper which require a lot of footwork but are decidedly worth the effort: The Academy of Fine Arts (Accademia), the world's finest collection of Venetian paintings, crammed with Titians, Tintorettos, Giorgiones and the whole Venetian school; the octagonal Church of Santa Maria della Salute, with paintings by Titian and Tintoretto; Santa Maria Formosa, built in 1492; Ca d'Oro and Ca' Rezzonico, two beautiful palaces on the Grand Canal housing interesting collections of art works; Santa Maria dei Miracoli, a 15th-century Renaissance masterpiece; Verrocchio's statue of Colleoni on horseback in front of the majestic Church of San Zanipolo; San Zaccaria with its 13th-century Romanesque belfry and paintings by Bellini, Tintoretto and Titian; and the magnificent Church of San Giovanni in Bragora, with art of Cima and Vivarini.

We almost forgot Santa Maria Gloriosa dei Frari (Titian and Bellini), the Church of San Rocco, with 6 Tintorettos, and the School of San Rocco, with its 56 Tintorettos! Escape from the crowds by wandering the less touristy districts around the Ghetto Nuovo, San Pietro in Castello or San Giacomo dell'Orio.

The Lido and Islands

By this time, you should be ready for a long rest. Every 20 minutes, steamers leave from Riva degli Schiavoni for the 15-minute trip across the Venetian Lagoon to the Lido, with its very smart beach hotels and not much else to recommend it as an excursion; it's very lazy and *very* expensive. The water, so shallow that you have to wade about half a mile before you swim, is as tepid as pea soup. The Municipal Casino is open at the Lido in summer (and from October 1-March 31 at Vendramin-Calergi Palace on the Grand Canal), and there are plenty of tennis courts, an 18-hole golf course, a riding school and everything else you could want if you can work up the energy.

The lagoon trips to Murano, Burano and Torcello, departing from the Fondamenta Nuova, are highly recommended. Murano, an ancient center of glass-blowing, is rather commercial. Visit the Museo Vetrario (Museum of Glass) here, and walk into any of the glass-blowing establishments on the Fondamenta dei Vetrai to watch this interesting procedure. Generally, glassware costs less here than in Venice. If possible, take it with you. Some tourists have been disappointed, to put it mildly, when the goods they received back home were inferior to what they ordered. Burano, more colorful and picturesque, is a small island fishing village, the center of the Venetian lace industry. Here, too, visitors are welcome to watch lacemakers at work. Torcello, a mile from Burano, was the first colony of the Venetian lagoon, established by the Venetians when they fled the barbarian hordes. It's a romantic, restful place with a cathedral dating from the 7th century, recommended for an hour, or a week, of complete repose. Take the regular public-service steamers, not organized boat tours, on which you're pressured to buy at each stop. Start at Torcello, then do Burano and Murano.

PRACTICAL INFORMATION FOR VENICE

HOTELS. These are no problem in Venice. The city sometimes seems to have no buildings which aren't palaces, and many of these have been converted into hotels —and when you stay in a palace hotel in Venice, you can take the term literally. Be sure to ask for the all-inclusive rates. You will probably have to take half pension terms during high season unless the hotel is *garni* (without restaurant). But Venice is Italy's most expensive tourist city, so be prepared! Complaints about over charging should be taken to the official tourist office in the Piazza San Marco.

Deluxe

Bauer, Campo San Moisè (tel. 707022). One of the finest hotels in Italy. The style is both elegant and contemporary and there's a terrace restaurant and roof garden for summer dancing.

Cipriani, Giudecca island (tel. 707744). Overlooks the lagoon and is quiet, smart and expensive—as might be expected. Airconditioning throughout and gardens, pool, terrace restaurant. Short boat ride from S. Marco and center.

Danieli Royal Excelsior, Riva degli Schiavoni (tel. 410077). Of the deluxe hotels in Venice, this seems to be the favorite, at least among Anglo Saxon visitors. Superb location and gourmet dining on a terrace commanding a wonderful view.

Gritti Palace, Campo S. Maria del Giglio (tel. 410125). Preferred by those who like a smaller and quieter base. It's distinctive, beautifully furnished and superbly run, with famed restaurant. Offers art, cooking courses.

Expensive

Cavaletto e Doge Orseolo, San Marco 1107 (tel. 700955). Recommended.

Gabrielli, Riva degli Schiavoni (tel. 5231580). All comforts in this elegant and historic palace.

Locanda Cipriani, on Torcello (tel. 730150). Expensive but unforgettable 6-room pension hideaway.

Londra, Riva degli Schiavoni (tel. 700533). Impeccable management; small but attractive rooms and terrace restaurant.

Luna, Calle dell'Ascensione 1243 (tel. 89840). An old favorite with old-fashioned décor, comfortable rooms.

Metropole, Riva degli Schiavoni (tel. 705044). Elegant and well-furnished; airconditioned throughout with excellent service.

Monaco e Grand Canale, Grand Canal (tel. 700211). Bright and comfortable rooms, some smallish; canal side dining and airconditioning.

Saturnia Internazionale, Via XXII Marzo (tel. 708377). Elegant Renaissance palace, central, quiet, well-kept, handsomely furnished; courteous service.

Moderate

Ala, San Marco 2494 (tel. 708333). Handsome, on pretty square.

Bisanzio, Calle della Pietà (tel. 703100). Small, comfortable and pleasant.

Bonvecchiati, San Marco 4488 (tel. 85017). Has a vine covered dining terrace.

Concordia, San Marco 367 (tel. 706866). Nicely furnished rooms and excellent location near St. Mark's.

La Fenice, San Marco 1936 (tel. 32333). Charming with attractive rooms and pretty garden terrace.

Flora, San Marco 2283 (tel. 705844). Delightful small hotel.

Do Pozzi, Calle XXII Marxo (tel. 707855). Small rooms but a pretty hotel.

Al Sole Palace, Fondamenta Minotto (tel. 32144). Santa Croce district; interesting location off the beaten track, all comforts.

Inexpensive

Accademia, Dorsoduro 1058 (tel. 5237846). Attractive pension in quiet old villa with garden.

Alla Fava, Castello 5525 (tel. 29224). Near the Rialto, reader-recommended for good atmosphere.

Bucintoro, Riva degli Schiavoni, near Arsenal (tel. 5223240). Overlooking lagoon.

Casa Frollo, Guidecca (tel. 5222723). A 17th-century villa on the other side of the lagoon; recommended.

La Forcola, Cannaregio 2356 (tel. 720277). Quiet; 10 min. from S. Marco and station.

Madonna dell'Orto, Cannaregio, next to church of same name (tel. 719955). Exceptional value, atmosphere. Few private baths. Off beaten track but handy to vaporetto.

Paganelli, Riva degli Schiavoni (tel. 5224324). Basic furnishings but fine location and pleasant restaurant.

San Fantin, at La Fenice (tel. 5231401). Clean and pleasant.

San Moise, near church of the same name (tel. 703755). Central, quiet.

Scandinavia, Santa Maria Formosa (tel. 5223507). Near S. Marco.

Seguso, Zattere 779 (tel. 22340). Good second class pension.

LIDO HOTELS. The Lido is more expensive than Venice proper and the hotels here, though for the most part extremely smart, are open only in summer. The beach is on the far side of this famous strip of land and 15 minutes by vaporetto from Venice.

Excelsior Palace (L), tel. 5260201. On the beach itself with 230 rooms and suites; private beach, nightclub, several restaurants.

Adria Urania, Villa Nora (E), Viale Dandolo 29 (tel. 5260120). Pleasant twin-villa hotels 5 minutes from the beach.

Grand Hôtel des Bains (E), tel. 765921. Behind the beach with park and gardens, tennis, pool and private beach; *Pagoda* restaurant and large, well furnished rooms.

Petit Palais (E), Lungomare Marconi (tel. 765993). Comfortable; with private beach.

Quattro Fontane (E), Via Quattro Fontane 16 (tel. 760227). Book ahead for this quiet, excellent hotel with country-house atmosphere.

Restaurants

Expensive

Antico Martini, Campo San Fantin 1981 (tel. 24121). Excellent restaurant with dancing and outdoor dining.

Caravella, Calle XXII Marzo (tel. 708901). In Hotel Saturnia Internazionale; exceptional cuisine and intimate atmosphere.

Cipriani, Giudecca (tel. 85068). Outstanding terrace restaurant in the hotel of the same name.

La Colomba, Frezzeria 1665 (tel. 21175). Efficient service and excellent seafood.

Il Cortile, Via XXII Marzo (tel. 708377). Pleasant outdoor dining. Delicious food and good atmosphere. Open Apr.–Oct.

Danieli, tel. 26480. Justly famous for incomparable view and generally superb food. Minimum of 80,000 lire per person for food, wine excluded.

Gritti Palace, on Grand Canal (tel. 26044). In hotel of the same name; considered by some to be Venice's very best restaurant.

Graspo de Ua, Calle Bombosieri (tel. 23647). Cordial Venetian inn near Rialto.

Harry's Bar, Calle Valleresso (tel. 36797). Nostalgic favorite still keeping up extremely high standards. Overly touristy at times.

Ivo, Ramo Fuseri (tel. 705889). Tiny, elegant, excellent.

Taverna La Fenice, Campiello Marinonio (tel. 23856). In a delightful square; serves splendid food.

Moderate

Ai Cugnai, San Vio (tel. 89258). Reasonable trattoria.

Antica Besseta, Calle Salvio (tel. 37687). Small; traditional specialties.

Al Conte Pescaor, Piscine San Zulian (tel. 21483). Good food and courteous service.

Corte Sconta, Calle del Pestrin, near S. Giovanni in Bragora (tel. 27024). Hard to find but well worth the trouble.

Fiaschetteria Toscana, Campo San Giovanni Crisostomo (tel. 85281). Very good food, courteous service, recommended. Reserve.

Harry's Dolci, at Sant'Eufemia on Giudecca; light meals, tea.

La Madonna, Calle delle Madonna 594 (tel. 23824). *The* place for excellent seafood. Crowded and touristy in high season, otherwise good.

Locanda Montin, Dorsoduro 1147 (tel. 23307). Historic trattoria.

Al Milion, San Giovanni Crisostomo 5481 (tel. 29302). A popular place where you can eat inexpensively and well.

Nono Risorto, San Cassiano (tel. 27630). Traditional Venetian cuisine.

Panada, Calle Larga (tel. 27358). Central, good.

Poste Vece, Pescheria 1608 (tel. 23822). Bustling trattoria, Venetian cuisine.

Vecia Cavana, Santi Apostoli 4624 (tel. 87106). Local specialties widely appreciated by those in the know.

GETTING ABOUT. Gondolas can be expensive; inquire at your hotel or at local tourist office for current rates, and come to terms with gondolier before you set out. Figure on at least 40,000 lire for one to six persons for 50 minutes minimum. Water taxis (motorboats) tend to overcharge. Short rides cost from 30,000 lire up. The vaporetto fare runs from 1,600 lire up; you can buy a tourist ticket for about 8,000 lire, valid 24 hours. After 10 P.M. a supplement of 25% applies to all public transport, including gondolas. If you're staying a few days, the *Carta Venezia* is a good buy (have extra passport photo handy). To and from airport, take bus (about 3,500 lire) or Cooperative San Marco motorboat (fixed charge of about 10,000 lire includes bags).

MUSEUMS. Though many insist the entire city of Venice is itself the finest museum, you will not want to miss the following outstanding collections. Hours are subject to change, so check at your hotel.

Accademia delle Belle Arti, in Convent and Church of Santa Maria Della Carità, on Grand Canal. The great Venetian painters. Closed Mon.

Ca d'Oro, right bank of Grand Canal. Splendid palace, artworks.

Correr Museum, entrance under portico dell' Ascensione, on west side of Piazza San Marco. History of Venice. Closed Tues.

Doges' Palace, at San Marco. Magnificent 14th-century palazzo decorated by Titian, Tintoretto and Veronese, with Porta della Carta and Scala dei Giganti. Book Secret Itineraries tour a day ahead. Ask for English commentary.

Fortuny Museum, Campo San Benedetto, near La Fenice. Offbeat collection of furnishings and fashion by designer Fortuny. Closed for structural repairs.

Museo del Merletto, on Burano. Lace museum, precious ancient and contemporary pieces.

Museo Navale, at the Arsenale. Maritime museum, with scale models.

Pesaro Palace, left bank of Grand Canal. Oriental and Modern art.

Querini-Stampalia Palace, near Church of Santa Maria Formosa. Art Gallery and library. Closed Mon.

Rezzonico Palace, left bank of Grand Canal. Decorative arts, works by Guardi, Longhi, Tiepolo. Closed Fri.

Scuola del Carmini, opposite church of same name, Tiepolo and others.

Scuola degli Schiavoni, far off in east section not far from Naval Museum. Carpaccio is the star here, in a Renaissance oratory. Closed Mon.

Scuola di San Rocco, opposite Santa Maria Gloriosa dei Frari, 56 works by Tintoretto in beautiful 16th-century building. Great Hall is masterpiece.

Venier dei Leoni Palace, left bank of Grand Canal. Magnificent home of the Peggy Guggenheim collection of modern art. Open Apr.–Oct. Closed Tues.

Museo Vetrario, Murano's glass museum displays glass objects from Roman times onward. Closed Wed.

SHOPPING. When you first see the displays of glassware around St. Mark's Square you may think that the Venetian glassmakers have had their day. Be patient. There's still some exquisite glass available; you just have to be discriminating enough to pick it out from the mass of mediocre stuff that the makers think will appeal to tourists.

If you have time to go to Murano, visit *Domus,* Pescheria 15A, on the main canal, for a discerning selection of the island's best. In Venice, *Salviati* at San Gregorio 195 and Piazza San Marco 79B and 110, has a huge collection including museum pieces, worth a visit even if you don't buy.

Venini. Piazzetta Leoncini, is famous for tasteful decorator objects in glass. For glass beads, go to *Mario Sanzogno,* Calle Canonica, or *Venezia Mario,* Campo SS. Filippo e Giacomo, or to *Domus* on Murano.

Venetian lace is as expensive as it is beautiful. If you want to buy or merely look, you can see how lace is made without going to Burano by visiting *Jesurum & Co.* behind St. Mark's cathedral. At 1091 Campo San Gallo is *Lorenzo Rubelli & Figlio's* luscious display of velvets and velvet brocades.

For stunning handbags go to *Roberta da Camerino,* Piazza S. Marco 127 and 5864 Campo S. Maria Formosa.

You'll have a wonderful time on that Rialto Bridge, which is lined with shops, and don't disdain the little portable stalls along the lagoon. Amid all the junk there are some nice novelty chokers of pastel-colored blown glass beads and some good toy gondolas and other amusing souvenirs.

The Veneto

Padua, about 20 miles west of Venice, has a famous university, founded in 1222; the 650-year-old Scrovegni Chapel, with frescos by Giotto; and the 13th-century Basilica of Sant' Antonio, built over the tomb of Saint Anthony of Padua, scene of an important pilgrimage every June 13. See the Donatello bronzes in this church and his celebrated statue of Gattamelata on the square nearby.

Vicenza, badly hit during the war, is still a treasure trove of Palladian architecture. Palladio's first major work, the Basilica Palladiana, dominates the Piazza dei Signori; the Corso Palladio is lined with palaces, and the beautiful Teatro Olimpico, Palladio's last work, is still intact.

Verona, a handsome medieval city, was the home of Romeo and Juliet, whose home and alleged tomb—as well as the impressive Castelvecchio and its art museum, the Piazza delle Erbe, the Piazza dei Signori and the Scaligeri Tombs, the churches of Sant'Anastasia and San Zeno—all should be seen. An unforgettable experience in this particularly attractive town is an open-air opera performance given in the Roman Arena. It seats 25,000 spectators and is so acoustically perfect that you can hear clearly from the last row. The performances are held in July and August.

For an unusual sidetrip, a comfortable excursion boat glides along the Brenta Canal between Padua and Venice, past the stately villas of 17th- and 18th-century Venetian nobles. The trip takes seven hours, includes a luncheon stop at Oriago and a visit to the Villa Nazionale, Stra, the most magnificent of them all. (Excursion starts alternately at Venice or Padua, with return trip by bus.) Off the beaten track and well worth a leisurely excursion by car through lovely countryside are the villas around Treviso, notably those by Palladio; CIT offers two all-day villa tours weekly from June 15-September 15.

PRACTICAL INFORMATION FOR THE VENETO

ASOLO. *Villa Cipriani* (E), tel. 55444. Aristocratic villa, a CIGA hotel. Excellent restaurant.
Restaurants. *Charly's One* (M), tel. 52201. *Ca'Derton* (M), tel. 52730. Simple.

LIDO DI JESOLO. *Bellevue* (E), tel. 961233. On Pineta beach with pool and terrace. *Las Vegas* (E), tel. 90731. Ultra modern hotel right on the beach; all rooms with balcony; pool. *Byron* (M), tel. 971023. On beach with comfortable rooms. *Galassia* (M), tel. 972271. Similar amenities.

PADUA. *Padovanelle* (E), at Ponte di Brenta (tel. 625622). On hippodrome grounds just outside the city; smart and modern with pool and good restaurant. *Plaza* (E), Corso Milano (tel. 656822). Central; recommended. *Donatello* (M), Piazza del Santo (tel. 36515). *Europa* (M), Largo Europa (tel. 661200). Central; all rooms with bath. *Majestic* (M), Piazzetta dell'Arco 2 (tel. 663244). Central.
Restaurants. *El Toulà* (E), Via Belle Parti 11 (tel. 26649). Tops for cuisine, ambience. *Isola di Caprera* (E), Via Marsilio 9 (tel. 39385). Favorite for seafood, game. *Giovanni* (M), Via Maroncelli 22 (tel. 772620). Classic, lively. *Cavalca* (M), Via Manin 8 (tel. 39244). *Pedrocchi* is historic, old-world café.

TREVISO. *Carlton* (M), tel. 55221. *Continental* (M), tel. 57216. *Fogher* (M), tel. 20686. In the outskirts; comfortable.
Restaurants. *El Toulà* (E), Via Collalto (tel. 40275). Superb food and atmosphere. *Beccherie* (M), Piazza Ancilotto (tel. 40871). Fine local cuisine.

VERONA. *Due Torri* (L), tel. 595044. Rebuilt on the site of an old hostelry and wholly delightful; central, quiet and with authentic period furnishings. *Colomba d'Oro* (E), Via Cattaneo (tel. 595300). Near the Arena with attractive terrace restaurant; good. *Vittoria* (E), Via Adua (tel. 590566). Central, smallish, quiet. *Accademia* (M), Via Scala (tel. 596222). Central and comfortable. *Firenze* (M), Corso Porta Nuova (tel. 590299). Near station, well-equipped. *Giuletta e Romeo* (M), Vicolo Tre Marchetti (tel. 23554). On medieval street, simple, small. *Torcolo* (I), Vicolo Listone (tel. 21512). Small.

Restaurants. *Dodici Apostoli* (E), Corticella San Marco (tel. 596999). Known for food and atmosphere; 14th-century building. *Le Arche* (E), Via Arche Scaligere (tel. 21415). Small, elegant seafood restaurant. *Il Desco* (E), Via San Sebastiano 7 (tel. 595358). Creative cuisine. *Marconi* (M), Via Fogge 4 (tel. 591910). Classic favorite. *Re Teodorico* (M), Castel San Pietro (tel. 49903). Good; wonderful view. *I Torcoloti* (M), Via Zambelli 24 (tel. 26777).

VICENZA. *Jolly* (E), Viale Roma (tel. 24560). Modern and all rooms with bath or shower. *Continental* (M), Via Trissino (tel. 505478). Comfortable. *Cristina* (M), Corso S. Felice (tel. 34280). *Basilica* (I), Piazza Erbe 9 (tel. 21204).

Restaurants. *De Remo* (M), at Ca'Impenta (tel. 500018). Delicious *risotto* and *baccalà*. *Gran Caffè Garibaldi* (M), Piazza Signori (tel. 44147). Upstairs, a good restaurant. *Al Pozzo* (M), Via Sant'Antonio 1 (tel. 21411). Good atmosphere. *Scudo di Francia* (M), Via Piancoli 4 (tel. 26284). Medieval setting, very good food. *Gran Caffè Garibaldi* (M), Piazza dei Signori (tel. 230066). Upstairs, a fine restaurant. *Al Pozzo* (M), Via Sant'Antonio 1 (tel. 2141). Good atmosphere.

The Dolomites

Increasingly, tourists are finding their way into the Alpine paradise of the Dolomites, a year-round mountain playground of unspoiled villages and unsurpassed scenery. An easy way to catch a glimpse of this country from Venice is to take the CIT bus trip that starts daily from the Piazzale Roma between June 1 and September 30, leaving at 8 A.M., passing through Treviso, Vittorio Veneto, Pieve di Cadore and Cortina d'Ampezzo, and returning at 6.30 P.M.

Cortina d'Ampezzo, scene of the 1956 Winter Olympics, is the jewel of the Dolomites. It has everything from the gentlest beginner slopes to spectacular jumps, a bobsled run, numerous cableways and chair lifts; in fact the complete works making it one of Italy's outstanding ski centers. If you've ever dreamed of a place where you could ski the year round, the Dolomites can make that dream come true—believe it or not, a giant slalom contest takes place every year at Solda, in the middle of July!

Among the highlights of this attractive region are: Trent (Trento), the area's southern bastion with a thousand years of history and art concentrated in its Piazza del Duomo; Bolzano, the heart of the Alto Adige, which to many Austrians is their lost province of South Tyrol; the famous Brenner Pass to Austria; Belluno, dating from pre-Roman days and surrounded by medieval castles and towers; and Merano, with its combination of skiing and sun bathing in mild winter temperatures and its world famous grape cure. Although the city has a definitely therapeutic effect, Merano nonetheless also offers many invigorating activities that are typical of the whole Dolomite region—tennis, polo, horse racing, swimming, trout fishing, canoe races, shooting the rapids, mountain climbing, golf.

PRACTICAL INFORMATION FOR THE DOLOMITES

BELLUNO. *Astor* (M), Piazza Martini (tel. 24921). All rooms with bath. *Dolomiti* (I), Via Carrera (tel. 27077). All rooms with bath. *Europa* (I), Via Vittorio Veneto (tel. 24705). A very superior (I).

Restaurants. *K2* (E), Via Cipro. Regional specialties. *Zumelle* (E). Romantic castle restaurant just out of town. *Cappello* (M), Via Ricci 8 (tel. 20122). Popular with locals. *Al Sasso* (M), Via Consiglio (tel. 22424). Near Piazza Erbe.

BOLZANO. *Grifone* (E), Piazza Walther (tel. 27057). Modern comfort, traditional hospitality; recommended. *Park Hotel Laurin* (E), Via Laurino (tel. 47500). Luxurious, a CIGA hotel; park, heated pool. *Alpi* (M), Via Alto Adige (tel. 25625). Modern and central. *Asterix* (M), Piazza Mazzini (tel. 43300). Comfortable, well-furnished, small hotel. *Città di Bolzano* (M), Piazza Walther (tel. 25221). Large rooms in period style, handsome salons and good service. *Scala* (M), Via Brennero (tel. 41111). Fine hotel with pool and park.

Restaurants. *Grifone* (E), in hotel of same name (tel. 27057). Excellent regional specialties. *Caterpillar* (M-E), Via Castel Flavon (tel. 44644). Good spot. *Abramo* (M), Piazza Gries 16 (tel. 30141). Excellent food, worth a visit. *Chez Frederic* (M), Via Armando Diaz (tel. 41411). Menu with French accent.

BRESSANONE. *Elefante* (E), tel. 22288. 16th-century villa with pool and memorable restaurant. *Dominik* (M), tel. 30144. Central, quiet, attractively modern. *Jarolim* (I), tel. 22230. Near the station with pool and garden.

CORTINA D'AMPEZZO. *Miramonti-Majestic* (L), tel. 4201. A luxurious hotel, expensive and posh; beautifully appointed with handsome salons and attractive alpine bar, tennis, pool and golf. Open Jul.–Aug., Dec. 20–end March. *Cristallo* (E), tel. 4281. Also top level with smart clientele and rustic-chic decor; very comfortable. Tennis, pool. *De la Poste* (E), tel. 4271. Central with large rooms and lively public rooms; *the* place to be seen. *Victoria* (E), tel. 3246. On main street; pleasant and attractive.

Ancora (E), tel. 3261. Close to cableway with attractive rooms and efficient service. *Cortina* (M), tel. 4221. Central and friendly with comfortable modern rooms. *Europa* (M), tel. 3221. Smallish rooms, good service and cuisine.

Al Larin (M), on Dobbiaco road (tel. 61341). Attractively furnished; good value. *Menardi* (M), tel. 2400. Rustic, attractive and comfortable; good value. *Montana* (M), tel. 3366. Central, basic and bustling.

Restaurants. *Caminetto* (☺), tel. 3525. Sunny terraces, great food. *Capannina* (E), tel. 2950. Delicious food in smart surroundings. *Fogher* (E), tel. 2702. Excellent. *El Toula* (E), tel. 3339. Elegant and expensive. *Da Melon* (M), tel. 61819. Smart but homey. *Meloncino* (M), tel. 61043. Excellent.

MADONNA DI CAMPIGLIO. *Golf* (E), tel. 41003. Just outside center with large well-appointed rooms and 9-hole golf course. *Savoia Palace* (E), tel. 41004. Comfortable, medium-size hotel. *Caminetto* (M), tel. 41242. Small and cozy, all rooms with bath. *St. Hubertus* (M), tel. 41144. A pleasant hotel.

MERANO. *Castel Freiberg* (E), Monte Franco (tel. 44196). Overlooking Merano, fine castle hotel with period furnishings, swimming pool. Open Apr.–Nov. *Meranerhof* (E), Via Manzoni (tel. 30230). Comfortable; all rooms with bath; pool. *Palace* (E), Via Cavour (tel. 34734). Very smart and expensive; town's leading spot. *Savoy* (E), Via Rezia (tel. 47600). Fine Swiss-type hotel. *Villa Mozart* (E), Via San Marco 26 (tel. 30630). Beautiful villa. Recommended for comfort, superb food, gourmet cooking school. *Anatol* (M), Via Castani (tel. 25511). Has thermal pool. *Juliane* (M), Via dei Campi (tel. 30195). Attractive, medium-range hotel with pool. *Schloss Labers* (M), Via Labers (tel. 34484). Pool, tennis.

Restaurants. *Andrea* (E), Via Galilei (tel. 37400). Small but excellent; book ahead. At *Villa Mozart* hotel (see above), same owner serves gala dinners for parties of 6 or more. Elegant, outstanding, *very* expensive. *Terlano Puts* (M), Via Portici 231 (tel. 35571). Good food, atmosphere.

STELVIO PASS. *Passo dello Stelvio* (M), tel. 903162. Remarkable location on the very summit of the pass; excellent service and fine restaurant.

TRENTO. *Castel Toblino* (E), tel. 44036. Elegant castle hotel outside Trento. *Everest* (M), tel. 986605. Good value. *Villa Madruzzo* (M), tel. 986220. First class comforts in handsome villa hostel at Cognola, 12 miles out of Trento. *Vittoria* (M), tel. 980089. Good.

Restaurants. *Accademia* (M), Vicolo Colica (tel. 981011). Good ambiance and food. *Chiesa* (M), Via San Marco (tel. 985577). Best in town; handsome old

dining room and fine cuisine. *Giulia* (M), Via Gazzoletti (tel. 984752). Good
value. *Villa Madruzzo* (M), tel. 980089. Good food in splendid surroundings.

The Trieste Area

Varied and off the beaten tract, Italy's easternmost provinces of
Udine, Gorizia and Trieste are worth exploring. The area, long part of
the Austro-Hungarian Empire, has a strong Slavic flavor while an
almost continuous border of sand sloping gently to the sea between
Venice and Trieste provides splendid beaches like Lignano Sabbiadoro.
Udine has a 13th-century cathedral standing on the Piazza della
Libertà, an arcaded square, one of the loveliest in Europe. If you like
Tiepolo, you should make an excursion to this town—his paintings are
everywhere, especially in the splendid Bishop's Palace.
Aquileia has an impressive basilica, built in 1061, and many relics
of Roman times, including a splendid forum. Grado is an unusual
island port with an attractive beach, a gridiron of quays and canals, a
harbor full of fishing boats and pleasure craft and a gem of a sixth-
century Byzantine cathedral.
Bustling Trieste, with its impressive Piazza della Libertà right on the
sea, is a center for yachting, horseracing and water sports. Its international samples fair each June is a big event, and the open-air opera given
each July in the 17th-century Castello di San Giusto rivals that of
Verona. The June-September Sound and Light spectacle at romantic
Miramare Castle is a must. Tarvisio, which stages various ski jumping
and racing competitions in January, is the chief resort for sportsmen
in this region, providing excellent hunting and fishing, too.
The summer resorts located in the hill and mountain areas of the
region are at their busiest from late June through August, while the
seaside resorts are filled up from the middle of June through August.
The winter sports season is at its height during December and January,
and some resorts continue to be active through February.

PRACTICAL INFORMATION FOR THE TRIESTE AREA

BIBIONE. *Principe* (E), Via Ariete 71 (tel. 43256). Large resort hotel on
beach. *Bembo* (M), Corso Europa 29 (tel. 43418). Modern, on beach. *Palace*
(M), Via del Leone 28 (tel. 43135). Bright, on beach.

GRADO. *Villa Bernt* (E), Via Colombo 5 (tel. 82516). Small, attractive. *Savoy*
(M), Via Carducci 33 (tel. 81171). Well-kept, with pool. *Tiziano Palace* (M),
Riva Slataper 8 (tel. 80965). Large, central.
Restaurants. *Da Nico* (E), Via Marina 10 (tel. 80470). Small place, inventive
fish dishes. Book. *Colussi* (M), Via Roma 2 (tel. 80110). Terrace dining.

LIGNANO SABBIADORO. *Eurotel* (E), tel. 428992. At smart Lignano Rivi-
era. *Grief* (E), tel. 422261. At Lignano Riviera, with pool and on the beach.
President (E), tel. 422537. Elegant and modern. *Bella Venezia* (M), tel. 422184.
Garden, beach. *Medusa Splendid* (M), tel. 72211. Medium range hotel at Lig-
nano Pineta.
Restaurants. *Bidin* (M), Viale Europa (tel. 71988). Reserve. *Alle Bocce* (M),
Via Platani 90 (tel. 71512). Country cooking.

TARVISIO. *Nevada* (M), tel. 2394. Good hotel.

TRIESTE. *Adriatico Palace* (E), tel. 224241. At the chic yachting port of
Grignano and with a private beach. *Duchi d'Aosta* (E), Piazza Unita (tel. 62081).
Best in town; modern and well appointed. *Jolly Cavour* (E), Corso Cavour (tel.
7694). Near the station; airconditioned. *Columbia* (M), Via della Geppa (tel.
69434). Comfortable and close to the station. *Continental* (M), Via San Nicolò
(tel. 65444). Very central.

Restaurants. *Harry's Grill* (E), Piazza Unita d'Italia 2 (tel. 62081). In Duchi d'Aosta Hotel, with elegant, old-world decor. *Birreria Dreher* (M), Via Giulia 75 (tel. 566286). Beer cellar with Austrian cuisine. *Granzo* (M), Piazza Venezia 7 (tel. 762332). Seafood. *Nastro Azzuro* (M), Riva Sauro 10 (tel. 755985). Seafood specialties, some dishes pricey. *Sacra Osteria* (M), Via Campo Marzio 13 (tel. 744968). One of city's best for local specialties. Book ahead. *Suban* (M), Via Comici 2 (tel. 54368). Fine Central European cuisine and nice view of city.

UDINE. *Astoria* (E), tel. 207091. Central, comfortable. *President* (M), tel. 292905. Fairly central, modern.

Restaurants. *Buona Vite* (E), Via Treppo 10 (tel. 21053). Elegant spot for seafood. *Alla Vedova* (M), Via Tavagnacco 9 (tel. 470291). Authentic regional cuisine. *Vitello d'Oro* (M), Via Valvason 4 (tel. 291982). Atmosphere, varied menu.

Liguria's Two Rivieras

Liguria is a strip of coastline stretching 217 twisting miles from the French border to Tuscany. Its seaside towns have been compared to a string of precious stones, the central pearl of which is Genoa. East of Genoa, the region is known as the Riviera di Levante; the western string is the Riviera di Ponente.

These twin rivieras are a popular year-round tourist area. It's carnival time here from January on. The spring opera season in Genoa, La Spezia and San Remo gets underway in February. Easter celebrations, flower parades, water games, regattas, motor races, tennis, golf, swimming, and skin diving—these are the diversions of Liguria. The safe, gently sloping fine sand beaches of the Riviera di Ponente are perfect for children. The best are San Remo, Imperia, Diano Marina, Laigueglia, Alassio, Finale Ligure, Spotorno, with rock bathing at Varigotti, sand at Noli.

After Genoa, the aspect of the coast changes, and the bathing here is generally for good swimmers who might prefer to dive from the rocks into deep water. Chief rendezvous for yachtsmen are Portofino, Pegli, San Remo, Santa Margherita Ligure and Genoa.

The Resorts, East and West

West of Genoa, the top resort is San Remo, which has a casino and a lively social and sports life. Bordighera, with its April parade of flowers, is quieter and prettier, and runs it a close second. Alassio, an international watering place, is a particular favorite of the English; it boasts an 18-hole golf course. Finale Ligure is attractive.

On the Riviera di Levante, Rapallo, also beloved by the English, is queen, followed closely by two beautiful small resorts, Santa Margherita Ligure and Portofino, most chi-chi spot on the Riviera. Camogli and Sestri Levante also are small and colorful.

La Spezia is a good excursion center for trips to such quaint towns as Portovenere, a fishing village on the site of an ancient Roman fortress. The Cinque Terre, five fishing towns with good swimming and magnificent scenery, are relatively unspoiled.

Genoa and the Ligurian Coast

Genoa is a handsome maritime city, set in a great semicircle around its busy port. The *Genovesi,* although they have the reputation in Italy of being *avari* (misers), have known how to spend money to beautify their city. The Via Garibaldi is typical, with its princely mansions and hidden gardens and its two important museums, the Palazzo Bianco and the Palazzo Rosso. The Via Venti Settembre is a rich example of art nouveau. The Church of Sant'Ambrogio was reconstructed in 1527 over a tiny 4th-century chapel.

This is one of 400 churches in Genoa, among the most interesting of which are the Cathedral of San Lorenzo, started in the 3rd century and rebuilt in its present Romanesque style in 1100, and Santo Stefano, where one of Genoa's most famous seafaring men, Christopher Columbus, was baptized. You can visit his home, and also the house of the great violinist Paganini, another famous native son.

To get the flavor of medieval Genoa, go to the Piazza San Matteo, where a group of ancient houses, belonging to the celebrated Doria family, dates from the 12th century. Many of the Dorias, including famous Andrea, were buried in the crypt of San Matteo, built in 1125, with its typical black-and-white marble façade. All the flavor of Genoa's mighty days of empire is summed up in the great palaces of the city—Palazzo Doria, Palazzo Ducale, Palazzo Reale and Palazzo San Giorgio.

Wander through the *carugi,* Genoa's picturesque old quarter, quietest (pedestrians-only) sector of a city plagued by traffic noise, and take the cablecar up to Monte Righi for some great views.

The bathing beaches of the Riviera di Levante (Ligurian coast *east* of Genoa) are apt to be most crowded in July and August. June and September are the best months in our opinion. The season on Riviera di Ponente (*west* of Genoa) is more staggered, but it is always best to reserve ahead. Beach charges are made generally (except by hotels with private beach): from 2,000 lire up for entry to beach, chair, changing facilities, umbrella. Off season (May, end September-end October) hotel rates are attractive.

Bear in mind that the waters of both Rivieras are polluted and that swimming in the immediate area of Genoa is highly risky, *when* permitted. In contrast, the hinterland offers unspoiled charms.

Avoid summer and weekend traffic back-ups into smaller resorts such as Portofino, which is pretty but touristy. Camogli is nicer.

PRACTICAL INFORMATION FOR LIGURIA

ALASSIO. *Diana* (E), tel. 42701. Posh and modern; on the beach with pool. *Mediterraneo* (E), tel. 42564. Most rooms with bath; private beach. *Spiaggia* (E), tel. 43403. On the beach. *Beau Sejour* (M), tel. 40303. *Ideale* (M), tel. 40376. *Majestic* (M), tel. 42721. *Eden* (I), tel. 40182. *Torino* (I), tel. 40616.

Restaurants. *La Palma,* (E), Via Cavour 5 (tel. 40314). Exceptional local cuisine and jovial atmosphere. *La Liggia* (M), Via Aleramo 3 (tel. 469076). Closed Nov.–Mar. Pleasant, good food. *La Capanna* (I), Via Genova 29 (tel. 44088).

BORDIGHERA. *Cap Ampelio* (E), tel. 264333. All rooms with balcony and sea view; pool. *Del Mare* (E), tel. 262202. With pool and on beach; tops for comfort. *Astoria* (M), tel. 262906. Quiet, well-furnished, garden. *Jean Pierre* (M), tel. 260668. Clean, pleasant, reader-recommended. *Villa Elisa* (M), tel. 261313. Above the town; good.

Restaurants. *Le Chaudron* (E), Piazza Bengasi 2 (tel. 263592). Italian food with masterful French touch. *Pinin* (E), Via Arziglia 20 (tel. 261322). On the San Remo road; recommended. *Piemontese* (M), Via Roseto 8 (tel. 261651).

CAMOGLI. *Cenobio dei Dogi* (E), tel. 770041. Best in town; attentive service, beautiful location; pool and tennis. *Le Ginestre* (M), tel. 770013. Bright and well-equipped.

Restaurants. *Gay* (E), Piazzeta Colombo (tel. 770242). Lively and pretty spot in the port. *Rosa* (E), Largo Casabona (tel. 771088). Attractive and reliable hotel restaurant. *La Camogliese* (M), Via Garibaldi 78 (tel. 771086). Varied menu.

FINALE LIGURE. *Moroni* (E), tel. 692222. Large and attractive. *Punta Est* (E), tel. 600612. Lovely villa hotel. *Colibri* (M), tel. 692681. Good but can be noisy.
 Restaurant. *Ai Torchi* (E), tel. 690531. Fine setting, good food.

GENOA. *Bristol Palace* (E), Via Venti Settembre 35 (tel. 592541). Traditional elegance. *Savoia Majestic* (E), Piazza Acquaverde (tel. 261641). Facing Principe station. Best in category.
 City (M), Via San Sebastiano (tel. 592595). Very central but very quiet. *Eliseo* (M), Via Piaggio (tel. 880210). Central, comfortable and well-furnished. *Sauli* (M), Viale Sauli 5 (tel. 16121). Near Brignole station; pleasant. *Vittoria-Orlandini* (M), Via Balbi 45 (tel. 261923). Near Principe station; good views.
 Restaurants. *Cardinali* (E), Via Assarotti 60 (tel. 870380). Excellent. *Gran Gotto* (E), Via Fiume 11 (tel. 564344). Regional specialties. *La Santa* (E), Vico Indorati (tel. 293613). Exclusive atmosphere. Reserve. *Zeffirino* (E), Via Venti Settembre 20 (tel. 591990). Central and good. *Mario* (E), Via Conservatori del Mare (tel. 298467). In old section.
 Centrally located are: *Da Nani e Mumo* (M), Salita del Fondaco 20 (tel. 205884). Central, good. Reserve. *Da Franco* (M), Archivolto Mongiardino 2 (tel. 203614). *Lino* (M), Via San Martino 11 (tel. 311052). *Pesce d'Oro* (M), Piazza Caricamento 65 (tel. 292539), for fish.
 At Boccadasse, fishing port suburb: *Le Ghiese* (E), Via Boccadasse 29 (tel. 310097). *Da Vittoria* (E), Belvedre Firpo (tel. 312872).

IMPERIA. *Corallo* (M), tel. 61980. Best in town. *Croce di Malta* (M), tel. 63847. On tiny beach.
 Restaurants. *Nannina* (E), Via Matteotti 56 at Porto Maurizio (tel. 20208). Seafood specialties. *Lanterna Blu* (M), Borgo Marina (tel. 63859).

LA SPEZIA. *Jolly* (E), tel. 27200. Very comfortable. *Royal* (E), tel. 900326. At Portovenere; good hotel.
 Restaurants. *La Loggia* (E), Corso Nazionale (tel. 501084). Smart, good. *Carlino* (M), Piazza Battisti 37 (tel. 32291). Local dishes. *Posta* (M), Via Don Minzoni 24 (tel. 34419). A classic.

LERICI. *Italia* (M), on central piazza (tel. 967108). Beautifully restored old hotel on port; no elevator. *Shelley* (M), tel. 967127. Good views.
 Restaurants. *Conchiglia* (M), Piazza del Molo (tel. 967344). Small; book ahead. *Da Paolino* (M), Via San Francesco 14 (tel. 967801). Cheery place.

OSPEDALETTI. *Rocce del Capo* (E), tel. 59733. Small with pool and gardens. *Petit Royal* (M), tel. 59026. Pleasant if a little old fashioned. *Alexandra* (PM), tel. 59031. Small pension with garden.

PORTOFINO. *Splendido* (L), tel. 69195. An outstanding hotel; smart clientele; tennis courts. *Nazionale* (E), tel. 69138. All rooms with bath or shower. *Portofino Vetta* (E), tel. 772281. On mountain top. *Eden* (M), tel. 69091. Small. All are booked a long way ahead in this exclusive resort.
 Restaurants. *Nazionale* (E), tel. 69138. In hotel of same name. *Pitosforo* (E), tel. 6902068. Good food on attractive terrace. *Splendido* (E), tel. 69195. Very splendido. *Navicello* (E), Salita della Chiesa (tel. 69471). Good. *Batti* (E), tel. 69379. Book ahead for all.

RAPALLO. *Eurohotel* (E), tel. 60981. On hillside overlooking the sea; airconditioning; pleasant pool in garden. *Astoria* (M), tel. 54577. Central, smallish. *Moderno* (M), tel. 50601. Beautiful old villa, modern rooms. *Riviera* (M), tel. 50248. Central, best in category. *Minerva* (I), tel. 50356. Garden.
 Restaurants. *Da Ardito* (E), Via Canale 9, at San Pietro di Novello (tel. 51551). Everything's good here. *Cuoco d'Oro* (M), Via Vittoria 5 (tel. 50745). *Romina* (M), Via Savagna 3 (tel. 64289). At edge of town, a good trattoria.

SAN REMO. *Royal* (L), tel. 79991. In park near the casino; elegant and comfortable; pool, tennis and garage. *Astoria West End* (E), tel. 70791. Old-world comfort in a palace hotel. *Colombia Majestic* (E), tel. 884884. Quiet location above the madding crowd. *Londra* (E), Corso Matuzia (tel. 79961). Traditional elegance. *Méditeranée* (E), Corso Cavalotti 76 (tel. 75601). Very comfortable, well-furnished rooms, in seaside park. *Montecarlo* (M), tel. 80766. Attractive hotel with pool. *Nazionale* (M), tel. 77577. Next to the casino. *Paradiso* (M), tel. 85112. Quiet location.

Restaurants. *Giannino* (E), Corso Trento Trieste (tel. 70843). Elegant, excellent. *Pesce d'Oro* (E), Corso Cavallotti 272 (tel. 66332). Fine for seafood. *Gambero Rosso* (E), Via Matteotti 71 (tel. 83037). Another top seafood restaurant. *Il Grottino* (M), Via Gaudio 47 (tel. 83178). Small, with pleasant veranda.

SANTA MARGHERITA LIGURE. *Imperial Palace* (L), tel. 88991. Largest and most expensive in town; with pool. *Continental* (E), tel. 86512. Handsomely furnished; on sea; gardens. *Miramare* (E), tel. 87014. Palatial; beach and 2 nightclubs. *Mediterraneo* (M), tel. 86881. Lovely villa. *Metropole* (M), tel. 86134. Beach facilities. *Conte Verde* (I), tel. 87139.

Restaurants. *All'Ancora* (E), Via Maragliano (tel. 80559). Fine family-run restaurant. *La Cambusa* (E), Via Bottaro (tel. 87410). *Simpatico* seafood place. *Basilico* (M), tel. 88812. *Faro* (M), tel. 86867. Spartan, good seafood. *Trattoria dei Pescatori* (M), Via Bottaro (tel. 86747).

SESTRI LEVANTE. *Dei Castelli* (E), tel. 41044. Quiet location by the sea; very comfortable; recommended. *Villa Balbi* (E), tel. 42941. *Mimosa* (M), tel. 41449. Small but good. *Miramare* (M), tel. 41055. *Vis à Vis* (M), tel. 42661. Basic rooms, but panoramic view and good restaurant.

Restaurants. *Angiolina* (E), Via Rimembranza 49 (tel. 41198). Fine seafood. *Sant'Anna* (E), Lungomare Descalzo 85 (tel. 41004). Elegant. *Schooner San Marco* (M), at marina (tel. 41459).

SPOTORNO. *Royal* (E), tel. 745074. Spacious and attractively decorated with pool and disco. *Pineta* (M), tel. 745412. On hill above town; quiet and pleasant with good views; short walk to the beach; low rates for category.

VENTIMIGLIA. *La Riserva* (M), at Castel d'Appio (tel. 39533). Delightful inn, seasonal.

Restaurants. *Balzi Rossi* (E), tel. 38132. Exceptional. *La Capannina* (M), tel. 351726. *Corsaro* (M), tel. 351874.

The Emilian Way

The region of Emilia is laid out for the most part along the famous old Roman road, the Emilian Way, which runs from Milan through Piacenza in the northwest to Rimini on the Adriatic. Among its chief tourist attractions are Bologna, one of the chief art and gastronomic cities of Italy; Parma, another place that combines these two pleasures; Ravenna, once the capital of the Byzantine Empire; Piacenza, a city of Gothic treasures; the art towns of Reggio Emilia and Ferrara, and a string of beaches, from the quieter, pollution-afflicted ones among the pine woods to the north, Marina di Ravenna, Marina Romea, Lido degli Estensi, and Lido delle Nazioni, to noisier, smart, but crowded Rimini, Cervia, Cesenatico, Bellaria, Riccione and Cattolica. These last-named beaches can be recommended for their fine sand, gentle slope and safe swimming. Salsomaggiore, the leading spa of Italy (except for Tuscany's Montecatini) is celebrated for its summer entertainment season and its battle of flowers in June.

Things to see: in Piacenza, the 16th-century Palazzo Farnese, the 12th-century Lombardian-Romanesque cathedral; the 13th-century Palazzo del Comune, and the Lombard Church of Sant' Antonino.

In Parma: the 12th-century Romanesque cathedral with Correggio's fresco of the Assumption decorating the dome, a masterpiece of Renaissance art; the churches of San Giovanni Evangelista and the

Madonna della Steccata; the Palazzo della Pilotta, containing one of Italy's greatest collections of art, superbly lighted in an airconditioned setting of luxurious comfort. In this same palazzo, don't miss the National Museum of Former Ages, with its valuable Etruscan and Roman antiquities and the remarkable wooden Farnese theater.

Reggio Emilia is worth a brief stop for its 16th-century cathedral and Parmeggiani Gallery of paintings (Veronese, El Greco and Van Dyck).

Modena has a world-famed collection of illuminated manuscripts in its Biblioteca Estense, and the city itself, once capital of the Duchy of Este, is charming, with its fountains and 12th-century bell tower, a rather incongruous background for the Communist posters all over the place.

Bologna

If you love art, architecture and good food, you will be in heaven wandering through the porticoed streets among the Renaissance palaces and fountains of Bologna. If you go to one of the city's famed restaurants for lunch, just ask for *un pranzo alla bolognese,* "a Bolognese luncheon" and leave the rest up to the waiter. When you stagger forth after your epic meal, visit the great Church of San Petronio, one of the most beautiful Gothic structures in Italy. Climb the 11th-century Torre degli Asinelli (350 ft. high) for a fine vista of Bologna's grandeur. Stroll through the Piazza del Nettuno and see Giambologna's Fountain of Neptune.

A walk down the Strada Maggiore, lined with medieval houses, will lead you to the 15th-century church of Santa Maria dei Servi, with its glowing Madonna by Cimabue. Other noteworthy churches include 4th- to 16th-century Santo Stefano, Santa Maria della Vita, and San Domenico, with sculpture by Michelangelo. The most beautiful private palaces in Bologna are on the Via Zamboni, and a fine collection of the Bologna School is on view in the city's Art Gallery, along with such outstanding examples of other work as Raphael's *Ecstasy of St. Cecilia* and Titian's *Crucifixion.*

Ravenna

Ravenna means mosaics, specifically the wonderful 5th- and 6th-century Byzantine mosaics in San Vitale, Sant'Apollinare Nuovo, the Cathedral baptistry, the tomb of Galla Placida and Sant'Apollinare in Classe. These alone would warrant a long journey, but you may want to make an excursion past the once-splendid pine forest along the shores to picturesque Comacchio and the nearby Abbey of Pomposa.

PRACTICAL INFORMATION FOR EMILIA

HOTELS. Emilia is well-provided with hotels, especially in the leading towns and resorts. Distances between the most rewarding places are short, so that you're sure to find a good place to stay the night. Reserve early for Parma in May and September, fair months, and for the coast resorts in the peak season of July-August. At beach resorts pension plan rates are very low, and include beach facilities. These resorts are especially favored by German and Scandinavian tourists.

BOLOGNA. *Royal Carlton* (L), Via Montebello (tel. 554141). Modern and elegant with airconditioning. *Elite* (E), Via Saffi (tel. 437417). On the outskirts; sleek and functional. *Garden* (E), Via delle Lame 109 (tel. 261861). Renovated monastery with pleasant garden; central. *Internazionale* (E), Via Independenza 60 (tel. 262685). Central, attractive and efficient. *Milano Excelsior* (E), Via

Pietramellara 52 (tel. 239442). Across from the station; reader-recommended for excellent service and pleasing atmosphere.

Alexander (M), Via Pietramellara 45 (tel. 270924). Near the station; excellent value and first class comforts. *San Donato* (M), Via Zamboni 16 (tel. 235397). Central and comfortable. *Nettuno* (M), Via Galleria 65 (tel. 260964). Central. *Roma* (M), Via d'Azeglio 9 (tel. 274400). Inconspicuous little hotel with aircondioning. *Tre Vecchi* (I), Via Independenza 47 (tel. 231991). Comfortable with good restaurant.

Restaurants. *Cordon Bleu* (E), in *Elite* Hotel, Via Saffi (tel. 437417). Outstanding. *Bacco* (E), Villa Orsi, Centergross (tel. 862551). Excellent cuisine, both classic and modern. *Dante* (E), Via Belvedere 2 (tel. 224464). Cuisine, atmosphere, prices, all at top level. *Franco Rossi* (E), Via Donzelle 1 (tel. 279959). Exceptional cuisine, wines. *Notai* (E), Via Pignattari 1 (tel. 228694). Elegant, *nuova cucina*. *Pappagallo* (E), Piazza Mercanzia (tel. 232807). Stunning ambiance, *nuova cucina*.

Bertino (M), Via della Lama 55 (tel. 522230), reasonable and good. *Birreria Lamma* (M), Via dei Giudei 4 (tel. 236537). Varied menu, good value. *Buca San Petronio* (M), Via dei Musei 4 (tel. 224589). Central location, classic local dishes. *Carlo* (M), Via Marchesana 6 (tel. 233227). Outdoor dining in summer. *Cesoia da Pietro* (M), Via Massarenti 90 (tel. 342854). Very good. *Duttuor Balanzon* (M), Via Fossalta 3 (tel. 232098). Fine restaurant, also *tavola calda*. *La Braseria* (M), Via Testoni 2 (tel. 264584). Good central trattoria. *Ruggero* (M), Via degli Usberti 6 (tel. 236056). *Silvio* (M), Via Valturini 4 (tel. 233424). Fine tortellini. *Serghei* (M), Via Piella 12 (tel. 232978). Classic cuisine.

CATTOLICA. *Caravelle* (E), tel. 962416. 45 rooms, all with balcony and bath; private beach. *Victoria Palace* (E), tel. 962921. Comfortable hotel. *Beau Rivage* (M), tel. 963101. Most rooms with bath or shower; on the beach. *Diplomat* (M), tel. 962200. Good hotel right on the beach.

Restaurant. *La Lampara* (E), Piazzale Darsena (tel. 963296). Exquisite seafood. *Moro-Osvaldo* (M), tel. 962438. Very good.

FERRARA. *Europa* (M), Corso Giovecca 49 (tel. 21438), attractive old hotel, period furnishings; closed Aug. *Ferrara* (M), Piazza della Repubblica (tel. 33015). Central; good. *De la Ville* (M), Piazza Stazione (tel. 53101), modern.

Restaurants. *Da Giovanni* (M), Largo Castello 32 (tel. 35775). Tasteful décor, tasty food. *Buca San Domenico* (M), Piazzetta Sacrati 32 (tel. 37006).

MODENA. *Canal Grande* (E), Corso Canalgrande (tel. 217160). Central, comfortable rooms, attractive decor. *Fini* (E), Via Emilia Est (tel. 238091). Excellent motor hotel. *Estense* (M), Viale Berengario 11 (tel. 242057). Central and unpretentious.

Restaurants. *Borso d'Este* (E), Piazza Roma (tel. 214114). Tops for atmosphere, cuisine. *Bianca* (M), Via Spaccini 24 (tel. 311524). *Da Enzo* (M), Via Coltellini (tel. 225117). Recommended. *Fini* (M), Largo San Francisco (tel. 223314). No exaggeration to describe this as one of the country's best restaurants.

PARMA. *Palace* (E), Viale Mentana (tel. 21032). Modern; best in town. *Park Stendhal* (E), Via Bodoni (tel. 208057). All rooms with shower. *Park Toscanini* (E), Viale Toscanini (tel. 29141). Old but comfortable. *Torino* (M), Via Mazza (tel. 21046). Central, all rooms with shower.

Restaurants. *La Filoma* (E), Via Venti Marzo (tel. 34269). A classic. *Canon d'Or* (M), Via Nazario Sauro 3 (tel. 25234). Good food, Verdi relics. *La Greppia* (M), Strada Garibaldi 39 (tel. 33686). Very good. *Leon d'Oro* (M), Viale Fratti 4 (tel. 35997). *Parizzi* (M), Strada della Repubblica 7 (tel. 25952). Local cuisine at its best. *Taverna Sant'Ambrogio* (M), Via S. Ambrogio 3 (tel. 34482).

PIACENZA. *Roma* (E), Via Cittadella (tel. 23201). Most rooms with bath or shower; airconditioned. *Cappello* (M), Via Mentana (tel. 25721). Traditional hotel. *Milano* (M), Viale Risorgimento (tel. 31419). Near the station; classic and comfortable.

Restaurant. *Il Teatro* (E), Via Verdi 16 (tel. 23777). Book ahead for one of Italy's best restaurants; excellent French and Italian cuisine.

RAVENNA. *Bisanzio* (E), Via Salara (tel. 27111). Very good hotel. *Jolly* (E), Piazza Mameli (tel. 35762). Best in town. *Park* (E), tel. 430184. At Marina di Ravenna resort with pool, tennis and private beach. *Argentario* (M), Via di Roma (tel. 22555). *Centrale Byron* (M), Via 4 Novembre 14 (tel. 22225). Central; simple but adequate rooms. At Marina Romea, *Romea Motel* (M), Via Romea (tel. 61247). 3 miles out of town. *Trieste* (M), Via Trieste (tel. 421566).

Restaurants. *Bella Venezia* (M), Via 4 Novembre 3 (tel. 22746). Good and not too expensive. *Torre* (M), Via Costa 3 (tel. 22098). *Tre Spade* (M), Via Rasponi (tel. 32382). Central; seasonal menu, very good. Some items pricey.

REGGIO EMILIA. *Astoria* (E), Via Nobili (tel. 35245). Best in town. *Posta* (M), Piazza Battisti (tel. 32944). Adequate.

Restaurants. *La Casseruola* (E), Via San Carlo. Tops. *Girrarosto* (E), Via Nobili 24 (tel. 37671). Hotel restaurant standing on its own merits. *Campana* (M), Via Simonazzi (tel. 39035). Regional dishes.

RICCIONE. *Abner's* (E), tel. 600601. Overlooks own private beach. *Atlantic* (E), tel. 601155. Posh and modern and on the beach. *Lido Mediterraneo* (E), tel. 42461. Big resort hotel with pool and disco among other facilities. *Savioli Spiaggia* (E), tel. 43252. On the sea front with pool and gardens. *Des Bains* (M), tel. 601650. Terraces, near beach. *Bel Air* (M), tel. 41998. Cheerful and comfortable. *Vienna Touring* (M), tel. 601700. Quiet location; modern and well run. *Alexandra Plaza* (I), tel. 615344. In quiet zone bordering on Misano; good value. *Dory* (I), tel. 40896. Pleasant and near the beach. *Flamengo* (I), tel. 41741. Attractive hotel near the beach.

Restaurants. *Calderone* (M), Viale d'Annunzio 72 (tel. 43222). Big, lively, good. *Pescatore* (M), Via Nievo 11 (tel. 42526), a touch of elegance.

RIMINI. *Grand* (L), tel. 24211. Topnotch palace type facing the sea; beach club, pool, tennis and kosher nosh on demand. *Ambasciatori* (E), tel. 27642. *Imperiale* (E), tel. 52255. *Savoia-Excelsior* (E), tel. 23801. Near the sea with tennis. *Aristeo* (M), tel. 81150. *Biancamano* (M), tel. 55491. *Ciotti* (I), tel. 80055. *Eurogarden* (I), tel. 80308. *Milton* (I), tel. 23456.

Restaurants. *Il Ristorantino* (E), Piazzale Independenza (tel. 24213). *Vecchia Rimini* (E), Via Cattaneo 7 (tel. 26610). Excellent and highly recommended. *Da Enzo* (M), Vicolo Santa Chiara (tel. 24148). Informal family-run place. *Tonino* (M), Via Ortaggi 7 (tel. 24834). Simple but good.

SALSOMAGGIORE. *Milano* (L), tel. 76141. Big and elegant with pool and spa. *Centrale* (E), tel. 771141. Traditional; with cure facilities. *Porro* (E), tel. 78221. Handsome. *Daniel* (M), tel. 76241. Modern and quiet. *Valentini* (M), tel. 78251.

Restaurants. *Alle Querce* (E), at Campore (tel. 771184). Exceptionally good. *Al Tartufo* (E), Viale Marconi 32 (tel. 72296). Tops in town.

San Marino

Not far from Rimini in northern Italy, on the eastern slopes of the Apennines overlooking the Adriatic, there is a small republic of 23 square miles and about 20,000 inhabitants which claims to be the oldest in the world. San Marino is the capital, and there are eight villages scattered around the surrounding hills, as well as the famous Castelli Sammarinesi.

The people of San Marino live on the income from postage stamps and tourists. Nearly a million of the latter come each year to admire San Marino's medieval fortresses, kept in a fine state of preservation and reconstruction. The effect is of time arrested.

The tourist trade is further encouraged by the complete absence of any border formalities. You don't need a visa to go there, not even a passport. If you want yours stamped for souvenir purposes, you'll have to request it. (For a really spectacular ride, take the helicopter service between San Marino and Rimini.)

PRACTICAL INFORMATION FOR SAN MARINO

HOTELS. *Grand Hotel San Marino* (E), tel. 992400. On top of Mount Titano and San Marino's best. *Joli* (E), tel. 991009. Near the station with a good restaurant. *Titano* (E), tel. 991007. Splendid view from the terrace restaurant of this good hotel. *Diamond* (M), tel 991003. Small, comfortable and reasonable. *Excelsior* (M), tel. 991163. *Tre Penne* (M), tel. 993437. Reasonable and with a fine restaurant.

Restaurants. *Buca San Francésco* (M), tel. 991462. *La Taverna* (M), tel. 991196.

SPECIAL EVENTS. In summer, usually July-September, *International Festival of Arts;* September, the *Palio dei Balestreri,* dating from the 16th century and with colorful crossbowmen in traditional dress. Check the dates with the Tourist Department, Palazzo del Turismo, San Marino or with the Rimini Tourist Office. A picturesque ceremony investiture of newly elected regents takes place on April 1 and October 1.

Florence

One of the world's great art cities, Florence isn't, however, just one big museum. Thanks to the initiative of its spirited inhabitants, it bustles with commerce and culture, and its monuments are a vital part of everyday life. The Palazzo Vecchio, for example, is *still* the town hall. But there are times when the city is overwhelmed by the thousands of tourists who invade it on day trips, all wanting to see the same things. Try to avoid crowds by visiting museums during off-peak hours.

The best place to begin a survey of the staggering riches of Florence is in the Piazza del Duomo. The facade of Florence cathedral (Santa Maria del Fiore) is faced with white, green and red marble. It may take some getting used to, but inside, the church is a stupendous example of Tuscan Gothic architecture. The giant dome, designed by Brunelleschi, is decorated by an immense fresco, *The Last Judgment,* by Vasari and Zuccaro. Over the entrance to the Sacrestia Vecchia is a terracotta by Luca della Robbia. The mosaic over the Porta della Mandorla along the north wall is by Ghirlandaio. Presently the dome is being reinforced and restored.

Next to the cathedral, Giotto's 14th-century Campanile rises to a height of 292 feet. It has been called the most beautiful bell tower in the world. Luca della Robbia did the first row of exterior bas reliefs with Andrea Pisano. Climb 414 steps for a superb view of Florence.

Directly in front of the cathedral, you will find the famous Baptistery of San Giovanni, with Ghiberti's greatest work, the East Door, or "Gate of Paradise" to use Michelangelo's phrase. It took the artist 27 years—from 1425 to 1452—to complete this matchless work in bronze. The North Door, representing the Life of Christ and the Evangelists, is also Ghiberti's work. Andrea Pisano is the sculptor of the South Door, completed in 1336.

Behind the cathedral is the Museo dell'Opera del Duomo, with a wealth of treasures including the charming panels from the choir loft by Luca della Robbia, and one of Michelangelo's three magnificent *Pietàs.*

Take the Via Calzaioli from the Piazza del Duomo to the Church of Orsanmichele. Its exterior niches hold statues by Nanni di Banco, Donatello and Verrochio, wonderful examples of early Renaissance sculpture. Inside, see the 14th-century tabernacle by Andrea Orcagna.

Resuming your walk along the Via Calzaioli, you will come to the Piazza della Signoria, in the center of which Savonarola was burned alive. The square is dominated by the Palazzo della Signoria, better known as the Palazzo Vecchio (The Old Palace). Built between 1298 and 1314, it is now the city hall. That Michelangelo David in the piazza is a copy; the original is in the Academy Gallery, safe from the ravages of the weather.

Next to the Palazzo Vecchio is the 14th-century Loggia della Signoria, with famous sculptures by Giambologna, Benvenuto Cellini and others. Nearby is the Piazza degli Uffizi, flanked by the Uffizi Palace, which houses what may be the most important collection of paintings in the world. Don't try to do it in less than half a day.

Other Highlights

Here are some other selected highlights of Florence—the Mercato Nuovo (New Market), covered by an arcade; the Ponte Vecchio (Old Bridge) across the Arno, spared by the Germans but hit hard by the 1966 flood and lined on both sides with goldsmiths, silversmiths and Florence's best jewelers; the Palazzo Pitti (Pitti Palace), a massive 15th-century building full of vast halls and salons, which in turn are full of tapestries, portraits, sculpture and an important collection of 16th- and 17th-century paintings which occupy 28 rooms of the palace; the finely planned Palazzo Strozzi, an outstanding Renaissance palace and courtyard; Brunelleschi's Church of San Lorenzo, with the adjoining New Sacristy by Michelangelo with its famous tombs of Giuliano and Lorenzo, Dukes of Medici; the Church of San Marco, with its museum containing the most important works of Fra Angelico: his *Annunciation* is here, and we recommend this particular visit even if it means giving up something else.

Incidentally, the best way to see the historic center of the city is on foot. For a rest, try a horse-carriage ride right through the Cascine, Florence's beautiful public park stretching for two miles along the Arno.

And what more? The Bargello Museum, with its fabulous collection of sculpture by Michelangelo, Verrocchio, Donatello and others; the Church of Santa Croce, the largest and most beautiful of all Italy's Franciscan churches, and the burial place of Michelangelo, Galileo, Machiavelli and many other illustrious Italians, and repository of priceless works of art, many of which were almost irreparably damaged in the floods. If it's open, visit the Palazzo Davanzati, a fully furnished Renaissance palace. For a refreshing change, stroll through the Boboli Gardens behind Pitti Palace.

By foot, car or bus, you should explore the lovely four mile promenade along the Viale dei Colli. The road winds outside and above Florence to a height of 340 feet at the Piazzale Michelangelo. The view here is superbly Tuscan—Florence, the plain beyond, Pistoia, and, in the far distance, the highest peaks of the Apennines. We almost hesitate to tell you while you're enjoying the view, but behind you at the top of the hill, there's the Romanesque church of San Miniato al Monte, built in 1013, one of the most beautiful and famous in Florence, and you really ought to climb that extra hundred feet and see it.

Environs of Florence

The villa towns just outside Florence are easily accessible by streetcar and bus. Many of the great Tuscan villas and their beautiful gardens are open to the public. Fiesole, with its 11th-century cathedral, Roman ruins and magnificent views, is 20 minutes by municipal bus from Florence. Inquire at Florence EPT about tours of outlying villas and the surrounding wine district, a pleasant way to break the monotony of city sightseeing.

PRACTICAL INFORMATION FOR FLORENCE

HOTELS AND RESTAURANTS. As an important tourist center, Florence naturally has many good hotels, but it's best to reserve well ahead at all times. Visitors to fashion shows crowd hotels at certain times of the year. Try to avoid the peak tourist seasons of Easter, May, and Jul.–Aug.

Deluxe

Excelsior-Italia, Piazza Ognissanti 3 (tel. 294301). It's big, it's posh and it's beautifully located on the Arno. Excellent restaurant.

Savoy, Piazza della Repubblica 7 (tel. 283313). More centrally located; barely a stone's throw from the cathedral and hardly less grand.

Villa Medici, Via del Prato 42 (tel. 261331). Between the station and Cascine park; well furnished, spacious; pool, garden and delightful rooftop restaurant.

Expensive

Augustus, Vicolo dell'Oro 5 (tel. 283054). Close to Ponte Vecchio, quiet, good value.

Baglioni, Piazza Unita (tel. 218441). Roof garden with exceptional view.

Croce di Malta, Via della Scala (tel. 282600). 120 compact and functional rooms; rooftop pool and sundeck.

De La Ville, Piazza Antinori (tel. 261805). Smart, medium sized hotel with marble floors and rich furnishings and spacious and quiet rooms.

Kraft, Via Solferino (tel. 284273). 70 small but well appointed rooms; rooftop terrace restaurant and swimming pool.

Lungarno, Borgo San Jacopo 14 (tel. 264211). Superior, quiet; smallish, well-decorated rooms, many with view.

Majestic, Via Melarancio (tel. 264021). Near the railway station; entirely renovated to provide modern comforts in a 16th-century Florentine idiom.

Minerva, Piazza Santa Maria Novella 16 (tel. 284555). Rather posh with comfortable rooms and pool.

Plaza Lucchesi, Lungarno della Zecca Vecchia (tel. 264141). A favorite for traditional decor, good service and front rooms with a view; just a short walk from the Uffizi.

Principe, Lungarno Vespucci (tel. 284848). Has a relaxed, private house atmosphere; 22 bright, airconditioned rooms, many looking over the river, others onto the tiny garden.

Regency, Piazza d'Azeglio (tel. 577728). Fairly central villa-hotel with a reputation for style, comfort, a Relais hotel.

Villa Cora, Viale Macchiavelli (tel. 2298451). Splendid neoclassical villa with period furnishings and modern comforts. Taxi ride to center.

Moderate

Berchielli, Lungarno Acciaioli 14 (tel. 211530). Very central and with smallish but spotless rooms and garden courtyard.

Continental, Lungarno Acciaoli (tel. 282392). Bright and cheery atmosphere; roofgarden but lots of traffic noise.

Jennings Riccioli, Lungarno delle Grazie (tel. 213724). Furnishings blend antique and functional; spacious front rooms have good view but rather a lot of traffic noise.

Laurus, Via Cerretani 8 (tel. 261752). Very central and brightly furnished in modern style; 94 compact and airconditioned rooms.

Mona Lisa, Borgo Pinti 27 (tel. 296213). Central pension in historic palazzo with garden and atmosphere.

Rivoli, Via della Scala (tel. 216988). 43 smallish but clean rooms with bath or shower; pleasant public rooms and garden courtyard.

Villa Azalee, Viale Fratelli Rosselli 44 (tel. 260353). Lovely old villa with garden, personalized atmosphere.

Inexpensive

Aprile, Via della Scala (tel. 216237). An historic palazzo converted into a comfortable hotel.

Columbia-Parlamento, Piazza San Firenze 29 (tel. 213150). Near most of the main tourist attractions.

Hermitage, Vicolo Marzio (tel. 287216). Central pension, book early.
Porta Rossa, Via Porta Rossa 19 (tel. 287551). Central; atmospheric.
Pendini, Via Strozzi 2. Central pension, recommended.
Rapallo, Via Santa Caterina (tel. 472412). 10 minutes from the cathedral.

Restaurants

Expensive

Barrino, Via dei Biffi 2/2, corner Via Ricasoli (tel. 215180). Elegant favorite of the smart set, excellent cuisine.
Le Cantine, Via di Pucci 4 (tel. 298879). *The* in place.
Da Noi, Via Fiesolana 40r (tel. 242917). Reservations a must for this little gem; creative cuisine.
Doney, Via Tornabuoni 46 (tel. 214348). Florentine classic.
Harry's Bar, Lungarno Vespucci 22 (tel. 296700). An American favorite; good drinks but pricey food.
Mamma Gina, Borgo San Jacopo 37 (tel. 296009). French cuisine for the most part.
Oliviero, Via delle Terme (tel. 287643). Excellent; with dinner dancing.
Pinchiorri, Via Ghibellina 87 (tel. 242777). Superb blend of food and wine in ancient palace; book ahead. Considered among Italy's top ten.
Le Rampe, Viale Poggi 1 (tel. 663063). Recommended.
Regency, Piazza d'Azeglio (tel. 587655). Elegant and excellent; in top hotel.
Sabatini, Via Panzani (tel. 211559). One of the absolute top places in the country; traditional atmosphere and superb food; book ahead.

Moderate

Antellesi, Piazza Santa Croce 21 (tel. 245698). Good food.
Buca Lapi, Via del Trebbia 1 (tel. 213768). A big favorite with Americans.
Cantinetta Antinori, Piazza Antinori (tel. 292234). Light meals or snacks accompanied by famous house wines.
Casa del Vin Santo, Via Porta Rossa 15r (tel. 216995). Book ahead.
Dino, Via Ghibellina 51 (tel. 241452). Food is an excuse in this wine-lovers' heaven.
Cibreo, Via dei Macci 118 (tel. 677394). Cordial service, unusual menu.
Frederigo, Pizza dell'Olio (tel. 212090). Good for Florentine specialties.
Lume di Candela, Via delle Terme 23r (tel. 294566). Romantic, pricey.
La Loggia, Piazzale Michelangelo (tel. 287032). Fine view, touristy.
La Maremma, Via Verdi 16r (tel. 218615). Excellent Tuscan cuisine.
Mario da Ganino, Piazza Cimatori 4r (tel. 214125). Popular, informal.
Paoli, Via dei Tavolini 12 (tel. 216215). Central with attractive Gothic decor and fine pasta.
La Sostanza, Via dei Porcellana 25 (tel. 212691). Plain and small; serves hearty steaks, salads and famous bean dishes; typical brusque service.

Inexpensive

Antico Barile, Via dei Cerchi 40r (tel. 213142).
Antico Fattore, Via Lambertesca (tel. 261215). Good spot behind the Palazzo Vecchio.
Buca Nicolini, Via Ricasoli. Does wonders with beans and rustic specialties.
Cantinone del Gallo Nero, Via Santo Spirito 6 (tel. 218898). Chianti cellar serving local dishes. Book for supper.
Di Fagioli, Corso dei Tintori 47 (tel. 244285). Typical Florentine cooking.
Latini, Via Palchetti 6r (tel. 210916). Near Palazzo Rucellai.
Mossacce, Via del Proconsolo 55 (tel. 294361). Tiny and busy and no lingering allowed, but the ready-to-eat food is fine and the atmosphere authentic.

NIGHTLIFE. Florence quiets down noticeably in the late evening, but there are a few spots for night owls. At *Oliviero* and the *Baglioni* you can dine and dance, and *Harry's Bar* remains a popular rendezvous. *George and the Dragon,* at Borso Apostoli, is a nice British-style pub; the *Red Garter,* Via Benci, offers beer and banjo music. *Caffè Voltaire,* Via Alfani 26, is a cosy, bohemian hangout.

MUSEUMS AND PLACES OF INTEREST. Below we list some of the outstanding museums and places of interest in Florence. Check with tourist offices for hours, as these can vary a great deal. You would be wise to plan your museum itinerary in advance (say the day before), so as to fit as many places grouped together as possible. Try to start as early as you can, to avoid the tourist busloads. At the time of writing, all museums open only until 2 P.M.

Accademia, Via Ricasoli. Michelangelo's *David* dominates, but there are others of his works as well.

Archeological Museum, Piazza SS. Annunziata 9. Important Etruscan antiquities.

Bargello, Via del Proconsolo. An exceptional collection of Renaissance sculptures.

Duomo, Piazza del Duomo. Santa Maria del Fiore, the cathedral, with Brunelleschi's dome, Giotto's belltower, Ghiberti's *Gate of Paradise* to the Baptistry.

Medici Chapels (Church of San Lorenzo), Piazza Madonna. Tombs by Michelangelo.

Museo dell'Opera del Duomo, Piazza Duomo 9. Outstanding pieces from the cathedral complex.

Museo di San Marco, Piazza San Marco. Houses most of Fra Angelico's principal works in the monastery where he lived.

Museum of Scientific History, Piazza dei Giudici 1. Scientific instruments, maps.

Stibbert Museum, Via Stibbert 26. Arms and armor.

Palazzo Davanzati, Piazza Davanzati. Furnished with authentic 14th to 17th-century pieces.

Palazzo Pitti, Via Guicciardini. Contains Renaissance and baroque art in its Palatina Gallery; also has Modern Art Gallery and Silver Museum.

Palazzo Medici-Riccardi, Via Cavour 1. Beautiful frescoes in chapel.

Palazzo Vecchio, Piazza della Signoria. Fulcrum of the city's history; was decorated by Vasari and Michelangelo.

Santa Croce, Piazza Santa Croce. Remarkable Florentine Gothic church; Michelangelo's tomb, Giotto frescoes.

Santa Maria Novella, Piazza Santa Maria Novella. Monumental cloisters, impressive art works and frescoes.

Uffizi, Piazza degli Uffizi. One of the world's most important museums, now going into its fourth century and displaying a breathtaking collection of Renaissance art.

SHOPPING. Most fashionable street is the Via Tornabuoni which runs from the Arno to the Piazza Antinori.

Don't miss that marvelous jumble of shops on the Ponte Vecchio. And by all means go to the Mercato Nuovo near Ponte Vecchio where various types of handicrafts are on display—straw, wood, leather, lace, and alabaster—a souvenir hunter's haven. Haggling is a fine art here; don't be shy. See Piazza San Lorenzo's big morning market.

USEFUL ADDRESSES. AAST, Via Tornabuoni 15, and Railway Station; *American Express,* SIT, Via Panzani 20R, tel. 283.825; CIT, Via Cerretani 59; *Cook's,* Via Tornabuoni 21; EPT, Via Manzoni 16.

Consulates: *American,* Lungarno Vespucci 38; *British,* Lungarno Corsini 2.

Tours: enquire at EPT for program of wine tours, or villa tours (April through June) which include tea at a pleasant inn, and (Saturdays only) a visit to *I Tatti,* villa of the late Bernard Berenson.

English-speaking churches: *Catholic,* the Cathedral, San Marco, Santa Maria Novella; *Church of England,* St. Mark, Via Maggio 9; *Protestant Episcopal,* Via Rucellai 5; *Christian Science,* Via della Spada 1; *Synagogue,* Via Farini 4.

Tuscany

Tuscany is a happy blend of high mountains, fertile valleys and long stretches of sandy beaches which curve along the west coast of Italy into the pine woods of La Maremma. But the magnet which has drawn people to this region for centuries is not the fabled green valleys of Tuscany, but the cities and towns, living symbols of the centuries-old Tuscan culture that brought forth the Renaissance and masters like Michelangelo, Dante, Leonardo da Vinci, Boccaccio and Petrarch. Florence, the Athens of Italy, Siena, Arezzo, Pisa—it is cities like these, with their atmosphere of antiquity almost intact, that have made Tuscany the most desirable destination in Italy.

The route down Tuscany's coast will take you to famed Carrara, where you can visit the marble quarries; Forte dei Marmi, with its pine-bordered beach of fine white sand, and Viareggio, the largest bathing resort on the Tyrrhenian coast.

West of Florence, the road out to Pisa passes through three remarkable cities—Prato, Pistoia and Lucca. Prato's 12th-century Romanesque cathedral contains works by almost all the major artists of Tuscany. If you're here on September 8, 9, 10 or 11, you'll be in the midst of an exciting fair combining entertainment with the chance to pick up a few bargains in wool and cotton goods, two famous Prato products. Eight miles beyond the art city of Pistoia is Montecatini, Italy's leading spa for afflictions of the stomach and liver. It's a charming hill town with enough hotels and swank restaurants to send you back to the waters; the season runs from April to November. Don't miss Lucca, one of Tuscany's most picturesque towns. Its 16th-century ramparts are delightful; as are its treeplanted promenades. Its cathedral, same epoch, is considered by many experts the most spectacular monument in Tuscany. Check the Della Robbias in the Church of San Michele, another extraordinary example of Tuscan architecture.

Pisa

Pisa's four major monuments are conveniently located in the Piazza del Duomo—the 900-year-old cathedral with its 69 antique columns; the 12th-century Baptistery, where you can admire the early Renaissance pulpit and the echo of your own voice; the extraordinary Camposanto (cemetery), and the Campanile, which is the famous Leaning Tower. Begun in 1173, the Leaning Tower sags about 14 feet off center because of a slight slip in the land during its construction. Some 294 steps spiral up to a terrace at the top, where the view of Pisa is worth the hike. Don't leave this beautiful Tuscan town without casting at least a brief glance at the Piazza dei Cavalieri, one of the finest squares in the region.

Elba

You won't miss too much if you skip the important commercial port of Leghorn (Livorno), but we heartily recommend a visit to Elba if you can fit it in. Aside from its Napoleonic connections, this little island has wonderful camping sites in the pines, lovely beaches you can call your own, a splendid round-the-island drive by car or bus through tremendous scenery, and tiny coastal towns where the sweet white wine of Elba comes cold and sparkling at roadside inns and restaurants. Be careful after the second glass or *you'll* be saying "Able was I ere I saw Elba". This delightful island, 18 miles long by 12 wide, is reached by steamer from Piombino several times a day. It's a 15-mile trip to Elba's biggest town, Portoferraio. There's also a hydrofoil service from Piombino. Like all Tuscan coastal resorts, it's overcrowded in August.

Siena and Arezzo

If you have time for only one town in Tuscany outside of Florence, make that town Siena. It retains more completely than any other Italian town both the look and spirit of the Middle Ages. The perfect time to visit Siena would be on July 2 or August 16, when the Corsa del Palio (Race of the Banner) has the whole town parading and competing in horse races in the beautiful Piazza del Campo in medieval costume. Highly recommended, but the race itself is over in a flash; it's the pre-race excitement and the celebrations afterward that are most interesting. The event draws huge crowds of tourists.

Off the beaten track between Florence and Siena is San Gimignano, medieval town of the towers, a charming place that is just being discovered by tourists. One other storehouse of Tuscan art treasures which should not be skipped is Arezzo, birthplace of Petrarch and home of the famous Guido of Arezzo, who invented the musical scale. Don't miss Piero della Francesca's series of frescos, *The Story of the True Cross*, in the 14th-century Church of San Francesco. They are a high point in the whole history of painting. The 12th-century Romanesque Santa Maria Church should also be visited here. To enjoy the full flavor of this wonderful town, just wander up and down its hilly streets, ending up at the medieval Piazza Grande, where there's an antique fair once a month. And if you're here on the first Sunday of September, you'll see the medieval Saracen's Joust, which rivals Siena's Palio in pageantry and thrills.

Porto Santo Stefano and Porto Ercole, on the Argentario Peninsula near Grosseto, are "in" resorts with the international set but are "out" in August, unless you have your own yacht to escape the crowds.

PRACTICAL INFORMATION FOR TUSCANY

 HOTELS. Avoid the central part of Tuscany in midsummer. The best seasons are spring and fall. The beach resorts are usually full-up from June through August and some beach hotels close November-April. Reserve well in advance if you want to stay overnight during such folklore festivals as Siena's *Palio* (July 2 and August 16), Arezzo's Joust of the Saracen (in September) and Viareggio's Carnival (February). Hotels are booked way ahead by out-of-towners coming to see these spectacular events.

AREZZO. *Continentale* (M), Piazza Guido Monaco (tel. 20251). Best in town center. *Europa* (M), Via Spinello (tel. 357701). Large modern hotel near the station. *Graverini* (M), Via Guido Monaco (tel. 21881). Near the station; reasonable. *Minerva* (M), Via Fiorentina (tel. 27891). Modern and functional hotel on the outskirts; good restaurant.

Restaurants. *Buca di San Francesco* (M), Via San Francesco (tel. 23271). Lots of atmosphere, good local cuisine. *Cantuccio* (M), Via Madonna del Prato 76 (tel. 26830). Attractive place for good food. *La Casentinese* (M), Viale Michelangelo (tel. 243105). Modest ambiance, reasonable and good. *Spiedo d'Oro* (M), Via Crispi (tel. 22873). Central, simple, *simpatico*. *Tastevin* (M), Via de Cenci (tel. 28304). Central, in historic palazzo, smart.

CASTIGLIONE DELLA PESCAIA. *Roccamare* (E), tel. 941124. Smart spot. *Riva del Sole* (E), tel. 933625. On the beach; tennis and all amenities. *David-Poggiodoro* (M), tel. 933030. With pool. *Park Zibellino* (M), tel. 941055. At the Roccamare holiday village.

CHIANCIANO. *Grand e Royal* (L), tel. 63333. Traditional and elegant; a fine hotel. *Excelsior* (E), tel. 64351. All comforts in this smart spot. *Michelangelo*

(E), tel. 64004. Very comfortable. *Capitol* (M), tel. 64681. Modern and good. *Fortuna* (M), tel. 64661. Good.

Restaurants. *Casanova* (E), Strada Vittoria (tel. 60449). Excellent. *Casale* (M), Via Cavine (tel. 30445). Rustic.

ELBA. At **La Biodola:** *Hermitage* (E), tel. 969932. On the beach with pool. At **Capoliveri:** *International* (M), tel. 968611. Modern and rather impersonal with pool. *Acacie* (M), tel. 968526. Friendly and attractive; on the beach. At **Cavoli:** *Bahia* (M), tel. 987055. Cottages overlooking beach. At **Magazzini:** *Fabricia* (M), tel. 966181. Modern and near the beach with pool. At **Marciano Marina:** *La Primula* (E), tel. 99010. In town; attractive. At **Marina di Campo:** *Montecristo* (E), tel. 976782. Pool and tennis among the facilities. At **Porto Azzurro:** *Cala di Mola* (M), tel. 95225. At **Procchio:** *Del Golfo* (E), tel. 907565. Modern resort hotel. *Desirée* (M), tel. 907502. Spacious rooms, private beach.

FIESOLE. *Villa San Michele* (L), tel. 59451. Top-level comfort and service in converted 15th-century monastery. Quiet luxury. A Relais hotel.

Restaurant. *Cave di Maiano* (M), tel. 59133. 2 km. away; rustic, very good.

FORTE DEI MARMI. *Augustus* (L), tel. 80202. All comforts in this outstanding hotel; beach club and disco among numerous splendors. *Hermitage* (E), tel. 80022. In quiet park with pool; mini-bus service to beach 2km. away. *Park* (E), tel. 81494. All resort facilities. *Astoria Garden* (M), tel. 80754. *Florida* (M), tel. 80266. Comfortable medium range hotel. Modern. *Villa Angela* (M), tel. 80652. With private beach. *Adam's Villa Maria* (M), tel. 80901. Garden, sea view.

GIGLIO. Island hideaway off Porto San Stefano. *Castello Monticello* (M), tel. 809252. With pool and tennis. *Demo's* (M), tel. 809235. Large and comfortable.

LUCCA. *Villa Principessa* (E), tel. 370037. Elegant villa-style hotel at Massa Pisana. *Napoleon* (M), tel. 53141. Good. *Universo* (M), tel. 49046. Classic.

Restaurants. *Solferino* (E), tel. 59118. A little outside town; highly recommended. *Buca di Sant'Antonio* (M), tel. 55881. Excellent. *La Mora* (M), tel. 57109. Outside town at Ponte a Moiano; outstanding, rustic. *Sergio* (M), tel. 49944. Fine food. *Il Punto* (M), tel. 46264. Central, varied menu. *Vipore* (M), tel. 59245. Pleasant country dining. *Delle Mura* (I), tel. 47962. Picturesque and inexpensive spot.

MONTECATINI TERME. *Grand Hotel et La Pace* (L), tel. 75801. Palace type hotel with traditional furnishings and secluded location. *Bellavista* (E), tel. 72122. Attractive. *Croce di Malta* (E), tel. 79381. Superior hotel with annex. *Tamerici e Principe* (E), tel. 71041. Good hotel. *Astoria* (M), tel. 71191. Good. *Capelli* (M), tel. 71151. Traditional type. *Pellegrini,* tel. 71241. Central.

Restaurants. *Giovanni* (M), Corso Roma (tel. 71695). Fine wining, dining. *Vittoria Hotel* (M), Via Liberta 2 (tel. 79271). Good. *Lido's* (E), Montecatini Alto (tel. 766378). Top-level cuisine, panorama.

ORBETELLO-MONTE ARGENTARIO. *Corte dei Butteri* (E), tel. 885546. On beach, pool, resort-style, quiet; at Fonteblanda. *Il Pellicano* (E), tel. 833801. Near Porto Ercole; chic, informal luxury. *Don Pedro* (M), tel. 833914. Modern and good value. At **Porto Santo Stefano:** *Filippo II* (E), tel. 812694. Smart. *Cala Piccola* (E). Exclusive resort hotel.

Restaurants. At Porto Ercole, *Lampara* (M), tel. 833024. Good trattoria on port. At Porto Santo Stefano, *La Formica* (M), on Pozzarello beach (tel. 814205). Very good.

PISA. *Dei Cavalieri* (E), Piazza Stazione (tel 43290). Large and well appointed; close to the station. *Duomo* (E), Via Santa Maria (tel. 27141). Central and quiet with comfortable rooms. *Arno* (M), Piazza Repubblica (tel. 22243). Central, smallish. *La Pace* (M), Via Gramsci 14 (tel. 502266). Near station, good.

Restaurants. *Al Ristoro dei Macelli* (E), Via Volturno (tel. 20424). Excellent cuisine. *Sergio* (E), Lungarno Pacinotti (tel. 48245). Very good food by the Arno. *Centrale-Spartaco* (E), Piazza Vittorio (tel. 23335), fine. *Emilio* (M), Via

Roma 28 (tel. 26028). *Nando* (M), Via Contessa Matilde (tel. 24291). *Santa Maria* (M), Via S. Maria (tel. 26206).

PRATO. *Palace* (M), tel. 592841. On outskirts; modern, well-equipped. *President* (M), tel. 30251. Sleek and modern. *Villa Santa Cristina* (M). Comfortable villa outside town.

Restaurants. *Baghino* (M), Via dell'Accademia 9 (tel. 27920). Attractive spot. *Pirana* (E), Via Valentini 110 (tel. 25746). Excellent. *Stella d'Italia* (M), Piazza Duomo 8. Central; pleasant.

PUNTA ALA. *Cala di Porto* (E), tel. 922455. Smart hotel with park and pool. *Gallia Palace* (E), tel. 922022. Elegant hotel with private beach. *Golf* (M), tel. 922026. Near the beach.

SAN GIMIGNANO. *La Cisterna* (M), tel. 940328. Fine view and good restaurant. *Bel Soggiorno* (I), tel. 940375. Renovated inn; all rooms with bath; rooftop restaurant.

SIENA. *Excelsior* (E), Piazza La Lizza (tel. 288448). A Jolly hotel. *Certosa* (E), at Maggiano (tel. 288180). Outside town, only 14 well-furnished rooms in old-world setting. No elevator. Closed in winter. *Park Hotel* (E), tel. 44803. On the outskirts; a handsome 15th-century palace with delightful grounds and pool. *Athena* (M), tel. 286313. Handy and comfortable. *Continentale* (M), tel. 286313. Old and central and very quiet. *Palazzo Ravizza* (M), Piano dei Mantellini (tel. 280462). Recommended for central location, period decor.

Restaurants. *Park Hotel* (E), Via Marciano (tel. 44803). Excellent dining in this CIGA hotel. *Da Guido* (M), Vicolo Pettinaio (tel. 200042). A favorite. *Al Mangia* (M), Piazza del Campo (tel. 281121). Classic view and food. *Medioeva* (M), Via Rossi (tel. 280315). *Nello* (M), Via Porrione 28 (tel. 289043). *Tre Campane* (M), Piazzetta Bonelli (tel. 286091). Central, modest, good. *Tullio Tre Cristi* (M), Vicolo Provenzano (tel. 280608). Longtime favorite.

VIAREGGIO. *Grand Royal* (E), tel. 45151. Central and imposing; front rooms can be noisy; well-furnished, pool, gardens and beach. *Principe di Piemonte* (E), tel. 50122. Fine hotel on the sea. *American* (M), tel. 47041. Well furnished. *Garden* (M), tel. 44025. Attractive small hotel.

Restaurants. *Astor* (E), tel. 50301. In hotel of the same name and an altogether excellent restaurant in modern surroundings. *Montecatini* (E), Viale Manin 8 (tel. 42129). Very fine food. *Tito del Molo* (E), Lungomolo Corrado del Greco (tel. 42016). Good seafood. *Patriarca* (E), Viale Carducci (tel. 53126). Excellent. *Romano* (E), Via Mazzini (tel. 31382). Tops; reserve.

VOLTERRA. *Nazionale* (M), tel. 86284. Basic but clean.

Restaurants. *Etruria* (M), Piazza Priori (tel. 86064). *Porcellino* (M), tel. 86392.

Umbria, the Mystic Province

Roughly half way between Florence and Rome is the mystic province of Umbria, wrapped in a strange bluish haze that gives an ethereal, painted look. Its three principal tourist centers—Assisi, Orvieto and Perugia—are all more than a thousand feet high, which helps cool them in the hot months of July and August, though May, June and September are more comfortable months to visit here. To the three cities just mentioned, a fourth can now be added—Spoleto, where Gian-Carlo Menotti's annual *Festival of Two Worlds* draws cosmopolitan crowds in June-July (information from the Festival Office, Via Margutta 17, Rome).

Assisi, Orvieto and Perugia

Assisi seems to be actually alive with the sweet personality of St. Francis, who is buried here in the huge 13th-century basilica on the Hill of Paradise. The Master of St. Francis, Cimabue, Giottino, Giotto and Pietro Cavallini are just a few of the great artists whose work glorifies this church and the dim lower level of the Basilica; two flights below is the crypt where you can see the tomb of St. Francis himself. In the Sacristy of the lower church to the left of the altar, you will see a number of relics of the saint, including the patched gray cassock and crude sandals which he is said to have been wearing when he received the Stigmata in 1224.

Orvieto stands dramatically on top of an island of volcanic rock in the middle of the Tiber Valley. Its chief attraction is the cathedral, a magnificent 13th-century church with a marble exterior of alternating stripes of black and white. Seen in that special net of Umbrian light, it is most impressive. In one of the side chapels are frescos by Luca Signorelli. Before exploring the rest of this atmospheric town, try a *fiasco* of Orvieto wine, at its best here at the source.

Perugia's contributions to the happiness of this world include Perugina chocolates, Luisa Spagnoli's angora sweaters, and the 15th-century Umbrian master, Perugino. He and his pupil, Raphael, decorated the Stock Exchange, which, with a chapel and art gallery are all included in Perugia's 13th-century Municipal Palace. We recommend a brief meander through Perugia's medieval streets, especially the Via delle Volte, a favorite photographic subject.

PRACTICAL INFORMATION FOR UMBRIA

ASSISI. *Subasio* (M), tel. 812206. Flowered terraces and good views from this fine hotel. *Fontebella* (M), tel. 812883. Pleasant hotel. *Giotto* (M), tel. 812209. *Umbra* (M), tel. 812240. Small and quiet.

Restaurants. *Buca San Francesco* (M), tel. 812204. Central, serving rustic and hearty fare. *La Fontana da Carletto* (M), tel. 812933. Local specialties. *Fortezza* (M), tel. 812418. Medieval setting, very good food. *Il Frantoio* (M), tel. 812977. Good atmosphere, local dishes. *Paradiso* (M), tel. 812843. Pleasant spot. *Taverna dell'Arco* (M), tel. 812383. Medieval atmosphere. *Umbra* (M), tel. 812240. Dining in the garden of the hotel of the same name is delightful.

GUBBIO. *Cappuccini* (E), tel. 922241. Below town; attractive, spacious rooms, tranquil atmosphere, adequate service. *Bosone* (M), tel. 923008. Central, modern and well-equipped.

Restaurants. *Dei Consoli* (M), tel. 922135. Hearty dishes. *Porta Tessenaca* (M), tel. 924365. Atmosphere, sometimes touristy. *Taverna del Lupo* (M), tel. 922968. Local specialties.

ORVIETO. *Badia* (E), tel. 90359. Converted abbey below town. *Maitani* (E), tel. 33001. Elegant and best in town. *Italia* (M), tel. 33045. Most rooms with bath or shower. *Virgilio* (M), tel. 35252. Delightful; on cathedral square.

Restaurants. *Maurizio* (E), tel. 34114. Good eating. *Morino* (E), tel. 35152. Renowned for fine food. *L'Ancora* (M), tel. 35446.

PERUGIA. *Brufani Palace* (L), tel. 20741. Elegant luxury hotel. *Perugia Plaza* (E), tel. 34643. Modern and good. *La Rosetta* (M), tel. 20841. Central, comfortable and cheerful.

Restaurants. *Ricciotto* (E), Piazza Dante (tel. 21956). Good. *Falchetto* (M), Via Bartolo (tel. 61875). Known for local specialties. *La Lanterna* (M), Via Rocchi 6 (tel. 66064). Umbrian cuisine.

At **Torgiano**, 8 miles from Perugia, *Tre Vaselle* (E), tel. 982447. A *Relais* hotel-restaurant, famous for excellent cuisine.

SPOLETO. *Gattapone* (E), tel. 36147. Reserve way ahead for this 8-room gem. *Clitunno* (M), tel. 38240. Central; attractive. *Dei Duchi* (M), tel. 35241. Modern with good restaurant and view. *Manni* (I), tel. 38135. Comfortable.

Restaurants. *Dei Duchi* (M), tel. 35241. In hotel of the same name. *Del Festival* (M), tel. 32198. *Taverna il Tartufo* (M), tel. 25136.

The Marches

The Marches constitute an unusual region for unusual travelers: those who have seen the showplaces—Rome, Tuscany, Venice—and want to get to know the unselfconscious heart of Italy. The country, bounded by the Apennines and the Adriatic, is full of isolated towns, rushing torrents, and mountains from 3,000 to 8,000 feet high.

The jewel of the Marches is Urbino, a living monument to the Renaissance. The great Ducal Palace of Frederick of Montefeltro, dominating the city from its rocky eminence, is worth a pilgrimage. Its library includes some of the finest illuminated manuscripts in existence; its art gallery, major works by Uccello, Piero, Signorelli and Titian. The whole castle will tell you more of the bursting wealth and energy of the Italian Renaissance than any history book. Raphael's birthplace is another attraction in an exceptionally attractive town.

Loreto and Ancona

Special trains bring sick pilgrims from all over Italy to the Holy House of Loreto, reputedly the Virgin's home at the time of the Annunciation, and transported by Angels to Loreto in the 13th century, when the Holy Land was overrun by Mohammedans. Special pilgrimage days are March 25, August 15, September 8, December 8 and December 10. On the last date, which celebrates the miraculous transference of the Holy House, bonfires are lit all over the region.

Pesaro, one of whose sons was Rossini, is a pleasant seaside town, perfect if you want to combine swimming with sightseeing.

Ancona, also on the sea, is a wonderful place for wandering, especially in the old town between cathedral and port, where you walk on ancient stone ramps under Gothic arches. The Romanesque cathedral has a commanding position with an excellent view of the town and its colorful harbor. The marble Arch of Trajan, just 300 yards as the crow flies from the cathedral's lovely white and rose stone door, remains intact. It is just about the finest Roman arch in Italy. Don't miss the toy-like church of Santa Maria della Piazza, the lacy arches of the Loggia dei Mercanti, or the powerful *Crucifixion* by Titian in the San Domenico Church.

PRACTICAL INFORMATION FOR THE MARCHES

ANCONA. *Grand Palace* (E), tel. 201813. About the best in town. *Jolly* (E), tel. 201171. Good hotel. *Passetto* (E), tel. 31307. *Emilia* (M), tel. 801117. At Portonovo beach. *Rome e Pace* (M), tel. 202007. Central, solid, traditional.

Restaurants. *Da Miscia* (E), Molo Sud (tel. 201376). Reserve for exquisite seafood. *Passetto* (E), Piazza IV Novembre (tel. 33214). Best. *Giardino* (M), Via Filzi (tel. 22998). Fine pastas and local specialties. *La Moretta* (M), Piazza Plebiscito (tel. 58382). Turn-of-the-century trattoria.

LORETO. *Giardinetto* (M), tel. 977135. Adequate overnight.
Restaurant. *Da Orlando* (M), tel. 977696. At Loreto Archi.

PESARO. *Victoria* (E), tel. 34343. Atmosphere, all comforts. *Caravan* (M), tel. 64513. 35 rooms. *Caravelle* (M), tel. 64078. Bright, modern and comfortable.

Mamiani (M), tel. 35541. Central for sightseeing. *Spiaggia* (M), tel. 32516. On beach, pool.

Restaurants. *Lo Scudiero* (E), Via Baldassini (tel. 64107). Classic cuisine in historic locale. *Da Carlo al Mare* (E), Viale Trieste 265 (tel. 31453). Admirable *zuppa di pesce. Della Posta* (M), Via Giordano Bruno (tel. 33292). Excellent.

SAN BENEDETTO & PORTO D'ASCOLI. Twin beach resorts. *Roxy* (E), tel. 4441. Good. *Calabresi* (M), tel. 60548. At resort center. At **Porto d'Ascoli:** *Ambassador* (M), tel. 659443. Seasonal resort hotel.

Restaurants. *Angelici* (M), tel. 3597. *Stalla* (M), tel. 4933.

URBINO. *San Giovanni* (M), tel. 2827. Central; spartan rooms in renovated medieval palace, good restaurant. *Montefeltro* (M), on outskirts, modern.

Restaurants. *Nuovo Coppiere* (M), Via Porta Maria (tel. 41350). Intimate, good. *San Giovanni* (M), Via Barocci (tel. 3486).

Scenic Campania

The Campania region of Italy stretches south from Capua and Caserta through a region of evocative names. Vesuvius, the destroyer of Pompeii and Herculaneum; the Cave of the Sibyls, near Lake Averno, one of the gates to hell; Capri, sybaritic playground of the emperors. The view of Naples from the Sorrento Peninsula is breathtaking—as, in a different way, are the hairpin bends of the Amalfi Drive.

The high season in the Campania is April, when the weather is ideal. The next best months are May, June, September and October. July and August are hot, but Capri, Ischia and the seaside resorts have their consolations during these big vacation months, and consequently they are apt to be crowded, as they are also at Easter.

Public transportation links the main sights: the Circumvesuviana railways runs every half-hour between Naples and Sorrento, via Herculaneum and Pompeii. SITA buses connect Sorrento with Positano, Amalfi, Ravello and Salerno. The Cumana railway links the Solfatara and Pozzuoli, Lake Averno and Cuma. A boat service goes to the islands of Capri, Procida and Ischia.

Naples

The greatest attraction of Naples is its extraordinary National Museum, chock full of beautiful Greek and Roman art, especially from Pompeii. The museum was spruced up after the terrible earthquake in 1980 and is much more pleasant than it used to be, although you may find sections are still closed off. See the colossal Farnese Bull statuary group and the mosaics from Pompeii. You will find ample evidence of the earthquake's damage coupled with urban decay in Naples' historic and picturesque center. These problems, together with chaotic traffic and virulent delinquency, have sadly diminished Naples' appeal.

By the way of contrast to the National Museum, the Capodimonte Royal Palace, atop the hill of the same name, is one of the most orderly and sumptuous museums in Europe, its armor, china and picture collections arranged with great taste.

The best view of the city and its marvelous bay is from the Carthusian Monastery (Certosa di San Martino), on the slopes of the Vomero. A fine example of Neapolitan baroque architecture, it contains the National Museum of San Martino, with priceless works of art and relics from the Kingdom of Naples. Step out on the balcony for a view you'll never forget. Another great view is from the terrace on top of Capodimonte Palace.

Attractions of the city proper include the Umberto Gallery; Via Santa Lucia, best shopping street for gifts, cameos, tortoise shell, coral and other Neapolitan specialties; the San Carlo Opera House, one of the most famous in the world; the massive Castel Nuovo, begun in 1282, with its Arch of Triumph. The Piazza del Mercato and the harbor are both worth a visit, for here you will be rubbing elbows with one of the chief attractions of this city, the exuberant, animated, spontaneous, effervescent, arm-waving Neapolitans. Remember, however, that you are easily recognizable as a tourist and are therefore a potential target for purse and camera snatchers.

Environs of Naples

On the western outskirts, near the Mergellina Station, the Tomb of Virgil is the starting point for explorations to the west. Solfatara, with its churning crater of boiling mud, can be visited. Don't miss the Roman amphitheater at Pozzuoli, smaller but far better preserved than the Colosseum at Rome; the ancient Temple of Serapis here should be seen too, for it's an indicator of volcanic activity.

Branching right from Pozzuoli along the Via Domiziana, you pass Lake Averno (Lago di Averno), an entrance to the underworld, through which Aeneas went to visit his dead father, Anchises, and, less than a mile further, the ancient Greek colony of Cuma, where you should visit the Antro della Sibilla, celebrated grotto of the Cumaean Sibyl. Turn south, after Cuma, to Baia, the luxury-loving Roman Baiae, whose hot springs made it the largest (and most dissolute) spa of the empire.

North of Naples (18 miles) is Caserta, whose greatest attraction is the royal palace, built in 1752 for the Bourbon kings of Naples and Sicily and intended to be more grand and beautiful than Versailles. It isn't; but then again, it isn't exactly a slum.

Herculaneum and Pompeii

East and south of Naples the first point of interest is Herculaneum (Ercolano). If your time is short, choose this even in preference to Pompeii. Like Pompeii, Herculaneum was buried by the eruption of Vesuvius in 79 A.D., but it was destroyed by a mass of volcanic mud that sealed and preserved wood and other materials which were consumed by red hot cinders at Pompeii. Smaller than its more famous neighbor, Herculaneum was wealthier, more select, and more has been left in place. There is more of a sense of a living community here than at Pompeii. A visit is highly recommended. To reach the summit of Vesuvius, with its splendid view of the Bay and Campania countryside, you can take a bus or drive up to the lower station of the presently defunct chair lift. To get there, take a local Circumvesuviana train to the Ercolano stop, where scheduled buses run up to the station plaza. From there it's a strenuous and dusty climb up to the crater. Details at EPT tourist offices at Via Partenope 10 and at central station or at Azienda Autonoma tourist office in the Royal Palace.

Pompeii is the most famous system of excavations anywhere in the world, and one of the largest. The city once housed 20,000 people and it is a fascinating place. Figure on at least a half-day visit; either book a guided tour or do it on your own with a good detailed guidebook and plan. If you're not with a group, the guardians stationed at the gates of the more important houses will probably insist on explaining the sights to you. Have lots of small change handy for tips (500 lire or so each time). Some rather mild ancient Roman pornography is kept under lock and key. There's a bar and quite satisfactory self-service restaurant within the excavations, along with tables for picnickers. Walk the extra bit to see the brilliant frescoes in the Villa dei Misteri.

The Amalfi Drive

One of the highlights of the entire Campania is the trip along the
Amalfi Drive as it twists and turns along the contours of the beautiful
southern coast of the Sorrento peninsula. Take the trip between Positano, Amalfi and Salerno by bus (the hairpin turns are hard on queasy
stomachs). Be sure to sit on the side of the bus flanking the sea for the
best views. The scenery is also superb from Ravello's belvederes and
from the steamers that ply the coast between Amalfi, Sorrento, Capri
and Naples. We rate Positano, Amalfi and Ravello way ahead of Sorrento, which is overwhelmingly touristy during high season.

Capri and Ischia

Capri continues to be one of the greatest playgrounds of Campania,
as it was when the Emperor Tiberius reputedly diverted himself by
flinging his former favorites off the cliffs. This pint-sized paradise is an
island four miles long, two miles wide and in spots more than 1,900 feet
high. It's as old as the Phoenicians; in fact they are supposed to have
cut a rock stairway that connects Marina Grande with the upper town
of Anacapri.

The town of Capri itself is afflicted with more than its quota of
perpetual tourists. But the beauties of the island more than compensate
for this. See the famed Gardens of Augustus, with views of Marina
Piccola and the Faraglioni shoals, or the Tiberius villa (on foot); also
the impressive medieval survivals: the 11th-century Byzantine Church
of San Costanzo; the 14th-century Carthusian monastery; the ruins of
the Castle of Castiglione, high up on the heights of San Michele; and
the fabulous Castello di Barbarossa, 800 steps up (worth every one of
them). Axel Munthe's house is a delightful spot to visit, also.

But Capri's most celebrated wonders are natural. The famed Blue
Grotto is as beautiful as they say. Boats visit only in calm weather and
the entrance is so small that everybody must duck his head; if there's
a queue of boats, the visit is brief and, frankly, disappointing. Take a
bus or open taxi to charming Anacapri to get away from the thickest
crowds, and set off on foot to Torre Damecuta and the ruins of an
imperial villa, or to the Migliara belvedere.

If the long established charms of Capri have become slightly stale
through long familiarity, those of the island of Ischia across the Bay
of Naples are equally under siege. The island is flooded by vacationers
seeking more elbow room than Capri affords, with the result that Ischia
is as crowded as its neighbor during the summer.

More than twice the size of Capri, Ischia is 40 minutes from Naples
by hydrofoil. Porto d'Ischia is the point of debarkation as well as being
the largest town, with a spa and many good hotels. Casamicciola and
Lacco Ameno are bustling beachside spas; Sant'Angelo is a former
fishing village and is quieter and a little more removed from the main
stream of tourism. There are fine beaches in the Forio area. A bus
makes an 18-mile circular tour of the island, but it's better to go by car.
From November to Easter most tourist-oriented shops and restaurants
are closed in coastal and inland resorts throughout the region.

Paestum

One final excursion south from Naples is to the old Greek colony of
Paestum which has some of the best-preserved Greek architectural
monuments in the world, not excepting Greece itself. The Temple of

Poseidon, a perfect example of Doric architecture, is one of many sights which more than warrant the 60-mile trip from Naples; see the recently excavated Greek frescoes in the museum.

Incidentally, the CIT agency offers a full day round trip from Naples to Paestum in addition to trips to Pompeii, Amalfi, Capri and other points of interest.

PRACTICAL INFORMATION FOR CAMPANIA

AMALFI. *Luna* (E), tel. 871002. In town; a converted convent, complete with cloisters. Seaside pool. *Santa Caterina* (E), tel. 871012. Lovely hotel with flowered terraces and lift to pool and private beach. *Dei Cavalieri* (M), tel. 871333. Bright and modern; short walk to town, stairs to tiny beach. *Miramalfi* (M), tel. 871247. Outside town; anonymous decor and private swimming area.

Restaurants. *Caravella* (M), tel. 871029. Fish specialties; one of the best spots in town. *Ciccio-Cielo Mare Terra* (M), on road toward Conca (tel. 871030). Both view and food are wonderful. *Da Gemma* (M), Via Cavalieri di Malta (tel. 871345). Authentic local cuisine. *Taverna del Doge* (M), Via Supportico (tel. 872303). Attractive seafaring atmosphere. *Lemon Garden* (I). Follow the signs; a long walk but worth it.

ANACAPRI. Upper town on the island of Capri. *Europa Palace* (E), tel. 8370955. Beautifully located, but some noisy rooms; attractive modern decor; pool, terrace and view. *Bellavista* (M), tel. 8371463. Small and good value. *San Michele* (M), tel. 8371427. Villa with view.

CAPRI. *Quisisana* (L), tel. 8370788. Luxurious and smart. *Regina Cristina* (E), tel. 8370303. 49 rooms; ultra modern. *Flora* (M), tel. 8370211. Villa; a honeymooner's dream. *La Floridiana* (M), tel. 8370713. Well situated. *La Pergola* (M), tel. 837000. *Semiramis* (M), tel. 8370833. *Villa Pina* (I), tel. 8377517. Pleasant inexpensive hotel.

Restaurants. *Canzone del Mare* (E), tel. 8370104. At Marina Piccola; swim, sun and then have lunch here. *La Capannina* (E), tel. 8370732. Chic and expensive tavern. *Casina della Rose* (E), tel. 8370200. Good, not exorbitantly priced. *Faraglioni* (E), tel. 8370320. Recommended. *Pigna* (E), tel. 8370280. Best on the island and very good indeed. *Gemma* (M), tel. 8370461. *Grottino* (M), tel. 8370584. Less expensive; good. *Paolino* (M), tel. 8376102.

ISCHIA. At **Casamicciola:** *Cristallo Palace* (E), tel. 994362. On hill. *Madonnina* (E), tel. 994062. On the beach. *Manzi* (E), tel. 994722. At **Ischia:** *Aragona Palace* (E), tel. 981383. *Excelsior Belvedere* (E), tel. 991020. Best. *Miramare Castello* (M), tel. 991333. At Ischia Ponte, attractive. *Regina Palace* (M), tel. 991344. *Villa Paradiso* (M), tel. 991501, and *La Villarosa* (M), tel. 991316, are small villa-hotels with pool, garden.

At **Lacco Ameno:** *Regina Isabella* (L), tel. 994322. Very elegant and expensive; beach, pool, tennis, spa. *La Reginella* (E), tel. 994300. Tennis and pool; good hotel. *San Montano* (E), tel. 994033. Modern and tranquil. At **Punta Molino:** *Grand Hotel Punta Molino* (E), tel. 991544. Airconditioned; with beach and pool. *Moresco* (E), tel. 991122. Hacienda-style hotel. At **Sant'Angelo:** *Vulcano* (E), tel. 999322. Pleasant with pool and spa.

Restaurants. *Gennaro* (M), tel. 992917. *Zi Nannina a Mare* (M), tel. 991350. Good. *Di Massa* (M), tel. 991402. All in the port.

NAPLES. *Excelsior* (L), tel. 417111. Airconditioned luxury hotel on the waterfront; finest in city. *Vesuvio* (L), tel. 417044. Elegant, palace-type hotel with attentive service. *Jolly* (E), tel. 416000. 30 story building with all the usual functional comforts plus a panoramic rooftop restaurant. *Majestic* (E), tel. 416500. Comfortable. *Mediterraneo* (E), tel. 312240. Roof restaurant with view of the bay; comfortable. *Britannique* (M), tel. 66933. Good views, clean, well-kept. *Paradiso* (M), Via Catullo 11 (tel. 660233). On Vomero; quiet. *Torino* (M), tel. 322410. Central for sightseeing.

Restaurants. *Arcate* (E), Via Aniello 249 (tel. 683380). Pleasant. *Casanova Grill* (E), of Hotel Excelsior, Via Partenope 48 (tel. 417111). Smart, very good.

Along the Santa Lucia waterfront: *Ciro* (M), tel. 415686, and *Scialuppa di Starita* (M), tel. 404349.

For food with a view, you have to travel farther. On the Posillipo hill are elegant *Galeone* (E), Via Posillipo 16 (tel. 684581) and excellent *Sacrestia* (E), Via Orazio 116 (tel. 664186). *Sbrescia* (E), Rampe Sant'Antonio (tel. 669140). Also has good view. *Al 53* (M), Piazza Dante 53 (tel. 341124). Classic trattoria, outdoors in summer. *D'Angelo* (M), Via Aniello 203 (tel. 365363). View. *Le Bergantino* (M), Via Torino (tel. 264746). Near station, vast menu, pizzeria annex around the corner. *Ciro a Santa Brigida* (M), Via Santa Brigida 71 (tel. 324072). Central, good, but can be pricey. *Dante e Beatrice* (M), Piazza Dante 44 (tel. 349905). Modest trattoria, longtime favorite. *Don Salvatore* (M), Via Mergellina 5 (tel. 681817). Good. *Il Faro* (M), at Marechiaro (tel. 7695142), in delightful location on sea. *Rugantino* (M), Via Fiorentini 45 (tel. 325491).

Pizzerias: all (M)— *Bellini*, Via Santa Maria di Constantinopoli 80; *Gorizia*, Via Bernini 29; *Lombardi*, Via Benedetto Croce 59; *Pizzicato*, Piazza Municipio; *Port'Alba*, Via Port'Alba 18.

PAESTUM. At temples: *Martini* (M), tel. 811020. Bungalows. *Villa Rita* (I), tel. 811081. Modest. On beach: *Le Palme* (M), tel. 843036.

POSITANO. *San Pietro* (L), tel. 875455. 1½ miles outside town; cliffside luxury with gorgeous views, beach and tennis. *Sirenuse* (E), tel. 875066. Modern comfort with period accents. *Covo di Saraceni* (M), tel. 875059. Large, pleasant and clean rooms; some noise from beach location. *Palazzo Murat* (M), tel. 875177. Handsome old villa with modern wing; in quiet garden but near beach. *Poseidon* (M), tel. 875014. Comfortable and tastefully furnished; terraces and pool. *Ancora* (M), tel. 875318. Cosy; terraces and view.

Restaurants. *Buca di Bacco* (E), tel. 875004. Terrace overlooking beach. *La Cambusa* (M), tel. 875432. Overlooking beach, seafood can be pricey. *Capurale* (M), tel. 875374. *Chez Black* (M), tel. 875036. On beach. *Covo dei Saraceni* (M), tel. 875059. Very good terrace restaurant, but can be pricey. *Taverna del Leone* (M), tel. 875474. On road toward Praiano.

RAVELLO. *Caruso Belvedere* (M), tel. 857111. Small with fine restaurant. *Palumbo* (M), tel. 857244. Excellent. *Rufolo* (M), tel. 857133. Very comfortable; pool. *Parsifal* (I), tel. 857144. Delightful hotel. *Villa Amore* (I), tel. 857135.

Restaurants. Those of *Caruso* and *Palumbo* hotels are outstanding, but can be expensive. Both (M). *Compa Cosimo* (M), tel. 857156. Popular trattoria. *Villa Maria* (M), tel. 857170. Attractive pension restaurant.

SORRENTO. *Cocumella* (E), tel. 8782933. Tops, beautiful villa in park with terraces, views, pool. *Imperial Tramontano* (E), tel. 8781940. Central, historic villa, gardens, views, pool. *Excelsior Grand Hotel Victoria* (E), tel. 8781900. Fine hotel with excellent service, cooking and accommodations; a little old fashioned. *Parco dei Principi* (E), tel. 8782101. Modern, lush park, terraces, pool. *Bellevue Syrene* (M), tel. 8781024. *Eden* (M), tel. 8781909. *Minerva* (M), tel. 8781011. On outskirts.

Restaurants. *Beppe* (M), Via Sant'Antonio 12 (tel. 8784176). Rustic, good. *Cattedrale* (M), Via Sersale 4 (tel. 8772584). Elegant, quiet. *Kursaal* (M), Via Fuorimura 7 (tel. 878126). Classy villa dining with view. *La Lanterna* (M), Via San Cesareo 23 (tel. 8781355). Off picturesque street, small, informal. *Parrucchiano* (M), Corso Italia 71 (tel. 8781321). A classic for local cuisine. *Zi 'Ntonio* (M), Via de Maio 11 (tel. 8781623). Pleasant.

Circolo dei Forestieri, Via de Maio. Kind of tourists' café with price-controlled drinks and good music in beautiful setting overlooking bay.

The Deep South

Off the beaten tourist track—though perhaps not for long—are the three southern provinces of the Italian boot—Apulia, the heel; Lucania, the instep; Calabria, the toe. Good new roads and the beginnings of new, modern, well-equipped resorts are attracting tourists to the region's extraordinarily beautiful shores and mountain valleys. Apulia (except for the Gargano) and Lucania have extremes of summer and winter climate that make it advisable to visit them between seasons. Calabria has more welcoming weather. You'll find forests and mountain scenery at Gambarie d'Aspromonte or San Giovanni in Fiore.

This is an old land, with literary and historical associations going back as far as Homer. Scilla in Calabria, for instance, is the famous Scylla facing the whirlpool of Charybdis, which menaced the ship of Ulysses. Lecce, one of the most strikingly beautiful cities of Italy, with its charming baroque palaces and churches, has recently been discovered touristically, and this fact suggests one of the appeals of the south—these regions offer a fascinating experience to the traveler who enjoys visiting places seldom seen by the average tourist.

The beaches along this coast are among the most beautiful in Italy. Names to remember among the newly popular resorts—off the beaten track, but with all the amenities of better-known, higher-priced places —are, in Basilicata-Lucania—Maratea; in Calabria—Praia, Tropea, Squillace, Stalleti, Copanello; in Apulia—Gallipoli, Ostuni, Barletta, Peschici and Vieste on the Gargano Peninsula, and San Domino in the Tremiti Islands.

PRACTICAL INFORMATION FOR THE DEEP SOUTH

 HOTELS. Accommodations in the south were not too good until the Jolly hotel chain got to work; it has done wonders in opening up a region hitherto poorly prepared to receive visitors. Resort hotels are usually open from May to October. Reserve in advance for Bari in September, the month of the Levant Fair.

ALBEROBELLO. *Trulli* (E), tel. 721130. Two score of cottages in the ancient local style; all rooms with bath; pool. Closed Nov.–March. *Astoria* (M), tel. 721190. Undistinguished but comfortable.

Restaurants. *Cucina dei Trulli* (M), tel. 721179. *Pugliese* (M), tel. 721437. *Trullo d'Oro* (M), tel. 721820. All serve local dishes.

BARI. *Jolly* (E), tel. 364366. Attractive and comfortable. *Palace* (E), tel. 216551. Good central location; airconditioned. *Boston* (M), tel. 216633. Central. *Grande Oriente* (M), tel. 544422. Large, central.

Restaurants. *La Panca* (E), Piazza Massari (tel. 216096). Highly recommended. *Pignata* (E), Via Melo 9 (tel. 232481). The best in town. *Sorso Preferito* (M), Via de Nicolò 44 (tel. 235747). Good food and wine. *Vecchia Bari* (M), Via Dante 47 (tel. 216496). Attractive, classic local cuisine.

BRINDISI. *Majestic* (E), tel. 222941. On station square. Medium size, best in town. *Mediterraneo* (M), tel. 82811. Modern and functional.

Restaurant. *La Botte* (M), Corso Garibaldi 72 (tel. 28400). *Giubilo* (M), Via del Mare 56, in Hotel Approdo (tel. 29668). Near ferry to Greece. Very good.

CATANZARO. *Guglielmo* (M), tel. 26532. Central and airconditioned. *Grand* (M), tel. 25605. *Motel AGIP* (M), tel. 51791. Just outside town. *Palace* (M), tel. 31344. A few miles away on beach.

Restaurants. *La Griglia* (M), Via Poerio (tel. 26883). *Uno Più Uno* (M), Galleria Mancuso (tel. 23180).

CETRARO. *San Michele* (E), tel. 91012. Palatial and isolated hotel; lift to private pebbly beach; tennis, pool.

COSENZA. *Centrale* (M), tel. 73681. All rooms with bath. Better hotel in Rende suburb: *Europa* (M), tel. 36531. *Motel AGIP* (M), tel. 839101, at Castiglione.

Restaurant. *Calavrisella* (M), Via De Rada (tel. 28012). Central, fine.

FOGGIA. *Cicolella* (M), tel. 3890. Airconditioned rooms and all with shower; best in town. *President* (M), tel. 79648. Modern; on the road to the airport.
Restaurants. *Cicolella* (E), has two branches: *In Fiera* (tel. 32166) and at *Hotel* (tel. 3890), both excellent. *Nuova Bella Napoli* (M), Via Callisto Azzarita (tel. 26188). In old town.

GALLIPOLI. *Costa Brada* (E), tel. 476396. Big resort hotel on sandy beach. *Le Sirenuse* (M), tel. 473441. View over sandy beach; large pool, tennis.

GARGANO. *Gusmay* (E), tel. 94032. Modern; long walk to private beach. *Pizzomunno* (E), tel. 78741. At Vieste. *Baia delle Zagare* (M), tel. 4155. On beautiful inlet at Mattinata; cottage-style; lift to beach. *Del Faro* (M), tel. 79011. Good resort hotel at Pugnochiuso; pool and beach. *Morcavallo* (M), tel. 94005. At Peschici. *Valle Clavia* (M), tel. 94209. Near Peschici.

LECCE. *President* (E), tel. 51881. Modern and efficient; on outskirts. *Risorgimento* (M), tel. 42125. Central, handsomely renovated, very good. *Patria* (M), tel. 29431. Central; old-fashioned comforts.

MARATEA. *Santavenere* (L), tel. 876160. All resort facilities in quiet location. *Villa del Mare* (M), tel. 878007. Peaceful and attractively furnished; lift to pebbly beach on pretty cove.

POTENZA. *Park* (M), tel. 22811. 3 miles outside town; modern and comfortable.
Restaurants. *Fuori le Mura* (M), Via IV Novembre (tel. 25409). *Da Peppe* (M), Largo San Michele (tel. 28030). Fine local specialties.

PRAIA A MARE. *Germania* (M), tel. 72016. *Mondial* (M), tel. 72214. Both unassuming, reasonable.

REGGIO CALABRIA. *Excelsior* (E), tel. 25801. Adequate in a city of undistinguished hotels. If driving, much better accommodations at attractive *Castello di Altafiumara* (M), at Cannitello (tel. 759061), near Villa San Giovanni and Sicily ferries.

TARANTO. *Delfino* (E), tel. 339981. Good, with pool and beach. *Jolly* (E), tel. 330861. Also good; pool. *Plaza* (M). Central, large.
Restaurants. *Al Gambero* (E), Via del Ponte (tel. 411190). Nice view. *Sirenetta* (M), Via Garibaldi (tel. 497657). Seafood. *Pizzeria Marcaurelio* (M), Via Cavour 17 (no phone). Good antipasto.

TROPEA. *Baia Parahelios* (M), tel. 61505. Large vacation village at nearby Parghelia. *Pineta* (M), tel. 61700. Modest hotel on sandy beach below town. *Virgilio* (M), tel. 61201. In town. *Sabbie Bianche* (I), tel. 61505. Vacation village at Parghelia.

Sicily, Southernmost Island

Sicily, tinged with color and subtlety, is quite unlike Italy. It is a unique land in which it is possible to ski on a snowy slope, stroll among palms and orange groves, and swim in the sea in sight of flowering almond trees— *all in the same day.* Spring is the best time to come, when the countryside is at its best, but Taormina is popular year round; its mild winters are renowned. Summers are hot and the *scirocco,* that hot wind from Africa, can make things pretty miserable and listless for periods of three days and more.

If you have the time, we recommend CIAT's two excellent five-day circuits of the island, the Golden Ribbon and the Sunshine Ribbon. Here are the high points of tourist interest as we see them, however: Palermo, an unforgettable city with its languor and monuments of all the civilizations that have enriched it; Monreale, with its cathedral's perfectly preserved mosaics, 6,000 dazzling square yards of them; Selinunte, with its colossal Temple of Apollo and other reminders of the glory that was Greece; Agrigento, at once a modern city and the site of some of the most stupendous Greek ruins in existence (many of them better preserved than the ones in Greece); Syracuse, with its fine Greek theater; Catania, handsome city, built on lava, and center of excursions to the craters of 10,000-foot-high Mt. Etna; Cefalù, whose 12th-century Norman cathedral has mosaics that almost approach those of Monreale; and finally, beautiful Taormina. Here the water is as clear as crystal at the lovely beaches below the town, and the town itself seems suspended in the air between the cobalt sea and snowy Etna.

You will enjoy walking down the Corso, the main street of Taormina, observing the ornate old palaces and the colorful throng of tourists promenading there. Sit at one of the cafés and look out at Etna. Go to the Greek Theater, if not for one of the splendid performances of Greek plays by the Italian Institute for Classical Drama, then at least for the view, which will remain with you always, a memory of the beauty of Sicily which is perhaps best epitomized by "the Circe-like enchantment of this magic town". But if you can, turn inland to Enna, Ragusa or Caltagirone for a clearer view of genuine Sicilian life and landscape. Seek out Noto, the beautiful baroque town near Syracuse, and Erice, a medieval citadel high above Trapani.

PRACTICAL INFORMATION FOR SICILY

HOTELS. Hotels in the island's main cities are generally fine, often top-notch. In smaller towns and off the beaten track they are usually limited and basic. All may be located on noisy streets or highways. Resort hotels and tourist villages are well-organized; they close during winter months.

AEOLIAN ISLANDS. Lipari: *Carasco* (M), tel. 9811605. Resort hotel. *Gattopardo* (M), tel. 9811035. **Vulcano:** *Arcipelago* (M), tel. 9852002. *Eolian* (M), tel. 9852152. *Sables Noir* (M), tel. 9852014. Simpler accommodations also on Panarea, Stromboli and Santa Maria Salina.

AGRIGENTO. *Jolly dei Templi* (E), tel. 76144. Near the temples. *Villa Athena* (E), tel. 23833. Best; beautiful location at the temples and fine ambiance. *Akrabello* (M), tel. 76277. Modern; pool.

Restaurants. Both in Valley of Temples: *Vigneto* (M), Via Magazzeni Cavalieri (tel. 44319). Rustic. *Taverna Mose* (M), tel. 26778. Local dishes.

CALTANISSETTA. Restaurant. *Cortese* (M), Viale Sicilia 166 (tel. 31686). Very good local dishes and wines.

CATANIA. *Central Palace* (E), Via Etnea (tel. 325344). Central, noisy. *Excelsior* (E), Piazza Verga (tel. 325733). Big, modern. *Sheraton* (E), at Venusilia, Acicastello (tel. 494000). Large, self-contained, beach. *Motel AGIP* (M), at Ognina (tel. 492233). Lovely, sea view. *Nettuno* (M), Via Lauria (tel. 493533).

Restaurants. *Pagano* (M), Via de Roberto 37 (tel. 322720). Exceptional local food. *Da Rinaldo* (M), Via Simili 59 (tel. 249335). Good trattoria. *La Siciliana* (M), Via Marco Polo 52 (tel. 376400). Family-run, excellent seafood. At Ognina, *Costa Azzurra* (E), tel. 494920. The tops.

CEFALU. *Baia del Capitano* (M), tel. 20003. Comfortable beach hotel. *Callette* (M), tel. 21856. Beach hotel. *Kalura* (M), tel. 21354. On beach. *Sabbie d'Oro* (M), tel. 21565. Big tourist village at Santa Lucia; pool.

EGADI ISLANDS. On Favignana: *L'Approdo di Ulisse* (M), tel. 921287. At Calagrand: *Punta Fanfalo* (M), tel. 921332. Tourist village.

ENNA. Best hotel in the area is at Lake Pergusa, 10 km. away: *La Giara* (M), tel. 36030.

Restaurants. *Centrale* (M), Via 6 Dicembre (tel. 21025). Small, good. *La Fontana* (M), Via Vulturo (tel. 25465). Local specialties.

MESSINA. *Jolly* (E), tel. 43401. Airconditioned; pool. *Riviera Grand* (E), tel. 57101. 140 rooms with bath; beach. *Royal Palace* (M), tel. 2928151. *Venezia* (M), tel. 718076. If driving, *Paradis* (M), in Paradiso suburb, is modern, comfortable, with good views.

Restaurants. *Alberto* (E), Via Ghibellina (tel. 710711). Superlative food and service. *Pippo Nunnari* (E), Via Bassi (tel. 2938584). Very good. *Donna Giovanna* (M), Via Risorgimento (tel. 718503).

PALERMO. *Villa Igeia* (L), tel. 543744. Luxurious and picturesque, with handsome salons and gardens; tennis, pool. *Delle Palme* (E), tel. 583933. Old-fashioned. *Politeama Palace* (E), tel. 322777. Recent, ultra-modern and comfortable. *Mediterraneo* (M), tel. 581133. *Motel Agip* (M), tel. 552033. Modern.

Restaurants. *Charleston* (E), Piazzale Ungheria (tel. 321366). Chic, tops; reserve. *Gourmand* (E), Via della Libertà (tel. 323431). Elegant. *La Scuderia* (M), Via del Fante (tel. 520323). Smart favorite, beautiful terrace. *Cuccagna* (M), Via Principe Granatelli (tel. 587267). Good central trattoria. *Ficodindia* (M), Via Amari (tel. 324214). Heavy on atmosphere. *La N'Grasciata* (M), Via Tiro a Segno (tel. 230947). Totally unpretentious seafood place. *Lo Scudiero* (M), Via Turati (tel. 581628).

PIAZZA ARMERINA. *Jolly* (E), tel. 81446. With good restaurant.

Restaurants. *Da Battiato* (M), Contrada Casale (tel. 82453). *Papillon* (M), Via Manzoni (tel. 82524). *Al Ritrovo* (M), Highway 117b (tel. 85282). Simple and inexpensive. *Da Totò* (M), Via Mazzini (tel. 81153).

RAGUSA. *Montreal* (M), tel. 21133. Central; adequate.

Restaurant. *Orfeo* (M), tel. 21035. Near cathedral.

SYRACUSE. *Jolly* (E), tel. 64744. Best in town. *Motel AGIP* (M), tel. 66944. Modern and reliable. *Villa Politi* (M), Via Politi 2 (tel. 32100). Quiet.

Restaurants. *Fratelli Bandiera* (E), Via Trieste (tel. 65021). Rustic, good. *Arlecchino* (M), Largo Empedocle (tel. 66386). Fine food, service. *Rutta e Ciauli* (M), Riviera Dionisio (tel. 65540). Terrace; recommended.

TAORMINA. *San Domenico* (L), tel. 23701. Dominican monastery, complete with Renaissance cloister, converted into a modern hotel; posh. *Bristol Park* (E), tel. 23006. Well furnished; pool. *Excelsior* (E), tel. 23976. Attractive and traditional. *Jolly Diodoro* (E), tel. 23312. Villa-type; pool. *Sea Palace* (E), at Mazzarò; attractive with pool and beach. *Timeo* (E), tel. 23801. Near Greek Theater; quiet, handsome and excellent. *Vello d'Oro* (E), tel. 23788. In the heart of town; garish but comfortable. *Villa Sant'Andrea* (E), tel. 23125. At Mazzarò; attractive traditional decor and friendly atmosphere; garden terraces directly on the beach. *Sirius* (M), tel. 23477. Attractive villa-type hotel with terraces. *Sole Castello* (M), tel. 23491. Attractive. *Villa Belvedere* (M), tel. 23791. *Villa Fiorita* (M), tel. 24122. Pleasant and well furnished. *Villa Paradiso* (M), tel. 23922. Central, comfortably furnished. *Villa Riis* (M), tel. 24875. *Villa San Pancrazio* (M), tel. 23252. Roman remains for archeology buffs.

Restaurants. *San Domenico* (E), tel. 23701. In famous hotel, top-level cuisine, beautiful setting. *Villa Le Terrazze* (E), tel. 23913. Elegant terrace dining, wonderful view. *Timeo* (E), tel. 23801. Excellent restaurant of lovely hotel. *Ciclope* (M), tel. 23263. Longtime favorite. *La Griglia* (M), tel. 23980.

On the beach at **Mazzarò**, both seasonal: *Oliviero* (E), at Hotel Sant'Andrea, tel. 23125; lovely seaside setting; *Pescatore* (M), tel. 23460; seafood.

At **Isola Bella:** *Da Giovanni* (E), tel. 23531. Small.

TRAPANI. *Ermione* (E), tel. 29400. At Erice, a picturesque town high above Trapani.

Restaurants. In Trapani, *Dell'Arco* (M), Via Nino Bixio 40 (tel. 27796). Modest but good. At Erice, *Taverna di Re Aceste* (M), tel. 869084. *Bettolaccia* (M), tel. 28380. 80 types of pasta.

LIECHTENSTEIN

To the east of the Rhine, between Lake Constance and the Swiss canton of the Grisons, is the pocket-sized Principality of Liechtenstein. Last remnant of the Holy Roman Empire, it is a prosperous, independent, hereditary monarchy of 61 square miles and about 26,500 loyal subjects. The current ruler is His Highness Franz Joseph II, Maria Alois Alfred Karl Johann Heinrich Michael Georg Ignatius Benediktus Gerhardus Majella, Prince von und zu Liechtenstein and Duke of Troppau and Jaegerndorf. The heir apparent is Prince Johann Adam Pius. His mother is Princess Gina, and Liechtensteiners fondly remember her during the war-time gas rationing, careening down from the castle on a bicycle to do her shopping.

Liechtenstein, which is united with Switzerland in a customs union and represented by Switzerland abroad, got its start as an independent nation when a wealthy Austrian prince, Johann Adam von Liechtenstein, bought up two bankrupt counts in the Rhine Valley, united their lands, and in 1719 obtained an imperial deed, creating the Principality of Liechtenstein.

Art connoisseurs will find a side trip to Liechtenstein rewarding. On exhibit every day in the Prince's Gallery above the National Tourist Office in the mini-capital of Vaduz is the Wiener Biedermeier collection from the Prince's famous private art collection. But sadly the stunning Rubens collection, back in Liechtenstein following its loan to the Metropolitan Museum in New York, is no longer on public display. On the second floor (the entrance fee covers both) is the Liechtenstein National Gallery which stages important loan exhibitions. There's an interesting Historical Museum, and philatelists shouldn't miss the Stamp Museum—Liechtenstein issues its own stamps and they are very popular among collectors.

PRACTICAL INFORMATION FOR LIECHTENSTEIN

 WHAT WILL IT COST. Liechtenstein prices (including postage) are roughly on a par with Switzerland. In Vaduz, hotel prices are about those of a Swiss budget resort. Full pension (bed, private bath or shower, all meals, tips and taxes) will cost about Fr.80 to 220 a day depending on the room and class of establishment. But in mountain villages hotel prices are appreciably less (except during the winter sports high season).

Swiss currency regulations and rates of exchange apply, the Swiss franc being Liechtenstein's legal tender (see *Switzerland* chapter). The Swiss National Tourist Office also serves Liechtenstein.

 WHEN TO COME. Like all Alpine resorts, Liechtenstein has two main seasons, from June to Sept., and (for skiing) from Dec. to Mar. Early May is especially attractive for then it is blossom time in the Rhine valley orchards. All the year round, art lovers will find a look at the fine collections in the *Liechtenstein Gallery,* Vaduz, richly rewarding.

Climate. Bracing; similar to Switzerland. Can be delightful in the summer.

NATIONAL HOLIDAYS. Jan. 1 (New Year's Day); Jan. 6 (Epiphany); Feb. 2 (Candlemas Day); Mar. 3 (Shrove Tuesday); Mar. 19 (Feast of St. Joseph); Mar. 25 (Lady Day); Apr. 17, 20 (Easter); May 1 (May Day); May 28 (Ascension); June 8 (Whit Monday); June 18 (Corpus Christi); Aug. 15 (Assumption); Nov. 1 (All Saints Day); Dec. 8 (Immaculate Conception); Dec. 25, 26.

 GETTING TO LIECHTENSTEIN. Although several of Europe's international trains, such as the Arlberg Express, cross Liechtenstein (and more pass within a few miles) none stops at the Principality's three small stations. It is best to use the Swiss border stations at Buchs (St. Gallen) or slightly farther-away Sargans, or the Austrian one at Feldkirch. All are well served by long-distance express trains and connected with Vaduz by bus. From Buchs it takes only about fifteen minutes by bus, ten minutes by taxi. Running along Liechtenstein's Rhine frontier is a motorway (N13) going to Lake Constance, Austria and Germany in the north, and southwards past Chur toward the San Bernardino. To the west, motorways go most of the way to Zurich, Berne and Basle.

CUSTOMS. There are no formalities for entering Liechtenstein from Switzerland; all travel documents valid for Switzerland are also valid here. If you come from Austria, frontier formalities are the same as if you were entering Switzerland. Swiss customs officials and border police do the checking.

 HOTELS. In the past, with a few notable exceptions the best hotels (although none were deluxe) have been in or near Vaduz. But new ones are now springing up along the Rhine valley and in the mountains. Some hotels of a certain price range may offer less expensive rooms, especially during the out-of-season period. A Liechtenstein specialty is its mountain inns, all at least 4,000 feet up but easily accessible by car. Ideal for those seeking quiet—and clean air.

BALZERS. *Post* (I), tel. 41208. Small, with bowling and garden. *Römerhof* (I), tel. 41960. Small and inexpensive.

BENDERN. *Deutscher Rhein* (I), tel. 31347. Central but quiet; views.

ESCHEN. *Brühlhof* (I), tel. 31566. Terrace restaurant.

MALBUN. *Gorfion* (M), tel. 24307. Garden. *Malbunerhof* (M), tel. 22944. Medium-sized hotel with indoor pool, sauna and bowling. *Alpenhotel Malbun* (I), tel. 21181. Indoor pool; facilities for children. *Montana* (I), tel. 27333. Small and central. *Walserhof* (I), tel. 23396. Small family hotel. No shower.

SCHAAN. *Sylva* (M), tel. 23942. Indoor pool and sauna; some (I) rooms available. *Dux* (I), tel. 21727. Garden; special facilities for children and the handicapped. *Linde* (I), tel. 21704. Quiet and central. *Schaanerhof* (I), tel. 21877. With indoor pool and sauna.

SCHELLENBERG. *Krone* (I), tel. 31168. Tranquil. Garden; indoor pool.

STEG. *Alpenhotel Steg* (I), tel. 22146. Very reasonably priced. No shower.

TRIESEN. *Meierhof* (I); tel. 21836. Views and a pool; facilities for the disabled. *Schäfle* (I), tel. 21502. Only 11 rooms; inexpensive. *Schatzmann* (I), tel. 29070. Central, with views.

TRIESENBERG. *Kulm* (I), tel. 28777. Good family hotel; excellent views. *Martha Büler* (I), tel. 25777. 8 rooms only. *Samina* (I), tel. 22339. Quiet; good food.

VADUZ. *Park-Hotel Sonnenhof* (E), tel. 21192. Quiet hotel with sauna and indoor pool 5 minutes from town; fine gardens and superb view. *Real* (M), tel. 22222. Central and small; excellent. *Schlössle* (M), tel. 25621. Quiet. *Adler* (I), tel. 22131. Central. *Au* (I), tel. 21117. Good, inexpensive country inn. No shower. *Engel* (I), tel. 21057. Central; dancing. *Garni Landhaus Prasch* (I), tel. 24663. Bed and breakfast only.

RESTAURANTS. The cuisine is Swiss with Austrian overtones. There are quite a few restaurants. In Vaduz, barely 5 minutes' walk from the center, try the *Torkel* restaurant, owned by the prince and surrounded by his vineyards. A good place to sample Vaduzer, the potent local red wine. Food at the *Engel* is highly thought of. Also atmospheric are *The Old Castle Inn* and *Linde's,* the latter for a reasonably priced meal. *Café Wolf,* snacks only. Avoid the restaurants near the castle as they are mostly very expensive. In Balzers: *Engel* and *Schlosshof-Gutenberg.* Also, *Post* in Hotel Post, very good and not expensive; and *Roxy,* a snack bar with dancing, no entrance fee and very reasonable prices. In Triesenberg: *Café Sele,* good food yet inexpensive, and *Edelweiss.* In Malbun: *Scesaplana.* In Eschen: the *Haldenruh* and *Hirschen.* In Triesen: the restaurant in the *Hotel Schäfle* is good. A good lunch or dinner ranges from about 12 francs in an unsophisticated spot to around 40 or so in the best.

ENTERTAINMENT. There is dancing at the *Maschlina* and *Mittagspitze* in Triesen, *Landhaus* in Nendeln, *Römerkeller* and *Roxy* in Balzers, *Tiffany* in Eschen and *Derby* in Schaanwald, as well as at Malbun's *Gorfion* and *Turna.* Liechtenstein is not a place for nightclubbing.

SHOPPING. Due to the customs union, prices are the same as in Switzerland and you get the same goods. Apart from the usual souvenirs (there are attractive dolls with local costumes), the hand-made ceramics and, of course, the Liechtenstein postage stamps, there is little to tempt you.

MUSEUMS. Largely as a result of the Prince's decision to allow part of his world-famous private collection to be on public display, visitors to Vaduz can always enjoy art exhibitions unmatched by any other community of similar size. Currently occupying the whole first floor of the National Gallery, above the Tourist Office, and beautifully lit and displayed, is a Wiener Biedermeier collection. On the second floor important loan exhibitions are held. Admission covering both galleries is Fr.3.

The Historical Museum and Postal Museum in Vaduz and Triesenberg's Walser Museum are also worth a visit.

 USEFUL ADDRESSES. *Tourist Office Vaduz,* Städtle 37, 9490 Vaduz (tel. 21443), for information and hotel bookings. *Tourist Office Malbun,* 9497 Malbun-Triesenberg (tel. 26577) for hotel bookings and information about the Liechtenstein alpine area. *Liechtenstein National Tourist Office,* P.O.B. 139, 9490 Vaduz (tel. 21443) for general information.

Exploring Liechtenstein

Begin in Vaduz, the attractive, 5,000-citizen capital to which low taxes lure the fortunate few who are not confined to a certain spot by their jobs. The little town is dominated by Vaduz castle, a princely looking edifice if ever there was one. Normally, the interior is out of bounds for tourists; even if you can't enter the castle, do go and see it. Originally built in the 13th century, it was frequently rebuilt over the years until the complete 20th-century overhaul which gave it its present form. Vaduz has another outstanding medieval building, the Rotes Haus, once a fortress for the bailiffs of a Swiss Benedictine monastery. If you're feeling energetic, a 40-minute climb northeast of Vaduz will take you to the romantic ruins of the Wildschloss.

From Vaduz, we strongly recommend a tour along the twisty, climbing road past Vaduz castle which has a succession of splendid views of the Rhine Valley, to the little town of Triesenberg. About a mile beyond the town, a turn-off on the left leads to the mountain hotels of Masescha and Gaflei. The latter, at 4,920 feet, is the starting point for the Fürstensteig, a path along the high ridge dividing the Rhine and Samina valleys. It does not involve any dangerous climbing. Masescha, Gaflei, nearby Silum and Triesenberg, are small, do-it-yourself skiing centers in winter and lovely spots for walking in summer.

But our road continues upwards and then plunges into a tunnel to emerge near the hamlet of Steg (4,200 ft.) in a high Alpine valley; wild, impressive and with rushing mountain streams. In summer, Steg is an excellent starting point for a wide choice of not over-strenuous mountain hikes, such as that up the Samina valley to the Bettlerjoch Pass (6,400 ft.). When the snow arrives, the hamlet becomes a no-frills skiing center which has particularly good cross-country skiing.

If you now take the excellent new road which continues beyond Steg you will find that, after a couple of miles, it ends abruptly at Malbun (5,200 ft.), a small higgledy-piggledy village nestling on the floor of a huge mountain bowl. Malbun is gaining in popularity on the international ski scene for its varied facilities.

There's a regular bus service between Vaduz and Malbun but, if possible, go by car. The return journey will take well under two hours including brief viewing stops en route, but leave more time if you can.

LUXEMBOURG

While the old idea of Luxembourg as a toyland monarchy still lives on, this little grand duchy is now a major center for tourism from North America, thanks in large part to Icelandair, whose services make this the starting point for many young people and other budget-minded visitors to Europe.

Squeezed in between Belgium, Germany and France, the Grand Duchy of Luxembourg is a thriving, Rhode-Island sized land whose 366,000 contented inhabitants offer the traveler one of the tourist bargains of Europe. Prices are 10 to 15% lower than in neighboring Belgium, whose currency is valid in Luxembourg. Typical of the country's tourist amenities are 50% weekend reductions on the National Railways. There are loads of villages with simple clean hotels and excellent country restaurants. Trout fishing is still possible at the lake, along the Moselle, or on the private reaches of friends. Apply for a special fishing permit to the District Commissioners or communal administrators before arriving in the Grand Duchy. This is a country of parades and processions, good cheer, and a hearty capacity for beer and Moselle wine.

PRACTICAL INFORMATION FOR LUXEMBOURG

 WHAT WILL IT COST. The rate of inflation in Luxembourg is one of the lowest in Europe. This may well have something to do with the small size of the country, which appears to enable rising costs to be limited more successfully than in neighboring countries.

The monetary unit is the franc, which is divided into 100 centimes. Belgian money is legal tender in Luxembourg, but Luxembourg francs can only be used within the confines of the Grand Duchy. Therefore, change all remaining Luxembourg banknotes before leaving the country.

At the time of writing, there were about 52 francs to the U.S. dollar and 73 francs to the pound sterling.

A typical day outside Luxembourg might cost two people:

Hotel, with breakfast	1,650	francs
Lunch, without wine	1,100	
Transportation (taxi for 5km)	350	
Coffee (4)	160	
Beer (4)	140	
Motor coach tour	900	
Dinner, including wine	1,900	
Miscellaneous 10%	600	
	6,800	francs

SOURCES OF INFORMATION. For information on all aspects of travel in Luxembourg, contact the Luxembourg National Tourist Office. Their addresses are:

In the U.S.: 801 Second Ave., New York, N.Y. 10017 (tel. 212–370–9850).
In the U.K.: 36 Piccadilly, London W.1 (tel. 01–434 2800).

WHEN TO COME. The tourist season runs from around Easter through to mid-September, though summer is the best time. However, there are numerous off-season attractions and price reductions to tempt the would-be visitor and these are worth checking out before you make any final decision. Write the ONT, B.P. 1001, Luxembourg, for details.

Climate. Temperate, with summer tending to be cool though winters are not severe. Rain is fairly frequent.

Average afternoon temperatures in Fahrenheit and centigrade:

Luxembourg	Jan.	Feb.	Mar.	Apr.	May	June	July	Aug.	Sept.	Oct.	Nov.	Dec.
F°	36	40	49	58	65	71	74	73	65	56	45	39
C°	2	4	9	15	18	22	23	23	18	13	7	4

SPECIAL EVENTS. Carnival is thoroughly celebrated with processions and balls. Many ancient traditions, neglected elsewhere, persist in Luxembourg. They include Candlemas, Wintersend, May Day and Harvest Home. On the third Sunday after Easter there is a great pilgrimage procession to Our Lady of Luxembourg; on Whit-Tuesday, the famous dancing procession of Echternach, the Springprozession in honor of St. Willibrord. Wiltz Genzefest; unique broom-flower festival with parades, pageant and dancing. *June,* international vintage car tour. *June-July,* International Festival of Classical Music at Echternach. *July,* open-air theater and music festival at Wiltz. Second weekend in *September,* Wine Festival and Folklore Parade at Grevenmacher. Many wine festivals and tasting days along the Moselle from May on. Bikers appreciate the almost monthly cross-country races, many being international events.

National Holidays. Jan. 1; Apr. 17, 20 (Easter); May 1 (May Day); May 28 (Ascension); June 8 (Whit Mon.); Jun. 23 (National Day); Aug. 15 (Assumption); Nov. 1 (All Saints); Dec. 25, 26. *In Luxembourg City:* Mar. 2 (Carnival Mon.); Sept. 1 (Braderie); Nov. 2 (All Souls).

VISAS. Nationals of the United States, Canada, Australia, New Zealand, EEC countries and practically all other European countries do not require visas for entry into Luxembourg. However, you must of course have a valid passport.

HEALTH CERTIFICATES. Not required for entry into Luxembourg from any country.

GETTING TO LUXEMBOURG. By Plane. *Icelandair's* budget flights via Reykjavik link New York and Chicago with Findel airport. There are direct flights from Detroit and Orlando. The Grand Duchy can also be reached by changing at London, Amsterdam, Brussels, or Paris where *Luxair* and other carriers have daily flights.

By Train. Frequent services from Brussels (3 hrs.); it is on the route of the *Edelweiss* (Brussels to Zurich) and the *Riviera Express* (Amsterdam to Italy).

CUSTOMS. There are two levels of duty-free allowance for goods imported to Luxembourg. Travelers coming from a country outside of the EEC may bring in 200 cigarettes or 50 cigars or 100 cigarillos or 250gr. of tobacco; 1 liter of spirits over 22% proof or 2 liters of sparkling wine plus 2 liters of other wine; 50gr. of perfume and .25 liter of toilet water; other goods to the value of 2,000 francs. Travelers coming from an EEC country may bring in 300 cigarettes or 75 cigars or 150 cigarillos or 400gr. of tobacco; 1.5 liters of spirits over 22% proof or 3 liters of sparkling wine plus 5 liters of other wine; 75gr. of perfume and ⅜ liter of toilet water; other goods to a total value of 15,800 francs.

HOTELS. Everywhere in Luxembourg you can be sure of finding clean accommodations with excellent and plentiful food. Most hotels have rooms with bath and all have bathrooms available on each floor. Many establishments encourage tourism by offering special off-season terms for a three-day stay.

Our hotel grading system is divided into four categories. All prices are for 2 people in a double room. Deluxe (L) 3,600–8,500 francs, Expensive (E) 2,400–3,600 francs, Moderate (M) 1,300–2,400 francs, Inexpensive (I) 900–1,300 francs. These prices apply to the capital, Luxembourg City, as this is still where most English-speaking people make their base.

CAMPING. There are numerous sites for tents or caravans. Ask for the *Office National de Tourisme* (ONT) camping guide.

RESTAURANTS. Finding a place to eat in the Grand Duchy is no problem. In addition to the many individual restaurants, most hotels also have restaurants. We have classified the establishments recommended in this chapter in three price categories. Expensive (E) 1,200–3,000 francs, Moderate (M) 700–1,200 francs, Inexpensive (I) 250–700 francs. These prices are for one person and are very much an average, as the range for many of the restaurants included is a wide one.

Food and Drink. Luxembourg cooking combines German heartiness with Franco-Belgian finesse. Smoked pork and broad beans or sauerkraut *(carré de porc fumé)* is of Teutonic origin, but *cochon de lait en gelée* (jellied suckling pig) is a more authentic local dish. The preparation of trout, pike and crayfish is excellent. You can get the famous smoked Ardennes ham *(jambon d'Ardennes)* all year round.

Pastry and cakes are excellent. Ask for *tarte aux quetsches.* Outstanding desserts are prepared with the aid of local liqueurs: the better restaurants will make to order the delicious *omelette soufflée au kirsch;* or a dollop of quetsch, mirabelle or kirsch may be added to babas or fruit cups.

Luxembourg's white Moselle wines are a drier hock than the wines of the Rhine which they resemble more than the fruitier wines of the French Moselle.

Brewing beer, another Luxembourg specialty, is an old-established, traditional industry. Among the best-known brands are *Mousel, Diekirch, Simon* and *B B B Bofferding*.

To round out a satisfying meal, there's nothing better than a local liqueur. When at Beaufort, try the blackcurrant wine *(cassis)*.

TIPPING. Service and taxes are included in the bill, but for especially good service you might give an extra 5%. Taxi drivers expect a tip, hairdressers appreciate one.

MAIL. Airmail to the U.S. and Canada 23 francs for the first 10 grams (one airmail sheet and envelope), 3 francs for each additional 10 grams. To England (automatically by airmail): 12 francs for the first 20 grams. Postcards: 19 francs to the U.S. by air, 10 to the U.K.

CLOSING TIMES. Shops are open from 8 A.M. to noon, and from 2 P.M. to 6 P.M., except on Monday, when most don't open before 2 in the afternoon. Bank hours are 8 to noon, and 1 to 4.30, Monday through Friday. Both shops and banks close on public holidays. Change windows at the airport and railway stations are open every day from 8 A.M. to 9 P.M.

USEFUL ADDRESSES. (Luxembourg City.) *American Embassy,* 22 blvd. Emmanuel Servais; *British Embassy,* 28/IV blvd. Royal; *Office National de Tourisme,* Air Terminal, pl. de la Gare, and at Airport; *Automobile Club of Luxembourg,* 13 rte. de Longwy; *Wagons Lits Tourisme,* 80 pl. de la Gare and 103 Grand'Rue, handle Cook's bookings.

GETTING AROUND LUXEMBOURG. By Train. Weekend return tickets, 1-day, 5-day and monthly network tickets (which include buses) and party tickets offer savings. Tourists over 65 years of age can obtain a 50% reduction upon showing their passport or ID card. *Circuits Trains-Pedestres* guides show how best to reach areas for beautiful walks. Services to most points in the country run nearly hourly all day.

By Car. Speed limit in towns is 60km./hr. (37mph), on the open road, 90km./hr. (56mph). Safety belts must be worn unless a medical certificate exempts one. A green card, though not obligatory, is recommended for British and other EEC nationals.

Blue-zone parking in Luxembourg City and other centers is supplemented by parking meters and a system of ticket dispensers allowing motorists to buy any time period desired for parking. Police are empowered to impose on-the-spot fines of up to 1000 francs for certain offences. Alcohol and blood tests are legal.

Premium petroleum at presstime was around 32 francs a liter.

For details of combined motoring/hiking holidays, see the *Circuits Auto-Pedestre* guides.

Car Hire. A daily cost of around 1,350 francs, plus 13.50 francs per km. and a refundable deposit of 10,500 francs upwards. Credit cards are preferred over cash. Try one of the following: *Avis,* 13 rue Duchscher; *Colux,* 24 Dernier Sol; *Inter Rent,* 88 rte. de Thionville; *Hertz,* 25 av. de la Liberté. All the aforementioned are in Luxembourg City and most with representation at the airport. Campers can await you by pre-arrangement with the *Kemwel (Europak) Group Inc.,* 247 W. 12th St., New York City, serviced in Luxembourg by *Auto Europa* and *Colux.*

Exploring the Capital

Luxembourg City will not disappoint you. The old town looks exactly like a setting for the operetta *The Count of Luxembourg,* and you would never suspect that the city is the judiciary and banking center of the European Economic Community, and the meeting place of its Council of Ministers for three months of the year. The visitor will not be conscious of the mighty steel foundries and model farms of this progressive duchy, but only of a pleasant world of castles, turrets and moats, especially on summer nights when the bridges, spires and ramparts reassert themselves in the stunning illumination of the floodlights.

The city itself is small (about 100,000 inhabitants) and a perfect place to explore on foot. With a little imagination, a walk outside over the ramparts will recreate the past when this was one of the impregnable bastions of Europe. The model of the citadel in its heyday displayed at the Municipal Center, rue du Curé, will help. Visit the late Gothic cathedral of Our Lady of Luxembourg, and take the guided tour through the nearby casemates (summer only). This is a veritable voyage into the past, when Luxembourg's three rings of defense included 53 forts linked by 16 miles of tunnels and casemates hewn into solid rock.

Don't miss the area around the Marché aux Poissons (Fish Market), site of the capital's oldest buildings, and the National Museum, which contains priceless works of art. Walk along the beautiful Promenade de la Corniche, with its magnificent view over the deep valley below. Especially recommended is a walk to the head of the Old Bridge, the Passerelle, and a descent into the valley by the Montée de la Petrusse. At the foot of the hill, partially cut into the rock, is the Chapel of Saint Quirinus, one of the oldest shrines in the country.

Of special interest to Americans is the United States Military Cemetery, three miles east from Luxembourg City. More than half of the 10,000 American soldiers who fell in Luxembourg during the Rundstedt offensive of World War II lie buried here. Among the thousands of graves is that of General George S. Patton, Jr., commander of the U.S. 3rd Army. A mile down the road is the German Military Cemetery.

PRACTICAL INFORMATION FOR LUXEMBOURG CITY

GETTING AROUND LUXEMBOURG. By Bus. From the airport bus no. 9 goes to town and to the main bus center near the rail station. From here the blue and yellow buses will take you anywhere in Luxembourg City and to places nearby. Buses 9 and 16 go to the Youth Hostel and nos. 2, 4, 11 and 12 to the town center. Tickets cost 25 fr. on the bus plus 25 fr. per piece of luggage (which may be refused during rush hours). You can buy a card giving you 10 trips for 175 fr. from rail station ticket windows and from some banks and bookstores. A *Luxair* bus (fare 120 fr.) also serves the airport and passengers traveling with luggage or in rush hours will find this easier than the no. 9. Information on buses to the countryside may be had from rail station information desks.

Hotels

Deluxe

Aerogolf-Sheraton, rte. de Trèves (tel. 3–45–71). 150 rooms, in delightful surroundings near the airport.

Cravat, 29 blvd. Roosevelt (tel. 2–19–75). 60 rooms. Overlooks the valley and Pont Adolphe.

Holiday Inn, rue du Fort Niedergrunewald (tel. 43–77–61). 260 rooms, fully airconditioned. Pool, sauna.

Inter-Continental, rue Jean Engling, Dommeldange (tel. 43781). 348 rooms. All amenities for conducting top-level business in idyllic surroundings; swimming pool, health club, all-weather tennis courts.

Royal, 12 blvd. Royal (tel. 4–16–16). 180 rooms. All luxury amenities. Quiet elegance in Luxembourg's mini Wall St.

Expensive

Central Molitor, 28 av. de la Liberté (tel. 48–99–11). 35 rooms. Long a favorite with business travelers.

Eldorado, 7 pl. de la Gare (tel. 48–10–71). 45 rooms. Offers stocked refrigerators in each room.

International, 20–22 pl. de la Gare (tel. 48–59–11). 60 rooms, and a fine restaurant.

Kons, 24 pl. de la Gare (tel. 48–60–21). 140 rooms; still uses pages!

Nobilis, 47 av. de la Gare (tel. 49–49–71). 50 rooms. Ample parking.

Novotel-Alvisse Parc, rte. d'Echternach, Dommeldange (tel. 43–56–43). 293 rooms. Outdoor and indoor swimming pools, tennis.

President Mapotel, 32 pl. de la Gare (tel. 48–61–61). 40 rooms; newly renovated, with a bright breakfast room.

Moderate

Airfield, 6 rte. de Trèves (tel. 43–19–34). 10 rooms. Convenient to Findel Airport.

Alfa, 16 pl. de la Gare (tel. 48–65–65). 100 rooms. Reliable ever since the days when Gen. Eisenhower stayed here.

Bristol, 11 rue de Strasbourg (tel. 48–58–29). 30 rooms. Can arrange fishing or hunting in the countryside.

Carlton, 9 rue de Strasbourg (tel. 48–48–02). 45 rooms. Parking.

Du Chemin de Fer, 4 rue Joseph Junck (tel. 49–35–28). 25 rooms.

Cheminée de Paris, 10 rue d'Anvers (tel. 49–29–31). 24 rooms; terrace.

City, 1 rue de Strasbourg (tel. 48–46–08). 30 rooms. Good homecooking at *City-Cave* downstairs.

Dauphin, 42 av. de la Gare (tel. 48–82–82). 35 rooms. Welcomes groups.

Delta, 74–76 rue Adolphe Fischer (tel. 49–30–96). 20 rooms. Garage.

Empire, 34 pl. de la Gare (tel. 48–52–52). 45 rooms; excellent restaurant.

Italia, 15–17 rue d'Anvers (tel. 48–66–26). 20 rooms. Italian specialty restaurant.

Schintgen, 6 rue Notre Dame (tel. 2–28–44). 35 rooms. A warm welcome to simple comforts.

Inexpensive

Beaumont, 11 rue Beaumont (tel. 2–52–37). 15 rooms. Chinese restaurant.

Elisabeth, 17 rue du Fort Elisabeth (tel. 49–23–10). 10 rooms.

Du Theatre, 3 rue Beaumont (tel. 2–53–37). 20 rooms.

Weber, 50 rue Zithe at the Place de Paris (tel. 48–92–39). 10 rooms. Rock bottom.

Zurich, 36 rue Jos. Junck (tel. 49–13–50). 13 rooms.

Restaurants

Expensive

Au Gourmet, 8 rue Chimay (tel. 2–55–61). Reserve a table to be sure.

Bouzonviller, 138 rue Albert Unden (tel. 47–22–59). Fresh seafood specialties; 200 wines.

Cordial, 1 pl. de Paris (tel. 48–85–38). Evenings only.

St. Michel, 32 rue de l'Eau (tel. 2–32–15). Try the *blanc de turbot au bourgeuil* or, for dessert, *désir de reine.*

Patin d'Or, Kockelscheuer (tel. 2–64–99). At skating rink.

Scandia Um Bock, 4–8 rue de la Loge (tel. 2–22–36). Gourmet restaurant (E) upstairs; grill (M), down.

Le Vert Galant, 23 rue Aldringer (tel. 47–08–22). For "new" French gourmet cuisine. Closed Sat. and Sun.

Moderate

Bella Napoli, 4 rue de Strasbourg (tel. 49–33–67). Italian and local cuisine.

Caesar, 18 av. Monterey (tel. 47–09–25). Franco-Italian cuisine.

Club 5, 5 rue Chimay (tel. 4–67–63). Good salads. Terrace in summer.

La Lorraine, 7 pl. d'Armes (tel. 47–14–36). Seafood specialties in luxury liner decor. Daily delivery of fish and shellfish from private fisheries in Brittany. Quiche, too.

Le Marronnier, 5 av. Marie-Thérèse (tel. 447–43–216). Fine view of the Pont Adolphe and valley of the Petrusses.

Osteria del Teatro, 21–25 allée Scheffer (tel. 2–88–11). Franco-Italian specialties.

Taverne du Passage, 18 rue du Curé—14 pl. Guillaume (tel. 4–06–63). *Raclette Grisons, fondues de fromage* and other Swiss dishes.

Inexpensive

Ancre d'Or, 23 rue du Fossé (tel. 47–29–73). Try the *riz du veau.*

Le Calao, 47 av. de la Gare (tel. 49–49–71). Try the *turbot au vinaigre de framboises* or *homard armoricaine.*

China Garden, 11 rue Beaumont (tel. 2–04–87). Chinese and local cuisine.

Du Commerce, 13 pl. d'Armes (tel. 2–69–30). Reliable everyday fare.

Maison des Brasseurs, 48 Grand 'Rue (tel. 47–13–71). Luxembourg grills. Try the *jambonneau choucroute.*

La Marée, 37 av. de la Liberté (tel. 49–08–99). Seafood specialties.

McDonald's, 49 av. de la Gare (tel. 49–63–47). Classic McDonald's.

Pole Nord, 2 pl. de Bruxelles (tel. 47–23–23). Luxembourg and French cuisine.

San Remo, 10 pl. Guillaume (tel. 47–25–68). Luxembourg, Italian, and international menu.

Star of Asia, 19 rue des Capucins (tel. 47–12–40). Eastern, vegetarian and diet menus.

Taverne Nobilis, 47 av. de la Gare (tel. 49–49–71). Convenient parking.

Taverne de la Poêle d'Or, 20 Marché-aux-Herbes (tel. 4–08–13). Try the *turbotin au blanc de poirot.*

Um Dierfgen, 6 côte d'Eich (tel. 2–61–41). Steaks (horse or beef) in a rustic Luxembourg village atmosphere.

NIGHTLIFE. As far as the capital, Luxembourg City, is concerned, the leading nightclub is the *Splendide,* which is at 18 rue Dicks. The floorshows are fair and the prices are not excessive. By law, all clubs must close by 3 in the morning. In fact, all nightlife rolls along relatively quietly in Luxembourg, except that is at the discos, which are both numerous and vibrant.

MUSEUMS. Castle of Sigefroi, founder of Luxembourg. Perpetually open. Remains of original fortification built 963.

Luxembourg Casemates, 10–5 seasonally. Unique, once impregnable, fortifications hand-hewn from solid rock.

Luxembourg Fortress Model, 10–12.30, 2–6 in season. Tickets at Tourist Office, pl. d'Armes.

Pescatore Museum, 2–6 seasonally. Dutch and French paintings.

Post and Telephone Museum, Tues., Thurs., Sat. 10–12, 2–5.

State Museums, daily (except Mon.) 9.30–11.30, 2–6. Paintings, sculpture, natural history and archeology.

The Countryside

There are many excursions out of Luxembourg City. One, by Route 7, will take you into the romantic winding valleys of the Ardennes, cut by swift streams that are ideal for angling. For hiking, there are well-marked trails through lovely forests.

Take route E 27 northeast from Luxembourg to Echternach with its lake and recreation center and the lovely region which the Luxembourgers call their Switzerland. Junglinster is the site of one of the most powerful transmitting stations in Europe, Radio Luxembourg.

The Moselle Valley is best reached by way of Route 1 out of Luxembourg City. It joins Route 10 at Grevenmacher, where you may visit the Cooperative of Vinegrowers' cellars or the celebrated caves of Bernard-Massard. At Remich, the Caves St. Martin, hewn from rock, may also be seen and their champagne sampled. Route 10 follows the Moselle south past Remich, a wine center of Roman origin, then leaves the river and brings you to Mondorf-les-Bains, a noted spa which, along with physical re-education and cures for the liver, features concerts and fireworks on the occasions of the Luxembourg, French, British and American national holidays.

A two-day tour of the Grand Duchy of Luxembourg which will touch all the major points of interest is as follows:

Depart Luxembourg City—Mondorf-les-Bains—Moselle Valley (Remich—Grevenmacher-Wasserbillig)—Echternach—Little Switzerland (Beaufort Castle—Müllerthal-Larochette)—Diekirch. Approximately 75 miles.

Diekirch—Vianden Castle—Stolzembourg—Clervaux Castle—Wiltz—Bavigne—Esch sur Sûre Castle—the Upper Sûre dam and lake (approximately 50 miles).

Upper Sûre Valley—Bourscheid Castle—Erpeldange—Ettelbruck—Berg—Mersch—Castles Hollenfels and Ansembourg—Septfontaines-Koerich—Steinfort—return to Luxembourg City (approximately 65 miles). Total about 190 miles.

PRACTICAL INFORMATION FOR THE REGIONS

BEAUFORT. Castles. "Little Swiss" scenery. *Meyer* (E), 120 Grand'rue (tel. 8–62–62), the best. *Binsfeld* (M), 1 montée du Château (tel. 8–60–13). *Thielen* (I), 11 Grand'rue (tel. 8–60–05). Clean, comfortable.

BERDORF. Central for walks through gulfs and chasms or to high viewpoints. *Parc* (L), 39 rte. de Grundhof (tel. 7–91–95). *Bisdorff* (E), 2 rue Heisbich (tel. 7–92–08). Indoor pool. *l'Ermitage* (M), 44 rte. de Grundhof (tel. 7–91–84). In the forest. Pool. *Kinnen* (M), 34 rte. d'Echternach (tel. 7–91–83). *Pittoresque* (I), 115A rue um Wues (tel. 7–95–97).

CLERVAUX. Castle, abbey, walks, fishing. *de l'Abbaye* (E), 80 Grand'rue (tel. 9–10–49). Fishing. *Claravallis* (E), 3 rue de la Gare (tel. 9–10–34). *International* (M), 10 Grand'rue (tel. 9–10–67). *Koener* (M), 14 Grand'rue (tel. 9–10–02). Hunting. *du Parc* (M), 2–4 rue du Parc (tel. 9–10–68). *St. Hubert* (M) (tel. 9–24–32). At nearby Reuler should Clervaux be full.

Restaurants. *les Écuries du Parc* (I), 4 rue du Parc (tel. 9–23–64). *du Vieux Château* (I), 4 rue du Château (tel. 9–20–12).

ECHTERNACH. *Bel-Air* (L), 1 rte. de Berdorf (tel. 72–93–83). The best. *Grand Hotel* (E), 27 rte. de Diekirch (tel. 72–96–72). *la Petite Marquise* (E), 18 pl. du Marché (tel. 7–23–82). *St. Hubert* (E), 21 rue de la Gare (tel. 7–23–06). *de la Sûre* (E), 49 rue de la Gare (tel. 72–94–14). Hunting, fishing. *Universal* (E), 40 rue de Luxembourg (tel. 72–99–91). Hunting, fishing. *du Commerce* (M), 16 pl. du Marché (tel. 7–23–01). Terrace. *du Parc* (M), 18 rue Hovelech/9 rue de l'Hôpital (tel. 72–94–81). *Petite Suisse* (I), 56 rue A.Duchscher (tel. 7–21–78).

Restaurants. *Bel-Air* (M), 1 rte. de Berdorf (tel. 72–93–83). Choice cuisine. *la Petite Marquise* (M), 18 pl. du Marché (tel. 7–23–82). *Parnass* (M), 7–8 pl. du Marché (tel. 72–94–83). *du Pont* (I), 34 rue du Pont (tel. 7–20–26).

ESCH-SUR-ALZETTE. *Acacia* (E), 10 rue de la Liberation (tel. 54–10–61). T.V. *Auberge Royale* (E), 19 rue des Remparts (tel. 5–26–30). Excellent restaurant. *Mercure* (M), 12 rue de l'Alzette (tel. 54–11–33). Central. *de a Poste* (M), 107 rue de l'Alzette (tel. 5–26–18).

Restaurants. *au Bec Fin* (E), 15 pl. N. Metz (tel. 5–21–41). *Pavilion Galgenberg* (M), Galgenberg (tel. 54–02–28). Terrace with wide outlook, play park for children.

ESCH-SUR-SÛRE. *des Ardennes* (M), 1 rue du Moulin (tel. 8–91–08). *Beau-Site* (M), 2 rue de Kaundorf (tel. 8–91–34). *du Moulin* (M), 6 rue du Moulin (tel. 8–91–07). Best situated of the three.

ETTELBRUCK. *Biver.* (I), 5 rue de Bastogne (tel. 8–22–44). Minimal but commendable. *Cames* (M), 45 rue Prince Henri (tel. 8–21–80). *Central* (M), 25 rue de Bastogne (tel. 8–21–16). *Solis* (M), 58 rue de Bastogne (tel. 8–23–93).

GAICHEL (EISCHEN). Restaurants. *de la Gaichel* (E), Maison 5 (tel. 3–91–29). Restaurant specializes in crustaceans. Reservations usually necessary. *à la Bonne Auberge* (M), Maison 7 (tel. 3–91–40). Restaurant specialty in season, wild young boar in wine sauce.

GREVENMACHER. *le Roi Dagobert* (E), 32 rue de Trèves (tel. 7–57–17). *de la Poste* (M), 28 rue de Trèves (tel. 7–51–36). *Govers* (I), 15 Grand'rue (tel. 7–51–37).
Restaurants. *Princesse Marie-Astrid* (I), 32 rte. de Thionville (tel. 75–82–75). Home port of this day-liner. Phone for reservations and dine on board. *Belle Vue* (I), 3 rue Kurzacht (tel. 7–56–14). Overlooks the Moselle. *Relais des Batéliers* (I), rte. du Vin (tel. 7–56–28). Overlooks the Moselle.

GRUNDHOF. Restaurant. *Brimer* (E), tel. 8–62–51. Splendid.

LAROCHETTE. *du Château* (M), 1 rue de Medernach (tel. 8–70–09). *de la Poste* (E), 11 pl. Bleich (tel. 8–70–06). *Résidence* (M), 14 rue de Medernach (tel. 8–73–91).

LEESBACH (SEPTFONTAINES). Restaurant. *Vieux Moulin* (E), tel. 3–05–27. Good food in the valley of the Seven Castles.

MONDORF-LES-BAINS. *Grand-Chef* (E), 36 av. des Bains (tel. 6–81–22). *Welcome* (E), 4 av. Marie-Adelaïde (tel. 66–07–85). *Beau-Séjour* (M), 3 av. Dr. Klein (tel. 6–81–08). *International* (M), 58 av. Fr. Clement (tel. 6–70–73). *Windsor* (M), 19 av. des Bains (tel. 6–72–03).
Restaurants. *Astoria* (M), 1 rte. de Remich (tel. 6–81–31). *Bristol* (M), 4 av. Dr. Klein (tel. 6–81–15). Fine kosher cooking. *Grand Chef* (M), 36 av. des Baines (tel. 6–81–22). Try the Crayfish.

MÜLLERTHAL. *Réserve du Müllerthal* (L), tel. 8–76–84. *Central* (M), 1 rue de l'Ernz Noire (tel. 8–72–88). Excellent restaurant.

REMICH. *des Ardennes* (M), 29 rue de la Gare (tel. 6–97–49). *Beau-Séjour* (M), 30 quai de la Moselle (tel. 69–81–26). *de l'Esplanade* (M), 5 Esplanade (tel. 6–91–71). *St. Nicolas* (M), 31 Esplanade (tel. 69–83–33). Good cheer overlooking the Moselle. Enormous towels!
Restaurant. *Belle Epoque* (E), quai de la Moselle (tel. 69–84–89). Dine well and watch the river.

VIANDEN. *du Château* (M), 74–78 Grand'rue (tel. 8–45–74). *Heintz* (M), 55 Grand'rue (tel. 8–41–55). *Hof van Holland* (M), 6 rue de la Gare (tel. 8–41–70). *The Nugget Gulch* (M), 2 rue de Bettel (tel. 8–42–66). *Oranienburg* (M), 126 Grand'rue (tel. 8–41–53). Fishing. *Victor Hugo* (M), 1 rue Victor Hugo (tel. 8–41–60).
Restaurants. *Hostellerie Trinitaires* (M), Hotel Heintz (tel. 8–45–59). An atmospheric restaurant of the first order. *Oranienburg* (M), 126 Grand'rue (tel. 8–41–53). *Veiner Stuff* (M), 26 rue de la Gare (tel. 8–41–74).

WILTZ. *du Commerce* (M), 9 rue des Tondeurs (tel. 9–62–20). *Beau-Séjour* (M), 21 rue du X Septembre (tel. 9–62–50). *du Vieux Château* (M), 1 Grand'rue (tel. 9–60–18). Excellent restaurant.
Restaurants. *des Ardennes* (M), 61 Grand'rue (tel. 9–61–52). *Belle-Vue* (I), 5–7 rue de la Fontaine (tel. 9–60–62).

MALTA

Malta, so fortunately situated in the middle of the Mediterranean, with its mild, sunny climate, is a perfect place for a holiday. Although a small island—including Gozo and Comino it covers only 122 square miles—its strategic position has always brought it fame. It tempted maritime nations since the Phoenicians sailed the seas. Indeed, they colonized it. It was later seized by the Carthaginians. Rome took the islands in 218 B.C.

From early days Malta has been a protagonist of Christianity. St. Paul was shipwrecked on the island and converted the inhabitants. In 1565 the Knights of Jerusalem held the island with a handful of men as a Christian stronghold against the Turks in one of the most spectacular sieges in history.

The Maltese are charming, religious and hard working. Without in any way detracting from the pride they have in their island home, the comings and goings of other nations have bequeathed an international veneer that makes them naturally gregarious and hospitable. Today, the overall population density exceeds 2,600 to the square mile.

There are religious festivals, richly-decorated churches and plenty of fascinating places for the sightseer and archeologist to visit. The Blue Grotto is reminiscent of the one in Capri. There are Crusader remains, Neolithic temples and an underground temple called the Hypogeum, cut deep into the rock—the only one of its kind in the world. Recently the vast hospital of the Order of St. John built by the Knights has been restored and converted into an international Conference Center to seat over 1,000 delegates. Here, you can see the Malta Experience, a spectacular multivision show highlighting 5,000 years of Maltese history.

Gozo is connected to Malta by ferry, and a helicopter service has recently been brought into use. It is a charming island studded with farms and fishing coves. It has more vegetation than Malta, but there are many flat-topped hills and craggy cliffs. Comino, the island between Gozo and Malta, provides splendid underwater hunting grounds, the aquamarine water being clear and unpolluted. Bathing is safe. There are no tides. Even Byron could not resist visiting Malta's sister islands —"not in silence pass Calypso's isles . . . ".

Valletta

From the air Valletta, Malta's capital, appears honey-colored, a stone city jutting into the Mediterranean wedged between two natural harbors. Where there are no flat-roofed houses, spires or baroque domes, the city is festooned with ramparts, walls, the castle of St. Angelo, now a tourist complex, and Fort St. Elmo left by the Knights of St. John of Jerusalem.

The main shopping street, Republic, serves as the city's spine. From it, other streets are laid out on a grid pattern, many sloping precipitously to the harbors on either side. Some of these streets are stepped, their facing houses with overhanging balconies nearly touching.

PRACTICAL INFORMATION FOR MALTA

WHAT WILL IT COST. Malta has a decimal currency, the Maltese Lira (Lm). The Lm is divided into 100 cents, each cent being subdivided into 10 mils. There are Lm10, Lm5, and Lm1 notes (due to be replaced by a coin); coins are for 50 cents, 10 cents, 5 cents, 1 cent, 5 mils, 3 mils, and 2 mils. Gold and silver coins are the legal tender. At the time of writing, the exchange rate for Lm1 was $2.34 and £1.60. You can take into the country any amount in travelers checks and other currency, but only up to Lm50. You may take out of the country currencies up to the amount imported and declared to Customs on arrival, also Maltese currency up to Lm25.

A typical day for two might cost:

Hotel, moderate, with breakfast	Lm10–12
Lunch at moderate restaurant	8
Coffee	.50
Transport (taxi ride)	1.50
Drinks	2
Dinner	10
Miscellaneous 10%	3
	Lm37.00

SOURCES OF INFORMATION. For information on all aspects of travel to Malta, contact the Malta Government Tourist Office. Its addresses are:

In the U.S.: Maltese Consulate, 249 East 35 St., New York, N.Y. 10016 (tel. 212–725–2345).

In the U.K.: College House, 2nd Floor, Suite 207, Wright's Lane, Kensington, London W.8 (tel. 01–938 2668).

WHEN TO COME. Summers are hot, though tempered by sea breezes. The archipelago is delightful the year round, but May through October is the high season, with April and May the months for spring freshness.

Average afternoon temperatures in degrees Fahrenheit and centigrade:

Malta	Jan.	Feb.	Mar.	Apr.	May	June	July	Aug.	Sept.	Oct.	Nov.	Dec.
F°	59	59	62	66	71	79	84	85	81	76	68	62
C°	15	15	17	19	22	26	29	29	27	24	20	17

 SPECIAL EVENTS. On Good Friday, solemn but colorful processions are held in several towns and villages. Carnival is held in the Capital, Valletta, and starts on the second Sunday in May. The "Mnarja" (folk festival) is held on the nearest weekend to the 28th of June and is an all night traditional festa with folk music, dancing and singing. Some 61 festi are held throughout the island between May and October. A water carnival is held on the first Sunday after September 8th, and boat races and band marches commemorate the Great Siege of 1565 and the lifting of the more recent one of 1940–43. Malta's National Day is March 31st—Freedom Day.

National Holidays. Jan. 1 (New Year's Day); Mar. 31 (Freedom); Mar. 28 (Good Fri.); May 1 (Workers' Day); Aug. 15 (Assumption); Dec. 13 (Republic); Dec. 25.

VISAS. Nationals of the United States, EEC and many other European countries do not require visas for entry into Malta. However, you must of course have a valid passport.

HEALTH CERTIFICATES. Not required to enter Malta.

 GETTING TO MALTA. By Plane. Malta's international airport of Luqa has air services with various European destinations by direct or through flights. These include London, Manchester, Paris, Frankfurt, Milan, Rome, Catania, Palermo, Tunis and Tripoli. *Air Malta* is the national carrier but *British Airways, Alitalia, Libyan Airlines, Lufthansa, KLM, Swissair,* and *Tunis Air* fly into and out of the island. Flying time from London is about 3 hours.

By Ferry. The *Gozo Channel Co. Ltd.* operates twice weekly from Syracuse in Sicily (summer only). The *Tirrenia Line* operates throughout the year from Naples via Reggio Calabria (once weekly) to Catania (3 times weekly). This crossing includes a call at Syracuse. Both ferries carry cars and have refreshment facilities.

 CUSTOMS. You may bring into the country 200 cigarettes or 250gr. of tobacco; spirits or cordials or liqueurs up to 1 full bottle and 1 bottle of wine; perfumery and/or toilet water not exceeding Lm2.00 in value. Importation of dogs and cats from rabies free countries may be allowed subject to certain health regulations.

 HOTELS AND RESTAURANTS. The island is well supplied with hotels and holiday complexes in all categories. Where service charge is not included 10% is adequate for tipping. Our hotel grading system is divided into four categories. All prices are for 2 people in a double room. Deluxe (L) Lm35 upwards, Expensive (E) Lm20–35, Moderate (M) Lm12–20, Inexpensive (I) Lm8–12.

There is a very good choice of restaurants from deluxe, expensive (Casino and Medina) down to fast food (hamburgers and fish and chips) and including Chinese, fish (Palazzo Pescatore), and beach (Luzzu) establishments. Local dishes include *Lampuki pie, Bragoli* and *Rikotta* but all the usual fare is available for the unadventurous with pork being the best bet.

Our grading system for restaurants is as follows—Expensive (E) Lm6 and up; Moderate (M) Lm2–6; Inexpensive (I) below Lm2.

GOLDEN BAY. *Golden Sands* (E), tel. 573961. 258 rooms with bath. Pool. Overlooking the bay.

MARSASCALA. *Jerma Palace* (E), tel. 823222. Over 200 rooms. A selection of small cafes and discos in this bay area.

MEDINA. *Xara Palace* (I), St. Paul's Sq. 18 rooms.
Restaurants. *Medina Restaurant* (E), Holy Cross St. (tel. 74004). *Fontanella Tea Rooms,* also serves snack lunches; near Bastion.

MELLIEHA BAY. *Mellieha Bay* (E), tel. 573844. 214 rooms with bath. A good base for lovers of water sports and fishing. *Maritim Selmun Palace Hotel* (M), overlooking St. Paul's Bay and Mellieha Bay (tel. 572455). 160 rooms.
Restaurants. *Arches* (E), 113 Main St. (tel. 573436). Openair roof restaurant in summer. *Tunny Net* (M), tel. 573135. Seafood restaurant set on the water's edge.

PARADISE BAY. *Paradise Bay* (E), tel. 573981. 211 rooms with bath. Air-conditioning, pool. Situated about 14 miles from Sliema.

RABAT. Restaurant. *Barrel & Basket* (M), St. Augustine Street (tel. 67426). Local food and music.

ST. ANTON. *Corinthia Palace* (L), tel. 40301. 156 rooms with bath, balcony. In the center of the island. Pools, health and sports center, *Al Hana* night club featuring Lebanese specialties.

ST. GEORGE'S BAY. *Villa Rosa* (M), tel. 511811. 154 rooms with bath. Two pools, boating, water-skiing, skin-diving facilities. Garden.

ST. JULIAN'S BAY. *Dragonara Hotel* (L), tel. 36421. 202 airconditioned rooms. Situated within the 15-acre grounds of Malta's only casino (of the same name). Excellent restaurant and cabaret. *Malta Hilton* (L), tel. 36201. 200 luxurious rooms with all amenities. Three pools, one heated in winter.

ST. PAUL'S BAY. Restaurants. *Gillieru* (E), tel. 573480. *Beachaven* (M), tel. 573682.

SALINA BAY. *Salina Bay* (E), tel. 573781. 107 rooms with bath. Airconditioning, pool. Facing the sea, about 6 miles from Sliema.
Restaurant. *Luzzu* (E), Qawra (tel. 573925). Italian cuisine, on the sea shore. Owned by Corinthia Palace Hotel.

TARXIEN. *Malta Health Farm* (M), tel. 823581. The only hydro in Malta. A converted hunting lodge surrounded by its own orchard. Fully-equipped gym, saunas and pool. Unusual disco called *Roots* housed in a disused water cistern and some old cellars.
Restaurant. *Il Kastell* (M), Health Farm, Main St. (tel. 823581). Flambé dishes, unusual underground disco.

VALLETTA. *Grand Hotel Excelsior* (L), Floriana (tel. 23661). *Phoenicia* (L), the Mall, Floriana (tel. 21211). The best known and longest established hotel. *British* (M), 267 St. Ursula St. (tel. 24730). View of harbor. *Castille* (M), St. Paul's St. (tel. 623677). View of harbor. *Osborne* (M), 50 South St. (tel. 623656).
Restaurants. *Bologna* (E), 59 Republic St. *Alexandra* (M), 35 South St. Cordon bleu cooking. *Barrakka* (M), Castille Pl. *The Manoel* (I), Marsamxetta Rd. *The Midland* (I), 25 St. Ursula St.

The Outer Islands

COMINO. *Comino* (E), tel. 573051. 160 rooms with bath. Two pools. The island is only 20 minutes by launch from Malta, has one hotel, one policeman, one postman, and no cars.

GOZO. *Ta'Cenc* (L), tel. 556819. 48 rooms, several bungalow suites. Openair restaurant, pools, lounge, bar. *Calypso* (M), Marsalform (tel. 556131). Overlooking an enclosed fishing harbor. *Cornucopia Hotel* (M), 10 Gnien Imrik St., Xaghra. Villas and apartments. *Duke of Edinburgh* (M), 113 Racecourse St., Victoria (tel. 76468). Victoria is Gozo's attractive capital, with over 7,000 inhabitants.

Museums

VALLETTA. St. John's Co-Cathedral contains Caravaggio's masterpiece *The Beheading of St. John.*

Palace of the Grand Masters. State apartments with tapestries and paintings. The Armoury of the Knights with arms and armor of various periods.

National Museum of Archeology. Examples of tomb furniture of the Punic and Roman periods, prehistoric pottery, etc.

National Museum of Fine Arts, South St. An 18th-cent. palace housing paintings, sculpture and furniture connected with the Order of St. John.

MARSAXLOKK. Close by museum of Ghar Dalam, a small building where you can see skeletons of pigmy hippopotami, stag, bear and elephant, the latter no larger than a St. Bernard dog. You can visit the cave where they were found.

MEDINA. Outside the city walls there is a Roman villa with wonderful mosaics and other treasures.

TARXIEN. Small museum at entrance to Hal Tarxien neolithic temples with exhibits from the excavations.

GETTING AROUND MALTA. Excellent bus service at about 12 cents covers the whole island. Avis, Hertz, and Europcar are represented and most garages are also in the car hire business. Prices are reasonable. You drive on the left as in Britain. Speed limits are 25 mph in built-up areas and only 40 elsewhere. Taxis can be identified by red number plates; they have meters but can omit to switch them on; about Lm1.0 per mile.

CLOSING TIMES. Shops are open from 9 to 7, Mon. to Fri.; 9 in the morning to 8 at night on Sat. There is usually a lunchhour closing for around 2 to 3 hours. Banking hours are from 8.30 to 12.30 Mon. to Fri.; 8.30 to 12 on Sat.

MAIL. Letters by air to North America cost 12 cents, postcards 8 cents, airletters to the U.K. and Europe 8 cents, postcards 7 cents.

USEFUL ADDRESSES. *American Embassy,* Development House, St. Anne St., Floriana (tel. 620424). *British High Commission,* 7 St. Anne St., Floriana (tel. 621285). *Malta Government Tourist Office,* 1 City Arcade, Valletta (tel. 24444). *Thomas Cook,* 20 Republic Street, Valletta.

MONACO

Between Nice and Menton, at the very heart of the French Riviera, lies the glittering principality of Monaco. An independent state, its frontiers controlled by France, Monaco consists of about 450 acres of expensive apartment buildings and beach clubs, cliffs and coastline. The Monégasques are easygoing and friendly, not without reason: they pay almost no taxes, have no military service, and live in a thoroughly prosperous enclave. The idyll was tragically shattered in September 1982 with the sudden death of Princess Grace, wife of Prince Rainier, hereditary ruler of Monaco. However, their three children, and the birth of a son to Princess Caroline in 1984, should ensure the continued rule of the family.

The principality consists of four towns: the ancient community of Monaco, high on a rock, with the prince's postcard palace, a modern cathedral in Romanesque style, and a world famous aquarium; La Condamine, where business thrives and the main port is; Monte Carlo, centered around the casino; and Fontvieille, rapidly coming up as an industrial center. The world-famous casino of Monte Carlo is the center of social life, scene of gala dinners, elegant parties and spectacular shows. The casino also houses the delightful Salle Garnier, a gilded theater which looks like a chocolate box version of the Paris Opéra. This theater, made famous by Diaghilev and the Ballets Russes, offers a glittering winter season of ballet, opera and drama. The old casino now has a rather gaudy rival in the gaming rooms in the Loew's Monte-Carlo hotel, and in the Monte Carlo Sporting Club.

Although gambling still brings a great deal of income to the principality, tourism is a very important industry here; and business tourism an increasingly major activity, especially since the building of a splendid conference center and auditorium in 1979. Reclaiming land from the sea has been a key priority. In fact, since World War II, Monaco has beaten all world records for peaceful territorial expansion, increasing the country's area by 20% through land reclamation. Beaches and hotels have been built with the purpose of attracting a wider range of visitors, middle and lower-income groups as well as the more affluent.

Discovering Monaco

First and foremost, visit the casino. Try your luck if you think it wise; otherwise, reserve in advance for dinner, take in a floorshow, have a drink, or just watch the suckers trying to break the bank.

Monaco has several museums (see end of section) but you shouldn't miss the splendid Exotic Gardens either. The Monte-Carlo Golf Club provides a magnificent mountainous course, but watch your step, or you'll end up in the Mediterranean several hundred feet below. There are golf and tennis tournaments all the year round and galas at the Sporting Club (December-April) and the Sporting d'Eté at Larvotto, during the summer season. The famous Monaco Grand Prix is in May, and an international bridge tournament is held each June. The summer calendar of events features a dazzling ball each Friday night at the Sporting d'Eté. There are the aquatic distractions of swimming, skindiving, water skiing, and yachting. The Monte-Carlo Country Club holds international tennis championships which attract the big names —one of them was the great Bjorn Borg, now a resident of Monaco along with many another who'd be crippled by tax if they stayed back home.

You will want to make short excursions to Beausoleil, a popular residential district linking Monaco to France; to the hilltop village of Eze; to the fortified village of Roquebrune, with its curious tangle of narrow stepped lanes, and the equally ancient village of La Turbie, with its magnificent view from the Grande Corniche (see France section).

PRACTICAL INFORMATION FOR MONACO

WHAT WILL IT COST. Monaco equates to an expensive French resort. As you will see from our section on France, this puts the hotels quite high in European costs. The hotel range is, approximately, (L) 900–1,600, (E) 500–850, (M) 300–500, (I) 180–300. (The currency in Monaco is the French franc.) Restaurant prices also follow the pattern for the more expensive cities of France—(E) 300–500, (M) 200–300, (I) 100–200.

WHEN TO COME. The temperature is roughly equivalent to that of southern California. Winter has traditionally been the smart season, but with the increase in the numbers of less wealthy tourists, the seasons extend to both winter and summer. However, the winter remains just a bit smarter, with ballet, opera, music festival, fancy dress balls, yachting regattas, and the Monte Carlo rally.

Average afternoon temperatures in degrees Fahrenheit and Centigrade:

Monaco	Jan.	Feb.	Mar.	Apr.	May	June	July	Aug.	Sept.	Oct.	Nov.	Dec.
F°	56	56	59	64	69	76	81	81	77	70	62	58
C°	13	13	15	18	21	24	27	27	25	21	17	14

SPECIAL EVENTS. Winter season: *Oct. thru Apr.,* galas at the Sporting Club; concerts by the Philharmonic Orchestra; *Nov.,* Fête Nationale Monégasque; *Dec.,* International Circus Festival; *Dec. thru Mar.,* Monte Carlo Arts Festival (ballet, concerts and theater), opera season; *Jan.,* Monte Carlo Auto Rally; *Easter,* International Tennis Championships; *Apr.,* sailing regattas; *May,* Monaco Grand Prix. **Summer season:** concerts in the Cour d'Honneur of the Prince's palace; Red Cross gala; Monte Carlo Arts Festival; gala dinners every Fri. at Sporting Club; Art and Antiques exhibit; fireworks festival.

Public Holidays. Same as for France, except that Nov. 19 (National Day) replaces July 14.

CUSTOMS. None if you enter from France; otherwise the same as for France.

 HOTELS. The top hotels of **Monte Carlo** are the last word in luxury and are correspondingly expensive. You can get a single room with bath at the fabulous *Hôtel de Paris,* pl. Casino (tel. 93–50–80–80), for about 1,000 francs, off-season, but you can pay all you have for a suite in which the management will obligingly change the furniture to suit your taste. This, the most famous of Monte Carlo's hotels, is diagonally across from the Casino. It has a swimming pool, heated in winter, and is airconditioned throughout. Its grill room has a magnificent view and the food is generally good, if overpriced (it has a second restaurant too); its *cave* of vintage wines is probably unequalled on the Côte d'Azur.

Most modern in the (L) category is *Loew's Monte-Carlo,* av. Spélugues (tel. 93–50–65–00), part of the giant Spélugues project of residential apartments, convention center etc., built on a concrete platform jutting into the sea below the Casino. The hotel has every amenity, plus two luxury restaurants: *Foie Gras* (E), no lunch (see below) and the livelier *Argentin* (E), serving South American cuisine late into the night.

Among the other (L) hotels are—the old-established but successfully modernized *Hermitage,* square Beaumarchais (tel. 93–50–67–31), which has good restaurants; and elegant *Mirabeau,* av. Princesse-Grace 1 (tel. 93–30–80–67), all the usual amenities plus gambling rooms and a good restaurant (closed July and Aug., when meals are served by the pool instead).

Alexandra (L), 35 blvd. Princesse-Charlotte (tel. 93–50–63–13), no restaurant, and the somewhat old-fashioned but friendly *Balmoral* (M), 12 av. Costa (tel. 93–50–62–37) are medium-size hotels.

Etoile (I), tel. 93–30–73–92, is very central; with restaurant. *Poste* (I), 5 rue Oliviers (tel. 93–30–70–56). Modest, in side street below casino, with restaurant.

At **Monte Carlo beach**—*Monte Carlo Beach* (L), tel. 93–78–21–40, peaceful, with pool, is exclusive and has been modernized throughout. *Beach Plaza* (E), tel. 93–30–98–80, is also on the beach, and has 3 pools as well as waterfront facilities.

At **Monaco** itself—*Terminus* (M), (tel. 93–30–20–70), airconditioned, with two restaurants. *France* (I), tel. 93–30–24–66, no restaurant.

 RESTAURANTS. Best place for classical cuisine is *Foie Gras* (E), in Loew's Hotel. *Grill* (E) and *Salle Empire* (E), in Hôtel de Paris, are elegant if overpriced, with classical cuisine and splendid wines. *Dominique Le Stanc* (E), is a welcome newcomer and very fashionable. Tiny and delightful, with successful *nouvelle cuisine* plus a collection of antique dolls to add to your enjoyment.

Bec Rouge (E), tel. 93–30–74–91, home-style cooking, and *Calanque* (E), tel. 93–50–63–19, good fish dishes, are a bit more reasonable. Also *Rampoldi* (E), tel. 93–30–70–65, brasserie-type, always crowded.

Pistou (M), in Loew's Hotel, serves regional dishes.

Café de Paris (M), tel. 93–50–57–75, very popular, right by the casino. *Pinocchio* (M), tel. 93–30–96–20, is good for Italian specialties, but gets very busy (no lunches). *Polpetta* (I), tel. 93–50–67–84, good Italian cooking, chic.

MAIL. Same rates as France, but you must buy special stamps.

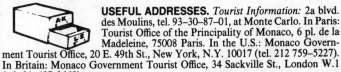

USEFUL ADDRESSES. *Tourist Information:* 2a blvd. des Moulins, tel. 93–30–87–01, at Monte Carlo. In Paris: Tourist Office of the Principality of Monaco, 6 pl. de la Madeleine, 75008 Paris. In the U.S.: Monaco Government Tourist Office, 20 E. 49th St., New York, N.Y. 10017 (tel. 212 759–5227). In Britain: Monaco Government Tourist Office, 34 Sackville St., London W.1 (tel. 01–437 3660).

Travel Agents: Havas-Voyages, 4 rue des Iris, *American Express,* 35 blvd. Princesse Charlotte, *Wagons Lits-Cook's,* av. des Spélugues. The *Société des Bains de Mer,* which controls the Hôtel de Paris, the Monte-Carlo Golf Club, the Country Club, Jimmy'z, not to mention the Casino and a few million other things, is a good source of information about events sporting and cultural and just plain fun. Write to them in Monaco (no address needed) or Paris: 24 Rue Marbeuf, 75008 Paris. Hotel reservations for the SBM hotels are handled in London by MMA Motivations Ltd, Society Hotels, 99 Regent St., W.1 (tel. 01–437 9918); and in the U.S. at 505 Park Avenue, New York 10022 (tel. 212–688–9890 or 800–221–4708).

Car Rental: Hertz, 57 rue Grimaldi (tel. 93–50–79–60); *Avis,* 9 av. d'Ostende (tel. 93–30–17–53).

MUSEUMS. The best known is the world-famous *Oceanographic Museum,* with its own aquarium, in Monaco itself. The prince's palace is open to the public; it has particularly interesting items connected with Napoleon. The *National Museum* in Monte Carlo specializes in dolls and automata.

NORWAY

Beautiful Norway is the northernmost country in Scandinavia. The country, about 1,100 miles long and about the size of New Mexico, is literally laced by the sea, which penetrates its western side with a series of *fjords* or inlets. These fjords have given the nation a coastline of more than 12,000 miles and some of the most magnificent scenery in the world. You should certainly try to get to the North Cape, extreme northern point of Europe, where, from May 14 until August 1, the sun stays above the horizon all night, for this is the luminous land of the Midnight Sun. Conversely, there is a period in midwinter with no daylight above the Arctic Circle when there appears the unforgettable and eerie brilliance of the aurora borealis (the Northern Lights).

There is a certain moral justice in the fact that Norway's scenic splendor is now attracting so much tourist business, for all this natural beauty has been of little economic value in the past; seven-tenths of Norway is bare rock, glaciers, and wild romantic mountains rising to heights of more than 8,000 feet. Less than four percent of the land is tilled and mineral resources are comparatively small. But more fish are brought ashore than in most other European countries and its merchant fleet is the fifth largest in the world. Royalties have begun to flow in from North Sea oil and Norway's economic prospects are brighter than most countries' in Western Europe (despite its non-membership in the Common Market).

Known as the land of Vikings, Ibsen and Grieg, Norway is not the enigmatic, introverted place of popular preconception; the Norwegians are full of good humor, friendly to foreigners and glad to exchange ideas—in English fortunately.

PRACTICAL INFORMATION FOR NORWAY

WHAT WILL IT COST. Inflation has hit Norway as it has so many other countries in the Western world, and you can expect a yearly increase of around 10%. Deluxe accommodations and restaurant prices in the capital, Oslo, and the other major cities come at truly deluxe price and are for expense accounts only. As elsewhere in Scandinavia, prices in the suburbs are rather more reasonable.

The unit of currency in Norway is the crown, or *krone* (NOK), which divides into 100 öre. At the time of writing, the exchange rate for the krone was NOK 7.50 to the U.S. dollar and 10.50 to the pound sterling, but these figures are very liable to change both before and during 1987.

A typical day in Oslo might cost two people:

Hotel, moderate, with breakfast (see special offers)	NOK 600
Lunch, moderate	160
Transportation (see Oslo Card)	100
Coffee and snack	60
Entertainment	100
Dinner	300
Miscellaneous 10%	150
	NOK 1,470

SOURCES OF INFORMATION. For any information regarding traveling in Norway, the Norwegian National Tourist Board is invaluable. You can contact them at the following addresses:

In the U.S.: 655 Third Ave., New York, N.Y. 10017 (tel. 212–949–2333).
In the U.K.: 20 Pall Mall, London S.W.1 (tel. 01–839 2650).

WHEN TO COME. Summer in Norway lasts from early May until mid-September. However, May and June are considered good months to visit, although the climate can vary considerably from year to year and place to place in this very long country. At the North Cape, the sun does not sink below the horizon from the second week in May until the last week in July. June through August the sea is at its warmest and this does attract both locals and tourists, with the result that some hotels are crowded.

September is the month for those seeking a mountain holiday: the autumn foliage is then at its beautiful best, though the weather can be variable. The winter-sports season runs from Christmas to late April.

Climate. Offshore Gulf Stream currents prevent extremes. The north averages ten degrees colder, but recent years have changed weather patterns here as elsewhere.

Average afternoon monthly temperatures are listed below.

Oslo	Jan.	Feb.	Mar.	Apr.	May	June	July	Aug.	Sept.	Oct.	Nov.	Dec.
F°	30	32	40	50	62	69	73	69	60	49	37	31
C°	−1	0	4	10	17	21	23	21	16	9	3	−1

SPECIAL EVENTS. *January,* Monolith Ski Race in Frogner park in Oslo; ski festival in Lillehammer. *March,* Holmenkollen Ski Festival in Oslo—world's largest skiing competitions; Winter Festival Week in Narvik beyond the Arctic Circle; Birkebeiner historical Viking ski race in Lillehammer. *April,* Easter religious festival in Oslo. *May,* Bergen International Festival of music, drama and folklore; May 17, Norway's national day. *June,*

Grieg Festival at Lofthus on the Hardanger fjord; cultural festival week in Harstad; North Sea Festival in Haugesund; jazz festival in Kongsberg. *July,* international yachting races in Oslo fjord; Viking festival at Stiklestad near Trondheim. *August,* international jazz festival in Molde. *October,* furniture fair in Oslo. *December 10,* Nobel Peace Prize presentation in Oslo.

National Holidays. Jan. 1; Apr. 16–20 (Easter); May 1 (May Day); May 17 (Constitution Day); May 28 (Ascension); June 7, 8 Whitsun (Pentecost); Dec. 25, 26.

VISAS. Nationals of the United States, Canada, Australia, New Zealand, EEC countries and practically all other European countries do not require visas for entry into Norway, provided their stay does not exceed 3 months in any 6-month period.

HEALTH CERTIFICATES. Not required for entry into Norway from any country.

RABIES WARNING. Owing to the risk of rabies, *very* stringent rules are in force for the import of dogs, cats and other animals into Norway. A prior permit *must* be obtained from the Ministry of Agriculture. The smuggling of animals into Norway incurs heavy fines, and the animals must be returned to their country of origin immediately, at their owner's expense, or destroyed. There are *no* exceptions.

GETTING TO NORWAY. By Plane. There are direct flights from New York to Bergen and Oslo by SAS; also from Minneapolis/St. Paul to Oslo by Northwest Orient Airlines; and from New York via Reykjavik to Oslo by Icelandair. Otherwise, there are good connecting services to Oslo, Bergen and Stavanger from Copenhagen, which in turn has direct flights to New York, Chicago, Los Angeles, Seattle and Anchorage by SAS.

In the U.K., there are direct flights from London to Oslo, Bergen and Stavanger; from Norwich to Stavanger; from Newcastle to Bergen and Stavanger; and from Aberdeen to Stavanger and Bergen.

Most European capitals and major cities are linked with Oslo by air, either direct or via Copenhagen.

By Boat. A new route, available all year round, is Harwich–Oslo; departures once a week, on Thursday. Summer-only sailings (June through September) Harwich–Kristiansand, Newcastle–Bergen and Newcastle–Stavanger.

By Train. If you're no sailor and would like to reduce the sea travel to a minimum, there is the Harwich–Hook of Holland boat service (6 hours), with train travel through Holland and Germany: The North West Express leaves London (Liverpool Street Station) in the morning and gets you to Copenhagen with connecting day trains to Oslo and Stockholm. The night boat train from London connects with the Holland-Scandinavian Express at Hook of Holland next morning and reaches Copenhagen—with connecting night trains to Oslo and Stockholm.

By Car. There are car ferry services from England to Norway, from Amsterdam to Kristiansand and to Stavanger/Bergen, and from Kiel to Oslo. From Denmark there are year-round ferry services from Copenhagen to Oslo, Frederikshavn to Oslo, Hanstholm to Bergen, Hirtshals to Kristiansand, Stavanger and Bergen, and from Frederikshavn to Larvik.

CUSTOMS. 1 liter of spirits, 1 liter of wine and up to 200 cigarettes may be brought in duty free (overseas visitors: 2 liters of spirits, 2 liters of wine and 400 cigarettes). You may bring in foreign currency in unlimited amounts, also Norwegian currency, but not notes of higher than NOK 100. You may be asked to declare this when you enter, and you cannot take out more than 2,000 kroner.

HOTELS. Norwegian hotels are spotlessly clean and comfortable, and the visitor receives value for his money. Inclusive pension stays are available for stays of 3–5 days or longer. Accommodations vary in size, of course, and in degree of comfort, but the hotel trade is protected by law in Norway, and every establishment calling itself a hotel must fulfill certain requirements with regard to size, standard of modern conveniences, etc. Resort hotels offering superior accommodation are called "tourist" or "mountain" hotels—the latter must be situated at least 2,500 feet above sea level.

There are few Norwegian hotels in the top luxury category or in the very lowest price group. Our grading system is divided into four categories. All prices are for single occupancy. Deluxe (L) NOK 800 and up, Expensive (E) NOK 600, Moderate (M) NOK 500, Inexpensive (I) NOK 300 and up.

Note. Hotels strictly enforce a noon checkout. If you want to keep your room until 1 or 2 P.M. it will mean an extra 25%, to 6 P.M. 50%.

CAMPING. Over 1400 camping sites have been established in Norway. The majority are run by Norway's A.A. and list of them in English can be obtained from corresponding associations abroad. Facilities vary according to grading (one, two or three stars).

RESTAURANTS. Our grading for restaurants in Norway is as follows—Expensive (E) from NOK 200 and upwards; Moderate (M) from NOK 100 upwards; Inexpensive (I) below NOK 75.

Food and Drink. Hearty is the word for Norwegian meals. Breakfasts are often enormous with a variety of fish, meats and cheese, and fine bread served from the cold buffet along with coffee and boiled or fried eggs. A smaller Continental breakfast is available at most city hotels. A national institution is the *koldtbord* (cold table) which will often be in evidence at lunch time, featuring smoked salmon, fresh lobster, shrimp and other products of the sea, also assorted meats, salads, cheese, desserts and hot dishes. The sandwiches are a meal in their own right. They are called *smörbröd*. Equally appreciated by Norwegians and their visitors are the roast venison, ptarmigan in cream sauce, wild cranberries and a special berry called *multer* with a flavor all its own. After that even the fiery Norwegian schnaps, *aquavit*, seems cool.

Liquor and wine are sold only at the state special monopoly stores—*Vinmonopolet*—and licensing laws are rather severe. You can't drink at a bar before 1 P.M. in resort hotels and before 3 P.M. in town restaurants, and they are closed on Sunday, but if you can afford it, you can buy more than enough at the liquor stores to tide you over those arid spells. Alcohol is scarce in most provinces, except at the top *høyfjells* and *turist* (mountain and tourist) hotels, and costs are high. However, most hotels and restaurants are licensed to sell alcohol at any time to residents.

TIPPING. Norway is not accustomed to much tipping, particularly outside the main centers. Service charge and VAT are always added to the bill in hotels, restaurants and bars. Round out this bill in the latter if you wish, and of course tip for special service. Porters are usually tipped 4 Nok. per bag. Beauty parlors do not expect tips. Taxi drivers don't expect tip either, but if in doubt add small amount. It is usual to tip tour guides if satisfied.

MAIL. Current airmail rates to the U.S. and within Europe are NOK 3.50 for up to 20 grams, NOK 6.00 for up to 50 grams. Postcards to the U.S., Canada, and the U.K. all go at NOK 3.00.

CLOSING TIMES. Shops from 9 to 5 (4 P.M. in summer). On Saturdays they may close as early as 2 P.M., especially in summer. Banking hours are 8.30 to 3.30, Monday through Friday, but closed on Saturdays. Museums, etc., are usually open until 6 P.M. in high season (June, July, August). Consult tourist offices, *Oslo Guide,* or *Oslo This Week* for exact times.

USEFUL ADDRESSES. *American Embassy,* Dramensveien 18; *British Embassy,* Ths Heftyesgate 8; *Canadian Embassy,* Oscarsgate 20. *Norwegian Tourist Board,* H. Heyerdahlsgate 1; *Oslo Tourist Information Office,* Oslo City Hall (harbor entrance); *Norwegian Mountain Touring Association,* Stortingsgate 28. *Royal Norwegian Automobile Club* (KNA), Parkveien 68; *Norwegian Automobile Association* (NAF), Storgaten 2.

All above addresses are in Oslo.

Bergen Festival Office, Grieghallen, Lars Hilles gt 3A, 5000 Bergen.

GETTING AROUND NORWAY. By Plane. In spite of (or perhaps because of) a difficult terrain and a comparatively small population Norway has a comprehensive air network serving even very small communities. These flights are operated by *SAS,* Braathens *SAFE* and *Widerøe,* the two latter being independently owned companies. Details of all services from local travel agents.

By Train. Norwegian railways go from Oslo to Kristiansand and Stavanger, to Bergen and north to Trondheim and on to Bodø. There is also the main line east to Stockholm and south to Gothenburg and Copenhagen. Most of the network is scenically attractive. The trains are clean, comfortable and carry restaurant, buffet and refreshment services on longer distance journeys. On overnight services there are 1st and 2nd class sleepers. Many local trains carry only 2nd class but this is of a high standard. Be sure to inquire about the *Nordturist* ticket which enables the holder to unlimited rail travel throughout Norway (and the rest of Scandinavia), as well as a substantial discount on a number of ferry services.

By Boat. An intricate network of ferries all the way up the fjord-indented coast links many settlements, villages and towns. They operate all the year round and where appropriate link in with train and bus services. Indeed, complete integration of all forms of public transport is an outstanding characteristic of Norway. Full information on ferries can be obtained from tourist information offices as well as the ferry operators themselves.

By Bus. Local and medium distance buses are an essential part of Norwegian transport. Some are operated by the railway, others by private enterprise and yet others by local communities. They are clean and comfortable and run throughout the year—even in mid-winter.

By Car. In Norway you drive on the right. Many roads are outstanding tourist attractions on their own merit—particularly in the Fjord Country—with hairpin bends and mountain passes, smiling lakes and thundering waterfalls. There is never a long tedious journey to reach your destination in Norway because you are there all the time. The scenery is constantly changing in all its breathtaking beauty. There are good hotels along every major tourist route. One word of warning, though: filling stations can be few and far between, so do stock up when you get the chance. Gasoline currently costs approximately NOK 5.00 per liter for all kinds, but these figures could change before and during 1987. Lead-free (*blyfri*) gasoline is being introduced all over the country from 1986. It is expected that this will be cheaper than normal gasoline so as to encourage its use where possible.

The official speed limit on the open road is 50mph, but in the context of the narrow, winding, mountainous nature of the routes this makes sense.

Car Hire. *Scandinavian Car Rental,* Fredensborgveien 33; *Bislett Car Rental,* Pilestredet 70; *Avis,* Munkedamsveien 27, also Fornebu, Bergen, Stavanger and other towns; *Center Car,* Drammensveien 126B. *Kjøles* (Hertz), General Birchsgt 16. All in Oslo.

Oslo, Norway's Capital

The bright, breezy and outdoorsy capital of Norway is a hospitable city of almost 450,000 people at the head of the Oslofjord. You may be surprised to know that in area it is one of the largest metropolises in the world (it was enlarged by 27 times its size in 1948, to include huge areas of surrounding country).

This usually begins on the main street, Karl Johansgate, which leads from the Central Station to the Royal Palace. Half of this street is now a pedestrian precinct. Below the Palace is a small green park, on the harbor side of which is the Stortingsgate and the National Theater, with its entrance flanked by statues of Norway's two great dramatists, Henrik Ibsen and Bjørnsterne Bjørnson. Despite the recent building of a splendid new concert hall, this is still the focal point of Oslo's cultural life. A stairway behind the theater leads to the underground station, departure point for excursions to the outlying sections of Oslo.

Visit the twin-towered red brick Rådhus or City Hall, the interior of which contains 2,000 square yards of bold-figured murals by Henrik Sørensen, Alf Rolfsen and other leading Norwegian artists, depicting all phases of life and work in Norway. Just beyond the City Hall are the romantic spires and ramparts of Akershus Fortress, which dates from about 1300. The occupying Nazis used it from 1940 to 1945, and, close beside the stone monument which honors the memory of the Norwegian patriots who were executed within these walls, is a very interesting and completely unembittered Resistance Museum. A military museum was also opened in 1978. Frogner Park is the scene of 150 groups of bronze and granite sculpture by Gustav Vigeland. Opinions vary as to the value of this huge concentration of sculpture. But see it for yourself—you can hardly avoid it—and if you like it, go to the artist's studio at Nobelsgate 32, now the Vigeland Museum (situated beside the park). For the best view of the city take the tram to Sjømannsskolen, the Merchant Marine Academy. From the front terrace there you can see the harbor, the two fjords, and the old and new towns. For a more distant panoramic view take the electric train to Holmenkollen and walk up to the ski jump.

The most rewarding of Oslo's many excursions is to Bygdøy. You take the boat from the quay marked "Bygdøy" in front of the City Hall and you dock in front of a wedge-shaped building that houses the famous polar ship, *Fram,* the vessel on which Fridtjof Nansen and Roald Amundsen traveled. Beside it, a museum built in 1957 contains another symbol of modern Viking courage, the famous *Kon Tiki* balsa raft, which carried Thor Heyerdahl, four of his countrymen, one Swede and one parrot (international type!) 4,800 miles from Peru to Polynesia and "Ra II," on which he drifted across the Atlantic in 1970. Apex of a seafaring triangle is the Maritime Museum. Farther inland is the greatest memorial of all to Norway's seafaring prowess, three original Viking vessels—the Tune ship, the Oseberg ship, and the Gokstad ship. Also at Bygdøy is the Folk Museum. In addition to over 80,000 exhibits there are 150 original houses, barns, *stabburs,* etc. Don't miss the Gol wooden stave church, built around 1200.

GETTING AROUND OSLO. By subway. The Oslo metro is divided into two halves covering the eastern and the western sectors. Western lines radiate from the National Theater station, eastern and northern from Jernbanetorget station.

By bus. Street car and bus stops are indicated by round metal indicators painted blue and showing the schedule. The single fare is NOK 10 but you can buy a *trikkekort* good for 12 trips at NOK 90, or a 24-hour tourist ticket for NOK 30. This gives unlimited travel by bus, tram, subway, local trains and ferry boats within the city boundaries. (See also *Oslo Card,* below.)

By taxi. Dial 38 80 90 to call a taxi, or look up the nearest taxi stand in the phone book under *drosjer.* Taxis can be hailed from the street as long as they are more than 100 meters from a taxi rank.

An *Oslo Card* entitles you to free travel on public transport, free admittance to museums and other places of interest, reduced rates on sightseeing coaches, ski hire, a rebate on car rental, and special offers in restaurants. The card is valid for 1–3 days and costs: NOK 60 (child NOK 30) for 1 day; NOK 90 (child NOK 45) for 2 days; NOK 120 (child NOK 60) for 3 days. *Note:* 1986 prices; expect slight increases for 1987. The card can be obtained from hotels, leading stores and the Tourist Information Office.

PRACTICAL INFORMATION FOR OSLO

HOTELS. By all means reserve your accommodations well in advance either through a travel bureau or by writing directly to the hotel of your choice. Consult the folder, *Hotels in Norway,* published annually by the Norwegian Tourist Board. Also useful is the *Oslo Guide* published by the Oslo Travel Association and available at their Information Office at Oslo City Hall, also at most hotels and from various travel agents. If you find yourself in Oslo with nowhere to stay, go to the Oslo Travel Association's billeting center at the Central station, through which you can obtain a room as late as midnight.

23 Oslo hotels offer *greatly* reduced rates at weekends throughout the year and at Christmas, New Year, Easter and Whitsun holidays. They cannot be booked more than 3 days in advance. Further information from the Tourist Information Office or travel bureaux.

Deluxe

Bristol, Kristian IV's gt 7 (tel. 02–415840). 215 beds. Centrally located on a quiet side street. With restaurant, bars, grill room, night club.

Continental, Stortingsgata 24/26 (tel. 02–419060). 318 beds in building set across the street from the National Theater. Top-grade restaurant, popular theater-cafe, grill, coffee shops, bar.

Grand, Karl Johansgate 31 (tel. 02–429390). 525 beds. On main street, with exclusive restaurant, also top-floor restaurant, night club, sandwich buffet, bar, swimming pool, sauna, solarium.

Holmenkollen Park, Kongevei 26 (tel. 02–146090). 350 beds, 200 rooms, all with facilities. New in 1982, on hillside overlooking fjord and city. Atrium restaurant, bar and gourmet restaurant; pools, sauna, sports.

Scandinavia, Holbergsgate 30 (tel. 02–113000). 967 beds. Facing Royal Palace, the largest hotel in Norway with 24 floors; 24-hour room service, restaurants, coffee shop, night club, bars, indoor pool, shopping arcade. Owned by SAS.

Sheraton Hotel Oslo Fjord, P.O. Box 160, 1301 Sandvika (tel. 02–545700). Opened in 1985. 384 beds, facilities in all rooms. 7 km from Fornebu airport, 15 km from Oslo. Restaurants, bar, next to Inforama Congress Center.

Expensive

Ambassadeur, Camilla Collettsvei 15 (tel. 02–441835). 54 beds, near the Royal Palace; several suites, sauna and pool.

Astoria, Akersgata 21 (tel. 02–426900). 175 beds, popular restaurant.

KNA, Parkveien 68 (tel. 02–562690). 228 beds, in a peaceful west-end street; restaurant. Run by the Royal Automobile Club.

Nye Helsfyr, Strømsveien 108 (tel. 02–672380). 225 beds, all rooms with facilities. Bar, restaurant.

Sara, Gunnerusgate 3, (tel. 02–429410). 470 beds, restaurant, bar. Near Central station.

SAS Park Royal, P.O. Box 185, 1324 Lysaker (tel. 120220). 500 beds. Near airport, 10 minutes from city center. New wing opened in 1985. All facilities, restaurant, night club.

Stefan, Rosenkrantzgate 1 (tel. 02–429250). 200 beds, all rooms with bath/shower. Popular restaurant, unlicensed.

Moderate

Akershus Hotel, Akerskaien (tel. 02–428680). 144 beds; boatel, restaurant.

Carlton Rica, Parkveien 78 (tel. 02–563090). 86 beds, all rooms with bath/shower. Rica restaurant, famous for fine food.

Hotel Europa, St. Olava gt 31 (tel. 02–209990). 280 beds; breakfast only.

Hotel Munch, Munchs gt 5 (tel. 02–424275). 285 beds; breakfast only. New.

Mullerhotel West, Skovveien 15 (tel. 02–562995). 76 beds, most rooms with bath. Bar, popular Coq d'Or grill.

Nobel, Karl Johansgate 33 (tel. 02–427480). 104 beds, most rooms with facilities. Bistro, bar. Somewhat faded; but excellent central location.

Norum, Bygdøy Alle 53 (tel. 02–447990). 90 beds, most rooms with facilities. Bistro with good food.

Triangel, Holbergs plass 1 (tel. 02–208855). 200 beds. Unlicensed.

Inexpensive

Anker, Storgata 55 (tel. 02–114005). Summer hotel only (June/Aug.) 500 beds. Cooking facilities, restaurant, cafeteria, supermarket.

Gyldenløve, Bogstadveien 20 (tel. 02–601090). 330 beds. Bed and breakfast hotel. Unlicensed.

Haraldsheim Youth Hostel, Haraldsheimveien 4 (tel. 02–218359). 270 beds, 6 in each room. International atmosphere, cafeteria, sauna.

IMI, Staffeldtsgate 4 (tel. 02–205330). 110 beds. Mission hotel, unlicensed.

Panorama, Sognsveien 218 (tel. 02–187080). Summer hotel only (June/Aug.). 770 beds, most rooms with facilities. Restaurant, cafeteria.

 RESTAURANTS. All the major hotels have restaurants where food and service are generally very good. The cream of the hotels offer outstanding restaurants of the highest quality. Licensing restrictions are apt to baffle visitors. Beer and wine are served any day of the week during opening hours, but hard liquor is available only after 3 P.M. and never on a Sunday.

Expensive

Blom, Karl Johansgt 41 (tel. 427300). Meeting place for artists for over a century. Norwegian and international cuisine. Lunch buffet, outdoor café in summer. Closed Sun.

Caravelle, Fornebu (tel. 120220). Sited at the airport. International menu.

De Fem Stuer, Holmenkollen Park Hotel, Kongevn 26 (tel. 02–146090). Exclusive gourmet restaurant in one of Norway's best-preserved timber buildings. Good parking facilities. Open daily.

Den Glade Laks-M/S Pibervigen, Rådhusbrygge 4 (tel. 419996). Fish and shellfish. Summer excursions on the fjord.

Frognerseteren, Frognerseteren (tel. 143736). Overlooking the city and fjord, reached by Holmenkollen tram from the National Theater underground station. A must for all visitors to Oslo, an old timber building in traditional Norse style, with a large open hearth and Norwegian specialties.

Holmenkollen, Holmenkollvn 119 (tel. 146226). Between station and ski jump. Panoramic view over Oslo. Hot and cold meals. Moderately-priced cafeteria. Open daily.

Najaden, Bygdøynes (tel. 554490). Overlooking the fjord. Good food. Reached by bus or ferry from City Hall—situated in Norwegian Maritime Museum.

Tre Kokker, Drammensveien 30 (tel. 442650). Near the Royal Palace, a charcoal grill and an outstanding kitchen run by Norway's top gourmet, Hroar Dege. Dancing in the bar. Closed Sunday.

Moderate

Bagatelle, Bygdøy Alle (tel. 446397). West of the Royal Palace, an intimate French restaurant. Closed Saturday and Sunday.

Bella Napoli, Storgt 26 (tel. 410052). Italian, same management as Mamma Rosa. Informal atmosphere, popular with young people.

La Brochette, Dronning Maudsgt 1–3 (tel. 416733). French food in a distinctive milieu.

Cheese Inn, Ruselokkveien 3 (tel. 419679). A small and intimate restaurant specializing in cheese dishes. Southwest of the Royal Palace.

Frascati's Little Kjøkken, Stortingsgt 20 (tel. 111228). Good for light meals, with an open sandwich buffet. Near City Hall.

Gallagher's Steak House, Karl Johansgate 10 (tel. 429651). Restaurant with pizza pub on main street. American-style steaks and pancakes; evening music.

Mamma Rosa, Øvre Slottsgt 12 (tel. 420130). Italian with pleasant atmosphere. Guitar music in evenings. Open daily.

La Mer, Pikestredet 31 (tel. 203445). Norway's only French fish restaurant. Closed Sunday.

Peking House, St. Olavsgt 23 (tel. 114878). Good Chinese food. Quick service, pleasant surroundings. Near SAS hotel.

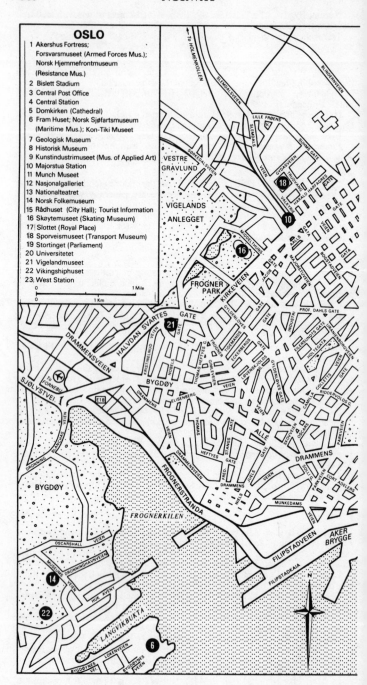

OSLO

1 Akershus Fortress;
   Forsvarsmuseet (Armed Forces Mus.);
   Norsk Hjemmefrontmuseum
   (Resistance Mus.)
2 Bislett Stadium
3 Central Post Office
4 Central Station
5 Domkirken (Cathedral)
6 Fram Huset; Norsk Sjøfartsmuseum
   (Maritime Mus.); Kon-Tiki Museet
7 Geologisk Museum
8 Historisk Museum
9 Kunstindustrimuseet (Mus. of Applied Art)
10 Majorstua Station
11 Munch Museet
12 Nasjonalgalleriet
13 Nationalteatret
14 Norsk Folkemuseum
15 Rådhuset (City Hall); Tourist Information
16 Skøytemuseet (Skating Museum)
17 Slottet (Royal Place)
18 Sporveismuseet (Transport Museum)
19 Stortinget (Parliament)
20 Universitetet
21 Vigelandmuseet
22 Vikingshiphuset
23 West Station

0   1 Mile
0   1 Km

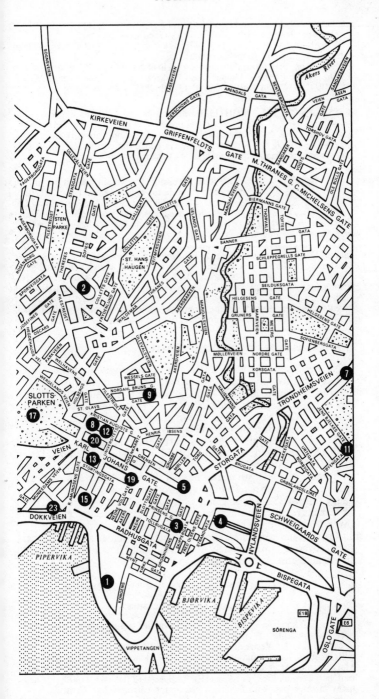

Inexpensive

Dampen, Torggata 8 (tel. 02–331783). Good cafeteria.

Vegeta, Munkedamsvn. 3B (tel. 428557). Vegetarian. Situated near National Theater, station and shopping centers.

Kaffistova, Grillstova, Torgstova—a chain of coffeeshops and restaurants run by the Young Farmers' Union. Good food, no alcohol. Rosenkranzgt. 8 (tel. 428837/429974) and Karl Johansgt. 13 (tel. 428839).

NIGHTLIFE. Several hotels and restaurants in Oslo present cabaret programs and floor shows, and the number of floor shows is rising. Some are very short-lived, however, so always check the current edition of *Oslo This Week* for details. Most night spots stay open until 4 A.M.

SHOPPING. Typically Norwegian handcrafts are on sale in workshops in the arcade behind Oslo Cathedral. Permanent sales exhibitions can be seen at *Norway Designs,* Stortingsgate 28, *Forum,* Rosenkrantzgate 7, and *Husfliden,* Møllergate 4. *Thorkildsen,* N. Slottsgate 9, specializes in Sage mink and Norwegian blue fox furs.

In the silver market, *David Andersen,* Karl Johansgate 20, makes the world-famous David Andersen Enamel. *J. Tostrup,* Karl Johansgate 25, features somewhat more modern pieces. For the very best in crystal and glass etching, go to *Christania Glasmagasin,* Stortorget 10. If it's pewter you're looking for, there's *Tinnboden,* Tordenskjoldsgate 7, where you can also see a splendid array of dolls in regional dress. Finally, knitwear can be found at the *Scandinavian Sweater Shop* in Hotel Scandinavia arcade, *Maurtua* opposite the City Hall, *William Schmidt & Co.,* Karl Johansgate 41, and in all the main stores.

Kristiansand—on the South Coast

Norway's sunny South Coast is a holiday paradise in its own right. It has a highly indented coastline, sheltered by myriad islands and skerries, which are ideal for bathing, boating and fishing. Its principal city is Kristiansand, founded in 1641, one of the four most important gateways to Norway, reached by car ferry from Harwich in 21 hrs and Hirtshals 4. The Sørland railroad takes you to Oslo in 5 hours, Stavanger 3 hours. Among the sights are Christiansholm fortress from about 1680, Oddernes church from about 1050, Kristiansand Cathedral from 1885, Gimle Estate Museum from 1820, with furniture and paintings from the 17th and 18th centuries, and the Vest-Agder Museum with many ancient timber dwellings and workshops. The veteran narrow-gauge railway (Setesdalsbanen), with a steam locomotive dating from 1895, runs regularly during the summer. Boat sightseeing with a guide (M/S Maarten) daily except Sunday among the islands.

Kristiansand also offers Norway's biggest animal and amusement park, covering approximately 100 acres, and a new Fun Center with sports activities, restaurant etc.

PRACTICAL INFORMATION FOR KRISTIANSAND

Hotels and Restaurants

Nearly all hotels in Kristiansand have lowpriced summer offers, with various hotel pass systems.

Caledonien (E), Vestre Strandgate 7 (tel. 042–29100). 400 beds, all in rooms with facilities. Restaurant, cafeteria, bar. Central location. *Christian Quart* (E), Markensgate 39 (tel. 042–22210). 230 beds, all in rooms with facilities. Restaurant, bar. Central. *Evenbye's Ernst* (E), Rådhusgate 2 (tel. 042–21400). 154 beds, many of the rooms with facilities. Restaurant, cafeteria, bar. Central.

Norge (M), Dronningensgate 5 (tel. 042–23320). 130 beds, all in rooms with facilities. Restaurant, cafeteria. Central. *Rica Fregatten* (M), Dronningensgate

66 (tel. 042–21500). 110 beds, many in rooms with facilities. Restaurant, bar. 800 m. from ferry harbor.

Bondeheimen (I), Kirkegaten 15 (tel. 042–24440). 47 beds, all rooms with facilities. Cafeteria. *Metropole* (I), Dronningensgate 8 (tel. 042–21465). 21 beds, restaurant.

Savoy Hotel (I), Kristian IV's gt 1 (tel. 042–24175). 40 beds, fun pub. Next to the harbor, bus and railway terminals.

Restaurants. You will find good restaurants in the hotels listed; the local city guide offers a complete list of restaurants and cafeterias.

Sjøhuset (M), Ø. Strandgt 12a (tel. 042–26260). Popular seafood restaurant on the waterfront. Openair section in summer. *Telford's Pub* (M), Caledonien Hotel, Vestre Strandgate 7 (tel. 042/29100), and the adjoining *Tartan Room* are popular among the younger set.

Stavanger—the "Oil City"

Stavanger, founded in the eighth century, is an interesting city with old streets and houses side by side with modern buildings. Norway's fourth largest city (after Oslo, Bergen and Trondheim), it used to be the fish-canning capital of Europe, but has now become the new "oil city", serving as a base for the oil rigs in the North Sea. The city has expanded considerably in recent years, but still retains its charm. Its pride is the Anglo-Norman cathedral of the late-11th century. Ledaal Museum is a fine patrician mansion, where the King resides when he visits Stavanger. Stavanger Museum has cultural and historical collections from the region, also a maritime museum.

Some of Stavanger's sights are outside the city boundary: Viste Cave, which is said to be 6,000 years old. Ullandhaug is an Iron Age farm, reconstructed from the Migration period. However, when it comes to excursions, there is nothing to beat the dramatic Lyse fjord.

PRACTICAL INFORMATION FOR STAVANGER

Hotels and Restaurants

Atlantic Hotel (L), Jernbaneveien 1 (tel. 04–527520). 536 beds in rooms with facilities. Several specialty restaurants, grill and coffee shop, bar, disco. Central location, facing lake.

SAS Royal Hotel (L), Løkkevn. 26. Opening 1987. 210 rooms with all facilities. Two restaurants, health club with swimming pool and sauna, business service center, airline check-in. Basement garage.

KNA (E), Lagårdsveien 61 (tel. 04–528500). 400 beds, most in rooms with facilities. Havestuen grill, Barbella bar. Central. *Victoria* (E), Skansegate 1 (tel. 04–520526). 200 beds, most in rooms with facilities; has the *Prinsen* restaurant and *Victoria* bar. Central.

Alstor (M), Tjensvoll (tel. 04–527020). 144 beds, all in rooms with facilities. Restaurant, bar, dancing in the evening. 3 km from the city center. *Scandic Hotel* (M), 4070 Madla (tel. 04–526500). 270 beds, all in rooms with facilities; *Scandic* piano bar. *Grand Hotel* (M), Klubbgate 3 (tel. 04–533020). Bed and breakfast. 110 beds, most in rooms with facilities. Cafeteria. Central. *Sola Strand Hotel* (M), Axel Lundsv. 1 (tel. 04–650222). Near the airport. 150 beds, most in rooms with facilities. *Viste Strand* (M), 4070 Randaberg (tel. 04–597022). 90 beds, 50 rooms with bath/shower. On beach, 17 km from city center. Restaurant, bar.

Mosvangen Youth Hostel (I), Tjensvoll (tel. 04–532976). 3 km from station, facing Lake Mosvangen. 120 beds.

Restaurants. *Atlantic* (E), Jernbaneveien 1 (tel. 04–527520), in Atlantic Hotel. Orchestra and dancing, fine food and select wine list.

Skagen (M), Skagenkaien (tel. 04–526190). *Straen,* N. Strandgt. 15, for fish specialties.

China Town House (I), Salvagergate 3 (tel. 04–520814). Near harbor, good selection of Oriental and European dishes. *Dickens* (I), Skagenkaien 6 (tel. 04–527324). Modern pub in a 17th-century wharf house; pizza bar. *Elisabeth* (I), Kongsgt 41 (tel. 04–532967). Exclusive. *La Gondola* (I), Nytorget 8 (tel. 04–534235). *Korvetten* (I), Torget 8 (tel. 04–521111). Three sections; intimate wine cellar with light music, a standard restaurant, and a pub (no food). *Mikado* (I), Østerväg 9 (tel. 04–561681). Japanese. *Moon House,* Sølvberggt. 9 (tel. 04–534343). Chinese. *De Røde Sjøhns,* N. Holmegt. 14–20 (tel. 04–520194).

Bergen—Gateway to the Fjord Country

Bergen (pop. 200,000) is Norway's second-largest city, founded in 1070. It faces a fjord and is surrounded by seven mountains. This ancient Hanseatic city has much to offer the visitor. The fish market and the adjoining flower and vegetable market near the city center are fascinating sights, and so are the surviving 17th-century warehouses and Bergenhus fortress. The Hanseatic Museum is rich in ancient equipment and furniture. St. Mary's church is the oldest edifice in Bergen, built in the 12th century. "Old Bergen" is an interesting collection of early-19th-century dwellings.

Edvard Grieg was born in Bergen, and his mansion is now a museum, beautifully situated, 8 km. south of Bergen, near the famous Fantoft stave church from the late Viking Age. It is one of the best-preserved stave churches in Norway. The Fløyen funicular railway starts in the city and goes to the very top of Mount Fløyen, 320 m. (1050 ft.) above sea level. It is a 10-minute trip full of scenic interest.

The annual Bergen International Festival of music, drama, ballet and folklore in May/June is one of the most outstanding cultural events in Scandinavia, with great emphasis on the music of Edvard Grieg and other Norwegian composers.

Bergen is the starting point for the famous coastal express steamers to North Cape and beyond, as well as boat trips to the Hardanger, Sogne, and Nord fjords. Special express boats connect with Stavanger.

PRACITCAL INFORMATION FOR BERGEN

Hotels and Restaurants

Norge (L), Ole Bulls plass 4 (tel. 05–323000). 498 beds, all in rooms with facilities, several suites. Several restaurants, garden room for summer dancing, bars, pub, disco pub, snack bar, etc. Excellent hotel, centrally located. *SAS Royal* (L), Bryggen (tel. 05–318000). 500 beds, all in rooms with facilities. Gourmet restaurant, dancing restaurant, wine bar, café. Faces harbor.
Neptun (E), Walckendorffsgate 8 (tel. 05–326000). 196 beds, all in rooms with facilities. Gourmet restaurant. Central. *Orion* (E), Bardbenken 3 (tel. 05–318080). 230 beds, most in rooms with facilities. Diningroom, bar, Galeien disco bar. Near Haakon's Hall, facing harbor. *Rosenkrantz* (E), Rosenkrantzgate 7 (tel. 05–315000). 155 beds, most in rooms with facilities. Restaurant. 400 m. west of flower market, overlooking harbor.
Toms (M), C. Sundtsgate 52 (tel. 05–232335). 78 beds, all in rooms with facilities, including refrigerator. Diningroom. 500 m. from station.
Augustin (I), C. Sundtsgate 24 (tel. 05–230025). 65 beds, 12 rooms with bath/shower. Breakfast room. Popular family hotel. *Fantoft* (I), 5036 Fantoft (tel. 05–282910). 668 beds, all rooms with facilities. Summer only (June/Aug.). *Hanseaten* (I), Sandbrugaten 3 (tel. 05–316155). 44 beds. Fully licensed, restaurant, dancing. *Montana* (I), Johan Blydtsvei 30 (tel. 05–292900). Excellent youth hostel. 250 beds, 5 in each room, all with hot & cold water.
Restaurants. *Bellevue* (E), Bellevuebakken 9 (tel. 05–310240). Formerly a 17th-century manor, fine views of city and fjord. Good food, friendly service. *Neptun* (E), Walckendorffsgate 8 (tel. 05–326000). Best gourmet food in town.
Bryggen Tracteursted (M), Bryggestredet (tel. 05–315785). You can buy live fish in the market and have it cooked as you like. *Chianti* (M), Strømgate 8 (tel. 05–226430). At central bus station. Specialty spaghetti and fish; dancing daily except Mon. *Excellent* (M), Torvgaten 1a (tel. 05–327735). Seafood specialties and dancing on showboat. *Fløyen Restaurant* (M), Fløyen (tel. 05–312624). At top of funicular; views of city and fjord. Openair restaurant in summer; dancing.
Bryggestuen (I), Bryggen 6 (tel. 05–310630). Popular for light lunch. *Holbergstuen* (I), Torvalmenning 6 (tel. 05–318015). Excellent fish. *Villa Amorini* (I),

Rasmus Meyers Alle 5 (tel. 05–310039). Modern decor, good food. *Wesselstuen* (I), Engen 14 (tel. 05–326972). Pot luck and fish; popular.

The Fjords

The spectacular fjords are Norway's top attractions, and Norwegians like to say that if Americans go to Europe without seeing the Norwegian fjords, it would be like going to Niagara without seeing the Falls. Although the coastline is indented by fjords all the way from Oslo to North Cape and beyond, the Fjord Country is usually considered to be the coastline between Stavanger and Trondheim, because this is where the greatest scenic attractions are seen at their best—particularly during "fjord blossom time" in May and June, when the countryside is ablaze with striking colors.

Stavanger's Hafrs fjord is famous for the Viking battle which took place over a thousand years ago. East of Bergen lies the giant Hardanger fjord with grand vistas of the Folgefonn glacier. North of Bergen is the great Sogne fjord, longest in Norway (110 miles) with several narrow inlets, including the Fjerland fjord, which provides views of the Jostedal glacier, largest icefield on the Continent of Europe. Further north are the smaller arms of Sunn fjord and Nord fjord, followed by the most fantastic of all fjords—the Geiranger with the famous Seven Sisters waterfalls, tumbling down the mountainside in a sheer fall of about 5,000 ft. Finally, among all of the other fjords there is the spacious Romsdal fjord with the panorama of 87 peaks.

The most comfortable way to see the magnificent fjord scenery is by boat from Bergen, or by a combination of boat, train, ferry and bus. Most travel agents offer package tours which take in the highlights of the Fjord Country.

PRACTICAL INFORMATION FOR THE FJORD COUNTRY

ÅLESUND. *Scandinavie* (E), Løvenvoldgate 8 (tel. 071–23131). 87 beds. Central. *Noreg* (M), Kongensgate 27 (tel. 071–22938). 131 beds. Central.

ÅNDALSNES. *Grand Bellevue* (M), tel. 072–21011. 88 beds, good restaurant. *Setnes Youth Hostel* (I), tel. 072–21382. 46 beds.

BALESTRAND. *Kvikne* (M), tel. 056–91201. 400 beds. On the fjord, modern and comfortable, run by the same family for generations.

GEIRANGER. *Union* (E), tel. 071–63000. 240 beds. Famous fjord hotel. *Geiranger* (M), tel. 071–63005. 151 beds. *Merok* (M), tel. 071–63002). 110 beds.

LOEN. *Alexandra* (E), tel. 057–77660. 340 beds in a large family-run hotel. Included in many package tours. *Richards* (M), tel. 057–77261. 38 beds in this small hotel.

LOFTHUS. *Ullensvang* (E), tel. 054–61100. 250 beds in a fine fjord hotel which features Grieg's composer cabin in the garden (there's an annual Grieg program June 15).

MOLDE. *Alexandra* (E), tel. 072–51133. 207 beds. *Romsdalsheimen* (M), tel. 072–51711. 50 beds. *Rimo Hostel* (I), tel. 072–54330. 232 beds.

OLDEN. *Olden Fjord* (M), tel. 057–73235. 77 beds. *Olden Krotell* (M), tel. 057–73296. 30 beds.

SOGNDAL. *Hofslund* (M), tel. 056–71022. 90 beds. *Sogndal* (M), tel. 056–72311. 190 beds, modern and comfortable.

STALHEIM. *Stalheim* (E), tel. 055–22122. 220 beds. Perched on top of Stalheim canyon, with a fantastic view painted by many 19th-century artists.

ULVIK. *Brakanes* (E), tel. 055–26105. 150 beds. On the fjord. *Strand* (M), tel. 055–26305. 94 beds. *Ulvik Hostel* (M), tel. 055–26200. 120 beds.

The Bergen Railroad—Oslo/Bergen

Railroads and scenery always go together in Norway—and the famous Bergen electric railroad probably provides the most scenic rail journey in Europe. Leaving Oslo at fjord level, it winds its way up Hallingdal valley and across the Hardanger mountain plateau before descending to Bergen at fjord level. The distance is 471 km. and the trip takes 7 to 9 hours. The highest point is 1,301 m. near Finse, with impressive views of the Hardanger glacier. It was here that *Scott of the Antarctic* and *The Empire Strikes Back* were made.

One of the highways between Oslo and Bergen runs almost parallel with the railroad, but it is blocked by snow in winter between Ustaoset and Fossli—whereas the highway through Telemark is open all the year, thanks to several tunnels under the mountain passes. This is a wonderful region for high-mountain cross-country skiing, with good snow conditions until June. The numerous resorts include some of the best ski centers in Norway.

PRACTICAL INFORMATION FOR THE BERGEN RAILROAD

GEILO. *Bardøla* (E), tel. 067–85400. 206 beds. *Highland* (E), tel. 067–85600. 172 beds. *Holms* (E), tel. 067–85622. 140 beds. *Geilo* (M), tel. 067–85511. 145 beds. *Ustedalen* (M), tel. 067–85111. 155 beds. *Geilo Hostel* (I), tel. 067–85300. 200 beds.

GOL. *Pers* (E), tel. 067–74500. 270 beds. *Gol Youth Hostel* (I). 40 beds.

USTAOSET. *Ustaoset Motel* (M), tel. 067–87123. 50 beds. 2 km. from the station. *Ustaoset Mountain Hotel* (M), tel. 067–87161. 145 beds.

VOSS. *Fleischers* (M), tel. 055–11155. 122 beds. Adjoins station. *Jarl* (M), tel. 055–11933, 130 beds. *Park* (M), 055–11322. 76 beds. *Voss Youth Hostel* (I), tel. 055–12017. 200 beds, 4 or 6 in each room. Modern and popular.

The Dovre Railroad—Oslo/Trondheim

This is another scenic railroad, which takes in the entire length of lake Mjøsa (largest in Norway) and the Gudbrandsdal valley, and runs right across the Dovre mountain plateau, descending to Trondheim, a distance of 553 km., a trip of around 8 hours. There are numerous resorts all along—particularly in the Gudbrandsdal valley—including some very good ski centers.

PRACTICAL INFORMATION FOR THE DOVRE RAILROAD

LILLEHAMMER. *Lillehammer Turisthotell* (E), tel. 062–54800. 330 beds, entirely modern and comfortable. *Victoria* (E), tel. 062–50049. 174 beds. *Oppland* (M), tel. 062–51528. 140 beds. *Birkebeiner Hostel* (I), tel. 062–51994, 88 beds.

On the mountain plateau behind Lillehammer: *Sjusjøen Mountain Hotel* (E), 2612 Sjusjøen (tel. 062–63401). 120 beds. *Hornsjø* (M), 2615 Hornsjø (tel. 062–64064). 401 beds. 27 km. by bus from town. *Nevra* (M), 2614 Nordseter (tel. 062–64001). 140 beds. 12 km. by bus from town. *Pellestua* (I), 2637 Hunder (tel. 062–64031). 80 beds.

TRETTEN. *Gausdal Mountain Hotel* (E), 2622 Guasa (tel. 062–28500). 250 beds. 16 km. from the station. *Skeikampen Mountain Hotel* (M), 2622 Gausa (tel. 062–28505). 120 beds. 17 km. from the station.

Trondheim

Trondheim is a delightful city with a colonial air about it. Its famous Nidaros cathedral, dating from 1150 and in the English Gothic style, is Scandinavia's largest medieval building. Also impressive is Stifts-goarden, or royal residence, a magnificent rococo structure dating from 1775, the second largest domestic wooden building in Scandinavia. The Bishop's Palace is a fine relic of Trondheim's medieval glory, and the whole city has an atmosphere worthy of its historic position as the coronation place of Norway's kings.

PRACTICAL INFORMATION FOR TRONDHEIM

Hotels

Ambassadeur (E), Elvegate 18 (tel. 07–527030). 85 beds, all in rooms with facilities, including color TV. Bistro, roof terrace. *Astoria* (E), Nordregate 24 (tel. 07–529550). 95 beds, most in rooms with facilities. Restaurant, bar, bistro, dancing. *Britannia* (E), Dronningensgate 5 (tel. 07–530040). 180 beds, most in rooms with facilities. Palm Court restaurant, Hjørnet lunch restaurant, bar dancing. *Prinsen* (E), Kongensgate 30 (tel. 07–530650). 115 beds. Restaurant, bar, grill and wine lounge, bistro, billiards. *Royal Garden* (E), Kjopmannsgt 73 (tel. 07–521100). Trondheim's newest hotel. 600 beds, all rooms with facilities. 3 restaurants, bar and nightclub.

Scandic Hotel (M), Brøsetveien 186 (tel. 07–539500). 210 beds, all in rooms with facilities. Restaurant, bar, sauna, car park. 3 km. from the city center. *Hotell IMI* (M), Kongensgate 26 (tel. 07–528348). 120 beds, all rooms with facilities. Diningroom, cafeteria, unlicensed.

Hotel Residence (I), Munkegate 26 (tel. 07–528380). 150 beds, most rooms with facilities. Restaurant, bar, dancing; open-air restaurant in summer. *Sing-saker* (I), Rogersgate 1 (tel. 07–520092). 200 beds. Restaurant, bodega, billiards, sauna. Summer only (June 15–Aug. 15).

North Norway—Land of the Midnight Sun

If you go to North Norway between May and August, there is continual daylight, because in certain areas the sun never dips below the horizon during this period. North Norway can also be surprisingly warm during the peak season. It is a region of great contrasts—rugged coastline, sheltered fjords, vast expanses of open moorland, reindeer herds and thriving urban centers. Thousands of houses were wilfully destroyed in 1944 by the retreating Germans during World War II, and most towns and villages have now been rebuilt on modern lines.

You may go north by air or sea, by rail and bus and car. The coastal express steamers which sail between Bergen and Kirkenes near the Russian frontier, provide one of the most unusual voyages in the world. Every day throughout the year a ship leaves Bergen to go north—and another ship leaves Kirkenes to go south, passing each other at different points during the voyage. It's a trip of 2,500 nautical miles, discovering magnificent fjords, 35 towns and villages, thousands of islands, also glaciers and waterfalls. The round trip takes 11 days, and bookings should be made in advance.

The Nordland railroad from Trondheim to Bodø was opened in 1961, and the 729-km.-long trip is crammed with scenic delight, crossing the Arctic Circle at Stødi. At Fauske, trains connect with the Polar express bus, which takes you to Kirkenes in four days. A cross-country road from Narvik to Kiruna was opened in 1984; its mountainous route includes some spectacular scenery. If you travel by car, the road distance from Oslo to North Cape is 2233 km. or 1,383 miles.

PRACTICAL INFORMATION FOR NORTH NORWAY

ALTA. *Alta Hotel* (M), tel. 084–35311. 105 beds.

BARDU. *Bardu Motor Hotel* (M), tel. 089–81022. 78 beds.

BODØ. *SAS Royal* (E), Storgaten 2, (tel. 081–24100). 425 beds, all in rooms with facilities. *SAS Norrøna* (I), Storgaten 4 (tel. 081–24100). 170 beds.

FINNSNES. *Finnsnes Hotel* (M), tel. 089–40833. 92 beds.

HAMMERFEST. *Grand Rica* (M), 7 Sørgt. 15 (tel. 084–11333). 117 beds. Restaurant with dancing, pizza house, bar. *Brassica* (I), tel. 084–11822. 30 beds. Cafeteria, disco.

HARSTAD. *Grand Nordic* (E), tel. 082–62170. 130 beds. *Viking Nordic* (M), Fjordgate 2, tel. 082–64080. 180 beds.

HONNINGSVÅG. *Nordkapp Hotel* (M), Nordkappgt. 4 (tel. 084–72333). 248 beds. Restaurant, cafeteria, pub. *Havly* (I), tel. 084–72966. 60 beds in this seamen's hostel that opens to visitors. Some rooms with facilities.

KARASJOK. *Karasjok Turist Hotel* (M), Storgt. 12A (tel. 084–66203). 76 beds. Dining room, pizza tavern, sauna. *Karasjok Turistsenter* (M), tel. 084–66446. 65 beds, café, sauna.

KAUTOKEINO. *Kautokeino Turisthotell* (M), tel. 084–56205. 116 beds. Restaurant, cafeteria. *Kautokeino Youth Hostel* (I), tel. 084–56016. 35 beds.

NARVIK. *Grand Royal* (E), Kongensgate 64 (tel. 082–41500). 230 beds. *Malm Pensjon* (I), Frydenlundsgate 28 (tel. 082–42383). 50 beds, some in rooms with facilities.

SJØVEGAN. *Sjøvegan Hotel* (I), tel. 089–71204. 60 beds.

SKJERVØY. *Skjervoy Sentrum Hotel* (I), tel. 083–60377. 46 beds.

SØRKJOSEN. *Sørkjos Hotel* (I), tel. 083–65277. 100 beds.

SØRREISA. *Sørreisa Hotel* (I), tel. 089–61201. 32 beds.

SVOLVAER. *Havly* (I), tel. 088–70344, 106 beds. *Lofoten Nordic* (M), tel. 088-71200. 93 beds, all in rooms with facilities. *Lofoten Motell & Veikro*, (I), Vesterålsvn. (tel. 088–70777). 100 beds. Comfortable and well equipped. *Vita Motell* (I), Damskipskaien (tel. 088–70378). 100 beds. Comfortable.

TROMSØ. *Grand Nordic* (E), tel. 083–85500. 290 beds. *SAS Royal* (E), tel. 083–56000. 340 beds, all in rooms with facilities. *Saga* (M), tel. 083–81180. 100 beds. *Tromso Youth Hostel* (I), tel. 083–85735. 64 beds.

POLAND

A country of some 120,000 square miles lying between East Germany and the Soviet Union and with no naturally defensible borders, Poland's geographical position has long made her history one of almost continuous warfare. Founded in the 10th century, her borders have advanced and receded under a succession of rules. She became a major power in the 14th century, while during the Jagellonian dynasty Poland expanded to become one of the largest states in Europe. The 16th century was the golden age of economic and cultural development. After the death without heir of Sigismund II Augustus in 1572, there was a period of elective monarchy, the rulers including those of the Swedish Vasa dynasty during which successful military campaigns were conducted against the strengthening power of Muscovy. In 1683, King John III Sobieski won great fame in his defeat of the Turks outside Vienna.

Under the last of Poland's kings, Stanislaus Augustus Poniatowski in the 18th century, there was a rich revival of economic and cultural life that had declined since the mid-17th century. But between 1772–1795 there came the First, Second and Third Partitions of Poland, and thereafter the country was carved up in varying packages between Russia, Austria and Prussia, only to regain independence at the end of the First World War. It was not to be for long. On September 1, 1939, the Nazi invasion began.

Today, Poland is about the size (121,000 square miles) of New Mexico or the British Isles, and its population has, since the territorial changes and human losses of World War II, consisted predominantly of Polish-speaking Roman Catholics. Due to the loss of some six million people (half of them Jews) during the war, followed by an extended baby boom, over half of the present population of 37 million is under thirty—making Poland one of the most youthful countries in Europe.

Every one of her major cities, with the exception of Cracow, has had to be rebuilt or restored after the wholesale destruction of the war. Particularly splendid restoration work has been done on Warsaw's Old Town and in Gdansk on the Baltic coast.

Poland offers a wide variety of outdoor holiday activities: excellent hunting and fishing in the lush lake and forest regions, first-class skiing in the dramatic Tatra and Karkonosze Mountains; swimming and sailing in the innumerable lakes or at the splendid Baltic beaches, where the sea may be a bit coolish for some tastes. Whatever your reason for going—be it to look up relatives or merely stop over on your way elsewhere—the Poles will be glad to see you.

Poland Today

Forced under communist rule in 1945, Poland in the last 40 odd years has undergone tremendous changes which have transformed an underdeveloped, war-torn and predominantly rural country into a modern industrialized state. Though the political system remained oppressive during the 50s, 60s and early 70s, the standard of living and material well-being of Poles improved significantly.

Since the mid-70s, however, the story has been rather different. Efforts to expand and modernize the economy further, through massive borrowing and the importation of Western technology, backfired and led to crisis. The program was overambitious and inefficiently implemented. Growing food shortages and disintegrating services fueled social unrest and led to strikes and political opposition. This culminated in the summer of 1980 in the formation, in the Baltic port of Gdansk, of Solidarity (*Solidarność*), the Communist bloc's first independent trade union. For 16 spectacular months, Solidarity struggled for greater democracy, while under its patronage the country witnessed a flowering of national culture. Solidarity's fundamental incompatibility with Soviet-style communism, however, led to the imposition of martial law in December 1981 and the smashing of the union and many of its achievements. Though martial law has since been lifted, the discontent that sparked the formation of Solidarity remains close to the surface in Polish life. In 1983, Pope John Paul II returned to visit his homeland. More than any other figure, the Pope, the first Pole to hold the office, can be said to embody the spirit of the Polish people. The awarding of the Nobel Peace Prize to the Solidarity leader, Lech Wałęsa, in 1983, was a tribute to the movement's ideals.

But despite these persistent and real difficulties, Poland remains an attractive country to visit and can provide a rewarding and very inexpensive vacation. The Poles themselves, a devoutly religious people—all the more so since the election of John Paul II in 1978—welcome visitors with an hospitality that can be almost overwhelming. They love to eat and drink—mostly in cafes and restaurants where you will have little difficulty in joining them—and have a passionate interest in all things Western, especially clothes and music. Similarly, the picturesque countryside (one of Poland's many peculiarities is that, despite its communist way of life, 85% of the land is privately owned) remains delightful and very traditional. Horses, for example, are used in the fields and as a means of transport to an extent now unknown in much of the rest of Eastern Europe.

Nonetheless, the political situation in Poland is still unstable and anyone planning a vacation or a visit should check with Orbis or a reliable travel agent to make sure of the latest situation. Continuing shortages of food and other goods may occasionally present the visitor with some inconvenience and discomfort.

PRACTICAL INFORMATION FOR POLAND

13.06
5.24
24.00
23.0

WHAT WILL IT COST. Group and individual tours to Poland are arranged by *Polorbis* and accredited travel agents representing *Polorbis* (addresses below), who will handle all arrangements, including visa, hotel accommodation and prepayment. *Polorbis* operates the best hotels and pensions in Poland. Examples of tour prices ex-UK, including return flight, are: from £145 for a weekend in Warsaw; or from £416 for a two-week tour of Poland (most meals included). Other arrangements include *à la carte* holidays for individuals, fly-drive, and a wide variety of budget packages primarily for young people.

The monetary unit is the *złoty*, which is divided into 100 *groszy* (rarely seen). Banknotes are issued in 50, 100, 500, 1,000, 2,000 and 5,000 złoty; coins in 1, 2, 5, 10, and 20 złoty.

The official rate of exchange is currently 155 złoty to the US$. This is certain to change so check before your trip.

All visitors must exchange foreign currency to the value of US$15.00 per person per day, or the equivalent in pounds sterling. Excepted are people under 21 years of age and students, and foreign passport holders and their families whose Polish descent has been recognized by the appropriate Polish consular office or diplomatic mission: they must exchange $7.00 per day. Exempt altogether from this obligatory currency exchange are children under 16, transit visitors to neighboring countries, and visitors who have prepaid for their stay through vouchers or package bookings. Vouchers may be used towards hotel costs which must be paid at the official exchange rates.

You may bring in any amount of foreign currency, including travelers' checks, and exchange it at border points, air, sea and road, in most hotels, and at any *Polorbis* exchange counter. Despite an active black market (in which the dollar can fetch up to five times its official value), changing money outside the official exchange offices is not permitted. Similarly, the import and export of Polish currency is *not* permitted. Foreign currency thus imported must be declared upon arrival and recorded in a special certificate. Outside banking hours, money can be changed at most international hotels.

The major credit cards including Access, Bank America, Eurocard, Master-Charge, American Express, Carte Blanche, Diners Club and Visa are accepted at all principal hotels, restaurants, Orbis services and selected stores in larger towns.

A typical day might cost two people (U.S.$):

Hotel (moderate)—with breakfast	$35
Lunch	16
Dinner with wine	20
Beer	2
Coffee	1
Tram (4 rides)	1
Taxi (about 5 km)	2.50
Theater	5
Miscellaneous 10%	10
	$92.50

SOURCES OF INFORMATION. For advice on all aspects of travel to Poland, the Polorbis organization is invaluable. Their addresses are:
    In the U.S.: 500 Fifth Ave., New York, N.Y. 10110 (tel. 212–391–0844).
    In the U.K.: 82 Mortimer St., London W.1 (tel. 01–637 4971).

WHEN TO COME. Spring and summer are pleasant for sightseeing, while fall is a good time for cultural events in the cities, and also an especially rewarding season to visit the Tatra Mountains. The winter sports season lasts from December to March.

Climate. The Polish climate is quite varied. The Tatra Mountains have alpine weather, with warm air currents (*halny*) in winter. Spring can be windy, fall long and sunny.

Average afternoon temperatures in Fahrenheit and centigrade:

Warsaw	Jan.	Feb.	Mar.	Apr.	May	June	July	Aug.	Sept.	Oct.	Nov.	Dec.
F°	30	32	41	54	67	72	75	73	65	54	40	32
C°	-1	0	5	12	19	22	24	23	18	12	4	0

SPECIAL EVENTS. *May,* International Chamber Music Festival, Łancut; Festival of Contemporary Polish Plays, Wrocław; International Book Fair, Warsaw. *May–December,* Symphonic and chamber music concerts in Wawel Castle courtyard (Cracow). *June,* International Trade Fair, Poznań; Polish Song Festival, Opole; Midsummer "wianki" celebrations on June 23 throughout Poland. *June–September,* Chopin recitals at composer's birthplace, Żelazowa Wola near Warsaw; *August,* Chopin festival in Duszniki Zdroj. International Song Festival, Sopot. *September,* Oratorio and Cantata Festival, Wrocław; International Festival of Highland Folklore, Zakopane; "Warsaw Autumn" International Festival of Contemporary Music, Feature Film Festival, Warsaw; International Festival of Song and Dance Ensembles, Zielona Góra. *October,* Jazz Jamboree, Warsaw. *November–December,* Presentation of year's most outstanding dramas, Warsaw. *December,* Competition for the best Christmas Crib, Cracow.

National Holidays. Jan. 1 (New Year's Day); Apr. 20 (Easter Mon.); May 1 (Labor Day); June 6; July 22 (National Day); Nov. 1 (Remembrance); Dec. 25, 26.

VISAS. In order to obtain a visa you must have: a) signed valid passport, valid for no less than 9 months from expected date of departure for Poland; b) duly executed application form with two signed photos; c) a declaration ensuring the coverage of all costs connected with the planned stay in Poland in the form of *Orbis* exchange orders or vouchers. No application is required by persons under 16 years of age and included in the family passport. Applications should be submitted at least 14 days before intended departure to any Polish consulate personally, by post, or through a travel agency. In New York the Polish consulate is at 233 Madison Avenue, New York, 10016; in London at 73 New Cavendish Street, W.1; in Glasgow at 26 Buckingham Terrace, Great Western Road, Glasgow G12. Visas are not issued at border points.

A visa costs $15 or the equivalent in any other Western currency; double, treble and quadruple transit visa, £10 or dollar equivalent.

All visitors must register within 48 hours at a hotel, campsite, or local administration authority.

These regulations and rates are subject to change.

HEALTH CERTIFICATES. International certificates of vaccination against *cholera* are required if arriving within 5 days after leaving or transiting an infected area.

GETTING TO POLAND. By Air. From Montreal and New York *LOT,* the Polish airline, flies regularly to Warsaw. From London, *LOT* and *BA* have almost daily flights to Warsaw. In addition, special cheaper flights are operated in summer from London; details from *Polorbis.*

By Train. From London to Warsaw via Hook of Holland takes about 32 hours. From Vienna, the *Chopin Express* takes 13 hours. Both have sleeping cars. There is also a special deal on rail services from London's Victoria Station from once monthly up to several times a month, according to season, offering substantial reductions. Details from *Polorbis.*

By Car. Best route from England is via Harwich to Hook of Holland by night. An early start next morning from the Hook will bring you to the Polish frontier soon after 7 P.M. *Prins Ferries* have a car service from Harwich to Hamburg, Germany. Car ferries cross from Copenhagen (Denmark) and Ystad (Sweden) to Świnoujście; from Helsinki (Finland) to Gdańsk.

Drivers' own licence is acceptable provided it is marked as valid for Poland; in addition, an International Green Card is necessary for insurance purposes.

CUSTOMS. Personal belongings may be brought in duty-free, including sports equipment (but guns and ammunition require a Polish permit), musical instruments, typewriter, radio, two cameras with 24 films or 10 rolls film for each as well as 10 rolls film for one movie camera (16 mm), one liter each of wine and spirits and 250 cigarettes, 50 cigars, or 250 gr tobacco.

Articles not exceeding 2,000 złoty can be taken out of Poland duty-free, but there are restrictions on certain items so check the latest regulations. Articles purchased at special Pewex shops for foreign currency may also be taken out on presentation of sales receipts. These regulations are subject to change.

HOTELS. Hotel accommodations in Poland are available in five categories: luxury, 4-star, 3-star, 2-star and 1-star. These correspond to our categories of Deluxe (L), Expensive (E), Moderate (M) and Inexpensive (I) in the following way: the approximate *Orbis* hotel costs per person in a double room with bath or shower and breakfast are for luxury (L) $100; 4-star (E) $45–$56; 3-star (M) $35–$45; 2- and 1-star (I) $18–$25. Rates are about 25% lower than these prices in low season. Many establishments include rooms of more than one category. Orbis hotels are usually the best for non-Polish-speaking visitors. There is a shortage of hotel accommodations, so advance bookings are strongly recommended.

As food supplies are unpredictable at present it is perhaps advisable to make reservations for the best hotels that the traveler can possibly afford.

Orbis hotels include a number of foreign-built luxury establishments such as *Intercontinental Hotels* and *Holiday Inns. Orbis* has built several motels *(Novotels)* along major routes. They also handle private accommodations. Other establishments, often of the older type but including rooms with bath or shower, are *Municipal Hotels,* run by local authorities; the hotel of the *PTTK* (the very old-established Polish Tourist Association), usually called *Dom Turysty;* and the hotels of various local tourist and sports associations. A number of roadside inns *(zajazdy),* often in attractive local style, offer inexpensive food and a few guest rooms. Information about all these can be obtained from *Orbis* offices abroad, and reservations can be made through *Polorbis* in the U.K. and *Polish Travel Bureau* in the U.S.

In addition, the *Polish Youth Hostels Association* operates about 1,200 hostels, open to all. It is best to join the association or belong to any other similar association of the *International Youth Hostels Federation,* thus entitling you to reductions. A list is included in the *IYHF* international register.

Self-catering accommodations are also available, but can only be arranged on the spot.

CAMPING. There are about 230 campsites in Poland, nearly 75% of them fitted with 220V power points and several with 24V points for caravans. Facilities also include washrooms, canteens and nearby restaurants and food kiosks. *Orbis* can give full details.

RESTAURANTS. The selection of restaurants is wide, but it should be noted that food supplies are currently erratic and that it is advisable to book meals in top-class hotel restaurants as they receive the best ingredients. A meal in a deluxe (L) restaurant will cost around $20, expensive (E) $15, moderate (M) $10, inexpensive (I) $5 or even less.

Roadside inns *(zajazdy)* are inexpensive and serve traditional Polish cuisine. Self-service snack and coffee bars are to be found in larger centers; cafés *(kawiarnia)*, a way of life in Poland, serve delicious pastries.

Food and Drink. Polish food is basically Slavic with Baltic overtones, meaning an interesting variety of soups and meats (with emphasis on pork) as well as fresh water fish. Frozen or packaged foods are not popular, so ingredients are usually fresh. Much use is made of cream, which is inexpensive, and pastries are rich, delectable.

Some of the best typically Polish meals are to be found in the villages and market towns where delicious *barszcz* (clear beetroot soup) is served in large helpings along with sausage, cabbage, potatoes, sour cream, *czarny chleb* (coarse rye bread) and beer. *Chłodnik* is a cold rich cream soup with crayfish. Other dishes are: *Pierogi* (a kind of tortellini), which can be stuffed with various savory fillings; *Gołabki*, cabbage leaves stuffed with minced beef; *Zrazy Zawijane,* a kind of beef rissole; *Flaki,* a very select dish of tripe, served boiled or fried; *Bigos,* sauerkraut with various meats; *Kołduny,* a kind of ravioli with lamb meat filling. Bottled *Zywiec* (beer) is delicious. Western drinks (whisky, gin, brandy) can be had at most bars, but are extremely expensive. *Wódka,* of course, is a Polish specialty, which is often drunk before, with and after meals; some brands are flavored with forest herbs (*Zubrówka*). And try Polish mead, a honey wine.

TIPPING. A service charge is usually added to restaurant bills; if not, add 10 percent. Tipping is not obligatory, but readily accepted. Cab drivers get 10 percent.

MAIL. An airmail letter to the U.S. costs 50 zł., a postcard 22 zł.; a letter to the U.K. and Europe costs 29 zł. (postcard 17 zł.), to the U.S. 30 zł. A letter sent by registered post costs 20–30 zł. more.

Telephones: older public call boxes take 2 zł. coin, newer ones 2 and 5 zł. coins. If you place a long-distance call from your hotel be sure to check the service charge.

Both postage and telephone charges will increase this year.

CLOSING TIMES. Food shops are open from 6 or 7 A.M. to 7 P.M., others from 11 A.M. to 7 P.M. Department stores are open from 9 A.M. to 8 P.M. and "Ruch" newspaper kiosks from 6 A.M. to 9 P.M. Offices and banks are generally open from 8 A.M. to 3 P.M. or from 9 A.M. to 4 P.M. Local tourist information centers can advise on up-to-date opening times of historic monuments and museums.

PHOTOGRAPHY. You may not take photographs from the air, nor of industrial and transport installations.

USEFUL ADDRESSES. *US Embassy,* al Ujazdowskie 29; *British Embassy,* al. Róż 1; *Canadian Embassy,* Katowicka 16 or 25; Polish Travel Office *(Orbis),* ul. Bracka 16 and ul. Stawki 2; *PZM* (Polish Motoring Association), ul. Krucza 14; *PTTK* (Polish Tourist Association), ul. Swiętokrzyska 36; *LOT* (Polish Airlines), al. Jerozolimskie 44, ul. Waryńskiego 9 and ul. Stycznia 39; *British Airways,* ul. Krucza 49; *Emergency* telephone 997 (police), 998 (ambulance) or 999 (anywhere in Poland).

GETTING AROUND POLAND. By Air. *LOT* operates daily flights linking 11 main cities. Warsaw's Okecie Airport (international and domestic flights) is about 6 miles (9 km) from the city center, with regular bus connections. Air fares are roughly double rail fares.

By Train. Internal rail travel in Poland is quite inexpensive so trains are always crowded. Travel 1st. class if possible and always get to the station well in advance of the departure time. Reservations are obligatory on certain express services such as those linking Warsaw with Katowice. On overnight trains there are 1st. and 2nd. class sleeping cars and 2nd. class couchettes. There is a runabout ticket called *Polrailpass* which costs $60 for 8 days' travel and $90 for 21 days, a really good bargain.

By Bus. Buses are a little more expensive than trains. There is a network of bus services linking main cities as well as smaller towns and villages off the rail network. Dual train/bus tickets can be bought from *Orbis;* good for visiting Zakopane in the Tatra Mountains via Cracow. Buses are always crowded.

By Car. Traffic drives on the right and the usual Continental rules of the road are observed. Drinking is absolutely prohibited. Horn blowing is prohibited in built-up areas. There is a speed limit of 90 kph (62 mph) on the open road and 50 kph (31 mph) in built-up areas.

Motor traffic is sparse and main routes often bumpy. Other roads are often narrow and in the country cluttered with horse-drawn carts. European (E) routes crossing Poland include E12 (W. Germany—Prague—Warsaw), E14 (Austria—Sweden) and E8 (E. Germany—Warsaw—USSR).

Foreign tourists can buy gasoline with special coupons. Foreign currency coupons are inexpensive, can buy unlimited gas, and are refundable if unused. They can be bought from travel agents in advance, at border points or from *Orbis* offices. The cost is £3.90 for 10 liters.

In case of accident or repair problems contact the Polish Motoring Association *(PZM),* ul. Krucza 14, Warsaw (tel. 29 62 52). Carry a spare parts kit.

Car hire. Cars are available for hire from *Avis* at Okecie international airport or through *Orbis* offices. High-season rates are from $15–$28 per day, according to car model, plus insurance and 17–28 cents per km, or $90–$180 one week with unlimited mileage. Fly-drive arrangements are also available ex-UK through *Polorbis.* Rented cars can be driven out of the country and left abroad, but an additional charge is made on the distance between the car's location and where it was rented from.

Taxis. Taxis start at 45 zł., increasing by 18 zł. per km. After 11 P.M. rates are 54 zł. and 27 zł. respectively. (Radio taxi tel. 919.)

Hitchhiking. Poland is one of the few countries that does not frown on this method of travel. Hitchhikers can buy special books of coupons at border points, tourist information centers, etc., and, on obtaining a lift, give drivers the appropriate coupons covering the distance they plan to ride. Drivers who collect the largest number of coupons during the year actually receive prizes. A system of inexpensive accommodation for hitchhikers has also been evolved. Directing this unusual aspect of travel is the Hitchhiking Committee *(Komitet Autostopu),* ul. Narbutta 27a, Warsaw.

Warsaw

In January 1945 Warsaw—Poland's capital since the 17th century—was a heart-breaking desert of ruin and rubble, a prostrate victim of systematic Nazi destruction. In that same year, only a third of its pre-war population remained; of its half-million Jews, some 200 were still alive. But Warsaw's survivors, determined to rebuild their ancient city, set about the task so energetically that today the new Warsaw is a city of one million-plus inhabitants.

The historic old districts have been painstakingly reconstructed according to old prints and paintings, including those of Belotto Canaletto in the 18th century, thus eliminating some of the later, less attractive buildings. The result, in warm and pastel colors, is quite remarkable, and the atmosphere is enhanced by the fact that the Old Town is closed to motorized traffic. Here you can visit the living replica of the city's old marketplace, the cobblestoned Rynek Starego Miasta, with its colorful house fronts, charmingly uneven roofs and wrought-iron grillwork; open-air exhibitions of modern paintings by local artists are held here. All over the Old Town, churches, palaces and lovely burghers' houses have been beautifully rebuilt, the last and largest of them being the Royal Palace, recently completed. In front of it rises the King Sigismund Column, the symbol of Warsaw.

The busy main thoroughfares, Krakowskie Przedmieście and Nowy Świat lead to the city's grandest open space, Łazienki Park, where the Polish kings built their "out of town" summer palaces in the 17th and

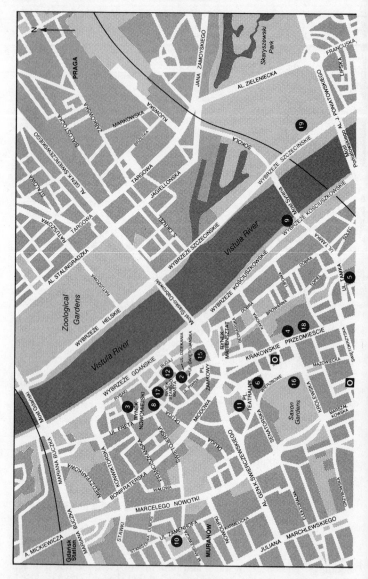

18th centuries, such as those of Belvedere and Łazienki, though today they are near the modern heart of the city. Near the Łazienki Palace is the charming 18th-century Theater on the Isle, and it is only a short stroll across the park from here to the Chopin monument, beside which concerts are held in summer on Sundays.

With ironic humor, Warsaw citizens will tell you that the best vantagepoint from which to admire the view of their rebuilt city is atop the 37-story Palace of Culture and Science. Why? Because it's the only spot from which you can avoid looking at the Palace of Culture and

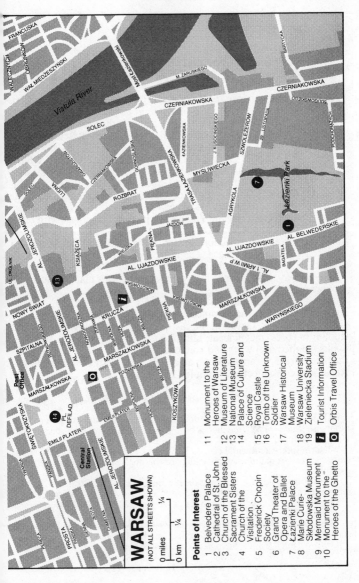

WARSAW
(NOT ALL STREETS SHOWN)

0 miles ¼ ¼
0 km ¼

Points of Interest

1 Belvedere Palace
2 Cathedral of St. John
3 Church of the Blessed Sacrament Sisters
4 Church of the Visitation
5 Frederick Chopin Society
6 Grand Theater of Opera and Ballet
7 Łazienki Palace
8 Marie Curie-Skłodowska Museum
9 Mermaid Monument
10 Monument to the Heroes of the Ghetto
11 Monument to the Heroes of Warsaw
12 Museum of Literature
13 National Museum
14 Palace of Culture and Science
15 Royal Castle
16 Tomb of the Unknown Soldier
17 Warsaw Historical Museum
18 Warsaw University
19 Zieleniecka Stadium
ℹ Tourist Information
◎ Orbis Travel Office

Science—a wedding-cake skyscraper, personal gift from Stalin. From this pinnacle you can see the river Vistula to the east, with two of its bridges, the Śląsko-Dąbrowski and the Poniatowskiego, crossing to the Praga side of the city. If you cross the Dąbrowski bridge near Rynek Starego Miasta, you come to the Zoological Gardens. Cross by the Poniatowskiego bridge to get to the giant Dziesieciolecia stadium. Along the river opposite the Stadium are many foreign embassies. The reconstructed Great Opera House is one of the finest in Europe and well worth visiting.

Warsaw's Hinterland

North: Seven miles north of Warsaw is Młociny with its Ethnographic Museum, situated in a beautiful old park on the banks of the Vistula.

West: Żelazowa Wola (40 miles from Warsaw) is the place where Chopin was born. The charming little country house with its lovely garden is now a museum. Each Sunday, from June to September Chopin's music is played by Poland's most famous pianists or guest artists from abroad. On your way back, drive through the primeval forest, an elk reserve near Kampinos, and visit Palmiry Cemetery, scene of mass executions of Poles by the Nazis.

South: At Wilanów southeast of Warsaw, visit the old palace of King Jan Sobieski, one of Poland's loveliest residences, now a museum with a rich collection of paintings and antiques. Here, too, is a Poster Museum. At Czersk, 30 miles south of Warsaw on the same road, is the lovely medieval castle of the Mazowiecki princes since 732. Kazimierz-Dolny, an hour out along the Vistula, is a picturesque village with relics of Polish Renaissance architecture. A favorite with artists. Łowicz, 50 miles from Warsaw, a folklore center, has a fascinating museum in a 17th-century Baroque Palace. The Palace of the Radziwill family, with original 17th-century furniture, is at Nieborów, 55 miles out. Arkadia, 57 miles away, has a lovely 17th-century park with many statues and monuments.

About 100 miles southeast of Warsaw is Lublin, one of the oldest cities in Poland. At the entrance to the old part of town is the curious Gothic Krakowski Gate and the castle which towers over the city. Old Lublin harbors magnificent churches, delightful houses, secretive nooks, vaulted archways and romantic courtyards. Nearby Pulawy is the site of the Czartoryski's palace. Zamość is the best preserved Renaissance architectural complex in Poland.

PRACTICAL INFORMATION FOR WARSAW

HOTELS. All hotels listed have all or some rooms with bath or shower unless otherwise stated. Most *Orbis* hotels have one or more shops, a hairdresser and laundry facilities.

Victoria Inter-Continental (L), ul. Królewska 11 (tel. 27–92–91). 360 rooms, suites, several restaurants, night club, indoor pool, sauna. Modern, in ideal location.

Orbis-Europejski (E), Krakowskie Przedmieście 13 (tel. 265051). 280 spacious rooms, suites. Best for food and service.

Orbis-Forum (E), ul. Nowogrodzka 24–26 (tel. 21019). 750 rooms. Informal gourmet meals.

Orbis-Grand (E), ul. Krucza 28 (tel. 294051). 430 rooms, suites, rooftop café-restaurant with glass-enclosed terrace, night club, indoor pool.

Orbis-Novotel (E), ul. Sierpnia 1 (tel. 464051). 150 rooms. Indoor pool.

Orbis-Solec (E), ul. Zagorna 1 (tel. 259241). 150 rooms.

Orbis-Vera (E), ul. Wery Kostrzewy 16 (tel. 227421). New, in west part of city on way to airport.

MDM (E-M), Pl. Konstytucji 1 (tel. 216211). 193 rooms.

Metropol (E-M), ul. Marszałkowska 99a (tel. 294001). 192 rooms.

Polonia (E-M), ul. Jerozolimskie 45 (tel. 287241).

Warszawa (E-M), Pl. Powstanców Warszawy 9 (tel. 269421).

Dom Turysty (M), Krakowskie Przedmieście 4–6 (tel. 263011). 72 rooms.

Saski (M), Pl. Dzierzynskiego 1 (tel. 204611). 106 rooms.

Private accommodations are available through *Syrena,* ul. Krucza 16 (tel. 257201).

RESTAURANTS. Warsaw has a variety of good restaurants. Current food shortages mean that the top hotels are the best supplied. Rynek Starego Miasta (Old Town Market) has several restaurants and cafés well worth patronizing.

Bazyliszek (E), Rynek Starego Miasta 7–9. One of the best restaurants in town. Serves very traditional Polish food in an attractive setting.

Canaletto (E), in Victoria Inter-Continental Hotel. One of the best hotel restaurants. Serves Polish specialties.

Forum (E), ul. Nowogrodzka 22–24. One of the best hotel restaurants.

Kongresowa (E), in the Palace of Culture. Frequented by Poland's rich and famous.

Krokodyl (E), Rynek Starego Miasta 19. For a meal with a view.

Napoleonski (E), ul. Plowiecka 83. Napoleonic style; private hotel and restaurant. Favorite among Western businessmen.

Retman Gdański (E), ul. Bednarska 9. Charming restaurant in Mariensztat district. Regional food.

Kamienne Schodki (M), Rynek Starego Miasta 26. Duck and wine specialty.

Murzynek (M), Rynek Starego Miasta. Excellent for quick, light meals.

Staropolska (M), Krakowskie Przedmieście 8. Informal, famous for its fish.

Brief details of other good moderate (M) restaurants: *Ambassador,* ul. Matejki 2, opposite the US Embassy; *Cristal-Budapest,* ul. Marszałkowska 21/25 (Hungarian); *Gościniec Opolski,* ul. Pulawska 102; *Kameralna,* Foksal 16; *Karczma Słupska,* ul. Czerniakowska 127; *Kurpiowska,* ul. Ciołka 20; *Rarytas,* Marszałkowska 15 (with floorshow); *Suwalska,* ul. Spokojna 4; *Zalipie,* ul. Filtrowa 83; *Zywiecka,* ul. Marszałkowska 66.

CAFES. Warsaw teems with cafés which move outdoors in summer. It is a way of life with the Poles. Coffee, tea and those luscious cakes can be found at: *Fukier,* Rynek Starego Miasta 27, popular wine bar-cum-coffee house. *Gong,* Al. Jerozolimskie 42, has a marvelous selection of imported tea. *Alhambra,* Al. Jerozolimskie 32, Turkish coffee. *Teatralna,* ul. Corazziego 12. *Telimena,* Krak. Przedmieście. *Trou Madame,* Łazienki Park, in a beautiful setting. *Hopfer,* ul. Krak. Przedmieście 53, with delicious ice cream.

 GETTING ABOUT. Tickets for trams (3 zł.) and buses (3 zł.; 6 zł. for express buses) must be bought in advance from "Ruch" newsstands. You cancel your own ticket in a machine on the tram or bus. Fares are doubled after 11 P.M.

Some horse cabs remain; fare to be agreed with driver (around 600 zł. per hour). On Sundays and holidays, a novel 45-minute trip is by 1908 tram, starting from Plac Starynkiewicza. Inexpensive sightseeing tours by mini Melex cars are also arranged by the *Warsaw Tourist Services Office Syrena,* ul. Krucza 16. *Orbis* runs sightseeing bus tours of the city throughout the year and more frequently, as well as into the surroundings, in summer. A half- or full-day excursion costs from $10–40, including meal and often traditional entertainment. Pleasure-boat trips on the river Vistula are also operated in summer, details from *Warsaw Navigation agency,* Dworzec Wodny.

 ENTERTAINMENT. The *National Philharmonic Hall,* ul. Sienkiewicza 12, puts on excellent concerts. Poland's 13 opera companies stage frequent operas and operettas. The famous dance troupes, *Mazowsze* and *Śląsk,* perform to full houses. Each Sunday, from June to September there are midday concerts at Zelazowa Wola, Chopin's birthplace 40 miles from Warsaw.

There are some 17 theaters in Warsaw, many with bold and original stage sets and excellent acting. Those which visitors might enjoy are *Teatr Wielki* (Grand Theater of Opera and Ballet); *Operetka* (Operettas), ul. Nowogrodzka 49; *Syrena* (revues), ul. Litewska 3; *Teatr Dramatyczny* and *Teatr Studio* (contemporary plays), both in the Palace of Culture and Science; *Ateneum* (traditional and contemporary drama), ul. Stafana Jaracza 2; *Wspołczesny* (contemporary), ul. Mokotowska 13; *Mały* (contemporary), ul. Marszałkoska 104. Tickets to the theater cost 60–210 zł. and to the cinema 150–230 zł.

For a different slant on the city, try *Wanda Warska's Modern Music Club,* a very popular, candle-lit jazz club. Must reserve. Or *Amfora,* on the East Wall, an intimate redecorated club with music and good food; romantic. The nightclub *Olimp,* on the 11th floor of the hotel Grand, provides a good meal and a strip show (costs 800 zł. on entry, food included). Warsaw's most famous cabaret is *Pod Egida* on Nowy Swiat, renowned for its political satire. Inexpensive favorites among the young are student clubs: *Hybrydy,* ul. Koniewskiego 7/8; *Riviera-Remont,* ul. Warynskiego 12; *Stodoła,* ul. Batorego 2; *Proxima,* ul. Zwirki i Wigury 95.

MUSEUMS. Open daily except Monday. Of Warsaw's many museums these perhaps are of most interest to out-of-town tourists: *Muzeum Narodowe* (National), a1. Jerozolimskie 3. Poland's main collection of ancient, classical and modern Polish art and handicraft, as well as other masters; *Muzeum Sztuki Ludowej* (Folk Art), a1. Na Skarpie 8; *Muzeum Historyczne Miasta Warszawy* (Warsaw Historical Museum), Rynek Starego Miasta 28. Don't miss the historical movie "Warsaw Prevails", graphically showing the destruction of the city in the last war; *Madame Curie Museum,* ul. Freta 16, in the house where she was born and lived for many years; *Muzeum Towarzystwa im. Fryderyka Chopina* (Frederic Chopin Museum), Ostrogski Palace, u1. Okolnik 1, closed Sun. (though the main museum is at the composer's birthplace, see below). In the city's lovely Łazienki Park, there are several former *royal summer residences,* including that of Poland's last king, Stanislaus Poniatowski in the 18th century, now a museum of palace interiors.

Zacheta (The Art Gallery), P1. Malachowskiego 3; *Sculpture Museum and Fine Art Gallery of the Union of Polish Painters & Sculptors,* ul. Marchlewskiego 36; *Modern Art Gallery,* Rynek Starego Miasta 23.

Wilanów Palace, former royal summer residence built by King Jan III Sobieski, with its beautiful antiques, and also housing exhibition of contemporary posters (10 km); *Łowicz Ethnographic Museum,* collection of folk costumes, also gallery of Polish 19th-century paintings (50 km); *Zelazowa Wola,* Chopin Museum in the house where he was born; Chopin concerts are held here every Sunday, June to Sept. (60 km).

SHOPPING. Opening hours tend to be long. Some food shops open at 7 A.M., others stay open until 8 P.M. Most shops, however, are closed three Saturdays in every month, except for some food shops open limited hours. Beautiful handicraft things and specialties are plentiful. Shop along Rynek Starego Miasta, Nowy Swiat, Krucza and Marszalkowska for all sorts of attractive local craftwork. Don't forget to take home some Polish *Zubrówska* or *Wyborowa*-brand vodka. Try the *Cepelia* stores for a wide range of Polish folkcraft, such as glass and enamelware, amber and lovely hand-woven woolen rugs; *Orno* shops for silverware and hand-made jewelry; and *Desa* and *Art* stores for works of art, ornaments and objets d'art. These accept local and foreign currency. *Pewex* hard currency shops sell local and imported items; here you find cigarettes, imported spirits, and especially vodka at very low prices, as well as imported chocolate, coffee, and a range of clothing. A visit to the *Flea Market* is highly recommended. Open Saturday mornings, it is atmospheric and full of bargains.

Cracow and the Southern Mountains

Medieval Cracow, ancient seat of Polish kings and Poland's oldest academic institution, the Jagiellonian University, is the only major city in the country that escaped devastation during the war. Today, its fine ramparts, towers, dungeons, and churches, summing up seven centuries of Polish architecture, as well as its lively theatrical and musical life, make Cracow once again a major attraction for tourists.

Cracow's main showpiece is its well-preserved 16th-century castle called Wawel, "Poland's Acropolis". A pre-Romanesque 10th-century rotunda, discovered within the walls of Wawel castle, is one of the city's oldest monuments. Pearls of Renaissance architecture are the arcaded castle courtyard and Sigismund's chapel. The castle has an exotic collection of Oriental art and 16th-century Flemish tapestries; of the original 356, 136 survive, having been smuggled across to Canada during the war. One of the castle's more curious exhibits is a huge four-room Turkish tent, captured in Vienna. Wawel cathedral, close by, shelters the delicately carved sarcophagi of many kings, and the building itself is a remarkable illustration of architectural styles across the centuries, each making its contribution since the cathedral was founded in the 10th century. Below Wawel hill in the heart of the city, you can wander through Cracow's medieval Town Square with its famous Cloth Hall, today housing an arcade of Cepelia folk art shops. Scattered throughout the town are 67 Romanesque, Gothic and baroque churches. Don't miss 12th-century Mariacki (St. Mary's) church with its 15th-century triptych by Wit Stwosz, a masterpiece of Gothic woodcarving. If you take a guided tour, you won't be allowed to miss Cracow's model industrial suburb of Nowa Huta. Puszcza Niepolomicka is a fine zoo in a forest game preserve.

Cracow's Hinterland

About 10 miles from Cracow is Wieliczka, the oldest salt mine in Europe. It has been exploited since the end of the 13th century and still produces 700 tons of pure salt a day. It is renowned for its sculptures, including a great underground chapel, hewn in crystal rock salt, and its concert hall in which performances are held from time to time. A fascinating museum illustrates the development of the salt mines, and three km. of the total of 300 km. of underground passages are open to the public. The therapeutic properties of this remarkable underworld have proved effective in the treatment of respiratory ailments and a section of the mine is now a unique underground spa. Between Cracow and Częstochowa (100 miles to the north) is an unusual group of 125 medieval castles, mostly in ruins, with a few restored. Visit the one at Pieskowa Skala, with a museum and café. Forty miles due west of Cracow is the former Nazi concentration camp of Oświęcim (Auschwitz), where some four million Nazi victims were put to death. Thirty five miles to the northwest of Cracow is the village of Wadowice, birthplace of Pope John Paul II.

Zakopane, Mountain Paradise

About 70 miles south of Cracow, Zakopane, 3,000 feet high in the dramatic Tatra mountains, along the Czechoslovak frontier, is Poland's most popular health and holiday resort. Native and foreign visitors flock to this mountain valley outpost for winter and summer sports and to witness ski-jumping and ice-skating competitions. There is a funicular to the top of Gubalowka, just above the town, and a cable car (be prepared for a long wait in the season, unless you have pre-booked) almost to the top of Kasprowy Wierch (nearly 6,500 feet) where there is a mountaintop restaurant right on the border with Czechoslovakia. Well worth a visit is Morskie Oko, a crater-like lake nestled among snowy, soaring peaks. Marked trails provide pleasant walks out of Zakopane and, in winter, a horse-drawn sleigh for local excursions is a thrilling experience. Zakopane has many hotels, a museum, theater, cafés, dance spots and restaurants. Krynica, in the nearby Beskid mountains, is also a winter sports center as well as a famous spa. Accommodations are inexpensive but satisfactory. Not far beyond the Tatras lie the picturesque Pieniny Mts., with 1000-foot deep canyons. For a different type of thrill, take the nerve-twisting half day raft ride down the sinuous turbulent Dunajec river from Czorsztyn.

Wrocław, the Young-Old City

Situated midway between Cracow and Poznań on the Odra River in Lower Silesia, this city dates back to the 10th century. The restored 13th-century Town Hall, in the Market Square, is regarded as a magnificent example of burgher architecture. Of equal interest are the Gothic cathedral, baroque university and Japanese garden. See also the Tomaszewski Mime Theater. Wrocław is a good launching point for the Karkonosze Mountains bordering Czechoslovakia.

PRACTICAL INFORMATION FOR CRACOW AND THE SOUTH

All hotels listed have some or all rooms with bath or shower unless otherwise stated. Most *Orbis* hotels have shops, a hairdresser and laundry facilities.

CRACOW. *Inter-Continental* (L), to open soon. Lovely position on banks of River Vistula.
Orbis-Cracovia (E), al. Puszkina 1 (tel. 64720). 427 rooms, suites, night club.
Orbis-Holiday Inn (E), ul. Koniewa 7 (tel. 75044). 306 rooms, indoor pool, sauna. About 2 miles from city center.
Dom Turysty (M), ul. Westerplatte 15–16 (tel. 29566). 187 rooms of various categories, very central and reasonably priced.
Orbis-Francuski (M), ul. Pijarska 13 (tel. 25122). 59 rooms, modernized.
pod Kopcem (M), al. Waszyngtona (tel. 22258). On city outskirts. Attractively converted from former barracks. Quiet location, but a long walk down into town.
Private accommodations are available through *Wawel Tourist,* Rynek Głwówny (tel. 26454).
Restaurants. The best in town are at the hotels: *Holiday Inn* and *Francuski,* also *Kaprys,* ul. Florianska 32. All (E). Others recommended are: *Wierzynek,* Rynek Główny 16, in beautiful historic buildings, very popular; *Balaton,* ul. Grodzka 37 (Polish and Hungarian food); *Ermitage,* ul. Karmelicka 3; *Staropolska,* ul. Sienna 4; *Kurza Stopka;* all (M).
Cafes and Cabarets. *Kaprys,* ul. Florianska 32; *Norworol,* rather elegant café in the old Cloth Hall; *Jama Michalikowa,* ul. Florianska 45, cabaret, has 19th- and 20th-century wall paintings; *Hawełka,* Rynek Główny 34; *Piwnica pod Baranami,* Rynek Główny 27, an ancient palace vault, cabaret weekends only; *Pod Jaszczurami,* Rynek Główny, student club, good jazz; *Wieza Ratuszowa,* in Town Hall tower, Rynek Główny. *Frant,* ul. Pijarska 2, with tasty ice cream.
Museums. Outstanding is the *Wawel Castle Museum* with its 71 rooms of treasures, Flemish tapestries and lovely furnishings. *National Gallery of Polish Painting* (Cloth Hall), Rynek Główny. Historical collection of Polish canvases; *Czartoryski Museum* (Collection of the Princes Czartoryski), ul. Pijarska 8. Canvases of old European masters, including some works of Rembrandt and a beautiful Da Vinci; *History Museum,* Sw. Jana; *Ethnographical Museum,* Pl. Wolnica, an excellent folk museum.
Theaters. *J. Slowacki Theater and Opera House,* Sw. Ducha 1, one of best in Poland, opera and drama; *Philharmonic,* ul. Zwierzyniecka 1. *H. Modrzejewska Stary Theater,* ul. Jagiellonska 1; *Groteska-Lalki* (Puppets), ul. Skarbowa 2; *Operetkowy* (light opera), ul. Lubicz 28.
Useful Addresses. *Orbis,* ul. Puszkina 1; *Polish Motoring Assoc.,* ul. Sławkowska 4; *LOT,* Basztowa 15. *Tourist Information Office,* ul. Pawia 8 (tel. 26091).

CZĘSTOCHOWA. *Orbis-Patria* (E), ul. Starucha 2 (tel. 47101). 107 rooms, suites, night club. *Centralny* (M), 62 rooms.

KARPACZ. Mountain resort. *Orbis-Skalny* (E), ul. Obrońców Pokoju 3 (tel. 721722). 154 rooms.

WROCŁAW. *Grand* (E), ul. Swierczewskiego 102 (tel. 44311). *Orbis-Novotel* (E), ul. Wyścigowa 31 (tel. 675051). 154 rooms, outdoor pool, on city outskirts. *Orbis-Panorama* (E), ul. Dzierżynskiego 8 (tel. 34681). 113 rooms, suites. *Orbis-*

Wroclaw (E), 307 rooms, indoor pool, sauna. *Orbis-Monopol* (M), ul. Modrzejewskiej 2 (tel. 37041). 86 rooms, old-fashioned, central.

Restaurants and cafés: *Lotos,* ul. Grabiszynska 9, and *Stylowa,* ul. Kościuszki, both (E); *Bieriozka,* ul. Nowotki 13 (Russian food), *Lajkonik,* ul. Nowowiejska 102, both (M); *Herbowa* (M) (tearoom-café), Rynek 19.

ZAKOPANE. Famous ski resort in Tatra Mountains south of Cracow. *Orbis-Kasprowy* (L), ul. Polana Szymoszkowa (tel. 4011). 288 rooms, night club, pool, sauna, sports facilities, glorious views, but a little outside resort. *Orbis-Giewont* (M), ul. Kościuszki 1 (tel. 2011). 48 rooms, central. *Gazda* (E–M), ul. Zaruskiego 1 (tel. 5011). *Morskie Oko* (M-I), ul. Krupówki 30 (tel. 5076/78). 43 rooms. For private accommodations contact *Tatry,* ul. Kościuszki 23 (tel. 2151). The *Orbis tourist information office,* ul. Krupówki 22 (tel. 5051) can also help find accommodations.

Restaurants, some with dancing, are: *Jedrus, U Wnuka* (regional), *Gubalówka, Watra,* and *Wierchy,* all (M-E). *Kmicic* is a pleasant café. *Siedem Kotów* and *Obrochtówka* have a good local atmosphere, both (I). Also *Murowana Piwnica* and *Europejska.*

Local sights include the *Tatra Museum,* covering all aspects of this beautiful area, and the *Kenar School of Carving.*

Poznań and the North

Poznań, halfway between Warsaw and Berlin, has been an East-West market place for a thousand years. The important International Trade Fair, held here since 1922, has become in recent years a major trading center between the communist and capitalist worlds. It regularly attracts American and British participation.

A look around the town is rewarding: Visit the Old Market Square with its decorated, Italian-style Town Hall and richly façaded burghers' houses. Poznań has numerous historical churches and palaces. Of particular interest are: Działynski Castle, with neo-Classic sculptures; Przemysław Castle, former seat of the Great Dukes of Poland; Franciscan Church, with an interior richly decorated with baroque stuccos; Raczynski Library, built in the 19th century with Paris' Louvre as its model; Górki Palace, unique Renaissance structure, with roof-garden-cum-fishpond; State Ballet school with a beautiful baroque arcaded courtyard; baroque Parish Church, with 17th-century stuccos and polychromy; Gothic cathedral, with 18th-century baroque spires and 10th- and 11th-century relics in special crypt.

The new town of Poznań houses the Mickiewicz University, Opera House, Academy of Medicine, Post Office buildings and many fine parks.

Poznań is the center for some interesting excursions, which include Kórnik, with its medieval castle library; Biskupin, a resurrected prehistoric fort, the 'Polish Pompeii'; and Romanesque Gniezno, ex-capital of Poland and legendary birthplace of the Polish state.

The Masurian Lake District

About 160 miles north of Warsaw, toward the Soviet border, the great water-laced landscapes of the Masurian lakes offer a whole range of possibilities for water sports enthusiasts, especially canoeing, sailing and fishing among the many large lakes linked by rivers and canals. Olsztyn is the principal city, and Gizycko, Mikolajki and Ruciane are among the main resorts. In addition to inexpensive hotels and boarding houses, self-catering cottages can be rented through the regional Mazur-Tourist Enterprise, who also arrange all kinds of special-interest facilities, such as boat or bicycle hire, photo safaris, sailing holidays.

The Baltic Coast

The climate may be on the brisk side, but the beaches, many backed by pine woods, are splendid. Gdańsk, formerly the "Free City" of Danzig, was 90% destroyed in World War II, but has been rebuilt and some areas have been beautifully restored in their original Gothic, Renaissance or baroque styles. Famous as the city which saw the birth of Solidarity in 1980, Gdańsk was also the scene of serious civil disturbances in 1970. The Three Crosses monument outside the gates of the Lenin ship yard commemorates those workers who died in the rioting. Sopot, between Gdańsk and Gdynia, is the most popular resort—and the most crowded.

PRACTICAL INFORMATION FOR POZNAŃ AND THE NORTH

All hotels listed have some or all rooms with bath or shower unless otherwise stated. Most *Orbis* hotels have shops, a hairdresser and laundry facilities.

GDAŃSK. *Novotel-Orbis* (E), ul. Pszenna 1 (tel. 315611/19). 154 rooms, 2 miles from city center. *Orbis-Hevelius* (E), ul. Heweliusza 22 (tel. 315631). 276 rooms. *Orbis-Marina* (E), ul. Jelitowska 20 (tel. 531246). 193 rooms. Newly completed. *Orbis-Posejdon* (E), ul. Kapliczna 33 (tel. 530227/8). 154 rooms, indoor pool, disco; a few miles away at the seaside resort of Gdańsk-Jelitkowo. *Orbis-Monopol* (M), ul. Gorkiego 1 (tel. 316851/5). 125 rooms, opposite railway station.

Useful addresses: *Tourist Information Office,* ul. Heweliusza 8 (tel. 310338).

OLSZTYN. Gateway to Masurian Lakes. *Novotel-Orbis* (E), ul. Sielska 4a (tel. 24081). 98 rooms, outdoor pool.

POZNAŃ. Note that hotels are heavily booked during the Fair. *Novotel-Orbis* (E), ul. Warszawska 64–6 (tel. 70041). 153 rooms, outdoor pool; on city outskirts. *Orbis-Merkury* (E), ul. Roosevelta 20 (tel. 40801). 351 rooms, suites, night club; near Fair grounds. *Orbis-Polonez* (E), al. Stalingradzka 54 (tel. 699141). 420 rooms, suites, night club; not far from center. *Orbis-Poznań* (E), pl. Gen. Dąbrowskiego 1 (tel. 332081). 490 rooms, suites, all facilities; central. *Orbis-Bazar* (M), ul. Marcinkowskiego 10 (tel. 51251). 98 rooms; old-fashioned but very central.

Restaurants: There is dancing at *Magnolia* (ul. Głogowska 40), *Adria* (ul. Głogowska 14), *Moulin Rouge* (ul. Kantaka 8–9), all (E-M). *Smakosz* (ul. 27 Grudnia 8) is (E-M), *Pod Koziolkami* (Stary Rynek 63) is (M-I).

Useful addresses: *Poznań Tourist Information Center,* Stary Rynek 77 (tel. 56156); *LOT,* ul. Czerwonej Armii 69 (tel. 52847).

SOPOT. Baltic beach resort. *Orbis-Grand* (E), Powstańców Warszawy 8/12 (tel. 510042). 130 rooms, suites, night club, beach-side location. One of the oldest and most elegant hotels in Poland.

Restaurants: Try *Ermitage,* Bohaterów Monte Cassino 23, and *Alga,* ul. Bohaterów Monte Cassino 62.

Useful addresses: *Tourist Information Office,* ul. Chopina 10 (tel. 510618).

PORTUGAL

Portugal is still something of an unknown quantity to many people and only those who have been here can truly appreciate the unique charm of this country which is really outside the mainstream of Europe. The pace of life is leisurely, punctuality is rare, and old-fashioned politeness essential. Human relations still count for much; residents shake the hands of those known to them in shops and on the street and tempers are almost never lost, at least in public, whatever the provocation.

However, for all their courtesy and dignity, the Portuguese have had a rough ride over the last ten years or so. They entered the 70s with one of the lowest standards of living of any West European country and had to endure a revolution in 1974 that, aside from severely disrupting the economy and precipitating the loss of the country's African colonies, also raised the specter of communism.

Today, however, the political situation has stabilized with membership of the Common Market, and Portugal can offer much to the tourist with an open mind and a taste for the new and the old side by side. Outside the cosmopolitan cities of Lisbon and Oporto, this land possesses a deeply individual national character, though each province has its own traditions and folklore; all, in their different ways, colorful and picturesque. Hospitality here is endemic, and beauty appreciated in the Latin sense—color everywhere and a fine disdain for plate glass and aluminum are the key notes.

The Portuguese have for some years now exploited their country's natural tourist charms intelligently and successfully, building a network of new roads and filling stations, constructing *pousadas* —state-run inns that offer comfort at rigorously controlled prices—and assisting in the development of many holiday resorts.

In short, Portugal has succeeded in reorganizing herself, and has done so with dignity and charm.

For the visitor, there is also the added bonus of being able to find many genuine bargains in hotels and restaurants that can only multiply the pleasures of a holiday here, though we would add that prices on the Algarve are no longer as amazingly low as they were.

PRACTICAL INFORMATION FOR PORTUGAL

WHAT WILL IT COST. Although prices have risen during the last few years, Portugal is still almost the least expensive country for tourists to visit in Europe. Deluxe and top class hotels do not offer pension terms, though outside Lisbon first class accommodations can be had at very reasonable prices. The *pousadas* around the country are government owned and offer accommodations and service which are first class. In general, apart from the main tourist spots in high season, Portugal offers fantastic value for money.

The monetary unit in Portugal is the escudo. It is divided into 100 centavos. The symbol for the escudo is a $ sign, written between the escudo and the centavo unit. It takes a little while to get used to it. When you see $50 in Portugal it means 50 centavos. The 50 centavo piece is now the lowest legal tender.

At the time of writing the exchange rate for the escudo was approaching 200$00 to the U.S. dollar and well over 200$00 to the pound sterling.

A typical day outside Lisbon might cost two people:

	Escudos
Hotel (moderate) double room, breakfast and taxes included	6,600
Lunch at restaurant (moderate)	4,200
Transportation (taxi and 2 buses)	720
Coffee	120
Beer and snack	840
Dinner (moderate)	4,200
Museum entrance fee	200
	16,880

SOURCES OF INFORMATION. For information on all aspects of travel in Portugal, the Portuguese National Tourist Office (Casa de Portugal) is invaluable. Their addresses are:

In the US. 548 Fifth Ave., New York, N.Y. 10036 (tel. 212–354–4403).
In the UK. 1–5 New Bond St., London, W.1 (tel. 01–493 3873).

WHEN TO COME. The main tourist season is in July and August when the weather is at its hottest. However, the climate is very good from March to October with almost no rain, except in winter and fall, though there is often a breeze in Estoril in July and August.

Climate. Winters are very mild in Portugal with some rain. In summer the temperature remains high, especially in the south of the country.

Average afternoon temperatures in degrees Fahrenheit and centigrade:

Lisbon	Jan.	Feb.	Mar.	Apr.	May	June	July	Aug.	Sept.	Oct.	Nov.	Dec.
F°	56	58	61	64	69	75	79	80	76	69	62	57
C°	13	14	16	18	21	24	26	27	24	21	17	14

Algarve												
F°	61	61	63	67	73	77	83	84	80	73	66	62
C°	16	16	17	19	23	25	28	29	27	23	19	17

SPECIAL EVENTS. The most outstanding folklore festivals are: June 13, 23 and 29, St. Anthony, St. John and St. Peter in Lisbon; June 23–24, St. John in Oporto and almost all over the country; Gulbenkian Festival of Music in Lisbon and principal cities, winter and spring; July, *Colete Encarnado* (bullfights), Vila Franca de Xira, usually second week; August 17–19, *Nossa Senhora da Agonia,* at Viana do Castelo; *Festa dos Tabuleiros,* Tomar, every second year in early July; August and September see the Arts and Crafts Fair at Estoril and the Gulbenkian sponsored Music and Ballet Season; September, festivities at Nazaré, with folklore groups and bullfights; Nov. 11, *São Martinho* at Golegã (lively horse fair); and the great religious pilgrimages to Fatima from May through October on the 12th and 13th of each month.

National Holidays. Jan. 1 (New Year's Day); Mar. 3 (Carnival); Apr. 17 (Good Fri.); Apr. 25 (Freedom Day); May 1 (Labor Day); Jun. 10 (National Day); Jun. 18 (Corpus Christi); Aug. 15 (Assumption); Oct. 5 (Day of the Republic); Nov. 1 (All Saints); Dec. 1 (Independence Day); Dec. 8 (Immaculate Conception); Dec. 25 (Christmas Day).

VISAS. Nationals of the United States, Canada, Australia, New Zealand, EEC countries and practically all other West European countries, do not require visas for a stay of less than 2 months. However, a valid passport is required.

HEALTH CERTIFICATES. These are not required for entry.

GETTING TO PORTUGAL. By Plane. From New York, *Air Portugal, TAP* and *TWA* fly to Lisbon, the former also to the Azores. From Montreal, *CP Air* and *Air Portugal* fly to Lisbon as well. From London, *Air Portugal* and *British Airways* fly a pool service to Lisbon, Oporto, and Faro (Algarve). There are many charter flights to the last from the U.K. Also services from major western European capitals to Lisbon.

By Train. From Paris to Lisbon and Oporto, sleeping-car and couchettes through Spain. The best train is the *Sud Express,* taking approx. 24 hrs.

By Sea. From Plymouth (England), *Brittany Ferries* will take you and your car to Santander (Spain), from where it is an easy two days' drive into Portugal.

CUSTOMS. You are allowed to bring in 200 cigarettes, a liter of spirits and 2 liters of wine, 50 grams of perfume and 0.25 grams of toilet water. Other goods to the value of esc. 3,000 may be imported by over 15 year olds.

HOTELS. The standard of hotels and pensions in Portugal is generally very good, if not quite as inexpensive as before. However, there is a good choice of accommodations from the deluxe hotels and *pousadas* down to the *Estalagems, Residencias* and pensions all over the country which are usually excellent and offer very reasonable rates.

A recent development has been the opening of several privately-owned country houses to paying guests, chiefly in the north. Particulars from: *Turismo de Habitacão,* Rua Alexandre Herculano 51–3D, 1200 Lisbon, tel. 681713 or Ponte de Lima, tel. 942335 for houses in the Minho.

Our hotel grading system is divided into four categories. All prices are for one person. Deluxe (L) 12,500$00, Expensive (E) 5,000$00 to 7,500$00, Moderate (M), 3,000$00 to 4,000$00, Inexpensive (I) 1,500$00 to 2,000$00. Pensions vary but expect to pay 1,250$00 to 2,000$00; *Residencias* and *Estalagems,* from 1,500$00 to 2,500$00. These prices usually include service, tourist taxes and breakfast.

CAMPING. Camping is on the upswing in Portugal and there are now many good sites all over the country. They are all graded, and are remarkably inexpensive. Largest is the *Monsanto Parque Florestal,* run by the Lisbon municipality. In general, camping is not restricted to official sites.

YOUTH HOSTELS. All over the country. For information apply to Rua Andrade Corvo 46, Lisbon 1000 (tel. 571054).

RESTAURANTS. The Portuguese prefer to do most of their eating at home, which may be a reason why every so often even really good restaurants become unpredictable. A return visit to a previously tried and liked eating place can result in disappointment. In the main, however, very good meals can be had at many a place. Restaurants are classified by us as Expensive (E) 4,500$00 and up, Moderate (M) 2,500$00 to 3,000$00, Inexpensive (I) 1,500$00 to 2,000$00. These prices are for one person with house wine—but note that expensive restaurants do not serve latter.

Food and Drink. Fish is one of the staples of Portugal, and you will find none finer, nor more of it. The Portuguese never tire of *bacalhau* (salt cod). According to legend there are 365 ways of preparing it, one for every day of the year. The whole gamut of shellfish is available at a price: so try the jugged lobster, stuffed crab *(santola),* and the big clams with pork. *Mexilhões* means mussels; *ameijoas* are small clams; both are excellent. If you're a real gourmet, try *polvo* (octopus), grilled, stewed or with rice. Then tackle *lulas* and *chocos,* squid and cuttlefish with red wine *en casserole.*

In the north, a great specialty is *caldo verde,* a delicious soup of potatoes, shredded cabbage and olive oil. River fish—salmon, lamprey, trout—are fine. Portuguese beef is not famous, but *bife na frigideira,* steak in a pottery dish, is very good. Pork, however, is always excellent. If you see cuts of pork or a suckling pig, or more often sardines, being roasted barbecue style, that should be your meat.

Caldeirada, a fish stew similar to *bouillabaisse,* can be found all along the coast from Aveiro to Algarve, with slight variations according to the region.

Sample all the cheeses, *cabreiro* (goat) and especially those made of ewe's milk, *queijo da Serra* and *queijo de Azeitão.* They have a highly distinctive and delicious flavor.

There are many pleasant wines apart from Mateus, which is ubiquitous outside the country but less regarded at home. For an apéritif Sercial (Madeira) is excellent, as is white port, and the white Colares and the red or white Dão are well worth trying. The Vinho Verde, 'green wine', is exquisite and lightly sparkling. The regional wines are usually delicious: Vidigueira, Evel and Borba from the Alentejo; Lagoa from Algarve; Nabantino from Tomar; and best of all Buçaco from Coimbra. But the greatest of Portuguese wines is port, and the greatest of all ports is vintage port, unblended and matured in the bottle; vintage port is not at its best until it is 15 to 20 years old.

Ruby port is a blend of different vintages bottled before it loses its red color, while tawny port usually has matured in the cask; white port, amber-colored and drier, can successfully compete with sherry as an elegant apéritif.

Madeira is the other great Portuguese wine, from vines on the island of Madeira. It is produced in four main types: Sercial, dry and usually drunk as an apéritif or with soup; Verdelho, a medium wine; Bual, rich with a bouquet of its own; and Malmsey, a sweet dessert wine.

TIPPING. Hotels and restaurants charge 10% service and 3.1% tourist tax included in the price list. Waiters will expect 5–10%. Taxis expect 15–20%. Minimum tip for small services: 50$00.

MAIL. Postal rates, both domestic and foreign, are prone to frequent increases in these times of economic uncertainty. For current rates consult the post offices or at hotel reception.

CLOSING TIMES. Shops open at 9, close at 7, with a usual closure from 1–3. Banks: weekdays 8.30–11.45 and 1–2.45. Closed on Saturdays.

USEFUL ADDRESSES. In Lisbon: *American Embassy and Consulate*, Av. das Forcas Armadas (tel. 725600). *US Library* (afternoons only), Av. Duque de Loulé 22–B (tel. 570102). *British Embassy and Consulate*, Rua S. Domingos à Lapa 37 (tel. 661191). *Canadian Embassy and Consulate*, Rua Rosa Aráujo 2 (tel. 563821). *British Institute Library*, Rua Luis Fernandes 3 (tel. 369208). *American Chamber of Commerce*, Rua Dona Estefania 155 (tel. 572561). *British-Portuguese Chamber of Commerce*, Rua Estrela 8 (tel. 661586).

Portuguese Tourist Offices, Palacio Foz, Praça dos Restauradores (tel. 363314), Av. Antonio Augusto Aguiar 86 (tel. 575091) and Airport (tel. 893689). *Automobile Club of Portugal*, Rua Rosa Aráujo 24 (tel. 563931). *American Express*, Av. Sidonio Pais 4 (tel. 539871). *Wasteels-Expresso*, Av. Antonio Augusto Aguiar 88–C (tel. 579180), for local and international rail reservations. *British Hospital*, Rua Saraiva de Carvalho 49 (tel. day 602020, night 603785). English speaking doctors and nurses. In and out-patients. English bank, *Lloyds Bank International*, Rua do Ouro 40–48 (tel. 361211), with branches in Monte Estoril, Parede, Oporto, Braga. Guided tours, *Citirama*, Av. Praia de Vitoria 12–B (tel. 575564). *Capristanos*, Av. Duque de Loulé 47–A (tel. 542973). *Rodoviaria Nacional*, Av. Casal Ribeiro 18 (tel. 577715) and Av. 5 de Outubro 75–C (tel. 559214) have buses all over the country.

GETTING AROUND PORTUGAL. By Plane. Domestic routes link Lisbon with Faro and Oporto, Funchal, Madeira and the Azores, all flown by *TAP* jets. Internal air fares are comparatively low in spite of recent increases.

By Train. The Lisbon-Oporto service is excellent, with certain trains taking cars at very low cost. Lisbon-Algarve is slower, with a faster afternoon train every day. Cars can be sent by train in the summer. The Lisbon-Castelo Branco-Guarda line also takes cars and the scenery along the banks of the River Tagus is lovely. The country is well served with trains, though they can be slow and run at inconvenient times to some of the more remote parts of the country such as the Sabor line to Miranda do Douro, where a few steam trains still run. Passengers over 65 years of age can get a 50% reduction on rail fares in Portugal by showing a Eurorail card. Sunday timetables are the same as weekdays. Frequent local electric trains from Lisbon to Estoril, Cascais and Sintra. Half fares on these only outside rush hours.

By Car. Roads are generally good but often narrow. Local drivers are notably rash and careless. Safety belts are obligatory in the country though not in towns. 90 octane fuel is well over 100$00 a liter, and will increase.

Car Hire. You can hire self-drive cars in Lisbon from *Avis*, *Contauto* (Carop), *Europcar*, *Hertz*, *Travelcar*, all with offices at the airport, as well as *InterRent* and many others. In Oporto, Cascais, Estoril, Faro and other major towns there are branches of these and local car hire agencies.

Lisbon, City of Hills and Views

Lisbon, set in a semi-circle that rises on the north bank of the great river Tagus, is Portugal's capital, chief seaport and nerve center. The view of the pale city glimmering in the setting sun, from the south bank of the river or from the great suspension bridge, which was thrown across the deep waters by American engineers some twenty years ago, is unforgettable. The lights come on gradually, porpoises sometimes play in the waves and you can have dinner in a restaurant on the river wall at Cacilhas with this stunning scene before you.

With over a million inhabitants, Lisbon is small compared to most capital cities, but its elongated shape and many hills make it seem larger. It is a fascinating combination of the new and old—in architecture, shops, people and even business. For human relationships count for much, as has been said, and more can be achieved by politeness and a smile than by firmness, however justified it appears.

There is little in Lisbon that dates from before the great earthquake of 1755, when the heart of the town was destroyed. Rebuilt by the

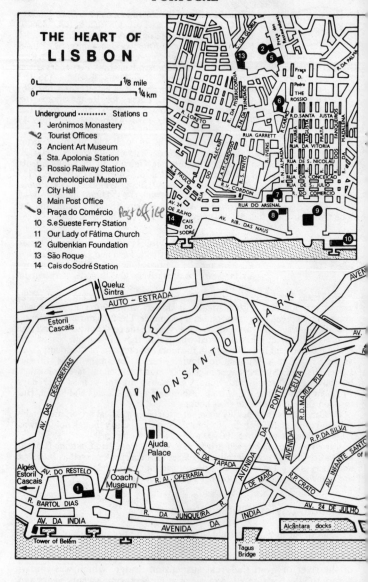

THE HEART OF LISBON

0 _____ ⅛ mile
0 _____ ¼ km

Underground ········· Stations □

1 Jerónimos Monastery
2 Tourist Offices
3 Ancient Art Museum
4 Sta. Apolonia Station
5 Rossio Railway Station
6 Archeological Museum
7 City Hall
8 Main Post Office
9 Praça do Comércio *Post office*
10 S. e Sueste Ferry Station
11 Our Lady of Fátima Church
12 Gulbenkian Foundation
13 São Roque
14 Cais do Sodré Station

Marquis of Pombal, the Prime Minister, in a satisfying, sober geometrical alignment of perfectly proportioned buildings, the *Baixa* or Low Town between the Tagus and the famous Rossio Square, is one of the earliest examples of town planning on a large scale.

Today, driving in from the airport, you will see wide avenues with new apartment houses, but few high-rise buildings, and a melee of traffic—rapid autobuses, some doubledeckers and endless private automobiles and taxis, distinguishable by their green roofs. The airport is only twenty minutes from the center so you soon get to the Avenida da Liberdade, the Champs Elysees of Lisbon, with new office blocks and hotels alongside art nouveau private houses.

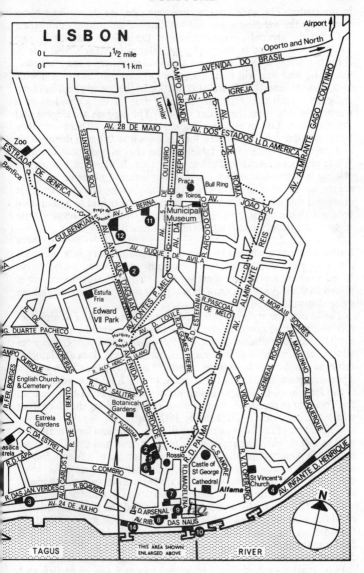

The Rossio, the heart of the capital, is a fascinatingly animated forum, in perpetual motion over the black and white waves of the inlaid pavement, with colorful flower stalls at one end. The columned National Theatre on the north side, is faced by a charming archway and flanked by Pombal's austere 18th-century facades. To the northwest rises one of the oddest railway stations in Europe, with a mock Moorish elevation, and travelers have to go up in lifts or else use the stairs to reach the trains which run to Sintra.

Good shopping streets lead from the Rossio to the lovely Praça do Comercio or Terreiro do Paço, known to foreigners in old days as Black Horse Square, owing to the splendid equestrian statue of King José I in the center. The wide river washes one side, the other three being flanked by the handsome arcaded buildings of government ministries.

Climb the ancient cobbled streets of the Alfama quarter beyond Lisbon cathedral up to the northeast. Glimpses of the Castelo de S. Jorge can suddenly be seen up a narrow alley or over a low tiled roof. Go on up and you will find this sprawling castle spread over a wide area. It dates from the Moorish occupation of the country, but has been endlessly rebuilt and restored since the days of the Crusaders who wrested the city from the Moors in 1147. The gardens are elegant and the view over Lisbon and the Tagus is magnificent. There are stone tables and stools for picnickers, for Lisboans love to eat in the open air and the city fathers provide tables and benches in every suitable spot. White peacocks, ducks and other birds strut about and it is a perfect place in which to laze on a warm day. But before strolling down again, see the medieval village of Santa Cruz that grew up between the great outer and inner walls of the castle. Narrow streets lead to a charming square with the parish church at one side, surrounded by houses, little shops and Michel's excellent French restaurant.

As you go down, look in at the *miradouro* or belvedere of Santa Luzia, where you can get an idea of the extraordinary way in which the early part of this city has been built up over the years. These *miradouros* are at strategic vantage points all over Portugal, sometimes placed so the traveler can draw in and perhaps eat a picnic overlooking some stupendous vista.

The Manueline style is Portugal's greatest contribution to architecture and is found nowhere else in the world. Inspired by the sea and the 15th-century discoveries of the Portuguese navigators, sculptors added richly carved motifs of seaweed, exotic corals, flora and knotted cables to Gothic buildings, thus creating a literally fantastic new style. There are examples all over the country, of which the most remarkable is the Jeronimos Church at Belem in the outskirts of Lisbon, near to the Tower of Belem on the banks of the Tagus, marking the place from which the discoverers sailed in the 15th century.

Cafés abound in Lisbon and they all serve wine and local brandy as well as soft drinks. The smart cafés in the Rossio and the Chiado are filled with men reading their paper or just chatting to a friend, indeed it sometimes seems surprising that any business ever gets done, as so much talk goes on all the time. The *vinho da casa,* or house wine, is usually good and those who like a dessert-type should try *abafado.*

It is round the castle and in the Alfama and the fishwives quarter of Madrogoa, on the other side of the city, that the great festivals of St. Anthony, St. John and St. Peter on June 13, 24 and 29, are still celebrated with nightly parades, singing and dancing in the streets and covered markets where fresh grilled sardines can be had with wine.

Food markets are all over Lisbon, open from 8 A.M., or earlier, to 1 or 2 P.M. The largest and best is across the road by Caes de Sodré station, with fish of every kind and fruit and vegetables piled in delicious mounds. Customers are allowed to pick out their fruit or vegetables from the abundance on view. At the entrance to this market there is a fascinating basket shop with every possible kind of basket on sale. The *Feira da Ladra* or Thieves Market is open on Tuesdays and Saturdays in the Campo de Sta. Clara behind the church of S. Vicente. There are now few antiques but a great deal of junk.

PRACTICAL INFORMATION FOR LISBON

Hotels

Deluxe

Altis, Rua Castilho 11 (tel. 522496). 219 rooms. Garage.

Meridien, Rua Castilho 149 (tel. 690900). 333 rooms, Lisbon's latest luxury hotel.

Ritz (InterContinental), Rua Rodrigo da Fonseca 88 (tel. 692020). 290 rooms, magnificent view, nightclub. Delicious food in the restaurant and grill-room. The rooms are spacious and elegantly furnished. Ample parking.

Sheraton, Rua Latino Coelho 1 (tel. 575757). 388 rooms, swimming pool, sauna, ballroom, restaurant and grillroom. Garage.

Tivoli, Av. da Liberdade 185 (tel. 530181). 344 rooms, fantastic view. Good restaurant and grillroom. Garage.

Expensive

Diplomatico, Rua Castilho 74 (tel. 562041). 90 modern rooms, terrace with fine view. 2 restaurants, excellent food; private parking.

Fenix, Praça Marques de Pombal 8 (tel. 535121). 116 very pleasant rooms with bath. Choice Spanish dishes in the grillroom.

Florida, Rua Duque de Palmela 32 (tel. 576145). 108 rooms with bath or shower, restaurant. Very popular with Americans.

Lisboa Penta, Av. dos Combatantes (tel. 7264554). 592 rooms. Restaurant. Pool. Very modern with parking. Some way from the center, near U.S. Embassy.

Lutecia, Av. Frei Miguel Contreiras 52 (tel. 803121). 151 airconditioned rooms with TV, top floor restaurant with panoramic view; parking for 200 cars. Some distance from center.

Tivoli Jardim, Rua Julio Cesar Machado 7 (tel. 539971). 119 rooms with bath, good restaurant, snack bar. Free parking area. Central.

Moderate

Capitol, Rua Eça de Queiroz 24 (tel. 536811). 50 rooms with bath or shower. Quiet. Restaurant. Snackbar.

Eduardo VII, Av. Fontes Pereira de Melo 5–C (tel. 530141). 68 rooms with bath. Attractive rooftop-restaurant terrace.

Embaixador, Av. Duque de Loulé 73 (tel. 530171). Near the U.S. Library, 96 rather small rooms with bath, restaurant.

Flamingo, Rua Castilho 41 (tel. 532191). Near Pombal Square. 39 rooms with bath. Restaurant. Friendly.

Impala, Rua Filipe Folque 49 (tel. 558914). 26 apartments with bath and kitchenette for up to 4 people.

Jorge V, Rua Mouzinho da Silveira 3 (tel. 562525). 49 airconditioned rooms with bath. Breakfast only.

Principe, Av. Duque d'Avila 201 (tel. 536151). 56 rooms with bath. Restaurant.

Reno, Av. Duque d'Avila 195, next to *Principe* (tel. 548181). 47 rooms with bath. German management. Breakfast only.

Rex, Rua Castilho 169 (tel. 682161). 41 rooms with bath.

Roma, Av. de Roma 33 (tel. 767761). 264 rooms with bath. Restaurant with view; snack bar, pool. Not central.

Inexpensive

Borges, Rua Garrett 108 (tel. 361951). 100 rooms, all with bath. Old fashioned, though on the main shopping street. Restaurant.

Lis, Av. da Liberdade 180 (tel. 563434). 62 rooms with bath. Only breakfast.

Miraparque, Av. Sidonio Pais 12 (tel. 578070). 96 rooms with bath.

Senhora do Monte, Calçada do Monte 39 (tel. 862846). In the oldest part of town. All 27 rooms with bath, balcony and fine views. Breakfast only.

Among the countless pensions *York House* (E) (Pensão Residencia Inglesa), Rua das Janelas Verdes 32 (tel. 662435), is charming. 46 rooms, most with bath. A former convent in a shady garden, up a long flight of steps. Annex at No. 47 in same street. Good restaurant. Book well in advance.

Residencia America (E), Rua Tomas Ribeiro 47 (tel. 531178). 55 rooms with bath. *Avenida Alameda* (M), Av. Sidonio Pais 4 (tel. 532186). 27 rooms with bath. *Avenida Parque* (M), Av. Sidonio Pais 6 (tel. 532181). 40 rooms with bath. *Horizonte* (M), Av. Antonio Augusto de Aguiar 42 (tel. 539526). 52 rooms with bath. *Nazareth* (M), Av. Antonio Augusto Aguiar 25 (tel. 542016). 32 rooms with bath. *Imperador* (M), Av. 5 de Outubro 55 (tel. 574884). 45 rooms with bath. *Canada* (I), Av. Defensores de Chaves 35 (tel. 538159). 40 rooms with bath. All these are central. Breakfast only.

 RESTAURANTS. Lisbon's biggest restaurants are of the international type. Since they depend largely on the unpredictable tourist trade, the smallest places are apt to change in quality, or even go out of existence, overnight. Only tables in first-class restaurants need to be reserved.

Expensive

Antonio Clara, Av. da Republica 38 (tel. 766380). Excellent food in large Edwardian house.

Aviz, Rua Serpa Pinto 12b (tel. 328391). Has the right atmosphere and the right food, excellent. Closed Sun., dinner Sat.

Casa da Comida, Trav. des Amoreiras 1 (tel. 685376). Set around flowered patio. Closed Sun., lunch Sat.

Gambrinus, Rua Portas de Santo Antão 23 (tel. 321466). Seafood.

Gondola, Av. Berna 64 (tel. 770426). Serves rich Italian food, and in fine weather you can eat in the garden. Closed Sun., dinner Sat.

Michel, Largo de Santa Cruz do Castelo 5 (tel. 864338). On small, elegant square inside castle walls. Serves classic French food. Closed Sun.

Pabe, Rua Duque de Palmela 27–A (tel. 535675). Political and big business clientele. Always open.

Tagide, Largo da Academia 18–20 (tel. 320720). Splendid view of Black Horse Square and River Tagus. Closed Sun., dinner Sat.

Tavares, Rua Misericordia 35 (tel. 321112). In a turn-of-the-century setting, the much praised cuisine is taken very seriously. Exceptional wine list. Closed Sat. and Sun. lunch.

Moderate

Bistro Breque, Rua Buenos Aires 28–B (tel. 607006). Good food and service. In diplomatic district. Closed Sun.

Forno da Brites, Rua Tomás Ribeiro 75 (tel. 542724). Excellent value, helpful service; halfway between the Sheraton and Edward VII Park.

O Paco, Av. Berna 44B (tel. 770642). Opposite the Gulbenkian Museum, amusing decor, literary clientele, regional dishes, good steaks. Closed Mon.

Petite Folie, Av. Antonio Augusto Aguiar 74 (tel. 41949). Good French food.

A Quinta, corner of Rua do Ouro and Rua Santa Justa, at the top of the elevator (tel. 365588). If you secure a table by the window you have the city at your feet. Country decor. No parking. Closed Sun., dinner Sat.

Solmar, Rua Portas de Santo Antão 108 (tel. 323371). A vast seafood restaurant. Check price before ordering lobster. Always open.

Inexpensive

Anarquistas, Largo de Trinidade 14 (tel. 323510). One of the oldest restaurants in Lisbon. Full of atmosphere. Closed Sundays in summer.

Atinel Bar, Cais dos Cacilheros (tel. 372419). Picture windows right onto the river Tagus. Also tables outside. Good unpretentious food and friendly service. Always open.

Bonjardim, Travessa Santo Antão 12 (tel. 324389). Very simple, very crowded, good food. Chicken and suckling pig, spit roasted. Always open.

Colombo, Av. da Republica 10H (tel. 555228). Pleasant food. Delicious cakes. Always open.

Porto de Abrigo, Rua de Remolares 16 (tel. 360873). Excellent Portuguese food at very reasonable prices. Specialties are duck and crab *(Santola)*. Very full at lunch, easy to get a table at dinner.

The Great American Disaster, Praça Marques de Pombal 1 (tel. 41266). Hamburger joint. Music. Always open.

CASAS DE FADO. These are restaurants where you listen to *fado* singers and eat Portuguese specialties. Meals are not obligatory; you can spend your time from after dinner until the wee hours on local red or white wine or whatever other drink you may favor. Guitars accompany the *fadistas* and when the mood calls for it, one or the other waitress joins in and a musical dialogue ensues made up entirely on the spur of the moment. Most genuine *fado* places are situated in the oldest parts of town, Alfama or Bairro Alto. *Parreirinha de Alfama,* Beco do Espirito Santo 1 (tel. 868209) and *Snr. Vinho,* Rua do Meio à Lapa 18 (tel. 672681) are among the most popular. Tourists are generally directed to *Machado,* Rua do Norte 91 (tel. 360095), a rather over-done place (closed Mon.); *Luso,* Trav. da Queimada 10 (tel. 362889), closed Sun., and *A Severa,* Rua das Gáveas 51 (tel. 364006), closed Thurs., always have very good singers. Perhaps the most unspoilt is *Lisboa a Noite,* Rua das Gaveas 69 (tel. 368557) which has an ancient wishing well on the premises; closed Sun. *Solar da Herminia,* Largo Trinidade Coelho 10 (tel. 320164) is another well known place. *O Faia,* Rua da Barroca 56 (tel. 326742) is favored by the locals. All these are in Bairro Alto.

NIGHTLIFE. Lisbon nightclubs in general don't rank international class. New ones open, fairly new ones fold: it's unpredictable.

Ad Lib, Rua Barata da Salgueiro 28–7.

Banana Power, Rua de Cascais, Alcantara. The most in-place of all.

Sheraton Hotel, top-floor restaurant; live band and dancing. Stunning view.

Stones, Rua do Olival 1. Smart and respectable.

GETTING AROUND LISBON. The *tram* service is one of the best in Europe, and is still cheap. Tourist one-week season tickets cost 1,000$00, good for unlimited travel on buses and trams. Books of 20 half-price tickets can be bought at Cais de Sodre and other terminals. Try routes 18, 28, 29 and 30 for an unusual tour of the city on one of the oldest tram networks in the world. *Subways,* called *Metropolitano,* connect the Rossio with the Zoological Gardens at Sete Rios and with Campo Grande, Entrecampos (site of the bull ring), also with Alvalade. Fare 45$00 to any point. A book of 10 tickets costs 350$00.

MUSEUMS. All museums are closed on Mondays and public holidays. Open 10–5. Entrance fees are between 100$00 and 150$00. Free on Sundays.

Ajuda Palace. Fine 19th-century royal rooms and furnishings.

Ancient Art Museum, Rua das Janelas Verdes. Good collection of paintings, ceramics, jewelry, tapestries etc. Has fine Portuguese primitives and works by Hieronymus Bosch, Zurbarán, Holbein, Durer, and many others, plus German silver. Entrance free Sat. and Sun. Snackbar.

Aquarium, Dafundo. Open Mon. to Sat., midday–6, Sun. 10–6. Entrance free Wed.

Botanical Gardens, Rua de Escola Politécnica. *Estufa Fria* is a vast greenhouse with a remarkable collection of semi-tropical plants and streams with fish and water lilies; *Estufa Quente* is a hothouse, reached through the cool house, and very large and filled with rare specimens. Open 10–5; in the Parque Eduardo VII. Entrance 50$00.

Contemporary Art, Rua Serpa Pinto. 19th- and 20th-century Portuguese painting and sculpture. The portraits by Columbano are a revelation. Closed 12.30–2.

Costume Museum, Lumiar, in the lovely old Palmela Palace. With superb gardens, and a good but expensive restaurant. **Theater Museum** next door. A fair distance out, so (unless you are eating) have your taxi wait. Closed 1–2.30.

Ethnological Museum, Praça do Império, Belém. Prehistoric, Greek and Roman relics. Closed 12.30–2. Also, splendid **Marine Museum** nearby.

Folk Art, Av. de Brasília, Belém. An eloquent showing of the provincial arts and artifacts of Portugal, many of which are fast disappearing. Closed 12.30–2.

Gulbenkian Foundation Museum, Av. Berna. A collection, acquired by oil millionaire Calouste Gulbenkian, of world-famous paintings—many from Leningrad's Hermitage Museum: centuries-old Persian prayer mats, Turkish textiles, Oriental art, tiles and early glass, coins, silver, 18th-century French paintings, sculpture and furniture, Italian primitives, French impressionists, and Art Nouveau jewelry.

The Foundation is set in a lovely park, and presents concerts and ballet in the two auditoria as well as special exhibitions. There is a library and cafeteria, and the place has become the main art center in Lisbon. The Modern Gallery has a good self-service restaurant.

Open Tues., Thurs., Fri., Sun., 10–5; Wed., Sat., 2–7. Closed Mon.

Lisbon City, Palacio do Pimenta, Campo Grande. Paintings, engravings, models and books relating to Lisbon, all beautifully displayed in a superb 18th-century house. Open 2–6. Entrance free.

Military Museum, Largo dos Caminhos de Ferro. Armor and weapons from the 15th century.

Religious Art, Largo Trindade Coelho. Next to the Church of S. Roque. Superb embroidered vestments, gold and silver ecclesiastical vessels, portraits.

Ricardo Espírito Santo Foundation, in an old palace at Largo das Portas do Sol 2. Museum-school of decorative arts. Workshops for the reproduction of antiques, for gold-beating and gilding, for tapestry work, and for bookbinding, etc. Closed 1–2.30.

Royal Coaches, Praça Afonso de Albuquerque, Belém. The richest collection of royal coaches and carriages in the world.

Tile Museum, Madre de Deus Convent, Rua da Madre de Deus. Glazed tiles, pictorial and decorative, from Moorish times to the present day.

Zoo, Parque das Larangeiras. Set in a lovely park. The animals grow sleek in the sun. Restaurants and snackbars. Open 9–sunset. Entrance 150$00.

SHOPPING. Lisbon offers the tourist a wide choice of hand-made goods. The best buys are shoes, leather goods, baskets, materials, glazed tiles, porcelain and pottery, hand embroidery, bookbinding and handicrafts in general. The traditional shopping streets in Lisbon are the Rua Garrett, commonly called the Chiado, the Rua do Ouro, the Rua Augusta and the Rua da Prata, running down to the river from the Rossio. But you will find good shops in all of Lisbon's residential districts.

Almost all stores shut from 1 to 3. To make up for this Latin lunch hour, they stay open until 7 in the evening, as they do in nearby Cascais and Estoril. Shops close at 1 P.M. on Saturdays. Shopping centers and supermarkets are now all over Lisbon; many are open until midnight and on Sundays.

Estoril and Cascais

Down the Tagus towards the sea, the Estrada Marginal and the electric railway line from Caes de Sodré lead through Alges, Caxias and attractive Paco d'Arcos to Estoril and Cascais. Estoril is pleasantly old-fashioned with a good sandy beach, and geometrically laid out gardens leading up to the casino. This is not unlike a comfortable club with deep sofas and armchairs around a flowered courtyard. There is a restaurant, night club, cinema, exhibitions of modern paintings and the gambling rooms—remember to take your passport if you wish to play any of the games of chance. The Casino opens from 3 P.M. to 3 A.M. There is no charge to go into the building, but if you wish to play there is an admission fee. A music and ballet festival is held here every August and September, subsidised by the Gulbenkian Foundation, so tickets are remarkably moderate in price. At the same time, an Arts and Crafts Fair takes place in a wood nearby. The golf club to the north has an excellent course, pool and restaurant open to the public.

Cascais, a couple of miles beyond Estoril, is much more up to date with a plethora of restaurants at all prices, night clubs and good shops and boutiques. There are long, sandy beaches for bathing and a fishermen's beach where the catch is landed and taken directly to the fish market for a Dutch Auction that takes place every day. In stormy weather the boats are drawn up on the beach which adjoins the Estrada Marginal, and there are always two or three booths selling strange sea shells. Beyond the ancient citadel, past the Castro Guimarães Museum set in a lovely park, and the Boca do Inferno, a hugh cavity in the rocks, where the sea rushes in to make a kind of whirlpool in rough weather, the road passes the newly opened Quinta da Marinha, with 18-hole golf course, tennis, and pool, etc. Then through a bare landscape of pines and sun-bleached dunes to the rocky spine of the Serra de Sintra, above the westernmost point of Europe—Cabo da Roca.

Queluz, Sintra and Mafra

The inland road from Lisbon to Sintra passes the gardens of Queluz, a rosy 18th-century royal palace (closed Tues.), as romantic as the castle of the Sleeping Beauty. It is a good curtain raiser for enchanting Sintra, one of the gems of Portugal. In the center of an open plain, a volcanic eruption thrust the spine of Sintra into being, with its mass of rocks from which burst thousands of springs. Around Sintra the vegetation combines jasmine, arbutus, bamboo, camellias, mimosa, tree ferns and 90 species of exotic flowering plants that are seldom found elsewhere in Europe. The famous gardens of Monserrate are open to the public.

Don't miss the old Palácio da Vila (closed Wed.), in the town, with its small Moorish garden and many tiles. Linked with every king of Portugal since John of Aviz, this palace is a lecture in stone on Portuguese architecture, combining Gothic, Moorish, Manueline and Victorian elements in a surprisingly harmonious way. Take a *fiacre* in the square to within reach of the ruined Moorish castle with its ramparts and dungeons and its sweeping panoramic view to the sea. This is the oldest castle in Sintra. The newest, Pena (closed Mon.), was built in 1840 for a German prince consort, Ferdinand of Saxe-Coburg. It is an architectural fantasy, ranging from genuine medieval to equally genuine Victorian, inspired by Balmoral. From the terraces and grounds there are superb views of the surrounding countryside and right back to Lisbon. The road to both castles is steep and tortuous. There is a big country fair on the second and fourth Sundays of every month at São Pedro de Sintra.

North of Sintra is a delightful area, highly agricultural and Lisbon's main source of vegetables. The farms are often hand cultivated and irrigated from wells. In the midst of such a pastoral setting, the monumental convent of Mafra (closed Tues.) rises up, built by King João V with the wealth of Brazil and the labor of 50,000 men. The pale, elegant, lichen covered facade is set on a wide square, so you can sit in one of the cafés opposite and take in the curiously satisfying mass of building stretching for over eight hundred feet from the great church in the center. The palace is worth seeing, particularly the grisaille rococo library and the Empire furnishings of the royal apartments. In the great park there are deer and wild boar, and a small museum with royal carriages and photographs of shooting parties of long ago. On Sunday afternoons in the summer there are often concerts on the huge carillons in the church towers.

Ericeira, a few miles from Mafra on the coast, is a charming town, famous for its lobsters and bracing Atlantic air. There is a large hotel and several good pensions and a general air of prosperous good cheer.

North of Lisbon

Obidos, snug within its encircling walls, is fascinating with its narrow streets, whitewashed houses and fine churches. The narrow, winding main street is rather misleadingly called Rua Direita (straight), but it does lead straight to the restored 15th-century castle now functioning as a tiny but inviting *pousada*. A walk along the top of the ramparts presents you with a marvelous view of the roof-tops of the town—as well as the multicoloured washing drying in the sun and wind.

A bronze statue of Queen Leonor stands at the entrance to Caldas da Rainha (literally, the Queen's Thermal Baths), a town which she made famous by promoting the ill-smelling springs which cured her rheumatism. Caldas is also a noted ceramic center, specializing in glazed earthenware pieces in human, animal and vegetable form.

In the midst of peach and apricot orchards at the confluence of the Alcoa and Baça streams is the town of Alcobaça. The chief attraction is the notable Monastery of Santa Maria, built by the Cistercians in 1152. The abbey church, with its breath-taking interior, is the largest in Portugal. See the Gothic tombs of Dom Pedro I and his murdered secret wife, Inês de Castro. They are splendid examples of Portuguese sculpture, despite their profanation by Napoleon's soldiers.

Another "must" to the north of Alcobaça is Batalha, with its celebrated monastery of Our Lady of Victory, built in the 14th and 15th centuries. The finest example of flamboyant Gothic in Portugal, it contains the impressive sarcophagus of João I and his English queen, Philippa of Lancaster and the tombs of Portugal's two unknown soldiers from World War I in the Chapter House.

About 10 miles east of Batalha is one of the famous shrines of Christendom, Fátima, where, on May 13, 1917 the Virgin is said to have appeared to three little shepherds. On the 12th and 13th of each month from May until October, huge crowds of pilgrims make their way to the shrine at Fátima. On these occasions, it is impossible to get a room without booking ahead; pilgrims pray all night in the open.

Southwest on the coast is the fishing town of Nazaré. Here the ocean hurls itself in fury on a dangerous beach, bounded to the north by a 300-foot cliff on top of which stands the Church of Our Lady of Nazaré, a shrine for fishermen. The fishing boats here are rounded and turned up at bow and stern to enable them to cut through the huge breakers. When the catch is good, the whole village harnesses itself to the dripping nets, sometimes so heavy that tractors are employed to pull them in, in place of the oxen which were formerly used. If you want to understand the primitive strength and dignity of Portugal, watch the fishing ships come in at Nazaré (very crowded in July and August).

Southward from Lisbon

The promontory that juts out between the estuaries of the Tagus and the Sado is a delightful area, easily explored from Lisbon in a day. You can take a car-ferry to Cacilhas or drive across the impressive suspension bridge built by an American engineer. A new motorway takes you to Setúbal.

Beyond Azeitão on the old road is the Serra da Arrabida, a great limestone ridge with, on the northern slopes, the original forest of the peninsular; today still thick with impenetrable undergrowth and tall specimens of the tree-heath. If you take the road to the right out of Azeitão, you will get to the turning to Sesimbra. This has a fine castle, but what was a delightful seaside resort has now, unlike other places in Portugal, been so built up that it is hard to find the still charming original fishing village. Another ten kilometers and you are at Cape Espichel. Ignore the lighthouse, but admire the arcaded 18th-century pilgrim houses on either side of the wide square in front of the pilgrimage church of Nossa Senhora do Cabo.

Outside Azeitão and long before the road to Sesimbra, a turning to the south will take you over the end of the Serra to one of the loveliest roads in Portugal which goes along the side of the hills, far above the river Sado, of which you have a bird's eye view. A road goes down to the long sickle-shaped beach of Portinho da Arrábida. This is a perfect place for lunch; try one of the little beach restaurants or the *estalagem* in an old fort. The bathing's good here, but parking is hell in summer.

A lower road to Setúbal has been excavated nearer to the seashore. It has less spectacular views than the top road, but is still beautiful and Setúbal, a big fishing and canning town on the Sado river, contains a museum and the earliest Manueline building, the Church of Jesus. Its strange twisting Arrabida marble pillars make it almost unique.

Return to Lisbon via Palmela where the huge Templar's Castle crowns a hilltop. Part of this fantastic aglomeration of building of every period up to the 18th century has been turned into a superb *pousada.* The vista embraces Lisbon to the north and Setúbal to the south.

Go back to Lisbon, not on the motorway, but by Vila Fresca de Azeitão. It was here that King Manuel built for his mother the first summer residence of Portugal, the manor of Bacalhoa. The gardens may be visited every afternoon from 1 to 5 P.M., except Sundays. They include a great water tank, and a pavilion in which is the earliest dated tile panel in Portugal—a scene of Susannah and the Elders.

PRACTICAL INFORMATION FOR ENVIRONS OF LISBON

ALCOBAÇA. *Hotel Santa Maria* (I), tel. 43295. 31 rooms with bath. Breakfast only.
Restaurant. *Coraçóes Unidos* (M), tel. 42142. Good country food and wine.

AZEITÃO. *Estalagem Quinta das Torres* (E), tel. 2080001. 12 rooms with bath. Charming private residence. Restaurant. Cottages in grounds. Pool.

BATALHA. *Pousada do Mestre Domingues* (L), tel. 96260. 21 rooms with bath, restaurant. *Motel São Jorge* (M), tel. 96186. 10 rooms.

CACILHAS. Restaurant. *Floresta do Ginjal* (M), tel. 275–0087. Immense dining rooms on the first and second floors, and a captivating view of Lisbon across the Tagus. Go for the view rather than the food. Always open.

CARCAVELOS. *Hotel Praia Mar* (E), tel. 2473131. 158 rooms with bath. Restaurant. Pool and sea view.

CASCAIS. *Albatroz* (L), tel. 282821. Right on the sea, 40 elegant rooms, with attractive bar and restaurant. Pool. *Estoril-Sol* (L), tel. 282831. 404 rooms with bath, and a huge pool. *Cidadela* (E), tel. 282921. Also has several self-contained flatlets, restaurant, supermarket and pool. *Albergaria Valbom* (M), tel. 2865801. 40 rooms with bath. Breakfast only. *Baia* (M), tel. 281033. 87 rooms with bath. Balconies giving view over the bay. Restaurant. *Hotel Apartamento Equador* (M), tel. 2840524. 117 apartments. Pool, supermarket, restaurant. Good value. Not in center.
Restaurants. *Dom Leitão* (E), tel. 2865487. Good food. Closed Wed. *João Padeiro* (E), tel. 280232. Fairly trendy. Closed Tues. *O Pipas* (E), tel. 2864501. Excellent seafood. *Pescador* (E), tel. 282054. Folksy and crowded, but good seafood and atmosphere. *O Batel* (M), tel. 280215. The last three are all in the Rua das Flores. *Burladero* (M), tel. 2868751. Under the bull ring. Excellent food in pleasant setting. *Duke of Wellington* (I), Rua Frederico Arouca 32, English owner. Simple menu. *Pigalo* (I), Trav. Frederico Arouca 12. Good value. You can listen to *fado* in the evenings at *Kopus,* Largo das Grutas 3.

ERICEIRA. *Estalagem Morais* (E), Rua Dr Miguel Bombarda 5 (tel. 62611). 40 rooms with bath. Pool. *Hotel de Turismo* (M), tel. 63545. 154 rooms with bath. Right on the sea with two swimming pools. Several restaurants.

ESTORIL AND MONTE ESTORIL. (All rooms with bath in the following hotels.) *Hotel Palácio* (L), tel. 268–0400. 174 rooms, a combination of modern comfort and old-fashioned elegance. Pool. *Atlántico* (E), Estrada Marginal 7–7A (tel. 268–0270). 183 rooms overlooking sea; huge pool; but railway between hotel and sea. *Belvedere* (E), Rua Dr. Antonio Martins 8–8A (tel. 268–9163). 16 rooms with bath. Well run, excellent food. Garden. *Cibra* (E), Estrada Marginal (tel. 2681811). 89 rooms, splendid view from top-floor dining room. *The Founder's Inn* (E), Rua D. Afonso Henriques 11 (tel. 2682221). English-owned, 12 rooms; breakfast only. *Grande Hotel* (M), Av. Saboia (tel. 268–4609). 72 rooms, pool and near the sea. *Lennox Country Club* (E), Rua Eng. Alvaro Pedro de Sousa 5 (tel. 2680424). 32 rooms, small pool. *Sintra-Estoril* (E), on the road between Estoril and Sintra (tel. 269–0720). 192 rooms, indoor pool, at Alcabideche. *Alvorada* (M), Rua de Lisboa 3 (tel. 268–0070). 51 rooms, service flatlets, faces casino. *Hotel Apartamento Touring Estoril* (M), Rua do Viveiro (tel. 2683385). 99 apartments. Some way from the sea. Pool. *Lido* (M), Rua do Alentejo (tel. 2684098). 62 rooms, very quiet, not near sea. Pool. *Londres* (M), Av. Fausto Figueiredo 17, (tel. 268–4245). 68 rooms, pool. *Paris* (M), Estrada Marginal (tel. 268–0018). 99 rooms, pool, noisy. *Pica-Pau* (M), (Woodpecker Inn), Av. D. Afonso Henriques 2 (tel. 268–0556). 34 rooms. Pool, guitar and dancing in the evening. *Zenith* (M), Rua Belmonte 1 (tel. 2680202). 48 rooms, top-floor restaurant. Pool. *Inglaterra* (I), Av. de Portugal 2 (tel. 2684461), 49 rooms. Pool, good family hotel.

Restaurants. *Choupana* (E), tel. 268–3099. Right on the sea just before you drive into Estoril. The three man band plays practically non-stop, food is good, and they also serve lunch. The *English Bar* (E), tel. 268–0413. Opposite Atlántico hotel. Very good food and wine. *Ronda* (E), tel. 268–0965. Dancing at this spot. *Golf Club* restaurant (M), open to non-members. Charming rooms. *Ray's Bar* (M), tel. 268–0106. American owner, friendly. Opens at 6 P.M. *Sinaleiro* (I), tel. 268–5439. Opposite Grande Hotel. Good food and decor.

Casino, tel. 268–8048, is not smart. Roulette, baccarat and chemin de fer are played and there is a restaurant (E) and floor shows. Also one-armed bandits. You will need your passport to get in to the gaming rooms. Cinema.

FATIMA. *Estalagem D. Gonçalo* (M), tel. 97262. 12 rooms with bath. Good food. *Fátima* (M), tel. 97751. 76 rooms with bath. *Santa Maria* (M), tel. 97615. 59 rooms with bath. *Hotel Três Pastorinhos* (M), tel. 97229. 92 rooms, all with bath. *Pax* (I), tel. 97812. 51 rooms with bath. Several other hotels and pensions and most of the religious houses receive visitors.

Restaurants. Fatima has a number of reasonable restaurants and cafés.

GUINCHO. *Hotel do Guincho* (L), tel. 2850491. 36 rooms with bath, in old fortress. Restaurant on sea. *Estalagem do Muchaxo* (L), tel. 285–0221. 24 rooms with bath, and an excellent, if somewhat overrated seafood restaurant. Pool. *Estalagem Mar do Guincho* (M), 13 rooms with bath, has another excellent restaurant. Several seafood restaurants at a price. Swimming is very dangerous on this long Atlantic beach.

NAZARÉ. *Nazaré* (M), tel. 46311. 50 rooms with bath. *Praia* (M), tel. 46423. 40 rooms with bath. *Dom Fuas* (I), tel. 46351. 32 rooms with bath.

Restaurant. *Mar Bravo* (E), tel. 46180. Splendid view.

OBIDOS. *Pousada do Castelo* (L), tel. 95105. 6 rooms with bath, located in medieval castle. *Estalagem do Convento* (E), tel. 95217. 14 rooms with bath. Is pleasant, just outside city walls.

PALMELA. *Pousada de Palmela* (L), tel. 2351226. 28 rooms with bath. Located in Templar's castle crowning a hill with stunning views to Lisbon and Setúbal.

PORTINHO D'ARRABIDA. *Residencia Santa Maria* (M), tel. 208–0527. 33 rooms with bath. Breakfast only. Several beach restaurants nearby.

QUELUZ. Restaurant. *Cozinha Velha* (L), tel. 950740. The most romantic restaurant in the Lisbon region. The original kitchen of the Queluz palace, it has retained its old fittings, gleaming copper pots and pans and even the spits on which oxen used to be roasted whole.

SESIMBRA. *Hotel do Mar* (E), tel. 223–3326. 120 rooms, pool. Good restaurant. *Espadarte* (I), tel. 223–3189. 80 rooms with bath. On the sea. Several restaurants.

SETÚBAL. *Pousada S. Felipe* (L), tel. 24981. Outside the town in old castle, 15 rooms with bath, atmospheric and a great view. *Hotel Esperança* (M), tel. 25151. 76 rooms with bath.
Restaurants. Good restaurants include *Bocage* and *O Tunel,* both in Praca Bocage. Both (M).

SINTRA. *Hotel Palácio de Seteais* (L), tel. 923–3200. 18 rooms with bath and lovely furnishings. Formerly the property of the Counts of Marialva, well worth at least a lunch visit. *Tivoli Sintra* (E), tel. 9233505. 77 rooms with bath. Good restaurant. *Central* (M), tel. 923–0963. 11 rooms with bath. Both in main square.
Restaurant. *Cantinho de S. Pedro* (M). Excellent food close to S. Pedro market. Very good house wine. Closed Mon. and Thurs. dinner. *Tulhas Bar* (I). Just off main square. Good food, friendly.

Ribatejo

If you follow the west bank of the Tagus north from Lisbon, you will enter the green pastures of Ribatejo. This is the country of the horses, bulls and *toureiros,* whom you will see in the highly expert spectacle of Portuguese bullfighting; the bull is not killed, and the horses—always stallions—are as highly trained as polo ponies and ridden superbly. The long-horned herds are led by *campinos,* or cowboys, armed with long, javelin-like staves, and wearing their striking costumes—blue knee-breeches, white hose, bolero, red waistcoat and green and red cap. The best time to visit the Ribatejo is during the bullfights at Vila Franca or Salvaterra, and certainly at the time of local *fêtes,* the "Colete Encarnado", at Vila Franca de Xira, the second weekend of July, or the "Barrete Verde", at Alcochete, the second Sunday in August. In all major towns, *feiras* are held on certain days of the year (check locally whether any are in the offing while you are there). Sometimes, as at Golegã, on November 10th to 12th, it is a horse fair; at others livestock, pottery and country produce abound.

Those travelers startled by the strong flavor of Ribatejan celebrations will be moved by the charm of Almourol. This was originally a strategic feudal castle, built on an island in the Tagus by the grand master of the Order of Knights Templar. In striking contrast to this medieval ruin is the great dam of Castelo de Bode, on the River Zêzere. Completed in 1950 by British engineers, it is a most impressive accomplishment.

But the treasure of Ribatejo is Tomar, built in a region of ravishing beauty, reminiscent of Tuscany. But one visits Tomar chiefly for the Convent of Christ. The Templars were installed there in the year 1160, and one can still see their original circular sanctuary, the Charola, with seven cloisters in the vast complex.

Out of gratitude, King Manuel gave to the Convent of Tomar a church of exquisite beauty. One comes first to a marvelous portal by João de Castilho, but, above all, see the famous window of the Chapter House, most fantastic example of Manueline art. The town on the river Nabão is prosperous and pleasant to walk in. The churches are elegant, the people are friendly and the river gardens add to the charm.

PRACTICAL INFORMATION FOR RIBATEJO

CASTELO DE BODE. *Estalagem da Ilha do Lombo* (E), tel. 37128. 15 rooms with bath. Pool. On an island on the lake. *Pousada de São Pedro* (E), tel. 38175. 14 rooms with bath. By the dam and huge lake.

CERNACHE DO BONJARDIM. *Estalagem Vale da Ursa* (M), tel. 67511. 12 rooms with bath. Pool, water sports. Charming, newly built inn overlooking lake. Excellent food.

TOMAR. *Hotel dos Templarios* (E), tel. 32121. 84 rooms with bath, pool. *Pensão Nuno Alvares* (I), tel. 32873. 12 rooms, good country food and local wine.

Restaurants. There are several places by the river Nabão to try the local Nabantino wine. *Bela Vista* (M), is by the bridge; good food. Closed Tues.

The Beiras

Watered by the Mondego River, Beira Litoral, with its population of peasants and fishermen, is a synthesis of Portugal. Pride of the area is Portugal's third city and former capital, Coimbra. This town, built on a steep hill above the river, is famous for its university. Founded in 1290, it is one of Europe's oldest. Its alumni roster includes Camões, Portugal's great epic poet; the novelist Eça de Queiroz; Saint Anthony of Padua; Antero de Quental, the philosopher, and António de Oliveira Salazar. Coimbra vibrates with life during the university year, and the *fado* is king of music here, more sophisticated than in Lisbon.

Take your children to Portugal dos Pequeninos, a charming park containing copies of many monuments and dwellings typical of the country and of the former overseas provinces, all built to scale for a child of five. The finest among the city's many churches are the Romanesque Sé Velha (Old Cathedral), and Santa Cruz, with its evocative cloister, Machado de Castro Museum, notable early sculpture. Across the river, the Convent of Santa Clara-a-Nova with Gothic, Renaissance and baroque features, should be seen. Figueira da Foz at the mouth of the Mondego is a popular resort, with a charming museum.

South of Coimbra are the splendid Roman remains at Conimbriga and the magnificent feudal castle of Queen Isabel and Dom Diniz at Leiria. The river Liz meanders through the town, which has a lovely arcaded square.

Aveiro, a provincial fishing town, is worth a visit, especially in late-March during the fair, when there is dancing on the brightly painted, flower-garlanded fishing boats. The museum in an old convent contains some memorable religious art. Aveiro's great sport is night fishing in the lagoons or *Ria* (a boat trip on them is recommended) and its great dish is the result—a delicious fish soup called Caldeirada à Pescadora. Near Ilhavo the 160-year-old *Vista Alegre* porcelain factory has a small museum containing many early pieces, and a shop, too.

Buçaco was the scene in 1810 of a ferocious battle in which Wellington defeated Napoleon's troops. On the eve of his victory, he slept in a cell of the Carmelite Monastery here. Take a walk through the mysteriously-lighted *mata,* the high cedar forest planted by the monks of Buçaco 300 years ago.

Once the hunting lodge of Portuguese royalty, the Buçaco Palace, situated within the forest, is a deservedly famous hotel. Luso and Curia, in the neighborhood, are both well-known and greatly frequented spas, with old-fashioned hotels and pensions suited to all tastes. The Serra da Estrela (up to 6,500 ft.) has fine winter skiing.

Viseu and Lamego, north west of Coimbra, are two entrancing baroque cities. The former—with a superb ensemble of the 12th-century cathedral facing the twin-towered facade of the Misericordia church across a wide, long space—is filled with 17th- and 18th-century houses and churches while the museum by the cathedral contains Portuguese primitive paintings and sculptures.

Further north, where baroque joy is toned down somewhat by the local gray granite, Lamego is a lovely place. The museum in the Bishop's palace has fine tapestries, early canvases and sculpture and the churches are also worth seeing. But Lamego is best known for the pilgrimage church of Nossa Senhora dos Remedios, set in an extraordinary architectural complex of stairs embellished by pillars, obelisks, arches and numerous gushing fountains. The whole fantastic creation, against a backdrop of wood-mantled hills, is not to be missed.

PRACTICAL INFORMATION FOR THE BEIRAS

AVEIRO. *Afonso V* (M), tel. 25191. 80 rooms with bath. Exceptionally good restaurant. *Hotel Imperial* (M), tel. 22141. 52 rooms with bath. *Arcada* (I), tel. 23001. 55 rooms with bath. Breakfast only.
Restaurants. *Cozinha do Rei* (E) is one of several possibilities.

BUÇACO. *Palace Hotel* (L), tel. 93101. Former royal hunting lodge in forest, 80 rooms with bath, quiet and restful. Outstanding service. Restaurant.

CANAS DE SENHORIM. *Hotel Urgeirica* (M), tel. 67267. 50 rooms with bath. Country setting. Pool.

COIMBRA. *Astoria* (M), tel. 22055. 70 rooms with bath. Good food and Buçaco wine, old-fashioned. *Bragança* (M), tel. 22171. 83 rooms with bath. *Oslo* (M), tel. 29071. 17 rooms with bath. Panoramic view. Several *residencias* and pensions.
Restaurants. *Piscinas* (M) is perhaps the best. Closed Mon. *Dom Pedro* (closed Mon.) and *Santa Cruz,* both (M), provide good local food.

CURIA. *Das Termas* (M), tel. 52185. 45 rooms with bath. Pool. *Palace* (M), tel. 52131. 122 rooms with bath. Pool. A famous spa resort.

FIGUEIRA DA FOZ. *Estalagem da Piscina* (E), tel. 22420. 20 rooms with bath. Pool. *Grande Hotel* (E), tel. 22146. 91 rooms with bath. *Aparthoteis Atlantico and Sotto-Mayor* (M), tel. 22539. Very good service flats with wonderful view. *Hotel da Praia* (I), tel. 22082. 65 rooms with bath. Breakfast only. Several other hotels and pensions. Splendid beach and casino.
Restaurants. *Calema* (E) is open for dinner only. Live music, floor show. *Abrigo da Montanha* (M) is situated just outside town. Superb view. Closed Mon.

GUARDA. *Hotel de Turismo* (M), tel. 22205. 105 rooms with bath, pool.

LAMEGO. *Estalagem do Lamego* (E), tel. 62162. 7 rooms with bath. *Hotel do Parque* (I), tel. 62105. 33 rooms. Near N.S. dos Remedios.

LEIRIA. *Hotel Euro-Sol* (M), tel. 24101. 54 rooms with bath. Pool. *Lis* (I), tel. 22108. 41 rooms with bath. Breakfast only, old-fashioned. In center of town.

LUSO. *Grande Hotel das Termas* (M), tel. 93450. 158 rooms with bath, magnificent spring-water pool. A famous spa near Buçaco. Several pensions.

SERRA DA ESTRELA. *Pousada de São Lourenço* (E), tel. 47150. Two miles from Penhas Douradas, between Manteigas and Gouveia, altitude 4,500 feet, picturesque and comfortable. 11 rooms all with bath. Check to see if it is open. *Hotel de Manteigas* (M), tel. 47114. 26 rooms with bath. Superb location.

VISEU. *Hotel Grão Vasco* (E), tel. 23511. 88 rooms with bath, attractive. Pool. *Avenida* (I), tel. 23432. 40 rooms with bath. Several pensions and restaurants.

Douro

Douro's capital is Oporto, and Oporto's capital is port. The whole province owes its wealth to that wonderful wine, made from the grapes that ripen all along the scorching, terraced slopes of the Douro River; Henry of Burgundy, a Duke of Portucale (hence the name), brought in the vines in the 11th century.

Try to visit this province of Portugal in late September, because this is the way you've always imagined a wine harvest. Watch the "must" poured into enormous casks and loaded on the lorries or, now more rarely, on the *rabelos,* strange, Phoenician-looking boats.

Oporto, though now surrounded by urban sprawl, is a thriving bourgeois city, grown rich on the grape and its natural harbor. For many years, a royal edict forbade nobles to build within the city walls, hence the ascendancy of commerce and artisanship. The chief ornaments of Oporto are its gardens, filled with roses and camellias, and the river Douro itself, with its golden green water speckled with white sails and spanned by three splendid bridges. Of these, the most interesting is the two-level Dom Luis Bridge. The Dona Maria Bridge, a filigree of steel, was built by Eiffel; the impressive Ponte da Arrabida was inaugurated in 1964.

See here the Romanesque church of São Martinho da Cedofeita, the oldest in Portugal, and the church of the Clerigos, which dominates the city with its 10-story tower. São Francisco's fantastic gilded woodcarvings are worth seeing as are those in Santa Clara. Museums worth a look include the charming Romantic, the Ethnographic, and the Soares dos Reis.

The wine lodges are across the river at Vila Nova de Gaia, on the slopes of which Wellington assembled his troops for the attack on Oporto in the Peninsular War against Napoleon.

Popular beach resorts in the environs of Oporto include Foz do Douro at the river mouth, Póvoa de Varzim, an exceedingly picturesque fishing community, Espinho, Ofir and Miramar, a pleasant little family beach with a few hotels and a golf course. All have pools as bathing in the Atlantic can be dangerous and the sea is polluted.

PRACTICAL INFORMATION FOR DOURO

ESPINHO. *Hotel Praia Golfe* (E), tel. 720630. 119 rooms with bath. On a scale seen nowhere else in Portugal except the Algarve. Pool. *Hotel Espinho* (M), tel. 720002. 32 rooms with bath in delightful art nouveau setting. Breakfast only. Several other hotels and pensions. Two superb golf courses, pool, conference rooms, casino and excellent restaurant (E).

MATOSINHOS. *Porto Mar* (I), tel. 932104. 32 rooms with bath, in this colorful fishing village near Oporto. Breakfast only.
Restaurants. *Majára* (E). Closed Wed. *Marajo* (M). Closed Tues.

MIRAMAR. *Hotel Mirasol* (M), tel. 9622665. 25 rooms with bath. Several good restaurants.

OFIR. *Estalagem Parque do Rio* (E), tel. 961521. 36 rooms. *Hotel de Ofir* (E), tel. 961383. 220 rooms. *Pinhal* (E), tel. 961473. 89 rooms. All have rooms with bath, heated pools, and are on or near the superb beach.

OPORTO. *Infante de Sagres* (L), tel. 28101. 82 rooms with bath. *Meridien* (L), tel. 668860. 227 rooms with bath. Oporto's latest luxury hotel. *Batalha* (E), tel. 20571. 147 rooms with bath. *Castor* (E), tel. 570014. 58 rooms with bath. *Dom Henrique* (E), tel. 25755. 102 rooms with a panoramic 15th floor roof restaurant. *Grande Hotel do Porto* (M), tel. 28176. 100 rooms with bath. *Imperio* (M), tel. 26861. 95 rooms with bath. *Residencias* and pensions all over town.

Restaurants. *Escondidinho* (E), a countrywide famous restaurant, unpretentious outside, tip-top cuisine. *Portucale* (E), the roof-top restaurant of Albergaria Miradouro, deluxe. *Acquario Marisqueiro* (M), mainly seafood. *Neptuno* (I), for good cheap seafood.

POVÓA DE VARZIM. *Vermar* (E), tel. 61041. 208 rooms with bath. Several restaurants; pool, many facilities. *Grande* (M), tel. 62061. 106 rooms with bath. On the sea. Casino.

Minho

For the tourist with the taste and leisure to explore out-of-the-way places, the lesser-known provinces of Portugal can be richly rewarding. Minho, bounded by Spain, the Atlantic and the Douro River, has the most colorful folk costumes, the loveliest landscapes, and the liveliest peasants of all. Their rapid whirling folk dances, the *Vira* and others, are performed to the strange music of various country instruments, the rhythm for which is provided by a split cane or *caninha*. Check with your hotel what local fairs are on and enjoy the good food of the Minho. Renaissance Viana, baroque Braga and medieval Guimarães all preserve their epochal charm intact, and all are worth a visit by the tourist in search of the unspoiled. The Peneda-Geres National Park extends over some 70,000 hectares along the Spanish frontier, where wild boar, wolves, civit cats and a unique breed of wild ponies roam in wooded valleys and golden eagles hover over the mountain summits.

Trás-os-Montes

If you have come as far as the Minho, venture into Portugal's least known province, Trás-os-Montes—Over the Mountains—which is bounded by the upper reaches of the Douro to the south, Spain to the east and north and the river Tamego to the west. It is beautiful in its wild grandeur and still remote from the rest of the country. The main roads are now good. Drive through Murça with its iron-age pig in the middle of town and on through the splendid high rolling country with groves of sweet chestnut and cherry trees to Braganza and Miranda-do-Douro, both fascinating and strange. They are so near to Spain that they both have frontier posts, the former at Quintanilha, some miles away, the latter almost in the city, but they are little used.

PRACTICAL INFORMATION FOR MINHO AND TRÁS-OS-MONTES

BRAGA (Minho Province). *Elevador* (E), tel. 25011. 25 rooms with bath at Bom Jesus do Monte outside the town. Pool. *Turismo* (E), tel. 27091. 132 rooms with bath. Pool. *Caranda* (M), tel. 97027. 100 rooms with bath. *Francfort* (I), tel. 22648. 16 rooms some with bath, good restaurant, central. Parking.

Restaurants. *Conde D. Henrique* (M). Closed Wed. *S. Frutuoso* (M). Closed Mon.

BRAGANZA (Trás-os-Montes Province). *Pousada de S. Bartolomeu* (E), tel. 22493. 15 rooms with bath, a few miles from the Spanish border. *Bragança* (M), tel. 22579. 42 rooms with bath.
Restaurant. *Restaurant Arca de Noé* (I), good local food.

CALDAS DE GERÊS (Minho Province). For the National Park. *Parque* (M), tel. 65112. 62 rooms, most with bath. Pool. *Termas* (M), tel. 65143. 31 rooms with bath. Several other (I) hotels and pensions.

GUIMARÃES (Minho Province). *Pousada de Sta. Maria da Oliveira* (L), tel. 412157. 16 rooms with bath. Situated in old palace. *Pousada de Sta. Marinha* (L), tel. 418380. 55 rooms with bath, in old convent. Lovely view; a bit out of town.

MIRANDA DO DOURO (Trás-os-Montes Province). *Pousada de S. Catarina* (L), tel. 42255. 12 rooms with bath. *Pensão Planalto* (M), tel. 42362. 43 rooms with bath.
Restaurant. *Virabar* (E), for good food.

POVÓA DAS QUARTAS (Beira Province). *Pousada de Santa Barbara* (E), tel. 52252. 16 rooms with bath near Oliveira do Hospital.

VALENÇA DO MINHO (Minho Province). *Pousada de São Teotónio* (E), tel. 22252. A mile from the Spanish border, 16 rooms with bath, inside castle walls.

VIANA DO CASTELO (Minho Province). *Afonso III* (E), tel. 24123. 89 rooms with bath. *Parque* (E), tel. 24151. 118 rooms with bath, pool. *Santa Luzia* (E), tel. 22192. 48 rooms with bath, in refurbished hotel set in extensive gardens. Pool. Reasonable restaurants all over the town.

VILA NOVA DE CERVEIRA. *Estalagem da Boega* (E), Quinta do Outeiral, Gondarem (tel. 951231). 30 rooms with bath. Pool. Excellent food. *Pousada de D. Diniz* (E), tel. 95601. 29 rooms with bath, in an old castle.

The Alentejo

Alentejo, the largest province, is the granary of Portugal. Her vast forests furnish the country's most important export product, cork. The country fairs in this hospitable region are especially animated. You might try the one at Estremoz, held every Saturday in the Rossio, the main square, or the great fair at Vila Viçosa at the end of May. In this city is the fine palace of the Dukes of Braganza which is open to the public. It contains beautiful porcelain, tapestries and furniture. Castelo de Vide and Marvão are both lovely, untouched hill towns with fine castles.

At Évora, you can trace the cycles of history in stone. The graceful columns and marble capitals of the temple of Diana will remind you that the Romans were firmly established in the peninsula. But Évora has in addition a fine Romanesque cathedral, a fortified Gothic chapel, and the ruins of the palace where Manuel the Fortunate received Vasco da Gama.

PRACTICAL INFORMATION FOR ALENTEJO

CASTELO DE VIDE. *Hotel Sol e Serra* (M), tel. 91301. 51 rooms with bath. Pool. Good food and local wine.
Restaurant. *D. Pedro V* (M).

ELVAS. *Estalagem D. Sancho II* (E), tel. 22686. 24 rooms with bath. *Pousada de Santa Luzia* (E), tel. 22194. 11 rooms, 9 with bath. Exceptional food. Just outside city walls and 4 miles from Spanish border. *Hotel D. Luis* (M), tel.

22756, 46 rooms with bath. Pool. *Restaurant Aqueduto* (I), near huge 15th cent. aqueduct.

ESTREMOZ. *Pousada Rainha Santa Isabel* (L), tel. 22618. In an old castle, 23 airconditioned rooms with bath. *Hotel Alentejano* (I), tel. 22717. 21 rooms. Breakfast only. In huge main square. *Pensão Restaurant Estremoz* (I), tel. 22834. 9 rooms. In same square.
Restaurant. *Restaurant Aguias D'Ouro* (M). In main square.

ÉVORA. *Pousada dos Lóios* (L), tel. 24051. In the romantic setting of an ancient convent by the ruins of the Temple of Diana. 28 rooms with bath. *Planicie* (M), tel. 24026. 33 rooms with bath. *Santa Clara* (I), tel. 24141. 21 rooms with bath. Central, quiet.
Restaurants. *Cozinha de Santo Humberto* (E). Good regional food. Closed Thurs. *Fialho* (E). Very good food and wine. Closed Mon. *O Gião* (M). Recommended for regional cuisine. Closed Mon.

MARVÃO. *Pousada de Santa Maria* (E), tel. 93201. 9 rooms with bath. Delicious Alentejo food. *Estalagem D. Dinis* (M). 8 attractive rooms with bath. Restaurant.

PORTALEGRE. *Hotel Dom João III* (M), tel. 21192. 56 rooms with bath. *Mansão Alto Alentejo* (I), tel. 22290. In old part of town. Breakfast only.
Restaurant. *O Alpendre* (M). Closed Mon.

VILA NOVA DE MILFONTES. *O Castelo* (L), tel. 96108. 12 rooms with bath in private castle overlooking the Mira estuary. *Moinho da Asneira* (M), tel. 96182. Service rooms and apartments. Pool, water sports.

The Algarve

The brilliantly tinted, aromatic Algarve is the exotic southernmost province, indelibly marked by centuries of Arab occupation. Sun worshippers love it in the almost tropical heat of summer. But the best time to come is at the beginning of February, when the whole place is a sea of white almond blossoms. The flat-roofed white houses, the fig and palm trees, will remind you of Morocco. The many excellent golf courses are very reasonable in price and set in lovely unspoilt country near first-class hotels or tourist complexes with fine pools, tennis, boating and other sports. The three casinos are located at Monte Gordo, Montes de Alvor and Vilamoura.

The port of Olhão, where sardine-canning is big business, is easy on the eye, though a bit hard on the olfactory senses. The entire Barlavento coast to the west of Faro is highly picturesque, ranging from golden, peaceful beaches to the jagged cliffs and roaring waves at Sagres.

Faro, the capital, with an international airport, is roughly in the center of the coast line which stretches a hundred miles in length from Sagres in the west to the Spanish frontier. Faro, now the seat of the bishop instead of the old city of Silves, was a great Moorish center until its capture by King Afonso III in 1249 ended Muslim rule in the country. The Praia de Faro, a long sandy islet, is reached by boat or road.

Other places of interest are Tavira, an enchanting town descending to the River Sequa which can be crossed by a Roman bridge; the 18th-century palace of Estoi near extensive Roman remains at Milreu, inland from Faro; Albufeira, still charming in spite of being the most popular resort in the Algarve; Lagos; and, finally, the focal points of Sagres and Cape St. Vincent on the extreme southwest corner of the province. It was at Sagres that Prince Henry the Navigator plotted and planned the sea routes taken in the 15th century by all the early Portuguese explorers down the then unknown western shores of Africa.

If the Algarve coast is too hot, you have only to mount to the cool heights of the Monchique Range a few miles inland, where there are quiet footpaths among waterfalls and an amazing variety of trees.

Algarve, Portugal's most developed tourist area, contains a huge selection of holiday accommodation, including rental villas with domestic service and pools. There are camping sites all along the coast.

PRACTICAL INFORMATION FOR THE ALGARVE

ALBUFEIRA. *Hotel da Balaia* (L), tel. 52681. 229 airconditioned rooms, bar, pool, nightclub, tennis, shops and furnished bungalows. Three miles east, on clifftop. *Aldeia das Acoteias* (E), tel. 66267. 302 apartments, 24 villas. Pool, tennis, nightclub. *Estalagem do Cerro* (E), tel. 52191. 51 lovely rooms. *Albufeira Jardim* (E), tel. 52092. 174 one-, two- and three-room apartments and a good restaurant. Heated pool. *Sol e Mar* (E), tel. 52121. 74 rooms, 2 bars, nightclub, pool, noisy but overlooks the beach. *Hotel da Aldeia* (M), tel. 55031. 99 rooms. Pool, nightclub. *Boavista* (M), tel. 52175, on hillside. Has rooms and apartments, restaurant with a glorious view. Pool. *Rocamar* (M), tel. 52611. 91 rooms. *Baltum* (I), tel. 52106. 26 rooms, noisy but near beach, with annexe of 23 rooms. All rooms have baths. There is a large number of apartments with swimming pools, pensions and restaurants etc.

Restaurants. Albufeira boasts a large number of restaurants; check out the price lists displayed in the windows. *O Cabaz da Praia* (M), tel. 52137. On clifftop, lovely sea view, very popular. Closed Sat. dinner, Sun. *Sir Harry's Bar* (M) off the main square, an English pub with a friendly owner. An international rendezvous. *A Ruina* (M), tel. 52094. Unusual setting, good seafood from the local fishmarket next door.

ARMAÇÃO DE PERA. *Hotel Garbe* (E), tel. 55187. 104 rooms. On the beach, good food. *Viking* (E), tel. 32336. 92 rooms, each with fridge. A bit out of town.

FARO. *Casa Lumena* (E), tel. 22028. 12 rooms with bath, in fine old house. Closed Sun. *Eva* (E), tel. 24054. 146 rooms, rooftop restaurant. Pool. Free bus to Faro Island beach. *Faro* (M), tel. 22076. 52 rooms with bath. Several pensions.

Restaurants. *Al-Faghar* (E), tel. 23740. Good food in an old house. *Cidade Velha* (E), Largo da Sé 19 (tel. 27145). Highly recommended. *Kappra* (E), tel. 23366. In town center. Closed Sat. and Sun. *Lady Susan* (E), tel. 28857. English-owned, popular.

LAGOS. *Golfinho* (E), Praia de Dona Ana (tel. 63001). 262 rooms with bath. Pool. Long flight of steps down to beach. *Hotel de Lagos* (E), tel. 62011. 273 rooms with bath. Pool. *Meia Praia* (M), tel. 62001. 66 rooms with bath. Pool. Out of town but near Palmares golf course. *São Cristovão* (M), tel. 63051. 77 rooms with bath. Modern, breakfast only.

Restaurants. *Alpendre* (E), tel. 62705. One of the best in Algarve; dinners only. *Kalunga* (E), Rua Marques de Pombal. Excellent fish.

MONCHIQUE. *Albergaria Lageado* (E), tel. 92206. 21 rooms with bath at Caldas de Monchique (spa) in a valley. *Estalagem Abrigo da Montanha* (E), tel. 92131. 6 rooms with bath. Superb views.

MONTECHORO. *Aldeamento Montechoro* (E), tel. 52651. 61 service villas and apartments. Pool, tennis. *Hotel Montechoro* (E), tel. 52651. 362 rooms with bath. Pool, 3 restaurants, excellent.

MONTE GORDO. Casino. *Hotel Alcazar* (E), tel. 42184. 95 rooms. *Vasco da Gama* (E), tel. 44321. 165 rooms. *Navegadores* (M), tel. 42490. 214 rooms. All rooms have baths, all hotels have pools.

MONTES DE ALVOR. *Penina Golf Hotel* (L), tel. 22051/8. 202 rooms with bath, excellent food, casino, Olympic-sized pool, tennis, bus to beach, 18-hole golf course (on Eurogolf Circuit), 2 nine-hole courses. Located between Portimão and Lagos.

OLHAS D'AGUA. Restaurant. *La Cigale* (E), tel. 52607. One of the best restaurants in the Algarve.

PORTIMÃO. *Estalagem Miradouro* (M), tel. 23011. 30 rooms with bath. *Globo* (M), tel. 22151/4. 68 rooms with bath. Several pensions.
Restaurants. *Alfredo's* (E). Dinner only. Closed Tues. *7 Mares* (M), good spot. A number of small, inexpensive places on the quay serve delicious grilled fresh sardines.

PRAIA DE ALVOR. *Hotel D. João II* (E), tel. 20135. 220 rooms with bath; 18 suites. Pool. *Torralta Holiday Club* (I), tel. 20511. 644 apartments, plus shopping center, nightclub, and pools; very good value.

PRAIA DO CARVOEIRO. *Hotel Dom Sancho* (E), tel. 57301. 47 rooms with bath. *Quinta do Paraíso* (E), tel. 57278. 116 superb service apartments. Pool, tennis.
Restaurant. *Castelo* (E), tel. 57218. Excellent food. Closed Thurs.

PRAIA DA FALÉSIA. *Hotel Alfamar* (E), tel. 66341. 264 rooms with bath. *Apartamentos* and *Villas Alfamar* (I), tel. 66351. 70 self-service villas and apartments with pool, tennis, riding, nightclub.

PRAIA DE LUZ. *Luz Bay Club* (E), tel. 63045. 131 service villas. Pool, tennis, nightclub, restaurant; very well managed.

PRAIA DA QUARTEIRA. *Hotel Quarteira Sol* (E), tel. 34421. 98 rooms with bath. Pool, nightclub. *D. José* (I), tel. 34310. 134 rooms with bath. Pool, nightclub. Several smaller hotels and pensions. *Apartamentos Quarteira Sol* (M), tel. 34421. 138 serviced apartments. Pool, tennis.

PRAIA DA ROCHA. *Algarve* (L), tel. 24001/8. 219 airconditioned rooms. Pool, etc. *Alealà* (M), tel. 24062. 20 rooms. *Jupiter* (M), tel. 22401/5. 144 rooms, pool and nightclub.

PRAIA DOS TRÊS IRMÃOS. *Hotel Alvor Praia* (L), tel. 24020/9. 201 rooms with bath. Pool, tennis, nightclub, airconditioning. *Delfim* (E), tel. 27171. 312 rooms with bath. Pool, tennis. *Aldeamento Prainha* (M), tel. 20561. 63 apartments. The finest pool in the Algarve, tennis.

SAGRES. *Pousada do Infante* (L), tel. 64222/3. 15 rooms with bath, high above the sea. *Hotel da Baleeira* (M), tel. 64212/3. 108 rooms with bath. Pool.

SANTA BARBARA DE NEXE. *Hotel La Reserve* (L), tel. 91474. 20 airconditioned suites with bath, kitchenette, terrace. 2 pools. Tennis. 5-star restaurant.

SÃO BRÁS DE ALPORTEL. *Pousada de Sao Brás* (E), tel. 42305. 21 rooms with bath, 8 in annex. Lovely view.

TAVIRA. *Hotel-Apartamento Eurotel* (M), tel. 22041. 75 service apartments. Pool, tennis.

VALE DO LOBO-ALMANSIL. *Dona Filipa* (L), Vale do Lobo (tel. 94141/2/3). 129 rooms with bath. Pool. 18-hole golf course on the Henry Longhurst Eurogolf Circuit. Superb golf club. *Aldeamento do Vale do Lobo* (L), tel. 94145. 161 service villas. Pool, tennis, nightclub.

VILAMOURA. Two 18-hole golf courses. Casino. *Atlantis* (L), tel. 32535. 305 rooms with bath. Pool, tennis. *Dom Pedro* (E), tel. 35450. 261 rooms with bath. Pool, tennis, near yachting marina. *Motel Vilamoura* (M), tel. 32321. 52 rooms with bath. Large number of service apartments, all with pools.

ROMANIA

There is much about Romania that is extremely unusual. Its culture, especially its peasant culture, is unique. Similarly, though the country bears many of the industrial and urban scars common to any European state, there are still many regions that boast a way of life that barely exists outside folklore museums elsewhere in Europe. The remoteness of this way of life naturally indicates much unspoilt and splendid scenery. Additionally, influences both external and internal have endowed Romania with a fine miscellany of monuments.

To deal first with the vital statistics, Romania has an area of 91,700 sq. miles (237,500 sq. km), and is the twelfth largest country in Europe, similar in size to Yugoslavia, Great Britain, West Germany (or Oregon). The "Latin island" is bounded by two seas, one actual and the other metaphorical. The first is, of course, the Black Sea, to which Romania contributes about 150 miles (245 km) of coastline. The other is the "sea" of non-Latin countries that hem in Romania on every side—Bulgaria to the south, Yugoslavia to the west, Hungary to the northwest and the USSR to the north and northeast.

Romania's history has been a troubled affair. Roman domination, barbarian invasions, Hungarian and Habsburg rule and Turkish incursions have all left their mark. Bitter struggles for independence in the 19th century won a considerable degree of autonomy and in 1878, full independence for much of the country, extending to the whole in 1918. Between the two World Wars, an embryonic democracy was established. After "liberation" by the Soviet Army at the end of World War II, Romania became a Communist republic. Despite some improvements in industry, medicine and education, foreign debts and an erratic economy have hampered progress. A concerted effort to reduce massive debts is meeting with some success, but has meant many restrictions for the Romanians. Western visitors, though receiving preferential treatment, can hardly remain unaware of shortages in shops and long lines for basic necessities; even more of streets unlit at night, the early closing of restaurants, and availability of hot water in hotels limited to certain hours. The vagaries of a mysterious bureaucracy, and all the manifold frustrations it engenders, also make themselves felt. Services can, and often do, lack polish. As a visitor to Romania, it is important to approach the country with an open mind. There is much here that is fascinating and beautiful.

PRACTICAL INFORMATION FOR ROMANIA

WHAT WILL IT COST. The monetary unit is the *leu* (plural *lei*), which is divided into 100 *bani*. Banknotes circulate in denominations of 5, 10, 25, 50 and 100 lei, and there are coins of 1, 3 and 5 lei and 5, 10, 15 and 25 bani.

At the present tourist rate of exchange there are 12.50 lei to the U.S.$, 16.20 to the pound sterling. Subject to change. Visitors must exchange a sum of $10 or its equivalent per person per day for the number of days for which they have requested a visa. Tourists with prepaid services and children under 14 years are exempt from this obligatory currency exchange.

Additional hard, freely convertible currency or travelers' checks may be exchanged inside Romania at the tourist rate. An unofficial exchange rate exists on the black market, but the risk of penalties and general unpleasantness resulting from being caught makes any involvement highly undesirable.

You may bring in any amount and kind of foreign currency, including travelers' checks, and freely exchange it at branches of the *National Bank of Romania,* at most border crossings, and at some hotels. The import and export of Romanian currency is not permitted. All exchanges beyond the minimum daily exchange rate will be refunded in hard currency on your departure.

Credit cards (American Express, Eurocard and the like) may be used to exchange currency and are accepted in most major hotels and restaurants.

A typical day might cost two people:

Hotel, moderate, with breakfast	500 lei
Lunch, moderate, excluding drinks	140
Dinner, moderate, with wine	250
2 coffees each	24
Tram (4 rides)	4
Taxi (about 5 km)	36
Theater or opera	50
Miscellaneous 10%	90
	1094 lei

HOW TO GO. All foreign travel to Romania is organized by the Romanian National Tourist Office, which is run by the Ministry of Tourism. They have a number of offices overseas (see below for addresses), but tours to Romania cannot be booked through them but must be made via a travel agent accredited by the National Tourist Office. There are a good many of these, however, so booking your vacation should prove no problem, and a list of all officially-approved agents is available free from the National Tourist Office. All these will also be able to arrange visas, for which there is a fee of a few pounds or dollars.

Romania is much better geared to the organized tour than to the independent traveler, for the tourist industry revolves around pre-paid vouchers. Without them you will need to exercise extra patience as well as fulfill the obligatory currency exchange of $10 per day. A few tour operators offer more flexible arrangements for individual travelers, especially motorists, with pre-paid vouchers for accommodations, meals and gasoline. Some agents make a point of featuring art-treasure, walking or other special-interest activities, and these will be indicated in the list from the National Tourist Office.

The addresses of Romanian National Tourist Offices overseas are:

In the US: 573 Third Ave., New York, NY 10016; and Romanian Commercial Office, 575–577 Third Ave., New York, NY 10016.

In Canada: Embassy of Romania and Consular Office, 655 Rideau St., KIN 6A3, Ottawa, Ontario.

In the UK: 29 Thurloe Place, London S.W.7 2HP.

 WHEN TO COME. Bucharest should be visited in the spring. The Black Sea coast season is from June to September. A skiing holiday in the Carpathians is best taken January through March, a walking holiday in summer. **Climate.** Moderate on coast, hot inland in summer though cooler in the mountains. Winters are coldest in mountains, warmest on the coast.

Average maximum daily temperatures in Fahrenheit and centigrade:

Bucha-rest	Jan.	Feb.	Mar.	Apr.	May	June	July	Aug.	Sept.	Oct.	Nov.	Dec.
F°	34	39	50	64	73	81	86	86	77	64	50	39
C°	1	4	10	18	23	27	30	30	25	18	10	4

 SPECIAL EVENTS. *March,* the Kiss Fair, Arad; *May,* Week of the Lads, Braşov; *July,* Young Girl's Fair, Mount Gaina; *August,* Celebrations at Mt. Cealău, Bukovina; *September,* Folklore Festival, Bucharest. **National Holidays.** Jan. 1 (New Year's Day); Jan. 2; May 1 (Labor Day); May 2; Aug. 23 (Liberation); Aug. 24.

HEALTH CERTIFICATES. Not required of foreign visitors.

 GETTING TO ROMANIA. By Plane. Both *Pan Am* and *Tarom,* the Romanian national airline, have flights from New York to Bucharest. From London, *Tarom* flies three times a week to Bucharest. Charters fly direct to Mamaia. There is a bus service from Bucharest airport to the town terminal costing 8 lei, and a public bus costing 2 lei from near the airport.

By Train. Bucharest can be reached via the *Balt-Orient Express* from Stockholm and Malmö via East Germany, Czechoslovakia and Hungary, by the *Wiener Walzer* from Vienna, the *Orient Express* from Paris, Munich and Vienna, etc. From London, the journey takes 2 days.

By Car. Romania may be entered by car from the USSR, Hungary, Yugoslavia and Bulgaria. The following are convenient border points and distances to Bucharest: (from Hungary) Borş, 400 miles on DN1–E15, or Nădlac, 392 miles on DN7; (from Yugoslavia) Moraviţa 389 miles; or the even shorter route over the new Iron Gates Dam bridge at Turnu Severin; (from Bulgaria) Calafat (via Danube ferry) 200 miles, Giurgiu (Danube bridge) 40 miles, Negru Vodă, 197 miles, or Vama Veche (on Black Sea coast) 194 miles; (from USSR) Albiţa, 261 miles or Siret, 296.

No customs documents are required. Green Card insurance is recognized, as are international or national drivers licenses.

By Boat. Although cruise ships call at Constanza on the Black Sea coast, there is no regular passenger ship service to Romania. On the Danube, cruises operate from Passau or Vienna to the Danube Delta.

 CUSTOMS. Personal belongings may be brought in duty-free, including such items as two cameras with black and white or color films, 24 rolls of film, two rolls of movie film, a small movie camera, portable radio, portable typewriter, etc. Each adult may also import duty-free 300 cigarettes or 300 gr. of tobacco, 2 liters of liquor and 5 liters of wine. Gifts to the value of 2,000 lei may be brought in tax-free.

Gifts and articles to the total value of 1,000 lei may be exported duty-free.

 HOTELS. Hotel rates are generally government controlled and standardized throughout. In due course, Romania will change to the international star system of hotel classification, but for the moment you are most likely to encounter the old system of Deluxe A and B, 1st category A and B, 2nd category, etc. This is misleading for most Western visitors whose expectations of 1st category will rarely be met, and we have therefore graded hotels in our lists with the following equivalents: Deluxe A, approximating to 5-star (L); Deluxe B, 4-star (E); 1st category A, 3-star (M); and 1st category B, 2-star (I). Prices for two people in a double room with bath or shower and including breakfast are as follows: (L) $75–94, (E) $54–75, (M) $30–54, (I) $20–30.

Standards are rarely comparable to those in the West, but neither are prices. Plumbing in particular can be erratic and, at the time of writing, economies also mean that hot water may only be available between certain hours. These should be posted up at reception or in the room; if not, make enquiries.

The national tourist offices, *Carpați* and *Litoral,* and their branches will arrange accommodations for those who have not booked in advance. Private accommodations are available in a limited number of places through local tourist offices.

 CAMPING. There are about 100 camp sites in Romania. All main towns and resorts have them. The best appointed are those for which the Romanian Automobile Club *(ACR)* issues prepaid tourist coupons (valid May through September).

 SPAS. The spas and health resorts of Romania are world famous, particularly for the "anti-aging" compounds and treatment available in Bucharest at the Flora Hotel and others. Of the 160 spas in the country, the most important include: (on the Black Sea coast) Eforie Nord, Mangalia and Neptun; (inland) Felix, Herculane, Calimanești and Vatra Dornei.

 RESTAURANTS. The cost of meals is most reasonable, and you will not often pay over 150 lei except at deluxe establishments, wine and tip included. Figure 70 to 90 lei for a moderate (M) restaurant and 40 to 70 lei for an inexpensive (I) one. You can eat for much less at a self-service *bufet express* or *lacto vegetarian* snack bar.

Food and Drink. There has been a noticeable, if patchy, improvement in standard and choice of late. Deep-fried food and "french fries with everything" still dominate too many menues, but a genuine effort to promote some of Romania's excellent specialties is also evident. Look out for soups such as *ciorba de perisoare,* a soup with meatballs, *ciorba taraneasca* with meat and lots of vegetables, *bors,* giblet soup, and richly varied fish soups. Sour cream or eggs are often added to soups.

The Romanians' all-purpose staple is *mamaliga,* a highly versatile cornmeal mush, which can be served in countless different ways. *Tocana* is a stew made with pork, beef or mutton, seasoned abundantly with onions, and served with mamaliga. *Ghiveci,* also called "monastic hodge-podge" when it has no meat, is a preparation of over twenty vegetables cooked in oil and served hot or cold. Another typical dish is Moldavian *parjoale*—flat meat patties, highly spiced, served with a wide variety of garnishes. Another entrée greatly in demand is *sarmale*—pork balls wrapped in cabbage leaves.

One great specialty of Romania is charcoal-grilled meat, often in the form of sausages. Among the countless varieties are *mititei,* highly seasoned mincemeat grilled to order in cafés and restaurants, and *patricieni,* resembling frankfurters.

Enormously popular are such marine savories as *nisetru la gratar* (grilled Black Sea sturgeon), *raci* (crayfish), and *scrumbii la gratar* (grilled herring).

Fruit and fruit juices are delicious and inexpensive, but not easily available. Among the Romanian desserts you will enjoy trying are *placinte cu poale in briu,* rolled cheese pies, and Moldavian *cozonac* (brioche) or *pasca,* a sweet cream cheesecake. *Baclava, cataiff* and other cakes of Oriental origin are now definitely part of Romanian cuisine.

Entrées are traditionally accompanied by a small glass of *tzuica*, the usually powerful plum brandy whose strength, dryness and aroma all vary according to region and locality. Of Romania's distinguished wines, best-known (and winners in international competition) are the *Pinot Noir* and *Chardonnay* from the Murfatlar vineyards near the Black Sea. Also highly recommended are the *Grasa* and *Feteasca* from Moldavia's Cotnari vineyards. The availability of coffee is erratic, and the Romanians can't make good tea!

 TIPPING. A 12% service charge is added to meals in most restaurants. Leave something extra (about 10%) if the service has been exceptionally good. Porters and taxi drivers should be given 5–10 lei.

 MAIL. Airmail rate to the US is 16 lei for a letter, 13 lei for a postcard; to Britain 11 lei for a letter, 8 for a postcard, but check before mailing.

If you wish to place a long-distance call from your hotel be sure to check the hotel's service charge.

 CLOSING TIMES. Shops usually open from 9 or 10 A.M. to 6 or 8 P.M.; food shops open earlier but close for some hours in the middle of the day. Supermarkets open daily 8 A.M. to 8 P.M. Most are open Saturday mornings and some also Sunday mornings. Banks are open 9 A.M. to 12 noon and 1 P.M. to 3 P.M. Mondays through Fridays, 9 A.M. to 12 noon Saturdays.

 USEFUL ADDRESSES. In Bucharest: *US Embassy,* Tudor Arghezi 7–9; *Canadian Embassy,* Nicolae Iorga 36; *British Embassy,* Strada Jules Michelet 24; *Tarom* (Romanian Airlines), Strada Brezoianu 10; *Carpati National Tourist Office,* Blvd Magheru 7; *Romanian Automobile Club (ACR),* Blvd Poligrafiei 3; *Navrom* (Danube river boat travel), Blvd Dinicu Goleseu 58; *Romanian National Bank,* Strada Lipscani 25.

In Mamaia: *Litoral National Tourist Office,* Hotel Bucharest.

 GETTING AROUND ROMANIA. By Plane. *Tarom* maintains regular services between Bucharest and most major towns and resorts. Fares are very reasonable. Flights leave from either Otopeni Airport (international and some domestic flights), 12 miles from city center, or from Băneasa Airport (domestic flights), 4½ miles from center. Regular airport buses.

By Train. The Romanian railway system radiates from Bucharest with the main lines going west to Timişoara, north and then west to Hungary, south to Bulgaria and north to the USSR. There is also a trunk route from the capital to the port of Constanza and the Black Sea resorts of Eforie and Mangalia. The service is partially electrified with more electrification under way.

Trains carry 1st. and 2nd. class carriages with dining and buffet cars on long distance routes. Certain expresses have obligatory reservation and require supplementary fare although the latter does not apply if tickets are purchased abroad. Getting tickets in Romania other than for local trains (simple there) is a time consuming process, so allow yourself plenty of time when buying a long distance ticket. Train travel is on the whole moderately priced.

By Car. The usual Continental rules of the road are observed, though speed limits are based on engine size. The speed limit for ordinary cars is 60 kph (37 mph) in built-up areas and 80–100 kph (50–62 mph) on all other roads. Drinking is absolutely prohibited.

There is a good and improving network of main roads—sometimes with frost damage in mountain areas. Secondary roads are good to atrocious, but take you into magnificent and unspoilt areas: keep your tank filled up and carry a spare parts kit. A thoroughly serviceable map showing roads and surfaces is available free from the tourist offices.

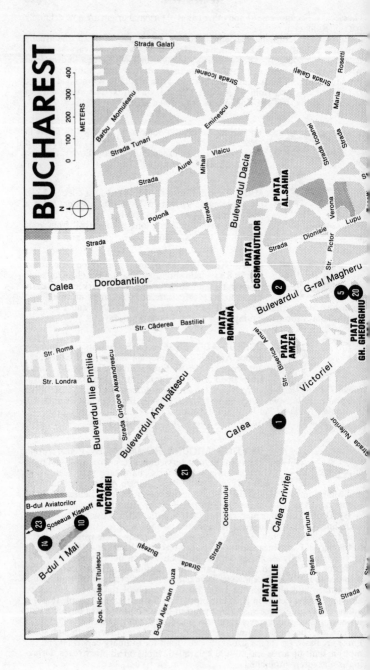

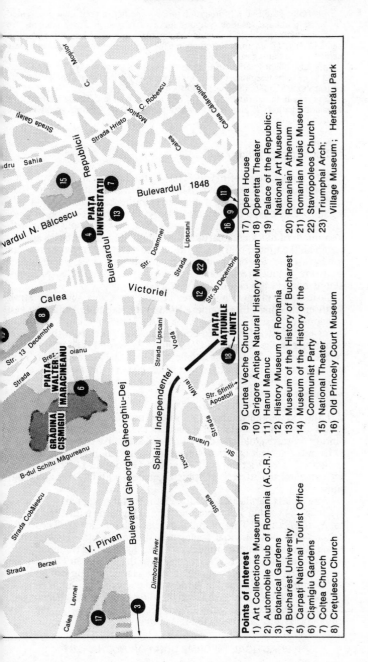

Points of Interest

1) Art Collections Museum
2) Automobile Club of Romania (A.C.R.)
3) Botanical Gardens
4) Bucharest University
5) Carpaţi National Tourist Office
6) Cişmigiu Gardens
7) Colţea Church
8) Creţulescu Church
9) Curtea Veche Church
10) Grigore Antipa Natural History Museum
11) Hanul Manuc
12) History Museum of Romania
13) Museum of the History of Bucharest
14) Museum of the History of the Communist Party
15) National Theater
16) Old Princely Court Museum
17) Opera House
18) Operetta Theater
19) Palace of the Republic; National Art Museum
20) Romanian Athenum
21) Romanian Music Museum
22) Stavropoleos Church
23) Triumphal Arch; Village Museum ; Herăstrău Park

Important: note that all foreign motorists, whether in their own or a rented car, *must* purchase gasoline coupons for hard currency. These coupons are available at border points, tourist offices and main hotels. The fly-drive arrangements of *ACR* (Romanian Automobile Club) are marketed overseas and some include a free daily gasoline allowance.

ACR also offers a variety of services to members of the AAA, AA, RAC, etc. Road signs show telephone numbers for emergency breakdown help. In Bucharest telephone 123456, outside 12345.

Cars may be hired through *Avis* at Otopeni Airport and Strada Cihoski 2, in association with *ACR* and from the main tourist offices. Charges are about $15 a day, plus mileage.

Discovering Bucharest

With a population of over 1,800,000, Bucharest can boast of being one of Europe's larger cities. Although it was inhabited more than 1,000 years ago, the hamlet of Bucharest in the vast Danube plain only began to take shape in the 14th century. From that time on, it grew rapidly. Today its 19th-century houses share the metropolis along with great modern blocks of apartment buildings, and new suburbs springing up all the time. From beside the cathedral on the city's one low hill you have a fine view of the city and the Dîmbovita River, which divides the town. A blue-green chain of park-rimmed lakes dotted with tiny islands borders the city on the northeast.

Busiest part of town is the area around the Calea Victoriei. Stroll north up this main thoroughfare from Piata Natiunile Unite and you will come to several landmarks such as the National History Museum; the charming little Cretulescu church; the headquarters of the Central Committee of the Romanian Communist Party; and the former Royal Palace, now the Socialist Republic of Romania Palace (built in 1933 and housing the fine National Art Museum). At this point you reach Piata Gheorghiu-Dej and Bucharest's grandest concert hall, the Romanian Atheneum.

For a complete contrast, turn off Calea Victoriei and into the old core of the city in the Lipiscani district, where you will find narrow shopping streets around the substantial remains of the Old Princely Court (15th century onwards), old churches and some attractive restaurants adapted from the ancient cellars of long ago. To the left along this southern section of Calea Victoriei you pass Blvd Gheorghiu-Dej from which you can enter the attractive Cişmigiu Gardens with its lakes and fountains.

More or less parallel with Calea Victoriei is the main artery formed by Blvd 1848, Blvd Balcescu, and Blvd Magheru, with their shops, hotels, the National Theater and the main office of Carpati. The northern end of Calea Victoriei comes into spacious Piaţa Victoriei from which Kiseleff Avenue continues on to the distinctive Triumphal Arch and beyond it, the extensive green spaces of the Herăstrău Park. In this municipal paradise on the shores of Lake Herastrau you can go boating, swimming, fishing or watch the world go by from pleasant lakeside restaurants. Here, too, is one of the oldest and most charming of Europe's "village" museums. Liberty Park and August 23 Park are among other pleasant oases for relaxation.

PRACTICAL INFORMATION FOR BUCHAREST

HOTELS. Note that hotels are often heavily booked in the tourist season. Apply to the *Carpaţi Tourist Office* for help if you have not booked. See page 614 for guidance on rates and categories of hotels. Those listed below have restaurants unless otherwise stated.

Bucuresti (L), Calea Victoriei 63–69 (tel. 154580). Biggest and most modern, with 442 rooms and suites, pools, keep-fit complex, sauna, and all the amenities of a top-class hotel.

Flora (L), Blvd Poligrafiei 3 (tel. 184640). 155 rooms, modern, with full facilities for geriatric (rejuvenation) program. Less central, but near Herastrau Park.

Intercontinental (L), Blvd N. Bălcescu 4 (tel. 140400). 417 rooms. Top facilities, central location.

Ambassador (E), Blvd Magheru 10 (tel. 110440). 233 rooms. Very central.

Athenée Palace (E), Strada Episcopiei 1–3 (tel. 140899). 306 rooms. A prewar *grande dame,* the most Parisian of Bucharest's hotels, central. Recently renovated.

Bulevard (E), Blvd Gh. Gheorghiu-Dej 1 (tel. 153300). 89 rooms, central.

Continental (E), Calea Victoriei 56 (tel. 145349). 53 rooms, central.

Dorobanţi (E), Calea Dorobanţi 5–9 (tel. 110860). 298 rooms, modern, central.

Lido (E), Blvd Magheru 5 (tel. 144930). 121 rooms. Another golden oldie that has well withstood the test of time, with open-air pool and terrace, very central. May be closed for restoration.

Manuc Inn (Hanul Manuc) (E), Strada 30 Decembrie 62, opposite the Old Princely Court. Built round courtyard and one of the most attractive hostelries in town, dating from early 19th century; 30 rooms.

National (E), Blvd Republicii 33 (tel. 130199). 196 rooms.

Capitol (M), Calea Victoriei 29 (tel. 140926). 80 rooms. Central.

Minerva (M), Strada Lt. Lemnea 2–4 (tel. 506010). 83 rooms. Central.

Negoiu (M), Strada 13 Decembrie 16 (tel. 155250). 90 rooms. Central.

Park (M), Blvd Poligrafiei 3 (tel. 180950). 270 rooms. Near Herăstrău Park.

Union (M), Strada 13 Decembrie 16 (tel. 132640). 220 rooms. Central.

 RESTAURANTS. In addition to hotel restaurants there is quite a wide selection, mostly at very reasonable prices, but the choice of dishes on the menu is often limited.

Berlin (E), C. Mille Str. 4. Excellent food.

Bucur (E), Poenaru Bordea Str. 2. Romanian food.

Capşa (E), Calea Victoriei 34. One of the best in town, plush and with *belle époque* atmosphere.

Mioriţa (E), Soseaua Kiseleff. Attractive situation in Herăstrău Park.

Pădurea Băneasa (E), in Baneasa Forest, towards the airport. Pleasant setting, folkloric shows.

Pescaruş (E), on lake shore in Herăstrău Park. Folk show.

Marul de Aur (M), Calea Victoriei 163. Reached through courtyard, a little less central.

Carul cu Bere (M-I), Strada Stavropoleos 5. Traditional late 19th century beer house, former meeting place of the artist set; lots of atmosphere; ground floor tavern and cellar restaurant below.

Crama Domnească (M-I), 13 Şelari St. Attractive setting in ancient cellars adjoining Old Princely Court; traditional food.

Doina (M-I), Şoseaua Kiseleff 4. Romanian food, garden terrace.

La doi Cocoşi (M-I), Şoseaua Străuleşti 6. Romanian food. About 15 km. from town.

Rapsodia (M-I), Strada Şelari 2. Another attractive cellar restaurant near Old Princely Court, decorated with old folk masks.

 CAFES. Romanians are cream cake addicts and you will find a mouthwatering selection in establishments bearing the name *cofetaria* (which do not, however, serve coffee, but usually soft drinks). For inexpensive snacks, try one of the *bufet expres* or *lacto vegetarian* (specialising in dairy products), self-service snack bars dotted about the city.

TRANSPORTATION. *Subway/underground:* the first two lines of the new subway system are now ready, totalling about 17 km. Cost is 1 leu for any distance; you insert the coin into a machine which opens a barrier. *Trams* cost 1 leu (pay as you enter); tickets for *buses* (1.75 lei) and *trolley buses* (1.50 lei) can be bought at kiosks. *Taxis* charge about 6 lei per km, plus 5 lei on starting. *Carpati* operate several *sightseeing tours* of Bucharest and surroundings.

NIGHTLIFE. Prewar Bucharest was one of Europe's most wide-open cities. After a postwar period of socialist puritanism nightlife shows definite signs of a comeback, but at the time of going to press, economic measures impose a closing time of 10.30 or 11 on restaurants. However, discos and nightclubs stay open until 1 A.M. and among the latter are the *Melody, Bucureşti* and facilities at the *Continental, Intercontinental, Athenee Palace* and *Doina.* Restaurants at most major hotels offer dancing to live (and usually very loud!) music. Parisian-type cafés and *brasseries* include the *Tosca, Ciresica, Tic-Tac,* and *Tomis* on Gheorghiu-Dej, the *Unic* on Balcescu, the *Turist* on Magheru, and the *Corso* at the Intercontinental Hotel. Also popular are the *Gradiniţa* and *Dunărea.*

ENTERTAINMENT. Opera is performed at the *Romanian Opera House* (Blvd Gheorghiu-Dej 70). The magnificent *Romanian Athenaeum* (Strada Franklin 1) is the home of two symphony orchestras. Folkloric entertainment can be enjoyed at the *Rapsodia Romana Artistic Ensemble Hall* (Strada Lipscani 53). Drama is performed at the *Caragiale National Theater* (Blvd Bălcescu 2) and at the *Comedy Theater* (Strada Mandineşti). There is also the *Tandarica Puppet Theater* (Calea Victoriei 50) and the *State Jewish Theater* (Strada Barasch 15) which gives performances in Yiddish.

MUSEUMS. The *Muzeul de Arta S.R.R.* (National Art Museum), in a former royal palace, has works by El Greco, Titian, Rembrandt, and by modern French and Romanian painters. The *Muzeul de Istoriei de România* (History Museum of Romania), in the former Central Post Office building, has beautiful displays illustrating Romanian life and history, from neolithic to modern times. The collection of objects in gold and precious stones (which can be visited separately) is quite stunning. These two museums, as well as the *Art Collections Museum* (combining several fine private collections of art treasures) are located on the Calea Victoriei. Outstanding of its kind is the *Village Museum* which has fully furnished genuine peasant houses from all parts of the country (Şoseaua Kiseleff, on the edge of Herăstrău Park). Also not to be missed is the fascinating ruined complex of the *Old Princely Court,* the *First Princely Court* in Bucharest, part of a very extensive site dating from the 15th century onwards. *Carpaţi* runs comprehensive museum tours.

SHOPPING. Comturist is the foreign trade agency for the sale of Romanian products and imported goods for hard currency only; it has many outlets in Bucharest, as well as in all towns and tourist centers. For souvenirs or simply window shopping stroll down Bucharest's main thoroughfares, Calea Victoriei and Blvd Magheru. Romania's superbly rich folk art includes rugs; embroidered sheepskin coats, blouses and scarves, and skirts; ceramics, pottery, hand-painted icons and carved wooden objects. The traditional shopping area of Lipscani boasts picturesque, varied and old-style shops within walking distance of central hotels. Look out for *Galerie de Artă* shops run by the Union of Plastic Artists *(Fondul Plastic).* Markets provide the only venue for private enterprise. The main one is at Piaţa Uniiri, open seven days a week, but best visited in the morning.

Some addresses: folk art shop at Strada Pictor Verona 1; *Bucureşti* department store, Strada Baraţiei 2; *Romarta,* Calea Victoriei 66–68, for readymade clothes, accessories, knitwear; *Melodia,* Blvd Magheru 16, sells records, wines and the famous *tzuica* liquor. Also *Bijuteria* for jewelry, *Arta Populara* for handicrafts, *Stirex* for glassware, *Dacia Bookshop* for foreign books, *Filatelia* for stamps, *Gioconda* for silks, *Hermes* for handicrafts, and *Electa* for woolens.

Discovering the Interior

Exploration of Romania will be greatly facilitated if one grasps some basic geographical distinctions. This doesn't mean that you have to memorize the names of her 39 counties, but you should broaden your focus and think in terms of six larger regions, the equivalent of such American entities as the Midwest and Deep South, or Britain's Lake District and West Country, etc. The regions in question are Wallachia, Transylvania, Moldavia, Dobrudja, Maramureș, and the Banat.

Without going into excessive detail, Wallachia (which contains Bucharest) is all Romania south of the lower range of the Carpathians except for the region fronting on the Black Sea. That is Dobrudja. Dobrudja has two other natural boundaries (the Danube to the west and its delta to the north) and one artificial one, the Bulgarian border to the south.

Moldavia, which includes Bukovina, is the Romanian northeast. It's bound on the west by the eastern range of the Carpathians and to the east by the Soviet border.

Transylvania is all Romania contained within the natural "amphitheater" of the Carpathians except for two regions. One is Maramureș, Romania's northwest corner that is bound by the U.S.S.R. and Hungary. The other is a level land called the Banat, bordering on Yugoslavia and Hungary and forming the extreme western part of the country.

The Black Sea and Danube Delta

Romanians can be justly proud of their splendid beaches, with their gentle surf and fine sands. Most popular seaside resort is Mamaia, three hours from Bucharest. Its nine-mile stretch of shore is lined with villas and hotels, well-equipped with sports facilities. As it caters mainly to group tours, you can get extremely good value here, at low cost. Constanza is a busy Black Sea port built on the ruins of the old Greek colony, Tomis, where Ovid spent his last years. Today, its narrow streets and five mosques add Oriental charm and color to an otherwise modern town. Its museums contain outstanding archeological finds. To the south lies a string of modern resorts, hardly typically Romanian but offering good amenities for a relaxed holiday, usually with a choice of sea or lake. Eforie, 14 km. from Constanza, has hotels of all categories, minigolf, tennis and other sports, with motorboat trips on Lake Techirghiol. It is a famous year-round health spa with well-equipped bathing pavilions, treating rheumatic ailments and skin diseases. Neptun, close to Comorova Forest, has a wide beach with dozens of modern hotels, good water skiing, tennis, etc., and is quieter than other seaside resorts.

In Jupiter there are several new high-rise hotels standing right on the beach. The newest resort is Venus, with neighboring Aurora, 43 kilometers from Constanza, with daring architecture. In most hotels, each room has a balcony. Farthest south, Mangalia (called Callatis in ancient times) is a town, port and resort at the same time. Two-thousand-year-old Greek and Roman remains, and old houses with wooden balconies stand next to streamlined hotels built in concrete, glass and ceramics.

Another of the region's attractions is the Danube delta, Europe's leading wildlife sanctuary. This mighty European river divides into three main arms on this final stage of its journey to the Black Sea, and the fascinating and primeval wilderness created by its waters plays host to over 300 species of birds, plus a wide variety of fish, crustaceans, mammals, and plant life. Excursions in the delta can be taken from Tulcea, the area's main population center, either by regular passenger boats, sightseeing tours or, best of all, by arrangement with the local fishermen.

PRACTICAL INFORMATION FOR THE BLACK SEA AND DANUBE DELTA

Hotels and Restaurants

CONSTANZA. Ancient and interesting Black Sea port. *Palace* (E), 132 rooms, recently renovated, with terrace overlooking the sea and tourist port of Tomis. *Continental* (M), 139 rooms. *Casa cu Lei* (House with Lions) is a restaurant in a charming converted old town house. The *Casino* (M), in ornate early 20th-century style with night bar, is by the sea.

EFORIE NORD. Beach and health resort. *Europa* (E), 242 rooms; high-rise building in small park near sea. *Delfinul, Meduza* and *Steaua de Mare,* each with 231 rooms, are all (E).

JUPITER. Offers a choice of sea or lake. *Capitol* (M), 220 rooms, open-air pool, by sea. *Cozia* (M), 200 rooms, open-air pool, by lake. *Olimpic* (M), 220 rooms, near sea. *Scoica* (M), 120 rooms, open-air pool, short stroll from sea or lakes. *Tismana* (M), 260 rooms, large complex near small lake Tisman. Restaurants include *Orizont,* open-air with folk music, and *Paradis* nightclub and disco.

MAMAIA. Top Black Sea resort. *International* (E), 100 rooms, outdoor pool, one of earliest and best, on beach. *Ambassador* (M), *Lido* (M) and *Savoy* (M) are the newest trio, grouped round open-air pools near beach, in north of resort. Next door, with similar layout, are *Amiral* (M), *Comandor* (M) and *Orfeu* (M). *București* (M), 60 rooms, open-air pool, is in resort center. *Dacia* (M), 370 rooms, near open-air pool and beach in south of resort. Nearby is high-rise *Parc* (M), 210 rooms, indoor pool. In addition, restaurants include rustic-style *Insula Ovidiu* on island; *Miorița,* Romanian food and attractive setting on lake shore; *Cherhana,* fish specialties served in Danube-delta style building on lake shore; *Satul de Vacanță* (Holiday Village), traditional Romanian architecture, featuring numerous small restaurants serving local specialties; and *Vatra,* garden restaurant in resort center.

MANGALIA. Southernmost beach and health resort on Black Sea. *Mangalia* (E), 293 rooms.

NEPTUN. Beach and health resort with lakes and extensive oak woods. *Neptun* (E), 126 rooms, pool, disco, good facilities, by one of lakes. *Doina* (M), 330 rooms, pool, full treatment facilities, some distance from sea or lakes. *Delta* (M), 94 rooms, *Dobrogea* (M), 110 rooms and *Sulina* (M), 110 rooms, are grouped near one of lakes, each with indoor pool and disco. In adjoining resort of **Olimp,** *Amfiteatru,* 330 rooms, *Belvedere,* 230 rooms, and *Panoramic,* 210 rooms, form an (E) complex with open-air pools and discos, terraced above beach. Restaurants include *Calul Balan,* with folkloric shows, and *Neptun* in typical Romanian style, both in nearby Comorova forest.

TULCEA. Modern main town of Danube delta, with ocean-going ships passing through. *Delta* (M), 117 rooms, overlooks Danube. *Egreta* (M-I), 116 rooms. A new hotel is under construction.

VENUS. Beach resort. *Cocurul* (M), 204 rooms, open-air pool, near small lake, short stroll from beach. *Raluca* (M), 132 rooms, short stroll from beach. *Silvia* (M), 128 rooms, open-air pool, near sea. The adjoining resort of Aurora rises in a series of pyramid-shaped hotels named after precious stones—such as *Agat, Coral, Diamant, Safir*—each with 100–120 rooms and with or near open-air pool, close to beach. *Cătunul* is a folk-style complex of restaurant, pastry shop and coffee house.

Museums

Constanza has some most interesting museums including the *National History and Archaeological Museum,* whose superb Treasury features unique statues, pottery, etc., from Greek, Roman and Daco-Roman cultures; the *Regional Museum, Navy Museum,* and the finest *Aquarium* in Eastern Europe. Don't miss the impressive Roman complex which includes a fabulous *Mosaic,* over 2,000 sq. meters, from the 4th century A.D. In Tulcea, the *Museum of the Danube Delta* gives an excellent introduction to this fascinating region.

The Bukovina Monasteries and Moldavia

The famed Bukovina painted monasteries are located in the northeast near the Russian border, and are most easily reached from Suceava, the regional capital. Built in the 15th and 16th centuries, the monasteries, painted with frescos inside and outside are: Voroneţ, Humor, Arbore, Suceviţa and Moldoviţa. They are each different and all enchanting, but the most exquisite is the Voronet church, with an outside wall entirely dedicated to the depiction of *The Last Judgment.* Wind and rain have slightly eroded some of the frescos, but the majority retain their vivid colors. The monastery of Putna, furthest from Suceava and extensively restored in modern times, is revered as the last resting place of Stephen the Great, the Moldavian prince who commissioned most of the monasteries and led the struggle against the Turks.

Northwest from Piatra Neamţ, the upper Bistriţa valley leads deep into the Carpathians and, especially above the man-made Bicaz Lake, brings you into a wild and lovely region full of folkloric interest. Modern hotels in small mountain resorts, such as Durău, make comfortable bases from which to explore.

Well worth visiting is the Moldavian capital of Iasi, Romania's third largest city. Iaşi has been an intellectual center since the 17th century when Moldavia was ruled by Prince Vasile Lupu, an outstanding sponsor of the arts. There is continuity in Iaşi's intellectual tradition and the palace once inhabited by the prince of Moldavia has, since 1907, been a Palace of Culture with sections devoted to art, history, ethnography, and technology. Moldavia is also home of the great Cotnari vineyards and Vaslui, 41 miles south of Iaşi, is the scene of Stephen the Great's 1475 victory over the Turks.

Transylvania

Transylvania, with the Carpathian "amphitheater" as a natural barrier, was less subject to Tartar and Turkish invasions from the east and south than were other parts of Romania. At the same time its western section—flat country—was open to Hungarian infiltration. Transylvania was occupied by Hungary as recently as 1940–44 and ethnic Hungarians are today a sizable minority. Transylvania's principal communities are Cluj-Napoca, a cultural and university center, and Brasov, an ancient city famous for its charming old center and Black Church (14th–15th centuries). Nearby is the scenic Carpathian resort of Poiana Brasov, while about 20 miles away is Bran castle of Dracula fame, well worth visiting even though the connections with that controversial prince are extremely tenuous. Two medieval jewels are Sighişoara, where the historical Dracula was reputedly born, and Sibiu, site of the magnificent Brukenthal museum. Other locales of interest are Alba Iulia, with its Roman roots; Hunedoara, with its astounding

14th-century castle incorporating many later styles; and the famous Felix spa, near the Hungarian border.

Maramureş

Though the smallest of Romania's traditional regions, Maramureş has made impressive contributions to industry, folklore, and tourism. Its largest city, Satu Mare, is a center for machine tools, textiles, furniture, and lumber. Baia Mare, second in population, is Romania's mining capital. The region is especially famous for its truly beautiful 18th-century wooden churches, especially in the Iza valley. Traditional architecture, folk costumes, crafts and customs survive to a remarkable degree in this area. Another of its better known attractions is the "Merry Cemetery" of Sapinţa, its graves enlivened by cheerful, brightly painted designs, each depicting the profession, trade and character of the occupant.

The Banat

Like many of Romania's border regions, the Banat has a racially mixed population. Bordering on both Hungary and Yugoslavia, it numbers ethnic Magyars and Slavs among its inhabitants. The capital, Timişoara is Romania's fourth largest city. Though a center of industry, Timişoara has good 18th-century architecture and lovely parks. Also of interest is the Herculane spa, in use as a thermal establishment since Roman days. Many Roman traces survive and the mountain setting is glorious. This southern region of the Carpathians includes the spectacular Iron Gate sector of the Danube, where the gigantic hydroelectric complex built in co-operation with the Yugoslavs, can be visited, and fascinating Roman remains, including traces of a mighty bridge across the Danube, can be seen at nearby Turnu Severin.

PRACTICAL INFORMATION FOR THE INTERIOR

Hotels and Restaurants

BAIA MARE. Main center for Maramureş. *Mara* (E), 120 rooms, recent, in newest part of town. *Bucureşti* (M), 74 rooms, in modern center of town, very good food; *Carpaţi* (M), 114 rooms, by river; *Minerul* (M), 48 rooms, turn-of-century building on main square of old town.

BRAŞOV. Gateway to central Carpathians. *Carpaţi* (L), 312 rooms, top facilities, central; *Capitol* (E), 180 rooms, central; *Parc* (M), 38 rooms, short stroll from center; *Postăvarul* (M), 167 rooms, restored late-19th-century building near center. Restaurants include the popular cellar restaurant *Cerbul Carpatin* (E-M) in 17th-century merchant's house, with excellent folk show; and *Cetăţuia* fortress where a restaurant complex includes one in Transylvanian style.

CLUJ. Transylvania. *Belvedere* (E-M), 150 rooms, located amongst 18th-century fortifications on hill, linked by steps to center. *Napoca* (E-M), 160 rooms, fairly modern, but not central. *Continental* (M), 50 rooms, old-fashioned, but central, opposite Cathedral. Restaurant *Transilvania* (M) serves specialties.

IAŞI. Moldavian capital, near Soviet border. *Traian* (M), 137 rooms. *Unirea* (M), 183 rooms.

ORADEA. Transylvania, near Hungarian border. *Dacia* (E-M), 170 rooms, short stroll from center. *Astoria* (M-I), central. *Transylvania* (I), 70 rooms, central.

PIATRA NEAMŢ. Moldavia. *Ceahlau* (E), 146 rooms. *Central* (E-M), 132 rooms, but avoid its annex, the *Bulevard.*

POIANA BRAŞOV. Major winter sports center, near Braşov. *Alpin* (E), 141 rooms, the best and quietest. *Teleferic* (E), 149 rooms, closest to the cable car station. *Sport* (M), 122 rooms, simple but good value and nearest to nursery slopes. There are several traditional-style restaurants.

PREDEAL. Major winter sports center in Prahova valley. *Cioplea* (E), 162 rooms. *Orizont* (E), 157 rooms. *Bulevard* (M), 43 rooms.

SIBIU. Lovely old town and gateway to Carpathians. *Continental* (E), 180 rooms, modern, near old town. *Bulevard* (E), 129 rooms, older but comfortable, at entrance to old town. *Impăratul Romanilor* (E), 96 rooms, attractively restored 18th-century building in old town. Two tavern-style restaurants in the old town are *Butoiul de Aur* (Golden Barrel) and *Sibiul Vechi* (Old Sibiu).

SIGHIŞOARA. Transylvania. *Steaua* (M), 54 rooms.

SINAIA. Mountain and ski resort. *Montana* (E-M), 180 rooms, modern and near cable car station. *Sinaia* (E-M), 248 rooms. *Palas* (E), 148 rooms. *Alpin* (M), 56 rooms, at 4,500 ft. with fine view over Prahova valley.

SUCEAVA. Gateway to painted churches of Moldavia. *Bucovina* (E-M), 130 rooms. *Arcasul* (E-M), 100 rooms.

TIMIŞOARA. Banat. *Continental* (E), 160 rooms, high rise, short stroll from central Opera Square. *Timişoara* (E-M), 240 rooms, very central. *Banatul* (M), 95 rooms. Restaurants include *Bastion* (E), in old Turkish fortifications, folk show, and *Faleza Bega* (M), with terrace by river.

TÎRGOVIŞTE. Ancient capital of Wallachia. *Dimboviţa* (M-I), 107 rooms. *Turist* (M-I), 29 rooms.

TURNU SEVERIN. On Danube, near Iron Gates. *Trajan* (E-M), the latest. *Parc* (M), 138 rooms, near banks of Danube.

Museums and Monuments

The *Brukenthal Museum* in Sibiu has a magnificent collection of paintings, furniture and superb folk costumes; the old walls, towers and many old buildings make this a particularly rewarding center. Braşov is another fine town with its remarkable *Black Church, Citadel Museum* and many charming corners. Yet another is Iaşi whose *Trei Ierarhi Church* (beautifully carved stonework) and *Palace of Culture* (several museums) are only some of the many fascinating sights. Timişoara's 14th-century *Iancu of Hunedoara's Castle* houses the *Museum of Banat.* Other museums of special interest are: the *Museum of Transylvanian Ethnography* at Cluj, *Museum of Petrol* at Ploeşti, *Museum of the Iron Gates* at Turnu Severin, *Peleş Castle* (art museum) at Sinaia, *County Museum* at Suceava, famous for its coin collection. And, of course, the Moldavian *painted monasteries* of Moldoviţa, Voroneţ, Humor, Suceviţa and Arbor are justifiably widely famed.

SPAIN

Spain has long had a rather schizophrenic reputation as a vacation destination among English-speaking tourists. On the one hand, as Europe's premier package-holiday destination, the country is almost instinctively associated in the minds of many with the worst excesses of the cheap-holiday-in-the-sun boom of the '60s and '70s. The vast numbers of faceless hotels along the Mediterranean coasts, for all the world like so many egg cartons staring blindly out to sea, stand today as eloquent and damning evidence of a hurried and poorly-regulated expansion into the brutal world of mass tourism.

The other half of the equation is infinitely more appealing. For Spain is also the land of the fountain-singing courtyards of Moorish Granada and Cordoba, dusty plains where Don Quixote rode to do battle with imaginary enemies, gaunt and somnolent hill-top towns little changed from the days when Spain was the preeminent power in Europe.

Still, if it's beaches you're after, there is the Costa del Sol in the south, where Marbella and Torremolinos have become a rendezvous for international society. A similar role has always been played in the north by San Sebastián, in the Basque country, formerly the summer capital of Spain. Farther west are the resort city of Santander and, over on Spain's strip of the Atlantic, La Coruña, a long-standing favorite of British visitors, and the island of La Toja, near Pontevedra. In the east is the enormously popular Costa Brava, the northernmost stretch of the Catalan coast, from the borderline between Barcelona and Gerona provinces to the French frontier. To the south, around Alicante, is the Costa Blanca, with its most popular tourist center at Benidorm; south of Huelva is the recently developed Costa de la Luz, with the beaches of Cadiz not far off.

When you tire of roasting in the sun, hire a car and head for one of the thousands of castles, ruins or bulging museums nearby. Perhaps the number one tourist attraction of Spain is the Alhambra at Granada. Following close behind it come the Mosque of Córdoba and the Alcazar and Cathedral of Seville. Santiago de Compostela, whose magnificent cathedral houses the shrine of St. James the Apostle, is a museum in itself. Avila is a historic walled town and Segovia boasts its Roman aqueduct and proud Alcazar. Madrid, the capital, contains some of the greatest art collections in the world, and the nearby Monastery of the Escorial is another of Spain's great sights; the excursion can be combined with a visit to the Valley of the Fallen Memorial. Towering above the Tagus, Toledo, home of El Greco, with its cathedral, synagogues and panoramas, is one of Spain's greatest treasures. Barcelona, the capital of Cataluña, has a charm and vitality quite its own.

The Country and the People

There are immense variations in climate, topography and regional personality within Spain itself. You would never confuse the treeless Mancha tableland of the austere Castilian plateau with the rice swamps and orange groves of Valencia, for example, nor the pink and olive hills of Andalusia with the snow-capped Pyrenees. And if you travel widely in Spain you will begin to note the differences between the dark-haired, white-skinned Castilians, proud, elegant, conservative and reserved; the up-and-coming "progresista" Catalans, often with blonde or reddish hair, an inheritance from the Visigoths; the exuberant, voluble Andalusians, whose dark and languorous eyes have that unmistakable Arabian Nights look, quite a contrast to the stocky, light-eyed Basques.

But there are also characteristics that all Spaniards seem to have in common, a kind of unifying quality, a national spirit. This is still evident despite the growth of political separatist movements all over the country. First of all there is the unity of religious sentiment. Despite certain exceptions, the majority of the Spanish people still maintain the religious enthusiasm that sustained them through eight centuries of Holy Wars against the Moorish Infidel, the Counter Reformation and the horrors of the Spanish Inquisition. There is something violent in this religious emotion. The thorns and blood are real in Spain.

Secondly, you will find the Spanish are proud with a pride of race. They carry themselves like a proud people. España, they will remind you, was a great nation for centuries during which Italy and Germany were a mere conglomeration of squabbling little duchies. If it is true that Spanish character oscillates between idealism and materialism, it is usually idealism that triumphs in the end, or at least until the advent of industrialism over the past fifteen years.

The greatest of Spanish national virtues is courage. This explains the popularity of Spain's most typical spectacle, the bullfight. The bullfight is basically an ordeal of courage.

To see a *corrida,* literally a "running" of the bulls, is to understand the violent smouldering heart of Spain. The bullfight season in Spain runs from Easter through October. Almost every town has its Plaza de Toros, the bullring. To see the most famous *toreros* (they're only called *toreadors* in *Carmen*), you should visit Madrid in May, Seville in Holy Week or the April Fair, and Pamplona in early July. Though soccer is more popular than bullfighting, in the last few years there has been a resurgence in the popularity of the *corrida,* especially among the young.

Spanish Folklore

If Spain is the home of the *siesta* (though in the big cities this is quickly disappearing), it is also, *par excellence,* the country of the *fiesta* which, except during Holy Week, is the reverse of solemn—and a local saint's day is apt to consist of a half-hour Mass in the church, followed by bullfights, dancing, music, fireworks and general rejoicing. There are countless *romerias* (picnic excursions to shrines), and these are extremely colorful with long cavalcades of beautifully caparisoned horses and carts. There are *verbenas,* night festivals on the eve of religious holidays, and there are *fallas,* which are celebrations of almost pagan revelry. *Ferias* are local fairs.

There are many extremely colorful folk dances in Spain, such as the *jota* of Aragon, the *fandango* of Andalusia, and the lively but subtle Catalan *sardana,* which last you will see danced in the streets of almost any Catalan town or village during its Fiesta Mayor. But the most famous of Spanish dances is the fiery, passionate Andalusian *flamenco,* strongly suggestive of Arab influence. When that rhythmic stamping and clapping starts and you hear the wail of the vocalist, you'll be close to the mystery of this Catholic-pagan country.

PRACTICAL INFORMATION FOR SPAIN

WHAT WILL IT COST. Costs in Spain have soared dramatically over the past decade. Yet despite an inflation rate currently touching 13%, the relative strength of the dollar and the pound against the peseta has kept prices within bounds for most visitors. However, Spain's entry into the EEC in January 1986 looks certain to spark off a significant series of new price rises. A new value added tax (IVA) and enforced price rises for several basic commodities, among them wine and liquor, have already helped push up the cost of hotels and restaurants.

Forecasting prices for 1987 is, therefore, a speculative business at best. It can only be hoped that though the cost of accommodations and dining-out in Spain may soon be on a par with that of many other European countries, the relatively low cost of transport (other than gas for private cars) and a still favorable exchange rate will continue to conspire that Spain retains its place among the more moderately-priced European destinations.

As in most countries, prices vary slightly from region to region and obviously the less visited and more out-of-the-way places will cost less than the more popular destinations. Top of the list for extravagance comes the international resort of Marbella, long the mecca of the rich and famous. Following close behind are the two leading cities of Madrid and Barcelona. Seville too, as a major tourist city, features high prices. As a general rule hotels on the north coast tend to be higher than average, whereas the little visited but delightful region of Extremadura, on Spain's western border with Portugal, offers some of the best value for money. In the highly developed coastal regions such as the Costa Brava, Costa Blanca or Costa del Sol, there is a proliferation of comfortable 3-star hotels (though some are now beginning to show their cracks) which offer extremely reasonable rates due to their close liaison with package tour agencies. These hotels may be fully booked for the high season but outside of July and August, you have a good chance of finding high standards of accommodations at a reasonable price.

Despite huge increases across the board in hotel rates in the last few years, Spain still scores in offering the visitor a wide choice of accommodations, from luxury 5-star hotel down to meager but often very comfortable 2-star hostel. The sheer number of hotels and restaurants is simply incredible. Though really good inexpensive restaurants are now few and far between, the huge number of medium-priced places to dine offers you a choice unmatched by most other European countries.

MONEY. You may not legally acquire more than 150,-000 pesetas outside of Spain, so you will not be able to bring more than that into the country; and you may take out only 20,000 ptas. in cash when you leave. You can bring in any amount of foreign currency but, in theory, you can only leave the country with the equivalent of 80,000 ptas. in foreign currency. It is generally better to change traveler's checks in banks than in hotels, restaurants and shops where the rate of exchange may not be quite as good; however, many Spanish banks take an enormous commission charge so it may not work out very much different. Always ask the bank what its commission is *before* you change money; if it exceeds 1% take your business elsewhere. Pay your bills in Spain in pesetas.

There are coins for 1, 5, 10, 25, 50 and 100 ptas.; bills are 200, 500, 1,000, 2,000, and 5,000 ptas. At presstime, the exchange rate was around 145 ptas. to the dollar and 215 ptas. to the pound sterling.

A typical day for two people might cost in pesetas:

Hotel (moderate) with bed and breakfast	5,000
Lunch at moderate restaurant	3,000
Dinner at moderate restaurant with wine	5,000
Transportation (2 taxis and 4 bus rides)	700
4 coffees	300
4 beers	350
Miscellaneous	650
	15,000

SOURCES OF INFORMATION. An invaluable source of information on all aspects of travel to Spain is the Spanish National Tourist Office, located:

In the U.S.: 665 Fifth Ave., New York, N.Y. 10022; 1 Hallidie Plaza, Suite 801, San Francisco, CA 94102; 845 North Michigan Ave., Chicago, IL 60611; 4800 The Galleria, 5085 Westheimer, Houston, TX 77056; Casa del Hidalgo, Hypolita St. George, San Agustin, FL 32084.

In Canada: 60 Bloor St. West, Suite 201, Toronto, Ontario M4W 3B8.

In the U.K.: 57 St. James's St., London S.W.1.

 WHEN TO COME. Tourist season is from April through October. Peak vacation months of July and August are apt to be too hot for comfort except at seaside resorts. Madrid should be visited in late spring or fall if possible. Seville is best in May, early June and September.

Climate. Hot and dry in summer; moderate in winter, except for bitter cold for some weeks on the central plateau.

Average afternoon temperatures in Fahrenheit and centigrade:

Madrid	Jan.	Feb.	Mar.	Apr.	May	June	July	Aug.	Sept.	Oct.	Nov.	Dec.
F°	47	51	57	64	71	80	87	86	77	66	54	48
C°	8	11	14	18	22	27	31	30	25	19	12	9

Barcelona												
F°	56	57	61	64	71	77	81	82	78	71	62	57
C°	13	14	16	18	22	25	27	28	26	22	17	14

 SPECIAL EVENTS. *Jan.,* commemoration of Granada's liberation from the Moors in 1492 (2nd); Day of the Kings (Epiphany) celebrations all over Spain (5th and 6th). *Mar.,* Fallas of San José in Valencia (12th-19th). *Apr., Easter,* Holy Week processions in Seville, Málaga, Granada, Córdoba, Valladolid, Cuenca. Seville Fair; Burial of the Sardine, Murcia. *May,* Decorated patios festival in Córdoba (1st–12th); Horse Fair in Jerez de la Frontera; Feast of San Isidro in Madrid with top bullfighting; *Whitsun,* Romería del Rocío pilgrimage in Almonte (Huelva); *Corpus Christi,* Processions at Toledo and

Sitges where the streets are carpeted with flowers. *June,* Granada International Music Festival, in the 14th-century Moorish Alhambra (through July). *July,* fiesta of San Fermín in Pamplona with the running of the bulls; Pilgrimage to the shrine of St. James in Santiago de Compostela (25th). *Aug.,* celebrations for the Feast of the Assumption at La Alberca (Salamanca); San Sebastián and Elche (Alicante) Mystery Play (14th and 15th); Music Festival, Santander; Málaga Fair; Fiesta de San Lorenzo in the Escorial (10th); Fiesta de San Miguel, Seville. *Sept.,* fiesta of the Virgen de las Angustias, Granada; Vintage Festival, Jerez de la Frontera; film festival, San Sebastián. *Oct.,* festival of the Virgen de El Pilar at Zaragoza. *Dec.,* Christmas is celebrated throughout the country from the 24th to January 6. Gifts are given on the 6th.

Best check on the spot as dates are liable to change from year to year.

National Holidays. Jan. 1 (New Year's Day); Jan. 6 (Epiphany); Mar. 19 (St. Joseph, Fathers' Day); Apr. 16, 17, 19 (Maundy Thurs., Good Fri., Easter Mon.—varies from city to city); May 1 (May Day); Corpus Christi (2nd Thurs. after Whitsun); Jun. 24 (St. John); Jul. 25 (St. James); Aug. 15 (Assumption); Oct. 12 (Virgin of El Pilar); Nov. 1 (All Saints); Dec. 8 (Immaculate Conception); Dec. 24 (P.M. only), 25. In addition, each town has its own fiesta, when it celebrates the feast day of its local saint.

VISAS. Neither American, British nor Canadian citizens need a visa to visit Spain. Visas are required for Australians. Americans and Britains are allowed a 90-day stay after each entry.

HEALTH CERTIFICATES. Not required for entry to Spain.

GETTING TO SPAIN By Plane from the U.S. From North America there are direct flights from New York, Miami and Montreal to Madrid, and from New York to Malaga and Barcelona by through plane service.

By Plane from the U.K. and the Continent. London and major European cities are linked not only with Madrid by the national carrier, *Iberia,* and reciprocal airlines, but also to Barcelona, Malaga, Seville, Alicante, Bilbao, Santiago, Valencia, the Canary Islands and the Balearics. Moreover, all these destinations are served by prolific charter flights based in Britain, Germany, Netherlands, Switzerland, France and Scandinavia.

By Train. Although the Spanish (and Portuguese) railway gauge is wider than that operating through much of the rest of Europe, getting to Spain by train is easy. There are now three through trains which change their wheels at the border or have "telescopic" bogies on the carriages which can be adjusted rapidly to suit the wider gauge of Spanish track. The first is the *Barcelona Talgo,* an overnight express which leaves the French capital about 9 P.M. and arrives in Barcelona at 9 A.M. the next day. It carries 1st and 2nd class sleepers with special four berth sleepers in 2nd class, a full dining car and a bar all the way. The second, which began in 1981, is the *Madrid Talgo,* again with sleeping cars, dining car and bar car. This time it leaves Paris (Gare Austerlitz) at 8 P.M. and arrives in Madrid (Chamartín) at about 9 A.M. the next day. The third is the *Puerta del Sol* which leaves Paris around 6 P.M., reaching Madrid at 10 A.M.; it has couchettes and carries cars, thus forming part of the Motor Rail service.

There is a similar train but operating during the day with 1st and 2nd class carriages and dining car—the *Catalan Talgo* running between Geneva and Barcelona, via Valence, Avignon, Nîmes, Narbonne, and Port Bou, taking around 9½ hours for the journey. The *Talgo* is a special type of train designed in Spain and used widely there. On good track it gives a very comfortable ride.

Of course there are many other trains running to the Franco-Spanish border with direct connecting trains in Spain. A lovely route not much used by tourists into Spain is from Toulouse through the foothills of the Pyrenees and through those mountains to La Tour de Carol where you change trains and then run through Catalonia down to Barcelona. 1st and 2nd class in France and 2nd class in Spain; you leave Toulouse at about 10.20 A.M., reaching La Tour about 1.20 P.M., allowing around 25 minute stop here to change trains and for refreshments, arriving in Barcelona at about 5.30 P.M.

Advance reservations for these long distance trains are essential, particularly for sleepers and couchettes.

SPAIN

631

By Bus. The main regular bus line operating between England and Spain is marketed under the name of *Supabus,* and is run by both British and Spanish bus companies out of London's Victoria Coach Station. Their main routes are to Gerona (for Costa Brava), Barcelona, Valencia, and Alicante, and to San Sebastián, Burgos, Madrid, Algeciras, and all intermediate destinations. For reservations and information, contact the Travel Center at Victoria Station (tel. 01–730 0202) or any *Supabus* or *National Express* agent in Britain. *Iberbus, Francebus* and *Via Tourisme* also have similar services to Spain originating in Paris, and *Intercar Alsa* runs a service from Paris through northern Spain to Salamanca and Santiago.

By Car. Direct to Santander from Plymouth by *Brittany Ferries,* a 24 hour voyage, or to St. Malo—also by Brittany Ferries—or to Le Havre by *Townsend Thoresen.* If making for Madrid or west of it, drive down the west side of France to enter at Irun. For eastern Spain slope across to Toulouse and enter through or near Andorra. In either case a night crossing and one hotel night will get you there.

CUSTOMS. You can bring in anything intended for personal use duty free, but be reasonable about it. Only 200 cigarettes duty free, 5 rolls of film, 1 liter of liquor and 2 of wine. You may take out purchases of up to 25,000 ptas. without payment of export duty. Luggage is rarely checked.

HOTELS. Spanish hotels, once an incredible bargain, have over the last three years raised their prices by some 25% or more. Service, also, is often less willing than it once was. Nevertheless, most hotels still offer relatively good value for money and rates are still far from the astronomical levels of some London or U.S. hotels. Hotels are officially classified from 5-star to 1-star; from 4 to 1-star for hotel apartments, and from 3 to 1-star for hostels and pensions. We use the following system: (L) for Deluxe; (E) for Expensive; (M) for Moderate; (I) for Inexpensive.

The rates for these grades (based on mid-1986 prices) are (L) 12,000 and up; (E) 7,500–11,500; (M) 4,750–7,450; (I) 3,000–4,700 for major centers; elsewhere (L) 10,000–14,000 (rare); (E) 6,250–9,500; (M) 4,250–6,000; (I) 2,500–4,000. These prices are for two people sharing a double room; one person occupying a double room is charged 80% of the full price. A further IVA tax will also be added to your bill. In most cases this will be around 6% though in the case of luxury hotels it may be as high as 12%. (Note that some hotels which we list in a certain category, say (E), will have a number of rooms at a cheaper rate.)

Hotel prices are registered with the Spanish National Tourist Office and must, by law, be prominently posted at the reception desk. Be sure to understand clearly whether meals are available (most hotels classed as *residencias* do not have restaurants), and whether you will be required to pay for any, particularly breakfast, even if you do not take them. At times of special fiestas rates can double or triple and you may well be obliged to take half-board terms (e.g. Seville *feria,* Pamplona *San Fermines*). In the less expensive hotels breakfast is not usually included in the price of the room.

PARADORES, ALBERGUES AND HOSTERIAS.
The government operates a number of hotels and hostelries called *paradores, albergues* and *hosterías.* The *paradores,* often historic castles in magnificent settings, all with restaurants, offer good accommodations, often with much local flavor and history, though readers are beginning to report that service can be impersonal. *Albergues,* principally for motorists, are more functional but very comfortable and they also have restaurants. *Hosterías* are rustic, local specialty restaurants in places of touristic interest. No sleeping accommodations.

CAMPING.
Camping sites are state-run and there are over 530 sites in Spain, nearly all of them with food supplies available. The season is long: many are open year-round, others April through September or October. The heaviest concentration of sites is along the Mediterranean coast. Foreigners must show their passport or identity card when registering at sites. Camping Carnets are not essential though they are recommended. Information can be obtained from *American Youth Hostels, Inc.,* 1332 I (Eye) St., N.W., 8th Floor, Washington

D.C. 20005; the *Canadian Youth Hostels Association,* National Office, 333 River Rd., Vanier City, Ottawa, Ont.; or the *Camping and Caravan Club Ltd.,* 11 Lower Grosvenor Place, London SW1. A useful handbook is the *Guia de Campings* published annually and available from bookstores.

RESTAURANTS. Spanish restaurants are designated by the official classification of 5-fork, 4-fork etc. Our grading system is slightly simpler . . . (E) for Expensive, (M) for Moderate and (I) for Inexpensive. The relative approximate cost of a meal for two comprising three courses, a bottle of house wine and coffee, would be: Major centers: (E) 8,000–10,000; (M) 5,000–7,500; (I) 3,500–4,750. Away from major centers prices could well be less.

Many restaurants, particularly in coastal resorts or business districts, offer a set menu which works out very much cheaper than choosing *à la carte.* This is generally known as the *menú del día* or sometimes the tourist menu, *menú turístico,* and usually includes soup or appetizer, one or two main courses, bread, dessert and sometimes a beverage. Prices vary with the class of the restaurant, but 1,000 ptas. is a fair average.

Meals are habitually taken much later in Spain than in any other country in Europe. It's hard to get lunch before 1.30 P.M., and 3 P.M. is considered quite normal. Dinner before 8.30 P.M. is almost unheard of; 10 P.M. is a usual hour. Madrid tends to keep even later house than the rest of the country. Hotel dining rooms work on earlier hours, usually 8 P.M. till 10 P.M.

Incidentally it is customary to give an additional tip of around ten per cent (no more) even if the tab says service is included. Service charges are never added to restaurant bills.

Food and Drink. Olive oil is at the base of Spanish cooking and contrary to expectation, Spanish cooking is not generally fiery and peppery like the Mexican cuisine. Don't hesitate to order seafood anywhere, even inland at Madrid. A fast service brings the fresh catch daily to the market, and the crabs, shrimps, prawns, crayfish and other crustaceans are excellent.

Here are some special dishes to look for: *Gazpacho,* a cold soup of tomatoes, garlic, bread crumbs, cucumber and green pepper with croutons, which is delicious and refreshing at the end of a long hot day. *Paella* delights most visitors, and is now so widely known outside Spain as to be thought of as the country's national dish. Try *jamon serrano,* sun-cured mountain ham, dark red in color and served in thin, translucent slices. The Basques are great eaters, and some of their specialties are *Bacalao a la Vizcaina,* salt codfish cooked in a tomato sauce; *angulas,* tiny eels cooked whole in olive oil with garlic and *merluza a la vasca,* white fish with clams, asparagus and hard-boiled eggs. Other specialties include: *almejas marinera,* steamed clams in garlic and wine sauce, and *calamares,* squid rings fried in batter with lemon wedges. In the Basque Country and Galicia, order *centollo,* a huge crab cooked in the shell with a spicy sauce. If all this sounds too exotic you can always have grilled meat by asking for *a la parrilla.*

Sherry is the most characteristic of Spanish drinks. There are the *finos,* pale, dry, and drunk widely as an aperitif; *amontillados,* medium dry, same purpose; *olorosos,* dark, sweet and heavy sherries; generally drunk as a dessert wine. *Manzanilla,* not technically a sherry, is popular in Spain; it has a higher alcoholic content than any sherry. Each region has its own table wines, *Rioja, Penedés,* and *Valdepeñas* being the best known. Try the unbottled wine of the house *(vino de las casa):* it is usually good, and inexpensive. Spanish beer is also good.

TIPPING. Spanish hotels rarely add a service charge to their bills, though remember to allow for the additional IVA tax. Leave the chambermaid around 300 ptas. a week and tip the porters 35 ptas. a bag. If you call a bellboy give him 30 ptas. Spanish restaurants never add a service charge to your tab but you should always leave about 10%, even when it says "service and tax included". Waiters in nightclubs will expect rather more. Doormen and hat-check girls get 25 ptas.

Station porters operate on a fixed rate, officially 40 ptas. a bag. The taxi drivers get 10% if they use the meter, otherwise *nothing.* Theater and movie ushers get 10 ptas. Restroom attendants everywhere get 5 ptas. (perhaps 10 in a very smart establishment).

MAIL. To the U.S. and Canada: 62 ptas.; to the U.K. and rest of Europe: 45 ptas. Postcards are 52 ptas. to the U.S. and 35 ptas. to Europe. (1986 prices.)

SHOPPING. There are many typical souvenirs that can be purchased at reasonable prices throughout Spain. But unfortunately you can't expect to find real bargains any longer. Don't try bargaining, except with gypsies and street vendors, as prices are fixed and you may well offend. However, in some of the more obvious tourist rip-off places, it will do no harm to suggest politely that perhaps you might be given a small discount when you are purchasing several items. Many of these shops automatically give tourists a 5 or 10% discount anyway, to encourage spending.

Some ideas for souvenirs to take home include damasquino jewelry, knives and swords from Toledo; ceramics—especially good around Toledo, Valencia, and Seville, though if you can't carry vases and plates, buy some of the decorative tiles found in the Barrio Santa Cruz in Seville; Don Quixote and Sancho Panza figures carved from olive wood; Lladró porcelain; marquetry boxes or chess sets from Granada; filigree silver from Cordoba; lace shawls, mantillas and tablecloths from Seville; esparto grass work *botas* (wine-skin bottles), castanets, fans, Spanish dolls and bullfight posters.

CLOSING TIMES. Shops are open in the morning from 9 or 10 to either 1.30 or 2. In the afternoons from around 4 to 7 in winter, and 5 to 8 in summer. In some cities, especially in summer, they close on Saturday afternoons. Tourist shops in seaside resorts and the *Corte Inglés* and *Galerías Preciados* department stores in major cities stay open throughout the siesta. Banks are open 9.30 to 2, Mon.-Fri., and 9.30 to 12.30 or 1 on Saturdays. Museum hours vary greatly from city to city and from summer to winter. Many open mornings only and all state-run museums are closed on Mondays.

TOURIST INFORMATION OFFICES. The Spanish State Tourist Office provides an excellent information service for tourists and has offices in all provincial capitals and many smaller towns of tourist interest. These offices are usually open from about 9.30 to 1 and 4.30 to 7, Mon.-Fri., and 9.30 to 1 on Sat., though some work 8.30 to 3. Staff speak English and will provide free maps and information. They will advise on (though not book) accommodations, bus and train timetables, restaurants, museums, guided tours and local fiestas. Look for signs saying *Información* or *Oficina de Turismo*.

GETTING AROUND SPAIN. By Plane. Both *Iberia* and *Aviaco* (Spain's second airline) operate a wide network of routes within Spain, linking all the main cities and the Balearics. These services are mainly by modern jet aircraft but with some prop-jet services to smaller airports. In the summer the routes to and within the Balearics are very popular and advance reservation is essential. Similarly the Malaga–Madrid route is frequently overbooked, especially at Easter and in high season.

By Train. The Spanish railway system known usually by its initials RENFE has been vastly improved in the last ten to 15 years. There are various types of train in Spain—Talgo, Inter-City, ELT (electric unit expresses), TER (diesel rail cars) and ordinary semi-fast and local trains. Airconditioned stock is now wide spread although by no means universal. Fares are determined by the kind of train you travel on rather than the distance traveled. Over-night trains carry 1st and 2nd sleeping cars and 2nd class couchettes as a rule. Dining, buffet and refreshment services are available on almost all long distance trains.

If you are traveling on a rail pass or ticket bought abroad you must have it endorsed before travel. It is advisable to purchase all tickets other than for local journeys in advance and not to wait until your day of travel. You can do this from all main railroad stations at the ticket window marked *Largo Recorrido, Venta Anticipada,* or from the downtown RENFE offices in main cities. Travel agencies displaying the blue and yellow RENFE sign also sell rail tickets at no extra cost, enabling you to avoid the endless high season lines at stations and RENFE offices; they can obtain your tickets on the same day, if not immediately. RENFE has a nationwide computer system and to purchase a ticket you need not be in the city where you will board your train.

By Bus. Spain has an excellent bus network. Some of the coaches on major routes are now quite luxurious although this isn't always the case in certain of the more rural areas. Buses offer a good means of transport; they tend to be more frequent than trains, they are much cheaper, and often you see more of the countryside. On major routes and at holiday times it is advisable to buy your ticket a day or two in advance. Some cities have central bus stations but in many, including Madrid and Barcelona, buses leave from various boarding points. Always check with the local tourist office.

By Car. Remember that Spain has its own special brand of heat, much more exhausting that that on the north side of the Pyrenees, so don't plan to drive very long distances. The roads are mostly straight, but narrow and not too smooth. Gasoline prices are on a par with Britain, high by American standards. Foreign drivers are advised to obtain a bail bond in case of accident. Beware of saints' days and football matches which can reduce everything to chaos.

Madrid

Madrid, capital of Spain, is one of the boom towns of Europe. On the direct firing line during the Spanish Civil War, it was badly damaged, and entire districts were destroyed. Reconstruction was undertaken and now skyscrapers, ministries, plush hotels, restaurants and cinemas are seen everywhere; the population more than doubled in 20 years to almost four million. Today it is a modern, 20th-century city built up around a 17th-century core.

The real life of Madrid can best be savored from the terrace of one of the numerous cafés in the Plaza Mayor where whilst enjoying a pre-lunch or dinner drink, you can watch the Madrileños pass—vivacious, handsome men and women, well-dressed, friendly and proud.

Aside from a view of the people's everyday life, the foremost tourist attraction of Madrid is the Prado Museum. Situated in a rose-colored palace, a stone's throw from the Ritz and Palace hotels, this is one of the world's greatest art museums. Even if your stay in Madrid is a short one, you should devote at least a morning or an afternoon to the incomparable El Grecos, Velázquezs, Murillos and Goyas in this collection. And don't forget that, thanks to the extraordinary taste and acquisitiveness of Charles V, Philip II, and Philip IV, the Prado is also rich in the works of Italian and Flemish masters—Titian, Raphael, Botticelli, Fra Angelico, Veronese, Tintoretto, Rubens, Van Dyck and Breughel, and a fine collection of Bosch paintings.

Nearby in the Casón del Buen Retiro you should not miss another of Spain's proud and recent acquisitions: Picasso's *Guernica* brought to Madrid in 1981 after 40 years in exile in New York's Museum of Modern Art. After the dazzling and staggering experience of the Prado, we recommend a rest cure in the nearby Retiro Park.

Outstanding among Madrid's smaller museums is the Lazaro Galdiano Museum with its magnificent collection of objets d'art, including Europe's best collection of ivory and enamel, and many fine works by Goya, El Greco, Zurbarán and Velázquez. You will also enjoy the tapestries, paintings and lovely old porcelain in the Cerralbo Museum. A worthwhile trip for Goya enthusiasts is to the Goya Pantheon in the Hermitage of San Antonio de la Florida. Here lies the great artist, headless, his head having inexplicably disappeared between his burial in Bordeaux in 1828 and the exhumation of his body for transfer to Spain in 1888.

To recuperate from *this* bout of museum crawling, take an *aperitivo* in one of the numerous sidewalk cafes or *tapas* bars, then an early Madrid dinner about 9:30 P.M., finishing just in time for the "evening" performance of a *flamenco* show in a club, which begins at 11:30 and lasts until at least 1:30 A.M. If these hours seem too outlandish, we remind you that there's an "afternoon" at 7 P.M.! Early or late, you should take in one of these exciting gypsy flamenco shows, which will bring you closer to the violent heart of Spain than even a bullfight.

Madrid's second greatest sight, the Royal Palace is worth an entire morning. One immense side of the building looks from the crest of a hill to the snow-capped Guadarrama Mountains, 40 miles away. The 30 main salons face east across an open square to the Royal Theater and a formal 18th-century garden. In the center of the square is a striking equestrian statue of Philip IV, from a design by Velázquez. The palace was spared by mutual agreement of both sides during the civil war. Inside the palace you will see Tiepolo frescos, porcelain clocks, about 800 tapestries, portraits by Goya, Mengs and Ribera, and roughly five miles of the most beautiful carpets you have ever seen. Also impressive are the palace's royal chapel, the armory with a fine collection of weapons and armor from the 15th through 18th centuries, and the royal pharmacy. Guides are available at the main entrance to show you around.

In addition to the Castellana, the wide avenue of Gran Via and the Puerta del Sol—Madrid's Times Square or Piccadilly Circus—you will want to see a little bit of "old" Madrid. From the Puerta del Sol turn up Calle Mayor, then left along Esparteros to the Palacio de Santa Cruz, now the Ministry of Foreign Affairs, but once the headquarters of the dreaded Spanish Inquisition. From this point, you can trace the steps of its victims to the Plaza Mayor where they underwent the terrible ordeal of the *auto da fé*. Built in 1619, this beautiful, partially-arcaded square is the point at which old Madrid begins. In the far left-hand corner, you will find a steep flight of stone steps cut into a section of the city's medieval walls, leading into Calle Cuchilleros. On the way down there are some atmospheric eating places. At the bottom, and to the right, begins as quaint a cobbled rabbit warren as you will find in any European town. A city map is useless, so follow your fancy and then get a cab to take you back to the 20th century.

Here are two highly recommended visits, not usually on the conventional tourist list for Madrid. The first is a visit to the Royal Tapestry Factory where, for two centuries, some of the world's most beautiful tapestries and carpets have been made. (Open mornings only, closed weekends and the whole of August.)

The second visit is to the Archeological Museum, Calle Serrano 13, which features a magnificent allround collection including Iberian vases and many porcelains. There is a huge assortment of Roman artifacts, medieval art and objects, Moorish rooms, Egyptian mummies, navigational instruments, jewelry, etc. Entrance fee includes the right to visit the excellent reproduction of the prehistoric Altamira Caves. The museum now houses the exquisite Iberian-carved bust *The Lady of Elche,* formerly in the Prado.

Excursions from Madrid

Thirty-one miles from Madrid, at the foot of the Guadarrama Mountains, is San Lorenzo del Escorial, burial place of Spanish kings and queens. The monastery, built by that religious fanatic, Philip II, as a memorial to his father, Charles V, is a vast rectangular edifice, conceived and executed with a monotonous magnificence worthy of the Spanish royal necropolis. The church, in the shape of a Greek cross, contains a famous cross by Benvenuto Cellini, and paintings by Velázquez, Ribera and El Greco. The spartan private apartment of Philip II and the bare cell in which he chose to die are in striking contrast

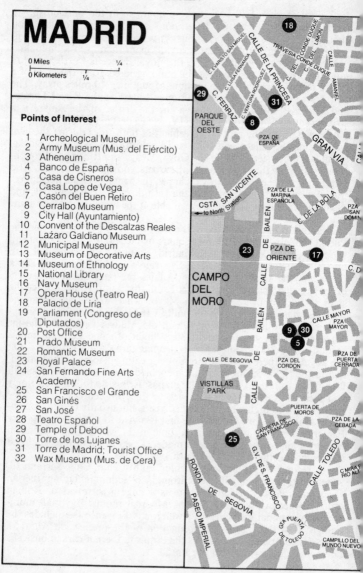

MADRID

0 Miles   ¼
0 Kilometers   ¼

Points of Interest

1   Archeological Museum
2   Army Museum (Mus. del Ejército)
3   Atheneum
4   Banco de España
5   Casa de Cisneros
6   Casa Lope de Vega
7   Casón del Buen Retiro
8   Cerralbo Museum
9   City Hall (Ayuntamiento)
10   Convent of the Descalzas Reales
11   Lazáro Galdiano Museum
12   Municipal Museum
13   Museum of Decorative Arts
14   Museum of Ethnology
15   National Library
16   Navy Museum
17   Opera House (Teatro Real)
18   Palacio de Liria
19   Parliament (Congreso de Diputados)
20   Post Office
21   Prado Museum
22   Romantic Museum
23   Royal Palace
24   San Fernando Fine Arts Academy
25   San Francisco el Grande
26   San Ginés
27   San José
28   Teatro Español
29   Temple of Debod
30   Torre de los Lujanes
31   Torre de Madrid; Tourist Office
32   Wax Museum (Mus. de Cera)

to the beautiful carpets, porcelain and tapestries with which his less austere successors decorated the rest of this monastery-palace.

It is possible to include in your trip to El Escorial a visit to the monumental Valle de los Caidos—Valley of the Fallen—a memorial to the million men who were slaughtered in Spain's civil war. A crypt, cut through 853 feet of rock, is surmounted by a 492-foot cross of reinforced concrete faced with stone. This somber and impressive monument is the last resting place of Jose Antonio, founder of the Falangists, and of General Franco.

Twenty-one miles east from Madrid is Alcalá de Henares, birthplace of Catherine of Aragon, Cervantes and other famous Spaniards. You

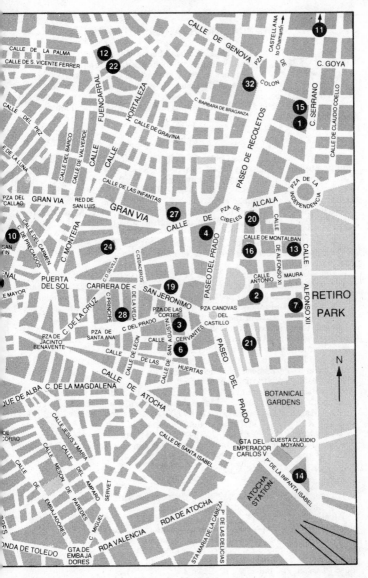

can visit the old university, the house where the author of *Don Quixote* was born, and the Church of Santa Maria la Mayor in which he was baptized. Dine in 15th-century cloisters in the Hostería del Estudiante.

Thirty miles south of Madrid is Aranjuez, an elegant arcaded town with a splendid palace. The gardens, with their cascade falling into the Tagus River, are delightful, the last word in formal landscape designing. Visit Charles IV's Casa del Labrador (farm worker's cottage), a sumptuous copy of the Trianon at Versailles, whose lavish decoration is a far cry from the picture conjured up by its humble name. In summer, lunch at one of the riverside restaurants; at Eastertime, sample Aranjuez's famous early strawberries and asparagus.

PRACTICAL INFORMATION FOR MADRID

 HOTELS. Madrid offers a wide range of hotels, all the way from the millionaire Villa Magna to modest little pensions where you can live, and eat remarkably well, on a modest budget. Accommodations are hardest to come by at Easter and in July and August. There are hotel accommodations services at Chamartin and Atocha stations and at the national and international airport terminals.

Deluxe

Holiday Inn, in the Azca Center off Calle Orense (tel. 456 70 14). This latest addition to Madrid's luxury hotels opened in 1985. 313 rooms, executive suites, banqueting salons, pool, sauna and gymnasium. Very comfortable.

Luz Palacio, Castellana 57 (tel. 442 51 00), is tastefully decorated, with restaurants, cocktail lounge etc.

Meliá Castilla, Capitán Haya 43 (tel. 270 84 00). 936 rooms. Madrid's largest hotel in the increasingly fashionable and gourmet area in the north of the city. Pool and *La Scala* nightclub.

Meliá Madrid, Princesa 27 (tel. 241 82 00), 25 stories, and 250 rooms featuring every modern convenience. Several restaurants, own garage; close to the Plaza España.

Miguel Angel, on Miguel Angel 31 off the Castellana (tel. 442 81 99), is modern and luxurious. Elegantly appointed public and private rooms. Conveniently located, hotel has fast become a favorite with discerning travelers.

Mindanao, San Francisco de Sales 15 (tel. 449 55 00). In residential area close to the University City in the northwest of town, with pools and sauna.

Monte Real, Arroyo Fresno 17 (tel. 216 21 40), located in the posh Puerta de Hierro section, out of town, is the last word in ritzy elegance. Quiet, dignified, with all amenities. 1 km. from Puerta de Hierro golf course.

Palace, Plaza de las Cortes 7 (tel. 429 75 51). Dignified turn-of-the-century hotel close to Parliament and the Prado. With a somewhat faded old-world charm; readers' reports have been mixed.

Ritz, Plaza de la Lealtad 5 (tel. 221 28 57), is conservative, aristocratic, very quiet, with beautiful rooms and large suites. Madrid's number one hotel.

Villa Magna, Castellana 22 (tel. 261 49 00). Modern and exclusive, and along with the Ritz, classed in "super deluxe" category.

Wellington. Velázquez 8 (tel. 275 44 00). Well located and attracting a solid, conservative clientele. Much favored by bullfighting *aficionados,* including the matadors themselves, during the May San Isidro festivals.

Expensive

Aitana, Castellana 152 (tel. 250 71 07). Popular with businessmen. Close to Orense shopping center and Bernabeu stadium.

Alcalá, Alcalá 66 (tel. 435 10 60). Convenient to Retiro Park and Goya shopping area. Well praised by readers for its good value.

Arosa, Salud 21 (tel. 232 16 00); central location on Gran Vía. Despite drab exterior, much praised by readers for comfort and friendly service.

El Coloso, Leganitos 13 (tel. 248 76 00). A small hotel in the heart of town, close to Gran Vía and Plaza de España.

Emperador, Gran Vía 53 (tel. 247 28 00). Its central location makes it popular with visitors. Roof top pool with good views.

Emperatriz, López de Hoyos 4 (tel. 413 65 11). Attractive, stylish hotel just off the Castellana.

Los Galgos, Claudio Coello 139 (tel. 262 42 27). Comfortable, well-appointed rooms, most with balcony. Near U.S. Embassy and Serrano shopping area.

Liabeny, Salud 3 (tel. 232 53 06). Modern hotel centrally located in the Plaza del Carmen close to main shopping streets.

Mayorazgo, Flor Baja 3 (tel. 247 2600). Pleasant hotel tucked away in side street off the Gran Vía.

Menfis, Gran Vía 74 (tel. 247 09 00). 122 pleasantly old-fashioned rooms.

Plaza, Plaza de España 8 (tel. 247 12 00). Centrally located at bottom of Gran Vía and overlooking Plaza de España. Americans are made very welcome.

Moderate

Abeda, Alcántara 63 (tel. 401 16 50). Pleasant; off Ortega y Gasset.

Carlos V, Maestro Vitoria 5 (tel. 231 41 00). Simple, old-world charm; very central location near main pedestrian shopping streets.

Inglés, Echegaray 10 (tel. 429 65 51). A long-standing favorite. Modernized, in narrow old street just off Puerta del Sol.

Moderno, Arenal 2 (tel. 231 09 00). Good hotel, in a very central, if rather noisy, location just off Puerta del Sol.

Principe Pio, Cuesta de San Vicente 16 (tel. 247 80 00). Pleasant and quiet. Dining room, food and service commended. Close to Palace.

Regina, Alcalá 19 (tel. 221 4725). Elegant, old-style hotel by Sevilla metro, half way between Cibeles and Puerta del Sol.

Rex, Gran Vía 43 (tel. 247 4800). On corner of Silva just down from Callao.

Victoria, Plaza del Angel 7 (tel. 231 45 00). In the heart of "old" Madrid close to Plaza Santa Ana. Old-world hotel which retains its faithful clientèle. Once a favorite of famous bullfighters and Hemingway.

Inexpensive

Asturias, Sevilla 2 (tel. 429 66 70). Renovated old hotel on a very busy intersection just up from Puerta del Sol.

Francisco I, Arenal 15 (tel. 248 02 04). Located mid-way between Puerta del Sol and Teatro Real. Good restaurant.

Internacional, Arenal 19 (tel. 248 18 00). Old world charm and friendly service. Some excellent rooms, others are rather scruffy. Be sure to check first.

Lar, Valverde 16 (tel. 221 65 92). A 3-star hotel, with good-value rates. Central location but on a rather noisy street.

Paris, Alcalá 2 (tel. 221 6496). A delightful hotel, full of elegant, old world charm, right on Puerta del Sol.

Regente, Mesonero Romanos 9 (tel. 221 29 41). Simple, old-fashioned hotel close to shopping streets around Callao. Good value for its price.

 RESTAURANTS. If Madrid is your first stop in Spain, you may feel ravenous before you see any signs of food on the way; normal meal hours in the capital are even later than in the rest of Spain, where they are already later than anywhere else in Europe. Though some work schedules now necessitate a 1 P.M. lunchtime, the normal lunch hour is 2 P.M. to 3 P.M., though 3.30, or even 4 on a Sunday, is not at all unusual. In the evening, whereas most Spanish restaurants begin to fill up around 9.30, 10 is the earliest for Madrileños, and 10.30 more the norm, especially in summer. If you can't wait, most hotels serve dinner from 8.30, and certain restaurants (*Botín* and *Edelweiss*) open early for the benefit of foreigners. Otherwise, you can obtain snacks, and even meals, in any of the many cafeterias around town which are open until midnight or later.

If you want to be really economical, choose restaurants offering a *menu del día* or look for a *restaurante económico.* At the bottom of the scale in price, but not in quality, many will give you a fine meal for 900 pesetas.

A word of warning: most restaurants, including all those in our Expensive category, close for a month in summer, usually in August, and many close in Easter week, too. Most close one day a week, so remember to check.

Expensive

El Amparo, Jorge Juan 10 (tel. 431 64 56). Elegant décor and imaginative dishes with emphasis on Basque cuisine. One of the best.

Bajamar, Gran Vía 78 (tel. 248 59 03), offers some of the best seafood in town in its downstairs dining room. But watch those prices!

Clara's, Arrieta 2 (tel. 242 00 71). Superb food in a lovely old house on the corner of Pza Isabel II. Clara's is now considered one of the very best in town.

Las Cuatro Estaciones, General Ibáñez Ibero 5 (tel. 253 6305). A choice of four menus, one for each season of the year, and sumptuous decor to match. Highly recommended.

Escuadrón, Tamayo y Baus 8 (tel. 419 28 30), is small, intimate and exclusive. Wonderful game in season. Châteaubriand etc. Impeccable service and food.

El Gran Chambelán, Ayala 46 (tel. 431 77 45). Elegant restaurant with superb cuisine. Try their *menu estrecho y largo,* literally "narrow and wide"—a little of everything, it's delicious.

Horcher, Alfonso XII 6, (tel. 222 07 31), is famous. Founded by an Austrian 40 years ago, its specialties are game, smoked fish and Central European dishes. Service is exquisite and so are the prices!

Jockey, Amador de los Rios 6 (tel. 419 24 35). Tops for food and prices. A long-standing favorite which ranks among Madrid's top three restaurants.

Nicolasa, Velázquez 150 (tel. 261 99 85). Top Basque food served by owners of its famous namesake in San Sebastian. Attractive decor; waitresses wear Basque costume.

Ritz Hotel, Paseo del Prado 5 (tel. 221 2857). The elegant dining room of this sumptuous hotel is a long standing favorite, as is its garden terrace in summer. We have had many delighted reports from readers.

Zalacaín, Alvarez de Baena 4 (tel. 261 48 40). In a private villa with elegant decor and topnotch food. Gourmets consider this Spain's best restaurant.

Moderate

Alkalde, Jorge Juan 10 (tel. 276 33 59). Cave-like rooms, pleasant atmosphere, excellent food and service. One of the best consistently good restaurants.

Botín, at Cuchilleros 17 (tel. 266 42 17), is always considered more or less a must for tourists. Located in the picturesque quarter back of the Plaza Mayor in a 17th-century building. Three floors of quaintness, though we recommend *upstairs* rather than the overrated cellar. Two sittings for dinner at 8 and 10.30. Reservations essential.

Casa Lucio, Cava Baja 35 (tel. 265 32 52), near the Plaza Mayor serves topnotch Spanish fare (steaks, lamb, eels etc.) in mesón setting in a maze of small rooms. Personalized service, excellent value.

Casa Paco, Puerta Cerrada 11 (tel. 266 3166). Crowded, atmospheric old tavern famous for its steaks; a perennial favorite.

El Cosaco, Alfonso VI 4 (tel. 265 35 48), offers Russian food. Charming Russian decor, portions a bit skimpy. Call for reservations. American owned.

Las Cuevas de Luis Candelas, Cuchilleros 1 (tel. 266 54 28), is actually built inside a part of the old walls of Madrid. Go down the flight of steps leading off the Plaza Mayor to reach it. A bit of a tourist trap, though.

Edelweiss, Jovellanos 6 (tel. 221 03 26), just behind Parliament. Substantial portions of German food. Opens at 7 P.M. Go early as reservations not accepted.

La Gran Tasca, Ballesta 1 (tel. 231 00 44). In a very unsalubrious street but do not let the surroundings put you off. Inside it is cozy and respectable and the food superb. Frequented by many famous figures, including Hemingway.

Los Siete Jardines, San Vicente Ferrer 86 (tel. 232 2519). Vogue restaurant in Malasaña with "Four Seasons" menus. Atmospheric turn-of-the-century decor.

Valentín, San Alberto 3 (tel. 221 16 38). Long-standing meeting place of influential and famous Spaniards from all walks of life ranging from bullfighters to literati. Intimate décor, good service, standard Spanish dishes.

Zarauz, Fuentes 13 (tel. 247 30 66). Just off Arenal, with superb displays of shellfish and exquisite fish dishes. Closed July and August.

Inexpensive

Dining in cafeterias is rather impersonal and will cost you a deal more than dining in good local restaurants. For the budget-minded, here is a list of acceptable places where you may not always find an English-language menu, but are sure to be served Spanish food at modest prices:

La Argentina, corner of Gravina and Valgame Díos. The setting is unpretentious, and the food simple and hearty.

La Bola, Bola 5. Plenty of old world charm with local specialties.

Casa Ciriaco, Mayor 84, open since 1917, an old stand-by. Popular for its good value, friendly service and traditional cooking.

Casa Domingo, Alcalá 99, is unpretentious enough, opposite the Retiro; sidewalk lunching. Meat dishes from north of Spain. Open every day.

Casa Ricardo, Fernando el Católico 31. Lunch only. Small, friendly, popular and crowded. Wine at the bar while you wait. 50 years of good home-cooking.

El Luarqués, Ventura de la Vega 16 (tel. 429 61 74). Decorated with photos of the picturesque port of Luarca in Asturias, this popular restaurant is always crowded with Madrileños who recognize its sheer good value.

Terra a Nosa, Cava San Miguel 3, just off the Plaza Mayor. Small, atmospheric bistro, specializing in dishes and wines from Galicia.

CAFETERIAS. For snacks of American-type meals cafeterias are the place to go. They are not self-service establishments as in the States but have tables with service or you can sit at the counter. They offer good sandwiches, fruit juices, savory snacks, coffee, pastries and light meals. The following are some of the most popular:

California, Goya 21, Goya 47, Gran Vía 39, Gran Vía 49, Salud 21.
Morrison, Gran Vía 43, Arapiles 13, Capitán Haya 78, Felipe II 18.
Nebraska, Alcalá 18, Gran Vía 32 and 55.

TRADITIONAL CAFÉS. For atmosphere of 50 years or so ago, try:
Café Comercial, Glorieta de Bilbao 7. Little has changed here in 30 years, though it is now in one of the "in" areas of Madrid.
Cafe Gijón, Paseo de Recoletos 21. The most famous of the cafés of old; a real Madrid tradition. Tables outside in summer.
Café Lyon, Alcalá 57. Charming, old-fashioned décor, just up from Cibeles.
La Mallorquina, Puerta del Sol between Mayor and Arenal. Old-world pastry shop with tea salon. Tea ritual (6–7 P.M.) is worth seeing.

BARS. To spend an enjoyable, really typical Spanish evening, you should go bar-hopping in any of the following areas:

The traditional **mesones area** between the Puerta Cerrada and Plaza Mayor has long been famous. Do the rounds of the mesones with names like *Tortilla, Champiñón, Gamba, Cochinillo,* etc. Guitars, singing, dancing and clapping may well accompany your *vino* or *sangría.* Best on Friday and Saturday nights.

The **Huertas** area around Calle de las Huertas leading from the Paseo del Prado to the Plaza del Angel is a popular night time area packed with colorful *tapas* bars and stylish cafes and wine bars offering live folk or chamber music. Two popular bars here are *El Elhecho* and *La Fidula.*

Explore the old narrow streets between **Puerta del Sol** and **Plaza Santa Ana:** Espoz y Mina, Victoria, Núñez de Arce, Echegaray. You'll be able to sample a different *tapa* in every bar.

The **Malasaña** area around Glorieta de Bilbao and Plaza Dos de Mayo is the popular "in" area with the young of Madrid. Bars, tea rooms, jazz cafés and pubs abound. Try especially *Café de Ruiz,* Ruiz 14; *Manuela, Mala Saña* and *Crêperie Ma Bretagne,* all on Vicente Ferrer; and *La Tetería de la Abuela,* Espíritu Santo 19.

GETTING AROUND MADRID. Airport to city. Taxis between the airport and city center will cost the meter fare (800–1000 ptas.) plus 150 ptas. surcharge and 30 ptas. per bag. Otherwise, take the excellent airport bus to the Colón terminal (underground Pl. Colon depot). Cost is around 170 ptas., time 30 mins. Departures every 10 to 20 min., depending on time of day.

By Subway. The subway is the easiest and quickest way of getting around Madrid. There are 10 lines and the whole system was renovated in 1982. At press-time flat-fare tickets cost 40 ptas. Buy a *taco* of 10 tickets to avoid standing in line each time. The metro runs from around 6 A.M. to 1 A.M.

By Rail. There are two main railroad stations: *Chamartín* at the northern end of the Castellana, departure point of trains to the north, northeast, and the Levante, including those to Paris, Irún-Hendaye, San Sebastián, Bilbao, Santander, Gijón, Oviedo, Valladolid, Burgos, Zaragoza, Barcelona, Valencia and Alicante. Trains to Andalusia, Extremadura and Lisbon leave from *Atocha* (Mediodia) station, at the far end of Paseo del Prado. An underground line connects *Chamartín* and *Atocha* stations, and a few trains run through the city, for example commuter trains to Avila, Segovia and El Escorial. Madrid's third station, *Estación del Norte,* has trains to Salamanca, Santiago de Compostela, La Coruña and all destinations in Galicia. **Note:** Always check carefully which station your train leaves from (some trains to Valencia/Alicante leave from Chamartín, others from Atocha).

For train information and advance tickets, go to the RENFE office at Alcalá 44, open 8 to 2 and 4 to 7, Mon.-Fri., and 8 to 1.30, Sat.

By Bus. Buses cost 45 ptas. or 70 ptas. for a transfer ticket (available on certain routes only). There is a collective ticket which is good for 10 rides called a *bono-bus.* It will save you almost a third on regular fares and can be bought from the EMT kiosks on Pza Cibeles, Callao or Puerta del Sol. The smaller micro-buses are more comfortable and less crowded. They charge 50 ptas. and a 20-ride ticket can be bought at considerable saving from EMT kiosks. A map of all bus routes is available from the EMT kiosk in Pza Cibeles.

A good way to get acquainted with the city is to ride the *Circular* bus, marked with a red C. Its route passes several monuments and a number of the main streets and a ride will only cost you one ticket. Another good ride is on bus number 27 along the Paseo del Prado, Paseo de Recoletos and Castellana.

Regular line bus service to Toledo, *Continental Auto,* from Estación Sur Autobuses, Canarias 17; to Avila, from Martín de los Heros 4 and Calle Toledo 143; to Segovia, *La Sepulvedana,* from Paseo de la Florida 11; to Aranjuez, *Empresa AISA,* from Estacíon Sur Autobuses, Canarias 17; to El Escorial, *Empressa Herranz,* from Isaac Peral 10 (via Galapagar) and from Paseo Moret 7 (via Guadarrama).

By Taxi. Taxi fares start at 65 ptas. and cost around 36 ptas. per kilometer. The average city ride will rarely cost you more than 300 ptas. Each suitcase is an additional 25 ptas. On Sundays, taxis add 50 ptas. to the fare. Cabs after 11 P.M. also cost 50 ptas. more. If a cab picks you up at a railroad station, that's 50 ptas. more, and if it takes you to or from the bullring or football match, that's an additional 50 ptas. Make sure the driver puts the meter on when you start your ride. When free for hire taxis display a *libre* sign in daytime and a green light at night.

NIGHTCLUBS. Since Franco's death, the nightclub scene has flung off all restraint and Madrid now abounds in shows featuring striptease, topless dancers, gay spectacles, transvestism and similar entertainments. Pick-up bars ranging from the old-time stand-bys to flashy, elegant new places in the Generalísimo area, have multiplied enormously over the past few years. Travelers who knew the tame Spain of a decade ago will be amazed at the difference, as all censorship has been discarded.

Madrid's Casino is 18 miles out on the N-VI road to La Coruña at Torrelodones. It's one of the largest in Europe, and offers roulette, chemin de fer, bacarrá and blackjack, plus three restaurants, six bars and a nightclub with cabaret. For reservations, call 859 0312. In the city the leading nightclub is **La Scala,** Rosario Pino 7 (tel. 450 45 00) in the Meliá Castilla hotel. Dinner, dancing and cabaret at 8.30 and a second, less expensive show at 12.45. Open till 4 A.M.

Florida Park in the Retiro Park (tel. 273 78 04). Open from 9.30–3.30 daily except Sun. and Mon. with shows at 11 P.M. You can have dinner here and the shows often feature ballet or Spanish dance.

Cleofás, Goya 7 (tel. 276 45 23), **Xairo,** Paz 11 (tel. 231 24 40) and **Xenon** in Plaza Callao (tel. 231 97 94) all offer early evening discothèque followed by orchestra, dancing and a show around 1 A.M.

Madrid abounds with discos. There are two sessions a day: *tarde* from around 7 to 10.30 and mainly for the younger set, and *noche* with doors opening as early (or as late!) as 11 P.M. though they won't fill up until at least 12.30. Most discos close around 3 or 4 A.M. Entrances vary between 700 and 1,500 ptas. Some special discos are: **Macumba,** trendy and popular at Chamartín station, with grill, pizzeria and crêperie. **Joy Eslava,** Arenal 11, in the converted Eslava theater. All the latest in trendy décor complete with lasers and special sound effects. **Marquee** and **Rock-Ola,** at Padre Xifre 3 and 5. Both feature live bands, Rock-Ola favors new wave and Marquee hard rock. **Mississippi,** Princesa 45, is another leading contender; open till 5 A.M. **Pacha,** Barceló 11, in the old Teatro Barceló, is decorated like New York's *Studio 54.*

ENTERTAINMENT. If your Spanish is not very good, the legitimate theater is likely to be a complete loss to you. However, you won't need Spanish to enjoy a *zarzuela* or a musical revue. They're good fun. The best bet for non-Spanish-speaking visitors is the **Zarzuela,** Jovellanos 4, where you may see dance groups, operas, operetta and, of course, *zarzuela,* if it's the season.

Flamenco. Madrid boasts several good *tablaos.* Entrance to show usually includes one drink and starts at around 1,700 ptas. Many of the clubs also serve dinner for which you should allow 4,000–5,000 ptas. Especially recommended are **Café de Chinitas,** Torija 7 (tel. 248 51 35). Excellent flamenco and top food, but much more expensive than most. **Corral de la Morería,** Morería 17 (tel. 265 84 46). Lots of atmosphere from resident flamenco troupe. A la carte dinners. Also good are **Arco de Cuchilleros,** Cuchilleros 7 (tel. 266 58 67); **Los Canasteros,** Barbieri 10 (tel. 231 81 63); **Torres Bermejas,** Mesonero Romanos 15 (tel. 232 33 22). **Corral de la Pacheca,** Juan Ramón Jiménez 26 (tel. 458 11 13) is touristy but fun for the uninitiated. **Venta del Gato,** Avda de Burgos 214 (tel. 202 34 27). 7 km. north on road to Burgos. Very authentic.

Music. The main concert hall is the **Teatro Real** in the Plaza Isabel II at the end of Arenal. Here also is the luxuriously decorated **Opera** whose performances (not in summer) are usually well worth seeing. Seats are not expensive by international standards. Concerts are also given occasionally in the **Teatro de la Zarzuela,** the **Fundación March,** Castelló 77, and the **Sala Fenix** on the Paseo de la Castellana. For details see the weekly *Guía del Ocio, El País,* and local papers.

Concerts are also often given at the foreign institutes, the ones at the **German Institute,** Calle Zurbarán 21, being especially fine. (Admission free.) At the **British Institute,** there are also sometimes concerts, plays and movies. Address is Almagro 5. Concerts of chamber music at musical conservatory, Plaza de Isabel II. The **Washington Irving Center,** San Bernardo 107, run by the U.S. government, often has interesting lectures and concerts and some films.

Cinema. Most foreign films are dubbed into Spanish but there are a few cinemas showing films in their original language with Spanish subtitles. Look in the newspaper *El País* or else in the weekly *Guía del Ocio,* where these films will be marked *v.o.* for *version original.* The official Filmoteca, with different films each day, mostly in their original language, is in the Bellas Artes complex in Marqués de Casa Riera.

Cinemas on the Gran Vía tend to be sold out, especially on weekend evenings so it is advisable to buy your numbered tickets in the morning. Ushers should be tipped 10 pesetas. The best seats are usually called *butacas.*

Parks. The huge Casa de Campo Park across the Manzanares River is popular with Madrileños, especially at weekends, for anything from jogging, swimming and sports to picnicking or visiting the **Amusement Park** or **Zoo.** To reach the park take bus 33 from Plaza Isabel II-Opera. The Amusement Park is open daily April through September, and on Sat. and Sun. only, Oct. through Mar. The Zoo (reached by bus 33 or metro: Batan) is open daily except Mondays in Nov. through Feb.

Another way of reaching the Casa de Campo is to take the cablecar, *teleférico,* running from Paseo de Rosales across to the park. Splendid views.

Information. By far the best guide to what's on in the capital, is the weekly *Guía del Ocio,* available from any newsstand, which gives a complete run-down of movies, theater, clubs, discos, restaurants, art shows, concerts, etc., though readers with limited Spanish may find it hard to follow.

 MUSEUMS. The times of opening given below hold good at time of publication, but are subject to frequent change. Best check with the Tourist Office. Admission charges to state-run museums now apply only to foreigners, most are free for Spaniards. Entrance fees are for the most part minimal, the Prado and Royal Palace being two exceptions. Remember museums of the Patrimonio Nacional (the State) are closed Mondays.

Archeological Museum, Serrano 13. Open 9.30–1.30 Closed Mon. Contains an excellent archeological collection; the Greek vases and Roman artifacts are particularly fine. Also includes large collection of medieval furniture and art: a good ceramics collection and the little-known (to tourists) treasures of Iberian Spain. Well worth a visit. Entrance fee entitles you to visit a replica of the Altamira Caves. Now houses the famous *Dama de Elche.*

Army Museum, Méndez Núñez 1, 10–5; 10–1.30 on Sun. Closed Mon. Contains a vast collection (three stories) of trophies, weapons and documents. A special section dedicated to the Civil War. This is one of the few museums in Spain where all articles are meticulously indexed and labeled.

Cerralbo Museum, Ventura Rodríguez 17. 10–2 and 4–7, 10–2 only on Sun. Closed Mon. and throughout August. Tapestries, painting and some of the loveliest old porcelain to be seen anywhere. Housed in the Cerralbo mansion, with many personal bric-à-brac still left in place.

Contemporary Art Museum. Located close to the University City, Avda. Juan de Herrera. 375 paintings, 200 sculptures, including Picassos and Mirós; set in pleasant gardens; well worth a visit. Open weekdays 10–6, Sundays 10–2. Closed Mon.

Goya Pantheon, in the Hermitage of San Antonio de la Florida, Paseo de la Florida, 11–1 and 3–6. Closed Wed. and Sun. P.M. Collection of works by Goya; the artist himself (albeit headless) is buried here. Worthwhile but not very clearly labeled for those with limited Spanish.

Lázaro Galdiano Foundation, Serrano 122. Open 10–2. Closed Mon. and in August. This museum is a 'must'. It is housed in an old, aristocratic mansion, and besides containing a magnificent collection of paintings, furniture, clocks, armor, jewels, artifacts, weapons etc., it is a delight, thanks to the impeccable arrangement. There is a sizeable collection of English painting, too. The best collection in Europe of ivory and enamel.

Lope de Vega's House, Cervantes 11. Open 11–2, closed Mondays. The great playwright's house and garden skillfully restored. Closed July 15 to Sept. 15.

Municipal Museum, Fuencarral 78. Several rooms depicting Madrid's past. Open 10–2 and 5–9; Sun. 10–3. Closed Sun. P.M. and Mon. A.M.

Naval Museum, Montalbán 2. 10.30–1.30; closed Mondays and in August. Ship models, nautical instruments etc. The most famous exhibit is Juan de Cosa's original map, used by Columbus on his first voyage to the New World.

Prado Museum, Paseo del Prado. Open 10–6, Tues.-Sat., Apr.-Sept.; 10–5, Oct.-Mar. Sundays and holidays, 10–2. Closed Mon. Admission includes entrance to **Casón del Buen Retiro,** too. This is a must. The Prado is universally acknowledged as one of the greatest art collections in the world. If your time is limited, you may be glad to know that the greatest treasures (Velázquez, El Greco, Murillo, Bosch though not Goya) are one floor up, with a direct entrance up a flight of steps from outside, so you can easily bypass the ground floor. The Prado annexe, the **Casón del Buen Retiro,** Felipe IV 13, has a collection of 19th-century Spanish art and is the home of Picasso's famous *Guernica.* Open same hours as Prado except Wed. when it opens 3–9.

Royal Academy San Fernando Museum, Alcalá 13. Open 10–2, closed Sun. and fiestas. Collection of Spanish paintings including works by Goya and Zurbarán.

Royal Coach Museum, Royal Palace gardens. Same hours as palace and closed when official functions are held in the Royal Palace.

Royal Palace, Plaza de Oriente. Open May-Sept., 10–12.45 and 4–5.45; Oct.-Apr., 10–12.45 and 3.30–5.15. Sun., 10–1.30 only. Tickets cost 310 ptas. for a full visit with admission to library, palace and chapel, pharmaceutical museum, armory etc. English-speaking guides are available. Especially notable is the collection of 800 tapestries, mostly Flemish, the Tiepolo ceiling of the throne room, the Gasparini room and the armory.

Royal Tapestry Works, Fuenterrabía 2. Open 9.30–12.30. Entrance 25 pesetas. Closed Sat. and Sun. and from Aug. 1 to Sept. 15. Highly recommended.

 BULLFIGHTING. Madrid has two bullrings so be careful you get the right one. The main ring at Ventas seats 25,000 and is something to see when it's packed to overflowing with an enthusiastic crowd. The other ring is at is the Vista Alegre in the Carabanchel Bajo region across the Manzanares river.

The season in Madrid runs from April to October. There is almost always a fight on Sunday, and often on Thursday as well. Starting times may vary from 4.30 P.M. until 7; bullfights and Mass are the only things in Spain that start on time, so be sure to be there early, for taxis are hard to get in the afternoon, and once the corrida has started, doors to the arena are closed. Pillows to sit on can be rented at the arena. Tickets for bullfights can be bought at Ventas or Vista Alegre rings on the day of the fight or in advance from the *taquillas* on the Calle de la Victoria, off the Carrera San Jerónimo. The average Sunday *corridas* are now little more than a tourist spectacle—and rarely very good at that—but if you are intent on seeing a really good fight, try to be in Madrid during the San Isidro festivals in mid-May when Spain's best *toreros* display their skills at Ventas. Tickets may be expensive and hard to obtain.

SHOPPING. Madrid is no longer the place it once was for unusually exciting buys, where treasures can be discovered and incredible bargains made. But if the thrill of the hunt has gone, the large number of well-stocked stores selling everything imaginable, the glittering curio shops with their wares piled helter-skelter on dusty shelves, the richness and abundance of authentic works of art and, above all, the love and pride with which local goods are manufactured, still makes shopping in Madrid one of the chief attractions for anyone visiting this booming capital. Foreign visitors are, in theory, entitled to 10% export duty on purchases costing over 10,000 ptas. per item, but don't expect all stores to be geared up to cope with this.

Business hours. The siesta lasts from 1.30 until 5 in the summer, 2 to 4.30 in the winter, but most department stores, including the *Corte Inglés* and *Galerías Preciados*, now stay open all day from 9–8.

Madrid has two main shopping areas. The first is in the center of town where the principal shopping streets are along the Gran Vía, the Calles de Preciados, del Carmen and Montera and the Puerta del Sol. The second, and more elegant area—and naturally more expensive—is in the Salamanca district bounded by Serrano, Goya and Conde de Peñalver. The new up-and-coming area is the Orense shopping center just off the Castellana in the north of the city.

One of the most interesting and colorful of the Madrid shopping areas is one you should save for a Sunday morning. It's the **Rastro** or Flea Market, which stretches down the Ribera de Curtidores from El Cascorro statue, and extends over a maze of little side streets branching out from either side. Here, on a Sunday morning, you'll see an incredible display of secondhand odds and ends, spread out artistically on blankets on the ground.

The central area, Curtidores, is rather less rundown. Here canvas booths have been set up to sell everything under the sun. Most of these, though, are cheap articles which are of little interest to the tourist, except for picture-taking.

If you want to try your hand at bargaining (which is a must here), there are booths selling everything conceivable. Buy with care, though, and don't carry money exposed. This place is an infamous hangout for pick-pockets.

From a buyer's viewpoint, the most interesting part of the Rastro is a series of galleries which line the street behind the booths. In dark shops built around picturesque patios, you can find all the antique dealers of Madrid represented. These shops, unlike the booths, are open all week during regular shopping hours, as well as on Sunday mornings.

For handicrafts and Toledo ware, you will find literally hundreds of shops all over Madrid, many of which are reliable, some less so. A sound bet, though very pricey, are the **Mercados Nacionales de Artesanía** run by the Spanish government, with branches at Gran Vía 32, Hermosilla 4, Don Ramon de la Cruz 33 and Plaza de las Cortes 3. They have a wonderful assortment of all things Spanish and will ship goods throughout the world.

Toledo wares are particularly good at **Artesania Toledana,** Paseo del Prado and at **El Escudo de Toledo,** next door in Plaza Canovas del Castillo. In both these stores you'll find a large selection of daggers, swords, chess boards, paintings, fans, Lladró porcelain, guns and leather wine bottles. For Granada wares, marquetry, inlain mother of pearl and so on, try **Artesania Granadina,** Marques de Casa Riera. For ceramics, **Cerámica Española,** Isabel la Católica 2

USEFUL ADDRESSES. *Spanish Tourist Office,* Torre de Madrid in the Plaza de España. *City Tourist Office,* Plaza Mayor 3. *U.S. Embassy,* Serrano 75, (tel. 276 36 00). *British Embassy,* Fernando el Santo 16, (tel. 419 15 28). *Main Post Office,* Plaza Cibeles. *Telephone Exchange,* Gran Vía at the Red San Luis. *Airport information,* (tel. 411 25 45). *Iberia,* Cánovas del Castillo 4, (tel. 411 20 11). *TWA,* Gran Vía 66 (tel. 248 00 04). *British Airways,* Gran Vía 66 (tel. 205 4212). *Hotel reservations,* in the national and international terminals at Barajas airport and at Chamartín and Atocha stations.

British-American Hospital, Juan XXIII 1, in the University City, (tel. 234 67 00). *American Express,* Plaza de las Cortes 2, (tel. 222 11 80). *Police station* (lost passports, muggings), Los Madrazo 9 (tel. 221 25 25). *RENFE office,* Alcalá 44.

Car hire: *Atesa,* Gran Vía 59, (tel. 248 97 93); *Avis,* Gran Vía 60, (tel. 248 42 03); *Europcar,* San Leonardo 8, (tel. 241 88 92); *Hertz,* Gran Vía 88, (tel. 248 58 03); *Ital,* Princesa 1, (tel. 241 22 90).

Toledo

Toledo, an hour and a half by bus southwest from Madrid, is like a living national monument, depicting all the elements of Spanish civilization in hand-carved, sun-mellowed stone. Set on a hill overlooking the Tagus River, this ancient city is a fascinating architectural blend of Christian and Moorish elements, especially rich in buildings of the late 15th and 16th centuries. The best time to visit Toledo is in the spring or fall, because in summer it is scorched by the sun and in winter it is swept by icy winds. But better to see this town and be uncomfortable than not to see it at all! The most important festivals take place during Easter Week and Corpus Christi with their stately religious processions; if you can schedule Toledo for either of those times, so much the better. The three main tour companies run daily tours to Toledo from Madrid by bus. Inquire of your hotel porter. Or take the train from Atocha Station or bus from Estación del Sur. At the height of the season be prepared for crowds of nightmare proportions.

For such a small city Toledo is richly endowed with magnificent historic buildings, but this is hardly surprising as the city was Spain's capital under both Moors and Christians. Begin your visit in the 13th-century cathedral, See of the Cardinal Primate of Spain. Somber but elaborate, it is blazing with jeweled chalices, gorgeous ecclesiastical vestments, hundreds of historic tapestries, 750 stained-glass windows and pictures by Tintoretto, Titian, Murillo, El Greco, Velázquez and Goya. But the real jewel of Toledo is the small Chapel of Santo Tomé, home of El Greco's *Burial of the Count of Orgaz.* Here you can capture the true spirit of the Greek painter who adopted Spain, and in particular Toledo, as his homeland. Not far away is a replica of El Greco's house, where you can see copies of the artist's work, and the splendid Sinagoga del Tránsito revealing Christian and Moorish as well as Jewish influences in its architecture and decoration. See also the church of Santa María la Blanca, another former synagogue. Two worthwhile museums are the beautiful Hospital de Santa Cruz and the former palace of the Duchess of Lerma, the Hospital de Tavera, just outside the walls. These monuments are just some of the reasons to spend the maximum time possible in this city with its Moorish houses, exquisite iron work, and tortuous network of cobbled alleys. Wear your most comfortable shoes. It is worth hiring a cab for a drive around the city on the Carretera de Circunvalación, across the Tagus. This gives you views of Toledo's striking silhouette from all sides, especially impressive at dusk.

PRACTICAL INFORMATION FOR TOLEDO

HOTELS. Parador Conde de Orgaz (E), tel. 22 18 50, is the best. A modern parador located on far side of Tagus with magnificent views.

Alfonso VI (M), tel. 22 26 00, fairly new, with Castillian-style decor. Next to the Alcazar.

Almazara (M), tel. 22 38 66. Charming setting, 3.5 km out of town. Great views, friendly service. Closed Nov. to March.

Cardenal (M), tel. 22 49 00. Ancient house built into the city wall with bags of character and outstanding restaurant.

Carlos V (M), tel. 22 21 00. Pleasant, modern hotel in heart of town.

Maravilla (I), tel. 22 33 04. In Barrio Rey, just off Plaza Zocodover.

Imperio (I), tel. 22 76 50. Very central, and ideal for budgeteers.

RESTAURANTS. Toledo has always had top eating places and the best is probably **Hostal del Cardenal** (E), Paseo de Recaredo, (tel. 22 08 62), managed by Botín of Madrid. Another excellent and highly recommended restaurant is **Venta de Aires** (E), Circo Romano 25 (tel. 22 05 45). Its specialty is partridge which is a specialty of the city in general. Cozy and rustic, indoors in winter, outdoors in large garden in summer.

Adolfo (M), La Granada 6 (tel. 22 73 21). Up an alleyway close to cathedral. Well restored interior; especially good for roasts.

Aurelio (M), Plaza del Ayuntamiento 8 (tel. 22 77 16). Typical and popular; something of a Toledan institution.

Casa Aurelio (M), Sinagoga 6 (tel. 22 20 97). Highly recommended by readers, especially for partridge or quail.

Siglo XIX (M), Cardenal Tavera 10 (tel. 22 51 83). Near the Hospital de Tavera just outside the city walls; its 19th-century decor makes a change from typical Toledo style. Excellent food.

La Tarasca (M), Comercio 8. Elegant restaurant in main shopping street; a little different from Toledo's typical restaurants.

Los Cuatro Tiempos (I), Sixto Ramón Parro 7 (tel. 22 37 82). Atmospheric with beautiful ceramics. Very popular with locals, excellent value.

For real budget dining go to the **Barrio Rey** just behind Plaza Zocodover which is packed with economical bars and diners.

There are many well-recommended restaurants just a little way out of town; to reach them you will need a car or to hire a cab. Two pleasant terraced restaurants on the Ctra Piedrabuena are **Cigarral Monterrey** and **Venta Carranza** at nos. 42 and 39 (tels. 22 69 50 and 22 30 69). Both are (M). Another is **Emperador** (M), Ctra del Valle 1 (tel. 22 46 91). Lashings of atmosphere and much praised by readers.

Castile and the Western Provinces

The provinces of Old Castile lie to the north and west of Madrid, and their three main centers, Avila, Segovia and Burgos, can be reached easily from the capital, though Burgos is usually included as a stop en route from Madrid to France or vice versa. New Castile is made up of the provinces of Madrid, Toledo, Cuenca, Guadalajara and Ciudad Real which lie mostly to the east and south of the capital.

Avila and Segovia

Avila, 4,000 feet above sea level, is the highest provincial capital in Spain. Alfonso VI rebuilt the town and walls in 1090, bringing it permanently under Christian control. It is these walls, the most complete military installations of their kind in Spain, that give Avila its special medieval quality. Thick and solid, they entirely enclose the city and you should begin your visit to Avila with a tour of these walls. The religious atmosphere of the city is as striking as the military. The personality of Saint Teresa, the Mystic to whom the city is dedicated, lives today as vividly as it did in the 16th century. Pilgrims to Avila can visit the Convent of the Augustine Nuns where she was educated; the Encarnación, where she made her profession and became Prioress; the convent of St. Joseph, first establishment of the Carmelite reform; and finally the monument to Saint Teresa, which stands on the site of her birth. The Cathedral of Avila, begun in the 12th and completed in the 15th century, is a fine example of Gothic Transition architecture. See the Church of San Pedro, a Romanesque gem with a beautiful rose window; it's in the center of the city. The Basilica of San Vicente, Romanesque and Gothic of the 12th to 14th centuries, stands outside the walls on the spot where the saint was martyred. More than a sightseeing experience, Avila is a spiritual and historic adventure.

Segovia is 60 miles from Madrid, over the 5,000-foot Navacerrada Pass of the Guadarrama Mountains, or more quickly through the Guadarrama Tunnel. It can also be reached in about an hour by car. High on its rock stands the romantic Alcazar fortress palace of the great Queen Isabella. Even more striking, however, is the undamaged Roman aqueduct, still in use, one of the best-preserved Roman remains in the world. The ancient, crooked streets of Segovia are picturesque beyond description. But the city's most subtle beauties are in its many Romanesque churches, untouched for six centuries. The finest examples are San Martin and San Millan, San Lorenzo and San Clemente. San Juan de los Caballeros is today a studio for ceramics, founded by the Spanish artist Zuloaga. Vera Cruz, just outside the town and affording a superb view of the Alcazar, is one of the most notable churches of the Knights Templar in Europe. It was consecrated in 1208. The 16th-century cathedral, one of the finest in Spain, rises in glory at the highest point in the town. It was the last Gothic building to be erected in Spain, and it's one of the newest buildings in Segovia!

Salamanca and Valladolid

Salamanca, 133 miles from Madrid, is an ancient and lovely city, and your first glimpse of it is bound to be unforgettable. Beside you flows the swift Tormes River and beyond it rise the old houses of the city, topped by the golden walls, turrets, domes and spires of the Plateresque cathedral. The name Plateresque comes from "plata" (silver) and implies that the soft stone is chiseled and engraved like that metal. Salamanca's cathedral and university buildings are among the finest examples of this style in existence. But undoubtedly the crowning glory of this lovely city, surpassing even its wealth of convents and churches, is its elegant 18th-century Plaza Mayor.

Valladolid is a province rich in castles and ancient buildings. The capital city (same name) is like an oasis in the arid landscape, thanks to its beautiful gardens, watered by the Pisuerga River. The *Ferias Mayores* or Great Fairs make a colorful diversion in September. The Easter processions of the *Semana Santa* are unusually impressive. Tourists in Valladolid will want to see the house where Columbus died in 1506; the old home of Cervantes, now a museum; the Casa de los Viveros, where Ferdinand and Isabella were married in 1469; the churches of San Benito and San Pablo; and the Oriental Museum with its magnificent collection of Chinese and Philippine art. And be sure not to miss the National Museum of Sculpture, housed in the College of San Gregorio; the best in Spain.

Burgos and Léon

One of those historic cities is Burgos, the city of El Cid, the national hero who embodies the Spanish idea of chivalry. You can visit El Solar del Cid, built on the site of a house where he once lived, and see his tomb in the transept of the cathedral. This Gothic cathedral, whose twin towers greet the visitor to Burgos from afar is of imposing grandeur and breathtaking richness. Don't miss the Condestable Chapel, the Golden Stairway, and the Flycatcher Clock high above the beginning of the nave. The 13th-century Gothic cloister contains many statues of interest; in fact, the whole cathedral is a treasure house of sculpture. The greatest treasures of all are locked up; engage a guide if you want to see them. Other highlights of Burgos are the churches of San Esteban, San Nicolas, and San Gil; the celebrated Casa del Cordon of the 15th century, where Columbus was received by Ferdinand and Isabella when he returned from his second voyage to America; and the Monasteries of Las Huelgas and La Cartuja, both a little way out of town.

León, almost 200 miles by road from Madrid, is the gateway to the northwestern provinces of Asturias and Galicia. León cathedral, with ts magnificent stained-glass windows, is justly famous. Also note-worthy is the Collegiate Church of San Isidoro, begun in 1005.

Cuenca

Cuenca, 102 miles southeast of Madrid, is a charming city long neglected by tourists, but now coming into its own due largely to the breathtaking beauty of its "hanging houses", which are literally sus-pended over a precipice, and in one of which a modern art museum, one of the finest in Spain, has been opened. A stroll through the old part of the town, with its cathedral (famous for its grillework) is a perennial delight. Some 25 miles away is the unforgettable Ciudad Encantada, the so-called "city" being in reality vast prehistoric rock formations which have been eroded by millions of years of wear into curious shapes.

Cáceres, Mérida and Badajoz

In little-visited Extremadura, the traveler comes upon extraordinary feudal towns, rich in medieval palaces, fortified houses and twisted streets. This is the land of the *conquistadores,* and ample evidence of them remains in the escutcheoned palaces they built with profits from gold brought back from the New World. Cáceres, with its Plaza Mayor, and right in its heart, the Old Town packed with fortified palaces and churches, will amply reward the tourist. Thirty miles east of Cáceres is the historic and picturesque hill-town of Trujillo, where Pizarro, conqueror of Peru, was born. His house still stands in the Plaza Mayor. At Yuste you can see the monastery where a world-weary Charles V died in 1558, and high in the mountains at Guadalupe, visit the shrine venerated since the 13th century.

Mérida is particularly famous for Roman ruins, which include a superb theater where classic dramas are performed at night, two aque-ducts, Trajan's Arch, a Circus and a brand new Museum of Archeolo-gy. At Medellín, Hernán Cortés was born in 1485, and Zafra, a charming town of arcaded streets and squares, boasts a splendid para-dor where he once stayed.

Badajoz, a border town between Spain and Portugal, southwest of Madrid, is situated on the left bank of the Guadiana River and is one of the oldest towns in the peninsula, though rather run-down. It resem-bles a huge fort, with its Moorish Alcazaba, sturdy cathedral, Vauban fortifications and an impressive bridge across the Guadiana.

PRACTICAL INFORMATION FOR CASTILE AND THE WESTERN PROVINCES

HOTELS AND RESTAURANTS. There are a number of government-operated establishments in this area, and they are always a good bet, often the best available. The **Paradores** are at: *Oropesa,* west of Talavera de la Reina, and *Ciudad Rodrigo,* both in old castles and on route to Portugal; *Segovia; Tordesillas,* 20 miles southwest of Valladolid; *Villafranca del Bierzo* in the province of León on the road to the Galician coast; *Alarcon; Avila; Mérida; Soria; Zamora; Guadalupe; Jarandilla; Santo Domingo de la Calzada; Calahor-a; Almagro; Benavente; Cervera de Pisuerga; Sierra de Gredos; Salamanca; Sigüenza; Zafra.* There are functional roadside paradores at *Manzanares, Pue-la de Sanabria* and *Santa María de la Huerta.*

ALMAGRO (Ciudad Real). *Parador Nacional* (E), tel. 86 01 00. Located in he 16th-century convent of Santa Catalina, with pool and gardens.

ALMURADIEL (Ciudad Real). *Los Podencos* (M), tel. 33 90 00. On Madrid-Cádiz road just before the Despeñaperros Pass; comfortable roadside inn.

ARANDA DE DUERO (Burgos). *Los Bronces* (M), tel. 50 08 50, recent, a mile out of town on N1. *Montehermoso* (M), tel. 50 15 50, also out of town—around 2½ miles north. Closer to town is *Tres Condes* (I), tel. 50 24 00. 35 rooms.
Restaurants. *Casa Florencio* (E), Arias de Miranda 14, tel. 50 02 30. Good roast lamb. *Méson de la Villa* (M), Plaza Mayor 1. Serving some of Castile's best roasts for over 25 years.

AVILA. *Palacio Valderrábanos* (E), tel. 21 10 23. 15th-century mansion opposite cathedral. Beautifully appointed, highly recommended. *Parador Raimundo de Borgoña* (E), tel. 21 13 40. In a reconstructed palace right on the city walls. *Don Carmelo* (M), tel. 22 80 50. Modern and pleasant, near station. *Cuatro Postes* (M-I), tel. 21 29 44. Modern with great views of town. *Rey Niño* (M-I), tel. 21 14 04. Good value in heart of town. Open May–Oct. only.
Restaurants. *El Rastro* (M), Plaza del Rastro 4. Typical Castilian inn built into old city walls. *El Torreón* (M), near the cathedral, with typical downstairs "cave" restaurant, is the best bet, though you might also enjoy local specialties served at the *Parador.*

BADAJOZ. *Gran Hotel Zurbarán* (E), tel. 22 37 41, modern with pool; the best. *Río,* tel. 23 76 00 and *Lisboa,* tel. 23 82 00, both (M) and across the river; *Lisboa* is well recommended by reader. *Conde Duque* (M-I), tel. 22 46 41, is the most central.
Restaurants. *Caballo Blanco* (E), tel. 23 42 21. Elegant dining, a little out of center. *Los Gabrieles* (M) and *El Sotano* (M) are both central and recommended by locals. *Manila* (I), good tapas and snacks or (M) dining upstairs.

BURGOS. *Landa Palace* (L), tel. 20 63 43. 2 miles out of town on the Madrid road. All amenities; reader-praised for its charm. *Almirante Bonifaz* (E), tel. 20 69 43, and *Condestable* (E), tel. 20 57 40, are both good comfortable hotels. *Fernán Gonzáles* (M), tel. 20 94 41, pleasant, modern hotel across river. *Mesón del Cid* (M), tel. 20 87 15. Magnificently located in a 15th-century house opposite cathedral, with atmospheric restaurant. *España* (I), tel. 20 63 40. Faded but friendly old hotel on the Espolón. *Norte y Londres* (I), tel. 20 05 45. Delightful, friendly service and old-world charm.
Restaurants. Dining at the *Landa Palace* (E) is excellent. *Arriaga* (E-M), on Lain Calvo, is old-fashioned, with linen tablecloths and ancient, respectful waiters. *Gaona* (E-M), on same street has more typical mesón ambience. *Casa Ojeda* (M), Victoria 5. Beautifully located in a Castilian house, part restaurant and, sadly, part cafeteria. *Rincón de España* (M), good food and smart dining room or outside on pleasant terrace. *Pinedo* (M) is a stylish, old-world tea room and bar with upstairs restaurant, on the Espolón opposite Hotel España.

CÁCERES. *Alcántara* (M), tel. 22 89 00, and *Extremadura* (M), tel. 22 16 00, both rather functional and a little out of center. We recommend *Alvarez* (M-I), tel. 24 64 00, a friendly older hotel right in center.
Restaurants. *Nuestra Señora de la Montaña* (M), 1 km. out at the shrine; magnificent food and views. *El Figón* (M), central with lots of local color.

CUENCA. *Torremangana* (E), tel. 22 33 51, has good restaurant. *Cueva del Fraile* (M), tel. 21 15 71. In 16th-century house 7 km. out. *Xucar* (I), tel. 22 45 11. Modern, simple and central, with excellent *Figon* restaurant next door.
Restaurants. *Mesón Casas Colgadas* (E), with fine views, in one of the "hanging houses". Exquisite dishes, great service. *Figón de Pedro* (M) and *Los Claveles* (M) are both long standing traditions in Cuenca, latter with game specialties.

LEÓN. *San Marcos* (L), tel. 23 73 00. In elegant and stupendous old palace. Antique furnishings. *Conde Luna* (E), tel. 20 65 12, with recommended *El Mesón* restaurant. *Quindos* (M), tel. 23 62 00, is very well recommended. *Ríosol* (I), tel. 22 36 50. Reader recommended, near the station.

Restaurants. *Novelty* (E), modern, central and the most luxurious. *Las Redes* (E-M), family-run with excellent shellfish fresh from Galicia. *Bodega Regia* (M), good cooking in a 13th-century house. *Casa Pozo* (M), popular with locals.

LOGROÑO. *Los Bracos* (E), tel. 22 66 08 is the most recent. *Carlton Rioja* (E), tel. 24 21 00, the most stylish. *Gran* (M), tel. 25 21 00, is an old-timer, but serviceable.
Restaurant. *Mesón de la Merced* (E), Marqués de San Nicolás 109, tel. 22 10 24. Outstanding restaurant, praised by readers.

MERIDA. (Badajoz). *Parador Via de la Plata* (E), tel. 31 38 00. In a magnificent old convent in the center of town. *Emperatriz* (M), tel. 30 26 40, a medieval palace on the Plaza de España. *Nova Roma* (M), tel. 31 12 01, near Roman theater.

NAVACERRADA (Madrid). *Arcipreste de Hita* (M), tel. 856 01 25, pool, garden and other amenities. *La Barranca* (M), tel. 856 00 00, is newest, with pool. *Dona Endrina* (M). Pleasant old-fashioned house; cafeteria. *Las Postas* (M). Good views.
All the above are in the village. Up at the pass are—*El Corzo* (I), small and friendly. Fair restaurant. *Pasadoiro* (I) is a bit bigger, 36 rooms. *Venta Arias* (I) probably the best of the three. All have good views.

SALAMANCA. *Gran Hotel Feudal* (E), tel. 21 35 00. Comfortable with plenty of old-world charm and a magnificent medieval dining room. *Monterey* (E), tel. 21 44 00. Comfortable older hotel, central. *Parador* (E), tel. 22 87 00. A modern parador on far side of river with views of town.
Alfonso X (M), tel. 21 44 01, and *Condal* (M), tel. 21 84 00, are both central and good. *Castellano III*, tel. 25 16 11, is new and good.
Ceylan (I), tel. 21 26 03; *Emperatriz* (I), tel. 21 92 00, in beautiful historic building near La Clerecía; *Pasaje* (I), tel. 21 20 03; all are reasonable.
Restaurants. *Chez Victor* (E), Espoz y Mina 26, tel. 21 31 23. Well-known for French cuisine. *Feudal* (E), in the Gran Hotel, tel. 21 35 00. Superb meals in a medieval dining hall. *Nuevo Candil* (E), Pza. de la Reina 2, tel. 21 90 27. One of Salamanca's best restaurants. *Venecia* (E), Plaza del Mercado 5, tel. 21 67 44, another leading restaurant. All (M) and well-recommended are *El Candil*, Ruiz Aguilera 10, tel. 21 72 39; *El Mesón*, Pza. Poeta Iglesias 3, tel. 21 72 22; *Río Plata*, Pza. del Peso 1, tel. 21 90 05. Excellent reputation.

SEGOVIA. *Los Linajes* (E), tel. 43 12 01. Delightful modern hotel in Castilian style with splendid views. *Parador Nacional* (E), tel. 43 04 62. 3 km out with superb views. *Acueducto* (M), tel. 42 48 00. Renovated older hotel, with balconies overlooking the famous aqueduct. *Las Sirenas* (M), tel. 43 40 11. A deluxe hostel in old house overlooking San Martín church.
3 km out at La Lastrilla is *Puerta de Segovia* (M), tel. 43 71 61. Modern and comfortable if rather functional.
Restaurants. *Mesón de Candido* (E), Plaza Azoguejo, tel. 42 59 11, in 15th-century building and one of the best-known restaurants in Spain, where you should reserve a table early to get a view of the famous aqueduct. *Mesón Duque* (E), Cervantes 12, one of the most agreeable places to dine. Dating back to 1985, it boasts fine food and several atmospheric dining rooms.
Also good are: *El Bernardino* (M), Cervantes 2, a pleasant intimate place with superb views, excellent paella, large portions, and friendly service. *Cesar* (M), Ruiz de Alda 10. Agreeable restaurant specializing in fish, a good contrast to other typical Segovian restaurants. *Mesón Don José María* (M), Cronista Lecea 11, is very popular; good food at reasonable prices. Opposite is *La Oficina*, another typical (M) spot with two delightful dining rooms. *La Taurina* (I) in the Plaza Mayor with typical Segovian decor, bullfight ambience.

SORIA. Best is the *Parador Antonio Machado* (E), tel. 21 34 45. Lovely views. *Alfonso VIII* (M), tel. 22 62 11, with character. Newest is *Caballero* (I), tel. 22 01 00. *Mesón Leonor* (I), tel. 22 02 50, on hill overlooking town.

VALLADOLID. *Felipe IV* (E), tel. 30 70 00, is modern and central, if a bit impersonal. *Meliá Parque* (E), tel. 47 01 00, is newest but in dull part of town. Best is *Olid Meliá* (E), tel. 35 72 00, close to historical section and Sculpture Museum.

Imperial (M), tel. 33 03 00 and *Roma* (M), tel. 35 46 66, are both oldish, comfortable hotels close to Plaza Mayor.

Restaurants. *El Hueco* (E), Campanas 4. Atmospheric restaurant below a lively mesón; superb daily specials. *Meson La Fragua* (E), Paseo de Zorilla 10. Top cuisine in magnificent mesón atmosphere. *El Figón de Recoletos,* stylish, good menu and wine list, and *Mesón Cervantes,* Rastro 6, close to Cervantes house, are high (M). *Atrio* (M), opposite Roma Hotel is very pleasant.

There is a whole cluster of good (M) restaurants on Marina Escobar, of which *Meson Panero* and *Tito's* are especially recommended.

For (I) dining, try *Machaquito,* C. Fernandez de la Torre 5, or any of the numerous taverns in nearby Calle Correos, *Mesón Combarro* at no. 3 being the most popular.

Pamplona and Zaragoza

The regions of Navarre and Aragon are generally neglected by visitors, except for Zaragoza (Saragossa), chief city of Aragon, which is on the Madrid-Barcelona route, and Pamplona, the famous Navarese city of the Running of the Bulls.

The Pamplona Fiesta de San Fermin, when the bulls are run, takes place annually between July 6 and 15. Hotel prices are doubled at this season, but even so it is very difficult to find accommodation unless you apply far in advance. The Spanish Tourist Bureau in Pamplona is at Duque de Ahumada 3. Don't expect to do much sleeping if you come to Pamplona for this vigorous affair. The climax is the running of the bulls which takes place early each morning. Ahead of them run the young men of Navarre—and an increasing number of misguided tourists—dodging the infuriated charges of the stampeding bulls for the edification of their girl friends. The San Fermines bullfights held in late afternoon offer a chance to see Spain's best *toreros* at work.

Zaragoza, capital of Aragon, has always been a city of great strategic importance, and today it is the home of the country's most famous officers' training academy. Equidistant between Madrid and Barcelona, it is an obvious stopping place for travelers, either by road or rail. Of tourist sights, there is the cathedral and even more important, the Basilica del Pilar, set upon the banks of the Ebro River. With its cupolas and blue tiling, its baroque magnificence seems at first sight to belong to Baghdad rather than Aragon. Its chief treasure is the tiny statue of the Virgin on a jasper pillar, much worn by 250 years of kisses from the devout. The other architectural highlight of Zaragoza is the Castle of the Aljaferia (11th century), which is situated on the outskirts. There is also a Museo de Pintura with some Goya paintings (the artist's home was close by), and El Greco's *St. Francis.*

PRACTICAL INFORMATION FOR PAMPLONA AND ZARAGOZA

PAMPLONA (Navarre). Be sure to book *long* in advance for the San Fermines. *Los Tres Reyes* (L), tel. 22 66 00. Pool, garden and many other facilities. *Nuevo Hotel Maisonnave* (M), tel. 22 26 00. *Orhi* (M), tel. 24 58 00, without restaurant. *Yoldi* (M), tel. 22 48 00, the least expensive, very pleasant.

Restaurants. *Hartza* (E), Juan de Lebrit 19. High standards and very popular. *Josetxo* (E), Estafeta 73. Famous for over 30 years, one of the best. *Las Pocholas-Hostal del Rey Noble* (E), Paseo de Saraste 6. Long-standing favorite in cozy setting. *Rodero* (M), Arrieta 3. Popular and very busy at lunchtime.

ZARAGOZA. *Corona de Aragón* (L), tel. 43 01 00, is tops. *Palafox* (L), tel. 23 77 00, is the newest. *Don Yo* (L), tel. 22 67 41, highly recommended, very central. *Gran* (L), tel. 22 19 01. Excellent old hotel, well modernized with lots of style. *Goya* (E), tel. 22 93 31. *Europa,* tel. 22 49 01 and *Oriente,* tel. 22 19 60 are both (M) and central. *Paris* (I), tel. 23 65 37, central. *Gran Vía* (I), tel. 22 92 13, smallish, central.

Restaurants. *Los Borrachos* (E), Paseo de Sagasta 64, tel. 27 50 36. Game and fish specialties. Recommended by one reader as "the best in Spain". *Costa Vasca* (E), Valenzuela 13, tel. 21 73 39. Top Basque and Aragonese dishes, specializing in fish. Recommended. *El Cachirulo* (E), tel. 33 16 74. 4 km. out on N232 to Logroño; superb food. Aragonese atmosphere and folk music.

Casa Tena (M), Plaza San Francisco 8, tel. 35 80 22. Famous for its variety of meat dishes, and its fish is excellent too. *Casa Colas* (M), Mátires 10, and opposite, *Casa Tobajas* (M), are just two of the many budget restaurants on and around this street. *Mesón del Carmen* (M), Hernán Cortes 4. An old favorite.

La Rinconada de Lorenzo (I), La Salle 3. Owned by a former *jota* singer, this friendly, personalized restaurant serves traditional Aragonese fare.

The North Coast and Hinterland

The northern coast of Spain is a rectangle that looks in two directions across the Atlantic. It embraces the Basque country (the section closest to France), Cantabria, Asturias and Galicia. The northern provinces present a charm all their own, yet just as "Spanish" as the better-known attractions of Andalusia and the south. Along the coast of Asturias and Galicia the sea is often rough and cold, though the deep Galician *rías,* or estuaries, are sheltered and calm, and the landscape is as green and lush as southern Ireland. Here you will find the snowy mountains of the Picos de Europa, variable skies, and ancient, gray stone towns rich in Romanesque architecture, nestled among tall trees.

There are three top tourist attractions in this area: the fabulous medieval town of Santillana del Mar and the neighboring caves of Altamira with their world-famous prehistoric paintings (now only open to visitors for very limited periods due to pollution problems); Santiago de Compostela; and San Sebastián, a leading international resort.

San Sebastián, 12 miles from the French frontier, was long the tourist capital of Spain and has two of the best beaches in Europe—La Concha, first, Ondarreta, a close second. San Sebastián is provided with all the luxury hotels, shops, restaurants, bars and nightclubs a tourist could desire. The climate is lovely, the city attractive and never excessively hot, thanks to the fresh Biscay breezes. An added bonus is a quaint fishermen's section with picturesque streets and excellent restaurants in all price ranges. Perhaps we should mention here that in recent years the Basque country, in particular San Sebastián, has been the scene of many violent acts of terrorism on the part of ETA, the Basque separatist movement. Such violence is directed at policemen and local dignitaries, however, not at visitors or holiday makers.

In the Basque provinces, beside San Sebastián, there are numerous points of great interest to be visited. In the province of Guipúzcoa, there is an uninterrupted chain of superb beaches which goes right to the French border. At Deva there is a fine bathing beach. The charming little port of Zumaya, and the tiny port of Guetaria are each well worth a visit. Nearby Zarauz is a fashionable bathing resort. Inland, near Azpeitia, you can visit the ornate baroque monastery built around the manorhouse of the family of San Ignacio de Loyola, founder of the Jesuit movement. The rooms in which the saint was born and where his conversion took place are now highly lavish chapels.

Bilbao is the largest city in the Basque country. It is an industrial center and port more than a tourist resort, but in the summer months the luxurious villas of the residential suburbs of Santurce and Portugalete fill with guests from Madrid. Iron ore is extracted in the locality and the largest blast furnaces in Spain are found around Bilbao.

Vitoria, in the province of Alava, is an interesting little town set in beautiful country. There are Van Dyck and Rubens paintings side by side with the 12th-century Virgin in the Cathedral of Santa María, but of greater importance to the locals is the jasper White Virgin of Vitoria in the equally old Church of San Miguel.

Santander has long been a cultural as well as a vacation center. Unfortunately most of the city was destroyed in a fire after the civil war, but Santander has come back into its own and in summer virtually every hotel (of which there are a great many) is jammed with Spanish and foreign tourists. El Sardinero beach and the Magdalena are justly famous for their fine sand. The promenade along the seashore in Santander is one of the prettiest in all Spain, and each August sees a music and art festival, with top international stars participating.

Since the Middle Ages Santiago de Compostela has been the holiest place in all Spain. In medieval times it was, with Rome and the Holy Land, one of the three great centers of pilgrimage in Christendom, and the Way of St. James, which can still be followed today, is lined with a chain of magnificent Romanesque monasteries and churches. The great nave of the 12th-century cathedral, said to have been built over the grave of St. James the Apostle, soberer in style than is common in Spain, is immensely impressive. The principal chapel, under whose altar St. James and two of his disciples are buried, is dazzlingly rich. The Archbishop's Palace is outstanding, even in this country of ancient palaces, and the entire town is ringed with historic monasteries, churches and pilgrims' hostels.

The feast day of St. James, July 25, is the great moment of Santiago de Compostela, but it is a protracted moment which actually begins on the night of the 24th and continues for a week. This is the time to come if you want to participate in the religious festivities, but make sure you have your hotel accommodation first. Other times are recommended if you want to move leisurely about the cathedral and along the arcaded streets of this ancient holy city.

North of Santiago de Compostela, La Coruña has become a popular seaside resort, while further south, the beauty of La Toja Island draws vacationers from all over.

PRACTICAL INFORMATION FOR NORTH COAST AND HINTERLAND

BILBAO. Tops is the *Villa de Bilbao* (L), tel. 441 60 00, with its excellent *Artagan* restaurant, elegant Spanish cuisine, *Aránzazu* (E), tel 441 32 00, and *Ercilla* (E), tel. 443 88 00, come next, latter with excellent *Bermeo* (E) restaurant. *Carlton* (E), tel. 416 22 00, older but still good.

Nervion (M), tel. 445 47 00, good in the middle range, and so is *Conde Duque* (M), tel. 445 60 00. N.B.: hotel prices in Bilbao are relatively high.

Restaurants. *Guria* (L), Gran Vía 66. Superb food, one of best restaurants in Basque Country. *Iturriaga* (E), Alameda Mazarredo 20. Fine food with a terrace overlooking the river. *Casa Vasca* (M), Ejército 13, and *Victor* (M) are other favorites.

LA CORUÑA. Top is *Finisterre* (E), tel. 20 54 00. Beautiful open location on the bay with sweeping views. *Atlántico* (E), tel. 22 65 00, is also good. *Riazor* (M), tel. 25 34 00. Comfortable; close to beach. *España* (I), tel. 22 45 06. Modern and central. *Mara* (I), tel. 22 18 02, is simple and small but good value.

Restaurants. Virtually all the restaurants are on Olmos, Galera and Estrella. *El Rápido* (E), Estrella 7, has one of the best displays of shellfish in all Galicia. *El Coral* and *Duna-2* are (E-M) and both on Estrella. Good for seafood and regional specialties from all over Spain. *Naveiro* (I), San Andrés 129. Traditional eating house serving good Galician specialties.

COVADONGA (Oviedo). *Pelayo* (E), tel. 84 60 00, an ideal mountain retreat; charming, reader-recommended. Excursions to mountain lakes leave here.

GIJÓN (Oviedo). *Principe de Asturias* (E), tel. 36 71 11, close to beach, cafeteria only. *Hernán Cortés* (E), tel. 34 60 00, rather elderly now. *Parador El Molino Viejo* (E), tel. 37 05 11. Modern copy of an old Asturian windmill. *Pathos* (M), is difficult to find. Tel. 35 25 46. Close to the port.

Restaurants. *Casa Victor* (M), Carmen 11. Some of the best fish in Asturias, all cooked to order. *Las Delicias* (M), a little way out in Somió. Well recommended, good fish and seafood. Outdoor dining on leafy terrace in summer. *Mercedes* (M), in Plaza Libertad, with wood-paneled rustic décor and family-type atmosphere. Not open evenings, Sun.-Wed.

OVIEDO. Far and away the best is *La Reconquista* (L), tel. 24 11 00. Lovely old house plus all amenities. *La Jirafa*, tel. 22 22 44, *Ramiro I*, tel. 23 28 50, and *Regente*, tel. 22 23 43, are all (E). *Barbón*, tel. 22 52 93, is (M), and *España*, tel. 22 05 96, is a reasonable (I).

Restaurants. Well recommended is *Marchica* (E), Dr. Casal 10. Also has excellent cider (an Asturian specialty) and shellfish bar. *Casa Fermín* (M), has a high reputation for good food. *La Goleta* (M), Covadonga 32, is a small restaurant specializing in seafood. Book ahead.

SAN SEBASTIÁN (Guipuzcoa). *Londres y de Inglaterra* (L), tel. 42 69 89. Gracious charm, splendid views, excellent restaurant and service. Newer is *Costa Vasca* (E), tel. 21 10 11. Up above Ondarreta beach, though rather lacking character. *Niza* (M), tel. 42 66 63, lots of oldworld charm. *Orly* (E-M), tel. 46 32 00, small and popular; cafeteria only. *Parma* (M), tel. 42 88 93. Sea views, excellent bathrooms, good value.

Restaurants. The best known is *Nicolasa* (E), Aldamar 4, tel. 42 17 16. Something of an institution in San Sebastián. Four elegant dining rooms serving Basque and French specialties. *Akelarre* (E), tel. 21 20 52, atop Mount Igueldo, has good food and magnificent view. *Txomín* (E), Infanta Beatriz 14, tel. 21 07 05. Elegant setting in a beautiful Ondarreta villa.

Juanito Kojua (M), Puerto 14, is famous throughout Spain for its succulent seafood dishes. Simple decor, with upstairs and downstairs dining areas. But expect to wait. For any number of typical seafood restaurants, stroll along the harbor or through the narrow streets of the old town.

Arzac (L), tel. 27 84 65, on the road to Fuenterrabía, is one of Spain's best. Unusual menu in an intimate cottage setting. Reserve long in advance.

SANTANDER. The *Real* (L), tel. 27 25 50, though once one of the best in Europe, and still with a fine location, is now rather outstripped by the *Bahia* (E), tel. 22 17 00.

Near the Sardinero beach, *Sardinero* (M), tel. 27 11 00, reader-recommended *Europa* (I), tel. 27 07 49, a value-for-money pension.

Restaurants. Dozens of good restaurants here. *Rhin* (M) faces the Sardinero beach. Also on Sardinero beach, *Chiqui* (M), at far end of second beach, is a long established popular restaurant. Also at Sardinero are *Piquío* (M), tel. 27 55 03, boasting one of the best chefs in town, and *Il Giardinetto* (M), an Italian restaurant serving pizzas, pasta, and zabaglione; very good value.

In town, one of the best is *Puerto* (E), Hernán Cortés 63. Also good is *Iris* (M), Castelar 5, close to Puerto Chico. Some excellent fish and inventive Cantabrian dishes. *Maclem* (M), Vargas 55. Generous servings. Especially good is the suckling pig, and in season, the eels, salmon, partridge and hare.

12 km. out at **Puente Arce** is *El Molino* (E), located in an old windmill with superb decor. Something of a legend for its setting and innovative cooking.

SANTIAGO DE COMPOSTELA (La Coruna). *Hostal de los Reyes Catolicos* (L), tel. 58 22 00, is a famous hotel located in a 15th-century pilgrim's hostel built by Ferdinand and Isabella. Lashings of atmosphere but standards are dropping. *Compostela* (E), tel. 58 57 00. Comfortable old hotel on edge of old town. *Los Tilos* (E), tel. 59 79 72, 2 km. out on La Estrada road. *Peregrino* (E), tel. 59 18 50. Modern, a little way out on Pontevedra road, pool and gardens but a bit austere. *Gelmirez* (M), tel. 56 11 00. Functional, adequate hotel not far from center. *Santiago Apostel* (M), tel. 58 71 38, recent, just out of town on Lugo road. *Rey Fernando* (I), tel. 59 35 50. A small new hotel. *Universal* (I), tel. 58 58 00. Near the *Compostela;* reader-recommended.

Restaurants. *Don Gaiferos* (E), Rua Nova 23, tel. 58 38 94. Elegant dining; one of the best. *Vilas* (E), tel. 59 10 00, a favorite since 1915. *Tacita de Oro* (M), Hórreo 31, is another long-standing favorite. *Alameda* (M), a glorified cafeteria, but good food; *El Caserio,* and *Victoria,* both (M) and in Calle Bautizados. *San Clemente* and *Trinidad,* both (M) and on San Clemente, with pleasant sidewalk tables. Most of the restaurants and bars are on Calle del Franco; take your pick of the hundreds of economical diners here. *San Jaime* (I), Raiña 4 overlooking Pza Fonseca, is delightful.

SANTILLANA DEL MAR (Santander). The excellent *Parador de Gil Blas* (E), tel. 81 80 00, in a lovely old house, comes first. Then *Los Infantes* (M), tel. 81 81 00, again a lordly spot. *Altamira* (I), tel. 81 80 25, is cozy and rustic.

Restaurant. *Los Blasones* (M), Plaza de Gandara, tel. 81 80 70. Open April-Oct. Reader-recommended, and serving delicious food at reasonable prices.

LA TOJA (Pontevedra). *Gran Hotel* (L), tel. 73 00 25. A hotel with everything, marvellous situation, great views, golf, pool, casino—the lot.

VIGO (Pontevedra). *Bahia de Vigo* (E), tel. 22 67 00, comfortable, well-equipped rooms. *Samil Playa* (E), tel. 23 25 30, about 6 km out of town on beach. *Ensenada* (M), tel. 22 61 00, *México* (M), tel. 41 40 22, and *Niza* (M), tel. 22 88 00, are all good bets. *Estación* (M), tel. 21 56 12, small, good value, near station. (All hotel prices in Vigo are high.)

Restaurants. *El Castro* (M), Manuel Olibie 31, attractively located. *El Mosquito* (M), Plaza Villavicencio 4, for good seafood.

VITORIA (Alava). Best is the *Gasteiz* (E), tel. 22 81 00. *Canciller Ayala* (E), tel. 22 08 00, is also good. *General Alava* (M), tel. 22 22 00, is reliable. 13 km. out is the *Parador of Argomaniz* (M), tel. 28 22 00, an ancient palace with wonderful views.

Restaurants. Tops are *Dickens* (E), San Prudencio 17, specializing in *nouvelle cuisine,* and *El Portalón* (E), Correría 151, tel. 22 49 89, in a 15th-century house. *Dos Hermanas* (M), Madre Pedruña 7, for traditional Basque cooking.

ZARAUZ (Guipuzcoa). **Restaurant.** *Karlos Arguiñano* (E), Mendilauta 13, tel. 83 01 78, is superb.

Barcelona

Barcelona, capital of the province and ancient country of Catalonia, is a big city (almost 3 million inhabitants), a flourishing Mediterranean port, and a great tourist center. It commands a glorious position, similar to that of Naples, with a beautifully carved-out gulf and harbor. It enjoys a climate milder than that of Naples or Rome, and is only rarely oppressive in summer. A lively, sophisticated city, it is fiercely proud of its strong Catalan traditions. Barcelona is not only the gateway to the Mediterranean, it is a center of tourist excursions to the Holy Grail Monastery of Montserrat, to La Molina, a top ski resort of the Spanish Pyrenees, to Tarragona and the castled towns of Catalonia, and to that 90-mile stretch of the Costa Brava.

To get the atmosphere of Barcelona, walk down the Ramblas, those wide promenades which in 1860 replaced the city walls which once encircled the old town. The Ramblas are alive into the wee hours of the morning, humming with the incessant murmur of voices. A word of warning, though: it is best not to carry purses or cameras in the lower reaches of the Ramblas as this area is alive with purse-snatchers.

In the more conventional sightseeing department, the cathedral has the place of honor, dominating the old town, known as the Gothic Quarter, which stretches from the Plaza de Cataluña to the Puerta de la Paz. Known to the local citizens as La Seu, it is a splendid creation of Catalan Gothic, at once strong and exquisite. The cloisters are among the best in Spain. The buildings in the cathedral area share the church's noble character—the Episcopal Palace; Palau de la Generalitat, the seat of the ancient parliament of Catalonia; and across the Plaça St. Jaume, the magnificent Ayuntamiento. On the nearby Plaza Real and in the Calle del Rech, the 14th- and 15th-century palaces have a grace and elegance reminiscent of Florence. Their severity contrasts with the stalactite-stalagmite fantasy of Gaudi's Church of the Sagrada Familia, started in 1881, and though still unfinished, one of Barcelona's most visited buildings.

Barcelona boasts some impressive museums, notably the Museum of Catalan Art on Montjuich and its adjoining Ceramics Museum, the modernistic Miró Foundation also on Montjuich, and the worthwhile Picasso collection housed in an ancient palace in the old town. Should you be in Barcelona over a summer weekend or on the celebration of a fiesta, check to see if the magnificent colored fountains at the Palacio Nacional on Montjuich are playing; they are an unforgettable sight.

Excursions from Barcelona

The Number 1 excursion from Barcelona is to the world-famous monastery of Montserrat, where medieval legend placed the Holy Grail. The fantastic, mystic mountain, jutting abruptly up to a height of 3,725 feet above the valley of the River Llobregat, inspired Wagner's consecrational play of *Parsifal.* Founded in 800 A.D., the monastery is still occupied by 300 Benedictine monks. The sanctuary as you see it today dates from 1410. See the Grotto of the Virgin, the Mirador, the Chapel of San Miguel, and the Chapel of Santa Cecilia (Romanesque, dating from 872). A funicular will take you to the Grotto of San Juan Garin, and a cablecar to the Hermitage of San Jeromino and a sweeping panoramic view.

South of Barcelona you will find Sitges, the seaside spot to which the people of Barcelona flock for bathing, fishing and golf. Thirty-four miles farther south, through vineyards and olive groves, is Tarragona, with its splendid vestiges of the Roman era. The famous aqueduct is 4 km. north of the city. Regarded as one of Rome's finest urban creations, it still keeps the stamp of Empire in the surviving Circus Maximus. The Middle Ages added city walls and citadels, and parts of the old town still exert the evocative charm of living history.

PRACTICAL INFORMATION FOR BARCELONA

Hotels

Deluxe

Avenida Palace, Gran Vía 605 (tel. 301 96 00). 1950s style, all amenities of a luxury hotel and much praised by readers; central.

Diplomatic, Vía Pau Claris 122 (tel. 317 31 00). Modern, central and favored by politicians and businessmen. Swimming pool.

Presidente, Diagonal 570 (tel. 200 21 11). Modern well-appointed rooms, with a splendid view over city.

Princesa Sofia, Pio XII (tel. 330 71 11). Largest of the deluxe hotels with pool, shops and all amenities; on the Diagonal some distance out.

Ritz, Gran Vía 668 (tel. 318 52 00). Once one of the most elegant hotels in Europe, but not recommended until its renovation program is completed.

Sarriá Gran Hotel, Avda. Sarriá 50 (tel. 239 11 09). Modern, in the Plaza Francesc Maciá area.

Expensive

Colón, Avda. Catedral 7 (tel. 301 14 04). On the edge of the Gothic Quarter overlooking the cathedral square. Garage and some suites.

Condor, Vía Augusta 127 (tel. 209 45 11). In elegant area just beyond Diagonal. Parking and good amenities.

Cristal, Diputación 257 (tel. 301 66 00). Good location, close to center, on corner of Rambla Cataluña.

Gala Placidia, Vía Augusta 112 (tel. 217 82 00). A luxurious, suites-only hotel, though officially classed only as 3-star.

Gran Hotel Calderón, Rambla de Cataluña 26 (tel. 301 00 00). A good modern hotel with parking, sun-terrace and cafeteria, on corner of Diputación.

Royal, Ramblas 117 (tel. 301 94 00). Good modern hotel right on top section of Ramblas. Reader-recommended.

Moderate

Covadonga, Avda Diagonal 596 (tel. 209 55 11). Stylish older hotel.

Expo, Mallorca 1–35 (tel. 325 12 12). Modern and professional but somewhat ascetic. Self-service cafeteria only. Close to Sants Station air terminal.

Gran Vía, Gran Vía de las Corts Catalanes 642 (tel. 318 19 00). Elegant old hotel between Paseo de Gracia and Pau Claris.

Habana, Gran Vía 647 (tel. 301 07 50). Genteel and old-fashioned establishment on an elegant street.

Montecarlo, Rambla de los Estudios 24 (tel. 317 58 00). Central, in an old building, with turn-of-the-century decor.

Suizo, Plaza del Angel 12 (tel. 315 41 11). Just off Via Layetana on the edge of the Gothic Quarter. Has had many good reports.

Terminal, Provenza 1 (tel. 321 53 50). Opposite Sants station. Pleasant service; comfortable and functional rooms.

Wilson, Diagonal 569 (tel. 209 25 11). Traditional hotel on the Diagonal between Aribau and Muntaner.

Inexpensive

Continental, Rambla de Canaletas 138 (tel. 301 25 08). At very top of Ramblas near Plaza Cataluña. Stylish period décor.

Internacional, Ramblas 78 (tel. 302 25 66). Friendly, old-fashioned hotel if somewhat faded; opposite Liceo Opera House.

Mesón Castilla, Valdoncella 5 (tel. 318 21 82). Pleasant old hotel centrally located in old part of town not far from university.

Paseo de Gracia, Paseo de Gracia 102 (tel. 215 58 24). Good location.

San Agustín, Plaza de San Agustín 3 (tel. 317 28 82). Centrally located in small pleasant square just off the Ramblas, not far from the Liceo.

 RESTAURANTS. Barcelona is rich in fine restaurants. Lunch is served from 1.30 to 3.30, and dinner, in theory, from 8.30 to 11, but if you're on the early side, you may have the dining room all to yourself. Better hold out until 9. Many restaurants close for a month in summer, usually August, and some close Sat. nights and Sun. Be sure to check.

Expensive

Agut d'Avignon, Trinidad 3 (tel. 302 60 34), for especially good Catalan food.

Ama Lur, Mallorca 275 (tel. 215 30 24). Luxurious restaurant in beautiful house with garden. Basque cuisine. Very famous.

Finisterre, Diagonal 469 (tel. 230 91 14). Catalan specialties served in style.

La Font del Gat, Paseo Santa Madrona (tel. 224 02 24). Magnificent setting on Montjuich, patio dining with fountains and flowers. Worth the price.

Quo Vadis, Carmen 7 (tel. 302 40 72). One of Barcelona's "musts." Highly original dishes; much praised.

Reno, Tuset 27 (tel. 200 91 29). Close to Plaza Francesc Maciá. Exquisite cuisine, very expensive. An ideal restaurant for business entertaining.

Via Veneto, Ganduxer 10 (tel. 250 31 00). Highly recommended.

La Venta, Plaza del Funicular 22 (tel. 212 64 55). One of Barcelona's most charming restaurants. Outdoor terrace with wonderful view.

Moderate

Can Sole, San Carlos 4 (tel. 319 50 12). Atmospheric, with superb seafood.

Caracoles, Escudillers 14 (tel. 301 20 41). Specialty is snails. Very atmospheric. A real Barcelona tradition.

Culleretes, Quintana 5 (tel. 317 64 85). Between Boquería and Fernando just off Ramblas. A real find. Plenty of atmosphere, interesting décor and good Catalan specialties.

La Dida, Roger de Flor (tel. 207 23 91). Strongly recommended restaurant with atmospheric decor; in vicinity of Plaça Joan Carlos.

Siete Puertas, Paseo Isabel II 14 (tel. 319 30 33). Near the waterfront, lots of atmosphere; one of Barcelona's all-time greats.

Inexpensive

Agut, Gignas 16, tel. 315 17 09. Now celebrating 50 years of good Catalan cooking; deep in the Gothic Quarter.

Can Lluis, Cera 49. Over 100 years old and very popular.

Flash Flash, La Granada 25. Serves 101 omelets till 1.30 A.M.

La Ponsa, Enrique Granados 89. Family-run, with good Catalan food.

Raco d'en Jaume, Provença 98 (tel. 230 00 29). Good down-to-earth Catalan cooking—an insight into the way Catalan families eat at home.

GETTING AROUND BARCELONA. A taxi from the airport to city center will cost around 1,500 ptas. or else take the airport train to Sants Station terminal. An average city taxi ride is unlikely to cost over 350 ptas.

The subway system, the "metro", covers the city fairly extensively and is the cheapest form of public transport. A flat fare system is in operation and a ride on the metro costs a little less than a bus ride. Most of the principal bus lines pass through the Plaza de Cataluña. Fares are a little higher on Sundays. To go up Mount Tibidabo, take bus 17 or the metro from Pza. de Cataluña to Avda. de Tibidabo, and from there a special tram *(tramvia blau)* runs to the funicular station. To reach the Parque Güell, take buses 10, 24 or 31. The transport kiosk in Plaza Cataluña opposite Calle Vergara will help with queries and supply maps of the bus and metro system. They also sell peseta-saving *tarjetas multiviaje* for both buses and metro.

ENTERTAINMENT. The best guide to all forms of nightlife, culture, cinema, eating out, etc. is the weekly *Guía del Ocio,* available at newsstands everywhere. Barcelona has long had a reputation for a somewhat dubious nightlife and it has not been slow to take advantage of the permissiveness of the post-Franco era. We do advise care in selecting nightspots as there are many which may offend.

For a city of its size, Barcelona has surprisingly few good **nightclubs.** Some you might like to try are:

Arnau, Para-lel 60 (tel. 242 24 08). Old-time music hall in heart of Barcelona's traditional nightlife area. Small, fun and quite popular; very inexpensive.

Belle Epoque, Muntaner 246 (tel. 209 73 85). Beautifully decorated music hall with good shows; worth it for decor.

Caesar's, Avda de Roma 2 (tel. 325 48 72). One of the few traditional cabaret restaurants in Barcelona.

El Molino, Vilá y Vilá 93 (tel. 241 63 83). Famous turn-of-the-century theater retaining some of its atmosphere, though contemporary shows have for the most part superceded its old-time music-hall burlesque.

For **flamenco,** try: **El Cordobés,** Rambla de Capuchinos 35, tel. 317 66 53; or **Los Tarantos,** Plaza Real 17, tel. 302 51 50. Both *tablaos* are quite good although they are put on purely for tourists as Catalans are not noted as flamenco aficionados.

What it lacks in nightclubs, Barcelona perhaps makes up in stunning **discos: Bocaccio,** Muntaner 505; **Duetto,** Consejo de Ciento 294; **Equilibrio,** Plaza del Funicular; **Studio 54,** Paral-lel 54; **Trauma,** Consejo de Ciento 228; **Up and Down,** Numancia 179, number among the best.

Theater. Much of the city's best theater is either in Catalan or mime; **Els Joglars** and **La Claca** are internationally renowned Catalan mime troupes. Barcelona hosts an International Mime Festival in March, an annual Puppet Festival, and an International Theater Festival in the **Teatre Grec** on Montjuich in July and Aug. The experimental **Teatre Lliure** is one of the best theaters.

Music. The **Gran Teatro del Liceo**, Rambla del Centro 2, tel. 318 91 22, is one of the world's finest opera houses. An international opera and ballet season is held here from Nov. through May. Concerts are held regularly in the **Palau de la Música,** just off Vía Layetana, and in summer there are weekly concerts in the patio of the **Antiguo Hospital de la Santa Cruz** on Calle Hospitalet.

Cinema. Although most international movies are dubbed into Spanish, about half-a-dozen *cines de arte y ensayo* show films in their original language. They are listed in *Guía del Ocio*. The official **Filmoteca** at Travesera de Gracia 63 shows 3 films a day, mostly in their original (often English) language.

MUSEUMS. Most museums charge admission, though many are free on Sundays. Most close Mondays. Opening times change frequently; always doublecheck.

Archeological, Parque de Montjuich. Tues.–Sat. 10–1, 5–7; Sun. 10–1. Display of finds from Ampurias. Also Roman mosaics.

Decorative Arts, Palacio de la Virreina, Rambla de las Flores 99. Houses the Cambó collection and various visiting exhibitions. Open Tues.–Sat. 9.30–2 and 4.30–9; Sun. 9.30–2; Mon. 4.30–9.

Federico Marés Museum, Calle de los Condes de Barcelona 8. Collections of Romanesque and Gothic wood-carvings, religious objects etc. Open Tues.–Sat. 9–2 and 4–7; Sun. 9–2.

Gaudí Museum, Parque Güell; intriguing exhibit of works by Gaudi and his associates. Open Sun. 10–2, 4–7.

Joan Miró Foundation, Montjuich Park. Works by Miró and young Catalan artists. Also many exciting, controversial temporary exhibitions. Open Tues.–Sat. 11–8, and Sun. 11–2.30.

Maritime Museum, Reales Atarazanas, Puerta de la Paz. Huge collection of naval souvenirs, and ship models including the first submarine and a map used by Amerigo Vespucci. Open Tues.–Sat. 10–2 and 4–7; Sun. 10–2.

Modern Art Museum in Ciudadela Park. Paintings from 18th- to early 20th-centuries. Many delightful turn-of-the-century pictures. Small patio makes an imaginative setting for contemporary works. Open Tues.-Sat. 9–7.30; Sun. 9–2; Mon. 3–7.30.

Municipal Museum of the History of Barcelona, in the Casa Padellás in the Plaza del Rey. Open Tues.-Sat. 9–2 and 5–8.30; Sun. 9–2; Mon. 5–8.30.

Museum of Catalan Art, Palacio Nacional, on Montjuich, Tues.–Sun. 9–2. The greatest collection of early Catalan art in existence. It also houses an interesting **Ceramics Museum** with a good collection of 15th- to 18th-century ceramics and terracota from Catalonia, Valencia and Aragón.

Pedralbes Monastery at end of Paseo Reina Elisenda. Founded by Queen Elisenda, fourth wife of Jaime II, in 1326. A good example of 14th-century Catalan architecture, with murals by Ferrer Bassa (1346). Sundays 10–1.

Picasso Museum, Montcada 15. Good collection of his work, many bequeathed to the city by the artist himself; housed in three historic palaces. Open Mon. 4–8.30; Tues.–Sat. 9–2 and 4–8.30; Sun. 9–2.

Sagrada Familia, Gaudi's still incomplete extravaganza, located between Provenza and Mallorca, Cerdeña and Marina. At present something more akin to a building site than a religious monument but nevertheless well worth a visit. Open weekdays 9.30–2 and 3–6.45; Sundays, 10–2 and 3–6.45.

Science Museum, Teodor Roviralta 55. Open daily 10–8. The first of its kind in Spain. Also includes a **Planetarium** with functions twice daily, Mon.–Sat., and half hourly on Sun.

Theater Museum, Nou de la Rambla 3. Collection of posters and theater memorabilia located in Gaudi's Palacio Güell just off Ramblas. Has been closed for restoration so check, but normally open Tues.–Sat. 11–2 and 6–8. Sun. 11–2 only.

Wax Museum, Rambla de Sta Monica 4. Open daily, 11–2 and 4.30–8.

BULLFIGHTING. Bullfights are held from Easter through October, usually on Sunday afternoons. Barcelona's main bullring is the Monumental on Gran Vía and Carlos I. The Las Arenas ring is rarely used now. Tickets can be bought from the ring itself on the day, or from the official ticket office at Muntaner 24 or from below the Teatro Principal in the Ramblas.

SHOPPING. The most elegant shops are along the Paseo de Gracia and the Diagonal around Plaza Francesc Maciá. Tuset off the Diagonal is good for small boutiques. But the most fascinating area for the tourist is the rabbit warren of narrow streets in the Gothic Quarter (but watch out for purse-snatchers) between the Ramblas and Vía Layetana. Calle Ferran is especially good. For antiques try the Calle de la Paja or Baños Nuevos. An antiques market is held on some Thursdays in the cathedral square.

Barcelona's **flea market**, known as Els Encants, sells a little bit of everything, and is held on Mon., Wed., Fri. and Sat. in the Plaza de las Glorias Catalanas.

The main **department stores** are the *Corte Inglés* in Plaza de Cataluña and a newer one on the Diagonal (metro: María Cristina); and *Galerías Preciados* in Puerta del Angel, Plaza Francesc Maciá and Avda Meridiana 352.

USEFUL ADDRESSES. *Spanish Tourist Office,* Gran Vía 658. *City Tourist Office,* Plaza San Jaime. *RENFE* information, at Sants-Central and Termino Stations. *Iberia,* Plaza de España (tel. 325 60 00) and Rambla de Cataluña 18 (tel. 325 71 00). *British Airways,* Paseo de Gracia 59 (tel. 215 21 12). *Bus Station,* buses for most destinations (but not Madrid) leave from Estación del Norte, Avda Vilanova. *U.S. Consulate,* Via Layetana 33 (tel. 319 95 50). *British Consulate,* Diagonal 477 (tel. 322 21 51). *Main Post Office,* Plaza Antonio López. *Telephone Exchange,* Plaza Cataluña corner Fontanella. *Car Hire: Atesa,* Balmes 141 (tel. 302 28 32); *Avis,* Casanova 209 (tel. 209 95 33); *Hertz,* Tuset 10 (tel. 217 80 76).

The Costa Brava

This is an extraordinarily beautiful stretch of jagged shoreline that begins at Blanes, 40 miles northeast of Barcelona, and continues with 90 miles of sun-drenched coves and beaches to the Franco-Spanish frontier town of Port Bou. Though for long it remained undiscovered, where once there were ten hotels along the coast, there are today thousands; apartment blocks have sprung up like mushrooms.

Such expansion of facilities for millions of visitors every year has inevitably encroached upon the natural beauty of the coast, yet the fantastically brilliant blue of the sea by day still contrasts with red-brown headlands and cliffs, as do the distant lights of the sardine fishing fleet that reflect across the wine-colored waters at dusk. Neat umbrella pines still march briskly to the fringes of white sandy beaches; at least when they can find their way through the concrete and cars.

If you're on the Costa Brava on July 24 don't miss the procession of garlanded fishermen's boats to the shrine of their patron saint at Santa Cristina. In Cadaqués you will find Salvador Dalí's unique house and garden, and inland, in Figueras, the renowned Dalí Museum.

PRACTICAL INFORMATION FOR THE COSTA BRAVA

BAGUR (Gerona). *Parador de la Costa Brava* (E), tel. 62 21 62, in idyllic setting at Aiguablava beach. Book early.

Aigua Blava (E), tel. 62 20 58, on the Fornells beach, one of Spain's loveliest hotels. *Bonaigua* (M), tel. 62 20 50, good view and good value.

BLANES (Gerona). *Park* (E), tel. 33 02 50, on the beach, with pool and tennis. *Horitzó* (I), tel. 33 04 00, also near beach, with views. In town are—*Ruiz* (I), tel. 33 03 00, and *S'Arjau* (I), tel. 33 03 21; both good value.

Restaurant. *Casa Patacano* (M), Paseo del Mar 12, tel. 33 00 02. On the seafront with fish and seafood goodies.

CADAQUÉS (Gerona). *Playa Sol* (E), tel. 25 81 00. Overlooking beach.

Restaurants. *Es Baluard* (M), Riba Nemesio Llorens 2, tel. 25 81 83. *Don Quijote* (M), Avda. Caridad Seriñana, tel. 25 81 41. Pleasant bistro with terrace and ivy-covered garden. *La Galiota* (M), Narciso Monturiol 14, tel. 25 81 87. Decorated with Dalí paintings; be sure to book.

CALONGE (Gerona). *Park Hotel San Jorge* (E), Ctra de Palamos, tel. 31 52 54. One of the best hotels on the Costa Brava. *Cap Roig* (E), Ctra de Palamos, tel. 31 52 16. Large hotel with pool and tennis.

FIGUERAS (Gerona). *President* (M), tel. 50 17 00, and *Durán* (M), tel. 50 12 50, are best. Outside town about 1 mile on the N-II is the delightful *Ampurdán* (M), tel. 50 05 62, a comfortable motel-type hotel with an outstanding restaurant.
Restaurants. The restaurant at the hotel *Ampurdán* (E) is justly famous. *Durán* hotel restaurant (M) is also a long-standing tradition.
5 km out on road to Olot is *Mas Pau* (E), tel. 54 61 54, in a lovely old farmhouse with charming garden; beautiful setting and superb food.

LLAFRANCH (Gerona). *Terramar* (E), tel. 30 02 00. Old but very reliable hotel with good views. *Levante* (M), tel. 30 03 66, smaller but good value.

LLORET DE MAR (Gerona). *Monterrey* (E), tel. 36 40 50. Pool, tennis, nice garden. *Roger de Flor* (E), tel. 36 48 00. Good views, pool, 15 mins. from beach and center.
At Fanals beach: *Rigat Park* (E), tel. 36 52 00. Spanish-style, pleasantly situated with beach and pool. At the Santa Cristina beach: *Santa Marta* (E), tel. 36 49 04, one of Spain's most luxurious hotels.
In an area that is bursting with budget hotels, try *Reina Isabel* (I), tel. 33 41 21, one of the better ones, overlooking beach, and *Tropicana* (I), tel. 33 41 30.
Restaurants. The panoramic restaurant of the *Santa Marta* hotel (L), boasts superb cuisine and impeccable service. In town *La Bodega Vella* (M) and *Taverna del Mar* (M) are both recommended.

PALAMOS (Gerona). *Trias* (E), tel. 31 41 00. One of the few Costa Brava old timers; pool and attractive gardens. Outstanding restaurant.
Restaurants. *María de Cadaqués* (E), Notarias 39, delicious fish. *Big Rock* (E), Plaça dels Arbres, tel. 31 63 45. Famous; reservations essential. *Refugio de Pescadores* (M), Paseo del Mar 44, in San Antonio de Calonge, great seafood.

PLAYA DE ARO (Gerona). *Columbus* (E), tel. 81 71 66. Garden, tennis and pool. *Rosamar* (M), tel. 81 73 04. *S'Agoita* (M-I), tel. 81 71 54. *Roura* (I), tel. 81 70 66, for fine service and budget prices.
Restaurants. 4 km out on road to Sta Cristina is *Mas Nou* (E), tel 81 78 53. In a lovely setting with bright, stylish decor, excellent food and wines and very good service.

ROSAS (Gerona). *Almadraba Park* (E), tel. 25 65 50. 5 km out on beautiful headland; good service and fine restaurant. *Terraza* (E), tel. 25 61 54, cafeteria, pool and tennis. *Coral Playa* (M), tel. 25 62 50; *Goya Park* (M-I), tel. 25 75 50.
Restaurants. *El Bulli* (E), tel. 25 76 51. A few km. southeast in Cala Montjoy, one of Catalonia's best restaurants. Also outstanding is *La Llar* (E), tel. 25 53 68, 5 km. out on Figueras road.

S'AGARO (Gerona). *Hostal de la Gavina* (L), tel. 32 11 00. Smart resort and one of the most deluxe Costa Brava hotels. Palatial setting, superb dining.

SAN FELIU DE GUIXOLS (Gerona). *Reina Elisenda* (E), Paseig Dels Guixols, tel. 32 07 00. Garden and good amenities. *Caleta Park* (E-M), on San Pol beach, tel. 32 00 12. *Montjoi* (M), San Elmo, tel. 32 03 00. Overlooking harbor, good service. *Gesoria* (I), Campmany 3, tel. 32 03 50. *Montecarlo* (I), Abad Sunyer 110, tel. 32 00 00. On a cliff with wonderful views.
Restaurants. *Eldorado Petit* (E), Rambla Vidal 11, tel. 32 18 18. The best on the Costa Brava if not all Catalonia. Two pleasant (M) restaurants are *S'Adolitx* and *Casa Buxo*, both on Calle Mayor.

SANTA CRISTINA DE ARO (Gerona). *Costa Brava Golf* (E), tel. 83 70 52. Great for golf in peaceful setting.

Restaurant. 2 km. out on C 250 is *Les Panolles* (M), tel. 83 70 11, a converted farm with local specialties.

TOSSA DE MAR (Gerona). *Reymar* (E), tel. 34 03 12, is far and away the best. *Mar Menuda* (M), tel. 34 10 00, comes next, close to sea. Of the numerous moderate hotels here *Ancora* (M), tel. 34 02 99, and *Vora Mar* (M), tel. 34 03 54, are both good bets.

Restaurants. *Es Moli* (M), tel. 34 14 14. Outdoor dining in delightful leafy patio. *Bahía* (M), tel. 34 12 91. Good food in a pleasant restaurant opposite the beach at the end of Paseo del Mar.

The Balearic Islands

Lying about 120 miles south of Barcelona, Majorca is as old as legend and just as fascinating. It was here that Hercules found the Golden Apples of the Hesperides in the mythical times of the Greek Argonauts. This island and 15 others are the fabled Islas Baleares. They have been occupied by Romans, Vandals, the Byzantine Empire under Belisarius, Moors and the English. The English are still there as tourists and residents. So are the Americans. And they couldn't be happier.

Prices have risen with the rapidly increasing popularity of the Balearics, and they are now somewhat higher than those on the Costa Brava. If you want a holiday that mixes rest with sociability, Palma is your best bet. Minorca and Ibiza are simpler and cheaper. The former has concentrated on villa developments rather than hotels and is more suited to a family holiday or those who like things very quiet. Ibiza, the one time hippy center of Spain, is the prettier of the two. Outside its brash package-tour resorts, the Balearic islands are still much favored by vacationers seeking the simplicity of island life.

PRACTICAL INFORMATION FOR THE BALEARICS

WHEN TO COME. All year round though April to October is best. Majorca has an especially fine climate, mild in winter and saved by sea breezes from oppressive heat in summer. Generally speaking, Ibiza is hotter and Minorca colder than Majorca in all seasons, but these are relative differences. Winter can be chilly though in the Balearics, and many hotels close November–March. The few that stay open often have many low-cost winter rate deals.

GETTING THERE. By Air. Most European capitals are connected by both scheduled and charter flights to Palma de Mallorca, and, to a lesser extent, to Ibiza and Minorca. British tour operators offer a wide range of inclusive package holidays from very inexpensive to luxury. *Iberia* has daily flights from London (Heathrow) to Palma and *Air Europe* several a week from Gatwick, with special excursion fares available. Low cost charter flights operate direct from most British airports.

Iberia flies direct from New York, Miami, and Los Angeles to Madrid where you can connect with the one hr. domestic flight to Palma. Iberia also offers domestic services from several Spanish cities (the flights from Barcelona or Valencia take around 35 mins.) and between the various Balearic islands.

All flights are heavily booked in high summer, at Christmas, and Easter.

By Boat. *Compañia Trasmediterránea* operates year-round passenger and car ferry services from the mainland to the Balearics. From Barcelona, during summer there are twice daily services to Palma (8 hrs.); 3 weekly to Ibiza (9 hrs.), and 2 weekly to Mahón (Minorca) (9 hrs.). There are also regular services from Valencia and Alicante. From Palma there are 2 sailings weekly to Ibiza (5 hrs.) and 1 weekly to Mahón (Minorca) (3 hrs.).

There is also a twice weekly car ferry link between Sète in France to Majorca and Ibiza in July, August and September.

HOTELS AND RESTAURANTS. It is essential to book hotels in advance. By the end of April all the best-known resorts are booked to capacity until mid-October. Such has been the building boom over the last decade or so that parts of the coast of Majorca have become impenetrable concrete jungles, with hotels outbidding each other with budget offers to try and entice the tourist into their look-alike palaces. Remember many hotels are closed Nov.–Mar.

Majorcan food is Catalan food, but richer and more highly seasoned. The best wines come from the Binisalem and Felanitx areas. The island also has an interesting apéritif called *palo,* a bitter-sweet concoction made from St. John's bread, and the unusual *hierbas,* a herb liqueur.

Majorca (Mallorca)

BAÑALBUFAR. *Mar y Vent* (M), Jose Antonio 49 (tel. 61 00 25). Tiny, only 15 rooms, but in a lovely spot.

CALA D'OR. *Cala Esmeralda* (E), tel. 65 71 11, on outskirts, pool, all amenities. *Cala d'Or* (M-I), Avda. Bélgica (tel. 65 72 49). Good swimming and sandy beach.

CALA MILLOR. *Osiris* (M), Na Peñal (tel. 56 73 25). A good choice near the beach. Not far away, in **Costa de los Pinos** is *Eurotel Golf Punta Rotja* (E), tel. 56 76 00, in very attractive setting with extensive sports facilities including a 9-hole golf course.

CALA RATJADA. *Aguait* (M), Avda. de los Pinos (tel. 56 34 08). Good pool, rocky bathing. *Son Moll* (M), Triton (tel. 56 31 00). *Serrano* (M), Son Moll (tel. 56 33 50). Andalusian-style wine cellar. *Carolina* (I), tel. 56 31 58, stands alone in a beautiful bay with sandy beach, 3 miles from town. *Cala Gat* (M), Ctra. Antonio Maura (tel. 56 31 66). Buried in pines near rock beach.
Restaurant. Try *Ses Rotges* (E), tel. 56 31 08, attractive French food; some rooms.

DÉYA. *Es Moli* (E), Ctra. Valldemosse a Deyá (tel. 63 90 00). Great views in the Chopin/Sand country; excellent food, too. *Costa d'Or* (I), tel. 63 90 25, at **Lluch Alcari,** delightfully budget villa in the trees.

FORMENTOR. *Formentor* (L), tel. 53 13 00. Wonderfully located, with lovely gardens and magnificent sea and mountain views. Attractive beach.

ILLETAS. *Mar-Sol* (L), tel. 40 25 11. Fine amenities; kosher and regular cuisine. *Bonanza Playa* (E), tel. 40 11 12. Large hotel plus bungalow complex, pool, golf, etc. *Albatros* (E), tel. 40 22 11, good views and all facilities.

MAGALLUF. *Barbados* (E), Notario Alemany (tel. 68 05 50). Pool and restaurant. *Coral Playa* (E), tel. 68 05 62; nice views and pool. *Atlantic* (M), Punta Ballena (tel. 68 02 08). By beach, surrounded by pines.

PAGUERA. *Sunna* (E), Gaviolas (tel. 68 67 50). Pool and tennis. *Villamil* (E), tel. 68 60 50, set in pines above the sea. *Gaya* (M), Calle Niza, is a good-value 3-star hotel by the beach with pool and garden. In nearby **Cala Fornells,** *Coronado* (E), tel. 68 68 00, with pool and gardens; more views.

PALMA. The area around the Majorcan capital is one vast hotel complex, most of which is identified by the names of former villages now engulfed. None of our three (L) hotels are actually in the center of the city. *Son Vida Sheraton* (L), tel. 45 10 11, is about 6 miles out of town, installed in an old castle, with some original furniture, extensive grounds, golf, riding. *Valparaiso Palace* (L), Francisco Vidal (tel. 40 04 11). Impressive garden and superb bay view. *Victoria-Sol* (L), Joan Miro 21 (tel. 23 43 42). Great views, pool, and cooking.

Belver-Sol (E), on the Paseo Maritimo (tel. 23 80 08). Nightclub. *Palas Atenea-Sol* (E), Paseo Ing. Gabriel Roca (tel. 28 14 00). *Raquet Club* (E), at Son Vida (tel. 28 00 50). A sportsman's mecca.

Bonanova (M), Francisco Vidal (tel. 23 59 48). Very reasonable rates for grade.

Club Nautico (M), on the harbor (tel. 22 14 05). Yachtmen's H.Q. *Drach* (M), Font y Monteros 21 (tel. 22 31 46). *Mirador* (M), Meques Cenia 27 (tel. 23 20 46). In town but with sea view. *Saratoga* (M), Paseo Mallorca (tel. 22 72 40).

Capitol (I), Plaza del Rosario (tel. 22 25 04). Central, near the cathedral.

Restaurants. *Ancora* (E), Joan Miró 137, tel. 40 11 61. One of the most attractive restaurants in the Balearics, with stylish décor typical of Palma and genuine Mallorquín cuisine. Closed Sun. and Mon. lunchtime.

Porto Nova (E), Paseo del Mar, tel. 68 17 16. One of Palma's most luxurious restaurants, out at Magalluf. The salmon and game specialties are especially recommended in season. Closed in November.

Le Bistrot (M), Teodoro Llorente 4, tel. 28 71 75. Typical French bistro. Very popular with the locals. Closed Sun. and in July. *C'an Nofre*, Manacor 27, tel. 46 23 55. Simple restaurant in town, noted for its Mallorquín specialties. Closed Wed. night and all day Thurs. and Feb. *Chez Sophie* (M), Apuntadores 24, tel. 22 60 86. Good French cooking. *Club Nautico Cala Gamba* (M), tel. 26 10 45. Excellent seafood. Closed Mon.

Gina's (M), Plaza de la Lonja 1 (tel. 22 64 84). Fine Italian and Spanish food. *Céller Sa Premsa* (I), Plaza Obispo de Palou, one of the oldest budget bargains. Simple Spanish food in congenial surroundings; atmospheric.

PALMA NOVA. The area around the bay which includes **Magalluf.** Among the dozens of hotels here are—*Comodoro* (E), Paseo Calablanca (tel. 68 02 00). *Delfín Playa* (E), tel. 68 01 00, good pool. *Punta Negra* (E), tel. 68 07 62, ideally sited near quiet cove, one of the better bets in the area.

Restaurant. Best in the area is *Portonova* (E), Paseo del Mar.

PUERTO DE POLLENSA. *Daina* (E), Atilio Boveri (tel. 53 12 50). *Miramar* (M), Anclada Camarasa (tel. 53 14 00). Friendly. *Raf* (M), Paseo Saralegui 84 (tel. 53 11 95). Good value.

PUERTO DE SOLLER. *Eden Park* (M), Es Traves (tel. 63 16 00). Overlooks harbor. *Es Port* (I), Antonio Montes (tel. 63 16 50). Old-world style hostel with many amenities; pool and tennis. *Esplendido* (I), Es Traves (tel. 63 18 50). Terraced dining.

Minorca (Menorca)

There are several beach resort hotels but they deal mainly with package tours and are accessible only by taxi, car or tour bus. If you are looking for a beach holiday, best go through a travel agent. The hotels below may be better suited to the independent traveler. We would emphasize the need to have your own transport in Minorca. The major car hire companies have desks at the airport.

CALA'N PORTER. **Restaurant.** *Cueva d'en Xoroi* (E). "Cave" restaurant with fine sea view and excellent fish.

CIUDADELA. *Esmeralda* (M), Paseo Nicolas (tel. 38 02 50). Overlooking the sea at the end of Paseo San Nicolás. Pool, tennis and garden. *Alfonso III* (I), Calvo Sotelo 53, tel. 38 01 50. Good and inexpensive. *Ciutadella* (I), San Eloy 10. Clean hostel with restaurant; right in town center.

Restaurants. Most are along Marina at the harbor side. The best is *Casa Manolo* (M), tel. 38 00 03. Tables outdoors on the quayside. Very popular, especially at lunch. *El Comilón* (M), on the Paseo Colón has a good choice of menu and a pleasant patio and décor. *Ca's Quintu* (I) on the corner of Plaza Alfonso III is a typical bar with an *económico* restaurant.

FORNELLS. A small fishing port on the north side of the island, well worth a visit for its four fish restaurants on the quayside; famous for their lobsters. *Es Pla* (E-M), tel. 37 51 55, is perhaps the best.

MAHON. *Capri* (M), San Esteban 8, tel. 36 14 00. *Port Mahón* (M), Paseo Marítimo, tel. 36 26 00. On a cliff overlooking the harbor.

Restaurants. Most are down at the port; the more expensive ones at the Villacarlos end on the Andén del Levante, and the more atmospheric, typically Spanish ones on the Andén del Poniente.

Up in town, *El Greco* (M), Dr. Orfila 49, tel. 36 43 67, just off the main square; good French cooking. *Chez Gaston* (I), Conde de Cifuentes 13, tel. 36 00 44, is well known to locals and tourists. Amazingly low prices for quite good food. There are two sittings for dinner (8 and 9.30) and it is essential to book.

The following restaurants are in the **Mahón area;** you will need a car: *De Nit* (M), Camino Ferranda 3, Llumesanas, tel. 36 30 30. Excellent cuisine and tasteful décor either indoors or outside in a patio bestrewn with foliage. The owner, a Frenchman, is friendly and speaks English. This is the best. Must book. *El Serreno* (M), tel. 36 32 68. Down a bumpy track between San Clemente and Alayor roads. English-owned, enormous help-yourself to all you can eat buffet of roast meats including wine at fixed price. Dining indoors or on long trestle tables in the garden.

San José (M), a pleasant farmhouse on your left, 2 km. out on road to Fornells. Indoor and outdoor dining. Closed Tues.

VILLACARLOS. *Del Almirante* (I), tel. 36 27 00. Small stylish hotel in 18th-century mansion with red façade. Overlooks the sea, set back from the Mahón-Villacarlos road.

Restaurants. Most are around the harbor in Cala Fons, including a pizzeria and crêperie. They are best at night, few are open for lunch. *La Lola* (M), Cala Fons 27, is pleasant; and serves Basque cuisine. *Ca's Pintor* (E-M), in Cala Corp, is a French restaurant with bistro-type décor. Set menu only and geared to tourists but atmospheric.

Ibiza

IBIZA (Town). *El Corsario* (M), Poniente 5 (tel. 30 12 48). On top of D'Alt Vila; great views, pleasant rooms.

At **Figueretas** beach—*Los Molinos* (E), Huntaner 60 (tel. 30 22 50). Pool, gardens and view. *Ibiza Playa* (M), tel. 30 28 04, close to beach.

At **Talamanca** beach, across the bay—*Argos* (M), tel. 30 10 62, again pool and good views.

Restaurants. *Formentera* (E-M), Eugenio Molina 4, tel. 30 00 54. Beside the port and something of a tradition in Ibiza, this restaurant has served good home cooking for over 40 years. Outdoor dining in summer. *Sal i Pebre* (E-M), Pou 9. In the port area with attractive dining room and some tables on the sidewalk. Friendly service. Its meat dishes are very good. *El Brasero* (M), Barcelona 4, tel. 30 71 68. Popular restaurant with lots of relaxed, friendly atmosphere, especially geared to the young. Good food and one of the "in" places to eat. *El Sausalito* (M), Plaza Garijo 5, facing the port. Try their *plato del día.*

PORTINATX PLAYA. *Cigueña Playa* (M), tel. 33 30 44. *El Greco* (M), tel. 33 30 48. *Presidente Playa* (M), tel. 33 30 14.

SAN ANTONIO ABAD. *Palmyra* (E), tel. 34 03 54, is on the beach, with pool. *Tanit* (M), tel. 34 13 00, out at Cala Gració. In town—*Excelsior* (I), tel. 34 01 85, fine value.

Restaurants. *S'Olivar* (M), San Mateo 9, tel. 34 00 10, with pleasant garden and Spanish food. 1 km north is *Sa Capella* (M), tel. 34 00 57, an old chapel decorated with works of art. Well recommended. *Racó d'es Pins* (M), in Port d'es Torrent. Particularly good for seafood. Dining in garden under the trees.

SAN MIGUEL. *Hacienda Na Xamena* (L-E), tel. 33 30 46. One of the best hotels in the Balearics. On its own, high up on a cliff overlooking the sea.

SANTA EULALIA DEL RIO. One of the best is the *Fenicia* (M), tel. 33 01 01, just across the river from town. *S'Argamasa* (M), Ca'n Fita, Urb. S'Argamassa (tel. 33 00 51). Six miles north, private beach, quiet location. (I) value is *Ses Roques,* tel. 33 01 00.

GETTING AROUND. Majorca. There are daily bus services between the resorts and Palma, which make a whole day excursion inexpensive and easy. There is a delightfully old-fashioned train that goes through the mountains to Sóller from Palma, and another to Inca.

For sightseeing, you can rent a car from *Atesa*, Antonio Ribas 33 (tel. 22 60 84), *Avis* (tel. 23 07 20), and *Hertz*, (tel. 23 48 33), the latter two both on Paseo Marítimo at nos. 16 and 13, all in Palma. There are also many local car hire firms; it will pay you to shop around. Note that most gas stations are closed Sundays.

Sightseeing coaches, run by reliable travel agencies such as Wagons-Lits/Cooks, Iberia, Marsans, Meliá etc., pick you up at your hotel and take you to Valldemosa Monastery, Formentor and Pollensa, the caves of Artá and Drach, Sóller, and the gardens of Raza etc. Boat excursions are available as well from such ports as Palma, Alcudia, Pollensa, and Soller.

The Other Islands. On the other islands it is simply a question of local bus or taxi, or renting a car or scooter. Scooters are especially popular in Ibiza and rental places are everywhere. All the important roads are good; but away from the few highroads, the road surfaces can be diabolical.

You can rent cars in the main towns. In **Ciudadela,** Minorca, *Avis* are in Conquistador 81 (tel. 38 11 74) and *Hertz* at Carni de Mao 40 (tel. 38 30 12). In **Mahón,** Minorca, *Avis* are at the airport. *Hertz* at Vassalló 14. In **Ibiza,** *Avis* and *Hertz* are at the airport and *Atesa* at Carni de Castell 41 (tel. 36 39 16).

SHOPPING. Majorca has a number of specialties that provide charming souvenirs to take home with you. Among them are Majorcan pearls, manufactured by **Majorica,** in Manacor; also ceramics, tiles, cups and plates, all brightly colored, with blue and red prevailing; embroidery; and wrought-iron articles of all kinds, from lamps to flower bowls. Perhaps the best buys of all are in leather: shoes, made largely in Inca, gloves, extremely reasonable and very soft, jackets and so on. The two main areas to explore are the winding streets and staircases around the Plaza Mayor and the smart Avenida Jaime III.

Markets are always great fun to visit. Palma is well supplied with them. *Mercado Pedro Garau* in the Plaza Pedro Garau is a riot of animals and food. The *Flea Market* on Saturdays is a maze of everything from wood and leather to cast-off clothes and furniture.

Minorca and Ibiza really don't have that much to offer the tourist. In Ibiza you might look out for embroidered cloths, silver *(plata de ley),* jewelry, gloves and trendy fashions. Minorca has a few ceramics and good shoes and gloves— but avoid those tourist-trap "leather factories" on the highway.

USEFUL ADDRESSES. *Tourist Offices.* Palma de Mallorca, Avda Jaime III 10, and at airport; Mahón (Minorca), Plaza del Generalísimo 13; Ibiza, Vara del Rey 15. *British Consulate* in Palma, Plaza Mayor 3D, tel. 21 24 45. *U.S. Consulate* in Palma, Jaime III 26, tel. 22 26 60.

Southeastern Spain

The most interesting provinces of southeastern Spain are Valencia and Alicante. The first place of note after entering Valencia is Sagunto, with its Roman theater big enough to hold 8,000 people. In 219 B.C. Sagunto, resisting Hannibal during the Punic Wars, knew one of the most violent and heroic moments in Spain's heroic and violent history. Rather than surrender, the inhabitants became cannibals, living on their own dead. Finally, when defeat was inevitable, they set the town on fire and all perished in mass suicide.

Only 14 miles away is Valencia. Famous for its orange groves which perfume the night with the heady scent of their blossoms, Valencia is popular with tourists despite its heat and noise. The port is about two miles from the center of the city. In the city, though 4 km. from the center, are the beaches of Malvarrosa, Arenas and Nazaret, though we recommend the Pinedo and Saler beaches a little to the south of town. The 13th-century cathedral of Valencia claims possession of the Holy Grail, the chalice used at the Last Supper (though this is also claimed by Montserrat, near Barcelona). See also the 15th-century bell, affectionately known as "Miguelito", and an extraordinary silver figure of the Virgin, dating from the fourth century. Other highlights of Valencia are the 15th-century Lonja del Mercado with its Orange Court, the Ceramics Museum in the fantastic palace of the Marqués de Dos Aguas, and the art gallery in the Convent of Pio V, one of the best in Spain. But Valencia's chief attraction for the tourist is its famous *fallas* from March 16–19, climaxing on the last night in a festival with the burning of hundreds of papier-maché figures of famous Spanish personalities, often embodying sharp satirical digs at the ruling powers.

Driving south from Valencia, the road skirts the vast lagoon of La Albufera where the permanently flooded land is Spain's most important rice-growing area. The abundance of rice in the region gave rise to Spain's national dish, the *paella valenciana*. But outstripping even rice in importance is the product for which Valencia is most famous: oranges. In spring the waves of perfume from the orange groves around Gandía are almost overpowering. The heady scent gave name to this stretch of coastline, the Orange Blossom Coast, or Costa del Azahar.

Just before you round Cape Não and catch your first glimpse of the Costa Blanca, you pass the small towns of Denia and Javea, both pleasant resorts with spectacular views.

The Costa Blanca stretches from Cape Não to Alicante and is so called—white coast—for the brilliance of the light that plays on its white cliffs. The hills leading down to the coast are dotted with extensive villa developments and though much of its natural beauty remains, the property developers have taken their toll. Calpe and Altea have some interesting old quarters, while just beyond them, the 1,000-foot Rock (Peñón) of Ifach rises sheer from the sea.

At the heart of the Costa Blanca lies Benidorm with its two magnificent beaches. Benidorm is the embodiment of the worst excesses of the '60s and '70s property developers, a concrete jungle, complete with amusement arcades, cocktail bars and endless hamburger joints.

Alicante, founded as a Carthaginian colony in the third century B.C. has that African look, with its superb avenue of date palms, its vast Moorish castle dominating the city from a rocky peak, and its palm-lined harbor from which ships sail to the Balearic Islands and Algiers. This town is torrid in the summer. If you get tired of 90 in the shade temperatures, you can cool off at Busot, 14 miles away and set among pine woods at a height of over 4,000 feet. Another excursion is the 26-mile bus trip to Elche with its famed palm forest and Mystery Play on the Feast of the Assumption on August 15.

PRACTICAL INFORMATION FOR SOUTHEASTERN SPAIN

ALICANTE. *Gran Sol* (E), Méndez Núñez 3, tel. 20 30 00. Central and one block away from seafront. *Meliá Alicante* (E), tel. 20 50 00. Vast apartment complex overlooking beach. All (M), all in the old town just off the Explanada, all full of old-world charm, are *Colegio Oficial Farmacéuticos*, tel. 21 07 00; *Palas*, tel. 20 93 10, and *Residencia Palas*, tel. 20 66 90. *Covadonga* (M), tel. 20 28 44, modern and pleasant in Plaza Luceros 17. *La Balseta* (I), Manero Molla 9, tel. 20 66 33, is central.

Out at the San Juan de Alicante beach—*Sidi Juan Palace* (L), tel. 16 13 00, beautiful location, and all amenities.

Restaurants. *Delfín* (E), Expl. de España 14. Modern and elegant. *Quo Vadis* (E), Plaza Santísima Faz 3. Atmospheric, in square in old town. Sidewalk dining in summer. *Goleta* (M), Expl. de España 8. Plain, simple décor with old-world air. *Rincón Castellano* (I), Manero Molla 12. Charming friendly mesón with excellent value *menu del día*. A real budget find.

BENIDORM (Alicante). Top is the *Gran Hotel Delfín* (E), tel. 85 34 00. Pool, tennis, gardens, old Spanish furniture.

Among the other (E) spots are:—*Cimbel,* tel. 85 21 00, pool and good range of rooms. *Los Dálmatas,* tel. 85 19 00, recent and one of the best in this grade.

Both (M) are: *Avenida,* tel. 85 41 08. A 4-star hotel with very reasonable rates; and *Belroy Palace,* tel. 85 02 03, also 4 stars, no restaurant.

There are a large number of (I) establishments. A good one is *Planesia,* tel. 85 54 66, modern, great views, food good and friendly service.

Restaurants. *I Fratelli* (E), Dr Orts Llorca, tel. 85 39 79. Excellent Italian restaurant with stylish turn-of-century decor. *Tiffany's* (E), Avda. del Mediterraneo, best in town.

ELCHE (Alicante). *Huerto del Cura* (E), tel. 45 80 40. Lovely setting in palm grove, with excellent *Els Capellans* restaurant. *Cartagena* (I), tel. 46 15 50.

Restaurant. *Parque Municipal* (M), is an open-air favorite in the park.

VALENCIA. *Rey Don Jaime* (L), Avda Baleares 2, tel. 360 73 00, in outskirts towards El Grao. Readers praise its delicious food. *Astoria Palace* (E), tel. 352 67 37. Modern and central in pleasant Plaza Rodrigo Botet. *Reina Victoria* (E), tel. 352 04 87. Central and elegant old-world style. *Excelsior,* Barcelonina 5, tel. 351 46 12, and *Inglés,* Marqués de Dos Aguas, tel. 351 64 26, are both (M) with lots of old-world charm. *Bristol* (M-I), Abadía San Martín, is well recommended. *Europa,* Ribera 4, and *Internacional,* beside railroad station, are both good (I)s.

On Saler beach, *Sidi Saler Palace* (L), tel. 367 41 00, with tennis and sauna.

Restaurants. *El Cachirulo* (E), tel. 361 13 15. Rustic Aragonese restaurant specializing in meat dishes. *El Condestable* (E), tel. 369 92 50. Small and intimate with superb medieval decor and high standards. *La Hacienda* (E), tel. 373 18 59. Stylish, with antique furniture and fine cuisine. *Ma Cuina* (E), tel. 341 77 99. Fine Basque cooking well known to local gourmets.

Les Graelles (M), tel. 360 47 00. Old farmhouse atmosphere; specializing in Valencian cooking. *Lionel* (M), Tel. 351 65 66. Attractively decorated and consistently reliable. *Meson Marisquero* (M), tel. 322 97 91. Atmospheric, with a superb display of seafood. For a good selection of (M) and (I) restaurants, try the Calle Moisén Femades. *Casa Cesáreo* (I), Guillén de Castro 15. Charming decor and good paella at lunchtime. *Venta del Toboso* (I), Mar 22. Rustic restaurant popular for over 60 years.

Moorish Spain

Andalusia is the heart of the mystery of Spain. The closest you can come to that heart is in Seville, 55 minutes from Madrid by air. This is the city of Don Juan and Carmen, the spiritual capital of Andalusia.

Seville's cathedral, begun in 1402, a century and a half after St. Ferdinand delivered the city from the Moors, can only be described in superlatives. It is the largest in Spain (and the largest Gothic building in the world), the highest, and the richest in great works of art. This immense monument to Christianity enshrines the mortal vestiges of St. Ferdinand and Christopher Columbus. Every day, characteristically, the bell that summons the faithful to prayer rings out from a Moorish minaret, relic of the Arab mosque whose admirable tower of Abou Yakoub the Sevillians could not bring themselves to destroy. Now topped by a five-story bell tower, called the Giralda (weathercock), this splendid example of Arabic art is one of the marvels of Seville.

Other sights which you should not miss are the Tower of Gold and the Alcazar, Mudejar palace of Pedro the Cruel, the fascinating quarter of Santa Cruz with its twisting byways, dignified old houses and flagstoned patios; the Casa Pilatos and the baroque Alms House of La Caridad with paintings by Murillo and Valdés Leal, the latter comissioned by Miguel de Mañara, the original Don Juan, who died within these walls.

There is no more pious and no more boisterous festival in all of Europe than Holy Week in Seville. The first procession begins Palm Sunday afternoon, the last ends with the final streaks of sunset on Good Friday. There are mummers dressed up as Roman centurions, gypsy songs and dances, firecrackers, barefoot penitents staggering under the weight of crosses, pious women actually bleeding under crowns of thorns; there are the improvised *saetas,* anguished songs inspired by the sufferings of Jesus, and there are dramatic prostrations before the Madonna, the thrusting of fingers into the wounds of Christ. You can watch this extraordinary exhibition of agony and joy from rented seats, but we must warn you that Seville is jammed at this time and that all hotel accommodations are heavily booked well ahead of this date.

Corboda is worth a visit even in the unrelenting heat of summer for its incomparable eighth-century mosque. Abd el Rahman, an emir of the great caliphate of Cordoba, intended it to surpass all other Arab mosques in grandeur. When you cross the threshold, you are immediately overwhelmed by the evidence of the rich Moorish civilization which was and still is the glory of this Spanish city. Even after Saint Ferdinand had driven out the Moors, the citizens of Cordoba refused to disturb a single stone of their wonderful mosque. They simply blessed the building and consecrated it to the Virgin.

Granada is another monument of Moorish Spain, perhaps the most impressive of all. When Boabdil, the last Moorish king, surrendered the city to Ferdinand and Isabella, his heartbroken sob found a lasting echo in Arab hearts. As for the Catholic Monarchs, they wept with joy, kneeling among their monks and soldiers on that January day in 1492 to thank God for victory as their flag was raised on the tower of the Alhambra. They lie side by side, Ferdinand and Isabella, in the Royal Chapel of the cathedral of Granada, immortalized in bas reliefs and glorified by paintings of El Greco and Ribera—but even this glory is dimmed by Granada's most famous monument, the dazzling Arabian Nights palace of the Alhambra. When you visit its filigree courtyards with their ornate stucco work as delicate as lace, you will retain a series of indelible images—the marble baths, perforated like incense burners, the turquoise green and black of the Pool of Myrtles, the Fountain of Lions into which once flowed the blood of 36 beheaded princes. The rose-red Alhambra and the nearby Generalife, summer residence of the caliphs, are sure to figure amongst your most vivid memories of Spain.

PRACTICAL INFORMATION FOR MOORISH SPAIN

CORDOBA. *El Gran Capitán* (E), tel. 47 02 50. Modern and well maintained, not far from station. Tops is the vast, airconditioned *Meliá Córdoba* (E), tel. 29 80 66, pleasant and central. *Parador de la Arruzafa* (E), tel. 27 59 00. Modern parador 4 km out to north. Readers' reports have been mixed. *Los Gallos* (M), tel. 23 55 00. Reasonable accommodations but rather geared to tour groups. *Maimónides* (M), tel. 47 15000. Lovely location right by mosque but some of the rooms are showing their age. *Colón* (I), Alhaken II, tel. 22 62 23, is excellent value. *Marisa* (I), tel. 47 31 42, is a charming Andalusian house near mosque.

Restaurants. Near the Mosque is *El Caballo Rojo* (E), Cardenal Herrero 28, delightfully atmospheric with superb food, a "must." *Castillo de la Albaida* (E), tel. 27 34 93. 4 km from center, in a 14th-century castle, though location is superior to cuisine.

Almudaina (M), Plaza del los Santos Mártires 1, tel. 47 43 42. Located in an old school on edge of Judería, and overlooking Alcázar walls. Delightful décor. *El Churrasco* (M), Romero 16, tel. 29 08 19. A favorite with the Cordobeses, especially for roast meats. *Mesón Bandolero* (M), Medina y Corella 8. Close to mosque and charmingly decorated. *El Patio Arabe* (I), Calle Manriquez. Simple and geared to tourists, but with a pretty outdoor patio. *Los Patios* (I), Cardenal Herrero 16. Self-service but worth a visit for its beautiful setting.

GRANADA. *Alhambra Palace* (E), tel. 22 14 68. Beautiful Moorish-style palace atop the Alhambra hill with magnificent views; standard of rooms variable. *Carmen* (E), José Antonio 62, tel. 25 83 00. Stylish and comfortable; in center of town. *Parador de San Francisco* (E), tel. 22 14 93. In an old convent within the Alhambra walls, Spain's most popular parador. You'll need to reserve 4–6 months in advance. Readers report curt, impersonal service.

America (M), tel. 22 74 71. Charming hostel within Alhambra grounds. Very popular, book ahead. *Guadalupe* (M), tel. 22 34 23, and *Generalife* (M), tel. 22 55 06, with pool, are both recent and comfortable; on Alhambra hill close to entrance to Generalife. *Kenia* (M), Molinos 65, tel. 22 75 06. Small, quiet, with personalized service; in a former private villa. *Victoria* (M), Puerta Real, tel. 25 77 00. Old-world charm, period dining room, in heart of town.

Inglaterra (I), Cetti Meriem 8, tel. 22 15 59. Old-world hotel with character. Outside somewhat shabby but rooms are modernized. *Maciá* (I), tel. 22 75 35. Modern and comfortable in pleasant Plaza Nueva.

Restaurants. *Baroca* (E), tel. 26 50 61. Considered one of Granada's best restaurants. *Cunini* (E), Pescadería 9, tel. 26 37 01. Long famous for its fish and seafood, but rather overpriced. *Colombia* (E-M), tel. 22 74 33. On Alhambra hill, stylish Arab decor, guitar music and splendid views. *Los Leones* (E-M), José Antonio 10, tel. 25 50 07. Smart and well recommended. *Sevilla* (M), Oficios 14. Beside cathedral in Alcaicería, picturesque decor. *Los Manueles* (I), Zaragoza 2. Atmospheric with smoked hams hanging from ceiling.

JAEN. A city that offers little to the tourist but a one-night stay in the beautiful *Parador Santa Catalina* (E), tel. 23 22 87, is a worthwhile delight. This converted medieval castle perched on a hill top has balconied rooms with breathtaking views for miles around.

SEVILLE. Hotel prices can double, even triple, during Holy Week and the Feria, when you will be obliged to take half board.

Alfonso XIII (L), tel. 22 28 50. Built for 1929 Exhibition, now renovated and still full of beauty and great style; mixed reports from readers.

Doña María (E), Don Remondo 19, tel. 22 49 90. Small, tasteful rooms furnished with antiques; rooftop pool with view of Giralda. *Inglaterra* (E), Pza Nueva 7, tel. 22 49 70. Renovated hotel in central square; good reputation. *Los Lebreros* (E), Luis Morales 2, tel. 57 94 00. Modern and luxurious, a little out of center. *Macarena* (E), San Juan Ribera 2, tel. 37 57 00. On edge of town; comfortable and stylish.

Good (M) are *Becquer*, Reyes Católicos 4, tel. 22 89 00. Pleasant and modern. *Fernando III*, San José 21, tel. 21 73 07. On edge of Barrio Sta Cruz; rooftop pool; recommended.

In the (I) range try—*Ducal*, tel. 21 51 07, simple old-world charm, and *Murillo*, tel. 21 60 95, picturesque and quiet in heart of Barrio Santa Cruz.

Restaurants. All (E) are—*Albahaca*, Plaza Santa Cruz, tel. 22 07 14. Beautifully located in heart of old Jewish quarter; creative dishes. *Mesón Don Raimundo*, Argote de Molina 26, tel. 22 33 55. Great atmosphere in an old convent. *Or-Iza*, Betis 61, tel. 27 95 85. Serves Basque *nouvelle cuisine. Paco Ramos*, Reyes Católicos 21, tel. 21 75 74. Excellent.

Bodegón Torre del Oro (M), Santander 15, tel. 21 31 69. Rustic atmosphere, good food, popular with locals and tourists. *La Isla* (M), Arfe 25. Readers praise its paella and fish dishes. *Rio Grande* (M), tel. 27 18 31. Huge riverside terrace across from Golden Tower.

La Cueva del Pez Espada (I), Rodrigo Caro 18. Colorful, fun tavern just off Plaza Doña Elvira in Barrio Santa Cruz. *El Giraldillo* (I). Picturesque mesón opposite entrance to cathedral. *El Mesón* (I), Dos de Mayo 26. Typical Sevillian *bodega* of James Michener fame; lashings of atmosphere.

Warning. Carry minimal cash, no jewelry or documents on you; Seville is notorious for street muggings.

The Costa del Sol and Cadiz

One of Europe's biggest resort areas, the Costa del Sol stretches from Almería in the east to Algeciras in the west. The beaches are frankly not that good, the sand being gray and shingly and the sea far from clean; its popularity undoubtedly stems from its hot climate. Places of interest include Almuñecar, a fishing village since Phoenician times 3,000 years ago; Nerja, with its fantastic lookout known as the Balcony of Europe high above the sea, and equally fantastic Neolithic caves; and Málaga, famous for its grapes, its seafood and a winter climate equalled in hours of sunshine only by Sicily.

Málaga claims the title of Capital of the Costa del Sol though most tourists stay in the beach resorts to its west such as Torremolinos, the magnet for a heterogeneous assortment of charterflight groups and vacationing sunseekers from all over Europe and America. Its streets are lined with a seemingly endless array of restaurants, cafés and boutiques. The construction of gigantic high-rise buildings has long since transformed what was once a poor fishing village into a concrete metropolis. Its existence now is solely to provide pleasure to the tourist. Continuing west, you come to Fuengirola, Marbella, the poshest of the Costa del Sol's resorts, with its elegant marina at Puerto Banús, Estepona, somewhat less touristy, and finally San Roque, a romantic-looking town built by the Spaniards when the British captured Gibraltar in 1704 and devoted until recently to the pursuit of smuggling.

From San Roque, it is only eight miles along a road winding through eucalyptus trees to the seedy port of Algeciras. From here there are regular crossings to Morocco and access, via La Linea, to Gibraltar. The drive from Algeciras to historic Cadiz by way of Tarifa takes you 75 miles along a beautiful road with views of the straits of Gibraltar, the coast of Africa and the Atlas Mountains of that dark continent looming black against the sky.

Cadiz, the brawling southern port destroyed by Drake in revenge for its contribution to the "Invincible Armada", is African in appearance, with palm trees, cupolas, and ancient shabby white houses atop a rocky peninsular surrounded on almost every side by sea. North of here are the orderly vineyards that signal your approach to a famous little town, Jerez de la Frontera, home of one of the world's great wines. Visit the *bodegas* of Gonzalez Byass or Pedro Domecq for a taste of some of the rarer vintages of sherry and for a look at the casks signed by royalty, bullfighters, writers, musicians and other distinguished admirers of this heady wine.

From Jerez to Seville is only 60 miles by a good highway, but if you are driving and haven't imbibed too much of that golden *Jerez,* we recommend the mountainous inland road cutting from Jerez to Málaga, through picturesque Arcos de la Frontera and ancient Ronda. One of the oldest towns in Spain, Ronda is perched above a rocky cleft, 1,000 feet deep, spanned by a Roman bridge. Practically untouched since the 18th century, this romantic kingdom of mountaineers and smugglers has long exerted a magnetic attraction for artists and bullfighting aficionados, Goya and Hemingway among them.

PRACTICAL INFORMATION FOR THE COSTA DEL SOL

ALGECIRAS (Cadiz). *Reina Cristina* (L-E), tel. 65 00 61, justly famous; tropical garden, views of Gibraltar and Africa. *Octavio* (E), tel. 65 24 61, with *Iris* restaurant; praised by readers. *Alarde* (M), Alfonso XI 4, tel. 66 04 08. Modern and central. *Anglo Hispano* (I), Avda Villanueva, tel. 67 15 90. Simple.

Restaurants. *Marea Baja* (M), Trafalgar 2, tel. 66 36 54. Small, attractive seafood restaurant, one of the best in town. *Pazo de Edelmiro* (I), Plaza Miguel Martin 1, good value.

ALMERIA. Dull town with little to offer the tourist. *Gran Hotel Almería* (E), tel. 23 80 11, good service and comfort. *Torreluz* (M), tel. 23 47 99, functional but adequate, right in center.
Restaurants. *Rincón de Juan Pedro* (M), Plaza del Carmen 6, tel. 23 53 79. Best in town, with charming typical decor and good food. *Imperial* (I), Puerta de Purchena 5, plain decor but incredible value.

ANTEQUERA (Málaga). Just north of town is the comfortable *Parador* (E), tel. 84 00 51, pleasant garden, good food and splendid views.

ARCOS DE LA FRONTERA (Cádiz). *Parador Casa del Corregidor* (E-M), tel. 70 05 00. In the picturesque Plaza de España in the heart of the old town.
Restaurant. *Mesón del Brigadier Curro El Cojo* (E-M), tel. 70 10 03, at the lake. Regional country cooking; pork and sausage specialties.

BENALMADENA COSTA (Málaga). *See also* Torremolinos. *Tritón* (L), tel. 44 32 40, pools, private beach, sauna. *Riviera* (E), tel. 44 12 40, well-maintained, some rooms overlooking beach. *Alay* (E), tel. 44 14 40, two pools, good service, recommended.
Restaurant. *El Castillito Bilbil* (M), tel. 44 18 12, for gourmet food and romantic atmosphere; reader-recommended.

CADIZ. *Atlántico* (E), tel. 21 23 01, magnificent headland location. *Francia y París* (M), tel. 22 23 48, in a quiet, charming square, highly recommended.
Restaurants. *Anteojo* (M), Alameda de Apodaca 22, tel. 21 36 39, dining room upstairs and terrace downstairs both with splendid views. *Curro El Cojo* (M), Paseo Marítimo 2, tel. 23 31 86. Offers meat specialties of Cádiz. Andalusian patio décor. *El Faro* (M), San Felix 15, tel. 21 10 68. Excellent seafood, typical décor in the picturesque old quarter.

ESTEPONA (Málaga). *Golf el Paraiso* (E), tel. 81 28 40, 7 miles out on the Málaga road. Disco, revolving restaurant; beach, golf and tennis. *Santa Marta* (M), tel. 81 13 40, 11 km. out. A little shabby but friendly.
Restaurants. *El Molino,* tel. 81 34 90, and *The Yellow Book,* tel. 80 04 84, both (E) with outstanding cuisine. *Costa del Sol* (M), reader-recommended.

FUENGIROLA (Málaga). *Las Palmeras* (E), tel. 47 27 00, overlooking front. *Florida* (M), tel. 47 61 00, with character, pleasant garden and pool. *Las Rampas* (I), tel. tel. 47 09 00. Central, excellent value.
Restaurants. *Monopol* (E), tel. 47 44 48, near central market; high standards. *La Cazuela* (M), Miguel Márquez 8. Small and popular in charming Andalusian house.

JEREZ DE LA FRONTERA (Cádiz). *Jerez* (L), Avda Alvaro Domecq 35. Recent state-owned hotel with all amenities. *Capele* (E), Gen. Franco 58, tel. 34 64 00. *Aloha Motel* (M), tel. 33 25 00, pleasant motel on Seville road.
Restaurants. *El Bosque* (E), tel. 33 33 33. Lovely setting in park. *Tendido 6* (E), tel. 34 48 35. Beside bullring; excellent seafood. *La Posada* (M), Arboledilla 2. **Warning: Take extra care with valuables; street robberies are common.**

MÁLAGA. *Malaga Palacio* (E), tel. 21 51 85. Very central, the best, but we have had reports of poor standards. The *parador* is currently closed for renovations. *Casa Curro* (M), tel. 22 72 00. Central and functional just off main street. *Los Naranjos* (M), Paseo de Sancha 29. Little way out on pleasant avenue. *Las Vegas* (M), Paseo de Sancha 22. One of the best.
Restaurants. *La Alegría* (E) Marín García 18, specializes in shellfish. *Skorpios* (E), tel. 25 84 94. On road up to Gibralfaro; recommended. *Antonio Martín* (M), tel. 22 21 13. Popular dining on terrace in Paseo Marítimo harbor

area. *Cortijo de Pepe* (M), good-value dining and charming décor in Plaza de la Merced. *Guerola* (M-I), Esparteros 8. An original menu.

Out in **El Palo** is the famous fish restaurant *Casa Pedro,* tel. 29 00 13, overlooking the sea, and *Mesón Los Machucao* (M), tel. 29 22 97, reader-recommended for food, service and ambience.

MARBELLA (Málaga). *Meliá Don Pepe* (L), tel. 77 03 00. Every possible amenity; ask for room facing sea, the other views are rather bleak. *Los Monteros* (L), tel. 77 17 00, on the outskirts. 18-hole golf course, tennis, pools, horses; an admirable hotel. Its *El Corzo Grill* (E) is an elegant gourmet spot. *Don Carlos* (L), tel. 83 11 40, former Hilton, 7 miles east of Marbella, set in 16 landscaped acres. *Puente Romano* (L), tel. 77 01 00, spectacular addition to area. Hotel/apartment complex; beautiful grounds, two pools, huge disco; stylish suites. *Marbella Club* (E), tel. 77 13 00, more lovely gardens, plus bungalow accommodation. Deluxe prices. *El Fuerte* (E), tel. 77 15 00. In town center overlooking Paseo Marítimo.

In the (M) range are—*Artola,* tel. 83 13 90, pool, tennis, about 7 miles east; *Estrella del Mar,* tel. 83 12 75, pool, sauna, etc., 5 miles east; *Baviera* (I), tel. 77 29 50, right by the bus station.

Restaurants. *La Hacienda* (L), tel. 83 12 67. 12 km. east and one of very best restaurants in Spain. *La Fonda* (E), Plaza Santo Cristo, in a stunningly beautiful Andalusian house; justly famous. Many colorful restaurants around the Plaza de los Naranjos and Virgen de los Dolores, notably *Mena* (M) right in the square; *Meson del Pasaje* (M), Pasaje 5, with charming Victorian decor; and *El Balcon de la Virgen* (I).

Chez Charlemagne (E), 5 miles out on the Málaga road, French specialties and lovely garden. *El Refugio* (M), tel. 77 18 48. Andalusian house with terrace on hill on road to Ojén, 1½ miles out. Well recommended. The **Puerto Banús** marina is packed with restaurants.

NERJA (Málaga). *Parador de Nerja* (E), tel. 52 00 50, pool and garden, views of the sea. *Portofino* (I), tel. 52 01 50, delightful little hotel, right in town center, with good food.

Restaurants. *Rey Alfonso* (E-M), Balcón de Europa. Recommended. *Pepe Rico* (M), off Calle Cristo, for good food and service.

RONDA (Málaga). *Reina Victoria* (E), Jerez 25, tel. 87 12 40. Spectacular location on rim of the gorge. Pool. *Polo* (M), tel. 87 24 47, pleasant, old-style hotel. *Royal* (M), tel. 87 11 41. Comfortable and friendly.

Restaurants. *Don Miguel* (M), Villanueva 4, tel. 87 10 90. Terrace overlooking Tagus gorge. *Mesón Santiago* (M), Marina 3. Atmospheric. *Pedro Romero* (M), opposite bullring. *Piccola Capri* (I), charming pizzeria.

TORREMOLINOS (Málaga). *Pez Espada* (L), tel. 38 03 00. Stylish older favorite, in Carihuela area. *Cervantes* (E), tel. 38 40 33. Elegant and cosmopolitan in town center. *Príncipe Sol* (E–M), tel. 38 41 00. With marvelous buffets at the end of Paseo Marítimo.

(M)s include *Don Pedro,* tel. 38 68 44, on Paseo Marítimo; *Amargua,* tel. 38 46 33, and *Jorge V,* tel. 38 11 00, both in Carihuela area.

In the (I) range are: *Blasón,* tel. 38 66 55, right on the central square, could be noisy; *Bristol,* tel. 38 28 00; *Los Nidos,* tel. 38 04 00, just beyond Carihuela; *Prammelinos,* tel. 38 19 55, in pleasant Andalusian house with garden and pool, on highway on Benalmadena side of town.

Restaurants. In the center: *Caballo Vasco* (E), Casablanca, tel. 38 23 36. Delicious Basque cuisine. Also in **Casablanca** are *Florida* (M), at no 15. Hot and cold buffet at fixed price. Eat as much as you can. *Viking* (M), at no. 1, has good Danish food, and next door is *El Establo* (M), serving mixed grills, steaks, barbecue and hamburgers. Good steaks also at *Las Pampas* (M), just round the corner. Nearby in the **Pueblo Blanco** are several good restaurants: *El Atrio* (M), delightful, small French bistro; *La Cava* (M), recent and stylish, the décor is elegant and the menu original; *León de Castilla* (M), rustic; good selection of Spanish dishes and wines; *La Rioja* (M), again with atmosphere and good wines. *Pizzería La Barraca* (I), on corner of Fandango and Casablanca.

On the **Bajondillo Beach** are several good fish restaurants. Two recommended by a reader are *Hawaii Playa* and *El Yate de Cordobés*.

The real gourmet area of Torremolinos is the **Carihuela.** Stroll along the promenade or the Calles Bulto and Carmen and make your own choice. But one you should not miss is *El Cangrejo* (M), Bulto 25, tel. 38 04 79, which has a wonderful display of seafood, though recent reports have complained of poor service. Much praised by a reader is *Antonio* (M), at the far end of the Carihuela. Also good are *Casa Guaquín, Casa Prudencio* and *El Roqueo,* all (M). The latter is now one of the most popular restaurants amongst locals; owned by two former fishermen, its fish and seafood are renowned on the Costa del Sol.

SWEDEN

Larger than California, nearly twice the size of the British Isles, Sweden is the biggest and richest of the Scandinavian nations. Its 175,000 square miles stretch from the sunny, fertile plains of the south to the frozen tundra of the Arctic Circle. It is a land of stunning contrasts. From the cobbled streets of Stockholm's old town you can look across the water to modern apartments equipped with individual yacht basins; not far from the medieval Riddarholm Church where Sweden's kings are buried, there is a modern hospital with a heliport on its roof. And in the far north, where Lapps still herd their reindeer as they have done for a thousand years, the iron ore city of Luleå has a civic center whose sidewalks are centrally heated.

The main sights to see are: the beautiful capital Stockholm; the medieval cities of Visby, Uppsala and Sigtuna; the chateau country of Skåne; folkloric Dalarna province; the resort town Båstad; Gripsholm and Skokloster castles near Stockholm. If you have more time, "midnight sun" excursions to the far north, and along the Göta Canal which runs the breadth of the country are also worthwhile.

There are 8,300,000 Swedes, descendants of those roving Vikings who conquered Russia in the ninth century, penetrated as far south as Constantinople, saved the Protestant Reformation with their intervention in the Thirty Years' War, and had all Europe in turmoil with the military exploits of their brilliant young warrior king, Charles XII, in the 18th century. After that the Swedes had had enough and for the last century and a half have pursued a policy of neutrality. Then, crop failures and near famine sent more than two million Swedes to the United States where they settled predominantly in Minnesota. Now, Sweden ranks as a leading industrial country. It is a parliamentary monarchy, following a middle course between capitalism and socialism.

676

PRACTICAL INFORMATION FOR SWEDEN

WHAT WILL IT COST. Sweden's reputation as an expensive country is not altogether justified, even though living standards are high. Hotel and restaurant costs in the larger cities can be expensive, but the price of gasoline is among the lowest in Europe, and visitors can take advantage of the many hotel discount schemes that operate during the summer. Many restaurants offer a reduced-price "dish of the day," and all major cities have budget transportation schemes which are often linked to discounted admission charges at tourist attraction.

The Swedish krona (abbreviated SEK; plural kronor) is divided into 100 öre. There are 10, 50, 100, 500, 1,000 and 10,000 SEK notes. 1- and 5-krona coins are very similar and are easily confused if you are not familiar with them. Exchange rate at presstime was 7.60 SEK to the U.S. dollar and 11.00 to the pound sterling.

A typical day in Sweden might cost two people:

	May—Sept.	Oct.—Apr.
Hotel (using hotel check) double room with breakfast	400 SEK	500 SEK
Lunch at restaurant	100	100
Transportation	80	80
Coffee and cake	40	40
Bottle of beer	40	40
Theater	150	150
Dinner	150	150
Miscellaneous 10%	90	120
	1,050 SEK	1,180 SEK

SOURCES OF INFORMATION. For information on all aspects of travel to Sweden, the Swedish National Tourist Office is invaluable. Their addresses are:
In the U.S.: 655 Third Ave., New York, N.Y. 10017.
In the U.K.: 3 Cork St., London, W.1.

WHEN TO COME. From the standpoint of summer weather, the best time to come is from late May through August. July is the Swedes' vacation month—there's a mass exodus of Stockholmers from Stockholm and a mass influx of people from elsewhere into the city. You can never depend on the weather, of course, but even early May, September, and October do offer some distinct advantages. You get beautiful sunny days, if a shade on the brisk side, and it is also easier to get hotel accommodations. For winter sports the season runs from Christmas to the beginning of June, depending on the region you choose. Except for Lapland, the peak period is generally February—March. You won't need floodlighting if you go to Lapland for skiing under the Midnight Sun. Major international trade fairs are held throughout the year, particularly in the purpose-built exhibition centers in Stockholm, Gothenburg and Malmö.

Climate. The winter tends to be bitter and the summer cool. However, you get 19 hours' daylight on a June day in Stockholm. Beyond the Arctic Circle the Midnight Sun reigns: from mid-May to mid-July the sun never sets.

Average afternoon temperatures in Fahrenheit and centigrade:

Stock-holm	Jan.	Feb.	Mar.	Apr.	May	June	July	Aug.	Sept.	Oct.	Nov.	Dec.
F°	31	31	37	45	57	65	70	66	58	48	38	33
C°	-1	-1	3	7	14	18	21	19	14	9	3	1

 SPECIAL EVENTS. *February:* Great Lapp Winter Fair in Jokkmokk; *March:* Vasa Ski Race, 55 miles cross-country Sälen to Mora; *April* 30: Walpurgis Night Festival all over Sweden; *June:* Ballet Festival at the Royal Opera in Stockholm; international tennis matches at Båstad; *July:* Visby Festival in medieval cathedral ruin; Swedish Derby at Jägersro, Malmö; *August:* Sweden-America Day in Skansen Park, Stockholm; Minnesota Day in Växjö, southern Sweden; *December:* Nobel Festivities in Stockholm (by invitation only); St. Lucia Day (13th) celebrated throughout.

National Holidays. Jan. 1 (New Year's Day); Jan. 6 (Epiphany); Apr. 17–20 (Easter); May 1 (Labor Day); May 28 (Ascension); June 8 (Whit Mon.); June 20 (Midsummer); Nov. 1 (All Saints); Dec. 25, 26.

 VISAS. Nationals of the United States, Canada, Australia, New Zealand, EEC countries and many other parts of the world do not require visas for entry into Sweden, provided a valid passport is held. No vaccination certificate is required to enter Sweden.

 GETTING TO SWEDEN. By Plane. On the North Atlantic routes there are direct flights from New York and Minneapolis to Stockholm and also from New York to Gothenburg. There are flights from other cities to Copenhagen, from where there are good connections by air, rail and ferry. Malmö and the southern part of Sweden are served by hovercraft which connect with flights at Copenhagen's Kastrup airport. There are nonstop flights from London and major Continental cities to Stockholm on a daily basis by *SAS* and other airlines. Also flights between Gothenburg and London.

By Boat. From the U.K. there are two routes. Both are *DFDS Seaways*, the first being from Harwich (direct train links from London and Manchester) to Gothenburg, taking 24 hours for the crossing. The second is from Newcastle upon Tyne to Gothenburg, taking around 25 hours. This is a summer only route (June to the end of August) twice weekly. And there are various ferry services from Denmark, Germany and Finland to Sweden.

By Train. There are through trains from Germany, France, the Benelux countries and of course Denmark and Norway into Sweden. From the U.K. the most convenient rail route is the crossing via Harwich to the Hook of Holland. With this you leave London (Liverpool St.) at around 9.40 A.M. for Harwich. At the Hook you join the *Nord West Express* with through carriages and couchettes to Copenhagen where there is a direct express link to Stockholm arriving there about 6.50 P.M.

 CUSTOMS. Non-European residents may bring in 400 cigarettes or 200 cigarillos or 100 cigars of 500 gr. of tobacco; 1 liter of spirits or wine and 2 liters of beer; a reasonable amount of perfume. Europeans are allowed 200 cigarettes or 100 cigarillos or 50 cigars or 250 gr. of tobacco; travelers 20 years or older, 1 liter of spirits, 1 liter wine and 2 liters beer; and, as with non-Europeans, a reasonable amount of perfume. Prohibited for all visitors: alcohol over 60° (120° proof).

 HOTELS. Many towns have a centrally located hotel booking office (*Hotellcentral* or *Rumsförmedling*). In almost every provincial town you will encounter a "Grand Hotell", "Stora Hotellet" or "Stadshotellet", and you may rest assured that they are invariably good. Advance reservations are recommended in hotels and motels, particularly in the larger towns, during the high season (May 15 to Sept. 30). A 15% service charge is included in the price of the room. Many hotels include breakfast in the rate.

Several chains of hotels operate in Stockholm and throughout the country, catering at different price levels. Two well-known state-supported companies have useful "initial" names—SARA and RESO. For the budget traveler there is the hotel check system (*Swed-cheque*) which makes a holiday simple and economic. There are two price groups: Quality checks, which work out at approximately 220 SEK, and Budget checks, around 160 SEK. The Quality check provides a night's accommodations for one person in a twin-bedded room with bath or shower and the price includes breakfast. The Budget check gives accommodations in a room without private bath or shower but does include breakfast. There is a surcharge for single rooms and also in some hotels in the major cities. Hotel checks can be used only from June 1 through August 31, but several Swedish hotel groups offer reduced prices during the summer which in some cases work out cheaper than the checks.

Note. Hotel checks can only be bought *outside* Sweden. Contact the Swedish Tourist Office in New York or London for travel agents selling the checks.

Bilturlogi is a hotel pass valid at 200 hotels during the summer months with which you can pay as little as 100 SEK per bed. Bookings are only accepted if made the day before. The pass costs 45 SEK and is available in bookshops and some hotels. For more information, write to Siljansgården, S–79303 Tällberg.

There are good pensions in all parts of the country as well as comfortable resort hotels often open all year round, that are especially prepared to cater to foreign visitors. At seaside resorts on the west coast in Bohuslän, you may rent rooms in a fisherman's cottage and take your meals at a restaurant; accommodations are clean, if primitive.

The hotels listed later in this chapter are graded in three price categories. In every case, the charge is for 2 people in a double room. Expensive (E) covers the 650–1,300 SEK range; Moderate (M) 500–700 SEK; and Inexpensive (I) 250–500 SEK. These prices apply to hotels in the main cities. Corresponding details for rural accommodations are somewhat lower.

 CAMPING. About 700 camping sites are approved by the *Swedish Tourist Board.* Of these, around 200 are rated 3-star (the highest standard). Some sites have cottages for overnight accommodation (2–4 beds) equipped with heating and electricity. There are about 4,000 cottages of this type. Sites are generally open June through August. A camping card is required at most sites, and this can be obtained at the site for 15 SEK.

A camping book with a map and all the sites is issued yearly. It is in Swedish with a key to the symbols in English, German and French. Contact the Swedish Tourist Board, too, for a free abbreviated list (in English) of camping sites.

 RESTAURANTS. Swedish restaurants are excellent, with hearty fare and lots of choice. We have graded those we carry in our listings as follows—Expensive (E) 120 SEK and up; Moderate (M) 70–120 SEK; Inexpensive (I) 40–70 SEK.

Food and Drink. The Swedish *smörgåsbord*, someone once said, is often abused in spelling, pronunciation, and preparation. Smörgåsbord is a large table which is usually placed in the middle of the dining room and is easily accessible to all guests. On it are placed a large variety of hors d'oeuvre type dishes and you help yourself—often several times—and take what you like of them. Traditionally, the order goes something like this: pickled herring (possibly more than one kind) with a boiled potato; a couple more fish courses, probably cold smoked salmon, fried Baltic Sea herring, and sardines in oil; the meats, liver paste, boiled ham, sliced beef, not uncommonly smoked reindeer; a salad, fruit and or vegetable; and finally the cheeses. Order *snaps* (the collective name for *aquavit* or *brännvin* liquors) with the meal, drink it neat and chase it with water or beer.

Other national dishes are: crayfish, pea soup and pork followed by pancakes, fried Baltic herring (*strömming*), and goose.

Liquor is served in two, four and six centiliter quantities; best specify the size you want or you may be served a stiff 6 cl. drink with an equally stiff check. Before noon (1 P.M. on Sundays) it's soft drinks only unless you buy your own bottle at one of the state-owned liquor shops which open at 9 A.M. At midnight everything is usually put away except wine and beer. Liquor stores are closed Sat. and Sun.

 TIPPING. Hotel prices include a 15% service charge. Bigger hotels also charge extra for the porter service, in which case porters do not have to be tipped. Inquire whether the porter service will be charged or not when you arrive at the hotel. A porter should be paid 5 SEK per bag. The service charge in restaurants is always included in the bill. Hatcheck girls and washroom attendants get 5 SEK. Cab drivers are always tipped at least 10% of the fare on the meter; 10 to 15% is paid in barber shops and beauty salons.

 MAIL. Letters to the U.S. and Canada by airmail under 20 grams cost 3.40 SEK. Airmail postcards cost 2.90 SEK. Postcards and letters within Europe cost 2.30 and 2.90 SEK respectively. For philatelists there is a special shop opposite the main post office at Vasagatan 28, Stockholm.

 **CLOSING TIMES.** Shops usually open 9–6 Mon. through Fri. Sat. and the day before a holiday closing time varies between 1 and 4 in the afternoon. Department stores and many other shops in the larger cities keep open until 8 or 10 one evening in the week (usually Mon. or Fri.), but *not* in June and July, and some stores open on Sun. Banks are open 9.30–3 Mon.–Fri.; many also open in the evening between 4.30 and 6. In many larger cities the banks are open for business from 9.30–6. The bank at Stockholm's Arlanda International Airport is open daily from 7 A.M. through 10 P.M.

 USEFUL ADDRESSES. *American Embassy*, Strandvägen 101. *British Embassy*, Skarpögatan 6. *Canadian Embassy*, Tegelbacken 4. *Tourist Center*, Sweden House, Kungsträdgården. *American Express*, Birger Jarlsgatan 1, *Wagons Lits/Cooks*, Vasagatan 22. The library of the *Swedish Institute*, Kungsträdgården. Books about Sweden at reasonable prices.

In case of emergency telephone 90 000. For tourist information about Stockholm in English call (08) 221840.

GETTING AROUND SWEDEN. By Plane. Both *SAS* and *Linjeflyg* (the leading domestic airline) have a wide network of services within Sweden. Their fare structure is such that flying at off-peak times is remarkably inexpensive. Apart from one or two smaller towns and cities all the services are by jet aircraft. All flights serving Stockholm operate from Arlanda airport, about 25 miles north of the city.

By Train. Swedish Railways are among the best in Europe; although the network is not as dense as in some countries, it does reach right up to the far north and is largely electrified. Trains are spotlessly clean, comfortable and offer two classes on all long distance trains. Overnight trains carry sleepers (1st and 2nd class) and 2nd class couchettes. Dining, buffet and refreshment services are also carried on all long distance trains.

Rail fares in Sweden are among the cheapest in Europe. All second-class fares were reduced by 25 percent as of November 1985 except for Friday and Sunday services, and at the same time the previous low-price railcard was discontinued. There is now a price ceiling for long-distance trips, with a flat-rate fare for all journeys of about 560 miles and over. Children under 16 travel at half the applicable fare. There is also a special fare for groups of between two and five passengers. The first adult pays the normal fare but additional adults qualify for a substantial discount and the first child travels free.

Sweden is also a partner in the *Scanrail Card* for unlimited travel. (See under Denmark for details.)

By Bus. *The Swedish State Railways* (SJ) operate a network of buses all over Sweden. In addition to this regular traffic, there are express coaches over longer distances. Several private companies operate weekend coach services to about 100 places.

By Boat. In summer, services ply from Stockholm and Gothenburg to the islands of the archipelagos; to the islands of Gotland and Öland (also inter-island services) and to Ven in Öresund. There are cruises on the famous Göta Canal, on the Dalsland and Kinda canals, and on several inland waterways.

By Car. Sweden drives on the right. Speed limits are 50km/hr (30mph) in built-up areas, 90km/hr (56mph) on rural roads; motorways 110km/hr (68mph). Third-party insurance is compulsory. Try to park your car in the parking lots or special places in the streets where there are meters. Wrongly parked cars are towed away in the larger cities. To get your car you have to pay a penalty of about 1000 SEK. Drivers must use dipped headlights even during daylight hours. In cars with seat belts, both the driver and front-seat passenger must wear them, as must front-seat passengers in taxis.

Gasoline *(bensin)* varies in price from one part of Sweden to another but ranges between about 4.40 and 4.60 SEK per liter. Lead-free gasoline is now readily available.

There are many wild animals on Sweden's roads: respect roadsigns indicating their presence by reducing your speed to suit visibility.

Note. Never drive after drinking. You can be prosecuted even if you have only a low level of alcohol in the blood, and the penalties if you are found to be over the limit are severe.

Car Hire. Information on hiring in the Stockholm area from *Avis,* Industrivägen 20, Solna; *Bonus Biluthyrning,* Östgötagatan 75; *Europcar,* Box 45066; *Hertz,* Odengatan 32; *InterRent,* Birger Jarlsgatan 32A; *OK,* Sveavägen 153–155. *Esso* (Exxon) rents cars at 70 service stations in 35 cities and its rates are low.

Stockholm and Environs

Stockholm has been called one of the world's most beautiful cities and few will deny that it is a handsome and civilized capital with a natural setting. Founded as a fortress on a little island in Lake Mälaren, over the centuries the town spread to nearby islands, and then to the mainland. Today, the "City on the Water" delights the visitor with its vistas over water, its parks, tree-lined squares and boulevards. Nature and city planning have combined to create a pleasing metropolis.

Since World War II increasing urbanization and traffic demands have caused extensive replanning and rebuilding. First came the two huge satellite city centers of Vällingby to the west and Farsta to the south, connected by a subway (T-banan). Next came the wholesale rebuilding of a vast area in the heart of the city (from the Hötorget market place to the "Sergels Torg") constituting an enormous yet compact trade and commerce center. The newest shopping area is the Arcade Gallerian near N.K. and the Sweden House.

May, June, July and August are the best months to visit here. Then you have the best weather and the greatest variety of sightseeing facilities. Bring reasonably warm clothing along.

For purposes of exploration, the city's island geography divides Stockholm into neat parcels. First, there's the city between the bridges, or the Old Town, site of the Royal Palace and its adjoining islands, Riddarholmen (Isle of Knights) and Helgeandsholmen (Island of the Holy Spirit). This is essentially the heart of the capital and the nation. Södermalm is the southern section, across the bridge leading from the Old Town. Norrmalm, north of the Old Town, is the business and financial district of Stockholm. Kungsholmen, a large island west of Norrmalm, is the site of the famous Town Hall and offices of the municipal government; Östermalm, east of Norrmalm, is mostly residential, full of embassies and consulates. Finally there is Djurgården, a huge island, projecting east toward the Baltic in the channels between Östermalm and Södermalm, with the marvelous park of Skansen, the openair museum, the Royal Flagship *Wasa* and her museum.

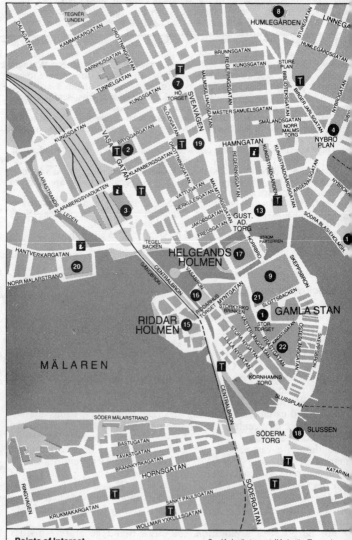

Points of Interest

1 Börsen (Stock Exchange)
2 Centralpostkontoret
  (Central Post Office)
3 Central Rail Station; Air Terminal
  (opposite)
4 Dramatiska Teatern
  (Royal Dramatic Theater)
5 Historiska Museet (Museum of
  National Antiquities)

6 Kaknästornet (Kaknäs Tower)
7 Konserthuset (Concert Hall)
8 Kungliga Biblioteket
  (Royal Library)
9 Kungliga Slottet (Royal Palace);
  Livrustkammaren (Royal Armory)
10 Moderna Museet (Museum of
   Modern Art)
11 Nationalmuseet
   (National Museum)

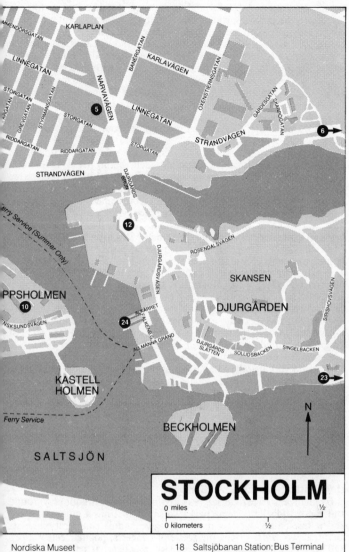

KARLAPLAN

MMENDÖRSGATAN

LINNEGATAN

STORGATAN

ARGATAN

GREVGATAN

STRUMGATAN

STORGATAN

NARVAVÄGEN

BANERGATAN

KARLAVÄGEN

5

LINNEGATAN

OXENSTIERNSGATAN

GARDESGATAN

SKARPÖGATAN

6

RIDDARGATAN

RIDDARGATAN

STORGATAN

STRANDVÄGEN

STRANDVÄGEN

DJURGÅRDS BRON

erry Service (Summer Only)

12

DJURGÅRDSVÄGEN

ROSENDALSVÄGEN

SKANSEN

DJURGÅRDEN

SIRISHOVSVÄGEN

PPSHOLMEN

10

NSKSUNDSVÄGEN

A. KARRET

FALKENB G.

24

ALLMÄNNA GRAND

DJURGÅRDS SLÄTTEN

SOLLIDSBACKEN

SINGELBACKEN

23

KASTELL HOLMEN

N

Ferry Service

BECKHOLMEN

SALTSJÖN

STOCKHOLM

0 miles   ½

0 kilometers   ½

Nordiska Museet
(Nordic Museum)

Operan (Royal Opera House)

Östasiatiska Museet (Museum of
Far Eastern Antiquities)

Riddarholmskyrkan
(Riddarholm Church)

Riddarhuset (House of Nobility);
Supreme Court

Riksdag (Parliament)

18 Saltsjöbanan Station; Bus Terminal
19 Sergels Torg
20 Stadshuset (Town Hall)
21 Storkyrkan (Cathedral)
22 Tyska Kyrkan (German Church)
23 Waldemarsudde
24 Wasavarvet (Wasa Museum)
T Subway Stations
i Tourist Information Offices

The Royal Palace is huge, and like so many royal properties in the democratic monarchies of Scandinavia, easy of public access; you can stroll into the inner courtyard any time during the day. Interior parts which may be visited are the Hall of State, containing the king's silver throne; the Chapel Royal with its historic and artistic treasures, the Festival and Bernadotte suites, and Gustav III's collection of classical sculpture, the palace museum and the Treasury with the crown jewels. The Royal Armory has objects associated with Swedish historical events. The changing of the guard takes place Wednesdays and Saturdays at noon and on Sundays at 1 P.M. (during July and August every day; on weekdays at noon and on Sundays at 1 P.M.). You can buy "royal" souvenirs at Slottsboden in the outer courtyard (closed Mondays).

Diagonally across from the south side of the palace is the Stockholm Cathedral, the national church of Sweden, dating from 1250. Also known as The Great Church, its chief treasure is a 15th-century statue of St. George and the Dragon, set up to commemorate a Swedish victory over the Danes in 1471. When you come out of the Great Church, turn right and walk down the Storkyrkobrinken, following a medieval route as do most of the lanes in the Old Town. Passing between centuries-old buildings you emerge in a little square called the Riddarhustorget. Here is the Riddarhuset, House of the Nobility, containing the crests of Swedish noble families. The bridge across the canal and railroad tracks will lead you to the famous Riddarholm Church, once part of a Franciscan monastery, the weathered red brick and open spire of which are symbolic of Sweden's ancient glory. Here lie Gustavus Adolphus, hero of the Thirty Years' War, and the brilliant, dashing Carolus Rex whose victories over the Russians and Continental Armies stunned the world until he fell in Norway in 1718. The last king to be buried in this ancient church was Gustav V in 1950.

Before leaving the Old Town, visit Stortorget, the oldest square in Stockholm with its tall old houses and the Stock Exchange, containing on its second floor the headquarters of the Swedish Academy which awards the Nobel Prize for literature. And don't miss the Marten Trotzigs Gränd, a tiny lane no more than three feet wide, and half of it a staircase. It connects the Prästgatan with Västerlånggatan, the latter something of a shopping street for over 200 years.

A renovated house of 1740, called Midas (after the king with the golden touch), has 15 boutiques and a deluxe restaurant, the Grappe d'Or; entrances at Mälartorget, Lilla Nygatan and Tyska Brinken.

Near Slussen you will find many small art galleries at Puckeln on Hornsgatan; some are open Sundays.

By all means go to Skansen, Stockholm's unique outdoor playground and the world's first theme park. To say that it has a museum, a zoo and a fascinating view is merely to give a dull enumeration of its facilities. To say that it is the scene of concerts, popular celebrations and folk dancing is merely to suggest its gaiety. It's full of openair dance floors, coffee shops and workshops (handcrafts and various peasant skills are demonstrated in the old buildings). It is the perfect place to get a real idea of the culture and traditions of Sweden. Whole estates, churches and farm houses have been moved here bodily from all over Sweden. You can even get married in the 18th-century church. When still at Djurgården, you should not miss the *Wasa*. This royal flagship sunk on her maiden voyage in 1628, was recovered from the Stockholm harbor and painstakingly preserved by a complex humidifying method.

Still another highlight is the Stockholm Town Hall, which has been called "the most beautiful building of this century in Europe". Built by Ragnar Östberg, dedicated in 1923, it has become a symbol of modern, progressive Stockholm. You should visit the Golden Hall with the ancient technique of mosaic work used to cover the high walls with boldly designed modern pictures; the Blue Hall, the Prince's Gallery with its large murals by Prince Eugen; the Terrace, a formal garden which seems to be floating on the water of Lake Mälar and which affords beautiful views of the Old Town and a chance to study the loggia and massive architecture of the Town Hall itself, and finally the Tower, partly accessible by elevator and providing a splendid view of Stockholm and the archipelago. You will get a still better view of Stockholm and surroundings from the viewing terraces of the Kaknäs Television Tower.

If you're interested in more modern architecture and the model housing developments with which Stockholm has earned its reputation for city planning, we recommend the following areas, apart from the new city center of Nedre Norrmalm, which you can hardly miss: Danviksklippan, skyscraper apartments overlooking the city from the south; the "star-type" apartment houses at Torsvikplatan, by subway, change to bus at end of line (Ropsten); for suburban planning, Vällingby, Farsta, Skärholmen and Kista.

Short Excursions from Stockholm

Drottningholm Palace (50 minutes by steamer from the Town Hall quay; 20 minutes by bus from subway station, Brommaplan) is one of the most charming royal residences in Europe. Inspired by Versailles, it is open to the public. The Court Theater, with its 18th-century scenery intact, is unique. Performances are given two to four times a week, late May until mid-September. There are beautiful gardens, as well as the charming little China Pavilion.

Saltsjöbaden (literally, Salt Sea Baths) is the principal winter and summer resort of the archipelago, 18 minutes by train from Stockholm (Slussen). In summer this is a rendezvous for yachtsmen and motorboat buffs. Among other amenities is an excellent harbor, 9-hole golf course, tennis courts, riding stables, and nude swimming in summer (but not mixed; a wooden wall separates the sexes). Skating, skate-sailing, ice-boating and crosscountry skiing are the winter sports.

The Haga Pavilion, located in the vast park surrounding the Haga Palace (at present uninhabited), is just a few minutes by bus no. 515 from Odenplan or bus no. 52 from Sergelstorg. It is an exquisitely furnished miniature 18th-century summer palace.

Another interesting excursion, 35 minutes by bus from Slussen, is Gustavsberg, where the noted ceramics works may be visited by groups on arrangement.

Longer Excursions from Stockholm

The Swedes call the great archipelago east of their capital, Skär-gården or Garden of Skerries. There are thousands of these islands, forming a unique summer playground for the Swedes who have summer cottages scattered all over the region or rent rooms. There are no resorts, only a few villages, among them Sandhamn (yachting center, sandy beaches, hotel and restaurants), three hours from Stockholm by boat from Grand Hotel quay, and Vaxholm (small town with fortress, tennis courts, hotel, restaurants), one hour from Stockholm.

West of Stockholm is the valley of Lake Mälar, the cradle of Swedish history. The following excursions can be completed in a day or less from Stockholm: Uppsala, ancient pagan and Christian capital of Sweden and site of Scandinavia's oldest university (celebrated its 500th anniversary in 1977), and largest cathedral. Visit the 16th-century castle where Queen Christina abdicated; Hammarby House, and some pagan burial mounds just outside the town.

Sigtuna is an idyllic little town with an 11th-century fortified church ruin and other monuments of Sweden's history.

Gripsholm, a 16th-century castle three and a half hours by steamer through the lovely scenery of Lake Mälar, has the largest collection of historical portraits in the world. Don't miss the little theater in the castle, better in some ways than the famous one at Drottningholm.

Skokloster is another impressive castle, about 45 miles by road from Stockholm; built in the 17th century it still has its original rich furnishings. There is also a veteran car museum.

PRACTICAL INFORMATION FOR STOCKHOLM

 GETTING AROUND STOCKHOLM. By underground and bus. There is a good underground system *(T-banan)* and many connecting bus routes. The transport area is divided into zones. Tickets may be bought from ticket counters or drivers. Children and senior citizens travel half fare. 20-coupon booklets are sold at Pressbyrån newspaper kiosks and give a considerable saving. The current price is 55 SEK (half price for senior citizens). A journey within one zone costs two coupons. Two children accompanied by a paying passenger may travel free.

There are three types of tourist ticket. One is valid for 24 hours within the inner city; another is valid for the whole transportation network; and a third gives you 72 hours unlimited travel. Prices vary from 18–60 SEK. Half-fare for senior citizens and the under-18s.

But the best bet is to buy a Key to Stockholm card *(Stockholmskortet)*. As well as providing free transportation throughout Greater Stockholm, it also offers free admission to 50 museums in the city plus free sightseeing trips. Cards valid for up to four days can be purchased at prices ranging from about 65 to 220 SEK. They can be bought at a number of outlets in the city, including the Tourist Center at Sweden House and the *Hotellcentralen* accommodation bureau at the central railroad station.

 HOTELS. It's recommended to reserve rooms in advance during the summer months. If you arrive without a reservation, consult the Hotellcentralen in the underground level of the Central Station. This room booking service is open in summer, weekdays from 8 A.M. to 9 P.M. (Sundays from 1 P.M.); shorter opening times in winter. A charge is made for each room reserved. There are several chain hotels and restaurants such as SARA, RESO, SCANDIC and OK offering a dependable, generally moderate standard.

Summer visitors to Stockholm can buy a "Stockholm Package" which offers three nights in top-class hotels at heavily discounted prices. The package price includes a Key to Stockholm card.

If you want to rent a private room write to Hotelltjänst, Vasagatan 38, 111 20 Stockholm or call 08–10 44 67. The price is from 125–150 SEK for two persons.

The *Swedish Touring Club (STF)* operates some 300 youth hostels and touring lodges throughout the country, some located in scenic spots or old, interesting houses. Open to all, charges are about 35–45 SEK per person per night. For further information contact: STF, Box 25, S–101 20 Stockholm.

Expensive

Amaranten, Kungsholmsgatan 31 (tel. 08–541060). 415 rooms with bath or shower. Restaurants, cocktail lounge, nightclub, conference rooms. Sauna, swimming pool, sunbathing terrace and exercise facilities. Bank and shops on the ground floor. Subway station in hotel. Garage.

Anglais, Humlegardsgatan 23 (tel. 08–249900). 211 rooms with bath. Restaurant, garage.

Birger Jarl, Tulegatan 8 (tel. 08–151020). 250 rooms with bath or shower. Coffee shop. Garage.

Carlton, Kungsgatan 57 (tel. 08–223400). 127 rooms. Situated near the Concert Hall and shopping district. Restaurant. Garage.

Continental, Klara Vattugränd 4 (tel. 08–244020). 250 rooms with bath. Convenient, opposite the Central Station. Elegant main restaurant; the café is popular for lunch and quick meals. *(RESO.)*

Diplomat, Strandvägen 7C (tel. 08–635800). 132 rooms with bath. Central, wonderful view of the harbor.

Esplanade, Strandvägen 7A (tel. 08–630740). 33 rooms, most with bath. Breakfast room. Nice atmosphere. Central.

Grand, S. Blasieholmshamnen 8 (tel. 08–221020). 350 rooms with bath or shower. Central. Terrace restaurants overlook the water.

Grand Hotel Saltsjöbaden, Saltsjöbaden (tel. 08–7170020). 101 rooms with bath. A castlelike place on the waterfront in this suburban resort. Restaurants.

Lady Hamilton, Storkyrkobrinken 5 (tel. 08–234680). 35 rooms, sauna. In the Old Town.

Lord Nelson, Västerlånggatan 22 (tel. 08–232390). 31 rooms. Nautical atmosphere. Also in the Old Town.

Mälardrottningen, Riddarholmen (tel. 08–243600). 59 cabins. Barbara Hutton's yacht converted into a floating hotel in the center of the city.

Malmen, Götgatan 49 (tel. 08–226080). 279 rooms with bath. Restaurant. On the southern heights, a few minutes from downtown by subway. *(RESO.)*

Mornington, Nybrogatan 53 (tel. 08–631240). 137 rooms with bath or shower. Central, quiet. Restaurant. Garage.

Palace, St. Eriksgatan 115 (tel. 08–241220). 215 rooms. Garage in the basement. Restaurant. (RESO)

Park, Karlavägen 43 (tel. 08–229620). 205 rooms with bath. Solarium and sauna. Restaurant.

Reisen, Skeppsbron 12–14 (tel. 08–223260). 125 rooms with bath. The hotel is built inside the setting of three 17th-century houses, facing the sea in the center of Stockholm. Sauna and pool in basement. *(SARA.)*

Royal Viking, Vasagatan 1 (tel. 08–141000). 350 rooms; close to rail station and air terminal. Duplex penthouse suites, glass-roofed wintergarden.

SAS-Hotel Arlandi, Arlanda (tel. 0760–61800). 300 rooms. Restaurant, bar, nightclub. Sauna and pool. Cinema and library. Tennis court. Soundproofing. Bus service from Arlanda airport (5 minutes).

Sergel Plaza Hotel, Brunkebergstorg 9 (tel. 08–226600). 407 rooms. Health club and sauna. In the city center.

Sheraton—Stockholm, Tegelbacken 6 (tel. 08–142600). 476 rooms with bath. Fine restaurant, popular cocktail lounge. Sauna. Garage. *SAS* office, shops. Air terminal nearby.

Strand, Nybrokajen 9 (tel. 08–222900). 134 rooms. Central.

Terminus, Vasagatan 20 (tel. 08–222640). 155 rooms. Restaurant, cocktail bar. Near Central Station and air terminal.

Moderate

Alexandra, Magnus Ladulasgatan 42 (tel. 08–840320). 90 rooms with bath.

Alfa Hotel, Marknadsvägen 6, Johanneshov (tel. 08–810600). Near Liljeholmen subway station. 104 rooms, sauna, restaurant, bar, outdoor cafeteria.

Bromma, Brommaplan (tel. 08–252920). 141 rooms with bath. Restaurant. 15 minutes by subway from downtown shopping area. Sauna. *(RESO.)* Direct bus to Arlanda airport.

Flamingo, Hotellgatan 11, Solna (tel. 08–830800). 130 rooms, most with bath. Restaurant, bar, grill. Located 10 minutes outside Stockholm by subway.

Flyghotellet, Brommaplan (tel. 08–262620). 68 rooms with bath. Only breakfast served. Direct bus to Arlanda airport.

Hotel City, Slöjdgatan 7 (tel. 08–222240). 300 rooms. Belongs to the Salvation Army.

Karelia, Birger Jarlsgatan 35 (tel. 08–247660). 87 rooms with bath. Central. Only breakfast served.

Scandic Hotell, on Highway E4, 4 miles southwest (tel. 08–462660). Motel, 125 rooms, most with bath. Cafeteria.

Scandic Motel, on Highway E4 to the south (tel. 7100460). Motel with 279 rooms with bath or shower. Restaurant. Sauna, gym, pool.

Scandic Motel, on Highway 18, 4 miles north (tel. 08–850360). 215 rooms with bath or shower in this motel. Sauna, pool. Two restaurants. The bus from Arlanda airport stops here on request.

Sjöfartshotellet, Katrinavägen 26 (tel. 08–226960). 184 rooms with bath or shower. Restaurant. *(RESO.)*

Stockholm, Norrmalmstorg 1 (tel. 08–221320). 93 rooms, most with bath. Situated on top floors of downtown office building. Only breakfast served.
Tegnérlunden, Tegnérlunden 8 (tel. 08–349780). 74 rooms. Quiet. Only breakfast served.

Inexpensive

af Chapman, Skeppsholmen (tel. 08–103715). Formerly a sailing ship, now operating as a Youth Hostel. Clean and very popular, so stays are limited to 5 nights. Closed mid-Dec. through mid-Jan. 136 beds.
Frescati, Professorsslingan 13–15 (tel. 08–155090). 168 rooms with shower. Open June through Aug. only. Restaurants, bars, lounges and reading rooms.
Hotelship Gustaf af Klint Stadsgården, Quay berth 153 (tel. 08–40 40 77). 28 cabins. Near Slussen subway station.
Kristineberg, Hj. Söderbergs väg 10 (tel. 08–130300). 143 rooms, 12 public baths. Ten minutes by subway from downtown shopping area. Pleasant restaurant.
Savoy, Bryggaregatan 12B (tel. 08–221280). 53 rooms. Only breakfast served.
Skeppsholmen Youthhostel (tel. 08–202506). Near the af Chapman. Open year-round. 140 beds.
Zinken, Pipmarkargränd 2 (tel. 08–585011). 28 rooms without bath. Close to subway. Breakfast only.

 RESTAURANTS. Although atmosphere varies greatly in Stockholm restaurants, the food is fairly standardized, making the distinction one of quality. The following is a representative selection.

Expensive

Aurora, Munkbron 15 (tel. 08–219359). Sited in a beautiful 300-year-old building in the Old Town with pleasant small rooms in cellar vaults. Excellent food. Closed Sunday. *(SARA.)*
Den Gyldene Freden, Österlånggatan 51 (tel. 08–101259). Stockholm's oldest restaurant with medieval cellars, historic traditions, atmosphere, lute singers some evenings.
Djurgårdsbrunns Värdshus (tel. 08–679095). A few minutes from downtown by taxi or bus. A 17th-century inn overlooking a meadow and canal.
Fem Små Hus, Nygränd 10 (tel. 08–100482). A charming spot located in the Old Town. Very good food. Its name means "five small houses".
Konstnärshuset, Smålandsgatan 7 (tel. 08–110232). Good food and drinks in intimate surroundings in the heart of town. Murals by Swedish painters. Service in the grill is better than average.
Operakällaren (tel. 08–111125). A famous restaurant located in the opera house, as its name suggests, and overlooking the harbor and the palace. It is under the same management as the Riche (see below) and thus excellent. The *Café Opera* retains its cozy atmosphere, while the *Bakfickan* snackbar is recommended for quick meals.
Östermalmskällaren, Storgatan 3 (tel. 08–677421). Quiet atmosphere, modern decor. *(SARA.)*
Riche, Birger Jarlsgatan 4 (tel. 08–107022). A plush institution with cocktail lounge, good food, good drinks, and music.
Solliden, Skansen (tel. 08–601055). On the heights of Stockholm's favorite pleasure grounds, ten minutes from the town center. Overlooks city and harbor. Vast enough for 600 guests. *(SARA.)*
Stallmästaregården, Norrtull near Haga (tel. 08–243910). An old inn on the outskirts of Haga. Historical traditions, modern management. Coffee in the court, a lovely garden, after a good meal of a summer evening can be a delightful experience. Same management as the Riche (see above), so good food, including smörgåsbord. Music. Haga air terminal nearby.
Stortorgskällaren, Stortorget 7 (tel. 08–105533). Located in a medieval cellar.
Teatergrillen, Nybrogatan 3 (tel. 08–107044). Intimate atmosphere. Steaks among the best in town. Closed July.
Victoria, Kungsträdgården (tel. 08–101085). Friendly place conveniently open to 3 in the morning.

Moderate

Bäckahästen, Hamngatan 2 (tel. 08–200136). Good food at a reasonable price. Openair summer service. Popular.

Brända Tomten, Stureplan 13 (tel. 08–114959). Delightful dining rooms with antique furnishings. Openair dining in summer.

La Brochette, Storgatan 27 (tel. 08–622000). Specializes in French dishes, spit and charcoal-grilled.

Cattelin, Storkyrkobrinken 9 (tel. 08–201818). One of the best places to eat in the Old Town.

Gondolen, Slussen (tel. 08–402021). Suspended high in the air at the top of the Katarina elevator. Magnificent view.

Sturehof, Stureplan 2 (tel. 08–142750). An unpretentious place, comparatively large, which makes good fish its business. Set in the heart of town.

In Kungshallen at Hötorget there are many small restaurants. The biggest is the *Musikcafé* on the second floor (tel. 08–119688).

Inexpensive

For sandwiches and other inexpensive snacks, the cafeterias and tearooms found in many of Stockholm's big department stores are one answer. For burgers and the like there's *Clock,* and of course the ubiquitous *McDonald's.* Also recommended:

Annorlunda, Malmskillnadsgatan 50 (tel. 08–219569). A small restaurant with a low-cost profile.

Cassi, Narvavägen 30 (tel. 08–617461).

Hamlet, Vasagatan 8–10 (tel. 08–101029).

Kristina, Västerlånggatan 68 (tel. 08–200529). In Old Town, a building dating from 1630. Evening music.

Lilla Falstaff, Sveavägen 8 (tel. 08–100966).

Michel Angelo, Västerlånggatan 62 (tel. 08–215099).

Örtagården, Nybrogatan 31 (tel. 08–671700). Vegetarian restaurant with an historic atmosphere. Closes at 7 P.M.

 NIGHTLIFE. For addresses, opening times etc., check *This Week in Stockholm* published by Stockholm Information Service. Most places are open from 9 in the evening to 3 in the morning and charge an entrance fee if there is a floorshow. In summer there is openair dancing at the Skansen and Gröna Lund amusement parks. The following are a selection of restaurant-nightclubs:

Long-established is *Bacchi,* Järntorgsgatan 5, popular with the expense account set.

Others include *Club Opera,* Operakajen 9; *Strand,* Nybrokajen; *Strömsborg,* on an island opposite Sheraton; *King Creole,* Kungsgatan 18; *Cabaret,* Barnhusgatan 12–14; *Grand Hotel Royal,* Blasieholmen; *Ritz,* Medborgarplatsen; *Alexandra,* in Stockholm Plaza Hotel; *Cindy,* in the Amaranten Hotel.

Youngsters favor the many clubs and "cellars" such as *Bobbadilla,* Svartmangatan 27; *Gamlingen,* Helga Lekamensgränd 10 (membership required); *Top Floor Club,* Sturegatan 10; *Tramps,* Sturegatan 12; *Kolingsborg* at Slussen.

MUSEUMS. Hallwyl Museum, Hamngatan 4. A palatial residence dating from about 1900. Guided tours only, in English at 1.15 P.M. daily June 12 through Aug. 31, except Saturdays. Closed Mon.

The Kaknäs Tower, Norra Djurgården, daily 9 to midnight. Bus 69. A unique view of Stockholm, with taped commentary in four different languages. Cafeteria and restaurant.

Millesgården, Lidingö, May to Oct. 10–5 daily, closed winter. Take the underground to Ropsten, then bus.

Museum of Modern Art, on Skeppsholmen island, a few hundred meters from the National Museum of Fine Arts, open daily from 11 A.M. Cafeteria.

National Museum of Antiquities and Royal Cabinet of Coins, at Narvavägen-Linnégatan, daily 11–4. Collections from prehistoric times and the Middle Ages.

National Museum of Fine Arts, near Grand Hotel, open daily 10–4 except Mon. Cafeteria with lunch service.

Nordic Museum, Djurgården, 10–4, closed Mon. Large collection of objects showing the progress of civilization in Sweden.

Skansen, Djurgården, 8 A.M.–11.30 P.M., buildings open summer 11–5. Buses 47 and 44, ferry from Slussen and in summer from Nybroplan. The world's first openair museum (opened 1891) with excellent view of both city and harbor. Also zoo with mostly Scandinavian animals and Sweden's largest aquarium.

Technical Museum at Museivägen, Norra Djurgården, close to the Kaknäs Tower, 10–4, Sat. and Sun. 12–4. Bus 69.

Wasa at Alkärret, Djurgårdsvägen, summer 9.30–7 daily, winter 10–5. In summer, films and guided tours around the ship; in winter, do enquire about tours schedule. Not to be missed, though. Cafeteria.

SHOPPING. You will find high-quality but not necessarily expensive goods everywhere. Of the main department stores, *Nordiska Kompaniet* (popularly known as N.K.) is the first one to head for and is open on Sundays. It has the best features of Neiman-Marcus and Harrods rolled into one plus a few specialties of its own, including a fine selection of Swedish glassware. You'll find it at Hamngatan 18–20. For inexpensive men's and women's clothing look for branches of *Hennes & Mauritz* (H. & M.). *P.U.B.* also offers a wide range of goods but less in the luxury class and at lower prices. Two branches, the older one at Hötorget, the other in a glass-walled building the corner of Kungsgatan and Drottninggatan. Another block down the street is *Åhlens,* the third of the main stores and also a fine place to shop. For a fine selection of Swedish crystal visit *Peter Casselryd* at Storholmsgatan 5, Skärholmen (subway). Tel. 08–710 51 16. He will ship anywhere. Call for free limo service.

For specialist tastes, *De Fyras Bod,* Birger Jarlsgatan 12, is the center for native arts and crafts created by handicapped artists: handwoven linen tablecloths, handloomed rugs, wrought iron etc. For all kinds of original ideas in interior decoration there's *Svenskt Tenn,* Strandvägen 5A.

Economy tip. Taxfree shopping is available in many shops. They display a sign. Ask for the procedure to be followed at the shop. The sales tax—less a service fee—will be refunded at the airport or port, though shops usually require that you buy goods worth a minimum of 200 SEK to qualify.

Gothenburg

Gothenburg, first port and second city of Sweden, may very well be your first port of call. It is a pleasing city with its leafy avenues, great sprawling harbor, network of canals, and combination of Dutch Renaissance and modern architecture. Its Liseberg amusement park is one of the most delightful in the world, more modern than Copenhagen's Tivoli Gardens, and a pleasant place to dine outdoors. See the magnificent City Theater and Concert House with fountain by Carl Milles; the performances in both are exceptionally good. The Stora Theater presents first-rate opera and musical comedy. A trip to the Elfsborg Fortress (1670) in the harbor is a must: there is a museum, church, and cafeteria. The city also has an airport, Landvetter.

Bohuslän, north from Gothenburg, is an archipelago with rocky islands, skerries and deep fjords. Among numerous resorts are popular Marstrand (1½ hours by bus from Gothenburg, hotels, restaurants, yachting center), Lysekil and Fiskebäckskil farther north, and near the Norwegian border, Strömstad. They are invaded by Swedish vacationers in July, but June and August offer a splendid season.

The Göta Canal

If you want to enjoy a completely relaxed three-day travel experience, the Göta Canal trip from Gothenburg to Stockholm or vice versa is highly recommended. The steamer ties up at some of the principal points of interest for brief guided tours (for a small extra cost) which you can take or leave, and you can always get off and stroll for awhile, while the boat is going through the little locks. Starting from Gothenburg, here are some of the highlights of this unique journey:

Bohus Fortress. As you steam up the majestic Göta River, you see the town of Kungälv, with medieval Bohus Fortress above it. It was built by the Norwegians in 1308.

Trollhättan Falls. These falls power one of the country's major hydroelectric stations but, although much of the power is harnessed, the water still hurtles wildly over the cliffs.

Läckö Castle. Shortly after entering Lake Vänern from the southeast, you arrive at this monument to Sweden's imperialistic 17th century. Across the bay is Kinnekulle, one of the "table mountains".

Vadstena. The steamer ties up almost in the shadow of the huge Vasa Castle. You have time to inspect it, as well as the medieval church and nunnery founded by St. Birgitta, mother of the Birgittine Order.

Vreta. On the days when the steamer is moving through the many sets of locks between Vadstena and Berg you can stop off to visit Vreta cloister, Sweden's first nunnery (1162).

The Baltic Coast. You come out on the island-strewn Baltic Sea south of Norrköping, and follow the coast north before turning into the Södertälje Canal. A lovely archipelago.

Lake Mälar. The Södertälje Canal carries you into Lake Mälar, which brings you, via the beautiful channel from the west, right to the heart of Stockholm. You tie up almost in the shadow of the characteristic profile of the Stockholm Town Hall. You can make the same trip in the opposite direction, from Stockholm to Gothenburg, as there are two or three sailings a week in each direction from late May until the beginning of September.

Daytrips are also available on these and other boats operating in Motala, Norrköping, Söderköping and Karlsborg.

PRACTICAL INFORMATION FOR GOTHENBURG

 HOTELS. Gothenburg is fairly well supplied with accommodation in all categories, but it is always a good idea to reserve ahead. If you happen to find yourself without a room, you can contact the Room Booking Service of the city's Tourist Office, Kungsportsplatsen 2, tel. 100740. Open June 1–Aug. 31 daily 10–8; Sept. 1–May 31 Mon.-Fri. 10–6, Sat. 10–2. Room booking service is also available at Nordstadstorget Mon.-Fri. 9.30–6, Sat. 9.30–3 all year, near the air terminal.

Expensive

Europa, Köpmansgatan 38 (tel. 031–801280). 480 rooms. Nightclub. Air terminal in same block, railway station opposite. *(SARA.)*

Hotel Panorama, Eklandagatan 51 (tel. 031–810880). 352 rooms.

SAS Park Avenue, Kungsportsavenyn 36 (tel. 031–176520). 320 rooms. Best in town. Many restaurants, nightclub, panorama lounge. SAS airline check-in.

Windsor, Kungsportsavenyn 6 (tel. 031–176540). 83 rooms. Cozy atmosphere—quiet, secluded.

Moderate

Hotel Liseberg Heden, Sten Sturegatan (tel. 031–200280). 160 rooms.

Hotel Lorensberg, Berzeliigatan 15 (tel. 031–810600). 125 rooms.

Hotel Örgryte, Danskavägen 68–70 (tel. 031–197620). 74 rooms.

Inexpensive

ME's Pensionat, Chalmersgatan 27 A (tel. 031–207030). 8 rooms.

Ostkupan Youthhostel, Mejerigatan 2 (tel. 031–401050). 150 beds. Open year round.

RESTAURANTS. Gothenburg has a number of restaurants offering good and varied food. Its specialty, however, is fish, fresh from the sea and ingeniously prepared. Ask the headwaiter what's best for the day. The Tourist Office regularly publishes a list of budget-price restaurants.

Expensive

Fiskekrogen, Lilla Torget (tel. 031–130730). Well-known fish restaurant.
Johanna, Södra Hamngatan 47 (tel. 031–112250). One of Sweden's best.
Valand, Vasagatan 41. Has casino.
Victors, Skeppsbroplatsen 1.

Moderate

Åtta glas, Kungsportsbron 1 (tel. 031–136015). On a boat opposite the tourist office.
Räkan, behind SAS Park Avenue Hotel (tel. 031–169839). You sit around a pool with "shrimp trawlers", which you guide to your table by radio. Dance floor in basement.
White Corner, Vasagatan 43B. Pub-cum-steakhouse.

Inexpensive

For an inexpensive meal or quick snack, try the hamburger chains or one of the main pizza restaurants (which also offer other dishes), or department store cafeterias.

Dalarna Province

Three or four hours by train northwest of Stockholm, Dalarna province is one of Sweden's major tourist attractions, a favorite holiday region, rich in history, local color, folk costumes, popular art and handicrafts. You can visit an old summer farm—called *fäbod*—up in the mountain and forest region where, in olden times, the cattle were driven on the arrival of summer. Industry also has an old tradition in Dalarna. The Stora Kopparberg Company is the world's oldest business company, with charters dating from 1288. The most interesting parts of the copper mine at Falun are open to visitors. The weekend celebration of Midsummer Eve is particularly vigorous and colorful here in the Lake Siljan area. The lakeshore resorts hold miniature Viking ship races, openair plays and many other folklore events. Best introduction to the marvelous arts and crafts of Dalarna is at Tällberg or at Rättvik, both with good rustic art museums, handicraft exhibits and tourist hotels. One of the most interesting provincial towns is Mora, with a superb collection of 40 timber buildings, some of them 600 years old, which constitute Zorn's Gammelgård, an outdoor museum. This is also the gateway to skiing country. The first Sunday in March attracts tens of thousands of spectators to Mora to see a great crosscountry race commemorating the 55-mile trip that two local skiers took in 1521 to inform Gustavus Vasa that the men of Dalarna would fight for his war of liberation against the Danes. Children will be delighted with the new Santaworld theme park nearby.

Recommended skiing centers in northern Dalarna: Sälen and Grövelsjön. In southern Dalarna: Leksand, Rättvik and Tällberg.

Visby and the Isle of Gotland

This historic island in the Baltic with its capital, Visby, is 30 minutes by air from Stockholm. It's a five-hour trip from Nynäshamn to Visby by comfortable car ferries, and you can drive or take a bus directly to the Nynäshamn pier in an hour or so from Stockholm. In summer there is a direct service from Stockholm to Visby.

Or take your car on a four-hour ferry trip from Oskarshamn to Visby, or from Västervik (summer only). No matter how you go, you'll be glad you did. The walled city of Visby is one of the medieval jewels of Europe, full of reminders of the Golden Age of the 12th and 13th centuries when this town was commercial queen of the Baltic. You'll have a wonderful time prowling around here, climbing the 700-year-old stairways to the watchtowers and battlements, admiring its medieval merchant palaces and churches. Visby is an excursion center too. There are 92 beautiful churches on Gotland, not one built later than 1361, innumerable prehistoric remains such as Viking "ship-burials" and prehistoric camps, well-preserved medieval farms and picturesque fishing villages. Interesting sights are also the stalactite caves at Lummelunda, the bird islands of Stora and Lilla Karlsö and the small "russ" horses, of which one species is half-wild and lives in the deep woods near Lojsta. All along Gotland's wonderful coasts you will find sandy beaches and excellent opportunities for swimming. On the coast you will also see fantastic stacks eroded by the sea.

Skåne, the Château Country

Southernmost province of Sweden, Skåne is the breadbasket of the country with its fertile agricultural plains. It also has many tourist attractions and if you are in Denmark without time for an extended visit to Sweden it's a good idea to make a day excursion here by hydrofoil to Malmö, returning by boat and train, or car via Helsingborg-Helsingör.

This is a prosperous area, and there are many châteaux and castles open to visitors. One-day excursions by bus into the "Château Country" operate daily during summer from Malmö and Helsingborg. The northwestern corner of Skåne is a popular resort area with Båstad, the most fashionable of the summer resorts here.

Northward from Båstad is Halmstad, capital of the province of Halland, and nearby is Tylösand, a big popular seaside resort (plenty of hotels, golf, tennis). Afterwards come Falkenberg and Varberg, with its imposing old cliff fortress; both have good beaches.

In Småland, the neighboring province, the city of Kalmar has a twin fascination for tourists. First, there is the magnificent Kalmar Castle with a highly recommended tour, which evokes the building's romantic past. Secondly, from Kalmar there are train and bus connections to some of the finest glassworks of Europe: *Orrefors, Kosta, Boda, Lindshammar,* and *Strömbergshyttan.* The region is not at all industrial looking; the plants are scattered through the wooded wilderness of Småland in a series of isolated villages. Watching the skilled craftsmen blowing and shaping the red-hot glass is a fascinating experience. Bus tours to the glassworks, where you can often buy "seconds" at a good price, operate from Växjö and Kalmar.

From Kalmar the longest bridge in Europe leads to the island of Öland.

PRACTICAL INFORMATION FOR DALARNA, GOTLAND, SKÅNE AND SMÅLAND

Dalarna

AVESTA. *Star Hotel* (M), tel. 0226–560–00. 80 rooms. Pool, sauna.

BORLÄNGE. *Scandic Gylle Wärdshus* (I), tel. 0243–119–00. 32 rooms. South of the city; color scheme follows traditional Dala patterns of red and blue.

FALUN. *Motor Hotel* (M), tel. 023–221–60. 106 rooms. *Grand Hotel* (M), tel. 023–187–00. 183 rooms.

LEKSAND. *Hotel Furuliden* (I), tel. 0247–114–05. 27 rooms.

MALUNG. *Hotel Skinnargården* (I), tel. 0280–117–50. 53 rooms.

MORA. *Scandic Hotel* (M), tel. 0250–150–70. 49 rooms. *Mora Hotel* (M), tel. 0250–117–50. 92 rooms. Traditional.

RÄTTVIK. *Gärdebygården* (I), tel. 0248–100–07. 50 rooms. *OK Motor Hotel* (M), tel. 0248–110–70. 32 rooms.

TÄLLBERG. *Klockargården* (M), tel. 0247–502–61. 37 rooms. *Siljansgården* (M), tel. 0247–500–40. 30 rooms. Both with a view over Lake Siljan.

Gotland

LJUGARN. *Lövängen* (I), tel. 0498–930 11. 50 rooms, some with shower and WC. Beautiful garden, tennis and windsurfing. 46 km. from Visby on the east coast of the island.

VISBY. *Snäck* (M), tel. 0498–600–00. Residential hotel. 102 flats, each one with two bedrooms and a huge balcony facing the Baltic Sea. Restaurants, sauna, tennis. Only 4 km. north of the city. Sometimes there are bargain packages by air from Stockholm. Enquire at the Gotland tourist office in Stockholm (tel. 08–236170). *Toftagården* (M), tel. 0498–654 00. 60 rooms. 20 km. south of Visby near a sandy beach. Tennis, minigolf. Walks through wooded areas. *Tofta Strandpensionat* (M), tel. 0498–650 09. 94 rooms. Sauna. Private parking. Near the center of the city.

Halland

FALKENBERG. *Grand* (M), Ågatan (tel. 0346–14450). 54 rooms with showers.

HALMSTAD. *Scandic Hotel Hallandia* (M), Rådhusgatan 4 (tel. 035–118800). 92 rooms with bath.

VARBERG. *Statt* (M), Kungsgatan 24 (tel. 0340–16100). 126 rooms.

Skåne

BÅSTAD. *Hallandsås Motel* (M), tel. 0430–242 70. 23 rooms. *Hemmeslövs Herrgårdspensionat* (M), tel. 0431–700–32. 150 rooms. Situated in a forest. Open Easter through August only.

HELSINGBORG. *Hotell Mollberg* (E), Stortorget 18 (tel. 042–120270). 72 rooms. Traditional, near harbor. *Hotel Magnus Stenbock* (M), L. Strandgatan 5 (tel. 042–126250). 25 rooms. Low summer rates. *Larödbaden Hotel and Restaurant* (M), 25 019 Helsingborg (tel. 042–92046). In Larod, 7 km. north, near Sofiero Castle. All rooms with sea view; known for good food.

MALMÖ. *Kramer* (E), tel. 040–701 20. 100 rooms. Traditional, central location. Nightclub. *Garden Hotel* (M), Baltzarsgatan 20 (tel. 040–10 40 00). 174 rooms. *Hotel Winn* (M), Jörgen Kocksgatan 3 (tel. 10–18–00). 100 rooms. Near the railway station, ferries and airport terminal. *Skyline Hotel* (M), Bisittaregatan 2 (tel. 040–803 00). 270 rooms. A new hotel with many facilities. On the outskirts of the city.

Restaurants. *Kockska Krogen at Stortorget* (E), tel. 040–70320. *Kronprinsen* (E), Mariedalsvägen 32 (tel. 040–77240). Dancing and floorshow. *Pers Krogle*

(E), Limhamnsvägen 2 (tel. 040–67011). *Margaretapaviljongen* (M), in Pildammsparken (tel. 040–962773).

Småland

BORGHOLM (on Öland island). *Strand Hotel* (M), tel. 0485–110 20. 135 rooms. View over the sound. Restaurant and dancing.

KALMAR. *Kalmarsund Hotel* (E), Fiskaregatan 5 (tel. 0480–181 00). 85 rooms. Low summer rates. Cosy atmosphere. *Hotel Witt* (E), tel. 0480–152 50. 112 rooms. Restaurant and dancing; central location. *Slottshotellet* (M), tel. 0480–882–60. 29 rooms. Elegant town house.

YSTAD. *Ystads Saltsjöbad* (M), tel. 0411–13630. 110 rooms. Golf, tennis. Restaurant overlooking the Baltic. *Prins Carl* (I), tel. 0411–100 35. 9 rooms. *Hotel Sekelgården* (I), Stora Västergatan 9 (tel. 0411–18752). 9 rooms in a charming old building. Breakfast only.

Värmland and the Highlands

Sweden's most celebrated region in song and legend is Värmland. Karlstad, the provincial capital, can be reached from three to six hours by train from Stockholm, Gothenburg or Oslo, also by plane from Stockholm in 40 minutes and by motor coach from Gothenburg in 4½ hours. From here in summer there are numerous guided bus tours that will take you through the lovely countryside around Selma Lagerlöf's home. The house, Marbacka, is now a museum, maintained as she left it at the time of her death in 1940. Just a few miles below nearby Sunne, you can wander freely through the grounds of Rottneros, a splendid example of an estate of the landed Swedish gentry. Safaris by bus or private car to watch moose are organized by the tourist office in Sunne. Hovfjället Nature Reserve at Vitsand is 16 miles north of Torsby. There are beautiful walks and panoramic views from an outlook tower. Each day there are short hiking tours with a guide. There is a restaurant open every day (June 20–Aug. 15) from 12–4 P.M. A few hours by train from Stockholm is the province of Hälsingland, where old time dancing and music has had a revival. A big folk-dance event is the Hälsinge Hambo at the beginning of July, when 1,500 pairs compete in the villages of Hårga, Bollnäs, Arbrå and Järvsö. You will find embroidery from the area at Järvsö Vävstuga (tel. 0651–405 34).

The Swedish highlands, ranging from central Sweden up beyond the Arctic Circle for a distance of 500 miles, offer you holidays unlike any others. Jämtland is skiing country—slalom and crosscountry—but this region is equally recommended in summer for hiking. Trails are well-marked for both skiing and mountaineering. Many come for the fishing, with rainbow trout, grayling and char as the leading attractions.

There are plenty of good, reasonable mountain resorts, all served by the railroad that goes west to the Norwegian border from Östersund. Östersund can also be reached by air (one hour from Stockholm), with further connection by bus or car to the different mountain resorts. Motorists reach them by following the Europe highway 75 which runs from Sundsvall, on the east coast, across middle Sweden via Östersund to Trondheim in Norway. Motorists are also urged to visit the mountain region of Härjedalen Province which lies south of Jämtland, a little off the beaten track. One of the country's most scenic roads is over the Flatruet mountain plateau (3,200 ft. above sea level).

North to Lapland

If you are looking for the sensation of being out of this world, the region north of the Arctic Circle will give it to you. The sun never sets from the end of May until the middle of July in this strange, unreal world, peopled by the Laplanders still pursuing their ancient way of life as they follow their reindeer from one grazing region to another. You can fly from Stockholm to Kiruna in 1½ hours or there's the Stockholm-Narvik express train which leaves Stockholm in the late afternoon. From Kiruna there are a number of fascinating excursions to make. An hour or so further on the main railway line north of Kiruna is Abisko, one of the most popular resorts of Lapland. An aerial ropeway, one and a half miles long, takes you up to Mount Nuolja. The very last resort before crossing into Norway is Riksgränsen; it's above the timberline, and there are ski instructors and guides. The skiing season runs to June, and it is here that you can enjoy the sensation of skiing in the light of the Midnight Sun. A new road from Kiruna to Narvik in Norway has now been opened. Near the Tärnafjällen mountain area in southern Lapland is the Vindel-Lais nature reserve, Hemavan and Tärnaby being tour centers. The inland railway (Inlandsbanan) runs for more than 800 miles from Kristinehamn to Gällivare; a discounted ticket of approximately 375 SEK gives you unlimited travel for two weeks, as well as hotel reductions, etc.

If you are short of time you could join a "Midnight Sun Excursion," operated by SAS and Scandinavian Express once weekly from the beginning of June through August 10. You take a morning flight from Stockholm to Kiruna, north of the Arctic Circle, where lunch is served. You then visit the Jukkasjäpvi Lapp Museum before continuing on the newly-opened road to Riksgränsen, from where you are taken on an evening excursion to Narvik on the Norwegian coast for a mountaintop view of the spectacular scenery. You stay overnight at Riksgränsen and arrive back in Stockholm the following afternoon.

If you don't mind missing a night's sleep, there is also a weekly "Midnight Light Adventure" trip. You take a late-evening flight from Stockholm to Luleå in the far north, where you board a bus which takes you on a trip along the coastal road and into the mountains. Later you'll have a midnight supper on the Arctic Circle and will be initiated into the Arctic Circle Club. Before returning to Luleå airport, you can take a spectacular trip down the Kamlunge rapids, with lifejackets and waterproofs provided. You're back at Stockholm's Arlanda Airport at 8.25 A.M.

PRACTICAL INFORMATION FOR THE HIGHLANDS

ÅRE. *Hotel Diplomat-Åregården* (M), tel. 0647–502–65. 107 rooms. *Sunwing Åre* (M), tel. 0647–504–30. 50 rooms, 142 flats. *Hotel Lundsgården* (I), tel. 0647–500–04.

BJÖRKLIDEN. *Hotel Fjället* (M), tel. 0980–41050. 66 rooms, bungalows available. Restaurant, sauna, skilifts. Midnight sun from nearby mountaintop, May 31–July 16.

JÄRVSÖ. *Järvsöbaden* (M), tel. 0651–40 400. 45 rooms. Outdoor pool, tennis, sauna, ski-lifts and golf nearby.

KALL. *Kallgårdens Turisthotel* (M), tel. 0647–41200. 55 rooms.

KARLSTAD. *Hotel Drott* (M), tel. 054–11 56 35. 76 rooms. Near the station. *Hotel Grand* (M), tel. 054–11 52 40. 70 rooms. *Stadshotellet* (M), tel. 054–11 52 20. 140 rooms. In the center of the city close to the River Klarälven.

KIRUNA. *Hotel Ferrum* (E), tel. 0980–18600. 170 rooms. *(RESO.) Vassijaure Fjällgård* (I), tel. 0920–42022. 24 rooms.

LULEÅ. *SAS Luleå Hotel* (E), tel. 0920–94000. 213 rooms. Nightclub. *Scandic Hotel* (M), tel. 0920–28360. 164 rooms. Solarium, pool, sauna.

ÖSTERSUND. *Hotel Winn* (M), tel. 063–127740. 138 rooms. (SARA.)

RIKSGRÄNSEN. *Sara Hotel Riksgränsen* (M), tel. 0980–400–80. 77 rooms and 66 flats.

STORLIEN. *Hotel Storlien* (M), tel. 0647–701–51. 14 rooms. *Storliens Högfjällshotel* (M), tel. 0647–701–70. 192 rooms. *Storvallens Stughotel* (M), tel. 0647–701–80. 54 rooms in cottages.

SUNNE. *Hotel Selma Lagerlöf* (M), tel. 0565–130 80. 156 rooms. View of Fryken Lake. *Länsmansgården* (M), tel. 0565–103 01. 30 rooms. Also view of the lake; local atmosphere.

TORSBY. *Torsby Herrgård* (M), tel. 0560–138–20. 34 rooms. *Hotel Björkarna* (I), tel. 0560–120–10. 30 rooms.

VÅLÅDALEN. *Vållådalens Turiststation* (M), tel. 0647–35110. 70 rooms.

VALLSTA. *Stiftsgården* (I), tel. 0278–470–47. 34 rooms.

SWITZERLAND

Switzerland is the heart of the matter of Europe. Not only is it geographically right in the center, but its network of roads-with-tunnels, plus telephone, telegraph and postal services and the Swiss Federal Railways, are firm spokes to all of the Continent. And its scenery is unmatched—with Alpine peaks, rolling fields, vast lakes with comfortable lakeboats, and a southern canton (the Ticino) where palm trees line the lakefront and Italian traditions give a new look to the Switzerland you have been led to expect.

Switzerland has for long been regarded as one of the most expensive holiday destinations in Europe, but that is no longer the case. Over the last few years, the Swiss have kept a tight rein on their prices, especially where hotels and restaurants are concerned, and, although it is certainly not a budget country, it no longer ranks among the most expensive for the visitor.

Modern tourism started in Switzerland and the country is still right at the top when it comes to the art of looking after people on holiday. You would be amazed how many hoteliers around the world have been trained in the demanding school of Swiss catering. But the Swiss approach to tourism has not rested on its considerable laurels. The National Tourist Office is always coming up with attractive new schemes to draw the people of the world to its clean and efficient country. Setting a precedent now followed by several of its neighbors, Switzerland was the first to offer its rail Holiday Card, which you may purchase in 8-day, 15-day and one-month versions, for 1st- or 2nd-class travel. Since the national network of trains, postal buses, trams and lakeboats ties the entire mountainous mass together, you can go anywhere at whatever time you wish, at a fee you have already paid.

Highlights

The highlights of Switzerland are first and foremost the Alps. Ever since the English "invented" tourism in the 19th century, people have traveled to Switzerland to admire, paint, climb and ski down Europe's mightiest mountain range. Of the many Alpine ascents perhaps the most spectacular is up the Jungfrau in the Bernese Oberland. But there are many, many others almost equally phenomenal: Mount Rigi in the Lucerne region, up the cogwheel railway from Zermatt to the top of the Kleintitlis and from Stechelberg to the Schilthorn to mention only a few. Among other top scenic excursions are those to the falls of the Rhine in northeast Switzerland and to the dramatic and awesome Rhône glacier in the south. The passes over the Alps—the Susten, the Furka, the Julier, the Simplon and the St. Gotthard—are all extraordinary triumphs of engineering, as well as providing incredible views of mountain scenery even if only glimpsed from the windows of a train as it snakes in and out of the many tunnels burrowing through the rocky masses. The efficiency and comfort of the Swiss railways are justly famous, but there is one train journey that should appeal even to those who regard trains merely as a means of getting from A to B. This is the aptly named Glacier Express which claws its way from Zermatt and Brig along the desolate Oberalp Pass, the backbone of Europe, to St. Moritz. The journey lasts 7½ hours, passing over 291 bridges and through 91 tunnels.

However, Switzerland does not consist entirely of mountains, even if it can seem that way at times. Many of its cities are remarkably beautiful and well worth visiting for their own sakes. The medieval charm of Berne with its arcades and fountains and world-famous performing clock is perhaps the most lovely of all, but little St. Gallen for example up in the northeast, positively exuding old world charm, or cosmopolitan Geneva in the southwest both attract a steady stream of admiring visitors. Switzerland is also a land of lakes and gentle valleys, and a trip on one of the many lake steamers or a stroll or drive in the lowlands are among the country's most potent charms.

But the greatest joy of Switzerland is that it really is a year-round holiday destination. The Alps are every bit as dramatic in summer as in winter, and though the multitude of flowers decorating their slopes may disappoint skiers, they provide an enchanting setting for walkers or those who merely want to look and admire. And it goes without saying that the Swiss winter sports resorts are among the finest, and in many cases the most famous, in Europe.

PRACTICAL INFORMATION FOR SWITZERLAND

WHAT WILL IT COST. Switzerland's current rate of inflation is around 3%, which makes it one of the lowest of all industrial countries, and their battle with inflation is unceasing. Swiss prices have certainly risen, but they've done so less rapidly than those of some other countries.

The strength of the Swiss franc means you get precious few of them for your dollar, pound or other currency, but Swiss stability means on the other hand that most prices, including hotel prices, remain more or less the same from year to year keeping costs within reach of the average traveler.

As in all countries, some areas are more expensive than others so outside major tourist centers your costs can be kept reasonably low. Full board in one of the big name resorts will necessarily run much higher than equivalent accommodations away from the jet set spots, and you'll still find Switzerland's dependable charm, cleanliness and civilized comfort, for which the country is justly famous. Try the small resorts of the Valais, northeastern Switzerland, the Jura and Ticino's beautiful valleys, where (depending on season and room) bed and breakfast can be had for upward of Fr.35 per person in a double room with bath or shower. If you hanker after town life, Berne, though the capital, is far from being the most expensive city. Or try St. Gallen in northeastern Switzerland, where bed and breakfast can be found in a 3-star hotel for around Fr.40 per person in a double room, or Fribourg where costs are similar.

The Swiss monetary unit is the franc, which is divided into 100 centimes (or Rappen). There are nickel-silver coins of 5, 10, 20 and 50 centimes (or ½ franc), 1 franc, 2 francs and 5 francs. There are notes of 10, 20, 50, 100, 500, and 1000 francs.

The rate of exchange at time of writing was Fr.2.70 to the US dollar, Fr.3.10 to the pound sterling.

A typical day outside a major resort might cost two people:

	Francs
Hotel (moderate) double room with bath and breakfast	120
Lunch at restaurant (moderate)	38
Transportation (2 bus or tram rides)	6
2 coffees	4
2 beers	3
Theater (good seats)	36
Dinner (including wine)	60
Miscellaneous 10%	25
	292

SOURCES OF INFORMATION. The incomparably efficient Swiss National Tourist Office is the major source of information on all aspects of travel to Switzerland. Their addresses are:

In the U.S.: Swiss Center, 608 Fifth Ave., New York, NY 10020 (tel. 212–757 –5944); 250 Stockton St., San Francisco, CA 94108 (tel. 415–362–2260).

In Canada: Commerce Court West, P.O. Box 215, Commerce Court Postal Station, Toronto, Ontario M5L 1E8 (tel. 416–868–0584).

In the U.K.: Swiss Center, 1 New Coventry St., London W.1 (tel. 01–734 1921).

WHEN TO COME. Summer tourist season from May through Sept. Winter sports season: December through April. Skiing into May and June if you go high enough, and throughout the summer in several places.

Climate. Moderate, changeable, naturally cooler in the mountains, but about 10 degrees warmer south of the Gotthard. In winter, below freezing in a substantial part of Switzerland.

Average afternoon temperatures in Fahrenheit and centigrade:

Geneva	Jan.	Feb.	Mar.	Apr.	May	June	July	Aug.	Sept.	Oct.	Nov.	Dec.
F°	39	43	51	58	66	73	77	76	69	58	47	40
C°	4	6	11	14	19	23	25	24	21	18	8	4

SPECIAL EVENTS. Switzerland has a vast, year-round program of cultural, folklore, sporting and traditional events, often big affairs of international renown, but frequently much smaller, simpler, and relatively local in character. The latter, although drawing fewer spectators, are often the most picturesque. A booklet *Events in Switzerland,* published twice yearly, is available free from the Swiss National Tourist Offices.

National Holidays. Jan. 1, 2 (New Year's); Apr. 17, 20 (Easter); May 1* (Labor Day); May 28 (Ascension); June 8 (Whit Mon.); Aug. 1* (National Day); Dec. 25, 26. * Not throughout the country.

VISAS. Nationals of the United States, Canada, Australia, New Zealand, EEC countries and practically all other European countries do not require visas for entry into Switzerland. However, you must of course have a valid passport.

HEALTH CERTIFICATES. Not required for entry into Switzerland from any country.

 GETTING TO SWITZERLAND. By Plane. There are direct flights to both Zurich and Geneva from New York and to Zurich only from Boston, Chicago and Montreal. There is also an airlink between Miami and Zurich. Practically all European capitals and major cities are linked to both Zurich and Geneva, and Basle airport (technically in France) also has good airlinks with London, Paris, Frankfurt, Brussels and Amsterdam to name only a few. There is a direct service to the small airport at Berne from London (Gatwick).

If you arrive at Zurich airport you can send your luggage to any railway or postal coach station in Switzerland for Fr.9 per piece. Check it in with the railway counter clerk just behind customs. Return service also available.

By Train. Switzerland is the railway crossroads of Europe, a sort of vast international rail junction. Consequently it is easily reached by train from all over Western and central Europe. There are through services, for example, from cities as far apart as Amsterdam and Barcelona, Rome and Copenhagen, Budapest and Brussels. From London, the fastest direct route is from Victoria—leaving at 2 P.M.—and via Folkestone and Calais. From here there is a through express (2nd. class couchettes and day carriages) to Basle with direct connections to Zurich, Berne, Lucerne, Interlaken and Lugano. Lucerne, for example, is reached around 7.45 A.M.

By Car. There are a great many drive-on-off car ferry services across the Channel, but only a few need be seriously considered as a means of getting to Switzerland. The routes from Dover or Folkestone to Boulogne and Calais by *Sealink* or *Townsend Thoresen* are the shortest sea crossings—and therefore the least expensive—but the landfall is not ideal for reaching Switzerland quickly; it is ideal, however, for getting there pleasantly on a judicious blend of French major and minor roads. This can be done easily with one overnight stop.

To reach Basle in one day, make for Dunkirk or Ostend by Sealink, or Zeebrugge by Townsend Thoresen, all from Dover; Flushing by Olau Line out of Sheerness; Hook of Holland from Harwich by Sealink; or by North Sea Ferries from Hull to Zeebrugge—then latch onto the European motorway network. The mileage to Basle from these ports ranges from 405 from Zeebrugge to 450 from The Hook. There are no road tolls in Holland, Belgium or Germany.

 CUSTOMS. Except for a restriction to 400 cigarettes or 500 grams of tobacco or 100 cigars plus 2 liters of wine (half these quantities for residents of European countries), plus 1 liter of spirits, all of which should be carried in your hand luggage, nothing intended for personal use is barred. As for exports, there are no limits on Swiss products. You may bring in and take out of the country any amount of any currency.

 HOTELS. Swiss hotels are perhaps the best in the world. At the top end of the scale, deluxe hotels provide a service that is unequalled in courtesy, efficiency, comfort and—above all perhaps—cleanliness. But even the most modest hotels are efficient and comfortable and—it really is a national vice—spotlessly clean. English is spoken in nearly all establishments.

Our hotel grading system is divided into four categories. Deluxe (L) Fr.240 and *up*, Expensive (E) Fr.160–240, Moderate (M) Fr.130–160 and Inexpensive (I) Fr.80–130. All prices are for two people in a double room and these categories largely coincide with Switzerland's own grading system which awards 5 stars to deluxe hotels, 4 stars to expensive hotels, 3 stars to moderate hotels and 1 or 2 stars to inexpensive spots. Shower and half-board (one full meal a day) are frequently included in the prices quoted above. In the lists that follow, we have indicated where this is the case by the term "all inclusive". (This does not, of course, refer to garni hotels, which serve breakfast only). Most Swiss hotels have a wide range of prices: for example, hotels in the (E) category will often also have accommodations in the (M) price range. Prices can be considerably higher in the smarter resorts, particularly in the more expensive categories. Similarly, you may find less expensive rates in some areas such as northeast Switzerland, Ticino, Fribourg or the Jura country. The rates we give are for the high season; big differences can be found at other times of the year.

RESTAURANTS. These are invariably of a high standard. The Swiss take food pretty seriously. Our restaurant grading system is divided into three categories. Expensive (E), Fr.30 and up, Moderate (M) Fr.15–25 and Inexpensive (I) Fr.8.50–15. These prices are for one person and do not include wine.

Food and Drink. Swiss cuisine (*Kochkunst* or *cucina,* if you prefer the German or Italian-speaking cantons) is varied, if not especially subtle. The great specialty is *fondue,* the delicious concoction of Gruyère or Emmentaler cheese melted and skillfully mixed with white wine, flour, kirsch and a soupçon of garlic. There are lots of cheeses and cheese specialties in this dairyland; two you ought to try are *Emmentaler* and *Tête de Moine.* The *Guide Fromage Suisse,* free from the Swiss Tourist Office, gives a list of restaurants serving cheese specialties. If you like pig's feet, don't leave Geneva without ordering *pieds de porc au madère,* a great specialty of this town. A Valais specialty is *viande séchée* (dried beef or pork). The meat is not cured, but dried in airy barns in Alpine valleys. It is also a specialty of the Grisons where it is called *Bündnerfleisch.* Cut wafer-thin, with pickled spring onions and gherkins, it makes a delectable, although somewhat expensive, hors d'oeuvre.

Pork meat in sausage form has a variety of names, each locality having a special recipe for their making: *Knäckerli* and *Päntli* (Appenzell), *Mostmöckli,* and *Kalbsleberwurst* (the latter made of calf's liver). The Grisons boasts of its *salsiz* (small salami), *Landjäger, Beinwurst, Engadiner Wurst,* and *Leberwurst.*

Cakes and sweetmeats are equally varied in this part of the world. *Leckerli* are Basel specialties: spiced honey cake, flat and oblong in shape, with a thin coating of sugar icing on top. In Berne, they are sold with a white sugar bear for decoration. *Fastnachtküchli* are sugar-dusted pastries, eaten everywhere during Mardi Gras. *Gugelhopf* are large, high, bunlike cakes with a hollowed center, useful for stuffing with whipped cream. *Schaffhauserzungen,* which as the name implies are made in Schaffhausen, are cream-filled cakes.

The Swiss, especially those of the west and the south, are great wine drinkers. White wine is appreciated as an appetizer in preference to spirits or vermouth and—if only for the sake of your budget—you should at least give it a try; start with the fuller, softer Valais whites (*Johannisberg* or *Fendant*), as some Swiss wines are rather on the dry side.

WINTER SPORTS. Almost year-round skiing is possible in the high Alpine regions of the Valais, Grisons, Vaud and the Bernese Oberland. The normal season around the well known resorts is from December to April, sometimes even into May. The best time of all is March and April when the days are longer, the *Sulz* (spring snow) fast, and the sun bright and warm, although February is also a popular month. If you are wondering about resorts and ski schools, your only problem will be one of elimination. If you want up-to-the-minute information on all aspects, from hotel availability to snow conditions, the Swiss National Tourist Office in New York, San Francisco, Chicago, London or Zürich will supply it.

Beginners should think first perhaps of Saas Fee as well as Lenk, Adelboden, Leysin and Wengen. For moderate skiers top choices would include Gstaad, Klosters, and Lenzerheide, while Davos, Pontresina, St. Moritz, Verbier and Zermatt would be high on the list of both moderate skiers and experts. Ski-bobbing, skijöring, acrobatic skiing (Leysin has an aero-ski school) are some of the extra-curriculars available, after which the charms of a toboggan may seem a little tame. Do bear in mind though that the St. Moritz Cresta Run is 1,327 yards long, that the record time from the top is barely 55 seconds, that speeds often exceed 80 m.p.h., and that the eight hairpin turns of the Cresta are guaranteed to keep you from worrying about your income tax, though the thought of inheritance taxes may flit through your mind from time to time.

TIPPING. By law, an automatic service charge of 15% is now included in all hotel, restaurant, café, bar and hairdressers' bills. This normally covers everything except that some people give the hotel baggage porter Fr.1, Fr.3 for much baggage. However, if anyone is especially helpful (e.g. the hotel desk porter in saving you money, or giving you advice on tours or nightlife) an appropriate reward would be appreciated. Station and airport porters get Fr.1.50 for each article plus 10%. In a cloakroom where no fixed charge is made give about 50 centimes per person to the attendant. 15% is already added to taxi fares in most towns. Ushers and washroom attendants may expect Fr.1; and if you feel that you have had special service from your hotel maid you can leave her about Fr.5 extra.

MAIL. Current rates for letters and postcards to the U.S. are: Fr.1.20 for up to 10 grams; Fr.1.50 for up to 20 grams. To the U.K. the rate is Fr.–.90 for up to 20 grams. These prices may well change during 1987.

CLOSING TIMES. Usual shop hours are from 8 A.M. to 12 noon and from 1:30 to 6:30 P.M. Banks: hours vary from place to place, but usually 8 A.M. to 4:30 or 5 P.M. Closed for lunch and on Saturdays and Sundays. Foreign currency exchange windows at airports and larger railway stations are open daily from 10 P.M.

USEFUL ADDRESSES. *Embassies:* American, Australian, British, Canadian, South African at Berne. *Consulates:* American and South African at Zurich; Australian and New Zealand at Geneva; British at Geneva, Lugano, Montreux and Zurich. *Swiss National Tourist Office,* Bellariastr. 38, Zurich, but local tourist office there at main station. Each locality has its well-run information office, called *Verkehrsbüro, Office du Tourisme* or *Ente Turistico,* usually in or very close to the railway station. For police, dial 117; fire brigade, 118.

GETTING AROUND SWITZERLAND. By Train. The Swiss railway system is unrivalled by any in the world. Its services are almost entirely electrified and are operated by the federally-run *Schweiz. Bundesbahnen* (SBB); or *Chemins de Fer Fédéraux* (CFF) and *Ferrovie dello Stato Svizzere* (FSS) in the French-speaking and Italian-speaking areas respectively. All three emblems are carried on most carriages and locomotives, but the same high standards apply everywhere. There are also a number of privately-owned lines, some, such as the *Berne-Lötschberg-Simplon* line (BLS) or the *Rhaetian Railway* (RhB), of considerable importance. Add to these many small local lines and mountain railways and a number of splendid steam locomotives and you have a railway traveler's paradise.

The Swiss Holiday Rail Card is perhaps the best runabout ticket of its type available. Not only does it give unlimited travel over the entire railway system, it also includes all the postal bus routes (see below), some 300 miles of lake steamer routes and is good for reductions of between 25% and 50% on most mountain and cable railways. Issued for 4, 8 and 15 days and for one month, it costs, in 1st class, Fr.215, Fr.250, Fr.300, and Fr.420 respectively. In 2nd class it costs Fr.145, Fr.170, Fr.205, and Fr.285 (these figures are approximate and subject to change). Children from 6 to 15 inclusive travel at half fare. The card can be purchased in your country of origin or at Zurich and Geneva airports and at Zurich, Geneva and Berne stations.

In addition to the Swiss Holiday Rail Card, there are a number of regional runabout tickets based on specific areas or resorts such as Interlaken, Lucerne or Lugano. Inquire locally for information at regional tourist offices. Cities in Switzerland all have excellent integrated local transport services and issue runabout tickets valid for a day, three days or one week.

By Bus. Apart from urban bus services, bus travel in Switzerland effectively means the postal coach system. This extends all over the country, is integrated with railway and lake steamer services and runs throughout the year. The buses are painted a bright yellow and are comfortable without being luxurious. They are punctual in the extreme. Costs are comparable to 2nd. class rail travel. In summer reservations are advisable and in some areas essential.

By Car. Swiss roads, including the principal mountain passes, are usually well-surfaced although heavy traffic can make driving on some main routes relatively slow. Motorways are excellent. Major mountain passes, although often steep, can be negotiated without difficulty by an average car, but care is needed. Uphill traffic has priority over that coming down. On mountain postal roads (indicated by a sign showing a posthorn against a blue background) the big yellow Swiss postal coaches can demand precedence in any situation. For information by telephone about Alpine road conditions, dial 163. In case of breakdown, dial 140 for road assistance. For police dial 117.

You drive on the right. There is a strictly enforced, absolute speed limit of 80 k.p.h. (50 m.p.h.) on all roads except motorways; latter usually 120 k.p.h. (75 m.p.h.). In built-up areas 50 k.p.h. (30 m.p.h.). *Heavy, on-the-spot fines for infringement.* Except on main roads, vehicles coming from the right have right of way. The international motoring code signs apply. Many towns have parking meters or "Blue Zones": discs for the latter obtainable from tourist offices, automobile clubs, some garages, banks etc. Motorways are identified by green directional signs. Motorists are required to display a special tax disc if they wish to drive on the motorways. Discs are good for one year, and are available at the border, at a cost of Fr.30. They are also available in the U.K. from the Swiss National Tourist Office, the A.A. and the R.A.C. at a cost of £10.

Special car-carrying trains through Alpine tunnels make year-round transit possible of the Albula and Lötschberg passes. Road tunnels go under the Grand St. Bernard, St. Gotthard and San Bernardino passes, as well as Mont Blanc (at Chamonix, 50 miles from Geneva), but east-west transit can pose problems.

Third party insurance is compulsory in Switzerland, and motorists are advised to carry an international insurance Green Card. Those without a Green Card (EEC nationals excluded) have to buy insurance cover at the frontier (about Fr.30 for 30 days). Safety belts are mandatory in front seats; children under 12 must sit in back. Gasoline costs about Fr.1.18 to Fr.1.28 per liter but prices change unpredictably. Gasoline stations everywhere.

CAR HIRE. Most travel agencies and car hire firms, several airlines, and Swiss railroads can arrange to have a self-drive or chauffeur-driven car awaiting your arrival in Switzerland. In Zurich are the head offices of *Budget,* PO Box 84, Scheideggstr. 72; *Europcar/National,* Badenerstr. 812; while *Avis* is at Flughofstr. 61, Glattbrugg. All have offices or agents at Basle, Geneva and Zurich airports and most large towns and resorts.

The Grisons and the Engadine

The canton of the Grisons (German: Graubünden) is often spoken of as "Switzerland in miniature" because of its concentration of high Alpine peaks, beautiful lakes and deep valleys. Along with the Bernese Oberland, this is the area most familiar to winter sports devotees. Here are places to which ski enthusiasts flock from all over the world, such as Arosa, Davos, Flims, Klosters, Lenzerheide, Pontresina, Savognin, Laax, Disentis, Splügen, San Bernardino, Sedrun, Bergün and the vast conglomeration of St. Moritz and its winter sports satellites. Here, peppered with all manner of winter and summer resorts, is the famous Engadine—the mountain-bordered valley of the river Inn and its chain of lovely lakes—which cuts a 25-mile-long swath across the southern part of the Grisons.

The resort seasons are June to September and December to April. In the winter high season, St. Moritz and other fashionable spots glitter with cosmopolitan sophistication, but you will find countless smaller resorts as well as unspoiled mountain and valley villages. So don't get the idea you can't enjoy yourself here on a limited budget. You can—and thousands do. However, the Grisons offers much more than winter sports. It is beautiful at most seasons—in the late spring, the summer and fall. Indeed, many consider the best time to be the latter part of

June or early July, for then the mountainsides come ablaze with wild flowers.

The variety of the Grisons will provide you with the excitement of many contrasts. Enjoy the medieval streets of Chur; the incomparable ski-runs of Klosters; the remarkable network of cablecars, chairlifts and ski lifts at nearby Davos, and its famous Parsenn run where, from a height of some 9,000 feet, you can ski down over vast open fields to the town, a drop of 3,500 feet or so; the beautiful village of Guarda (Engadine), under federal protection to ensure that its peasant dwellings with their striking *sgraffiti* ornamentation remain unchanged. Or try the adjoining resorts of Scuol, Vulpera and Tarasp with their healthful waters (good for the liver), worth discovering, especially for the pure white, 11th-century dream castle of Tarasp, perched on top of a sheer cliff some 500 feet above the valley floor.

For two modest resorts, try the charming Engadine villages of Celerina and Samedan, the latter noted for its splendid views of the Bernina mountain chain—Piz Palü (12,900 ft.) and Piz Bernina (13,300 ft.), just a couple of peaks to give you an idea of the scale. Celerina, nearby St. Moritz's kid brother, is first-rate for skiing, with easy access to all of the more celebrated resort's winter sports facilities. The famous Cresta bobsled run has its terminus here. Not to be missed from either Celerina or Samedan is the trip up the Muottas Muragl funicular with its marvelous view of the upper Inn Valley and the chain of lovely lakes starting at St. Moritz.

St. Moritz itself, at an altitude of 6,000 feet and on the shores of the sky-blue lake of the same name, has all the cachet of a world capital. Before the rise of Rome, even before the fall of Troy, the healing qualities of its waters were known. Many Europeans still take these waters or soak themselves in baths to cure a wide range of ailments. But these days the waters are almost forgotten in the flurries of snow and the glitter of international society on the ski slopes. This is the winter playground of the fashionable world, and if you come here to see statesmen, film stars, what remains of European nobility, and Arab oil sheiks worth their weight in diamonds, you won't be disappointed. In summer, when prices are appreciably below winter levels, it is lovely, too, with facilities for swimming, sailing, riding, mountain climbing, golf, tennis and some of the best fishing in Switzerland in the River Inn.

Some of the smart set feel that St. Moritz has become too popular. Their answer is Arosa (5,900 ft.), with every facility for summer and winter sports and even horseracing on the snow and ice. Dressy, smart and elegant, it is less expensive than St. Moritz. It also has a bathing beach on the little lake, one of the largest ski schools in Switzerland (with 100 instructors), heated swimming pool, ice rink and, winter or summer, some of the most magnificent mountain scenery in the world.

PRACTICAL INFORMATION FOR THE GRISONS AND ENGADINE

AROSA. (All inclusive.) *Arosa Kulm Hotel* (L), tel. 310131. At the top end of town and well placed for Hörnli gondolas and Carmenna lift. *Eden* (L), tel. 311877. Very comfortable. *Excelsior* (L), tel. 311661. With indoor pool. *Golfhotel Hof Maran* (L), tel. 310185. Every sporting facility, including golf as the name suggests. *Park-Hotel* (L), tel. 310165. Grand and comfortable. *Savoy* (L), tel. 310211. Indoor pool. *Waldhotel-National* (L), tel. 311353. Pre-war atmosphere; a favorite of Thomas Mann's. *Alpensonne* (E), tel. 311547. *Alpina* (E), tel. 311658. *Belri* (E), tel. 311237. In quiet location. *Streiff* (E), tel. 311117. In garden, *Vetter* (E), tel. 311702. At Ramoz, *Litzirüti* (I), tel. 311063.

Restaurants. *Central* (M), tel. 311513. Try the Scampi Maison or the rack of lamb *à la Sarladaise*. *Kursaal-Casino* (M), tel. 311261.

CELERINA (All inclusive). *Cresta Palace* (L), tel. 33564. Indoor pool and many winter sports facilities. *Cresta Kulm* (E), tel. 33373. Quiet location. *Misani* (E), tel. 33314. With good restaurant. *Posthaus* (M), tel. 32222.

CHUR. *Duc de Rohan* (I), tel. 221022. Indoor pool and elegant restaurant; best in town. *Drei Könige* (I), tel. 221725. Central. *Romantik Hotel Stern* (I), tel. 223555. Atmospheric historic building with good restaurant; central.

Restaurants. There are several (E) restaurants in the *Duc de Rohan* hotel (see above). Specialties include *Crevettes Pisani,* veal kidneys à la Palmir. They also serve a Graubünder Rhine wine. *Bahnhof-Buffet* (I), tel. 223013. Good, like so many of its kind.

DAVOS. (All inclusive). In Davos Platz: *Morosani's Posthotel* (L), tel. 21161. Highly recommended. *Steigenberger Belvedere* (L), tel. 21281. All facilities in this luxurious spot. *Schweizerhof* (L), tel. 21151. Central; recommended. *Bellavista Sporthotel* (E), tel. 54252. In garden.

In Davos Dorf: *Derby* (L), tel. 61166. Comfortable and quiet. *Fluela* (L), tel. 61221. Extremely grand with every amenity. *Montana Sporthotel* (E), tel. 53444. *Parsenn* (E), tel. 53232. Central location; skittle alley. *Bristol* (M), tel. 53033. Good restaurant.

Restaurants. In Davos Dorf: *Meierhof* (M), tel. 61285. In Davos Laret: *Tschiery's Landhaus* (E), tel. 52121. Try the *Menu Campagnard*—country fare at its expensive best!

FLIMS. (All inclusive). *Adula* (L), tel. 390161. Indoor pool, gardens and good restaurant. *Parkhotel* (L), tel. 390181. In beautiful grounds with many sports facilities and all comforts. *Schweizerhof* (L), tel. 391212. Sporting facilities and attractive grounds. *Schlosshotel* (E), tel. 391245. Central with good restaurant. *National* (M), tel. 391224. Comfortable and central. *Cresta* (I), tel. 391302. Central but quiet location.

Restaurants. In Flims Dorf: *Stiva,* with an open fireplace, and *Las Valettas* (both E, both in Hotel Crap Ner, tel. 392626). *Albana Sporthotel* (I): three restaurants, plus pizzeria, terrace and pub, near ski lifts and cableways; tel. 392333.

KLOSTERS. (All inclusive). *Aaba Health* (L), tel. 48111. Indoor pool, sauna, cure facilities; vegetarian. *Steinbock* (L), tel. 44545. Highly recommended. *Vereina* (L), tel. 41161. Tennis in grounds; indoor pool and sauna. *Kurhotel Bad Serneus* (E), tel. 41444. Cure facilities; quiet location. *Büel* (I), tel. 42669. Simple but central. *Silvapina* (I), tel. 41468. In own garden; ideal for children.

Restaurants. *Steinbock* (M), tel. 44545. *Rufinis* (I), tel. 41371. *Surval* (I), tel. 41121.

LAAX. (All inclusive). *Crap Sogn Gion* (E), tel. 392192. Indoor pool, sauna and skittle alley. *Happy Rancho Sporthotel* (E), tel. 390131. Exceptionally well equipped with 2 pools, tennis, sauna and solarium. *Sporthotel Signina* (E), tel. 390151. Indoor pool and tennis; dancing. *Sporthotel Larisch* (M), tel. 22126. Indoor pool and sauna.

Restaurant. *Sporthotel Larisch* (I), in hotel of same name (see above). Large rustic restaurant and Bündnerstube, garden terrace. Fondues, "Larisch-Topf", fresh trout.

LENZERHEIDE. (All inclusive). *Grand Hotel Kurhaus Alpina* (L), tel. 341134. Comfortable and smart; central. *Guarda Val* (L), tel. 342214. Great rustic charm. *Sunstar* (L), tel. 340121. Central with all comforts; also (E) rooms. *Lenzerhorn* (M), tel. 341105. Central with gardens. *Sporz-Davains* (I), tel. 341218. Family run.

Restaurants. *Guarda-Val* (E), in hotel (see above). Atmospheric. *Cafe Kurhaus* (I), tel. 343665. 16 different sorts of tea.

PONTRESINA. (All inclusive). *Grand Hotel Kronenhof* (L), tel. 60111. Expensive and grand; good restaurant. *Walther* (L), tel. 66471. Ice rink, tennis and sauna among the facilities. *Bernina* (E), tel. 66221. Central; in own grounds with good restaurant. *Rosatsch* (E), tel. 67777. Sauna; centrally located. *Sporthotel Pontresina* (E), tel. 66331. *Bahnhof-Chesa Briotta* (I), tel. 66242. Simple hotel.

ST. MORITZ. (All inclusive). *Badrutt's Palace Hotel* (L), tel. 21101, central, but with spacious ground and marvelous views at the back; *very* expensive. *Carlton Hotel* (L), tel. 21141. Long famed for its quiet elegance and service; very expensive. *Crystal* (L), tel. 21165. Central; with sauna. *Schweizerhof* (L), tel. 22171. Gymnasium among the many facilities. *Suvretta House* (L), tel. 21121. About a mile out of town in marvelous grounds; very pricey. *Chantarella* (E), tel. 21185. Good for children; in own grounds. *Bellevue* (E), tel. 22161. Riding and sauna. *Soldanella* (E), tel. 33651. In own grounds; reasonable hotel. *National* (M), tel. 33274. *Sonne* (M), tel. 33527. With some cheaper rooms.

Restaurants. *Rôtisserie des Chevaliers* (E), tel. 21151. Graded "excellent" in the *Passeport Bleu* Swiss gastronomic guide. In St. Moritz Bad: *Steinbock* (I), tel. 36035. Specialties include French onion soup *au gratin*, lamb chops *à l'estragon, risotto capuccino. Sonne* (M), see hotel above. Good Italian restaurant.

SAMEDAN. (All inclusive). *Bernina* (E), tel. 65421. Tennis and dancing. *Quadratscha* (E), tel. 64257. Indoor pool. *Donatz* (M), tel. 64666. Golf, ice rink and curling among the facilities. *Hirschen* (M), tel. 65274. In historic building in the center of town. Some cheaper rooms. *Sporthotel* (M), tel. 65333. In own grounds.

Restaurant. *Le Pavillon* (M), in Bernina hotel (see above). Boletus mushrooms prepared at the table, fresh homemade goose liver pâté, calves' liver *à la Veneziana.*

SCUOL. (All inclusive). *Guarda Val* (E), tel. 91321. Historic and atmospheric building; central but quiet. *Parkhotel Tarasp* (E), tel. 91221. Tennis and dancing. *Bellaval* (M), tel. 91481. Good family hotel. *La Staila* (M), tel. 91483. Ideal for children.

Restaurant. *Filli* (M), tel. 99927.

SILS-MARIA, BASELGIA. (All inclusive). At Sils-Maria: *Waldhaus* (L), tel. 45331. Indoor pool and tennis; quiet. *Maria* (E), tel. 45317. Sailing school as well as ice rink and curling. *Privata* (M), tel. 45247. Central; good for children.

At Sils-Baselgia: *Margna* (L), tel. 45306. Many facilities but rather expensive. *Chesa Randolina* (E), tel. 45224. Quiet. *Chasté* (I), tel. 45312. Small and simple inexpensive hotel.

At Sils-Fextal: *Fex* (I), tel. 45356.

SILVAPLANA. (All inclusive). *Albana* (L), tel. 49292. Sauna and gymnasium. *Arlas* (E), tel. 48148. Small hotel. *Sonne* (E), tel. 48152. Sailing, skating, and dancing; in quiet surroundings. *Chesa Grusaida* (M), tel. 48292. *Corvatsch* (I), tel. 48162. No showers.

TARASP-VULPERA. (All inclusive). *Schweizerhof* (L), tel. 91331. Excellent value; (E) rooms available. *Waldhaus* (L), tel. 91112. Cure facilities, tennis, golf and pool in this quiet hotel. *Villa Silvana* (M), tel. 91354. Sports and cure facilities. *Tarasp* (I), tel. 91445. Ice rink; central but quiet.

Restaurant. *Chasté* (E), tel. 91775. Rated in *Passeport Bleu* as "excellent". Try the sole fillets *à la Champs Elysées.*

Northeastern Switzerland

This is an area that is rich in variety, rich in tradition—and just plain rich! Yet despite its prosperity, evident throughout the region, it retains an air of other-worldliness. Everywhere you see past and present interwoven: houses, new as well as old, with frescoes and carved-wood balconies, or turrets, roofs and entire walls of wood shingles—so delicate that, when weathered, they look like fur. Old customs are as alive today as they were centuries ago. Yet St. Gallen's textile industry leads in technical development, and some of her new public buildings achieve dizzy heights of modernity. Because tourists have been slow to appreciate northeastern Switzerland's widely differing attractions, it has kept its personality intact, unharried by tourism with a capital 'T'. Consequently its prices are often lower than in some more famous parts of Switzerland.

The region lies to the east of Zurich and to the north of the Grisons and roughly comprises the cantons of Glarus, St. Gallen and—cocooned within the latter—Appenzell plus Thurgau and Schaffhausen. This area has many faces ranging all the way from snowcapped 8,200-foot Mt. Säntis to the shores of Lake Constance. Its many mutations include the rolling hills of Appenzell; a host of lakes, from ten-mile-long Walensee to little mountain gems like Seealpsee; the vast Rhine valley plain and a mountain valley for every mood. To the east, the Rhine separates Switzerland from the little principality of Liechtenstein, and from Austria with the mountains of Vorarlberg and the charm of Bregenzerwald within easy reach.

Towns range from St. Gallen, whose magnificent rococo library is generally considered the most beautiful room in Switzerland, to spas such as Bad Ragaz, and scores of summer and winter resorts. Some smaller towns, notably Appenzell, played a big part in the development of the Swiss Confederation. Both halves of Appenzell, and Glarus, still have their picturesque *Landsgemeinde*, or open-air parliament.

PRACTICAL INFORMATION FOR THE NORTHEAST

APPENZELL. *Romantik Hotel Säntis* (M), tel. 878722. Historic building; riding. *Hecht* (I), tel. 871025. Central; bowling. *Taube* (I), tel. 871149. Small and inexpensive with sauna; central but quiet.
  Restaurant. *Säntis* (M), in hotel (see above). Local specialties, river trout, Appenzell wine. Excellent.

BAD RAGAZ. (All inclusive). *Grand Hotel Hof Ragaz* (L), tel. 90131. Cure facilities; comfortable. *Quellenhof* (L), tel. 90111. In park with cure facilities, golf and tennis. *Lattmann* (E), tel. 91315. Cure facilities; central. *Sandi* (E), tel. 91756. Quiet, facilities for handicapped, some (M) rooms. *Ochsen* (M), tel. 92451. Central, gymnasium, TV in all rooms. *Ursalina* (I), tel. 92588. Central; breakfast only. Garden.
  Restaurants. *National* (M), tel. 91304. The veal soufflé is famous—and there's game during the open season. *Wartenstein* (M), see hotel above.

BRAUNWALD. (All inclusive). *Alpina* (E), tel. 843284. Marvelous view from the restaurant; quiet. *Bellevue* (E), tel. 843843. Tennis, sauna, indoor pool; good for children. *Tödiblick* (E), tel. 841236. Quiet hotel in park; some (M) rooms.
  Restaurants. *Alpenblick* (I-M), tel. 841544. Scampi, snails, frogs' legs *à la provençale*, porterhouse T-bone steak. *Rübschen* (I-M), tel. 841534. French cuisine.

RAPPERSWIL. *Schwanen* (M), tel. 219181. Centrally located in historic building; some (I) rooms. *Schiff* (I), tel. 283888. Delightful small hotel in attractive building.
  Restaurants. *Eden* (E), tel. 271221. Graded "excellent" in *Passeport Bleu*. Fish and meat specialties. Gastronomic menus Fr.60 to Fr.80. *Hirschen* (I-M), tel. 276624. Fillets of perch, *Hainanese Mah Mee*, soufflé Grand Mariner.

ST. GALLEN. *Walhalla beim Bahnhof* (E), tel. 222922. Near the station; comfortable. *Hecht am Marktplatz* (M), tel. 226502. Attractive hotel with dancing and excellent restaurant; central. *Dom* (I), tel. 232044. Breakfast only; comfortable and friendly hotel near the cathedral. *Ekkehard* (I), tel. 224714. Central; with bowling. *Sonne Rotmonten* (I), tel. 244342. Quiet and comfortable.
  Restaurants. *Schnäggehüsli* (Snail Shell) (E), tel. 256525. Snail soup, salmon trout, homemade pâté. *Walhalla* (E), in hotel (see above). Graded "excellent" in *Passeport Bleu*. *Schwarzer Bären* (M), tel. 353055.

WILDHAUS. (All inclusive). *Acker* (E), tel. 59111. Indoor pool, sauna and gymnasium; good for children. *Hirschen* (E), tel. 52252. Pool and sauna. *Toggenburg* (M), tel. 52323. Sauna. Panoramic view from restaurant.

Zurich

Zurich, with some 380,000 inhabitants, is one of the most beautifully situated cities in Switzerland, as well as being the largest. It's the industrial heart of the nation, but you'd never know it. There's no smoke, no smog. The industries are all electrified, and the buildings in which they are housed look more like sanatoria or college dormitories than factories. There are no slums. The workers live in pretty little villas with flowers round the door, or in apartment blocks. And beneath the staid pavement of Bahnhofstrasse lie the gold-filled vaults of the banks whose famous numbered accounts have made Zurich a world financial center.

Zurich is Protestant. On a high pedestal beside the Grossmünster, a church said to have been founded by Charlemagne, stands the statue of Ulrich Zwingli. In 1519, defying the Pope, he started preaching the Reformation there, almost splitting the Swiss Confederation in two. His bronze effigy looks out toward the Niederdorf. Even today his spirit tends to live on in Zurich. Ironically, the cathedral's splendid Romanesque architecture dominates the city's most swinging quarter, that same Niederdorf over which Zwlingli presides. But if the Zurichers have a streak of puritanism, they are also scrupulously honest, fastidiously clean, generous, and truly remarkable for their genuine kindness.

Zurich's weather, to quote James Joyce, who is buried in Zurich and who wrote many pages of his *Ulysses* in the Pfauen Restaurant, is "as uncertain as a baby's bottom". A rare crystal-clear day providing a wonderful vista of snow-capped mountains rising from the lake is, according to Zurichers, a guarantee that it's going to rain. April and May are almost certain to be rainy and cold, although you may get some blissfully warm, sunny days. But from early summer through the fall, the odds are with you.

PRACTICAL INFORMATION FOR ZURICH

 HOTELS. If you want the best—and can afford it— Zurich offers a bewildering choice of superb hotels. The city also has a large number of more moderately priced establishments that still maintain the very highest standards of Swiss hoteliers. However, as Zurich is generally rather on the expensive side, there unfortunately is something of a lack of inexpensive hotels.

Deluxe

Atlantis Sheraton, Döltschiweg 234 (tel. 4630000). With indoor pool, sauna and considerable luxury; quiet location.

Baur au Lac, Talstr. 1 (tel. 2211650). Stands in its own lakeside minipark near the end of the Bahnhofstr; an elegant establishment.

Carlton Elite, Bahnhofstr. 41 (tel. 2116560). In the heart of chic downtown Zurich.

Dolder Grand Hotel, Kurhaustr. 65 (tel. 2516231). Up among the pinewoods, but only about 10 minutes from the city center; outdoor pool and superb views.

Savoy Baur en Ville, Poststr. 12 (tel. 2115360). Situated in the middle of the exclusive shopping center on Bahnhofstr.

Zum Storchen, Weinplatz 2 (tel. 2115510). Historic building in the heart of town; splendid view from the first-class restaurant.

Expensive

Ascot, Lavaterstr. 15 (tel. 2011800). In business area; very smart. With some (M) rooms.

Continental, Stampfenbachstr. 60 (tel. 3633363). All rooms airconditioned; dancing; central.

Florhof, Florhofgasse 4 (tel. 474470). Central but quiet; elegant mansion hotel. Some (M) rooms.

Glärnischof, Claridenstr. 30 (tel. 2024747). Smart grill restaurant and all the expected comforts.

Moderate

Schifflände, Schifflände 18 (tel. 694050). Fairly new but lacks nothing in plush comfort.

Trümpy, Limmatstr. 5 (tel. 425400). Central, with good grill restaurant and TV in all rooms.

Inexpensive

Bahnpost, Reitergasse 6 (tel. 2413211). Central but quiet and very reasonably priced. No shower.

Buchzelg, Buchzelgstr. 50 (tel. 538200). A rather superior hotel for this category; in own grounds.

Fischer, Schaffhauserstr. 520 (tel. 3012755). Very inexpensive.

Franziskaner, Stüssihofstatt 1 (tel. 2520120). Small and central.

Leonhard, Limmatquai 136 (tel. 2513080). In the heart of town.

Limmathof, Limmatquai 142 (tel. 474220). Simple, but central.

Rothaus, Langstr. 121 (tel. 2412451). Recommended.

Spirgarten, Lindenplatz 5 (tel. 622400). With good restaurant and skittle alley.

Splendid, Rosengasse 5 (tel. 2525850). Central. No shower.

Du Théâtre, Seilergraben 69 (tel. 2526062). Breakfast only; central.

Restaurants

Expensive

Baur au Lac Grill, Talstr. 1 (tel. 2211650), not to be confused with the main dining room of that hotel. French cuisine at its best plus an excellent selection of regional dishes.

Bauschänzli, near Quai Bridge (on its own island in the River Limmat) (tel. 2112862). With concerts.

Chez Max, Seestr. 53 (tel. 3918877). Just outside Zurich; one of Switzerland's most famous restaurants.

Fischstube Zürichhorn, built on piles over the Lake at Bellerive 160 (tel. 552520). Excellent food.

Rôtisserie Côte d'Or (at the Goldenes Schwert Hotel), Marktgasse 14 (tel. 2525944). Reader-recommended.

Seiler's Ermitage, Seestr. 80, Küsnacht (tel. 9104441). Eat on the garden terraces; very famous.

Veltliner Keller, Schlüsselgasse 8 (tel. 2213228). Hard to find but worth the effort. Superbly prepared regional specialties served amid splendid carved-wood decor in the dining rooms.

The guildhall restaurants are all famed for good food and atmosphere.

Haus zum Rüden (the Gothic restaurant of the Society of Noblemen), Limmatquai 42 (tel. 479590).

Kronenhalle, Rämistrasse 4 (tel. 2510256). Recommended.

Zunfthaus zur Safran (Spice Merchants' Guildhall), Limmatquai 54 (tel. 476722).

Zunfthaus zur Schmieden (Blacksmiths' Guildhall), Marktgasse 20 (tel. 2515287). Good food.

Zunfthaus zur Zimmerleuten (Carpenters' Guildhall), Limmatquai 40, (tel. 2520834).

Moderate

Bahnhofbuffet (Main Rail Station restaurant). Good, if a bit noisy; specialties tend to be expensive.

Bodega Española, Münstergasse 15 (tel. 2512310). Spanish.

Chianti-Quelle, Stampfenbachstr. 38 (tel. 3623509).

Ciro's, Militärstr. 16 (tel. 2417841). Italian specialties.

Emilio, Müllerstr. 5 (tel. 2418321). Spanish specialties.

Hongkong, Seefeldstr. 60 (tel. 2518202). Outstanding Chinese food.

Kropf, Gasenstr. 16 (near Paradeplatz) (tel. 2211805). First-rate meal for around Fr. 18.

Mövenpick, chain of good restaurants; see the phone book for details.

Napoli, Sandstr. 7 (tel. 4620764). Also Italian.

Piccoli-Accademia, Rotwandstr. 48 (tel. 2416243).

Widder, Widdergasse 6 (tel. 2113150). Excellent, reserve in advance; delightful atmosphere, entertainment and good food.

Inexpensive

Gleich, Seefeldstr. 9 (tel. 2513203). Excellent vegetarian restaurant

Hilti-Vegis, Sihlstr. 28 (tel. 2213870). Also vegetarian and good value.

The Migros chain of self-service restaurants is also good value; you will find them in all the larger Migros stores.

The Zurich Frauenverein (Women's Institute) runs a string of good-value, wholesome-if-simple-food places including the *Seidenhof, Mensa, Rütli, Volkshaus, Kehlhof, Im Grüf, Zürichberg, Rigiblick* and *Olivenbaum.*

University cafeterias include *The Mensa,* Rämistr. 71; *The Mensa, Polyterrasse,* Leonhardstr. 34; and *Culmann,* Culmannstr. 1. The *Olivenbaum, 4-Linden, Frohsinn* and *Seidenhof* are all run by temperance leagues and offer plain, substantial food at very attractive prices.

ENTERTAINMENT. Zurich nightspots can best be described as undistinguished. Striptease/hostess: *Maxim, La Puce* (in the small bar), *Terrasse,* and *Red House.* Dancing: *Mascotte* (usually, fine jazz), *La Ferme* (rustic style), *Bellerive, Diagonal* of the Baur au Lac (chic), *Hazyland* (good music; western saloon decor). And at *Kindli* there's Swiss folklore and a good, musical stage show.

The *Schauspielhaus* presents one of the best classical repertoires in Europe. The *Opernhaus* (grand opera, light opera, operetta) produces topnotch performances for the annual June festival. The *Bernhard* theater plays broad farce, the small *Theater am Hechtplatz* is an experimental stage for all sorts of acted entertainment, and presents plays mainly in German.

MUSEUMS. Centre Le Corbusier, Bellerivestrasse at Hoschgasse. Last building designed by the great Swiss architect. It is devoted largely to his paintings, which, though not as well-known as his architectural work, are surprisingly good.

Museum of Applied Arts (Kunstgewerbemuseum), Ausstellungstrasse 60. Graphic and applied arts; there is a fine library.

Rietberg Museum, Gablerstr. 15. Admirable collection of primitive and Oriental sculptures.

Swiss National Museum. (Landesmuseum), Museumstrasse 2. Just behind the main rail station. Especially good for students of Swiss history.

Wohnkultur, Barengasse 20–22. Two marvelous patrician homes dating from 1650 and decorated in styles current between then and the mid-19th century.

Zurich Art Museum (Kunsthaus), Heimplatz. Small but outstanding permanent collection, especially strong on French moderns. Exhibitions here are often excellent.

Lucerne and Central Switzerland

Few cities are more beloved by tourists than Lucerne, with its 15th- and 16th-century houses, its medieval covered bridges, and its dreamy old world atmosphere contrasting with the liveliest interest in modern art, music and other expressions of 20th-century culture. April through October is the season here. The August/September music festival is an international event with its topflight orchestras, conductors, singers and soloists. If you want to come for that, it would be wise to make hotel reservations and procure tickets *at least six months in advance.*

You'll have the most fun shamelessly crossing and recrossing those two wonderful 14th- and 15th-century wooden bridges, the Kapellbrücke and the Spreuerbrücke, inspecting the paintings under the roof.

The renovated Kapellbrücke, the larger and most famous of the two, leads diagonally across the swiftly-flowing River Reuss from the old St. Peter's chapel, past the picturesque Wasserturm (water tower) to the southern bank. The paintings here depict scenes from Lucerne's history. Those on the Spreuerbrücke portray the Totentanz, a grim medieval dance of death. Wander through the picturesque old quarters on the north bank, inspect the ancient city walls, take a look at the quaint Weinmarkt, and you could almost be back in the Middle Ages.

You must, of course, see the famous Lion of Lucerne, designed by Thorwaldsen, carved in stone by Ahorn in the early 19th century, and dedicated to the heroic Swiss Guards of Louis XVI, who defended the Tuileries when the French Revolution broke out in 1792. The Lion lies in a niche hewn out of the cliffside near the celebrated Glacier Gardens, a unique collection of huge potholes created by glacier water during the Ice Age but not unearthed until 1872.

Excursions from Lucerne are delightful. Lake Lucerne, or the Vierwaldstättersee (Lake of the Four Forest Cantons) as the Swiss call it, is in the very heart of the country. In addition, it is idyllically beautiful. The lake boat tour from Lucerne to Flüelen, stopping at many little resorts en route, is highly recommended, and you should also get up above the lake for one of the sweeping, overall views of this region. See it, for example, from Mount Pilatus south of Lucerne, a 7,000-foot triangular crag accessible by an aerial cableway from Kriens, or by cogwheel railway from Alpnachstad. The Rigi, although only 5,900 feet, will give you further splendid views. It's more gentle, more friendly than Pilatus and has green turf on top. Although the skiing here is excellent, it lasts for only a few weeks in January/February. Three mountain railways go to the summit; one from the pretty little resort of Vitznau, the second from Arth-Goldau, near Lake Zug and only about 14 miles from Lucerne itself, and the third is an aerial cable way from Weggis. From Küssnacht, a lakeside resort between Lucerne and Arth-Goldau, to Immensee on Lake Zug, you can take the historic Hohle Gasse or "Sunken Lane", along which the tyrannical Austrian bailiff, Gessler, was riding when William Tell's arrow struck him down. You'll hear much more of this legendary hero at Altdorf, where William Tell is reputed to have shot an arrow through an apple on his little boy's head. At nearby Bürglen (his birthplace) you'll find a vast William Tell collection housed in a tower. You can go from Lucerne to Altdorf in one hour by rail; the boat takes about three hours via Flüelen. Schwyz, between Lucerne and Altdorf on the St. Gotthard line, is one of the oldest towns in Switzerland. But its claim to fame lies in the fact that it is the place from which Switzerland (in German, Schweiz) derives both its name and its flag. Here, in the impressive archives building, you may see that precious document, the Oath of Eternal Alliance, which, in 1291, became Switzerland's Declaration of Independence.

Zug, an ancient walled city with much modern development, can be reached from Zurich by rail. It has an interesting museum of gold and silver work and other handicrafts and there are also splendid views, from the hill overlooking the town, of the Jungfrau and other great peaks. Einsiedeln, the birthplace of Paracelsus and home of the celebrated Black Madonna of Einsiedeln, performs every 5 years (ending in 5 or 0) *The Great World Theater* by Calderón, a spectacular religious melodrama in which 700 local residents take part. The Abbey Church forms a splendid baroque backcloth.

The ski resorts in this area are Engelberg (3,500 ft.), but with lifts rising to 9,900 ft.; Stoos (4,200 ft.), with lifts to 6,300 ft., and Andermatt, all old-established and popular.

PRACTICAL INFORMATION FOR CENTRAL SWITZERLAND

ALTDORF. *Goldener Schlüssel* (I), tel. 21002. Historic building in the heart of this historic town. *Bahnhof* (I), tel. 21032. Central and very inexpensive. No shower.
Restaurant. *Höfli* (I), tel. 22197. Closed Wednesday.

ANDERMATT. *Bergidyll* (I), tel. 67455. Quiet and ideal for children, central. *Krone* (I), tel. 67206. Sauna and gymnasium; central. *Monopol-Metropol* (I), tel. 67575. Indoor pool and facilities for the handicapped. *Schlüssel* (I), tel. 67198. Small and central.
Restaurant. *Drei Könige* (M), tel. 67203. Lantern-lit grill room. Cheese, Chinese and Bourguignonne fondues.

BRUNNEN. *Seehotel Waldstätterhof* (E), tel. 331133. Lakeside location with tennis, good restaurant and extensive grounds; facilities for children. *Bellevue au Lac Kursaal* (M), tel. 311318. On lakeside; quiet and comfortable. *Parkhotel Hellerbad* (M), tel. 311681. Cure facilities, tennis and gardens; central but quiet. *Elite & Aurora* (I), tel. 311024. Splendid views. *Weisses Rössli* (I), tel. 311022. Good family hotel in historic building; central.
Restaurant. *Weisses Rössli* (I), in hotel of same name (see above). Indonesian specialties.

BÜRGENSTOCK. *Grand Hotel* (L), tel. 641212. Golf, tennis, pool, skittle alley; on the expensive side. *Park Hotel* (E), tel. 641331. Many facilities; in own grounds. *Waldheim* (I), tel. 641306. In own grounds with pool and great view. Reader-recommended.

ENGELBERG. *Ring-Hotel* (E), tel. 941822. Good family hotel in own grounds. *Bellevue Terminus* (M), tel. 941213. Quiet, in own grounds with indoor tennis court. *Alpenklub* (I), tel. 941243. Central and rather superior inexpensive hotel; breakfast only. *Crystal* (I), tel. 942122. Central and quiet family hotel. *Maro* (I), tel. 941076. Very quiet; own garden.
Restaurant. *Hess* (M), tel. 941366. Recommended.

LUCERNE. *Carlton-Hotel Tivoli* (L), tel. 513051. Looks out over the water; considerable comfort offered by this splendid hotel. *Palace* (L), tel. 502222. Spacious hotel that faces lake across a tree-lined promenade; famous and luxurious. *Schweizerhof* (L), tel. 502211. Traditional elegance in this old hotel. *Europe Grand Hotel* (E), tel. 301111. View over the lake; comfortable. *Montana* (E), tel. 516565. Situated on hillside with magnificent views and private cable car. Editor-recommended.
Astoria (M), tel. 244466. Panoramic rooftop terrace and bar; facilities for the handicapped; recommended. *Des Alpes* (I), tel. 515825. Close to the river and with excellent restaurant. *Park* (I), tel. 239232. Central but quiet; close to the station. *Schiff* (I), tel. 513851. Very superior hotel for this category; attractive building.
Restaurants. *Arbalète French Restaurant* (E), in Hotel Monopol and Metropole, Pilatusstr. 1 (tel. 230866). Very good. *Von-Pfyffer-Stube* (E), in Grand Hotel National, Haldenstr. 4 (tel. 501111). Excellent. *Li Tai Pe* (E), Furrengasse 14 (tel. 511023). Also very good. *Old Swiss House* (E), Lowenplatz 4 (tel. 516171). Excellent grading. *Zum Raben* (M), Kornmarkt 5 (tel. 515135). Recommended. *Hubertus* (M), Hertensteinstr. 32 (tel. 222550). Very good. *Wilden Mann* (M), Bahnhofstr. 30 (tel. 231666).

PILATUS. *Bellevue* (I), tel. 961255. Near the summit of the mountain at nearly 7,000 ft.; modern, circular and very quiet. *Pilatus-Kulm* (I), tel. 961255. Even less expensive, but much older, a little lower down. No shower.

RIGI. At Rigi-Kaltbad: *Hostellerie Rigi* (E), tel. 831616. Indoor pool and sauna. *Bellevue* (M), tel. 831351. Less swanky but the same fantastic view.

WEGGIS. (All inclusive). *Albana* (E), tel. 932141. Ideal family hotel. *Beau-Rivage* (E), tel. 931422. Pool among the many facilities. Reader-recommended. *Central am See* (E), tel. 931252. Some (M) rooms. Swimming pool and quiet location. Recommended. *Rigi am See* (E), tel. 932151. Comfortable hotel by lake. Some (M) rooms. *Waldstätten* (E), tel. 931341. Golf; ideal for children. *Mirabell* (I), tel. 931131.

ZUG. *City Hotel Ochsen* (E), tel. 213232. In the heart of town in an historic building. Highly recommended. *Rosenberg* (M), tel. 214343. Quiet; in own grounds with good view. *Löwen au Lac* (I), tel. 217722.

Restaurants. *Aklin* (I–E), Am Zytturm (tel. 211866). Excellent. *Hirschen* (I–M), tel. 212930. *Rosenberg* (I–M), tel. 217171. Very good.

Basle and the Swiss Rhineland

Basle, astride the Rhine, sheltered by the Vosges and the German Black Forest to the north, and the Swiss Jura in the south and west, is the northern gateway of Switzerland. With about 191,000 people, it is Switzerland's second largest city, and an important commercial center. One of Europe's greatest inland ports, it is a lively city rich in interest and culture; one in which elements of quaint medievalism and bustling modernity are commingled. Baslers love fun—their carnival is one of the most uproarious in Europe and they are, perhaps, the friendliest people in Switzerland.

The best way to capture the atmosphere of Basle is to sit at a terrace café beside the Rhine, or stroll along Rheinweg, a pleasant riverside esplanade backed by old houses squeezed one against the other. Overlooking the river is the cathedral (Münster) which has all the considerable charm of Rhenish architecture. And beside it is the exquisite Münsterplatz, justly renowned for the perfection of its proportions. Inside are the tombs of Queen Anne (wife of Rudolf of Habsburg) and Erasmus of Rotterdam, one of many brilliant scholars whose names have lent luster to Basle's great university through the centuries. Don't miss the marvelous panorama of the city on both sides of the Rhine from the Wettstein Bridge.

A few paces from Barfüsserplatz is the Freie Strasse, Basle's biggest shopping street, leading to the attractive market place and its colorful 16th-century town hall. From the nearby fishmarket, with its Gothic fountain, by climbing up narrow medieval streets, you will come to St. Peter's Place and the New University, hallowed by memories of Erasmus, Burckhardt (historian of the Renaissance), and other great scholars who came here.

There are pleasant daily riverboat excursions in summer, leaving from the embankment behind the Three Kings Hotel. The river is navigable as far as Rheinfelden, about two hours upstream.

Basle is the gateway to the Swiss Rhineland, a beautiful region stretching to Lake Constance and beyond; one in which the river meanders past rich agricultural land, orchards, a sprinkling of castles, medieval towns with the stepped gables typical of the Rhineland, and several resorts and spas. For good measure, near Schaffhausen the river tumbles over the famous Rhine Falls.

PRACTICAL INFORMATION FOR BASLE AND THE SWISS RHINELAND

BADEN. *Staadhof* (L), tel. 225251. Indoor pool and cure facilities in this luxury hotel. *Verenahof* (L), tel. 225251. In own grounds with indoor pool and cure facilities. *Hirschen* (I), tel. 226966. Gymnasium and cure facilities. No shower.

Restaurants. *Bodega Grill Room* (M), tel. 226217. Rôtisserie, grill, bar, garden. Recommended: tartare steak, scampi. *Kursaal Casino* (M), tel. 227188.

BASLE. *Basle Hilton* (L), Aeschengraben 31 (tel. 226622). Near the main station; indoor pool. *Drei Könige am Rhein* (L), Blumenrain 8 (tel. 255252). Its Rhine terrace is as famous as its cuisine. *Euler* (L), Centralbahnplatz 14 (tel. 234500). Elegant; with the best food in town. *Basle* (E), Münzgasse 12 (tel. 252423). Central but quiet.

Bristol (M), Centralbahnstr. 15 (tel. 223822). Some (I) rooms. *City-Hotel* (M), Henric-Petristr. 12 (tel. 237811). Airconditioning throughout. Recommended; good restaurants. *Drachen* (M), Aeschenvorstadt 24 (tel. 239090). Centrally located with facilities for children. Quiet. *Gotthard-Terminus* (M), Centralbahnstr. 13 (tel. 225250). Simple; central. Some (I) rooms available. *Steinenschanze* (I), Steinengraben (tel. 235353). *Vogt-Flügelrad* (I), Küchengasse 20 (tel. 234241). Good family hotel; quiet.

Restaurants. *Bruderholz* (E), Bruderholzallee 42 (tel. 358222). French, Swiss, Indonesian specialties. Closed Sunday, Monday. *Schützenhaus* (E), Schützenmatt 56 (tel. 236760). Strongly recommended.

Chez Pepino (M), Hammerstr. 87 (Kleinbasel), tel. 339415. Homemade pasta. *Escargot* (M), tel. 225333. At main rail station. *Holbeinstube* (M), Dufourstr. 42 (tel. 223600). *Pagode* (M), Steinenvorstadt 32 (tel. 238077). 140 Chinese specialties. *Pfauen* (M), St. Johanns-Vorstadt 13 (tel. 253267). For fresh and salt water fish. *Safran Zunft* (M), Gerbergasse 11 (tel. 251959). Fondue "Bacchus" with all the trimmings (14 of them!), trout. *St. Alban-Eck* (M), St. Alban-Vorstadt 60 (tel. 230320). Excellent.

OLTEN. *Europe* (I), tel. 323555. *Schweizerhof* (I), tel. 264646. Central.

Restaurants. *Zollhaus* (E), tel. 263628. Closed after 9.30 Sunday evenings. Rated "very good". *Felsenburg* (M), tel. 262277. Also rated "very good". Closed Tuesday.

RHEINFELDEN. *Schwanen Solbad* (E), tel. 875344. Sauna, gymnasium, cure facilities. *Goldener Adler* (I), tel. 875332. Central, in historic building. No shower. *Schiff am Rhein* (I), tel. 876087. Quiet rooms; bowling.

SCHAFFHAUSEN. *Kronenhof* (M), tel. 56631. *Bahnhof* (I), tel. 54001. Quiet hotel with facilities for the disabled. Excellent value. *Parkvilla* (I), tel. 52737. Sailing and tennis; peaceful location.

Restaurants. *Fischerzunft* (E), tel. 53281. Specializes in fish from the Rhine. "Excellent" rating. *Gerberstube* (M), tel. 52155. Homemade pasta; scampi. *Theater* (E), tel. 50558. *Ticino* (E), tel. 51907. Rated "very good". *Friede* (M), tel. 54715. Dates back to 1445. Closed Wednesday.

Museums

BASLE. Antiken-Museum, St. Albangraben 5. Opened in 1966, it is the only one of its kind in Switzerland, with Greek art 2,500 to 100 BC, Italian art 1,000 BC to AD 300.

Basler Papiermühle, St. Alban-Tal 35. 9–5; closed Mon. Located in 15th-century papermill. Includes water-driven stamping mill plus many exhibits on paper-making, typography and book binding through the ages.

Ethnological Museum, Augustinerstrasse 2. Large and remarkable museum with some 100,000 exhibits from all corners of the globe; those from New Guinea and the South Seas are the pride and joy of the collection.

Kirschgarten, Elisabethenstrasse 27. Museum of 18th-century Basle life contained in an old house. Furniture, costume, clocks, porcelain, silver, toys, etc.

Kunstmuseum, St. Albangraben. Weekdays 10–5 (May-Oct. closed 12–2). Entrance fee, but Wed. pm and Sat. and Sun. free. Splendidly interesting enjoyable museum, with an impressive collection of works beautifully displayed, from 13th-century triptychs to modern paintings.

Jewish Museum of Switzerland, Kornhausgasse 18. An appropriate collection; this is the city where Herzl organized the first Zionist congress in 1897.

Museum of Contemporary Art, St. Alban-Tal 2. Considerable collection of modern works by Ernst, Giacometti and Sutherland, among others.

Berne

Berne, the seat of government of the Swiss Confederation, ascribes an exact date to its foundation—1191. It also possesses a legend of how it came about, and how the city got its name. According to one version, Berthold V, Duke of Zähringen, had decided to build a city on the bend of the River Aare where Berne stands today. He was hunting in the forest, which at that time stretched on both sides of the river, and told his followers that the new city would be named after the first animal he killed. It happened to be a bear. Coincidence it may be, but the name of Berne differs only slightly from the German word for bear, and to this day a bear is the principal feature on the city's coat of arms. (Don't miss the famous bears themselves in their pit at the far end of the Nydegg Bridge.)

It is not difficult to cover the principal attractions of Berne in a comparatively short time, since the geography of the city has compressed its sights into a restricted area, albeit a hilly one. The old town is perched on a high rock that juts into a loop of the River Aare. Most of what the visitor wants is contained within this loop, and the few places outside it lie just on the far side of the bridges.

As you stroll through the streets of the capital, three architectural features will almost certainly impress you—arcades, fountains and towers. The arcades, which roof the sidewalks of so many of Berne's streets, are one of the city's chief characteristics. These *Lauben,* as they are called, are a welcome asset in the main shopping streets. With their low, vaulted roofs, they extend to the edge of the pavement, where they are supported on sturdy 15th-century pillars.

The brilliantly colored and skilfully carved fountains, their bases surrounded by flowers, are for the most part the work of Hans Gieng, and were set up between 1539 and 1546. Witty and joyful, they provide light relief from the often severe structure of the medieval houses that form their background. The Fountain of Justice might seem less than original with its figure of the blindfolded goddess, with her sword and scales, perched on a high column, until you glance at the severed heads that lie at the base—not only those of the emperor, the sultan and the Pope, but even, striking nearer home, of the mayor of Berne! The Ogre Fountain bears a giant enjoying a meal of small children. Then there are the Bagpiper, the Messenger, Moses, the Zähringer Fountain (with its harnessed bear and its cubs feasting on a bunch of grapes), Samson (overcoming a lion), and many others, some of them sculptured references to historical events.

Of the towers, the most famous is the Zytgloggeturm, as it is called in the local dialect. Originally built as a city gate in 1191, though much rebuilt and restored since, the Zytgloggeturm has been providing hourly entertainment since 1530 when the astronomical clock and various mechanically operated puppet figures in a pulpit-like structure beside it were installed on its eastern side. Here the hour is not merely struck (by a knight in golden armor at the top of the tower), it is performed— and performed by a large and varied cast of characters.

Berne is an excellent center from which to tour. You can reach the Lake of Thun by train in 20 minutes and the Bernese Oberland in an hour. A host of other resorts are within easy reach.

PRACTICAL INFORMATION FOR BERNE

Hotels

Deluxe

Bellevue Palace, Kochergasse 3–5 (tel. 224581). High above the River Aare with a superb view of the Alps; very much a hotel in the grand tradition; excellent restaurant. Has some rooms in (E) price range.

Schweizerhof, Schweizerhoflaube 11 (tel. 224501). Another fine hotel; splendid decor and memorable cuisine; opposite the station. Some cheaper rooms.

Moderate

Alfa, Laupenstr. 15 (tel. 253866). A quiet hotel a few minutes from the station.

Bären, Schauplatzgasse 4 (tel. 223367). Large and plush with good, if expensive, restaurant.

Bristol, Schauplatzgasse 10 (tel. 220101). Breakfast only; comfortable and central. Sauna.

City-Mövenpick, Bubenbergplatz 7 (tel. 225377). Central but with very quiet rooms; facilities for the handicapped.

Metropole, Zeughausgasse 26–28 (tel. 225021). Comfortable modern hotel in the center of town.

Savoy, Neuengasse 26 (tel. 224405). Breakfast only; central and with facilities for the handicapped.

Wächter-Mövenpick, Genfergasse 4 (tel. 220866). Central and quiet family hotel near the station.

Inexpensive

Bahnhof-Süd, Bümplizstr. 189 (tel. 565111). Quiet; with bowling. Very inexpensive.

Continental, Zeuhausgasse 27 (tel. 222626). Near the Kornhausplatz.

Goldener Adler, Gerechtigkeitsgasse 7 (tel. 221725). In historic building with facilities for children and the disabled.

Hospiz z. Heimat, Gerechtigkeitsgasse 50 (tel. 220436). Atmospheric and central.

Krebs, Genfergasse 8 (tel. 224942). Breakfast only; quiet rooms.

Nydegg, Gerechtigkeitsgasse 1 (tel. 228686). In the old town; simple and very inexpensively priced.

Regina-Arabelle, Mittelstr. 6 (tel. 230305). In own grounds and quiet.

Zum Goldenen Schlüssel, Rathausgasse 72 (tel. 220216). Historic building in the heart of the old town.

 RESTAURANTS. The standard of Berne's cooking is high and there are a great many restaurants in all price categories. The city has a reputation for giving better than average value for money.

Expensive

Bären, Schauplatzgasse 4 (tel. 223367). First-class.

Bellevue Palace, Kochergasse (tel. 224581). Also Grill (E) and City Restaurant (I–M) in same establishment.

Commerce, Gerechtigkeitsgasse 74 (tel. 221161). Spanish cuisine—paella, scampi, zarzuela. A Berne institution.

Della Casa, Schauplatzgasse 16 (tel. 222142). Quietly elegant.

Du Théâtre, Theaterplatz 7 (tel. 227177). Excellent food, formal atmosphere.

Ermitage, Amthausgasse 10 (tel. 223541). Tabatière, Bonbonnière, Carnotzet. Bar. Recommended.

Mistral, Kramgasse 42 (tel. 228277). Closed Sunday.

Räblus, Zeughausgasse 3 (tel. 225908). Very distinguished.

Schultheissenstube, in Schweizerhof hotel (see above). Outstanding; very expensive.

Zum Rathaus, Rathausplatz 5 (tel. 226183). Very fine, expensive though.

Moderate

Hong Kong, Hodlerstr. 16 (tel. 222649). Chinese specialties. Recommended.
Kornhauskeller, Kornhausplatz 18 (tel. 221133). Cellar restaurant specializing in good, no-nonsense Swiss food. Closed Monday.
Le Mazot, Bärenplatz 5 (tel. 227088). Swiss specialties.
Pinocchio, Aarbergergasse 6 (tel. 223362). Italian specialties.
Taverne Valaisanne, Neuengasse 40 (tel. 227766). Fondue, raclette, wafer-thin mountain-dried beef.

Inexpensive

EPA, Marktgasse 24. Department store restaurant. No alcohol, but excellent value.
Gfeller Rindlisbacher, Bärenplatz 21 (tel. 226944). All kinds of quiches and fruit tarts. Cheapest coffee in town but no alcohol.
Loeb, Spitalgasse 47–57. 2nd floor of store; good value. No alcohol.
Migrolino, in Marktgasse over Migros chainstore. No alcohol.
Mövenpick, branches at Aarbergergasse 30 (tel. 226414); Bubenbergplatz 5a (tel. 224713); Neuengasse 44 (tel. 220866); and Waisenhausplatz 28 (tel. 224563). All have more expensive menus as well.
Vegetaris, Neuengasse 15. A first-floor restaurant where, surprisingly, you can eat outside in a quiet, first-floor garden. Sumptuous breakfasts are served Saturdays. Succulent salads and imaginative vegetarian food. No alcohol.

 ENTERTAINMENT. Unless you understand German, the theater in Berne will be pretty well lost on you, except for the *Municipal Theater* which stages opera, operetta, ballet and plays. Berne is noted for its "cellar theaters," frequently fascinating, often outstanding. Some are inclined to be ephemeral, but there are usually at least half a dozen. Nightspots in Berne are far from spectacular, but they allow you to while away an evening and get in some dancing. *Mocambo* has two good floorshows and is the most elegant spot in town. *Chikito* also has its *Frisco-Bar* and caters to a very young crowd. You can dance at the *Kursaal* (and, if you wish, fritter away your money at boule). Dance bars include the vast *Babalu* and (mainly for young people) *Happy Light.* *Restaurant zum Schwert,* Rathausgasse 66, is a popular local drinking place.

 MUSEUMS. Art Museum (Kunstmuseum), Hodlerstrasse 12. Only a small part of the collection is presently exhibited because of reconstruction of the Museum. This includes works by Cézanne, Hodler, Braque, Picasso, Klee and other artists of the 19th and 20th centuries.
Historical Museum, Helvetiaplatz 5. Entrance free. One of Switzerland's most important historical museums with internationally renowned collections on Bernese history and prehistoric times, applied art, ethnology and coin and medal engraving. A major attraction is the fine collection of 15th-century tapestries from the heyday of Burgundian-Dutch culture.
Käfigturm Museum (Prison Tower). Information and exhibition center devoted to the economic and cultural life of Berne. Permanent sound/slide show illustrating the Canton's history, tourism and other cultural and economic aspects.
Municipal Art Gallery (Kunsthalle), Helvetiaplatz 1. Temporary exhibitions of national and international art.
Natural History Museum, Bernastrasse 15. One of Europe's major natural history museums. 220 dioramas showing Swiss and foreign mammals and birds. Extensive collection of minerals, crystals and precious stones from the Swiss Alps. Most popular exhibit is the perfectly preserved St. Bernard rescue dog, Barry.
PTT Museum, Helvetiaplatz 4. Entrance free. Houses one of the most extensive collections of rare stamps open to the public in the world.
Swiss Alpine Museum, Helvetiaplatz 4 (see PTT Museum above; same address). Scenery and cultural life in the Swiss Alps, history of mountaineering, collection of reliefs, cartography.

The Bernese Oberland

The Bernese Oberland is a magnificent area of 1,800 square miles comprising nine valleys, the lovely lakes of Thun and Brienz and a number of little lakes in the heart of the mountains. Its wild mountain scenery acted as a magnet for tourists in the 19th century after its sublime grandeur was first "discovered" by that arch propagator of the Romantic sensibility, Jean-Jacques Rousseau.

The gateway to the Bernese Oberland is Interlaken. For generations, it had one purpose only, to attract summer visitors. In winter most of its great hotels, tearooms and bars closed down. But today, more and more are open all year as winter sports enthusiasts begin to realize just how many superb facilities are readily accessible.

Interlaken, as its name implies, is situated "between the lakes"— those of Thun and Brienz. It is also surrounded by a superb mountain panorama. The west and east sections of the town are connected by the Höheweg, the central boulevard lined with trees, formal gardens, hotels and shops. A quaint touch is given by the horse drawn carriages as they clip-clop alongside modern coaches, but it's a nostalgic touch, too, as they are among the few remaining relics of 19th-century and Edwardian Interlaken. The older hotels have been pulled down or modernized, and new ones have arisen such as the skyscraper Hotel Métropole with its breathtaking views from the upper floors.

During the summer, Interlaken has a tradition of openair performances (but the audience sits in a fine covered grandstand) of Schiller's *William Tell,* a drama with many actors which perpetuates the story of the legendary hero and the historic overthrow of the house of Habsburg. The resort also has an outstandingly fine 18-hole golf course, but golfers claim that they are put off by the magnificent scenery!

Of Interlaken's many splendid excursions, the most spectacular, given the right weather, is the famous trip to Jungfraujoch (11,333 ft.). From Interlaken east station you go by rail to Lauterbrunnen where, in the green cogwheel train of the Wengenernalp Railway, the steep climb really begins. The train twists and turns through tunnels and over viaducts, giving a succession of camera-clicking views of mountains, valleys and waterfalls. At Kleine Scheidegg (6,760 ft.) you change to the smart little brown and cream train of the Jungfrau railway which in six miles climbs more than 4,500 feet to the summit station. The line took 16 years to build, was opened as long ago as 1912, and is still one of the world's railway marvels.

Beyond Kleine Scheidegg there are wonderful views of Mönch (13,-450 ft.) as well as of the treacherous North Wall of the Eiger. You do go up it, but in safety and comfort and on the inside! Just beyond Eigergletscher station (7,610 ft.) the train plunges into the 4½ mile long tunnel through the Eiger and Mönch mountains up to Jungfraujoch station. On the way it stops twice: at Eigerwand station (9,400 ft.) just inside the North Wall and at Eismeer (10,370 ft.). At each, enormous windows have been cut in the mountainside, and the train waits long enough for you to get out and peer at the fabulous views.

From the underground Jungfraujoch summit station a free elevator will take you to the 11,720 ft. high Sphinx terrace to gaze at an Alpine panorama that is one of Europe's wonders, and to look down to the 10-mile-long Aletsch glacier. You can visit the ice palace, glacier exhibition, souvenir shop or post office, have a sleigh ride or skiing lesson, or eat a meal in the new mountainside restaurant.

On the homeward journey you can descend by the alternative Grindelwald route giving superb views of the North Wall towering above. Back at Interlaken you can reflect that you've been on the highest railway in Europe to the world's highest underground station; stood on Europe's highest mountain observation terrace; looked down on the greatest glacier in the Alps; been, in short, on what is almost certainly Europe's finest and most spectacular excursion—and traveled on the world's most expensive railway. But, like some 400,000 people every year, it's a fair bet that you'll think it worth every franc.

PRACTICAL INFORMATION FOR THE BERNESE OBERLAND

ADELBODEN. (All inclusive). *Beau-Site* (E), tel. 732222. Quiet. Fitness center. Facilities for the disabled. *Parkhotel Bellevue* (E), tel. 731621. Quiet with indoor pool and sauna and facilities for children. *Alpenrose* (M), tel. 731161. Comfortable. *Kreuz* (M), tel. 732121.

   Restaurant. *Die Alte Taverne,* tel. 732131. Six Bernese farmsteads united in one restaurant.

BEATENBERG. *Jungfraublick* (I), tel. 411581. Centrally located small hotel with magnificent view. *Kurhaus Silberhorn* (I), tel. 411212. In own grounds; sauna.

BRIENZ. *Bären* (I), tel. 512412. Quiet hotel by lake. *De La Gare* (I), tel. 512712. Small, very inexpensive hotel.

GRINDELWALD. *Grand Hotel Regina* (L), tel. 545455. Indoor and outdoor pools, tennis and sauna; dancing in the evenings. *Parkhotel Schoenegg* (E), tel. 531853. Indoor pool, gymnasium and sauna; quiet hotel in own grounds. *Silberhorn* (E), tel. 532822. Quiet with facilities for children; kosher food. *Alpina* (M), tel. 533333. Comfortable and quiet. *Schweizerheim* (I), tel. 531058. Simple and small but very reasonably priced.

GSTAAD. *Bellevue Grand Hotel* (L), tel. 83171. 2 restaurants; facilities for children and quiet location. *Olden* (L), tel. 43444. Central; dancing in the evenings. *Palace* (L), tel. 83131. Expensive; cure facilities. *Alphorn* (E), tel. 44545. Quiet hotel with indoor pool and ideal for children. *Posthotel Rössli* (E), tel. 43412. Atmospheric and attractive.

INTERLAKEN. *Metropole* (L), tel. 212151. 18-story building with superb views from the top. Also (E) rooms. *Victoria-Jungfrau Grand Hotel* (L), tel. 212171. Indoor pool, tennis. *Bellevue-Garden-Hotel* (E), tel. 224431. Quiet and comfortable. *Du Lac* (E), tel. 222922. Near Lake Brienz boat landing stage; recommended. *Stella* (E), tel. 228871. Exceptionally pleasant and highly recommended; indoor pool. *Oberland* (M), tel. 229431. Recommended. *Park-Hotel Mattenhof* (M), tel. 216121. Tennis, pool, facilities for children. *Alpina* (I), tel. 228031. Simple but inexpensive. *Gasthof Hirschen* (I), tel. 221545. In historic and attractive building. (No shower at last two.)

   Restaurants. *La Terrasse* (E), at Victoria-Jungfrau Grand Hotel (see above). Very good food. *Schuh* is the best place in Interlaken for morning coffee and afternoon tea.

KANDERSTEG. (All inclusive). *Royal-Bellevue* (L), tel. 751212. Riding, tennis, water skiing, 2 pools; very quiet. *Victoria & Ritter* (E), tel. 751444. Indoor pool and tennis; ideal for children. *Alpenrose* (I), tel. 751170. Quiet and comfortable.

LENK. *Crystal* (E), tel. 32206. Small and caring. *Kreuz* (E), tel. 31387. Indoor pool and sauna and facilities for the handicapped. *Parkhotel Bellevue* (E), tel. 31761. Pool and own grounds. *Sternen* (I), tel. 31509. Centrally located.

MÜRREN. *Eiger* (E), tel. 551331. Indoor pool, gymnasium and sauna. *Murren* (E), tel. 552424. Center of winter social life. *Alpina* (M), tel. 551361. Tennis and marvelous views. Some (I) rooms. *Edelweiss* (M), tel. 552612.

SAANENMÖSER. (All inclusive). *Golf & Sport Hotel* (L), tel. 43222. Curling, tennis, skating and golf. *Hornberg* (L), tel. 44440. Indoor pool and sauna in this quiet and comfortable hotel.

SPIEZ. *Belvédère* (E), tel. 543333. Quiet hotel with marvelous views. *Edenhotel* (M), tel. 541154. Pool and tennis. *Bellevue* (I), tel. 542314. Good views; quiet.

THUN. *Freienhof* (M), tel. 215511. Much modernized 14th-century building in old town; quiet. *Krone* (M), tel. 228282. Historic building with indoor pool and facilities for children. Both have (I) rooms. *Beau Rivage* (I), tel. 222236. Indoor pool.
Restaurants. *Casa Barba* (M), tel. 222227. Spanish specialties. *Steinbock* (M), tel. 224051. Also very good.

WENGEN. (All inclusive). *Park* (L), tel. 565161. Indoor pool and sauna. *Regina* (L), tel. 551512. Splendid family hotel. (E) rooms available. *Alpenrose* (E), tel. 553216. Unequalled views. *Belvédère* (E), tel. 552412. Good family hotel. *Eiger* (E), tel. 551131. Central with good restaurant.

ZWEISIMMEN. *Krone* (I), tel. 22626. Ideal family hotel. *Rawyl-Sternen* (I), tel. 21251. With skittle alley. *Sport-Motel* (I), tel. 21431. Quiet location; golf.

The Swiss Jura, Canton Fribourg and Gruyère

This whole area is one of the most unusual in Switzerland. For one thing, it embraces both mountains and lowlands, as well as having more than its fair share of lakes. For another, it has the distinction of being Switzerland's only bilingual region. Roughly speaking, west here *est ouest* and east *ist ost*, that is, the French-speaking half is to the west and the German-speaking area is to the east. But it is not unusual to hear towns referred to both by their German and French names, thus Biel for Bienne, Murten for Morat, Neuenburg for Neuchâtel, Solothurn for Soleure; or vice versa of course.

The Jura runs northeast from Lake Geneva with Lake Neuchâtel and Lake Biel, lying in the same direction, in its center. To the southwest are the rich pasture lands of the Swiss plateau and to the northwest the Jura mountains, a considerable range in length though puny in height by Alpine standards.

The region's two principal cities are Fribourg and Neuchâtel. Fribourg sits just a little to the north of the foothills of the Bernese Alps. The city has an air of happy satisfaction, as well it might having been both a prosperous city and an important Catholic center for many centuries. Like many of Switzerland's historic cities, its considerable medieval charm mingles discreetly with an up-to-date and modern approach. Apart from the ancient and beautifully preserved patrician houses, the fountains dotted around the winding streets and the splendid 16th-century town hall, the city's principal treasures are the 13th-century Cathedral of St. Nicholas and the Church of the Augustines which has a magnificent 17th-century altar by Peter Spring, the sculptor-monk.

Neuchâtel is similarly prosperous, but has an air of greater reserve, an almost tangible dignity. It sits on the northwestern corner of its lake of the same name with a fabulous view to the southeast of the whole crowded range of the middle Alps—all the way from the majestic mass of Mont Blanc to the Bernese Oberland—stretching away in the far distance. Its inhabitants boast that they speak the "best French in Switzerland," one reason for the city's preeminence as a center of learning. But it is also the watchmaking capital of Switzerland—another way of saying of the world. Among its highlights are the Collegiate Church, a handsome Romanesque and Gothic structure dating from the 12th century, and many elegant town houses, almost a common-place in this prosperous and harmonious town. But almost anywhere in the Old Town you'll find picturesque buildings. And when you've had your fill of sightseeing, relax in the shade of the trees lining the quays with that incredible Alpine panorama stretched before you.

Behind Neuchâtel are the Jura mountains themselves, reaching from Geneva in the southwest to Basel in the northeast. This is a region of pine forests, lush pastureland, and deeply cleft, craggy valleys. Despite its relative lack of height—no peak is over 5,000 ft.—some parts of the Jura can be bitterly cold in winter. La Brévine, a windswept hamlet on the French border, is sometimes called the Swiss Siberia. Temperatures here often drop as low as 15°F below.

The Jura's highlights include the watchmaking town of La Chaux-de-Fonds, where there is an interesting underground museum with over 3,000 timepieces, and Mount Soleil which, at 4,200 ft. is not quite the highest mountain in the range but is nonetheless the Jura's most popular skiing resort. Saignelégier, to the north of Mount Soleil, is Switzerland's leading horse-breeding region and every August holds a fascinating horse show and market with races that attract large crowds. It is set in typical Jura scenery: rolling hills, long valleys and ridges dotted with pine-capped hummocks.

PRACTICAL INFORMATION FOR THE JURA, CANTON FRIBOURG AND GRUYERES

BULLE. *Des Alpes & Terminus* (I), tel. 29292. Central and quiet. Facilities for the disabled.

Restaurants. *Café de la Gare* (M), tel. 27688. Try the *fondue au Vacherin. De l'Hôtel de Ville* (M), tel. 27888.

CHATEL-ST.-DENIS/LES-PACCOTS. *Corbetta* (I), tel. 567120. Quiet and attractive. No shower. *Ermitage* (I), tel. 567541. Indoor pool and bowling.

Restaurant. *Tivoli* (M), tel. 567039. *Fondue fribourgeoise.*

LA-CHAUX-DE-FONDS. *Fleur-de-Lys* (M), tel. 233731. Quiet; some (I) rooms available. *Moreau* (M), tel. 232222. Good family hotel with facilities for the handicapped.

Restaurants. *Aérogare* (M), tel. 268266. *La Provençale* (M), at Hotel de la Poste (tel. 222203). Very good.

ESTAVAYER-LE-LAC. *Du Château* (I), tel. 631049. Very small but attractive. No shower. *Du Port* (I), tel. 631032. Central.

Restaurants. *Du Lac* (E), tel. 631343. Excellent. *Hostellerie des Chevaliers* (E), tel. 61933. First class. *Hostellerie St. Georges* (M), tel. 62246. For *quiche gruyèrienne.* Also very good.

FRIBOURG. *Duc Bertold* (M), rue des Bouchers 112 (tel. 811121). One of the town's best, in historic building. Excellent food. Some (I) rooms. *Eurotel* (M), Grand' Place 14 (tel. 813131). Centrally located with golf and indoor pool. Good restaurant. *Alpha* (I), rue de Simplon 13 (tel. 227272). Gymnasium and quiet rooms. *De la Rose* (I), pl. Notre-Dame (tel. 224607). Charming rooms. *Touring* (I), rue de Lausanne 25 (tel. 223219). Modest and central. The restaurant serves good food.

Restaurants. Apart from those in all the hotels listed above, which are good, there are: *Restaurant Français* (upstairs at the main railway station), tel. 222816. Reserve in advance; excellent. *L'Aigle Noir* (E), rue des Alpes 58 (tel. 224977). Recommended. *Café du Midi* (M), rue de Romont 25 (tel. 223133). Highly recommended for all cheese specialties, dried meat dishes and other regional specialties. *Frascati* (M), rue de Romont 3 (tel. 228256). Italian specialties; excellent pizzas.

GRUYÈRES. *Hostellerie des Chevaliers* (M), tel. 61933. Quiet. *Hostellerie St. Georges* (M), tel. 62246. Both have (I) rooms. *Hôtel de Ville* (I), tel. 62424. Historic building in the heart of town.

MORAT. *Bonne Auberge au Bains* (M), tel. 712262. At Muntelier. Recommended; has (I) rooms. *Schiff* (M), tel. 712701. Quiet and comfortable; (I) rooms. *Krone* (I), tel. 715252. Central, but with quiet rooms. *Weisses Kreuz* (I), tel. 712641. Bowling and facilities for the handicapped.

NEUCHÂTEL. *Beaulac* (M), tel. 258822. Splendidly situated by the lake; quiet but central. *Eurotel* (M), tel. 212121. Modern and a little antiseptic; indoor pool and sauna. *City* (I), tel. 255412. In the lower town. *Touring* (I), tel. 255501. Quiet.
Restaurants. *Buffet de la Gare* (M), main station (tel. 254853). Excellent station restaurant. *La Prairie* (M), Grand rue 8 (tel. 255757). Open from 11 A.M. to 1 A.M.; central. *Palais du Peyrou* (M), av. du Peyrou (tel. 251183). Regional specialties. *Au Vieux Vapeur* (M), Port Centre Ville (tel. 243400). Floating restaurant with bar and dancing; very romantic.

ST. URSANNE. *Deux Clefs* (I), tel. 553110. Old and atmospheric, overlooks River Doubs; excellent restaurant.

Geneva

Geneva is handsomely situated at the western end of Lake Geneva (in French, Lac Léman), where the River Rhône leaves the lake en route to France and the Mediterranean. The river and lower basin of the lake divide the city into northern and southern sectors, joined by bridges. There are delightful promenades, and lovely views across the water towards the famous fountain—symbol of the city—and Mont Blanc beyond it. An ancient city, Geneva was controlled from 58 B.C. to 443 A.D. by the Romans, who had their citadel on the crest of the hill where the Cathedral of St. Peter now dominates the old town. Irrevocably associated with the famous 16th-century French Huguenot reformer, John Calvin, Geneva became a rather staid and melancholy city, thanks to the Protestant sumptuary laws. Understandably, many citizens fled from its drab life, but far more English, French and Italian refugees came in, bringing with them new crafts, trades, and a keen sense of business, a heritage which remains in evidence even today. Today, Geneva has an atmosphere of cosmopolitan sophistication. Although the International Red Cross was founded in the city in 1864, it was the establishment of the ill-fated League of Nations here after the First World War which put Geneva firmly on the map as an international center of major importance. Today, with about 155,400 inhabitants, it is the third-largest city in Switzerland.

You can see many of the attractions of Geneva in a single walk by starting from the rail station down the rue du Mont-Blanc. At the lakeside, turn right along the Quai des Bergues flanking the Rhône, crossing the river on the Pont de l'Isle to the Place Bel-Air from which you follow the rue de la Corraterie to the place Neuve with its Grand Théâtre, and the Conservatory of Music. From here, you enter the park, which contains the university and Geneva's gigantic international memorial to the Reformation.

Leaving the park, turn left up the rue St. Léger into the charming old place Bourg-de-Four, and then take any of the narrow streets that lead up to St. Peter's Cathedral where you may be stirred or unmoved by the sight of the pulpit from which Calvin preached. Or rather you won't, as the interior of the cathedral has been completely gutted as part of a major restoration project which is liable to last some years. However, you can still go up the North Tower from where there is a sweeping view of Geneva and the lake—and of course the brooding masses of the Alps.

The winding, cobbled streets leading down from the cathedral to the modern city have considerable picturesque charm. The Grand-rue is the oldest of them; Jean-Jacques Rousseau was born at No. 40 on June 28, 1712. Also in this neighborhood is the 12th-century house at No. 6, rue du Puits-St.-Pierre, and the 17th-century houses built by Italian religious refugees on the rue de l'Hôtel-de-Ville.

For an interesting contrast to these ancient attractions, go back across the Rhône and out to Ariana Park, where the handsome Palais des Nations, now the European Office of the United Nations, the W.H.O. headquarters and other international buildings can be visited by guided tours throughout the year.

PRACTICAL INFORMATION FOR GENEVA

 WHEN TO COME. Geneva is a summer city when, of course, it is inevitably crowded. The four-day fête of Geneva, with fireworks, street dancing, parades of flower-covered floats, etc., occurs in the middle of August, and there is much jollification during the mid-December festival of Escalade. For events at the time of your visit, get a copy of *La Semaine à Genève* (This Week in Geneva) from your hotel. Also, all tourist information from Geneva Tourist Office, 2 Rue des Moulins.

 **HOTELS.** Hotel rooms are at a premium throughout the year. Book in advance if you possibly can or you may well be in trouble. There is a reservation service at the main rail station.

Deluxe

Beau Rivage, 13 quai du Mont Blanc (tel. 310221). Fine grill room and famous terrace; airconditioning throughout.

Des Bergues, 33 quai des Bergues (tel. 315050). A decidedly distinguished atmosphere pervades this luxury spot.

Intercontinental, 7–9 petit Saconnex (tel. 346091). With private suites, pool, sauna and smart shops; 18 storys and 400 rooms.

De la Paix, 11 quai Mont Blanc (tel. 326150). Small but attractive.

Président, 47 quai Wilson (tel. 311000). Delightfully decorated; airconditioning throughout.

La Réserve, 41 route des Romelles (tel. 741741). In pleasant park with lakeside terrace and outdoor pool; quiet, elegant and luxurious.

Le Richemond, Jardin Brunswick (tel. 311400). Famous family-run hotel overlooking river.

Expensive

Amat-Carlton, 22 rue Amat (tel. 316850). Quiet; TV in all rooms.

California, 1 rue Gevray (tel. 315550). Breakfast only; central but quiet. Some (M) rooms.

Cornavin, 33 blvd. James-Fazy (tel. 322100). Breakfast only; central and close to station. Some (M) rooms.

Grand-Pré, 35 rue de Grand-Pré (tel. 339150). Quiet, central, breakfast only.

Rex, 44 av. Wendt (tel. 457150). Medium-sized hotel; central.

Royal, 41 rue de Lausanne (tel. 313600). Airconditioning throughout; good restaurant.

Moderate

Athénée, 6 route de Malagnou (tel. 463933). Good value; central.

Drake, 7 rue Butini (tel. 316750). Quiet and central.

Eden, 135 rue de Lausanne (tel. 326540). Near the Palais des Nations.

Inexpensive

Astoria, 6 place Cornavin (tel. 321025). Breakfast only; handy for the station.

Bernina, 22 place Cornavin (tel. 314950). Opposite station and good value; breakfast only. Recommended.

Lido, 8 Chantepoulet (tel. 315530). Breakfast only; centrally located but quiet.

International et Terminus, 20 rue des Alpes (tel. 328095). With good grill restaurant.

Mon Repos, 131 rue de Lausanne (tel. 328010). Quiet with good restaurant.

Rivoli, 6 rue des Pâquis (tel. 318550). Breakfast only; central, well-managed, comfortable.

 RESTAURANTS. Geneva is full of good restaurants, with French cooking dominant, though there are plenty of places that provide the mixed Swiss cuisine, and a number specialize in the dishes of other countries.

Expensive

Le Béarn, quai de la Poste 4 (tel. 210028). Classic French cuisine.

Les Continents, ch. Petit Sacconex 9 (tel. 346091). In the Intercontinental hotel. Dine by candlelight on the 18th floor with a superb view of the lake. First class.

Le Duc, quai Mont-Blanc 7 (tel. 317330). Outstanding seafood.

Au Fin Bec, rue de Berne 55 (tel. 322919). One of Geneva's best.

Le Gentilhomme, in Le Richemond hotel (see above).

Le Neptune, in Du Rhône hotel (see above). Local dishes and seafood.

La Perle du Lac, 128 rue de Lausanne (tel. 317935). A joy for summer dining.

Moderate

Le Bateau, an old paddle steamer converted and moored at the south end of the pont du Mont-Blanc, Jardin des Anglais (tel. 213288).

Du Grand Pré, rue Hoffmann 15 (tel. 333219).

Inexpensive

Chez Bouby, 1 rue Grenus (tel. 310927). Reader-recommended.

Migros, chain store cafeterias—a good bet for inexpensive meals.

Mövenpick, on place de la Fusterie, and a big branch on the Right Bank. Also has a more expensive part.

 ENTERTAINMENT. Geneva is not Paris, but it comes closer to it than any other city in Switzerland, and can be fairly lively in the evening. There are two theaters, the *Grand Théâtre* and the *Comédie,* where you may see opera, operetta, or plays. You may have a chance to see experimental productions at the *Théâtre de Poche.* In summer, concerts and plays are given in the courtyard of the Hôtel de Ville.

Concert halls are *Victoria Hall,* rue Général Dufour, where the Orchestre de la Suisse Romande gives its concerts; *Conservatoire de Musique,* pl. Neuve; *Radio Geneva,* 66 bd. Carl-Vogt.

 NIGHTCLUBS. With a good floorshow, entrance will be around Fr.25; a Scotch, rather more. If a "hostess" joins you at your table or at the bar and suggests you buy her a drink, she means champagne (she gets a percentage from the house). Don't be afraid to say no—you won't be the first.

The liveliest is perhaps the *Ba-Ta-Clan,* 15 rue de la Fontaine; other lively spots are *Le Grillon* and *Piccadilly. The Pussy Cat Saloon,* 15 rue des Glacis de Rive, puts on two first class international shows and striptease nightly. In the same building, *Club 58* with excellent disco and band.

Probably the best spot in town, and the place to go if you want to avoid striptease, is *Maxim's,* pl. des Alpes. There's neither strip nor floorshow at *La Tour,* 6 rue Tour-de-Boël, but it always has two bands.

MUSEUMS. Ariana, avenue de la Paix. Headquarters of International Ceramics Academy. Collection of European and Oriental china and earthenware.

Art and History, rue Charles-Galland. Fine permanent collection of archeological objects, painting and sculpture; particularly strong in decorative art, with emphasis on Genevese enamels.

Baur Collection, rue Munier-Romilly 8, not far from the Art and History Museum. In a former private house, a fine collection of Chinese and Japanese ceramics, jades, prints, etc. Open daily except Mon. 2–6.

History of Science Museum, 128 rue de Lausanne; good display of scientific instruments. Open 2–6; also Sun., 10–12.

Horological Museum, 15 route de Malagnou (beside Natural History Museum). Fine collection of timepieces.

Natural History, 11 route de Malagnou. 10–12, 2–5, entrance free. Splendidly arranged collection in new building. There is also a Botanical Museum and Conservatory near the United Nations buildings.

Palais des Nations, Parc de l'Ariana; European Office of the United Nations. Guided tours of the building at least twice daily throughout year except Dec. 21–Jan. 2.

Palais Wilson, 51 quai Wilson. 9–12, 2–6, free. Educational exhibition of the International Education Bureau.

Petit Palais, 2 terrasse Saint-Victor, has modern art from 19th century onwards, and also loan exhibitions. Open daily except Mon.

Voltaire, 25 rue des Délices, 2–5 Mon. to Fri. Entrance free. Exhibits on Voltaire and his times—portraits, busts, furniture, etc.

SHOPPING. This is still the watchselling center of the world. All the leading Swiss manufacturers have offices and outlets here. When you see the array of jewelry in the shops along the rue du Rhône, du Marché and rue de la Croix d'Or, or look at the many haute couture boutiques in the rue du Rhône, you'll know that Calvin's sumptuary laws are a dead letter in this town today. If you're looking for antiques, you'll have a field day in those little narrow streets that tumble down from the old quarters clustered around the cathedral.

The Circuit of Lake Geneva

One of the joys of Lake Geneva is that the old road along the northern (Swiss) side is never far from its picturesque shore, although if you are in a hurry take the faster but less interesting motorway almost all the way from Geneva to Villeneuve. If you prefer the prettier but slower road along the lake, you will pass through Coppet, with its lovely château which belonged to Louis XVI's financial adviser Jacques Necker (a Swiss) and his daughter Madame de Staël; attractive Céligny; Nyon, founded by Julius Caesar as a camp for war veterans in 56 B.C. and subsequently (17th and 18th centuries) the center of a flourishing chinaware craft whose flowersprigged productions are still in demand; Morges, a popular yachting and sailing center with a 13th-century castle and a statue of Paderewski, who spent his last years on his beautiful estate at nearby Tolochenaz.

Lausanne, nearly 40 miles from Geneva on the northern shore of the lake, calls itself "Switzerland's city of the future". A great favorite with such distinguished foreigners as Voltaire and Gibbon in the 18th century, this hilly city, rising in tiers from the lakeside, is the prosperous, business center of western Switzerland, and a pleasant resort.

Sightseeing in Lausanne should include the Cathedral of Notre Dame, a fine example of Burgundian Gothic, restored since vandal Reformation days; the Castle of St. Maire; the 17th-century city hall; and the handsome, modern Federal Palace of Justice. The wooded Jorat heights above the city are ideal for walking tours. Lausanne-Ouchy, an elegant resort, is a good place of embarkation for short, pleasant excursions on the smart white steamers that shuttle across the lake all summer long. Try the half hour trip to St. Sulpice to see the best-preserved 11th-century Romanesque church in Switzerland. A dozen miles north of Lausanne is La Sarraz, whose castle, on a rocky promontory, is a national monument and contains a splendid furniture collection.

The circuit of Lake Geneva continues east of Lausanne along a beautiful 15-mile stretch past the steep vineyards of Lavaux, which produce excellent vintages, much in demand. Harvest time here in mid-October is very boisterous on these precipitous slopes. At Pully, five miles east of Lausanne, you have a choice of roads just before entering the village. Take the one which leads away from the lake for the breathtaking Corniche Road that winds through the vineyards to Chexbres, 2,000 feet above sea level, then descends to the lake highway again just before Vevey.

Vevey, with its inspiring view across the lake to the lofty peak of Dent d'Oche, has been, with Montreux, a popular resort with the English since the early 19th century. Today, many famous foreigners live hereabouts. At the eastern end of its lovely lakeside promenade is La Tour de Peilz, a resort-suburb named after its 13th-century castle—all of which reminds us that it was in this region that Jean-Jacques Rousseau set his *Nouvelle Héloïse,* that 18th-century European best seller which set the fashion for Swiss travel. In nearby Gruyère you can visit the cheese factory.

Even more romantic than Vevey is Montreux, one of Europe's most beautifully situated resorts. A French-style Edwardian town, now much modernized, it caters largely to foreigners, and is famed alike for its mild climate, lush vegetation and well-tended gardens.

There are some wonderful trips to be taken from Montreux. One is by mountain railroad to the Rochers de Naye. Here, at 6,700 feet above sea level, you will have a view over Lake Geneva, the Savoy and the southern Swiss Alps. As late as May you'll be able to enjoy excellent skiing. A second excursion from Montreux is the ride to Glion and Caux with its celebrated "Mountain House", headquarters of the Moral Rearmament movement. Not least, and a mere 1½ miles by trolley bus from Montreux, there is one of Europe's most famous sights, the castle of Chillon. Immortalized by Byron, the island castle (although it's only a few feet from the shore) was built in the 13th century under the direction of Duke Peter of Savoy. The dungeon's most famous prisoner was François Bonivard who, as Prior of St. Victor in Geneva, had supported the Reformation, conduct which infuriated the Catholic Duke of Savoy. Bonivard spent six gloomy years here until the Bernese freed him in 1536.

The Swiss tour of Lake Geneva really ends here at Chillon, though you can continue to Villeneuve and the Rhône estuary, or even strike north to Col du Pillon to take the marvelous cablecar ride up to the perpetual snow of the Diablerets glacier with its panoramic restaurant. But if you cross the Rhône and start back to complete the circuit of the lake, you'll soon find yourself in another country, for much of the southern shore of Lake Geneva is French. If you have a sudden inclination to gamble, you can stop on your way at the popular French thermal resort of Evian.

PRACTICAL INFORMATION FOR THE LAKE GENEVA REGION

CHEXBRES. *Du Signal* (M), tel. 562525. Quiet with splendid view and tennis and pool. *Cécil* (I), tel. 561292. Pool.

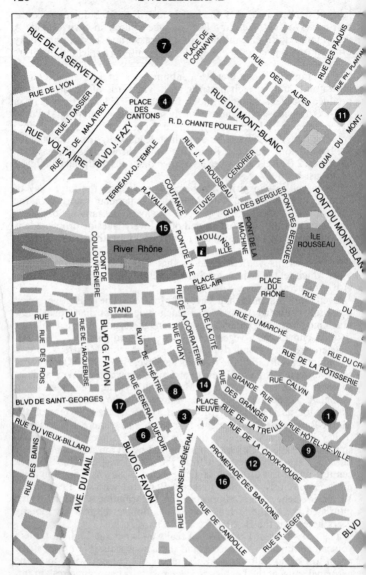

LES DIABLERETS. *Eurotel* (E), tel. 531721. Indoor pool and sauna. *Ermitage et Meurice* (E), tel. 531551. Sauna gymnasium and indoor pool. *Les Lilas* (I), 531134. Small. *Mon Abri* (I), tel. 531481. Comfortable and quiet.

LAUSANNE. *Le Beau Rivage* (L), tel. 263831. Splendid hotel, very much in the grand manner, at Ouchy overlooking the lake; tennis, indoor pool and sauna; ideal for children. *Alpha* (E), tel. 230131. In center with two good restaurants; quiet. *Bellerive* (E), tel. 269633. Down the hill between the city center and Ouchy; quiet and with facilities for the handicapped. *Continental* (E), tel. 201551. Near the station; quiet and good. *Angleterre* (M), tel. 264145. Quiet hotel overlooking the lake. *Regina* (I), tel. 202441. Breakfast only; central but quiet.

GENEVA

N

| 0 Miles | ¼ |
| 0 Kilometers | ¼ |

Lac Léman

Points of Interest

1 Cathédrale de St. Pierre
2 Collège Calvin
3 Conservatoire de Musique
4 Église de Notre Dame
5 Église de St. Joseph
6 Église du Sacre Coeur
7 Gare de Cornavin (rail station)
8 Grand Théâtre
9 Hôtel de Ville (City Hall)
10 Jet d'Eau
11 Monument Brunswick
12 Monument de la Reformation
13 Musée d'Art et d'Histoire;
   Russian Church
14 Musée Rath
15 Tour de l'Île
16 Université
17 Victoria Hall

ℹ️ Tourist Information

PROMENADE DE LAC

QUAI GUSTAVE ADOR

GÉNÉRAL-GUISAN

RUE P. FATIO

RUE VERSONNEX

RUE DES EAUX VIVES

AVE PICTET DE ROCHEMONT

RUE DE RIVE

RUE DE LA RIVE

R. DE LA TERRASSIÈRE

JAQUES-DALCROZE

HELVETIQUE

R. D. GLACIS-DE-RIVE

RUE DE VILLEREUSE

BLVD

RUE DE MALAGNOU

ROUTE

Restaurants. *La Grappe d'Or* (E), Cheneau de Bourg 3 (tel. 230760). Excellent. *Le Relais,* in Lausanne Palace hotel, rue du Grand-Chêne 7 (tel. 203711). Also excellent. *Du Mont d'Or* (E), Contigny 1 (tel. 267460). Very good. *Il Grottino* (M), rue Grand-Chêne 4 (tel. 227658). Italian. *Le Chalet Suisse* (I), Sauvabelin (tel. 222312). *Le Mandarin* (I), av. du Théâtre 7 (tel. 237484). Chinese.

At Crissier, near Lausanne: *Girardet* (E), tel. 341514. One of Switzerland's truly great restaurants and super-expensive (you won't get away for less than Fr.150 a head if you let Girardet have his tempting way with you!). A gastronomic experience not to be missed. Essential to book a long way ahead.

At Ouchy: *Grill Wellingtonia,* in Le Beau Rivage hotel (see above), tel. 263831. *Le Château d'Ouchy* (M), place du Port (tel. 267451). *Le Voile d'Or* (M), av. Delacroze 9 (tel. 278011).

At St. Sulpice: *L'Abordage* (E), tel. 247138. Excellent. *Le Débarcadère* (E), tel. 351068. Also excellent rating.

MONTREUX. *Excelsior* (L), tel. 633231. Pool, sauna and gym; three excellent restaurants. Also has (E) rooms. *Le Montreux Palace* (L), tel. 635373. Vast hotel with golf, tennis and outdoor pool. *Eurotel* (E), tel. 634951. Lakeside hotel with indoor pool; kitchenette in every room. *Suisse et Majestic* (E), tel. 635181. Sauna and gymnasium; facilities for children. *Bon Accueil* (M), tel. 630551. Breakfast only; central. *Masson* (I), tel. 631537. Facilities for children; quiet.

Restaurants. *Au Vif Argent Rôtisserie* (E), tel. 635053. Elegant restaurant in the Montreux Palace hotel. *Brasserie Bavaria* (M), tel. 632545. *Le Clou* (M), tel. 632044. Well recommended. *Au Parc* (M), tel. 634658. Fine Italian restaurant.

NYON. *Du Clos de Sadex* (E), tel. 612831. Small hotel on the lake; quiet and with waterskiing. *Beau Rivage* (E), tel. 613231. Splendid view; some (M) rooms.

Restaurant. *Le Léman* (E), tel. 612241. Excellent.

VEVEY. *Trois Couronnes* (L), tel. 513005. Sumptuous Victorian interior full of character and comfort; open air restaurant overlooking lake. *Comte* (E), tel. 541441. By the lake; (M) rooms available. *Du Lac* (E), tel. 511041. With swimming pool; lakeside location. *De Famille* (I), tel. 513931. Indoor pool and sauna; central. *Touring & Gare* (I), tel. 510647. Central.

Restaurants. *Du Raisin* (E), tel. 511028. Known as "chez Pierre" to the regulars. First class. *Le Chandelier* (M), tel. 528837.

VILLARS. *Grand Hôtel du Parc* (L), tel. 352121. Quiet with indoor pool and tennis; ideal for children. *Eurotel* (E), tel. 353131. Central with indoor pool and sauna. *Du Golf-Marie-Louise* (M), tel. 352477. Quiet and central; tennis. *Chalet Henriette* (I), tel. 352163. Facilities for the handicapped.

The Valais (Zermatt and the Matterhorn)

Following a roughly L-shaped section of the Rhône between Lake Geneva and the Canton of Ticino, the Valais, Wallis in German, has long been famous as one of Europe's most magnificent regions. The backbone of the canton is the fertile and impressive Rhône Valley, off which an incomparable network of lesser valleys, mostly steep, narrow and often little-known to tourists, leads into superb mountain scenery. Swiss engineers have achieved the near-impossible by building roads up most of these valleys; but you'll see much more, and probably worry less, if you leave the driving to an expert on one of Switzerland's ubiquitous postal buses. The Valais has numerous famous and fashionable resorts, but even more that are quiet, charming and noticeably cheaper than is usual in Switzerland. We list some of the better known resorts, but off-the-beaten-track exploration is very rewarding.

Here's news: *you* can climb the Matterhorn! If you can walk, are tolerably sound in wind and limb, have a few days to spare to get in condition, and can afford to hire one of Zermatt's expert guides, he'll get you to the top of that formidable lump of rock and bring you down again in one piece. The expedition will take about a couple of days and on the way you will come across nothing less than the world's highest (12,000 ft.) public conveniences! You need have no qualms about your guides either; those at Zermatt are famous and many have accompanied scientific expeditions to the Himalayas and other mountain ranges around the world.

With less effort, you can get almost the same sensation (though not the same satisfaction) by taking one of the highest cogwheel railroads in Europe from Zermatt to Gornergrat. Here, at a mere 10,200 feet (the Matterhorn is 14,690), you will have a view over shimmering glaciers and 50 or more king-size peaks.

Zermatt is the leading winter sports center of the Valais, with cog-wheel railways, cable cars, chair and ski lifts, skating and curling rinks galore. Skiing often lasts into late spring here, and right through summer in the Theodul Pass area. Saas-Fee, a bit less crowded, is also a first-rate summer and winter resort. Besides ski lifts, there are gondolas and cable cars going to Felskinn, Langefluh and Plattjen, all at dizzy heights. The Sion and Sierre areas, especially the Crans-Montana-Vermala resort complex, are equally lovely in summer and winter. Crans has the distinction of having the first golf course ever installed on the Continent. It's still one of the best. Verbier is another well-known winter sports center, while the secluded little Val d'Anniviers has a number of charming winter sports resorts at Grimentz, St. Luc, Chandolin and Zinal which have managed to retain the rustic character of these typical Valaisan mountain villages, with their chalets and raised wooden barns (known locally as *mazots*).

An up-and-coming summer and winter resort is Grächen, a sunny village in the St. Niklaus valley, situated at an altitude of 5,305 feet. You can reach it by car or mail-bus from St. Niklaus Station. It has an aerial cableway which takes you up to the splendid skiing fields on the Hannigalp (6,950 ft.).

PRACTICAL INFORMATION FOR THE VALAIS

ANZÈRE. *Des Masques* (E), tel. 382651. (M) rooms available. *Grand Roc* (I), tel. 383535.

BRIG. *Schlosshotel* (M), tel. 236455. Also (I) rooms. Breakfast only; quiet and with facilities for the handicapped. *Gliserallee* (I), tel. 231195. Very small and inexpensive.
Restaurant. *Schlosskeller* (M), tel. 233352.

CHAMPÉRY. *Beau-Séjour Vieux Chalet* (I), tel. 791701. Quiet. *Rose des Alpes* (I), tel. 791218.
Restaurant. *Des Alpes* (M–I), tel. 791222. Excellent.

CHAMPEX. *Des Alpes et Lac* (M), tel. 41151. Tennis and facilities for children. *Du Glacier Sporting* (I), tel. 41402. Quiet and ideal for children.

CRANS. *Alpine et Savoy* (L), tel. 412142. Gymnasium, indoor pool and sauna. *Excelsior* (L), tel. 401161. Quiet and comfortable; also some (E) rooms. *Elite* (E), tel. 414301. Pool and facilities for the handicapped; ideal for children. *Des Mélèzes* (E), tel. 431812. Quiet hotel in own grounds. *Tourist* (E), tel. 413256. Breakfast only; central and in own grounds. All three have (M) rooms. *Centrale* (I), tel. 413767. Central. *Du Téléférique* (I), tel. 413367. Small.
Restaurant. *Rôtisserie de la Channe* (E), tel. 411258.

EVOLÈNE. *D'Evolène* (I), tel. 831151. Tennis and pool. No showers. *Hermitage* (I), tel. 831232. Quiet.

GRÄCHEN. (All inclusive). *Alpina* (I), tel. 562626. Central, but quiet rooms. *Hannigalp & Valaisia* (I), tel. 562555. Indoor pool, gymnasium and sauna.

LEUKERBAD. (All inclusive). *Badehotel Bristol* (L), tel. 611833. Riding, tennis, indoor pool and gymnasium as well as cure facilities. *Badehotel Grand-Bain* (E), tel. 621161. Spa hotel; tennis. *Walliserhof* (M), tel. 611424. Centrally located and with facilities for the disabled. *Zayetta* (M), tel. 611646. Central and quiet and with sauna. *Dala* (I), tel. 611213. Breakfast only; central; facilities for the handicapped.

SAAS-FEE. (All inclusive). *Grand Hotel* (L), tel. 571001. Comfortable. *Saaserhof* (L), tel. 571551. Facilities for the handicapped along with sauna and quiet rooms in this the smartest hotel in town. *Allalin* (E), tel. 571815. Central and quiet with marvelous view. *Burgener* (E), tel. 571522. Central but quiet and with superb view. *Britannia* (M), tel. 571616. Sauna. *Des Alpes* (I), tel. 571555. Quiet rooms; sauna; breakfast only.

SION. *Du Rhône* (I), tel. 228291. Central but quiet. *Touring* (I), tel. 231551. Facilities for the handicapped and quiet rooms.

 Restaurants. *Caves de Tous Vents* (E), tel. 224684. Very good. *Big Ben Pub* (M), tel. 227977.

VERBIER. (All inclusive). *Rhodania* (L), tel. 70121. Comfortable and central; (E) rooms available. *Grand-Combin* (E), tel. 75515. Central and quiet and with facilities for the handicapped. *Le Mazot* (E), tel. 76812. Sauna. *Rosa-Blanche* (E), tel. 74472. (M) rooms as well.

 Restaurant. *Rosalp* (E), tel. 76323. Outstanding.

ZERMATT. (All inclusive). *Mont Cervin* (L), tel. 661121. Famous and luxurious; tennis, indoor pool, sauna; central. *Nicoletta* (L), tel. 661151. Comfortable and friendly; quiet. *Alphubel* (E), tel. 673003. Central and quiet; (M) rooms available. *Touring* (E), tel. 671177. Quiet; also (M) rooms. *Gabelhorn* (I), tel. 672235. Breakfast only; quiet. *Tannenhof* (I), tel. 673188. Breakfast only; reasonable.

 Restaurants. *Seilerhaus + Otto-Furrer-Stube* (E), tel. 671996. *Tenne* (E), tel. 671801. Excellent. *Nicoletta* (M), tel. 661151. First class.

Ticino, Southernmost Canton

South of St. Gotthard is Ticino, the odd-man-out of the Swiss cantons partly because it is the only Italian-speaking one. It projects like a spearhead into Italy and it is hardly surprising that this part of Switzerland has a distinctly Italian flavor not only in its food, but also in its buildings, people, atmosphere and climate. In the lake district, December and January can admittedly be cold and wet, but the rest of the year is normally blissfully warm and sunny except for occasional stormy spells—usually shortlived. And summer can be downright hot.

But don't be fooled by Ticino's appearance. You are still very much in Switzerland! Like many another Swiss canton it has winter sports, Alpine scenery, lakes, and plenty of mountain transport as well as typical Swiss efficiency and hospitality. But as a free bonus Ticino throws in its almost Mediterranean climate at lower levels, some lovely unspoiled valleys, and three world-famous resorts—Lugano, Locarno and Ascona. Prices in Ticino, away from the big resorts, are a trifle below those elsewhere in the country.

Just as the three resorts have their distinctive personalities, so do Ticino's many valleys, each vying with the other for scenery and charm. Like many other unsung attractions in Ticino, these lovely valleys are missed by most tourists, although they are nearly all easy to reach, as the canton is endowed with a fine network of public transport. Good, if sometimes narrow, roads lead everywhere, in several cases almost to the summit of fair-sized mountains.

Lugano

Set around a large bay in Lake Lugano, with the green heights of Monte San Salvatore and Monte Brè as sentinels at each end, the city of Lugano rises from the shore up the sides of gently rolling hills. Forming, with its suburbs of Paradiso and Castagnola, an almost unbroken line of hotels and elegant villas around the bay, Lugano has a rather opulent air of pleasantly self-conscious sophistication. And not without reason. For with its mild climate and magnificent setting it is

virtually a year-round resort; one with everything in the way of entertainment, sport, sidewalk cafés, lakeside promenades, to say nothing of
an enviable selection of shops to suit millionaires (and they are frequently around in Lugano) as well as travelers on a shoestring budget.

Art lovers will find much to interest them in Lugano and its neighborhood. In the town itself, the old Franciscan church of Santa Maria
degli Angeli has the famous *Crucifixion* fresco and other smaller ones
which Bernardino Luini painted in 1529. The cathedral of San Lorenzo, up the hill to the station, is notable for its 16th-century Renaissance
façade, and for the splendid lake and city view from its terrace. Beside
the lake in Castagnola is the beautiful mansion, La Villa Favorita,
bought in 1932 by the late Baron Heinrich von Thyssen. In its
Pinacoteca—a specially built wing—are over twenty superbly lit and
arranged salons containing his priceless art collection as well as additions made by the present Baron. Probably Europe's finest private
collection, and a must for all art lovers, the Pinacoteca is normally open
Easter to mid-October.

Outside Lugano itself, you can best get your bearings by taking a
funicular to the top of Monte San Salvatore (2,995 ft.) or Monte Brè
(3,053 ft.). Either will give you an eagle's eye view of Lugano and its
irregularly shaped lake, and the hills, valleys and mountains of the
region. Better still is the ascent of Monte Generoso (5,590 ft.). Take a
boat to Capolago at the southern end of the lake (about 50 minutes
from Lugano) where, beside the jetty, the little, red cogwheel-train will
take you on its 40-minute climb to the top station. The grassy summit
is about 250 feet higher, but there is a prepared path, steep and rough
but not too difficult. From the top, on a clear day you'll see the Po
valley and Apennines in the south, the snow-capped Alps to the north,
and much of Ticino in between. Choose good weather for these ascents
and go before the clouds have begun to gather around the peaks as they
often do about mid-day.

There are many lake excursions from Lugano. An amusing, 20-
minute trip (it's rather less by bus) is to Campione d'Italia on the
opposite shore, a square mile of Italian territory entirely surrounded
by Switzerland. Campione's chief attraction is a large, glamorous and
glittering casino. Being Italian, although Swiss money is used, the
maximum stakes are high and you can fritter away your fortune on
roulette, chemin-de-fer and what-have-you in a fraction of the time it
takes in Lugano where stakes are limited by Swiss law. Another 20-
minute boat trip from Lugano, or better still a delightful half-hour
lakeside walk from the Castagnola trolley stop, is to the picturesque
village of Gandria whose cottages rise straight from the water's edge.

For contrast, take the lovely drive from Lugano, past a succession
of spectacular lake and mountain views, along the high ridge which
leads to the village of Carona, then on through the equally charming
village of Vico Morcote and steeply down to the waterside townlet of
Morcote. If you return to Lugano along the lake shore road, stop for
a while at Melide to visit "Swissminiatur", a vast exhibition of typical
or famous Swiss houses, churches, castles, villages, trains, ships, the
lot—all at 1/25th life size.

Locarno and Ascona

More relaxed than Lugano and only half the size, Locarno, on the
shore of Lake Maggiore, is an international resort, but in the old part
of the town, with its attractive, narrow streets of arcaded houses, you
will soon realize its age. The 16th century was a bad one for Locarno.
First, about 60 of its most distinguished Protestant families were exiled,
fleeing to Zurich, where they helped to establish that city's prosperous

silk trade. Then the town was struck by the Black Plague, which cut its population from 4,800 to 700. At the beginning of the 20th century, it was still a place of no great note despite its beautiful situation. But in 1925 it suddenly leapt to world fame when Briand, Stresemann, Mussolini and Chamberlain met here to sign the Locarno Pact.

Today, Locarno is a go-ahead resort which has somehow managed to remain almost unspoiled by popularity; it is sunny, spacious, with a subtle air of dignity and sophistication. From the middle of the town itself, and only a few paces from the tree-shaded waterfront, you can be whisked by cable railway, cablecar and chair lift up to Cardada (4,050 ft.) and Cimetta (4,950 ft.). Both have magnificent views of Lake Maggiore and the Alps, and towards the end of winter you can ski on the snowy slopes while others bask in the sun by the lake below.

Only 2½ miles from Locarno is the small resort-town of Ascona. What gives Ascona a character of its own is its charming and relaxed atmosphere—and more particularly its contrast. For almost hidden behind the lively, colorful cafés which line the tree-bordered shore promenade is Ascona's other face—an intriguing muddle of quaint old streets and twisting alleys surrounding the eye-catching church tower; streets and alleys filled with boutiques, antique shops, bookbinders, art galleries and other craft shops.

Locarno and Ascona are alike in being first-rate centers for excursions by road, rail or on the lake. From either, smart white boats, and even hydrofoils, give plenty of opportunities to explore the beauties of Lake Maggiore and its islands. You can make the trip of half-an-hour or so to the minuscule Brissago islands with their lovely sub-tropical gardens. Or, if you can spare a day or half-day you can go further afield to the Italian resort of Stresa or the beautiful Borromean Islands. From both Locarno and Ascona, too, it's a quick, easy drive to valleys which are wild and secluded; Valle Verzasca and Valle Maggia are two of the best.

PRACTICAL INFORMATION FOR TICINO

ASCONA. *Castello del Sole* (L), tel. 350202. Lakeside hotel with indoor and outdoor pools, tennis, gymnasium and sauna; comfortable and quiet. *Delta* (L), tel. 351105. All facilities in this excellent hotel. *Europe au Lac* (L), tel. 352881. Quiet lakeside hotel with 2 pools; (E) rooms available. *Monte Verita* (E) tel. 350181. In huge hilltop park; views, pool. *Acapulco au Lac* (E), tel. 354521. Quiet hotel by lake with waterskiing and indoor pool. *Tamaro au Lac* (M), tel. 350282. Atmospheric and quiet. Most hotels close for 2–4 months in the winter.
    Restaurants. *Al Faro* (M), p. Motta (tel. 358515). Delightful meals indoors and outdoors. *Da Ivo* (M), v. Collegio (tel. 351031). Local color. *Monte Verità* (M), tel. 351281. Recommended. *Otello–La Creperia* (M), vl. Papio, tel. 353307.

LOCARNO. *La Palma au Lac* (L), tel. 330071. Beautiful situation on lake; waterskiing, indoor pool and sauna. *Arcadia al Lago* (E), tel. 310282. Modern, central, garden with pool. *Muralto* (E), tel. 330181. Fine view of the lake; central; facilities for the handicapped. *Quisisana,* (E), tel. 330141. High above town with splendid view, indoor pool and gymnasium. *Beau-Rivage* (M), tel. 331355. Central and quiet. *Remorino* (M), tel. 331033. In Minusio. Breakfast only; quiet in own grounds with pool; ideal for children. *Du Lac* (I), tel. 312921. Central; breakfast only; facilities for the disabled.
    Restaurants. *Centenario* (L), v. dei Muralti 1 (tel. 338222). *Coq d'Or* grill-room at La Palma au Lac (E), vl. Verbano 29, Muralto (tel. 330171). Another of Switzerland's outstanding restaurants. *Mövenpick-Oldrati* (M), Lungolago, Muralto (tel. 338544).

LUGANO. *Eden Grand Hotel* (L), riva Paradiso 1 (tel. 550121). Cure facilities, airconditioning, indoor pool, waterskiing and sauna in this quiet lakeside hotel. *Admiral* (E), tel. 542324. 2 pools, sauna and gymnasium; facilities for the handicapped. *Alba* (E), v. della Scuole 11 (tel. 543731). Breakfast only; central but quiet. *Béha* (M), v. Mazzini 22 (tel. 541331). Central and with facilities for the handicapped. *Meister* (M), v. San Salvatore 11 (tel. 541412). Fine family hotel with pool. *Nizza* (M), v. Guidino 1 (tel. 541771). Park with heated pool. Excellent cuisine; panorama bar. Budget rooms too. Recommended. *Cristina* (I), v. Zorzi 28 (tel. 543312). Tropical garden with heated pool. Tennis, water sports and San Salvatore funicular nearby. Budget rooms too. *Rio* (I), v. Cantonale 9 (tel. 228144). Small, simple and very reasonably priced; breakfast only. *Walter au Lac* (I), v. Rezzonico 7 (tel. 227425). Central; reasonable.

Restaurants. *Bianchi* (E), v. Via Pessina 3 (tel. 228479). *Al Portone* (E), vl. Cassarate 3 (tel. 235995). Excellent. *Grotto Grillo* (E), v. Ronchetto 6 (tel. 511801). *Cina* (M), p. Riforma 9 (tel. 235173). First class Chinese restaurant. *Locanda del Boschetto* (M), v. Casserinetta 40 (tel. 542493). Very good. *Mövenpick - Parco Ciani* (M), tel. 238656. Indoors and outdoors.

TURKEY

This country, spanning two continents, offers an abundance of magnificent beaches, exciting historical sites, art treasures and a myriad of exotic mosques. Roughly 296,000 square miles in size, it has a population of over 49,000,000. Because it is still relatively undeveloped with regard to hotels and related facilities, visitors concentrate mostly on Istanbul, Ankara and the Aegean coast. But the Turquoise Coast farther south has the best beaches and the most interesting archaeological sites; the beautiful Black Sea coast is unspoiled and unpretentious; and the vast highlands of eastern Turkey can still provide free adventure for those less-demanding of the creature comforts. (In the latter region organized travel is the most advantageous way of exploring the widely scattered sites and taking care of the formidable accommodation and language problems.)

In general, the best time of year to visit Turkey is between April and November, and the primary objectives are: Istanbul, one of the most beautifully sited cities in the world; the ancient Greek towns of Pergamon, Ephesus and Side; the renowned "Seven Churches of Asia" from the journeys of St. Paul; the underground cities and rock churches of Cappadocia.

A Bit of History

From the beginning Asia Minor has been rich in legend. Noah's Ark is claimed to have come to rest on Mount Ararat, Homer to have been born in Izmir (the ancient Greek Smyrna), and the Virgin Mary to have spent her last days on earth at Ephesus. Turkey as a nation came into existence only in 1923, through the efforts of Mustafa Kemal Atatürk after the collapse of the Ottoman Empire and foreign intervention. After two army coups, democracy returned in 1973 but proved to be unable to deal with mounting terrorism so that the armed forces once again intervened in September 1980 to the general relief of the population. The economy greatly improved under the National Security Council, whose head was elected President for seven years in November 1982. In the simultaneous plebiscite, over 90% approved the new constitution. One year later, the free-enterprise Motherland Party obtained a majority in the election for the Grand National Assembly. A third attempt at democracy got off to a promising start by a radical shake-up of the civil service. Municipal elections in 1984 confirmed the preeminence of the Motherland Party, which has kept Turkey a faithful NATO ally.

PRACTICAL INFORMATION FOR TURKEY

WHAT WILL IT COST. Though well below the 120% it was before the military takeover, inflation is again hovering near the 40% mark. Frequent small devaluations keep prices fairly stable in foreign currencies. In this edition prices are, therefore, quoted in dollars and indicate the real cost for tourists more accurately than if given in Turkish *lira* (TL). The country is inexpensive and prices outside the main cities and resorts can be rock bottom, though you should remember that the food and accommodation can be correspondingly simple.

The monetary unit is the Turkish *lira*. At the time of writing the rate is TL530 to the U.S. dollar, TL750 to the pound sterling. Tourists may import and export the equivalent of up to $100 in Turkish currency. Banknotes and traveler's checks can be changed at banks, travel agencies, and major hotels. Exchange slips should be retained to reconvert TL into foreign currency. Likewise, if the value of purchases to be taken out exceeds TL40,000.

A typical Moderate day might cost two people:

Hotel (double room with breakfast)	US $30
Lunch at a Turkish restaurant	20
Transportation	10
Light refreshment	5
Evening entertainment	12
Dinner (set menu at a hotel)	15
Miscellaneous 10%.	9
	101

SOURCES OF INFORMATION. For information on all aspects of travel in Turkey, the Turkish Tourism Information Office is invaluable. Their addresses are:

In the U.S.: 821 United Nations Plaza, New York, N.Y. 10017 (tel. 212-687-2194).

In the U.K.: 170–73 Piccadilly, London W.1 (tel. 01-734 8681).

WHEN TO COME. The tourist season lasts from the beginning of April to the end of October. It is at its height during July and August. In many ways though, the best times of the year to be there are from April to June and later in September and October. This is particularly true if you intend to travel inland where it can become unbearably hot during high summer.

Climate. The climate in Turkey varies a great deal according to the time of year and place. On the Anatolian plain summer is hot and dry (up to 102° Fahrenheit) and winter snowy and cold. The coast of the Black Sea is mild and damp with the rainfall falling at over 90 inches a year. The Mediterranean coast has a moderate climate all the year round with the temperature averaging 75°.

Average afternoon temperatures in Fahrenheit and centigrade:

Ankara	Jan.	Feb.	Mar.	Apr.	May	June	July	Aug.	Sept.	Oct.	Nov.	Dec.
F°	39	42	51	63	73	78	86	87	78	69	57	43
C°	4	6	11	17	23	26	30	31	26	21	14	6

SPECIAL EVENTS. *May,* festivals in the ancient amphi-theaters of Ephesus, Pergamon (Bergama near Izmir) and Silifke; *June,* Mediterranean Festival, Izmir; *June/July,* Istanbul Art Festival; Festival of Bursa; *August/September,* International Fair, Izmir, Festival of Bodrum.

National Holidays. Jan. 1 (New Year's Day); Apr. 23 (National Independence and Children's Day); May 19 (Youth and Sports Day); sunset May 31 to sunset Jun. 2 *(Seker Bayram);* sunset Aug. 6 to Aug. 9 *(Kurban Bayram);* Aug. 30 (Victory Day); Oct. 29 (Republic Day).

VISAS. Nationals of the United States, Canada, Australia, New Zealand, EEC countries and practically all other European countries do not require visas for entry into Turkey.

Health Certificates. Not required for entry into Turkey.

CUSTOMS. A traveler may import 200 cigarettes or 50 cigars or 200 gr. of tobacco; 1 liter of alcoholic beverage in opened bottles; a reasonable amount of perfume and 1 liter of eau de Cologne. Objects up to a value of $1,000 can be exported on production of a currency exchange slip. For new carpets the limit is $3,000, while old ones also require a special permit.

GETTING TO TURKEY. By Plane. There are daily flights from New York and all major European and Middle East cities to Istanbul, with onward services to Ankara by *THY,* the Turkish national airline. There are also some direct flights to Ankara and Izmir; charter flights in summer to Antalya and Dalaman.

By Train. There is one through train from Western Europe to Istanbul—called the *Istanbul Express*—which has 2nd class couchettes and 1st and 2nd class day carriages. This train leaves Munich at about 5.30 P.M. and travels via Salzburg, Zagreb, Belgrade and Sofia, reaching Istanbul some 42 hours later (that is with two nights travel). Dining car in the Turkish section of the route. There are also services from Athens via Thessaloniki to Istanbul, and from Moscow via Romania and Bulgaria. In Asia Minor there is the *Toros Express* from Baghdad to Ankara and Haydarpasa (for Istanbul) running twice a week depending on local conditions.

HOTELS. Hotels in Turkey are among Europe's cheapest, but the standards are lower and in many the whole concept of comfort leaves much to be desired. Deluxe and Expensive hotels are airconditioned, and even Moderate and Inexpensive hotels have all rooms with baths or showers, but in the last category hardly any have a restaurant, though they serve breakfast. Luxury hotels are only to be found in or around big cities like Ankara, Istanbul and Izmir, while a few Expensive hotels, modest by Western standards, have been opened in coastal resorts. Off the tourist beat there are many hotels which have not been officially classified. We have omitted these establishments but it must be pointed out that they are usually clean and that the willing service often makes up for the lack of amenities.

Our hotel grading system is divided into four categories. All prices are for two people in a double room. Except in Istanbul and Ankara, Turkish luxury rating fails to come up to our deluxe, while Expensive is not really expensive by general standards. Deluxe (L) 75–130 dollars, Expensive (E) 35–60 dollars, Moderate (M) 22–35, Inexpensive (I) 10–20.

CAMPING. There are organized campsites along the main roads in western, southern and central Turkey. The Ministry of Tourism and Information issues a multilingual folder, *Camping-Turkey,* which contains all that you might wish to know.

RESTAURANTS. The official classifications, I, II and III, correspond roughly to our Expensive (E), Moderate (M), and Inexpensive (I). Avoid the international-style restaurants, especially in the motels, where the food is indifferent. Instead, you should go to Turkish restaurants where the food is usually tasty. You will, in addition, pay considerably less. In most restaurants you can go into the kitchen and choose your own food and you will find that the service in most is about the fastest in the world.

It is possible to get an adequate meal at a Turkish restaurant for around $7, without wine. For a superb Turkish repast, representative of the best in Turkish cooking, with wine, don't expect to pay less than $30. Leave 10% tip for the waiter and something for the boy who brings the wine. Check your bill: honesty often fails to make up for mathematical deficiencies.

Food and Drink. Turkish cuisine isn't all that exotic, as it is based on age-old recipes common to the eastern Mediterranean from Greece to Egypt. It's a good idea to remember a few Turkish names for dishes so you won't be limited to eating *shish kebabs* (meat, usually lamb, roasted on a spit): *Kadin Budu* is meatballs with rice; *kiliç* is a swordfish with bay leaves, spit-roasted; *çerkes tavugu,* chicken cooked with a red pepper and walnut sauce; *dolmas,* vine leaves stuffed with black currants, pine nuts and rice, cooked in olive oil. The yogurt is superb, but the honey-and-nut pastries are excessively sweet. Snacks from street stands are tasty but not recommended unless you have a strong stomach.

The Turkish national drink is *raki,* a potent potion which the Turks drink as an apéritif. There are some very drinkable wines and a variety of sweet liqueurs. Coffee is nearly always of the Turkish variety, except in the top establishments. But it is relatively expensive and has been replaced as national drink by rather insipid tea grown along the Black Sea.

TIPPING. A service charge of 15% is added to the bill but it does not always find its way to the personnel. Keep this in mind and tip those who have looked after you. Waiters expect about 10%. Washroom attendants, movie and theater ushers will be thankful for a tip in the region of the equivalent of about 25 cents. For taxi drivers, round up the fare to the next TL50.

MAIL. Post offices are recognizable by the yellow sign *PTT.* Postage rates are frequently adjusted in order to keep pace with inflation, so find out from your hotel porter or the post office itself.

CLOSING TIMES. Shops are open from 9 to 7 P.M. with a break for lunch; closed Saturday afternoon and Sunday. Banks and Public Offices open Monday to Friday 8.30 to 12, 1.30 to 5. Small shops, especially in tourist resorts, stay open later, and also often open on weekends.

HEALTH There is a risk of malaria in a number of provinces between July and October; consult local health authorities.

Water is safe to drink in all the main cities. In remote places it is best to stick to bottled mineral water. The non-fizzy *Kizilay* is particularly pleasant.

USEFUL ADDRESSES. In Istanbul: Consulates: *U.S.,* Mesrutiyet Cad. 106; and *British,* Mesrutiyet Cad. 34. Tourist Information: Mesrutiyet Cad. 57, Sultan Ahmet Square, Atatürk Airport and Hilton Hotel; *American Express,* Hilton Hotel entrance; *Wagons-Lits/Cook,* Cumhuriyet Cad. 22. *The American Hospital,* Güzelbahçe Sok., Nişantaşi. In Ankara: Embassies: *U.S.,* Atatürk Blvd. 110; *British,* Şehit Ersan Caddesi 46A, Çankaya; *Canadian,*

Nenehatun Caddesi 75, Kücükesat. Tourist Information: Gazi Mustafa Kemal Blvd. 26, Maltepe. *American Hospital,* Güniz Sok. 30, Kavaklidere.

 GETTING AROUND TURKEY. By Plane. Turkey is a large country where distances are made even greater by the mountain ranges. *Turkish Airlines (THY)* flies to all provincial capitals, 8 times daily between Istanbul and Ankara in both directions, Istanbul–Izmir 3 flights daily. Fares are low and there are reductions for married couples, students and children.

By Train. A network of 5,160 miles connects all the principal towns but leaves large stretches on both coasts unserved. Travel is slow however. From Istanbul to Ankara (360 miles), for instance, takes 9½ hours. Second class is grim, but fares are low enough to allow you to travel first class. The faster diesel trains (one class only) are the most satisfactory though they operate only during the daytime.

By Boat. All towns on the coasts can be reached by *Turkish Maritime Lines.* The Black Sea line *(Karadeniz)* sails from Istanbul to Hopa near the Russian border; the fast 6-day roundtrip in summer touches the main ports; the all-year round slow run calls in addition at the smaller ports. The Mediterranean line *(Akdeniz)* offers a good choice of cruises as well as regular services. There are numerous ferries across the Bosphorus, the Sea of Marmara and the Dardanelles.

By Car. Drive on the right. The international (green) card is valid for European Turkey (Thrace) only so that you will have to take out insurance at the border for Anatolian Turkey. Traffic in the cities is well regulated, though less so in Istanbul. In the country, trucks, bicycles, and flocks of animals act as constant hazards. Just remember that Turkey has a high accident rate.

By Bus. Private companies provide frequent and inexpensive day and night services between all towns. For a short stay, organized tours are by far the best way to see the most.

Car Hire. Companies have desks at airports and major hotels; only locally made Murats (Fiats) and Renaults available. Rates are slightly higher than in Western Europe.

Taxis. Plentiful and cheap, distinguished by a black-and-yellow checkered band round the middle. Dolmuş (shared) minibuses run along fixed routes in major towns and travel to the neighboring countryside.

Istanbul

Istanbul is Turkey's traditional gateway from the West, and the traveler in a hurry is bound to concentrate his time here. It's worth fitting a stop at Istanbul into even the tightest of schedules, because few places can offer so much impact in so little time. The Turks rightly claim that you haven't seen Turkey when you've seen Istanbul alone . . . but it's still unique.

With a population of over 5,000,000, Greater Istanbul sprawls over the northern European and Asian shores of the Sea of Marmara. Founded in 658 B.C. by a Megarian Greek named Bysas (hence the name of Byzantium) it became in A.D. 330 the capital of the Roman Empire as Constantinople (from the Roman emperor Constantine). After the Fourth Crusade in 1204 it became the seat of Latin emperors, but reverted to the Greeks before being captured in 1453 by the Turks, who gradually imposed the name of Istanbul.

All these ups and downs have left their traces on the old section of Istanbul—the walled city between the sea and the Golden Horn is still partially spared by the bulldozers of progress.

Crammed into the old city are its marvelous mosques and palaces, which rise up like a vision from the Arabian Nights. In the center of the sightseeing area stands St. Sophia, built by the Emperor Constantine in 347, destroyed by fire and then rebuilt in the sixth century by Emperor Justinian. The Turks converted the world-famous basilica into a mosque with four minarets instead of tearing it down. It's now a museum so some mosaics can again be seen, giving an idea of the former splendor. Beyond the graceful fountain of Ahmed III stands the Mosque of Sultan Ahmed, known as the Blue Mosque from the colored tilework in its interior, a fascinating lesson in abstract design. Just don the oversized slippers at the door to cover your shoes and you can enter any mosque in Istanbul.

You go back to the Romans at the partly reconstructed imperial stables, now the Museum of Mosaics. But within the Hippodrome are two imported landmarks, the Serpentine Column which came from Delphi and the Obelisk, from Egypt. Something really unusual near St. Sophia is the "sunken palace" of Istanbul, actually a cistern built almost 1450 years ago through whose 336 columns boats can row.

From here, you can go to lunch or to the Grand Bazaar, depending upon your stamina. At any rate, take a breather before visiting the old palace of the Sultans. The three vast courtyards of what is now the Topkapi Palace Museum spread over the walled town's eastern promontory jutting out into the water. The view of the Bosphorus, the Golden Horn, and Asia beyond is incomparable. The main sights are: 6th-century St. Irene, used as a concerthall for the Istanbul Art Festival; the treasury with unbelievably enormous emeralds; the harem, through which you must take a guided tour; and the pavilion housing several relics sacred to Islam. At the archaeological museum you can say "sic transit gloria" in front of the supposed sarcophagus of Alexander the Great.

You should visit the Suleymaniye Mosque built in the 16th century by Sinan, the greatest of Turkish architects. From here, you will probably return to your hotel in the new town over the Atatürk Bridge, which gives you a chance to take in the aqueduct built by Valens 1,700 years ago.

On the shores of the Bosphorus is the Dolmabahçe Palace, constructed in the 19th century, where the sultans lived after abandoning the Topkapi Palace and like the smaller Beylerbey Palace on the Asiatic shore surpassing anything that Hollywood might have dreamt up.

The Grand Bazaar

There are some four thousand tiny shops under one roof in a complex that dates back to the 16th century, although it has been partly burned down a goodly number of times since then, the 1954 reconstruction being itself severely damaged in a 1975 fire. The Grand Bazaar of Istanbul offers everything from hair curlers to TV sets, but for the visitor the fine craftwork is more important that the mass-produced junk. No matter what the price asked, you are expected to bargain— even if you find the first price reasonable. Bargaining is simply part of the game. If you don't buy, no one will be offended.

Our best advice to you is to look around and absorb the local color instead of buying in a hurry. Best buys: leather coats and jackets, copper and brass ware, rugs and embroideries, onyx jewelry, and Turkish slippers. Don't get conned into buying any so-called antiques whose provenance is not even doubtful in most cases, while the rare genuine article is not allowed to be exported. Remember that because Turkey is considered a developing country, many of the things you buy there may be exempt from U.S. Customs duties under the G.S.P. plan, as explained in the section on Customs in Facts at Your Fingertips, at the beginning of this volume.

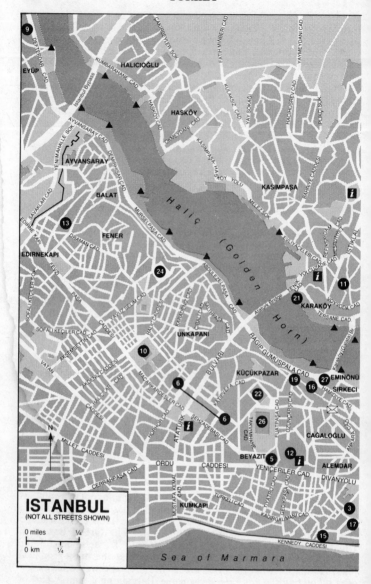

Environs of Istanbul

A good plan is to cruise along the Bosphorus. The ferryboats leave from the Galata Bridge and zigzag between Europe and Asia until they reach the Black Sea (with the Soviet Union across the water beyond the horizon). On this trip, you sail past Rumelihisar castle, under Europe's longest suspension bridge, 3,540 feet, connecting two continents, and between charming little villages serving delectable seafood.

Points of Interest

1 Archeological Museum; Museum of the Ancient Orient
2 Atatürk Museum
3 At Meydani (Hippodrome)
4 Ayasofya (St. Sophia)
5 Bayezit II Cami
6 Bozdoğan Kemeri (Aqueduct of Valens)
7 Çinili Köşk (Tiled Pavilion)
8 Dolmabahçe Palace
9 Eyüp Sultan Cami
10 Fatih Cami
11 Galata Tower
12 Kapalı Çarsı
13 Kariye Museum
14 Kız Kulesi (Tower of Leander)
15 Küçük Ayasofya (Small St. Sophia)
16 Mısır Carsısı
17 Museum of Mosaics
18 Museum of Turkish and Islamic Art
19 Rüstem Pasa Cami
20 St. Irene
21 Sokollu Mehmet Paşa Cami
22 Süleymaniye Cami
23 Sultan Ahmet Cami (Blue Mosque)
24 Sultan Selim Cami
25 Topkapı Saray
26 University
27 Yeni Cami

🄸 Tourist Information
▲ Ferry Terminal
✉ Post Office

At Sariyer, you can get a bus or a taxi back (the round trip by boat takes seven hours).

More relaxing can be done on an excursion by boat, also from Galata Bridge, to the Princes' Islands, six miles from the southern end of the Bosphorus in the Sea of Marmara. There are nine islands, but only four are inhabited. They are pleasant wooded resort spots with open-air restaurants and the easy pace of the horse-and-buggy age (no cars are allowed). The ferry takes you to Büyük Ada, the biggest of the islands with simple hotels.

PRACTICAL INFORMATION FOR ISTANBUL

GETTING AROUND ISTANBUL. By Bus. The trolley-bus service is efficient but limited. Ordinary buses are antiquated and usually overcrowded. The biggest bus terminals are on Taksim Square and at the Sirkeci Rail Station.

By Minibus. Privately owned, but barely more expensive than the buses, they run along fixed routes with frequent stops. Signposts at Taksim Square and the Sirkeci Rail Station indicate the various routes and destinations; elsewhere it is difficult to discover the route. No tipping or talking to other passengers.

By Train. Electric trains from Sirkeci Rail Station to Ataköy and Florya beaches on the Sea of Marmara.

By Boat. Terminals at both ends of the Karaköy Bridge. Car ferry from Kabatas, near the Dolmabahçe Palace, to Üsküdar.

HOTELS. You will be wise to book well in advance, especially during the summer season, but it is doubtful if private bookings will be confirmed by (M) or (I) hotels; you might try through an agency. Though most top hotels are located in the new town, mostly around Taksim Square, the most up-to-date in the two lower categories are in the old town.

New Town

Deluxe

Hilton, Cumhuriyet Cad. (tel. 1467 050). 418 rooms. Situated in ample grounds, it has a large swimming pool. There are several restaurants and the hotel houses Turkey's only casino.

Marmara Etap, Taksim (tel. 1448 850). 424 rooms. Heated swimming pool; shopping arcade.

Sheraton, Mete Cad. Taksim (tel. 1489 000). 460 rooms. Turkey's largest hotel in Istanbul's tallest building; splendid view, all amenities.

Expensive

Dedeman, Yildiz Posta Cad. (tel. 1728 800). 261 rooms, 15 suites. Pool, sauna; off-center, in residential area.

Divan, Cumhuriyet Cad. (tel. 1464 020). 98 rooms, excellent service, fine restaurant.

Etap, Mesrutiyet Cad. (tel. 1448 880). 200 rooms, pool. Centrally placed.

Macka, Eytam Cad. (tel. 1401 053). 184 rooms, away from the center.

Moderate

Bale, Refik Saydam Cad., Tepebasi (tel. 1504 912). 63 rooms, very central.

Dilson, Siraselviler Cad., Taksim (tel. 1432 032). 90 rooms.

Keban, Siraselviler Cad., Taksim (tel. 1433 310). 87 rooms, garage.

Pera Palas, Mesrutiyet Cad., Tepebasi (tel. 1452 230). 110 rooms, survivor of the opulent days of the Ottoman Empire; exceptionally good restaurant.

T.M.T., Buyukdere Cad., Gayrettepe, off center (tel. 1673 334). 103 rooms.

Inexpensive

Çiragan, Müvezzi Cad., Beşiktaş (tel. 1600 230). 64 rooms. A little far out but very pleasant.

Kavak, Mesrutiyet Cad. (tel. 1445 844). 42 rooms; central.

Opera, Inönü Cad., Taksim (tel. 1435 527). 59 rooms.

Oriental, Cihangir Cad., Taksim (tel. 1451 067). 30 rooms.

Santral, Billurcu Sok. (tel. 1454 120). 114 rooms.

Old Town

Deluxe

Yesil Ev, Sultanahmet Square (tel. 528 67 64). Converted Ottoman mansion. 20 rooms, some (E).

Moderate

Akgün, Ordu Cad., Haznedar Sok. (tel. 5280 261). 87 rooms.
Anka, Molla Gurani Cad., Findikzade (tel. 5256 002). 65 airconditioned rooms.
Kalyon, Sahilyolu (tel. 5266 250). 40 rooms; overlooks the Sea of Marmara.
Olcay, Millet Cad. (tel. 5853 220). 134 rooms, only pool in Old Town, garage; on the main thoroughfare to the airport.
Sözmen, Millet Cad. (tel. 5234 006). 74 rooms.
Toro, Koska Cad., Laleli (tel. 5280 273). 54 airconditioned rooms; close to main sightseeing area.

Inexpensive

Astor, Laleli Cad., Aksaray (tel. 5224 423). 42 rooms.
Bern, Millet Cad., Muratpasa Sok., Aksaray (tel. 5232 462). 46 rooms.
Ebru, Gazi Mustafa Kemal Bul., Aksaray (tel. 5233 119). 35 rooms.
Kilim, Millet Cad., Findikzade (tel. 5860 880). 72 rooms, restaurant.
Topkapi, Oguzhan Cad., Findikzade (tel. 5254 240). 45 rooms, restaurant.

Istanbul Environs

Cinar (E), tel. 5732 910. 201 airconditioned rooms, dinner dancing, pool, beach. Conveniently close to the airport at Yesilköy. **Tarabya** (E), Kefeliköy Cad., Tarabya (tel. 1621 000). 262 rooms, excellent food; most reasonably priced of the official deluxe class. **Ataköy Motel** (M), tel. 5720 802. 206 rooms, pool; on beach. **Demirköy** (M), tel. 5724 945. 289 rooms, pool; on same beach as Ataköy Motel. **Turban Carlton** (M), Köybasi Cad., Yeniköy (tel. 1621 020). 120 rooms; pool, beach.

 RESTAURANTS. The restaurants of the *Hilton, Marmara Etap, Sheraton* and *Divan* hotels provida a home from home for the foreign palate, but also authentic local dishes in their Turkish-style dining rooms; dinner dancing and floorshows too. Below listed are the better-known expensive and moderate spots; there are dozens of inexpensive *lokanta* serving excellent dishes, though the choice is limited.

Expensive

Abdullah, has lately not quite lived up to its reputation; on Emirgan hills halfway along the Bosphorous; seafood specialties.
Cinar, in hotel near airport, has smart open-air dinner dancing on terrace and beach-side American bar.
Galata Tower has a terrific view, so-so food; floorshow in nightclub.
Liman Lokantasi, Rihtim Cad., Karaköy, open lunch only for excellent seafood.

Moderate

Bab Kafeterya, Yeşilçam Sok. Beyoglu, central.
Bar Servis, Tünel Cad., Karaköy. Splendid view from the large terrace over the Galata Bridge.
Dört Mevsim (*Four Seasons*), Istiklal Cad. 509. Good food in pleasant surroundings.
Geçit, Yeralti Geçiti Üstü, Karaköy. Overlooking the Karaköy Bridge.
Haci Salih, Sakizagaci Sok. Beyoglu. Large and serves no alcohol.
Malta Köşkü, Yildiz Park. Stunning view of the Bosphorus.
Pandrossa, Cumhuriyet Cad., Taksim.
Restoran 1001, Siraselviler Cad., conveniently central near Taksim Square.
Sempati, Halaskargazi Cad. 27, Pangalti. Also pub and café.
Topkapi Sarayi, in the palace gardens, is a blessing to the hungry sightseer.

On the Bosphorus

The European shore of the Bosphorus is lined with excellent restaurants and nightspots. Closest to town, **Motorest** (M), Domabahçe Cad., Beşiktaş; followed by **Süreyya** (E), Bebek Cad., Arnavutköy, **Şamdan** and **Sardunya,** both (M), Nisbetiye Cad. 28 and 30, Etiler. **Balikcil, Facyo, Garaj, Kösem Bistro,**

Palet 1 and **2** and **Zarifler,** all (M), are outstanding in Tarabya. Farther away, but worth the journey, is **Canli Balik,** Mesar Burnu Cad., Sariyer.

ENTERTAINMENT. Theater. Straight plays in Turkish need the special setting of St. Irene or Rumeli Hisar Castle during the Istanbul Art Festival, June/July. Concerts, opera and ballet in the 1,300-seat Atatürk Cultural Palace on Taksim Square. Sound and Light nightly May to October in front of the Blue Mosque.

Nightlife. Turkish cabarets, even the floorshows in the luxury hotel nightclubs, are sorely disappointing, as the belly dancing is hardly more than provincial striptease. The *Gazino* and *Külüp* bear little resemblance to American casinos or clubs, but merely offer dancing of sorts. Prices are well below international levels; appropriately so.

Beside the leading hotel nightclubs and the floorshow in the Galata Tower, the leading cabarets are *Kervansaray* and *Parizien,* both (E), Cumhuriyet Cad. 30 and 18. Other western style entertainment on this main avenue are *Külüp* 33, *Regine Gazinosu* and *Yeni Hydromel,* all (M), at Nos. 18, 16 and 12. Nearby, in the Taksim garden, *Taksim Belediye* (M), and across the square, *Büyük Maksim* (E), Siraselviler 17. Popular along the Bosphorus nightspots are *Bebek Asiyan* and *Bebek Park,* both (E), at Bebek.

MUSEUMS AND PALACES. For visits to mosques, felt slippers must be worn over the shoes, or shoes must be left outside. The Topkapi Museum is closed on Tuesday, all others on Monday. Opening times around 8.30 or 9.30, closing at 5.

Archeological Museum (Greek and Roman) and **Museum of the Ancient Orient** (Mesopotamia and Hittite), below the Topkapi Palace. Opposite is the **Çinili Köşk** (Tiled Kiosk), summer residence of Mehmet the Conqueror; now the Museum of Tiles.

Atatürk Museum, Kemal Atatürk's house, unchanged, with documents charting the history of the Turkish Republic.

Beylerbeyi Sarayi, on the Asian entrance to the Bosphorus Bridge. Built in 1865, it conforms exactly to Hollywood's ideal of an Oriental palace.

Dolmabahçe Sarayi, on the European entrance to the Bosphorus. An overwhelming medley of white marble Turkish-Indian-Baroque worthy of the Arabian Nights, built by Sultan Abdul Mecit in 1853.

Kariye Museum (Church of the Holy Savior of the Chora Monastery), near the Edirne Gate. Fine Byzantine mosaics and frescos.

Museum of Aya Sofya (St. Sophia). Awe-inspiring Byzantine architecture, with traces of magnificent mosaics.

Museum of Mosaics, in the stables of the Imperial Palace. Outstanding mosaics.

Museum of Turkish and Islamic Art, in a restored palace facing the Hippodrome. Turkish religious art, illuminated Korans, prayer rugs.

Topkapi Palace Museum. The maze of the restored harem; a dazzling display of the Sultans' treasure; armor and weapons, china and earthenware, enamels and miniatures, plus some of Islam's holiest relics.

Around the Sea of Marmara

Further afield, there are daily flights or a drive shortened by a ferry crossing to Anatolian Turkey's loveliest town: Bursa, first capital of the Osmanli Turks in the 14th century when the Green Mosque and the splendid tombs of the sultans were built. Bursa is famous for its handmade carpets. 4,000 feet up Mount Uludag are several Swiss-chalet type hotels where people go in summer to escape the heat and in winter to ski.

Troy itself is disappointing. Recollections of Homer might tempt you close to the entrance of the Dardanelles by ferry to Bandirma or Çanakkale, but only an archeologist would be able to conjure up

Priam's mighty palace from the mound of rubble left by nine subsequent cities over a period of some 3,500 years.

If you are driving through Thrace from Greece, though it means a detour of 65 miles, or on the E5 from Bulgaria, don't miss Edirne (Adrianople), whose central square is framed by three particularly lovely mosques.

PRACTICAL INFORMATION FOR THE SEA OF MARMARA

BURSA. *Akdogan* (E), Murat Cad. (tel. 24 755), 118 rooms, thermal pool. *Celik Palas* (E), Cekirge Cad. (tel. 19 600), 131 rooms, thermal pool. *Acar* (M). 47 rooms. *Dilmen* (M). 88 rooms. *Gönlü Ferah* (M). 63 rooms. *Yat* (M). 47 rooms.

ÇANAKKALE. Near Troy. *Bakir* (M) 35 rooms (tel. 4088). *Truva* (M). 66 rooms (tel. 10 24). *Motel Tusan-Truva* (M). 64 rooms (tel. Intepe 14 61).

EDIRNE. *Sultan* (M), Talat Pasa Cad. (tel. 13 72), 83 rooms, 66 showers. *Kervan* (I), Talat Pasa Cad. (tel. 13 82), 48 rooms.

MOUNT ULUDAG. Near Bursa. *Panorama* (E), 98 rooms. *Uludag* (E). 127 rooms. *Iffet* (M). 44 rooms. *Oberj Fahri* (M). 65 rooms.

The Aegean and Turquoise Coasts

Along the eastern shore of the Aegean the wealth and liberality of the Hellenistic kings and Roman emperors were lavished for centuries. The most extensive ruins of Graeco-Roman antiquity, palaces, temples and theaters in magnificent settings bear mute witness to a great past.

Pergamon was the center of the cult of Aesculapius, god of medicine. In his honor, the town built the *Asklepieion,* a temple with a medical library and a theater holding 3,500 spectators, restored for the annual Theatrical Festival held in May.

In the modern town of Bergama, you will come upon the Basilica, whose red brick has given it the name of Kizilavlu (the Red Courtyard). Over the centuries it has housed a succession of religious practices, from those of the Egyptian God Serapis to those of Christ and Mohammed. Across the stream flowing by the basilica is a beautiful Roman bridge with three arches.

After the Basilica, turn to the left—by car if possible, you have two miles to go—and upwards towards the Acropolis. At the end of the road, park you car and take the path leading to the gateway or Royal Door of the town's first wall. Inside and facing you are the remains of the world-renowned library of Pergamon, which once held 200,000 books gathered in the third century B.C. These books were written on parchment, a word deriving from the Greek root, *pergamene,* meaning of Pergamon—a paper made here from sheepskin. The whole grandiose complex is fascinating and evokes memories of the Hellenistic Attalid dynasty (214–133 B.C.) and the Romans who inherited their kingdom.

Izmir

The fire of 1922 destroyed almost all of the old town, only sparing the colorful sprawl of houses on the hillside surrounding the bay. Highlights are the Agora (ancient Greek marketplace); the fortress of Kadifekale, on Mount Pagos, with its beautiful view over the bay of Izmir; and the Archeological Museum in the center of the modern town. Opposite the Clock Tower, built in the beginning of the century, it is well worth taking a look at the small mosque of Konak, with its fine glazed tiles.

For a rest from sightseeing, you might go for a swim at Inciralti, about seven miles out of town, towards the beach resort of Çeşme. A pleasant outing is to take the ferry-boat across the bay, towards Karşiyaka. Visit too the acropolis of old Smyrna, dating from the 1st century B.C., at Tepekale in the Bayrakli suburb.

Selçuk (Ephesus)

Throughout its long history, the town has been rebuilt so often and has changed so much that it has lost its very name. On arriving, you stop at a signpost—Selçuk, while the guide says, "You are in Ephesus".

Mounts Pion and Koressos, Greco-Roman remains, a Byzantine basilica, and a Seljuk mosque constitute a hodge-podge of history. The pride of the museum is two splendid marble statues of Artemis, Greek in name but unmistakably Anatolian in appearance, with a triple row of breasts and a strange assortment of monsters on the garments.

For ancient paganism as for the beginnings of Christianity, Ephesus was an important center, second only to Athens, and later, to Jerusalem. The cult of Artemis changed into the cult of the Virgin Mary, as St. Paul and St. John both preached in the town. Up to the Middle Ages, Ephesus kept its standing till the silting up of its port. The world's first bank—run on the lines of today's banks, that is—opened here. A car is essential to visit the scattered sites, which include the water-logged remains of the Temple of Artemis, one of the Seven Wonders of the World, and vast Hellenistic and Roman ruins, many laced with memories of the early Christian church.

Driving out of town, from the Manisa Gate, views over the plain of Selçuk are revealed at every turn of the mountain road to Meryemana. Here is the simple House of Mary, thought to have been the place where St. John brought the mother of Christ after the Crucifixion, and from which, some believe, the Virgin ascended to heaven. Visited by Pope Paul VI in 1967 and Pope John Paul II in 1979, the number of pilgrims is constantly increasing.

When you have done with the sightseeing, relax on the sea only 12 miles away. Kuşadasi lies in the middle of a huge landlocked gulf divided by promontories into a series of fine beaches, each provided with modern hotels. This is an ideal center for excursions not only to nearby Priene, Miletus and Didyma, but also to Bodrum, ancient Halicarnassus further south, and inland to Pamukkale, the hot springs and pools above a petrified Niagara at the ancient city of Hierapolis.

The Turquoise Coast

Few shores can rival the profusion of natural and artistic beauties found along the 400 miles from the Bay of Antalya to the Bay of Mersin.

Antalya is the queen city of this Riviera—it was a summer resort in the days of the Seljuk Turks 800 years ago—and it offers an imposing portal built for the entry of the Emperor Hadrian in A.D. 130, a grooved minaret dating back to 1230, and the Karatay Mosque of 1250. And, best of all, the spectacular view over the gulf to the wild Lycian mountains jutting into the sea beyond the miles of pebble beach (lined with fish restaurants) at Konyaalti. Eight miles east is the fine sandy beach of Lara in a semi-tropical setting of banana plantations and orange groves. Further south is Turkey's largest beach resort, Alanya. It's ideal for early or later sunshine; July and August are advisable only if you really like heat.

When you get tired of sunning and swimming, there is plenty to see. Near Antalya lie the vast ancient ruins of Perge. The best-preserved amphitheater of the ancient world (seating capacity 15,000, still used for performances of classical tragedies during the annual late summer Festival) is at Aspendos, 31 miles to the east. There's an even bigger amphitheater at Side, 19 miles on. To the west an excellent road hugs the gulf and continues by the open sea all the 94 spectacular miles to Demre, the Myra of old, where you can see the church and the sarcophagus of the fourth-century Saint Nicholas, Bishop of Myra, who later became known as Santa Claus.

To the east, the 800 foot cliff at Alanya is crowned by an enormous fortress, its outer wall five miles in circumference.

Adana, Turkey's fourth city, lies on the Seyhan River 25 miles inland, in the middle of a fertile plain of cotton fields and orange groves. At the head of the southernmost gulf lies Iskenderun (Alexandretta), a busy port and industrial center as well as a banana-growing region.

Thirty-five miles south is Antakya, the ancient Antioch, where the followers of Jesus were first called Christians in the grotto of St. Peter. The town was founded in 301 B.C. and the first Christian church was established here. The Archeological Museum contains a collection of magnificent Roman mosaics, but the huge medieval fortifications on the mountain top are crumbling away.

PRACTICAL INFORMATION FOR THE AEGEAN AND TURQUOISE COASTS

ADANA. *Büyük Sürmeli* (E), Özler Cad. 170 rooms (tel. 21 944). *Divan* (E), Inönü Cad. 116 rooms (tel. 22 701). *Ipek Palas* (M), Inönü Cad., 84 rooms (tel. 18 743). *Koza* (M), Özler Cad., 66 rooms (tel. 18 853). All airconditioned.

ALANYA. Turkey's largest beach resort. *Alantur* (E), directly on the beach, 145 rooms, pool. *Alaadin* (M), 108 rooms. *Banana* (M), 142 rooms, pool. *Büyük* (M), 64 rooms. At Incekum beach to the west, three (M) motels: *Aspendos,* 83 rooms, pool; *Incekum,* 82 rooms; *Yalihan,* 50 rooms.

ANTAKYA. *Atahan* (M). 28 rooms. *De Liban* (M), 29 rooms. *Hidro* (M), 16 rooms. In the cooler Harbige suburb. *Divan* (I), 25 rooms.

ANTALYA. *Talya* (E). 150 airconditioned rooms. On a cliff above the beach; pool, sauna, disco. *Turban Adalya* (E), 28 airconditioned rooms in converted old mansion in restored port area. *Bilgehan* (M). 88 airconditioned rooms. *Büyük* (M). 42 rooms. *Tatoglu* (I). 36 rooms.

AYVALIK. Attractive village on the coast. *Büyük Berk* (M). 97 rooms. *Murat Reis* (M). 87 rooms and a pool. *Ankara* (I). 57 rooms.

BERGAMA. The site of ancient Pergamon. *Tusan Motel* (M). 2 miles from the town. 42 rooms. *Afacan Motel* (I). 16 rooms.

ÇEŞME. Seaside resort 53 miles west of Izmir. *Golden Dolphin* (E). 515 rooms; all sports facilities. *Turban Çeşme* (M). 216 rooms, thermal pool, large pool, fine beach, disco. *Ertan* (I). 60 rooms.

EDREMIT. Beach resort. *Çavuşoğlu* (M). 76 rooms, pool. *Akçam* (I). 33 rooms. *Aşiyan* (I). 45 rooms. *Beyaz Saray* (I). 26 rooms. *Öge* (I). 66 rooms.

EPHESUS (EFES). *Tusan* (M). 12 rooms, near the ruins. *Aksoy* (I). 21 rooms.

GÜMÜLDÜR. *Sultan* (M). 110 rooms. A motel on a good beach.

ISKENDERUM. *Hatayli* (M). 60 airconditioned rooms. *Hitit* (I). 40 rooms. *Mari Yali Motel* (I). 30 rooms. 7 miles out of town on a beach.

IZMIR. *Büyük Efes* (E), Cumhuriyet Mey. (tel. 144300). 296 rooms, 24 suites. Roof restaurants, nightclubs and pool. *Etap* (E), Cumhuriyet Bul. (tel. 144290). 128 rooms. *Izmir Palas* (E), Atatürk Bul. (tel. 215583). 148 rooms.

Anba (M), Cumhuriyet Bul. (tel. 144 380). 53 rooms. *Karaca* (M), 1379 Sok. (tel. 144445). 68 rooms. *Kilim* (M), Atatürk Bul. (tel. 145340). 88 rooms. *Kismet* (M), 1377 Sok. (tel. 217050). 68 rooms. *Babadan* (I), Gaziosman Paşa Bul. (tel. 139 640). 37 rooms. *Kaya* (I), Gaziosman Paşa Bul. (tel. 139771). 52 rooms.

Restaurants. In the Kültürpark, where the *Mediterranean Festival*, 10 days of folklore, is held in June, and the annual *Industrial Fair* in Aug./Sept., the *Golf* and *Park*, both (E), are complemented by four nightclubs: *Kübana* (E), *Ada, Göl*, and *Mogambo*, all (M). *Cafe Plaza* (E), Mustafa Bey Cad., serves international food. Among the several seafood restaurants along the waterfront, *Bergama, Deniz, Imbat* and *Palet*, all (M). *Sato* (E), located in the hills, has both good food and an excellent view.

KUŞADASI. *Imbat* (E). 140 rooms, pool. *Tusan* (E). 70 rooms, on a private beach; pool. *Akdeniz* (M). 181 rooms. *Kismet* (M). 65 rooms. *Marti* (M). 59 rooms, beach. *Ömer* (M). 109 rooms; on the beach. *Kustur Tatil Köyü* (I). 400 tiny bungalows in a holiday village.

MARMARIS. An attractive fishing village with a good beach. *Lydia* (M). 220 rooms in a self-contained complex. *Atlantik* (M), 40 rooms; *Marmaris* (I), 63 rooms. Both on the seafront. *Marti Tatil Köyü* (E), 213 rooms; *Turban Marmaris Tatil Köyü* (M), 246 bungalows. Both holiday villages on good beach.

MERSIN. *Mersin* (E). 105 airconditioned rooms, bay views. *Atlihan* (M), 93 airconditioned rooms. *Türkmen* (M). 54 rooms, pool. *Toros* (M). 62 rooms.

SIDE. *Defne* (E). 90 airconditioned rooms, pool, beach, tennis. *Cennet* (M), 63 rooms. *Turtel* (M), 66 rooms, above average. *Tusan Akdeniz* (M), 40 rooms; situated on a lonely beach.

Ankara

From a typical Anatolian town of 75,000 inhabitants, Ankara has grown since 1923 into a modern, westernized capital with a population of over three million. Atatürk called in leading European town planners, swamps were drained, malaria vanished, huge government buildings were raised and wide, airy boulevards and parks were laid out. Spreading out over a ring of hills commanding the Anatolian plateau, Ankara is still expanding.

The most imposing structure in Ankara is the Atatürk Mausoleum, a vast soaring hall surrounded by colonnades. But the citadel of old Angora still stands, too, with its inner fortress and its white tower. At this crossroads of history, there are the Temple of Augustus, Roman baths and an aqueduct, the Alâeddin and Aslahane mosques, a model farm founded by Atatürk, the National Opera House and the Turkish National Theater. And last, but not least. the Museum of Anatolian Civilizations adroitly housed in a former *bedesten* (bazaar), where you can admire the most important collection of Hittite art in existence. If you want to know more about these mysterious people and their civilization, take a day-excursion to Bogazkale and Yazilikaya, where the quotations from the ancient testament concerning the Hittites will spring to life.

Cappadocia

Ankara can be your base for excursions into Anatolia, notably to
Göreme (center of Cappadocia), Kayseri and Konya.

The Göreme valley is easily accessible, a site unparalled on earth
with its fairy chimneys and honeycombed rocks. This was once a
monastic center with 365 churches. You can see rupestral "houses"
(dwellings of three and four stories, sometimes higher). Nearly all the
churches have frescos, the most important lately restored, depicting an
endless series of biblical scenes, painted in a rather simple, childlike
way. Tokali Kilise is the largest of the churches, the Karanlik (Dark)
Kilise needs a flashlight, and the newest (13th century) frescos are in
the Elmali Kilise.

Four miles west of Ürgüp, from whose hotel windows you look
straight into the cataclysmic landscape, the gigantic rocky needle of
Ortahisar thrusts up, bearing a citadel hewn out of its sugarloaf point,
which you may climb to the railed-in top, though the cave-dwellers
have been removed to ordinary houses on the safer ground below. At
Uchisar a serrated escarpment pitted with crumbling dwellings dominates the horizon. It is an extraordinary setting—the village is still
inhabited, and if picturesqueness is what you're after, this is it—plus
a magnificent view from the citadel out over the countryside.

To complete this visit, don't miss the underground cities, where the
ingenuity of persecuted men created in the 8th century an underworld
with ominous overtones of the shape of things to come. Eight spacious
floors, each offering accommodation for 200 people, were carved into
the bowels of the earth. At Kaymakli, 7 miles south of Nevşehir, a
central airshaft assures perfect ventilation all the 250 feet down to the
bottom, from which a tunnel runs 6 miles south to another self-contained city at Derinkuyu.

Kayseri, the ancient Caesarea, is a 40 minute flight or a 200-mile
drive from Ankara and lies at an altitude of 3,270 feet. It offers remains
of the civilization of the Seljuk Turks, including the Great Mosque of
1136.

Konya lies 160 miles from Ankara. The monastery round the tomb
of the founder of the Whirling Dervishes is now a religious museum.
The 13th-century Karatay Medrese is a ceramics museum; and the Ince
Minaret Medrese, with its superb portal, is a museum of stone and
wood carvings.

PRACTICAL INFORMATION FOR ANKARA AND CAPPADOCIA

ANKARA. *Büyük Ankara* (L), Atatürk Bul. (tel. 344925). 180 rooms, 14
suites, 3 restaurants, nightclub, pool. *Dedeman* (E), Büklüm Sok. (tel. 344980).
252 rooms. *Kent* (E), Mihat Pasa Cad. (tel. 312111). 120 rooms. *Etap Mola* (E),
Izmir Cad. (tel. 339065). 57 rooms. All airconditioned.

Altinisik (M), Necatibey Cad. (tel. 291185). 55 rooms. *Apaydin* (M), Bayindir
Sok. (tel 333135). 50 airconditioned rooms. *Bulvar Palas* (M), Atatürk Bul. (tel.
342180). 170 rooms, good restaurant. *Keykan* (M), Fevzi Çakmak Sok. (tel.
302195). 50 rooms. *Stad* (M), Baruthane Meyd., Ulus (tel. 124220). 217 rooms.
Sultan (M), Bayindir Sok. (tel. 315980). 40 rooms.

Anit (I), Gazi Mustafa Bul. (tel. 292385). 91 rooms, sauna. *Ergen* (I), Ka-
ranfil. Sok. (tel. 344622). 52 rooms. *Hanecioglu* (I), Ulucanlar Cad. (tel.
202572). 54 rooms. *Yeni* (I), Sanayi Cad., Ulus (tel. 243220). 66 rooms.

Restaurants. The hotel restaurants are as good as any. *Altinnal, Bizon* and
Panorama, all in Çankaya Cad., Çankaya, are top. The two Chinese establishments, *China Town,* Köroglu Sok., Gazi Osman Paşa, and *Çin,* Portakal Cicegi
Sok., are popular. *Kristal,* Bayindir Sok., Kizilay, specializes in seafood. *R. V.*
is good for international dishes. All (E).

Anadolu Çiçek Pasaji, Izmir Cad., *Damla,* Yüksel Cad., Kizilay, *Hülya,* Hoşdere Cad., Çankaya, and *Kral Çiftligi,* Tunali Himli Cad., Kavaklidere, are more oriental oriented. *Liman Lokantasi,* Izmir Cad., Kizilay. All (M).

Patisserie Tuna, Atatürk Bul; *Piknik Club,* Tuna Cad., Kizilay; *Pizza Pino,* Tunali Hilmi Cad., and *Yakamoz,* Bayindir Sok, Kizilay, are all (I).

AVANOS. *Venessa* (M). 72 comfortable rooms.

KAYSERI. *Hattat* (M). 67 rooms. *Turan* (I). 70 rooms.

KONYA. *Özkaymak Park* (M), Otogar Cad. (tel. 33770). 90 rooms. *Yeni Sema* (M), Meram Yolu (tel. 13279). 30 rooms. *Konya* (I), Mevlana Alani (tel. 21003). 29 rooms, sauna.

NEVŞEHIR. *Göreme* (M). 72 rooms. *Orsan Kapadokya* (M). 80 rooms, pool. *Làle* (I). 21 rooms. *Viva* (I). 24 rooms.

ORTAHISAR. *Motel Paris* (M). 24 rooms. Pool.

UÇHISAR. *Kaya* (M). 60 rooms, pool; superb view over the valley; part of the Club Med.

ÜRGÜP. *Büyük* (M). 54 rooms. *Tepe* (M). 36 rooms. *Turban Motel* (M). 160 small apartments in bungalows; pool.

YUGOSLAVIA

In every sense, Yugoslavia is a country of fantastic variety. Its scenery varies from rich Alpine valleys, superbly fertile vast plains, and rolling green hills to bare, rocky, lowering gorges up to 3,000 feet deep, forests where you can still shoot bears and wolves, and huge expanses of gaunt limestone mountains dropping suddenly down to the coast, where a thousand-odd islands betray the summits of submerged mountain ranges.

The climate varies enormously with altitude and location. You can swelter on the coast in late October while snow lies a foot deep ten miles inland, on the nearest mountains' further slopes. Politically, Yugoslavia is Communist—or so Yugoslavs say. Yet it retains many incentives for the characteristically independent initiative that made possible the remarkable recovery from the destruction of World War II, a recovery aided enormously by Yugoslavia's early stand against influence of its affairs by the Soviet Union. Considerable economic success in the '60s and early '70s provided clear evidence of the value of this independence from the Soviet bloc.

The Country and the People

As the Turks were gradually driven out of much of the country in the 19th century, the map of Yugoslavia began to change. There emerged the independent kingdoms of Serbia and Montenegro. Bosnia-Hercegovina was transferred to the administration of Austro-Hungary in 1878. Macedonia remained under Turkish domination until the Balkan Wars of 1912/13. Slovenia in the northwest and Croatia, including the entire Dalmatian coast, stayed under Austro-Hungarian rule. This accounts for the difficulty in shaping such disparate parts into an entity. When the Kingdom of Yugoslavia was formed in 1918, rivalries between the formerly independent components remained acute. The complexity of the situation persists even today, with 22½ million people, descended from five main and many minor nationalities, dispersed among six republics in an area of 98,725 square miles. Although Yugoslavia's main language is Serbo-Croat, there are two other major ones (Slovenian and Macedonian). There are also two alphabets (Roman and Cyrillic) and three major religions (Orthodox, Catholic and Moslem). In fact, there is unity only in the people's independent spirit.

In the Second World War a fifth of the country's entire population was killed fighting—but one-third of the dead fell at the hands of fellow-Yugoslavs. Marshal Tito, commander of the victorious Partisan army, granted autonomy to each major ethnic group after the war. So modern Yugoslavia is a federation made up of six independent republics: Serbia, Slovenia, Croatia, Bosnia-Hercegovina, Macedonia, and Montenegro, with two autonomous regions, the Vojvodina and Kosovo, inside Serbia. Under the federal government in Belgrade, decentralization of political and economic power has continued. Legislation is controlled as much by chambers representing trades and professions as by politicians, and all representatives are subject to recall by electors.

A major characteristic of the Yugoslav system is workers' self-management, by which most enterprises are run by the people who work for them. This gives rise to an unexpected degree of competition, since rival organizations operate bus services, hotels, travel agencies, shops, etc. in opposition to each other in any given area.

But rampant inflation, low productivity, rising unemployment and a huge trade deficit are a source of great concern in the post-Tito era. Now strong measures to reduce inflation, rationalize imports and control investments have been introduced to reverse the situation. The nation is being asked to tighten its belt and roll up its sleeves, a need recognized by most Yugoslavs.

PRACTICAL INFORMATION FOR YUGOSLAVIA

WHAT WILL IT COST. The rate of inflation is currently very high, so all prices quoted here may well have doubled by the summer of 1987. However, the rate of exchange will reflect such changes and, for the Western visitor, Yugoslavia remains a good bargain. You can make major economies by traveling out of season when hotel prices are cheaper. In a major tourist area such as Dubrovnik, for example, the cheaper rooms in a hotel may be double in price during July, August and September, and the more expensive rooms will go up by between 30 and 50%. Transportation is cheap, and you can eat well at modest prices away from the obvious tourist haunts.

The monetary unit is the *dinar* divided into 100 *paras.* The rate of exchange at the time of writing is 350 dinars to the US dollar and 450 dinars to the pound sterling, but this is constantly changing, so only exchange sums to meet your immediate needs. Dinar checks, which can be purchased from many outlets in Yugoslavia and used as money, give a small discount on accommodations, meals, and some goods and services. Only unused dinar checks, not dinars, can be re-exchanged on leaving the country.

A typical day might cost two people:

Hotel (moderate) with breakfast, tax and service charges included	6000 D
Lunch (moderate restaurant) with wine	2500
Local bus/tram (2 trips each)	200
Light refreshment	1200
Theater	600
Dinner (set menu at a hotel) with wine	3500
Miscellaneous 10%	1000
	15,000 D

SOURCES OF INFORMATION. For information on all aspects of travel to Yugoslavia, the Yugoslav National Tourist Office is an invaluable source of information. Their addresses are:

In the U.S.: 630 Fifth Ave., Rockefeller Center, Suite 210, New York, N.Y. 10111 (tel. 212-757 2801).

In the U.K.: 143 Regent St., London W.1 (tel. 01–734 5243).

WHEN TO COME. July and August are the most popular months for holidays along the coast. They are also the hottest and the most crowded. Bathing is possible on the coast from May to early October. Winters are pleasant, though the sky may be overcast up to about May. Summers can be very hot indeed inland, unless you contrive to spend part of your time up in the mountains. Spring and fall are decidedly the best times for the interior. Winters there can be extremely cold. Winter sports in the mountain regions last from November through to May.

Climate. Winter temperatures on Dalmatian coast are higher than those of French and Italian Rivieras. Spring and summer delightful. Inland can be torrid in summer and very cold in winter.

Average afternoon temperatures in Fahrenheit and centigrade:

Belgrade	Jan.	Feb.	Mar.	Apr.	May	June	July	Aug.	Sept.	Oct.	Nov.	Dec.
F°	37	41	53	64	74	79	84	83	76	65	52	40
C°	3	5	12	18	23	26	29	28	24	18	11	4

Dubrovnik												
F°	50	52	58	63	70	76	80	79	75	69	60	52
C°	10	11	14	17	21	24	27	26	24	21	16	11

SPECIAL EVENTS. Among a crowded calendar of events, some of the major festivals held each year are: *May,* Peasant Wedding folklore event, Plitvice; *June,* Festival of traditional songs in several centers on Istrian and Croatian Littoral; *June-Aug./Sept.,* summer festivals in many centers, notably Belgrade, Ljubljana, Ohrid, Sibenik, Split, Zagreb, Opatija; *July,* Festival of Yugoslav Folk Music in Ilidza, Galicnik Wedding folklore event, International Review of Original Folklore in Zagreb, (27th) Moreska Sword Dance in Korcula (main performance but also held at other times), Peasant Wedding folklore event in Bohinj; Festival of Yugoslav Films in Pula; *July 10-August 25,* Dubrovnik Summer Festival, Yugoslavia's main cultural event; *August,* Sinj Equestrian tournament; *September,* Belgrade International Theater Festival; Festival of Yugoslav Folk songs, Ilidza; *October,* Belgrade festival of music; *October-December,* concert and theater season in all main cities.

National Holidays. Jan. 1 (New Year's Day); Jan. 2; May 1 (Labor Day); May 2; Jul. 4 (Veterans); Nov. 29, 30 (Republic). In addition, in *Serbia:* Jul. 7; in *Macedonia:* Aug. 2, Oct. 11; in *Montenegro:* Jul. 13; in *Slovenia:* Jul. 22, 23; and in *Croatia* and *Bosnia-Hercegovina:* Jul. 27.

VISAS. Nationals of the U.S., Canada, Australia and New Zealand all require visas to enter Yugoslavia, available free at any frontier post or airport. Nationals of Great Britain and the other EEC countries do not require visas. All visitors must have a valid passport.

HEALTH CERTIFICATES. Not required for entry into Yugoslavia from any country.

GETTING TO YUGOSLAVIA. By Plane. There are flights by *JAT* (Yugoslav Airlines) from New York and Chicago to Belgrade, Ljubljana and Zagreb. In addition, there are services from many European cities to Belgrade with some flights also serving Zagreb. In summer there are additional services to holiday areas such as Pula, Split, Dubrovnik and Ljubljana.

By Train. There are several express trains from Western Europe to Yugoslavia with through trains (or through carriages) from places as far away as Hamburg, Zurich and Brussels. Some expresses go to Belgrade (via Munich, Salzburg, and Zagreb), others to Split. From the U.K. a good route is on the *Tauern Express.* This leaves London (Victoria) around 1.40 P.M. and travels via Dover to Ostend, thence Munich, Salzburg and Zagreb where it arrives the following evening. In addition, there are express trains from Milan to Yugoslavia via Venice.

By Bus. Some privately operated bus routes from Western Europe (including the U.K.) to Greece may take passengers to Yugoslavia, but be sure they are properly licensed. There is no *Europabus* service to Yugoslavia.

CUSTOMS. Travelers over the age of 16 may import 200 cigarettes or 50 cigars or 250 gr. of tobacco; 1 liter of spirits; ¼ liter of eau de cologne and a reasonable quantity of perfume. Items such as sporting or camping equipment, camera, tape recorder, portable radio, etc., may also be brought in on verbal declaration.

HOTELS. Hotel prices are low for Mediterranean countries. On the other hand, accommodations, service and food standards especially are not strictly comparable with similar categories in Western European countries. Though hotels are officially classified Deluxe, A, B, C, these are not always indicative of prices; for example you will get a higher-category hotel in inland centers and less popular resorts for the same price as a lower category one in better known places. Likewise, standards of service and maintenance in the less affluent inland areas of the center and south of the country do not compare with those of the north and the coast. Our grading system is therefore indicative of prices; a free list of hotels available from the Yugoslav National Tourist Office gives the facilities of each establishment. All prices are for 2 people in a double room. Deluxe (L) $80–130, Expensive (E) $45–80, Moderate (M) $30–50, Inexpensive (I) $20–35. These prices are for the high season. Many hotels grant up to 50% reduction during the off season, many others close altogether in winter. Unless you are prepared to take pot luck, book as far ahead as possible if you are visiting the coast at the height of the summer.

Guesthouses, particularly prevalent in Slovenia and Croatia, offer good value. Farmhouse accommodations are now available in Slovenia, and self-catering apartments and bungalows are increasing in popular coastal areas. Private accommodations are well organized throughout the country and priced very reasonably. Local tourist offices provide information.

HOSTELS. Student hostels, without age restrictions, are very low-priced in all main cities and towns (summer only). Tourist offices can advise. There are also youth hostels, including some excellent international youth centers (age group 16–31 years), such as at Rovinj, Becici and Dubrovnik.

CAMPING. Sites are numerous in all tourist areas and growing in number elsewhere. A list is available from the Yugoslav National Tourist Office, indicating the facilities available at each.

RESTAURANTS. If you use the restaurants frequented by tourists, whether in hotels or in restaurants proper, you can expect to pay 500–2000 dinars, depending on category for a 3-course meal without drinks, less for a fixed-price meal. We have graded the restaurants expensive (E) 1500–2000 dinars, moderate (M) 800–1500 dinars, and inexpensive (I) from 500–800 dinars.

Food and Drink. Yugoslav cooking shows considerable regional differences. Bosnian and Macedonian dishes have the greatest Turkish influence; Slovenian ones have similarities with those of neighboring Austria. Along the Dalmatian coast there is a distinctly Mediterranean flavor. On the whole, meat specialties are better prepared than fish. Here are a few national favorites: *piktije,* jellied pork or duck; *prsut,* smoked ham; *cevapcici,* charcoal-grilled minced meat, and *raznjici,* skewered meat; *sarma* or *japrak,* vine or cabbage leaves stuffed with meat and rice; *Bosanski lonac,* an excellent Bosnian meat and vegetable hot-pot. Desserts are heavy and sweet: *strukli,* nuts and plums stuffed into cheese balls, then boiled; *lokum,* Turkish delight, and *alva,* nuts crushed in honey, are very sweet indeed.

This is a great wine-growing country and wine flows cheaply everywhere. Slovenia's wines are best known: *Ljutomer, Traminer* and *Riesling.* Red Dalmatian wines, such as *Dingac* and *Plavac,* are excellent, as is the white *Vugava* grown on Vis. Potent *slivovica* (slivovitz) plum brandy is the national liquor, and *maraskino,* made of morello cherries, the tastiest liqueur.

TIPPING. Generally expected, about 10% in hotels, restaurants and for taxi drivers.

MAIL. Airmail letters to the U.S. and Canada cost 110 dinars up to 20 grams; to the U.K. 80 dinars up to 20 grams. Postcards to the U.S. 60 dinars, to the U.K. 55 dinars. But check before mailing.

CLOSING TIMES. Business hours in Yugoslavia vary from season to season and from region to region. But in Belgrade business hours are as follows: banks 8 to 2; stores 8 to 12 and 4 to 8, though quite a few are now non-stop; restaurants 7 A.M. to midnight; cafes 6 A.M. to 11 P.M. (later for those with music); cinemas 3 P.M. to 11 P.M. and from 10 A.M. on Sundays.

USEFUL ADDRESSES. *Embassies:* American, Kneza Milosa 50, British, Generala Zdanova 46, Canadian, Proleterskih Brigada 69, all Belgrade. *Consulates:* American, Brace Kavurica 2, British, Ilica 12, both Zagreb. *Tourist Association of Yugoslavia,* Mose Pijade 8, Belgrade. Every town and main resort has a tourist information center or bureau. There are also several major Yugoslav travel agencies with offices in many towns and resorts; their services include excursions and various special-interest activities.

GETTING AROUND YUGOSLAVIA. By Plane. *JAT* (Yugoslav Airlines), plus one or two other lines owned by corporations within some of the Yugoslav republics, operate an extensive network of domestic air services that link over 20 cities and towns. Flights are frequently booked to capacity, so reserve well ahead.

By Train. With a substantial section of its network now electrified and with the promise of more electrification to come, *Yugoslav Railways* provide an inexpensive if generally rather crowded method of travel around the country. Trains are classed as *Ekspresni* (Express), *Poslovni* (rapid), *Brzni* (fast) and *Putnicki* (slow). Supplementary fares are charged for the first two, unless your tickets were purchased outside the country. Buffet cars are carried on a number of express trains, but always make a point of checking this. Sleeping cars and couchettes are carried on the principal overnight routes.

By Bus. A comprehensive bus network covers the country, and main routes are serviced by modern, comfortable express buses. They can, however, be crowded, especially during public holidays, so get your ticket in advance and arrive early. In remoter areas or on slower services, buses may well be of rather venerable vintage and some of the roads may be less than smooth. But it's a good way to see the countryside and meet the people—and the fares are low.

By Car. No international documents are required for the entry of your car: its registration certificate and your home driving permit are sufficient. Drive on the right hand side of the road. Third party insurance is compulsory; those without must obtain it at frontier posts. Visitors can buy gasoline coupons in hard currency abroad or at border points, and these entitle you to 5% more fuel at all gasoline stations than the value indicated on the coupons; otherwise gasoline can be purchased in dinars from all the normal outlets.

All main roads are surfaced, but the two principal highways, the *autoput* from Austria via Ljubljana to Zagreb, Belgrade and Nis, as well as the scenically magnificent Adriatic coastal road the *jadranska magistrala* from the Italian border to the frontier of Albania, are narrow and overcrowded except for stretches of toll motorway. The latter are gradually being extended and are indicated on the annually revised map available at Yugoslav National Tourist Offices. In case of emergency, dial 987 throughout the country.

Slovenia

Set in Yugoslavia's northwest corner, against Italian and Austrian frontiers, Slovenia is the part of Yugoslavia seen first by most visitors entering the country by road or rail. The north is a continuation of Austria's Alpine region, while rolling hill country begins south of the Julian Alps, and extends to a tiny section of the large Istrian Peninsula's coast south of the Italian border near Trieste.

The thickly-wooded Alpine regions contain many charming lakes, notably Lake Bled, with its 11th-century castle, romantic island, splendid golf course, and fine modern hotels, and Lake Bohinj, quieter and higher. In the southern inland area are the Postojna Caves, Europe's most striking series of vast interconnected underground caverns. Also worth visiting is Lipica where the famous stud for Lippizaner horses, founded 400 years ago, was re-established some years ago. Riding is available. As you approach Slovenia's short section of coast, the vegetation changes abruptly to vines, olives and figs and the climate becomes wholly Mediterranean. Here sophisticated, old-established Portoroz rubs shoulders with the newer coast resorts of Koper and Piran, based on old fishing ports. All, however, have many modern hotels and all the facilities that tourists expect.

Ljubljana, Slovenia's capital, is built around its hilltop castle. The city offers fine museums and baroque churches. Its summer festival, with open-air performances of opera and ballet, is well worth a visit. So is the autumn Wine Fair, when anyone can sample, without charge, hundreds of varieties of Yugoslav wines. From here you can visit Ptuj and Celje, the latter with discoveries of Roman art treasures. Maribor, near the Austrian border, is the main center for the Pohorje mountains.

Slovenia is Yugoslavia's best-known winter sports area, largely because the resorts are easily accessible. There are ski lifts at Kranjska Gora to the best slopes of the Vitranc Mountains and lifts at Bohinj to the vast terrain of the Vogel Plateau. The Pokljuka region provides perfect conditions for beginners. In the Pohorje the ground is even easier—and the prices reasonable. In summer, climbing and walking attract visitors to the same mountains. For kayak enthusiasts Slovenia offers splendid descents from Dravograd to Maribor on the Drava or from Zuzemberk on the Krka River. All forms of water sports are practiced on the coast.

PRACTICAL INFORMATION FOR SLOVENIA

Hotels and Restaurants

BLED. Delightful lake-side resort in Julian Alps. *Golf* (E), 150 rooms. Modern, central, with pool, saunas. *Grand Hotel Toplice* (E), 121 rooms. Grand old-style hotel by lake, pool, keep-fit facilities. *Park* (E), 186 rooms. Modern, near lake, pool, disco. *Jelovica* (M), 146 rooms. Short stroll from lake shore. *Kompas* (M), 92 rooms. *Krim* (M), 99 rooms. On main street.

BOHINJ. Near Bled, but much quieter. *Bellevue* (M). On slopes above lake. *Jezero* (M), 31 rooms, renovated. Near small shopping center. *Pod Voglom* (M), 28 rooms, few baths, quiet position near lake. *Zlatorog* (M), 43 rooms. At far end of lake on the shore, pool.

KOPER. Picturesque seaside resort and port. *Triglav* (E), 80 rooms, terrace overlooking sea; *Zusterna* (E), 154 rooms, pool. Shore-side across the bay.

KRANJSKA GORA. Summer mountain resort and winter sports center. *Kompas* (E), 155 rooms, pool; *Alpina* (M), 101 rooms; *Larix* (M), 130 rooms, pool; *Lek* (M), 75 rooms, pool; *Prisank* (M), 64 rooms.

LIPICA. Famous Lippizaner stud farm and riding center. *Lipica* (M), 102 rooms. *Maestoso* (M), 84 rooms, pool.

LJUBLJANA. Pleasant capital of Slovenia. *Holiday Inn* (L), Miklosiceva 3 (tel. 211434), 132 airconditioned rooms, pool, central; *Lev* (E), Vosnjakova 1 (tel. 310555), 209 airconditioned rooms, near Tivoli Park and a little less central; *Slon* (M), Titova 10 (tel. 211232), 185 rooms, those overlooking main street not recommended for light sleepers; *Union* (M), Miklosiceva 1 (tel. 212133), 270 rooms; *Ilirja* (I), Trg prekomorskih brigad 4 (tel. 551245), 136 rooms; *Turist* (I), Dalmatinova 13 (tel. 322043), 192 rooms. Also a good selection of inns and guest houses.

Restaurants. *Emonska klet* (M), Plecnikov trg. Cellar restaurant with music; *Macek* (M), Cankarjevo nbr. 15. Fish restaurant, near river in old town; *Maxim* (M), Trg. revolucije 1, traditional style with music; *Na Brinju* (M), Vodovodna 4, excellent food, small summer garden; *Pod Velbom* (M), Breg 18–20; near river, in old town; part of Hotel and Catering School, Slovene specialties.

MARIBOR. Main gateway to the Pohorje mountains. *Habakuk* (M), 40 rooms; *Orel* (M), 150 rooms; *Turist* (M), 133 rooms.

PORTOROZ. Long-established seaside resort. The following all have pools: *Grand Hotel Emona* (E), 254 rooms; *Grand Hotel Metropol* (E), 104 rooms; *Grand Hotel Palace* (E), 207 rooms; *Palace* (M), 165 rooms; *Mirna* (M), 89 rooms; *Neptun* (M), 89 rooms; *Riviera* (M), 204 rooms.

POSTOJNA. Site of some of Europe's most spectacular caves. Both (M) are *Jama,* 143 rooms, *Kras,* 54 rooms. *Sport* (I), 24 rooms.

Sights and Museums

LJUBLJANA. The Castle mainly 15th- to 16th-century, offering splendid views; Krizanke, a 16th-century monastery complex on earlier foundations, adapted in the 1930s for the Ljubljana Festival; many fine baroque buildings rebuilt in medieval Old Ljubljana at the foot of Castle Hill, with Mestni trg (square) as the focal point, dominated by the elaborate Town Hall.

Croatia (excluding Dalmatia)

The rich rolling farmlands of the Zagorje lie to the north of Zagreb. South of Zagreb an upland region, the Gorski Kotar, leads into the still remote Lika, separated from the sea by the gaunt 50-mile-long, 5,000-foot-high Velebit Range. Almost all Istria's coastline as well as the 600 miles of the Croatian Littoral and Dalmatia, the narrow beautiful coastal strip and its hundreds of islands extending all the way to south of Dubrovnik, belong to Croatia, with the exception of the Bosnian port of Kardeljevo.

In Istria, the 400 years of Venetian rule are evident in most coastal towns and villages, while the succeeding century of Austrian dominion shows clearly in the main coastal resort of Opatija. Tourist complexes (villas, chalets, hotels, bars, restaurants, campsites and trailer parks, beaches, etc.) have grown up around many previously tiny villages. Being so accessible, this part of the coast is extremely popular. Its beaches are safe for children and good underwater fishing can be had, as along all Yugoslavia's coast (but check local regulations first).

The lovely islands of Krk and Losinj are well-provided with accommodation. Beautiful Rab, a popular holiday spot for generations, can boast in its capital (of the same name) one of Yugoslavia's loveliest Venetian towns.

Zagreb, the capital, on the fringe of a fertile plain, is the capital of Croatia and rivals Belgrade in artistic achievements. It is largely central European in appearance due to the fact that during the historical see-saw of past centuries, Croatia formed an autonomous part of Austria and, later, of Hungary. Perched on the summit of a hill lies the old town, known as Gornji Grad; its patrician palaces are dominated by St. Mark's Church. On the outskirts of Zagreb is a cable-car which carries you up to Mount Sljeme, and beyond it there is the whole of the lovely Zagorje region with its old castles and churches, spas and quaint villages, in an unspoiled rural setting. Tito's childhood home at the village of Kumrovec is now a museum.

The most popular inland resort in Croatia is Plitvice, with its 16 lakes lying like terraces, one higher than the other, one of nature's wonders.

Dalmatia is dealt with in the next section.

PRACTICAL INFORMATION FOR CROATIA

Hotels and Restaurants

CRES. On island of the same name in the Gulf of Kvarner. *Kimen* (M). 226 rooms, by beach about a mile from town.

KRK. This island has an international airport and is connected to the mainland by a bridge. *Haludovo* (E), near Malinska. A fine complex with villas and apartments as well as hotel accommodations. Some of it is in the (M) range. *Adriatic* (M), at Omisalj. Modern hotel and annexes on shore below lovely hill village. *Corinthia* (M), near charming old port of Baska. With annexes, 290 rooms. *Drazica* (M), shore-side near Krk town. *Malin* (M), at Malinska. This hotel has cheaper annexes. *Park* (M), 268 rooms, at Punat, quiet resort with large marina.

LOVRAN. A beach resort just south of Opatija. *Beograd* (E-M). In a fine park on the seafront. *Miramare* (M). 32 rooms. *Park Villa Marina* (M), 74 rooms. *Splendid* (M). 83 rooms. Situated on the seafront.

MALI LOSINJ. Lively little commercial and pleasure port. Main tourist area is Cikat, 15 minutes' walk through pinewoods, where hotels include: *Alhambra* (M), built 1909 and the most charming; *Aurora* (M), 404 rooms, pool; *Bellevue* (M), 226 rooms, pool. All near rocky shore with good bathing.

OPATIJA. Large beach resort with old-world atmosphere. Newest is *Admiral* (E), 168 rooms. Shore-side by large marina, pools, varied amenities. *Ambassador* (E), 271 rooms, has similar facilities. *Adriatic* (M), 33 rooms, modern, own beach, night club; *Belvedere* (M), on sea shore, pool, tennis; *Imperial* (M), 129 rooms, central, traditional style, night club; *Kvarner* (M), 84 rooms, central, built in 1880s but modernized, fine gardens, pools, famous ballroom; *Slavija-Bellevue* (M), 150 rooms, traditional style, pool, night club, near sea; *Zagreb-Esplanade* (M), 110 rooms, near sea with garden terraces.

Restaurants. *Bevanda* (E), at Volosko, fish specialties. *Lido* (E), on Kvarner Beach, has terrace with dance floor. *Ariston* (M). *Plavi Podrum* (M), Volosko. *Zelengaj* (M).

PLITVICE. National Park featuring the Plitvice lakes. *Jezero* (E), 250 rooms, pool; *Plitvice* (E), 70 rooms, with annex; *Bellevue* (M), 90 rooms.

POREC. Lovely old town with famous Byzantine basilica. Istria's largest beach resort and scattered over several beaches. *Diamant* (M), *Neptun* (M), *Pical* (M), *Porec* (M), *Riviera* (M) are in or near town. There are a number of larger complexes some distance from the town, all (M): *Bellevue, Plava Laguna, Spadici, Lanterna, Zelena Laguna.*

PULA. There are remarkable Roman ruins including a 23,000-seat amphitheater. *Brioni* (E), 223 rooms. About 5 km. away on pine-clad point, own beach, pool. *Park* (M), 141 rooms, near Brioni. Sports facilities at nearby Verudela Center. *Riviera* (M), only centrally-located hotel. *Splendid* (M), 364 rooms. On outskirts, pool, by rocky shore. Some big tourist complexes at Medulin, 11 km. south.

RAB. A very lovely, densely wooded island. *International, Imperial* and *Istra,* all (M), in Rab town. *San Marino* (M), at Lopar. *Carolina* (M), at Suha Punta, has pool.

RABAC. A fishing port and major resort. *Apollo* (M), 54 rooms, is in town. Beyond town, near beach and with recreation facilities, are *Girandella* complex (M), *Lanterna* (M) and *Marina* (I). On outskirts, mammoth *Mimosa-Hedera-Narcis* complex (M), has sports facilities, pool.

RIJEKA. The country's main port and a partly industrial area. *Bonavia* (E), in town, old established and best. *Jadran* (M), in the Susak district. Located by the sea, it has a private beach. *Park* (I), in the Susak district.

Restaurants. *Gradina* (M) in Trsat Castle has fine views. On the wharf are *Gradski Restoran* (M), and *Zlatna Skoljka* (M), sea food.

ROVINJ. An attractive old town and a lively resort. *Rovinj* (M) is in town. A little south of town is the *Park* (E) and, in pinewoods beyond, *Eden* (E), pool, *Montauro* (E), *Monte Mulin* (M) and *Lone* (M), all with own beach and sports facilities. Nearby is entertainment center *Monvi* with restaurants, bars, disco and openair theater. Out-of-town complexes are at *Polari* to the south, and *Monsena* and *Valalta* to the north. There are also good accommodations on the islets of Crveni Otok and Katarina.

ZAGREB. *Esplanade* (L), Mihanoviceva 1 (tel. 512222). Imposing, modernized turn-of-century structure opposite main rail station; night club, dancing on terrace makes some rooms noisy in summer. *Inter-Continental Zagreb* (L), Krsnjavoga 1 (tel. 443411). 457 rooms, casino, night club, pool, national-style restaurant. *Palace* (E), Strossmayerov Sq. 10 (tel. 449211), near main rail station. *Dubrovnik* (M), Gajeva 1 (tel. 446666), recently renovated, very central overlooking Republic Square, 279 rooms, beer tavern but no restaurant. *Bristol*

(I), Gajeva 12 (tel. 410322), 30 rooms, very central, no restaurant. *Jadran* (I), Vlaska 50 (tel. 414257), near Cathedral, 32 rooms. Also good selection of *guest houses.*

Restaurants. *Korcula* (E-M), N. Tesle 17, fish and Dalmatian specialties. *Okrugljak* (E-M), Mlinovi 28, pleasant setting a little out of town. *Kaptolska klet* (M), Kaptol 5, central and good. *Pod mirnim krovovima* (M), Fijanova 7, excellent lamb on spit and freshwater fish. Many self-service restaurants at low prices include: *Medulic,* Meduliceva 2; *Splendid,* Zrinjevac 15; and *Corso,* Gunduliceva 2, all central.

Museums

ZAGREB. The Archeological Museum covers prehistoric to medieval times, including a massive coin collection; the Ethnographic Museum has interiors of peasant homes and folk collections; the Gallery of Old Paintings concentrates mainly on Italian Renaissance paintings while the Gallery of Primitive Art houses a fascinating selection of the works of the "naive" Croat peasant painters, now world famous; you can see some of the works of Yugoslavia's best-known sculptor in the Mestrovic Gallery. Mirmara Gallery, in a former Jesuit monastery, is a notable private collection. The Museum of the City of Zagreb is a model of its kind.

Dalmatia

This long stretch of coast and its numerous islands forms a separate entity, though administratively and ethnically, it is part of Croatia. The coastal regions present important differences from the interior, due to geography and still more to their separate historical background. While the Turks or the Habsburgs occupied much of the present-day Yugoslavia, Venice mostly ruled the Adriatic coast until the Napoleonic Wars. Only one Dalmatian city remained independent throughout these stormy centuries, namely Ragusa, today Dubrovnik.

The Dalmatian coast possesses not only dozens of seaside resorts, but also many historic towns. The whole of the walled city of Dubrovnik is an exquisite example of late Renaissance architecture. Split's old center lies within the walls of the monumental palace built by the Roman Emperor Diocletian. Trogir is an unspoilt medieval town and the historic city of Zadar contains impressive Roman and Romanesque remains. In addition there are scores of ancient little towns, some on the islands, where Venice left her imprint, such as Brac, Hvar, Ston, Sibenik and Korcula. For peace and quiet, try the islands of Kolocep, Lopud, Brac or Solta. Main centers like Dubrovnik and Split become very crowded in summer. Dalmatia possesses several old colorful traditional ceremonies and customs; if you are in the vicinity, don't miss the Moreska, at Korcula, July 27 (also every Thursday in summer), or the Alka, at Sinj, in August.

Thanks to the indented coastline and the large number of islands, this part of the Adriatic is of some interest to fishermen. Travel agencies at main centers organize fishing expeditions.

PRACTICAL INFORMATION FOR DALMATIA

Hotels and Restaurants

BRAC. A large island rather less developed than some others. In the small main coastal town of Bol are *Elaphusa* (upper M), 350 rooms, pool, with pavilion annex; *Borak* (upper M), 148 rooms; *Bijela Kuca* (M), with dependencies, 200 rooms. All with own beach. 3 km. from town is *Bretanide* (M), attractively designed to resemble a Dalmatian village.

CAVTAT. Old village and summer resort in beautiful bay near Dubrovnik. *Croatia* (L), 480 rooms, casino, own beaches, pools, disco. *Albatros* (E), 246 rooms, pool. *Adriatic* (M), 54 rooms. *Cavtat* (M), 109 rooms. *Epidaurus* (M), 192 rooms, older but well modernized. All with own beach.

DUBROVNIK. Exquisite walled town of international fame. Within strolling distance of the walls are the *Excelsior* (E-M), 211 rooms, pool; *Argentina* (E-M), 155 rooms, pool, and *Villa Dubrovnik* (E), all with rocky beach in the Ploce district; and *Imperial* (E), 108 rooms, in grand old style, but no beach, in the Pile district. The *Dubravka* (M), 22 rooms, is the only hotel within the walls. Most of the others are in the peninsula district of Lapad (3 km., good bus service). They include *Dubrovnik Palace* (E), own pool, nudist beach; nearby smaller *Splendid* (M) in pine wood with own beach, and *Kompas* (M) overlooking public beach of Sumratin. A little further is the fine Babin Kuk development with shopping precinct and restaurants, its several hotels including the impressive modern *Dubrovnik President* (L) soaring up from its own bathing area.

Restaurants. All (M) are *Dubravka,* near Pile Gate; *Gradska Kavana,* popular café rendezvous in the old city, but prices sometimes erratic; *Jadran* in cloisters of former monastery in the old town; *Mimosa,* charming, good value, opposite Imperial Hotel; *Prijeko,* intimate atmosphere, local specialties in the old town; *Riblji,* Dalmatian and fish specialties in the old town.

HVAR. Lovely main town on Hvar Island. Best is *Amfora,* 370 rooms, pool. Others in upper (M) price category include *Adriatic, Palace,* and *Sirena,* all with pools, and the slightly lower priced *Bodul.*

KORCULA. Gorgeous capital of the island of the same name. *Korcula* (M), 26 rooms, renovated, good value, is the only hotel in the old town. A short stroll away along the waterfront is *Park* (M), 275 rooms and, next door, the *Marko Polo* (M), 110 rooms, pool; both have their own bathing area. The *Bon Repos* complex (M), 329 rooms, is on the shore about 1 km. further.

Restaurants. All (M) are *Gradski podrum* in the old town, *Planjak* just outside the walls, *Mornar* near the waterfront, and *Adio Mare.*

MAKARSKA. A fine old coastal town and resort. *Dalmacija* (E), 190 rooms. Highrise hotel with pool, beach. With some lower-priced rooms, as is *Meteor* (E), 280 rooms. Near town, beach, pool, night club. *Riviera* (E), 265 rooms. *Park* (M-I), 70 rooms.

OREBIC. Old seafaring community on Peljesac Peninsula with lovely views to Korcula island. *Bellevue* (M), *Orsan* (M), *Ratheneum* (M), all with own beach.

PRIMOSTEN. Charming fishing village near Sibenik. *Adriatic-Raduca* (M), *Adriatic-Slava* (M), *Adriatic Zora* (M). The last two have pools; all have own beach.

SIBENIK. Fine old coastal town and resort with glorious cathedral. The *Solaris* complex 6 km. (3½ miles) from town, includes *Ivan* (E), indoor pool, and *Adrija* (M), *Jure* (M), *Niko* (M). Hydrotherapy treatment and extensive sports facilities. In town is *Jadran* (I), 48 rooms.

SPLIT. Major historic city and port. *Marjan* (E), 331 rooms, on sea front, rather noisy, night club, pools. *Bellevue* (M), 50 rooms, elegantly renovated, central. *Park* (M), 60 rooms in pleasant Bacvice district. *Central* (I), 40 rooms, in very heart of old city. *Lav* (M), 375 rooms, disco, pool. Beautifully situated beach in quiet, wooded bay 8 km. (5 miles) southeast, but erratic standards.

Restaurants. *Adriano* (M), pavement terrace on waterfront; Serbian specialties. *Dva Goluba* (M), beyond Marjan hotel, good views, seafood and national specialties. *Ero* (M), on Marmontova, by old town. National dishes. *Konoba Adriatik* (M), in heart of old city, national dishes. *MAK* (M), in ultra modern Koteks shopping center east of old town. *Sarajevo* (M), in old town. Bosnian specialties.

TROGIR. Fine medieval walled town. *Jadran* and *Medena,* both (M), latter with pool and about a mile from town. *Motel Trogir* (M), nearer town.

ZADAR. Historic city and port. *Barbara* (E), *Slavija* (M) and *Zadar* (M) are in the Borik district (3½ km.) and have their own beaches. *Zagreb* (M) is in town.

Museums and Sights

DUBROVNIK. Allow at least an hour to tour the splendid undamaged medieval walls on foot (nominal fee; access closed at 6 or 7 P.M.)—the roofscapes are stunning; the two most important buildings are the Sponza Palace and the Rector's Palace, the first housing the City Archives and the second the City Museum. There are many churches and monasteries; particularly notable are the Franciscan and Dominican Monasteries with their beautiful cloisters. Fort St. John houses the Ethnographic Museum, Maritime Museum and Aquarium, and gives marvelous views over the old harbor.

SPLIT. The whole of the old city within the walls of Diocletian's Palace, and the Underground Halls which provide a carbon copy of the original layout of the Palace; 15th-century Papalic Palace housing the excellent Municipal Museum; Ethnographic Museum in the 15th-century Old Town Hall; Cathedral of St. Doimus; the Baptistry (originally Temple of Jupiter); Mestrovic Gallery in this famous sculptor's former summer residence west of the city; nearby is excellent new Croat Antiquities Museum.

ZADAR. Many Roman remains, notably in the great Forum; massive St. Donat's Church, dating from the early 9th-century and incorporating much Roman stonework; the beautiful Romanesque Cathedral of St. Anastasia, and many other medieval and later churches; the remains of medieval and later fortifications and several town gates, including a monumental Roman triumphal arch.

Bosnia-Hercegovina

The domes and slender minarets scattered across the towns of this Republic give them an oriental air, hardly to be wondered at when you recall that they formed part of the Ottoman Empire for four centuries. The Turkish heritage is evident not only in the architecture, for a good many of the inhabitants have kept the faith of their former rulers. Although readily accessible, Bosnia-Hercegovina provides a stimulating contrast to the traveler coming from the Adriatic coast. Between them, they comprise a region of bare rocky hills, deep gorges, and vast game forests. The province offers excellent rock climbing and hunting. The rivers contain trout while trips can be made by kayak or raft down the exciting rapids of the Drina Gorge (several major travel firms arrange excursions). The Sutjeska National Park is a particularly wild and beautiful region.

The capital of the combined province is the picturesquely situated city of Sarajevo, a blend of East and West, and scene of the 1984 Winter Olympics. Mostar, Hercegovina's principal town, features its humpbacked stone bridge over the Neretva, built by the Turks in 1556, around which are clustered houses and mosques from the Turkish era. Other towns in Bosnia are Banja Luka, Jajce, built around an impressive waterfall, and Travnik, the residence of the Turkish vizirs (governors) from 1700 until 1852.

PRACTICAL INFORMATION FOR BOSNIA-HERCEGOVINA

BANJA LUKA. Modern town with picturesque districts from Turkish era. *Bosna* (M), 200 rooms, is the largest. *Slavija* (M), 45 rooms. *Motel International* (I). *Palace* (I).

JAJCE. Beautifully situated old town with typical Bosnian houses and dramatic waterfalls. *Jajce* (I), indoor pool. *Turist* (I).

MOSTAR. Interesting old town with famous 16th century bridge. Fine new *Ruza* (M), 75 rooms, near bridge and old quarters. *Bristol* (I), 56 rooms, and *Neretva* (I), 40 rooms, Moorish style, face each other across river, but some rooms are noisy.

Restaurants. *Labirint* (M), very popular with terrace overlooking river. *Pecina,* a tavern in a natural cave. *Stari Most* (I) by the old bridge. *Ascinica* (I) in town center, offers national dishes.

SARAJEVO. Amenities in this fascinating capital of the Republic were much boosted by preparations for the 1984 Winter Olympics. *Holiday Inn* (E), near rail station and spanking new. *Evropa* (M), Jugoslovenske Narodne Armije (tel. 532722), 225 rooms, old-established but renovated and best placed for exploring old town; service is a bit erratic. *National* (M), Obala Pariske komune 5 (tel. 532266), 73 rooms, just across river from center. *Central* (I), Zrinjskog 8 (tel. 533655) and *Stari Grad* (I), Marsala Tita 126 (tel. 533394), have no private baths but are central, adequate and inexpensive.

Restaurants. *Daira* (E-M), Halaci 5, in charmingly converted 17th century Turkish storehouse. *Morica Han* (E-M), Saraci bb, formerly old inn. Both serve national dishes. *Dalmacija* (M), Marsala Tita 45, fish specialties. *Lovacki Rog* (M), Nicole Tesle 24. Two handy self-service restaurants are *Bosna* and *Marin Dvor,* both in Marsala Tita street and central. Look out for *ascinica,* small eating places serving tasty local specialties which make quick inexpensive snacks.

TJENTISTE. Located in the beautiful Sujteska National Park. *Mladost* (I). *Sujteska* (I).

TREBINJE. Small town with Oriental atmosphere not far from Dubrovnik. *Leotar* (M). *Villa Lastva* (M).

Sights and Museums

SARAJEVO. The Bascarsija district or Old Turkish Quarter where the daily open-air market takes place among a maze of narrow streets bordered by craftsmen's shops; in the same area, Begova Mosque, the largest and most famous, and the nearby 17th-century Clock Tower; the Ali Pasha Mosque; the House of Svrzo and Despic House, respectively a Muslim and Orthodox Serb home from the 18th and 19th centuries; the old Serbian Orthodox Church with beautifully carved 18th-century iconostasis; National Museum with especially rich archeological and ethnographic sections; the Young Bosnia Museum by the spot from which Archduke Franz Ferdinand was shot, leading to World War I, and telling the story of the young revolutionaries.

Montenegro

Shut in between Bosnia-Hercegovina, Serbia and Albania, this smallest republic of the federation possesses some 60 miles of coastline dotted with rapidly developed seaside resorts, backed by rocky hills. The interior is dominated by the rugged Black Mountains, the Venetian's Montenegro, which the Yugoslavs call Crna Gora. In the north are some green valleys, and in the south huge Lake Skadar is shared with Albania.

Montenegro's history is one of unceasing struggle ever since the foundation of the medieval Serb state, of which it was a province until 1389. Then, following the Turkish victory at Kosovo, Serbia shrank northwards and finally disappeared. Though isolated, Montenegro resisted all foreign invaders. Its remoteness now made accessible by modern transport and better roads, this region offers a large choice for holiday activities.

From nearby walled Kotor, set on the splendid triple bay, a breath-taking road zigzags up Mount Lovcen, offering one of the most star-tling panoramas in Europe, over the fjord-like Gulf of Kotor, the successive mountain ranges and including a distant view of Albania. The former capital Cetinje, which still preserves its pre-World War I atmosphere, lies in a fertile bowl amid soaring bare mountains. In the mighty Durmitor Range to the northeast is the Tara Canyon—55 miles long—one of the most remarkable in Europe. Raft trips can be ar-ranged. Modern beach resorts stretch from Hercegnovi to Ulcinj, from which 11 miles of continuous sand run to the Albanian border. Mon-tenegro's developing port of Bar is now linked by a spectacular railway route with Belgrade, boring its way through dramatic mountainscapes and along the rim of precipitous gorges.

A violent earthquake hit the coast on Easter Sunday, 1979, causing very extensive damage. All the tourist amenities have now been re-stored or replaced, but the architectural treasures will take longer. The walled towns of Budva and Kotor were particularly badly affected.

PRACTICAL INFORMATION FOR MONTENEGRO

BUDVA. Charming walled town and popular resort with several beaches. Just outside walls, *Avala* (E), completely rebuilt, with 220 rooms, pool, night-club. About 1 km. away by extensive Slovenska Plaza beach, a major new holiday center (E-M) recreates a charming small-village atmosphere and offers top facilities with wide range of sports and entertainment. Other hotels are by large Becici beach, a few km. south, set in pleasant gardens. They include: *Bellevue* (E), 200 rooms; *International* (E), with own pool; *Mediteran* (E), 220 rooms, pool, nightclub; *Montenegro* (E-M), 550 rooms, pool, nightclub; *Splendid* (E), 190 rooms; all have good water sports facilities. *Mogren* (M), 46 rooms, just outside the town walls, next to *Avala,* with pool, nightclub.

HERCEG-NOVI. Attractive resort with splendid gardens set steeply by Gulf of Kotor. Rebuilt *Plaza* (E), 320 rooms, pool, rising like massive glasshouse from own bathing areas. *Topla* (M), pavilion-type villas on terraces by sea. *Rent-a-Villa* (M), modern self-catering accommodations near town center. The *Riviera* at Njivice (M) is reached in a few minutes by motor boat across bay.

Restaurants. *Gradski Restoran,* central, shady terrace. *Skver,* central, fish specialties.

MILOCER. Former residence of Yugoslav royal family, linked with Sveti Stefan (see below). *Milocer* (E), former summer royal residence, small, gracious, in extensive grounds and nearby new *Villa Milocer* (E). Modern *Maestral* (E-M), 160 rooms, pool, casino.

PETROVAC. Pleasant resort with good facilities. *Palas* (E), 185 rooms, rebuilt, pool, own beach. *Castellastva* (M), 175 rooms, friendly atmosphere. *Oliva Villas* (M), 110 rooms. *Rivijera* (M), 88 rooms.

SVETI STEFAN. Former fishing village within medieval walls on tiny island linked to coast and Milocer (see above) by modern causeway. Now luxury holiday village, 110 apartments with casino, pool, new sports center and sum-mer theater.

TITOGRAD. Capital of Montenegro, entirely rebuilt since World War Two. Attractive stone *Podgorica* (M), 60 rooms, on river bank. Older *Crna Gora* (I), 130 rooms, modernized.

Restaurant. *Mareza,* 10 km. from town towards Cetinje, fish specialties.

ULCINJ. Yugoslavia's southernmost seaside resort with distinct oriental at-mosphere. In town, best is *Galeb* (E), reconstructed, 153 rooms, pool. About 4 km. south of town is the 12 km.-long Velika Plaza (Long Beach) of gently shelving sands, with cluster of modern hotels including *Grand Hotel Lido* (E),

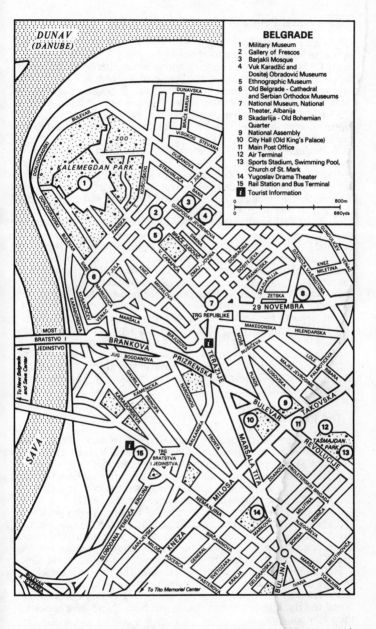

BELGRADE

1 Military Museum
2 Gallery of Frescos
3 Barjakli Mosque
4 Vuk Karadžić and Dositej Obradović Museums
5 Ethnographic Museum
6 Old Belgrade - Cathedral and Serbian Orthodox Museums
7 National Museum, National Theater, Albanija
8 Skadarlija - Old Bohemian Quarter
9 National Assembly
10 City Hall (Old King's Palace)
11 Main Post Office
12 Air Terminal
13 Sports Stadium, Swimming Pool, Church of St. Mark
14 Yugoslav Drama Theater
15 Rail Station and Bus Terminal
ℹ️ Tourist Information

best placed, 52 rooms and many bungalows. Also *Olympic* (E), 130 rooms, pool, and *Bellevue* (M), 370 rooms, beach-side restaurant.

ZABLJAK. Mountain resort at 4,700 ft. in magnificent Durmitor range. New *Planinka* (M), 105 rooms. Recent *Jezero* (M), 103 rooms, pool. Older *Zabljak* (I).

Serbia and Belgrade

Serbian national history begins with the establishment of a kingdom by Stefan Nemanja at the end of the 12th century. Under Tzar Dusan, in the first half of the 14th century, Serbia became the dominant power in the Balkans. However, at the Battle of Kosovo in 1389, it was overwhelmed by the greater numbers of the Turks and came under their control for five centuries. Serbia regained semi-independence in 1815 and full independence in 1878. Her growing importance, and influence upon the other Slavs under Habsburg rule, contributed to the sparking off of World War I.

In Belgrade (Beograd), you are really in the heart of the Balkans. Since its near-destruction in 1941, it has grown into a modern city of one and a half million inhabitants, but few cities boast as romantic a city park as the Kalemegdan, formerly a Turkish fortress built on a still more ancient Roman one. The National Museum is well worth a visit. Belgrade is the seat of the Patriarchate of the Serbian Orthodox Church; its Cathedral of the Holy Archangel Michael contains monuments to many heroes of Serbian history. Across the Sava River from the main part of the city lies Novi Beograd, whose unimaginative blocks of cement have risen out of what was formerly swamp land. Two modern architectural highlights are the Sava Center (congress and concert hall complex) and the Modern Art Museum.

In Topola, just south of Belgrade, is the home of Karageorge, the instigator of the first Serbian Insurrection against the Turks in 1804, and ancestor of the Serbian Karageorge dynasty. In town remain several buildings from Karageorge's time. On Oplenac hill, above the town, is the family mausoleum, walls of which are completely covered with fantastic mosaic reproductions of old Serbian frescos. To the southeast is Kragujevac, where over 7,000 of the inhabitants were shot in one day by the Germans as reprisals in the last war. There is a very moving memorial park.

The Iron Gates

North of the Danube are the plains of the Vojvodina, whose mixed population of Serbs, Hungarians, Croats, Slovaks, Montenegrins, Ruthenians, Macedonians, Austrians, and others testifies to the frequent and drastic political changes and struggles which this valuable farming area has undergone through its history. Downstream from Belgrade, the Danube flows through a spectacular gorge, the Djerdap (Iron Gates), one of the great natural wonders of Europe. At this point, the Danube forms the frontier between Yugoslavia and Romania, and the two nations jointly have constructed a vast hydroelectric, irrigation and navigation scheme, which has tamed these formerly treacherous waters. The all-day hydrofoil trip from Belgrade is well worth the time.

Hidden away in the interior of Serbia, in the remote areas of the Morava and Ibar valleys, you will come upon beautiful medieval Serb-Orthodox churches and monasteries, containing exquisite frescos that reveal the Byzantine influence. Cities like Novi Pazar have preserved their Eastern character.

The extreme southwestern part of Serbia, known as Kosovo, is an autonomous region administratively. The older districts of Pec, Pristina and Prizren have a Turkish appearance. The majority of the people of Kosovo are Albanians and there is a colorful mixture of costumes and traditions here. Despite a high degree of autonomy and economic support from the rest of the country, there was a recent period of strife because of minority demands to join with Albania, but all is reported to be normal once more. With its dramatic mountains, ancient monasteries and mosques, this is a very rewarding off-beat area, which now has several reasonable hotels.

PRACTICAL INFORMATION FOR BELGRADE

HOTELS. It is absolutely essential to book hotels in advance in Belgrade.

Deluxe

Beograd Inter-Continental (tel. 134760). 420 rooms, pool, adjoining glossy new Sava Center in New Belgrade and very elegant, though a fair trek from the city center.

Jugoslavija, Bulevarda Edvarda Kardelia 3 (tel. 600222). 577 rooms, pool, top facilities, by the Danube in New Belgrade, and further still from the city center, but lower prices.

Metropol, Bulevarda Revolucije 69 (tel. 330910). 220 rooms; sumptuous old style, now renovated; very central.

Moskva, Balkanska 1 (tel. 686255). 140 rooms, modernized, central, but does not fully warrant price category.

Expensive

Excelsior, Kneza Milosa (tel. 331381). 80 rooms.

Majestic, Obilicev Venac 28 (tel. 636022). 92 rooms.

Palace, Toplicin Venac 23 (tel. 637222). 78 rooms, some (M). Central.

Slavija, Svetog save 1 (tel. 450842). Over 500 rooms, mostly located in skyscraper and particularly good value, though less central. Some moderate rooms.

Moderate

Astorija, Milovana Milovanovica 1 (tel. 645422). 77 rooms. Older establishment, but central.

Balkan, Prizrenska 2 (tel. 687466). 95 rooms, central.

Kasina, Terazije 25 (tel. 335574). 96 rooms, very central.

Prag, Narodnog fronta 27 (tel. 687355). 118 rooms, central.

Splendid, Dragoslava Jovanovica 5 (tel. 335444), 50 rooms, no restaurant.

Srbija, Ustanicka 127 (tel. 413255). 337 rooms, modern, a little away from center.

Turist, Sarajevska 37 (tel. 682855). 97 rooms, near main rail station.

Union, Kosovska 11 (tel. 341055). 74 rooms, central.

RESTAURANTS. Belgrade's restaurants, outside the hotels, are as varied as you would expect in a capital city. The most popular ones are those in the city's old Bohemian quarter centered on a street called Skadarska, close to the city center. Though listed as Expensive, it is quite possible to eat moderately, depending on quantity and choice.

Expensive

Dva Jelena, Skadarska. Offers musical entertainment.

Ima Dana, Skadarska. This restaurant heads the list. It has entertainment other than just music and also has open-air dining.

Tri Sesira, Skadarska. Attractive bohemian atmosphere.

Vinogradi at Grocka (25 km.), roast-on-the-spit specialties, overlooking Danube.

Moderate

Dva Ribara, Narodnog fronta 23. Pleasant atmosphere.

Romani Tar, Terazije 27. An outstanding gipsy restaurant.

Trojka, Trise Kaclerovica 24, Russian food.

Inexpensive

Dunavski cvet, T. Koscuskog 63, fish specialties.

Dusanov Grad, Terazije. A safe if not a terribly exciting restaurant.

Three useful central self-service restaurants are **Zagreb,** Obilicev unac 29; **Kasina,** Terazije 25; **Atina,** Terazije 28. There are cafés everywhere. A historic one is the **Cafe of the Question Mark,** 7. jula 6, opposite Orthodox Cathedral and typical of Serbian homes two centuries ago.

SIGHTS AND MUSEUMS. The ancient fortress of Kalemegdan is a "must" for its interest and superb views over the confluence of the Sava and Danube rivers, and across the city. Bajrakli Dzamija, the only mosque left in the city, dates from the 17th century and was converted into a church in the 19th. The Ethnographic Museum illustrates costumes, household articles and typical peasant house interiors from different parts of the country, while the Fresco Gallery shows copies of the finest frescoes of the medieval Serbian and Macedonian monasteries. In a suitably modern building by the Sava in New Belgrade, the Modern Art Museum displays 20th-century Serb painting and sculpture. Fine religious works of art and vestments may be seen in the Museum of the Serbian Orthodox Church. The National Museum has outstanding archeological and medieval sections, including stunning neolithic gold jewelry, statuettes and the famous Duplja cart. In a quiet suburb to the south of the center is the Josip Broz Tito Memorial Center, with the tomb of the late President in his former home and museums closely connected with his life.

PRACTICAL INFORMATION FOR SERBIA

KRAGUJEVAC. *Kragujevac* (M), *Sumarice* (M), *Zelengora* (M).

NIS. High-rise *Ambassador* (M), 170 rooms, in center. *Nis* (M), quiet location.

NOVI SAD. Capital of Vojvodina on the Danube. *Park* (M), 315 rooms, modern, pool, nightclub. *Trdjava Varadin* (M), good hotel in ancient fortress overlooking river. *Novi Sad* (I).

PEC. Interesting capital of Kosovo. *Korzo* (I), very low-priced, adequate. *Metohija* (I), modern.

PRISTINA. Kosovo. *Grand Hotel Pristina* (M), 369 rooms, modern. *Kosovski Bozur* (I).

PRIZREN. Kosovo. *Motel Vlazrimi* (I).

SMEDEREVO. Town with huge ancient fort by the Danube. *Smederevo* (I).

Macedonia

The main attraction of this southernmost province is medieval Ohrid, in its lovely lakeside setting. Capital of Tsar Samuel, the medieval churches contain some extraordinary frescos and icons. There are two other large lakes, Prespa and Dojran, and the countryside holds countless reminders of Greek and Roman times. As in Serbia, there are a great number of Byzantine monasteries. From the summit of Mt. Solunska Glava, you can see as far as the Aegean and the Greek islands.

A disastrous earthquake in July 1963 destroyed the center of Skopje, a city of 200,000 inhabitants and the capital of Macedonia. However, thanks to the help and cooperation of many nations and organizations, Skopje was rebuilt rapidly; its monuments from Roman times (when it also suffered earthquake destruction) and its medieval treasures were restored, among them the church of the Holy Savior, with its famous woodcarvings, the Turkish Bath of Daut Pasha, now an art gallery, and the vast Turkish caravanserai.

PRACTICAL INFORMATION FOR MACEDONIA

OHRID. Beautiful old town with ancient monasteries by Lake Ohrid. Best is *Metropol* (M), 125 rooms, pool but no beach, on lake a few km. outside town. *Slavija* (M), 61 rooms. At Gorica, 3 km. south, *Gorica* (M), 60 rooms, pool, and *Park* (M), 37 rooms; both part of Inex enterprise on wooded peninsula, one of best locations on lake, with bathing beaches. Also 20 chalets (M), with pool. In town, on the lake-side, are *Grand Hotel Palace* (I), 134 rooms, and *Palace Annex* (I), 88 rooms; service is erratic.

SKOPJE. Macedonia's interesting capital. Best are *Continental* (E-M), 200 rooms, and *Grand Hotel Skopje* (M), 180 rooms, beside Vardar river. *Turist* (M), 80 rooms, on main business street. *Bellevue* (M), 65 rooms. Nearby but in much quieter location is *Jadran* (M), built in Turkish style, 23 rooms. *Olympic* tourist village (M), 260 rooms in hotel and chalets.

STARI DOJRAN. Summer resort on lake which has some of the best fishing in Yugoslavia. *Stari Dojran* (I), low priced but adequate.

STRUGA. Small resort on Lake Ohrid close to Albanian border. *Biser* (E), attractive local style, own beach, nightclub.

INDEX

(The letters H and R indicate hotel and restaurant listings.)

GENERAL

(See also "Practical Information" sections under each country for additional, detailed information.)

773

780 INDEX

GREECE

MAP
OF
EUROPE

EUROPE

Speak a foreign language in seconds.

Now an amazing space age device makes it possible to speak a foreign language *without* having to learn a foreign language.

Speak French, German, or Spanish.
With the incredible Translator 8000—world's first pocket-size electronic translation machines—you're never at a loss for words in France, Germany, or Spain.

8,000-word brain.
Just punch in the foreign word or phrase, and English appears on the LED display. Or punch in English, and read the foreign equivalent instantly.

Only 4¾" x 2¾", it possesses a fluent 8,000-word vocabulary (4,000 English, 4,000 foreign). A memory key stores up to 16 words; a practice key randomly calls up words for study, self-testing, or game use. And it's also a full-function calculator.

150,000 sold in 18 months.
Manufactured for Langenscheidt by Sharp/Japan, the Translator 8000 comes with a 6-month warranty. It's a valuable aid for business and pleasure travelers, and students. It comes in a handsome leatherette case, and makes a super gift.

Order now with the information below.

To order, send $69.95 plus $3 p&h ($12 for overseas del.) for each unit. Indicate language choice: English/French, English/German, English/Spanish. N.Y. res. add sales tax. MasterCard, Visa, or American Express card users give brand, account number (all digits), expiration date, and signature. SEND TO: Fodor's, Dept. T-8000, 2 Park Ave., New York, NY 10016-5677, U.S.A.

Make Your Trip More Enjoyable

"Try to speak the local language; it's really great fun. . . .

"The natives, who may not speak your language, will be proud and appreciative of your efforts to use *their* language.

"I can't think of a better way to break the ice---"

—Eugene Fodor

Fodor's / McKay has a wide list of Teach Yourself language and phrase books and foreign-language dictionaries. Most cost only a few dollars. If your local bookstore doesn't have the language book you need, write to us for a complete list of titles and prices.

Write to:
Sales Director
FODOR'S / McKAY
2 Park Avenue
New York, NY
10016